FIFTH EDITION

BIOLOGY

Sylvia S. Mader

WCB **Wm. C. Brown Publishers**

Dubuque, IA Bogota Boston Buenos Aires Caracas Chicago
Guilford, CT London Madrid Mexico City Sydney Toronto

Book Team

Editor *Carol J. Mills*
Developmental Editor *Connie Balius-Haakinson*
Production Editor *Carla D. Kipper*
Designer *Christopher E. Reese*
Art Editor *Kathleen M. Timp*
Photo Editor *Lori Hancock*
Permissions Coordinator *Vicki Krug*
Art Processor *Brenda A. Ernzen*

Wm. C. Brown Publishers

Vice President and Chief Executive Officer *Beverly Kolz*
Vice President, Publisher *Kevin Kane*
Vice President, Director of Sales and Marketing *Virginia S. Moffat*
Vice President, Director of Production *Colleen A. Yonda*
National Sales Manager *Douglas J. DiNardo*
Marketing Manager *Craig Johnson*
Advertising Manager *Janelle Keeffer*
Production Editorial Manager *Renée Menne*
Publishing Services Manager *Karen J. Slaght*
Royalty/Permissions Manager *Connie Allendorf*

A Times Mirror Company

Copyedited by *Moira Urich*

Cover photo: © Manfred Danegger/Peter Arnold, Inc.

The credits section for this book begins on page C-1 and is considered
an extension of the copyright page.

Copyright © 1996 Times Mirror Higher Education Group, Inc.
All rights reserved.

Library of Congress Catalog Card Number: 95–77804

ISBN 0–697–21819–8 (Paper)
ISBN 0–697–21818–X (Case)

Printed in the United States of America by Times Mirror Higher Education Group, Inc.,
2460 Kerper Boulevard, Dubuque, IA 52001

10 9 8 7 6 5 4 3 2 1

BRIEF CONTENTS

CONTENTS

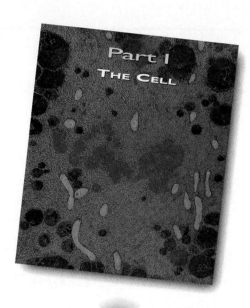

Part I
THE CELL

Part II
GENETIC BASIS OF LIFE

21
ORIGIN AND HISTORY OF LIFE

22
HUMAN EVOLUTION

23
CLASSIFICATION OF LIVING THINGS

24
VIRUSES AND KINGDOM PROKARYOTAE

33
GROWTH AND DEVELOPMENT IN PLANTS

34
REPRODUCTION IN PLANTS

35
ANIMAL ORGANIZATION AND HOMEOSTASIS

Part VII
BEHAVIOR AND ECOLOGY

READINGS

A CLOSER LOOK

RESEARCH REPORTS

OF HUMAN INTEREST

BIOLOGY AND TECHNOLOGY

📼 LIFE SCIENCE ANIMATIONS

The following illustrations in *Biology* are correlated to the *Life Science Animations* videotapes by Wm. C. Brown Publishers.

📼 Tape 1
Chemistry, the Cell, and Energetics

1. Formation of an Ionic Bond (fig. 3.7)
2. Journey into a Cell (figs. 5.3–5.8, 5.11, 5.12, 6.3, 6.14, 6.15, 8.3)
3. Endocytosis (figs. 5.8, 6.12, 6.13)
4. Cellular Secretion (fig. 5.8)
5. Glycolysis (figs. 9.2, 9.4)
6. Oxidative Respiration (including Krebs cycles) (figs. 9.3, 9.7)
7. The Electron Transport Chain and the Production of ATP (figs. 7.7, 7.10, 9.4, 9.8, 9.9, 9.10)
8. The Photosynthetic Electron Transport Chain and Production of ATP (figs. 7.8, 8.5, 8.6, 8.7)
9. C_3 Photosynthesis (Calvin Cycle) (figs. 7.8, 8.9, 8.10)
10. C_4 Photosynthesis (fig. 8.10)
11. ATP as an Energy Carrier (figs. 7.10, 9.3, 9.11)

📼 Tape 2
Cell Division/Heredity/Genetics/Reproduction and Development

12. Mitosis (figs. 10.3–10.8, 10.10, 11.6, 11.7)
13. Meiosis (figs. 11.2, 11.5–11.8)
14. Crossing Over (figs. 11.3, 11.4)
15. DNA Replication (figs. 15.7, 15.8, 15A)
16. Transcription of a Gene (figs. 16.5, 16.6, 16.11, 17.2, 17.3, 17.6, 17.7)
17. Protein Synthesis (figs. 16.8–16.11, 17.2, 17.8)
18. Regulation of *Lac* Operon (fig. 17.1)
19. Spermatogenesis (figs. 11.8, 45.7)
20. Oogenesis (figs. 11.8, 45.10)
21. Human Embryonic Development (figs. 46.9–46.12)

📼 Tape 3
Animal Biology I

22. Formation of Myelin Sheath (fig. 41.3)
23. Saltatory Nerve Conduction (fig. 41.6)
24. Signal Integration (figs. 41.4, 41.5, 41.7)
25. Reflex Arcs (fig. 41.9)
26. Organ of Static Equilibrium (figs. 42.11–42.13)
27. The Organ of Corti (fig. 42.13)
28. Peptide Hormone Action (cAMP) (fig. 44.2)
29. Levels of Muscle Structure (fig. 43.13)
30. Sliding Filament Model of Muscle Contraction (figs. 43.12, 43.14)
31. Regulation of Muscle Contraction (fig. 43.15)
32. The Cardiac Cycle and Production of Sounds (fig. 36.7)
33. Peristalsis (fig. 38.7)
34. Digestion of Carbohydrates
35. Digestion of Proteins

📼 Tape 4
Animal Biology II

36. Digestion of Lipids
37. Blood Circulation (figs. 36.2–36.4, 36.6, 36.8)
38. Production of Electrocardiogram (figs. 36.7, 36.9, 36.10)
39. Common Congenital Defects of the Heart (fig. 36.12)
40. A, B, O Blood Types (figs. 36.15, 36.16)
41. B-Cell Immune Response (fig. 37.6)
42. Structure and Function of Antibodies (fig. 37.7)
43. Types of T-cells (figs. 37.8, 37.9)
44. Relationship of Helper T-cells and Killer T-cells (figs. 37.8, 37.9)
45. Life Cycle of Malaria (fig. 25.13)

📼 Tape 5
Plant Biology/Evolution/Ecology

46. Journey into a Leaf (figs. 31.4b, 31.18, 31.19)
47. How Water Moves Through a Plant (figs. 31.2, 31.6, 32.1–32.5)
48. How Food Moves from a Source to a Sink (figs. 31.2, 31.7, 32.1, 32.12)
49. How Leaves Change Color and Drop in Fall
50. Mitosis and Cell Division in Plants (figs. 10.10, 33.11)
51. Carbon and Nitrogen Cycles (figs. 50.9, 50.10)
52. Energy Flow through an Ecosystem (figs. 1.4, 50.1, 50.7, 50.8, 50.9)
53. Continental Drift and Plate Tectonics (figs. 21.7, 21.8)

💿 CD-ROM CORRELATIONS

The following illustrations in *Biology* are correlated to the sixteen topic modules in *Explorations in Human Biology CD-ROM* by George B. Johnson:

1. Cystic Fibrosis (figs. 6.5, 14.7)
2. Active Transport (figs. 6.10–6.12)
3. Life Span and Lifestyle (figs. 36B, 36.9, 39.10, 48A)
4. Muscle Contraction (figs. 43.11–43.15)
5. Evolution of the Heart (figs. 36.5–36.8)
6. Smoking and Cancer (fig. 39.10)
7. Diet and Weight Loss (fig. 38.11)
8. Nerve Conduction (figs. 41.2–41.6, 41.9)
9. Synaptic Transmission (figs. 41.7, 41.10, 43.15)
10. Drug Addiction
11. Hormone Action (figs. 44.1–44.3, 44.8)
12. Immune Response (figs. 37.3–37.9)
13. AIDS (figs. 37B, 37.10)
14. Constructing a Genetic Map (p. 205, figs. 18.3, 18.4, 18.9)
15. Heredity in Families (figs. 14.6a, 14.7a, 14.9, 14.12, 14.13)
16. Pollution of a Freshwater Lake (figs. 51.1, 52.7, 52.8)

The following illustrations in *Biology* are correlated to the second CD-ROM by George B. Johnson entitled *Explorations in Cell Biology, Metabolism, and Genetics:*

1. How Proteins Function: Hemoglobin (figs. 16.2, 36.2, 39.8, 39.9)
2. Cell Size (figs. 5.3–5.5)
3. Active Transport (figs. 6.10–6.12)
4. Cell-Cell Interactions (figs. 6.5, 6.13, 17.11)
5. Mitosis: Regulating the Cell Cycle (figs. 10.3–10.8, 10.10, 11.6, 11.7)
6. Cell Chemistry: Thermodynamics (figs. 7.3–7.6)
7. Enzymes in Action: Kinetics
8. Oxidative Respiration (figs. 7.10, 9.2, 9.4, 9.6–9.9)
9. Photosynthesis (figs. 8.2, 8.3, 8.5–8.7)
10. Exploring Meiosis (figs. 11.2, 11.3, 11.5, 11.7)
11. Three-Point Genetic Cross (figs. 12.7, 13.5)
12. Heredity in Families (figs. 14.6, 14.7, 14.9, 14.12, 14.13, 14B)
13. Gene Segregation Within Families (figs. 14.6, 14.7)
14. DNA Fingerprinting: You Be the Judge (fig. 18.4)
15. Reading DNA (figs. 15.6, 15.7, 16.5)
16. Gene Regulation (figs. 16.5, 16.6, 16.11, 17.1, 17.2, 17.5)
17. Making a Restriction Map (p. 205, figs. 18.3, 18.4, 18.9)

PREFACE

Biology is an introductory college text that covers the concepts and principles of biology from the structure and function of the cell to the organization of the biosphere. It draws upon the entire world of living things to bring out an evolutionary theme that is introduced from the start. The writing style and clarity of the text make it appropriate for use by the liberal arts student but it is also comprehensive enough for the science major.

Biology demonstrates and in addition has the reader participate in the scientific process. Not only are notable contributors mentioned, significant experiments in the history of science are fully explained. Chapter 2, which discusses the scientific method, also illustrates this method by walking students through experiments in the current literature. As before, each part ends with a case study which encourages students to use scientific methodology in order to think critically. New to this edition are the Research Reports written by contemporary biologists who tell us how they go about doing their research and how their findings can be applied to human beings.

TEXT AND ILLUSTRATION COORDINATION

In this edition, you will find that all major topics begin at the top of a page and that each illustration is on the same or facing page with its text. Just glancing through the text verifies that the illustrations are on the same two page layout as their reference. This was achieved because the author was involved in deciding the layout of the book from the writing of the very first word! Coordination of text and illustration goes beyond simple placement, however. It also means making sure that the text and illustration together teach the concept under discussion. Contributors have helped improve the text and an excellent team of artists have assisted in creating the very best illustrations.

CHAPTERS NEW TO THIS EDITION

Evolution, which is the topic of Part III, includes two new chapters. The "Origin and History of Life" gives an overview of major evolutionary events since life evolved. "Human Evolution" is a chapter that includes the very latest information about recent discoveries.

Classification of plants and animals has been greatly influenced by cladistics, the most widely accepted school of systematics today. The various schools of systematics, including cladistics, are reviewed in the first of the diversity chapters. The diversity chapters received special attention and there is now a separate chapter for each of the kingdoms. New illustrations appear on nearly every page.

The part devoted to botany was expanded for this edition and recent research, especially concerning growth and development, is emphasized. These chapters have been carefully addressed. A new reading is devoted to the use of plants by human beings.

READINGS FOR THIS EDITION

The readings for this edition have been organized into several different types. We have already mentioned the "Research Reports," in which research biologists invite us to share in the excitement of their current findings. The "Of Human Interest" readings show how biology is applicable to the concerns of human beings. "A Closer Look" expands in an interesting way on the core information presented in the text. Some of these are about the research done by well-known biologists. Many chapters end with a section called "Biological Relationships" because students need to see how the various biological concepts are interrelated.

CLARITY IN WRITING AND NEW PEDAGOGY

Biology is as up to date as it possibly can be but is still retains its clarity and readability. The goal, as always, is to explain each concept without the use of jargon and in a way that is understandable to the beginning student.

Although the pedagogy in *Biology* has been praised by many, we have been able to make improvements. The micrographs are accompanied by a magnification bar that allows one to better judge the size of an organism. The use of these bars is explained in a reading entitled "The Microscopic Scale" found in chapter 5. Greek and Latin derivatives now accompany many boldfaced terms in order to give students a basis for learning and understanding scientific terminology. These are also included in the end-of-chapter glossary, which in this edition includes a full definition for each key term listed.

Even more significant, perhaps, are the new part introductions that review the central concepts of that part and how they relate to biology in general. At the start of each chapter, the chapter outline and learning objectives have been integrated so that learning objectives are listed under, and page referenced to, the major topics within that chapter. Students will appreciate that the heads for each chapter have been rewritten in an interesting way that highlights the significance of the material that follows. We continued to include the useful in-chapter summary statements that provide a synopsis of these same topics.

ORGANIZATION OF THE TEXT

The text has the following parts, which have been revised as discussed.

Introduction

An essay written by J. William Schopf, University of California—Los Angeles, which introduces the introductory chapter, shows how the unity and diversity of life is rooted in the evolutionary process. The chapter itself discusses the characteristics of life and at the same time introduces biological concepts that serve as an overview for the rest of the book.

Chapter 2, as mentioned, explains the scientific method and gives examples of both experimental and observational biological research.

Part I: The Cell

Cell structure and function and energy metabolism are presented in this part. Human applications are stressed throughout; for example, there is a reading about the new nutrition labels in the organic chemistry chapter. Cellular metabolism has been simplified, and there are many new illustrations to clarify cellular processes.

Part II: Genetic Basis of Life

This part is given a strong historical approach but practical aspects are not neglected. Students are given an opportunity to test their ability to do problems as they proceed. The cell cycle, human genetics, cancer coverage, and biotechnology have all been updated.

Part III: Evolution

This new part presents evolutionary tenets and serves as a springboard for the diversity chapters that follow. New chapters are provided on the process of evolution, the history of life, and human evolution. Many new findings have been included.

Part IV: Diversity of Life

The diversity chapters have been placed in a new part which begins with a chapter on systematics and classification of organisms. Special care was taken to introduce and explain the cladistic school of systematics. Each kingdom is assigned its own chapter which has been written anew. Almost every illustration in this part has been reworked and redrawn.

Part V: Plant Structure and Function

Four chapters are devoted to flowering plant anatomy and physiology. The first chapter provides a foundation for the others that discuss nutrition and transport, growth and development, and reproduction. The chapters in this part were expanded, rewritten and updated. Many new and interesting topics, illustrating the vitality of this area of biology, have been added.

Part VI: Animal Structure and Function.

This part, which begins with a chapter on animal organization and homeostasis, contains separate chapters on the various animal systems. The comparative approach has been strengthened and as requested by adopters, there is additional material on the reproductive methods of various animals.

Part VII: Behavior and Ecology

A behavior chapter precedes those devoted to ecology because behavior pertains to the interactions of organisms within ecosystems. The behavior chapter was completely rewritten and it now has an experimental approach. The ecology chapters balance traditional ecology with environmental concerns. Some instructors may wish to begin the year's work with this part, which is certainly a workable alternative.

AIDS TO THE READER

Biology was written to provide students with the opportunity to enjoy, appreciate, and come to understand the concepts of biology and the scientific process. The following text features are especially designed to assist student learning.

Part Introduction and Technology Correlation Lists

An introduction for each part highlights the central ideas of that part and specifically tells the student how the topics within each part contribute to biological knowledge.

At the beginning of each part are listings from *Explorations in Human Biology* and *Explorations in Cell Biology, Metabolism, and Genetics*, and from the *Life Science Animations* videotapes. The CD-ROM modules and the animations have been carefully correlated to figures in the chapters.

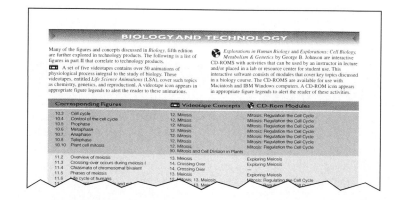

2 Learning Objectives

The Learning Objectives provide a framework for the content of each chapter. Note that the objectives are listed under the appropriate A-heads and are page referenced for student study.

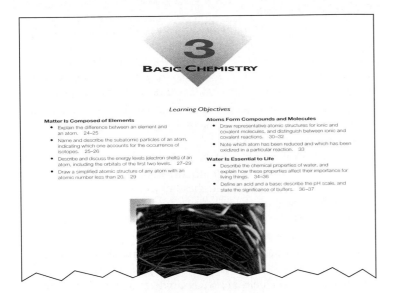

3 Internal Summary Statements

Internal summaries are highlighted and enlarged to illustrate the chapter's key concepts. These appear at the ends of major sections and help students focus their study efforts on the basics.

> The chemical properties of atoms differ because the number and the arrangement of their electrons are different.

4 Illustrations and Tables

The illustrations and tables in *Biology* have been designed to help students learn basic biological concepts as well as the specific content of the chapters, and are consistent with multicultural educational goals. Often it is easier to understand a given process by studying a drawing, especially when it is carefully coordinated with the text, as is the case here. New to this edition are integrative illustrations where both a photograph and a drawing are combined. Several new illustrations include information formerly found in tables.

5 Customization Option

The pages are double-numbered for full-color customization. An instructor can order a customized textbook to suit their course needs.

6 Figures Referenced On-page

Textual references and figures are found on the same page spread in the fifth edition. That means a student never has to turn the page to see the referenced figure.

7 Figures Correlated to Technology

Figures are correlated to the *Explorations* CD-ROMs and the *Life Science Animations* videotapes. Two icons, ▄▄ and ◉, are placed by figures that can be further enhanced with the multimedia products.

8 Boxed Features

Each chapter contains one or more readings. *Research Reports* are written by contemporary scientists and tell us about a particular aspect of their field of study. *Of Human Interest* highlights topics of special interest and ties biological principals to student concerns. *A Closer Look* expands on the core information presented in each chapter.

9 Chapter Summaries

The summary is a numbered list of statements that follow the organization of the chapter and helps students to identify the concepts and focus on important topics discussed in each chapter.

10 Chapter Questions

Three kinds of questions—study questions, objective questions, and critical thinking questions—appear at the close of each chapter. They allow students to test their ability to fulfill the study objectives. The study questions review the chapter, and their sequence follows that of the chapter. The critical thinking questions are based on biological concepts found in the chapter. They verify that knowledge of a biological concept allows one to reason about some particular aspect of biology. The objective questions allow students to test their ability to answer recall-based questions. The types of objective questions have been expanded in this edition to include questions that require the completing or labeling of diagrams. Answers to the objective questions and critical thinking questions appear in appendix D.

Writing across the curriculum recognizes that students need an opportunity to practice writing in all courses. When students write out the answers to the study questions, they are writing while studying biology. Writing out the answers to the critical thinking questions also fulfills writing across the curriculum requirements.

11 Selected Key Terms

Each chapter ends with a selected key term list. Key terms are boldfaced in the chapter, defined in context, and also appear in the end-of-text glossary. Especially significant key terms appear in the selected key term list. Each term is accompanied by its phonetic spelling, if needed, a definition, and in many cases, the Greek or Latin derivation.

12 Suggested Readings

The list of readings at the end of each part suggests references that can be used for further study of the topics covered in the chapters of that part. The references listed in this section were carefully chosen for readability and accessibility. New to this edition, references are followed by a short description and an indication of their level of rigor.

13 Critical Thinking Case Studies

Each part ends with a case study designed by Dr. Robert D. Allen, Victor Valley College, to help students think critically by participating in the process of science. At many institutions, instructors are encouraged to develop the writing skills of their students. In such cases, instructors could require students to write out their answers to the questions in each case study. Suggested answers for each of these questions appear in the Instructor's Manual.

14 Appendices and Glossary

The appendices contain optional information. Appendix A is an expanded table for classification of organisms; appendix B is an expanded table of chemical elements; appendix C is a new presentation of the metric system; and appendix D gives the answers to the objective questions and critical thinking questions found at the end of each chapter.

The glossary defines all the boldface terms in the text. These terms are the ones most necessary for the successful study of biology. Terms that are difficult to pronounce have a phonetic spelling.

ADDITIONAL AIDS

Instructor's Manual/Test Item File

The *Instructor's Manual,* revised by the author, is designed to assist instructors as they plan and prepare for classes using *Biology.* An expanded chapter outline which could be used as a lecture outline, is also available on disk. The outline includes the learning objectives and bold faced terms for each major section of the chapter. Lecture enrichment ideas are given and there is a listing of the transparencies and micrograph slides available for lecture hall use. A listing of videotape and CD-ROM ancillaries available from the publisher is followed by a listing of other audiovisual and computer software.

Suggested answers for the critical thinking case studies that appear at the end of each part in the text are placed at the end of the corresponding parts in the *Instructor's Manual.*

The Test Item File was revised by Dr. John Richard Schrock, Emporia State University, and now also includes higher level objective questions. The test item file questions are sequenced according to the learning objectives, and include objective, true/false, and critical thinking essay questions. Microtest III, a computerized test bank of the test items, is available in Dos, Windows, and Macintosh formats.

Study Guide

To ensure close coordination with the text, the author has written the *Study Guide* that accompanies the text. Each text chapter has a corresponding *Study Guide* chapter that includes a listing of learning objectives, study questions, puzzles and games, and a chapter test. Answers to the study questions and the chapter test are provided to give students immediate feedback. New to this edition is the KeyWord Crossword puzzle, an intriguing, new way to study glossary terms.

The learning objectives in the *Study Guide* are the same as those in the *Instructor's Manual*, and the study questions in the *Study Guide* are sequenced to these objectives. Instructors who make their choice of learning objectives known to the students can thereby direct student learning in an efficient manner. Instructors and students who make use of the *Study Guide* should find that student performance increases dramatically.

Microguide, a computerized study guide, is also available for students. This electronic study guide features chapter objectives, quiz questions, chapter summaries, and selected key terms. The questions are page referenced to the text.

Laboratory Manual

The author has also written the *Laboratory Manual to accompany Biology.* Most chapters in the text have an accompanying laboratory exercise in the manual (some chapters have more than one accompanying exercise). In this way, instructors are better able to emphasize particular portions of the curriculum. Every laboratory has been rewritten to further help students appreciate the scientific method and to learn the fundamental concepts of biology and the specific content of each chapter.

Customized Laboratory Manual-Full Color

All thirty-five exercises are now available as individual "lab separates" in full color, so instructors can order a customized manual to suit their particular course needs.

Laboratory Resource Guide

More extensive information regarding preparation is found in the *Laboratory Resource Guide.* The guide includes suggested sources for materials and supplies, directions for making up solutions and otherwise setting up the laboratory, expected results for the exercises, and suggested answers to all questions in the laboratory manual. It is available for free to all adopters of the laboratory manual.

Student Study Art Notebook

A full-color, lecture-time notepad containing all transparency images with space for notes, so students can spend more time paying attention and less time scrambling to sketch images. Packaged free with each new text.

Electronic Image Bank

Nearly all text illustrations will be available on CD-ROM with a presentation software that allows the user to manipulate the images and the labels.

Micrograph Slides

A boxed set of 100 slides of photo micrographs and electron-micrographs is available to adopters.

Transparencies

A set of 300 transparency acetates features key illustrations from the text in two- and full-color and now have upsized labels. A boxed set of slides containing the transparency images is also available.

Art Masters

A set of 250 art masters consisting of one-color line art with labels can be used for additional transparencies or can be copied and used for student hand-outs.

NEW TECHNOLOGY

Several new state-of-the-art technology products are available that are correlated to this textbook. These useful and enticing supplements can assist you in teaching and can improve student learning.

Explorations in Human Biology and Explorations in Cell Biology, Genetics, Metabolism, and CD-ROMs

Each of these interactive CDs by Dr. George B. Johnson comprise sixteen modules, featuring fascinating topics in biology. These interactive investigations are correlated to appropriate topical material in *Biology*. The multimedia figures are identified with a CD-ROM icon (🔅). Each text part opens with a list of *Explorations* topics correlated to those chapters.

Life Science Animations Videotapes

Fifty-three animations of key physiological processes are available on videotapes. The animations, correlated to this text by a videotape icon, bring visual movement to biological processes that are difficult to understand on the text page. The figures correlated to these videotapes are identified with a videotape icon (📼).

Life Science Living Lexicon CD-ROM

This new interactive CD-ROM, by Will Marchuk of Red Deer College, offers students a glossary of over 1,200 key science terms and definitions; word construction through the use of prefixes, root words, and suffixes; descriptions of eponyms; more than 1,000 full-color images for selected terms; and over 200 questions for student quizzing.

Other Technology Products that are Excellent Complements to *Biology*

BioSource videodisc, by Wm. C. Brown and Sandpiper Multimedia, Inc., features twenty minutes of moving animations and nearly ten thousand full-color illustrations and photos, many from leading WCB biology textbooks.

Biology StartUp, a five-disk set of Macintosh tutorials by Myles C. Robinson and Kathleen Hakola Pace, Grays Harbor College, is designed to help nonmajor students master challenging biological processes like chemistry and cell biology. This set can be a valuable addition to a resource center and is especially helpful to students enrolled in developmental education courses or those who need additional assistance to succeed in an introductory biology course.

OTHER TITLES OF RELATED INTEREST FROM WM. C. BROWN PUBLISHERS

You Can Make a Difference
Judith Getis

This short, inexpensive supplement offers students practical guidelines for recycling, conserving energy, disposing of hazardous wastes, and other pollution controls. It can be shrink-wrapped with the text at minimal additional cost. (ISBN 0–697–13923–9)

How to Study Science
Fred Drewes, Suffolk County Community College

This useful workbook offers students helpful suggestions for meeting the challenges of a college science course. It offers tips on how to take notes, how to get the most out of laboratories, and how to overcome science anxiety. The book's unique design helps students develop critical thinking skills while facilitating careful note taking. (ISBN 0–697–14474–7)

The Life Science Lexicon
William N. Marchuk, Red Deer College

This portable, inexpensive reference helps introductory-level students quickly master the vocabulary of the life sciences. Not only a dictionary, it carefully explains the rules of word construction and derivation, in addition to giving complete definitions of all important terms. (ISBN 0–697–12133–X)

Biology Study Cards
Kent Van De Graaff, R. Ward Rhees, and Christopher H. Creek, Brigham Young University

This boxed set of 300 two-sided study cards provides a quick yet thorough visual synopsis of all key biological terms and concepts in the general biology curriculum. Each card features a masterful illustration, pronunciation guide, definition, and description in context. (ISBN 0–697–03069–5)

The Gundy-Weber Knowledge Map of the Human Body

G. Craig Gundy, Weber State University

The 13-disk Mac-Hypercard program is for use by instructors and students alike. It features carefully prepared computer graphics, animations, labeling exercises, self-tests, and practice questions to help students examine the systems of the human body. Contact your local Wm. C. Brown representative or call 1–800–351–7671.

The Knowledge Map Diagrams

1. Introduction, Tissues, Integument System (ISBN 0–697–13255–2)
2. Viruses, Bacteria, Eukaryotic Cells (ISBN 0–697–13257–9)
3. Skeletal System (ISBN 0–697–13258–7)
4. Muscle System (ISBN 0–697–13259–5)
5. Nervous System (ISBN 0–697–13260–9)
6. Special Senses (ISBN 0–697–13261–7)
7. Endocrine System (ISBN 0–697–13262–5)
8. Blood and the Lymphatic System (ISBN 0–697–13263–3)
9. Cardiovascular System (ISBN 0–697–13264–1)
10. Respiratory System (ISBN 0–697–13265–X)
11. Digestive System (ISBN 0–697–13266–8)
12. Urinary System (ISBN 0–697–13267–6)
13. Reproductive System (ISBN 0–697–13268–4)

Demo—(ISBN 0–697–13256–0)
Complete Package—(ISBN 0–697–13269–2)

Critical Thinking Case Study Workbook

Written by Robert Allen, this ancillary includes 34 additional critical thinking case studies of the type found in the text. Like the text case studies, they are designed to immerse students in the "process of science" and challenge them to solve problems in the same way biologists do. The case studies here are divided into 3 levels of difficulty (introductory, intermediate, and advanced) to afford instructors greater choice and flexibility. An answer key accompanies this workbook.

ACKNOWLEDGMENTS

Many persons have helped me make this edition our best yet. My editor, Carol Mills, directed the efforts of all. Connie Haakinson, my developmental editor, served as a liaison between the editor, me, and many other people. She met each new challenge in a prompt and most professional way.

The production team at Wm. C. Brown Publishers worked diligently toward the success of this edition: Carla Kipper, the production editor; Kathleen Timp, the art editor; Lori Hancock, the photo researcher; and Chris Reese, the designer. My thanks to each of them for a job well done!

The Contributors

I wish to express my deep appreciation to the contributors. They critically reviewed my revised chapters, and told me how they could be improved. With their expertise, it was easier to make certain the content was complete, accurate, and up to date. The contributors were:

Part I: The Cell
  Roger Leslie, University of California, Davis
Part II: Genetic Basis of Life
  Robert H. Tamarin, Boston University
Part III: Evolution
  Emily Giffin, Wellesley College
Part V: Plant Structure and Function
  Donald Briskin and Margaret Gawienowski, University of Illinois at Urbana-Champaign
Part VII: Behavior and Ecology
  John Alcock, Arizona State University (Animal Behavior)
  George Cox, San Diego State University (Ecology chapters)

The Research Reports

I would also like to gratefully acknowledge and thank the scientists who wrote about their research and shared their fascinating studies of biology.

Life After Photosynthesis
  W. Dennis Clark
  Arizona State University

Reflections of a Cancer Researcher
  Thomas Gilmore
  Boston University

Origin and Adaptive Radiation of the Hawaiian Silversword Alliance
  Gerald D. Carr
  University of Hawaii at Manoa

Origin of the Genus Homo
  Steven Stanley
  The Johns Hopkins University

Spider Webs and Spider Classification
  William A. Shear
  Hampden-Sydney College

Competition for Resources and Biodiversity
  G. David Tilman
  University of Minnesota

Husband and Wife Team Explores Signal Transduction in Plants
  Donald Briskin and Margaret Gawienowski
  University of Illinois at Urbana-Champaign

Ion Channels and Vision
  Anita Zimmerman
  Brown University

Microscopes, Yeasts, and Membrane Synthesis
  Robin Wright
  University of Washington

The PCB Menace
  Ric Garcia
  Clemson University

Behavior in a Unicellular Alga
  Susan K. Dutcher
  University of Colorado, Boulder

Reviewers

I want to especially thank James Averett, Nassau Community College, who read every page of the fifth edition and had many helpful suggestions. Many other instructors of introductory biology courses around the country reviewed portions of the manuscript. Others assisted by taking the time to fill out survey forms that helped us make important decisions about content. With many thanks, we list their names here.

First Edition

A. Lester Allen   *Brigham Young University*
William E. Barstow   *University of Georgia*
Lester Bazinet   *Community College of Philadelphia*
Eugene C. Bovee   *University of Kansas*
Larry C. Brown   *Virginia State University*
L. Herbert Bruneau   *Oklahoma State University*
Carol B. Crafts   *Providence College*
John D. Cunningham   *Keene State College*
Dean G. Dillery   *Albion College*
H. W. Elmore   *Marshall University*
David J. Fox   *University of Tennessee*
Larry N. Gleason   *Western Kentucky University*
E. Bruce Holmes   *Western Illinois University*
Genevieve D. Johnson   *University of Iowa*
Malcolm Jollie   *Northern Illinois University*
Karen A. Koos   *Rio Honda College*
William H. Leonard   *University of Nebraska—Lincoln*
A. David Scarfe   *Texas A & M University*
Carl A. Scheel   *Central Michigan University*
Donald R. Scoby   *North Dakota State University*
John L. Zimmerman   *Kansas State University*

Second Edition

David Ashley   *Missouri Western State College*
Jack Bennett   *Northern Illinois University*
Oscar Carlson   *University of Wisconsin-Stout*
Arthur Cohen   *Massachusetts Bay Community College*
Rebecca McBride DeLiddo   *Suffolk University*
Gary Donnermeyer   *St. John's University (Minnesota)*
D. C. Freeman   *Wayne State University*
Sally Frost   *University of Kansas*
Maura Gage   *Palomar College*
Betsy Gulotta   *Nassau Community College*
W. M. Hess   *Brigham Young University*
Richard J. Hoffmann   *Iowa State University*
Trudy McKee
Brian Myres   *Cypress College*
John M. Pleasants   *Iowa State University*
Jay Templin   *Widener University*

Third Edition

Wayne P. Armstrong   *Palomar College*
Mark S. Bergland   *University of Wisconsin-River Falls*
Richard Blazier   *Parkland College*
William F. Burke   *University of Hawaii*
Donald L. Collins   *Orange Coast College*
Ellen C. Cover   *Manatee Community College*

John W. Crane   *Washington State University*
Calvin A. Davenport   *California State University-Fullerton*
Robert Ebert   *Palomar College*
Darrell R. Falk   *Pt. Loma Nazarene College*
Jerran T. Flinders   *Brigham Young College*
Sally Frost   *University of Kansas*
Elizabeth Gulotta   *Nassau Community College*
Madeline M. Hall   *Cleveland State University*
James G. Harris   *Utah Valley Community College*
Kenneth S. Kilborn   *Shasta College*
Donald R. Kirk   *Shasta College*
Jon R. Maki   *Eastern Kentucky University*
Ric Matthews   *Miramar College*
Joyce B. Maxwell   *California State University-Northridge*
Leroy McClenaghan   *San Diego State University*
Leroy E. Olson   *Southwestern College*
Barbara Yohai Pleasants   *Iowa State University*
David M. Prescott   *University of Colorado*
Robert E. Rinehart   *San Diego State University*
Mary Beth Saffo   *University of California—Santa Cruz*
Walter H. Sakai   *Santa Monica College*
Frederick W. Spiegel   *University of Arkansas-Fayetteville*
Gerald Summers   *University of Missouri-Columbia*
Marshall Sundberg   *Louisiana St. University*
Kathy S. Thompson   *Louisiana State University*
Anna J. Wilson   *Oklahoma City Community College*
Timothy S. Wood   *Wright State University*

Fourth Edition

W. Sylvester Allred   *Northern Arizona University*
Michael S. Gaines   *University of Kansas*
Helen L. Grierson   *Morehead State University*
Kerry S. Kilburn   *West Virginia State College*
Gail Kingrey   *Pueblo Community College*
Deborah K. Meinke   *Oklahoma State University*
Eugene Nester   *University of Washington*
Barbara Yohai Pleasants   *Iowa State University*
Robert Snetsinger   *Queens University*

Survey Respondents

Sister Julia Van Demack   *Silver Lake College*
Ken Beatty   *College of the Siskiyous*
John W. Metcalfe   *Potsdam College at the State University of New York*
Brenda K. Johnson   *Western Michigan University*
Tom Dale   *Kirtland Community College*
Marlene Kayne   *Trenton State College*
Peter M. Grant   *Southwestern Oklahoma State University*
Janet Carter   *Delaware Technical & Community College*
Frank F. Escobar   *Holyoke Community College*
John A. Chisler   *Glenville State College*
Nancy Goodyear   *Bainbridge College*
John F. Lyon   *University of Lowell*
Rob Snetsinger   *Queens University*
Fred Stevens   *Schreiner College*
Paula H. Dedmon   *Gaston College*

Bruce G. Stewart   *Murray State College*
Leo R. Finkenbinder   *Southern Nazarene University*
Mary P. Greer   *Macomb Community College*
Kenneth M. Allen   *Schoolcraft College*
Robert Cerwonica   *SUNY-Potsdam*
Darcy Williams   *Cecil Community College*
Dave McShaffrey   *Marietta College*
Elizabeth L. Nebel   *Macomb Community College*
Jal S. Parakh   *Western Washington University*
Dwight Kamback   *Northampton Community College*
David L. Haas   *Fayetteville State University*
A. Quinton White   *Jacksonville University*
Paul J. Hummer, Jr.   *Hood College*
Dee Forrest   *Western Wyoming College*
Linden C. Haynes   *Hinds Community College*
John De Banzie   *Northeastern State University*
Anne T. Packard   *Plymouth St. College*
L. H. Buff, Jr.   *Spartanburg Methodist College*
Dennis Vrba   *North Iowa Area Community College*
Donald L. Collins   *Orange Coast College*
Larrie E. Stone   *Dana College*
Brian K. Mitchell   *Longview College*
Dennis M. Forsythe   *The Citadel*
Bonnie S. Wood   *University of Maine at Presque Isle*
Eunice R. Knouso   *Spartanburg Medical College*
Larry C. Brown   *Virginia State University*
Clyde M. Senger   *Western Washington University*
James V. Makowski   *Messiah College*
James R. Coggins   *University of Wisconsin-Milwaukee*
Roland Vieira   *Green River Community College*
Donna Barleen   *Bethany College*
S. M. Cabrini Angelli   *Regis College*
W. Brooke Yeager, III   *Penn State-Wilkes-Barre*
Diana M. Colon   *Northwest Technical College*
Carolyn K. Jones   *Vincennes University*
Rita M. O'Clair   *University of Alaska Southeast*
Fred M. Busroe   *Morehead State University*
Edward R. Garrison   *Navajo Community College*
Joseph V. Faryniarz   *Maitatuck Community College*
K. Dale Smoak   *Piedmont Technical College*
Donald A. Wheeler   *Edinboro University of Pennsylvania*
W. Lee Williams   *Alamance Community College*
Eugene A. Oshima   *Central Missouri State University*

Richard C. Renner   *Laredo Junior College*
Peggy Rae Doris   *Henderson State University*
Charles H. Owens   *Virginia Highlands Community College*
Jeanette Oliver   *Flathead Valley Community College*
E. L. Beard   *Loyola University*
Monica Macklin   *Northeastern State University*

Fifth Edition

W. Sylvester Allred   *Northern Arizona University*
Dennis Anderson   *Oklahoma City Community College*
Rodney P. Anderson   *Ohio Northern University*
James Averett   *Nassau Community College*
Iona Baldridge   *Lubbock Christian University*
Reuben Barrett   *Prairie State College*
Steven Bassett   *Southeast Community College*
William J. Brett   *Indiana State University*
Carl D. Frailey   *Johnson City Community College*
Wayne Frair   *The King's College*
Harvey P. Friedman   *University of Missouri-St. Louis*
Clarence Fouche   *Virginia Intermont College*
David Fulford   *Edinboro University of Pennsylvania*
Peter M. Grant   *Southwestern Oklahoma State University*
John P. Harley   *Eastern Kentucky University*
George L. Harp   *Arkansas State University*
Wahid Hasan   *Bergen Community College*
Charles N. Horn   *Newberry College*
Harold N. Horn   *Lincoln Land Community College*
Andrew H. Lapinski   *Reading Area Community College*
Allan Larson   *Washington University*
James C. Lin   *Northwestern State University of Louisiana*
Gregory J. McConnell   *Emory Henry College*
Chuck Paulson   *Lake Forest College*
Tim Ruhnke   *East Stroudsburg University*
J. John Sepkoski, Jr.   *University of Chicago*
Florence Slater   *Glendale Community College*
Paul Keith Small   *Eureka College*
Kingsley R. Stern   *California State University*
Kathy Talaro   *Pasadena City College*
William A. Thomas   *Colby-Sawyer College*
Ann Vernon   *St. Charles County Community College*
Alan Walker   *Pennsylvania State University*
Tina Walls   *Howard Community College*
Joanne Westin   *Case Western Reserve*

1

A VIEW OF LIFE

Learning Objectives

How to Define Life
- List and explain the characteristics of life.   3–5
- Relate the concept of emergent properties to the increasingly complex levels of biological organization.   3

Life Has Unity and Diversity
- Use the theory of evolution to explain the unity and diversity of life.   6

Ecosystems Contain Populations
- Describe the organization of an ecosystem in terms of chemical cycling and a flow of energy.   6
- Discuss the characteristics of life that contribute to the organization of an ecosystem.   6–9

How Living Things Are Classified
- Describe classification categories and list (with examples) the kingdoms recognized by this text.   10

All living things on planet earth share the same characteristics of life.

EVOLUTION
THE GUT OF BIOLOGY

J. William Schopf
Director, UCLA Center for the Study of Evolution and the Origin of Life

Living Things Are Simple

From bacteria to bats, toadstools to trees, whippoorwills to whales—the diversity of the living world boggles the mind! Yet living things are not nearly as complicated as you might think. All are basically alike. All are made of cells. All have genes. And all are made up almost entirely of the same four chemical elements—carbon, hydrogen, oxygen, and nitrogen—known as "CHON,"—the elements of life. Why CHON? Why not a more exotic mixture, such as europium, gold, krypton, and thulium? The answer is simple. Life is composed of CHON because these elements were abundant when life first began. CHON is the stuff of which stars and galaxies are made—four little elements that are among the five most abundant in the entire universe. Moreover, all are able to combine with one another to form small, sturdy molecules (carbon dioxide, CO_2; water, H_2O; methane, CH_4; ammonia, NH_3; and many others). Some can even pair with atoms of their same type to make up common gases like oxygen, O_2, and nitrogen, N_2. Because all of these simple compounds dissolve in water, all can play an active role in the chemistry of life.

The Ecosystem Is Simple

Thus, we and everything else alive are made of the same simple "starstuff." But don't things get terribly complicated when we examine how living things interact to form the ecosystem of the living world? Not at all. In fact, though there are nearly 2 million living species known to science (and perhaps three to five times that many as yet undiscovered), all live by exactly the same rules. To stay alive, all of these different organisms need to satisfy just two basic necessities. Because all are made of CHON, all need a source of these building blocks of life. And in order to make use of CHON, all need a source of energy. Moreover, for all life, from microbes to man, there are just two strategies to meet these needs: the animal-like strategy of feeding on others (known as *heterotrophy*), and the self-feeding strategy of plants, algae, and plantlike microbes (*autotrophy*). The ecosystem of the entire world is just that simple. There are only two necessities—CHON and energy. And there are only two strategies—heterotrophy and autotrophy. This earth of ours is a planet of the eaters and the eatees!

Although you would not expect it, birds and humans share many characteristics in common. Descent from a common ancestor explains how this came about.

Why Is a Bird Like a Human?

Why is biology this thrifty? Once again, the answer is simple—evolution! Evolution is the *GUT* of biology, the *GRAND UNIFYING THEORY* that links all of life. All organisms, over all of time, are united by a common bond. Just as you are descended from your parents, grandparents, and so forth, going back for many generations, *all* forms of life that have ever lived are tied together by an unbroken evolutionary thread that can be traced back through geologic time to the infancy of our planet.

This linkage of all of life, surmised even by the ancient Greeks, can be seen by comparing the bone structure of a bird and a human. Why should a bird be like a human? After all, birds fly. Rather than having coarse, brittle bones like ours, maybe they would be better served by some strong, lightweight alloy such as titanium. And why do birds have ribs, knees, backbones, and eyeballs in the front of their heads? Are all those necessary for flight? Some, perhaps, but most, probably not. The answer is evolution. Today's life is a product of an unimaginably long evolutionary history, the result of life's development over hundreds and thousands of millions of years. Birds, just like us mammals, are descended from reptiles (lizards, dinosaurs, and the like). Reptiles evolved from amphibians (frogs and salamanders), and amphibians are descendants of fish. As it happened, early evolving fish, more than half a billion years ago, had bones made of bone-stuff (technically, hydroxyapatite). Titanium bones for birds (or even for us) might be great, but because of evolutionary ties to earth's earliest living things, it was hydroxyapatite bones or no bones at all. And so it was also for CHON, cells, genes, and even the structure of the world's ecosystem. Our modern world is just a scaled-up version of a microbial menagerie that originated literally billions of years ago!

Because evolution is the *GUT* of biology, the familiar biologic present is firmly rooted in the remote biologic past. But amazingly, recent advances in the life sciences have placed the biologic future in human hands. What evolution accomplished over hundreds of millions—even billions—of years, can now be manipulated and modified in laboratory test tubes within months or even weeks! Heady stuff. We are in the driver's seat, but which of many roads will we take? The future of life on planet earth is in our hands.

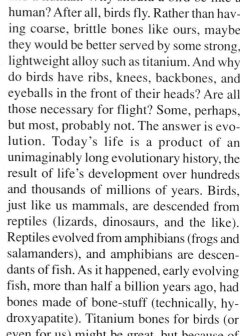

Through evolutionary descent all living things have the same fundamental characteristics. And these characteristics, which are often used to define life, also review the unifying concepts of biology, a science that seeks to understand what life is and how it functions. Therefore, it is appropriate to begin by examining the characteristics of life.

HOW TO DEFINE LIFE

Living things are organized, take materials and energy from the environment, respond to stimuli; reproduce and develop; and adapt to the environment.

Living Things Are Organized

The complex organization of living things begins with the cell, the basic unit of life. Cells are made up of molecules that contain atoms, which are the smallest units of matter that can enter into chemical combination. In multicellular organisms, similar cells combine to form a tissue—nerve cells form nerve tissue, for example. Tissues make up organs, as when various tissues combine to form the brain. Organs, in turn, work together in systems; for example, the brain works with the spinal cord and a network of nerves to form the nervous system. A multicellular individual has many organ systems.

There are levels of biological organization that extend beyond the individual organism. All organisms of one type in a particular area belong to a **population.** In a temperate deciduous forest, there is a population of gray squirrels and a population of oak trees. The populations of various animals and plants in the forest make up a community (fig. 1.1). The populations interact among themselves and with the physical environment (soil, atmosphere, etc.) forming an **ecosystem** [Gk. *eco,* house, and *sys,* together].

Summing the Parts

In the living world, the whole is more than the sum of its parts. Each new level of biological organization has emergent properties that are due to interactions between the parts making up the whole. For example, when cells are broken down into bits of membrane and oozing liquids, these parts themselves cannot carry out the business of living. Slice a frog and arrange the slices, and the frog cannot flick out its tongue and catch flies.

> Living things have levels of organization from cells to ecosystems. Each level of organization has emergent properties that cannot be accounted for by a sum of the parts.

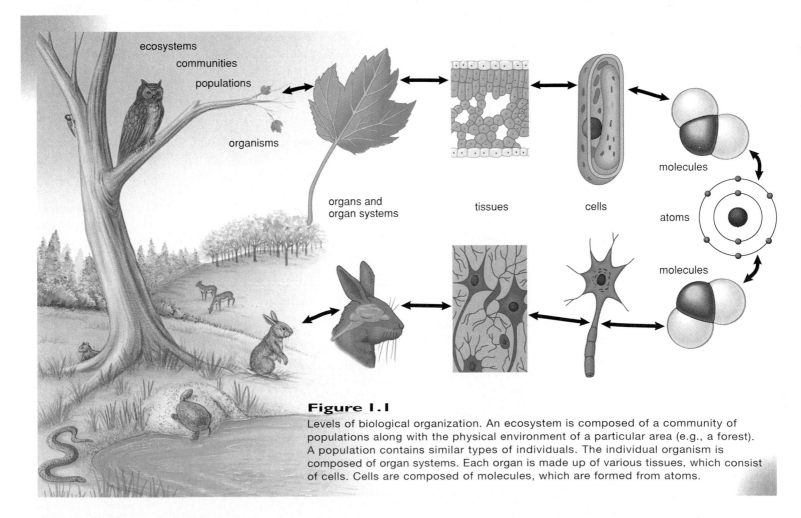

Figure 1.1

Levels of biological organization. An ecosystem is composed of a community of populations along with the physical environment of a particular area (e.g., a forest). A population contains similar types of individuals. The individual organism is composed of organ systems. Each organ is made up of various tissues, which consist of cells. Cells are composed of molecules, which are formed from atoms.

a.

b.

Acquire Materials and Energy

Living things cannot maintain their organization or carry on life's activities without an outside source of materials and energy (fig. 1.2). Food provides nutrient molecules, which are used as building blocks or for energy. **Energy** is the capacity to do work, and it takes work to maintain the organization of the cell and the organism. When nutrient molecules are used to make their parts and products, cells carry out a sequence of synthetic chemical reactions. **Metabolism** [Gk. *metab,* change] is all the chemical reactions that occur in a cell.

The ultimate source of energy for all life on earth is the sun. Plants and plantlike organisms are able to capture solar energy and carry on **photosynthesis,** a process that lets them store solar energy by converting carbon dioxide and water into energy-rich sugars. Animals get energy by eating plants or other animals.

> An intake of materials and energy is needed if an organism's organization is to be maintained. The ultimate source of energy for life on earth is the sun.

Remaining Homeostatic

For metabolic processes to continue, living things need to keep themselves stable in temperature, moisture level, acidity, and other physiological factors. This is **homeostasis** [Gk. *homeo,* like, and *stasis,* standing]—the maintenance of internal conditions within certain boundaries.

Many organisms depend on behavior to regulate their internal environment. A chilly lizard may raise its internal temperature by basking in the sun on a hot rock. When it starts to overheat, it scurries for cool shade. Other organisms have control mechanisms that do not require any conscious activity. When a student is so engrossed in her textbook that she forgets to eat lunch, her liver releases stored sugar to keep the blood sugar level within normal limits. Hormones regulate sugar storage and release, but in other instances the nervous system is involved in maintaining homeostasis.

Living Things Respond

Living things find energy and nutrients by interacting with their surroundings. Even unicellular organisms can respond to their environment. In some, the beating of microscopic hairs, and in others, the snapping of whiplike tails, moves them toward or away from light or chemicals. Multicellular organisms can manage more complex responses. A vulture can smell meat a mile away and soar toward dinner. A monarch butterfly can sense the approach of fall and begin its flight south where resources are still abundant.

The ability to respond often results in movement: the leaves of a plant turn toward the sun and animals dart toward safety. The ability to respond helps ensure survival of the organism and allows it to carry on its daily activities. All together, we call these activities the behavior of the organism.

Figure 1.3

Adaptations of rockhopper penguins, *Eudyptes*. **a.** Male and female rockhoppers courting on the rocks of their breeding ground. Their stubby forelimbs are modified as flippers for fast swimming. Only a little over a half meter tall, these penguins are named for their skill in leaping from rock to rock. **b.** Rockhoppers greet each other by braying: the sound has been likened to the screech of a rusty wheelbarrow.

a.

Living Things Reproduce and Develop

Life comes only from life. Every type of living thing can **reproduce,** or make a copy like itself (fig. 1.3). Bacteria, protozoa, and other unicellular organisms simply split in two. In most multicellular organisms, the reproductive process begins with the pairing of a sperm from one partner and an egg from the other partner. The union of sperm and egg cells results in an immature individual, which grows and develops through various stages to become the adult.

Embryos develop into a sperm whale or a yellow daffodil because of a blueprint inherited from their parents. The instructions for their organization and metabolism are encoded in the genes. The **genes,** which contain specific information for how the organism is to be ordered, are made of long molecules of DNA (deoxyribonucleic acid). All cells have a copy of the hereditary material, DNA, whose shape resembles a spiral staircase with thousands of steps.

Living Things Have Adaptations

Adaptations [L. *ad,* toward, and *apt,* adjust] are modifications that make an organism suited to its way of life. For example, penguins are adapted to an aquatic existence in the Antarctic (fig. 1.3). Most birds have forelimbs proportioned for flying, but a penguin has stubby, flattened wings suitable for swimming. Their feet and tails serve as rudders in the water, but the flat feet also allow them to walk on land. Rockhopper penguins have a bill adapted to eating small shellfish. Their eggs—one, or at most two—are carried on their feet, where they are protected by a pouch of skin. This allows the birds to huddle together for warmth while standing erect and incubating eggs.

The process by which organisms can become modified over time is called *natural selection.* Certain members of a **species** [L. *speci,* a kind], defined as a group of interbreeding individuals, may inherit a genetic change that causes them to be better suited to a particular environment. These members can be expected to produce more surviving offspring who also have the favorable characteristic. In this way, the attributes of the species' members change over time.

LIFE HAS UNITY AND DIVERSITY

All living things share the same basic characteristics discussed in this chapter. They are all composed of cells organized in a similar manner. Their genes are composed of DNA, and they carry out the same metabolic reactions to acquire energy and maintain their organization. This unity suggests that all living things are descended from a common ancestor—the first cell or cells. However, **evolution** [L. *evolut,* an unrolling] is descent with modification. One species can give rise to several species, each adapted to a particular set of environmental conditions. Specific adaptations allow species to play particular roles in an ecosystem. The diversity of organisms is best understood in terms of the many different ways in which organisms carry on their life functions within an ecosystem where they live, acquire energy, and reproduce.

> Descent from a common ancestor explains the unity of life. Adaptations to different ways of life account for the great diversity of life forms.

ECOSYSTEMS CONTAIN POPULATIONS

Adaptations include those features that allow populations to interact with themselves and with the physical environment within an ecosystem (fig. 1.4). All ecosystems taken together make up the **biosphere** [Gk. *bio,* life, and *spher,* ball], the network of life on earth. The interactions between populations in an ecosystem tend to keep the system relatively stable. Although a forest or pond changes—trees fall, ducks come and go, seeds sprout—each ecosystem remains recognizable year after year. We say it is in dynamic balance. In many cases, even the extinction of species (and their replacement by new species through evolution) still allows the dynamic balance of the system to be maintained.

If the ecosystem is big enough, it needs no raw materials from the outside. A big ecosystem just keeps cycling its raw materials, like water and nitrogen. The only input it needs is energy.

> Living things have various adaptations that help keep an ecosystem in dynamic balance and assure its continued existence.

Figure 1.4

Ecosystem organization. Within an ecosystem, chemicals cycle (see blue arrows): plants take in inorganic nutrients and produce organic food, which is used by themselves and various levels of animal consumers. When these organisms die and decay, inorganic nutrients are made available to plants once more. Energy flows (see yellow to red arrows): solar energy used by plants to produce organic food is eventually converted to heat by all members of an ecosystem (therefore a constant supply of solar energy is required for life to exist).

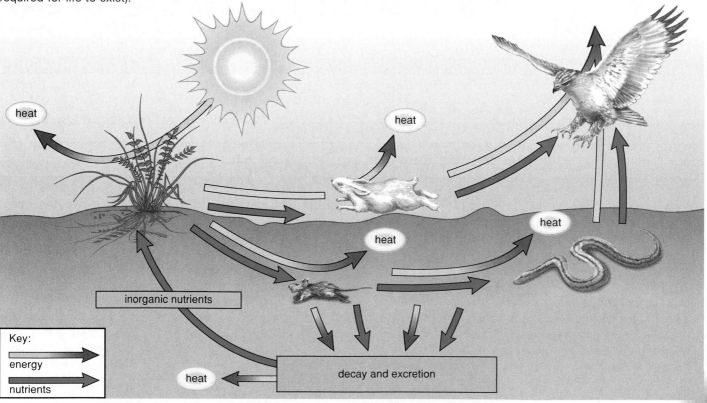

Key:
energy
nutrients

heat
heat
heat
heat
heat
inorganic nutrients
decay and excretion

What are those little icons in this book?

like this

This text is linked to great—and INEXPENSIVE—multimedia products. Where you see a little CD, the material is tied to the "Explorations" CD-ROM series.

Investigate biology as it *should* be explored—with movement. Color. And sound.

Explorations in Human Biology CD-ROM

George B. Johnson
Macintosh ISBN 0-697-22964-5
Windows ISBN 0-697-22963-7

Examine issues related to the human side of biology with this set of 16 interactive animations. Want to know how your habits will affect how long you'll live? Try Exploration 3, *"Life Span and Lifestyle."* **Interested in diet and weight loss?** See Exploration 7. These and other timely topics—like "AIDS," *"Smoking and Cancer,"* and *"Drug Addiction"*—are what you'll find.

Explore issues that affect you. Your friends. Your family.

With these *interactive animations* on CD-ROM, you set the variables and then evaluate how *you* affect the results.

Explorations in Cell Biology, Metabolism, and Genetics CD-ROM

George B. Johnson
Macintosh ISBN 0-697-29214-2
Windows ISBN 0-697-29215-0

These 17 interactive animations include subjects relevant to real-life people. Learn about **"DNA Fingerprinting: You Be the Judge"** in Exploration 14. You can investigate this and other topics with this CD-ROM. You'll find that you'll understand the subject matter even more in the process.

Delve into the world of cell structure and processes.

This cutting-edge software has a lot of *great features*—like clear topic information, colorful graphics and animated illustrations, a glossary with written and oral pronunciations, and narration in English and Spanish.

Are they affordable?

YES!

See for yourself.

For information or to order, contact your bookstore. Or call WCB toll-free:
800-338-5578.

WCB Wm. C. Brown Publishers

System requirements

IBM/PC or compatible

386 CPU or better
640 X 480 X 256 color
8 MB RAM
CD-ROM drive *(transfer rate of 300 KB recommended)*
mouse
DOS 5.0 or higher
Windows 3.1 or newer
Sound Blaster or compatible card optimal for audio

Macintosh

Macintosh LC III or greater
640 X 480 X 256 color
8 MB RAM
System 7.1 or newer
CD-ROM drive *(transfer rate of 300 KB recommended)*

Coral Reefs, a Marine Ecosystem

Coral reefs are found in clear, shallow tropical waters. Nowhere else in the sea is there such an abundance of living things (fig. 1.5). The reef consists of the skeletons of stony corals, colonial animals that form deposits of calcium carbonate. Only the outer layer of the reef is alive; the rest is an inert structure full of nooks and crannies, where fish can hide from their predators. Some types of fish venture out of hiding only at night, when they feed on plankton, the microscopic organisms that drift through the ocean. The coral animals themselves often feed at night also, taking in whatever comes within reach of their extended tentacles. Other fish are active during the day. These hover near the surface of the coral, grazing on algae and worms or on shrimp and crabs if their jaws, like those of lionfishes, are able to crunch through shells. Parrot fish even grind the stony coral skeletons themselves. All the smaller fishes are prey to large carnivores like groupers, moray eels, and barracudas.

Figure 1.5
Coral reef organization, featuring various animals.

red grouper, *Epinephelus*

coral, *Tubastrea*

lionfish, *Pterois*

moray eel, *Gymnothorax*

Palau coral reef

Tropical Rain Forests, a Terrestrial Ecosystem

Tropical rain forests are the most complex ecosystems in the world. They are found at low altitudes near the equator where there is plentiful sun and rainfall the entire year. Major rain forests are located in South America (fig. 1.6), central and west Africa, and Southeast Asia. Rain forests can be divided into several layers. In the top layer the highest trees rise above the canopy, which is a continuous layer of evergreen trees with broad leaves. If light penetrates through the canopy, there is an understory which con-

sists of shrubs and an undergrowth of ferns and herbs. Most animals live in the canopy where brightly colored birds, such as toucans and macaws, fly around eating fruit, buds, and pollen. Others birds, such as hummingbirds with long bills, feed from nectar often taken from the epiphytes that grow on the trees. Many mammals, such as tree sloths and spider monkeys, which also live in the canopy, are preyed upon by jaguars. Other canopy animals include butterflies, tree frogs, and dart-poison frogs. Snakes, spiders, and ants live on the ground. Many animals, such as bats, are active only at night.

Figure 1.6
Tropical rain forest organization, featuring plants and animals of the Amazon basin.

morpho butterfly, *Morpho*

toucan, *Ramphastos*

jaguar, *Panthera*

dart-poison frog, *Dendrobates*

cpiphytic orchid, *Lycaste*

Tropical Rain Forests: Can We Live Without Them?

So far, nearly 2 million species of organisms have been discovered and named. Two-thirds of the plant species, 90% of the nonhuman primates, 40% of birds of prey, and 90% of the insects live in the tropics. Many more species of organisms (perhaps as many as 30 million) are estimated to live in the tropical rain forests but have not yet been discovered.

Tropical forests span the planet on both sides of the equator and cover 6–7% of the total land surface of the earth—an area roughly equivalent to our contiguous forty-eight states. Every year humans destroy an area of forest equivalent to the size of Oklahoma. At this rate, these forests and the species they contain will disappear completely in just a few more decades. Even if only the forest areas now legally protected survive, 56–72% of all tropical forest species would still be lost.

The loss of tropical rain forests results from an interplay of social, economic, and political pressures. Many people already live in the forest, and as their numbers increase, more of the land is cleared for farming.

People move to the forests because internationally financed projects build roads and open the forests up for exploitation. Small-scale farming accounts for about 60% of tropical deforestation, and this is followed by commercial logging, cattle ranching, and mining. International demand for timber promotes destructive logging of rain forests in Southeast Asia and South America. A market for low-grade beef encourages their conversion to pastures for cattle. The lure of gold draws miners to rain forests in Costa Rica and Brazil.

The destruction of tropical rain forests produces only short-term benefits but is expected to cause long-term problems. The forests act like a giant sponge, soaking up rainfall during the wet season and releasing it during the dry season. Without them, a regional yearly regime of flooding followed by drought is expected to destroy property and reduce agricultural harvests. Worldwide, there could be changes in climate that would affect the entire human race. On the other hand, the preservation of tropical rain forests offers benefits. For example, the rich diversity of plants and animals would continue to exist for scientific and pharmacological study. One-fourth of the medicines we currently use come from tropical rain

forests. The rosy periwinkle from Madagascar has produced two potent drugs for use against Hodgkin disease, leukemia, and other blood cancers. It is hoped that many of the still-unknown plants will provide medicines for other human ills.

Studies show that if the forests were used as a sustainable source of nonwood products, such as nuts, fruits, and latex rubber, they would generate as much or more revenue while continuing to perform their various ecological functions. And biodiversity could still be preserved. Brazil is exploring the concept of "extractive reserves," in which plant and animal products are harvested but the forest itself is not cleared. Ecologists have also proposed "forest farming" systems, which mimic the natural forest as much as possible while providing abundant yields. But for such plans to work maximally, the human population size and the resource consumption per person must be stabilized.

Preserving tropical rain forests is a wise investment. Such action promotes the survival of most of the world's species—indeed, the human species, too.

The Human Population

The human population continuously increases and encroaches on natural ecosystems so they do not function as they once did. As more and more of the biosphere is converted to towns and cities, fewer of the natural cycles are able to function adequately to sustain the human population. It is important to do all we can to preserve the biosphere, because only then can we be assured that we will continue to exist. Presently, there is great concern about preserving the biodiversity (wide range of living things) in the world's tropical rain forests, as discussed in the reading on this page.

The preservation of biodiversity is extremely important, but we should also be aware that tropical rain forests perform services for us. They act like a giant sponge and absorb carbon dioxide, a pollutant that pours into the atmosphere from the burning of fossil fuels such as oil and coal. If the rain forests continue to be depleted as they are now, an increased amount of carbon dioxide in the atmosphere is expected to cause an increase in the average daily temperature. Problems with acid rain are also expected to increase, since carbon dioxide combines with water to form carbonic acid, a component of acid rain.

How Living Things Are Classified

Since life is so diverse (there are over 900,000 known types of insects alone!) it is helpful to have a classification system to group organisms according to their similarities. **Taxonomy** [Gk. *taxis,* arrangement, and *nomy,* science of] is the discipline of identifying and classifying organisms according to certain rules. In keeping with a practice started by the Swedish taxonomist Linnaeus, biologists give each living thing a binomial [L. *bi,* two, and *nom,* name], or two-part name. For example, the scientific name for the garden pea is *Pisum sativum.* The first word refers to the genus and the second word is the specific epithet of a species within that genus. The members of a species have similar characteristics and reproduce with one another. Similar species are placed in the same genus, then similar genera go into families, families

into orders, and so on into five kingdoms (fig. 1.7). The organizational levels of our taxonomic system are as listed next:

Levels of Classification		Human	Corn
	Kingdom	Animalia	Plantae
	Phylum*	Chordata	Magnoliophyta
	Class	Mammalia	Magnoliopsida
	Order	Primates	Commelinales
	Family	Hominidae	Poaceae
	Genus	*Homo*	*Zea*
	Species	*H.sapiens*	*Z.mays*

* Division in kingdoms Plantae and Fungi

Figure 1.7

Classification of organisms.
a. Representatives of the five kingdoms. **b.** Brief descriptions of the five kingdoms.

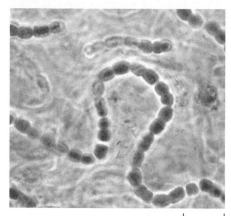

20 μm

Kingdom Prokaryote:
Cyanobacterium, *Nostoc*

Kingdoms of Life

Kingdom	Organization	Type of Nutrition	Representative Organisms
Prokaryotae (prokaryotes)	Small, simple single cell (sometimes in chains or mats)	Absorb food (some photosynthetic)	Bacteria, including cyanobacteria
Protoctista (protoctists)	Complex single cell (sometimes filaments, colonies, or multicellular)	Absorb, photosynthesize, or ingest food	Protozoa and algae of various types
Fungi	Mostly multicellular and filamentous with specialized, complex cells	Absorb food	Molds and mushrooms
Plantae (plants)	Multicellular with specialized, complex cells	Photosynthesize food	Mosses, ferns, and woody and nonwoody flowering plants
Animalia (animals)	Multicellular with specialized, complex cells	Ingest food	Sponges, worms, insects, fish, amphibians, reptiles, birds, and mammals

b.

10 μm

a. Kingdom Protoctista:
Unicellular organism,
Euglena

Kingdom Fungi:
Shaggy mane mushroom,
Coprinus comatus

Kingdom Plantae:
Flowering plant, *Rosa hybrid*

Kingdom Animalia:
African lynx, *Felix caracal*

Biological Relationships

Living things are diverse because they are adapted to particular roles in ecosystems. Their adaptations include a way of capturing materials and energy from the environment. Tubular corals extend tentacles to sweep up minute particles; groupers spring forward with open mouths to suck in small fish, and lionfish use colorful fins to attract unsuspecting crabs. Energy and materials are needed to maintain the structure and the function of the individual. Life is organized at various levels above and below the level of the individual. Individuals are interbreeding members of species, which live in ecosystems. When they reproduce, they pass on their organization to offspring. Over time, a species can change and evolve so that the specific adaptation of a few be-comes the adaptation of many. This is how species become as different as tubular corals, groupers, and lionfish. Evolution not only accounts for the diversity of life, it also accounts for its unity. All living things have the same levels of organization and function similarly because they are related—even back to the first living cell or cells on earth.

The concepts in this chapter apply to human beings also. Humans, too, are dependent on a cycling of materials and a flow of energy in natural ecosystems. Because humans have a highly developed culture, they tend to forget about this dependence. Only now are we becoming aware of how important it is to protect and preserve the natural world so that our own existence is assured.

Summary

1. Although living things are diverse, they share certain characteristics in common.

2. All living things are organized; the cell is the smallest unit of life. Cells form tissues, tissues form organs, organs form systems in individuals, individuals are members of populations, and populations make up communities in ecosystems.

3. Each level of organization has emergent properties that cannot be accounted for by simply adding up the properties of the previous level.

4. Living things need an outside source of materials and energy. These are used during metabolism for repair and growth of the organism.

5. Organisms differ as to how they acquire materials and energy. Plants photosynthesize and make their own food; animals eat either plants or other animals.

6. Living things need a relatively constant internal environment and have various mechanisms and strategies for maintaining homeostasis.

7. Living things respond to external stimuli; taken together, these reactions constitute the behavior of the organism.

8. Living things reproduce and pass on genes, hereditary factors that control organization and metabolism. Genetic changes allow evolution to occur.

9. The process of evolution explains both the unity and the diversity of life. Descent from a common ancestor explains why all organisms share the same characteristics, and adaptation to various ways of life explains the diversity of life forms.

10. Within an ecosystem, populations interact with one another and with the physical environment. Chemicals cycle through an ecosystem, but energy does not cycle, and eventually becomes heat.

11. Two examples of ecosystems, the coral reef and the tropical rain forest, show that the adaptations of organisms allow them to play particular roles within an ecosystem.

12. Living things are classified into groups from species to genus, family, order, class, phylum and kingdom. The text recognizes five kingdoms; prokaryotes are the unicellular bacteria; protoctists include protozoa and algae of varying complexity; fungi are multicellular photosynthesizers; and animals organisms that absorb food; plants are multicellular are multicellular ingest their food.

Writing Across the Curriculum

In order to practice writing skills, students should write out the answers to any or all of the study questions and the critical thinking questions. The study questions are sequenced in the same order as the text. Answers to the objective questions, and suggested answers to the critical thinking questions, are in appendix D.

Study Questions

1. What are the common characteristics of life listed in the text?   3

2. What evidence can you cite to show that living things are organized?   3

3. Why do living things require an outside source of materials and energy?   4

4. What is passed from generation to generation when organisms reproduce? What has to happen to the hereditary material DNA in order for evolution to occur?   5

5. How does evolution explain both the unity and the diversity of life?   6

6. What is an ecosystem, and why should human beings preserve ecosystems?   6

7. Choose an organism from a coral reef or a tropical rain forest and explain how it is adapted to its way of life.   7–8

8. What kingdoms are used in the classification system adopted by this text? What types of organisms are found in each kingdom?   10

Objective Questions

For questions 1–5, match the statements in the key with the sentences below.

Key:

  a. Living things are organized.
  b. Living things metabolize.
  c. Living things respond.
  d. Living things reproduce.
  e. Living things evolve.

1. Genes made up of DNA are passed from parent to child.

2. Zebras run away from approaching lions.

3. All organisms are composed of cells.

4. Cells use materials and energy for growth and repair.

5. There are many different kinds of living things.

6. Evolution from the first cell(s) best explains why

  a. ecosystems have populations of organisms.

  b. photosynthesizers produce food.

  c. diverse organisms share common characteristics.

  d. All of these are correct.

7. Adaptation to a way of life best explains why living things

  a. display homeostasis.

  b. are diverse.

  c. began as single cells.

  d. are classified into five kingdoms.

8. Into which kingdom would you place a multicellular land organism that carries on photosynthesis?

  a. Protoctista

  b. Fungi

  c. Plantae

  d. Animalia

9. Place the following labels on this diagram of chemical cycling and energy flow in an ecosystem: plants, animals, death and decay, nutrients (e.g., water, fertilizer) for plants.

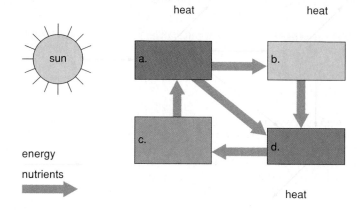

Concepts and Critical Thinking

1. *All living things evolved from a common ancestor.*

How does this concept explain the unity of life forms?

2. *Organisms are adapted to particular ways of life.*

How does this concept explain the diversity of life?

3. *Each level of biological organization has emergent properties.*

How does this concept help explain the difference between the living and the nonliving?

Selected Key Terms

adaptation An organism's modification in structure, function, or behavior suitable to the environment. [L. *ad,* toward, and *apt,* adjust]   5

biosphere The thin shell of air, land, and water around the earth that supports life. [Gk. *bio,* life, and *spher,* ball]   6

ecosystem A biological community together with the associated abiotic environment. [Gk. *eco,* house, and *sys,* together]   3

energy The capacity to do work and bring about change; occurs in a variety of forms.   4

evolution Changes that occur in populations of organisms with the passage of time, often resulting in increased adaptation of organisms to the prevailing environment. [L. *evolut,* an unrolling]   6

gene The unit of heredity passed on to offspring. [Gk. *gene,* origin]   5

homeostasis The maintenance of internal conditions in a cell or in organisms; for example, relatively constant temperature, pH, and blood sugar. [Gk. *homeo,* like, and *stasis,* standing]   4

metabolism All of the chemical reactions that occur in a cell during growth and repair. [Gk. *metab,* change]   4

photosynthesis A process by which plants utilize solar energy to make their own organic food.   4

reproduce To produce a new individual of the same kind.   5

species A taxonomic category that is the subdivision of a genus; its members can breed successfully with each other but not with members of another species. [L. *speci,* a kind]   5

taxonomy The branch of biology concerned with identifying and naming organisms. [Gk. *taxis,* arrangement, and *nomy,* science of]   10

2

THE SCIENTIFIC METHOD

Learning Objectives

Many biological experiments are performed in the laboratory where conditions can be more easily controlled. This technician is inserting liquid into a test tube using a pipette.

S cience helps human beings understand the natural world and is concerned solely with information gained by observing and testing that world. Scientists, therefore, ask questions only about events in the natural world and expect that the natural world in turn will provide all the information needed to understand these events. It is the aim of science to be objective rather than subjective, though it is very difficult to make objective observations and to come to objective conclusions because human beings are often influenced by their particular prejudices. Still, anything less than a completely objective observation or conclusion is not considered scientific. Finally, the conclusions of science are subject to change. Quite often in science, new studies, which might utilize new techniques and equipment, reveal that previous conclusions need to be modified or changed entirely.

The ultimate goal of science is to understand the natural world in terms of **theories,** concepts based on the conclusions of experiments and observations (fig. 2.1). A detective might have a theory about a crime, or a baseball fan might have a theory about the win-loss record of the home team, but in science, the word *theory* is reserved for a conceptual scheme supported by much research and not yet found lacking. Some of the unifying theories of biology are:

Name of Theory	Explanation
Cell	All organisms are composed of cells.
Biogenesis	Life comes only from life.
Evolution	All living things have a common ancestor and are adapted to a particular way of life.
Gene	Organisms contain coded information that dictates their form, function, and behavior.

You can see that, in general, biological theories pertain to various aspects of life. The theory of evolution enables scientists to understand the history of life, the variety of living things, and the anatomy, physiology, and development of organisms—even their behavior. Because the theory of evolution has been supported by so much research for over a hundred years, some biologists refer to the *principle* of evolution. They believe this is the appropriate terminology for any theory that is generally accepted as valid by an overwhelming amount of scientific evidence.

> Biologists ask questions and carry on investigations that pertain to the natural world. The conclusions of these investigations may eventually enable biologists to arrive at a theory that is generally accepted by all.

SCIENTISTS HAVE A METHOD

Scientists, including biologists, employ an approach for gathering information that is known as the **scientific method.** Although the approach is as varied as scientists themselves, there are still certain processes that can be identified as typical of the scientific method. Figure 2.1 outlines the primary steps in the scientific method. On the basis of **data** (factual information), which may have been collected by someone previously, a scientist formulates a tentative statement, called a **hypothesis** [Gk. *hypothesis,* foundation]. This is used to guide his or her observations and experimentation, which produce new data.

The new data may support the hypothesis; but if it does not, the hypothesis has to be rejected. Knowing that some future observation and/or experiment might falsify the hypothesis, a scientist never says that the data "prove" the hypothesis. Although a hypothesis cannot be proven true, it can be shown to be false.

It is customary for an investigator to report findings in a scientific journal so that the design and results of an experiment are available to all. This is important because all experimental results *must be repeatable;* that is, other scientists using the same procedures should get the same results. If they do not, the original data cannot be considered to support the hypothesis.

Figure 2.1

The scientific method. Accumulated scientific data are used to formulate the hypothesis. Observations and experiments test the hypothesis. The new data allow researchers to come to a general conclusion about the phenomenon being studied. Several such conclusions (labeled 1, 2, 3) enable scientists to develop a comprehensive theory. For example, studies in comparative embryology, comparative anatomy, and paleontology all support the theory of evolution.

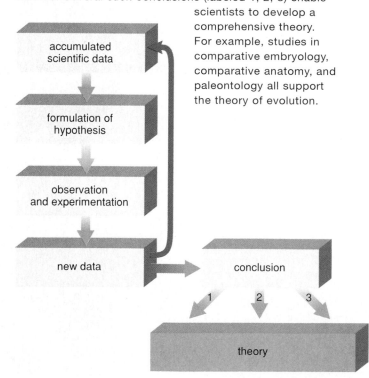

Often the authors of a report suggest other experiments that could be done to clarify or broaden the understanding of the matter under study. Science is an ongoing endeavor. Because hypotheses are never proven true, they are reviewed constantly. In particular, new procedures and instruments facilitate the process of revision. Previous data are used as a starting point, and then new data are collected. The new data may require a new conclusion and the formulation of revised hypotheses, which will then be tested.

> The scientific method consists of forming a hypothesis, testing it, and coming to a conclusion.

Example of Scientific Method

As an example, let us consider research performed by the British scientist H.B.D. Kettlewell:

Accumulated scientific data. Scientists had observed the prevalence of dark-colored peppered moths on trees in polluted areas (where tree trunks are darker) and the prevalence of light-colored peppered moths on trees in nonpolluted areas (where tree trunks are lighter).

Hypothesis. Formulating the hypothesis involves **inductive reasoning;** that is, scientists often use isolated facts to arrive at a possible explanation of the observed phenomenon. In this case the hypothesis was that predatory birds are responsible for the unequal distribution of moths because they feed on moths they can see.

Observation and experimentation. Once the hypothesis has been stated, deductive reasoning comes into play. **Deductive reasoning** begins with a general statement that infers a specific conclusion. It often takes the form of an "if . . . then" statement: *If* predatory birds are responsible for the unequal distribution of dark- and light-colored moths, *then* we should see birds feeding primarily on light-colored moths in polluted areas and on dark-colored moths in nonpolluted areas.

To see if this deduction was correct, Kettlewell performed an experiment. He released equal numbers of the two types of moths in the two different areas. He observed that birds captured more dark-colored moths in nonpolluted areas and more light-colored moths in polluted areas.

New data. From the unpolluted area, Kettlewell recaptured 13.7% of the light-colored moths and only 4.7% of the dark form. From the polluted area, he recaptured 27.5% of the dark form and only 13% of the light-colored moths (fig. 2.2). Mathematical data like these are preferred because they are objective and cannot be influenced by the scientist's subjective feelings.

Conclusion. In this instance, the data supported the hypothesis that predatory birds are responsible for the unequal distribution of light- and dark-colored moths.

Figure 2.2

Kettlewell experiment. Kettlewell hypothesized that in nonpolluted areas, predatory birds fed on dark-colored moths resting on light tree trunks, and in polluted areas, predatory birds fed on light-colored moths resting on dark tree trunks. After releasing the same number of each type of moth in the two areas, he was able to recapture the percentages of each type noted.

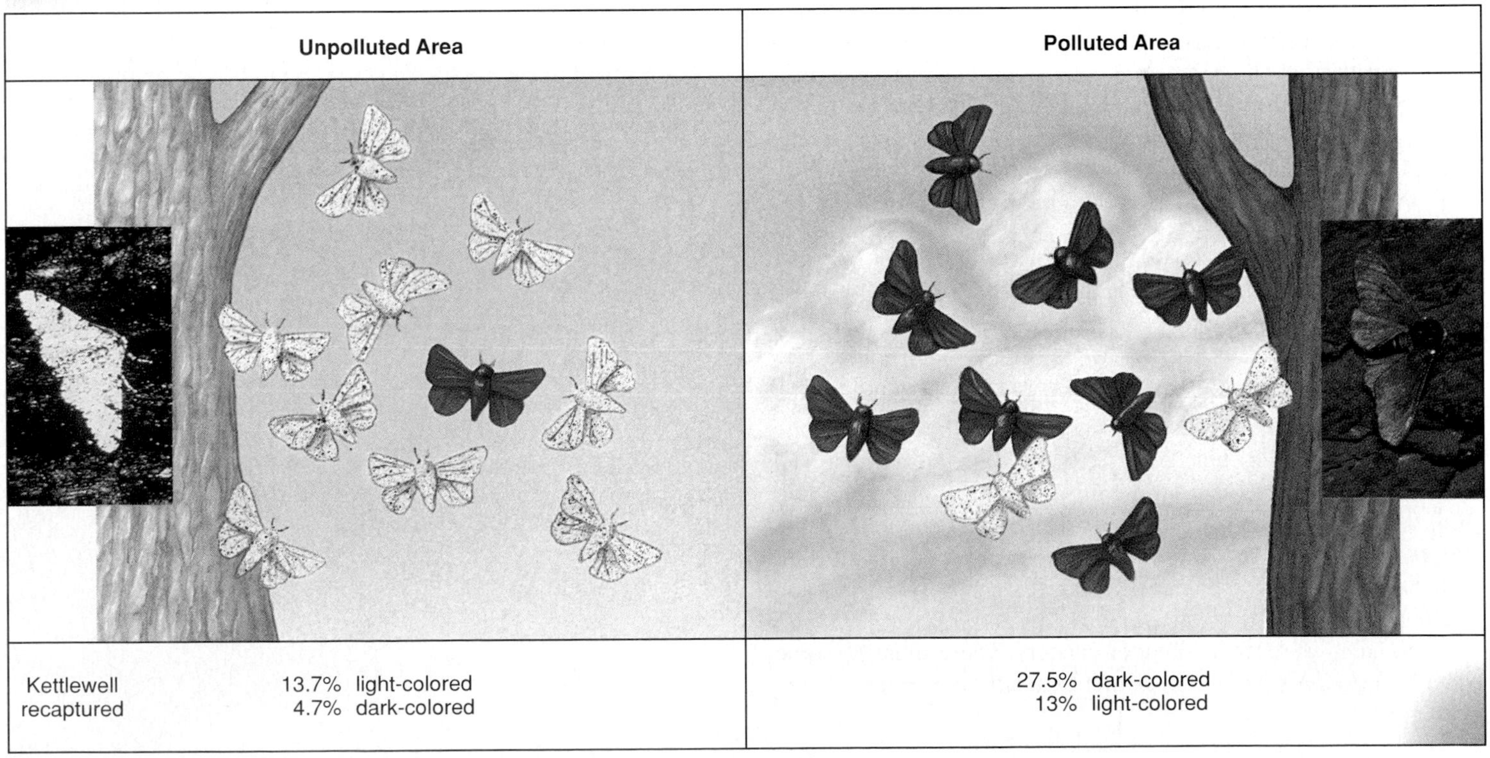

Unpolluted Area	Polluted Area
Kettlewell recaptured 13.7% light-colored 4.7% dark-colored	27.5% dark-colored 13% light-colored

SOME EXPERIMENTS HAVE A CONTROL

In a controlled experiment there is a **control group** that does not experience the component of the experiment being tested. The component of the experiment being tested is called the **experimental variable;** in other words, the investigator deliberately manipulates this component of the experiment. Then the investigator observes the effects of the experiment; in other words, he or she observes the **dependent variable:**

Experimental Variable	Dependent Variable
Component of the experiment being tested	Result or change that occurs due to the experimental variable

Example of a Controlled Experiment

As an example of a controlled experiment, suppose physiologists hypothesized that sweetener S is a safe food additive. They then design an experiment in which there are two groups of mice:

Experimental Group	Control Group
sweetener S in diet	no sweetener S in diet

To help ensure that the two groups are identical, inbred (genetically identical) mice are randomly placed into the two groups—say, ten mice per group. It is hoped that if any of the mice are different from the others, random placement will distribute them evenly between the groups. The experimenters also make sure that all environmental conditions—such as availability of water, cage conditions, and temperature of surroundings—are the same for all groups. The food for each group is exactly the same, except for the amount of sweetener S.

At the end of the experiment, both groups of mice are examined for bladder cancer. Let's suppose that 50% of the mice in the experimental group are found to have bladder cancer, while none in the control group have bladder cancer. The results of this experiment do not support the hypothesis that sweetener S is a safe food additive.

Use of a control group gives greater validity to the results of the experiment. In the described experiment, the control group did not show cancer, but the experimental group did. We can conclude that sweetener S in the diet must have brought about the cancer because this was the only difference between the two groups. Suppose, however, that both the experimental and control groups showed bladder cancer. If so, we could not conclude that sweetener S in the diet produced the effect (bladder cancer). There must be some other components of the experiment causing the cancer.

At this point, the physiologists might decide to do more experiments. They might hypothesize that sweetener S is safe if the diet contains less than 50% sweetener. They might decide to feed sweetener S to groups of mice at ever-greater percentages of the total intake of food:

Group 1 : no sweetener S in food (control group)

Group 2 : sweetener S in 5% of food

Group 3 : sweetener S in 10% of food

↓

Group 11 : sweetener S in 50% of food

Usually the data from experiments such as these are presented in the form of a table or graph (fig. 2.3). A statistical test may be run to determine if the difference in the number of cases of bladder cancer among the various groups is significant. After all, if a significant number of mice in the control group develop cancer, the results may be invalid. On the basis of the results, the experimenters try to develop a recommendation concerning the safety of adding sweetener S to the food of humans. They may determine, for example, that ever-larger amounts of the sweetener—over 10% of food intake—are expected to cause a progressively increased incidence of bladder cancer.

> Controlled experiments have a control group, which is not exposed to the experimental variable.

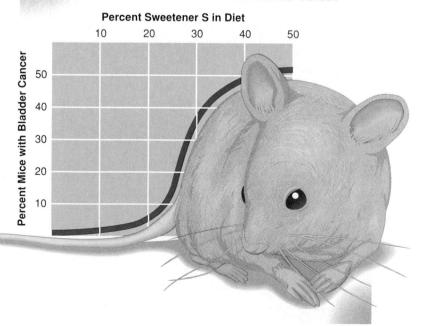

Figure 2.3
Hypothetical results of sweetener S study. The graph shows a positive correlation between increased amounts of sweetener S and increased incidence of bladder cancer.

SOME INVESTIGATIONS ARE OBSERVATIONAL

Scientists don't always gather data by experimenting. Much of the data they gather is purely observational, but even so, the steps described for the scientific method are still applicable: observations are made, a hypothesis is formulated, predictions are made on the basis of the hypothesis, and data are collected that support or disprove the hypothesis.

Example of Observational Data

Brian C. R. Bertram investigated the reproductive behavior of ostriches, *Struthio camelus,* in East Africa, where as many as seven female ostriches share the same nest. A resident male builds a nest which consists of only a scrape in the ground. He then mates with a female, called the major hen, and she starts to lay eggs. After a few days, other females which may not have mated with the resident male (called minor hens) add their eggs to the nest, and the major hen allows this. However, only the major hen incubates and guards the nest, which eventually can contain up to forty eggs—far too many for her to incubate. She keeps about twenty eggs in the center of the nest, and she pushes the others out to form an outer ring (fig. 2.4*a*).

Bertram knew of two hypotheses attempting to explain how the eggs in the outer ring could protect the eggs in the center of the nest. If there is a benefit, this would explain the permissive attitude of the major hen toward the minor hens. Local natives thought that, in the case of a savannah fire, the eggs surrounding the nest would rupture and the liquid would prevent the fire from damaging the eggs in the nest. In contrast, two previous investigators thought that these eggs may help to regulate egg temperature.

Bertram carefully studied three ostriches' nests. Every egg was numbered, weighed, measured, photographed, and examined for surface characteristics. He was able to determine which eggs were major hens' eggs by observing the birds laying, using time-lapse photography, and depending on knowledge of egg characteristics. He found that the major hen is able to recognize her own eggs and that she usually pushes only minor hens' eggs into the outer ring (fig. 2.4*b*). Bertram then observed that predators such as jackals and vultures normally eat only a few eggs during an attack, and that they tend to choose eggs in the outer ring rather than in the center. Therefore, the major hen is protecting her own eggs by pushing minor hens' eggs out to form a ring!

Neither of the original hypotheses was supported, but Bertram used his observations to formulate and support a hypothesis of his own. So far no one has hypothesized why major hens allow some minor hens' eggs to remain in the center of the nest, where they will hatch. Can you formulate a possible hypothesis based on Bertram's data in figure 2.4*b*? What further observations need to be made?

> Much scientific information is based on purely observational (descriptive) data, but the steps previously listed for the scientific method still apply.

Figure 2.4

Observational data. Major hen ostrich, *Struthio camelus,* rolls eggs out of a communal nest because they belong to other hens. The table shows that her eggs are kept in the center of the nest, where they are protected from predators who choose eggs in the outer ring. This is a benefit to the major hen who, like all organisms, wants to leave as many offspring as possible.

Position of Eggs in Three Incubating Ostrich Nests		
Eggs Laid by	No. of Eggs in Center (being incubated)	No. of (doomed) Eggs in Outer Ring
Nest A		
Major hen	9	0
Four other hens	10	8
Nest B		
Major hen	13	0
Two other hens	6	5
Nest C		
Major hen	9	1
Four other hens	9	10

Bertram, B.C.R. 1979. Ostriches recognize their own eggs and discard others. <u>Nature</u> 279: 233.

WHAT SCIENCE DOESN'T DO

Science is objective, not subjective. Science assumes that each person is capable of collecting data and seeing natural events in the same way. Assuming that our eyesight is normal, any one of us can observe how many times predatory birds eat moths or how often ostrich hens push eggs out of a nest. Any one of us can perform a controlled experiment in order to determine if a food additive is safe.

Science is founded in the belief that events can be explained fully by natural causes. Kettlewell concluded that moths disappear because they are eaten by predatory birds, and Bertram concluded that female ostriches push eggs out of the nest as a way to protect their own eggs. Science never seeks data or makes a conclusion that cannot be collaborated by any other person.

Science assumes that the same theories and principles are applicable to past, present, and future events. The data collected by scientists today can be used to explain past events. It follows, then, that science seeks a natural cause for the origin and history of life. The theory of evolution, which is supported by data collected by myriads of scientists, explains observations in all fields of biology and is especially applicable to the origin and history of life.

Doctrines of creation, which have a mythical, philosophical, or theological basis, are not a part of science because they are not subject to objective observations and experimentation by all persons. Many cultures have their own particular set of supernatural beliefs, and even various religions within a culture differ as to the application of these beliefs. Such approaches to understanding the world are not within the province of science. Similarly, **scientific creationism,** which states that God created all species as they are today, cannot be considered science because creationism upholds a supernatural cause rather than natural causes for events. When faith is involved, a hypothesis is not subjected to being proven false in a purely objective way.

Just as science does not test religious beliefs, it does not make ethical or moral decisions. The general public may want scientists to label certain research as "good" or "bad" and may want them to predict whether any resulting technology will primarily benefit or harm humanity. Yet science, by its very nature, is impartial and simply attempts to study natural phenomena. When we wish to make value judgments, we must go to other fields of study to find the means to make those judgments. And these judgments must be made by all people. The responsibility for how we use the fruits of science—including a given technology—must rest with people from all walks of life, not upon scientists alone. Scientists should provide the public with as much information as possible when such issues as fetal research, genetic engineering, and use of atomic energy are being debated. Then they, along with other citizens, can help make decisions about the future role of these technologies in our society. All of us have a responsibility to decide how to use scientific knowledge so that it benefits the human species and all living things.

Summary

1. Scientific investigations always pertain to the natural world, and the conclusions of the investigations are always subject to change.

2. The goal of science is to understand the natural world in terms of theories, which can be used to explain diverse observations and experiments. Some theories, such as the theory of evolution, are so well supported that many suggest they should be called principles.

3. In general, scientists use the scientific method. Based on their own observations or on those in the scientific literature, scientists formulate a hypothesis, carry out a plan of action, and come to a conclusion that either supports or fails to support the hypothesis.

4. It is possible to prove a hypothesis false, but it can never be proven true. Future observations and experimentations may prove a hypothesis false.

5. Inductive reasoning is used to formulate the hypothesis, and deductive reasoning is used to decide how to test the hypothesis.

6. Mathematical data are preferred for their pure objectivity.

7. Scientists often undertake controlled experiments. Controlled experiments require that (1) the environmental conditions are held constant, (2) there is a control group that goes through all the steps of the experiment except the one being tested, and (3) one or more experimental groups are involved.

8. In a controlled experiment, the experimental variable is that portion of the experiment being manipulated and the dependent variable is the change due to the experimental variable.

9. Much biological investigation is observational rather than experimental. Observational investigations also use the steps of the scientific method.

10. Religious beliefs, such as those forming the basis of scientific creationism, are not within the province of science. In science, explanations or conclusions must be based on natural causes in order to be considered legitimate.

11. Science comes to conclusions based on observations and experimentation; it does not make moral or ethical decisions. Such decisions are the obligations of *all* persons, including scientists.

Writing Across the Curriculum

In order to practice writing skills, students should write out the answers to any or all of the study questions and the critical thinking questions. The study questions are sequenced in the same order as the text. Answers to the objective questions, and suggested answers to the critical thinking questions, are in appendix D.

Study Questions

1. What is the day-to-day purpose of science, and what is the overall goal of science?   14

2. List biological theories that pertain to all living things.   14

3. There is no standard scientific method, but still it is possible to identify certain steps that are commonly accepted as components of this method. What are these steps?   14

4. For what purposes are scientific journals useful?   14

5. Apply the steps of the scientific method to Kettlewell's experiment regarding the distribution of dark- and light-colored moths.   15

6. Which of the steps in question 3 require(s) the use of inductive reasoning? Which require(s) the use of deductive reasoning?   15

7. Why do scientists prefer mathematical data?   15

8. Design a controlled experiment, using an example other than the one given in the text.   16

9. What is an observational investigation, and how does it differ from an experimental investigation?   17

10. Why is scientific creationism not within the province of science?   18

11. Explain why you would not expect science to make moral or ethical decisions.   18

12. An investigator spills dye on a culture plate and then notices that the bacteria live despite exposure to sunlight. He hypothesizes that the dye protects bacteria against death by ultraviolet (UV) light. To test this hypothesis, he decides to expose two culture plates to UV light. One plate contains bacteria and dye; the other plate contains only bacteria. Result: after exposure to UV light, the bacteria on both plates die. Fill in the right-hand portion of this diagram.   14

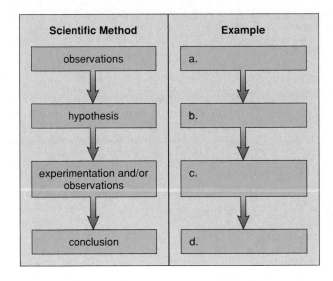

Objective Questions

For questions 1–3, refer to the following steps in the scientfic method.

    a. experimentation

    b. conclusion

    c. researching the scientific literature

    d. formulating the hypothesis

1. Place these items in the correct sequence.

2. With which of these steps would you associate inductive reasoning?

3. With which of these steps would you associate deductive reasoning?

4. Which is the experimental variable in the experiment concerning sweetener S?

    a. Conditions like temperature and housing are the same for all groups.

    b. The amount of sweetener S in food.

    c. Two percent of the group fed food that was 10% sweetener S got bladder cancer, and 90% of the group fed food that was 50% sweetener S got bladder cancer.

    d. The data were presented as a graph.

5. Which is the control group in this same experiment?

    a. All mice in this group died because a lab assistant forgot to give them water.

    b. All mice in this group received food that was 10% sweetener S.

    c. All mice in this group received no sweetener S in food.

    d. Some mice in all groups got bladder cancer; therefore, there was no control group.

6. Which is an example of an observational investigation?

    a. Jones put broken eggshells in the nest of some gulls and watched their behavior.

    b. Smith measured the length of the twigs of all trees in the designated area.

    c. Green put pesticide into one jar of amoebas but not into the other jar.

    d. Kettlewell counted how many moths the birds did not eat.

7. Which of these statements is correct?

    a. Because scientists speak of the "theory of evolution," they believe that evolution does not have much merit.

    b. A theory is simply a hypothesis that needs further experimentation and observation.

    c. Theories are hypotheses that have failed to be supported by experimentation and observation.

    d. The term theory in science is reserved for those hypotheses that have proven to have the greatest explanatory power.

Concepts and Critical Thinking

1. Scientists use the scientific method to gather information about the natural world.

   When utilizing the scientific method, hypotheses can be proven false but not true. Explain.

2. There are several underlying theories in biology.

   What is the difference between the use of the word theory in the everyday sense and in the scientific sense?

3. All persons—not just scientists—should decide on the role of various technologies in society.

   Science is not obligated to make policy decisions. Why not?

Selected Key Terms

control group A sample that goes through all the steps of an experiment except the one being tested; a standard against which results of an experiment are checked. 16

datum (pl., data) A fact or a piece of information collected through observation and/or experimentation. [L. *datum,* gift] 14

deductive reasoning A process of logic and reasoning, using "if . . . then" statements. 15

dependent variable A result or change that occurs when an experimental variable is utilized in an experiment. 16

experimental variable The condition that is tested in an experiment by manipulating it and observing the results. 16

hypothesis A supposition that is established by reasoning after consideration of available evidence; it can be tested by obtaining more data, often by experimentation. [Gk. *hypothesis,* foundation] 14

inductive reasoning A process of logic and reasoning, using specific observations to arrive at a hypothesis. 15

scientific method A step-by-step process for discovery and generation of knowledge—ranging from observation and hypothesis to theory and principle. 14

theory A conceptual scheme arrived at by the scientific method and supported by innumerable observations and experimentations. 14

Part I

THE CELL

A cell is the basic unit of life and all living things are composed of cells. Therefore, our knowledge of the structure and function of a cell can be applied directly to the organism, whose organization is maintained only by an input of matter and energy. Metabolic pathways carry out the transformations needed to change this input into the structure of the cell. In the end, the energy needed to maintain life comes from the sun. Plant cells capture solar energy and store it in molecules that later are utilized by all living cells. Knowledge of chemistry, energy transformations, and metabolic pathways increases our understanding of the essence of life.

Electron micrograph of a plant cell reveals its inner complexity.

Many of the figures and concepts discussed in *Biology*, fifth edition, are further explored in technology products. The following is a list of figures in part I that correlates to technology products.

A set of five videotapes contains 53 animations of physiological processes integral to the study of biology. These videotapes, entitled *Life Science Animations* cover such topics as chemistry, genetics, and reproduction. A videotape icon appears in appropriate figure legends to alert the reader to these animations.

Explorations in Human Biology and *Explorations in Cell Biology, Metabolism, and Genetics* by George B. Johnson are interactive CD-ROMs with activities that can be used by an instructor in lecture and/or placed in a lab or resource center for student use. This interactive software consists of modules that cover key topics discussed in a biology course. The CD-ROMs are available for use with Macintosh and IBM Windows computers. A CD-ROM icon appears in appropriate figure legends to alert the reader to these activities.

Corresponding Figures		Videotape Concepts	CD-Rom Modules
1.4	Ecosystem organization	52. Energy Flow Through an Ecosystem	—
3.7	Ionic reaction	1. Formation of an Ionic Bond	—
5.3	Prokaryotic cell	2. Journey into a Cell	Cell Size
5.4	Animal cell anatomy	2. Journey into a Cell	Cell Size
5.5	Plant cell anatomy	2. Journey into a Cell	Cell Size
5.6	Anatomy of the nucleus	2. Journey into a Cell	—
5.7	Rough endoplasmic reticulum	2. Journey into a Cell	—
5.8	Golgi apparatus	2. Journey into a Cell 3. Endocytosis 4. Cellular Secretion	—
5.11	Chloroplast structure	2. Journey into a Cell	—
5.12	Mitochondrion structure	2. Journey into a Cell	—
6.3	Fluid-mosaic model of plasma membrane	2. Journey into a Cell	—
6.5	Membrane protein diversity	—	Cell-Cell Interactions; Cystic Fibrosis
6.10	Facilitated transport	—	Active Transport
6.11	Sodium-potassium pump	—	Active Transport
6.12	Three methods of endocytosis	3. Endocytosis	Active Transport
6.13	Receptor-mediated endocytosis	3. Endocytosis	Cell-Cell Interactions
6.14	Plant cell wall	2. Journey into a Cell	—
6.15	Junctions between cells of the intestinal wall	2. Journey into a Cell	—
7.3	Energy of activation	—	Cell Chemistry: Thermodynamics
7.4	Enzymatic action	—	Cell Chemistry: Thermodynamics
7.5	Rate of enzymatic reaction	—	Cell Chemistry: Thermodynamics
7.6	Feedback inhibition	—	Cell Chemistry: Thermodynamics
7.7	Electron transport system	7. The Electron Transport Chain and the Production of ATP	—
7.8	Metabolic reaction	8. The Photosynthetic Electron Transport Chain and Production of ATP 9. C_3 Photosynthesis (Calvin Cycle)	—
7.10	Chemiosmotic ATP synthesis	7. The Electron Transport Chain and the Production of ATP 11. ATP as an Energy Carrier	Oxidative Respiration
8.2	Electromagnetic spectrum and chlorophylls *a* and *b*	—	Photosynthesis
8.3	Chloroplast structure and function	2. Journey into a Cell	Photosynthesis
8.5	Cyclic electron pathway	8. The Photosynthetic Electron Transport Chain and Production of ATP	Photosynthesis
8.6	Noncyclic electron pathway	8. The Photosynthetic Electron Transport Chain and Production of ATP	Photosynthesis
8.7	Chloroplast and thylakoid organization	8. The Photosynthetic Electron Transport Chain and Production of ATP	Photosynthesis
8.9	Light-independent reactions	9. C_3 Photosynthesis (Calvin Cycle)	—
8.10	Carbon dioxide fixation	9. C_3 Photosynthesis (Calvin Cycle) 10. C_4 Photosynthesis	—
9.2	Cellular respiration overview	5. Glycolysis	Oxidative Respiration
9.3	Relationship of glucose breakdown to the body proper	6. Oxidative Respiration (including Krebs Cycles) 11. ATP as an Energy Carrier	—
9.4	Glycolysis	5. Glycolysis 7. The Electron Transport Chain and the Production of ATP	Oxidative Respiration
9.6	Mitochondrion structure and function	—	Oxidative Respiration
9.7	Krebs cycle	6. Oxidative Respiration (including Krebs Cycles)	Oxidative Respiration
9.8	Electron transport system	7. The Electron Transport Chain and the Production of ATP	Oxidative Respiration
9.9	Organization of cristae	7. The Electron Transport Chain and the Production of ATP	Oxidative Respiration
9.10	Summary of complete glucose breakdown	7. The Electron Transport Chain and the Production of ATP	—
9.11	Metabolic pool concept	11. ATP as an Energy Carrier	—

3

BASIC CHEMISTRY

Learning Objectives

Matter Is Composed of Elements

- Explain the difference between an element and an atom.   24–25

- Name and describe the subatomic particles of an atom, indicating which one accounts for the occurrence of isotopes.   25–26

- Describe and discuss the energy levels (electron shells) of an atom, including the orbitals of the first two levels.   27–29

- Draw a simplified atomic structure of any atom with an atomic number less than 20.   29

Atoms Form Compounds and Molecules

- Draw representative atomic structures for ionic and covalent molecules, and distinguish between ionic and covalent reactions.   30–32

- Note which atom has been reduced and which has been oxidized in a particular reaction.   33

Water Is Essential to Life

- Describe the chemical properties of water, and explain how these properties affect their importance for living things.   34–36

- Define an acid and a base; describe the pH scale, and state the significance of buffers.   36–37

Inorganic versus organic molecules. The nonliving egg shell is largely composed of calcium carbonate, an inorganic substance. The living redwing blackbird chick, *Agelaius,* contains many varied organic molecules.

S ometimes it is difficult to realize that life has a chemical basis. Maybe this is because we usually deal with whole objects, such as trees, dogs, and people, and do not often consider their minute composition. If we did consider it, though, we would soon learn that the structure and the function of living things are dependent upon chemicals. The body of the cheetah that darts across the plain to capture a gazelle is composed of chemicals, and its success is dependent upon the chemical reactions that allow its eyes to see and its muscles to contract. Also, the cells of the bittersweet vine are made of chemicals, and it can climb a fence only because of the chemical reactions that permit growth to occur.

As recently as the nineteenth century, scientists believed that only nonliving things, like rocks and metals, consisted of chemicals alone. They thought that living things, such as the cheetah and the bittersweet vine, were different and had a special force, called a vital force, necessary for life. Scientific investigation, however, repeatedly has shown that both nonliving and living things have a chemical and physical basis. Therefore, it is appropriate for us to study chemical principles as an introduction to our study of life.

First we will look at the basic elements of matter and learn how these elements react with one another to form molecules. Then we will examine the complex molecules that characterize living things and eventually examine how they interact in the metabolic pathways of a cell. Our study will allow you to appreciate that life has a chemical basis.

MATTER IS COMPOSED OF ELEMENTS

Matter refers to anything that takes up space and has mass. It is helpful to remember that matter can exist as a solid, a liquid, or a gas. Then we can realize that not only are we matter but so too are the water we drink and the air we breathe.

All matter, both nonliving and living, is composed of certain basic substances called **elements.** It is quite remarkable that there are only ninety-two naturally occurring elements (see appendix B). We know these are elements because any particular element cannot be broken down to substances with different properties (a property is a chemical or physical characteristic, such as density, smell, taste, and reactivity).

Both the earth's crust and organisms are made up of elements, but they differ as to which ones (fig. 3.1). Only six elements—carbon, hydrogen, nitrogen, oxygen, phosphorus, and sulfur—make up most (about 98%) of the body weight of organisms. The acryonym CHNOPS helps us remember these six elements. These elements make up the complex molecules that are especially associated with living things.

> All living and nonliving things are matter composed of elements. Six elements in particular are commonly found in living things.

Figure 3.1

Elements of earth's crust and organisms. **a.** The earth's crust primarily contains oxygen, silicon, and aluminum. **b.** Living things primarily contain the elements hydrogen, oxygen, carbon, and nitrogen. Along with phosphorus and sulfur, these elements make up most biological molecules.

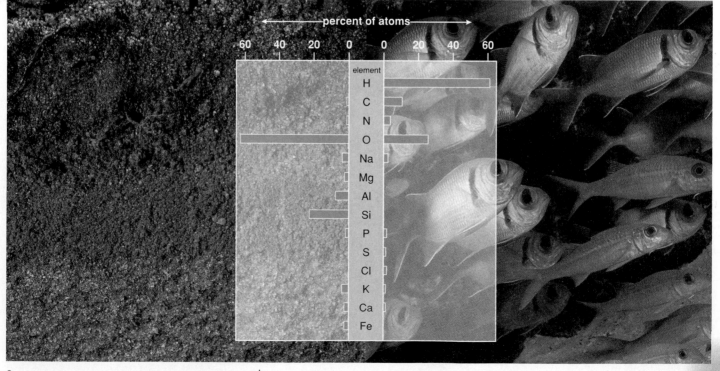

Elements Contain Atoms

In the early 1800s, the English scientist John Dalton proposed that elements actually contain tiny particles called **atoms** [Gk. *atomos,* individual]. He also deduced that there is only one type of atom in each type of element. You can see why, then, the name assigned to each element is the same as the name assigned to the type of atom it contains. Some of the names we use for the elements (atoms) are derived from English and some are derived from Latin. One or two letters create the *atomic symbol,* which stands for this name. For example, the symbol H stands for a hydrogen atom, and the symbol Na (for *natrium* in Latin) stands for a sodium atom. Table 3.1 gives the atomic symbols for the other elements (atoms) commonly found in living things.

From our discussion of elements, we would expect atoms to have a certain weight. The weight of an atom is in turn dependent upon the presence of certain subatomic particles. Although physicists have identified a number of subatomic particles, we will consider only the most stable of these: **protons, neutrons,** and **electrons** [Gk. *electr,* amber, electricity]. Protons and neutrons are located within the nucleus of an atom, and electrons move about the nucleus. Figure 3.2 shows the arrangement of the subatomic particles in helium, an atom that has only two electrons.

Our concept of an atom has changed greatly since Dalton's day. If we could draw an atom the size of a football field, the nucleus would be like a gumball in the center of the field and the electrons would be tiny specks whirling about in the upper stands. Most of an atom is empty space. We should also realize that we can only indicate where the electrons are expected to be most of the time. In our analogy, the electrons may even stray outside the stadium at times.

Atoms contain protons, neutrons, and electrons, all arranged in a definite manner.

The subatomic particles are so light that their weight is indicated by special units called atomic mass units (table 3.2). Protons and neutrons each have about one atomic unit of weight. In comparison, electrons have almost no weight; an electron weighs about $1/1,800$ that of a proton or neutron. Therefore, it is customary to disregard the combined weight of the electrons when calculating the total weight, called the *atomic weight,* of an atom.

All atoms of an element have the same number of protons. This is called the atom's *atomic number.* In table 3.1, atoms are listed according to increasing atomic number, as they are in the periodic table of the elements found in appendix B. This indicates that it is the number of protons (i.e., the atomic number) that makes an atom unique. The number of protons not only contributes to the physical properties (weight) of an atom, it also *indirectly* determines the chemical properties, which we will discuss in a later section.

Table 3.1

Common Elements in Living Things

Element*	Atomic Symbol	Atomic Number	Atomic Weight**
Hydrogen	H	1	1
Carbon	C	6	12
Nitrogen	N	7	14
Oxygen	O	8	16
Sodium	Na	11	23
Magnesium	Mg	12	24
Phosphorus	P	15	31
Sulfur	S	16	32
Chlorine	Cl	17	35
Potassium	K	19	39
Calcium	Ca	20	40

*A periodic table of the elements appears in appendix B.

**Average of most common isotopes.

Note: The atomic number gives the number of protons (and electrons in electrically neutral atoms). The number of neutrons is equal to the atomic weight minus the atomic number.

Figure 3.2

Model of helium (He), a simple atom. Atoms contain subatomic particles, which are located as shown. Protons and neutrons are found within the nucleus, and electrons are outside the nucleus. **a.** The stippling shows the probable location of the electrons in the helium atom. **b.** The average location of electrons is sometimes represented by a circle.

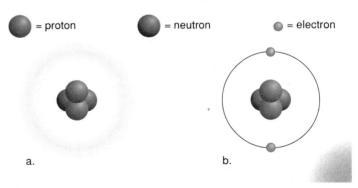

= proton   = neutron   = electron

a.   b.

Table 3.2

Subatomic Particles

Name	Charge	Weight
Electron	One negative unit	Very, very little
Proton	One positive unit	One atomic mass unit
Neutron	No charge	A little more than one atomic mass unit

Imaging the Body

X rays, which are produced when high-speed electrons strike a heavy metal, have long been used to image body parts. Dense structures like bone absorb X rays well and show up as light areas, whereas soft tissues absorb X rays to a lesser extent and show up as dark areas on photographic film. During CAT (computerized axial tomography) scans, X rays are sent through the body at various angles, and a computer uses the information to form a series of cross sections (fig. 3A). CAT scanning has all but eliminated the need for exploratory surgery.

PET (positron emission tomography) is a variation of CAT scanning. Radioactively labeled substances are injected into the body; metabolically active tissues tend to take them up and then emit gamma rays. This information is used by a computer to again generate cross-sectional images of the body, but this time the image indicates metabolic activity, not structure. PET scanning is used to diagnose brain disorders such as tumor of the brain, where a stroke has occurred, or whether the person has Alzheimer disease or epilepsy.

During MRI (magnetic resonance imaging), the patient lies in a massive, hollow, cylindrical magnet and is exposed to short bursts of a powerful magnetic field. This causes the protons (nuclei of hydrogen atoms) to align; then, when exposed to strong radio waves, they come out of alignment and produce a signal. A computer changes these signals into an image (fig. 3B). Tissues that have a lot of hydrogen atoms (such as fat) show up as bright areas, and those that contain little hydrogen (such as bone) appear black. Since this is the opposite of an X ray, you can see why MRI is more useful than an X ray for imaging soft tissues. However, many people cannot undergo MRI, since the magnetic field can actually pull metal objects out of the body, such as a tooth filling, a prosthesis, or a pacemaker!

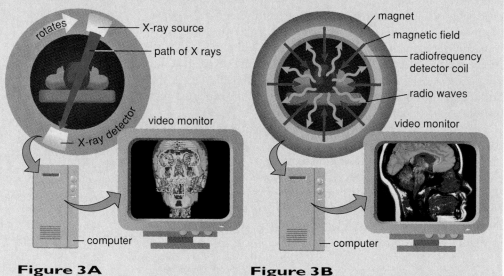

Figure 3A
CAT scan

Figure 3B
MRI

Isotopes Have Many Uses

All atoms of an element have the same number of protons but may differ in the number of neutrons. A carbon atom, for instance, may have more or less than its usual six neutrons. Atoms that have the same atomic number and differ only in the number of neutrons are called **isotopes** [Gk. *iso,* equal, and *topos,* place] (fig. 3.3). Isotopes have many uses. Because proportions of isotopes in various food sources are known, biologists can now determine the proportion of isotopes in mummified or fossilized human tissues to know what ancient peoples ate. Most isotopes are stable, but *radioactive isotopes* break down and emit radiation in the form of radioactive particles or radiant energy. It is the custom to use radioactive isotopes as tracers in biochemical experiments. For example, they were used to detect the sequential biochemical steps that occur during photosynthesis. And because carbon 14 (^{14}C) breaks down at a known rate, the amount of ^{14}C remaining is often used to determine the age of fossils. Radioactivity is also used in medical diagnostic procedures, as discussed in the reading on this page.

Figure 3.3

All atoms of a prticular element have the same atomic number, which tells the number of protons. This number is often written as a subscript to the lower left of the atomic symbol. The atomic weight (mass) is often written as a superscript to the upper left of the atomic symbol. For example, the carbon atom can be noted in this way:

atomic weight ——— $^{12}_{6}$**C** ——— atomic symbol
atomic number ———

Isotopes are atoms of the same element that differ in weight. The number of protons stays the same, but the number of neutrons can vary. The above configuration is the most common isotope of carbon; other isotopes are:

$$^{13}_{6}\text{C} \quad ^{14}_{6}\text{C} \quad ^{15}_{6}\text{C}$$

Figure 3.4

Electron energy levels. **a.** Electrons possess stored energy to different degrees. Those with the least amount of energy are found closest to the nucleus, and those with more energy are found farther from the nucleus. These energy levels are also called electron shells. **b.** An electron can absorb energy from an outside source, such as sunlight, and then move to a higher energy level. **c.** An electron can later give up the energy absorbed and drop back to its former energy level. This ability of an electron to absorb energy is important during photosynthesis.

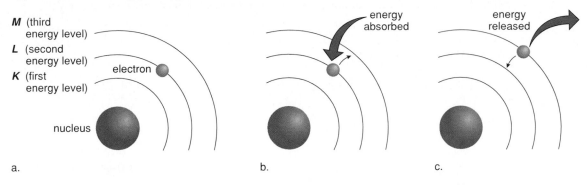

Atoms Have Chemical Properties

Protons and electrons carry a charge; protons have a positive (+) electrical charge and electrons have a negative (−) electrical charge. When an atom is electrically neutral, the number of protons equals the number of electrons. Therefore, in electrically neutral atoms, the atomic number tells you the number of protons and the number of electrons. For example, a carbon atom has an atomic number of six (table 3.1) and when electrically neutral, it has six protons and six electrons. Atoms have different chemical properties (the way they react with other atoms) because they each have a different number of electrons arranged about the nucleus.

> The chemical properties of atoms differ because the number and the arrangement of their electrons are different.

How do you know how electrons are to be placed in an atom? We will primarily use a simplified diagram of an atom called the Bohr model (see fig. 3.2b). In the Bohr model, electrons are placed in concentric energy levels, often called *electron shells,* about the nucleus. The Bohr model allows you to see how many electrons are in the outer shell, a characteristic that determines the reactivity of an atom.

A Bohr model provides a useful but very simplified diagram of the structure of an atom. As figure 3.2a shows, we can know only the probable location of electrons. The volumes of space where electrons are predicted to be found are termed **orbitals.** An electron shell can have one or more orbitals.

Electrons Move About the Nucleus

Why do electrons occupy different shells? All electrons have the same weight and charge, but they vary in energy content. **Energy** is defined as the ability to do work. Electrons differ in the amount of their *potential energy,* that is, stored energy ready to do work. The relative amount of stored energy is designated by placing electrons in electron shells about the nucleus (fig. 3.4). Electrons with the least amount of potential energy are located in the shell closest to the nucleus, called the *K* shell. Electrons in the next higher shell, called the *L* shell, have more energy, and so forth as we proceed from shell to shell outside the nucleus. An analogy may help you appreciate that the farther electrons are from the nucleus, the more potential energy they possess. Falling water has energy, as witnessed by how it can turn a waterwheel connected to a shaft that transfers the energy to machinery for grinding grain, cutting wood, or weaving cloth. The higher the waterfall, the greater the amount of energy released per unit amount of water.

Our analogy is not exact because the potential energy possessed by electrons is not due to gravity; it is due to the attraction between the positively charged protons and the negatively charged electrons. It takes energy to keep an electron farther away from the nucleus as opposed to closer to the nucleus. You have often heard that sunlight provides the energy for photosynthesis in green plants, but it may come as a surprise to learn that when a pigment such as chlorophyll absorbs the energy of the sun, electrons move to higher energy levels about the nuclei. An electron can become so energized that it actually leaves an atom and joins another one. Later, the electron releases energy when it drops back to a lower energy level.

Figure 3.5

Electron orbitals. Each electron energy level (see fig. 3.4) has one or more orbitals, a volume of space in which the rapidly moving electrons are most likely found. The nucleus is at the intersection of axes *x*, *y*, and *z*. **a.** The first energy level (electron shell) has only one orbital, which has a spherical shape. Two electrons can occupy this orbital. **b.** The second energy level has one spherical-shaped orbital and three dumbbell-shaped orbitals at right angles to each other. Since two electrons can occupy each orbital, there are a total of eight electrons in the second electron shell. Each orbital is drawn separately here, but actually the second spherical orbital surrounds the first spherical orbital, and the dumbbell-shaped orbitals pass through the spherical ones.

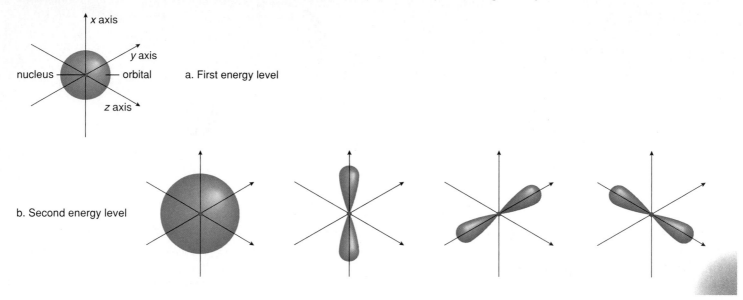

Electrons Occupy Orbitals

Although it is not possible to determine where rapidly moving electrons are from moment to moment, it is possible to describe the pattern of their motion. As mentioned, these volumes of space are called orbitals. Each shell of the Bohr model has one or more orbitals that depict the probable location of electrons as they move about the nucleus (fig. 3.5).

An orbital has a characteristic energy state and a characteristic shape. At the first energy level, there is only a single spherical orbital, where at most two electrons are found about the nucleus (fig. 3.5). The space is spherical shaped because the most likely location for each electron is a fixed distance in all directions from the nucleus. At the second energy level, there are four orbitals; one of these is spherical shaped but the other three are dumbbell shaped. This is the shape that allows the electrons to be most distant from one another. Since each orbital can hold two electrons, there are a maximum of eight electrons in this shell. Higher shells can be more complex and contain more orbitals if they are an inside shell. If such a shell is the outer shell, it too has only four orbitals and a maximum number of eight electrons.

Atomic Configurations

Since the manner in which atoms react with one another is dependent upon the number of electrons in the outer shell, it is helpful to have a convenient way to determine and to show this number. The examples of electrically neutral atoms in figure 3.6 will help you learn to do this. The first shell of an atom can contain up to two electrons; thereafter, each shell of those atoms, up to and including atom 20, calcium, can contain eight electrons. For these atoms, each lower shell is filled with electrons before the next higher shell contains any electrons.

The hydrogen atom shown in figure 3.6 is the smallest atom and has only one proton and one electron; therefore, the outer shell has only one electron. Carbon, on the other hand, has an atomic number of 6. It has six protons in the nucleus and six electrons in the shells (two electrons in the first shell and four electrons in the second, or outer, shell). Magnesium, with an atomic number of 12, has three shells (two electrons in the first shell, eight electrons in the second shell, and two electrons in the third, or outer, shell).

Figure 3.6

Bohr models of atoms most characteristic of biological molecules. Electrons are placed in energy levels (electron shells) according to certain rules: the first shell can contain up to two electrons and each shell thereafter can contain up to eight electrons as long as we consider only atoms with an atomic number of 20 or below. Each shell is to be filled before electrons are placed in the next shell.

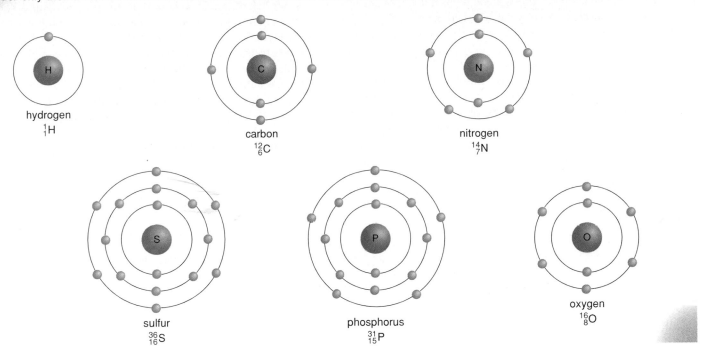

hydrogen
$^{1}_{1}H$

carbon
$^{12}_{6}C$

nitrogen
$^{14}_{7}N$

sulfur
$^{36}_{16}S$

phosphorus
$^{31}_{15}P$

oxygen
$^{16}_{8}O$

In the periodic table (see appendix B) elements are vertically arranged according to the number of electrons in the outer shell. If an atom has only one shell, the outer shell is complete when it has two electrons. Otherwise, *the octet rule,* which states that the outer shell is complete when it has eight electrons, holds. Atoms with eight electrons in the outer shell do not react at all; they are said to be inert. Atoms with fewer than eight electrons in the outer shell react with other atoms in such a way that after the reaction, each has a completed outer shell. Atoms can give up, accept, or share electrons in order to have a completed outer shell.

> **The number of electrons in the outer shell determines the manner in which atoms react with one another.**

Writing Chemical Formulas and Equations

When writing chemical formulas, atomic symbols are used to represent the atoms, and subscripts are used to indicate how many atoms of each type there are in a substance. For example, the chemical formula H_2O (read as H-two-O) indicates that a water molecule contains two hydrogen atoms and one oxygen atom. The chemical formula for glucose contains many atoms:

one molecule

$$C_6 H_{12} O_6$$

indicates 6 atoms of carbon | indicates 12 atoms of hydrogen | indicates 6 atoms of oxygen

Formulas are used in chemical equations to represent chemical reactions that occur between atoms and molecules:

$$6CO_2 + 6H_2O \longrightarrow C_6H_{12}O_6 + 6O_2$$

carbon dioxide   water   glucose   oxygen

In this equation, which is often used to represent photosynthesis, six molecules of carbon dioxide react with six molecules of water to yield one glucose molecule and six molecules of oxygen. The reactants (molecules that participate in the reaction) are shown on the left of the arrow and the products (molecules formed by the reaction) are shown on the right. Notice that the equation is "balanced," that is, there are the same number of each type of atom on both sides of the arrow.

ATOMS FORM COMPOUNDS AND MOLECULES

Simple molecules form when two or more atoms of the same element react with one another. Atmospheric oxygen does not exist as a single atom, O; instead, two oxygen atoms are joined as O_2. When atoms of two or more different elements react or bond together, a **compound** results. Water (H_2O) is a compound that contains the elements hydrogen and oxygen. We can also speak of H_2O as a **molecule** [L. *moles*, mass], because a molecule is the smallest part of a compound that still has the properties of that compound.

Electrons possess energy; therefore, the bonds that exist between atoms in molecules are energy relationships. Organisms are dependent upon chemical bond energy to maintain their organization. When a chemical reaction occurs electrons shift in their relationship to one another and energy may be given off. This is the energy that we make use of to carry on our daily lives.

Opposite Charges in Ionic Bonding

Ionic bonds form when electrons are transferred from one atom to another. For example, sodium (Na), with only one electron in its third shell, tends to be an electron *donor* (fig. 3.7). Once it gives up this electron, the second shell, with eight electrons, becomes its outer shell. Chlorine (Cl), on the other hand, tends to be an electron *acceptor*. Its outer shell has seven electrons, so it needs only one more electron to have a completed outer shell. When a sodium atom and a chlorine atom come together, an electron is transferred from the sodium atom to the chlorine atom. Now both atoms have eight electrons in their outer shells.

This electron transfer, however, causes a charge imbalance in each atom. The sodium atom has one more proton than it has electrons; therefore, it has a net charge of +1 (symbolized by Na^+). The chlorine atom has one more electron than it has protons; therefore, it has a net charge of −1 (symbolized by Cl^-).

Figure 3.7

During an ionic reaction, an electron is transferred from one atom to another. **a.** Formation of sodium chloride, an ionic compound. Here a single electron passes from sodium (Na) to chlorine (Cl). At the completion of the reaction, each atom has eight electrons in the outer shell, but each also carries a charge. Sodium now has a net charge of +1, symbolized as Na^+, and chlorine has a net charge of −1, symbolized as Cl^-. An ionic bond is the attraction between ions that carry a charge. **b.** Ionic bonding between Na^+ and Cl^- causes the atoms to assume a three-dimensional lattice in which each sodium ion is surrounded by six chlorine ions, and each chlorine ion is surrounded by six sodium ions. **c.** The crystals of table salt can vary in size, but their structure still is due to the lattice formation.

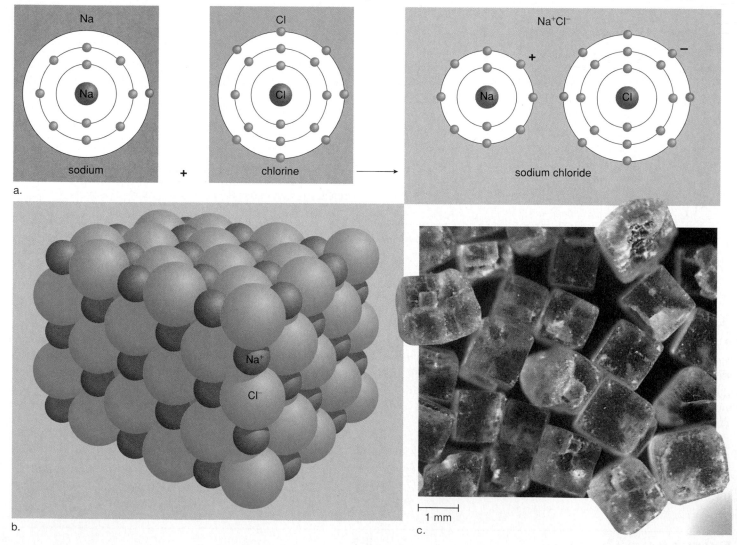

Such charged particles are called **ions.** Sodium (Na⁺) and chlorine (Cl⁻) are not the only biologically important ions. Some, such as potassium (K⁺), are formed by the transfer of a single electron to another atom; others, such as calcium (Ca⁺⁺) and magnesium (Mg⁺⁺), are formed by the transfer of two electrons.

Ionic compounds are held together by an attraction between the charged ions called an **ionic bond.** When sodium reacts with chlorine, an ionic compound called sodium chloride (Na⁺Cl⁻) results, and the reaction is called an ionic reaction. Sodium chloride is a salt commonly known as table salt because it is used to season our food (fig. 3.7c). Salts can exist as dry solids, but when such a compound is placed in water, the ions separate as the salt dissolves, as when Na⁺Cl⁻ separates into Na⁺ and Cl⁻. Ionic compounds are most commonly found in this dissociated (ionized) form in biological systems because these systems are 70–90% water (fig. 3.8).

> The transfer of electron(s) between atoms results in ions that are held together by an ionic bond, the attraction of negative and positive charges.

Figure 3.8
Killer whale, *Orcinus,* emerges from the sea. Seawater and the blood of vertebrates are strikingly similar in terms of the kinds of salts present and the relative concentrations of these salts. Life is believed to have originated in the sea, and the first organisms were adapted to a seawater environment. Since then, life forms have also become adapted to the freshwater and land environments. Even so, vertebrate blood has something of the same relative salt concentrations as the sea.

Sharing in Covalent Bonding

A **covalent bond** [L. *co,* with, and *valent,* strength] results when two atoms *share* electrons in such a way that each atom has a completed outer shell. Consider the hydrogen atom, which has one electron in the first shell—a shell that is complete when it contains two electrons. If hydrogen is in the presence of a strong electron acceptor, it gives up its electron to become a hydrogen ion (H⁺). But if this is not possible, hydrogen can share with another atom and thereby have a completed outer shell. For example, a hydrogen atom can share with another hydrogen atom. In this case, the two orbitals overlap and the electrons are shared between them (fig. 3.9a). Because they share the electron pair, each atom has a completed outer shell. When a reaction results in a covalent molecule, it is called a covalent reaction.

Figure 3.9
Covalently bonded molecules. In a covalent bond, atoms share electrons so that each atom has a completed outer shell. **a.** A molecule of hydrogen (H_2) contains two hydrogen atoms sharing a pair of electrons. This single covalent bond can be represented in any of the three ways shown. **b.** A molecule of oxygen (O_2) contains two oxygen atoms sharing two pairs of electrons. This results in a double covalent bond. **c.** A molecule of methane (CH_4) contains one carbon atom bonded to four hydrogen atoms. By sharing, each has a completed outer shell.

Electron Model	Structural Formula	Molecular Formula
a. H H	H–H	H_2
b. O O	O=O	O_2
c. H, H, C, H, H	H–C–H (with H above and H below)	CH_4

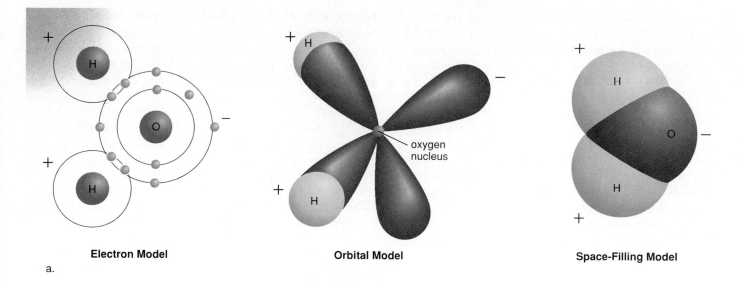

Electron Model   **Orbital Model**   **Space-Filling Model**

a.

oxygen
nucleus

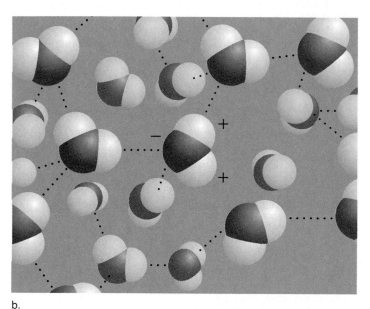

b.

Figure 3.10

Water molecule. **a.** Three models of the structure of water. The two-dimensional electron model of the structure of water does not tell anything about the shape of the molecule. The orbital model shows that when an atom of two energy levels (such as oxygen) combines with other atoms, the four orbitals of the outer shell (fig. 3.5*b*) rearrange to produce tear-shaped orbitals that point toward the corners of a tetrahedron; however, in water only two of the orbitals are utilized in covalent bonding. The space-filling model shows that the water molecule has a V shape. Water is a polar molecule, and because the oxygen attracts the electrons more strongly than do the hydrogens, there is a partial positive charge on each hydrogen and a partial negative charge on the oxygen. **b.** Hydrogen bonding between water molecules. A hydrogen bond is the attraction of a partially positive hydrogen to a partially negative atom in the vicinity. Each water molecule can bond to four other molecules in this manner. When water is in its liquid state, some hydrogen bonds are forming and others are breaking at all times.

A more common way to symbolize that atoms are sharing electrons is to draw a line between the two atoms as in the structural formula H–H. In a molecular formula, the line is omitted and the molecule is simply written as H_2.

Like a single bond between two hydrogen atoms, a double bond can also allow two atoms to complete their octets. In a double covalent bond, two atoms share two pairs of electrons (fig. 3.9*b*). In order to show that oxygen gas (O_2) contains a double bond, the molecule can be written as O=O.

It is even possible for atoms to form triple covalent bonds as in nitrogen gas (N_2), which can be written as N≡N. Single covalent bonds between atoms are quite strong, but double and triple bonds are even stronger.

> In a covalent molecule, atoms share electrons; not only single bonds but also double and even triple bonds are possible.

Some Covalent Bonds Are Polar

Normally, the sharing of electrons between two atoms is fairly equal, and the covalent bond is nonpolar. All the molecules in figure 3.9, including methane (CH_4), are nonpolar. In the case of water (H_2O), however, the sharing of electrons between oxygen and each hydrogen is not completely equal. The larger oxygen atom, with the greater number of protons, dominates the H_2O association. Electronegativity is a relative measure of the power of an atom in a covalent molecule to attract electrons to itself. The oxygen atom is more electronegative than the hydrogen atom, and it can attract the electron pair to a greater extent. In a water molecule, this causes the oxygen atom to assume a slightly negative charge and it causes the hydrogen atoms to assume a slightly positive charge. The unequal sharing of electrons in a covalent bond creates a **polar covalent bond,** and the molecule itself is a polar molecule (fig. 3.10).

> The water molecule is a polar molecule, the oxygen atom carries a slight negative charge and the hydrogen atoms carry a slight positive charge.

Hydrogen Bonding

Polarity within a water molecule causes the hydrogen atoms in one molecule to be attracted to the oxygen atoms in other molecules (fig. 3.10*b*). This attractive force creates a weak bond called a **hydrogen bond.** This bond is often represented by a dotted line because a hydrogen bond is easily broken. Hydrogen bonding is not unique to water. A biological molecule can contain many polar covalent bonds involving hydrogen and usually oxygen or nitrogen. The electropositive hydrogen atom of one bond is attracted to the electronegative oxygen or nitrogen atom of another bond within the same or different molecules.

Although a hydrogen bond is more easily broken than a covalent bond, many hydrogen bonds taken together are quite strong. Hydrogen bonds between parts of cellular molecules help maintain their proper structure and function. We will see that some of the important properties of water are also due to hydrogen bonding.

> A hydrogen bond occurs between a slightly positive hydrogen atom of one molecule and a slightly negative atom of another molecule or between parts of the same molecule.

Ionization Releases Ions

Covalently bonded molecules sometimes ionize; the atoms dissociate into ions. Water is one of these molecules; but in any quantity of water only a few molecules ionize. When water ionizes, it releases hydrogen ions (H^+) and hydroxyl ions (OH^-) in equal number:

$$H-O-H \rightleftharpoons H^+ + OH^-$$
$$\text{water} \qquad \text{hydrogen} \quad \text{hydroxyl}$$
$$\text{ion} \qquad \text{ion}$$

This equation is written with a double arrow because the reaction is reversible. Just as water can release hydrogen and hydroxyl ions, these same ions can also join to form water.

Ionization occurs because a hydrogen already engaged in a hydrogen bond splits off, and a hydroxyl ion remains. Ionization is not unique to small molecules; some of the larger molecules characteristic of living things also ionize. These are the cellular macromolecules that best interact with water because their unlike charges are attracted to one another. Such molecules are termed hydrophilic.

Reactions in Cells

Certain reactions are seen quite often in cells, and two of these are discussed here.

Oxidation Is the Opposite of Reduction

Oxidation-reduction reactions are an important type of reaction in cells, but the terminology was derived from studying reactions outside of cells. When oxygen combines with a metal, oxygen receives electrons and becomes negatively charged and the metal loses electrons and becomes positively charged.

Today, the terms **oxidation** and **reduction** are applied to many ionic reactions, whether or not oxygen is involved. Very simply, *oxidation refers to the loss of electrons, and reduction refers to the gain of electrons.* In our previous ionic reaction, $Na + Cl \rightarrow Na^+Cl^-$, the sodium has been oxidized (loss of electron) and the chlorine has been reduced (gain of electron).

The terms oxidation and reduction are also applied to certain covalent reactions. In this case, however, oxidation is the loss of hydrogen atoms, and reduction is the gain of hydrogen atoms. A hydrogen atom contains one proton (symbolized as H^+) and one electron (symbolized as e^-). Therefore, when a molecule loses a hydrogen atom, it has lost an electron, and when a molecule gains a hydrogen atom, it has gained an electron.

WATER IS ESSENTIAL TO LIFE

Life evolved in water, and living things are 70–90% water. What are the unique properties of water making it essential to the continuance of life (fig. 3.11)? Water is a polar molecule and water molecules are hydrogen bonded to one another (fig. 3.10). A hydrogen bond is much weaker than a covalent bond within a water molecule, but taken together, hydrogen bonds cause water molecules to cling together. Without hydrogen bonding between molecules, water would boil at −80° C and freeze at −100° C, making life as we know it impossible. But because of hydrogen bonding, water is a liquid at temperatures suitable for life. It boils at 100° C and freezes at 0° C. Water also has other important properties (table 3.3).

Water Has Unique Properties

1. *Water is the universal solvent and facilitates chemical reactions both outside of and within living systems.* Water is the universal solvent in that it dissolves a great number of solutes. When a salt, such as sodium chloride (Na^+Cl^-), is put into water, the negative ends of the water molecules are attracted to the sodium ions, and the positive ends of the water molecules are attracted to the chloride ions. This causes the sodium ions and the chloride ions to separate and to dissolve in water:

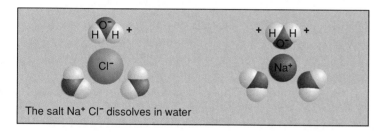

The salt Na^+ Cl^- dissolves in water

Water is also a solvent for larger molecules that contain ionized atoms or are polar molecules:

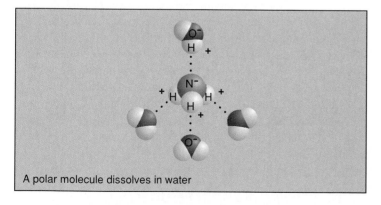

A polar molecule dissolves in water

When ions and molecules disperse in water, they move about and collide, allowing reactions to occur. Those molecules that can attract water are said to be **hydrophilic** [L. *hydr,* water, and Gk. *phil,* loving].

Figure 3.11

Properties of water. **a.** The temperature of water changes slowly, and a great deal of heat is needed for vaporization to occur. **b.** Ice is less dense than liquid water and, therefore, bodies of water freeze from the top down, making ice fishing possible after a hole is drilled through the ice. **c.** The heat needed to vaporize water can help animals in a hot climate maintain internal temperatures.

a.

b.

c.

Table 3.3

Water

Properties	Chemistry	Result
Universal solvent	Polarity	Facilitates chemical reactions
Adheres and is cohesive	Polarity; hydrogen bonding	Serves as transport medium
Resists changes in temperature	Hydrogen bonding	Helps keep body temperatures constant
Resists change of state (from liquid to ice and from liquid to steam)	Hydrogen bonding	Moderates earth's temperature
Less dense as ice than as liquid water	Hydrogen bonding changes	Ice floats on water

Nonionized and nonpolar molecules that cannot attract water are said to be **hydrophobic** [L. *hydr*, water, and Gk. *phobos*, dreading].

2. *Water molecules are cohesive.* Water flows freely, yet water molecules do not break apart. They cling together because of hydrogen bonding. Water molecules also adhere to surfaces, particularly polar surfaces. Therefore, water can fill a tubular vessel and still flow so that dissolved and suspended molecules are evenly distributed throughout a system. For these reasons, water is an excellent transport system both outside of and within living organisms. One-celled organisms rely on external water to transport nutrient and waste molecules, but multicellular organisms often contain internal vessels in which water serves to transport nutrients and wastes.

3. *The temperature of liquid water rises and falls more slowly than that of most other liquids.* A calorie of heat energy is needed to raise the temperature of one gram of water 1° C. This is about twice the amount of heat required for other covalently bonded liquids. The many hydrogen bonds that link water molecules help water absorb heat without a great change in temperature. Because water holds heat so effectively, its temperature falls more slowly. This property of water is important not only for aquatic organisms but also for all living things. Water protects organisms from rapid temperature changes and helps them maintain their normal internal temperatures.

4. *Water has a high heat of vaporization.* Converting one gram of the coldest liquid water to ice requires the loss of 80 calories of heat energy. Converting one gram of the hottest water to steam requires an input of 540 calories of heat energy (fig. 3.12). Hydrogen bonds must be broken to change water to steam; this accounts for the very large amount of heat needed for evaporation. This property of water helps moderate the earth's temperature so that it permits the continuance of life. It also gives animals in a hot environment an efficient way to release excess body heat. When an animal sweats, body heat is used to vaporize the sweat, thus cooling the animal.

Figure 3.12

Water properties. Water is the only common molecule that can be a solid, a liquid, or a gas according to the environmental temperature. At ordinary temperatures and pressure, water is a liquid, and it takes a large input of heat to change it to steam. (When we perspire, our body heat is causing water to vaporize; therefore, sweating causes us to cool off.) In contrast, water gives off heat when it freezes, and this heat will keep the environmental temperature higher than expected. Can you see why there are less severe changes in temperature along the coasts?

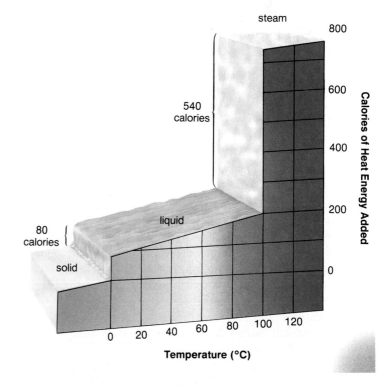

Figure 3.13

Most substances contract when they solidify, but water expands. Water is most dense at 4° C and becomes less dense as it either cools or warms. At 0° C water freezes, forming a lattice structure in which the hydrogen bonds are fixed. The water molecules in the lattice are further apart than in liquid water. Therefore, ice is less dense than liquid water and ice floats on liquid water. When water vaporizes at 100° C, all the hydrogen bonds are broken, and the molecules move away from one another.

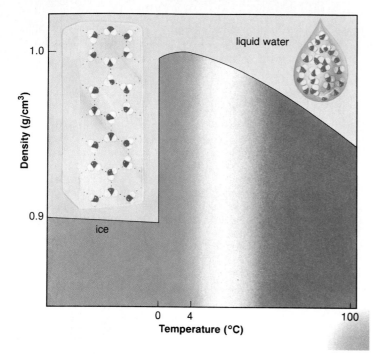

5. *Frozen water is less dense than liquid water.* As water cools, the molecules come closer together. They are densest at 4° C, but they are still moving about (fig. 3.13). At temperatures below 4° C, there is only vibrational movement, and hydrogen bonding becomes more rigid but also more open. This makes ice less dense than liquid water, which is why ice floats on liquid water. Bodies of water always freeze from the top down. When a body of water freezes on the surface, the ice acts as an insulator to prevent the water below it from freezing. This protects many aquatic organisms so that they can survive the winter.

> **Water has unique properties that allow cellular activities to occur and that make life on earth possible.**

Water and Acids and Bases

As previously mentioned, when water ionizes, it releases an equal number of hydrogen ions (H^+) and hydroxyl ions (OH^-):

$$H-O-H \rightleftharpoons H^+ + OH^-$$

water   hydrogen   hydroxyl
ion   ion

Only a few water molecules at a time are dissociated, and the actual number of these ions is very small (10^{-7} moles/liter).

There are many other substances that also dissociate and contribute ions to a given solution, which is a liquid containing a dissolved substance. **Acids** [L. *acidus,* sour] are molecules that release hydrogen ions when they dissociate. A strong acid, such as hydrochloric acid (HCl), dissociates almost completely when put into water:

$$HCl \longrightarrow H^+ + Cl^-$$

hydrochloric   hydrogen   chloride
acid   ion   ion

In contrast, **bases** are molecules that can take up hydrogen ions. When sodium hydroxide (NaOH) dissociates, hydroxyl ions are added in great numbers thereby decreasing the relative concentration of hydrogen ions. Sodium hydroxide is termed a strong base because it dissociates almost completely when put into water:

$$NaOH \longrightarrow Na^+ + OH^-$$

sodium   sodium   hydroxyl
hydroxide   ion   ion

pH Scale

Acids and bases affect the hydrogen ion concentration [H^+] in a solution. These concentrations are usually very small numbers and cumbersome to work with, so they are converted to their negative logarithms, p, and symbolized as pH:

[H^+] (moles per liter)	pH
1×10^{-5}	5
1×10^{-6}	6
1×10^{-7}	7

Notice that because the **pH scale** gives the negative logarithm of the [H^+], the scale is in positive numbers and a change of one unit involves a tenfold change in hydrogen ion concentration. Therefore, pH 6 has 10 times the [H^+] of pH 7, and pH 5 has one hundred times the [H^+] of pH 7.

Figure 3.14 illustrates the pH scale and the relative [H^+] and [OH^-] for each unit of the scale, which ranges from 0 to 14. *The pH of pure water is 7; this is neutral pH when [H^+] = [OH^-].* Acids have a pH from 0 to 7 and bases have a pH from 7 to 14. Therefore, pH 6.9 is acidic, while pH 7.1 is basic.

Figure 3.14

The pH scale. The proportionate amount of hydrogen ions to hydroxide ions is indicated by the diagonal line. Any pH above 7 is basic, while any pH below 7 is acidic.

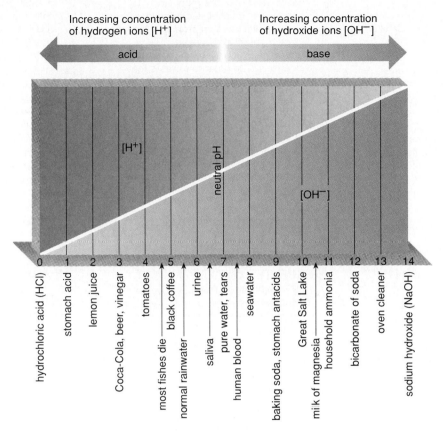

Buffers

Human blood has a pH of about 7.4, and a much higher or lower pH causes illness. Normally, pH stability is possible because organisms have built-in mechanisms to prevent pH changes. Buffers are the most important of these mechanisms. A **buffer** is a chemical or a combination of chemicals that can both take up and release hydrogen ions. Carbonic acid (H_2CO_3) helps buffer human blood because it is a weak acid that does not totally dissociate:

$$H_2CO_3 \rightleftharpoons H^+ + HCO_3^-$$

carbonic   hydrogen   bicarbonate
acid   ion   ion

When excess hydrogen ions are present in blood, the reaction goes to the left, and carbonic acid forms to maintain the pH. If hydroxyl ions are added to blood, water will form, effectively removing hydrogen ions. Other types of bases can directly combine with hydrogen ions. When a base removes hydrogen ions, the reaction goes to the right, and the pH is maintained.

It is possible to overcome an organism's buffering ability. Usually, however, buffers keep the pH within normal limits despite the many biochemical reactions that either release or take up hydrogen or hydroxyl ions.

Acids have a pH that is less than 7, and bases have a pH that is greater than 7. Organisms contain buffers that help maintain the pH within a normal range.

Summary

1. Both living and nonliving things are composed of matter consisting of elements. Each element contains atoms of just one type. The acronym CHNOPS tells us the most common elements (atoms) found in living things.

2. Atoms contain subatomic particles. Protons and neutrons in the nucleus determine the weight of an atom. Electrons are outside the nucleus and have almost no weight.

3. The atomic number indicates the number of protons and the number of electrons in electrically neutral atoms. Protons have a positive charge and electrons have a negative charge. Before atoms react, the charges are equal.

4. Isotopes are atoms of the same type that differ in their number of neutrons. Radioactive isotopes are used as tracers in biological experiments and medical procedures.

5. Electrons occupy energy levels (electron shells) at discrete distances from the nucleus. When electrons absorb energy from an outside source, they move to a higher level, and when they release energy, they drop back to a lower level.

6. Electron shells have orbitals. The first shell has a single spherical-shaped orbital. The second shell has four orbitals: the first is spherical shaped and the others are dumbbell shaped.

7. The number of electrons in the outer shell determines the reactivity of an atom. The first shell is complete when it has two electrons; in atoms up through calcium, number 20, every shell thereafter is complete with eight electrons. The octet rule states that atoms react with one another in order to have a completed outer shell that contains eight electrons.

8. Most atoms, including those common to living things, do not have completed outer shells. This causes them to react with one another to form compounds and/or molecules. Following the reaction, the atoms have completed outer shells.

9. When an ionic reaction occurs, one or more electrons are transferred from one atom to another. The ionic bond is an attraction between the resulting ions.

10. When a covalent reaction occurs, atoms share electrons. A covalent bond is the sharing of these electrons. There are single, double, and triple covalent bonds.

11. In polar covalent bonds, the sharing of electrons is not equal; one of the atoms exerts greater attraction for the electrons than the other and a slight charge results on each atom. A hydrogen bond is a weak attraction between a slightly positive hydrogen atom and a slightly negative oxygen or nitrogen atom within the same or a different molecule. Hydrogen bonds help maintain the structure and function of cellular molecules.

12. Chemical equations are used to symbolize chemical reactions. An atom that has lost electrons (or hydrogen atoms) has been oxidized, and an atom that has gained electrons (or hydrogen atoms) has been reduced.

13. Water is a polar molecule, and hydrogen bonding occurs between water molecules. These two features account for the unique properties of water, which are summarized in table 3.3. These features allow cellular activities to occur and life to exist on earth.

14. Water dissociates to produce an equal number of hydrogen ions and hydroxyl ions. This is termed neutral pH. In acidic solutions, there are more hydrogen ions than hydroxyl ions; these solutions have a pH less than 7. In basic solutions, there are more hydroxyl ions than hydrogen ions; these solutions have a pH greater than 7. Cells are sensitive to pH changes, and biological systems tend to have buffers that help keep the pH within a normal range.

Writing Across the Curriculum

In order to practice writing skills, students should write out the answers to any or all of the study questions and the critical thinking questions. The study questions are sequenced in the same order as the text. Answers to the objective questions, and suggested answers to the critical thinking questions, are in appendix D.

Study Questions

1. Name the kinds of subatomic particles studied; list their weight, charge, and location in an atom. Which of these varies in isotopes?   25–26

2. Define energy level and orbital. What is their relationship?   27–28

3. Draw a simplified atomic structure for a carbon atom that has six protons and six neutrons.   28

4. Draw an atomic representation for the molecule $Mg^{++}Cl_2^-$. Using the octet rule, explain the structure of the compound.   30

5. Explain whether CO_2 (O=C=O) is an ionic or a covalent compound. Why does this arrangement satisfy all atoms involved?   31–32

6. Explain why water is a polar molecule. What is the relationship between the polarity of the molecule and the hydrogen bonding between water molecules?   33

7. Define oxidation and reduction and note which has been oxidized and which reduced in this equation:

$$4 \, Fe + 3 \, O_2 \rightarrow 2 \, Fe_2O_3$$

Explain why this equation is balanced.   33

8. Name five properties of water and relate them to the structure of water, including its polarity and hydrogen bonding between molecules.   34–35

9. Define an acid and a base. On the pH scale, which numbers indicate an acid, a base, and a neutral pH?   36

1. An atom that has two electrons in the outer shell would most likely
   a. share to acquire a completed outer shell.
   b. lose these two electrons and become a negatively charged ion.
   c. lose these two electrons and become a positively charged ion.
   d. form hydrogen bonds only.

2. The atomic number tells you the
   a. number of neutrons in the nucleus.
   b. number of protons in the atom.
   c. weight of the atom.
   d. All of these are correct.

3. An orbital
   a. has the same volume and charge as an electron shell.
   b. has the same space and energy content as the energy level.
   c. is the volume of space most likely occupied by an electron.
   d. causes an atom to react with another atom.

4. A covalent bond is indicated by
   a. plus and minus charges attached to atoms.
   b. dotted lines between hydrogen atoms.
   c. concentric circles about a nucleus.
   d. overlapping electron shells or a straight line between atomic symbols.

5. An atom has been oxidized when it
   a. combines with oxygen.
   b. gains an electron.
   c. loses an electron.
   d. Both a and c are correct.

6. In which of these are the electrons shared unequally?
   a. double covalent bond
   b. triple covalent bond
   c. hydrogen bond
   d. polar covalent bond

7. In the molecule

$$\begin{array}{c} H \\ | \\ H - C - H \\ | \\ H \end{array}$$

   a. all atoms have eight electrons in the outer shell.
   b. all atoms are sharing electrons.
   c. carbon could accept more hydrogen atoms.
   d. All of these are correct.

8. Which of these properties of water is not due to hydrogen bonding between water molecules?
   a. stabilizes temperature inside and outside cell
   b. molecules are cohesive
   c. is a universal solvent
   d. ice floats on water

9. Acids
   a. release hydrogen ions.
   b. have a pH value above 7.
   c. take up hydroxyl ions.
   d. Both a and b are correct.

10. Complete this diagram of a nitrogen atom by placing the correct number of protons and neutrons in the nucleus and electrons in the shells. Explain why the correct formula for ammonia is NH_3 and not NH_4.

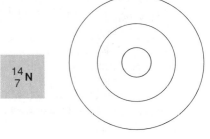

$$^{14}_{7}N$$

1. *Life has a chemical and physical basis.*
   Give an example from your knowledge of nutrition, medicine, or the environment to show that this concept has an everyday application.

2. *Atomic structure involves electronic energy levels.*
   Show that living things are dependent upon the energy relationships of electrons.

3. *Life is dependent upon the special properties of water.*
   Show that living things are absolutely dependent upon a particular property of water by explaining what would happen if water didn't have this property.

acid A compound tending to raise the hydrogen ion concentration in a solution and to lower its pH numerically. [L. *acidus,* sour]   36

atom The smallest particle of an element that displays its properties. [Gk. *atomos,* individual]   25

base A compound tending to lower the hydrogen ion concentration in a solution and raise its pH numerically.   36

buffer A substance or group of substances that tend to resist pH changes in a solution, thus stabilizing its relative acidity.   37

compound A substance having two or more different elements united chemically in fixed ratio.   30

covalent bond (koh-VAY-lent) A chemical bond in which atoms share one pair of electrons. [L. *co,* with, and *valent,* strength]   31

electron A negative subatomic particle, moving about in an energy level around the nucleus of an atom. [Gk. *electr,* amber, electricity]   25

energy Ability to do work and bring about change; occurs in a variety of forms.   27

hydrogen bond A weak bond that arises between a slightly positive hydrogen atom of one molecule and a slightly negative atom of another molecule or between parts of the same molecule.   33

hydrophilic (hy-druh-FIL-ik) A type of molecule that interacts with water by dissolving in water and/or forming hydrogen bonds with water molecules. [L. *hydr,* water, and Gk. *phil,* loving]   34

hydrophobic (hy-druh-FOH-bik) A type of molecule that does not interact with water because it is nonpolar. [L. *hydr,* water, and Gk. *phobos,* dreading]   35

ion Charged derivative of an atom—positive if the atom loses electrons and negative if the atom gains electrons.   31

ionic bond A chemical bond in which ions are attracted to one another by opposite charges.   31

isotopes Atoms having the same atomic number but a different atomic weight due to the number of neutrons. [Gk. *iso,* equal, and *topos,* place]   26

molecule The smallest part of a compound that retains the properties of the compound; also the union of two or more atoms of the same element. [L. *moles,* mass]   30

orbital A volume of space around a nucleus where electrons can be found most of the time.   27

oxidation (ahk-sih-DAY-shun) A loss of one or more electrons from an atom or molecule with a concurrent release of energy; in biological systems, generally the loss of hydrogen atoms.   33

pH scale A measurement scale for the hydrogen ion concentration [H^+] of a solution.   36

polar covalent bond A bond in which the sharing of electrons between atoms is unequal.   33

reduction A gain of electrons by an atom or molecule with a concurrent storage of energy; in biological systems, generally the gain of hydrogen atoms.   33

4

THE CHEMISTRY OF LIFE

Learning Objectives

Cells Contain Organic Molecules

- Explain and demonstrate the bonding patterns of a carbon atom.   42
- Recognize the various functional groups found in small organic molecules.   43
- Distinguish between condensation of monomers and hydrolysis of polymers.   44

Simple Sugars to Polysaccharides

- Recognize the molecular and structural formulas for glucose.   45
- Give examples of monosaccharides, disaccharides, and polysaccharides, and state their functions.   45–47

Fatty Acids to Lipids

- Give examples of various lipids, and state their functions.   48
- Recognize the structural formula for a saturated fatty acid, an unsaturated fatty acid, and the structural formula for a fat.   48–49

Amino Acids to Proteins

- Give examples of proteins, and state their functions.   52
- Recognize an amino acid, and demonstrate how a peptide bond is formed.   52
- Relate the four levels of protein structure to the bonding patterns observed at each level.   52–54

Nucleotides to Nucleic Acids

- State the two main types of nucleic acids and list their functions.   56
- Explain the structure of a nucleotide and tell how nucleotides are joined to form a nucleic acid.   57
- Compare the structures of DNA and RNA.   57
- Describe the structure and the function of ATP.   57

Atoms join to form small molecules and small molecules join to form macromolecules such as DNA, the substance of genes.

iving things are highly organized; therefore, it is easy for us to differentiate between the plant, the animal, and the bacterium in figure 4.1. We might even be inclined to think that these organisms are so different that they must contain entirely different types of chemicals. But this is not the case. Instead, they and all living things contain the same classes of primary molecules: carbohydrates, proteins, lipids, and nucleic acids. But within these classes there is molecular diversity among organisms. For example, the plant, the animal, and the bacterium all utilize a carbohydrate molecule for structural purposes, but the exact carbohydrate is different in each of them.

The most common elements in living things are carbon, hydrogen, nitrogen, and oxygen, which constitute about 95% of your body weight. But we will see that both the sameness and the diversity of life are dependent upon the chemical characteristics of carbon, an atom whose chemistry is essential to living things.

The bonding of hydrogen, oxygen, nitrogen, and other atoms to carbon creates the molecules known as **organic molecules**. Lay people sometimes use the word organic to mean wholesome. To biologists, organic molecules are those that always contain carbon and hydrogen. It is the organic molecules that characterize the structure and the function of living things like the primrose, the blueshell crab, and the bacterium in figure 4.1. **Inorganic**

Table 4.1

Inorganic versus Organic Molecules

Inorganic Molecules	Organic Molecules
Usually contain positive and negative ions	Always contain carbon and hydrogen
Usually ionic bonding	Always covalent bonding
Always contain a small number of atoms	May be quite large with many atoms
Often associated with nonliving elements	Usually associated with living organisms

molecules constitute nonliving matter, but even so, inorganic molecules like salts (e.g., Na^+Cl^-) also play important roles in living things. Table 4.1 contrasts inorganic and organic molecules.

Of the elements most common to living things, the chemistry of carbon allows the formation of varied organic molecules. This accounts for both the sameness and the diversity of living things.

Figure 4.1

Use of carbohydrate to provide structure. **a.** Plants are held erect partly by the incorporation of the polysaccharide cellulose into the cell wall, which surrounds each cell. **b.** The shell of crabs contains chitin, a different type of polysaccharide. **c.** Most bacterial cells, like plant cells, are enclosed by a cell wall, but in this case the wall is strengthened by another type of polysaccharide known as peptidoglycan.

250 nm

a.   b.   c.

CELLS CONTAIN ORGANIC MOLECULES

Carbon has four electrons in its outer shell, and this allows it to bond with as many as four other atoms. Moreover, because these bonds are covalent, they are quite strong. Usually carbon bonds to hydrogen, oxygen, nitrogen, or another carbon atom. The ability of carbon to bond to itself makes carbon chains of various lengths and shapes possible. Long chains containing fifty or more carbon atoms are not unusual in living systems. Carbon can also share two pairs of electrons with another atom, giving a double covalent bond. Carbon-to-carbon bonding sometimes results in ring compounds of biological significance.

Small Molecules Have Functional Groups

Carbon chains make up the skeleton or backbone of organic molecules. The small organic molecules in living things—sugars, fatty acids, amino acids, and nucleotides—all have a carbon backbone, but in addition they have characteristic functional groups (fig. 4.2). *Functional groups,* which are clusters of atoms with a certain pattern, always behave in a certain way. Therefore, functional groups help determine the characteristics of organic molecules.

One characteristic of an organic molecule of some importance is whether it is hydrophilic or hydrophobic. A polar molecule with plus and minus charges is **hydrophilic** [L. *hydr,* water, and Gk. *phil,* loving] and is attracted to water because water is also a polar molecule. A hydrocarbon (a molecule with only carbon and hydrogen) is always **hydrophobic** [L. *hydr,* water, and Gk. *phobos,* dreading], unless there is an ionized functional group.

For example, the carboxyl (acid) functional group, —COOH, can give up a hydrogen ion (H^+) and become ionized to —COO⁻. Then the molecule becomes hydrophilic.

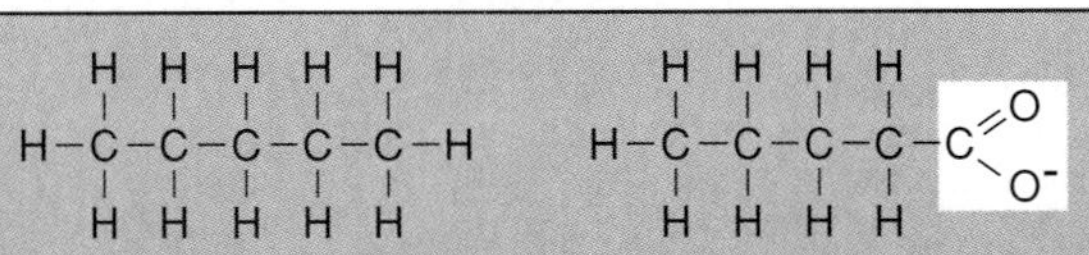

hydrocarbon
nonpolar
(hydrophobic)

acid in ionized form
polar
(hydrophilic)

Other functional groups (—OH, —CO, and —NH₂) are also polar even though they do not ionize. Since cells are 70–90% water, the ability or inability to interact with water profoundly affects the function of organic molecules in cells.

Functional groups add diversity to organic molecules. Another factor contributing to the diversity of organic molecules is the existence of isomers. **Isomers** [Gk. *iso,* equal, and *meris,* part] are molecules that have identical molecular formulas because they contain the same numbers and kinds of atoms, yet they are different molecules because the atoms in each isomer are arranged differently. For example, compounds with the molecular formula $C_3H_6O_3$ are assigned their own chemical name because the molecules differ structurally (fig. 4.3).

Figure 4.2

Functional groups. Molecules with the same type of backbone can still differ according to the type of functional group attached to the backbone. Many of these functional groups are polar, helping to make the molecule soluble in water. In this illustration, the remainder of the molecule (aside from the functional groups) is represented by an *R*.

Functional Groups		
Name	**Structure**	**Found in**
hydroxyl (alcohol)	$R-OH$	sugars
carboxyl (acid)	$R-C\begin{smallmatrix}O\\OH\end{smallmatrix}$	sugars fats amino acids
ketone	$R-\overset{O}{\underset{\|\|}{C}}-R$	sugars
aldehyde	$R-C\begin{smallmatrix}O\\H\end{smallmatrix}$	sugars
amine (amino)	$R-N\begin{smallmatrix}H\\H\end{smallmatrix}$	amino acids proteins
sulfhydryl	$R-SH$	amino acids proteins
phosphate	$R-O-\overset{O}{\underset{\underset{OH}{\|}}{\overset{\|\|}{P}}}-OH$	phospholipids nucleotides nucleic acids

R = remainder of molecule

Figure 4.3

Isomers. Isomers have the same molecular formula but different configurations. Both of these compounds have the formula $C_3H_6O_3$. **a.** In glyceraldehyde, oxygen is double-bonded to an end carbon. **b.** In dihydroxyacetone, oxygen is double-bonded to the middle carbon.

a. glyceraldehyde

b. dihydroxyacetone

Large Organic Molecules Have Monomers

Each of the small organic molecules already mentioned can be a unit of a large organic molecule, often called a *macromolecule*. A unit is called a *monomer*, and the macromolecule is called a **polymer** [Gk. *polus*, many, and *meris*, part]. Simple sugars (monosaccharides) are the monomers within polysaccharides; fatty acids and glycerol are found in fat, a lipid; amino acids join to form proteins; and nucleotides are the subunits of nucleic acids:

Polymer	Monomer
polysaccharide	monosaccharide
lipid (e.g., fat)	glycerol and fatty acid
protein	amino acid
nucleic acid	nucleotide

Cells contain only these four classes of macromolecules, and each has just this type monomer. Yet the macromolecules of each class can be quite varied. This is because the same type of monomer occurs in different varieties: there are different types of monosaccharides, fatty acids, amino acids, and nucleotides. Also, the same type of monomer can be joined in a way characteristic for a particular macromolecule, or it can have different functional groups. This is why macromolecular carbohydrates (i.e., polysaccharides) can have different characteristics as mentioned in the opening paragraph of this chapter. In the pages that follow, note the names of the various macromolecules, the monomers they contain, and how the monomers are joined. You will also want to know the functions of each type of macromolecule discussed.

> There are only a few types of molecules in cells, but these molecules still have great variety and therefore play different roles in cells.

Macromolecules are so named because they are very large; for example, the nucleic acid of a single cell can reach a length of about two meters. How do macromolecules get so large? Cells use the modular approach when constructing macromolecules, and the size of a macromolecule is dependent on the number of monomers it contains. In cellulose, a polysaccharide, thousands of glucose molecules are joined by the same type of bond. Regardless of the particular macromolecule and the type of bond that results, monomers are joined by an identical mechanism, which is described in the next section.

Condensation Is the Reverse of Hydrolysis

All macromolecules are made within a cell in essentially the same way. Two monomers join when a hydroxyl (—OH) group is removed from one monomer and a hydrogen (—H) is removed from the other (fig. 4.4*a*). This **condensation** of monomers is a *dehydration synthesis* because water is removed (dehydration) and a bond is made (synthesis). Condensation does not take place unless the proper enzyme (a molecule that speeds up a chemical reaction in cells) is present.

Polymers are broken down by **hydrolysis** [Gk. *hydr*, water, and *lysis*, loosening, dissolving], which is essentially the reverse of condensation; an —OH group from water attaches to one monomer and a —H attaches to the other (fig. 4.4*b*). This is a hydrolysis reaction because water is used to break a bond. Again, the proper enzyme is required.

Cells are constructed of macromolecules, and it is the macromolecules that perform the work of the cell. Macromolecules are therefore routinely built up and broken down in cells. Also, polysaccharides, in particular, serve as energy sources for cells. Their breakdown provides the energy needed by the cell to carry out dehydration synthesis and specialized activities such as muscle cell contraction or nerve cell conduction of impulses.

Figure 4.4

Synthesis and breakdown of polymers. **a.** In cells, synthesis often occurs when monomers are joined by condensation (removal of H_2O). **b.** Breakdown occurs when the monomers in a polymer are separated by hydrolysis (addition of H_2O).

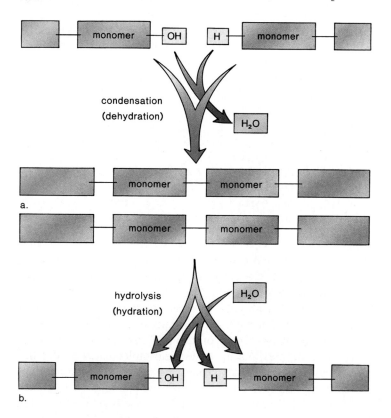

SIMPLE SUGARS TO POLYSACCHARIDES

Sugars and polysaccharides belong to a class of compounds called **carbohydrates** [L. *carbo*, charcoal, and Gk. *hydr*, water]. Simple sugars are *monosaccharides* (one sugar) with a carbon backbone of three to seven carbon atoms. The best known sugars are those that have six carbons (*hexoses*). **Glucose** [Gk. *gluco*, sweet, and *ose*, full of] is in the blood of animals, and *fructose* is frequently found in fruits. These sugars are isomers of each other. They all have the molecular formula $C_6H_{12}O_6$, but they differ in structure (fig. 4.5). Structural differences cause molecules to vary in shape, which is best seen by using space-filling models. Shape is very important in determining how molecules interact with one another.

Ribose and *deoxyribose* are two five-carbon sugars (*pentoses*) of significance because they are found respectively in the nucleic acids RNA and DNA. RNA and DNA are discussed later in the chapter.

A *disaccharide* contains two monosaccharides that have joined by condensation. *Sucrose* is a disaccharide that contains glucose and fructose (fig. 4.6). Sugar is transported within the body of a plant in the form of sucrose, and this is the sugar we use at the table to sweeten our food. We acquire this sugar from plants, such as sugar cane and sugar beets.

Lactose is a disaccharide that contains galactose and glucose and is found in milk. *Maltose* (composed of two glucose molecules) is a disaccharide of interest because it is found in our digestive tract as a result of starch digestion.

The most common *polysaccharides* in living things are starch, glycogen, and cellulose. Each of these is a polymer of glucose.

Figure 4.5
Two common six-carbon sugars. **a.** Glucose is a six-carbon sugar that usually exists as a ring compound in cells. The shape of glucose is indicated in the space-filling model. **b.** Fructose is an isomer of glucose. It too has the molecular formula $C_6H_{12}O_6$. Notice, though, that the atoms are bonded in a slightly different manner. The carbon atoms in glucose and fructose are numbered.

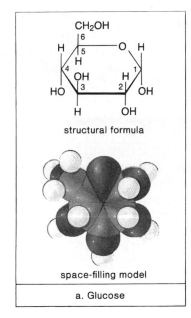

structural formula

space-filling model

a. Glucose

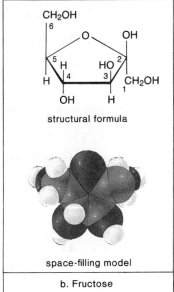

structural formula

space-filling model

b. Fructose

Figure 4.6
The sweetener sucrose. **a.** Most table sugar comes from sugar cane shown here or sugar beets. **b.** During condensation, a bond forms between the glucose and fructose molecules as the components of water are removed. During hydrolysis, the components of water are added as the bond is broken.

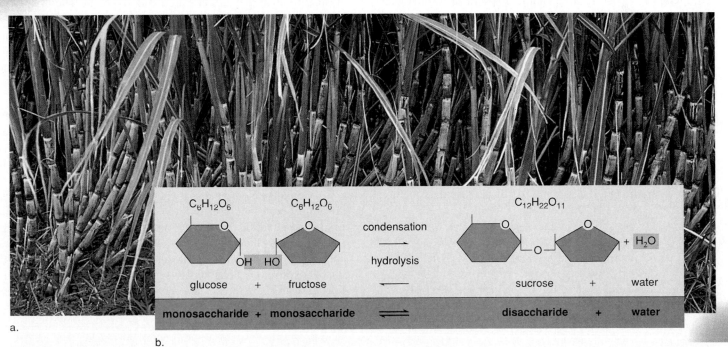

a.

b.

Figure 4.7

Starch and glycogen structure and function. **a.** Starch is a relatively straight chain of glucose molecules. (It may also branch as shown.) The electron micrograph shows starch granules in plant cells. Glucose is stored in plants as starch. **b.** Glycogen is a highly-branched polymer of glucose molecules. The branching allows breakdown to proceed at several points simultaneously. The electron micrograph shows glycogen granules in liver cells. Glucose is stored in animals as glycogen.

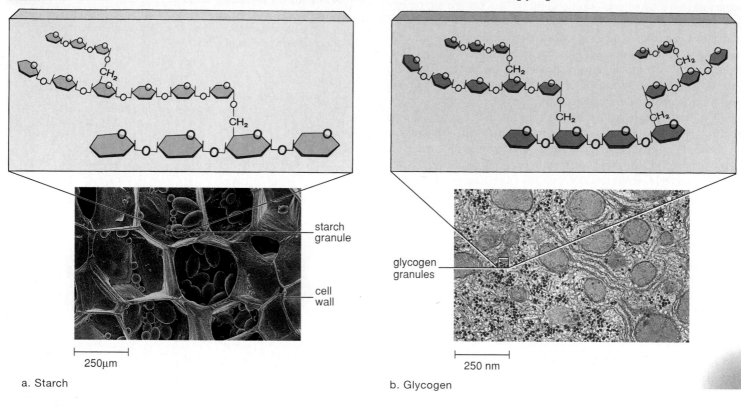

a. Starch

b. Glycogen

Starch and Glycogen Are Similar

The structures of starch and glycogen differ only slightly (fig. 4.7). **Glycogen** [Gk. *glyc*, sweet, and *gen*, produce] is characterized by many side branches, which are chains of glucose that go off from the main chain. **Starch** has few of these chains.

Plant cells store extra carbohydrates as complex sugars or starches. When leaf cells are actively producing sugar by photosynthesis, they store some of this sugar within the cell in the form of starch granules (fig.4.7a). Roots also store sugars as starch, and so do seeds. During seed germination, starch is broken down into maltose, which is used as an energy source.

Animal cells store extra carbohydrate as glycogen, sometimes called "animal starch." After a human eats, the liver stores glucose as glycogen (fig. 4.7b). Between meals, the liver releases glucose to keep the blood concentration of glucose near the normal 0.1%.

> Cells use sugars, especially glucose, as an immediate energy source. Glucose is stored as starch in plants and as glycogen in animals.

Cellulose and Chitin Are Similar

Cellulose contains glucose molecules that are joined together differently than they are in starch and glycogen. The orientation of the bonds in starch and glycogen allows these polymers to form compact spirals, making these polymers suitable as storage compounds. The orientation of the bond in cellulose causes the polymer to be straight and fibrous, making it suitable as a structural compound.

As shown in figure 4.8, the long, unbranched polymers of cellulose are held together by hydrogen bonding to form microfibrils. Several microfibrils, in turn, make up a fibril. Layers of cellulose fibrils are formed in plant cell walls. The cellulose fibrils are parallel within each layer, but the layers themselves lie at angles to one another to give added strength.

Humans have found many uses for cellulose. Cotton fibers are almost pure cellulose, and we often wear cotton clothing. Furniture and buildings are made from wood, which contains a high percentage of cellulose. Most animals, however, including humans, cannot digest cellulose because the enzymes that digest starch are unable to break the linkage between the glucose molecules in cellulose. Even so, cellulose is a recommended part of our diet because it provides bulk (also called fiber or roughage) that helps the

Figure 4.8

Cellulose fibrils. In plant cell walls, each fibril contains several microfibrils, and each microfibril contains many chains of glucose hydrogen-bonded together. Finally, we have a close-up view of three cellulose polymers, each made up of glucose molecules.

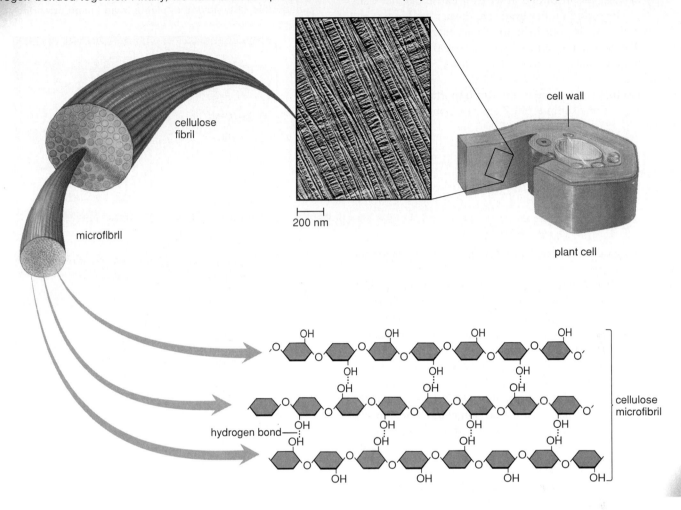

body maintain regularity of elimination. For humans, plants are a source of starch, and also fiber.

Cattle and sheep receive nutrients from grass because they have a special stomach chamber, the rumen, where bacteria that can digest cellulose live. Unfortunately, cattle are often kept in feedlots, where they are fed grains instead of grass. This practice wastes fossil fuel energy because it takes energy to grow the grain, to process it, to transport it, and finally to feed it to the cattle. Also, range-fed cattle move about and produce a leaner meat than do cattle raised in a feedlot. There is growing evidence that lean meat is healthier for humans than fatty meat.

Chitin [Gk. *chit,* a tunic], which is found in the exoskeleton of crabs and related animals like lobsters and insects, is also a polymer of glucose. Each glucose, however, has an amino group attached to it. The linkage between the glucose molecules is like that found in cellulose; therefore, chitin is not digestible by humans. Recently, scientists have discovered how to turn chitin into thread that can be used as suture material. They hope to find other uses for treated chitin. If so, all those discarded crab shells that pile up beside crabmeat processing plants will not go to waste.

Plant cell walls contain cellulose. The shells of crabs and related animals contain chitin.

FATTY ACIDS TO LIPIDS

A variety of organic compounds are classified as **lipids** [Gk. *lipos,* fat]. Many of these are insoluble in water because they lack any polar groups. The most familiar lipids are those found in fats and oils. Fat is utilized for both insulation and energy reserves by organisms. Fat below the skin of whales is called blubber; in humans it is given slang expressions such as "spare tire" and "love handles."

Phospholipids and steroids are also important lipids found in living things. For example, they are components of plasma membranes.

> Lipids are quite varied in structure, but they tend to be insoluble in water.

Fats and Oils Are Similar

Fats and **oils** contain two types of unit molecules: fatty acids and glycerol.

Each *fatty acid* consists of a long hydrocarbon chain with a carboxyl (acid) group at one end. Because the carboxyl group is a polar group, fatty acids are soluble in water. Most of the fatty acids in cells contain sixteen to eighteen carbon atoms per molecule, although smaller ones are also found. Fatty acids are either saturated or unsaturated (fig. 4.9). *Saturated* fatty acids have no double bonds between the carbon atoms. The carbon chain is saturated, so to speak, with all the hydrogens that can be held. *Unsaturated* fatty acids have double bonds in the carbon chain wherever the number of hydrogens is less than two per carbon atom:

saturated

unsaturated

Diets high in saturated (animal) fat have been associated with circulatory disorders. Replacement of saturated fat whenever possible with unsaturated (plant) oils such as peanut oil and sunflower oil has been suggested.

Glycerol is a compound with three hydroxyl groups (fig. 4.10). Hydroxyl groups are polar; therefore, glycerol is soluble in water. When fat is formed, the acid portions of three fatty acids react with these hydroxyl groups so that fat and three molecules of water form. Again, the larger fat molecule is formed by condensation, and a fat can be hydrolyzed to its components. Since there are three fatty acids per glycerol molecule, the fat molecule is sometimes called a *triglyceride*. Triglycerides are often referred to as neutral fats because they, unlike their components, lack polar groups that can hydrogen-bond

Figure 4.9

Fatty acid structure. Fatty acids are long hydrocarbon chains ending in a carboxyl (acid) group. Stearate is a saturated fatty acid, and oleate is an unsaturated fatty acid.

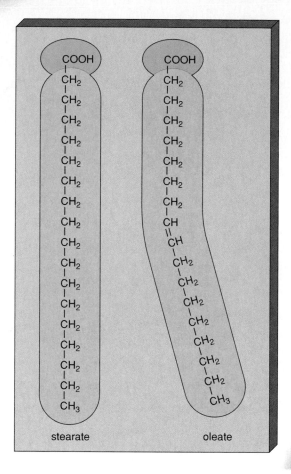

with water. Therefore, for example, cooking oils do not mix with water even though they are both liquids. Even after shaking, the oil simply separates out.

Triglycerides containing unsaturated hydrocarbon chains melt at a lower temperature than those containing saturated chains. This is because a double bond makes a kink that prevents close packing among the chains (fig. 4.9). We can reason, then, that butter, which is a solid at room temperature, must contain saturated hydrocarbon chains and that corn oil, which is a liquid even when placed in the refrigerator, must contain unsaturated chains. This difference is useful to living things. For example, the feet of reindeer and penguins contain unsaturated triglycerides, and this helps protect these exposed parts from freezing.

Nearly all organisms use fats for long-term energy storage. Fats have mostly C–H bonds, making them a richer supply of chemical energy than carbohydrates, which have many C–OH bonds. Molecule to molecule, animal fat contains over twice as

Figure 4.10

Formation of a neutral fat. Three fatty acids plus glycerol react to produce a fat molecule and three water molecules. A fat molecule plus three water molecules react to produce three fatty acids and glycerol.

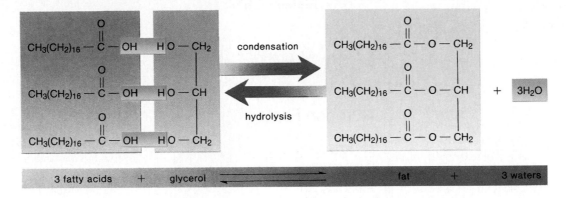

| 3 fatty acids | + | glycerol | ⇌ | fat | + | 3 waters |

much energy as glycogen; gram to gram, though, fat stores six times as much energy as glycogen. This is because fat droplets, being nonpolar, do not contain water. Small birds, like the broad-tailed hummingbird (fig. 4.11a), store a great deal of fat before they start their long spring and fall migratory flights. About 0.15 g of fat per gram of body weight is accumulated each day. If the same amount of energy were stored as glycogen, a bird would be so heavy it would not be able to fly.

Fats and oils are triglycerides (one glycerol plus three fatty acids). They are used as long-term energy storage compounds in plants and animals.

Waxes Are Different

In *waxes,* a long-chain fatty acid bonds with a long-chain alcohol. Waxes are also solid at normal temperatures because they have a high melting point. Being hydrophobic, they are also waterproof and resistant to degradation. In many plants, waxes form a protective covering that retards the loss of water for all exposed parts. In animals, waxes are involved in skin and fur maintenance. In humans, wax is produced by glands in the outer ear canal. Here its function is to trap dust and dirt particles, preventing them from reaching the eardrum.

A honeybee produces wax in glands on the underside of its abdomen. The wax is used to make the six-sided cells of the comb where honey is stored (fig. 4.11b). Honey contains the sugars fructose and glucose, breakdown products of the sugar sucrose.

Figure 4.11

Use of lipids. **a.** Because fat can be concentrated in droplets, it is the preferred way to store energy by broad-tailed hummingbirds, *Selasphorus,* and other birds that migrate long distances. **b.** The comb of a honeybee, *Apis,* is composed of wax, a compound consisting of fatty acids and alcohols. The wax is secreted by the bees' special abdominal glands.

a.

b.

Nutrition Labels

As of May 1994, packaged foods must be labeled as depicted in figure 4A. The nutrition information given here is based on the serving size (i.e., 1 ¼ cup, 57 g) of a cereal. A Calorie* is a measurement of energy. One serving of the cereal provides 220 Calories, of which 20 are from fat. At the bottom of the label, the recommended amounts of nutrients are based on a typical diet of 2,000 Calories for women and 2,500 Calories for men. Fats are the nutrient that has the highest energy content: 9 Cal/g compared to 4 Cal/g for carbohydrate and protein. The body stores fat for later use under the skin and around the organs. It is recommmended that a 2,000-Calorie diet contain no more than 65 g (595 Calories) of fat. Dietary fat has been implicated in cancer of the colon, pancreas, ovary, prostate, and breast. Although saturated fat and cholesterol are essential nutrients, dietary consumption of saturated fat and cholesterol should especially be watched and controlled. Cholesterol and saturated fat contribute to the formation of deposits called plaque, which clog arteries and lead to cardiovascular disease, including high blood pressure. Therefore, it is important to know how a serving of the cereal will contribute to the maximum recommended amount of fat, saturated fat, and cholesterol for the day. You can find this out by looking at the listing under % *Daily Value:* the total fat in one serving of the cereal provides 3% of the recommended amount of fat for the day. How much will a serving of the cereal contribute to the maximum recommended amount of saturated fat? cholesterol?

Carbohydrates (sugars and polysaccharides) are the quickest, most readily available source of energy for the body. Carbohydrates aren't usually associated with health problems, and it is recommended that the largest proportion of the diet be carbohy-

drates. Complex carbohydrates in breads and cereals are preferable to simple carbohydrates in candy and ice cream because they are likely to contain dietary fiber (nondigestible plant material). Insoluble fiber has a laxative effect and seems to reduce the risk of colon cancer; soluble fiber combines with the cholesterol in food and prevents the cholesterol from entering the body proper.

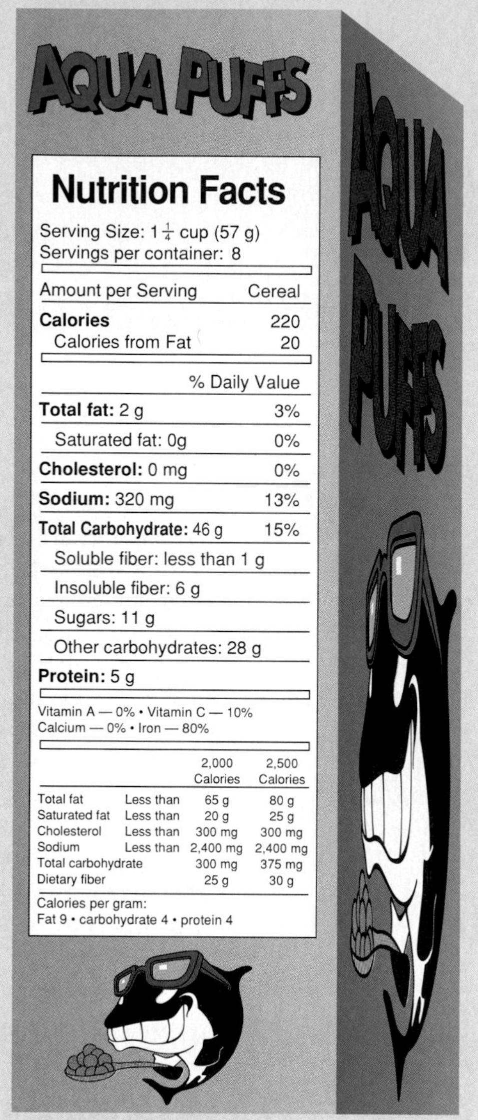

The body does not store amino acids for the production of proteins, which are found particularly in muscles but also in all cells of the body. Although it is not stated on the label, a woman should have about 44 g of protein per day and a man should have about 56 g of protein a day. Red meat is rich in protein, but it is usually also high in saturated fat. Therefore, it is considered best to rely more on protein from plant origins (e.g., whole-grain cereals, dark breads, legumes) more than is customary in the United States.

The amount of dietary sodium (as in table salt) is of concern because excessive sodium intake has been linked to high blood pressure in some people. It is recommended that the intake of sodium be no more than 2,400 mg per day. A serving of this cereal provides what percent of this maximum amount?

Vitamins are essential requirements needed in small amounts in the diet. Each vitamin has a recommended daily intake, and the food label tells what percent of the recommended amount is provided by a serving of this cereal.

* A calorie is the amount of heat required to raise the temperature of 1 g of water 1° C. Food energy is measured in Calories (the capital C means 1,000 calories).

Figure 4A

AQUA PUFFS

Nutrition Facts

Serving Size: 1 ¼ cup (57 g)
Servings per container: 8

Amount per Serving	Cereal
Calories	220
Calories from Fat	20

	% Daily Value
Total fat: 2 g	3%
Saturated fat: 0g	0%
Cholesterol: 0 mg	0%
Sodium: 320 mg	13%
Total Carbohydrate: 46 g	15%
Soluble fiber: less than 1 g	
Insoluble fiber: 6 g	
Sugars: 11 g	
Other carbohydrates: 28 g	
Protein: 5 g	

Vitamin A — 0% • Vitamin C — 10%
Calcium — 0% • Iron — 80%

		2,000 Calories	2,500 Calories
Total fat	Less than	65 g	80 g
Saturated fat	Less than	20 g	25 g
Cholesterol	Less than	300 mg	300 mg
Sodium	Less than	2,400 mg	2,400 mg
Total carbohydrate		300 mg	375 mg
Dietary fiber		25 g	30 g

Calories per gram:
Fat 9 • carbohydrate 4 • protein 4

Figure 4.12

Phospholipid structure and shape. Phospholipids are constructed like fats, except that they contain a phosphate group. **a.** Lecithin, shown here, has a side chain that contains both a phosphate group and a nitrogen-containing group. **b.** The polar portion of the phospholipid molecule (head) is soluble in water, whereas the two hydrocarbon chains (tails) are not. This causes the molecule to arrange itself as shown.

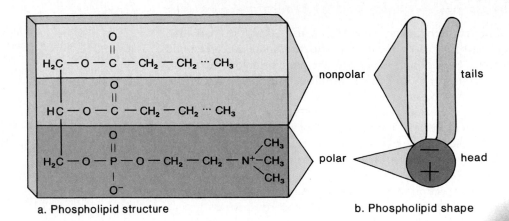

a. Phospholipid structure

b. Phospholipid shape

Phospholipids Have a Polar Group

Phospholipids [Gk. *phos,* light, and *lipar,* oil], as implied by their name, contain a phosphate group. A phosphate group is a polar group that can ionize and therefore is hydrophilic:

nonionized phosphate   ionized phosphate

Essentially, phospholipids are constructed like neutral fats, except that in place of the third fatty acid, there is a phosphate group or a grouping that contains both phosphate and nitrogen. This group becomes the polar head of the molecule, while the hydrocarbon chains of the fatty acids become the nonpolar tails (fig. 4.12). When phospholipid molecules are placed in water, they form a double layer in which the polar heads face outward and the nonpolar tails face each other. This property of phospholipids means that they can form an interface or separation between two solutions such as the interior and exterior of a cell. The plasma membrane of cells is basically a phospholipid bilayer.

> Phospholipids have a polar head and nonpolar tails. They arrange themselves in a double layer in the presence of water, and the plasma membrane of cells is essentially a phospholipid bilayer.

Steroids Have Carbon Rings

Steroids are lipids that have an entirely different structure from neutral fats. Each steroid has a backbone of four fused carbon rings and varies from other steroids primarily by the type of functional groups attached to the rings (fig. 4.13). Cholesterol is the precursor of several other steroids, including the vertebrate hormones such as aldosterone, which helps regulate the sodium content of the blood, and the sex hormones, which help maintain

male and female sex characteristics. Their functions vary due primarily to the different attached groups.

As previously mentioned, nutritionists have evidence that a diet high in saturated fats and cholesterol can lead to reduced blood flow caused by the deposit of fatty materials on the linings of blood vessels.

> Steroids are ring compounds that have a similar backbone but vary according to the attached groups. This causes them to have different functions in the bodies of humans and other animals.

Figure 4.13

Steroid diversity. **a.** Cholesterol, like all steroid molecules, has four adjacent rings, but their effects on the body largely depend on the attached groups indicated in red. **b.** Testosterone is the male sex hormone.

a. cholesterol

b. testosterone

AMINO ACIDS TO PROTEINS

Amino acids are the monomers that condense to form **proteins,** which are very large molecules with structural and metabolic functions. For example, in animals the proteins myosin and actin are the contractile components of muscle; insulin is a hormone that regulates the sugar content of the blood; hemoglobin transports oxygen in the blood; and collagen fibers support many organs. Proteins are present in the membrane that surrounds each cell, and they also exist within the cell. The cellular proteins called **enzymes** are organic catalysts that speed up chemical reactions within cells.

In this section we will point out that the role a protein plays in cells is dependent on its biological properties, which in turn are dependent on its structure.

Peptide Bonds Join Amino Acids

All amino acids contain two important functional groups: a carboxyl (acid) group (—COOH) and an amino group (—NH₂), both of which ionize at normal body pH in this manner. Therefore, amino acids are hydrophilic:

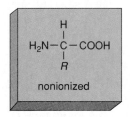 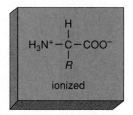

A **peptide** is two or more amino acids joined together, and a *polypeptide* is a chain of many amino acids joined by peptide bonds. A protein may contain more than one polypeptide chain; therefore, you can see why a protein could have a very large number of amino acids.

Figure 4.14 shows how two amino acids are joined by a condensation reaction between the carboxyl group of one and the amino group of another. The resulting covalent bond between two amino acids is called a **peptide bond.** The atoms associated with the peptide bond share the electrons unevenly because both oxygen and nitrogen atoms are electronegative. The hydrogen attached to the nitrogen is electropositive. The polarity of the peptide bond means that hydrogen bonding is possible between parts of a polypeptide.

Amino acids differ in the nature of the *R* group (*R*emainder of the molecule), which ranges in complexity from a single hydrogen to complicated ring compounds. The unique chemical properties of an amino acid depend on those of the *R* group. For example, some *R* groups are polar and some are not. Also, the amino acid cysteine has an *R* group that ends with a sulfhydryl (—SH) group that often serves to connect one chain of amino acids to another by a disulfide bond, —S—S.

Figure 4.14
Synthesis of a peptide. The peptide bond forms as the components of water are removed. There is a partial negative charge on the oxygen and nitrogen and a partial positive charge on the hydrogen within the peptide bond.

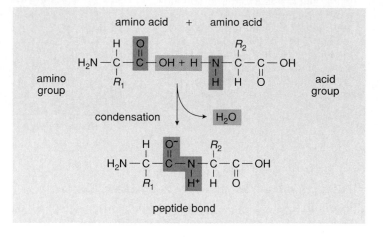

peptide bond

There are twenty different amino acids commonly found in cells, and figure 4.15 gives several examples.

> **Amino acids are joined by peptide bonds in polypeptides and proteins. Proteins have structural and metabolic functions in cells. Some proteins are enzymes that speed up chemical reactions.**

Proteins Can Be Denatured

Both temperature and pH can bring about a change in polypeptide shape. For example, we are all aware that the addition of acid to milk causes curdling; heating causes egg white, a protein called albumin, to congeal, or coagulate. When a protein loses its normal configuration, it is said to be denatured. Denaturation occurs because the normal bonding patterns between parts of a molecule have been disturbed. Once a protein loses its normal shape, it is no longer able to perform its usual function.

If the conditions that caused denaturation were not too severe, and if these are removed, some proteins regain their normal shape and biological activity. This shows that the sequence of amino acids forecasts the protein's final shape (fig. 4.16).

> **The final shape of a protein is dependent upon the sequence of amino acids in the polypeptide(s).**

Figure 4.15

Representative amino acids; the *R* groups are in the contrasting color. Some *R* groups are nonpolar and hydrophobic, some are polar and hydrophilic, and some are ionized and hydrophilic.

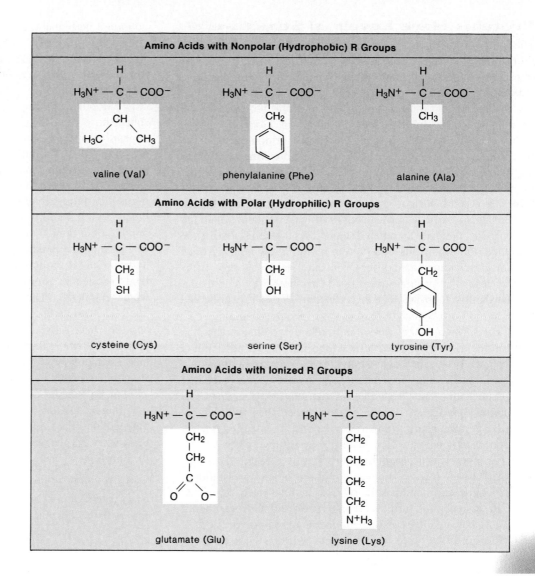

Amino Acids with Nonpolar (Hydrophobic) R Groups

valine (Val)   phenylalanine (Phe)   alanine (Ala)

Amino Acids with Polar (Hydrophilic) R Groups

cysteine (Cys)   serine (Ser)   tyrosine (Tyr)

Amino Acids with Ionized R Groups

glutamate (Glu)   lysine (Lys)

Figure 4.16

Denaturation and reactivation of the enzyme ribonuclease. When a protein is denatured, it loses its normal shape and activity. If denaturation is gentle and if the conditions are removed, some proteins regain their normal shape. This shows that the normal conformation of the molecule is due to the various interactions among a set sequence of amino acids. Each type of protein has a particular sequence of amino acids.

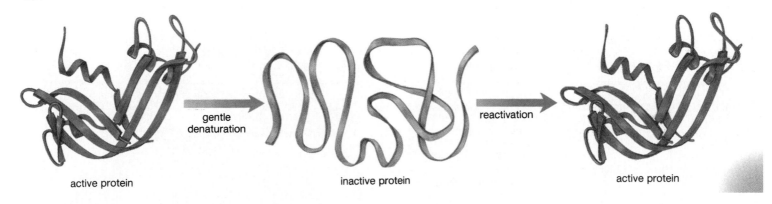

active protein

gentle denaturation

inactive protein

reactivation

active protein

Proteins Have Levels of Structure

The final shape of a protein in large measure determines the function of a protein in the cell or body of an organism. An analysis of protein shape shows that proteins can have up to four levels of structure (table 4.2).

The *primary structure* of a protein is the sequence of the amino acids joined by peptide bonds. In 1953, Frederick Sanger determined the amino acid sequence of the hormone insulin, the first protein to be sequenced. He did it by first breaking insulin into fragments and then determining the amino acid sequence of the fragments before determining the sequence of the fragments themselves. It was a laborious ten-year task, but it established for the first time that a particular protein has a particular sequence of amino acids. Today, there are automated sequencers that tell scientists the sequence of amino acids in a protein within a few hours. Notice that since each amino acid differs from another by its *R* group, it is correct to say that proteins differ from one another by a particular sequence of the *R* groups. The fact that some of these are polar and some are not influences the final shape of the polypeptide.

The *secondary structure* of a protein comes about when the polypeptide takes a particular orientation in space. Linus Pauling and Robert Corey, who began studying the structure of amino acids in the late 1930s, concluded about twenty years later that polypeptides must have particular orientations in space. They said that the α (alpha) helix and the β (beta) sheet were two possible patterns of amino acids within a polypeptide. They called it the α helix because it was the first pattern they discovered and the β sheet because it was the second pattern they discovered. Hydrogen bonding between oxygen and nitrogen atoms of amino acid monomers, in particular, stabilizes the α helix. In the β sheet, or pleated sheet, the polypeptide turns back upon itself and hydrogen bonding occurs between these extended lengths of the polypeptide.

Keratin is the type of protein found in hair, wool, feathers, hooves, claws, beaks, skin, scales and horns (fig. 4.17). The keratin in hair and wool is called α keratin because the polypeptides form an α helix. The α helices are bonded to one another by disulfide (S—S) linkages between two cysteine amino acids. When you get a permanent, the linkages are broken and then they are allowed to reform so hair becomes curly. The keratin in the other structures mentioned is called β keratin because the polypeptides form a β sheet. Silk is another protein in which the polypeptides are β sheets.

Globular proteins, so called because they have a globular shape, have regions of both α helix and β sheet arrangements depending upon the particular amino acids in the primary structure (fig. 4.18). The polypeptide of a globular protein folds and twists into a *tertiary structure* that is maintained by various types of bonding between the *R* groups. Indeed, the folding and twisting is determined by those *R* groups that can bond with one another, giving stability to the shape of the molecule. Hydrogen bonds, ionic bonds, and covalent bonds are seen. Again, disulfide linkages help maintain the tertiary shape. On the other hand, hydrophobic R groups do not react with other R groups and they tend to collect in a common region where they are not exposed to water (fig. 4.18). (These are called hydrophobic interactions.)

The various enzymes of a cell are generally globular proteins and they have only a tertiary level structure. Some other types of proteins with more than one polypeptide have a *quaternary structure*. Each polypeptide has its own primary, secondary, and tertiary structure and then these polypeptides are arranged to give a fourth level of structure termed the *quaternary structure*. Hemoglobin is a much studied globular protein that has a quaternary structure of four polypeptides. Each polypeptide has a heme group associated with it that carries oxygen reversibly. Various types of interactions between the polypeptide chains are observed.

> A protein has up to four levels of structure that account for its final three-dimensional shape. The shape of a protein determines its function in cells.

Table 4.2

Levels of Protein Structure

Level of Structure	Description	Type of Bond
Primary	Sequence of amino acids	Covalent (peptide) bond between amino acids
Secondary	Alpha helix and beta sheet	Hydrogen bond between members of peptide bond
Tertiary	Folding and twisting of polypeptide	Hydrogen, ionic, covalent (S—S), hydrophobic interactions* between *R* groups
Quaternary	Several polypeptides	Hydrogen, ionic bonds between polypeptide chains

* Strictly speaking, these are not bonds, but they are very important in creating and stabilizing tertiary structure.

Figure 4.17

Bighorn sheep, *Ovis canadensis*. The horns of antelope, sheep, and cattle have a bony core surrounded by a keratin sheath.

Figure 4.18

Levels of protein structure for a globular protein. **a.** The primary structure is the sequence of amino acids. **b.** The secondary structure contains helix segments and ß sheet segments. **c.** The tertiary structure is a twisting and turning of the polypeptide molecule. **d.** The quaternary structure contains more than one polypeptide, each with its own levels of structure.

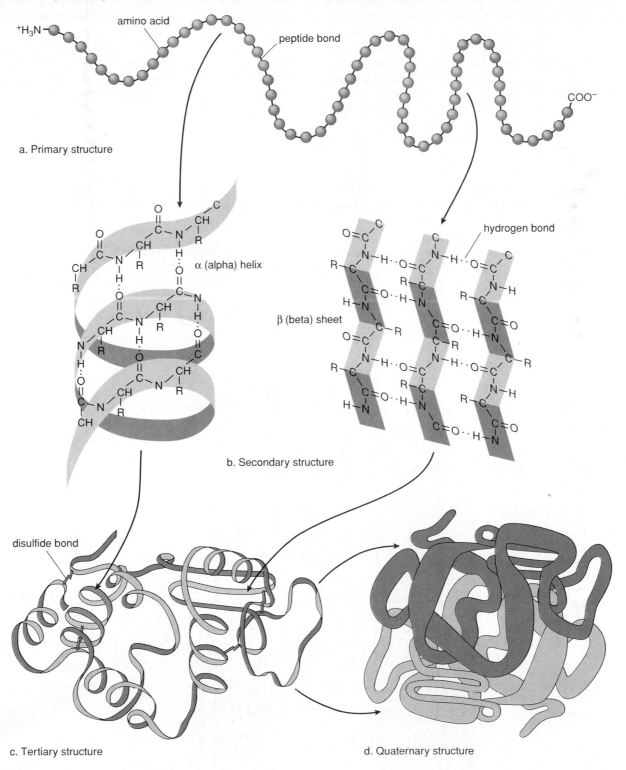

a. Primary structure

α (alpha) helix

β (beta) sheet

b. Secondary structure

c. Tertiary structure

d. Quaternary structure

NUCLEOTIDES TO NUCLEIC ACIDS

Every **nucleotide** is a molecular complex of three types of unit molecules: phosphate (phosphoric acid), a pentose sugar, and a nitrogen-containing base (fig. 4.19). Nucleotides have metabolic functions in cells. For example, some are components of coenzymes, which facilitate enzymatic reactions. ATP (adenosine triphosphate) is a nucleotide used in cells to supply energy for synthetic reactions and for various other energy-requiring processes. Nucleotides are also monomers in nucleic acids.

Nucleic acids are huge polymers of nucleotides with very specific functions in cells; for example, **DNA** (deoxyribonucleic acid) is the genetic material that stores information regarding its own replication and the order in which amino acids are to be joined to make a protein. Another important nucleic acid, **RNA** (ribonucleic acid), works in conjunction with DNA to bring about protein synthesis.

In DNA the sugar is deoxyribose, and in RNA the sugar is ribose; the difference accounts for their respective names (table 4.3). There are four different types of nucleotides in DNA and RNA. Figure 4.19 shows the types of nucleotides that are present

Figure 4.19

DNA structure. **a.** There are four different nucleotides in DNA; each contains phosphate, the pentose sugar deoxyribose, and a nitrogen-containing organic base. Two bases are purines: adenine (A) and guanine (G); two bases are pyrimidines: thymine (T) and cytosine (C). **b.** DNA has a ladder structure; the sugar-phosphate molecules make up the sides and the hydrogen-bonded bases make up the rungs. **c.** Actually, DNA is a double helix in which the two strands twist about each other.

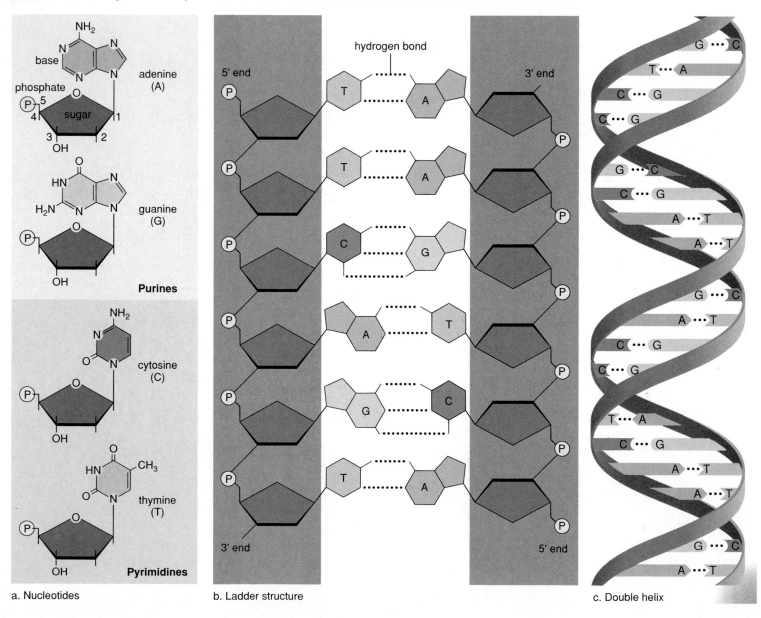

a. Nucleotides

b. Ladder structure

c. Double helix

in DNA. The base can be one of the purines, adenine or guanine, which have a double ring, or one of the pyrimidines, thymine or cytosine, which have a single ring. These structures are called bases because their presence raises the pH of a solution. In RNA, the base uracil occurs instead of the base thymine.

Nucleotides join in a definite sequence when DNA and RNA form by condensation. The nucleotides form a linear molecule called a strand in which the backbone is made up of phosphate-sugar-phosphate-sugar, with the bases projecting to one side of the backbone. Since the nucleotides occur in a definite order, so do the bases.

RNA is single stranded, but DNA is double stranded, with the two strands usually twisted about each other in the form of a double helix. The two strands are held together by hydrogen bonds between purine and pyrimidine bases. When unwound, DNA resembles a ladder. The sides of the ladder are made entirely of phosphate and sugar molecules, and the rungs of the ladder are made only of the complementary paired bases. The bases can be in any order within a strand, but between strands, thymine (T) is always paired with adenine (A), and guanine (G) is always paired with cytosine (C). This is called **complementary base pairing.** Therefore, regardless of the order or the quantity of any particular base pair, the number of purine bases always equals the number of pyrimidine bases.

> DNA has a structure like a twisted ladder: sugar and phosphate molecules make up the sides, and hydrogen-bonded bases make up the rungs of the ladder.

ATP (Adenosine Triphosphate)

ATP is a nucleotide. It derives its name from the three phosphate groups that are attached to the five-carbon sugar portion of the molecule (fig. 4.20). ATP is a high-energy molecule because the last two phosphate bonds are unstable and are easily broken. Usually in cells the terminal phosphate bond is hydrolyzed, leaving the molecule **ADP** (adenosine diphosphate) and a molecule of inorganic phosphate $\textcircled{P}$.

The energy that is released by ATP breakdown is used by all cells to synthesize macromolecules like carbohydrates and proteins. In muscle cells, the energy is used for muscle contraction, and in nerve cells, it is used for the conduction of nerve impulses. ATP is called the energy currency of cells because when cells carry out an activity or build molecules, they spend ATP.

> ATP is a high-energy molecule. ATP breaks down to ADP + $\textcircled{P}$, releasing energy, which is used for all metabolic work done in a cell.

Table 4.3

DNA Structure Compared to RNA Structure

	DNA	RNA
Sugar	Deoxyribose	Ribose
Bases	Adenine, guanine, thymine, cytosine	Adenine, guanine, uracil, cytosine
Strands	Double stranded with base pairing	Single stranded
Helix	Yes	No

Figure 4.20

ATP reaction. ATP, the universal energy currency of cells, has two phosphate bonds that are unstable and represented by wavy lines. When cells require energy, ATP usually becomes ADP + $\textcircled{P}$ and energy is released.

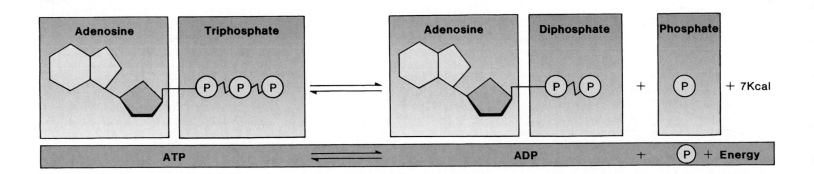

Table 4.4

Organic Molecules in Cells

	Categories	Examples	Functions
Carbohydrates	Monosaccharides 6-carbon sugar	Glucose	Immediate energy source
	Disaccharides 12-carbon sugar	Sucrose	Transport sugar in plants

	Polysaccharides
	  polymer of glucose
		Starch, glycogen,
		  cellulose
			Energy storage
			Plant cell wall structure

Lipids	Triglycerides 1 glycerol + 3 fatty acids	Fats, oils	Long-term energy storage

	Waxes
	  fatty acid + alcohol
		Cuticle,
		  ear wax
			Protective covering in plants
			  Protective in ears

	Phospholipids
	  like triglyceride except
	  the head group
	  contains phosphate
		—	Plasma membrane component

	Steroids
	  backbone of 4 fused rings
		Cholesterol,
		  testosterone
			Plasma membrane component
			Male sex hormone

Proteins	Polypeptides
	  polymer of amino acids;
	  3 levels of structure –
	  some proteins have
	  4 levels
		Enzymes
		Myosin and actin
		Insulin
		Hemoglobin
		Collagen
			Speed up cellular reactions
			Muscle cell components
			Regulates sugar content of blood
			Oxygen carrier in blood
			Fibrous support of body parts

Nucleic Acids	Nucleic acids
	  polymer of nucleotides
		DNA,
		  RNA
			Genetic material
			Protein synthesis

	Nucleotides	ATP, coenzymes	Energy carrier Assist enzymes

Summary

1. The chemistry of carbon accounts for the diversity of organic molecules found in living things. Carbon can bond with as many as four other atoms. It can also bond with itself to form both chains and rings. These are called the backbone of the molecule.

2. Each type of small molecule in living things—simple sugars, fatty acids, amino acids, and nucleotides—has a carbon backbone and is characterized by the presence of functional groups. Some functional groups are hydrophobic and some are hydrophilic.

3. Differences in the carbon backbone and attached functional groups cause molecules to have different chemical properties, and these determine how a molecule interacts with other molecules in cells.

4. The large organic molecules in cells are macromolecules, polymers formed by the joining together of monomers. Enzymes carry out both condensation (building up) and hydrolysis (breaking down) of macromolecules. For each bond formed, a molecule of water is removed, and for each bond broken, a molecule of water is added in these reactions.

5. Monosaccharides, disaccharides, and polysaccharides are all carbohydrates. Therefore, the term *carbohydrate* includes both the monomers (e.g., glucose) and the polymers (e.g., starch, glycogen, and cellulose). Starch and glycogen are energy-storage compounds, but cellulose has a structural function in plants.

6. Lipids include a wide variety of compounds that are insoluble in water. Fats and oils allow long-term energy storage and contain one glycerol and three fatty acids. Fats tend to contain saturated fatty acids, and oils tend to contain unsaturated fatty acids. In a phospholipid, one of the fatty acids is replaced by a phosphate group. In the presence of water, phospholipids form a double layer because the head of each molecule is polarized and the tails are not. Waxes and steroids are also lipids.

7. Proteins are polymers of amino acids. Some proteins are enzymes, and other proteins have structural roles in cells and organisms.

8. A polypeptide is a long chain of amino acids joined by peptide bonds. There are twenty different amino acids in cells that differ only by their *R* groups. Polarity and nonpolarity are important aspects of the *R* groups.

9. The shape of a protein influences its biological activity. A protein can be denatured and lose its normal shape and activity but, if reactivation conditions are appropriate, it assumes both again. This shows that the final shape of a protein is dependent upon the primary sequence of amino acids.

10. A protein has three levels of structure: the primary level is the sequence of the amino acids; the secondary level contains α (alpha) helices and ß (beta) sheets held in place by hydrogen bonding between peptide bonds; and the tertiary level is the final folding and twisting of the polypeptide that is held in place by bonding and hydrophobic

interactions between *R* groups. Proteins that contain more than one polypeptide have a quaternary level of structure.

11. Nucleic acids are polymers of nucleotides. Each nucleotide has three components: a sugar, a base, and phosphate (phosphoric acid). DNA, which contains the sugar deoxyribose, is the genetic material that stores information for its own replication and

for the order in which amino acids are to be sequenced in proteins. DNA, with the help of RNA, controls protein synthesis.

12. ATP, with its unstable phosphate bonds, is the energy currency of cells. ATP breaks down to ADP + Ⓟ, releasing energy that is used by the cell to do metabolic work.

13. Table 4.4 summarizes our coverage of organic molecules in cells.

Writing Across the Curriculum

In order to practice writing skills, students should write out the answers to any or all of the study questions and the critical thinking questions. The study questions are sequenced in the same order as the text. Answers to the objective questions, and suggested answers to the critical thinking questions, are in appendix D.

Study Questions

1. How are the chemical characteristics of carbon reflected in the characteristics of organic molecules? 42–43

2. Give examples of functional groups, and discuss the importance of their being hydrophobic or hydrophilic. 43

3. What molecules are monomers of the polymers studied in this chapter? How are monomers joined to produce polymers, and how are polymers broken down to monomers? 44

4. Name several monosaccharides, disaccharides, and polysaccharides, and give a function of each. How are these molecules structurally distinguishable? 45–46

5. Name the different types of lipids, and give a function for each type. What is the difference between a saturated and unsaturated fatty acid? Explain the structure of a fat molecule by stating its components and how they are joined together. 48–49

6. How does the structure of a phospholipid differ from that of a fat? How do phospholipids form a double layer in the presence of water? 51

7. Draw the structure of an amino acid and a dipeptide, pointing out the peptide bond. 52

8. How is the tertiary structure of a polypeptide related to its primary structure? Mention denaturation as evidence of this relationship. 52–54

9. Discuss the four levels of structure of a protein and relate each level to particular bonding patterns. 54–55

10. How are nucleotides joined to form nucleic acids? Discuss the structure of DNA, and name several differences between the structure of DNA and that of RNA. 56–57

11. Discuss the structure and function of ATP. 57

Objective Questions

1. Which of these is not a characteristic of carbon?
   a. forms four covalent bonds
   b. bonds with itself
   c. is sometimes ionic
   d. forms long chains

2. The functional group —COOH is
   a. acidic.
   b. basic.
   c. never ionized.
   d. All of these are correct.

3. A hydrophilic group is
   a. attracted to water.
   b. a polar or ionized group.
   c. found in fatty acids.
   d. All of these are correct.

4. Which of these is an example of hydrolysis?
   a. amino acid + amino acid → dipeptide + H_2O
   b. dipeptide + H_2O → amino acid + amino acid
   c. Both of these are correct.
   d. Neither of these is correct.

5. Which of these makes cellulose nondigestible?
   a. a polymer of glucose subunits
   b. a fibrous protein
   c. the linkage between the glucose molecules
   d. the peptide linkage between the amino acid molecules

6. A fatty acid is unsaturated if it
   a. contains hydrogen.
   b. contains double bonds.
   c. contains an acidic group.
   d. bonds to glycogen.

7. Which of these is not a lipid?
   a. steroid
   b. fat
   c. polysaccharide
   d. wax

8. The difference between one amino acid and another is found in the
   a. amino group.
   b. carboxyl group.
   c. *R* group.
   d. peptide bond.

9. The shape of a polypeptide is
   a. maintained by bonding between parts of the polypeptide.
   b. important to its function.
   c. ultimately dependent upon the primary structure.
   d. All of these are correct.

10. Which of these is the peptide bond?

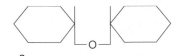

    a.

    b. c.

11. Nucleotides
    a. contain a sugar, a nitrogen-containing base, and a phosphate molecule.
    b. are the monomers for fats and polysaccharides.
    c. join together by covalent bonding between the bases.
    d. All of these are correct.

12. Label the following diagram using the terms monomer, hydrolysis, condensation, and polymer, and explain the diagram:

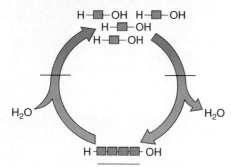

13. Label the levels of protein structure in this diagram of hemoglobin:

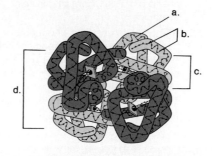

14. ATP
   a. is an amino acid.
   b. has a helical structure.
   c. is a high-energy molecule, which breaks down to ADP + Ⓟ.
   d. provides enzymes for metabolism.

Concepts and Critical Thinking

1. *The unity and the diversity of life begin at the molecular level of organization.*

   How do the organisms in figure 4.1 demonstrate this biological concept?

2. *The atoms and bonds within a molecule determine its chemical and physical properties.*

   Compare fats that largely contain either saturated or unsaturated fatty acid to demonstrate this concept.

3. *The properties of a molecule determine the role that the molecule plays in the cells or the body of an organism.*

   Choose either a phospholipid or the protein keratin to demonstrate this biological concept.

Selected Key Terms

amino acid An organic molecule having an amino group and an acid group, that covalently bonds to produce protein molecules.   52

carbohydrate A class of organic compounds consisting of carbon, hydrogen, and oxygen atoms; includes monosaccharides, disaccharides, and polysaccharides. [L. *carbo,* charcoal, and Gk. *hydr,* water]   45

condensation The joining of monomers by covalent bonding with the accompanying loss of water molecules.   44

DNA (deoxyribonucleic acid) A polymer produced from covalent bonding of nucleotide monomers that contain the sugar deoxyribose; the genetic material of nearly all organisms.   56

enzyme An organic catalyst, usually a protein molecule, that speeds chemical reactions in living systems.   52

hydrolysis (hy-DRAH-lih-sis) Splitting of a compound by the addition of water, with the H⁺ being incorporated in one fragment and the OH⁻ in the other. [Gk. *hydr,* water, and *lysis,* loosening, dissolving]   44

hydrophilic (hy-druh-FIL-ik) A type of molecule that interacts with water by dissolving in water or by forming hydrogen bonds with water molecules. [L. *hydr,* water, and Gk. *phil,* loving] 43

hydrophobic (hy-druh-FOH-bik) A type of molecule that does not interact with water because it is nonpolar. [L. *hydr,* water, and Gk. *phobos,* dreading]   43

inorganic molecule A type of molecule that is an organic molecule; not derived from a living organism.   42

isomers (EYE-suh-mur) Molecules with the same molecular formula but different structure and, therefore, shape. [Gk. *iso,* equal, and *meris,* part]   43

lipid (LIP-id) A class of organic compounds that tend to be soluble in nonpolar solvents such as alcohol; includes fats and oils. [Gk. *lipos,* fat]   48

nucleic acid A polymer of nucleotides; both DNA and RNA are nucleic acids.   56

nucleotide Monomer of DNA and RNA consisting of a five-carbon sugar bonded to a nitrogenous base and a phosphate group.   56

organic molecule A type of molecule that contains carbon and hydrogen; it may also have oxygen attached to the carbon(s).   42

peptide Two or more amino acids joined together by covalent bonding.   52

phospholipid (fahs-foh-LIP-id) A molecule having the same structure as a neutral fat except one bonded fatty acid is replaced by a group that contains phosphate; an important component of plasma membranes.   51

polymer Macromolecule consisting of covalently bonded monomers; for example, a protein is a polymer of monomers called amino acids. [Gk. *polus,* many, and *meris,* part]   44

protein A polymer having, as its primary structure, a sequence of amino acids united through covalent bonding.   52

RNA (ribonucleic acid) A nucleic acid produced from covalent bonding of nucleotide monomers that contain the sugar ribose; RNA helps DNA carry out protein synthesis.   56

steroid A type of lipid molecule having four interlocking rings; examples are cholesterol, progesterone, and testosterone.   51

5

CELL STRUCTURE AND FUNCTION

Learning Objectives

Cells Make Up Living Things

- State two tenets of the cell theory.   62
- Give several differences between bright-field light microscopy and transmission electron microscopy. Name several other types of microscopes that are available today.   64–65
- Explain, on the basis of cell-volume-to-cell-surface relationships, why cells are so very small.   63

Prokaryotic Cells Are Less Complex

- Describe the structure of a prokaryotic cell, and give a function for each part mentioned.   66

Eukaryotic Cells Are More Complex

- Describe the structure of the nucleus of a eukaryotic cell, and give a function for each part mentioned.   67, 70
- Name the structures that form the endomembrane system, and explain how they are related to one another.   71, 73–74
- Explain the relationship between chloroplasts and mitochondria, and describe the structure and function of each.   75–76
- Name the components of the cytoskeleton, and describe the structure and the functions of each component.   76–78
- Contrast the structures of prokaryotic cells, eukaryotic animal cells, and eukaryotic plant cells.   80

Scanning electron micrograph of nuclear pores. Nuclear pores allow molecules to pass between the nucleus and the cytoplasm of the cell.

100 nm

few cells, like a hen's egg or a frog's egg, are large enough to be seen by the naked eye, but most are not. This is the reason the study of cells did not begin until the invention of the first microscopes in the seventeenth century. It is not known exactly who was the first to see cells, but Antonie van Leeuwenhoek of Holland is famous for observing tiny, unicellular living things that no one had seen before. Leeuwenhoek sent his findings to an organization of scientists called the Royal Society in London. Robert Hooke, an Englishman, confirmed Leeuwenhoek's observations and was the first to use the term *cell*. The tiny chambers he observed in the honeycomb structure of cork reminded him of the rooms, or cells, in a monastery. Naturally, then, he referred to the boundaries of these chambers as walls.

CELLS MAKE UP LIVING THINGS

Although early microscopists had seen cells, it was more than a hundred years—in the 1830s—before Matthias Schleiden published his theory that all plants are composed of cells and Theodor Schwann published a similar proposal concerning animals. These Germans based their ideas not only on their own work but on the work of all who had studied tissues under microscopes. Today we recognize that virtually all the organisms we see about us are made up of cells (fig. 5.1). A **cell** is the smallest unit of living matter.

There are unicellular organisms but most, including ourselves, are multicellular. A cell is not only the structural unit, it is also the functional unit of organs and, therefore, organisms. This is very evident when you consider certain illnesses of the human body such as diabetes or prostate cancer. It is the cells of the pancreas or the prostate that are malfunctioning, rather than the body itself.

> All organisms are made up of cells, and a cell is the structural and functional unit of organs and, ultimately, organisms.

Soon after Schleiden and Schwann, another German scientist, Rudolf Virchow, used a microscope to study the life of cells. He came to the conclusion that "every cell comes from a preexisting cell." By the middle of the nineteenth century, biologists clearly recognized that all organisms are composed of self-reproducing cells.

> Cells are capable of self-reproduction. Cells come only from preexisting cells.

Figure 5.1
All organisms, whether plants or animals, are composed of cells. This is not readily apparent because a microscope is usually needed to see the cells. **a.** Corn. **b.** Light micrograph of corn leaf showing many individual cells. **c.** Rabbit. **d.** Light micrograph of a rabbit's intestinal lining showing that it, too, is composed of cells. The dark-staining bodies are nuclei.

a.   Corn, *Lea mays*

c.   Rabbit, *Oryctolagus* sp.

b.   200 μm   d.   200 μm

Figure 5.2

The sizes of living things and their components (1 meter = 10^2 cm = 10^3 mm = 10^6 μm = 10^9 nm). It takes a microscope to see cells and lower levels of biological organization. Cells are visible with the light microscope, but not in much detail. It takes an electron microscope to detect the intricate structure of cells. On this scale each unit is 10 times greater than the lower unit.

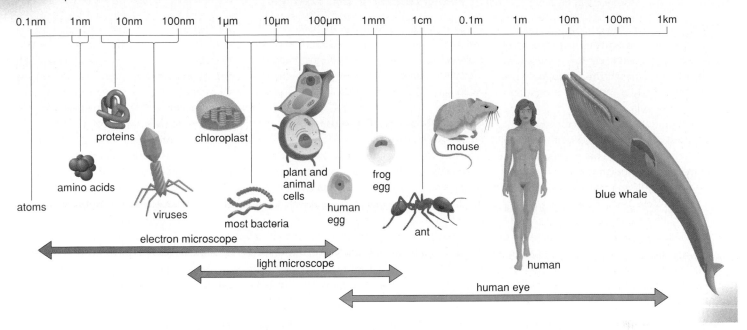

The previous two highlighted statements are often called the **cell theory**, but sometimes they are called the *cell doctrine*. Those who use the latter terminology want to make it perfectly clear that there are extensive data to support the cell theory and that it is universally accepted by biologists.

Cells Are Small

Cells are quite small. A frog's egg, at about one millimeter (mm) in diameter, is large enough to be seen by the human eye (fig. 5.2). Most cells are far smaller than one millimeter; some are even as small as one micrometer (μm)—a thousand times smaller than one millimeter—but even so they are still within the range of the light microscope. Cell inclusions and macromolecules are even smaller still than a micrometer and are measured in terms of nanometers (nm). There are a thousand nanometers in one micrometer.

An explanation for why cells are so small and why the body of a plant or an animal is multicellular is found by considering that nutrients enter a cell and wastes exit a cell at its surface. A large cell requires more nutrients and produces more wastes than a small cell. Therefore, a large cell that is actively metabolizing cannot make do with proportionately less surface area than a small cell. Yet, as cells get larger in volume, the proportionate amount of surface area actually decreases. A cube that is 1 mm tall has a surface area of 6 mm² and a volume of 1 mm³, or a ratio of 6:1. A cube that is 2 mm tall has a surface area of 24 mm² and a volume of 8 mm³, or a ratio of 3:1.

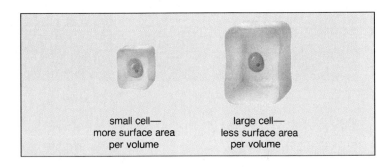

small cell—
more surface area
per volume

large cell—
less surface area
per volume

We would expect, then, that there would be a limit to how large an actively metabolizing cell can become. A chick's egg is several centimeters in diameter, but the egg is not actively metabolizing. Once the egg is fertilized and metabolic activity begins, the egg divides repeatedly without growth. Cell division restores the amount of surface area needed for adequate exchange of materials. Further, cells that specialize in absorption have modifications that greatly increase the surface area per volume of the cell. The columnar cells along the surface of the intestinal wall have surface foldings called villi (sing., villus), which increase their surface area.

A cell needs a surface area that can adequately exchange materials with the environment. Surface-area-to-volume considerations require that cells stay small.

Microscopy of Today

Cells were not discovered until the invention of the microscope in the seventeenth century. Since that time, various types of microscopes have been developed for the study of cells and their components.

In the *bright-field light microscope*, light rays passing through a specimen are brought into focus by a set of glass lenses, and the resulting image is then viewed by the human eye. In the *transmission electron microscope*, electrons passing through a specimen are brought into focus by a set of magnetic lenses, and the resulting image is projected onto a fluorescent screen or photographic film. In the *scanning electron microscope* (SEM), a narrow beam of electrons is scanned over the surface of the specimen,

which is coated with a thin metal layer. The metal gives off secondary electrons that are collected by a detector to produce an image on a television screen. The SEM permits the development of three-dimensional images (fig. 5A).

Magnification, Resolution, and Contrast

Almost everyone knows that the magnifying capability of a transmission electron microscope is greater than that of a light microscope. A light microscope can magnify objects a few thousand times, but an electron microscope can magnify them hundreds of thousands of times. The difference lies in the means of illumination. The path of light rays and electrons moving through space is wavelike, but the wavelength of electrons is much shorter than

the wavelength of light. This difference in wavelength accounts for the electron microscope's greater magnifying capability and its greater resolving power. The greater the resolving power, the greater the detail eventually seen. Resolution is the minimum distance between two objects before they are seen as one larger object. If oil is placed between the sample and the objective lens of the light microscope, the resolving power is increased, and if ultraviolet light is used instead of visible light, it is also increased. But typically, a light microscope can resolve down to 0.2 μm, while the electron microscope can resolve down to 0.0001 μm. If the resolving power of the average human eye is set at one, then that of the typical light microscope is about 500, and that of

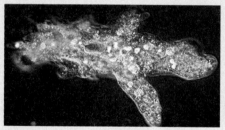

50 μm

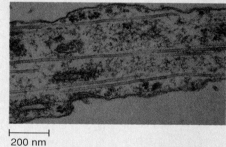

200 nm

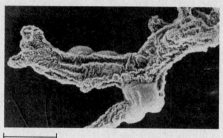

500 μm

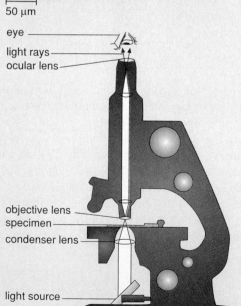

eye
light rays
ocular lens

objective lens
specimen
condenser lens

light source

a. Compound light microscope

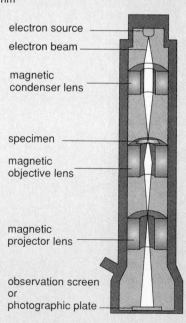

electron source
electron beam

magnetic condenser lens

specimen

magnetic objective lens

magnetic projector lens

observation screen
or
photographic plate

b. Transmission electron microscope

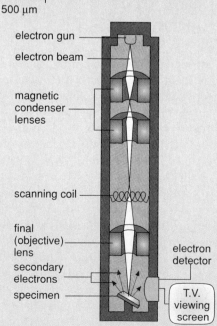

electron gun

electron beam

magnetic condenser lenses

scanning coil

final (objective) lens

secondary electrons
specimen

electron detector

T.V. viewing screen

c. Scanning electron microscope

Figure 5A

Diagram of microscopes with accompanying micrographs of *Amoeba proteus*.

the electron microscope is 100,000. This means that the electron microscope distinguishes much greater detail (fig. 5A).

Some microscopes view living specimens, but often specimens are treated prior to observation. Cells are killed, fixed so they do not decompose, and embedded into a matrix. The matrix strengthens the specimen so that it can be thinly sliced. These sections are often stained with colored dyes (light microscopy) or with electron-dense metals (electron microscopy) to provide contrast. Another way to increase contrast is to use optical methods such as phase contrast and differential interference contrast (fig. 5B). In addition to optical and electronic methods for contrasting transparent cells, there is a third very prominent research tool called *immunofluorescence microscopy*, so-called because it uses fluorescent antibodies to reveal the location of a pro-tein in the cell (see fig. 5.13). The importance of this method is that the cellular distribution of a single type of protein can be examined.

Illumination, Viewing, and Recording

Light rays can be bent (refracted) and brought to a focus as they pass through glass lenses, but electrons do not pass through glass. Electrons have a charge that allows them to be brought into a focus by magnetic lenses. The human eye utilizes light to see an object but cannot utilize electrons for the same purpose. Therefore, electrons leaving the specimen in the electron microscope are directed toward a screen or a photograph plate that is sensitive to their presence. Humans can view the image on the screen or photograph.

The major advancement in illumination has been the introduction of *confocal microscopy*, which uses a laser beam scanned across the specimen to focus on a single shallow plane within the cell. The microscopist can "optically section" the specimen by focusing up and down, and a series of optical sections can be combined in a computer to create a three-dimensional image, which can be displayed and rotated on the computer screen.

An image from a microscope may be recorded by replacing the human eye with a television camera. The television camera converts the light image into an electronic image which can be entered into a computer. In *video-enhanced contrast microscopy*, the computer makes the darkest areas of the original image much darker and the lightest areas of the original much lighter. The result is a high-contrast image with deep blacks and bright whites. Even more contrast can be introduced by the computer if shades of gray are replaced by colors.

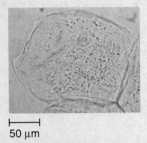

50 μm

Bright-field. Light passing through the specimen is brought directly in to focus. Usually, the low level of contrast within the specimen interferes with the specimen interferes with viewing all but its largest components.

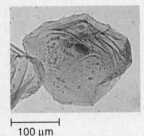

100 μm

Bright-field (stained). Dyes are used to stain the specimen. Certain components take up the due more than other components, and therefore contrast is enhanced.

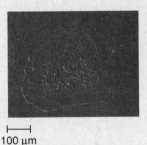

100 μm

Differential interference contrast. Optical methods are used to enhance density differences within the specimen so that certain regions appear brighter than others. It is used to view living cells, chromosomes, and organelle masses.

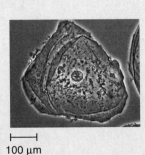

100 μm

Phase Contrast. Density differences in the specimen cause light rays to come out of "phase." The microscope enhances these phase differences so that some regions of the specimen appear brighter or darker than others. It is widely used to observe living cells and organelles.

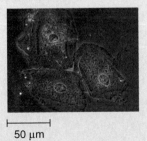

50 μm

Darkfield. Light is passed through specimen at an oblique angle so that the objective lens receives only light diffracted and scattered light by the object. Used to view organelles which appear quite bright against a dark field.

Figure 5B

Photomicrographs of cheek cells, illustrating different types of light microscopy.

PROKARYOTIC CELLS ARE LESS COMPLEX

Bacteria [Gk. *bact*, rod] are **prokaryotic cells** [Gk. *pro*, before, and *kary*, nucleus] in the kingdom Prokaryotae. Most bacteria are between 1–10 μm in size; therefore, they are just visible with the light microscope.

Figure 5.3 illustrates the main features of bacterial anatomy. There is a *cell wall* containing peptidoglycan, a complex molecule that contains chains of a unique amino disaccharide joined by peptide chains. In some bacteria, the cell wall is further surrounded by a capsule and/or gelatinous sheath called a slime layer. Motile bacteria usually have long, very thin appendages called *flagella* that are composed of subunits of the protein called flagellin. The flagella, which rotate like propellers, rapidly move the bacterium in a fluid medium. Bacteria also have *fimbriae*, which are short appendages that help them attach to an appropriate surface.

A membrane called the **plasma membrane** regulates the entrance and exit of molecules into and out of the cytoplasm, the interior of the cell. **Cytoplasm** in a prokaryotic cell consists of **cytosol**, a semifluid medium, and thousands of granular inclusions called *ribosomes* that coordinate the synthesis of proteins. In prokaryotes, most genes are found within a single chromosome (loop of DNA, or deoxyribonucleic acid) located within the **nucleoid** [L. *nucle*, nucleus], but they may also have small accessory rings of DNA called *plasmids*. In addition, the photosynthetic cyanobacteria have light-sensitive pigments, usually within the membranes of flattened disks called *thylakoids*.

Although bacteria seem fairly simple, they are actually metabolically diverse. Bacteria are adapted to living in almost any kind of environment and are able to live off almost any type of organic matter. Given an energy source, most bacteria are able to synthesize any molecule they may need. Therefore, the cytoplasm is the site of thousands of chemical reactions and bacteria are more metabolically competent than are human beings. Indeed, the metabolic capability of bacteria is exploited by humans who use them to produce a wide variety of chemicals and products for human use.

Bacteria are prokaryotic cells with these constant features.	
Outer boundary:	cell wall
	plasma membrane
Cytoplasm:	ribosomes
	thylakoids (cyanobacteria)
	innumerable enzyme
Nucleoid:	chromosome (DNA only)

Figure 5.3

Prokaryotic cells. **a.** Generalized nonphotosynthetic bacterium. **b.** Generalized cyanobacterium, a photosynthetic bacterium, formerly called blue-green alga.

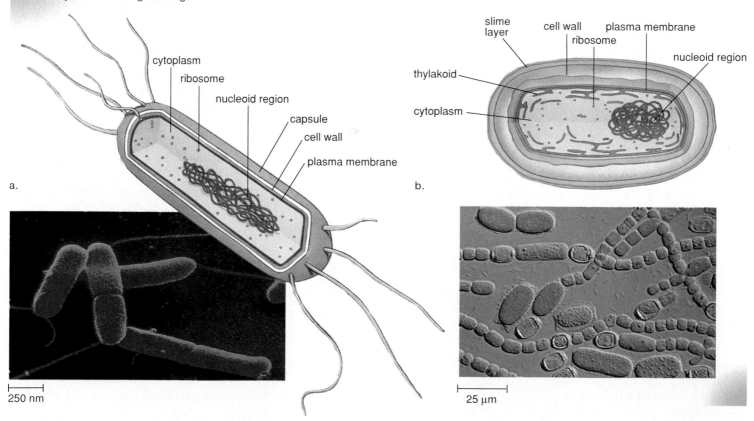

a.

250 nm

b.

25 μm

EUKARYOTIC CELLS ARE MORE COMPLEX

Eukaryotic cells are ten to one hundred times larger than prokaryotic cells. In contrast to prokaryotic cells, **eukaryotic cells** [Gk. *eu,* good, well, and *kary,* nucleus] have a true nucleus. A nucleus is a membrane-bounded structure where DNA is housed within chromosomes, which are complex threadlike structures.

> **Eukaryotic cells have a membrane-bounded nucleus, and prokaryotic cells lack a nucleus.**

Membrane is a phospholipid bilayer with embedded proteins.

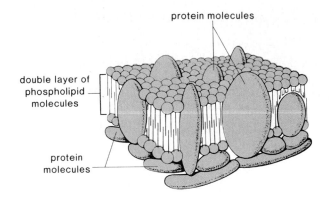

In eukaryotic cells, membrane not only surrounds the nucleus, it is also a major part of various **organelles**—small bodies, each with a specific structure and function (table 5.1). The cytosol, which is a semifluid medium outside the nucleus, is divided up and compartmentalized by these membranous organelles. Compartmentalization keeps the cell organized and keeps its various functions separate from one another. Just as prokaryotic cells lack a nucleus, so they also lack organelles. The cytosol in eukaryotic cells has an organized lattice of protein filaments appropriately called the *cytoskeleton.*

Eukaryotic cells, like prokaryotic cells, have a plasma membrane that separates the contents of the cell from the environment and regulates the passage of molecules into and out of the cell. Some eukaryotic cells, notably plant cells, also have an outer boundary called a **cell wall.** A plant cell wall contains cellulose fibrils and therefore has a different composition than that of prokaryotic cells. A cell wall supports and protects the cell but does not interfere with the movement of molecules across the plasma membrane.

Figure 5.4 shows the structure of an animal cell, and figure 5.5 shows the structure of a plant cell.

Table 5.1

Eukaryotic Structures in Animal Cells and Plant Cells

Name	Composition	Function
Cell wall*	Contains cellulose fibrils	Support and protection
Plasma membrane	Phospholipid bilayer with embedded proteins	Selective passage of molecules into and out of cell
Nucleus	Nuclear envelope surrounding nucleoplasm, chromatin, and nucleoli	Storage of genetic information
Nucleolus	Concentrated area of chromatin, RNA, and proteins	Ribosomal formation
Ribosome	Protein and RNA in two subunits	Protein synthesis
Endoplasmic reticulum (ER)	Membranous flattened channels and tubular canals	Synthesis and/or modification of proteins and other substances, and transport by vesicle formation
Rough ER	Studded with ribosomes	Protein synthesis
Smooth ER	Having no ribosomes	Various; lipid synthesis in some cells
Golgi apparatus	Stack of membranous saccules	Processing, packaging, and distributing molecules
Vacuole and vesicle	Membranous sacs	Storage of substances
Lysosome	Membranous vesicle containing digestive enzymes	Intracellular digestion
Microbody	Membranous vesicle containing specific enzymes	Various metabolic tasks
Mitochondrion	Inner membrane (cristae) within outer membrane	Cellular respiration
Chloroplast*	Inner membrane (grana) within two outer membranes	Photosynthesis
Cytoskeleton	Microtubules, intermediate filaments, actin filaments	Shape of cell and movement of its parts
Cilia and flagella	9 + 2 pattern of microtubules	Movement of cell
Centriole[d]	9 + 0 pattern of microtubules	Formation of basal bodies

*Plant cells
[d]Animal cells

Figure 5.4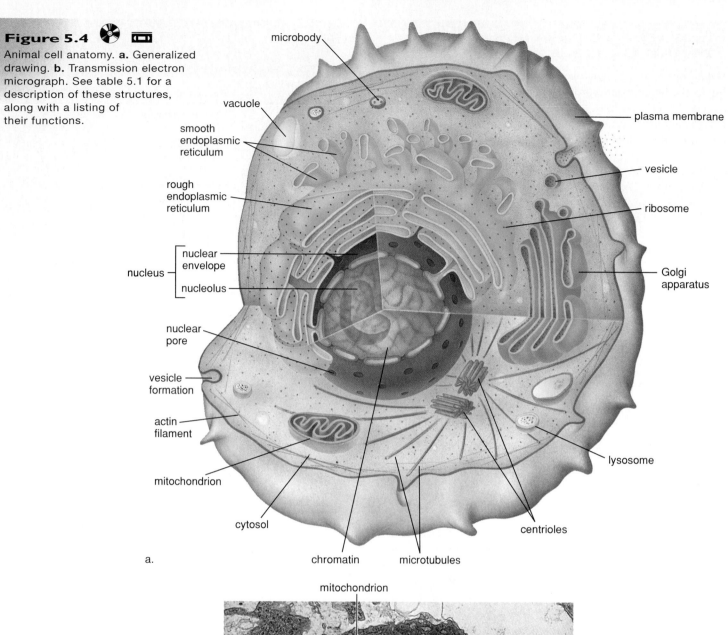

Animal cell anatomy. **a.** Generalized
drawing. **b.** Transmission electron
micrograph. See table 5.1 for a
description of these structures,
along with a listing of
their functions.

microbody

vacuole

smooth
endoplasmic
reticulum

rough
endoplasmic
reticulum

nucleus
{
nuclear
envelope

nucleolus
}

nuclear
pore

vesicle
formation

actin
filament

mitochondrion

cytosol

plasma membrane

vesicle

ribosome

Golgi
apparatus

lysosome

centrioles

chromatin

microtubules

a.

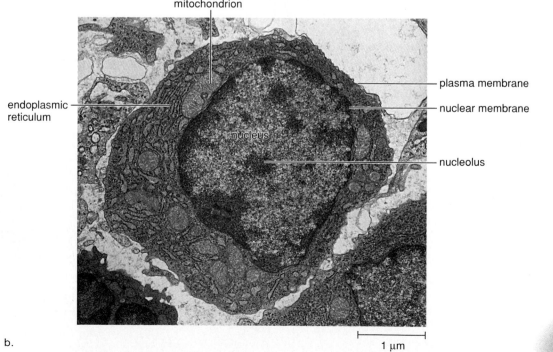

mitochondrion

endoplasmic
reticulum

nucleus

nucleolus

plasma membrane

nuclear membrane

b.

1 μm

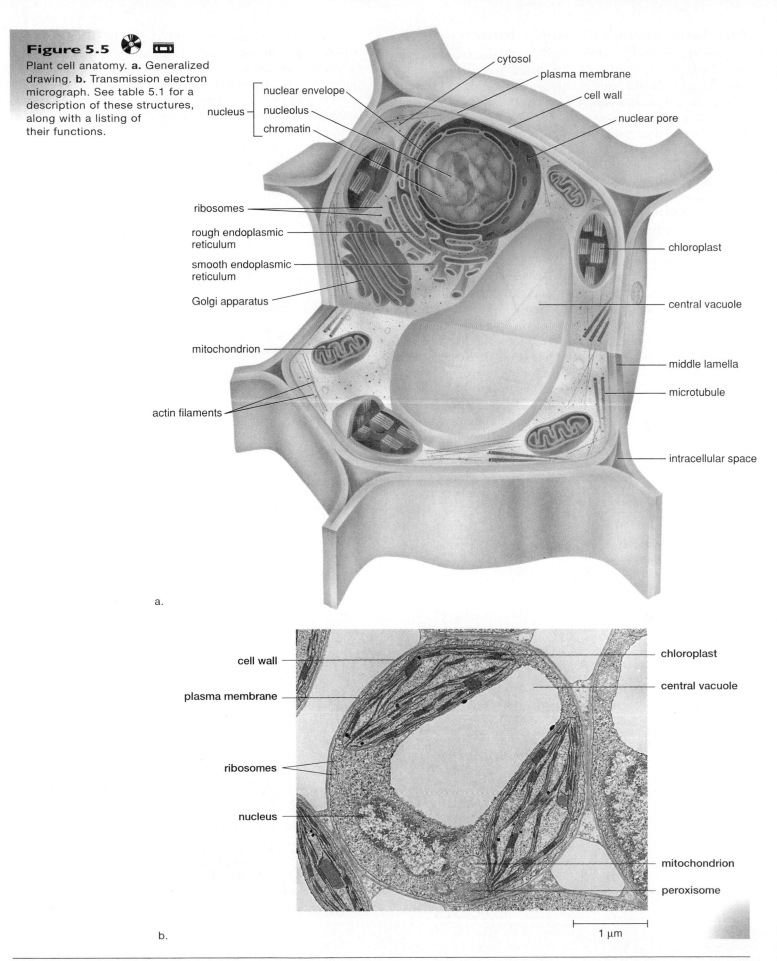

Figure 5.5

Plant cell anatomy. **a.** Generalized drawing. **b.** Transmission electron micrograph. See table 5.1 for a description of these structures, along with a listing of their functions.

a.

cytosol

plasma membrane

cell wall

nuclear pore

nuclear envelope

nucleolus

nucleus

chromatin

chloroplast

ribosomes

rough endoplasmic reticulum

smooth endoplasmic reticulum

Golgi apparatus

central vacuole

mitochondrion

middle lamella

microtubule

actin filaments

intracellular space

b.

cell wall

plasma membrane

ribosomes

nucleus

chloroplast

central vacuole

mitochondrion

peroxisome

1 μm

Nucleus Stores Genetic Information

The **nucleus,** which has a diameter of about 5 μm, is a prominent structure in the eukaryotic cell. The nucleus is of primary importance because it stores genetic information about the characteristics of the body's cells and their metabolic functioning. Every cell contains a complex copy of genetic information, but each cell type has certain genes, or segments of DNA, turned on, and others turned off. Which particular genes are active in a cell is controlled at least in part by cytoplasmic molecules capable of entering the nucleus. Activated DNA, with the help of RNA (ribonucleic acid), governs the sequencing of amino acids during protein synthesis. The proteins of a cell determine its structure and the functions it can perform.

When you look at the nucleus, even in an electron micrograph, you cannot see DNA molecules but you can see chromatin. **Chromatin** [Gk. *chrom,* color, and *tin,* stretch] looks grainy, but actually it is a threadlike material that undergoes coiling into rodlike structures called **chromosomes** [Gk. *chrom,* color, and *soma,* body], just before the cell divides. Chemical analysis shows that chromatin, and therefore chromosomes, contains DNA and much protein, and some RNA. Chromatin is immersed in a semifluid medium called the *nucleoplasm.* Nucleoplasm has a different pH from the cytosol, and this suggests that it has a different composition.

Most likely, too, when you look at an electron micrograph of a nucleus, you will see one or two regions that look darker than the rest of the chromatin. These are **nucleoli** [L. *nucleol,*

little nucleus], where another type of RNA, called ribosomal RNA (rRNA), is produced and where rRNA joins with proteins to form the subunits of ribosomes. (Ribosomes are small bodies in the cytoplasm that contain rRNA and proteins.)

The nucleus is separated from the cytoplasm by a double membrane known as the **nuclear envelope** (fig. 5.6). A layer of protein fibers associated with the inner membrane of the nuclear envelope (called the nuclear lamina) helps maintain the shape of the nucleus, organizes chromatin by providing chromatin attachment sites, and may funnel substances toward or away from the nuclear pores. The nuclear envelope has *pores* of sufficient size (100 nm) to permit the passage of proteins into the nucleus and ribosomal subunits out of the nucleus. High-power electron micrographs show that the pores have nonmembranous components associated with them that form a nuclear pore complex.

The structural features of the nucleus include the following.

Chromatin: (chromosomes)	DNA and proteins
Nucleolus:	chromatin ribosomal subunits
Nuclear envelope:	double membrane with pores

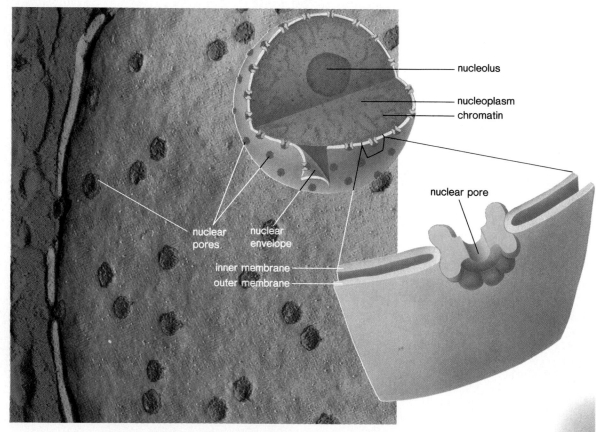

Figure 5.6

Anatomy of the nucleus. The nucleoplasm contains chromatin. Chromatin has a special region called the nuceolus, which is where rRNA is produced and ribosomal subunits are assembled. The nuclear envelope contains pores, as is shown in this micrograph of a freeze-fractured nuclear envelope. Each pore is lined by a complex of eight proteins.

nucleolus

nucleoplasm

chromatin

nuclear pore

nuclear pores

nuclear envelope

inner membrane

outer membrane

Ribosomes Coordinate Protein Synthesis

Ribosomes, as mentioned, are small particles composed of rRNA and proteins. Unlike many of the organelles discussed in this chapter, ribosomes are found in both prokaryotes and eukaryotes. In eukaryotes, ribosomes are 20 nm by 30 nm, and in prokaryotes they are slightly smaller. In both types of cells, ribosomes are composed of two subunits, one large and one small (fig. 5.7). Each subunit has its own mix of proteins and rRNA. Ribosomes perform a very important function because they coordinate protein synthesis.

Several ribosomes synthesizing the same protein are called a *polysome*. Polysomes can lie free within the cytosol, or they can be attached to the endoplasmic reticulum, a membranous system of saccules and channels in the cytoplasm.

> Ribosomes are small organelles involved in protein synthesis. A polysome is a group of ribosomes, each one involved in producing a copy of the same protein.

The Endomembrane System Is Elaborate

The endomembrane system consists of an elaborate series of intracellular membranes that compartmentalize the cell. Many types of enzymatic reactions occur all the time in cells, and the endomembrane system keeps each reaction restricted to a particular region. The membranes that make up the endomembrane system are connected by direct physical contact and/or by the transfer of vesicles (tiny membranous sacs) from one part to the other.

Endoplasmic Reticulum

The **endoplasmic reticulum** (ER), [Gk. *endo,* within, *plasm,* something molded, and L. *reticul,* network], a complicated system of membranous channels and saccules (flattened vesicles), is physically continuous with the outer membrane of the nuclear envelope. Rough ER is studded with ribosomes on the side of the membrane that faces the cytoplasm (fig. 5.7). Here proteins are synthesized and enter the ER lumen where processing and modification begin. Smooth ER, which is continuous with rough ER, does not have attached ribosomes. Smooth ER can have various functions depending on the particular cell. Sometimes it specializes in the production of lipids, such as steroid hormones. Smooth ER is abundant in cells of the testes and the adrenal cortex, both of which produce steroid hormones. In the liver it helps detoxify drugs; in muscle cells it acts as a storage site for calcium ions that are released when contraction occurs. Regardless of any specialized function, smooth ER also forms *transport vesicles* in which large molecules are moved within the cell. Often transport vesicles are on their way to the plasma membrane or another part of the endomembrane system, particularly the Golgi apparatus.

> ER is involved in protein synthesis (rough ER) and various other processes such as lipid synthesis (smooth ER). Molecules moving through the ER are eventually enclosed in vesicles that usually move to the Golgi apparatus.

Figure 5.7

Rough endoplasmic reticulum (ER). **a.** Electron micrograph of a mouse hepatocyte (liver cell) shows a cross section of many flattened vesicles with ribosomes attached to the side that abuts the cytosol. **b.** The three dimensions of the organelle. **c.** Model of a single ribosome illustrates that each one is actually composed of two subunits. **d.** Method by which the ER acts as a transport system.

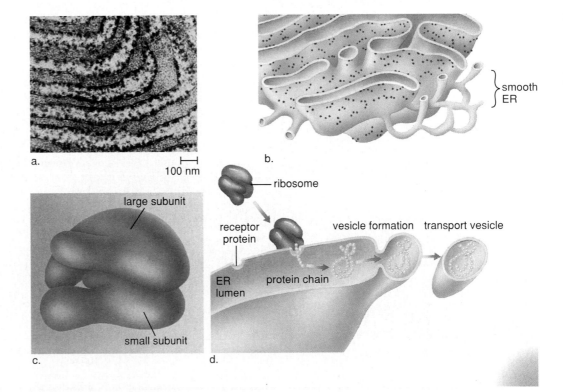

a.

100 nm

b.

smooth ER

ribosome

large subunit

small subunit

receptor protein

ER lumen   protein chain

vesicle formation   transport vesicle

c.

d.

The Microscopic Scale

When we view the world, we rely on past experiences to make decisions concerning the relative sizes and positions of things around us. Though these relationships are altered in photographs, we can judge the size of things if an object of familiar size is placed in the photograph. A human being might be placed next to an elephant, or a meter stick might be placed next to a snake, to provide familiar references of size. Microscopists use familiar references such as "the head of a pin" or "a human hair." But these references are inadequate when discussing cells and molecules, because they are so small that their sizes seem abstract to humans. We have no practical knowledge of what it is like to be the size of a virus. For example, a single water molecule is small and insignificant to a human, but it is relatively large and sticky to a virus.

Microscopists can make great use of quantitative measurements of cells, organelles, and molecules despite our inability to be intuitive about microscopic size. Knowledge of size relationships helps identify subcellular structures; for example, intermediate filaments are so called because their diameter is intermediate between the diameters of actin filaments and microtubules. Size is particularly characteristic of macromolecular assemblies such as viruses and ribosomes, where the numbers and types of constituent molecules are tightly controlled. Measurement of distances in cells is important to scientists studying movement of subcellular organelles. By measuring the distance an organelle moves over time, scientists can infer which molecules are causing the movement. The size of a cell and the distance between cells have important implications for the role that molecular diffusions can play in cell physiology. These are a few examples of the importance of quantitative measurements of size in cell biology; there are many more.

Measuring a common object with a ruler is quite simple, but how does a microscopist measure a mitochondrion? Everyone knows that meters, centimeters, and millimeters are units of a scale used to measure common structures. The microscopist has analogous measuring scales called stage micrometers and diffraction gratings, which can be used as micro-rulers. Both of these measuring devices are manufactured using a diamond cutting point whose motion is directed by an elaborate machine to cut lines on glass at precise spacings. The stage micrometer (used with light microscopes) is typically a line 1 mm in length, which is cut on a glass slide with divisions marked every 100 µm and subdivisions every 10 µm. Diffraction gratings (used with electron microscopes) are sold as thin metal replicas of the pattern cut on glass and appear to be miniature waffles. They come in many different scales, but 0.5 µm between lines is common.

A light microscopist measures a cell by first taking a photograph of the cell (generally called a micrograph) through the microscope. Then, without changing any of the settings of the microscope, the slide with the cell is replaced with the stage micrometer, and a second micrograph is taken. The negatives of both the cell and the micrometer are printed using a photographic enlarger. The microscopist then measures the distance between the centers of two adjacent divisions on the micrograph of the micrometer. The ratio of the measured line spacing on the enlarged photographic print to the actual spacing on the micrograph gives the amount of magnification.

Each micrograph in this book is accompanied by a black bar (black line) representing a certain distance. For example, a line with 10 µm written below it represents a distance of ten micrometers. You may develop a better understanding of scale by comparing the following micrographs along with their scale bars. The true size of a ribosome remains the same but why does it apparently get smaller as you go from free ribosome on the left to a ribosome attached to the ER to one that is shown in a cell (fig. 5C)?

Roger Leslie, University of California, Davis

Figure 5C

Size of ribosome using three different scales.

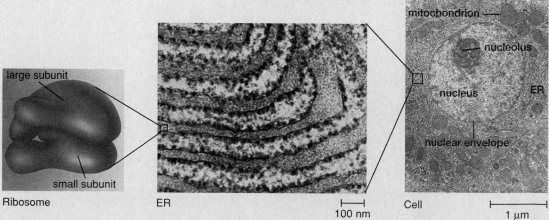

large subunit

small subunit

Ribosome

ER

100 nm

mitochondrion

nucleolus

nucleus

ER

nuclear envelope

Cell

1 µm

Golgi Apparatus

The **Golgi apparatus** is named for the person who first discovered its presence in cells. It consists of a stack of three to twenty slightly curved saccules whose appearance can be compared to a stack of pancakes (fig. 5.8). In animal cells, one side of the stack (the inner face) is directed toward the ER and the other side of the stack (the outer face) is directed toward the plasma membrane. Vesicles occur at the edges of the saccules.

The Golgi apparatus receives protein-filled vesicles that bud from the ER. Some biologists believe that these fuse to form a saccule at the inner face and that this saccule remains as a part of the Golgi apparatus until the proteins are repackaged in new vesicles at the outer face. Others believe that the vesicles from the ER proceed directly to the outer face of the Golgi apparatus, where processing and packaging occurs within its saccules. The Golgi apparatus contains enzymes that modify proteins; for example, it can add a chain of sugars to proteins, thereby making them glycoproteins.

The vesicles that leave the Golgi apparatus move to different locations in the cell. Some vesicles proceed to the plasma membrane, where they discharge their contents. Because this is *secretion*, it is often said that the Golgi apparatus is involved in processing, packaging, and secretion. Other vesicles that leave the Golgi apparatus are lysosomes.

> The Golgi apparatus processes, packages, and distributes molecules about or from the cell. It is also said to be involved in secretion.

Lysosomes

Lysosomes [Gk. *ly*, loose, and *soma*, body] are membrane-bounded vesicles produced by the Golgi apparatus that contain hydrolytic digestive enzymes.

Sometimes macromolecules are brought into a cell by vesicle formation at the plasma membrane (fig. 5.8). A lysosome can fuse with such a vesicle and can digest its contents into simpler subunits that then enter the cytoplasm. Some white blood cells defend the body by engulfing bacteria that are then enclosed within vesicles. When lysosomes fuse with these vesicles, the bacteria are digested. It should come as no surprise, then, that even parts of a cell are digested by its own lysosomes (called autodigestion). Normal cell rejuvenation most likely takes place in this matter, but autodigestion is also important during development. For example, when a tadpole becomes a frog, lysosomes are utilized to digest away the cells of the tail. The fingers of a human embryo are at first webbed, but they are freed from one another following lysosomal action.

Occasionally, a child is born with a metabolic disorder involving a missing or inactive lysosomal enzyme. In these cases, the lysosomes fill to capacity with macromolecules that cannot be broken down. The cells become so full of these lysosomes that the child dies. Someday soon it may be possible to provide the missing enzyme for these children.

> Lysosomes are membrane-bounded vesicles that contain specific enzymes. Lysosomes are produced by a Golgi apparatus, and their hydrolytic enzymes digest macromolecules from various sources.

Figure 5.8
Golgi apparatus.

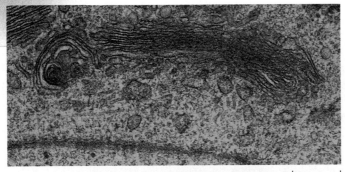

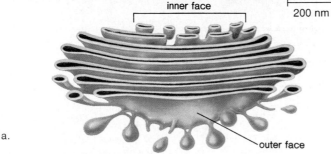

inner face

200 nm

a.

outer face

Structure of Golgi Apparatus

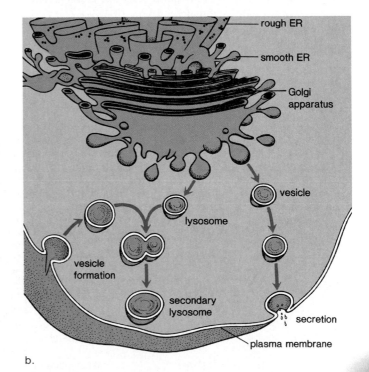

rough ER

smooth ER

Golgi apparatus

vesicle

lysosome

vesicle formation

secondary lysosome

secretion

plasma membrane

b.

Function of Golgi Apparatus

Figure 5.9

Peroxisome in a tobacco leaf. The crystalline, squarelike core of this microbody cross section is believed to contain the enzyme catalase, which breaks down hydrogen peroxide to form water.

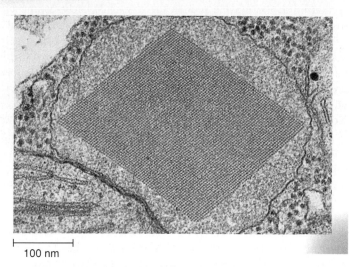

100 nm

Microbodies [Gk. *micr,* small], similar to lysosomes, are membrane-bounded vesicles but they contain only certain specific enzymes (fig. 5.9). Two types of microbodies are noteworthy: peroxisomes and glyoxysomes.

Peroxisomes are microbodies that have enzymes for transferring hydrogen atoms to oxygen. They form hydrogen peroxide (H_2O_2), a toxic molecule that is immediately broken down to water by the enzyme catalase. Peroxisomes are abundant in cells that metabolize lipids and in liver cells that metabolize alcohol. They are believed to help detoxify the alcohol.

Glyoxysomes have been observed in leaves that are carrying on photosynthesis. Here they contain enzymes that can metabolize some of the molecules involved in the photosynthetic process. They are also seen in germinating seeds, where they are believed to convert oils into sugars, which are used as nutrients by the growing plant.

Vacuoles

A **vacuole** is a large membranous sac. A vesicle is smaller than a vacuole. Animal cells have vacuoles, but they are much more prominent in plant cells. Typically, plant cells have one or two large vacuoles so filled with a watery fluid that they give added support to the cell (see fig. 5.5).

Vacuoles are most often storage areas. Plant vacuoles contain not only water, sugars, and salts but also pigments and toxic substances. The pigments are responsible for many of the red, blue, or purple colors of flowers and some leaves. The toxic substances help protect a plant from herbivorous animals. The vacuoles present in protozoans are quite specialized, and they include contractile vacuoles and digestive vacuoles.

> **The organelles of the endomembrane system are as follows.**
>
> **Endoplasmic reticulum (ER):** synthesis and modification and transport of proteins and other substances
>
> **Rough ER:** protein synthesis
>
> **Smooth ER:** lipid synthesis, in particular
>
> **Golgi apparatus:** processing, packaging, and distribution of protein molecules
>
> **Lysosomes:** intracellular digestion
>
> **Microbodies:** various metabolic tasks
>
> **Vacuoles:** storage areas

Figure 5.10 shows how organelles are mechanically separated from one another in the laboratory so their function can be determined.

Figure 5.10

Cell fractionation. Cell fractionation is a means to separate cell components so that their individual biochemical composition and function can be determined. Disrupted cells are subjected to a spinning action known as centrifugation. At a low speed, large particles, like cell nuclei, settle out and are found in the sediment. Smaller particles are still in the fluid (supernatant), which can be poured into a fresh tube and subjected to centrifugation at a higher speed until the smallest particles have been separated out. Even these can be separated by putting them in a sucrose gradient. The concentration of sucrose decreases from top to bottom and centrifugation causes the components to collect in the region of the gradient equal to their density. Once separated, the various cell fractions can be biochemically analyzed.

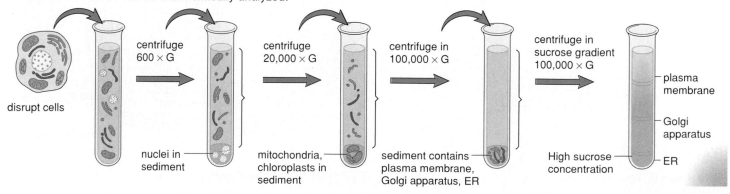

disrupt cells

centrifuge 600 × G — nuclei in sediment

centrifuge 20,000 × G — mitochondria, chloroplasts in sediment

centrifuge in 100,000 × G — sediment contains plasma membrane, Golgi apparatus, ER

centrifuge in sucrose gradient 100,000 × G — High sucrose concentration

plasma membrane
Golgi apparatus
ER

Energy-Related Organelles

Life is possible only because of a constant input of energy used to maintain the structure of cells. Chloroplasts and mitochondria are the two eukaryotic membranous organelles that specialize in converting energy to a form that can be used by the cell.

Photosynthesis, which occurs in **chloroplasts** [Gk. *chlor,* green, and *plast,* formed, molded], is the process by which solar energy is converted to chemical energy within carbohydrates. Photosynthesis can be represented by this equation:

> light energy + carbon dioxide + water ⟶ carbohydrate + oxygen

Here the word *energy* stands for solar energy, the ultimate source of energy for cellular organization. Only plants, algae, and cyanobacteria are capable of carrying on photosynthesis in this manner.

Cellular respiration, which requires **mitochondria** [Gk. *mito,* thread, and *chondro,* grain], is the process by which the chemical energy of carbohydrates is converted to that of ATP (adenosine triphosphate), the common carrier of chemical energy in cells. Cellular respiration can be represented by this equation:

> carbohydrate + oxygen ⟶ carbon dioxide + water + energy

Here the word *energy* stands for ATP molecules. When a cell needs energy, ATP supplies it. The energy of ATP is used for synthetic reactions, active transport, and all energy-requiring processes in cells. All organisms carry on cellular respiration, and all organisms except bacteria have mitochondria. Chloroplasts use the sun's energy to produce carbohydrates, and carbohydrate-derived products are broken down in mitochondria to build up ATP molecules.

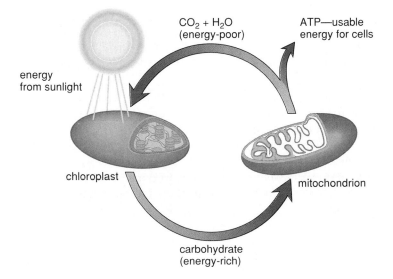

energy from sunlight

$CO_2 + H_2O$ (energy-poor)

ATP—usable energy for cells

chloroplast

mitochondrion

carbohydrate (energy-rich)

Figure 5.11 🎞

Chloroplast structure. **a.** Electron micrograph.**b.** Generalized drawing in which the outer and inner membrane has been cut away to reveal the grana.

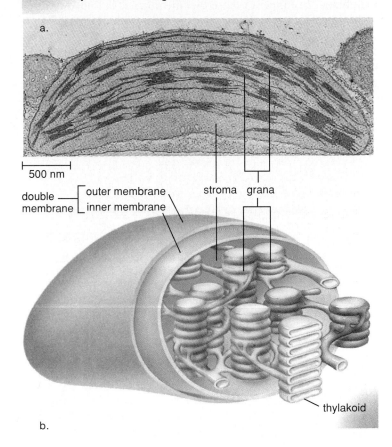

a.

500 nm

double membrane ⎰ outer membrane
⎱ inner membrane

stroma   grana

b.

thylakoid

Chloroplasts

Chloroplasts are about 4–6 μm in diameter and 1–5 μm in length; they belong to a group of plant organelles known as plastids. Among the plastids are also the *amyloplasts,* which store starch, and the *chromoplasts,* which contain red and orange pigments.

A chloroplast is bounded by a double membrane, and inside there is even more membrane, organized into flattened sacs called **thylakoids** [Gk. *thylac,* sack, and *oid,* like]. In certain regions, the thylakoids are piled up like stacks of coins, and each stack is called a **granum**. The fluid-filled space about the thylakoids is called the **stroma** (fig. 5.11).

Photosynthesis requires pigments that capture solar energy and enzymes that synthesize carbohydrate. Chlorophyll, green pigment, is located within the thylakoid membranes of grana. Enzymes are found within stroma. This is the way chloroplasts are organized to carry out photosynthesis. There are no chloroplasts in cyanobacteria, which are prokaryotic. Instead, chlorophyll is bound to cytoplasmic thylakoids.

Mitochondria

Most mitochondria are usually 0.5–1.0 μm in diameter and 7 μm in length, although the size and the shape can vary.

Mitochondria, like chloroplasts, are bounded by a double membrane. The inner of these two membranes is folded to form little shelves, called **cristae,** which project into the **matrix,** an inner space filled with a semifluid (fig. 5.12) medium. Analysis reveals that the matrix contains enzymes that break down carbohydrate-derived products, while ATP production occurs at the cristae.

Both mitochondria and chloroplasts contain their own DNA and ribosomes and can produce a few of their own proteins. They reproduce themselves by division.

> Chloroplasts and mitochondria are membranous organelles whose structure lends itself to the processes that occur within them.

Figure 5.12

Mitochondrion structure. **a.** Electron micrograph. **b.** Generalized drawing in which the outer membrane and portions of the inner membrane have been cut away to reveal the cristae.

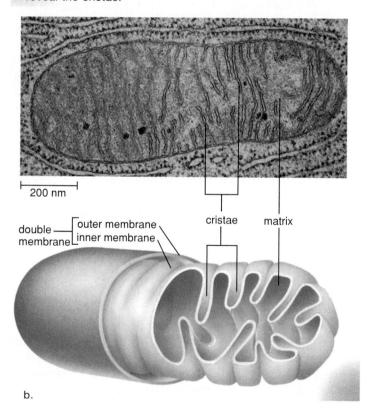

200 nm

double membrane — outer membrane, inner membrane   cristae   matrix

b.

Cytoskeleton Contains Filaments and Microtubules

The **cytoskeleton** [Gk. *cyt,* cell, and *skelet,* dried body] is a network of interconnected filaments and tubules that extends from the nucleus to the plasma membrane in eukaryotic cells. Prior to the 1970s, it was believed that the cytosol was an unorganized mixture of biomolecules. Then, high-voltage electron microscopes, which can penetrate thicker specimens, showed that the cytosol was instead highly organized. And the technique of immunofluorescence microscopy identified the makeup of specific protein fibers within the cytoskeletal network (fig. 5.13).

The name *cytoskeleton* is convenient in that it allows us to compare the cytoskeleton to the bones and muscles of an animal. Bones and muscles give an animal structure and also allow it to move. Similarly, we will see that the elements of the cytoskeleton maintain cell shape and allow it and the organelles to move. The cytoskeleton is dynamic; elements undergo rapid assembly and disassembly by monomers continuously entering or leaving the polymer. These changes occur at rates that are measured in seconds and minutes. The entire cytoskeletal network can even disappear and reappear at various times in the life of a cell. Before a cell divides, for instance, the elements disassemble and then reassemble into a structure called a spindle that distributes chromosomes in an orderly manner. At the end of cell division, the spindle disassembles and the elements reassemble once again into their former array.

The cytoskeleton contains three types of elements: actin filaments, intermediate filaments, and microtubules, which are responsible for cell shape and movement.

Actin Filaments for Structure and Movement

Actin filaments (formerly called microfilaments) are long, extremely thin fibers (about 7 nm in diameter) that occur in bundles or meshlike networks. The actin filament contains two chains of globular actin monomers twisted about one another in a helical manner.

Actin filaments can play a structural role as when they form a dense complex web just under the plasma membrane, to which they are anchored by special proteins. They are also seen in the microvilli that project from intestinal cells, and their presence most likely accounts for the ability of microvilli to alternately shorten and extend into the intestine. In plant cells, they apparently form the tracts along which chloroplasts circulate or stream in a particular direction.

How are actin filaments involved in the movement of the cell and its organelles? It is well known that myosin interacts with actin filaments in muscle cells to bring about contraction. Actin filaments move because they interact with myosin.

Figure 5.13

Immunofluorescence. This microscopy technique is based on the binding of fluorescent antibodies to specific proteins in the cell and is used to localize the components of the cytoskeleton.

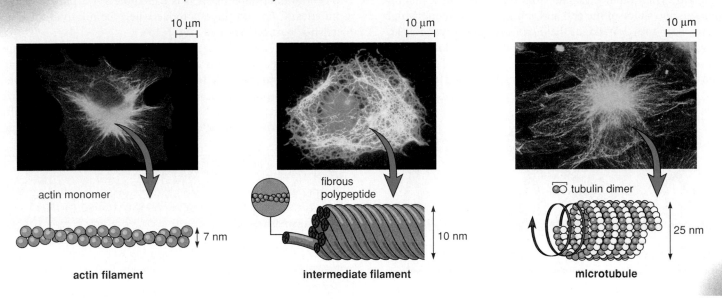

Myosin consists of a head plus a tail. After the head combines with and splits ATP, it binds to actin and undergoes a change in configuration which pulls the actin filament forward:

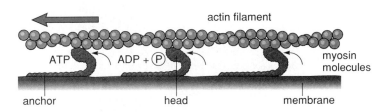

In muscle cells, the tails of several muscle myosin molecules are joined to form a thick filament. In nonmuscle cells, cytoplasmic myosin tails are bound to membranes but the heads still interact with actin. For instance, when daughter cells form during animal cell division, actin filaments (in conjunction with myosin) pinch off the two cells from one another. Also, it has been discovered that the presence of a network of actin filaments lying beneath the plasma membrane accounts for the formation of pseudopodia, extensions that allow certain cells to move in an amoeboid fashion.

Intermediate Filaments Are Diverse

Intermediate filaments (8–11 nm in diameter) are intermediate in size between actin filaments and microtubules. They are a ropelike assembly of fibrous polypeptides, but the specific type varies according to the tissue. There are intermediate filaments that support the nuclear envelope (called nuclear lamina) and others that support the plasma membrane and take part in the formation of cell-to-cell junctions. In the skin, the filaments, which are made of the protein keratin, give great mechanical strength to skin cells. Recent work has shown intermediate filaments to be highly dynamic. They also assemble and disassemble but need to have phosphate added first by soluble enzymes.

Microtubules Have Tubulin Subunits

Microtubules [Gk. *micr,* small, and L. *tubul,* little pipe] are small hollow cylinders about 25 nm in diameter and from 200 nm–25 μm in length.

Microtubules are made of a globular protein called tubulin, which occurs as λ tubulin and β tubulin. When assembly occurs, these tubulin molecules come together as dimers and the dimers arrange themselves in rows so that an λ tubulin is always adjacent to a β tubulin. Microtubules have thirteen rows of tubulin dimers about what appears to be an empty central core in electron micrographs.

In many cells the regulation of microtubule assembly is under the control of a microtubule organizing center, called the **centrosome** [Gk. *centr*, center, and *soma*, body], which lies near the nucleus. Microtubules radiate from the centrosome, helping to maintain the shape of the cell and acting as tracts along which organelles can move. Whereas the *motor molecule* myosin is associated with actin filaments, the motor molecules kinesin and dynein are associated with microtubules. One type of kinesin is responsible for moving vesicles, including those that arise from the ER along microtubules.

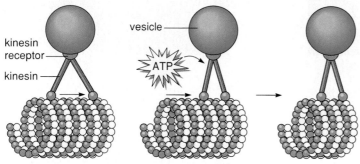

vesicle moves, not microtubule

There are different types of kinesin proteins, each specialized to move one kind of vesicle or cellular organelle. A second type of cytoplasmic motor molecule has been discovered and is called cytoplasmic dynein because it is closely related to the molecule dynein found in flagella.

Centrioles

In animal cells, the centrosome contains two centrioles lying at right angles to each other. **Centrioles** [Gk. *centr*, center] are short cylinders with a 9 + 0 pattern of microtubule triplets—that is, a ring having nine sets of triplets with none in the middle (fig. 5.14). Before an animal cell divides, the centrioles replicate and the members of each pair are at right angles to one another. Then each pair becomes part of a separate centrosome. During cell division the centrosomes move apart so that each new cell has its own centrosome. Plant cells have the equivalent of a centrosome but it does not contain centrioles. It would appear then that centrioles are not necessary to the assembly of cytoplasmic microtubules.

Cilia and Flagella

Cilia and **flagella** [L. *flagell*, whip] are hairlike projections that can move either in an undulating fashion, like a whip, or stiffly, like an oar. Cells that have these organelles are capable of movement. For example, unicellular paramecia move by means of cilia; sperm cells move by means of flagella. The cells that line our upper respiratory tract have cilia that sweep debris trapped within mucus back up into the throat, where it can be swallowed. This action helps keep the lungs clean.

Cilia are much shorter than flagella, but they have a similar construction and this construction is quite different from that of prokaryotic flagella. Eukaryotic cilia and flagella are membrane-bounded cylinders enclosing a matrix area. In the matrix are nine microtubule doublets arranged in a circle around two central microtubules. This is called the 9 + 2 pattern of microtubules. Cilia and flagella move when the microtubule doublets slide past one another (fig. 5.15).

Each cilium and flagellum has a basal body lying in the cytoplasm at its base. Basal bodies have the same circular arrangement of microtubule triplets as centrioles and are believed to be derived from them. It is possible that basal bodies organize the microtubules within cilia and flagella, but we know that cilia and flagella grow by the addition of tubulin dimers to their tips.

Centrioles have a 9 + 0 pattern of microtubules and give rise to basal bodies that organize the 9 + 2 pattern of microtubules in cilia and flagella.

Figure 5.14
Centrioles. **a.** Drawing of centrioles showing their 9 + 0 arrangement of microtubule triplets. (The 0 in this equation means that there are no microtubules in the center of the organelle.) **b.** A pair of centrioles is found in the centrosome where they lie at right angles to each other. Also, note the large number of free microtubules that radiate out of the centrosome, a microtubule organizing center.

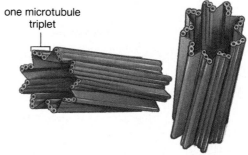

one microtubule triplet

a. Centrioles

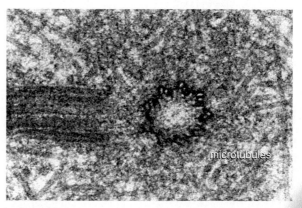

microtubules

b. Centrosome

Figure 5.15

Structure of cilium or flagellum. A cilium has a basal body with a 9 + 0 pattern of microtubule triplets. (Notice that there is a ring of nine triplets, but no central microtubules.) The shaft of the cilium has a 9 + 2 pattern (a ring of nine microtubule doublets surrounds a central pair of single microtubules). Also, compare the cross section of the basal body to the cross section of the cilium shaft and note that in place of the third microtubule, the outer doublets have dynein side arms. (Dynein is a motor molecule.) In the presence of ATP, the dynein side arms reach out and attempt to move along their neighboring doublet. Because of the radial spokes connecting the doublets to the central microtubules, bending occurs.

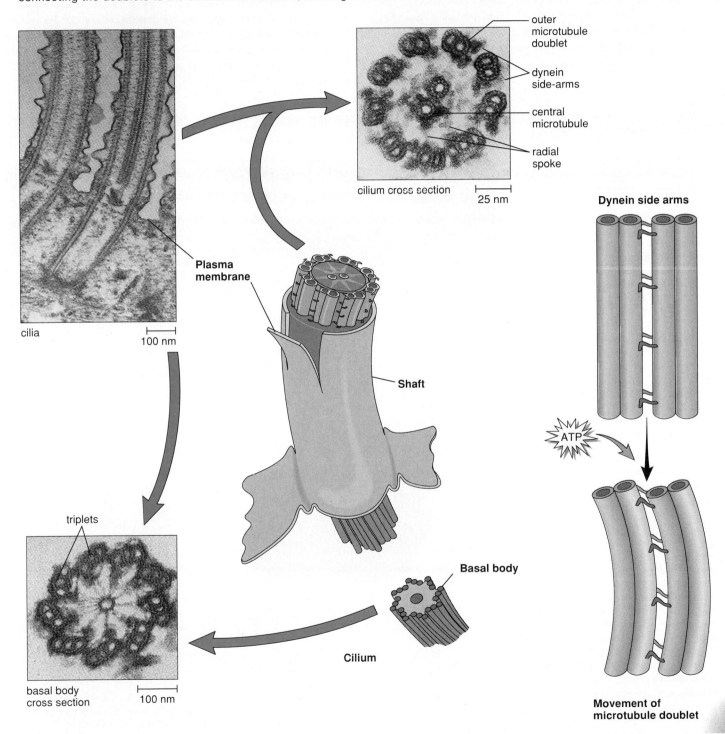

outer microtubule doublet

dynein side-arms

central microtubule

radial spoke

cilium cross section

25 nm

cilia

100 nm

Plasma membrane

Shaft

triplets

basal body cross section

100 nm

Basal body

Cilium

Dynein side arms

ATP

Movement of microtubule doublet

Biological Relationships

A cell carries on the functions and characteristics of living things. Look again at figures 5.4a and 5.5. Imagine nutrient molecules entering at the plasma membrane and being used as either energy sources or building blocks by the organelles, which are specialized for particular functions. In the mitochondria, glucose products are being broken down to supply the cell with ATP molecules. At rough ER, amino acids are being linked together to produce proteins. This synthetic reaction requires ATP energy. The proteins can be used for growth and repair of the cell or packaged in a secretory vesicle by the Golgi apparatus.

The nucleus is the control center of the cell; it contains DNA, the hereditary material that determines the sequence of amino acids in proteins. When a cell divides, a copy of the hereditary material is passed on to the daughter cells.

Compartmentalization keeps the various cellular functions regionally separated. Just as organelles are specialized, so are the various types of cells and tissues of the organism. Organisms, too, have evolved into particular types and are adapted to a particular way of life. A form-function relationship is therefore apparent at all levels of biological organization.

Summary

1. All organisms are composed of cells, the smallest units of living matter. Cells are capable of self-reproduction, and existing cells come only from preexisting cells.

2. Cells are very small and are measured in small units of the metric system. The plasma membrane regulates exchange of materials between the cell and the external environment. Cells must remain small in order to have an adequate amount of surface area per cell volume.

3. There are two major groups of cells: prokaryotic and eukaryotic. Both types have a plasma membrane and cytoplasm. Eukaryotic cells also have a nucleus and various organelles. Prokaryotic cells have a nucleoid that is not bounded by a nuclear envelope. They also lack most of the other organelles that compartmentalize eukaryotic cells. Table 5.2 summarizes the similarities and differences between prokaryotic and eukaryotic cells.

4. The nucleus of eukaryotic cells, represented by animal and plant cells, is bounded by a nuclear envelope containing pores. These pores serve as passageways between the cytoplasm and the nucleoplasm. Within the nucleus, the chromatin undergoes coiling into chromosomes at the time of cell division. The nucleolus is a special region of the chromatin where rRNA is produced and where proteins from the cytoplasm gather to form ribosomal subunits. These subunits are joined in the cytoplasm.

5. Ribosomes are organelles that function in protein synthesis. They can be bound to ER or exist free within the cytosol. Several ribosomes involved in synthesizing the same type of protein are called a polysome.

6. The endomembrane system includes the ER (both rough and smooth), the Golgi apparatus, the lysosomes, and other types of vesicles and vacuoles. The endomembrane system serves to compartmentalize the cell and keep the various biochemical reactions separate from one another. Newly produced proteins enter the ER lumen, where they may be modified before proceeding to the lumen of the smooth ER. The smooth ER has various metabolic functions depending on the cell, but it also forms vesicles that carry

Table 5.2

Comparison of Prokaryotic Cells and Eukaryotic Cells

		Eukaryotic Cells	
	Prokaryotic Cells	*Animal*	*Plant*
Size	Smaller (1–10 μm in diameter)	Larger (10–100 μm in diameter)	
Plasma membrane	Yes	Yes	Yes
Cell wall	Usually (peptidoglycan)	No	Yes (cellulose)
Nuclear envelope	No	Yes	Yes
Nucleolus	No	Yes	Yes
DNA	Yes (single loop)	Yes (chromosomes)	Yes (chromosomes)
Mitochondria	No	Yes	Yes
Chloroplasts	No	No	Yes
Endoplasmic reticulum	No	Yes	Yes
Ribosomes	Yes (smaller)	Yes	Yes
Vacuoles	No	Yes (small)	Yes (usually large, single vacuole)
Golgi apparatus	No	Yes	Yes
Lysosomes	No	Always	Often
Microbodies	No	Usually	Usually
Cytoskeleton	No	Yes	Yes
Centrioles	No	Yes	No
9 + 2 cilia or flagella	No	Often	No (in flowering plants) Yes (in ferns, cycads, and bryophytes)

proteins and other substances to different locations, particularly to the Golgi apparatus. The Golgi apparatus processes proteins and repackages them into lysosomes, which carry out intracellular digestion, or into vesicles that fuse with the plasma membrane. Following fusion, secretion occurs. The endomembrane system also includes microbodies that have special enzymatic functions, and the large single plant cell vacuole, which not only stores substances but lends support to the plant cell.

7. Cells require a constant input of energy to maintain their structure. Chloroplasts capture the energy of the sun and carry on photosynthesis, which produces carbohydrate. Carbohydrate-derived products are broken down in mitochondria as ATP is produced. This is an oxygen-requiring process called cellular respiration.

8. The cytoskeleton contains actin filaments, intermediate filaments, and microtubules. These maintain cell shape and allow it and the organelles to move. Actin filaments, the thinnest filaments, interact with the motor molecule myosin in muscle cells to bring about contraction; in other cells, they pinch off daughter cells and have other dynamic functions. Intermediate filaments support the nuclear envelope and the plasma membrane and probably participate in cell-to-cell junctions. Microtubules radiate out from the centrosome and are present in centrioles, cilia, and flagella. They serve as tracts along which vesicles, etc., move due to the action of specific motor molecules.

Writing Across the Curriculum

 In order to practice writing skills, students should write out the answers to any or all of the study questions and the critical thinking questions. The study questions are sequenced in the same order as the text. Answers to the objective questions, and suggested answers to the critical thinking questions, are in appendix D.

Study Questions

1. What are the two basic tenets of the cell theory?   62

2. Why is it advantageous for cells to be small?   63

3. What are the contrasting advantages of light microscopy and electron microscopy?   64–65

4. What similar features do prokaryotic cells and eukaryotic cells have? What is their major difference?   66–67

5. Roughly sketch a prokaryotic cell, label its parts, and state a function for each of these.   66

6. Distinguish between the nucleolus, rRNA, and ribosomes.   70–71

7. Describe the structure and the function of the nuclear envelope and the nuclear pores.   70

8. Trace the path of a protein from rough ER to the plasma membrane.   71

9. Give the overall equations for photosynthesis and cellular respiration, contrast the two, and tell how they are related.   75

10. What are the three components of the cytoskeleton? What are their structures and functions?   76–77

Objective Questions

1. The small size of cells is best correlated with
   a. the fact they are self-reproducing.
   b. their prokaryotic versus eukaryotic nature.
   c. an adequate surface area for exchange of materials.
   d. All of these are correct.

2. Which of these is not a true comparison of the light microscope and the transmission electron microscope?
   Light——Electron
   a uses light to "view" object—uses electrons to "view" object
   b. uses glass lenses for focusing—uses magnetic lenses for focusing
   c. specimen must be killed and stained—specimen may be alive and nonstained
   d. magnification is not as great—magnification is greater

3. Which of these best distinguishes a prokaryotic cell from a eukaryotic cell?
   a. Prokaryotic cells have a cell wall, but eukaryotic cells never do.
   b. Prokaryotic cells are much larger than eukaryotic cells.
   c. Prokaryotic cells have flagella, but eukaryotic cells do not.
   d. Prokaryotic cells do not have a membrane-bounded nucleus, but eukaryotic cells do have such a nucleus.

4. Which of these is not found in the nucleus?
   a. functioning ribosomes
   b. chromatin that condenses to chromosomes
   c. nucleolus that produces rRNA
   d. nucleoplasm instead of cytoplasm

5. Vesicles from the smooth ER most likely are on their way to the
   a. rough ER.
   b. lysosomes.
   c. Golgi apparatus.
   d. plant cell vacuole only.

6. Lysosomes function in
   a. protein synthesis.
   b. processing and packaging.
   c. intracellular digestion.
   d. lipid synthesis.

7. Mitochondria
   a. are involved in cellular respiration.
   b. break down ATP to release energy for cells.
   c. contain grana and cristae.
   d. All of these are correct.

8. Which organelle releases oxygen?
   a. ribosome
   b. Golgi apparatus
   c. mitochondrion
   d. chloroplast

9. Which of these is not true?
   a. Actin filaments are in muscle cells.
   b. Microtubules radiate out from the ER.
   c. Intermediate filaments sometimes contain keratin.
   d. Motor molecules use microtubules as tracts.

10. Cilia and flagella
    a. bend when microtubules try to slide past one another.
    b. contain myosin which pulls on actin filaments.
    c. are organized by basal bodies derived from centrioles.
    d. Both a and c are correct.

11. Study the example given in (a) below. Then for each other organelle listed, state another that is structurally and functionally related. Tell why you paired these two organelles.
    a. The nucleus can be paired with *nucleoli* because nucleoli are found in the nucleus. Nucleoli occur where chromatin is producing rRNA.
    b. mitochondria
    c. centrioles
    d. ER

12. Label these parts of the cell that are involved in protein synthesis and modification. Give a function for each structure.

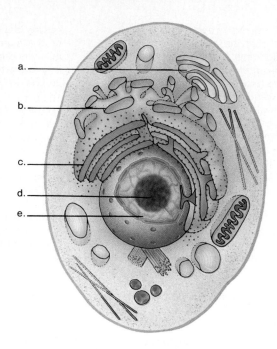

a. _____
b. _____
c. _____
d. _____
e. _____

Concepts and Critical Thinking

1. *All organisms are made up of cells.*
   What data would you use to convince someone that all organisms are composed of cells? What data would you have to find to nullify the cell theory?

2. *Cells are compartmentalized and highly organized.*
   Substantiate this concept by referring to table 5.1.

3. *Life begins at the cellular level of organization.*
   Which organelles contribute to the ability of the cell to maintain its structure and grow? What are the functions of these organelles?

Selected Key Terms

cell The smallest unit that displays the properties of life; composed of cytoplasm surrounded by a plasma membrane. 62

chromatin (KROH-mut-un) Complex of DNA and associated proteins observed within a nucleus that is not dividing. [Gk. *chrom,* color, and *tin,* stretch] 70

cilium (pl., cilia) Short, hairlike projection from the plasma membrane, occurring usually in larger numbers. 78

cytoplasm Contents of a cell between the nucleus (nucleoid) and the plasma membrane. [Gk. *cyt,* cell, and *plasm,* something modeled] 66

cytoskeleton Internal framework of the cell, consisting of microtubules, actin filaments, and intermediate filaments. [Gk. *cyt,* cell, and *skelet,* dried body] 67, 76

endoplasmic reticulum (en-doh-PLAZ-mik reh-TIK-yoo-lum) A system of membranous saccules and channels in the cytoplasm. [Gk. *endo,* within, and *plasm,* something molded, and L. *reticul,* network] 71

eukaryotic cell (yoo-kair-ee-AHT-ik) Typical of most types of organisms, except bacteria, having a well-defined nucleus and organelles. [Gk. *eu,* good, well, and *kary,* nucleus] 67

flagellum (pl., flagella) Slender, long extension used for locomotion by some bacteria, protozoa, and sperm. [L. *flagell,* whip] 78

Golgi apparatus An organelle consisting of saccules and vesicles that processes, packages, and distributes molecules about or from the cell. 73

lysosome Membrane-bounded vesicle that contains hydrolytic enzymes for digesting macromolecules. [Gk. *ly,* loose, and *soma,* body] 73

microtubule Small cylindrical organelle composed of tubulin dimers about an empty central core present in the cytoplasm, centrioles, cilia and flagella. [Gk. *micr,* small, and L. *tubul,* little pipe] 77

nucleoid Area in prokaryotic cell where DNA is found. [L. *nucle,* nucleus] 66

nucleolus (pl., nucleoli) Dark-staining, spherical body in the cell nucleus that produces ribosomal subunits. [L. *nucleol,* little nucleus] 70

nucleus (NOO-klee-us) Region of a eukaryotic cell, containing chromosomes, that controls the structure and function of the cell. 70

organelle A small, often membranous structure in the cytoplasm having a specific function. 67

prokaryotic cell (proh-kair-ee-AHT-ik) Typical of bacteria lacking a membrane-bounded nucleus and most organelles. 66

ribosome RNA and protein in two subunits; site of protein synthesis in cytoplasm. 71

6

MEMBRANE STRUCTURE AND FUNCTION

Learning Objectives

Membrane Models Have Changed

- Contrast the sandwich model of membrane structure with the fluid-mosaic model, and cite the evidence supporting these models.   84–85

The Plasma Membrane Is Complex

- Describe the arrangement of the lipid component, and give a function for each type of lipid in the membrane.   86–87

- Describe the arrangement of the protein component, and give several functions for these proteins.   87

How Molecules Cross the Plasma Membrane

- Define diffusion and osmosis, and explain their relevance to cell biology.   91–92

- Describe the appearance of a plant cell and an animal cell in isotonic, hypotonic, and hypertonic solutions.   92–93

- Name two types of transport by carrier proteins, and give an example for each.   94–95

- Contrast endocytosis and exocytosis. Name three types of endocytosis and differentiate among them.   96–97

The Cell Surface Is Modified

- Describe the dynamic nature of the extracellular matrix.   98

- Describe the composition of the plant cell wall.   98

- List and describe three types of junctions that occur between animal cells, Name and describe one type of junction between plant cells.   98–99

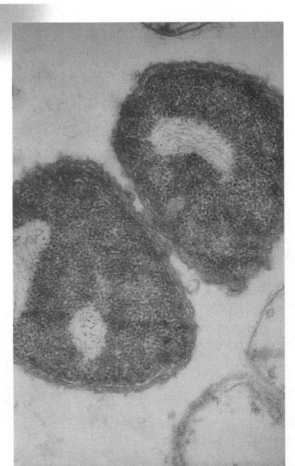

100 nm

All cells have a plasma membrane which regulates the entrance and exit of molecules into and out of the cell. Some, like these bacteria, *Neisseria,* also have a cell wall.

ll cells have a plasma membrane that serves as an interface between the interior, which is alive, and the exterior, which is nonliving. An intact plasma membrane is absolutely essential to a cell, and if by chance the plasma membrane is disrupted, the cell loses its contents and dies. In addition, the plasma membrane was absolutely essential to the evolution of the first cell or cells. Only when a membrane is present can there be a cell at all.

The interior and exterior environments of a living cell are largely fluids, even if the cell is within a multicellular organism. Quite often the composition of intracellular fluid (i.e., cytosol) is not quite the same as that of the extracellular fluids. The plasma membrane functions to keep the intracellular fluid relatively constant, despite the fact that molecules such as nutrients and wastes are continually moving into and out of the cell. This membrane regulates the entrance and exit of molecules into and out of the cell, and in this way the intracellular fluid remains compatible with the continued existence of the cell.

Another important function of membranes is communication. The components of a membrane signal other cells as to what type cell this is and/or also serve as receptors for various signal molecules that affect the cell's metabolism. Some take part in junctions that allow molecules to pass from cell to cell.

MEMBRANE MODELS HAVE CHANGED

At the turn of the century, investigators noted that lipid-soluble molecules entered cells more rapidly than water-soluble molecules. This prompted them to suggest that lipids are a component of the plasma membrane. Later, chemical analysis disclosed that the plasma membrane contains phospholipids (fig. 6.1). In 1925, E. Gorter and G. Grendel measured the amount of phospholipid extracted from red blood cells and determined that there is just enough to form a bilayer around the cells. They further suggested that the nonpolar (hydrophobic) tails are directed inward and the polar (hydrophilic) heads are directed outward:

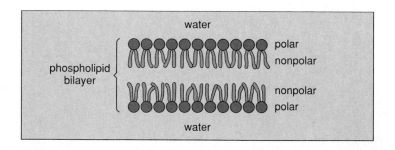

The presence of lipids cannot account for all the properties of the plasma membrane. For example, to account for the permeability of the membrane to certain nonlipid substances, J. Danielli and H. Davson suggested in the 1940s that globular proteins are also a part of the membrane. They proposed the *sandwich model*

Figure 6.1

Membrane structure. **a.** The red blood cell plasma membrane typically has a three-layered appearance in electron micrographs. **b.** Robertson's unit membrane model proposed that the outer dark layers in electron micrographs were made up of protein and polar heads of phospholipid molecules, while the inner light layer was composed of the nonpolar tails. The Singer and Nicolson fluid-mosaic model put protein molecules within the lipid bilayer. **c.** A technique called freeze-fracture allows an investigator to view the interior of the membrane. Cells are rapidly frozen in liquid nitrogen and then fractured with a special knife. The fracture often splits the membrane in the middle of the lipid bilayer. Platinum and carbon are applied to the fractured surface to produce a faithful replica that is observed by electron microscopy. **d.** The electron micrograph is not as smooth; the micrograph shows the presence of particles, consistent with the fluid-mosaic model.

a. Electron micrograph of red blood cell plasma membrane

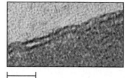

20 nm

b. Two possible models

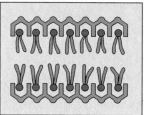 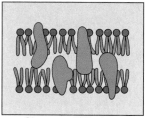

Robertson unit membrane   Singer and Nicolson fluid-mosaic model

c. Freeze-fracture of membrane

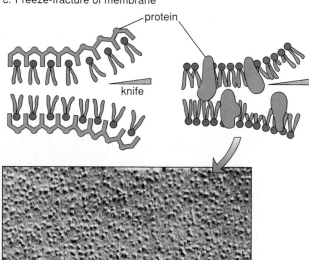

d. Electron micrograph of freeze-fractured membrane shows presence of particles

of membrane structure, later rejected, in which the phospholipid bilayer is a filling between two layers of proteins arranged to produce channels through which polar substances may pass:

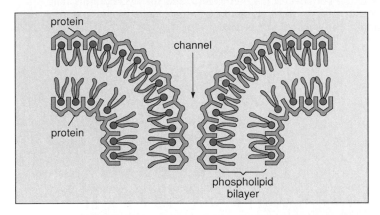

By the late 1950s, electron microscopy had advanced to allow viewing of the plasma membrane and other membranes in the cell. Since the membrane has a sandwichlike appearance, J. D. Robertson assumed that the outer dark layer (stained with heavy metals) contained protein plus the hydrophilic heads of the phospholipids (fig. 6.2). The interior was simply the hydrophobic tails of these molecules. Robertson went on to suggest that all membranes in various cells have basically the same composition. This proposal was called the unit membrane model.

This model of membrane structure was accepted for at least ten years, even though investigators began to doubt its accuracy. For example, not all membranes have the same appearance in electron micrographs, and they certainly do not have the same function. The inner membrane of a mitochondrion is coated with rows of particles and functions in cellular respiration; it therefore has a far different appearance and function from the plasma membrane. Finally, in 1972, S. Singer and G. Nicolson introduced the **fluid-mosaic model** of membrane structure, which proposes in part that the membrane is a phospholipid bilayer in which protein molecules are either partially or wholly embedded. The proteins are scattered throughout the membrane in an irregular pattern that can vary from membrane to membrane. The fluid-mosaic model of membrane structure is supported especially by electron micrographs of freeze-fractured membranes (see fig. 6.1).

The fluid-mosaic model of membrane structure is widely accepted at this time.

Our knowledge of the plasma membrane has increased over the years. There were a series of models, each one developed to suit the evidence available at that time. This illustrates that scientific knowledge is always subject to change, and modifications are made whenever new data are presented. A model is useful because it pulls together the available data and suggests new avenues of research.

Figure 6.2

The plasma membrane contains phospholipid molecules. Each phospholipid molecule is composed of glycerol bonded to two fatty acid chains and a chain that contains a phosphate group and a nitrogen group. The molecule arranges itself in such a way that the phosphate- and nitrogen-containing chain forms a polar (hydrophilic) head, and the fatty acid chains form nonpolar (hydrophobic) tails. The presence of a double bond causes a "kink" in a fatty acid tail. **a.** General appearance. **b.** Structural detail.

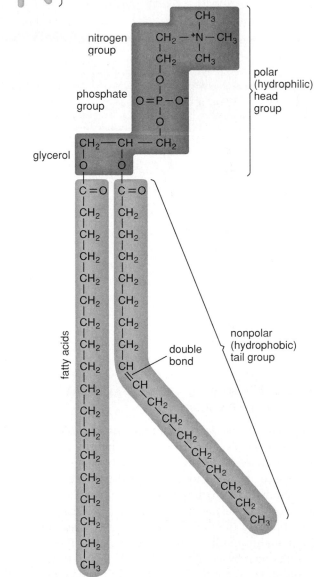

Figure 6.3 🔲

Fluid-mosaic model of an animal cell plasma membrane. The plasma membrane is composed of a phospholipid bilayer with embedded proteins. The hydrophilic heads of the phospholipids are at the surfaces of the membrane, and the hydrophobic tails make up the interior of the membrane. Note the asymmetry of the membrane; for example, carbohydrate chains project externally and cytoskeleton filaments attach to proteins on the cytoplasmic side of the plasma membrane.

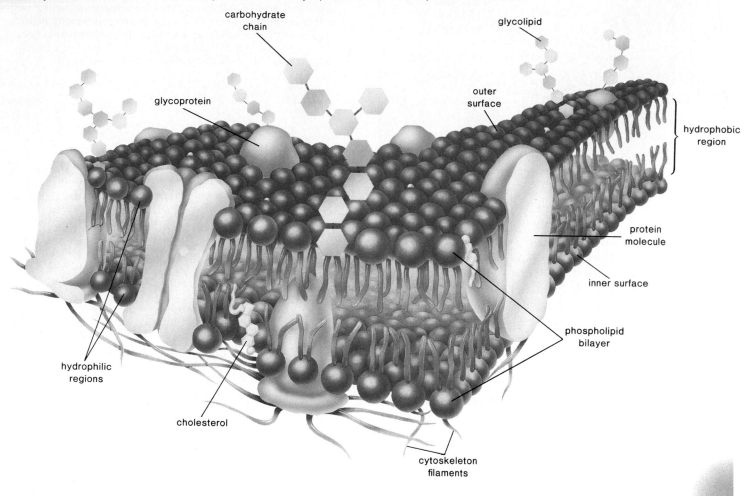

THE PLASMA MEMBRANE IS COMPLEX

The *fluid-mosaic model* of membrane structure has two components, lipids and proteins. Most of the lipids in the plasma membrane are **phospholipids** [Gk. *phos,* light, and *lipar,* oil], which are known to spontaneously arrange themselves into a bilayer. In a membrane, the hydrophilic (polar) heads of the phospholipid molecules face the intracellular and extracellular fluid and the hydrophobic (nonpolar) tails face each other (fig. 6.3). In addition to phospholipids, there are two other types of lipids in the plasma membrane. *Glycolipids* have a structure similar to phospholipids except that the hydrophilic head is a variety of sugars joined to form a straight or branching carbohydrate chain. **Cholesterol** is a lipid that is found in animal plasma membranes; related steroids are found in the plasma membrane of plants.

Cholesterol, which also has a hydrophilic and a hydrophobic end, arranges itself in this manner:

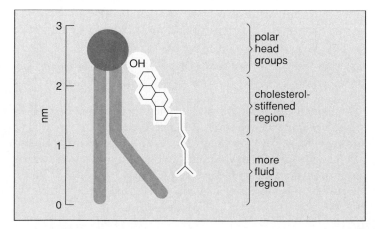

Cholesterol reduces the permeability of the membrane to most biological molecules.

> **Phospholipids form the matrix of the plasma membrane but glycolipids and cholesterol are also present. These are arranged to form a bilayer.**

Proteins are the other major component of membranes. Transmembrane proteins which are found within the membrane, often have hydrophobic regions embedded within the membrane and hydrophilic regions that project from both surfaces of the bilayer:

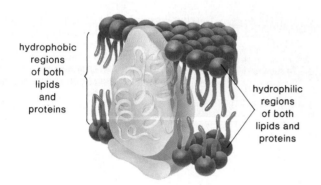

hydrophobic regions of both lipids and proteins

hydrophilic regions of both lipids and proteins

Many transmembrane proteins are *glycoproteins,* which have an attached carbohydrate chain. As with glycolipids, the carbohydrate chain projects externally.

Other proteins occur either on the cytoplasmic side or the outer surface side of the membrane. Some of these are anchored to the membrane by a covalently attached lipid or are covalently bonded to the carbohydrate chain of a glycolipid. Still others are held in place by noncovalent interactions which can be disrupted by gentle shaking or by a change in the pH.

The plasma membrane is asymmetrical; the two halves are not identical. The lipid and protein composition of the inside half differs from the outside half. The carbohydrate chains of the glycolipids and glycoproteins form a carbohydrate coat that envelops the outer surface of the plasma membrane. On the inside some proteins serve as links to the cytoskeletal filaments and on the outside some serve as links to an extracellular matrix. The extracellular matrix is discussed on page 98.

> **Transmembrane proteins span the lipid bilayer and often have attached carbohydrate chains. Proteins are also found on the cytoplasmic side or the outer surface side of the membrane.**

The Membrane Is Fluid

At body temperature, the phospholipid bilayer of the plasma membrane has the consistency of olive oil. The greater the concentration of unsaturated fatty acid residues, the more fluid the bilayer. In each monolayer, the hydrocarbon tails wiggle, and the entire phospholipid molecule can move sideways at a rate averaging about 2 µm—the length of a prokaryotic cell—per second. (Phospholipid molecules rarely flip-flop from one layer to the other, because this would require the hydrophilic head to move through the hydrophobic center of the membrane.) The fluidity of a phospholipid bilayer means that cells are pliable. Imagine if they were not—the nerve cells in your neck would crack whenever you nodded your head!

Although some proteins are often held in place by cytoskeleton filaments, in general they are observed to drift laterally in the fluid lipid bilayer. This has been demonstrated by fusing mouse and human cells, and watching the movement of tagged proteins (fig. 6.4). Forty minutes after fusion, the proteins are completely intermixed.

> **The fluidity of the membrane is dependent on its lipid components, phospholipids and glycolipids.**

Figure 6.4
Experiment to demonstrate lateral drifting of plasma proteins. After human and mouse cells fuse, the plasma proteins are intermixed within a short time.

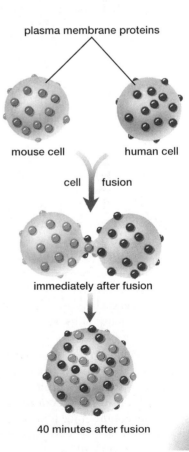

plasma membrane proteins

mouse cell   human cell

cell   fusion

immediately after fusion

40 minutes after fusion

The Membrane Is a Mosaic

The plasma membrane and the membranes of the various organelles each have their own unique collections of proteins. The proteins form different patterns according to the particular membrane and also within the same membrane at different times. When you consider that a red blood cell plasma membrane contains over fifty different types of proteins, you can see how this would be possible and why the membrane is said to be a mosaic.

The proteins within a membrane determine most of its specific functions. As we will discuss in more detail, certain plasma membrane proteins are involved in the passage of molecules through the membrane. Some of these have a *channel* through which a substance simply can move across the membrane; others are *carriers* that combine with a substance and help it to move across the membrane. Still other proteins are *receptors;* each type of receptor has a shape that allows a specific molecule to bind to it. The binding of a molecule, such as a hormone (or other signal molecule), can cause the protein to change its shape and bring about an intracellular response. Some plasma membrane proteins have an *enzymatic function* and carry out metabolic reactions directly. The extrinsic proteins associated with the membrane often have a structural role in that they help stabilize and shape the plasma membrane.

Figure 6.5 depicts the various functions of membrane proteins.

> The mosaic pattern of membrane is dependent on proteins, which vary in structure and function.

Cell-Cell Recognition

The carbohydrate chains of glycolipids and glycoproteins serve as the "fingerprints" of the cell. The possible diversity of the chain is enormous; it can vary by the number of sugars (fifteen is usual, but there can be several hundred), by whether the chain is branched, and by the sequence of the particular sugars. Recalling that glucose has many isomers will help you appreciate how one carbohydrate chain can vary from another.

Glycolipids and glycoproteins vary from species to species, from individual to individual of the same species, and even from cell to cell in the same individual. Therefore, they make cell-cell recognition possible. Researchers working with mouse embryos have shown that as development proceeds, the different type cells of the embryo develop their own carbohydrate chains and that these chains allow the tissues and cells of the embryo to sort themselves out.

As you probably know, transplanted tissues are often rejected by the body. This is because the immune system is able to recognize that the foreign tissue's cells do not have the same glycolipids and glycoproteins as the rest of the body's cells. We now know that a person's particular blood type is due to the presence of particular glycoproteins in the membrane of red blood cells.

Figure 6.5

Membrane protein diversity. These are some of the functions performed by proteins found in the plasma membrane.

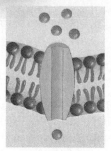

Channel Protein
Allows a particular molecule or ion to cross the plasma membrane freely. Cystic fibrosis, an inherited disorder, is caused by a faulty chloride (Cl⁻) channel; a thick mucus collects in airways and in pancreatic and liver ducts.

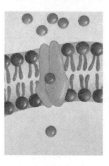

Carrier Protein
Selectively interacts with a specific molecule or ion so that it can cross the plasma membrane. The inability of some persons to use energy for sodium – potassium (Na⁺ – K⁺) transport has been suggested as the cause of their obesity.

Cell Recognition Protein
The MHC (major histocompatibility complex) glycoproteins are different for each person, so organ transplants are difficult to achieve. Cells with foreign MHC glycoproteins are attacked by blood cells responsible for immunity.

Receptor Protein
Is shaped in such a way that a specific molecule can bind to it. Pygmies are short, not because they do not produce enough growth hormone, but because their plasma membrane growth hormone receptors are faulty and cannot interact with growth hormone.

Enzymatic Protein
Catalyzes a specific reaction. The membrane protein, adenylate cyclase, is involved in ATP metabolism. Cholera bacteria release a toxin that interferes with the proper functioning of adenylate cyclase; sodium ions and water leave intestinal cells and the individual dies from severe diarrhea.

Microscopes, Yeasts, and Membrane Synthesis

Looking through a microscope has always made me feel a bit like an explorer in uncharted territory. In fact, my first fascination with cells began in elementary school with an experiment that used only hay, water, and a magnifying glass. For that experiment, we chopped up bits of dried hay into a glass bowl, poured hot water over it, and set the mixture on a windowsill. Several days later, to my astonishment, the water was filled with all kinds of single-celled organisms—paramecia, vorticellae, and amoebas. As I watched these amazing creatures, my mind raced with questions. Where did they come from? How did they eat, move, reproduce? Why could these single cells do all the things necessary for life, even though I needed billions of cells to do the same things? Now, as I look back on my scientific career, I find that most of my work has focused on various aspects of these basic questions.

For the past eight years, first as a postdoctoral fellow and then in my own laboratory, I have been asking a very simple cell how it makes membranes. As you might expect, the synthesis of membrane is complicated—because the cell must coordinate synthesis of specific proteins and lipids in both time and space within the cell. Understanding this process will tell us how cells work in general, and help us understand processes such as photosynthesis, drug detoxification, and transmission of nerve impulses.

My immediate goal is to persuade a cell to tell me how it "realizes" that new membranes are needed, how it makes the new membranes, and how it destroys the membranes when they are no longer needed. How can I accomplish this? First, I would like to turn on the synthesis and degradation of a specific membrane in the laboratory. Second, I would like the cell to be amenable to a wide variety of experimental approaches. As a postdoctoral fellow, I discovered that HMG-CoA reductase (HMGR) protein was a molecular switch that causes yeast cells to synthesize stacks of paired membranes near the nucleus. By using mo-

Robin Wright
University of Washington

lecular tricks, I can make yeast cells alter the amount of HMGR protein, and in this way I can induce yeast cells to synthesize or destroy this particular type of membrane.

But why yeast—*Saccharomyces cerevisiae*, the same organism that makes bread rise and beer bubble? Yeast has become one of the most popular organisms for biological research because it is relatively easy for researchers to change its genes. If you want to know if a gene is important, it can simply be removed. Or, if you only want to alter a protein, you can change its gene in some particular way. Because yeast grows so rapidly, such experiments can be done quickly. Another reason yeast is so popular is that many of its genes and metabolic pathways are nearly the same as in humans. Therefore, the experimental results can sometimes be applied to humans. For example, yeast reproduction studies have provided insights into how human cells regulate their division rates. This is critical information for understanding cancer.

Currently in my lab, undergraduate and graduate students are working with me to determine all the molecular events that occur when yeast responds to HMGR. We approach this goal using a multifaceted research program that includes biochemical experiments and both light and electron microscopy studies. One approach we use is to identify mutant yeast cells that

cannot make inducible membrane, even though the HMGR level is high. Such cells are either unable to "realize" when HMGR is elevated or cannot turn on membrane synthesis in response to this elevation. The defective gene in these mutant cells can be rapidly isolated and sequenced to determine its specific function. Another approach is to isolate a membrane, identify its protein components, and then isolate the genes that encode these proteins.

Why do we put so much effort into isolating and sequencing genes? There are computer databases that list all the previously identified yeast genes. If other scientists have isolated and studied a gene, their work may help us quickly understand the role of these genes in membrane protein synthesis. Even if we are the first to isolate a gene, we can then do additional experiments ourselves to study its function. For example, we can determine whether the gene encodes a protein essential to life in general or only for a particular membrane protein.

To complement our search for genes involved in membrane synthesis, we are also using genetic techniques to alter the HMGR itself. We hope to identify the regions of HMGR that serve as a membrane-inducing signal in yeast. We think that this work may have important applications, since HMGR has a critical role in control of cholesterol production. Therefore, understanding HMGR structure and function may help clinicians understand the development of heart disease.

Finally, we spend many hours just looking at yeast cells under a variety of conditions, in order to try to understand how membranes are formed and degraded. How are cells put together and why? That question—simple and yet very complex—has fascinated me since I first saw unicellular organisms cavorting in hay-fertilized water. Obviously, our research can't answer the whole question. However, results from our studies of an inducible membrane in a simple cell should help us understand how cells of all types regulate the synthesis of specific membranes.

Table 6.1

Passage of Molecules into and out of Cells

	Name	Direction	Requirements	Examples
Passive Transport Means	Diffusion	Toward lower concentration	Concentration gradient	Lipid-soluble molecules, water, and gases
	Facilitated transport	Toward lower concentration	Carrier and concentration gradient	Sugars and amino acids
Active Transport Means	Active transport	Toward greater concentration	Carrier plus energy	Sugars, amino acids and ions
	Exocytosis	Toward outside	Vesicle fuses with plasma membrane	Macromolecules
	Endocytosis Phagocytosis	Toward inside	Vacuole formation	Cells and subcellular material
	Pinocytosis (includes receptor-mediated endocytosis)	Toward inside	Vesicle formation	Macromolecules

HOW MOLECULES CROSS THE PLASMA MEMBRANE

A permeable membrane allows all molecules to pass through; an impermeable membrane allows no molecules to pass through; and a semipermeable membrane allows some molecules to pass through. The plasma membrane is not freely permeable; some molecules enter cells and others do not. In this regard, then, the plasma membrane can be called semipermeable. Certain small molecules can cross a plasma membrane, while large molecules cannot. However, some small molecules pass through the plasma membrane quickly, while others have difficulty in passing through or fail to pass through at all. Therefore, a plasma membrane is often regarded as **differentially permeable** (or selectively permeable) as well.

The structure of the plasma membrane affects which types of molecules can freely pass through it. Small noncharged molecules, particularly if they are lipid soluble, have no difficulty crossing the membrane. Macromolecules cannot freely cross a plasma membrane, and charged ions and molecules have difficulty. The membrane is usually positively charged outside and negatively charged inside. (Negatively charged ions tend to move through channels from inside to outside the cell, and positively charged ions tend to move through channels in the opposite direction.)

> The plasma membrane is differentially permeable. Only certain molecules can pass through freely; the others must be assisted across.

There are both passive and active ways of getting molecules across the plasma membrane. The active ways use energy (ATP, or adenosine triphosphate, molecules), while the passive ways do not. The *passive ways* involve diffusion and facilitated transport. The *active ways* involve active transport, endocytosis, and exocytosis.

Table 6.1 summarizes the various ways that molecules pass into and out of cells.

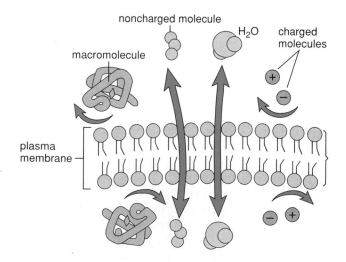

Figure 6.6

Process of diffusion. Diffusion is spontaneous; no energy is required. **a.** When dye crystals are placed in water, they are concentrated in one area. **b.** The dye dissolves in the water, and there is a net movement of dye molecules from higher to lower concentration. There is a net movement of water molecules in the opposite direction. **c.** Eventually, the water and the dye molecules are equally distributed throughout the container.

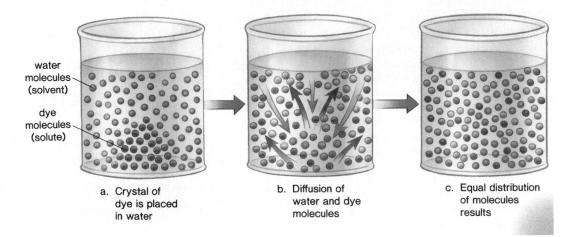

water molecules (solvent)

dye molecules (solute)

a. Crystal of dye is placed in water

b. Diffusion of water and dye molecules

c. Equal distribution of molecules results

Use of Diffusion and Osmosis

Diffusion is a physical process that can be observed with any type of molecule. During **diffusion,** molecules move from higher to lower concentration—that is, down their *concentration gradient*—until they are distributed equally. For example, when a few crystals of dye are placed in water (fig. 6.6), the dye and water molecules move in various directions, but their net movement is toward the region of lower concentration. Eventually, the dye is dissolved in the water, resulting in a colored solution. A solution contains both a solute, usually a solid, and a solvent, usually a liquid. In this case, the **solute** is the dye molecules and the **solvent** is the water molecules. Once the solute and solvent are evenly distributed, they continue to move about, but there is no net movement of either one in any direction.

Diffusion

The chemical and physical properties of the plasma membrane allow just a few types of molecules to enter and exit by diffusion. Lipid-soluble molecules, such as alcohols, can diffuse through the membrane because lipids are the membrane's main structural components.

Gases can also diffuse through the lipid bilayer; this is the mechanism by which oxygen enters cells and carbon dioxide exits cells. As an example, consider the movement of oxygen from the air sacs (alveoli) of the lungs to blood in the lung capillaries (fig. 6.7). After inhalation (breathing in), the concentration of oxygen in the alveoli is higher than that in the blood; therefore, oxygen diffuses into blood. A new way has been found to treat human disorders caused by a lack of some particular substance. Cells that produce the substance, like dopamine needed to treat Parkinson disease, are placed in a plastic capsule and the capsule is implanted in the patient's body. The substance diffuses out of the capsule into the body.

Water passes into and out of cells with relative ease. It probably moves through *channels* (see fig. 6.5), with a pore size large enough to allow the passage of water and prevent the passage of other molecules. The fact that water can penetrate a plasma membrane has important biological consequences, as described in the discussion that follows.

Figure 6.7

Gas exchange in lungs. Oxygen (O_2) diffuses into the capillaries of the lungs because there is a higher concentration of oxygen in the alveoli (air sacs) than in the capillaries.

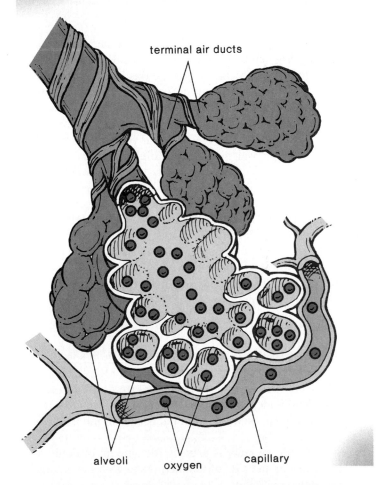

terminal air ducts

alveoli   oxygen   capillary

Molecules diffuse down their concentration gradients. A few types of small molecules can simply diffuse through the plasma membrane.

Figure 6.8

Osmosis demonstration. **a.** Thistle tube, covered at the broad end by a differentially permeable membrane, contains a 10% sugar solution. The beaker contains a 5% sugar solution. **b.** The solute (green circles) is unable to pass through the membrane, but the water passes through in both directions. There is a net movement of water toward the inside of the thistle tube, where there is a higher percentage of solute. **c.** In the end, the level of the solution rises in the thistle tube until a hydrostatic pressure increases to the level of osmotic pressure.

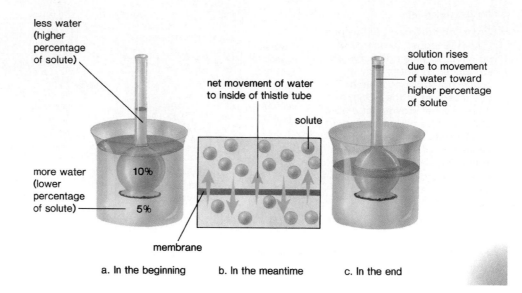

less water (higher percentage of solute)

more water (lower percentage of solute)

net movement of water to inside of thistle tube

solute

solution rises due to movement of water toward higher percentage of solute

membrane

a. In the beginning   b. In the meantime   c. In the end

Osmosis

The diffusion of water across a differentially permeable membrane has been given a special name; it is called **osmosis** [Gk. *osmo*, pushing]. To illustrate osmosis, a thistle tube containing a 10% sugar solution[1] is covered at one end by a differentially permeable membrane and is then placed in a beaker containing a 5% sugar solution (fig. 6.8). The beaker contains more water molecules (lower percentage of solute) per volume, and the thistle tube contains fewer water molecules (higher percentage of solute) per volume. Under these conditions, there is a net movement of water from the beaker to the inside of the thistle tube across the membrane. The solute is unable to pass through the membrane; therefore, the level of the solution within the thistle tube rises (fig. 6.8*c*). As water enters the thistle tube, a pressure called hydrostatic pressure builds up and the net movement of water ceases. The hydrostatic pressure is equivalent to the **osmotic pressure** of the solution inside the thistle tube.

Notice the following in this illustration of osmosis:

1. A differentially permeable membrane separates two solutions.

2. The beaker has more water (lower percentage of solute), and the thistle tube has less water (higher percentage of solute).

3. The membrane does not permit passage of the solute.

4. The membrane permits passage of water, and there is a net movement of water from the beaker to the inside of the thistle tube.

5. An osmotic pressure is present: the amount of liquid increases on the side of the membrane with the greater percentage of solute.

---

[1] Percent solutions are grams of solute per 100 ml of solvent. Therefore, a 10% solution is 10 g of sugar in 100 ml of water.

These considerations will be important as we discuss osmosis in relation to cells placed in different solutions. The plasma membrane allows such solutes as sugars and salts to pass through, but the difference in permeability between water and these solutes is so great that cells in sugar and salt solutions have to cope with the osmotic movement of water.

> **Osmosis is the diffusion of water across a differentially permeable membrane. Osmotic pressure develops on the side of the membrane that has the higher solute concentration.**

Osmosis occurs constantly in living organisms. For example, due to osmosis, water is absorbed from the human large intestine, is retained by the kidneys, and is taken up by blood. Since living things contain a very high percentage of water, osmosis is an extremely important physical process that can affect health.

Tonicity

Tonicity refers to the strength of a solution in relationship to osmosis. Cells can be placed in solutions that have the same percentage of solute, a higher percentage of solute, or a lower percentage of solute than the cell. These solutions are called isotonic, hypertonic, and hypotonic, respectively. Figure 6.9 depicts and describes the effects of these solutions on cells.

In the laboratory, cells are normally placed in solutions that cause them to neither gain nor lose water. Such solutions are said to be **isotonic solutions**; that is, the solute concentration is the same on both sides of the membrane, and therefore there is no net gain or loss of water (fig. 6.9*a, d*). The prefix *iso* means *the same*

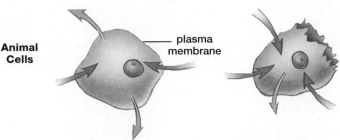

Figure 6.9

Osmosis in animal and plant cells. The arrows indicate the net movement of water. In an isotonic solution, a cell neither gains nor loses water; in a hypotonic solution, a cell gains water; and in a hypertonic solution, a cell loses water.

Animal Cells

plasma membrane

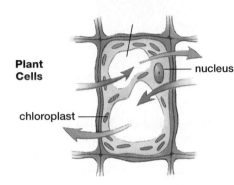

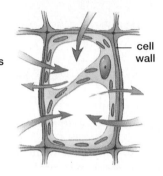

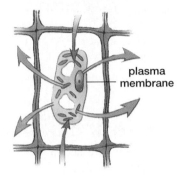

a. **Under isotonic conditions, there is no net movement of water.**

b. **In a hypotonic environment, water enters the cell, which may burst (lysis) due to osmotic pressure.**

c. **In a hypertonic environment, water leaves the cell, which shrivels (crenation).**

Plant Cells

nucleus

chloroplast

cell wall

plasma membrane

d. **Under isotonic conditions, there is no net movement of water.**

e. **In a hypotonic environment, vacuoles fill with water, turgor pressure develops, and chloroplasts are seen next to the cell wall.**

f. **In a hypertonic environment, vacuoles lose water, the cytoplasm shrinks (plasmolysis), and chloroplasts are seen in the center of the cell.**

as and the term *tonicity* refers to the strength of the solution. A 0.9% solution of the salt sodium chloride (Na^+Cl^-) is known to be isotonic to red blood cells because the cells neither swell nor shrink when placed in this solution (fig. 6.9*a*).

Solutions that cause cells to swell, or even to burst, due to an intake of water are said to be **hypotonic solutions**. The prefix *hypo* means *less than* and refers to a solution with a lower percentage of solute (more water) than the cell. If a cell is placed in a hypotonic solution, water enters the cell; the net movement of water is from the outside to the inside of the cell.

Any concentration of salt solution lower than 0.9% is hypotonic to red blood cells. Red blood cells placed in such a solution expand and sometimes burst due to the buildup of pressure (fig. 6.9*b*). The term *lysis* is used to refer to disrupted cells; hemolysis, then, is disrupted red blood cells.

The swelling of a cell in hypotonic solution creates **turgor pressure** [L. *turg,* swell]. When a plant cell is placed in a hypotonic solution, we observe expansion of the cytoplasm because the large central vacuole gains water and the plasma membrane pushes against the rigid cell wall (fig. 6.9*e*). The plant cell does not burst because the cell wall does not give way. Turgor pressure in plant cells is extremely important to the maintenance of the plant's erect position.

Solutions that cause cells to shrink or to shrivel due to a loss of water are said to be **hypertonic solutions**. The prefix *hyper* means *more than* and refers to a solution with a higher percentage of solute (less water) than the cell. If a cell is placed in a hypertonic solution, water leaves the cell; the net movement of water is from the inside to the outside of the cell.

A 10% solution of sodium chloride (Na^+Cl^-) is hypertonic to red blood cells. In fact, any solution with a concentration higher than 0.9% sodium chloride is hypertonic to red blood cells. If red blood cells are placed in this solution, they shrink (fig. 6.9*c*). The term *crenation* refers to red blood cells in this condition.

When a plant cell is placed in a hypertonic solution, the plasma membrane pulls away from the cell wall as the large central vacuole loses water. This is an example of plasmolysis, a shrinking of the cytoplasm due to osmosis. (fig. 6.9*f*).

In an isotonic solution, a cell neither gains nor loses water. In a hypotonic solution, a cell gains water. In a hypertonic solution, a cell loses water and the cytoplasm shrinks.

Figure 6.10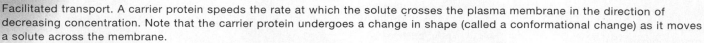

Facilitated transport. A carrier protein speeds the rate at which the solute crosses the plasma membrane in the direction of decreasing concentration. Note that the carrier protein undergoes a change in shape (called a conformational change) as it moves a solute across the membrane.

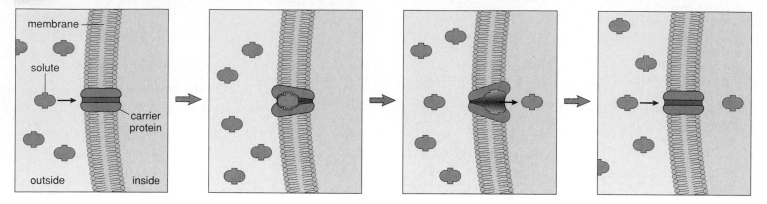

Use of Transport by Protein Carriers

The plasma membrane impedes the passage of all but a few substances. Yet, biologically useful molecules do enter and exit the cell at a rapid rate because there are carrier proteins in the membrane. **Carrier proteins** are specific; each can combine with only a certain type of molecule, which is then transported through the membrane. It is not completely understood how carrier proteins function, but after a carrier combines with a molecule, the carrier is believed to undergo a change in shape that moves the molecule across the membrane. Carrier proteins are required for facilitated transport and active transport (see table 6.1).

> Some of the proteins in the plasma membrane are carriers. They transport biologically useful molecules into and out of the cell.

Facilitated Transport

Facilitated transport explains the passage of such molecules as glucose and amino acids across the plasma membrane even though they are not lipid soluble. The passage of glucose and amino acids is facilitated by their reversible combination with carrier proteins, which in some manner transport them through the plasma membrane. These carrier proteins are specific. For example, various sugar molecules of identical size might be present inside or outside the cell, but glucose can cross the membrane hundreds of times faster than the other sugars. As stated earlier, this is the reason that the membrane can be called differentially permeable.

A model for facilitated transport (fig. 6.10) shows that after a carrier has assisted the movement of a molecule to the other side of the membrane, it is free to assist the passage of other similar molecules. Neither diffusion, explained previously, nor facilitated transport requires an expenditure of energy because the molecules are moving down their concentration gradient in the same direction they tend to move anyway.

Active Transport

During **active transport**, molecules or ions move through the plasma membrane, accumulating either inside or outside the cell. For example, iodine collects in the cells of the thyroid gland; glucose is completely absorbed from the gut by the cells lining the digestive tract; and sodium can be almost completely withdrawn from urine by cells lining the kidney tubules. In these instances, molecules have moved to the region of higher concentration, exactly opposite to the process of diffusion.

Both carrier proteins and an expenditure of energy are needed to transport molecules against their concentration gradient. In this case, energy (ATP molecules) is required for the carrier to combine with the substance to be transported. Therefore, it is not surprising that cells involved primarily in active transport, such as kidney cells, have a large number of mitochondria near a membrane where active transport is occurring.

Proteins involved in active transport often are called *pumps* because, just as a water pump uses energy to move water against the force of gravity, proteins use energy to move a substance against its concentration gradient. One type of pump that is active in all cells, but is especially associated with nerve and muscle cells, moves sodium ions (Na^+) to the outside of the cell and potassium ions (K^+) to the inside of the cell. These two events are presumed to be linked, and the carrier protein is called a **sodium-potassium pump.** A change in carrier shape after the attachment and again after the detachment of a phosphate group allows it to alternately combine with sodium ions and potassium ions (fig. 6.11). The phosphate group is donated by ATP when it is broken down enzymatically by the carrier.

Figure 6.11 📀

The sodium-potassium pump. The same carrier protein transports sodium ions (Na⁺) to the outside of the cell and potassium ions (K⁺) to the inside of the cell because it undergoes an ATP-dependent conformational change. The result is both a concentration gradient and an electrical gradient for these ions across the plasma membrane. Three sodium ions are carried outward for every two potassium ions carried inward; therefore, the inside of the cell is negatively charged compared to the outside.

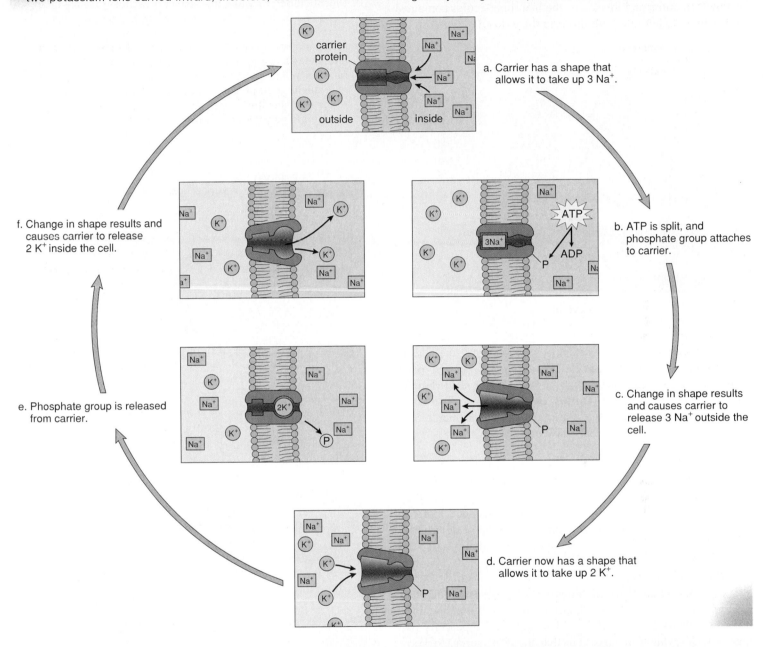

a. Carrier has a shape that allows it to take up 3 Na⁺.

b. ATP is split, and phosphate group attaches to carrier.

c. Change in shape results and causes carrier to release 3 Na⁺ outside the cell.

d. Carrier now has a shape that allows it to take up 2 K⁺.

e. Phosphate group is released from carrier.

f. Change in shape results and causes carrier to release 2 K⁺ inside the cell.

The passage of salt (Na⁺Cl⁻) across a plasma membrane is of primary importance in cells. The chloride ion (Cl⁻) usually crosses the plasma membrane because it is attracted by positively charged sodium ions (Na⁺). First sodium ions are pumped across a membrane and then chloride ions simply diffuse through channels that allow their passage. As noted in figure 6.5, the chloride ion channels malfunction in persons with cystic fibrosis, and this leads to the symptoms of this inherited (genetic) disorder.

During facilitated transport, small molecules follow their concentration gradient. During active transport, small molecules move against their concentration gradient.

Use of Membrane-Assisted Transport

Macromolecules such as polypeptides, polysaccharides, or polynucleotides are too large to be transported by carrier protein. Instead, macromolecules are transported in or out of the cell by vesicle formation, and this keeps the macromolecules contained so that they do not mix with those in the cytosol.

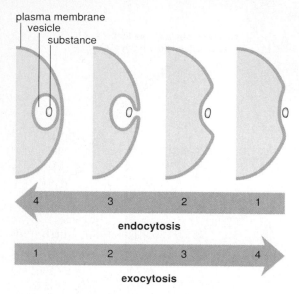

Exocytosis

During **exocytosis** [Gk. *exo,* outside, and *cyt,* cell], the vesicle often formed by the Golgi apparatus fuses with the plasma membrane as secretion occurs. This is the way that insulin leaves insulin-secreting cells, for instance. During cell growth, exocytosis is probably used as a means to enlarge the plasma membrane, whether or not secretion is also taking place.

Endocytosis

During **endocytosis** [Gk. *endo,* within, and *cyt,* cell], cells take in substances by vesicle formation (fig. 6.12). A portion of the plasma membrane invaginates to envelop the substance, and then the membrane pinches off to form an intracellular vesicle. There are three types of endocytosis: phagocytosis, pinocytosis, and receptor-mediated endocytosis

When the material taken in by endocytosis is large, such as a food particle or another cell, the process is called **phagocytosis** [Gk. *phag,* eat, and *cyt,* cell]. Phagocytosis is common in unicellular organisms like amoebas and in ameboid-type cells like macrophages, which are large cells that engulf bacteria and worn-out red blood cells in mammals. When the endocytic vesicle fuses with a lysosome, digestion occurs.

Pinocytosis [Gk. *pin,* drink, and *cyt,* cell] occurs when vesicles form around a liquid or very small particles. Blood cells, and cells that line the kidney tubules or intestinal wall, and plant root cells all use this method of ingesting substances. Whereas phagocytosis can be seen with the light microscope, the electron microscope must be used to observe pinocytic vesicles which are no larger than 1–2 μm.

Figure 6.12

Three methods of endocytosis. **a.** Phagocytosis occurs when the substance to be transported into the cell is large: white blood cells can engulf bacteria by phagocytosis. Digestion occurs when the resulting vacuole fuses with a lysosome. **b.** Pinocytosis occurs when a macromolecule such as a polypeptide is to be transported into the cell. The result is a small vacuole or vesicle. **c.** Receptor-mediated endocytosis is a form of pinocytosis. The substance to be taken in (a ligand) first binds to a specific receptor, which migrates to a pit or is already in a pit. The vesicle that forms contains the ligand and its receptor. Sometimes the receptor is recycled, as shown in figure 6.13.

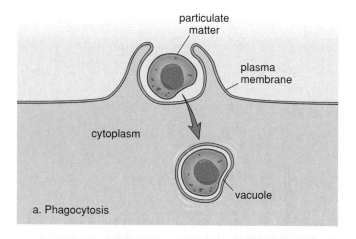

a. Phagocytosis

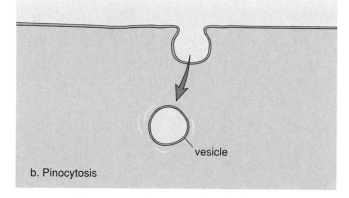

b. Pinocytosis

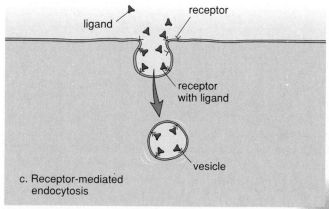

c. Receptor-mediated endocytosis

Figure 6.13

Receptor-mediated endocytosis. **a.** (1) The receptors in the coated pits combine only with a specific substance, called a ligand. (2) The vesicle that forms is at first coated with the structural protein clathrin, but soon the vesicle loses its coat. (3) Ligands leave the vesicle. (4) When exocytosis occurs, membrane and therefore receptors are returned to the plasma membrane. **b.** Electron micrographs of a coated pit in the process of forming a vesicle.

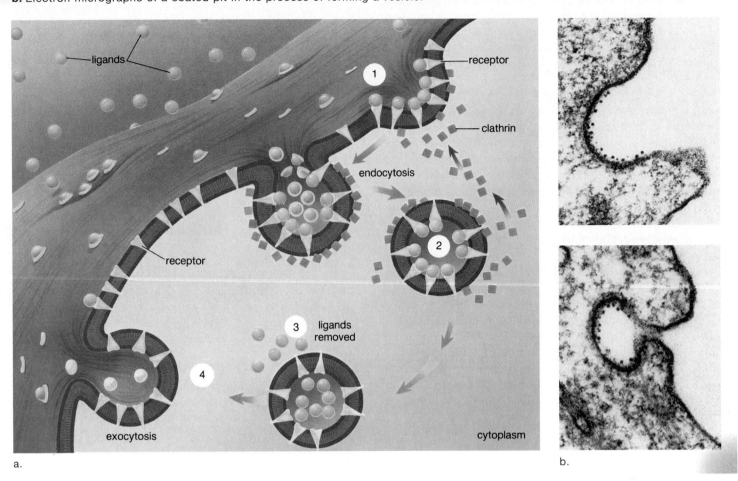

Receptor-mediated endocytosis is a form of pinocytosis that is quite specific because it involves the use of plasma membrane receptors. A macromolecule that binds to a receptor is called a ligand; peptide hormones and cholesterol are two well-known ligands. The binding of ligands to their receptors causes the receptors to gather at one location. This location is called a coated pit because there is a layer of fibrous protein, called clathrin, on the cytoplasmic side (see step 1, fig. 6.13). Clathrin is a protein that also coats at least some, if not all, of the vesicles that leave the Golgi apparatus. Clathrin seems to somehow facilitate the formation of a vesicle. Once the vesicle is formed, the clathrin coat is released and the vesicle appears uncoated (see step 2). The fate of the vesicle and its contents depends on the particular ligand. After reception of a peptide hormone brings about a change in the metabolism of the cell, the hormone and its receptors are digested when the vesicle fuses with a lyso-some. On the other hand, cholesterol is freed from its receptor by the creation of acidic conditions within the vesicle. Then the membrane of the vesicle and therefore the receptors are returned to the plasma membrane (step 4), or the vesicle can go to other membranous locations.

The role of coated pits in the sorting of molecules is only beginning to be appreciated. They appear to play a key role in the selective transfer and exchange of substances between membranes, such as when antigens from maternal blood pass into fetal blood at the placenta where such transfers take place.

> Receptor-mediated endocytosis allows cells to receive specific molecules and then sort them within the cell.

THE CELL SURFACE IS MODIFIED

The plasma membrane is the outer living boundary of the cell, but many cells have an additional component that is formed outside the membrane. Animal cells have an extracellular matrix and plant cells have a cell wall. These do not impede coordination of cell functions, and indeed they may assist the process by which cells function as a part of an organism.

The Extracellular Matrix Plays a Dynamic Role

An extracellular matrix is a meshwork of insoluble proteins and carbohydrates that is laid down by cells. It fills the spaces between animal cells and helps support them. The carbohydrate coat, consisting of the carbohydrate chains that protrude from the plasma membrane, is a part of the extracellular matrix. The carbohydrate chains allow cells to recognize one another, and they serve as receptors for molecules that affect cell metabolism. Similarly, the molecules within the extracellular matrix seem to play a dynamic role in dictating a tissue's shape and function. Fibronectins and laminins are sticky proteins that bind to receptors and thereby interlock cells. Fibronectins also form well-defined "highways" that direct the migration of cells during development. Recently, laminins were found to be necessary to the differentiation and milk-producing function of cells taken from the mammary glands of a mouse. It could be that the laminins are signalling proteins that turn on cellular metabolism and/or they may work via the cytoskeleton to affect the genes of cells! More work will be needed to determine the functions of the molecules in the extracellular matrix and how these functions are carried out.

Plant Cells Have Cell Walls

In addition to a plasma membrane, plant cells are surrounded by a porous cell wall that varies in thickness, depending on the function of the cell (fig. 6.14). All plant cells have a primary cell wall, whose best-known component is cellulose polymers united into threadlike microfibrils that form fibrils. The cellulose fibrils form a framework whose spaces are filled by noncellulose molecules. Among these are found pectins, which allow the wall to stretch when the cell is growing, and hemicelluloses, which harden the wall when the cell is mature. Pectins are especially abundant in the middle lamella between plant cells. Some cells in woody plants have a secondary wall that forms inside the primary cell wall. The secondary wall has a greater quantity of cellulose fibrils than the primary wall, and these layers are laid down at right angles to one another. Lignin, a substance that adds strength, is a common ingredient of secondary cell walls in woody plants.

Figure 6.14 📼

Plant cell wall. All plant cells have a primary cell wall and some have a secondary cell wall. The cell wall, which lends support to the cell, is freely permeable.

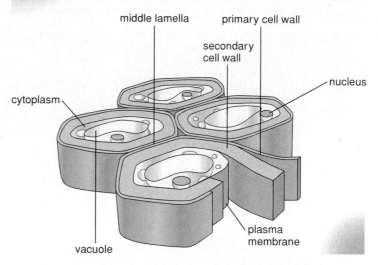

middle lamella — primary cell wall — secondary cell wall — nucleus — cytoplasm — plasma membrane — vacuole

The extracellular matrix of animal cells influences their shape and function. The cell wall of a plant cell supports the cell.

Tissue Cells Have Junctions

For the cells of a tissue to act in a coordinated manner, it is beneficial for the plasma membrane of adjoining cells to interact. The junctions that occur between cells are an example of such cellular interactions.

Junctions in Animal Cells

Three types of junctions are seen between animal cells: adhesion junctions (desmosomes), tight junctions, and gap junctions (fig. 6.15).

In *adhesion junctions* (desmosomes), internal cytoplasmic plaques, firmly attached to the cytoskeleton within each cell, are joined by intercellular filaments. In some organs—like the heart, stomach, and bladder, where tissues get stretched—adhesion junctions hold the cells together.

Adjacent cells are even more closely joined by *tight junctions,* in which plasma membrane proteins actually attach to each other, producing a zipperlike fastening. The cells of tissues that serve as barriers are held together by tight junctions; in the intestine the gastric juices stay out of the body, and in the kidneys the urine stays within kidney tubules, because the cells are joined by tight junctions.

Figure 6.15 [icon]

Junctions between cells of the intestinal wall. Tight junctions cause cells to form an impermeable barrier when adjacent plasma membranes are joined. Adhesion junctions (desmosomes) are where intracellular filaments run between two cells. Gap junctions are communication junctions where two identical plasma membrane channels join.

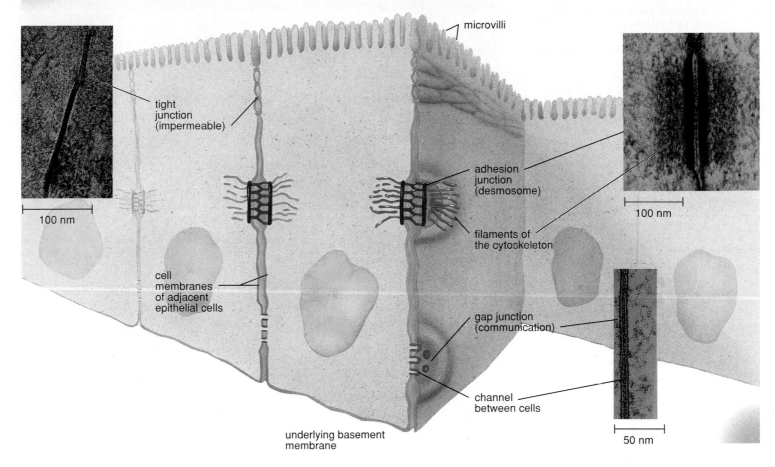

A *gap junction* allows cells to communicate. A gap junction is formed when two identical plasma membrane channels join. The channel of each cell is lined by six plasma membrane proteins. A gap junction lends strength to the cells, but it also allows small molecules and ions to pass between them. Gap junctions are important in heart muscle and smooth muscle because they permit a flow of ions that is required for the cells to contract.

Plant Cells

In plant tissues, the cytoplasm of neighboring cells can be connected by numerous narrow channels that pass through the cell wall. These channels are bounded by plasma membrane and contain cytoplasmic strands, called **plasmodesmata** [Gk. *plasm,* something molded, and *desm,* band, ligament], plus a tightly constricted tubular portion of endoplasmic reticulum. Plasmodesmata allow direct exchange of materials between neighboring plant cells, just as gap junctions do in animal cells.

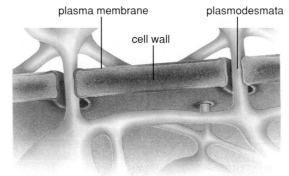

The activities of cells within a tissue are coordinated in part because cells are linked and directly communicate with one another.

Summary

1. The fluid-mosaic model of membrane structure developed by Singer and Nicolson was preceded by several other models. Electron micrographs of freeze-fractured membranes support the fluid-mosaic model, and not Robertson's unit membrane concept based on the Danielli and Davson sandwich model.

2. There are two components of the plasma membrane, lipids and proteins. In the lipid bilayer, phospholipids are arranged with their hydrophilic (polar) heads at the surfaces and their hydrophobic (nonpolar) tails in the interior. The lipid bilayer has the consistency of oil but acts as a barrier to the entrance and exit of most biological molecules. Glycolipids and glycoproteins are involved in marking the cell as belonging to a particular individual and tissue.

3. The hydrophobic portion of a transmembrane protein lies in the lipid bilayer of the plasma membrane, and the hydrophilic portion lies at the surfaces. Proteins act as receptors, carry on enzymatic reactions, join cells together, form channels, or act as carriers to move substances across the membrane.

4. Some molecules (lipid-soluble compounds, water, gases) simply diffuse across the membrane from the area of higher concentration to the area of lower concentration. No metabolic energy is required for diffusion to occur.

5. The diffusion of water across a differentially permeable membrane is called osmosis. Water moves across the membrane into the area of higher solute (less water) content. When cells are in an isotonic solution, they neither gain nor lose water; when they are in a hypotonic solution, they gain water; and when they are in a hypertonic solution, they lose water (table 6.2).

Table 6.2

Effect of Osmosis on a Cell

Tonicity of Solution	Concentrations		Net Movement of Water	Effect on Cell
	Solute	Water		
Isotonic	Same as cell	Same as cell	None	None
Hypotonic	Less than cell	More than cell	Cell gains water	Swells, turgor pressure
Hypertonic	More than cell	Less than cell	Cell loses water	Shrinks, plasmolysis

6. Other molecules are transported across the membrane by carrier proteins that span the membrane.

7. During facilitated transport, a carrier protein carrier assists the movement of a molecule down its concentration gradient. No energy is required.

8. During active transport, a carrier protein acts as a pump that causes a substance to move against its concentration gradient. The sodium-potassium pump carries Na^+ to the outside of the cell and K^+ to the inside of the cell. Energy in the form of ATP molecules is required for active transport to occur.

9. Larger substances can enter and exit a membrane by exocytosis and endocytosis. Exocytosis involves secretion. Endocytosis includes phagocytosis and pinocytosis (which includes receptor-mediated endocytosis).

10. Receptor-mediated endocytosis makes use of receptor molecules in the plasma membrane. Once specific substances (e.g., ligands) bind to their receptors, the coated pit becomes a coated vesicle. After losing the coat, the vesicle can join with the lysosome, or after freeing the ligand, the receptor-containing vesicle can fuse with the plasma membrane.

11. Plant cells have a freely permeable cell wall, with cellulose as its main component.

12. Junctions between animal cells include adhesion junctions and tight junctions, which help to hold cells together, and gap junctions, which allow passage of small molecules between cells. Plant cells are joined by small channels that span the cell wall and contain plasmodesmata, which are strands of cytoplasm that allow materials to pass from one cell to another.

Writing Across the Curriculum

In order to practice writing skills, students should write out the answers to any or all of the study questions and the critical thinking questions. The study questions are sequenced in the same order as the text. Answers to the objective questions, and suggested answers to the critical thinking questions, are in appendix D.

Study Questions

1. Describe the fluid-mosaic model of membrane structure as well as the models that preceded it. Cite the evidence that either disproves or supports these models. 84–85

2. Tell how the phospholipids are arranged in the plasma membrane. What other lipids are present in the membrane, and what functions do they serve? 86–87

3. Describe how proteins are arranged in the plasma membrane. What are their functions? Describe an experiment that indicates that proteins can laterally drift in the membrane. 87

4. What is diffusion, and what substances can diffuse through a differentially permeable membrane? 91

5. Describe an experiment that measures osmotic pressure. 92

6. Tell what happens to an animal cell and a plant cell when placed in isotonic, hypotonic, and hypertonic solutions. 92–93

7. Why do substances have to be assisted through the plasma membrane? Contrast movement by facilitated transport with movement by active transport. 94–95

Objective Questions

1. Electron micrographs following freeze-fracture of the plasma membrane indicate that
   a. the membrane is a phospholipid bilayer.
   b. some proteins span the membrane.
   c. protein is found only on the surfaces of the membrane.
   d. glycolipids and glycoproteins are antigenic.

2. A phospholipid molecule has a head and two tails. The tails are found
   a. at the surfaces of the membrane.
   b. in the interior of the membrane.
   c. spanning the membrane.
   d. Both a and b are correct.

3. Energy is required for
   a. active transport.
   b. diffusion.
   c. facilitated transport.
   d. All of these are correct.

4. When a cell is placed in a hypotonic solution,
   a. solute exits the cell to equalize the concentration on both sides of the membrane.
   b. water exits the cell toward the area of lower solute concentration.
   c. water enters the cell toward the area of higher solute concentration.
   d. solute exits and water enters the cell.

5. When a cell is placed in hypertonic solution,
   a. solute exits the cell to equalize the concentration on both sides of the membrane.
   b. water exits the cell toward the area of lower solute concentration.
   c. water exits the cell toward the area of higher solute concentration.
   d. solute exits and water enters the cell.

6. Active transport
   a. requires a carrier protein.
   b. moves a molecule against its concentration gradient.
   c. requires a supply of energy.
   d. All of these are correct.

7. The sodium-potassium pump
   a. helps establish an electrochemical gradient across the membrane.
   b. concentrates sodium on the outside of the membrane.
   c. utilizes a carrier protein and energy.
   d. All of these are correct.

8. Receptor-mediated endocytosis
   a. is no different from phagocytosis.
   b. brings specific substances into the cell.
   c. helps to concentrate proteins in vesicles.
   d. All of these are correct.

9. Plant cells
   a. always have a secondary cell wall, and the primary one may disappear.
   b. have channels between cells that allow strands of cytoplasm to pass from cell to cell.
   c. develop turgor pressure when water enters the nucleus.
   d. do not have cell-to-cell junctions like animal cells.

10. Write *hypotonic solution* or *hypertonic solution* beneath each cell. Justify your conclusions.

a. _____

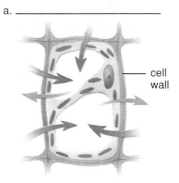

— cell wall

b. _____

Concepts and Critical Thinking

1. *All cells have a plasma membrane that separates their contents from the extracellular environment and serves to maintain their integrity.*

In a structural sense, how does the plasma membrane maintain the integrity of the cell? In a functional sense, how does the plasma membrane maintain the integrity of the cell?

2. *To remain alive, cells must have an extracellular environment that is compatible with their continued existence.*

How does the phenomenon of osmosis demonstrate this concept?

3. *Cells of multicellular organisms function as a unit.*

For cells to function as a unit, communication is necessary. How does the plasma membrane help distantly located cells communicate with each other? How does the plasma membrane help adjacent cells communicate with each other?

Selected Key Terms

active transport Use of a plasma membrane carrier protein to move particles from a region of lower to higher concentration; it opposes equilibrium and requires energy. 94

carrier protein A protein that combines with and transports a molecule across the plasma membrane. 94

cholesterol One of the major lipids found in animal plasma membranes; makes the membrane impermeable to many molecules. 86

differentially permeable Ability of plasma membranes to regulate the passage of substances into and out of the cell, allowing some to pass through and preventing the passage of others. 90

diffusion The movement of molecules from a region of higher to lower concentration; it requires no energy and tends to lead to an equal distribution. 91

endocytosis (en-doh-sy-TOH-sis) A process by which particles or debris are moved into the cell from the environment by phagocytosis (cellular eating) or pinocytosis (cellular drinking; includes receptor-mediated endocytosis). [Gk. *endo,* within, and *cyt,* cell] 96

exocytosis (ek-soh-sy-TOH-sis) A process by which particles or debris are moved out of the cell by vesicles that fuse with the plasma membrane. [Gk. *exo,* outside, and *cyt,* cell] 96

fluid-mosaic model Model for the plasma membrane based on the changing location and pattern of protein molecules in a fluid phospholipid bilayer. 85

hypertonic solution Higher solute concentration (less water) than the cytoplasm of a cell; causes cell to lose water by osmosis. [Gk. *hyper,* over, and *ton,* tension] 93

hypotonic solution Lower solute (more water) concentration than the cytoplasm of a cell; causes cell to gain water by osmosis. [Gk. *hypo,* under, and *ton,* tension] 93

isotonic solution A solution that is equal in solute concentration to that of the cytoplasm of a cell; causes cell to neither lose nor gain water by osmosis. [Gk. *iso,* equal, and *ton,* tension] 92

osmosis The diffusion of water through a differentially permeable membrane. [Gk. *osmo,* pushing] 92

osmotic pressure Measure of the tendency of water to move across a differentially permeable membrane; visible as an increase in liquid on the side of the membrane with higher solute concentration. 92

phagocytosis (fag-oh-suh-TOH-sis) A process by which amoeboid-type cells engulf large substances forming an intracellular vacuole. [Gk. *phag,* eat, and *cyt,* cell] 96

phospholipid (fahs-foh-LIP-id) A molecule having the same structure as a neutral fat except one bonded fatty acid is replaced by a group that contains phosphate; an important component of plasma membranes. [Gk. *phos,* light, and *lipar,* oil] 86

pinocytosis (pin-oh-suh-TOH-sis) A process by which vesicles form around and bring macromolecules into the cell. [Gk. *pin,* drink, and *cyt,* cell] 96

sodium-potassium pump A transport protein in the plasma membrane that moves sodium ions out of and potassium ions into animal cells; important in nerve and muscle cells. 94

turgor pressure The pressure of the cell contents against the cell wall, in plant cells, determined by the water content of the vacuole; gives internal support to the plant cell. [L. *turg,* swell] 93

7

CELLULAR ENERGY

Learning Objectives

Work Requires Energy

- State two energy laws that have important consequences for living things.   105
- Explain, on the basis of these laws, why living things need an outside source of energy.   106

Metabolism Involves Energy Exchanges

- Describe two types of metabolic reactions (pathways) that are found in all cells.   107
- Describe the structure and the function of enzymes and the conditions that affect the yield of enzymatic reactions.   107–10
- Describe the regulation of enzymatic reactions (pathways) by the process of inhibition. Compare competitive inhibition, noncompetitive inhibition, and feedback inhibition.   110–11

- Describe the relationship of the coenzymes NAD$^+$ and FAD to the electron transport system in mitochondria and NADP$^+$ to the electron transport system in chloroplasts.   112
- Describe with the aid of a diagram how degradative pathways drive synthetic pathways.   113

ATP Is Metabolic Energy

- Describe how ATP is built up and how ATP is used by cells. Explain why the energy released by ATP breakdown cannot then be used for ATP buildup.   114–15

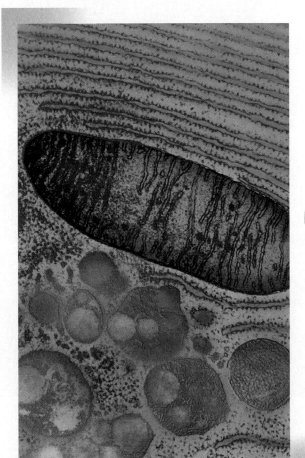

Mitochondria are the powerhouses of the cell. They convert nutrient molecules into supply ATP molecules that supply energy for cellular reactions.

1 µm

e can readily see that a butterfly's wing (fig. 7.1) is highly organized, but it takes a knowledge of cells to realize that they, too, are organized. All cells contain the same type of carbon-based molecules, and in eukaryotic cells, some of these molecules make up the organelles. It is the organelles that show us that a cell is just as organized in its own way as the butterfly's wing. Such organization cannot be maintained without a supply of energy. As an analogy, consider that your room quickly becomes a total mess unless you continually work to keep it straight (organized). Similarly, a cell must continually use energy to first form macromolecules from unit molecules and to then arrange the macromolecules into its structural components.

WORK REQUIRES ENERGY

Energy is defined as the capacity to do work—that is, to bring about a change. There are several different forms of energy. You use your own mechanical energy to straighten up your room; light energy allows you to see what you are doing; electrical energy makes the motor turn in your vacuum cleaner; and heat energy maintains a comfortable room temperature.

Another form of energy, not as obvious as these, is chemical energy, the energy that is stored in the bonds that hold atoms together. The chemical energy in food provides the energy for your muscles to do mechanical work. Just as chemical energy in food can be transformed into the mechanical energy used by your muscles, other forms of energy can be

Figure 7.1

Life's organization. The complex organization of living things is dramatized by the pattern of color in the wing of this painted lady butterfly, *Vanessa cardui*. But the unseen cells that make up the wing are also highly organized, and the nectar the butterfly obtains from the flower is needed to maintain the organization of both the cells and the wing.

similarly transformed. Electrical energy is transformed into light energy within a lightbulb, and the chemical bond energy of oil is transformed into electrical energy at a power plant.

A power plant does not create energy, it merely transforms it. Do transformations ever cause energy to be used up? We realize that matter is never created or destroyed. When we take materials and build a vacuum cleaner, we know that even if we throw the vacuum cleaner away, the materials are still not used up. It has been mentioned that chemical equations must always be balanced—the same number of atoms are present before and after a reaction—because mass cannot be used up. But what about energy? Can it ever be used up?

Energy Can Be Exchanged

As you have probably guessed, not only can energy never be created, it also can never be used up. The same amount of energy has always been present in the universe and will always be present. The first energy law states:

> Energy can be transformed from one form into another, but it cannot be created or destroyed.

We have what appears to be a paradox, however, because it often seems as if energy has been "lost" when transformations occur. For example, cars need to be refueled and animals must continue eating. The answer to the paradox is that neither automobiles nor organisms are isolated. It is said that they are a *system* that has *surroundings*. The surroundings supply the gasoline (or the food), and when the gasoline is used to do work, it results in heat that is accepted by the surroundings:

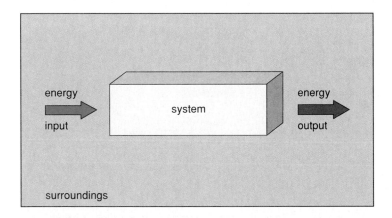

The first energy law can be interpreted to mean that if we put X amount of energy into a system (automobile, organism), then eventually X amount of energy will leave the system even if work has been done. Energy usually leaves in the form of heat.

Energy Cannot Be Recycled

Although energy was not lost in our examples, something seems to have been lost. To determine what this is, consider that gasoline can be burned to power a car, but the heat given off is no longer able to perform this task. The amount of *useful* energy, then, has changed. Similarly, once food energy is used to power muscles, this energy is no longer available because it has been converted to heat. The second energy law states:

> When one form of energy is transformed into another form, some useful energy is always lost as heat; therefore, energy cannot be recycled.

The second energy law implies that only processes that decrease the amount of useful energy occur naturally, or spontaneously. The word *spontaneous* does not mean that the process has to happen all at once; it simply means that it happens naturally over time. Your room tends to become messy, not neat; water tends to flow downhill, not up; and after death, organisms decay and eventually disintegrate. In other words, the amount of disorder (i.e., entropy) is always increasing in the universe. If this is the case, how do we account for an orderly room or the presence of highly organized structures, such as living cells and organisms? Obviously, these systems must have a continual input of energy, and this continual input of energy eventually increases the entropy of the universe.

While we have been drawing an analogy between nonliving systems (a car, your room) and a living system (a cell or an organism), there is a remarkable difference between the two types of systems. Although living things are continually taking in useful energy and putting out heat just like the nonliving system, the work performed in between these two events maintains their organization and even allows them to grow. A living organism represents stored energy in the form of chemical compounds:

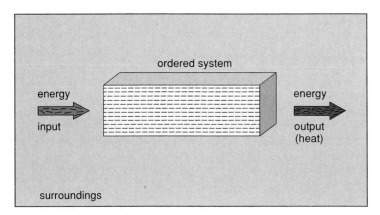

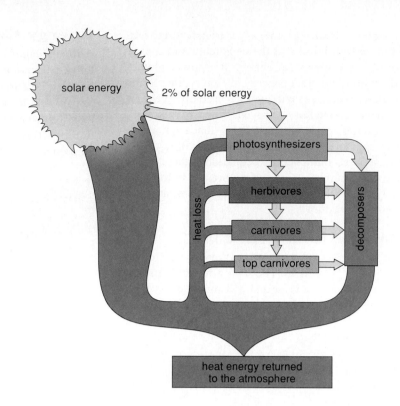

Figure 7.2

The loss of useful energy in a community of organisms. About 2% of the solar energy reaching the earth is taken up by photosynthesizers (plants and algae). This is the energy that allows them to make their own food. Herbivores obtain their food by eating plants, and carnivores obtain food by eating other animals. Whenever the energy content of food is used by organisms, it is eventually converted to heat. With death and decay, all the energy temporarily stored in organisms returns as heat to the atmosphere.

Living Things Obey Energy Laws

Life does not violate the energy laws discussed earlier, since each living thing merely represents a temporary storage area for useful energy. The useful energy stored in one organism can be used by another to maintain its own organization. Because of this, energy flows through a community of organisms (fig. 7.2). As transformations of energy occur, useful energy is lost to the environment in the form of heat, until finally useful energy is completely used up. Since energy cannot recycle, there is a need for an ultimate source of energy. This source, which continually supplies all living things with energy, is the sun. The entire universe is tending toward disorder, but in the meantime, solar energy is sustaining all living things. Photosynthesizing organisms like plants and algae are able to capture less than 2% of the solar energy that reaches the earth. They use this energy to make their own organic food, which then becomes the food for all other types of living things. Without photosynthesizing organisms, life as we know it could not exist.

Living things continually lose useful energy to the environment, but a new supply comes to them in the form of organic food produced by photosynthesizing organisms.

Energy-Balance Sheet

Only 42% of solar energy directed toward earth actually reaches the earth's surface; the rest is absorbed by or reflected into the atmosphere and becomes heat.

Of this usable portion, only about 2% is eventually utilized by plants; the rest becomes heat.

Of this, only 0.1–1.6% is ever incorporated into plant material; the rest becomes heat.*

Of this, only 20% is eaten by herbivores; a large proportion of the remainder becomes heat.*

Of this, only 30% is ever eaten by carnivores; a large proportion becomes heat.*

Conclusion: Most of the available energy is never utilized by living things.

* Plant and animal remains became the fossil fuels that we burn today to provide energy. So eventually this energy becomes heat.

METABOLISM INVOLVES ENERGY EXCHANGES

The food an organism eats becomes nutrient molecules for cells. Within cells, these molecules take part in a vast array of chemical reactions, collectively termed the **metabolism** [Gk. *metab*, change] of the cell. So far, we have stressed that nutrient molecules can be used as a source of energy. For this to occur, they have to be broken down, and in fact, they have to be oxidized. Oxidation is the removal of an electron either alone or in the form of a hydrogen atom. As oxidation occurs, energy is released:

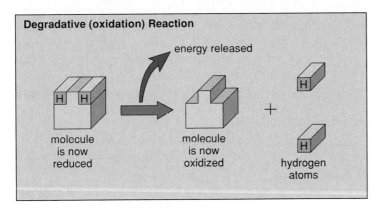

Degradative (oxidation) Reaction

energy released

molecule is now reduced

molecule is now oxidized

+

hydrogen atoms

We have already indicated that a cell needs energy to maintain its structure and to grow. In other words, some of the nutrient molecules present in cells are used to form the structure of the cell. To make membrane, amino acids are joined to form proteins, and fatty acids become a part of lipid molecules. There are also *synthetic* reactions in which reduction, the gain of electrons, occurs. Reduction can occur when hydrogen atoms are added to a molecule:

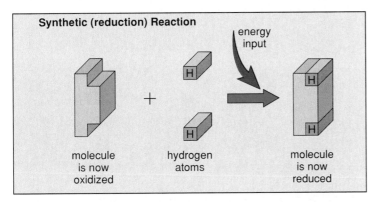

Synthetic (reduction) Reaction

energy input

molecule is now oxidized

+

hydrogen atoms

molecule is now reduced

In the reaction depicted energy is added as reduction occurs. Do you suppose it would be possible to take the energy released by degradative reactions and use it for synthetic reactions? Further, would it be possible to use the hydrogen atoms produced in certain degradative reactions for certain synthetic reactions? The answer to these questions is *yes,* and we are now going to explore how these processes occur inside cells.

Metabolism Utilizes Pathways

At any one time there are thousands of reactions occurring in cells. Compartmentalization, in the form of organelles, helps to segregate different types of reactions, but more segregation is needed. Within the different organelles, reactions are organized into *metabolic pathways*. Some of these pathways are largely degradative ones that release energy, as when carbohydrates are broken down in mitochondria. Other pathways are largely synthetic ones that require energy input, as when lipids are synthesized in smooth endoplasmic reticulum (ER).

In general, metabolic pathways can be represented by this diagram:

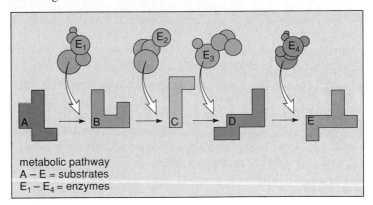

metabolic pathway
A – E = substrates
$E_1 – E_4$ = enzymes

In this pathway, B–D are products of the previous reaction and reactants of the next reaction, while $E_1–E_4$ identify different enzymes. A reactant in an enzymatic reaction is a **substrate** for that enzyme. The beginning substrate is A, and E is the end product of the pathway.

This simplified representation of a metabolic pathway does not indicate that the intermediate molecules (B–D) can also be starting points for other pathways. Degradative pathways can even interconnect with synthetic pathways, and in this way degradative pathways sometimes provide not only the energy but also the molecules needed for synthesis of cell components.

> Some pathways (reactions) in cells are degradative ones that release energy, and some are synthetic ones that require energy input.

Enzymes Speed Reactions

As indicated previously, every reaction within a metabolic pathway requires an enzyme. **Enzymes** are organic catalysts, usually globular protein molecules, that speed chemical reactions without being permanently changed. In addition some RNA (ribonucleic acid) molecules, particularly in the nucleus, can be enzymes, and these are called *ribozymes*. Every enzyme is very specific in its action and can speed only one particular reaction or one type of reaction. The name of an enzyme is often formed by adding *ase* to the name of its substrate, as in the following example:

Substrate	Enzyme
Lipid	Lipase
Urea	Urease
Maltose	Maltase
Ribonucleic acid	Ribonuclease
Lactose	Lactase

Some enzymes are named for the action they perform: a dehydrogenase is an enzyme that removes hydrogen atoms from its substrate.

Almost no reaction can occur in a cell unless its own enzyme is present and active. If enzyme 2 (i.e., E_2) in the diagram on page 107 is missing or not functioning, the pathway shuts down at B. Since enzymes are so necessary in cells, their mechanism of action has been studied extensively.

Enzymes Lower the Energy of Activation

Molecules frequently do not react with one another unless they are activated in some way. In the laboratory, activation is very often achieved by heating the reaction flask to increase the number of effective collisions between molecules. The energy that must be added to cause molecules to react with one another is called the *energy of activation* (E_a). Figure 7.3 compares E_a when an enzyme is not present to when an enzyme is present, illustrating that enzymes lower the amount of energy required for activation.

In baseball, a home-run hitter not only must hit the ball to the fence, the ball must also clear the fence. When enzymes lower the energy of activation, it is like removing the fence; then it is possible to get a home run hit by simply hitting the ball to the fence.

As an example, consider that the hydrolysis of casein (the protein found in milk) requires an energy of activation of 20,600 kcal/mole[1] in the absence of an enzyme, but only 12,600 kcal/mole in the presence of an enzyme. Enzymes lower the energy of activation by forming an enzyme-substrate complex.

---

1 The kcal (Kilocalorie) is a common way to measure heat, and a mole is the number of molecules present in the molecular weight of a substance (in grams).

Figure 7.3

Energy of activation (E_a). Enzymes speed the rate of chemical reactions because they lower the amount of energy required to activate the reactants.

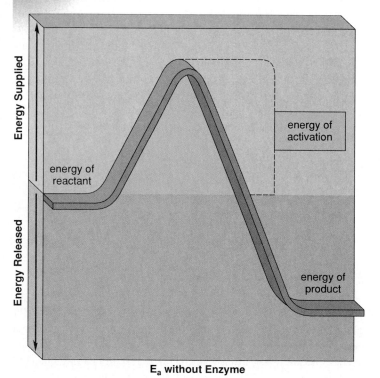

E_a without Enzyme

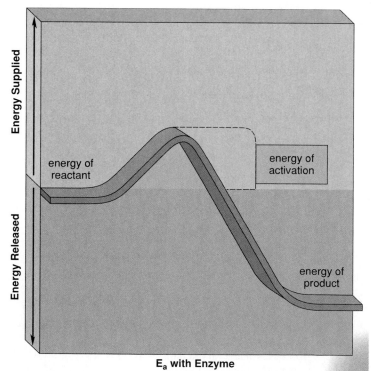

E_a with Enzyme

Figure 7.4

Enzymatic action. An enzyme has an active site, which is where the substrates and enzyme fit together in such a way that the substrates are oriented to react. Following the reaction, the products are released and the enzyme assumes its original shape. **a.** Enzymes carry out degradative reactions. **b.** Enzymes carry out synthetic reactions.

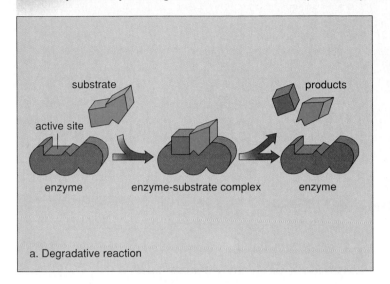

a. Degradative reaction

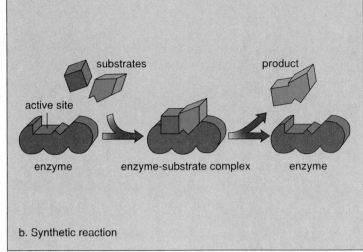

b. Synthetic reaction

Enzyme-Substrate Complexes

The following equation, which is pictorially shown in figure 7.4, is often used to indicate that an enzyme forms a complex with its substrate, which is the material that undergoes a change:

$$E + S \longrightarrow ES \longrightarrow E + P$$

| enzyme | substrate | enzyme-substrate complex | | product |

In most instances only one small part of the enzyme, called the **active site,** complexes with the substrate(s) (fig. 7.4). It is here that the enzyme and substrate fit together, seemingly like a key fits a lock; however, it is now known that the active site undergoes a slight change in shape in order to accommodate the substrate(s) more perfectly. This is called the *induced fit model* because the enzyme is induced to undergo a slight alteration to achieve an optimum fit. The change in shape of the active site facilitates the reaction that now occurs. After the reaction has been completed, the product(s) is released, and the active site returns to its original state. Only a small amount of enzyme is actually needed in a cell because enzymes are used repeatedly.

Some enzymes do more than simply complex with their substrate(s); they actually participate in the reaction. Trypsin digests protein by breaking peptide bonds. The active site of trypsin contains three amino acids with R groups that actually interact with members of the peptide bond—first to break the bond and then to introduce the components of water. This illustrates that the formation of the enzyme-substrate complex is very important in speeding up the reaction.

Sometimes it is possible for a particular reactant(s) to produce more than one type of product(s). The presence or absence of an enzyme determines which reaction takes place. If a substance can react to form more than one product, then the enzyme that is present and active determines which product is produced:

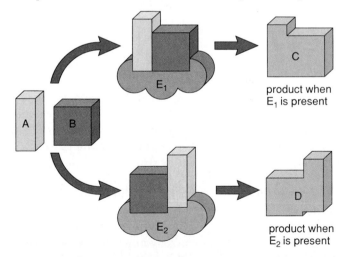

product when E_1 is present

product when E_2 is present

Most enzymes are protein molecules. Enzymes speed chemical reactions by lowering the energy of activation. They do this by forming an enzyme-substrate complex.

Figure 7.5

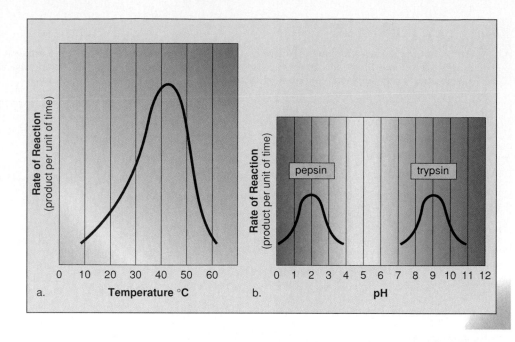

Rate of an enzymatic reaction as a function of temperature and pH. **a.** At first, as with most chemical reactions, the rate of enzymatic reaction doubles with every 10° C rise in temperature. In this graph, the rate of reaction is maximum at about 40° C; then it decreases until the reaction stops altogether, indicating that the enzyme is denatured. **b.** Pepsin, an enzyme found in the stomach, acts best at a pH of about 2, while trypsin, an enzyme found in the small intestine, performs optimally at a pH of about 8. The shape that enables these proteins to bind with their substrates is not properly maintained at other pHs.

Factors That Affect Enzymatic Speed

Enzymatic reactions proceed quite rapidly. For example, the breakdown of hydrogen peroxide into water and oxygen can occur 600,000 times a second when the enzyme catalase (an enzyme found in peroxisomes) is present. How quickly an enzyme works, however, is affected by how much enzyme and substrate are present. To achieve maximum product per unit time, substrate should fill active sites most of the time. Other factors are also important, as shown in the following discussion.

Moderate Temperature and Optimal pH Is Best

A higher temperature generally results in an increase in enzyme activity. As the temperature rises, the movement of both enzyme and substrate molecules increases, and there are more effective collisions between them. If the temperature rises beyond a certain point, however, enzyme activity eventually levels out and then declines rapidly because the enzyme is **denatured** (fig. 7.5a). An enzyme's shape changes during denaturation, and then it can no longer bind substrate molecules efficiently.

A change in pH can also affect enzyme activity (fig. 7.5b). Each enzyme has an optimal pH that helps maintain its normal configuration. Recall that the tertiary structure of a protein is dependent on interactions, such as hydrogen bonding, between R groups. A change in pH can alter the ionization of these side chains and disrupt the normal interactions, and denaturation eventually occurs. Again, the enzyme is then unable to combine efficiently with its substrate.

> Optimal temperature and pH increase the speed of enzyme activity.

Amount of Enzyme Affects Speed

While these factors affect enzyme productivity cellular mechanisms control both enzyme concentration and activity. Concentration increases when genes are turned on and protein (enzyme) production occurs. Concentration decreases when genes are turned off and protein production does not occur. A way to regulate the activity of enzymes is by phosphorylation. Molecules received by membrane receptors often turn on kinases, which then phosphorylate certain enzymes. Other molecules called phosphatases remove phosphate groups from enzymes. Processes regulated by phosphorylation include protein synthesis, cell division, activity of motor molecules, nuclear envelope breakdown, and development. Many of the genes that, when mutated, convert normal cells to cancerous cells code for kinases. The toxin produced by dinoflagellates that causes the often fatal, paralytic seafood poisoning is a potent phosphatase inhibitor.

Enzymes Can Be Inhibited

Inhibition is a common means by which cells regulate enzyme activity. In *competitive inhibition*, another molecule is so close in shape to the enzyme's substrate that it can compete with the true substrate for the enzyme's active site. This molecule inhibits the reaction because only the binding of the true substrate results in a product. In *noncompetitive inhibition*, a molecule binds to an enzyme but not at the active site. This other binding site is called the *allosteric site* (*allo*—other; *steric*—space or structure). In this instance, also, the molecule is an inhibitor because when it binds there is a shift in the three-dimensional structure of the enzyme that prevents the substrate from binding to the active site. In cells, however, inhibition is usually reversible; that is, the inhibitor is not permanently bound to the enzyme.

The activity of almost every enzyme in a cell is regulated by feedback inhibition. **Feedback inhibition** is an example of a

Figure 7.6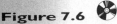

Feedback inhibition. The amino acid aspartate becomes the amino acid threonine by a sequence of five enzymatic reactions. When threonine, the end product of this pathway, is present in excess, it binds to an allosteric site on enzyme 1 and inhibits continued substrate binding.

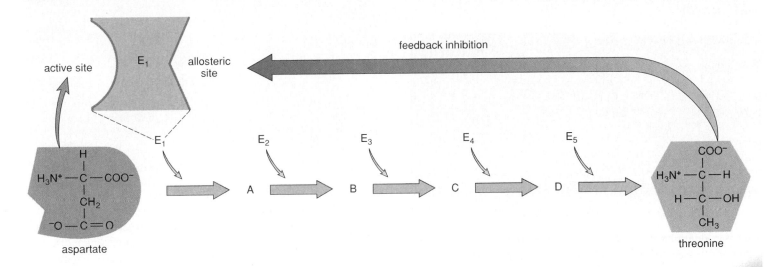

common biological control mechanism called negative feedback. Just as excessively high temperature can cause a furnace to shut off, so a product produced by an enzymatic reaction can inhibit its activity. When the product is in abundance, it binds competitively with its enzyme's active site (fig. 7.4); as the product is used up, inhibition is reduced and more product can be produced. In this way, the concentration of the product is always kept within a certain range.

Most enzymatic *pathways* are regulated by feedback inhibition, but the end product of a pathway binds at an allosteric site on the *first* enzyme of the pathway (fig. 7.6). This binding shuts down the pathway, and no more product is produced.

> In inhibition, a product binds to the active site or binds to an allosteric site on an enzyme.

Cofactors and Coenzymes Help Enzymes

Many enzymes require a nonprotein *cofactor* to assist them in carrying out their function. Some cofactors are ions; magnesium (Mg^{++}), potassium (K^+), and calcium (Ca^{++}) are often involved in enzymatic reactions. Some other cofactors, called **coenzymes,** are organic molecules that bind to enzymes and serve as carriers for chemical groups or electrons.

Usually coenzymes participate directly in the reaction. The coenzyme tetrahydrofolate works in conjunction with the enzyme

thymidylate synthase and donates a methyl group (CH_3) to form thymine, one of the bases found in DNA (deoxyribonucleic acid). In humans, this coenzyme is not present unless the diet includes the vitamin folic acid. **Vitamins** [L. *vit*, life] are relatively small organic molecules that are required in trace amounts in our diet and in the diet of other animals for synthesis of coenzymes that affect health and physical fitness.

The presence of other coenzymes in cells is similarly dependent on our intake of vitamins. These vitamins are of particular cellular interest:

VITAMIN	COENZYME
Niacin	NAD^+
B_2 (riboflavin)	FAD
B_1 (thiamine)	Thiamine pyrophosphate
Pantothenic acid	Coenzyme A (CoA)
B_{12} (cobalamin)	B_{12} coenzymes

A deficiency of any one of these vitamins results in a lack of the coenzyme listed and therefore a lack of certain enzymatic actions. In humans, this eventually results in vitamin-deficiency symptoms; niacin deficiency results in a skin disease called pellagra, and riboflavin deficiency results in cracks at the corners of the mouth.

> Coenzymes are nonprotein molecules that assist enzymes in performing their reactions.

How Energy Exchanges Occur in Cells

NAD^+ (nicotinamide adenine dinucleotide) is a coenzyme that carries electrons and quite often works in conjunction with enzymes called dehydrogenases. An enzyme of this type removes two hydrogen atoms ($2e^- + 2H^+$) from its substrate; both electrons but only one hydrogen ion are passed to NAD^+, and it becomes NADH:

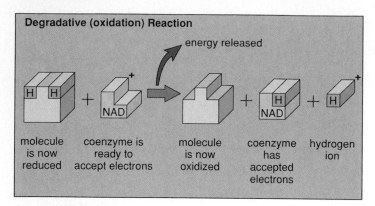

Degradative (oxidation) Reaction

energy released

molecule is now reduced | coenzyme is ready to accept electrons | molecule is now oxidized | coenzyme has accepted electrons | hydrogen ion

This is a degradative (oxidative) reaction that releases energy. Compare this equation to the similar one on page 109 and note that much less energy has been lost—the red arrow is smaller. The energy has been transferred to NAD^+ in the form of high-energy electrons. Another coenzyme called **FAD** (flavin adenine dinucleotide) also carries high-energy electrons, but it accepts both hydrogen ions (to become $FADH_2$).

Both NAD^+ and FAD are involved in **aerobic respiration** [Gk. *aer,* air], a metabolic pathway in mitochondria by which substrates are oxidized in a step-by-step manner to carbon dioxide and water. At various junctions along the way, these coenzymes accept electrons from certain substrates and carry them to an **electron transport system** consisting of membrane-bound carriers that pass electrons from one carrier to another. High-energy electrons are delivered to the system and low-energy electrons leave it. Every time electrons are transferred to a new carrier energy is released; this energy is ultimately used to produce ATP (adenosine triphosphate) molecules (fig. 7.7).

> NAD^+ and FAD are electron carriers that take electrons to the electron transport system in mitochondria. This system releases energy that is used to produce ATP molecules.

Chloroplasts also have an electron transport system for producing ATP. In this case the electrons that enter the system are taken from water. Solar energy energizes these electrons, and as they pass from carrier to carrier, energy is released and ATP is built up. In the end, the coenzyme $NADP^+$ accepts energized electrons and an H^+ become NADPH.

$NADP^+$ (nicotinamide-adenine dinucleotide phosphate) has a structure similar to NAD^+, but it contains a phosphate group that is lacking in NAD^+. This may signal an enzyme that its function is slightly different. It does carry electrons and a hydrogen ion just like NAD^+, but its electrons are used to bring about reduction during synthesis:

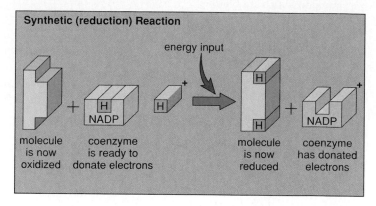

Synthetic (reduction) Reaction

energy input

molecule is now oxidized | coenzyme is ready to donate electrons | molecule is now reduced | coenzyme has donated electrons

During **photosynthesis** [Gk. *photo,* light, and *synthesis,* putting together] within chloroplasts, carbon dioxide is reduced to a carbohydrate. NADPH supplies the necessary electrons and ATP supplies the necessary energy to bring about this reduction.

NADPH also functions outside of chloroplasts. Within the cytosol, plant and animal cells use a special degradative pathway to produce NADPH. This NADPH is used during the synthesis of many necessary molecules in cells. Energy too is required, but for this purpose, ATP produced by mitochondria is utilized.

> $NADP^+$ is an electron carrier that participates, along with ATP, in synthetic reactions.

Figure 7.7

Electron transport system in which electrons pass from carrier to carrier. With each transfer, some energy is released and a portion of it is trapped for the purpose of producing ATP molecules.

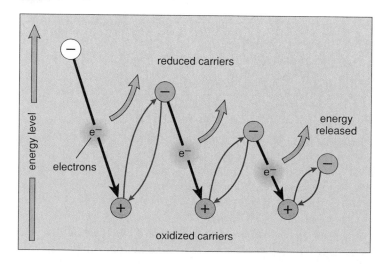

energy level

electrons

reduced carriers

energy released

oxidized carriers

How Degradation Is Linked to Synthesis

We stated it is possible to harness the energy and hydrogens provided by metabolic degradative reactions for synthetic reactions. This is possible *only* because ATP carries energy and NADPH carries electrons between degradative pathways and synthetic pathways (fig. 7.8).

Degradative pathways do run synthetic pathways in cells as long as the cell receives an outside source of energy and matter. The energy laws discussed earlier in this chapter tell us that life is possible only because organisms (cells) are able to temporarily *store* some of the energy that flows through them.

Of all the organisms, only photosynthesizers such as plants are able to make organic food by utilizing solar energy. In chloroplasts, solar energy is used to produce the ATP and the NADPH that are used to reduce carbon dioxide to a carbohydrate. These, and the other macromolecules produced by plants, supply plants and eventually all other living things with a source of organic food.

Plants and animals use organic food as both an energy source and a source of unit molecules. When used as an energy source, carbohydrates are degraded (oxidized) to carbon dioxide and water, which are excreted. Although heat is given off in the process, some of the energy is used to produce ATP in mitochondria.

Outside the mitochondira, degradation sometimes produces a supply of NADPH. Again ATP is a carrier for energy and NADPH is a carrier for electrons utilized in synthetic reactions. In this way, the flow of energy through the organism (cells) is utilized for growth and maintenance of the organism.

The role of enzymes in metabolism must not be forgotten. They make "warm chemistry" possible. Degradative reactions occur spontaneously (naturally), but only if sufficient energy of activation is supplied. Enzymes lower the energy of activation, making it possible for these reactions to occur very quickly at body temperature. Since the enzymes involved in synthesis are not the same as those used for degradation, however, the cell needs the coenzyme $NADP^+$ to carry electrons and ATP to carry energy from degradative to synthetic reactions.

> **Living things are all powered by the sun. Chloroplasts (plants only) produce carbohydrates, which are degraded in mitochondria (plants and animals) to produce ATP and otherwise to produce NADPH to allow growth and repair of the organism.**

Figure 7.8

Metabolic reactions. The degradative part of photosynthesis drives the synthetic part, and the degradative part of general metabolism drives the synthetic part. Degradation provides electrons and energy that are carried to synthetic reactions by NADPH and ATP, respectively.

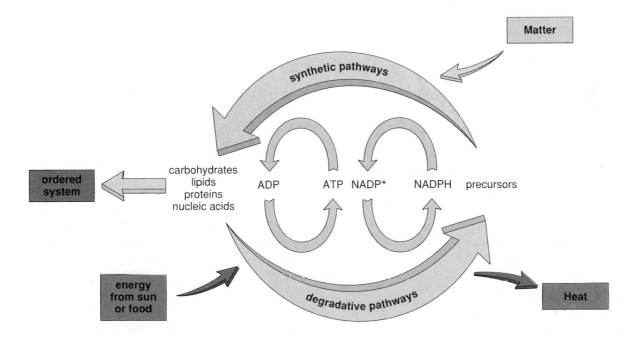

ATP Is Metabolic Energy

Organisms need a constant supply of energy because:

1. energy cannot be created;
2. useful work requires the conversion of energy from one form to another, causing some of the energy to be lost to the environment; and
3. maintenance of the high degree of cellular organization (not to mention growth and reproduction) constantly requires a large amount of work.

ATP (adenosine triphosphate) is the common energy currency of cells; when cells require energy, they "spend" ATP. You may think that this causes our bodies to produce a lot of ATP, and it does; the average male needs to produce about 8 kg (over 17 lb) of ATP an hour! Obviously, it would be impossible to carry around even a few hours' supply of ATP, and indeed the body has on hand only a limited amount at any time. The answer to the paradox is that ATP is constantly being recycled from **ADP** (adenosine diphosphate) and (P). The cell's entire supply of ATP is recycled about once each minute. Figure 7.9 shows the ATP cycle that occurs in cells. First, let's consider the left-hand side of this illustration—in other words, the buildup of ATP.

How ATP Is Built Up

Essentially, cells have two ways to make ATP. The first, called **substrate-level phosphorylation** [Gk. *phos,* light, and *phor,* movement], occurs in the cytosol. During this process, energy and a phosphate group is transferred from a substrate to ADP, forming ATP:

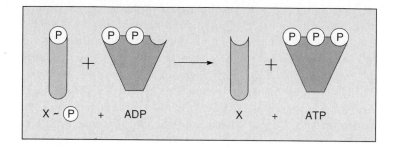

Substrate-level phosphorylation is not the primary way of forming ATP, however; most ATP is made within mitochondria and chloroplasts by way of the electron transport system mentioned earlier (see fig. 7.7). In this case, the phosphorylation that occurs is called **chemiosmotic phosphorylation**.

Chemiosmotic ATP Synthesis

For many years, it was known that ATP synthesis was somehow coupled to the electron transport system, but the exact mechanism could not be determined. Peter Mitchell, a British biochemist, received a Nobel prize in 1978 for his *chemiosmotic theory* of ATP production in both mitochondria and chloroplasts.

In mitochondria and chloroplasts, the carriers of the electron transport system are located within a membrane. According to the chemiosmotic theory, hydrogen ions (H⁺), which are often referred to as protons in this context, tend to collect on one side of the membrane because they are pumped there by certain carriers. This establishes an electrochemical gradient across the membrane that can be used to provide energy for ATP production. Particles, called *ATP synthase complexes,* span the membrane. Each complex contains a channel that allows hydrogen ions to flow down their electrochemical gradient. The flow of hydrogen ions through the channel provides the energy for the ATP synthase enzyme to produce ATP from ADP + (P) (fig. 7.10).

> Energy for ATP synthesis is derived from a hydrogen ion gradient established across a membrane by an electron transport system.

Figure 7.9
The ATP cycle. ATP is continually made and remade in cells. When ATP is formed, energy is added along with a phosphate group to ADP. When ATP breaks down to ADP + (P) energy is released.

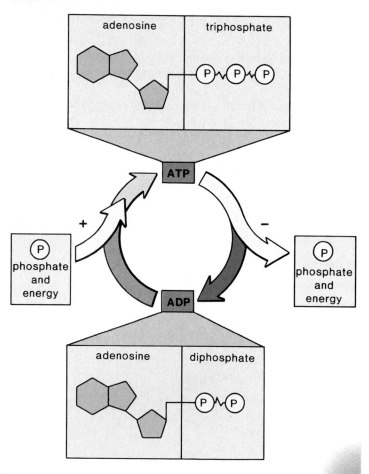

Figure 7.10

Chemiosmotic ATP synthesis. Carriers in the electron transport system pump hydrogen ions (H⁺) across a membrane in mitochondria and chloroplasts. When the hydrogen ions flow back across the membrane through a protein complex, ATP is synthesized by an enzyme called ATP synthase.

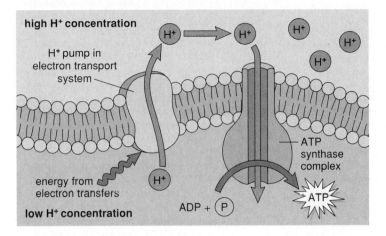

How ATP Is Used

Now, let's turn our attention to the right-hand side of figure 7.9. When ATP becomes ADP + ⓅP, the amount of energy released is just about enough for most biological reactions. ATP breakdown is coupled to the reaction that requires energy; that is, the two reactions take place at the same time and in the same place, and they usually utilize the same enzyme. During the coupling process, a phosphate group is often transferred to an intermediate compound. For example, during active transport, a phosphate group is transferred to a membrane-bounded protein.

ATP is utilized for all these purposes:

- Chemical work. Supplies the energy needed to synthesize macromolecules that make up the cell.
- Transport work. Supplies the energy needed to pump substances across the plasma membrane.
- Mechanical work. Supplies the energy needed to cause muscles to contract, cilia and flagella to beat, organelles to move, and so forth.

Energy Flows Through Systems

The energy released by ATP breakdown is used by the cell to do various types of work, and eventually it becomes nonusable heat. It cannot be used to reform ATP. Energy does not cycle in cells, organisms, or the biosphere; rather, it flows through them.

Consider this analogy. The sun's rays evaporate water from the seas and help create the winds which blow the clouds to the mountains where water falls in the form of rain and snow. The water in clouds is at a higher potential energy than is the water in the oceans, and this energy is stored in a mountain reservoir that has been dammed. Now the potential energy is converted to kinetic energy as the water is released, and to electrical energy as the falling water turns a turbine. This same process is repeated several times as the water moves from the mountain to the ocean. Finally, the energy produced by the hydroelectric dam system is lost into space as heat and other forms of radiation.

Similarly, the sun's energy is collected by plants and placed in chemicals that represent a form of potential energy. The potential energy is converted to the energy of ATP molecules. ATP is produced because the inner mitochondrial membrane acts like a dam to maintain an energy gradient in the form of a concentration gradient of hydrogen ions. The hydrogen ions flow through membrane channels that couple the flow of hydrogen ions to the formation of ATP, like the turbines in a dam couple the flow of water to the formation of electricity. The chemiosmotic synthesis of ATP was supported by a now-famous experiment performed by Andre Jagendorf of Cornell University utilizing chloroplasts (fig. 7.11). The experiment shows that ATP production is indeed tied only to a hydrogen ion gradient.

> ATP is an energy carrier in cells. It is the common energy currency because it supplies energy for many different types of reactions.

Figure 7.11

An experiment performed by Andre Jagendorf in 1966 supports the chemiosmotic theory. An electrochemical gradient was established by first soaking isolated chloroplasts in an acid medium and then the pH was abruptly changed to basic. ATP production occurred after ADP and ⓅP were added. This all occurred in the dark, proving that ATP synthesis is not directly linked to the chloroplast electron transport system, which works only in the light.

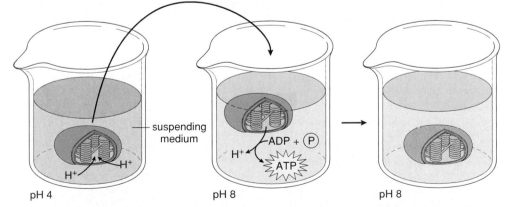

pH 4

H⁺ diffuses into chloroplasts so that they become pH 4.

pH 8

ADP and ⓅP are added to beaker. As H⁺ diffuses out of chloroplasts, ATP is produced.

pH 8

Chloroplast and medium have same pH. H⁺ electrochemical gradient no longer exists, and ATP production ceases.

Summary

1. There are two energy laws that are basic to understanding energy-use patterns in organisms at the cellular level. The first states that energy cannot be created or destroyed, and the second states that some useful energy is always lost when one form of energy is transformed into another form.

2. In keeping with these laws, living things need an outside source of energy. Plants capture the energy of sunlight to make their own food, and animals eat either plants or other animals to obtain food.

3. Metabolism includes two kinds of reactions, degradative and synthetic. During degradation, organic molecules derived from food are broken down and energy is released; oxidation occurs and electrons are removed from substances. During synthesis, an energy-requiring process, molecules derived from food are used as starting materials; when reduction occurs electrons are added to substances.

4. There are degradative metabolic pathways and synthetic metabolic pathways. Each reaction in a pathway requires its own enzyme. Enzymes speed up chemical reactions because they lower the energy of activation. They can do this because they form a complex with their substrate(s) at the active site.

5. Various factors affect the yield of enzymatic reactions, such as the temperature and the pH. A high temperature or a pH outside the optimum range for that enzyme can lead to denaturation, a change in structure that prevents the enzyme from functioning.

6. Cellular mechanisms regulate enzyme quantity and activity. Often, addition of phosphate activates enzymes and removal deactivates them.

7. The activity of most enzymes is regulated by inhibition. During competitive inhibition, a molecule competes with the substrate for the active site. During noncompetitive inhibition, a molecule binds to an allosteric site. During feedback inhibition, the product of an enzymatic reaction binds to the enzyme; for metabolic pathways, the end product usually binds to an allosteric site on the first enzyme in the pathway.

8. Many enzymes have cofactors or coenzymes that help them carry out a reaction. Coenzymes are nonprotein, organic molecules often derived at least in part from vitamins. NAD⁺ and FAD are coenzymes that carry high-energy electrons to an electron transport system that is usually located in mitochondria. Here electrons are transferred from one carrier to the next one. At the same time, energy is released and is used to produce ATP molecules. Chloroplasts also contain an electron transport system that receives electrons energized by the sun.

9. NADPH is a carrier of electrons, but it carries them to various synthetic reactions that involve reduction. ATP is a carrier of energy for synthetic reactions and other types of work performed by cells.

10. Degradative pathways drive synthetic pathways. Degradative pathways supply the ATP and the NADPH that is needed during synthesis. We must never forget, however, that in order for this to occur, the cell needs an outside source of energy and matter. Only a flow of energy through the organism allows it to sustain itself and to grow.

11. ATP is a high-energy molecule that serves as a common carrier of energy in cells. When ATP becomes ADP + Ⓟ, the right amount of energy is provided for many reactions. In order to produce ATP, the energy from carbohydrate breakdown is coupled to ATP production, and in order to pass this energy to synthetic reactions, coupling again occurs.

12. The chemiosmotic hypothesis explains just how the electron transport system produces ATP. The carriers of this system deposit hydrogen ions (H⁺) on one side of a membrane. When the ions flow down an electrochemical gradient through an ATPase complex, an enzyme utilizes the release of energy to make ATP from ADP and Ⓟ.

Writing Across the Curriculum

In order to practice writing skills, students should write out the answers to any or all of the study questions and the critical thinking questions. The study questions are sequenced in the same order as the text. Answers to the objective questions, and suggested answers to the critical thinking questions, are in appendix D.

Study Questions

1. Explain the first energy law using the terms *system* and *surroundings* in your explanation. Explain the second energy law using the term *useful energy* in your explanation.   105

2. Discuss the importance of solar energy, not only to plants but to all living things.   106

3. Contrast a degradative reaction with a synthetic reaction.   107

4. Diagram a metabolic pathway and use this to explain the terms *substrate* and *product* and the need for various enzymes.   107

5. In what way do enzymes lower the energy of activation? What does the induced fit model say about formation of the enzyme-substrate complex?   108–9

6. In what ways do temperature and pH affect the yield of enzymatic reactions? In what ways does a cell control enzyme activity?   110

7. Explain competitive inhibition, noncompetitive inhibition, and feedback inhibition of enzyme activity.   110–11

8. Contrast the function of NAD⁺ and FAD with that of NADP⁺.   112

9. In what way do degradative reactions drive synthetic reactions? Why is there still a need for an outside source of energy and matter?   113

10. Tell how cells form ATP, including the process of chemiosmotic phosphorylation. Tell how ATP is used and explain why the energy released from ATP breakdown cannot be used for ATP buildup.   114–15

Objective Questions

1. Degradative reactions
   a. can be oxidation reactions.
   b. are the same as synthetic reactions.
   c. require a supply of NADPH molecules.
   d. Both a and c are correct.

2. Enzymes
   a. make it possible for cells to escape the need for energy.
   b. are nonprotein molecules that help coenzymes.
   c. are not affected by a change in pH.
   d. lower the energy of activation.

3. An allosteric site on an enzyme is
   a. the same as the active site.
   b. where ATP attaches and gives up its energy.
   c. often involved in feedback inhibition.
   d. All of these are correct.

4. A high temperature
   a. can affect the shape of an enzyme.
   b. lowers the energy of activation.
   c. makes cells less susceptible to disease.
   d. Both a and c are correct.

5. Electron transport systems
   a. are found in both mitochondria and chloroplasts.
   b. release energy as electrons are transferred.
   c. are involved in the production of ATP.
   d. All of these are correct.

6. The difference between NAD$^+$ and NADP$^+$ is
   a. only NAD$^+$ production requires niacin in the diet.
   b. one contains high-energy phosphate bonds and the other does not.
   c. one carries electrons to the electron transport system and the other carries them to synthetic reactions.
   d. All of these are correct.

7. ATP
   a. is used only in animal cells and not in plant cells.
   b. carries energy between degradative pathways and synthetic pathways.
   c. is needed for chemical work, mechanical work, and transport work.
   d. Both b and c are correct.

8. Chemiosmotic phosphorylation is dependent upon
   a. the diffusion of water across a differentially permeable membrane.
   b. an outside supply of phosphate and other chemicals.
   c. the establishment of an electrochemical hydrogen ion (H$^+$) gradient.
   d. the ability of ADP to join with $\textcircled{P}$ even in the absence of a supply of energy.

9. Label this diagram that gives an overview of metabolism. Label the arrows either degradative reactions or synthetic reactions. Label the long lines either macromolecules or small molecules. Label the short lines ADP + $\textcircled{P}$, ATP, NADP, NADPH.

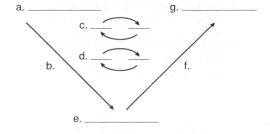

10. Label this diagram describing chemiosmotic phosphorylation.

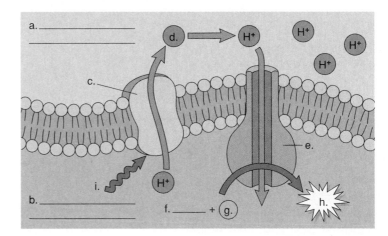

Concepts and Critical Thinking

1. *A constant input of energy is required to maintain the organization of the cell.*

   In reference to work performed by the rough ER and the Golgi apparatus, explain specifically why a cell needs energy to maintain its organization.

2. *In keeping with the first and second laws of thermodynamics, a cell takes in useful energy and gives off heat.*

   Explain why you would expect both parts of the ATP cycle to be responsible for the loss of useful energy through heat.

3. *The actions of enzymes allow the cell to maintain itself and grow.*

   Explain why most reactions do not occur in a cell unless a specific enzyme is present.

active site That part of an enzyme molecule where the substrate fits and the chemical reaction occurs.   109

ADP (adenosine diphosphate) (ah-den-ah-SEEN dy-FAHS-fayt) One of the products of the hydrolysis of ATP, a process that liberates energy.   114

aerobic respiration Metabolic reactions that require oxygen and provide energy to cells by the step-by-step oxidation of substrates in mitochondria with the concomitant build of ATP molecules. [Gk. *aer,* air]   112

ATP (adenosine triphosphate) (ah-den-ah-SEEN try-FAHS-fayt) A compound containing adenine, ribose, and three phosphates. The breakdown of ATP to ADP makes energy available for energy-requiring processes in cells.   114

chemiosmotic phosphorylation (kem-ee-ahz-MAHT-ik fahs-for-ah-LAY-shun) The production of ATP by utilizing the energy released when H$^+$ flows through an ATP synthase complex in mitochondria and chloroplasts. [Gk. *chem,* juice, *osmo,* pushing, *phos,* light, and *phor,* movement]   114

coenzyme A nonprotein organic part of an enzyme structure, often with a vitamin as a subpart.   111

denatured The condition of an enzyme when its shape is changed so that its active site cannot bind substrate molecules.   110

electron transport system A mechanism whereby electrons are passed along a series of carrier molecules, releasing energy for the synthesis of ATP.   112

energy Capacity to do work and bring about change; occurs in a variety of forms.   104

enzyme An organic catalyst, usually a protein molecule, that speeds chemical reactions in living systems.   107

FAD (flavin-adenine dinucleotide) (FLAY-vun AD-un-een dy-NOO-klee-uh-tyd) A coenzyme that functions as an electron acceptor in cellular oxidation-reduction reactions.   112

feedback inhibition A process by which a substance, often an end product of a reaction or a metabolic pathway, controls its own continued production by binding with the enzyme that produced it.   110

metabolism All of the chemical reactions that occur in a cell during degradation and synthesis which involve and produce metabolites. [Gk. *metab,* change]   107

NAD$^+$ (nicotinamide adenine dinucleotide) (nik-uh-TEE-nuh-myd AD-un-een dy-NOO-klee-uh-tyd) A coenzyme that functions as an electron carrier in cellular oxidation-reduction reactions of glycolysis and cellular respiration.   112

NADP$^+$ (nicotinamide-adenine dinucleotide phosphate) (nik-uh-TEE-nuh-myd AD-un-een dy-NOO-klee-uh-tyd FAHS-fayt) A coenzyme that functions as an electron carrier in cellular oxidation-reduction reactions of photosynthesis.   112

photosynthesis A process occurring within chloroplasts whereby chlorophyll traps solar energy and carbon dioxide is reduced to a carbohydrate. [Gk. *photo,* light, and *synthesis,* putting together]   112

substrate The reactant in an enzymatic reaction; each enzyme has a specific substrate. [L. *sub,* below, and *strat,* layer]   107

substrate-level phosphorylation (fahs-for-ah-LAY-shun) An enzymatic process in which ATP is formed by transferring a phosphate from a metabolic substrate to ADP. [Gk. *phos,* light, and *phor,* movement]   114

vitamin An organic molecule that is required in small quantities for various biological processes and must be in an organism's diet because it cannot be synthesized by the organism; often becomes part of coenzyme structure. [L. *vit,* life]   111

PHOTOSYNTHESIS

Learning Objectives

A frond of a fan palm tree, *Washingtonia*, collects the light that provides energy for photosynthesis.

ave you thanked a green plant today? Plants dominate our environment, but most of us spend little time thinking about the various services they perform for us and for other living things. Chief among these is their ability to carry on **photosynthesis** during which they use sunlight (*photo*) as a source of solar energy to produce carbohydrate (*synthesis*):

| solar energy | + | carbon dioxide | + | water | → | carbohydrate | + | oxygen |

Other organisms, called algae, also carry out photosynthesis in this manner. Algae are a diverse group, but many are water-dwelling, microscopic organisms related to plants. Food chains often start with photosynthesizers because they convert solar energy into chemical energy which is stored in the form of plant and animal matter. Plants and algae serve as the ultimate source of food for all other living things: the squirrel in figure 8.1 is feeding on nuts that were produced by a tree.

Figure 8.1

This North American red squirrel, *Tamiasciurus,* is a herbivore. It feeds directly on plant material produced by a photosynthesizer. Carnivores, such as a hawk that may feed on this squirrel, are also dependent, although indirectly, on food produced by photosynthesizers.

Photosynthesis has produced most of the oxygen in our atmosphere. When organisms oxidize carbohydrate to produce ATP molecules (adenosine triphosphate) they make use of oxygen (O_2) given off by photosynthesis. Nearly all living things are dependent on atmospheric oxygen derived from photosynthesis.

At one time in the distant past, plant and animal matter accumulated without totally decomposing. This matter became the fossil fuels (e.g., coal, oil, and gas) that we burn today for energy. This source of energy, too, is due to photosynthesis.

> **Photosynthesis is absolutely essential for the continuance of life because it is the source of food and oxygen for nearly all living things.**

SUNLIGHT IS SOLAR ENERGY

Photosynthesis is an energy transformation in which solar energy in the form of light is used to make carbohydrate molecules. Therefore, we will begin our discussion of photosynthesis with the energy source—sunlight.

Solar radiation can be described in terms of its energy content and its wavelength. The energy comes in discrete packets called **photons** [Gk. *photo,* light]. So, in other words, you can think of radiation as photons that travel in waves:

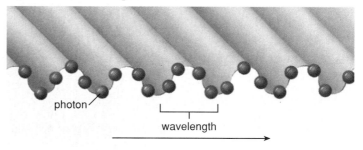

Figure 8.2*a* illustrates that solar radiation, or the **electromagnetic spectrum,** can be divided on the basis of wavelength—gamma rays have the shortest wavelength and radio waves have the longest wavelength. The energy content of photons is inversely proportional to the wavelength of the particular type of radiation; that is, short-wavelength radiation has photons of a higher energy content than long-wavelength radiation. High-energy photons, such as those of short-wavelength ultraviolet radiation, are dangerous to cells because they can break down organic molecules. Low-energy photons, such as those of infrared radiation, do not damage cells because they only increase the vibrational or rotational energy of molecules; they do not break bonds. But photosynthesis utilizes only the portion of the electromagnetic spectrum known as *visible light.* (It is called visible light because it is the part of the spectrum that the eye can see.) Photons of visible light have just the right amount of energy to promote electrons to a higher electron shell in atoms without harming cells. Visible or white light is actually made up of a number of different wavelengths of radiation;

Figure 8.2

The electromagnetic spectrum and chlorophylls *a* and *b*. **a.** The electromagnetic spectrum contains forms of energy that differ according to wavelength. Visible light is only a small portion of the electromagnetic spectrum. **b.** Chlorophylls *a* and *b* absorb certain wavelengths within visible light, which accounts for the action spectrum of (wavelengths necessary for) photosynthesis.

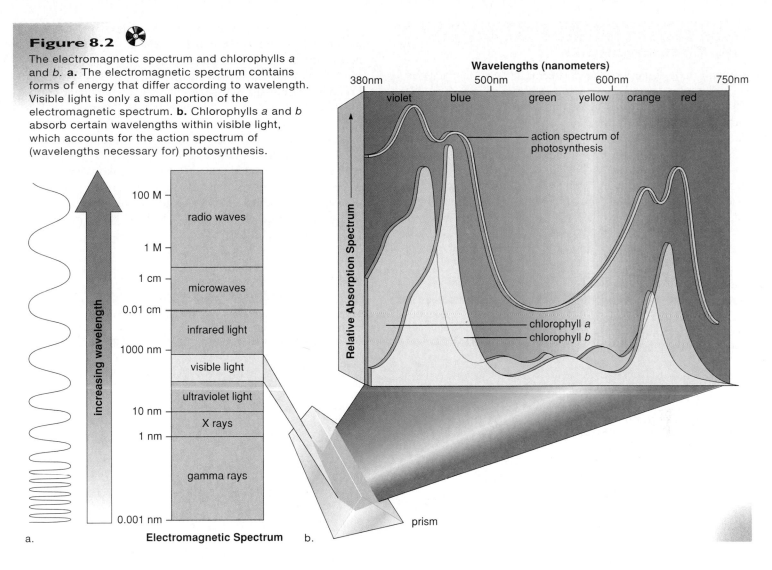

when it is passed through a prism (or through raindrops), we see these wavelengths as different colors of light.

Only about 42% of the solar radiation that hits the earth's atmosphere ever reaches the surface, and most of this radiation is within the visible-light range. Higher energy wavelengths are screened out by the ozone layer in the atmosphere, and lower energy wavelengths are screened out by water vapor and carbon dioxide before they reach the earth's surface. The conclusion is, then, that both the organic molecules within organisms and certain life processes, such as vision and photosynthesis, are chemically adapted to the radiation that is most prevalent in the environment.

The pigments found in photosynthesizing cells are capable of absorbing various portions of visible light. These pigments include chlorophyll *a* and chlorophyll *b* whose absorption spectra are shown in figure 8.2*b*. Both chlorophyll *a* and chlorophyll *b* absorb violet, blue, and red light better than the light of other colors. Because green light is only minimally absorbed, leaves appear green to us. There are other pigments, such as the carotenoids, in plants that are yellow-orange and are able to absorb light in the violet-blue-green range. These pigments become noticeable in the fall when chlorophyll breaks down.

To identify the absorption spectrum of a particular pigment, a purified sample is exposed to different wavelengths of light inside an instrument called a spectrophotometer. A spectrophotometer measures the amount of light that passes through the sample, and from this it can be calculated how much was absorbed. The amount of light absorbed at each wavelength is plotted on a graph, and the result is what we call the absorption spectrum (fig. 8.2*b*). How do we know that the peaks shown in chlorophyll's absorption spectrum indicate the wavelengths used for photosynthesis? Photosynthesis, of course, produces oxygen, and therefore we can use the production rate of oxygen as a means to measure the rate of photosynthesis at each wavelength of light. When such data are plotted, the resulting graph, called the *action spectrum*, is very similar to the absorption spectrum of the chlorophylls. Therefore, we are confident that the light absorbed by the chlorophylls does contribute extensively to photosynthesis.

> Photosynthesis utilizes the portion of the electromagnetic spectrum (solar radiation) known as visible light.

PHOTOSYNTHESIS OCCURS IN CHLOROPLASTS

It wasn't until the end of the nineteenth century that scientists knew that photosynthesis occurred in **chloroplasts** [Gk. *chlor,* green, and *plast,* formed, molded] and that the reaction was as shown on page 120. A seventeenth-century Dutchman, Van Helmont, grew a tree in a large pot and found that after five years, the amount of the soil in the pot had not changed. He concluded that the increase in weight was due to the addition of *water.* Joseph Priestley (English, 1733–1804) put a plant and a lit candle under a bell jar and found that after the candle had gone out, the plant could "renew" the air in such a way that the candle would burn if lit again. The science of chemistry was just emerging at this time, and Jan Ingenhousz (Dutch, 1730–99) identified the gas given off by plants as *oxygen.*

It was Nicholas de Saussure (Swiss, 1767–1845) who found that an increase in the dry weight of a plant was dependent upon the presence of *carbon dioxide.* Julius Sachs (German, 1832–97) noted that the green substance named chlorophyll is confined to the chloroplasts. In one experiment with a whole plant, he coated a few leaves with wax and observed that after exposure to *sunlight,* only the uncoated leaves, which could take in carbon dioxide, increased in *starch* content. Since these early days, many sophisticated experiments have been done to determine exactly how plants carry on photosynthesis. Some of these are described in the rest of the chapter.

Figure 8.3

Chloroplast structure and function. Thylakoids (flattened sacs) are stacked like poker chips into grana (one stack is a granum). Each thylakoid consists of a thylakoid membrane surrounding a thylakoid space. The thylakoid membrane contains chlorophyll and other pigments that absorb solar energy. The light-dependent reactions occur here. The fluid-filled stroma contains enzymes that reduce carbon dioxide (CO_2) to carbohydrate (CH_2O) during the light-independent reactions.

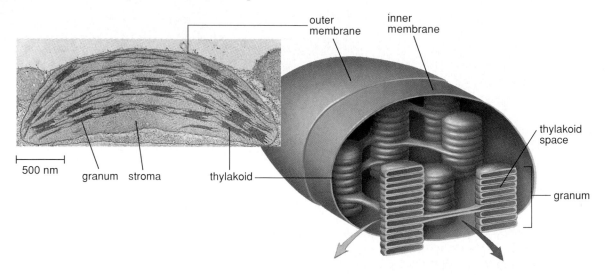

outer membrane · inner membrane · thylakoid space · granum · 500 nm · granum · stroma · thylakoid

thylakoid membrane: pigments that absorb solar energy

stroma: enzymes that catalyze reduction of CO_2

H_2O · ADP + P · ATP · NADP$^+$ · CO_2 · O_2 · NADPH · CH_2O

Light-Dependent Reactions **Light-Independent Reactions**

Chloroplasts Have Two Parts

In a chloroplast, a double membrane surrounds a large central compartment called the **stroma** [Gk. *stroma,* spread out]. The stroma encloses an enzyme-rich solution. A membrane system within the stroma forms flattened sacs called **thylakoids** [Gk. *thylac,* sack, and *oid,* like] which in some places are stacked to form *grana* [L. *gran,* grain], so called because they looked like piles of seeds to early microscopists. The space within each thylakoid is thought to be connected to the space within every other thylakoid, thereby forming an inner compartment within chloroplasts called the thylakoid space (fig. 8.3).

Chlorophyll [Gk. *chlor,* green, and *phyll,* leaf] and the yellow-orange pigments called carotenoids are found within the membranes of the thylakoids. As illustrated in figure 8.4, a chlorophyll molecule has a large hydrophilic head (porphyrin ring), which contains magnesium (Mg), and a long hydrophobic tail. The head, which absorbs solar energy, is believed to be associated with membrane proteins, while the tail anchors the molecule in the thylakoid membrane.

Photosynthesis Has Two Sets of Reactions

An overall equation draws only the beginning reactants and the end products of a metabolic pathway. Therefore, the probability of two sets of reactions was suggested by F. F. Blackman in 1905 after he discovered that when light is being absorbed maximally, a rise in temperature still increases the rate of photosynthesis.

The first set of reactions that takes place in the thylakoid, where chlorophyll and other pigments are located, is called the **light-dependent reactions** because they cannot take place unless light is present. They are the *energy-capturing reactions* — as water is split and oxygen is released, NADPH and ATP are made. The second set of reactions, called the **light-independent reactions** because they can take place in the dark, occur in the stroma. They are the *synthesis reactions*—they incorporate carbon dioxide (CO_2) into an organic molecule and use the NADPH and ATP produced by the energy-capturing reactions to reduce it to a carbohydrate (CH_2O).

The two sets of reactions are:

1. light-dependent: energy capturing
   reactions   reactions
2. light-independent: sythesis
   reactions   reactions

> Photosynthesis takes place in chloroplasts. Energy-capturing reactions take place in the thylakoids and synthesis reactions occur in the stroma.

Figure 8.4

Molecular structure of chlorophylls *a* and *b*. The ring structure is hydrophilic and the long hydrocarbon chain is hydrophobic. Note the similarity in structure to a phospholipid.

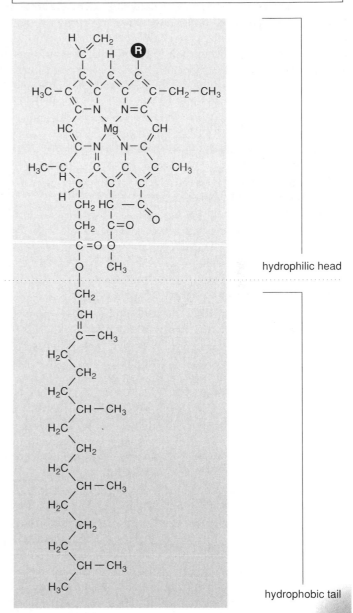

R = CH_3 in chlorophyll *a*   **R** = CHO in chlorophyll *b*

hydrophilic head

hydrophobic tail

SOLAR ENERGY IS CAPTURED

The light-dependent reactions require the participation of two light-gathering units called photosystem I (PS I) and photosystem II (PS II). The photosystems are named for the order in which they were discovered and not for the order in which they occur in the thylakoid membrane. Each **photosystem** has a pigment complex composed of chlorophyll *a* and chlorophyll *b* molecules (green pigments) and accessory pigments, such as carotenoid molecules (primarily red and orange but also yellow pigments). The closely packed pigment molecules in the photosystems serve as an "antenna" for gathering solar energy. Solar energy is passed from one pigment to the other until it is concentrated into one particular chlorophyll *a* molecule, the reaction-center chlorophyll. Electrons in the reaction-center chlorophyll *a* molecule become so excited that they escape and move to a nearby electron-acceptor molecule.

> In a photosystem, the light-gathering antenna absorbs solar energy and funnels it to a reaction-center chlorophyll *a* molecule, which then sends energized electrons to an electron-acceptor molecule.

Electrons Have Two Pathways

Electrons can follow a cyclic electron pathway or a noncyclic electron pathway during the first phase of photosynthesis. The cyclic electron pathway generates only ATP, while the noncyclic pathway results in both NADPH and ATP.

Cyclic Electron Pathway

The *cyclic electron pathway* (fig. 8.5) begins after the PS I pigment complex absorbs solar energy. In this pathway, high-energy electrons (e⁻) leave the PS I reaction-center chlorophyll *a* molecule but eventually return to it. Before they return, however, the electrons enter an **electron transport system,** a series of carriers that pass electrons from one to the other. Some of the carriers are cytochrome molecules; for this reason, the electron transport system is sometimes called a *cytochrome system* in chloroplasts. As the electrons pass from one carrier to the next, energy that will be used to produce ATP molecules is released and stored.

Some photosynthetic bacteria utilize the cyclic electron pathway only; therefore, this pathway probably evolved early in the history of life. It is possible that in plants, the cyclic flow of electrons is utilized only when carbon dioxide (CO_2) is in such

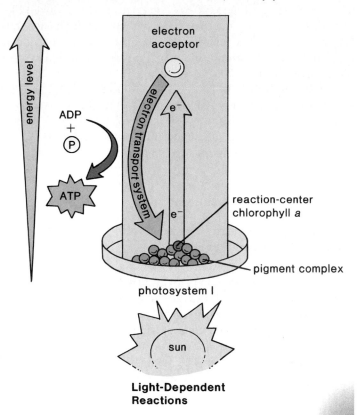

Figure 8.5

The cyclic electron pathway. Energized electrons (e⁻) leave the photosystem I (PS I) reaction-center chlorophyll *a* and are taken up by an electron acceptor, which passes them down an electron transport system before they return to PSI. Only ATP production results from this pathway. y.

Light-Dependent Reactions

limited supply that carbohydrate is not being produced. At this time, there would be no need for additional NADPH, which is produced by the noncyclic electron pathway.

It should also be noted that the second phase of photosynthesis, which occurs in the stroma, requires a larger number of ATP than NADPH. Perhaps the cyclic electron pathway routinely provides the extra ATP molecules required by reactions that occur in the stroma.

> The cyclic electron pathway, from PS I back to PS I, has only one effect: production of ATP.

Figure 8.6

The noncyclic electron pathway. Electrons, taken from water, move from photosystem II (PS II) to photosystem I (PS I) to NADP⁺. The ATP and NADPH produced will be used by the light-independent reactions to reduce carbon dioxide (CO_2) to a carbohydrate (CH_2O).

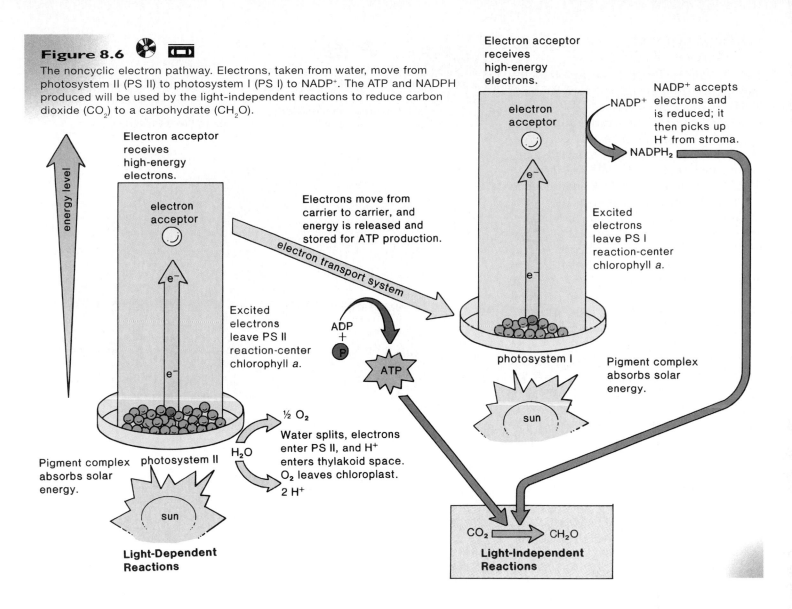

Noncyclic Electron Pathway

During the *noncyclic electron pathway,* electrons move from water (H_2O) through PS II to PS I and then on to NADP⁺ (fig. 8.6). This pathway begins when the PS II pigment complex absorbs solar energy and high-energy electrons (e⁻) leave the reaction-center chlorophyll *a* molecule. PS II takes replacement electrons from water, which splits, releasing oxygen:

$$H_2O \longrightarrow 2\,H^+ + 2\,e^- + \tfrac{1}{2}\,O_2$$

This oxygen evolves from the chloroplast and the plant as oxygen gas. The hydrogen ions (H⁺) temporarily stay in the thylakoid space.

The high-energy electrons that leave PS II are captured by an electron acceptor, which sends them to an electron transport system. As the electrons pass from one carrier to the next, energy that will be used to produce ATP molecules is released and stored. Low-energy electrons leaving the electron transport system enter PS I.

The PS I pigment complex absorbs solar energy, and high-energy electrons leave the reaction-center chlorophyll *a* and are captured by an electron acceptor. This time, the electron acceptor passes the electrons on to NADP⁺. NADP⁺ now takes on an H⁺ and becomes NADPH:

$$NADP^+ + 2\,e^- + H^+ \longrightarrow NAPDH$$

The NADPH and ATP produced by the noncyclic flow of electrons in the thylakoid membrane are used by enzymes in the stroma during the light-independent reactions.

Results of noncyclic electron flow: Water is split, yielding H⁺, e⁻, and O_2; ATP is produced; and NADP⁺ becomes NADPH.

Chemiosmosis Produces ATP

The thylakoid space acts as a reservoir for hydrogen ions (H⁺). First, each time water is split, two H⁺ remain in the thylakoid space. Second, as the electrons move from carrier to carrier in the electron transport system, they give up energy, which is used to pump H⁺ from the stroma into the thylakoid space. Therefore, there is a large number of H⁺ in the thylakoid space compared to the number in the stroma. The flow of H⁺ (often referred to as protons in this context) from high to low concentration across the thylakoid membrane provides the energy that allows an *ATP synthase enzyme* to enzymatically produce ATP from ADP + Ⓟ. (ADP is adenosine diphosphate.) This method of producing ATP is called *chemiosmotic ATP synthesis* because ATP production is tied to an electrochemical gradient.

ATP production during photosynthesis is sometimes called photophosphorylation because light is involved. If so, the production of ATP during the cyclic electron pathway is called *cyclic photophosphorylation,* and during the noncyclic electron pathway is called *noncyclic photophosphorylation.*

The Thylakoid Membrane Is Organized

Both biochemical and structural techniques have been used to determine that there are intact complexes (particles) in the thylakoid membrane (fig. 8.7):

PS II consists of the particle colored dark green, and the light-gathering pigment complex shown to one side. PS II splits water and produces oxygen.

The cytochrome complex is colored blue. This complex acts as the transporter of electrons between PS II and PS I. The pumping of H⁺ occurs during electron transport.

PS I consists of the particle colored light green and the light-gathering pigment complex to one side. Notice that PS I is associated with the enzyme that reduces NADP⁺ to NADPH.

ATP synthase complex has an H⁺ channel and a protruding ATP synthase. As H⁺ flows down its concentration gradient through this channel, ATP is produced from ADP + Ⓟ.

Figure 8.7 🔴 ▭

Organization of the chloroplast and thylakoid. **a.** The products of the light-dependent reactions, which occur in the thylakoid, are used by the light-independent reactions, which occur in the stroma. **b.** The functions of the protein complexes in the thylakoid membrane are listed to the left. Pq is a mobile carrier that transfers hydrogen ions (H⁺) from the stroma to the thylakoid space.

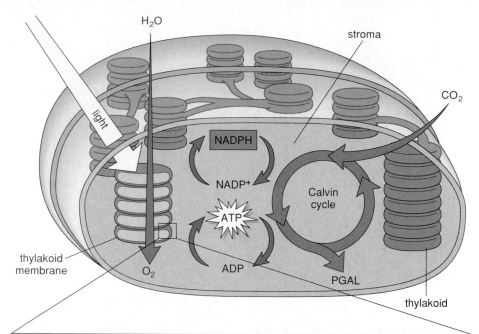

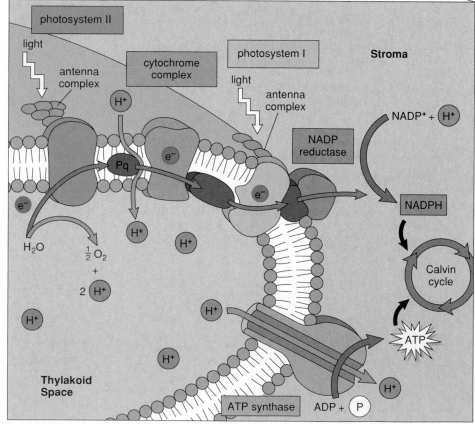

CARBOHYDRATE IS SYNTHESIZED

The light-independent reactions are the second stage of photosynthesis. They take their name from the fact that light is not directly required for these reactions to proceed. In this stage of photosynthesis, the NADPH and ATP produced by the noncyclic electron pathway during the first stage are used to reduce carbon dioxide: CO_2 becomes CH_2O within a carbohydrate molecule. Hydrogen atoms (e^- + H^+) and energy are needed for this reduction synthesis, and these are supplied by NADPH and ATP.

The reduction of carbon dioxide occurs in the stroma of a chloroplast by means of a series of reactions known as the **Calvin cycle**. Although this cycle does not require light, it is most likely to occur during the day, when a plant is producing high levels of ATP and NADPH. PS I has been found to set in motion a regulatory mechanism by which the enzymes of the Calvin cycle are turned on.

> **The light-independent reactions use the ATP and NADPH from the light-dependent reactions to reduce carbon dioxide.**

The Calvin Cycle Has Three Stages

The Calvin cycle is named for one of the individuals who was instrumental in identifying the reactions that make up the cycle (fig. 8.8). Melvin Calvin received a Nobel prize in 1961 for his part in determining these reactions. The Calvin cycle includes 1) carbon dioxide fixation, 2) carbon dioxide reduction, and 3) regeneration of **RuBP (ribulose bisphosphate).**

Figure 8.8

Identifying of the reactions involved in carbon dioxide fixation and reduction. **a.** Calvin and his colleagues used the apparatus shown; algae (*Chlorella*) were placed in the flat flask, which was illuminated by two lamps. Radioactive carbon dioxide ($^{14}CO_2$) was added, and the algae were killed by transferring them into boiling alcohol (in the beaker below the flask). This treatment instantly stopped all chemical reactions in the cells. Carbon-containing compounds were then extracted from the cells and analyzed. **b.** By tracing the radioactive carbon, Calvin and his colleagues were able to trace the reaction series, or pathway, by which CO_2 was incorporated. They found that the radioactive carbon (shown in boxes) is first added to RuBP and that the resulting molecule immediately splits to form two molecules of PGA. By gradually increasing the exposure of the algae to $^{14}CO_2$ before killing, they were able to identify the rest of the molecules in the cycle that is now called the Calvin cycle (see fig. 8.9).

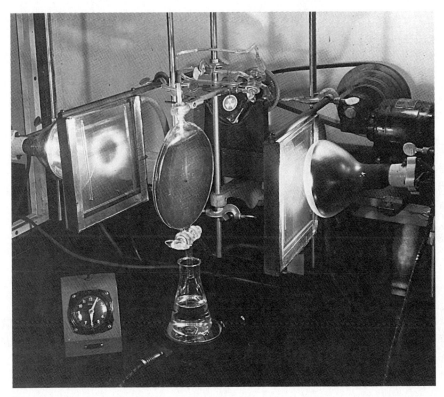

a.

b.

Fixing Carbon Dioxide

Carbon dioxide (CO_2) fixation, the attachment of carbon dioxide to an organic compound, is the first event in the Calvin cycle (fig. 8.9). At that time, **RuBP, (ribulose biphosphate)** a five-carbon molecule, combines with carbon dioxide. The enzyme that speeds up this reaction is called RuBP carboxylase, a protein that makes up about 20–50% of the protein content in chloroplasts. The reason for its abundance may be that it is unusually slow (it processes only about three molecules of substrate per second compared to about one thousand per second for a typical enzyme), and so there has to be a lot of it to keep the Calvin cycle going.

Carbon dioxide fixation occurs when carbon dioxide combines with RuBP.

The six-carbon molecule resulting from carbon dioxide fixation immediately breaks down to form two *PGA* (*phosphoglycerate*) three-carbon molecules. Because the first detectable molecule in the Calvin cycle is a three-carbon (C_3) molecule, it is also known as the C_3 cycle.

Figure 8.9

Light-independent reactions. The Calvin cycle uses ATP and NADPH to produce PGAL. Because five PGAL are needed to re-form three RuBP, it takes three turns of the cycle to have a net gain of one PGAL, which can be used to form glucose ($C_6H_{12}O_6$).

Metabolites of the Calvin Cycle	
RuBP	ribulose bisphosphate
PGA	phosphoglycerate
PGAP	diphosphoglycerate
PGAL	phosphoglyceraldehyde

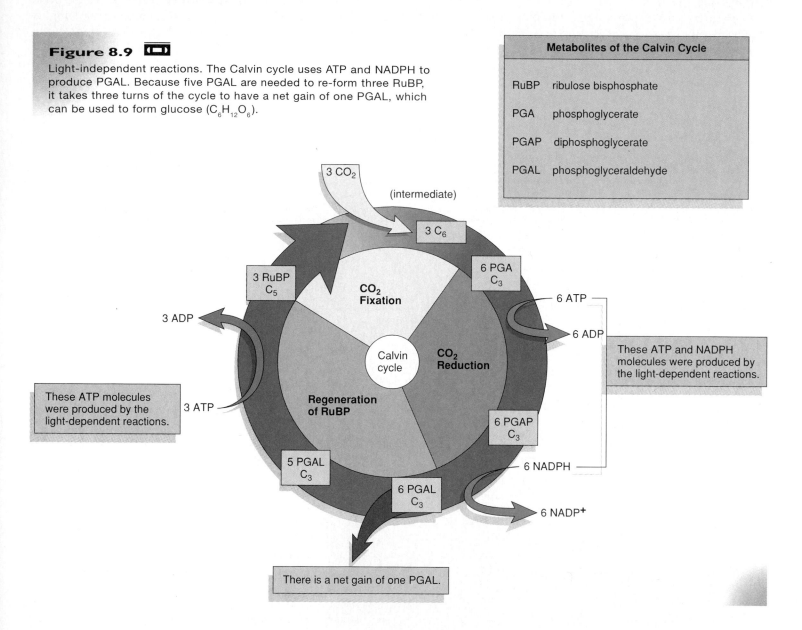

3 CO_2

(intermediate)

3 C_6

3 RuBP
C_5

6 PGA
C_3

CO_2 Fixation

3 ADP

6 ATP

6 ADP

Calvin cycle

CO_2 Reduction

These ATP and NADPH molecules were produced by the light-dependent reactions.

These ATP molecules were produced by the light-dependent reactions.

3 ATP

Regeneration of RuBP

6 PGAP
C_3

5 PGAL
C_3

6 NADPH

6 PGAL
C_3

6 NADP⁺

There is a net gain of one PGAL.

Reducing Carbon Dioxide

Each of the two PGA molecules undergoes reduction to PGAL (phosphoglyceraldehyde) in two steps:

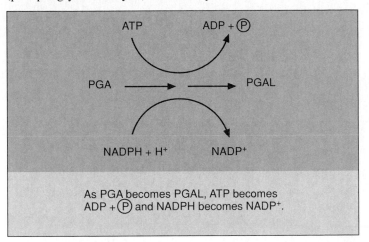

As PGA becomes PGAL, ATP becomes ADP + ℗ and NADPH becomes NADP⁺.

This is the actual reaction that uses NADPH and ATP from the light-dependent reactions, and it signifies the reduction of carbon dioxide (CO_2) to a carbohydrate (CH_2O). Hydrogen atoms and energy are needed for this reduction reaction, and these are supplied by NADPH and ATP, respectively.

PGAL, the end product of the Calvin cycle, is converted to all sorts of organic molecules. Compared to animal cells, algae and plants have enormous biochemical capabilities. They use PGAL for these purposes:

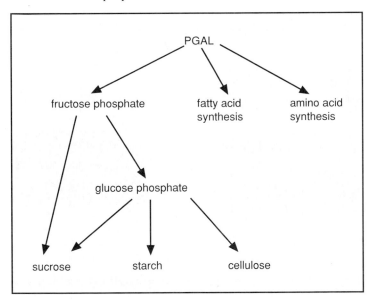

As shown here, glucose phosphate is among the organic molecules that result from PGAL metabolism. This is of interest to us because glucose is the molecule that plants and animals most often metabolize to produce the ATP molecules they require for their energy needs.

Regenerating RuBP

For every three turns of the Calvin cycle, five molecules of PGAL are used to re-form three molecules of RuBP so that the cycle can continue:

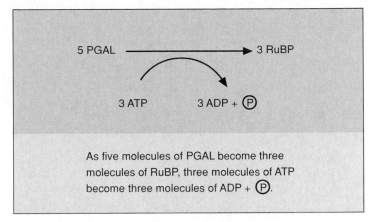

As five molecules of PGAL become three molecules of RuBP, three molecules of ATP become three molecules of ADP + ℗.

The net gain of three turns of the Calvin cycle is one PGAL molecule. This reaction also utilizes some of the ATP produced by the light-dependent reactions.

Five out of every six PGAL molecules of the Calvin cycle are used to regenerate three RuBP molecules, and the cycle begins again.

Environmental Effects on Photosynthesis

Modern society burns much fossil fuel (gasoline, coal, oil, gas) and, as a consequence, the amount of carbon dioxide in the atmosphere is rising. Just like the panes of glass in a greenhouse, carbon dioxide allows the sun's rays to pass through but then traps the heat given off. Global warming of a few degrees due to the increase in carbon dioxide and other identified "greenhouse gases" is expected. Scientists are now asking if an increase in atmospheric carbon dioxide and an increase in the daily temperature will affect photosynthesis and the metabolism of plants in general.

Another major area of concern is the depletion of the ozone (O_3) shield high above the earth's surface in the upper atmosphere. Near the earth's surface, ozone is a poison for both animals and plants, but in the upper atmosphere, ozone blocks ultraviolet radiation and safeguards all living things from its dangerous effects on DNA (deoxyribonucleic acid). Many are aware that severe depletion of ozone due to pollutants (particularly chlorofluorocarbons, CFCs) is expected to cause a steep rise in the incidence of human skin cancer. But what effect will ozone holes have on plant metabolism?

There have been no definitive answers to these questions, but studies are being done. The reading on page 132 discusses these concerns and the work of one investigator in this area.

Figure 8.10

Carbon dioxide fixation. Plants can be categorized according to the type of carbon dioxide fixation.

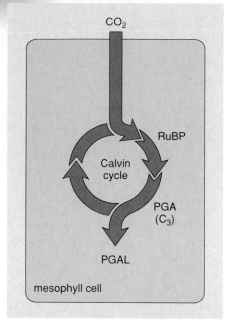

CO₂ fixation in a C₃ plant

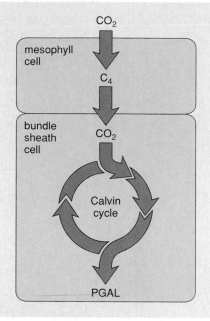

CO₂ fixation in a C₄ plant

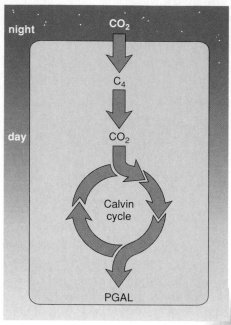

CO₂ fixation in a CAM plant

PHOTOSYNTHESIS TAKES OTHER ROUTES

Three modes of photosynthesis are known (fig. 8.10). In **C₃ plants,** the Calvin cycle fixes carbon dioxide (CO_2) directly, and the first detectable molecule following fixation is PGA, a C_3 molecule. **C₄ plants** fix CO_2 by forming a C_4 molecule prior to the involvement of the Calvin cycle. **CAM plants** fix CO_2 by forming a C_4 molecule *at night* when stomates can open without much loss of water.

C₄ Plants Flourish When It Is Hot and Dry

C_3 plants use RuBP carboxylase to fix CO_2 to RuBP, and the first detected molecule following fixation is PGA. C_4 plants use the enzyme PEP carboxylase (PEPCase) to fix CO_2 to PEP (phosphoenolpyruvate) and the result is oxaloacetate, a C_4 molecule.

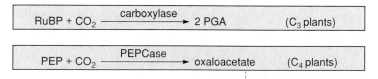

The structure of a leaf from a C_3 plant is different from that of a C_4 plant. In a C_3 plant, the *mesophyll cells* contain well-formed chloroplasts and are arranged in parallel layers. In a C_4 leaf, the

bundle sheath cells, as well as the mesophyll cells, contain chloroplasts. Further, the mesophyll cells are arranged concentrically around the bundle sheath cells:

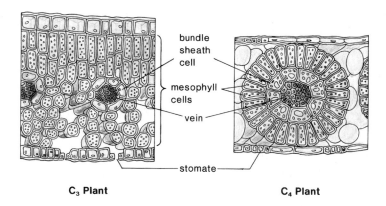

In a C_4 plant, CO_2 is taken up in mesophyll cells and then a reduced form of oxaloacetate (C_4 molecule) is pumped into the bundle sheath cells (fig. 8.10). Here, CO_2 enters the Calvin cycle. It takes energy to pump molecules, and you would think that the C_4 pathway would be disadvantageous. Yet in hot, dry climates, the net photosynthetic rate of C_4 plants such as sugar cane, corn, and Bermuda grass is about two to three times that of C_3 plants such as wheat, rice, and oats.

Photorespiration

Notice in the diagrams of leaves, there are little openings called stomates (sing., stomate) in the surfaces of leaves through which water can leave and carbon dioxide (CO_2) can enter. If the weather is hot and dry, these openings close in order to conserve water. (Water loss might cause the plant to wilt and die.) When stomates are closed, the concentration of CO_2 decreases in leaves, while oxygen, a by-product of photosynthesis, increases. In C_3 plants, oxygen competes with CO_2 for the active site of RuBP carboxylase (rubisCO) and the result is only one molecule of PGA:

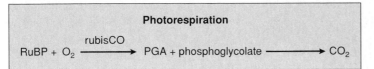

Photorespiration

$$RuBP + O_2 \xrightarrow{\text{rubisCO}} PGA + phosphoglycolate \longrightarrow CO_2$$

RuBP carboxylase is often called *rubisCO* because it has both a carboxylase and oxygenase activity. Further, this reaction is named *photorespiration* because in the presence of light (*photo*), oxygen is taken up and CO_2 is produced (*respiration*). Photorespiration wastes energy since it produces only one PGA.

Photorespiration does not occur in C_4 leaves even when stomates are closed because CO_2 is delivered to the Calvin cycle in the bundle sheath cells. When the weather is moderate, C_3 plants have the advantage, but when the weather becomes hot and dry, C_4 plants have the advantage, and we can expect them to predominate. In the early summer, C_3 plants such as Kentucky bluegrass and creeping bentgrass predominate in lawns in the cooler parts of the United States, but by midsummer, crabgrass, a C_4 plant, begins to take over.

C_4 plants have an advantage over C_3 plants when the weather is hot and dry because photorespiration does not occur to any extent.

CAM Plants Have an Alternative Way

CAM plants use PEPCase to fix some CO_2 *at night*, forming a C_4 molecule, which is stored in large vacuoles in their mesophyll cells until the next day. CAM stands for crassulacean-acid metabolism; the Crassulaceae is a family of flowering succulent plants that live in warm, arid regions of the world. CAM was first discovered in these plants, but now it is known to be prevalent among most succulent plants that grow in desert environments, including the cacti.

Whereas a C_4 plant represents partitioning in space—carbon dioxide fixation occurs in mesophyll cells and the Calvin cycle occurs in bundle sheath cells—CAM is an example of partitioning by the use of time. The C_4 formed at night releases CO_2 during the day to the Calvin cycle within the same cell, which now has NADPH and ATP available to it from the light-dependent reactions. The primary reason for this partitioning again has to do with the conservation of water. CAM plants open their stomates only at night, and therefore only at that time is atmospheric CO_2 available. During the day, the stomates close to conserve water and CO_2 cannot enter the plant.

Photosynthesis in a CAM plant is minimal because of the limited amount of CO_2 fixed at night, but it does allow CAM plants to live under stressful conditions (table 8.1).

CAM plants use PEPCase to carry on carbon dioxide fixation at night when the stomates are open. During the day, the stored carbon dioxide can enter the Calvin cycle.

Table 8.1

The Three Pathways of Carbon Dioxide Fixation

Feature	C_3	C_4	CAM
Leaf structure	Bundle sheath cells lacking chloroplasts	Bundle sheath cells having chloroplasts	Large vacuoles in mesophyll cells
Enzyme utilized	RubisCO	PEPCase	PEPCase
Optimum temperature	15–25° C	30–40° C	35° C
Productivity rate (tons/hectare/year)	22 ± 0.3	39 ± 17	Low—variable

Source: Data from Black, 1973; Salisbury and Ross, 1978.

Life After Photosynthesis

carbon dioxide (CO_2) from the atmosphere is the primary source for almost all of the organic carbon in the tissues of plants, animals, fungi, bacteria, and other organisms on earth. Plants fix CO_2 during photosynthesis, and other organisms get along by eating or absorbing plant material. It has long been known that the amount of CO_2 in the atmosphere influences how fast photosynthesis can occur. Generally, the more CO_2 available to a plant, the faster it photosynthesizes. These observations are becoming more important because it is predicted that the concentration of CO_2 in the atmosphere, which is currently about 0.04%, will double within the coming century.

My research is concerned primarily with "life after photosynthesis," meaning the metabolism of plants after CO_2 is incorporated into organic molecules. Such metabolism is often referred to as secondary metabolism, partly because it begins several steps beyond primary pathways like photosynthesis and cellular respiration, and partly because it produces metabolites that were once thought to be secondary—that is, chemicals that are not common and do not usually have a clear role in the life of a plant. Familiar secondary metabolites include such chemicals as nicotine, caffeine, menthol, strychnine, morphine, and rubber. They are familiar to us because of their importance in medicine or industry, but their roles in the life of a plant are not well known.

The plant I work with most is the sour orange (*Citrus aurantium*). I collaborate with Sherwood Idso and Bruce Kimball of the U.S. Department of Agriculture. Idso and Kimball have been growing enriched-CO_2 sour orange trees at their laboratory in Phoenix, Arizona, since 1987. They plant these trees in large, open-top chambers that are kept at about 0.07% CO_2 (not quite double the amount in the atmosphere). Periodically, I collect leaves and fruits from these trees, and from trees grown in similar chambers that are not CO_2-enriched, and bring them to my laboratory for various chemical analy-

W. Dennis Clark
Arizona State University

ses. The main comparisons I make are between the amounts of secondary metabolites in the enriched versus the unenriched trees.

Plant metabolism in general increases when photosynthetic rates increase. This is apparently the case in the secondary metabolic pathways that produce cardiac glycosides (heart-stimulating steroids) in purple foxglove (*Digitalis purpurea*), phenolics (phenol-containing chemicals) in wheat (*Triticum aestivum*), and flavonoids (ultraviolet [UV]-absorbing pigments) in rice (*Oryza sativa*) and in sour orange. (However, the same pathways either are not affected or are even inhibited by increased photosynthetic rates in other plants.)

My interest in this area of research began when I came across an article in *Science* in 1989[1] that described the changes in insects that were fed plants grown in an enriched-CO_2 environment. Overall, the growth and development of these insects were retarded by a diet of such plants. My mind jumped to the hypothesis that these unfavorable effects were caused by the accumulation of secondary metabolites in the enriched-CO_2 plants. And could it be, I wondered, that the rising amount of atmospheric CO_2 will alter the interactions between plants and herbivores by accelerating

1 Fajer, E.D., Bowers, M.D., and Bazzaz, F.A. 1989. The effects of enriched carbon dioxide atmospheres on plant-insect herbivore interactions. *Science* 243:1198-1200.

the buildup of secondary metabolites? It has been several years since I first asked this question, and the jury is still out. However, the verdict appears to be yes, in some cases. In other cases, altered plant-herbivore interactions may have little to do with secondary metabolism. Recent studies show that for grasshoppers the digestibility of enriched-CO_2 sagebrush (*Artemisia tridentata*) is improved, probably because of high starch content. Flavonoids, my favorite plant chemicals, are UV-absorbing pigments that may play a significant role in defending plants against damaging UV radiation. More UV radiation is reaching the earth from the sun because pollutants are causing our protective ozone (O_3) shield, which ordinarily absorbs UV radiation, to develop holes. Experiments in 1991 showed that the concentrations of flavonoids in rice leaves were highest in plants that were grown in a combination of high CO_2 and high UV radiation. Work in 1994 showed that flavonoids prevent UV radiation from harming the DNA of leaf cells. At this point it seems that plants, unlike ourselves and other animals, just might be able to cope quite well with these human-caused environmental changes.

Finally, any effects that rising atmospheric CO_2 has on secondary metabolism will also affect our diet and health. Most of the flavors and many of the nutrients, as well as numerous toxins, in fruits and vegetables are secondary metabolites. We don't know yet if growth in an enriched-CO_2 environment will make broccoli taste better in the future, or if it will contain more of the cancer-fighting nutrients that were recently discovered in it. And we don't know yet if toxins in potato skins will be more abundant in our high-CO_2 future. We are still on the forefront of this kind of research into the secondary metabolism of plants. It is clear, though, that such work will be helpful for understanding how environmentally induced changes in plant metabolism might affect everything from plant ecology to human health.

1. Photosynthesis (a) provides food either directly or indirectly for most living things, (b) produces oxygen, and (c) provided the energy to create today's fossil fuels.

2. Photosynthesis uses solar energy in the visible-light range; the photons of this range contain the right amount of energy to energize the electrons of chlorophyll molecules. Specifically, chlorophylls a and b absorb violet, blue, and red wavelengths best. This causes chlorophyll to appear green to us.

3. A chloroplast is bounded by a double membrane and contains two main portions: the liquid stroma and the membranous grana made up of thylakoid sacs. The light-dependent reactions take place in the thylakoids, and the light-independent reactions take place in the stroma.

4. In the cyclic electron pathway, electrons energized by the sun leave PS I. But instead of being sent to $NADP^+$ they pass down the electon transport system back to PS I again. It is possible the cyclic pathway occurs only if there is no free $NADP^+$ to receive the electrons; this is a way to prevent an energy overload of PS I. It serves to generate ATP, and in keeping with its name, it probably evolved first and is the only photosynthetic pathway present in certain bacteria today.

5. The noncyclic electron pathway of the light-dependent reactions begins when solar energy enters PS II. PS II energized electrons leave and go to an electron acceptor. The splitting of water replaces these electrons in the reaction-center chlorophyll a molecules; releases oxygen to the atmosphere; and donates hydrogen ions (H^+) to the thylakoid space. An acceptor molecule passes electrons to PS I by way of an electron transport (cytochrome) system. When solar energy is absorbed by PS I energized electrons leave and are ultimately received by $NADP^+$, which also combines with H^+ from the stroma to become NADPH.

6. The energy made available by the passage of electrons down the electron transport system allows carriers to pump H^+ into the thylakoid space. The buildup of H^+ establishes an electrochemical gradient. When H^+ flows down this gradient through the channel present in ATP synthase complexes, ATP is synthesized from ADP and Ⓟ by ATP synthase.

7. The thylakoid membrane is highly organized. (a) PS II functions to split water; (b) the cytochrome complex transports electrons and pumps H^+; (c) PS I is associated with an enzyme that reduces $NADP^+$; and (d) ATP synthase produces ATP.

8. The energy yield of the light-dependent reactions is stored in ATP and NADPH. These molecules are now used by the light-independent reactions to reduce carbon dioxide (CO_2) to carbohydrate.

9. During the light-independent reactions, the enzyme RuBP carboxylase fixes CO_2 to RuBP, producing a six-carbon molecule that immediately breaks down to two C_3 molecules. This is the first stage of the Calvin cycle. During the second stage, CO_2 is incorporated into an organic molecule and is reduced to carbohydrate (CH_2O). This step requires the NADPH and some of the ATP from the light-dependent reactions. For every three turns of the Calvin cycle, the net gain is one PGAL molecule; the other five PGAL molecules are used to re-form three molecules of RuBP. This step also requires ATP for energy. PGAL is then converted to all the organic molecules a plant needs.

10. In C_4 plants, as opposed to the C_3 plants just described, the enzyme PEPCase fixes carbon dioxide to PEP to form a four-carbon molecule, oxaloacetate, within mesophyll cells. A reduced form of this molecule is pumped into bundle sheath cells where CO_2 is released to the Calvin cycle. C_4 plants avoid photorespiration by a partitioning of pathways in space: carbon dioxide fixation occurs in mesophyll cells and the Calvin cycle occurs in bundle sheath cells.

11. During CAM photosynthesis, PEPCase fixes CO_2 to PEP at night. The next day, CO_2 is released and enters the Calvin cycle within the same cells. This represents a partitioning of pathways in time: carbon dioxide fixation occurs at night and the Calvin cycle occurs during the day. The plants that carry on CAM are desert plants, in which the stomates only open at night in order to conserve water.

Writing Across the Curriculum

In order to practice writing skills, students should write out the answers to any or all of the study questions and the critical thinking questions. The study questions are sequenced in the same order as the text. Answers to the objective questions, and suggested answers to the critical thinking questions, are in appendix D.

Study Questions

1. Why is it proper to say that ultimately all living things are dependent on solar energy? 120

2. Discuss the electromagnetic spectrum and the absorption spectrum of chlorophyll. Why is chlorophyll a green pigment? 120–21

3. Name the two major portions of chloroplasts and associate each portion with the two sets of reactions that occur during photosynthesis. How are the two pathways related? 123

4. What role do PS I and II play during the light-dependent reactions? 124

5. Trace the cyclic electron pathway, naming and explaining all the events that occur as the electrons cycle. 124

6. Trace the noncyclic electron pathway, naming and explaining all the events that occur as the electrons move from water to $NADP^+$. 125

7. Explain what is meant by chemiosmotic ATP synthesis, and relate this process to the electron transport system present in the thylakoid membrane. 126

8. How is the thylakoid membrane organized? Name the main complexes in the membrane and give a function for each. 126

9. Describe the three stages of the Calvin cycle. Which stage utilizes the ATP and NADPH from the light-dependent reactions? 127–29

10. Explain C_4 photosynthesis, contrasting the actions of rubisCO and PEPCase. 130–31

11. Explain CAM photosynthesis, contrasting it to C_4 photosynthesis in terms of partitioning of a pathway. 131

Objective Questions

1. The absorption spectrum of chlorophyll
   a. approximates the action spectrum of photosynthesis.
   b. explains why chlorophyll is a green pigment.
   c. shows that some colors of light are absorbed more than others.
   d. All of these are correct.

2. The final acceptor of electrons during the noncyclic electron pathway is
   a. PS I.
   b. PS II.
   c. ATP.
   d. $NADP^+$.

3. A photosystem contains
   a. pigments, a reaction center, and an electron acceptor.
   b. ADP, Ⓟ, and hydrogen ions (H^+).
   c. protons, photons, and pigments.
   d. Both b and c are correct.

4. Which of these should not be associated with the electron transport system?
   a. cytochromes
   b. movement of H^+ into the thylakoid space
   c. formation of ATP
   d. absorption of solar energy

5. PEPCase has an advantage compared to rubisCO. The advantage is that
   a. PEPCase is present in both mesophyll and bundle sheath cells, but rubisCO is not.
   b. rubisCO fixes carbon dioxide (CO_2) only in C_4 plants, but PEPCase does it in both C_3 and C_4 plants.
   c. rubisCO is subject to photorespiration, but PEPCase is not.
   d. Both b and c are correct.

6. The NADPH and ATP from the light-dependent reactions are used to
   a. cause rubisCO to fix CO_2.
   b. reform the photosystems.
   c. cause electrons to move along their pathways.
   d. convert PGA to PGAL.

7. CAM photosynthesis
   a. is the same as C_4 photosynthesis.
   b. is an adaptation to cold environments in the Southern Hemisphere.
   c. is prevalent in desert plants that close their stomates during the day.
   d. occurs in plants that live in marshy areas.

8. Chemiosmotic ATP synthesis depends on
   a. an electrochemical gradient.
   b. a difference in H^+ concentration between the thylakoid space and the stroma.
   c. ATP breaking down to ADP + Ⓟ.
   d. Both a and b are correct.

9. Label this diagram of a chloroplast.

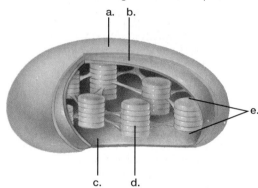

   f. The light-dependent reactions occur in which part of a chloroplast?
   g. The light-independent reactions occur in which part of a chloroplast?

10. Label this diagram using these labels: water, carbohydrate, carbon dioxide, oxygen, ATP, ADP + Ⓟ, NADPH, and $NADP^+$.

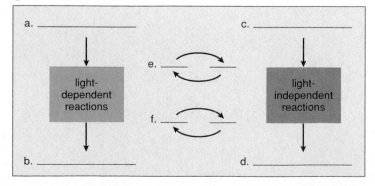

Concepts and Critical Thinking

1. *Virtually all living things are dependent on solar energy.*

What data would you use to convince a friend that the lives of human beings are dependent on solar energy?

2. *Photosynthesis makes solar energy available to living things.*

Explain how photosynthesis makes solar energy available by explaining the roles of chlorophyll, ATP, NADP$^+$, and carbon dioxide (CO_2) in photosynthesis.

3. *The cell and the organelles themselves are compartmentalized, and this assists their proper functioning.*

Name two major compartments (separate areas) of a chloroplast, and tell how photosynthesis is dependent on keeping the areas separate.

Selected Key Terms

C$_3$ plant A plant that directly uses the Calvin cycle; the first detected molecule during photosynthesis is PGA, a three-carbon molecule.   130

C$_4$ plant A plant that does not directly use the Calvin cycle; the first detected molecule during photosynthesis is a four-carbon molecule.   130

Calvin cycle A series of photosynthetic reactions in which carbon dioxide is fixed and reduced in the chloroplast.   127

CAM plant A plant that fixes carbon dioxide at night to produce a C$_4$ molecule that releases carbon dioxide to the Calvin cycle during the day; CAM stands for crassulacean-acid metabolism.   130

chlorophyll A green pigment that absorbs solar energy and is important in photosynthesis; occurs as chlorophyll *a* and chloroplast *b*. [Gk. *chlor,* green, and *phyll,* leaf]   123

chloroplast A membrane-bounded organelle with chlorophyll-containing membranous thylakoids; where photosynthesis takes place. [Gk. *chlor,* green, and *plast,* formed, molded]   122

electromagnetic spectrum Solar radiation divided on the basis of wavelength, with gamma rays having the shortest wavelength and radio waves having the longest wavelength.   120

electron transport system The passage of electrons along a series of carrier molecules from a higher to a lower energy level; the energy released is used for the synthesis of ATP.   124

granum (pl., grana) (GRAY-num) A stack of chlorophyll-containing thylakoids in a chloroplast.   123

light-dependent reactions The energy capturing portion of photosynthesis that takes place in thylakoid membranes and cannot proceed without solar energy; it produces ATP and NADPH.   123

light-independent reactions The synthesis portion of photosynthesis that takes place in the stroma and does not directly require solar energy; it uses the products of the light-dependent reactions to reduce carbon dioxide to a carbohydrate.   123

photon A discrete packet of solar energy; the amount of energy in a photon is inversely related to the wavelength of the photon. [Gk. *photo,* light]   120

photosynthesis A process occurring within chloroplasts whereby chlorophyll-containing organisms trap solar energy to reduce carbon dioxide to carbohydrate. [Gk. *photo,* light, and *synthesis,* putting together]   120

photosystem A photosynthetic unit where solar energy is absorbed and high energy electrons are generated; contains a pigment complex and an electron acceptor; occurs as PS (photosystem) I and a PS II.   124

RuBP (ribulose bisphosphate) A five-carbon compound that combines with and fixes carbon dioxide during the Calvin cycle and is later regenerated by the same cycle.   127

stroma (STROH-muh) A large, central compartment in a chloroplast that is fluid filled and contains enzymes used in photosynthesis. [Gk. *stroma,* spread out]   123

thylakoid (THY-luh-koyd) A fattened sac within a granum whose membrane contains chlorophyll and where the light-dependent reactions of photosynthesis occur.   123

9

CELLULAR RESPIRATION

Learning Objectives

Energy flows from the sun to the leaf and then on to these grasshoppers, *Romalea,* which feed on the leaf.

t is common knowledge that human beings eat food, which they digest to nutrient molecules, but you may not be aware that most other organisms, including plants and animals (fig. 9.1a), also use organic molecules as a source of building blocks and energy. Carbohydrate molecules (e.g., glucose) are a primary energy source because they are often broken down to acquire a supply of ATP (adenosine triphosphate) molecules. We can write the overall equation for cellular respiration in this manner:

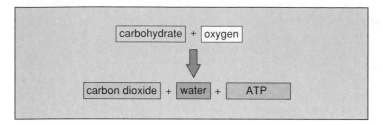

ATP, the energy currency of cells, provides the energy that cells need for transport work, mechanical work, and chemical work. Why do living things convert the chemical bond energy of carbohydrate to that of ATP? Why not, for example, use glucose energy directly, thereby bypassing mitochondria? The answer is that the energy content of glucose is too great for individual cellular reactions; ATP contains the right amount of energy, and enzymes are adapted through evolution to couple ATP breakdown with energy-requiring cellular processes.

Chloroplasts produce the energy-rich carbohydrates that typically undergo aerobic respiration in mitochondria. Cellular respiration, then, is the link between the solar energy captured by plants and the chemical energy utilized by both plants and animals (fig. 9.1b). Photosynthesis and cellular respiration are the means by which energy flows from the sun through all living things.

Usable energy is always lost when one form of energy is transformed into another form. Eventually, the energy content of food is completely dissipated, but the chemicals themselves cycle. When carbohydrate is broken down, the low-energy molecules carbon dioxide and water are given off, and these are the raw materials for photosynthesis (fig. 9.1b).

The energy of carbohydrates, which was originally provided by solar energy, is converted to ATP molecules in cells .

Figure 9.1

Aerobic respiration overview. **a.** Both plants and animals carry on aerobic respiration. **b.** Aerobic respiration and photosynthesis are related in the manner shown.

a.

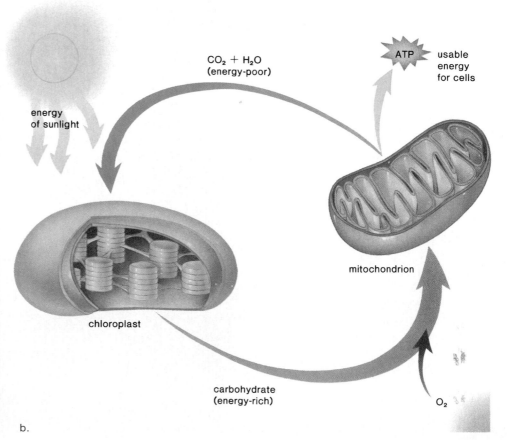

b.

How Cells Acquire ATP

Cellular respiration includes the various metabolic pathways by which carbohydrates and other metabolites are broken down with the concomitant buildup of ATP. Figure 9.2 shows how glucose is completely metabolized to carbon dioxide and water with the resulting buildup of usually 36 ATP molecules. The complete breakdown of glucose is **aerobic** [Gk. *aer,* air] and requires oxygen. It is possible to write an overall equation for the complete breakdown of glucose in this manner:

$$C_6H_{12}O_6 + 6\ O_2 \rightarrow 6\ CO_2 + 6\ H_2O + energy$$

The pathways illustrated in figure 9.2 allow the energy within a glucose molecule to be released slowly, step by step. Cells would lose a tremendous amount of energy if they used glucose directly—it contains far too much chemical energy for individual reactions, and therefore much energy would become nonusable heat. Also, the cell is far too delicate to utilize all the energy released in one burst. A gradual breakdown allows a concomitant gradual buildup of ATP molecules. If glucose is metabolized completely to carbon dioxide and water, the cell usually realizes a yield of 36 ATP molecules. The energy in 36 ATP molecules is equivalent to 39% of the energy that was available in glucose.

The complete breakdown of glucose requires three individual pathways: glycolysis, the Krebs cycle, and an electron transport system. In addition, the transition reaction acts like a bridge connecting glycolysis with the Krebs cycle. During these reactions, oxidation occurs by the removal of hydrogen atoms ($e^- + H^+$) from metabolites. Electrons are carried by the coenzyme NAD^+ (and FAD) from glycolysis and the Krebs cycle to the electron transport system, where they are eventually transferred to oxygen molecules. Oxygen then accepts hydrogen ions and water results. Notice that glycolysis, the breakdown of glucose to pyruvate, does not require oxygen. *Pyruvate* is a pivotal metabolite and if oxygen is not available to the cell, fermentation, an anaerobic process, occurs. Fermentation is a series of enzymatic reactions by which glucose is incompletely metabolized to lactate (animals) or carbon dioxide and alcohol (yeast). As you can see from figure 9.2, fermentation results in a net gain of only two ATP. If oxygen is available, aerobic respiration occurs and pyruvate enters the mitochondria, where the Krebs cycle and electron transport chain are located.

> Cellular respiration includes glycolysis and fermentation which are anaerobic and aerobic respiration which takes place in mitochondria when oxygen is available to the cell.

Figure 9.2

Cellular respiration overview. Glycolysis in the cytosol produces pyruvate, a key intermediary metabolite. If oxygen is not available, anaerobic metabolism continues and pyruvate is reduced to either alcohol or lactate, depending on the type of cell. If oxygen is available, aerobic respiration begins in a mitochondrion and pyruvate is metabolized completely to carbon dioxide and water. The net gain of ATP for glycolysis (and fermentation) is two ATP; the net gain of ATP for aerobic respiration is often 34 ATP; the net gain of ATP for the complete breakdown of glucose is then 36 ATP.

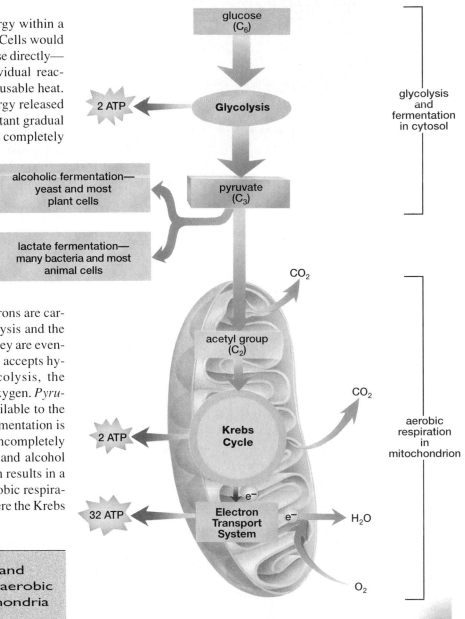

Figure 9.3

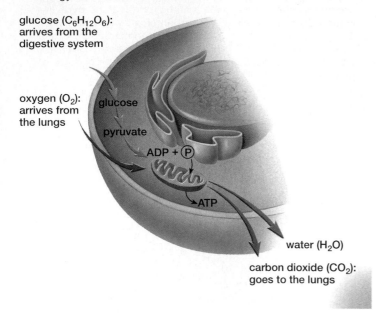

Relationship of glucose breakdown to the body proper. Glucose and oxygen are delivered to the cells by the bloodstream. Carbon dioxide and water are removed by the bloodstream. ATP remains in the cytoplasm as a source of energy for the cell to do work.

glucose ($C_6H_{12}O_6$): arrives from the digestive system

oxygen (O_2): arrives from the lungs

glucose

pyruvate

ADP + P

ATP

water (H_2O)

carbon dioxide (CO_2): goes to the lungs

Cellular Respiration Requires Breathing

The respiratory system of the body takes oxygen into the lungs and removes carbon dioxide. Therefore, the word *respiration* is sometimes used to mean breathing. However, this chapter discusses cellular respiration, the breakdown of nutrient molecules such as glucose with the concomitant buildup of ATP.

Breathing and cellular respiration are related. The air we breathe contains *oxygen* (O_2), and the food we eat contains glucose. These enter the bloodstream, and are carried about the body, until they diffuse into each and every cell. Glycolysis occurs in the cytosol and the end product, pyruvate, enters the mitochondria (fig. 9.3). In mitochondria, pyruvate is broken down to carbon dioxide (CO_2) and water (H_2O) as ATP is produced. All three of these diffuse out of the mitochondria into the cytoplasm. ATP is utilized inside the cytosol for energy-requiring processes. Carbon dioxide diffuses out of the cell, enters the bloodstream, and is taken to the lungs, where it is exhaled. The water molecules, called metabolic water, become important in a desert animal such as the kangaroo rat which drinks no water. All of its water intake is derived from food—only 10% is from the food's moisture and 90% is metabolic water.

GLYCOLYSIS AND FERMENTATION ARE ANAEROBIC

Glycolysis and fermentation occur in the cytosol outside the mitochondria. They are anaerobic pathways that do not require oxygen. Oxidation by removal of hydrogen atoms ($e^- + H^+$) does occur, though, and enough energy is released to generate a net gain of two ATP molecules. ATP production occurs by a process called **substrate-level phosphorylation** [Gk. *phos,* light, and *phor,* movement] in which a phosphate is enzymatically transferred from a substrate to ADP (adenosine diphosphate).

Glycolysis Takes Glucose to Pyruvate

During **glycolysis** [Gk. *glyc,* sweet, and *lys,* loosening], a series of enzymatic reactions, glucose is broken down to two molecules of **pyruvate** (fig. 9.4). Since glycolysis is universally found in organisms, it most likely evolved before the Krebs cycle and the electron transport system. This may be why glycolysis occurs in the cytosol and does not require oxygen. Bacteria evolved before other organisms, and there are some bacteria today that are anaerobic; they die in the presence of oxygen.

As glycolysis begins, the addition of two phosphate groups activates glucose C_6, a six-carbon molecule, to react. This requires two separate reactions and uses two ATP. Also, at one point, hydrogen atoms ($e^- + H^+$) are removed from the substrates of the pathway and are picked up by NAD^+.

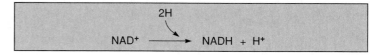

$$NAD^+ \xrightarrow{\text{2H}} NADH + H^+$$

Since this reaction occurs twice, two NADH are produced. Enough energy is released to allow the formation of four ATP. Subtracting the two ATP that were used to get started, glycolysis results in a net gain of two ATP.

When glycolysis is followed by aerobic respiration, pyruvate enters the mitochondria, where oxygen (O_2) is utilized. However, glycolysis does not have to be followed by aerobic respiration. Instead, it can be a part of fermentation.

Altogether the inputs and outputs of glycolysis are as follows:

Glycolysis	
inputs	outputs
glucose	2 pyruvate
2 NAD^+	2 NADH
2 ADP + 2 P	4 ATP (net 2)
2 ATP	

Figure 9.4

Glycolysis is a metabolic pathway that begins with glucose and ends with pyruvate. Net gain of two ATP molecules can be calculated by subtracting those expended from those produced. Text in boxes to the right explains the reactions.

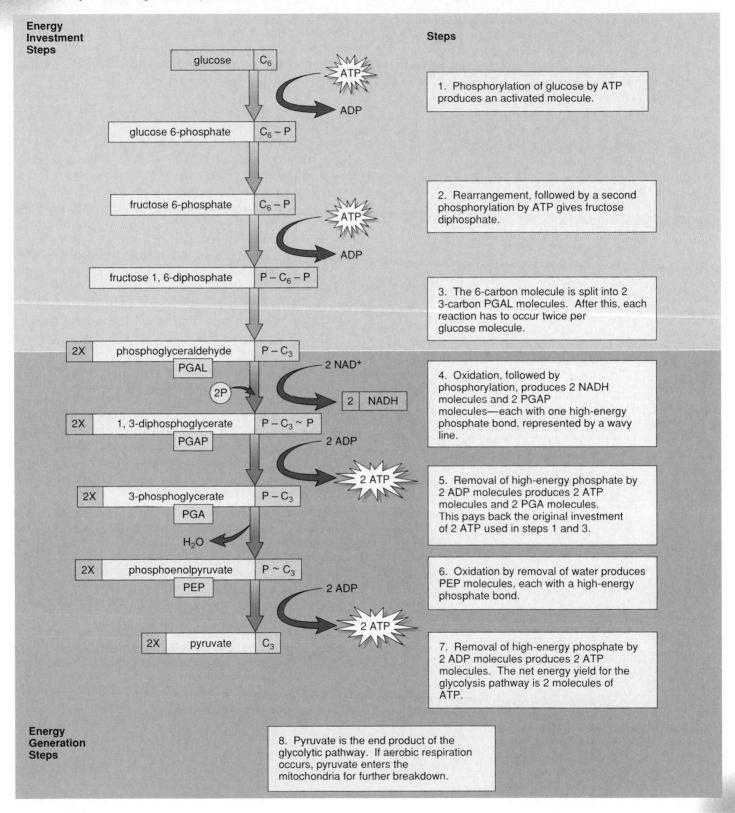

Energy Investment Steps

Steps

glucose | C_6

ATP → ADP

1. Phosphorylation of glucose by ATP produces an activated molecule.

glucose 6-phosphate | $C_6 - P$

fructose 6-phosphate | $C_6 - P$

ATP → ADP

2. Rearrangement, followed by a second phosphorylation by ATP gives fructose diphosphate.

fructose 1, 6-diphosphate | $P - C_6 - P$

3. The 6-carbon molecule is split into 2 3-carbon PGAL molecules. After this, each reaction has to occur twice per glucose molecule.

2X | phosphoglyceraldehyde | $P - C_3$
PGAL

2P

2 NAD⁺ → 2 | NADH

4. Oxidation, followed by phosphorylation, produces 2 NADH molecules and 2 PGAP molecules—each with one high-energy phosphate bond, represented by a wavy line.

2X | 1, 3-diphosphoglycerate | $P - C_3 \sim P$
PGAP

2 ADP → 2 ATP

5. Removal of high-energy phosphate by 2 ADP molecules produces 2 ATP molecules and 2 PGA molecules. This pays back the original investment of 2 ATP used in steps 1 and 3.

2X | 3-phosphoglycerate | $P - C_3$
PGA

H_2O

2X | phosphoenolpyruvate | $P \sim C_3$
PEP

6. Oxidation by removal of water produces PEP molecules, each with a high-energy phosphate bond.

2 ADP → 2 ATP

2X | pyruvate | C_3

7. Removal of high-energy phosphate by 2 ADP molecules produces 2 ATP molecules. The net energy yield for the glycolysis pathway is 2 molecules of ATP.

Energy Generation Steps

8. Pyruvate is the end product of the glycolytic pathway. If aerobic respiration occurs, pyruvate enters the mitochondria for further breakdown.

Fermentation Is Wasteful

Fermentation [L. *ferment,* yeast] is an anaerobic process that does not require oxygen. It consists of glycolysis plus one other reaction—the reduction of pyruvate to either lactate in animal cells or alcohol and carbon dioxide in yeast cells (fig. 9.5). Other end products are possible, depending on the type of enzyme in the particular organism.

If oxygen (O_2) is not available to cells, the electron transport system soon becomes inoperative. Electrons back up in the system when oxygen, the final acceptor, is not present. In this case, cells can still produce ATP by resorting to fermentation. However, fermentation results in only two ATP per glucose molecule and the organic products still contain much chemical energy.

When a cell is fermenting, glycolysis continues because NADH passes its electrons to pyruvate instead of to the electron transport system. Now NAD^+ is "free" to return and pick up more electrons. However, the end products of the process (e.g. lactate or alcohol) are toxic to cells, and high concentrations can eventually result in the death of the organism.

Fermentation Has Advantages and Disadvantages

Despite its low yield, fermentation is important because it can provide a rapid burst of ATP. In our own bodies, muscle cells more than other cells are apt to carry on fermentation. When our muscles are working vigorously over a short period of time, as when we run, fermentation is a way to produce ATP even though oxygen is temporarily in limited supply. At first, blood carries away all the lactate formed in the muscles. Eventually, however, lactate begins to build up in the muscles, changing the pH and causing the muscles to fatigue so that they no longer contract. When we stop running, our bodies are in **oxygen debt,** as signified by the fact that we continue to breathe very heavily for a time. Recovery is complete when the lactate is transported to the liver, where it is reconverted to pyruvate. Some of the pyruvate is respired completely, and the rest is converted back to glucose ($C_6H_{12}O_6$).

Because of fermentation, yeast cells are capable of growing and dividing anaerobically for a time. If the initial glucose level is high, however, the cells are eventually killed by the very alcohol they produce. Presumably, human beings were delighted to discover this form of fermentation—the ethyl alcohol produced has been consumed in great quantity for thousands of years.

How Efficient Is Fermentation?

A high-energy phosphate bond in an ATP molecule has an energy content of 7.3 kcal, and two ATP are produced per glucose molecule during fermentation. This is equivalent to 14.6 kcal. Complete glucose breakdown to carbon dioxide and water represents a possible energy yield of 686 kcal per molecule. Therefore, the efficiency for fermentation is only 14.6/686, or 2.1%. This is much less efficient than the complete breakdown of glucose. The inputs and outputs of fermentation are as follows:

Figure 9.5
Fermentation consists of glycolysis followed by a reduction of pyruvate. This "frees" NAD^+ and it returns to the glycolytic pathway to pick up more electrons.

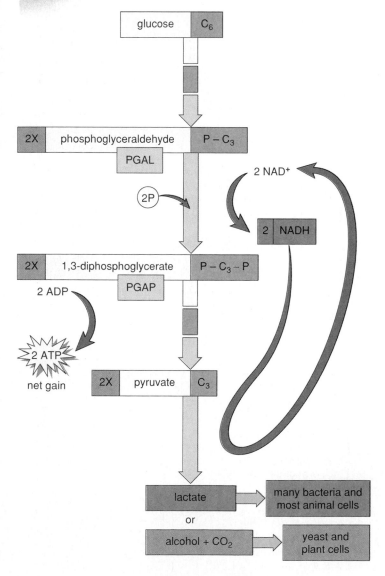

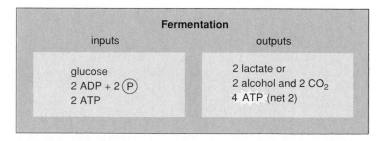

Fermentation	
inputs	outputs
glucose 2 ADP + 2 ⓟ 2 ATP	2 lactate or 2 alcohol and 2 CO_2 4 ATP (net 2)

Exercise: A Test of Homeostatic Control

Exercise is a dramatic test of the body's homeostatic control systems—there is a large increase in muscle oxygen (O_2) requirement, and a large amount of carbon dioxide (CO_2) is produced. These changes must be countered by increases in breathing and blood flow to increase oxygen delivery and removal of the metabolically produced carbon dioxide. Also, heavy exercise can produce a large amount of lactic acid due to the utilization of fermentation, an anaerobic process. Both the accumulation of carbon dioxide and lactic acid can lead to an increase in intracellular and extracellular acidity. Further, during heavy exercise, the working muscles produce large amounts of heat that must be removed to prevent overheating. In a strict sense, the body rarely maintains true homeostasis while performing intense exercise or during prolonged exercise in a hot or humid environment. However, a better maintenance of homeostasis is observed in those who have had endurance training.

The number of mitochondria increases in the muscles of persons who train; and, therefore, there is greater reliance on the Krebs cycle and the electron transport system to generate energy. Muscle cells with few mitochondria must have a high ADP concentration to stimulate the limited number of mitochondria to start consuming oxygen. After an endurance training program, the large number of mitochondria start consuming oxygen as soon as the ADP concentration starts rising due to muscle contraction and subsequent breakdown of ATP. Therefore, a steady state of oxygen intake by mitochondria is achieved earlier in the athlete. This faster rise in oxygen uptake at the onset of work means that the oxygen deficit is less, and the formation of lactate due to fermentation is less. Further, any lactate that is produced is removed and processed more quickly.

Training also results in greater reliance on the Krebs cycle and increased fatty acid metabolism, because fatty acids are broken down to acetyl-CoA, which enters the Krebs cycle. This preserves plasma glucose concentration and also helps the body maintain homeostasis.

Source: Scott K. Powers and Edward T. Howley, *Exercise Physiology*, 2d ed., 1994, Times Mirror Higher Education Group, Inc., Dubuque, Iowa.

In athletes, there is:
- a smaller oxygen deficit due to a more rapid increase in oxygen uptake at the onset of work;
- an increase in fat metabolism that spares blood glucose;
- a reduction in lactate and hydrogen ion (H^+) formation;
- an increase in lactate removal.

Figure 9.6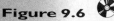

Mitochondrion structure and function. The mitochondrion is bounded by a double membrane with an intermembrane space. The inner membrane invaginates to form the shelflike cristae. Glycolysis is located outside mitochondria. The Krebs cycle occurs within the matrix, the fluid-filled interior. The electron transport system is located on the cristae of a mitochondrion.

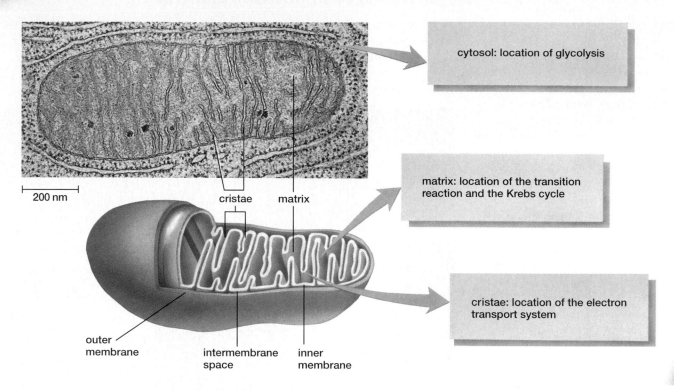

cytosol: location of glycolysis

matrix: location of the transition reaction and the Krebs cycle

cristae: location of the electron transport system

200 nm

cristae   matrix

outer membrane

intermembrane space

inner membrane

AEROBIC RESPIRATION OCCURS IN MITOCHONDRIA

During **aerobic respiration** [Gk. *aer,* air], pyruvate from glycolysis is broken down completely to carbon dioxide and water. Altogether, there is a gain of 36 ATP for the complete breakdown of glucose. This is far more than the two ATP that result from fermentation, an anaerobic process.

Aerobic respiration requires three different events: the oxidation of pyruvate to an acetyl group (called the transition reaction), the Krebs cycle, and the passage of electrons down an electron transport system. Aerobic respiration occurs in mitochondria, whose structure is shown in figure 9.6. A mitochondrion has a double membrane, with an intermembrane space (between the outer and inner membrane). Cristae are folds of inner membrane that jut out into the matrix, the innermost compartment, which is filled with a gel-like fluid. The transition reaction and the Krebs cycle enzymes are located in the matrix and the electron transport system is located in the cristae. Most of the ATP produced during cellular respiration is produced in mitochondria; therefore, mitochondria are often called the powerhouses of the cell.

Transition Reaction Is the First Step

The **transition reaction** is so called because it connects glycolysis to the Krebs cycle. In this reaction pyruvate is converted to a two-carbon *acetyl group* attached to *coenzyme A,* or CoA, and carbon dioxide is given off. This is an oxidation reaction in which hydrogen atoms ($e^- + H^+$) are removed from pyruvate by a dehydrogenase that uses NAD^+ as a coenzyme. The reaction occurs twice for each original glucose molecule.

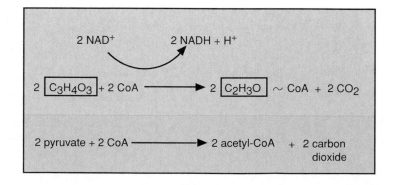

$2\ NAD^+ \qquad 2\ NADH + H^+$

$2\ \boxed{C_3H_4O_3} + 2\ CoA \longrightarrow 2\ \boxed{C_2H_3O} \sim CoA + 2\ CO_2$

2 pyruvate + 2 CoA ⟶ 2 acetyl-CoA + 2 carbon dioxide

Figure 9.7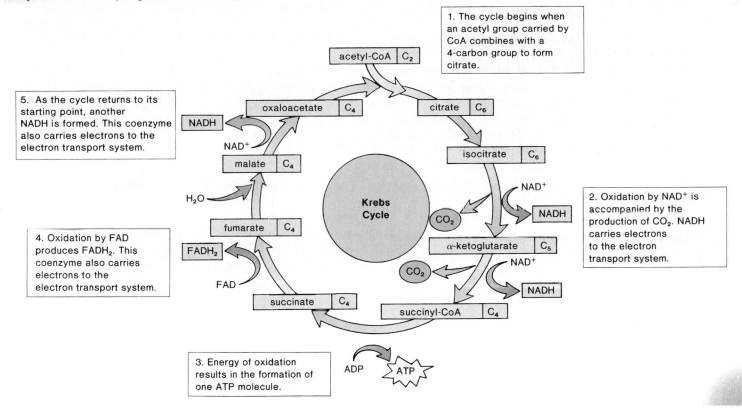

Krebs cycle. The net result of this cycle is the oxidation of an acetyl group to two molecules of carbon dioxide (CO_2). There is a gain of one ATP during the cycle but much energy still resides in the electrons that were removed by three molecules of NAD^+ and one molecule of FAD. NADH and $FADH_2$ then take the electrons to the electron transport system. (Keep in mind that the Krebs cycle turns twice per glucose molecule.)

1. The cycle begins when an acetyl group carried by CoA combines with a 4-carbon group to form citrate.

5. As the cycle returns to its starting point, another NADH is formed. This coenzyme also carries electrons to the electron transport system.

2. Oxidation by NAD^+ is accompanied by the production of CO_2. NADH carries electrons to the electron transport system.

4. Oxidation by FAD produces $FADH_2$. This coenzyme also carries electrons to the electron transport system.

3. Energy of oxidation results in the formation of one ATP molecule.

The Krebs Cycle Finishes Glucose Breakdown

The **acetyl-CoA** produced by the transition reaction enters the **Krebs cycle,** a cyclical metabolic pathway located in the matrix of mitochondria. The Krebs cycle is named for Sir Hans Krebs, a British scientist who received the Nobel prize for his part in identifying these reactions in the 1930s. The first metabolite of the cycle is citrate; for this reason, it is also known as the *citric acid cycle* (fig. 9.7).

The acetyl group that enters the Krebs cycle is oxidized to two molecules of carbon dioxide (CO_2). During the oxidation process most of the hydrogen atoms ($e^- + H^+$) are accepted by NAD^+, but in one instance they are taken by FAD. Some of the energy released when oxidation occurs is used immediately to form ATP by substrate-level phosphorylation, as in glycolysis.

$$R \sim \text{P} + ADP \longrightarrow ATP + R$$

R = rest of molecule

During the Krebs cycle, the C_2 acetyl group is oxidized to two molecules of CO_2. Oxidation results in NADH and $FADH_2$ molecules. Substrate-level phosphorylation yields an ATP molecule.

The Krebs cycle turns twice for each original glucose molecule. Therefore, the input and output of the Krebs cycle per glucose molecule are as follows:

Krebs Cycle	
inputs	outputs
2 acetyl groups	4 CO_2
2 ADP + 2 (P)	2 ATP
6 NAD^+	6 NADH
2 FAD	2 $FADH_2$

The Electron Transport System Produces Most ATP

The **electron transport system** located in the cristae of the mitochondria is a series of carriers that pass electrons from one to the other. Some of the protein complexes of the system are cytochrome molecules; therefore, the system is also termed a *cytochrome system.*

The electrons that enter the electron transport system are at first a part of hydrogen atoms (e^- + H^+) that were removed by NAD^+ and FAD from the substrates of glycolysis and the Krebs cycle. Figure 9.8 illustrates that these carriers deliver high-energy electrons to the system, and low-energy electrons leave the system. As a pair of electrons is passed from carrier to carrier, energy is released and used to form generally three ATP molecules. This process is sometimes called **oxidative phosphorylation** [Gk. *phos,* light, and *phor,* movement] because oxygen receives the energy-spent electrons from the last of the carriers. After accepting electrons, oxygen combines with hydrogen ions from the matrix, and water forms:

$$\tfrac{1}{2}O_2 + 2e^- + 2H^+ \longrightarrow H_2O$$

The hydrogen ions (H^+), released by the oxidation of NADH and $FADH_2$, are pumped from the matrix into the intermembrane space, which lies between the outer and inner membranes surrounding the mitochondrion. The accumulation of hydrogen ions in this space results in a notable electrochemical gradient. As the hydrogen ions move down their concentration gradient across the membrane, energy is provided for ATP production. As in photosynthesis, this method of producing ATP is called chemiosmotic ATP synthesis because ATP production is tied to an electrochemical gradient.

> **Each pair of electrons that passes from carrier to carrier of the electron transport system releases enough energy to allow the production of three ATP.**

The cell needs only a limited supply of the coenzymes NAD^+ and FAD because they are constantly being recycled and reused. Therefore, once NADH has delivered electrons to the electron transport system, it is "free" to return and pick up more hydrogens. In the same manner, the components of ATP are recycled in cells. Energy is required to join ADP + (P); then when ATP is used to do cellular work, ADP and (P) are made available once more. The recycling of coenzymes and ADP increases cellular efficiency since it does away with the need to synthesize NAD^+, FAD, and ADP anew.

Figure 9.8

The electron transport system. NADH and $FADH_2$ bring electrons to the electron transport system. As the electrons move down the system, energy is released and used to form ATP. For every pair of electrons that enters by way of NADH, three ATP result. For every pair of electrons that enters by way of $FADH_2$, two ATP result. Oxygen, the final acceptor of the electrons, becomes a part of water.

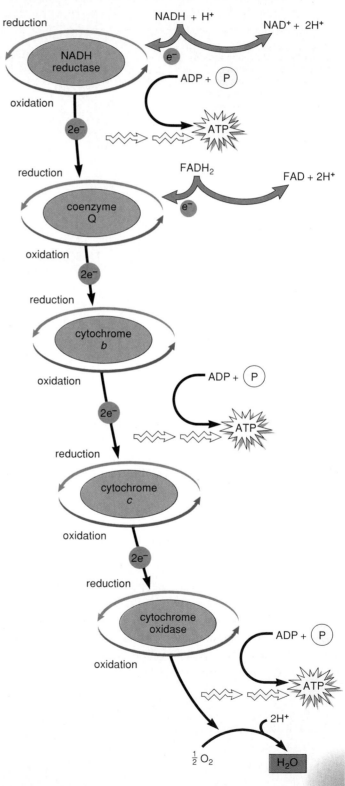

The Cristae Are Organized

The carriers of the electron transport system and those concerned with ATP synthesis and diffusion are spatially arranged in a particular manner in the cristae of mitochondria (fig. 9.9). Essentially the electron transport system consists of three protein complexes (particles) and two mobile carriers. The mobile carriers transport electrons between the complexes. The complexes are:

NADH dehydrogenase complex, which carries out oxidation of NADH; the electrons enter the electron transport system and when they are passed on energy becomes available to pump hydrogen ions (H⁺) into the intermembrane space;

cytochrome b-c complex, which receives electrons and also pumps H⁺ into the intermembrane space;

cytochrome oxidase complex, which receives electrons and passes them on to oxygen. Once again, energy is made available to pump hydrogen ions (H⁺) into the intermembrane space.

The cristae also contain an *ATP synthase complex* and a channel protein for ATP. As H⁺ flow from high to low concentration through the ATP synthase complex, ATP is synthesized from ADP +Ⓟ. Just how H⁺ flow drives ATP synthesis is not known; perhaps the H⁺ participate in the reaction or perhaps they cause a change in the shape of ATP synthase and this brings about protein synthesis. The finding of respiratory poisons has lent support to the chemiosmotic theory of ATP synthesis. When one poison inhibits ATP synthase, the H⁺ gradient becomes larger than usual, and when another type makes the membrane leaky to H⁺, no ATP is made because of a lack of a H⁺ gradient.

Once formed, ATP molecules diffuse out of the mitochondrial matrix by way of a channel protein.

Figure 9.9

Organization of cristae. The electron transport system is located in the cristae. As electrons move from one complex to the other hydrogen ions (H⁺) are pumped from the matrix into the intermembrane space. As hydrogen ions flow down their concentration gradient from the intermembrane space into the matrix, ATP is synthesized by an ATP synthase. ATP leaves the matrix by way of a channel protein.

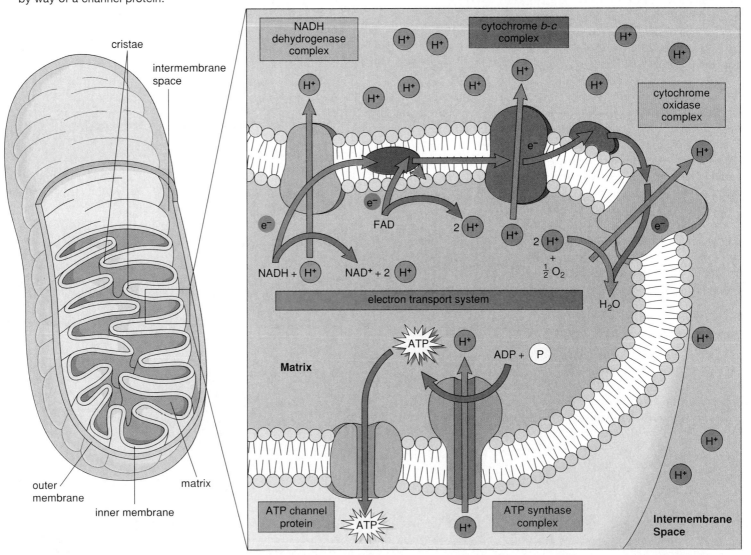

Calculating the Energy Yield from Glucose Metabolism

Figure 9.10 calculates the ATP yield for the complete breakdown of glucose to carbon dioxide and water.

Substrate-Level Phosphorylation: Small Yield

Per glucose molecule, four ATP molecules are formed directly by substrate-level phosphorylation: two during glycolysis and two during two turns of the Krebs cycle.

Oxidative Phosphorylation:Great Yield

Per glucose molecule, ten NADH molecules and two $FADH_2$ molecules take electrons to the electron transport system. For each molecule of NADH formed *inside* the mitochondria by the Krebs cycle, three ATP molecules result, but for each $FADH_2$, there are only two ATP produced. Figure 9.9 explains the reason for this difference: $FADH_2$ delivers its electrons to the transport system after NADH dehydrogenase complex has pumped hydrogen ions (H^+) into the intermembrane space. Since NADH utilizes all three complexes that pump hydrogen ions into the intermembrane space, three ATP result. Since FAD utilizes only two complexes that pump hydrogen ions into the intermembrane space, only two ATP result.

What about the ATP yield of NADH generated *outside* the mitochondria by the glycolytic pathway? NADH cannot cross mitochondrial membranes, but there is a "shuttle" mechanism, which allows its electrons to be delivered to the electron transport system inside the mitochondria. In most types of cells, the shuttle consists of an organic molecule, which can cross the outer membrane, accept the electrons, and deliver them to an FAD molecule in the inner membrane. This use of FAD, however, results in only two ATP molecules; therefore, in most cells the NADH produced in the cytosol results in the production of only two ATP instead of three ATP.

How Efficient Is Aerobic Respiration?

It is interesting to consider how much of the energy in a glucose molecule eventually becomes available to the cell. The difference in energy content between the reactants (glucose and oxygen) and the products (carbon dioxide and water) is 686 kcal. In other words, this is the total amount of energy available for the production of ATP molecules. An ATP phosphate bond has an energy content of 7.3 kcal, and 36 of these are produced during glucose breakdown; 36 phosphates are equivalent to a total of 263 kcal. Therefore, 263/686, or 39%, of the available energy is transferred from glucose to ATP. The rest of the energy is lost in the form of heat. In birds and mammals, in particular, some of this heat is used to maintain a body temperature above that of the environment. In other organisms, including plants, there are few if any measures to conserve heat, and the body temperature generally fluctuates according to the external environment.

> The energy yield of 36 ATP molecules represents 39% of the total energy that is available in a glucose molecule.

Figure 9.10 🎞

Summary of complete glucose breakdown with an accounting of the energy yield in terms of ATP molecules.

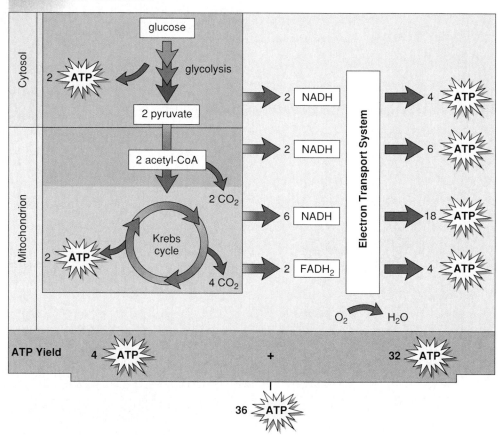

METABOLIC PATHWAYS ARE INTERRELATED

Degradative reactions break down molecules and synthetic reactions build them up. It is correct to say that degradative reactions drive synthetic reactions because the ATP that results from degradative reactions are used during metabolism when molecules, including macromolecules, are synthesized. Synthetic reactions produce cellular structural components, such as membranous organelles, and secretory products, such as hormones or digestive enzymes.

Degradation Provides Metabolic Energy

We already know that when glucose is broken down, ATP is generated. Other molecules can also undergo degradation to produce ATP. When a fat is used as an energy source, it breaks down to glycerol and three fatty acids. As figure 9.11 indicates, glycerol is converted to PGAL, a metabolite in glycolysis. The fatty acids are converted to acetyl-CoA, which enters the Krebs cycle. An eighteen-carbon fatty acid results in nine acetyl-CoA molecules. Calculation shows that respiration of these can produce a total of 108 ATP, a very large number. For this reason, fats are an efficient form of stored energy—there are three long fatty acid chains per fat molecule.

The carbon skeleton of amino acids can also be broken down. First, amino acids undergo deamination, or the removal of the amino group in the liver. The amino group becomes ammonia (NH_3), which enters the urea cycle. Urea is the primary nitrogenous excretory product of humans. The length of the carbon skeleton for degradation is dependent on the length of the R group, since this determines the number of carbons left after deamination.

Anabolic Reactions Use Metabolic Energy

The ATP produced during degradation drives synthetic reactions. But there is another way degradation is related to synthesis. The substrates making up the pathways in figure 9.11 can be used as starting materials for synthetic reactions. In other words, compounds that enter the pathways are oxidized to substrates that can be used for synthesis. This is the cell's **metabolic pool** [Gk. *metab,* change], in which one type of molecule can be converted to another. In this way, carbohydrate intake can result in the formation of fat. PGAL molecules can be converted to glycerol molecules, and acetyl groups can be joined to form fatty acids. Fat synthesis follows. This explains why you gain weight from eating too much candy, ice cream, and cake.

Some metabolites of the Krebs cycle can be converted to amino acids through transamination, the transfer of an amino group from one amino acid to another. Plants are able to synthesize all of the amino acids they need. Animals, however, lack some of the enzymes necessary for synthesis of all amino acids. Adult humans, for example, can synthesize eleven of the common amino acids, but they cannot synthesize the other nine. The amino acids that cannot be synthesized must be supplied by the diet; they are called the essential amino acids. The nonessential amino acids can be synthesized. It is quite possible for animals to suffer from protein deficiency if their diet does not contain adequate quantities of all the essential amino acids.

During times of fasting or whenever the diet does not contain enough glucose, the synthetic process called gluconeogenesis—production of new glucose   occurs.

Figure 9.11 📼

The metabolic pool concept. Carbohydrates, fats, and proteins can be used as energy sources, and they enter degradative pathways at specific points. Degradation (green arrows) produces metabolites that can also be used for synthesis of other compounds (blue arrows).

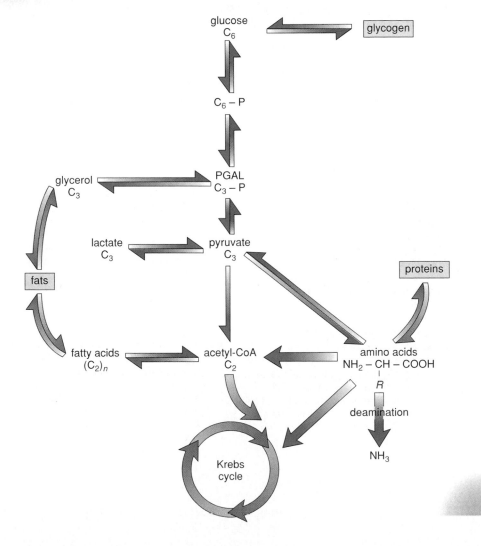

Gluconeogenesis is required in humans because the brain and certain other organs are unable to degrade any other metabolite but glucose. The principal substrates for gluconeogenesis are lactate from anaerobic metabolism in muscles, amino acids from the diet, and glycerol from fatty acid metabolism. The body is unable to convert acetyl-CoA molecules to glucose.

> All the reactions involved in cellular respiration are a part of a metabolic pool; the metabolites of the pool can be degraded or can be used for synthesis.

Biological Relationships

The unity of living things is most apparent at the biochemical level of organization. Organelles as dissimilar as chloroplasts and mitochondria are organized similarly and use similar processes for different purposes. Both have an electron transport system tied to the chemiosmotic synthesis of ATP, for example. The evolution of one pathway from the other can explain such unity.

Ultimately, living things are similar because of their common origin and common needs. Energy must be captured and utilized to maintain the structural organization of the individual. The organelles are simply the transformers by which this need is met. Solar energy is captured in chloroplasts and then flows from photosynthesizers to consumers, all of which contain mitochondria. Energy transformations always result in the loss of useful energy in the form of heat; therefore, energy cannot cycle and the biosphere requires a continual input of solar energy.

Human civilization gets a boost from solar energy that reached our planet long ago. At times in the past, conditions have favored burial rather than decomposition of plant and animal remains. These buried carbon compounds became the fossil fuels (oil, coal, gas) that we burn today. The stored solar energy of yesterday is running our high-tech society of today. Even agriculture is dependent on an infusion of fossil-fuel energy, for how bountiful would the harvest be without power machinery? But there is no free lunch, and our way of life is subject to ecological limitations, as witnessed by increasing air pollution.

Summary

1. In cells, the energy of carbohydrate molecules, in particular, is converted to ATP energy.

2. When glucose is completely oxidized, at least 36 ATP molecules are produced. Three events are required: glycolysis, the Krebs cycle, and passage of electrons along the electron transport system. Oxidation involves the removal of hydrogen atoms ($e^- + H^+$) from substrate molecules, usually by the coenzyme NAD^+.

3. Glucose metabolism often provides energy. Glycolysis anaerobically produces pyruvate, which either becomes reduced within the cytosol (fermentation) or becomes fully oxidized in mitochondria. Animal cells carry on lactate fermentation; yeast cells carry on alcoholic fermentation. Both kinds of fermentation produce only a net yield of two ATP molecules.

4. Glycolysis is the breakdown of glucose to two molecules of pyruvate. This pathway is a series of enzymatic reactions that occurs in the cytosol. Two NAD^+ accept two electons and become NADH. Then substrate-level phosphorylation produces a net gain of two ATP molecules. The NADH either gives electrons to pyruvate or takes them to a mitochondrion.

5. Fermentation involves glycolysis, followed by the reduction of pyruvate by NADH to either lactate or alcohol and carbon dioxide (CO_2). The reduction process "frees" NAD^+ so that it can accept more hydrogen atoms from glycolysis.

6. Although fermentation results in only two ATP molecules, it still serves a purpose. In vertebrates, it provides a quick burst of ATP energy for short-term, strenuous muscular activity. The accumulation of lactate puts the individual in oxygen debt because oxygen is needed when lactate is completely metabolized to CO_2 and water (H_2O).

7. Pyruvate from glycolysis can enter the mitochondrion, where the transition reaction takes place. During this reaction, oxidation occurs as CO_2 is removed. NAD^+ is reduced, and CoA receives the C_2 acetyl group that remains. Since the reaction must take place twice per glucose molecule, two NADH result.

8. The acetyl group enters the Krebs cycle, a cyclical series of reactions located in the mitochondrial matrix. Complete oxidation follows, as two CO_2 molecules, three NADH molecules, and one $FADH_2$ molecule are formed. The cycle also produces one ATP molecule. The entire cycle must turn twice per glucose molecule.

9. The final stage of pyruvate breakdown involves the electron transport system located in the cristae of the mitochondria. The electrons received from NADH and $FADH_2$ are passed down a chain of carriers until they are finally received by oxygen, which combines with H^+ to produce water. As the electrons pass down the chain, ATP is produced. The term *oxidative phosphorylation* is sometimes used for ATP production by the electron transport system.

10. The cristae of the mitochondria contain protein complexes that pass electrons from one to the other and pump H^+ into the intermembrane space, setting up an electrochemical gradient. When H^+ flows down this gradient through the ATP synthase complex, energy is released and used to form ATP molecules from ADP and Ⓟ.

11. Of the 36 ATP formed by complete glucose breakdown, four are the result of substrate-level phosphorylation and the rest are produced by oxidative phosphorylation. The energy for the latter comes from the electron transport system.

12. In the mitochondria, for each NADH molecule donating electrons to the electron transport system, three ATP molecules are produced. Each NADH formed in the cytosol, however, results in only two ATP molecules. This is because the hydrogen atoms must be shuttled across the mitochondrial membrane by a molecule that can cross it. In most cells, these hydrogen atoms are then taken up by FAD. Each molecule of $FADH_2$ results in the formation of only two ATP because its electrons enter the electron transport system at a lower level.

13. Carbohydrate, protein, and fat can be broken down by entering the degradative pathways at different locations. These pathways also provide metabolites needed for the synthesis of various important substances. Degradation and synthesis, therefore, both utilize the same metabolic pool of reactants.

Writing Across the Curriculum

In order to practice writing skills, students should write out the answers to any or all of the study questions and the critical thinking questions. The study questions are sequenced in the same order as the text. Answers to the objective questions, and suggested answers to the critical thinking questions, are in appendix D.

Study Questions

1. What types of organisms carry on cellular respiration? What is the function of this process?   138

2. Glycolysis results in pyruvate molecules. Contrast the fate of pyruvate under anaerobic conditions and aerobic conditions.   139

3. What are the three pathways involved in the complete breakdown of glucose to carbon dioxide (CO_2) and water (H_2O)? What reaction is needed to join two of these pathways?   139

4. What is the overall chemical equation for the complete breakdown of glucose to CO_2 and H_2O? How does a human cell acquire the needed substrates, and what happens to the products?   139

5. Outline the main reactions of glycolysis, emphasizing those that release energy.   140

6. Contrast glycolysis with fermentation. What is the benefit of pyruvate reduction during fermentation? What types of organisms carry out lactate fermentation, and what types carry out alcoholic fermentation?   142

7. Give the substrates and products of the transition reaction. Where does it take place?   144

8. What happens to the acetyl group that enters the Krebs cycle? What are the other steps in this cycle?   145

9. What is the electron transport system, and what are its functions?   146

10. Describe the organization of protein complexes within the cristae. Which complexes are a part of the electron transport system, and which have to do with ATP synthesis and diffusion out of the mitochondrial matrix? Explain how the complexes are involved in chemiosmotic ATP synthesis.   147

11. Calculate the energy yield of glycolysis and complete glucose breakdown. Distinguish between substrate-level phosphorylation and oxidative phosphorylation.   148

12. Give examples to support the concept of the metabolic pool.   149

Objective Questions

For questions 1–8, identify the pathway involved by matching them to the terms in the key.

Key:
   a. glycolysis
   b. Krebs cycle
   c. electron transport system
1. carbon dioxide (CO_2) given off
2. water (H_2O) formed
3. PGAL
4. NADH becomes NAD^+
5. oxidative phosphorylation
6. cytochrome carriers
7. pyruvate
8. FAD becomes $FADH_2$

9. Which of these is not true of fermentation?
   a. net gain of only two ATP
   b. occurs in cytosol
   c. NADH donates electrons to electron transport system
   d. begins with glucose

10. The transition reaction
   a. connects glycolysis to the Krebs cycle.
   b. gives off CO_2.
   c. utilizes NAD^+.
   d. All of these are correct.

11. The greatest contributor of electrons to the electron transport system is
   a. oxygen.
   b. glycolysis.
   c. the Krebs cycle.
   d. the transition reaction.

12. Substrate-level phosphorylation takes place in
   a. glycolysis and the Krebs cycle.
   b. the electron transport system and the transition reaction.
   c. glycolysis and the electron transport system.
   d. the Krebs cycle and the transition reaction.

13. Fatty acids are broken down to
    a. pyruvate molecules, which take electrons to the electron transport system.
    b. acetyl groups, which enter the Krebs cycle.
    c. amino acids, which excrete ammonia.
    d. All of these are correct.

14. Of the 36 ATP molecules that are produced during the complete breakdown of glucose, most are due to the action of
    a. chemiosmotic phosphorylation.
    b. the electron transport system.
    c. substrate-level phosphorylation.
    d. Both a and b are correct.

For questions 15–20, match the items below to one of the locations in the key.

Key:
    a. matrix of the mitochondria
    b. cristae of the mitochondria
    c. between the inner and outer membranes of the mitochondria
    d. in the cytosol

15. electron transport system
16. Krebs cycle
17. glycolysis
18. transition reaction
19. hydrogen ion (H^+) reservoir
20. ATP synthase complex

21. Label this diagram of a mitochondrion:

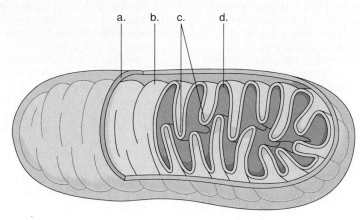

22. Label this diagram of complete glucose breakdown using these terms: glucose, electron transport system, Krebs cycle, pyruvate, acetyl-CoA, NADH (3 times), 2 ATP (twice), 32 ATP, H_2O, CO_2 (twice).

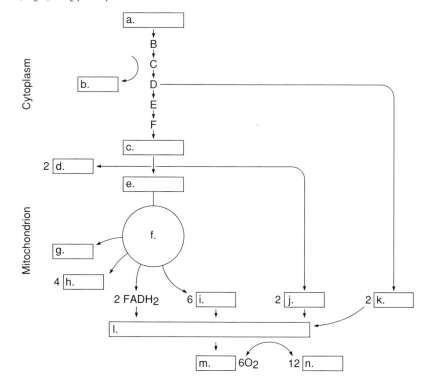

Concepts and Critical Thinking

1. *Photosynthesis and aerobic respiration permit a flow of energy and a recycling of matter.*

   Explain this concept by referring to figure 9.1.

2. *Solar energy first stored in nutrient molecules is transformed into a form that can be "spent" by the cell.*

   How are nutrient molecules utilized by cells as a source of energy?

3. *Certain metabolic pathways are virtually universal and thereby demonstrate the unity of living things.*

   In what way does glycolysis demonstrate the unity of living things and support the theory of evolution?

Selected Key Terms

acetyl-CoA A molecule made up of a two-carbon acetyl group attached to coenzyme A. The acetyl group enters the Krebs cycle for further oxidation. 145

aerobic Referring to a process in which oxygen is required. [Gk. *aer,* air] 139

aerobic respiration The aerobic breakdown of pyruvate within mitochondria; results in 34 ATP, carbon dioxide, and water. [Gk. *aer,* air] 144

cellular respiration Metabolic reactions that use the energy from carbohydrate or fatty acid or amino acid oxidation to produce ATP molecules; includes glycolysis, fermentation, and aerobic respiration. 139

electron transport system The passage of electrons along a series of carrier molecules from a higher to a lower energy level; the energy released is used for the synthesis of ATP. 124

fermentation The anaerobic breakdown of glucose that results in two ATP and products such as alcohol and lactate. [L. *ferment,* yeast] 142

glycolysis (gly-KAHL-uh-sis) An anaerobic pathway of metabolism converting glucose to pyruvate; resulting in a net gain of two ATP and two NADH molecules. [Gk. *glyc,* sweet, and *lys,* loosening] 140

Krebs cycle A cycle of reactions in mitochondria that begins with citric acid; it produces CO_2, ATP, NADH, and $FADH_2$; also called the citric acid cycle. 145

metabolic pool Metabolites that are the products of and/or the substrates for key reactions in cells allowing one type of molecule to be changed into another type, such as the conversion of carbohydrates to fats. [Gk. *metab,* change] 149

oxidative phosphorylation (fahs-for-ah-LAY-shun) The process by which ATP production is tied to an electron transport system that uses oxygen as the final receptor; occurs in mitochondria. [Gk. *phos,* light, and *phor,* movement] 146

oxygen debt The use of oxygen to metabolize lactate, which builds up due to anaerobic conditions, to pyruvate. 142

pyruvate (py-ROO-vayt) The end product of glycolysis; its further fate, involving fermentation or entry into a mitochondrion, depends on oxygen availability. 140

substrate-level phosphorylation (fahs-for-ah-LAY-shun) The process in which ATP is formed by transferring a phosphate from a metabolic substrate to ADP. [Gk. *phos,* light, and *phor,* movement] 140

transition reaction A reaction that oxidizes pyruvate with the release of carbon dioxide; results in acetyl-CoA and connects glycolysis to the Krebs cycle. 144

Suggested Readings for Part I

Becker, W. M., and Deamer, D. W. 1991. *The world of the cell.* 2d ed. Redwood City, Calif.: Benjamin/Cummings Publishing. Presents an overview of cell biology.

Bugg, C. E., et al. 1993. Drugs by design. *Scientific American* 269(6):92. Outlines an innovative approach to developing drugs, which has given rise to many promising new therapeutic agents.

Cross, P. C., and Mercer, K. L. 1993. *Cell and tissue ultrastructure: A functional perspective.* New York: W. H. Freeman and Company. Provides a detailed look at the ultrastructure and function of most body cells.

DeDuve, Christian. 1991. *Blueprint for a cell: The nature and origin of a cell.* Burlington, NC: Neil Patterson Publ. Defines life, origin of life, and elegant chemistry of cell processes; combines synthesis of modern views of cell chemistry with perspectives of evolutionary origin of those metabolic pathways; for advanced students.

Devlin, T. 1992. *Textbook of biochemistry: With clinical correlations.* 3d ed. New York: John Wiley & Sons. Presents the biochemistry of mammalian cells in detail, with emphasis on the processes of human disease.

Govindjee, and Coleman, W. J. 1990. How plants make oxygen. *Scientific American* 262(2):50. Discusses the mechanism that enables plants and some bacteria to make oxygen.

Hoffmann, R. 1993. How should chemists think? *Scientific American* 268(2):66. Concerns the chemist's role in the synthesis of useful vs. possibly useless, but esthetically pleasing, compounds.

Howells, M. R., et al. 1991. X-ray microscopes. *Scientific American* 264(2):88. X-ray microscopes have a better resolution than optical microscopes for seeing minute structures.

Lea, P., and Leegood, R. 1993. *Plant biochemistry and molecular biology.* Chichester, England: John Wiley & Sons. Gives an overview of plant metabolism.

Lichtman, J. W. 1994. Confocal microscopy. *Scientific American* 271(2):40. A confocal microscope focuses at different depths in an organic specimen.

Lienhard, G., et al. 1992. How cells absorb glucose. *Scientific American* 266(1):86. Explains the mechanism by which glucose is channeled through the plasma membrane.

Neher, E., and Sakmann, B. 1992. The patch clamp technique. *Scientific American* 266(3):44. Scientists can manipulate the pore-forming proteins that permit ions to enter or leave cells.

Olson, A. J., and Goodwill, D. S. 1992. Visualizing biological molecules. *Scientific American* 267(5):76. Computer images of biological molecules are important tools in protein research.

Sharon, N., and Lis, H. 1993. Carbohydrates in cell recognition. *Scientific American* 268(1):82. Discusses the role of carbohydrates in cell recognition and embryonic cellular organization.

Snyder, S. H., and Bredt, D. S. 1992. Biological roles of nitric oxide. *Scientific American* 266(5):68. Nitric oxide is a versatile, nonpersistent regulatory chemical in the body.

Stevens, A., and Lowe, J. 1992. *Histology.* London: Gower Medical Publishing. This text and color atlas discusses the relationship of human tissue structure to function, cell biology, and diseases.

Stossel, T. P. 1994. The machinery of cell crawling. *Scientific American* 271(3):54. Discusses how cells move.

Tedeschi, H. 1993. *Cell physiology.* 2d ed. Dubuque, Iowa: Wm. C. Brown Publishers. Examines the cell as an energy converter.

Welch, W. J. 1993. How cells respond to stress. *Scientific American* 268(5):56. Outlines mechanism by which cells protect themselves from heat damage, toxins, and disease.

Part I

THE PROCESSING OF INSULIN

An active insulin molecule is composed of two polypeptides linked by disulfide chemical bonds. It is known that the original protein, produced at the ribosomes, is a larger molecule than active insulin, which is secreted into the blood. Therefore, it is hypothesized that protein processing occurs within the organelles of the cell before active insulin is secreted.

To test the hypothesis, pancreatic tissue, which produces insulin, was subjected to autoradiography. Pancreatic tissue was immersed for a short time in a solution containing radioactive amino acids and then, at regular intervals, tissue was sectioned and placed on slides for autoradiography photography, a process which will show the location of radioactivity over time. Where do you predict the radioactivity will be as time elapses?

Prediction 1 Radioactive protein will appear in different organelles of the cell as time elapses.

Result 1 Within five minutes, the labeled protein moved to the inside of the endoplasmic reticulum (ER). After fifteen minutes, the labeled protein appeared in the Golgi apparatus, and after sixty minutes, it had moved to the secretory vesicles between the Golgi apparatus and the plasma membrane. These findings indicate that the protein moved from the ER to the Golgi apparatus and then to the secretory vesicles.

> **Question 1.** In keeping with these results, would an autoradiograph produced after sixty minutes show any sign of remaining radioactivity? Why or why not?

If the tissue had been exposed to radioactive amino acids for a considerable length of time (instead of a short time), how might the results differ from those described? These re-

sults tell us the pathway of protein movement, but they do not indicate where protein processing occurred. Where do you predict protein processing might occur?

Prediction 2 Protein processing might occur inside the ER or in the Golgi apparatus. Most likely, active insulin is in the secretory vesicles.

Result 2 Chemical analysis of organelle contents showed that a small amino acid chain is removed from the protein as soon as it enters the ER. The remaining molecule is called proinsulin.

> **Question 2.** Molecules that cross membranes usually combine with receptor sites in a lock-and-key manner. What might have been the purpose of the small amino acid chain that was removed in the ER?

Researchers then turned their attention to the vesicles. Using electron microscopy they observed vesicles coated with protein bristles close to the Golgi saccules, and uncoated vesicles were some distance away. Then they continued the autoradiography experiment. What do you predict regarding the movement of protein via these vesicles?

Prediction 3 Protein will be found first in the coated vesicles near the Golgi apparatus and then later in the uncoated vesicles some distance away.

Result 3 The results showed radioactivity first in the coated vesicles and then about thirty minutes later in the uncoated vesicles.

> **Question 3.** Is it possible that the protein might move from one type of vesicle to the other or that the coated vesicles might become uncoated vesicles? Why does the latter possibility seem more logical?

Another series of experiments was done to identify whether the protein in the vesicles was proinsulin or active insulin. Antibodies,

molecules that bind to specific molecules, were prepared for proinsulin or active insulin. Fine gold particles, which can be detected by electron microscopy, were linked to these antibodies. Pancreatic tissue slices were exposed to *either* proinsulin antibody or active insulin antibody and then examined using the electron microscope. What do you predict in regard to binding of the antibodies to the vesicles?

Prediction 4 Since coated vesicles precede uncoated vesicles and proinsulin precedes active insulin, proinsulin antibody will bind to coated vesicles and active insulin antibody will bind to uncoated vesicles.

Result 4 Results showed that proinsulin antibody binds only to the coated vesicles. Active insulin antibody binds only to the uncoated vesicles. These results strongly suggest that proinsulin is converted to active insulin as coated vesicles develop into uncoated vesicles.

> **Question 4.** **(a)** Why did the researchers prepare antibodies to proinsulin and active insulin? Why not just continue with radiography?
>
> **(b)** Why did the researchers choose to apply the two different types of antibodies separately? Why not apply them together?

The results of these experiments provide strong support for the hypothesis that protein processing occurs within the organelles of the cell before active insulin is secreted. Understanding the complete pathway of the formation of the active insulin molecule required a variety of techniques, each of which made an essential contribution to understanding the process.

Source: Orci, L., et al. 1988. The insulin factory. *Scientific American* 259(3):85.

Part II
GENETIC BASIS OF LIFE

The information that controls an organism's traits is stored in DNA, molecules that compose the genes located within chromosomes. The chromosomes duplicate prior to cell division when they are distributed so that each and every body cell contains a complete set. Sexual reproduction requires that the sex cells contain half the number of chromosomes, and there is a mechanism to ensure this.

Principles of inheritance include those that allow us to predict the chances that an offspring will inherit a particular characteristic from a parent. These apply especially to the breeding of plants and animals and the study of human genetic disorders. But to go further, and to control characteristics, it is necessary to understand how DNA and RNA function in protein synthesis. The human endeavor known as biotechnology is based on our newfound knowledge of nucleic acid biochemistry.

The principles of inheritance are central to understanding many other topics in biology—from the evolution and diversity of life to the reproduction and development of the organism. There is no topic in biology that stands alone; they are all interrelated!

Polar bear (*Ursus*) and cubs.

BIOLOGY AND TECHNOLOGY

Many of the figures and concepts discussed in *Biology,* fifth edition, are further explored in technology products. The following is a list of figures in part II that correlates to technology products.

A set of five videotapes contains 53 animations of physiological processes integral to the study of biology. These videotapes, entitled *Life Science Animation,* cover such topics as chemistry, genetics, and reproduction. A videotape icon appears in appropriate figure legends to alert the reader to these animations.

Explorations in Human Biology and *Explorations in Cell Biology, Metabolism, and Genetics* by George B. Johnson are interactive CD-ROMs with activities that can be used by an instructor in lecture and/or placed in a lab or resource center for student use. This interactive software consists of modules that cover key topics discussed in a biology course. The CD-ROMs are available for use with Macintosh and IBM Windows computers. A CD-ROM icon appears in appropriate figure legends to alert the reader to these activities.

Corresponding Figures		Videotape Concepts	CD-Rom Modules
10.3	Cell cycle	12. Mitosis	Mitosis: Regulation the Cell Cycle
10.4	Control of the cell cycle	12. Mitosis	Mitosis: Regulation the Cell Cycle
10.5	Prophase	12. Mitosis	Mitosis: Regulation the Cell Cycle
10.6	Metaphase	12. Mitosis	Mitosis: Regulation the Cell Cycle
10.7	Anaphase	12. Mitosis	Mitosis: Regulation the Cell Cycle
10.8	Telophase	12. Mitosis	Mitosis: Regulation the Cell Cycle
10.10	Plant cell mitosis	12. Mitosis; 50. Mitosis and Cell Division in Plants	Mitosis: Regulation the Cell Cycle
11.2	Overview of meiosis	13. Meiosis	Exploring Meiosis
11.3	Crossing-over occurs during meiosis I	14. Crossing Over	Exploring Meiosis
11.4	Chiasmata of chromosomal bivalent	14. Crossing Over	—
11.5	Phases of meiosis	13. Meiosis	Exploring Meiosis
11.6	Life cycle of humans	12. Mitosis; 13. Meiosis	Mitosis: Regulating the Cell Cycle
11.7	Comparison of meiosis and mitosis	12. Mitosis; 13. Meiosis	Mitosis: Regulating the Cell Cycle; Exploring Mitosis
11.8	Spermatogenesis and oogenesis in mammals	13. Meiosis; 19. Spermatogenesis; 20. Oogenesis	—
12.7	Dihybrid cross	—	Three-Point Genetic Cross
13.5	Polygenic inheritance	—	Three-Point Genetic Cross
P.205	Mapping the chromosomes	—	Making a Restriction Map; Constructing a Genetic Map
14.6	Pedigree chart for autosomal dominant disorders	—	Heredity in Families; Gene Segregation Within Families
14.7	Pedigree chart for autosomal recessive disorders	—	Heredity in Families; Gene Segregation Within Families; Cystic Fibrosis
14.9	Inheritance of sickle-cell disease	—	Heredity in Families
14B	Fragile-X syndrome inheritance	—	Heredity in Families
14.12	Cross involving X-linked allele	—	Heredity in Families
14.13	Pedigree chart for X-linked recessive disorders	—	Heredity in Families
15.6	Watson and Crick DNA model	—	Reading DNA
15.7	Semiconservative replication (simplified)	15. DNA Replication	Reading DNA
15.8	Meselson and Stahl DNA replication experiment	15. DNA Replication	—
15A	DNA replication (in depth)	15. DNA Replication	—
16.2	Sickle-cell disease in humans	—	How Proteins Function: Hemoglobin
16.5	Transcription of DNA	16. Transcription of a Gene	Gene Regulation; Reading DNA
16.6	RNA polymerase	16. Transcription of a Gene	Gene Regulation
16.8	Polysome structure	17. Protein Synthesis	—
16.9	Structure of tRNA molecule	17. Protein Synthesis	—
16.10	Translation	17. Protein Synthesis	—
16.11	Protein synthesis	16. Transcription of a Gene; 17. Protein Synthesis	Gene Regulation
17.1	*Lac* operon model	18. Regulation of *Lac* Operon	Gene Regulation
17.2	Levels of control of genetic expression	16. Transcription of a Gene; 17. Protein Synthesis	Gene Regulation
17.3	Nucleosome structure	16. Transcription of a Gene	—
17.5	Lampbrush chromosome	—	Gene Regulation
17.6	Transcription factors	16. Transcription of a Gene	—
17.7	Alternative splicing of identical primary mRNA transcripts	16. Transcription of a Gene	—
17.8	Posttranslational control	17. Protein Synthesis	—
17.11	Regulatory pathway/*ras* protein	—	Cell-Cell Interactions
18.3	PCR amplification and analysis	—	Making a Restriction Map; Constructing a Genetic Map; DNA Fingerprinting: You Be the Judge
18.4	RFLP analysis	—	Making a Restriction Map; Constructing a Genetic Map
18.9	Mapped human X chromosome	—	Making a Restriction Map; Constructing a Genetic Map

10

CELL REPRODUCTION: MITOSIS

Learning Objectives

Cell Division Occurs in All Organisms

- Relate cell division to the reproduction of unicellular organisms and the growth and repair of multicellular organisms. 158
- Name two general functions of cell division. 158
- Describe a duplicated eukaryotic chromosome. 159

How Eukaryotic Cells Cycle

- State the stages of the cell cycle, and describe what happens during each stage. 160
- Describe how the cell cycle is believed to be controlled, and relate this mechanism to the development of cancer. 160–61

How Eukaryotic Cells Divide

- Draw a series of diagrams illustrating the phases of mitosis in animal cells, and tell what happens during each phase; describe cytokinesis in animal cells. 162–64
- State at least one difference between plant and animal cell mitosis; describe cytokinesis in plant cells. 165

How Prokaryotes Reproduce

- Describe the prokaryotic chromosome and the process of binary fission. 166

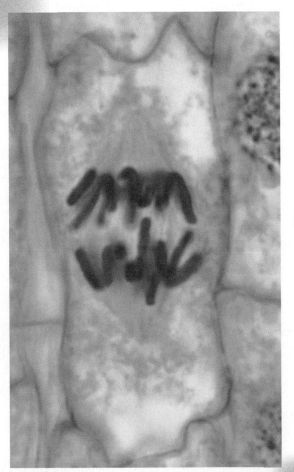

The mitotic spindle. During nuclear division, the chromosomes are attached to microtubules, which collectively assume the shape of a spindle. The spindle brings about the movement and distribution of a full set of daughter chromosomes to each of its poles.

20 μm

e have a tendency to think of reproduction in terms of multicellular organisms, but even multicellular organisms begin life as a single cell. New cells can come only from preexisting cells. The organization of a cell is such that it is very unlikely that the coming together of macromolecules would spontaneously produce a new cell. Instead, cell division accounts for *cell reproduction*, the process by which cells make a copy of themselves. Cell division is critically important in the life cycle of all organisms.

CELL DIVISION OCCURS IN ALL ORGANISMS

Cell division in unicellular (single-celled) organisms produces two new individuals that are like the parent. In multicellular organisms, cell division is a part of the growth process that produces the multicellular form we recognize as the organism (fig. 10.1). Cell division is also important in multicellular forms for renewal and repair. Our own body makes skin cells and about a million new red blood cells per minute to replace those that are worn out or damaged. In summary, then, the function of cell division varies according to the organism:

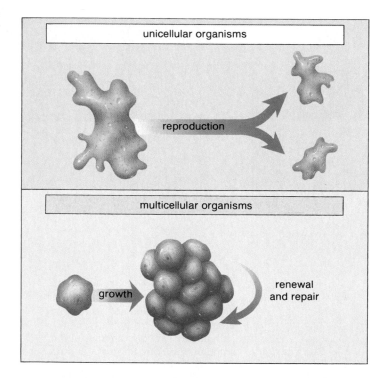

Cell Division Serves Two Functions

Cells grow larger and then they divide. What is the benefit of cell division in relation to growth? A small cell has a more adequate surface-area-to-volume ratio than a large cell. Everything that enters and exits a cell must cross the plasma membrane, and as the cell increases in size, there comes a point when the plasma

membrane surface area is not adequate to meet the needs of the cell. Cell division ensures that the surface-area-to-volume ratio will remain favorable.

Cell division helps cells maintain a favorable surface-area-to-volume relationship.

Cells are totipotent—each one contains a full complement of DNA (deoxyribonucleic acid), the genetic material. Simple cell division distributes the **chromosomes** [Gk. *chrom,* color, and *soma,* body], structures that contain the genetic material, in such a way that each and every cell gets a full number. Indeed, this chapter is principally about the way in which copies of chromosomes are passed from parent cell to daughter cells so that the daughter cells receive a copy of each and every chromosome. In this way the daughter cells receive a complete copy of the genes.

As a result of simple cell division, daughter cells have a complete copy of chromosomes and, therefore, genes.

Figure 10.1

Cell division and growth. Cell division maintains a favorable surface-area-to-volume relationship. It also follows growth and occurs in such a way that each cell is given a full complement of genes.

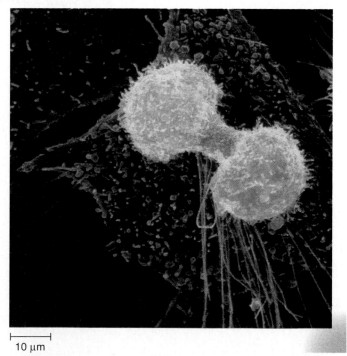

10 µm

The Chromosomes Are Numbered

When a eukaryotic cell is not undergoing division, the DNA (and associated proteins) within a nucleus is a tangled mass of thin threads called **chromatin** [Gk. *chrom*, color, and *tin*, stretch]. At the time of division, chromatin becomes highly coiled and condensed, and it is easy to see the individual chromosomes. In addition to chromatin, the nucleus contains at least one nucleolus that is attached to, and formed by, special regions of particular chromosomes. The nucleolus is involved in the production of ribosomes, which are small cytoplasmic particles involved in protein synthesis.

When the chromosomes are highly coiled and condensed at the time of cell division, it is possible to photograph and count them. Each species has a characteristic chromosomal number (table 10.1); for instance, human cells contain 46 chromosomes, corn has 20 chromosomes, and a crayfish has 200! This is called the full or **diploid (2n) number** [Gk. *dipl*, double, and *oid*, form] of chromosomes that is found in all cells of the body. The diploid number includes two chromosomes of each kind. Half the diploid number, called the **haploid (n) number** [Gk. *hapl*, single, and *oid*, form] of chromosomes, contains only one of each kind of chromosome. In the life cycle of many animals, only sperm and eggs have the haploid number of chromosomes.

> Each type eukaryote has a characteristic number of chromosomes in the nucleus of each cell.

Cell division in eukaryotes involves nuclear division (karyokinesis) and **cytokinesis** [Gk. *cyt*, cell, and *kine*, movement], which is division of the cytoplasm. Somatic, or body, cells undergo **mitosis** [Gk. *mito*, thread, and *sis*, the act of]—that is, nuclear division in which the chromosomal number stays constant. A 2n nucleus divides to produce daughter nuclei that are also 2n. Mitosis is the type of nuclear division that is involved in growth and repair of the body. Before nuclear division takes place, DNA replicates; thereafter, each chromosome is duplicated and has two identical parts called **sister chromatids** (fig. 10.2). Sister chromatids are genetically identical; that is, they contain exactly the same genes. Sister chromatids are constricted and attached to each other at a region called the **centromere** [Gk. *centr*, center, and *mer*, part]. During nuclear division the centromeres divide, and in this way each duplicated chromosome gives rise to two daughter chromosomes. These chromosomes, which have only one chromatid, are distributed equally to the daughter cells. In this way, each daughter cell gets a copy of each chromosome.

> DNA replicates prior to mitosis, nuclear division in which the chromosomal number stays constant.

Figure 10.2

Duplicated chromosomes. A duplicated chromosome contains two sister chromatids, each with copies of the same genes. **a.** Electron micrograph of a highly coiled and compacted chromosome, typical of a nucleus about to divide. **b.** A chromosome that is not condensed. One chromatid is indicated by the box. The chromatids are held together at a region called the centromere.

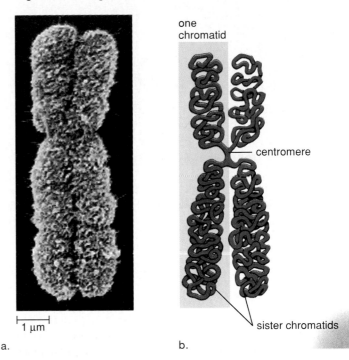

one chromatid

centromere

sister chromatids

1 μm

a.

b.

Table 10.1

Diploid Chromosomal Number of Some Eukaryotes

Type of Organism	Name of Organism	Chromosomal Number
Fungi	*Aspergillus nidulans* (mold)	8
	Neurospora crassa (mold)	14
	Saccharomyces cerevisiae (yeast)	34
Plants	*Vicia faba* (broad bean)	12
	Zea mays (corn)	20
	Solanum tuberosum (potato)	48
	Nicotiana tabacum (tobacco)	48
Animals	*Musca domestica* (housefly)	12
	Rana pipiens (frog)	26
	Felis domesticus (cat)	38
	Homo sapiens (human)	46
	Pan troglodytes (chimp)	48
	Equus caballus (horse)	64
	Gallus gallus (chicken)	78
	Canis familiaris (dog)	78

Figure 10.3

The cell cycle consists of four stages (G_1, S for synthesis, G_2, and M for mitosis). The length of the different stages varies both among species and among different cell types in the same individual. The approximate lengths of the phases for the broad bean (*Vicia faba*) and humans (*Homo sapiens*) are given.

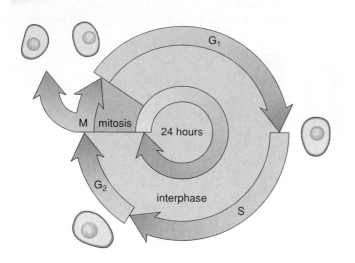

Stage	Main Events	Length of time (hours)	
		Vicia faba	*Homo sapiens* (cultured fibroblasts)
G_1	Organelles begin to double in number	4.9	6.3
S	Replication of DNA	7.5	7.0
G_2	Synthesis of proteins	4.9	2.0
M	Mitosis	2.0	0.7
	Total:	19.3	16.0

(G_1, S, and G_2 constitute Interphase.)

HOW EUKARYOTIC CELLS CYCLE

By the 1870s, microscopy could provide detailed and accurate descriptions of chromosomal movements during mitosis, but there was no knowledge of cellular events between divisions. Because there was little visible activity between divisions, this period of time was dismissed as a resting state termed **interphase** [L. *inter*, between, and Gk. *phase*, appearance]. When it was discovered in the 1950s that DNA replication occurs during interphase, the cell cycle concept was proposed.

Cells grow and divide during a cycle that has four stages (fig. 10.3). The entire cell division stage, including both mitosis and cytokinesis, is termed the *M stage* (M = mitosis). The period of DNA synthesis when replication occurs is termed the *S stage* (S = synthesis) of the cycle. The proteins associated with DNA in eukaryotic chromosomes are also synthesized during this stage. There are two other stages of the cycle. The period of time prior to the S stage is termed the G_1 *stage*, and the period of time prior to the M stage is termed the G_2 *stage*. At first, not much was known about these stages, and they were thought of as G = gap stages. Now we know that during the G_1 stage, the cell grows in size and the cellular organelles increase in number. During the G_2 stage, various metabolic events occur in preparation for mitosis. Some biologists today prefer the designation G = growth for these two G stages. In any case, interphase consists of G_1, S, and G_2 stages.

> Cells undergo a cycle that includes the G_1, S, G_2, and M stages.

How the Cycle Is Controlled

Some cells, such as skin cells, divide continuously throughout the life of the organism. Other cells, such as skeletal muscle cells and nerve cells, are arrested in the G_1 stage. If the nucleus from one of these cells is placed in the cytoplasm of an S-stage cell, it starts to finish the cell cycle. Cardiac muscle cells are arrested in the G_2 stage. If this type cell is fused with a cell undergoing mitosis, it too starts to undergo mitosis. It appears, then, that there are stimulatory substances that cause the cell to proceed through two critical checkpoints:

$$G_1 \text{ stage} \longrightarrow S \text{ stage}$$
$$G_2 \text{ stage} \longrightarrow M \text{ stage}$$

Over the past few years biologists have made remarkable progress in identifying the molecules that drive the cell cycle. Many groups, some of whom worked with frog eggs, others with yeast cells, and still others who used cell cultures as their experimental material, have shown that the activity of enzymes known as *cyclin-dependent kinases* (*Cdks*) regulates the passage of cells through these checkpoints. A **kinase** is an enzyme that removes a phosphate group from ATP (adenosine triphosphate, the form of chemical energy used by cells) and adds it to another protein. The phosphorylated molecule, which may also be a kinase, is now activated. Evidently, activation by kinases is a common way by which the cell can turn on various metabolic pathways.

The kinases involved in the cell cycle are called cyclin-dependent because they are activated when they combine with a protein called a **cyclin.** Cyclins are so named because their quantity is not constant. They increase in amount until they combine with a kinase, but this is a suicidal act because now the kinase activates various enzymes, one of which destroys the cyclin.

10-4

Figure 10.4

Control of the cell cycle. At two critical checkpoints a kinase combines with a cyclin, and this moves the cell cycle forward. Just before the S stage, S-kinase combines with S-cyclin and synthesis (replication) of DNA takes place; and just before the M stage, M-kinase combines with M-cyclin and mitosis occurs. When kinases phosphorylate proteins, they are activated and produce effects appropriate to the particular stage.

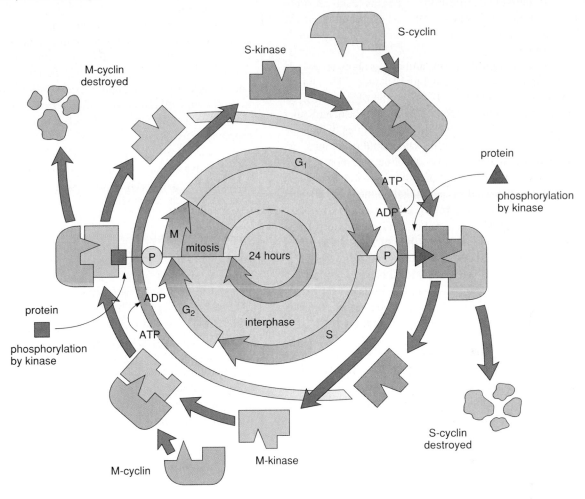

Figure 10.4 shows how the process works. In the diagram, S-kinase is capable of starting the process of DNA replication after it has combined with S-cyclin. S-cyclin is now destroyed and S-kinase is no longer active. M-kinase is capable of turning on mitosis after it has combined with M-cyclin. It is known that this particular kinase starts the process of (1) chromosome condensation, (2) nuclear envelope breakdown, and (3) spindle assembly. (The spindle is the structure involved in chromosome movement during mitosis.) Now M-cyclin is destroyed.

Until recently, the mechanics of the cell cycle and the causes of cancer were thought to be distantly related. Now they appear to be intimately related. For example, oncogenes are cancer-causing genes, and it is possible that they code for cyclins that have gone awry. Growth factors are molecules that attach to plasma membrane receptors and thereby bring about cell growth. Ordinarily, a cyclin might combine with its kinase only when a growth factor is present. But a cyclin that has gone awry might combine with its kinase even when a growth factor is not present. The result would be a tumor. On the other hand, tumor suppressor genes usually function to prevent cancer from occurring. It has been shown that the product of one major tumor-suppressor gene (*p53*) brings about the production of a protein that can combine with a cyclin-kinase complex and prevent that kinase from becoming active. There is much excitement in the scientific community because the work of cell biologists and geneticists is coming together to provide long-sought answers to certain questions in biology. And they are finding that the basic protein machinery of the cell cycle is similar in many different types of organisms.

> Kinases are activated by combination with a cyclin at two critical checkpoints in the cell cycle: the beginning of the S phase and the M phase.

HOW EUKARYOTIC CELLS DIVIDE

Mitosis is *division of the eukaryotic nucleus so that the daughter cell nuclei acquire the same number and kinds of chromosomes as the parent cell nucleus.* Before mitosis begins, each chromosome is duplicated and is composed of two chromatids; at the completion of mitosis each chromosome is composed of a single chromatid once more.

During mitosis, the **spindle** forms and brings about an orderly distribution of chromosomes to the daughter cell nuclei. The spindle contains many fibers, each composed of a bundle of microtubules. Microtubules are hollow cylinders found in the cytoplasm and other structures such as flagella and centrioles. Microtubules, which are made up of the protein tubulin, assemble when tubulin subunits join and disassemble when tubulin subunits become free once more. Microtubules of the cytoskeleton which is a network of interconnected filaments and tubules begin to disassemble when the spindle fibers begin forming, probably providing material for spindle formation.

The **centrosome** [Gk. *centr,* center, and *soma,* body], the main microtubule organizing center of the cell, has divided before mitosis begins. It's believed that these centrosomes are responsible for organizing the spindle. Each centrosome contains a pair of barrel-shaped organelles called **centrioles** [Gk. *centr,* center]; however, the fact that plant cells lack centrioles suggests that centrioles are not required for spindle formation.

How Animal Cells Divide

Mitosis, also called *karyokinesis,* is a continuous process that is arbitrarily divided into five phases for convenience of description. These phases are prophase, prometaphase, metaphase, anaphase, and telophase.

Prophase

It is apparent during *prophase* that nuclear division is about to occur because the chromatin has condensed and the chromosomes are visible structures (fig. 10.5). As the chromosomes continue to compact, the nucleolus disappears and the nuclear envelope fragments.

The already duplicated chromosomes are composed of two sister chromatids held together at a centromere. Counting the number of centromeres in diagrammatic drawings gives the number of chromosomes for the cell depicted. During prophase, the chromosomes have no apparent orientation within the cell. However, specialized structures called *kinetochores* develop on either side of each centromere, and these are important to future chromosome orientation.

The spindle begins to assemble as pairs of centrosomes migrate away from one another. Short microtubules radiate out in a starlike **aster** [Gk. *aster,* star] from the pair of centrioles located in each centrosome.

Prometaphase

As prometaphase (not depicted) begins, the spindle consists of poles, asters, and fibers, which are bundles of parallel microtubules. An important event during prometaphase is the attachment of the chromosomes to the spindle and their movement as they align at the metaphase plate (equator) of the spindle. The kinetochores of sister chromatids capture spindle fibers coming from opposite poles. Such spindle fibers are called *kinetochore fibers.* In response to attachment by first one kinetochore and then the other, a chromosome moves first toward one pole and then toward the other until the chromosome is aligned at the metaphase plate of the spindle.

Figure 10.5

Prophase drawing and micrograph of whitefish (animal) embryonic cell.
- chromatin condenses and chromosomes are visible
- chromosomes are duplicated
- nucleolus disappears
- nuclear envelope fragments
- centrosomes migrate away from each other
- spindle fibers are assembling

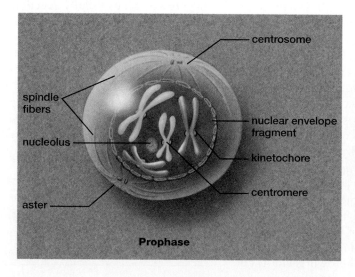
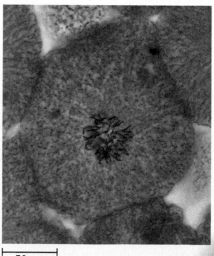

50 µm

Metaphase

During metaphase, the chromosomes, attached to kinetochore fibers, are aligned at the metaphase plate (fig. 10.6). There are many nonattached spindle fibers called *polar fibers,* some of which reach beyond the metaphase plate and overlap.

Anaphase

At the start of *anaphase,* the centromere of each duplicated chromosome divides (fig. 10.7). Daughter chromosomes, each with a centromere and single chromatid, begin to move toward opposite poles.

What accounts for the movement of the daughter chromosomes? It's known that the motor molecule dynein present in flagella is responsible for the movement of microtubules in flagella. Dynein has also been found in kinetochores and it's thought that these motor molecules assist chromosome movement along the microtubules of kinetochore fibers. As the daughter chromosomes move toward their respective poles, the kinetochore fibers disassemble at the ends closest to the kinetochore:

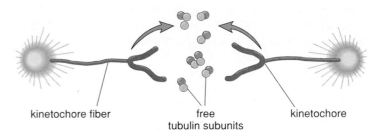

kinetochore fiber   free tubulin subunits   kinetochore

During anaphase the spindle also lengthens, placing greater distance between the poles. The polar fibers, which overlap at the metaphase plate of the spindle, are believed to be involved in this process. Again, motor molecules most likely allow the polar fibers to slide past one another, perhaps in relation to components of the cytoskeleton.

Figure 10.6

Metaphase drawing and micrograph of whitefish (animal) embryonic cell.
- nuclear envelope fragmentation is complete
- spindle formation is complete
- duplicated chromosomes are aligned at metaphase plate
- kinetochore fibers point to opposite poles

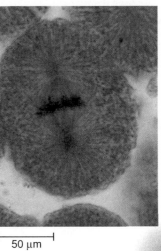

50 μm

Figure 10.7

Anaphase drawing and micrograph of whitefish (animal) embryonic cell.
- centromeres divide
- spindle lengthens
- diploid set of daughter chromosomes move toward each pole
- cytokinesis begins

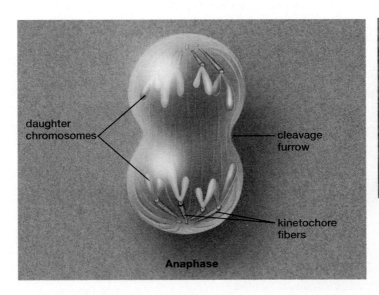

daughter chromosomes

cleavage furrow

kinetochore fibers

Anaphase

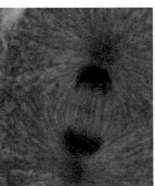

20 μm

Telophase

During *telophase*, the spindle disappears as new nuclear envelopes form around the daughter chromosomes (fig. 10.8). Each daughter nucleus contains the same number and kinds of chromosomes as the original parent cell. Remnants of the polar fibers are still visible between the two nuclei.

The chromosomes become more diffuse chromatin once again, and a nucleolus appears in each daughter nucleus. Cytokinesis is nearly complete, and soon there will be two individual daughter cells.

> Telophase is recognized by two clusters of daughter chromosomes within newly forming daughter nuclei.

Cytokinesis in Animal Cells

Cytokinesis, or cytoplasmic cleavage, usually accompanies mitosis. A cleavage furrow, which is an indentation of the membrane between the two daughter nuclei, begins as anaphase draws to a close. The cleavage furrow deepens when a band of actin filaments, called the contractile ring, slowly forms a constriction between the two daughter cells. The action of the contractile ring can be likened to pulling a drawstring ever tighter about the middle of a balloon. As the drawstring is pulled tight, the balloon constricts in the middle.

A narrow bridge between the two cells can be seen during telophase, and then the contractile ring continues to separate the cytoplasm until there are two daughter cells (fig. 10.9).

> Cytokinesis in animal cells is accomplished by a furrowing process.

Figure 10.8

Telophase drawing and micrograph of whitefish (animal) embryonic cell.
- chromosomes uncoil to chromatin
- nuclear envelopes reform
- nucleoli reappear
- daughter nuclei are diploid
- cytokinesis is nearly complete

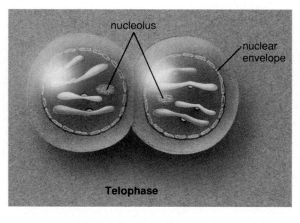

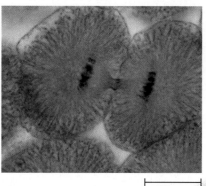

Figure 10.9

Cytokinesis in an animal cell. A single cell becomes two cells by a furrowing process. A contractile ring composed of actin filaments gradually gets smaller, and the cleavage furrow pinches the cell into two cells.

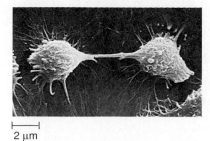

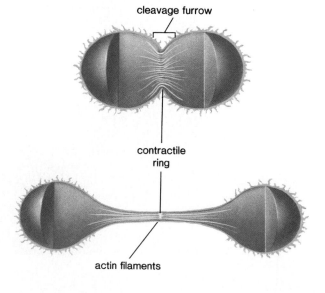

How Plant Cells Divide

Figure 10.10 illustrates mitosis in plant cells. Note that there are exactly the same stages in plant cells as in animals cells. As mentioned previously, plant cells have a centrosome, but there are no centrioles, and asters do not form during cell division.

Certain plant tissue, called meristematic tissue, retains the ability to divide throughout the life of a plant. Meristematic tissue is found in the root tip and shoot tip of stems. Lateral meristem accounts for the ability of trees to grow wider each growing season.

Cytokinesis in Plant Cells

Cytokinesis in plant cells occurs by a process different from that seen in animal cells. The rigid cell wall that surrounds plant cells does not permit cytokinesis by furrowing. Instead, the Golgi appa-

ratus, a membranous organelle in cells, produces membranous sacs called vesicles, which move along microtubules to the midpoint between the two daughter nuclei. These vesicles fuse, forming a **cell plate.** Their membrane completes the plasma membrane for both cells. They also release molecules that signal the formation of plant cell walls. These walls are later strengthened by the addition of cellulose fibrils.

> A spindle forms during mitosis in plant cells, but there are no centrioles or asters. Cytokinesis in plant cells involves the formation of a cell plate.

Figure 10.10

Plant cell mitosis. Note the absence of centrioles and asters and the presence of the cell wall. In telophase, a cell plate develops between the two daughter cells. The cell plate marks the boundary of the new daughter cells, where new plasma membrane and a new cell wall will form for each cell.

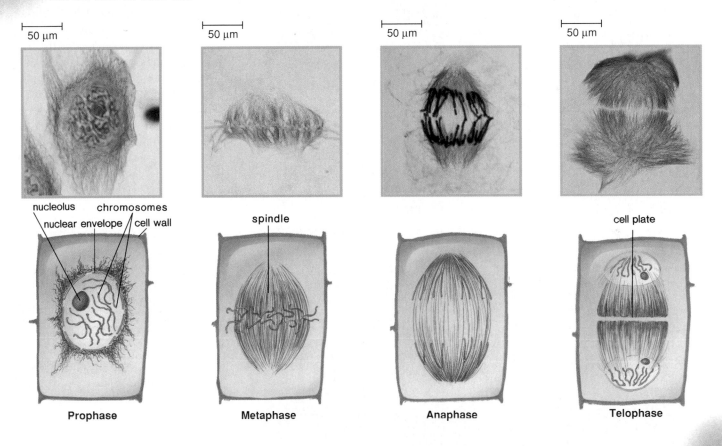

nucleolus   chromosomes
nuclear envelope / cell wall

spindle

cell plate

Prophase   Metaphase   Anaphase   Telophase

HOW PROKARYOTES REPRODUCE

Prokaryotic cells lack a nucleus and other membranous organelles found in eukaryotic cells. Prokaryotes include only the bacteria, which are usually unicellular.

The Chromosome Is Singular

Prokaryotes have a single chromosome that is tightly coiled to fit inside the cell. In electron micrographs the chromosome appears as an electron-dense, irregularly-shaped region called the **nucleoid** [L. *nucle,* nucleus, and Gk. *oid,* form], which is not enclosed by a membrane. When stretched out, the chromo- some is seen to be a circular loop attached to the inside of the plasma membrane. Its length may be about five hundred times the length of the cell, which is why it needs to be coiled inside the cell.

The chromosome of a typical bacterial cell is not like the eukaryotic chromosome because it lacks associated proteins. It consists simply of the genetic material, DNA.

> **The prokaryotic chromosome is a single loop of DNA that is tightly coiled into a region called the nucleoid.**

Division Is by Fission

Asexual reproduction requires a single parent, and the offspring are identical to the parent because they contain the same genes. Prokaryotes reproduce asexually by cell division. The process is termed **binary fission** [L. *bi,* two, and *fiss,* cleft] because division (fission) produces two (binary) daughter cells that are identical to the original parent cell. Before division takes place, the DNA is replicated so that there are two chromosomes attached to the inside of the plasma membrane. Following replication, the two chromosomes separate by an elongation of the cell that pulls the chromosomes apart. When the cell is approximately twice its original length, the plasma membrane grows inward and a cell wall forms, dividing the cell into two approximately equal portions (fig. 10.11).

> **Asexual reproduction in prokaryotes is by binary fission. DNA replicates and the two resulting chromosomes separate as the cell elongates. Unicellular eukaryotes reproduce asexually by mitosis. Mitosis and not binary fission involves the formation of a spindle.**

Figure 10.11

Binary fission. In electron micrographs, it is possible to observe a bacterium dividing to become two bacteria. The diagrams depict chromosomal duplication and distribution. First DNA replicates, and as the plasma membrane lengthens, the two chromosomes separate. Upon fission, each bacterium has its own chromosome.

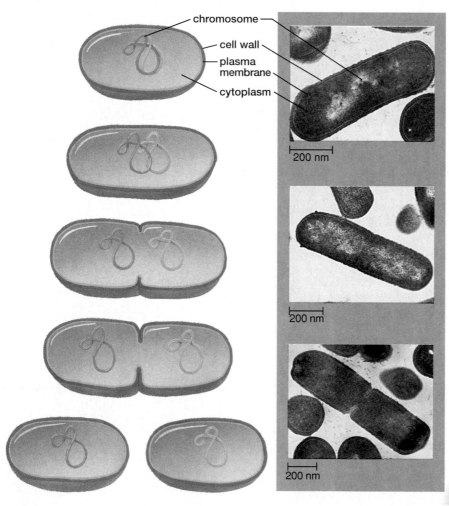

chromosome
cell wall
plasma membrane
cytoplasm

200 nm

200 nm

200 nm

1. In unicellular organisms, cell division allows the organism to reproduce. In multicellular organisms, cell division is necessary for growth and repair of tissues.

2. Cell division keeps the surface area-to-volume ratio at a level appropriate to the life of the cell. It also ensures that daughter cells have a complete copy of chromosomes and, therefore, genes.

3. Between nuclear divisions, the chromosomes are not distinct and are collectively called chromatin. Each eukaryote species has a characteristic number of chromosomes. The total number is called the diploid number, and half this number is the haploid number.

4. Among eukaryotes, cell division involves nuclear division (karyokinesis) and division of the cytoplasm (cytokinesis). Mitosis is nuclear division in which the chromosomal number stays constant.

5. Replication of DNA precedes cell division. The duplicated chromosomes are each composed of two sister chromatids held together at a centromere.

6. The cell cycle has four stages. During the G_1 stage the organelles increase in number; during the S stage, DNA replication occurs; during the G_2 stage, various proteins are synthesized; and during the M stage, mitosis occurs.

7. Biologists have made great strides in understanding how the cell cycle is controlled. Kinases that combine with cyclins become activated and regulate the passage of cells through the various stages. Two critical checkpoints in particular are known: the passage from the G_1 to the S stage, and the passage from the G_2 stage to the M stage.

8. Mitosis, nuclear division by which the daughter nuclei receive the same number and kinds of chromosomes as the parent cell, has five phases, which are described here for animal cells.

   Prophase—duplicated chromosomes are distinct; the nucleolus is disappearing; the nuclear envelope is fragmenting; and the spindle is forming between centrosomes. Asters radiate from the centrioles within the centrosomes.

   Prometaphase—the kinetochores of sister chromatids attach to spindle fibers extending from opposite poles. The chromosomes move back and forth until they are aligned at the metaphase plate.

   Metaphase—the spindle is fully formed and the duplicated chromosomes are aligned at the metaphase plate.

   Anaphase—daughter chromosomes move toward the poles. Most likely motor molecules, perhaps a dynein, are involved in chromosomal movement. Cytokinesis by furrowing begins.

   Telophase—nuclear envelopes reform, chromosomes begin changing back to chromatin, the nucleoli reappear, and

the spindle disappears. Cytokinesis completes the furrowing process that divides the cytoplasm.

9. Mitosis in plant cells is somewhat different from mitosis in animal cells because plant cells lack centrioles and, therefore, asters. Even so, the mitotic spindle forms and the same five phases are observed. Cytokinesis in plant cells involves the formation of a cell plate from which the plasma membrane and cell wall are completed.

10. The prokaryotic chromosome is a single long loop of DNA attached to the inside of the plasma membrane. Binary fission involves replication of DNA, followed by an elongation of the cell that pulls the chromosomes apart. Ingrowth of the plasma membrane and formation of new cell wall material divide the cell in two.

11. Binary fission (in unicellular prokaryotes) and mitosis (in unicellular eukaryotic protoctists and fungi) allow organisms to reproduce asexually. Mitosis in multicellular eukaryotes is primarily for the purpose of growth and repair of tissues.

Writing Across the Curriculum

In order to practice writing skills, students should write out the answers to any or all of the study questions and the critical thinking questions. The study questions are sequenced in the same order as the text. Answers to the objective questions, and suggested answers to the critical thinking questions, are in appendix D.

> **Study Questions**

1. What benefits are associated with cell division?   158

2. Describe the eukaryotic chromosome and the significance of the duplicated chromosome.   158

3. Describe the cell cycle, including a description of interphase.   160

4. How are the two critical checkpoints in the cell cycle controlled? How is this control mechanism apparently related to the development of cancer?   160–61

5. Define the following words: chromosome, chromatin, chromatid, centriole, cytokinesis, centromere, and kinetochore.   158–62

6. Describe the events that occur during the phases of mitosis.   162–64

7. By what mechanism do daughter chromosomes apparently move toward opposite poles of the spindle?   163

8. Contrast cytokinesis in animal cells with that in plant cells.   164–65

9. Describe the prokaryotic chromosome and the process of binary fission.   166

10. Why are binary fission in prokaryotes and mitosis in unicellular eukaryotes forms of asexual reproduction?   166

Objective Questions

1. What feature in prokaryotes substitutes for the spindle action in eukaryotes?
   a. centrioles with asters
   b. fission instead of cytokinesis
   c. elongation of plasma membrane
   d. looped DNA

2. How does a prokaryotic chromosome differ from a eukaryotic chromosome? A prokaryotic chromosome
   a. is shorter and fatter.
   b. is a single loop of DNA.
   c. never replicates.
   d. All of these are correct.

3. The diploid number of chromosomes
   a. is the 2n number.
   b. was in the parent cell and is in the two daughter cells following mitosis.
   c. varies according to the particular organism.
   d. All of these are correct.

For questions 4–6, match the descriptions that follow to the terms in the key.

Key:
   a. centriole   c. chromosome
   b. chromatid   d. centromere

4. point of attachment for sister chromatids

5. found at poles in the center of asters

6. coiled and condensed chromatin

7. If a parent cell has fourteen chromosomes prior to mitosis, how many chromosomes will the daughter cells have?
   a. twenty-eight
   b. fourteen
   c. seven
   d. any number between seven and twenty-eight

8. In which phase of mitosis are the chromosomes moving toward the poles?
   a. prophase   c. anaphase
   b. metaphase   d. telophase

9. Interphase
   a. is the same as prophase, metaphase, anaphase, and telophase.
   b. includes stages G_1, S, and G_2.
   c. requires the use of polar fibers and kinetochore fibers.
   d. rarely occurs.

10. Cytokinesis
    a. is mitosis in plants.
    b. requires the formation of a cell plate in plant cells.
    c. is the longest part of the cell cycle.
    d. is half a chromosome.

11. Label this diagram of prophase.

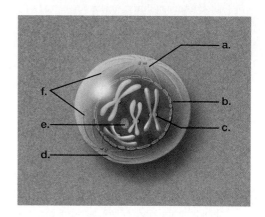

Concepts and Critical Thinking

1. *All cells come only from preexisting cells (the principle of biogenesis).*
   Cells can grow and reproduce. How is cell growth related to cell reproduction?

2. *Cells are totipotent—that is, each body cell contains a full complement of genes.*
   Explain why skin cells arise only from skin cells, and so forth for other tissues.

3. *Most eukaryotic cells reproduce by means of mitosis.*
   For the cell, what are the benefits of dividing by mitosis?

Selected Key Terms

binary fission Splitting of a parent cell into two daughter cells; serves as an asexual form of reproduction in bacteria. [L. *bi,* two, and *fiss,* cleft]   166

cell plate The structure across a dividing plant cell that signals the location of new plasma membranes and cell walls.   165

centriole Cell organelle, existing in pairs, that possibly helps organize a mitotic spindle for chromosome movement during animal cell division.   162

centromere (SEN-truh-mir) A constriction where sister chromatids of a chromosome are held together. [Gk. *centr,* center, and *mer,* part]   159

centrosome (SEN-truh-sohm) The central microtubule organizing center of cells consisting of granular material. In animal cells, it contains two centrioles. [Gk. *centr,* center, and *soma,* body]   162

chromatin (KROH-mut-un) The mass of DNA and associated proteins observed within a nucleus that is not dividing. [Gk. *chrom,* color, and *tin,* stretch]   159

cyclin A protein that cycles in quantity as the cell cycle progresses; combines with and activates the kinases that function to promote the events of the cycle.   160

cytokinesis (syt-oh-kuh-NEE-sus) The division of the cytoplasm following mitosis and meiosis. [Gk. *cyt,* cell, and *kine,* movement]   159

interphase The stage of the cell cycle during which DNA synthesis occurs and the nucleus is not actively dividing. [L. *inter,* between, and Gk. *phase,* appearance]   160

kinase (KY-nays) Any one of several enzymes that phosphorylate their substrates.   160

mitosis (my-TOH-sus) A process in which a parent nucleus produces two daughter nuclei, each having the same number and kinds as the parent nucleus. [Gk. *mito,* thread, and *sis,* the act of]   159

sister chromatid (KROH-muh-tud) One of two genetically identical chromosomal units that are the result of DNA replication and are attached to each other at the centromere.   159

spindle A microtubule structure that brings about chromosomal movement during cell division.   162

11

CELL REPRODUCTION: MEIOSIS

Learning Objectives

Halving the Chromosomal Number

- State the general role of meiosis in plant, animal, and fungal life cycles.   170
- Describe and state the significance of homologous chromosome pairs.   170

How Meiosis Occurs

- Give an overview of the process of meiosis and its stages, emphasizing the main events.   172
- Describe synapsis (bivalent formation), and tell how crossing-over occurs.   172–73

Meiosis Has Phases

- Describe the phases of meiosis I and meiosis II in detail.   174–75

Viewing the Human Life Cycle

- Describe the human life cycle, and compare the process of meiosis to that of mitosis.   176–77
- Compare the process of spermatogenesis to that of oogenesis.   178

Meiosis Is Important

- Describe the manner in which sexual reproduction brings about variation and contributes to the evolutionary process.   179

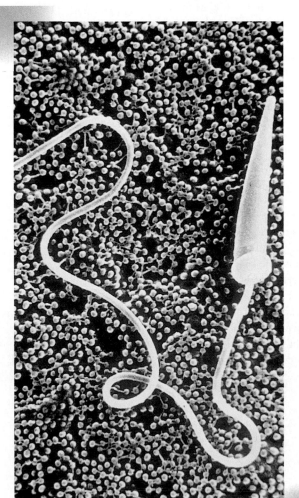

Sea star sperm on egg. Production of sperm and egg includes the process of meiosis, the type of cell division that reduces the chromosome number.

1 µm

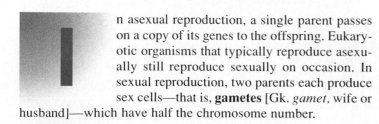

In asexual reproduction, a single parent passes on a copy of its genes to the offspring. Eukaryotic organisms that typically reproduce asexually still reproduce sexually on occasion. In sexual reproduction, two parents each produce sex cells—that is, **gametes** [Gk. *gamet,* wife or husband]—which have half the chromosome number.

HALVING THE CHROMOSOMAL NUMBER

Gamete formation and then fusion of gametes to form a cell called a *zygote* are integral parts of **sexual reproduction** (fig. 11.1). Obviously, if the gametes contained the same number of chromosomes as the body cells, the number of chromosomes would double with each new generation. Within a few generations, the cells of the individual would be nothing but chromosomes! The early cytologists (biologists who study cells) realized this, and Pierre-Joseph van Beneden, a Belgian, was gratified to find in 1883 that the sperm and the egg of the worm *Ascaris* each contained only two chromosomes, while the zygote and subsequent embryonic cells always have four chromosomes.

Life Cycles Vary

The term *life cycle* refers to all the reproductive events that occur from one generation to the next similar generation. A zygote always has the full or **diploid (2n) number** [Gk. *dipl,* double, and *oid,* form] of chromosomes. *Mitosis* is the type of nuclear division that maintains a constant chromosomal number. **Meiosis** [Gk. *mei,* less, and *sis,* the act of], the topic of this chapter, is the type of nuclear division that reduces the chromosomal number from the diploid (2n) number to the haploid (n) number. The **haploid (n) number** [Gk. *hapl,* single, and *oid,* form] of chromosomes is half the diploid number.

Meiosis occurs at different points during the life cycle of various kinds of organisms (fig. 11.1). In animals, it occurs during the production of the gametes. In plants, meiosis produces spores that divide mitotically to become a haploid generation. The haploid generation produces the gametes. In certain fungi, like black bread mold and also some algae, meiosis occurs directly after zygote formation, and the organism is always haploid. This organism produces the gamete nuclei.

Notice in figure 11.1 that all three types of life cycles have both a diploid stage and a haploid stage. In animals, the adult is always diploid and the haploid stage consists only of the gametes. In plants, the haploid stage, which produces the gametes, may be more substantial or less substantial than the diploid stage. In fungi (and some algae) only the zygote is diploid and the gamete nuclei are derived from an organism whose cells contain haploid nuclei.

Chromosomes Come in Homologous Pairs

In a diploid cell, the chromosomes occur in pairs. The members of each pair are called **homologous chromosomes** or **homologues** [Gk. *homo,* alike]. The homologues look alike; they have the same length and centromere position.

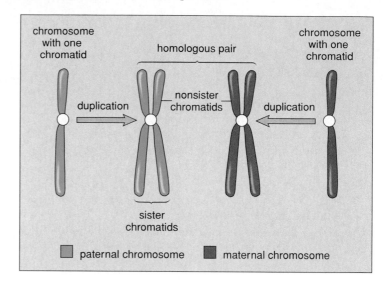

When stained, homologues have a similar banding pattern because they contain the same types of genes. If a gene for length of fingers occurs at a particular locus (location) on one homologue, it also occurs at the same locus on the other homologue. In the one instance, however, the gene might call for short fingers and in the other for long fingers.

The chromosomes in the diagram are duplicated as they would be just before nuclear division. When duplicated, a chromosome is composed of two identical parts called sister chromatids. The sister chromatids are held together at a region called the centromere. Notice that nonsister chromatids do not share the same centromere.

Why does the zygote with the diploid number of chromosomes contain homologous pairs? One member of each homologous pair was inherited from the male parent and the other was inherited from the female parent by way of the gametes. We will see that gametes contain one of each type of chromosome—derived from either the paternal or maternal homologue.

The zygote, which is always diploid, contains homologous chromosomes. Gametes are haploid due to meiosis, which occurs at varied times according to the life cycle.

Figure 11.1

Life cycles of an animal, a plant, and a fungus. While meiosis always reduces the number of chromosomes, it occurs at a different point in each life cycle. Therefore, in animals, the haploid stage consists only of the gametes; in plants, there is both a diploid and a haploid adult; and in fungi, the adult is always haploid because the zygote undergoes meiosis.

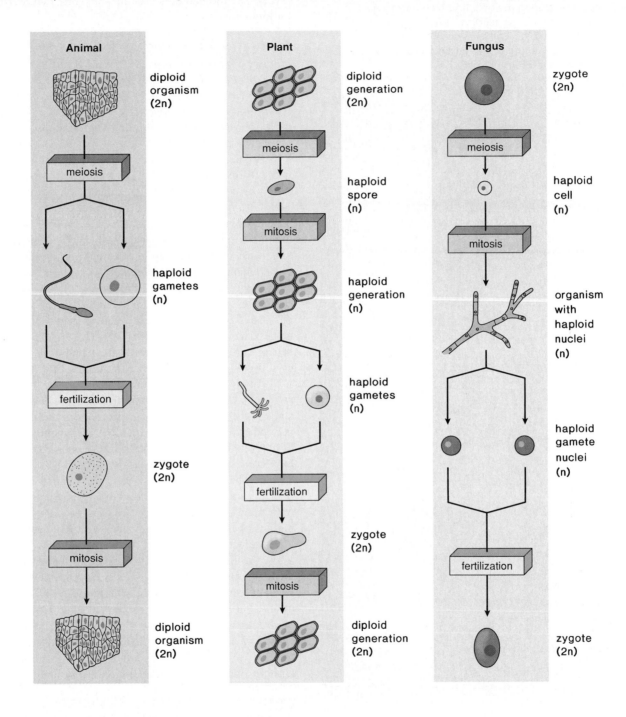

Figure 11.2

Overview of meiosis. Following DNA replication, each chromosome is duplicated. During meiosis I, the homologous chromosomes first pair, forming bivalents, and then *they* separate. During meiosis II, the *centromeres divide* and the daughter chromosomes separate. The four daughter cells are haploid. (The blue chromosomes were inherited from one parent, and the red chromosomes were inherited from the other parent.)

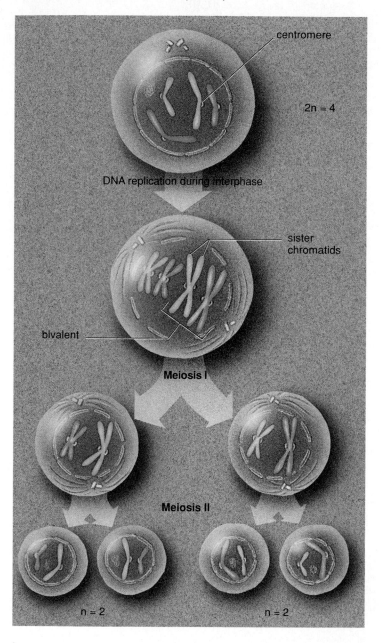

centromere

2n = 4

DNA replication during interphase

sister chromatids

bivalent

Meiosis I

Meiosis II

n = 2   n = 2

HOW MEIOSIS OCCURS

Meiosis keeps the chromosomal number constant from one generation to the next. It reduces the chromosomal number in such a way that the gametes contain only one member of each homologous pair.

Meiosis Has Two Divisions

Meiosis requires two nuclear divisions and produces four haploid daughter cells, each having one of each kind of chromosome and therefore half the total number of chromosomes present in the diploid parent nucleus. The parent cell has the diploid number of chromosomes, while the daughter cells have the haploid number of chromosomes.

Figure 11.2 presents an overview of meiosis, indicating the two cell divisions, *meiosis I* and *meiosis II*. Prior to meiosis I, DNA (deoxyribonucleic acid) replication has occurred; therefore, each chromosome has two sister chromatids. During meiosis I, something new happens that does not occur in mitosis. The homologous chromosomes come together and line up side by side due to a means of attraction still unknown. This so-called **synapsis** [Gk. *synap,* union] results in **bivalents** [L. *bi,* two, and *valent,* strength]—that is, two chromosomes that stay in close association during the first two phases. Sometimes the term **tetrad** [Gk. *tetr,* four] is used instead of bivalent because, as you can see, a bivalent contains four chromatids. Exchange of genetic material, called *crossing-over,* may occur between the nonsister chromatids of a tetrad. After crossing-over occurs, the sister chromatids of a chromosome are no longer identical.

Following synapsis during meiosis I, the homologous chromosomes separate. This separation means that only one chromosome from each homologous pair reaches a daughter nucleus. It is important for daughter nuclei to have a member from each pair of homologous chromosomes because only in that way can there be a copy of each kind of chromosome in the daughter nuclei. The members of the homologous pairs separate independently of one another; any particular kind of chromosome can be with any other kind in the daughter nuclei. Therefore, all possible combinations of chromosomes can occur within the gametes that result after meiosis is complete.

No replication of DNA is needed between meiosis I and meiosis II because the chromosomes are already duplicated; they already have two sister chromatids. During meiosis II, the centromeres divide and daughter chromosomes derived from sister chromatids separate. Therefore, the chromosomes in the four daughter cells have only one chromatid. You can count the number of centromeres to verify that the parent cell has the diploid number of chromosomes and each daughter cell has the haploid number.

> Following meiosis I and II, there are four haploid daughter cells, each having one copy of each kind of chromosome. All possible combinations of chromosomes occur.

Figure 11.3

Crossing-over occurs during meiosis I. **a.** The homologous chromosomes pair up, and a nucleoprotein lattice, called the synaptonemal complex, develops between them. This is an electron micrograph of the complex, which zippers the members of the bivalent together so that corresponding genes are in alignment. **b.** This diagrammatic representation shows only two places where nonsister chromatids 1 and 3 have come into contact. Actually, the other two nonsister chromatids most likely are also crossing-over. **c.** Chiasmata indicate where crossing-over has occurred. The exchange of color represents the exchange of genetic material. **d.** Following meiosis II, daughter chromosomes have a new arrangement of genetic material due to crossing-over, which occurred between nonsister chromatids during meiosis I.

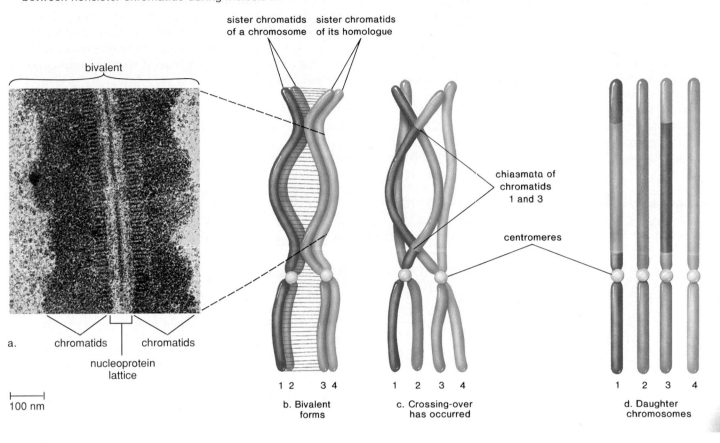

sister chromatids
of a chromosome

sister chromatids
of its homologue

bivalent

chiasmata of
chromatids
1 and 3

centromeres

a.   chromatids   chromatids

nucleoprotein
lattice

100 nm

1 2   3 4

**b. Bivalent
forms**

1   2   3   4

**c. Crossing-over
has occurred**

1   2   3   4

**d. Daughter
chromosomes**

Figure 11.4

Chiasmata (arrows) of a chromosomal bivalent, from a testis cell of a grasshopper. The chiasmata mark the places where crossing-over between nonsister chromosomes of the bivalent has occurred. The chiasmata hold the members of the bivalent together until separation of homologues occurs.

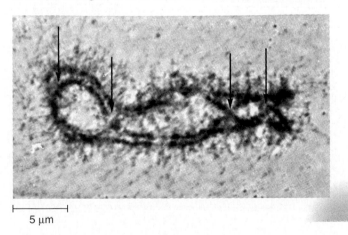

5 μm

Crossing-Over Introduces Variation

Crossing-over is an exchange of genetic material between nonsister chromatids of a bivalent during meiosis I. At synapsis, homologues line up side by side, and a nucleoprotein lattice (called the synaptonemal complex) appears between them (fig. 11.3). This lattice holds the bivalent together in such a way that the DNA of the nonsister chromatids is aligned. Now crossing-over occurs. As the lattice breaks down, homologues are temporarily held together by chiasmata (sing., chiasma), regions where the nonsister chromatids are attached due to crossing-over (fig. 11.4). Then, homologues separate and are distributed to different daughter cells.

Centromeres divide during meiosis II. Due to crossing-over, the daughter chromosomes derived from sister chromatids have a different combination of genes.

> Crossing-over is a way to increase genetic variation in the gametes.

MEIOSIS HAS PHASES

Both meiosis I and meiosis II have four phases: prophase, metaphase (preceded by prometaphase), anaphase, and telophase.

Prophase I

It is apparent during prophase I that nuclear division is about to occur because a spindle forms as the centrosomes migrate away from one another. The nuclear envelope fragments, and the nucleolus disappears.

The homologous chromosomes, each having two sister chromatids, undergo synapsis to form bivalents. As depicted in figure 11.5 by the exchange of color, crossing-over between the nonsister chromatids may occur at this time. After crossing-over, the sister chromatids of a duplicated chromosome are no longer identical.

Throughout prophase I, the chromosomes have been condensing so that by now they have the appearance of metaphase chromosomes.

Metaphase I

During prometaphase I, the bivalents held together by chiasmata (see fig. 11.4) have moved toward the metaphase plate (equator of the spindle). Metaphase I is characterized by a fully formed spindle and alignment of the bivalents at the metaphase plate. *Kinetochores*, regions just outside the centromeres, are seen, and these are attached to spindle fibers called kinetochore spindle fibers.

Bivalents independently align themselves at the metaphase plate of the spindle. The maternal homologue of each bivalent may be orientated toward either pole, and the paternal homologue of each bivalent may be aligned toward either pole. This means that all possible combinations of chromosomes can occur in the daughter cells.

Anaphase I

During anaphase I, the homologues of each bivalent separate and move to opposite poles. Notice that each chromosome still has two chromatids.

Figure 11.5

Phases of meiosis. Meiosis consists of two divisions, meiosis I and meiosis II, and each of these has four phases. Members of homologous pairs have different colors to indicate that one member of each pair is a maternal chromosome and the other is a paternal chromosome.

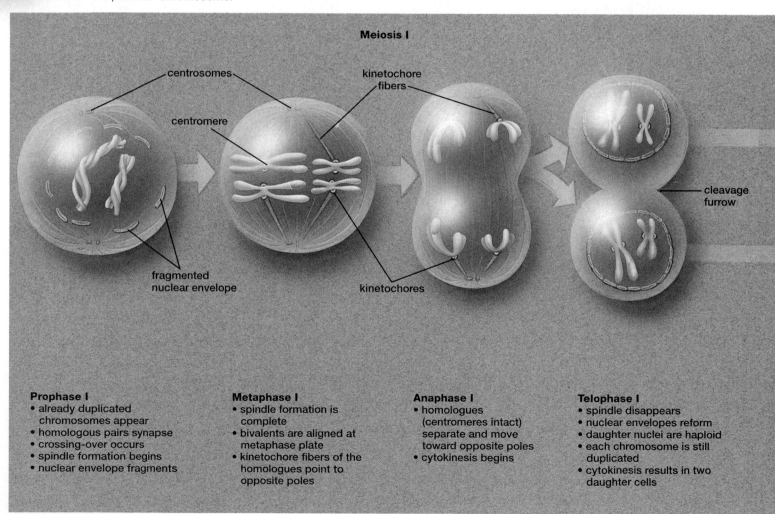

Meiosis I

centrosomes

kinetochore fibers

centromere

cleavage furrow

fragmented nuclear envelope

kinetochores

Prophase I
- already duplicated chromosomes appear
- homologous pairs synapse
- crossing-over occurs
- spindle formation begins
- nuclear envelope fragments

Metaphase I
- spindle formation is complete
- bivalents are aligned at metaphase plate
- kinetochore fibers of the homologues point to opposite poles

Anaphase I
- homologues (centromeres intact) separate and move toward opposite poles
- cytokinesis begins

Telophase I
- spindle disappears
- nuclear envelopes reform
- daughter nuclei are haploid
- each chromosome is still duplicated
- cytokinesis results in two daughter cells

Telophase I

In some species, there is a telophase I stage at the end of meiosis I. If so, the nuclear envelopes reform and nucleoli appear. This phase may or may not be accompanied by cytokinesis, which is separation of the cytoplasm. Figure 11.5 shows only two of the four possible combinations of haploid chromosomes when the parent cell has two homologous pairs of chromosomes. Can you determine what the other two possible combinations of chromosomes are?

Interkinesis

Interkinesis is similar to interphase between mitotic divisions except that DNA replication does not occur—the chromosomes are already duplicated.

Meiosis II

During metaphase II, the haploid number of chromosomes which are still duplicated align at the metaphase plate. During anaphase II, the centromeres divide and the daughter chromosomes move toward the poles. At the end of telophase II and cytokinesis, there are four haploid cells. Due to crossing-over of chromatids, each gamete can contain chromosomes with different types of alleles.

Following meiosis II, the haploid cells mature and become gametes in animals. In plants, they become spores that divide to produce a haploid adult generation. Plants also have a diploid adult generation (see fig. 11.1). In some fungi and some algae, the zygote that results from gamete fusion immediately undergoes meiosis, and therefore the adult is always haploid.

There are three ways by which genetic recombination comes about:

1. Independent alignment of bivalents at the metaphase plate means that gametes have a different combinations of chromosomes.
2. Crossing-over means that the chromosomes in one gamete have a different combination of genes than chromosomes in another gamete.
3. Upon fertilization, recombination of chromosomes occurs.

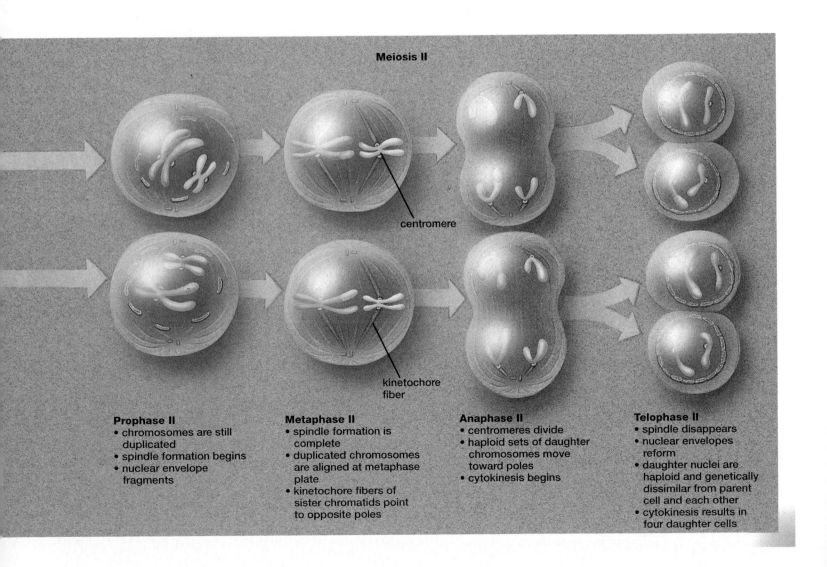

Meiosis II

centromere

kinetochore fiber

Prophase II
- chromosomes are still duplicated
- spindle formation begins
- nuclear envelope fragments

Metaphase II
- spindle formation is complete
- duplicated chromosomes are aligned at metaphase plate
- kinetochore fibers of sister chromatids point to opposite poles

Anaphase II
- centromeres divide
- haploid sets of daughter chromosomes move toward poles
- cytokinesis begins

Telophase II
- spindle disappears
- nuclear envelopes reform
- daughter nuclei are haploid and genetically dissimilar from parent cell and each other
- cytokinesis results in four daughter cells

VIEWING THE HUMAN LIFE CYCLE

Mammals, including humans, have a life cycle that requires both meiosis and mitosis (fig. 11.6). In males, meiosis is a part of **spermatogenesis** [Gk. *sperm,* seed, and *gene,* origin] which occurs in the testes and produces sperm. In females, meiosis is a part of **oogenesis** [Gk. *oo,* egg, and *gene,* origin], which occurs in the ovaries and produces eggs. A sperm and egg join at fertilization and the resulting zygote undergoes mitosis during development of the newborn child. After birth, mitosis is involved in the continued growth of the child and repair of tissues at any time.

Comparison of Meiosis with Mitosis

The following lists and figure 11.7 will allow you to compare meiosis to mitosis.

Occurrence

Meiosis occurs only at certain times in the life cycle of sexually reproducing organisms. In humans, meiosis occurs only in the sex organs and produces the gametes. Mitosis is more common because it allows growth and repair of body tissues in multicellular organisms, including humans.

Process

The following are distinctive differences between the processes of meiosis and mitosis.

1. DNA is replicated only once before both meiosis and mitosis; but there are two nuclear divisions during meiosis and only one nuclear division during mitosis.
2. Homologous chromosomes pair and undergo crossing-over during prophase I of meiosis but not during mitosis.
3. Paired homologous chromosomes (bivalents) align at the metaphase plate during metaphase I in meiosis; individual (duplicated) chromosomes align at the metaphase plate during metaphase in mitosis.
4. Homologous chromosomes (with centromeres intact) separate and move to opposite poles during anaphase I in meiosis; centromeres divide and daughter chromosomes move to opposite poles during anaphase in mitosis.
5. The events of meiosis II are just like those of mitosis except that meiosis II nuclei are always haploid.

Daughter Nuclei and Cells

The genetic consequences of meiosis and mitosis are quite different as well.

1. Four daughter cells are produced by meiosis; mitosis results in two daughter cells.
2. The four daughter cells formed by meiosis are haploid; the daughter cells produced by mitosis have the same chromosomal number as the parent cell.
3. The daughter cells from meiosis are not genetically identical to each other or to the parent cell. The daughter cells from mitosis are genetically identical to each other and to the parent cell.

Figure 11.6

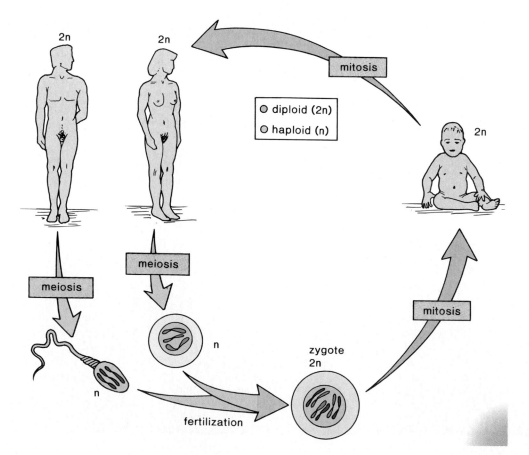

Life cycle of humans. Meiosis in males is a part of sperm production, and meiosis in females is a part of egg production. When a haploid sperm fertilizes a haploid egg, the zygote is diploid. The zygote undergoes mitosis as it develops into a newborn child. Mitosis continues after birth until the individual reaches maturity; then the life cycle begins again.

Figure 11.7

Comparison of meiosis and mitosis. (The blue chromosomes were inherited from one parent, and the red chromosomes were inherited from the other parent.)

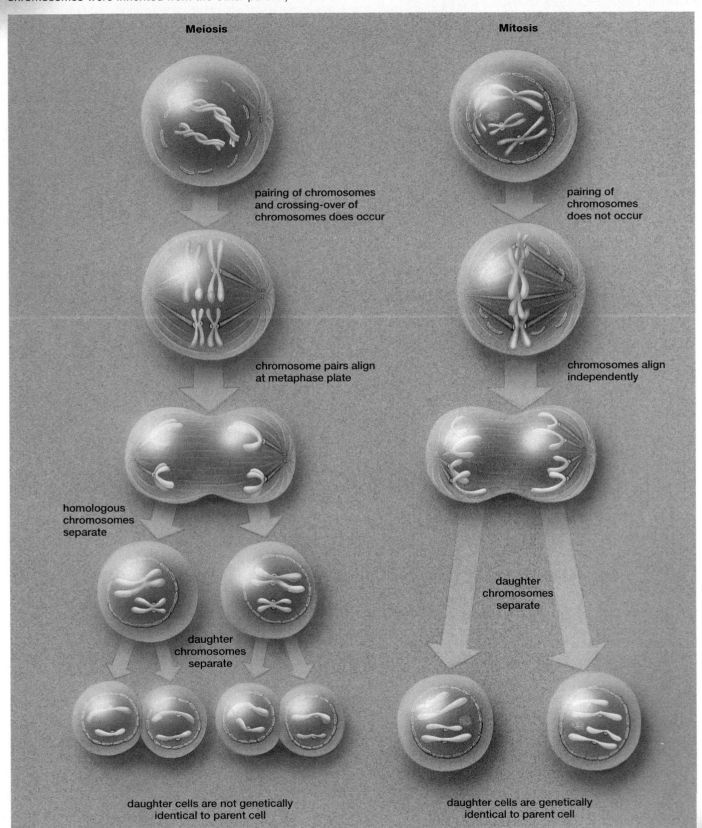

Meiosis

Mitosis

pairing of chromosomes and crossing-over of chromosomes does occur

pairing of chromosomes does not occur

chromosome pairs align at metaphase plate

chromosomes align independently

homologous chromosomes separate

daughter chromosomes separate

daughter chromosomes separate

daughter cells are not genetically identical to parent cell

daughter cells are genetically identical to parent cell

Oogenesis and Spermatogenesis Produce the Gametes

Figure 11.8 contrasts spermatogenesis with oogenesis, processes that produce the gametes in mammals, including humans. In the testes of males, primary spermatocytes with forty-six chromosomes divide to form two secondary spermatocytes, each with twenty-three duplicated chromosomes. Secondary spermatocytes divide to produce four spermatids, also with twenty-three daughter chromosomes. Spermatids then differentiate into sperm (spermatozoa). The processs of meiosis in males always results in four cells that become sperm.

In the ovaries of females, a primary oocyte has forty-six chromosomes and divides meiotically into two cells, each having twenty-three chromosomes. One of these cells, termed the **secondary oocyte** [Gk. *oo,* egg, and *cyt,* cell], receives almost all the cytoplasm (fig. 11.8). The other is a **polar body** that may disintegrate or may divide again. The secondary oocyte begins meiosis II and then stops at metaphase II. Then it leaves the ovary and enters an oviduct where it may be approached by a sperm. If a sperm does enter the oocyte, the oocyte is activated to continue meiosis II to completion. The mature egg has twenty-three daughter chromosomes. Meiosis in females produces only one egg and possibly three polar bodies. The polar bodies are a way to discard unnecessary chromosomes while retaining much of the cytoplasm in the egg. The cytoplasm serves as a source of nutrients for the developing embryo.

The Sperm and Egg Differ

From figure 11.9, it is apparent that the sperm and egg differ in their functions. The sperm is a tiny flagellated cell that is adapted for swimming to the egg. The egg is a large cell that awaits the arrival of the sperm and contributes most of the cytoplasm and nutrients to the zygote. Regardless, both gametes contribute twenty-three chromosomes and one member of each homologous pair of chromosomes to the new individual.

> In the human life cycle, only the gametes are haploid.

Figure 11.8 📷

Spermatogenesis and oogenesis in mammals. Spermatogenesis produces four viable sperm, whereas oogenesis produces one egg and at least two polar bodies. In humans, both sperm and egg have twenty-three chromosomes each; therefore, following fertilization, the zygote has forty-six chromosomes.

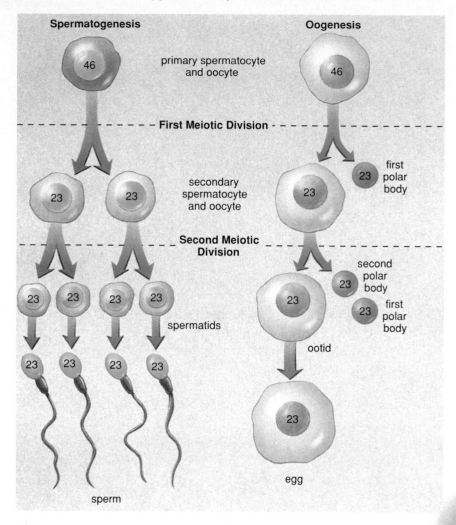

Figure 11.9

Anatomy of sperm and egg.

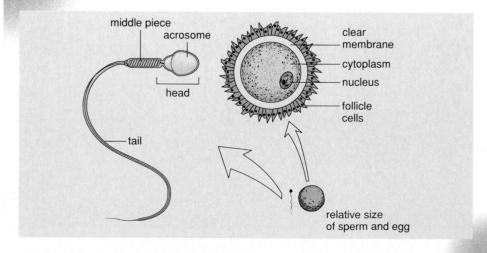

MEIOSIS IS IMPORTANT

In all sexually reproducing organisms, meiosis provides a way to keep the chromosomal number constant generation after generation. Without meiosis, the chromosomal number of the adult stages depicted in figure 11.1 would continually increase. Not only is the chromosomal number halved precisely, each daughter cell receives a copy of each kind of chromosome. This ensures that each daughter cell receives one of each kind of gene.

Meiosis also helps ensure that genetic recombination occurs with each generation. As a result of *independent assortment of chromosomes,* the chromosomes are distributed to the daughter cells in various combinations. The total number of possible combinations is 2^n, where n is the haploid number of chromosomes. In humans, where $n = 23$, the number of possible chromosome combinations produced by meiosis is a staggering 2^{23}, or 8,388,608. And this does not even consider the variations that are introduced due to *crossing-over.* For example, if we assume only one crossover occurs within each bivalent (actually many crossovers usually occur), then in humans crossing-over and independent alignment and separation will generate 4^{23} different kinds of gametes, or 70,368,744,000,000.

This is just the variation introduced by meiosis, but if the entire sexual reproductive process is considered, there is another element that introduces variation. Due to *fertilization,* the chromosomes donated by the parents are combined, and in humans, this means that $(2^{23})^2$, or 70,368,744,000,000, chromosomally different zygotes are possible, even assuming no crossing-over. If crossing-over occurs once, then $(4^{23})^2$, or 4,951,760,200,000,000,000,000,000,000, genetically different zygotes are possible for every couple.

If the diploid zygote becomes a diploid adult, the variability of recessive genes may remain hidden and is not subject to direct testing by the environment. If there is a haploid stage as there is in plants and fungi, any variability present is tested immediately by the environment.

In any case, a sexually reproducing population has a tremendous storehouse of genetic recombinations, which may be advantageous for evolution, particularly when the environment is changing. Asexually reproducing organisms, like prokaryotes, depend primarily on mutations to generate variation. This is sufficient because they produce great numbers of offspring within a limited amount of time. Mutation is still the raw material for variation among sexually reproducing organisms, but the shuffling of genetic material due to sexual reproduction may better allow adaptation to a changing environment. If the environment is not changing, the genetic makeup of the parents is most likely still adaptive.

> Meiosis promotes genetic recombination; the more chromosomes there are, the greater the recombinations possible.

Biological Relationships

All living things have a life cycle that includes cell division. In asexual reproduction, the life cycle includes only mitosis or its equivalent, and the offspring have the same genes as the parents. In sexual reproduction, the life cycle includes both mitosis and meiosis. Meiosis assures that offspring will have a different combination of genes than the parents.

Like begets like because the chromosomes are the depository of hereditary information that is passed from generation to generation. The genes are on the chromosomes and, like the chromosomes, genes also come in pairs, segregate, and assort independently. Only one gene of each pair is in a gamete. We should never forget that the genes consist of DNA and, while it may be convenient to speak of genes as if they are particles, that is not the case since they are very long DNA molecules. DNA can replicate; without this property chromosome duplication and, in turn, cell division as described would be impossible.

In multicellular forms, mitosis is prominent in life processes like growth, repair, and development. Mitosis distributes the chromosomes to the daughter cells in like measure, and all cells of the body have the same number and kinds of genes. They are said to be totipotent because each one could possibly give rise to a completely new individual. Cloning experiments (producing exact copies of the parent individual) have been successful only with embryonic cells because it has not been possible to stimulate mature nuclei to begin the developmental process.

Certain cells of the body divide more frequently than other cells. Those that do keep undergoing the cell cycle are more likely to become cancer cells, which never become mature and instead keep on dividing. In this regard, aging and cancer seem to represent opposite sides of a coin. As cells age, they reach a point when they no longer divide. No doubt knowledge of how the cell cycle is regulated will contribute to our understanding of both these phenomena. Again, we have to expect that this will require us to understand the makeup and workings of particular genes and the DNA that composes these genes.

The unity and diversity of life is dependent upon DNA, which is passed from generation to generation. In organisms that reproduce asexually, gene mutation is the only means to introduce variation, but genetic recombination is as significant as mutation in those that reproduce sexually. Variation allows evolution to occur. Ultimately, then, evolution itself is dependent upon the reproductive process and, therefore, cell division!

Summary

1. Meiosis is involved in any life cycle that involves sexual reproduction. Meiosis ensures that the chromosomal number in offspring stays constant generation after generation.

2. In the animal life cycle, only the gametes are haploid; in plants and fungi, there is a multicellular haploid adult that produces the gametes.

3. The nucleus contains pairs of chromosomes, called homologous pairs (homologues). During meiosis, the haploid daughter cells receive one of each kind of chromosome.

4. Meiosis requires two cell divisions and results in four daughter cells. Replication of DNA takes place before meiosis begins. During meiosis I, the homologues undergo synapsis (resulting in a bivalent) and crossing-over between nonsister chromatids occurs before they independently separate. The daughter cells receive one member of each pair of homologous chromosomes. There is no replication of DNA during interkinesis. During meiosis II, the daughter chromosomes separate in a manner similar to that in mitosis. The four resulting daughter cells are not genetically identical to the parent cell; they are haploid, and due to crossing-over, their chromosomes carry a different combination of genes.

5. Meiosis I is divided into four phases:
   Prophase I—Bivalents form, and crossing-over occurs as chromosomes condense; the nuclear envelope fragments.
   Metaphase I—Bivalents independently align at the metaphase plate.
   Anaphase I—Homologous chromosomes separate.
   Telophase I—Nuclei become haploid, having received one duplicated chromosome from each homologous pair.

6. Meiosis II is divided into four phases:
   Prophase II—Chromosomes condense and the nuclear envelope fragments.
   Metaphase II—The haploid number of still duplicated chromosomes align independently at the metaphase plate.
   Anaphase II—Daughter chromosomes separate.
   Telophase II—Four haploid daughter cells are genetically different from the parent cell.

7. During the life cycle of humans and many other animals, only the gametes are haploid. Meiosis is involved in spermatogenesis and oogenesis. Fertilization restores the diploid number of chromosomes.

8. Both mitosis and meiosis occur in the human life cycle. They can be compared in this manner:

Mitosis	Meiosis I
Prophase	
No pairing of chromosomes	Pairing of homologous chromosomes
Metaphase	
Duplicated chromosomes at metaphase plate	Bivalents at metaphase plate
Anaphase	
Daughter chromosomes separate	Homologous chromosomes separate
Telophase	
Daughter nuclei have the parent cell chromosomal number	Daughter nuclei are always haploid

Meiosis II is like mitosis except the nuclei are haploid.

9. Whereas spermatogenesis produces four sperm per meiosis, oogenesis produces one egg and two to three nonfunctional polar bodies. Spermatogenesis occurs in males and oogenesis occurs in females.

10. Mutations are the primary source of genetic variation among asexually reproducing organisms. But among sexually reproducing organisms, meiosis produces variation by independent assortment of homologous chromosomes and crossing-over. Fertilization also contributes to variation. Variation is important to the process of evolution; it promotes the possibility of adaptation to a changing environment.

Writing Across the Curriculum

In order to practice writing skills, students should write out the answers to any or all of the study questions and the critical thinking questions. The study questions are sequenced in the same order as the text. Answers to the objective questions, and suggested answers to the critical thinking questions, are in appendix D.

Study Questions

1. Why did early investigators predict that there must be a reduction division in the sexual reproduction process?   170

2. Compare the animal, plant, and fungal life cycles by indicating when meiosis occurs in each.   170

3. Define homologous chromosomes.   170

4. What are the events of meiosis that account for the production of four daughter cells with the haploid number of chromosomes having a different genetic makeup than in the parent cell?   172

5. Draw and explain a series of diagrams that illustrate synapsis and crossing-over. Indicate in your drawings what holds the sister chromatids together. Indicate what holds the homologues together.   172–73

6. Draw and explain a series of diagrams that illustrate the events of meiosis I.   174

7. Draw and explain a series of diagrams that illustrate the events of meiosis II. 175

8. Draw a diagram to illustrate the life cycle of humans. Compare spermatogenesis to oogenesis. 176–78

9. Construct a chart to describe the many differences between meiosis and mitosis. 177

10. What accounts for (1) the genetic similarity between daughter cells and the parent cell following mitosis and (2) the genetic dissimilarity between daughter cells and the parent cell following meiosis? 176

11. List the ways in which sexual reproduction contributes to variation among members of a population. What is the evolutionary significance of this variation? 179

Objective Questions

1. A bivalent (tetrad) is
   a. a homologous chromosome.
   b. the paired homologous chromosomes.
   c. a duplicated chromosome composed of sister chromatids.
   d. the two daughter cells after meiosis I.

2. If a parent cell has twelve chromosomes, then the daughter cells following meiosis will have
   a. twelve chromosomes.
   b. twenty-four chromosomes.
   c. six chromosomes.
   d. Any one of these could be correct.

3. At the metaphase plate during metaphase I of meiosis, there are
   a. single chromosomes.
   b. unpaired duplicated chromosomes.
   c. bivalents (tetrads).
   d. always twenty-three chromosomes.

4. At the metaphase plate during metaphase II of meiosis, there are
   a. single chromosomes.
   b. unpaired duplicated chromosomes.
   c. bivalents (tetrads).
   d. always twenty-three chromosomes.

5. Gametes contain one of each kind of chromosome because
   a. the homologous chromosomes separate during meiosis.
   b. the chromatids never separate during meiosis.
   c. two replications of DNA occur during meiosis.
   d. crossing-over occurs during prophase I.

6. Crossing-over occurs between
   a. sister chromatids of the same chromosomes.
   b. two different bivalents.
   c. nonsister chromatids of a bivalent.
   d. two daughter nuclei.

7. During which phase of meiosis do homologous chromosomes separate?
   a. prophase II
   b. telophase II
   c. metaphase I
   d. anaphase I

8. Fertilization
   a. is a source of variation during sexual reproduction.
   b. is fusion of the gametes.
   c. occurs in both animal and plant life cycles.
   d. All of these are correct.

9. Which of these is not a difference between spermatogenesis and oogenesis in humans?

	Spermatogenesis	**Oogenesis**
a.	occurs in males	occurs in females
b.	produces four sperm per meiosis	produces one egg per meiosis
c.	produces haploid cells	produces diploid cells
d.	always goes to completion	does not always go to completion

10. Which of these drawings represents meiosis I? How do you know?

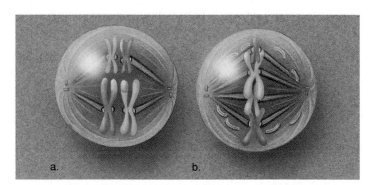

a.   b.

Concepts and Critical Thinking

1. *Methods of reproduction support the cell theory (i.e., all organisms are composed of cells).*

In what way do both asexual and sexual reproduction support the cell theory?

2. *Variation among offspring is greater with sexual reproduction than with asexual reproduction.*

How does asexual reproduction introduce variation among offspring? How does sexual reproduction introduce variation?

3. *Meiosis is an essential part of the life cycle of eukaryotes.*

If the zygote undergoes meiosis, the adult is haploid. Haploidy has what advantage and disadvantage?

Selected Key Terms

bivalent (by-VAY-lent) Homologous chromosomes, each having sister chromatids that are joined by a nucleoprotein lattice during meiosis; also called tetrad. [L. *bi*, two, and *valent*, strength] 172

crossing-over An exchange of segments between nonsister chromatids of a bivalent during meiosis. 173

diploid (2n) number A cell condition in which two of each type of chromosome is present. [Gk. *dipl*, double, and *oid*, form] 170

gamete (GAM-eet) Haploid sex cell. [Gk. *gamet*, wife or husband] 170

haploid (n) number A cell condition in which only one of each type of chromosome is present. [Gk. *hapl*, single, and *oid*, form] 170

homologous chromosome (hoh-MAHL-uh-gus) A member of a pair of chromosomes that carry genes for the same traits and synapse during prophase of the first meiotic division. [Gk. *homo*, alike] 170

homologue (HOH-muh-log) A member of a homologous pair of chromosomes. [Gk. *homo*, alike] 170

meiosis (my-OH-sus) The type of nuclear division that occurs as part of sexual reproduction in which the daughter cells receive the haploid number of chromosomes. [Gk. *mei*, less, and *sis*, the act of] 170

oogenesis (oh-uh-JEN-uh-sus) The production of eggs in females by the process of meiosis and maturation. [Gk. *oo*, egg, and *gene*, origin] 176

polar body In oogenesis a nonfunctional product three of the four meiotic products are of this type. 178

secondary oocyte (OH-uh-syt) In oogenesis the functional product of meiosis I; becomes the egg. [Gk. *oo*, egg, and *cyt*, cell] 178

sexual reproduction Reproduction involving meiosis, gamete formation, and fertilization; produces offspring with chromosomes inherited from each parent. 170

spermatogenesis (spur-mat-uh-JEN-uh-sus) The production of sperm in males by the process of meiosis and maturation. [Gk. *sperm*, seed, and *gene*, origin] 176

synapsis The pairing of homologous chromosomes during meiosis I. [Gk. *synap*, union] 172

tetrad Following synapsis, the set of four chromatids of a homologous chromosome pair, visible during prophase of meiosis I; also called a bivalent. [Gk. *tetr*, four] 172

12

MENDELIAN PATTERNS OF INHERITANCE

Learning Objectives

Introducing Gregor Mendel

- Discuss the ideas about heredity that were prevalent when Mendel began his experiments.   184
- Outline the general methodology that Mendel used for his experiments.   184

Mendel Did a Monohybrid Cross

- Diagram the type of monohybrid cross Mendel did, using words to indicate the phenotype and letters to indicate the genotype.   186–87
- State Mendel's law of segregation, and describe the reasoning he used to arrive at this law.   186

- Solve one-trait genetics problems utilizing the laws of probability.   188–89
- Explain the use of a testcross to determine the genotype of an individual.   190

Mendel Did a Dihybrid Cross

- Diagram the type of dihybrid cross Mendel did, and analyze the results.   191
- State Mendel's law of independent assortment, and describe the reasoning he used to arrive at this law.   191
- Solve two-trait genetics problems utilizing the laws of probability.   192–93

Diversity as in the tomatoes shown here is dependent upon the inheritance of different combinations of genes.

Zebras always produce zebras, never bluebirds, and poppies always produce seeds for poppies, never dandelions. Almost everyone who observes such phenomena reasons that parents must pass hereditary information to their offspring. Many also observe, however, that offspring rarely resemble either parent exactly. After all, black-coated mice occasionally produce white-coated mice.

The laws of heredity must explain not only the stability but also the variation that is observed between generations of organisms. The inheritance of chromosomes can explain the genetic stability seen in the passage of chromosomes (via the egg and sperm) from parent to offspring, and it can also explain variation if we can show that the chromosomes differ from one another in some way.

Gregor Mendel was an Austrian monk who formulated two fundamental laws of heredity in the early 1860s (fig. 12.1). Previously, he had studied science and mathematics at the University of Vienna, and at the time of his genetic research he was a substitute natural science teacher at a local technical high school.

INTRODUCING GREGOR MENDEL

Various theories about heredity had been proposed before Mendel began his experiments. In particular, the blending theory of inheritance was believed by many at this time.

Blending Theory of Inheritance

When Mendel began his work, most plant and animal breeders believed in the *blending theory of inheritance* because it acknowledged that both sexes contribute equally to a new individual. They felt that parents of contrasting appearance always produce offspring of intermediate appearance. Therefore, according to this theory, a cross between plants with red flowers and plants with white flowers would yield only plants with pink flowers. When red and white flowers reappeared in future generations, the breeders mistakenly attributed this to an instability in the genetic material.

The blending theory of inheritance offered little help to Charles Darwin, the father of evolution, who wanted to give his ideas a genetic basis. If populations contained only intermediate individuals and normally lacked variations, how could diverse forms evolve? Only a particulate theory of inheritance, as proposed by Mendel, can account for the presence of discrete variations (differences) among the members of a population generation after generation. Because Mendel's work went unrecognized until 1900, Darwin was never able to make use of it to support his theory of evolution.

> At the time Mendel began his study of heredity, the blending theory of inheritance was popular.

Figure 12.1
Gregor Mendel.

Mendel Breaks with Past

Most likely his background in mathematics prompted Mendel to add a statistical basis to his breeding experiments. He prepared for his experiments carefully and conducted preliminary studies with various animals and plants. He then chose to work with the garden pea, *Pisum sativum* (fig. 12.2a).

The garden pea was a good choice. The plants were easy to cultivate and had a short generation time. And although the peas normally self-pollinate, they could be cross-pollinated for the sake of the experiment. Many varieties of peas were available, and Mendel chose twenty-two for his experiments. When these varieties self-pollinated, they were *true-breeding*—the offspring were like the parent plants and like each other. In contrast to his predecessors, Mendel studied the inheritance of relatively simple and distinguishable traits—seed shape, seed color, and flower color (fig. 12.2b).

As Mendel followed the inheritance of individual traits, he kept careful records of the numbers of offspring that expressed each characteristic. And he used his understanding of the mathematical laws of probability to interpret the results. In other words, Mendel simply wanted to objectively observe facts, and if he did have personal beliefs, he set them aside for the sake of the experiment. This is one of the qualities that make his experiments as applicable today as they were in 1860.

> Mendel carefully designed his experiments and gathered mathematical data.

Figure 12.2

Garden pea anatomy and traits. **a.** In the garden pea, *Pisum sativum*, each flower produces both male and female gametes. The pollen grains, which upon maturity give rise to sperm, are produced within the anther of the stamen. The ovule, within the ovary of the pistil, eventually contains an egg. Following pollination—when pollen is deposited on the stigma (the top portion of the pistil)—the pollen grain develops a tube through which a sperm reaches the egg. Self-pollination is the rule in the garden pea because the sexual structures of the plant are entirely enclosed by petals. Sometimes Mendel allowed the plant to self-pollinate so that the male and female gametes of the same flower produced offspring. At other times, he performed cross-pollination, so that male and female gametes from different flowers produced offspring. He did this by removing the pollen-producing anthers of one plant and brushing the pollen on the stigmas of another plant.

Once the ovules had developed into seeds (peas), they could be observed or planted if necessary to observe the results of a cross. The open pod shows the results of a cross between plants with round, yellow seeds and plants with wrinkled, green seeds. **b.** Other crosses done by Mendel.

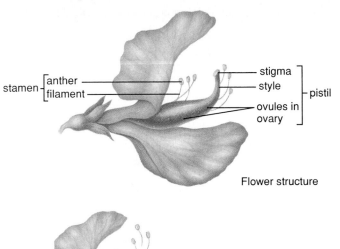

Flower structure

Cutting away anthers

Brushing on pollen from another plant

Results of cross:
round yellow seeds x wrinkled green seeds

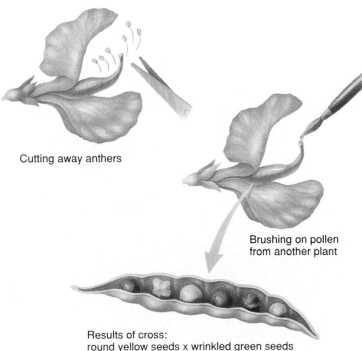

a.

Trait	Characteristics		F₂ Results*	
			Dominant	Recessive
Stem length	Tall	Short	787	277
Pod shape	Inflated	Constricted	882	299
Seed shape	Round	Wrinkled	5,474	1,850
Seed color	Yellow	Green	7,022	2,001
Flower position	Axial	Terminal	651	207
Flower color	Purple	White	705	224
Pod color	Green	Yellow	428	152

*All of these produce approximately a 3:1 ratio. For example,

$$\frac{787}{277} \cong \frac{3}{1}$$

b.

MENDEL DID A MONOHYBRID CROSS

After ensuring that his pea plants were true-breeding, Mendel was then ready to perform a cross-pollination experiment between two strains. The initial experiments were monohybrid crosses, so-called because the offspring are hybrid—they are the product of two different strains that differ in regard to only one trait. If the blending theory of inheritance were correct, then the cross should yield offspring with an intermediate appearance compared to the parents. For example, the offspring of a cross between a tall plant and short plant should be intermediate in height.

Mendel called the original parents the *P generation* and the first-generation offspring the *F_1* (for filial) *generation* (fig. 12.3). He performed *reciprocal crosses:* first he dusted the pollen of tall plants on the stigmas of short plants, and then he dusted the pollen of short plants on the stigmas of tall plants. In both cases, all F_1 offspring resembled the tall parent.

Certainly, these results were contrary to those predicted by the blending theory of inheritance. Rather than being intermediate, the offspring were tall and resembled only one parent. Did these results mean that the other characteristic (i.e., shortness) had disappeared permanently? Apparently not, because when Mendel allowed the F_1 plants to self-pollinate, $3/4$ of the *F_2 generation* were tall and $1/4$ were short, a 3:1 ratio (fig. 12.3).

Mendel counted many plants. For this particular cross, he counted a total of 1,064 plants, of which 787 were tall and 277 were short. In all crosses that he performed, he found a 3:1 ratio in the F_2 generation. The characteristic that had disappeared in the F_1 generation reappeared in $1/4$ of the F_2 offspring.

His mathematical approach led Mendel to interpret these results differently from previous breeders. He knew that the same ratio was obtained among the F_2 generation time and time again for each trait, and he sought an explanation for these results. A 3:1 ratio among the F_2 offspring was possible if:

1. the F_1 generation contained two separate copies of each hereditary factor, one of these being dominant and one being recessive;
2. the factors separated when the gametes were formed, and each gamete carried only one copy of each factor; and
3. random fusion of all possible gametes occurred upon fertilization.

In this way, Mendel arrived at the first of his laws of inheritance:

> **Mendel's law of segregation:**
> Each organism contains two factors for each trait, and the factors segregate during the formation of gametes so that each gamete contains only one factor for each trait.

Mendel's law of segregation is in keeping with a particulate theory of inheritance because many individual factors are passed on from generation to generation. It is the reshuffling of these factors that explains how variations come about and why offspring differ from their parents.

Figure 12.3

A monohybrid cross done by Mendel. The P generation plants differ in one regard—length of the stem. The F_1 generation are all tall, but the factor for short has not disappeared because $1/4$ of the F_2 generation are short. The 3:1 ratio allowed Mendel to deduce that individuals have two discrete and separate genetic factors for each trait.

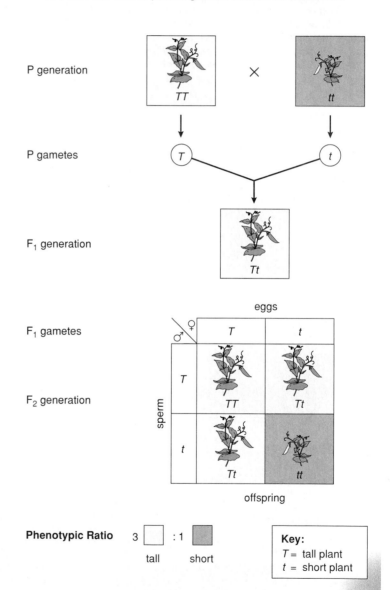

Phenotypic Ratio 3 ☐ : 1 ▨
tall short

Key:
T = tall plant
t = short plant

12-4

Modern Genetics Has an Explanation

Figure 12.3 also shows how we now interpret the results of Mendel's experiments on inheritance of stem length in peas. Each trait in a pea plant is controlled by two **alleles** [Gk. *allelo,* one another, parallel], alternate forms of a gene that in this case control the length of the stem. In genetic notation, the alleles are identified by letters, the **dominant allele** (so named because of its ability to mask the expression of its allele) with an uppercase (capital) letter and the **recessive allele** with the same but lowercase (small) letter. With reference to the cross being discussed, there is an allele for tallness (*T*) and an allele for shortness (*t*). Alleles occur on a homologous pair of chromosomes at a particular location that is called the **gene locus** (fig. 12.4).

During meiosis, the type of cell division that reduces the chromosomal number, the homologous chromosomes of a bivalent separate and then the daughter chromosome derived from the sister chromatids of separate. Therefore, the process of meiosis gives an explanation for Mendel's law of segregation and for why there is only one allele for each trait in the gametes.

In Mendel's cross, the original parents (P generation) were true-breeding; therefore, the tall plants had two alleles for tallness (*TT*) and the short plants had two alleles for shortness (*tt*). When an organism has two identical alleles, as these had, we say it is **homozygous** [Gk. *homo,* alike, and *zyg,* yoke]. Because the first parents were homozygous, all gametes produced by the tall plant contained the allele for tallness (*T*), and all gametes produced by the short plant contained an allele for shortness (*t*).

After cross-pollination, all the individuals of the resulting F_1 generation had one allele for tallness and one for shortness (*Tt*). When an organism has two different alleles at a gene locus, we say that it is **heterozygous** [Gk. *heter,* different, and *zyg,* yoke]. Although the plants of the F_1 generation had one of each type of allele, they were all tall. The allele that is expressed in a heterozygous individual is the dominant allele. The allele that is not expressed in a heterozygote is a recessive allele.

Genotype versus Phenotype

It is obvious from our discussion that two organisms with different allelic combinations for a trait can have the same outward appearance (*TT* and *Tt* pea plants are both tall). For this reason, it is necessary to distinguish between the alleles present in an organism and the appearance of that organism.

The word **genotype** [Gk. *geno,* race, and *typos,* image] refers to the alleles an individual receives at fertilization. Genotype may be indicated by letters or by short, descriptive phrases. Genotype *TT* is called homozygous dominant, and genotype *tt* is called homozygous recessive. Genotype *Tt* is called heterozygous.

The word **phenotype** [Gk. *pheno,* appear, and *typos,* image] refers to the physical appearance of the individual. The homozygous dominant individual and the heterozygous individual

Figure 12.4
Homologous chromosomes before and after replication.
a. The letters represent alleles; that is, alternate forms of a gene. Each allelic pair, such as *Gg* or *Tt,* is located on homologous chromosomes at a particular gene locus.
b. Following DNA replication, each sister chromatid carries the same alleles in the same order.

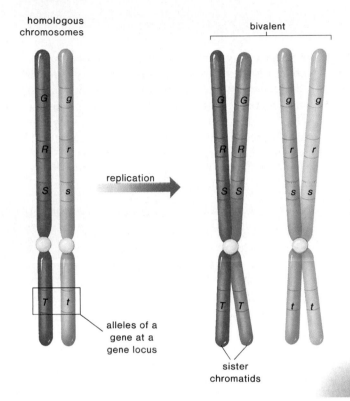

homologous chromosomes

bivalent

replication

alleles of a gene at a gene locus

sister chromatids

Table 12.1

Genotype versus Phenotype

Genotype	Genotype	Phenotype
TT	Homozygous dominant	Tall plant
Tt	Heterozygous	Tall plant
tt	Homozygous recessive	Short plant

both show the dominant phenotype and are tall, while the homozygous recessive individual shows the recessive phenotype and is short (table 12.1).

A homozygous dominant plant can pass on only a *T.* Why?
A heterozygous plant can pass on a *T* or a *t.* Why?
A homozygous recessive plant can pass on only a *t.* Why?

Doing Monohybrid Genetics Problems

When solving genetics problems, it is first necessary to know which characteristic is dominant. For example, the following key indicates that unattached earlobes are dominant over attached earlobes:

Key: *E* = unattached earlobes
e = attached earlobes

Suppose a homozygous man with unattached earlobes reproduces with a woman who has attached earlobes. What type of earlobe will the child have? In row 1, P represents the parental generation, and the letters in this row are the genotypes of the parents. Row 2 shows that the gametes of each parent have only one type of allele for earlobes; therefore, the child (F generation) will have a heterozygous genotype and unattached earlobes:

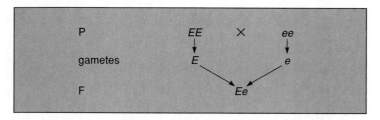

If the heterozygotes (F generation) reproduce with one another, will the child have unattached or attached earlobes? In the P generation there was only one possible type of gamete for each parent because they were homozygous. Heterozygotes, however, can produce two types of gametes; $^1/_2$ of the gametes will contain an *E*, and $^1/_2$ will contain an *e*.

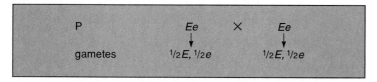

When determining the gametes, it is necessary to keep in mind that although an individual has two alleles for each trait, *each gamete has only one allele for each trait*. This is true of single-trait crosses as well as multiple-trait crosses.

When doing genetics problems, first decide on the appropriate key, and then determine the genotype and gametes for both parents.

Practice Problems 1 will help you learn to designate the gametes.

Figuring the Probable Results

When we calculate the expected results of the cross under consideration, or any genetic cross, we utilize the laws of probability. Imagine flipping a coin; *each time* you flip the coin there is a 50% chance of heads and a 50% chance of tails. In like manner, if the parent has the genotype *Ee*, what is the chance of any child inheriting either an *E* or *e* from that parent?

The chance of $E = ^1/_2$
The chance of $e = ^1/_2$

But in the cross *Ee* x *Ee*, a child will inherit an allele from both parents. The multiplicative law of probability states that *the chance, or probability, of two or more independent events occurring together is the product (multiplication) of their chance of occurring separately*. Therefore, the probability of receiving these genotypes is as follows:

1. The chance of $EE = ^1/_2 \times ^1/_2 = ^1/_4$
2. The chance of $Ee = ^1/_2 \times ^1/_2 = ^1/_4$
3. The chance of $eE = ^1/_2 \times ^1/_2 = ^1/_4$
4. The chance of $ee = ^1/_2 \times ^1/_2 = ^1/_4$

Now we have to consider the additive law of probability: *the chance of an event that can occur in two or more independent ways is the sum (addition) of the individual chances*. Therefore,

The chance of a child with unattached earlobes (*EE*, *Ee*, or *eE*) is $^3/_4$ (add **1, 2,** and **3**), or 75%.

The chance of a child with attached earlobes (*ee*) is $^1/_4$ (only **4**), or 25%.

Punnett Square Figures for You

The **Punnett square** was introduced by a prominent poultry geneticist, R.C. Punnett, in the early 1900s as a simple method to figure the probable results of a genetic cross. Figure 12.5 shows how the results of the cross under consideration (*Ee × Ee*) can be determined using a Punnett square. In a Punnett square all possible types of sperm are lined up vertically and all possible types of eggs are lined up horizontally (or vice versa), and every possible combination of alleles is placed within the squares. In our cross each parent has two possible types of gametes (*E* or *e*), so these two types of gametes are lined up vertically and horizontally.

The results of the Punnett square calculations show that the expected genotypes of offspring are $\frac{1}{4}$ *EE*, $\frac{1}{2}$ *Ee*, and $\frac{1}{4}$ *ee*, giving a 1:2:1 genotypic ratio. Since $\frac{3}{4}$ have unattached earlobes and $\frac{1}{4}$ have attached earlobes, this is a 3:1 phenotypic ratio.

The gametes combine at random, and in practice it is usually necessary to observe a very large number of offspring before a 3:1 ratio can be verified. Only if many offspring are counted can it be assured that all genetically different sperm have had a chance to fertilize all genetically different eggs. If a number of heterozygotes produced 200 offspring, approximately 150 of these would have unattached earlobes and approximately 50 would have attached earlobes (a 3:1 ratio). In terms of genotypes, approximately 50 would be *EE*, about 100 would be *Ee*, and the remaining 50 would be *ee*.

We cannot arrange crosses between humans in order to count a large number of offspring. Therefore, in humans the phenotypic ratio is used to estimate the chances any child has for a particular characteristic. In the cross under consideration, each child has a $\frac{3}{4}$ (or 75%) chance of having unattached earlobes and $\frac{1}{4}$ (or 25%) chance of having attached earlobes. And we must remember that *chance has no memory:* if two heterozygous parents already have a child with attached earlobes, the next child still has a 25% chance of having attached earlobes.

You will note that the Punnett square makes use of the laws of probability we mentioned in the previous section. First, we recognize there is a $\frac{1}{2}$ chance of a child getting the *E* allele or the *e* allele from a parent. In this way we are able to designate the possible gametes. What operation is in keeping with the multiplicative law of probability? The operation of combining the alleles and placing them in the squares. What operation is in keeping with the additive law of probability? The operation of adding the results, and arriving at the phenotypic ratio.

Mendel was quite familiar with the laws of probability and was able to make use of them to see that inheritance of traits depended upon the passage of discrete factors from generation to generation.

> The laws of probability allow one to calculate the probable results of one-trait genetic crosses.

Figure 12.5

Use of a Punnet square to determine the results of a genetic cross. When the parents are heterozygous, each child has a 75% chance of having the dominant phenotype and a 25% chance of having the recessive phenotype.

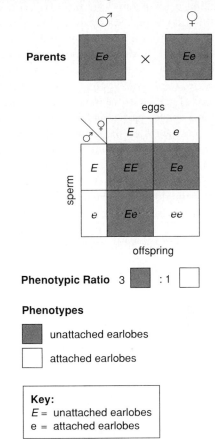

Phenotypic Ratio 3 ▨ : 1 ☐

Phenotypes

▨ unattached earlobes

☐ attached earlobes

Key:
E = unattached earlobes
e = attached earlobes

Practice Problems 2*

1. In rabbits, if *B* = dominant black allele and *b* = recessive white allele, which of these genotypes (*Bb, BB, bb*) could a white rabbit have?
2. In pea plants, yellow seed color is dominant over green seed color. When two heterozygote plants are crossed, what percentage of plants would have yellow seeds? green seeds?
3. In humans, freckles is dominant over no freckles. A man with freckles reproduces with a woman having freckles, but the children have no freckles. What chance did each child have for freckles?
4. In horses, trotter (*T*) is dominant over pacer (*t*). A trotter is mated to a pacer, and the offspring is a pacer. Give the genotype of all horses.

*Answers to Practice Problems appear in appendix D.

Mendel Did a Testcross

To test his idea about the segregation of alleles—in modern terms, that the F_1 was heterozygous—Mendel crossed his F_1 generation tall plants with true-breeding, short (homozygous recessive) plants. He reasoned that half the offspring should be tall and half should be short, producing a 1:1 phenotypic ratio (fig. 12.6*a*). He obtained these results; therefore, his hypothesis that alleles segregate when gametes are formed was supported. It was Mendel's experimental use of simple dominant and recessive traits that allowed him to formulate and to test the law of segregation.

In figure 12.6, the homozygous recessive parent can produce only one type of gamete—*t*—and so the same results would be obtained if the Punnett square had only one column. This is logical because the *t* means all the gametes that carry a *t*.

Today, a monohybrid **testcross** is used to determine if an individual with the dominant phenotype is homozygous dominant or heterozygous for a particular trait. Since both of these genotypes produce the dominant phenotype, it is not possible to determine the genotype by inspection. Figure 12.6*b* shows that if the F_1 in Mendel's cross had been homozygous dominant, then all the offspring would have been tall.

> **The results of a testcross indicate whether an individual with the dominant phenotype is heterozygous or homozygous dominant.**

Figure 12.6

Representation of a testcross to determine if the individual showing the dominant trait is homozygous or heterozygous. **a.** Because the offspring shows a 1:1 ratio of phenotypes, the individual is heterozygous, as shown. **b.** Because all offspring show the dominant characteristic, the individual is most likely homozygous, as shown.

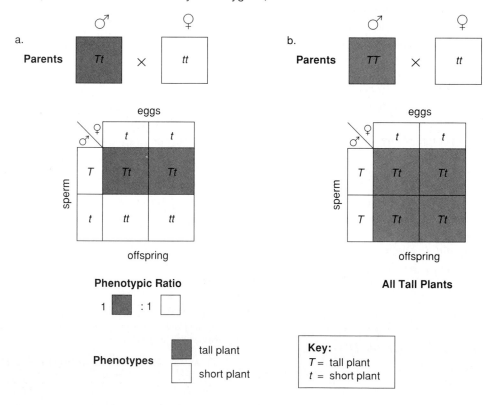

MENDEL DID A DIHYBRID CROSS

Mendel performed a second series of crosses that are called dihybrid crosses because the offspring are dihybrid—they are the product of two different strains that differ in regard to two traits. For example, he crossed tall plants having green pods with short plants having yellow pods (fig. 12.7). The F_1 plants showed both dominant characteristics. As before, Mendel then allowed the F_1 plants to self-pollinate. Two possible results could occur in the F_2 generation:

1. If the dominant factors (*TG*) always segregate into the gametes together, and the recessive factors (*tg*) always stay together, then there would be two phenotypes among the F_2 plants—tall plants with green pods and short plants with yellow pods.

2. If the four factors segregate into the gametes independently, then there would be four phenotypes among the F_2 plants—tall plants with green pods, tall plants with yellow pods, short plants with green pods, and short plants with yellow pods.

Figure 12.7 shows that Mendel observed four phenotypes among the F_2 plants, supporting the second hypothesis. Therefore, Mendel formulated his second law of heredity:

> **Mendel's law of independent assortment:** Members of one pair of factors separate (assort) independently of members of another pair of factors. Therefore, all possible combinations of factors can occur in the gametes.

Practice Problems 4*

1. For each of the following genotypes, give all possible gametes, noting the proportion of each gamete for the individual.
   a. *TtGG*
   b. *TtGg*
   c. *TTGg*
2. For each of the following, state whether a genotype or a gamete is represented.
   a. *Tg*
   b. *WwCC*
   c. *TW*

*Answers to Practice Problems appear in appendix D.

Figure 12.7

A dihybrid cross done by Mendel. P generation plants differ in two regards—length of the stem and color of the pod. The F_1 generation shows only the dominant traits, but all possible phenotypes appear among the F_2 generation. The 9:3:3:1 ratio allowed Mendel to deduce that factors segregate into gametes independently of other factors.

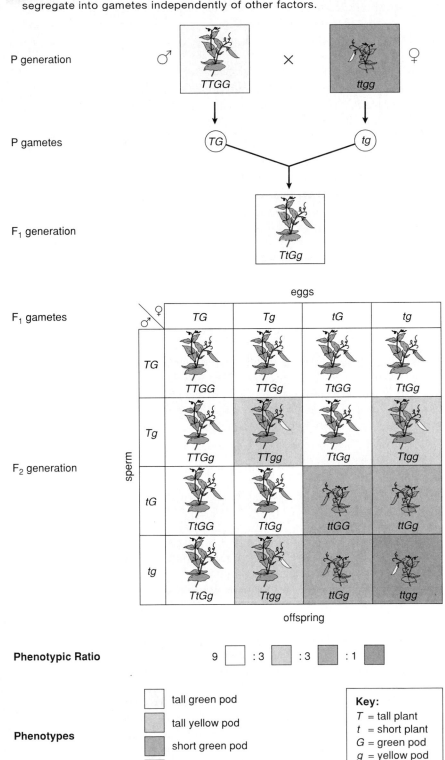

Phenotypic Ratio   9 ☐ : 3 ☐ : 3 ☐ : 1 ☐

Phenotypes
☐ tall green pod
☐ tall yellow pod
☐ short green pod
☐ short yellow pod

Key:
T = tall plant
t = short plant
G = green pod
g = yellow pod

Doing Dihybrid Genetics Problems

The fruit fly, *Drosophila melanogaster*, less than one-fifth the size of a housefly, is a favorite subject for genetic research because it has mutant characteristics that are easily determined. A "wild-type" fly has long wings and a gray body. There are mutant flies with short (vestigial) wings and black (ebony) bodies. The key for a cross involving these traits is L = long wing, l = short wing, G = gray body, and g = black body.

Figuring Probable Results Again

If two flies heterozygous for both traits are crossed, what are the probable results? Since each characteristic is inherited separately from any other, it is possible to apply again the laws of probability mentioned on page 188. For example, we know the F_2 results for two separate monohybrid crosses are as listed here:

1. The chance of long wings = $^3/_4$
   The chance of short wings = $^1/_4$
2. The chance of gray body = $^3/_4$
   The chance of black body = $^1/_4$

Using the multiplicative law, we know that:

The chance of long wings and gray body = $^3/_4 \times ^3/_4 = ^9/_{16}$
The chance of long wings and black body = $^3/_4 \times ^1/_4 = ^3/_{16}$
The chance of short wings and gray body = $^1/_4 \times ^3/_4 = ^3/_{16}$
The chance of short wings and black body = $^1/_4 \times ^1/_4 = ^1/_{16}$

Using the additive law, we conclude that the phenotypic ratio is 9:3:3:1. Again, since all genetically different male gametes must have an equal opportunity to fertilize all genetically different female gametes to even approximately achieve these results, a large number of offspring must be counted.

Punnett Square

In figure 12.8, the flies of the P generation have only one possible type of gamete because both are homozygous. All the F_1 flies are heterozygous ($LlGg$) and have the same phenotype (long wings, gray body).

The Punnett square in figure 12.8 shows the expected results when the F_1 flies are crossed, assuming that all genetically different sperm have an equal opportunity to fertilize all genetically different eggs. Notice that $^9/_{16}$ of the offspring have long wings and a gray body, $^3/_{16}$ have long wings and a black body, $^3/_{16}$ have short wings and a gray body, and $^1/_{16}$ have short wings and a black body. This phenotypic ratio of 9:3:3:1 is expected whenever a heterozygote for two traits is crossed with another heterozygote for two traits and simple dominance is present in both genes.

A Punnett square can also be used to predict the chances of an offspring having a particular phenotype. What are the chances of an offspring with long wings and gray body? The chances are $^9/_{16}$. What are the chances of an offspring with short wings and gray body? The chances are $^3/_{16}$, and so forth.

Today, we know that these results are obtained and the law of independent assortment holds because of the events of meiosis. The gametes contain one allele for each trait and in all possible combinations because homologues separate independently during meiosis I.

Figure 12.8

Mendel's law of independent assortment illustrated in a fruit fly cross. Each F_1 fly ($LlGg$) produces four types of gametes because all possible combinations of alleles can occur in the gametes. Therefore, all possible phenotypes appear among the F_2 offspring.

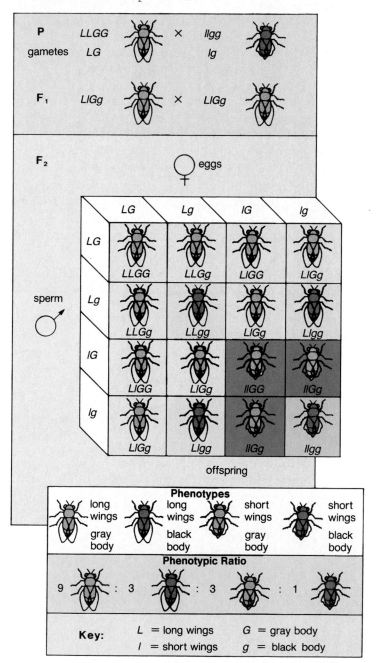

Dihybrids Can Be Tested Also

A dihybrid testcross is used to determine if an individual is homozygous dominant or heterozygous for either of the two traits. Since it is not possible to determine the genotype of a long-winged, gray-bodied fly by inspection, for example, the genotype may be represented as $L\_\_^{1}G\_\_$.

Figure 12.9

Representation of a dihybrid testcross to determine the genotype of a fly showing two dominant characteristics. If a fly that is heterozygous for both traits is crossed with another that is recessive for both traits, the expected ratio of phenotypes is 1:1:1:1. What would the result be if the test individual were homozygous dominant for both traits? homozygous dominant for one trait but heterozygous for the other?

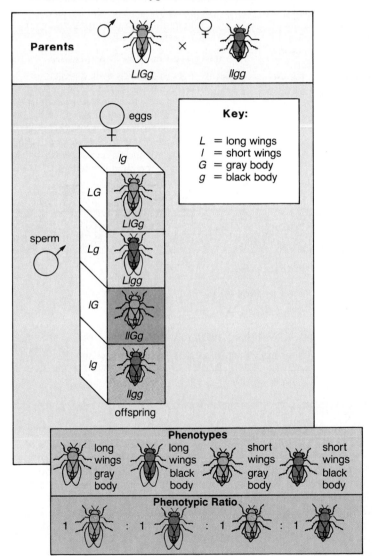

When doing a dihybrid testcross, an individual with the dominant phenotypes is crossed with an individual with the recessive phenotypes. For example, a long-winged, gray-bodied fly is crossed with a short-winged, black-bodied fly. A long-winged, gray-bodied fly heterozygous for both traits will form four different types of gametes. The homozygous fly with short wings and a black body can form only one kind of gamete:

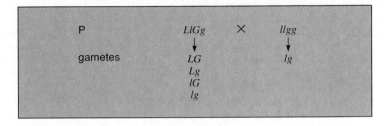

Figure 12.9 shows that ¹/₄ of the expected offspring have long wings and a gray body; ¹/₄ long wings and a black body; ¹/₄ have short wings and a gray body; and ¹/₄ have short wings and a black body. This is a 1:1:1:1 phenotypic ratio. The presence of offspring with short wings and a black body shows that the $L\_\_G\_\_$ fly is heterozygous for both traits and has the genotype $LlGg$.

If the $L\_\_G\_\_$ fly is homozygous for both traits, then no offspring will have short wings and/or a black body. If the $L\_\_G\_\_$ fly is heterozygous for one trait but not the other, what is the expected phenotypic ratio among the offspring?

Practice Problems 5*

1. In horses, B = black coat, b = brown coat, T = trotter, and t = pacer. A black pacer mated to a brown trotter produces a black trotter offspring. Give all possible genotypes for this offspring.

2. In fruit flies, long wings (L) is dominant over short wings (l), and gray body (G) is dominant over black body (g). In each instance, what are the most likely genotypes of the previous generation if a student gets the following phenotypic results?

   a. 1:1:1:1 (all possible combinations in equal number)

   b. 9:3:3:1 (9 dominant; 3 mixed; 3 mixed; 1 recessive)

3. In humans, short fingers and widow's peak are dominant over long fingers and continuous hairline. A heterozygote in both regards reproduces with a similar heterozygote. What is the chance of any one child having the same phenotype as the parents?

*Answers to Practice Problems appear in appendix D.

---

1 The blank means that a dominant or recessive allele can be present.

Summary

1. At the time Mendel began his hybridization experiments, the blending theory of inheritance was popular. This theory stated that whenever the parents were distinctly different, the offspring would be intermediate between them.

2. Mendel, unlike preceding plant breeders, decided to do a statistical study, most likely because he had a mathematical background.

3. Mendel chose the garden pea for several reasons: many true-breeding varieties were available, they were easy to cultivate, they had a short generation time, and they could be cross-pollinated even though they normally self-pollinated. He studied only distinctly different traits, kept careful records, and interpreted his results mathematically.

4. When Mendel did his monohybrid crosses, he found that the F_1 plants resembled only one of the parents; however, the characteristic of the other parent reappeared in about $1/4$ of the F_2 plants. Mendel saw that these 3:1 results were possible if the F_1 hybrid contained two factors for each trait, one being dominant and the other recessive, and if the factors segregated into the gametes.

5. Mendel's law of segregation states that there are two factors for each trait in the individual, and these separate into gametes that then have only one factor for each trait.

6. The laws of probability can be used to calculate the expected phenotypic ratio of a cross. In practice, a large number of offspring must be counted in order to observe the expected results, because only in that way can it be ensured that all possible types of sperm have fertilized all possible types of eggs.

7. Because humans do not produce a large number of offspring, it is best to use a predicted ratio as a means of estimating the chances of an individual inheriting a particular characteristic.

8. Mendel also crossed his F_1 plants with homozygous recessive plants. The results indicated that the recessive factor was present in the F_1 plants (i.e., that they were heterozygous). Today, we call this a testcross, because it is used to test whether an individual showing the dominant characteristic is homozygous dominant or heterozygous.

9. Mendel did dihybrid crosses, in which the F_1 individuals were dominant in both traits, but there were four phenotypes among the F_2 offspring. This allowed Mendel to deduce the law of independent assortment, which states that the members of one pair of factors separate independently of those from another pair. Therefore, all possible combinations of factors can occur in the gametes.

10. In regard to Mendel's dihybrid crosses, the laws of probability show that $9/16$ of the F_2 offspring have the two dominant traits, $3/16$ have one dominant trait with one recessive trait, $3/16$ have the other dominant trait with the other recessive trait, and $1/16$ have both recessive traits, for a 9:3:3:1 ratio.

11. The dihybrid testcross allows an investigator to test whether an individual showing two dominant characteristics is homozygous dominant for both traits or for one trait only, or is heterozygous for both traits.

12. Table 12.2 lists the most typical crosses and the expected results. Learning these saves the trouble of working out the results repeatedly for each of these crosses.

Writing Across the Curriculum

In order to practice writing skills, students should write out the answers to any or all of the study questions and the critical thinking questions. The study questions are sequenced in the same order as the text. Answers to the objective questions, and suggested answers to the critical thinking questions, are in appendix D.

Table 12.2

Common Crosses Involving Simple Dominance

Examples	Phenotypic Ratios
$Tt \times Tt$	3:1 (dominant to recessive)
$Tt \times tt$	1:1 (dominant to recessive)
$TtYy \times TtYy$	9:3:3:1 (9 dominant; 3 mixed; 3 mixed; 1 recessive)
$TtYy \times ttyy$	1:1:1:1 (all possible combinations in equal number)

Study Questions

1. How did Mendel's procedure differ from that of his predecessors? In what way did he set aside any personal beliefs he may have had?   184

2. How did the monohybrid crosses performed by Mendel refute the blending theory of inheritance?   186

3. Using Mendel's monohybrid cross as an example, trace his reasoning to arrive at the law of segregation.   186

4. Define these terms: allele, dominant allele, recessive allele, genotype, homozygous, heterozygous, and phenotype.   186

5. Use a Punnett square and the laws of probability to show the results of a cross between two individuals who are heterozygous for one trait. What are the chances of an offspring having the dominant phenotype? the recessive phenotype?   189

6. In what way does a monohybrid testcross support Mendel's law of segregation?   190

7. How is a monohybrid testcross used today?   190

8. Using Mendel's dihybrid cross as an example, trace his reasoning to arrive at the law of independent assortment.   191

9. Use a Punnett square and the laws of probability to show the results of a cross between two individuals who are heterozygous for two traits. What are the chances of an offspring having the dominant phenotype for both traits? having the recessive phenotype for both traits?   192

10. What would the results of a dihybrid testcross be if an individual was heterozygous for two traits? heterozygous for only one trait? homozygous dominant for both traits?   193

Objective Questions

For questions 1–4, match the cross with the results in the key:

Key:
   a. 3:1
   b. 9:3:3:1
   c. 1:1
   d. 1:1:1:1

1. $TtYy \times TtYy$
2. $Tt \times Tt$
3. $Tt \times tt$
4. $TtYy \times ttyy$

5. Which of these could be a gamete?
   a. *GgRr*
   b. *GRr*
   c. *Gr*
   d. None of these are correct.

6. Which of these properly describes a cross between an individual who is homozygous dominant for hairline but heterozygous for finger length and an individual who is recessive for both characteristics? (*W* = widow's peak, *w* = continuous hairline, *S* = short fingers, *s* = long fingers)
   a. *WwSs × WwSs*
   b. *WWSs × wwSs*
   c. *Ws × ws*
   d. *WWSs × wwss*

7. In peas, yellow seed (*Y*) is dominant over green seed (*y*). In the F_2 generation of a monohybrid cross in which a dominant homozygote is crossed with a recessive homozygote, you would expect
   a. plants that produce three yellow seeds to every green seed.
   b. plants with one yellow seed for every green seed.
   c. only plants with the genotype *YY* or *yy*.
   d. Both a and c are correct.

8. In humans, pointed eyebrows (*B*) are dominant over smooth eyebrows (*b*). Mary's father has pointed eyebrows, but she and her mother have smooth. What is the genotype of the father?
   a. *BB*
   b. *Bb*
   c. *bb*
   d. Any one of these is correct.

9. In guinea pigs, smooth coat (*S*) is dominant over rough coat (*s*) and black coat (*B*) is dominant over white coat (*b*). In the cross *SsBb × SsBb,* how many of the offspring will have a smooth black coat on average?
   a. 9 only
   b. about $^9/_{16}$
   c. $^1/_{16}$
   d. $^6/_{16}$

10. In horses, *B* = black coat, *b* = brown coat, *T* = trotter, and *t* = pacer. A black trotter that has a brown pacer offspring is
   a. *BT.*
   b. *BbTt.*
   c. *bbtt.*
   d. *BBtt.*

11. In tomatoes, red fruit (*R*) is dominant over yellow fruit (*r*) and tallness (*T*) is dominant over shortness (*t*). A plant that is *RrTT* is crossed with a plant that is *rrTt*. What are the chances of an offspring being heterozygous for both traits?
   a. none
   b. $^1/_2$
   c. $^1/_4$
   d. $^9/_{16}$

12. In the cross *RrTt × rrtt,*
   a. all the offspring will be tall with red fruit.
   b. 75% ($^3/_4$) will be tall with red fruit.
   c. 50% ($^1/_2$) will be tall with red fruit.
   d. 25% ($^1/_4$) will be tall with red fruit.

Additional Genetics Problems*

1. If a man homozygous for widow's peak (dominant) reproduces with a woman homozygous for continuous hairline (recessive), what are the chances of the children's having a widow's peak? a continuous hairline?

2. John has unattached earlobes (recessive) like his father, but his mother has attached earlobes (dominant). What is John's genotype?

3. In humans, the allele for short fingers is dominant over that for long fingers. If a person with short fingers who had one parent with long fingers reproduces with a person having long fingers, what are the chances of each child having short fingers?

4. In a fruit fly experiment (see key on page 192), two gray-bodied fruit flies produce mostly gray-bodied offspring, but some offspring have black bodies. If there are 280 offspring, how many do you predict will have gray bodies and how many will have black bodies? How many of the 280 offspring do you predict will be heterozygous? If you wanted to test whether a particular gray-bodied fly was homozygous dominant or heterozygous, what cross would you do?

5. In rabbits, black color (*B*) is dominant over brown (*b*) and short hair (*S*) is dominant over long (*s*). In a cross between a homozygous black, long-haired rabbit and a brown, homozygous short-haired one, what would the F_1 generation look like? the F_2 generation? If one of the F_1 rabbits reproduced with a brown, long-haired rabbit, what phenotypes and in what ratio would you expect?

6. In horses, black coat (*B*) is dominant over brown coat (*b*) and being a trotter (*T*) is dominant over being a pacer (*t*). A black pacer is crossed with a brown trotter. The offspring is a brown pacer. Give the genotypes of all these horses.

7. The complete genotype of a long-winged, gray-bodied fruit fly is unknown. (See key on page 192.) When this fly is crossed with a short-winged, black-bodied fruit fly, the offspring all have a gray body but about half of them have short wings. What is the genotype of the long-winged, gray-bodied fly?

8. In humans, widow's peak hairline is dominant over continuous hairline, and short fingers are dominant over long fingers. If an individual who is heterozygous for both traits reproduces with an individual who is recessive for both traits, what are the chances of a child's also being recessive for both traits?

---
*Answers to Additional Genetic Problems appear in Appendix D.

Concepts and Critical Thinking

1. *The laws of heredity explain genetic stability and variation between generations.*

   Explain why you are similar in appearance to your parents but do not resemble either one exactly.

2. *The laws of heredity are the same for all organisms.*

   Why would you expect the same laws of heredity to apply to both plants and animals?

3. *Alleles, carried by way of gametes from generation to generation, are not affected by the phenotype.*

   Explain why an individual, deformed by accident, can have children who have no such deformities.

Selected Key Terms

allele (uh-LEEL) Alternative forms of a gene—which occur at the same locus on homologous chromosomes. [Gk. *allelo,* one another, parallel] 187

dominant allele (uh-LEEL) An allele that exerts its phenotypic effect in the heterozygote; it hides the expression of the recessive allele. 187

gene locus The specific location of a particular gene on homologous chromosomes. 187

genotype The genes of an organism for a particular trait or traits; for example, *BB* or *Aa*. [Gk. *geno,* race, and *typos,* image] 187

heterozygous Possessing unlike alleles for a particular trait. [Gk. *heter,* different, and *zyg,* yoke] 187

homozygous Possessing two identical alleles for a particular trait. [Gk. *homo,* alike, and *zyg,* yoke] 187

phenotype The visible expression of a genotype—for example, brown eyes or attached earlobes. [Gk. *pheno,* appear, and *typos,* image] 187

Punnett square A grid that enables one to calculate the results of simple genetic crosses by lining up alleles within the gametes of two parents on the outside margin and their recombination in boxes inside the grid. 187

recessive allele (uh-LEEL) An allele that exerts its phenotypic effect only in the homozygote; its expression is masked by a dominant allele. 187

testcross A cross between an individual with the dominant phenotype and an individual with the recessive phenotype to see if the individual with the dominant phenotype is homozygous or heterozygous. 190

13
CHROMOSOMES AND GENES

Learning Objectives

Going Beyond Mendel

- Recognize and solve genetics problems involving degrees of dominance, interactions multiple alleles, and polygenes.   198–201
- Discuss, with examples, the relative influence of the genotype and the environment on the phenotype.   200

Chromosomes Contain Genes

- Support the chromosomal theory of inheritance by listing similarities in the behavior of chromosomes and genes.   202
- Explain the normal sex chromosome makeup of human males and females and how the sex of the individual is determined.   202
- Describe the experiment that allowed investigators to determine the existence of X-linked genes.   202

- Solve genetics problems involving x–linked alleles.   203
- Explain why linked genes do not obey Mendel's laws, and solve genetic linkage problems.   204
- Use the results of crosses involving linked genes to determine the order of genes on a chromosome.   205

Chromosomes Undergo Mutations

- Give examples of chromosomal mutations caused by a change in chromosomal number, and explain how such mutations could occur.   206
- Give examples of chromosomal mutations caused by a change in chromosomal structure, and explain how such mutations could occur.   207

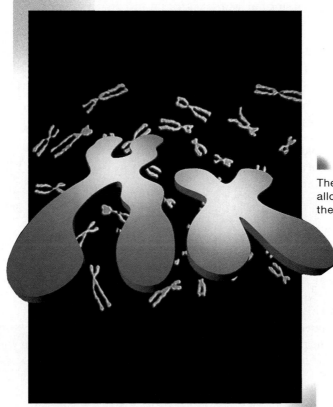

The sex chromosomes X and Y first allowed investigators to show that the genes are on the chromosomes.

rom his experiment with the garden pea, Gregor Mendel concluded that an organism inherits two factors for every trait and that one factor can be dominant over the other factor. Since that time, many exceptions to these fundamental ideas have been discovered and a few of these are discussed here.

GOING BEYOND MENDEL

Since Mendel's day patterns of inheritance in addition to simple dominance have been discovered.

Dominance Has Degrees

Mendel always observed simple dominance of one characteristic over another in his experiments. If Mendel had chosen other characteristics, he most likely would have observed **incomplete dominance,** in which neither allele if fully dominant. In a cross between a true-breeding, red-flowered four o'clock strain and a true-breeding, white-flowered strain, the offspring have pink flowers (fig. 13.1). This is not an example that supports the blending theory of inheritance prevalent when Mendel did his work, however. If these F_1 plants self-pollinate, the F_2 generation has a phenotypic ratio of 1 red-flowered : 2 pink-flowered : 1 white-flowered plant. Because the parental phenotypes reappear in the F_2 generation, it is obvious that we are still dealing with an example of particulate inheritance of the type described by Mendel.

There are also examples of **codominance,** in which both alleles are fully expressed. An individual with the blood type AB is exhibiting codominant characteristics. We know this because there are also some individuals who have blood type A and others who have blood type B. The recessive individual has blood type O and exhibits neither dominant characteristic.

With codominance, both alleles produce an effective product. In an individual with blood type AB, two different types of glycoproteins appear on the red blood cells. With simple dominance, the level of a gene-directed protein product is often in between that of the two homozygotes. In other words, the dominant allele is coding for the production of a protein, while the recessive allele is not coding for an effective protein.

A Gene That Controls Many Traits

The term *pleiotropy* is used to describe a gene that affects more than one characteristic of the individual. Individuals with Marfan syndrome tend to be tall and thin with long legs, arms, and fingers. They are nearsighted, and the wall of the aorta is weak, causing it to enlarge and, eventually, to split. All of these effects are caused by an inability to produce normal connective tissue. The difficulty stems from an allele that directs the production of an abnormal polypeptide for collagen. Both the mutant allele and a normal allele are both active.

Figure 13.1

Incomplete dominance illustrated by a cross between red- and white-flowered four o'clocks, *Mirabilis*. The F_1 plants are pink, a phenotype intermediate between those of the P generation; however, the F_2 results show that neither the red nor the white allele has disappeared. Therefore, this is still an example of particulate inheritance, though the heterozygote *Rr* is pink.

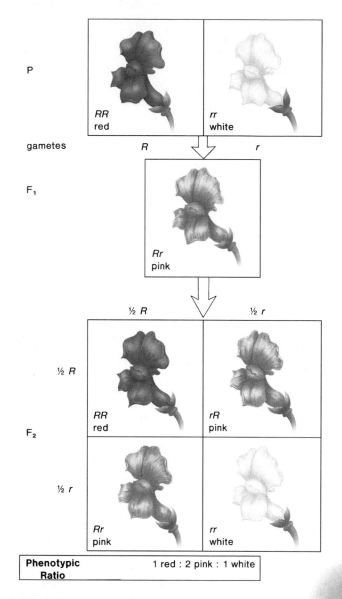

In pleiotropy, an allele affects more than one phenotypic characteristic.

Genes That Interact

Genes often interact to produce the phenotype. Sometimes a recessive pair of alleles at one locus prevents the expression of a dominant allele at another locus. This is called *epistasis*, meaning a "covering-up." For example, if two plants that produce white corn ears are crossed, the F_1 have purple kernels, but among the F_2, $^9/_{16}$ have purple kernels and $^7/_{16}$ have white kernels. Since the ratio is in sixteenths, the F_1 plants must have been dihybrids as shown in figure 13.2. The 9:7 ratio appeared instead of 9:3:3:1 because the homozygous recessive causes the kernels to be white even when there is a dominant allele for purple.

How can epistasis in this case be explained? The production of plant pigments involves a metabolic pathway in which each reaction is catalyzed by a particular enzyme. The presence of a dominant allele results in a functional enzyme for one reaction; the presence of two recessive alleles results in a nonfunctioning enzyme for another reaction. If any reaction of the metabolic pathway is blocked, the plant lacks pigment. A somewhat similar situation occurs in humans and other animals. If individuals inherit the allelic pair (*aa*) that causes albinism, they are unable to produce the normal pigment melanin. Therefore, it does not matter what genes they may have inherited for color of eyes and hair. These genes will not be expressed, and the individual will be an albino lacking pigment in all parts of the body.

Several Alleles for One Trait

Sometimes there are more than two alleles for a given chromosomal locus, in which case a trait is controlled by **multiple alleles.** Each individual has only two of all the available alleles.

In rabbits there are four alleles for coat color, and there is a dominance sequence that may be described like this:

$$C > c^{ch} > c^h > c$$

Therefore, there are four genotypes and phenotypes, as shown in figure 13.3.

Inheritance by multiple alleles causes a trait to exhibit more than two possible phenotypes. Blood type in humans is controlled by three alleles, and there are four possible phenotypes: A, B, AB, and O.

Figure 13.3

Inheritance by multiple alleles explains inheritance of coat color in these rabbits. Because there are four alleles that range in dominance (each individual has only two), there are four different genotypes and phenotypes.

genotypes: *CC, Cc^ch, Cc^h, Cc*
phenotype: wild type or agouti coat

genotypes: *c^chc^ch, c^chc^h, c^chc*
phenotype: chinchilla or light gray coat

genotypes: *c^hc^h, c^hc*
phenotype: Himalayan coat (albino with black extremities)

genotype: *cc*
phenotype: albino

Figure 13.2

Epistasis in color production in corn.

	♂		♀
Parents	AAbb	×	aaBB
	first white variety		second white variety

F_1

AaBb

purple

F_2

eggs

♀ sperm / ♂	AB	Ab	aB	ab
AB	AABB	AABb	AaBB	AaBb
Ab	AABb	AAbb	AaBb	Aabb
aB	AaBB	AaBb	aaBB	aaBb
ab	AaBb	Aabb	aaBb	aabb

offspring

Phenotypic Ratio   9   purple   7   white

Environment Affects the Phenotype

There is no doubt that both the genotype and the environment affect the phenotype. The relative importance of genetic and environmental influences on the phenotype can vary, but in some instances the environment seems to have an extreme effect.

In the water buttercup, *Ranunculus peltatus* (fig. 13.4), the submerged part of the plant has a different appearance from the part above water. Apparently, the presence or absence of an aquatic environment dramatically influences the phenotype.

In humans, if the drug thalidomide is taken during the second month of pregnancy, the newborn can be seriously malformed—either without arms or legs or with stublike appendages. This phenotype can be due to a rare recessive mutation in humans, but in this instance it is caused by the environmental effect of thalidomide—the genotype is normal!

> The relative effect of genes and the environment on the phenotype varies; there are examples of extreme environmental influence.

Figure 13.4

Environmental influence on the phenotype of the water buttercup *Ranunculus pelatus* is obvious. The submerged leaves are thin and finely divided, whereas those that lie above water are broad and flat.

Genes That Add Up

Polygenic inheritance [Gk. *poly,* many, and *genic,* producing] occurs when one trait is governed by several genes occupying different loci on the same homologous pair of chromosomes or on different homologous pairs of chromosomes. Each gene has a contributing and noncontributing allele. The contributing allele is represented by a capital letter and the noncontributing allele is represented by a small letter. Each contributing allele has a quantitative effect on the phenotype, and therefore the allelic effects are additive.

For example, H. Nilsson-Ehle studied the inheritance of seed color in wheat. After he crossed plants that produced white and dark red seeds, the F_1 plants were allowed to self-pollinate. The F_2 seeds have seven phenotypes ranging from white to dark red:

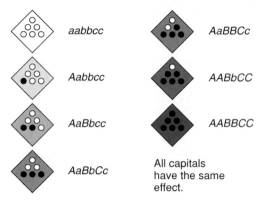

aabbcc   AaBBCc

Aabbcc   AABbCC

AaBbcc   AABBCC

AaBbCc   All capitals have the same effect.

Notice that each contributing allele has a small but equal quantitative effect, and that this accounts for the various degrees of color and the observed range in F_2 phenotypes. The proportions of the phenotypes can be graphed as in figure 13.5, and these proportions can be connected to form a bell-shaped curve.

If we were observing the phenotypes in nature, we would probably arrive directly at a bell-shaped curve because environmental effects cause many intervening phenotypes. Consider the inheritance of skin color or height in humans, which are believed to be examples of polygenic inheritance. In the first instance, exposure to sun can affect skin color and increase the number of phenotypic variations. In the second instance, nutrition can affect height, resulting in many more phenotypes than those expected.

> In polygenic inheritance, each contributing allele adds to the phenotype. A bell-shaped curve of phenotypes is due also to environmental effects.

Figure 13.5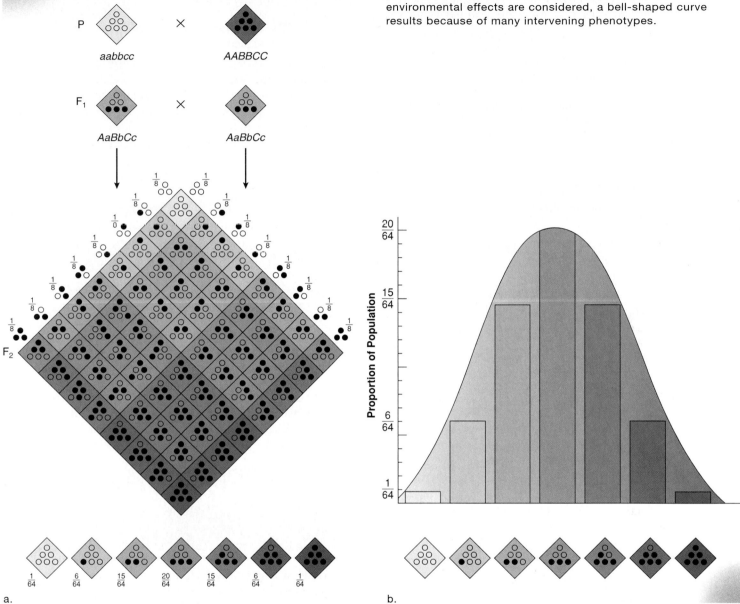

Polygenic inheritance. **a.** In this example, a trait is controlled by three genes; only the alleles represented by a capital letter are contributing alleles. When two intermediate phenotypes are crossed, seven phenotypes and genotypes are seen among the F$_2$ generation. **b.** The phenotype proportions are graphed. If environmental effects are considered, a bell-shaped curve results because of many intervening phenotypes.

a.

b.

Practice Problems 1*

1. What genotypes and phenotypes are possible among the offspring if a rabbit with the genotype Cc^h is mated to a rabbit with the genotype $c^{ch}c^h$?

2. What are the results of a testcross involving incomplete dominance when pink-flowered four o'clocks are crossed with white-flowered ones?

3. Breeders of dogs note various colors among offspring that range from white to black. If the coat color is controlled by three pairs of alleles, how many different shades are possible if all dominant genes have the same effect?

4. Investigators note that albino tigers usually have crossed eyes. What two inheritance patterns can account for a phenotype such as this?

*Answers to Practice Problems appear in appendix D.

CHROMOSOMES CONTAIN GENES

The behavior of chromosomes was described for mitosis by 1875, and for meiosis in the 1890s. By 1902, both Theodor Boveri, a German, and Walter S. Sutton, an American, had independently noted the parallel behavior of genes and chromosomes and had proposed the **chromosomal theory of inheritance**, which states that the genes are located on the chromosomes. This theory is supported by the following observations:

1. Both chromosomes and factors (now called alleles) are paired in diploid cells.

2. Both homologous chromosomes and alleles of each pair separate during meiosis so that the gametes have one-half the total number.

3. Both homologous chromosomes and alleles of each pair separate independently so that the gametes contain all possible combinations.

4. Fertilization restores both the diploid chromosomal number and the paired condition for alleles in the zygote.

> The genes are on the chromosomes; therefore, they behave similarly during meiosis and fertilization.

Sex Chromosomes Determine Gender

In animal species, the autosomes, or nonsex chromosomes are the same between the sexes. The members of each pair of autosomes are homologous. One special pair of chromosomes is called the sex chromosomes because this pair determines the sex of the individual. The sex chromosomes in the human female are XX and those in the male are XY. Because males can produce two different types of gametes—those that contain an X and those that contain a Y—normally males determine the sex of the new individual.

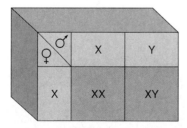

As you would suspect, the sex chromosomes carry genes that determine sex. In 1991, Robin Lovell-Badge and Peter Goodfellow and their colleagues in England isolated a gene called *sex-determining region Y* (*SRY*), which, when injected into XX mice, caused them to develop as males. It is believed that embryos develop ovaries unless the *SRY* gene switches the developmental process to one that leads to testes formation.

In addition to genes that determine sex, the sex chromosomes carry genes for traits that have nothing to do with the sex of the individual. By tradition, the term sex-linked or **X-linked** is used for alleles carried on the X chromosome. The Y chromosome is blank for these alleles.

Genes That Are on the X Chromosomes

The hypothesis that genes are on the chromosomes was substantiated by experiments performed by a Columbia University group of *Drosophila* geneticists, headed by Thomas Hunt Morgan. Fruit flies are even better subjects for genetic studies than garden peas: they can be easily and inexpensively raised in simple laboratory glassware; females mate only once and then lay hundreds of eggs during their lifetimes; and the generation time is short, taking only about ten days when conditions are favorable (fig. 13.6).

Drosophila flies have the same sex chromosome pattern as humans, and this facilitates our understanding of a cross performed by Morgan. Morgan took a newly discovered mutant male with white eyes and crossed it with a red-eyed female:

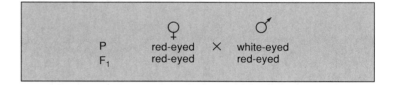

From these results, he knew that red eyes are dominant over white eyes. He then crossed the F_1 flies. In the F_2 generation, there was the expected 3 red-eyed : 1 white-eyed ratio, but it struck him as odd that all of the white-eyed flies were males:

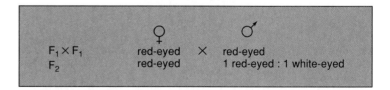

Obviously, a major difference between the male flies and the female flies was their sex chromosomes. Could it be possible that an allele for eye color was on the Y chromosome but not on the X? This idea could be quickly discarded because normal females have red eyes and they have no Y chromosome. Perhaps an allele for eye color was on the X, but not on the Y, chromosome. Figure 13.6*b* indicates that this explanation would match the results obtained in the experiment. These results support the chromosomal theory of inheritance by showing that the behavior of a specific allele corresponds exactly with that of a specific chromosome—the X chromosome in *Drosophila*.

> **X**-linked alleles are on the X chromosome and the Y chromosome is blank for these alleles.

Figure 13.6

Drosophila cross. **a.** Both males and females have eight chromosomes, three pairs of autosomes (II–IV), and one pair of sex chromosomes (I). Males are XY and females are XX. **b.** When solving X-linked genetics problems, males do not have a superscript attached to the Y chromosome because they lack the gene for eye color on that chromosome. Among the offspring in this cross, 50% of the males have white eyes. Because the males receive a Y chromosome from the male parent, they express whichever X chromosome is inherited from the female parent. In contrast, 50% of the female offspring are red-eyed heterozygotes—when an X^r is received from the female parent, it is masked by an X^R received from the male parent.

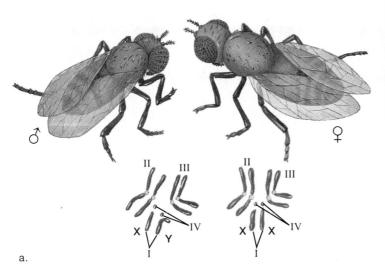

a.

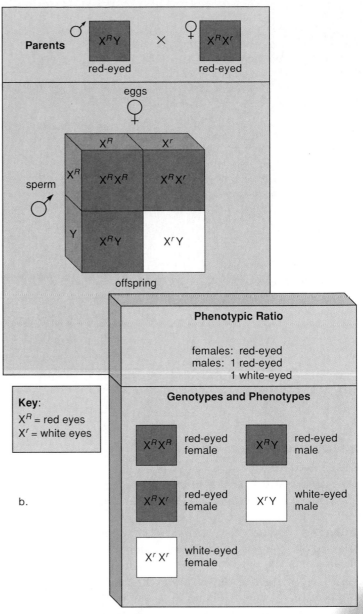

b.

Doing X-Linked Problems

Recall that when solving autosomal genetic problems, the key and genotypes are represented as follows:

KEY:

L = long wing

l = short wings

GENOTYPES:

LL, Ll, ll

As noted in figure 13.6, however, the key for an X-linked gene shows the allele attached to the X:

KEY:

X^R = red eyes

X^r = white eyes

Notice, too, that there are three possible genotypes for females, but only two for males. Females can be heterozygous $X^R X^r$, in which case they are carriers. Carriers usually do not show an abnormality, but they are capable of passing on an allele for an abnormality. Males cannot be carriers; if the normal allele is on the single X chromosome, they appear normal, and if the mutated allele is on the single X chromosome, they show the abnormality.

Practice Problems 2*

1. Using the key for *Drosophila* eye color shown in figure 13.6, give the three possible genotypes for females and the two possible genotypes for males. What are the possible gametes for these males?

2. Which *Drosophila* cross would produce white-eyed males? in what ratio?
   a. $X^R X^R \times X^r Y$
   b. $X^R X^r \times X^R Y$

3. A woman is color blind (recessive). What are the chances of her sons being color blind? If she reproduces with a man having normal vision, what are the chances of her daughters being color blind? being carriers?

*Answers to Practice Problems appear in appendix D.

Figure 13.7

Complete linkage versus incomplete linkage. **a.** Hypothetical cross in which genes for body and eye color on chromosome 2 of *Drosophila* are completely linked. Instead of the expected 1:1:1:1 ratio among the offspring, there would be a 1:1 ratio. **b.** Crossing-over occurs, and 6% of the offspring show recombinant phenotypes. The percentage of recombinant phenotypes is used to map the chromosomes (1% = 1 map unit).

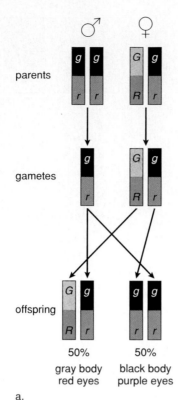
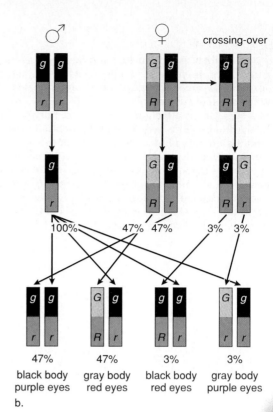

Key:
G = gray body
g = black body
R = red eyes
r = purple eyes

Genes Are Linked

Drosophila probably has thousands of different genes controlling all aspects of its structure, biochemistry, and behavior. Yet it has only four pairs of chromosomes. This paradox led investigators like Sutton to conclude that each chromosome must carry a large number of alleles. For example, it is now known that genes controlling eye color, wing type, body color, leg length, and antennae type are all located on the chromosomes numbered II in figure 13.6. The alleles for these genes are said to form a **linkage group** because they are found on the same chromosome.

It is easy to predict that crosses involving linked genes will not give the same results as those involving unlinked genes (fig. 13.7). Suppose you are doing a cross between a gray-bodied, red-eyed heterozygote and a black-bodied, purple-eyed fly. Since the alleles governing these traits are both on chromosome II, you predict that the results will be 1:1 instead of 1:1:1:1, as is the case for unlinked genes. The reason, of course, is that linked alleles tend to stay together and do not separate independently as predicted by Mendel's laws because they are on the same chromosome. Under these circumstances, the heterozygote forms only two types of gametes and produces offspring with only two phenotypes (fig. 13.7a).

When you do the cross, however, you find that a very small number of offspring show recombinant phenotypes (i.e., those that are different from the original parents). Specifically, you find that 47% of the offspring have black bodies and purple eyes, 47% have gray bodies and red eyes, 3% have black bodies and red eyes, and 3% have gray bodies and purple eyes (fig. 13.7b). What happened?

Crossing-over can occur between homologous chromosomes when they are paired during meiosis, and crossing-over produces recombinant gametes (fig. 13.8). In this instance, crossing-over produced a very small number of *recombinant gametes* (fig. 13.8) and when these were fertilized, *recombinant phenotypes* were observed in the offspring. An examination of chromosome II shows that these two sets of alleles are very close together. Doesn't it stand to reason that the closer together two genes are, the less likely they are to cross over? This is exactly what various crosses have repeatedly shown.

> All the genes on one chromosome form a linkage group that tends to stay together, except when crossing-over occurs.

Figure 13.8

Crossing-over. When homologous chromosomes are in synapsis, the nonsister chromatids exchange genetic material. Following crossing-over, recombinant chromosomes occur.

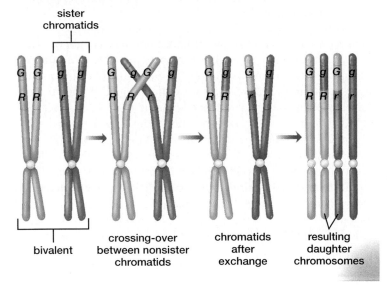

sister chromatids

bivalent

crossing-over between nonsister chromatids

chromatids after exchange

resulting daughter chromosomes

Practice Problems 3*

1. When *AaBb* individuals are allowed to self-breed, the phenotypic ratio is just about 3:1. What ratio was expected? What may have caused the observed ratio?

2. In two sweet pea strains, *B* = blue flowers, *b* = red flowers, *L* = long pollen grains, and *l* = round pollen grains. In a cross between a heterozygous plant with blue flowers and long pollen grains and a plant with red flowers and round pollen grains, 44% of offspring are blue, long; 44% are red, round; 6% are blue, round; and 6% are red, long. How many map units separate these two sets of alleles?

3. Investigators performed crosses that indicated bar-eyed and garnet-eyed alleles are thirteen map units apart, scalloped-winged and bar-eyed alleles are six units apart, and garnet-eyed and scalloped-winged alleles are seven units apart. What is the order of these alleles on the chromosome?

*Answers to Practice Problems appear in appendix D.

Mapping the Chromosomes

You can use the percentage of recombinant phenotypes to map the chromosomes, because there is a direct relationship between the frequency of crossing-over and the percentage of recombinant phenotypes. In our example, a total of 6% of the offspring are recombinants, and for the sake of mapping the chromosomes, it is assumed that 1% of crossing-over equals one map unit. Therefore, the allele for black body and the allele for purple eyes are six map units apart.

Suppose you want to determine the order of any three genes on the chromosomes. To do so, you can perform crosses that tell you the map distance between all three pairs of alleles. If you know, for instance, that:

1. the distance between the black-body and purple-eye alleles = 6 map units,
2. the distance between the purple-eye and vestigial-wing alleles = 12.5 units, and
3. the distance between the black-body and vestigial-wing alleles = 18.5 units, then the order of the alleles must be as shown here:

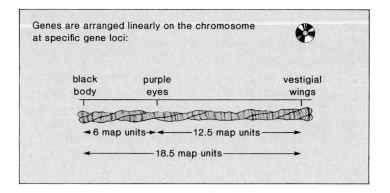

Genes are arranged linearly on the chromosome at specific gene loci:

black body   purple eyes   vestigial wings

◄6 map units►◄—12.5 map units—►

◄—18.5 map units—►

Of the three possible orders (any one of the three genes can be in the middle), only this order gives the proper distance between all three allelic pairs. Because it is possible to map the chromosomes, we conclude that genes are indeed located on chromosomes, they have a definite location, and they occur in a definite order.

> The crossing-over frequency is proportional to the recombinant phenotypic frequency, which, in crosses involving linked genes, indicates the distance between genes on the chromosomes.

CHROMOSOMES UNDERGO MUTATIONS

Mutations [L. *muta,* change] are permanent changes in genes or chromosomes that can be passed to offspring if they occur in cells that become gametes. Like crossing-over, recombination of chromosomes during meiosis, and gamete fusion during fertilization, mutations increase the amount of variation among offspring. *Chromosome mutations* include changes in chromosomal number and changes in chromosomal structure.

Changing Chromosomal Number

Changes in the chromosomal number include monosomies, trisomies, and polyploidy.

Monosomy and Trisomy

Monosomy occurs when an individual has only one of a particular type of chromosome (2n − 1), and *trisomy* occurs when an individual has three of a particular type of chromosome (2n + 1). The usual cause of monosomy and trisomy is nondisjunction during meiosis. *Nondisjunction* can occur during meiosis I if members of a homologous pair fail to separate, and during meiosis II if the daughter chromosomes fail to separate and instead go into the same daughter cell. Nondisjunction is more common during meiosis I than during meiosis II. Nondisjunction can also occur during mitosis.

Monosomy and trisomy occur in both plants and animals. In animals, autosomal monosomies and trisomies are generally lethal, although a trisomic individual is more likely to survive than a monosomic one. The survivors are characterized by a distinctive set of physical and mental abnormalities called a syndrome. In humans, Turner syndrome is a monosomy involving the sex chromosomes—the individual inherits a single X chromosome. The most common trisomy among humans is Down syndrome, which involves chromosome 21. Individuals with Turner syndrome and Down syndrome are expected to live a full lifespan.

Polyploidy

Some mutant eukaryotes have more than two sets of chromosomes. They are called **polyploids** [*poly*, many, and *ploid*, sets]. Polyploid organisms are named according to the number of sets of chromosomes they have. Triploids (3n) have three of each kind of chromosome, tetraploids (4n) have four sets, pentaploids (5n) have five sets, and so on.

While polyploidy is not a means to increase variation among animals because they have sex chromosomes, it is a major evolutionary mechanism in plants. It is estimated that 47% of all flowering plants are polyploids. Among these are many of our most important crops, such as wheat, corn, cotton, sugarcane, and fruits such as watermelons, bananas, and apples (fig. 13.9). Also many attractive flowers, such as chrysanthemums and daylilies, are polyploids. Polyploidy generally arises following hybridization. When two different species reproduce, the resulting plant, called a hybrid, may have an odd number of chromosomes. If so, the chromosomes cannot pair evenly during meiosis, and the hybrid plant will not be fertile. If the chromosomal number doubles, however, there will be an even number of chromosomes, and the chromosomes will be able to undergo synapsis during meiosis.

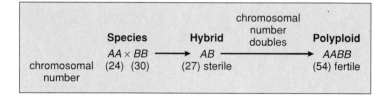

Monosomies (2n − 1) and trisomies (2n + 1) cause abnormalities. In plants, hybridization followed by polyploidy is a positive force for change.

Figure 13.9
Many food sources are specially developed polyploid plants. **a, b.** Among these are seedless watermelons and bananas. They are infertile (seeds poorly developed) triploids, but they can be propagated by asexual means. **c.** Polyploidy makes plants and their fruits larger, such as these jumbo McIntosh apples.

a.

b.

c.

Changing Chromosomal Structure

There are various agents in the environment, such as radiation, certain organic chemicals, or even viruses, that can cause chromosomes to break. Sometimes, however, the broken ends of one or more chromosomes do not rejoin in the same pattern as before, and this results in a change in chromosomal structure.

An *inversion* occurs when a segment of a chromosome is turned around 180° (fig. 13.10). You might think this is not a problem because the same genes are present, but the new position might lead to altered gene activity.

A *translocation* is the movement of a chromosomal segment from one chromosome to another, nonhomologous chromosome. Translocation heterozygotes usually have reduced fertility due to production of abnormal gametes.

A *deletion* occurs when an end of a chromosome breaks off or when two simultaneous breaks lead to the loss of a segment. Even when only one member of a pair of chromosomes is affected, a deletion often causes abnormalities. An example is cri du chat (cat's cry) syndrome. The affected individual has a small head, is mentally retarded, and has facial abnormalities. Abnormal development of the glottis and larynx results in the most characteristic symptom—the infant's cry resembles that of a cat.

A *duplication* is the doubling of a chromosomal segment. There are several ways a duplication can occur. A broken segment from one chromosome can simply attach to its homologue, or unequal crossing-over may occur, leading to a duplication and a deletion:

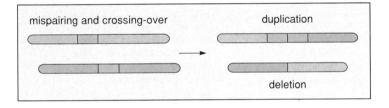

Multiple copies of genes can mutate differently and thereby provide additional genetic variation for the species. For example, there are several closely linked genes for human globin (globin is a part of hemoglobin, which is present in red blood cells and carries oxygen). This may have arisen by a process of duplication followed by different mutations in each gene.

> Chromosomal mutations include various changes in structure, which can lead to abnormal gametes and offspring.

Figure 13.10

Types of chromosomal mutations. **a.** Inversion occurs when a piece of chromosome breaks loose and then rejoins in the reversed direction. **b.** Translocation is the exchange of chromosomal pieces between nonhomologous pairs. **c.** Deletion is the loss of a chromosomal piece. **d.** Duplication occurs when the same piece is repeated within the chromosome.

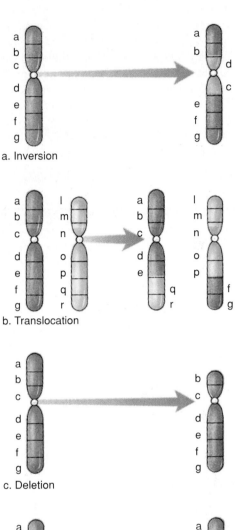

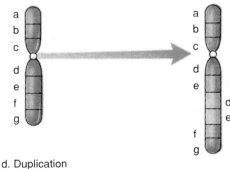

Biological Relationships

Mendel's statistical studies allowed him to formulate patterns of inheritance that are still used today to predict the chances of certain phenotypes among offspring. The many other patterns of inheritance that have been discovered since Mendel's time expand on his original contribution. The term phenotype is often used to mean some particular characteristic such as tall, short, or attached or unattached earlobes. But phenotype can also mean all the characteristics of an organism including its outward appearance, internal makeup, physiology, and behavior. Similarly, the term genotype can refer to a single gene locus or all the genes of an organism. In the end, the phenotype is influenced by the genotype plus the environment in which the organism grows and develops. Considering this, it is remarkable that Mendel arrived at a particulate theory of inheritance that still serves as a foundation for modern-day genetics and also evolutionary theory. Variations must arise and be present in each population if evolution is to occur.

It is important to realize that human beings are like, not dissimilar from, other organisms. Human genetics is also founded in Mendelian genetics and we, too, have an evolutionary history that ties us to all other living things. Mendel's laws of inheritance helped establish the chromosomal theory of inheritance, which states that the genes are on the chromosomes. This was a very fruitful theory because it not only led to the discovery that DNA (deoxyribonucleic acid) is the genetic material, it also set the stage for our ability to manipulate the genes. Gene therapy for some human disorders is now a reality.

Science progresses. The history of genetics shows that an original discovery can be modified and built upon as more and more research is done in that area. Mendel formulated laws that hold because of the behavior of chromosomes during meiosis. Still, the genes are not particles on the chromosomes and instead are DNA molecules located within the chromosomes. DNA directs protein synthesis and many proteins are enzymes that participate in the metabolism of the cells. It is cellular metabolism that makes us what we are and determines whether we are sick or healthy. Modern therapies are based on the recognition that living things have a cellular basis. Human genetics and biochemical genetics are discussed in subsequent chapters.

Summary

1. Different degrees of dominance have been observed. With incomplete dominance, the F_1 individuals are intermediate between the parental types; this does not support the blending theory because the parental phenotypes reappear in F_2. With codominance, the F_1 individuals express both alleles.

2. On the genotype level, the action of a dominant allele usually makes up for a noneffective recessive allele, but in the case of pleiotropy, a dominant allele causes an effect that drastically alters the phenotype in many regards.

3. Genes interact. The homozygous recessive condition can mask the effect of a dominant allele at another locus (epistasis).

4. Some genes have multiple alleles, although each individual organism has only two alleles. Coat color in rabbits is controlled by multiple alleles, and four different type coats are possible.

5. The relative influence of the genotype and the environment on the phenotype can vary. There are examples of extreme environmental influence.

6. Polygenic traits are controlled by genes that have an additive effect on the phenotype, resulting in quantitative variations. A bell-shaped curve is seen because environmental influences bring about many intervening phenotypes.

7. The chromosomal theory of inheritance says that the genes are located on the chromosomes, which accounts for the similarity of their behavior during meiosis and fertilization.

8. Sex determination in animals is dependent upon the chromosomes. Usually females are XX and males are XY.

9. Solid experimental support for the chromosomal theory of inheritance came when Morgan and his group were able to determine that the white-eye allele in *Drosophila* is on the X chromosome.

10. Alleles on the X chromosome are called X-linked alleles. Therefore, when doing X-linked genetic problems, it is the custom to indicate the sexes by using sex chromosomes and to indicate the alleles by superscripts attached to the X. The Y is blank because it does not carry these genes.

11. All the alleles on a chromosome form a linkage group. Linked alleles do not obey Mendel's laws because they tend to go into the gametes together. Crossing-over can cause recombinant gametes and recombinant phenotypes to occur. The percentage of recombinant phenotypes is used to measure the distance between genes and to map the chromosomes.

12. Chromosomal mutations fall into two categories: changes in chromosomal number and changes in chromosomal structure.

13. Monosomy occurs when an individual has only one of a particular type of chromosome ($2n - 1$); trisomy occurs when an individual has three of a particular type of chromosome ($2n + 1$). Polyploidy occurs when the eukaryotic individual has more than two complete sets of chromosomes.

14. Changes in chromosomal structure include inversions, translocations, deletions, and duplications.

Writing Across the Curriculum

In order to practice writing skills, students should write out the answers to any or all of the study questions and the critical thinking questions. The study questions are sequenced in the same order as the text. Answers to the objective questions, and suggested answers to the critical thinking questions, are in appendix D.

Study Questions

1. Compare the F_2 phenotypic ratio for a cross involving a dominant allele, an incompletely dominant allele, and codominant alleles.   198

2. If you were studying a particular population of organisms, how would you recognize that several traits are being affected by a pleiotropic gene?   198

3. Show that if a dihybrid cross between two heterozygotes involves an epistatic gene, you do not get a ratio of 9:3:3:1.   199

4. Explain inheritance by multiple alleles. List the human blood types and give the possible genotypes for each.   199

5. Give examples to show that the environment can have an extreme effect on the phenotype despite the genotype.   200

6. Explain why traits controlled by polygenes show continuous variation that can be measured quantitatively, have many intermediate forms, and produce a distribution in the F_2 generation that follows a bell-shaped curve.   200

7. What is the chromosomal theory of inheritance? List the ways in which genes and chromosomes behave similarly during meiosis and fertilization.   202

8. How is sex determined in humans? Which sex determines the sex of the offspring?   202

9. How did a *Drosophila* cross involving an X-linked gene help investigators show that certain genes are carried on certain chromosomes?   202

10. Show that a dihybrid cross between a heterozygote and a recessive homozygote involving linked genes does not produce the expected 1:1:1:1 ratio. What is the significance of the small percentage of recombinants that occurs among the offspring?   204

11. What are the two types of chromosomal mutations? What two types of changes in chromosomal number were discussed? What four types of changes in chromosomal structure were discussed?   206–7

12. What is a monosomy? a trisomy? Why would you expect a monosomy to be more lethal than a trisomy? Why is polyploidy not generally found in animals? In what way may polyploidy have assisted plant evolution?

Objective Questions

For questions 1–4, match the statements that follow to the items in the key:

Key:
- a. multiple alleles
- b. incomplete dominance
- c. polygenes
- d. epistatic gene
- e. pleiotropic gene

1. A cross between oblong and round squash produced oval squash.

2. Although most people have an IQ of about 100, IQ generally ranges from about 50 to 150.

3. Investigators noted that whenever a particular species of plant had narrow instead of broad leaves, it was also short and yellow, instead of tall and green.

4. In rabbits, the allele C is dominant to the allele c^{ch}, which is dominant to the allele c^h, which is dominant to the allele c. Each individual has only two of these alleles.

5. When a white-eyed *Drosophila* female occurs,
   a. both parents could have red eyes.
   b. the female parent could have red eyes but the male parent has to have white eyes.
   c. both parents must have white eyes.
   d. Both a and b are correct.

6. Investigators found that a cross involving the mutant genes *a* and *b* produced 30% recombinants, a cross involving *a* and *c* produced 5% recombinants, and a cross involving *c* and *b* produced 25% recombinants. Which is the correct order of the genes?
   a. *a, b, c*
   b. *a, c, b*
   c. *b, a, c*

7. A boy is color blind (X-linked recessive) and has a continuous hairline (autosomal recessive). Which could be the genotype of his mother?
   a. *bbww*
   b. X^bYWw
   c. bbX^wX^w
   d. X^BX^bWw

8. Which two of these chromosomal mutations are most likely to occur when homologous chromosomes are undergoing synapsis?
   a. inversion and translocation
   b. deletion and duplication
   c. deletion and inversion
   d. duplication and translocation

9. Investigators do a dihybrid cross between two heterozygotes and get about a 3:1 ratio among the offspring. The reason must be due to
   a. polygenes.
   b. pleiotropic genes.
   c. linked genes.
   d. epistatic genes.

10. In snakes, the recessive genotype *cc* causes the animal to be albino despite the inheritance of the dominant allele (B = black). What would be the results of a cross between two snakes with the genotype *CcBB*?
    a. all black snakes
    b. all white snakes
    c. 9:3:3:1
    d. 3 black : 1 albino

Additional Genetics Problems*

1. Chickens that are homozygous for the frizzled trait have feathers that are weak and stringy. When raised at low temperatures, the birds have circulatory, digestive, and hormonal problems. What inheritance pattern explains these results?

2. Chickens having black feathers are crossed with chickens having white feathers, and the result is chickens that appear to have blue feathers. What inheritance pattern explains these results, and what key do you suggest for this cross?

3. In radish plants, the shape of the radish may be long (*LL*), round (*ll*), or oval (*Ll*). If oval is crossed with oval, what proportion of offspring will also be oval?

4. If blood type in cats were controlled by three codominant and multiple alleles, how many genotypes and phenotypes would occur? Could the cross *AC* × *BC* produce a cat with AB blood type?

5. In *Drosophila*, S = normal, s = sable body; W = normal, w = miniature wing. In a cross between a heterozygous normal fly and a sable-bodied, miniature-winged fly, the results were 99 normal flies, 99 with a sable body and miniature wings, 11 with a normal body and miniature wings, and 11 with a sable body and normal wings. What inheritance pattern explains these results? How many map units separate the genes for sable body and miniature wing?

6. In *Drosophila*, the gene that controls red eye color (dominant) versus white eye color is on the X chromosome. What are the expected phenotypic results if a heterozygous female is crossed with a white-eyed male?

7. Bar eyes in *Drosophila* is dominant and X-linked. What phenotypic ratio is expected for reciprocal crosses between pure-breeding flies?

8. In *Drosophila*, a male with bar eyes and miniature wings is crossed with a female who has normal eyes and normal wings. Half the female offspring have bar eyes and miniature wings and half have bar eyes and normal wings. What is the genotype of the female parent?

9. In cats, S = short hair, s = long hair, X^C = black coat, X^c = yellow coat, and $X^C X^c$ = tortoiseshell (calico) coat. If a long-haired yellow male is crossed with a tortoiseshell female homozygous for short hair, what are the expected phenotypic results?

Concepts and Critical Thinking

1. *Genes often work together to produce the phenotype.*

   To demonstrate that the phenotype is controlled by the entire genome, give examples of human traits controlled by more than one pair of alleles.

2. *Genes are located on the chromosomes.*

   Give evidence that the genes are on the chromosomes and that the genes are linearly arranged.

3. *Genes on sex chromosomes determine the sex of the individual.*

   What evidence suggests that alleles on the Y chromosome determine maleness in humans? Considering the degrees of dominance discussed in the chapter, how do you think these alleles might relate to sex-determining alleles on the X chromosome?

Selected Key Terms

autosome Any chromosome other than a sex chromosome. [Gk. *aut,* self, and *soma,* body]   202

chromosomal theory of inheritance Theory that the genes are on the chromosomes, accounting for their similar behavior.   202

codominance A pattern of inheritance in which both alleles of a gene are expressed.   198

incomplete dominance A pattern of inheritance in which the offspring shows characteristics intermediate between two extreme parental characteristics—for example, a red and a white flower producing pink offspring.   198

linkage group Alleles of different genes that are located on the same chromosome and tend to be inherited together.   204

multiple allele A pattern of inheritance in which there are more than two alleles for a particular trait.   199

mutation An alteration in chromosome structure or number and also an alteration in a gene due to a change in DNA composition. [L. *muta,* change]   206

polygenic inheritance A pattern of inheritance in which a trait is controlled by several allelic pairs; each dominant allele contributes in an additive and like manner. [Gk. *poly,* many, and *genic,* producing]   200

polyploid (polyploidy) A condition in which an organism has more than two complete sets of chromosomes. [Gk. *poly,* many, and *ploid,* sets]   206

sex chromosome A chromosome that determines the sex of an individual; in animals, females have two X chromosomes and males have an X and Y chromosome.   202

X-linked gene Gene located on the X chromosomes that does not control a sexual feature of the organism.   202

---

*Answers to Additional Genetic Problems appear in Appendix D.

14
HUMAN GENETICS

Learning Objectives

Counting the Chromosomes

- Describe how a karyotype is prepared, what it consists of, and how it is used.   212

- Describe Down syndrome, its symptoms, its causes, and its relation to the age of the mother.   214

- List and describe different types of sex chromosomal abnormalities seen in humans.   215

Considering Autosomal Traits

- Recognize the autosomal dominant versus the autosomal recessive pattern of inheritance in a human pedigree chart.   218–19

- Give examples of and describe the most common autosomal genetic disorders in humans.   220–25

Considering Sex-Linked Genes

- Recognize the X-linked pattern of inheritance in a human pedigree chart.   226–27

- Give examples of and describe the most common X-linked genetic disorders in humans.   226–27

- Distinguish between sex-linked and sex-influenced traits.   226–27

Considering Polygenic Inheritance

- Describe the polygenic inheritance pattern and give examples of traits that are most likely controlled by polygenes.   228

The shape of the red blood cells in persons with sickle-cell disease is disadvantageous because it leads to a myriad of body disorders.

he concept that units of inheritance, called genes, are located on the chromosomes is applicable to human beings. Sometimes we tend to think that academic research done with other organisms will be of little direct value to us. However, Gregor Mendel's work with peas and Thomas Hunt Morgan's research with fruit flies does have relevance to ourselves. An understanding of human genetics can improve our own lives and the lives of our children.

COUNTING THE CHROMOSOMES

It has now been established that somatic (body) cells in humans have forty-six chromosomes. To view the chromosomes, cells can be treated and photographed just prior to dividing, as described in figure 14.1 for white blood cells. The chromosomes are then sorted and arranged by homologous pairs either by hand or today by computers that have special photometric capabilities. The mem-

bers of a pair not only have the same size and shape, they also have the same banding pattern. The resulting display of pairs of chromosomes is called a **karyotype.** Both males and females normally have twenty-three pairs of chromosomes, but one of these pairs is of unequal length in males. The larger chromosome of this pair is the X chromosome and the smaller is the Y chromosome. These are called the **sex chromosomes** because they contain the genes that determine sex. The other chromosomes, known as **autosomes,** include all the pairs of chromosomes except the X and Y chromosomes. In a karyotype, autosomes are usually ordered by size and numbered from the largest to smallest; the sex chromosomes are identified separately.

A normal human karyotype shows twenty-two pairs of autosomes and one pair of sex chromosomes. Males have an X and a Y chromosome; females have two X chromosomes.

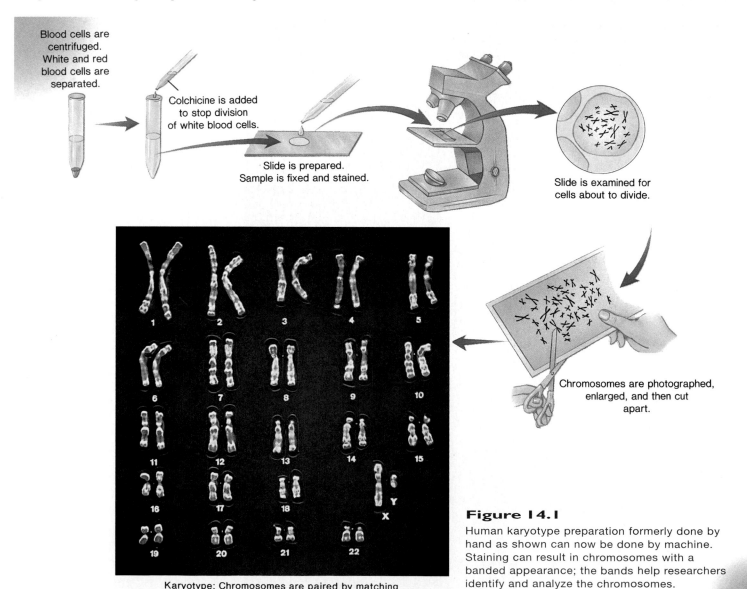

Blood cells are centrifuged. White and red blood cells are separated.

Colchicine is added to stop division of white blood cells.

Slide is prepared. Sample is fixed and stained.

Slide is examined for cells about to divide.

Chromosomes are photographed, enlarged, and then cut apart.

Karyotype: Chromosomes are paired by matching banding and are arranged by size and shape.

Figure 14.1

Human karyotype preparation formerly done by hand as shown can now be done by machine. Staining can result in chromosomes with a banded appearance; the bands help researchers identify and analyze the chromosomes.

Nondisjunction Causes Abnormalities

Gamete formation in humans involves meiosis, the type of cell division that reduces the chromosomal number by one-half because the homologous chromosomes separate. When members of a homologous chromosome pair fail to separate during meiosis I, called **nondisjunction,** gametes with too few (n−1) or too many (n+1) chromosomes result. Nondisjunction can also occur during meiosis II if daughter chromosomes fail to separate and instead go into the same daughter cell (fig. 14.2a).

When the abnormal gametes shown are fertilized by normal gametes, a monosomy (2n − 1) or a trisomy (2n + 1) can result. A study of spontaneous abortions suggests that many trisomies and nearly all monosomies are fatal. The most common autosomal trisomy seen among humans is trisomy 21 (Down syndrome), which occurs in one out of seven hundred live births (fig. 14.2b). Individuals with trisomy 13 (Patau syndrome) and trisomy 18 (Edward syndrome) have an average life span of less than one year. Heart and nervous system defects prevent normal development.

Nondisjunction of the sex chromosomes in humans also occurs. Four common, but abnormal, chromosomal types are XO, XXX, XXY, and XYY. The symbol O means that a sex chromosome is missing.

> Nondisjunction causes an abnormal chromosomal number in the gametes. Offspring inherit an extra chromosome (trisomy) or are missing a chromosome (monosomy).

Figure 14.2

Nondisjunction and resulting syndromes. **a.** Nondisjunction occurring in meiosis I and in meiosis II, with the resulting gametes (asterisks mark points of nondisjunction). **b.** Frequency of syndromes.

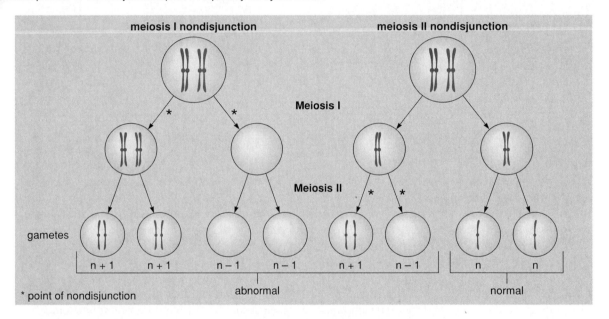

a.   * point of nondisjunction

Syndrome	Sex	Chromosomes	Frequency	
			Abortuses	*Births*
Down	M or F	Trisomy 21	1/40	1/700
Patau	M or F	Trisomy 13	1/33	1/15,000
Edward	M or F	Trisomy 18	1/200	1/5,000
Turner	F	XO	1/18	1/5,000
Metafemale	F	XXX (or XXXX)	0	1/700
Klinefelter	M	XXY (or XXXY)	0	1/2,000
XYY	M	XYY	?	1/2,000

b.

Figure 14.3

Down syndrome. **a.** Characteristics include a wide, rounded face and narrow, slanting eyelids. Mental retardation, along with an enlarged tongue, makes it difficult for a person with Down syndrome to speak distinctly. **b.** Karyotype of an individual with Down syndrome shows an extra chromosome 21. More sophisticated technologies allow investigators to pinpoint the location of specific genes associated with the syndrome. An extra copy of the *Gart* gene, which leads to a high level of purines, may account for the mental retardation of persons with Down syndrome.

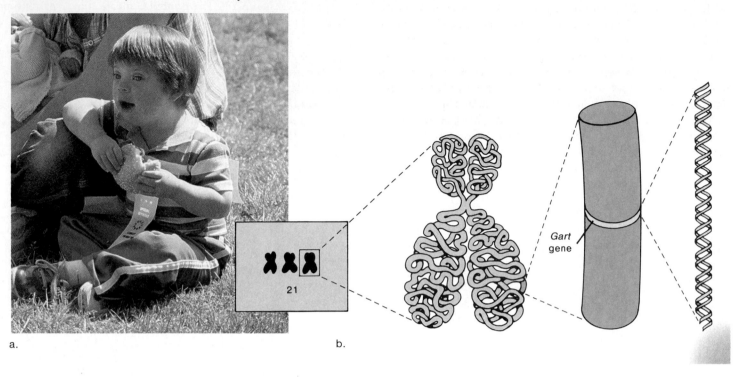

a.

b.

Gart gene

Down Syndrome

Persons with Down syndrome, described in figure 14.3, usually have three copies of chromosome 21 in their karyotype because the egg had two copies instead of one. The chances of a woman having a Down syndrome child increase rapidly with age, starting at about age forty. As a possible explanation, researchers suggest that older women may be more likely to carry a Down syndrome child to term because their bodies fail to recognize and abort abnormal embryos. In 23% of the cases of *Down syndrome* studied, the sperm, rather than the egg, had the extra chromosome 21. In about 5% of cases in either the sperm or the egg, the extra chromosome is attached to another chromosome, often chromosome 14. This abnormal chromosome arose because a translocation occurred between chromosomes 14 and 21 in one of the parents or even in a relative who lived generations earlier. Therefore, when Down syndrome is due to a translocation, it is not age related and instead tends to run in the family of either the father or the mother.

Although an older woman is more likely to have a Down syndrome child, most babies with Down syndrome are born to women younger than age forty because this is the age group having the most babies. As discussed in the reading on page 216,

chorionic villi testing and amniocentesis followed by karyotyping can detect a Down syndrome child. However, young women are not encouraged to undergo such procedures because the risk of complications resulting from these tests is greater than the risk of having a Down syndrome child. Fortunately, there is now a test based on substances in the blood that can identify mothers who might be carrying a Down syndrome child, and only these individuals need to undergo further testing.

It is known that the genes that cause Down syndrome are located on the bottom third of chromosome 21 (fig. 14.3*b*), and extensive investigative work has focused on discovering the specific genes responsible for the characteristics of the syndrome. Thus far, investigators have discovered several genes that may account for various conditions seen in persons with Down syndrome. For example, they have located genes most likely responsible for the increased tendency toward leukemia, cataracts, accelerated rate of aging, and mental retardation. The gene for mental retardation, dubbed the *Gart* gene, causes an increased level of purines in blood, a finding associated with mental retardation. It is hoped that someday it will be possible to control the expression of the *Gart* gene even before birth so that at least this symptom of Down syndrome can be suppressed.

X and Y Numbers Also Change

Sex chromosome abnormalities are often due to nondisjunction of these chromosomes during meiosis. Therefore, the gametes contain an abnormal number of sex chromosomes.

XYY males have two Y chromosomes instead of one. Affected males usually are taller than average, suffer from persistent acne, and tend to have barely normal intelligence. At one time, it was suggested that these men were likely to be criminally aggressive, but it has since been shown that the incidence of such behavior among them is no greater than among XY males.

From birth, an XO individual with *Turner syndrome* has only one sex chromosome, an X; the O signifies the absence of a second sex chromosome. Turner females are short, have a broad chest, and may have congenital heart defects. The ovaries never become functional, and in many individuals they are simply white streaks. Turner females do not undergo puberty or menstruate, and there is a lack of breast development (fig. 14.4a). Although no overt mental retardation is reported, Turner females show reduced skills in interpreting spatial relationships.

A male with *Klinefelter syndrome* has two or more X chromosomes in addition to a Y chromosome. Affected individuals are sterile males; the testes are underdeveloped and there may be some breast development (fig. 14.4b). These phenotypic abnormalities are not apparent until puberty, although some evidence of subnormal intelligence may be apparent before that time.

A *metafemale* is an individual with more than two X chromosomes. It might be supposed that the XXX female is especially feminine, but this is not the case. In some cases there is a tendency toward physical abnormalities and there may be menstrual irregularities, including early onset of menopause.

Years ago, Canadian scientist Murray Barr observed a consistent difference between human female and male nondividing cells. Females, but not males, have a small, dark staining mass of condensed chromatin adhering to the inner edge of the nuclear envelope (fig. 14.5). The dark-staining spot is called a *Barr body* after its discoverer. In 1961, English geneticist Mary Lyon suggested that the Barr body is an inactive X chromosome. Normal males with only one X chromosome do not have a Barr body; XXY individuals have one; XXX individuals have two; and so on. Counting the Barr bodies is another way to determine an abnormal number of sex chromosomes.

> One sex chromosome monosomy (Turner syndrome) and three trisomies (Klinefelter syndrome, metafemale, and XYY male) are known in human beings.

Figure 14.4

Abnormal sex chromosome inheritance. **a.** A female with Turner syndrome (XO) is distinguished by a thick neck, short stature, and immature sexual features. **b.** A male with Klinefelter syndrome (XXY) has immature sex organs and shows breast development.

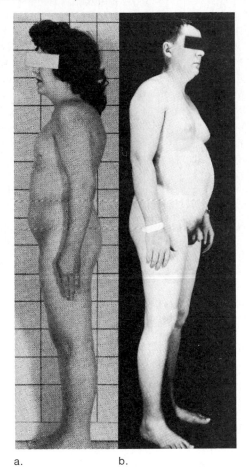

a.   b.

Figure 14.5

Cell Barr bodies. **a.** A normal male (XY) with no Barr bodies. **b.** A normal female (XX) with one Barr body. **c.** An XXX female with two Barr bodies (*see arrows*).

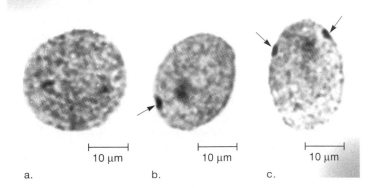

| 10 μm | 10 μm | 10 μm |

a.   b.   c.

Detecting Genetic Disorders

Genetic counseling can be more extensive today because of the availability of so many prenatal tests to detect chromosomal and gene mutations. Karyotyping of fetal or embryonic cells can indicate whether a developing child has Down syndrome or one of the other chromosomal abnormalities listed in figure 14.2. Also, the appropriate chromosome can be tested for the presence of a mutant allele for cystic fibrosis, neurofibromatosis, and sickle-cell disease, among others. For example, neural tube defect occurs early when the nervous system is first forming, and the presence of a chemical called α-fetoprotein indicates that the fetus has this condition. Biochemical tests are available for dozens of enzymes such as hexosaminidase A, the missing enzyme in persons with Tay-Sachs disease.

Amniocentesis is one way to obtain fetal cells for testing of chromosomal abnormalities and genetic disorders (fig. 14A*a*). In amniocentesis, a long needle is passed through the abdominal wall, the uterus, and the membranes surrounding the fetus; then a small amount of amniotic fluid, along with fetal cells, is removed. These fetal cells have been sloughed off from the skin or the respiratory or urinary systems. Since there are only a few cells in the fluid and they are nondividing (dividing cells are needed for karyotyping), it may be necessary to culture the cells. If so, it might be four weeks until the cells have grown and multiplied in cell culture in adequate numbers for testing purposes. This is a distinct disadvantage to those who wish to have the option of aborting the pregnancy if an abnormality is found, as it might be too late for a safe abortion.

There is a new technique, however, that can be used to detect many chromosomal abnormalities just one or two days after cells are obtained by amniocentesis. Fluorescent probes specific for certain regions of chromosomes can be applied to amniotic cells, and they will bind to and light up these regions. For example, a probe for the X chromosome can indicate how many X chromosomes are present in each cell.

Amniocentesis is considered more than 99% safe when done by an experienced physician. However, couples might want to know that the procedure does carry a possible risk to the fetus, as well as to the mother.

Chorionic villi sampling is a way to obtain embryonic cells for testing as early as the fifth week of pregnancy (fig. 14A*b*). The doctor inserts a long, thin tube through the vagina and into the uterus. With the help of ultrasound imaging, which gives a picture of the uterine contents, the tube is placed between the lining of the uterus and the chorion, a membrane that surrounds the embryo and has projections called chorionic villi. Suction is used to remove a sampling of the chorionic villi cells. Or alternately, a needle is inserted through the abdominal and uterine walls as is done with amniocentesis, except that the needle does not penetrate the fetal membranes. The chorionic villi contain cells with the same chromosomal and genetic makeup as the fetus, and therefore these cells can be tested to obtain information about possible fetal abnormalities.

The advantage of chorionic villi sampling is that testing can be done much earlier and an abortion, if desired, can be done during the first trimester when it is considered medically safer for the mother. Chorionic villi sampling has been done routinely for ten years and, thus far, the safety of the procedure seems to be comparable to that of amniocentesis.

Screening eggs for genetic defects is a new technique. Preovulation eggs are removed by aspiration after a telescope with a fiber–optic illuminator, called a laparoscope, is inserted into the abdominal cavity through a small incision in the region of the navel. The prior administration of the appropriate sex hormones ensures that several eggs are available for screening. Only the chromosomes within the first polar body are tested because if the woman is heterozygous for a genetic defect, and it is found in the polar body, then the egg must be normal. Normal eggs undergo in vitro (in an artificial environment) fertilization and are placed in the prepared uterus. At present, only one in ten attempts results in a birth, but it is known ahead of time that the child will be normal.

Recently, each year has seen the discovery of more and more genetic mutations associated with disorders ranging from Alzheimer disease to psychological disorders to colon cancer. Expectant couples sometimes ask for genetic tests even when there is little known about the medical risk involved with the potential disorder—and even when the potential disorder is apt to occur in middle age or even later in life. Consequently, many are beginning to question the degree to which prenatal genetic testing should be done, especially when the presence of a mutation may only indicate a *possible* risk of developing the condition. The general public thinks in terms of either/or—either the newborn will develop the disorder or it will not. It is difficult to come to a conclusion when the results indicate a 50% risk of developing a disorder. As a society we have not yet decided how many and what types of genetic tests should be done and how to interpret some of the results once they are done. Therefore, genetic counselors and physicians, too, don't always know how to present the results to patients or if the results should be made known at all. For example, suppose one prenatal twin is XY and the other is XYY—do you think the parents should be informed? Many XYY individuals live a normal life, and revealing the chromosomal abnormality might cause the parents to abort the pregnancy or to treat the XYY child differently. If you were one of the parents, would you want to be told?

Figure 14A

a. Amniocentesis is used to obtain fetal cells for testing. **b.** Chorionic villi sampling is used earlier in the pregnancy to obtain embryonic cells. **c.** A laparoscope is used to obtain eggs for genetic and biochemical testing prior to pregnancy.

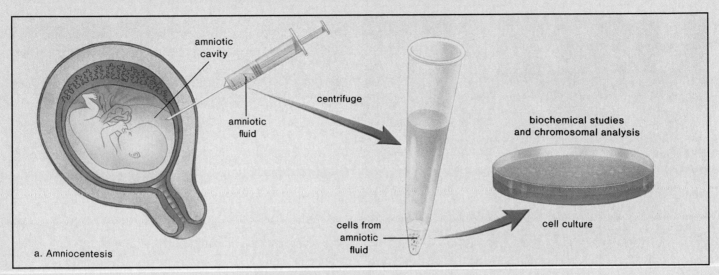

a. Amniocentesis

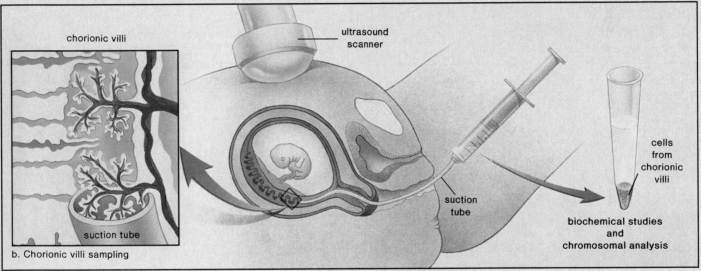

b. Chorionic villi sampling

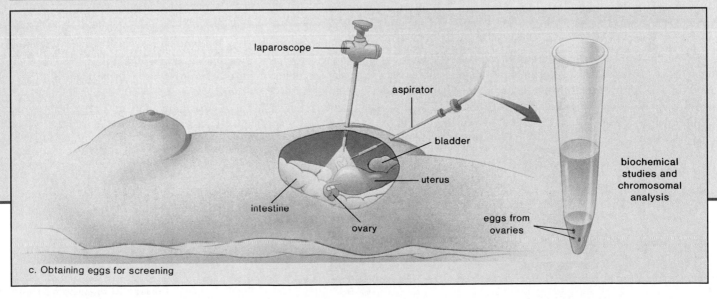

c. Obtaining eggs for screening

Figure 14.6 ⊙

Autosomal dominant disorders. **a.** Sample pedigree chart. **b.** Ways to recognize autosomal dominant disorders. **c.** Listing of common dominant disorders.

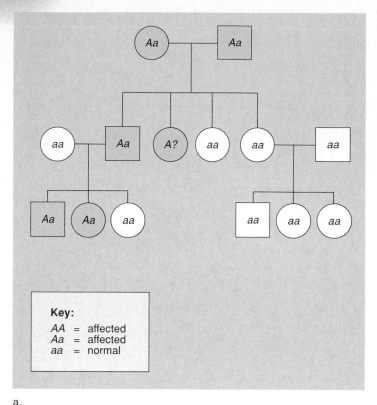

Key:
AA = affected
Aa = affected
aa = normal

a.

Autosomal Dominant Disorders
- Affected children usually have an affected parent.
- Heterozygotes *Aa* are affected.
- Two affected parents can produce an unaffected child.
- Two unaffected parents will not have affected children.
- Both males and females are affected with equal frequency.

b.

Currently, some 1,489 autosomal dominant disorders have been catalogued. Examples include:
- Neurofibromatosis—benign tumors in skin or deeper
- Achondroplasia—a form of dwarfism
- Chronic simple glaucoma (some forms)—a major cause of blindness if untreated
- Huntington disease—progressive nervous system degeneration
- Familial hypercholesterolemia—high blood cholesterol levels, propensity to heart disease
- Polydactyly—extra fingers or toes

c.

CONSIDERING AUTOSOMAL TRAITS

Just as individuals receive pairs of chromosomes (one from the egg and one from the sperm), they receive pairs of alleles. An allele is an alternate form of a gene. One allele can be dominant to the other, called the recessive allele. Many common human characteristics, such as presence of freckles, widow's peak, cleft chin, and tone deafness, are inherited as an autosomal dominant characteristic and therefore are presumed to be controlled by a dominant allele.

There Are Patterns of Inheritance

When a genetic disorder is an autosomal dominant, an individual with the alleles *AA* or *Aa* will have the disorder. When a genetic disorder is recessive, only individuals with the alleles *aa* will have the disorder. Genetic counselors often construct pedigree charts to determine whether a condition is dominant or recessive.

A pedigree chart shows the pattern of inheritance for a particular condition. Consider these two possible patterns of inheritance:

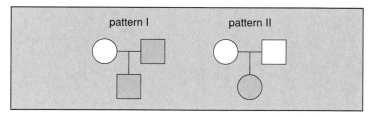

In both patterns, males are designated by squares and females by circles. Shaded circles and squares are affected individuals. A line between a square and a circle represents a union. A vertical line going downward leads, in these patterns, to a single child. (If there are more children, they are placed off a horizontal line.) Which pattern of inheritance do you suppose represents an autosomal dominant characteristic, and which represents an autosomal recessive characteristic?

Figure 14.7

Autosomal recessive disorders. **a.** Sample pedigree chart. **b.** Ways to recognize autosomal recessive disorders. **c.** Listing of common recessive disorders.

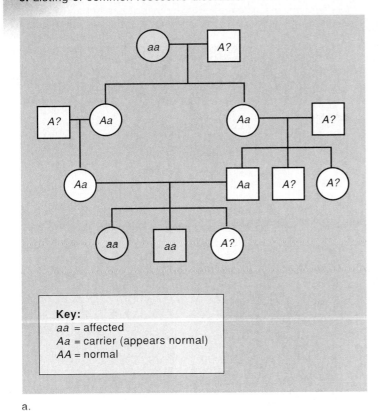

Key:
aa = affected
Aa = carrier (appears normal)
AA = normal

a.

Autosomal Recessive Disorders

- Most affected children have normal parents.
- Heterozygotes (*Aa*) have a normal phenotype.
- Two affected parents will always have affected children.
- Affected individuals with homozygous normal mates will have normal children.
- Close relatives who reproduce are more likely to have affected children.
- Both males and females are affected with equal frequency.

b.

Among 1,117 autosomal recessive disorders catalogued are:

- Cystic fibrosis—disorder affecting function of mucous and sweat glands
- Galactosemia—inability to metabolize milk sugar
- Phenylketonuria—essential liver enzyme deficiency
- Thalassemia—blood disorder primarily affecting persons of Mediterranean ancestry
- Tay-Sachs disease—lysosomal storage disease leading to nervous system destruction

c.

In pattern I, the child is affected, as is one of the parents. When a disorder is dominant, an affected child usually has at least one affected parent. Of the two patterns, this one shows a dominant pattern of inheritance. Figure 14.6 illustrates other ways to recognize an autosomal dominant pattern of inheritance. The figure also lists common autosomal disorders in humans.

If we know the pattern of inheritance and the genotype of the parents, it is possible to predict the chances of inheriting the condition. For example, if the disorder is dominant, and the cross is *Aa* x *aa*, the chances are 50% of inheriting and 50% of not inheriting the disorder.

In pattern II, the child is affected but neither parent is; this can happen if the condition is recessive and the parents are *Aa*. Notice that the parents are **carriers** because they appear to be normal but are capable of having a child with a genetic disorder. See figure 14.7 for other ways to recognize an autosomal recessive pattern of inheritance.

Again, we can predict the chances of inheriting the disorder. If the cross is *Aa* x *Aa* and the disorder is recessive, the chance of inheriting the disorder is 25%. It is important to remember that chance has no memory, and that each child born to this couple has a 25% chance of inheriting the disorder. This means that if a couple had four children, any number of them could have the disorder.

Dominant and recessive alleles have different patterns of inheritance.

Some Disorders Are Dominant

Of the many autosomal dominant disorders, some of which are listed in figure 14.6, we will discuss only two.

Neurofibromatosis

Neurofibromatosis, sometimes called von Recklinghausen disease, is one of the most common genetic disorders. It affects roughly one in 3,000 people, including an estimated 100,000 in the United States. It is seen equally in every racial and ethnic group throughout the world.

At birth or later, the affected individual may have six or more large, tan spots on the skin. Such spots may increase in size and number and may get darker. Small benign tumors (lumps) called neurofibromas may occur under the skin or in various organs. Neurofibromas are made up of nerve cells and other cell types.

This genetic disorder shows *variable expressivity.* In most cases, symptoms are mild and patients live a normal life. In some cases, however, the effects are severe. Skeletal deformities, including a large head, are seen, and eye and ear tumors can lead to blindness and hearing loss. Many children with neurofibromatosis have learning disabilities and are hyperactive.

In 1990, researchers isolated the gene for neurofibromatosis, which was known to be on chromosome 17. By analyzing the DNA (deoxyribonucleic acid), they determined that the gene was huge and actually included three smaller genes. This was only the second time that *nested genes* have been found in humans. The gene for neurofibromatosis is a tumor-suppressor gene active in controlling cell division. When it mutates, a benign tumor develops.

Huntington Disease

One in 20,000 persons in the United States has *Huntington disease,* a neurological disorder that leads to progressive degeneration of brain cells, which in turn causes severe muscle spasm and personality disorders (fig. 14.8). Most people appear normal until they are of middle age and have already had children who might also be stricken. Occasionally, the first signs of the disease are seen in these children when they are teenagers or even younger. There is no effective treatment, and death comes ten to fifteen years after the onset of symptoms.

Several years ago, the gene for Huntington disease was found to be located on chromosome 4, and a test was developed to determine if the disorder has been inherited. Because treatment is not available, however, few may want to have this information. In 1993, the gene itself was finally isolated and an analysis produced surprising results—the gene contains many repeats of the base triplet AGC (adenine, guanine, cytosine). Normal persons have 11 to 34 copies of the triplet and affected persons tend to have 42 to more than 120 copies. The more repeats present, the earlier the onset of Huntington disease and the more severe the symptoms. Further, it also appears that persons most at risk have inherited the disorder from their fathers.

Figure 14.8

Huntington disease. Persons with this condition gradually lose psychomotor control of the body. At first there are only minor disturbances, but the symptoms become worse over time.

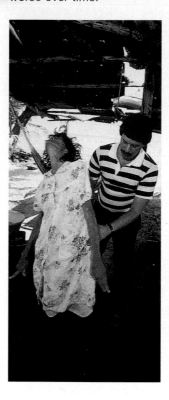

Since these findings, other genetic disorders have been found whose severity and time of onset depend on the number of triplet repeats present within the gene; these disorders are discussed in the reading on page 222. Triplet repeat mutations are more properly termed an *expanded trinucleotide repeat.* The observation that such repeats are likely to have been inherited from only the paternal or maternal parent is consistent with a new hypothesis given the name *genomic imprinting.* Genomic imprinting is also discussed in the reading on page 222.

Practice Problems 1*

1. A woman who is heterozygous for an autosomal dominant disorder reproduces with a normal man. What are the chances the child will develop the disorder?
2. A child has neurofibromatosis. The mother appears normal. What is the genotype of the father?

*Answers to Practice Problems appear in appendix D.

Sickle-Cell Is Partly Dominant

The field of human genetics also has examples of incomplete dominance and codominance. For example, when a curly-haired Caucasian person reproduces with a straight-haired Caucasian person, their children will have wavy hair.

Sickle-cell disease is an example of a human disorder that is controlled by incompletely dominant alleles. Individuals with the $Hb^A Hb^A$ genotype are normal, those with the $Hb^S Hb^S$ genotype have sickle-cell disease, and those with the $Hb^A Hb^S$ genotype have the *sickle-cell trait*. Two individuals with sickle-cell trait can produce children with all three phenotypes, as indicated in figure 14.9.

In persons with sickle-cell disease, the red blood cells aren't biconcave disks like normal red blood cells; they are irregular. In fact, many are sickle shaped. The defect is caused by an abnormal hemoglobin that accumulates inside the cells. Because the sickle-shaped cells can't pass along narrow capillary passageways like disk-shaped cells, they clog the vessels and break down. This is why persons with sickle-cell disease suffer from poor circulation, anemia, and poor resistance to infection. Internal hemorrhaging leads to further complications, such as jaundice, episodic pain of the abdomen and joints, and damage to internal organs.

Persons with sickle-cell trait do not usually have any sickle-shaped cells unless they experience dehydration or mild oxygen deprivation. Although a recent study found that army recruits with sickle-cell trait are more likely to die when subjected to extreme exercise, previous studies of athletes do not substantiate these findings. At present, most investigators believe that no restrictions on physical activity are needed for persons with the sickle-cell trait.

Among regions of malaria-infested Africa, infants with sickle-cell disease die, but infants with sickle-cell trait have a better chance of survival than the normal homozygote. Their sickled cells provide protection against the malaria-causing parasite, which uses red blood cells during its life cycle. The parasite dies when potassium leaks out of the red blood cells as the cells become sickle shaped. The protection afforded by the sickle-cell trait keeps the allele prevalent in populations exposed to malaria. As many as 60% of blacks in malaria-infected regions of Africa have the allele. In the United States, about 10% of the black population carries the allele.

Innovative therapies are being attempted in persons with sickle-cell disease. For example, persons with sickle-cell disease produce normal fetal hemoglobin during development, and drugs that turn on the genes for fetal hemoglobin in adults are being developed. Mice have been genetically engineered to produce sickled red blood cells in order to test new antisickling drugs and various genetic therapies.

> Sickle-cell disease is an example of a human genetic disorder that is controlled by incompletely dominant alleles.

Figure 14.9

Inheritance of sickle-cell disease. **a.** In this example, both parents have the sickle-cell trait. Therefore, each child has a 25% chance of having sickle-cell disease or of being perfectly normal and a 50% chance of having the sickle-cell trait. **b.** Sickled cells. Individuals with sickle-cell disease have sickled red blood cells as illustrated here.

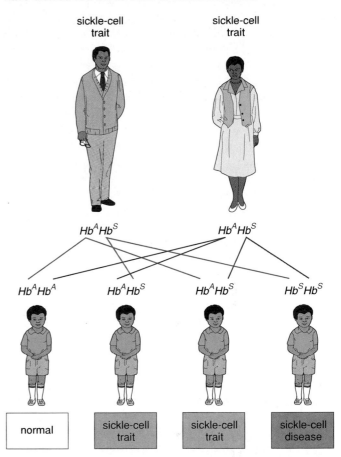

a.

b.

Unexpected Repeats

Fragile X syndrome is one of the most common genetic causes of mental retardation, second only to Down syndrome. It affects about one in 1,500 males and one in 2,500 females and is seen in all ethnic groups. It is called fragile X syndrome because its diagnosis used to be dependent upon observing an X chromosome whose tip is attached to the rest of the chromosome by a thin thread.

The inheritance pattern of fragile X syndrome is not like any other pattern we have studied (fig. 14B). The chance of being affected increases in successive generations almost as if the pattern of inheritance switches from being a recessive one to a dominant one. Then too, an unaffected grandfather can have grandchildren with the disorder; in other words he is a carrier for an X-linked disease. This is contrary to normality—we have learned that males with mutant alleles on the X chromosome always show the disorder!

In 1991, the DNA sequence at the fragile site was isolated and found to have trinucleotide repeats. The base triplet, CCG, was repeated over and over again. There are about 6–50 copies of this repeat in normal persons and over 230 copies in persons with fragile X syndrome. Carrier males have what is now termed a premutation; they have between 50 and 230 copies of the repeat and no symptoms. Both daughters and sons receive the premutation but only the daughters pass on the full mutation; that is, over 230 copies of the repeat. Any male, even those with fragile X syndrome and over 230 repeats, passes on at most the premutation number of repeats. It is unknown what causes the difference between males and females.

This type of mutation—called by some a dynamic mutation, because it changes, and by others an expanded trinucleotide repeat, because the number of triplet copies increases— is now known to characterize other conditions (table 14A). With Huntington disease, the age of onset of the disorder is roughly correlated with the number of repeats, and the disorder is more likely to have been inherited from the paternal parent. In keeping with Mendel's findings, we would expect the sex of the parent to play no role in inheritance. The present exceptions have led to the genomic imprinting hypothesis—that the sperm and egg carry chromosomes that have been "imprinted" differently. Imprinting is believed to occur during gamete formation, and thereafter the genes are expressed one way if donated by the father and another way If donated by the mother. Perhaps when we discover why more repeats are passed on by one parent rather than the other, we will discover the cause of so called genomic imprinting.

What might cause repeats to occur in the first place? Something must go wrong during DNA replication prior to cell division. The cell must find it difficult to correctly copy triplets that contain CG or GC combinations because all of the repeats so far noted have such combinations. What difficulty arises because of triplet repeats? DNA codes for cellular proteins and the presence of repeats undoubtedly leads to nonfunctioning or malfunctioning proteins.

Scientists have developed a new technique that can identify repeats in DNA, and they expect that this technique will help them find the genes for other human disorders. They expect expanded trinucleotide repeats to be a very common mutation indeed.

Table 14A

Human Genetic Disorders Caused by Base Triplet Repeats

Disease	Chromosome	Sex Bias of Parent Donating Severe Form	Repeated Sequence	Normal Number of Copies	Number of Copies Associated with the Disease
Fragile X syndrome	X chromosome	Maternal	CCG	6–50	Premutation = 50–230 Full mutation = 230–2,000
Spinobulbar muscular atrophy (Kennedy disease)	X chromosome	?	AGC	11–40	40–62
Myotonic dystrophy	Chromosome 19	Maternal	AGC	5–50	Premutation = 50–80 Full mutation = 80–2,000
Huntington disease	Chromosome 4	Paternal	AGC	11–34	Premutation = 34–42 Full mutation = 42–121
Spinocerebellar ataxia type 1	Chromosome 6	Paternal (possibly)	AGC	25–43	43–81

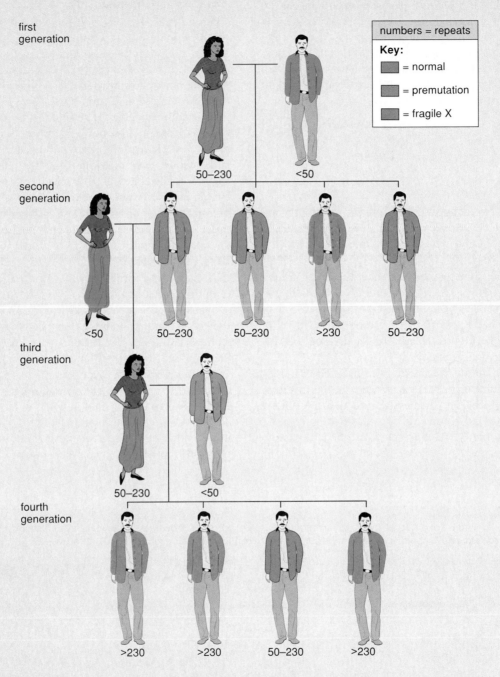

first
generation

second
generation

third
generation

fourth
generation

numbers = repeats

Key:

■ = normal

■ = premutation

■ = fragile X

50–230   <50

<50   50–230   50–230   >230   50–230

50–230   <50

>230   >230   50–230   >230

Figure 14B

Pattern of inheritance for fragile X syndrome, a disorder caused by the presence of base triplet repeats at a particular locus. Affected persons have over 230 repeats, a premutation is 50–230 repeats, and normal persons have fewer than 50 repeats. In each successive generation there are more affected individuals, usually males. The mutation is passed on by women with only a premutation number of repeats; men, even if affected, do not pass on the mutation.

Blood Type Is by Multiple Alleles

Some traits are controlled by **multiple alleles,** that is, more than two alleles. However, each person inherits only two of the total possible number of alleles. Three alleles for the same gene control the inheritance of ABO blood types: *A* = A antigen on red blood cells; *B* = B antigen on red blood cells; *O* = no antigens on red blood cells. Both *A* and *B* are dominant over *O*; therefore, there are two possible genotypes for type A blood and two possible genotypes for type B blood. If a person inherits one of each of these alleles, the blood type will be AB. Type O can only result from the inheritance of two *O* alleles:

PHENOTYPE	POSSIBLE GENOTYPE
A	*AA, AO*
B	*BB, BO*
AB	*AB*
O	*OO*

An examination of possible matings between different blood types sometimes produces surprising results. For example, if the cross is *AO* x *BO*, the possible genotypes of children are *AB, OO, AO,* and *BO.*

Blood typing can sometimes aid in paternity suits. A man with type A blood (having genotype *AO*) could possibly be the father of a child with type O blood. On the other hand, a man with type AB blood cannot possibly be the father of a child with type O blood. Therefore, blood tests are legally used only to exclude a man from possible paternity.

The Rh factor is inherited separately from A, B, AB, or O blood types. In each instance, it is possible to be Rh positive (Rh$^+$) or Rh negative (Rh$^-$). It can be assumed that the inheritance of this antigen on red blood cells is controlled by a single allelic pair in which simple dominance prevails: the Rh-positive allele is dominant over the Rh-negative allele.

Some Disorders Are Recessive

Of the many autosomal recessive disorders, some of which are listed in figure 14.7, we will discuss only three.

Tay-Sachs Disease

Tay-Sachs disease is a well-known genetic disease that usually occurs among Jewish people in the United States, most of whom are of central and eastern European descent. At first, it is not apparent that a baby has Tay-Sachs disease. However, development begins to slow down between four months and eight months of age—neurological impairment and psychomotor difficulties then become apparent. The child gradually becomes blind and helpless, develops uncontrollable seizures, and eventually becomes paralyzed. There is no treatment or cure for Tay-Sachs disease, and most affected individuals die by the age of three or four.

So-called late-onset Tay-Sachs disease occurs in adults. The symptoms are progressive mental and motor deterioration, depression, schizophrenia, and premature death. The gene for late-onset Tay-Sachs disease has been sequenced, and this form of the disorder apparently is due to one changed pair of bases in the DNA of chromosome 1.

Tay-Sachs disease results from a lack of the enzyme hexosaminidase A (Hex A) and the subsequent storage of its substrate, a glycosphingolipid, in lysosomes (fig. 14.10). Although more and more lysosomes build up in many body cells, the primary sites of storage are the cells of the brain, which accounts for the onset and the progressive deterioration of psychomotor functions.

There is a test to detect carriers of Tay-Sachs. The test uses a sample of serum, white blood cells, or tears to determine if Hex A activity is present. Affected individuals have no detectable Hex A activity. Carriers have about half the level of Hex A activity found in normal individuals. Prenatal diagnosis of the disease also is possible following either amniocentesis or chorionic villi sampling.

Figure 14.10

Tay-Sachs disease. **a.** When Hex A is present, glycosphingolipids are broken down. **b.** When Hex A is absent, these lipids accumulate in lysosomes and lysosomes accumulate in the cell. **c.** Electron micrograph of a cell crowded with lysosomes.

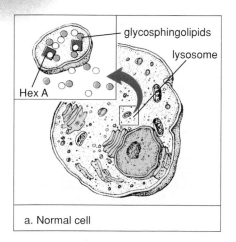

a. Normal cell

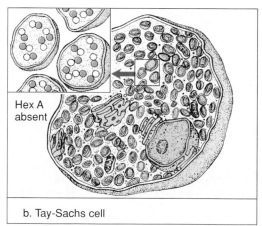

b. Tay-Sachs cell

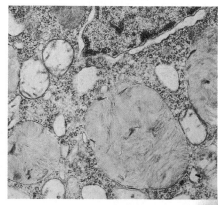

c.

Cystic Fibrosis

Cystic fibrosis is the most common lethal genetic disease among Caucasians in the United States. About one in five Caucasians is a carrier, and about one in 2,500 children born to this group has the disorder. In these children, the mucus in the lungs and the digestive tract is particularly thick and viscous. In the lungs, the mucus interferes with gas exchange (fig. 14.11).

In the past few years, much progress has been made in our understanding of cystic fibrosis, and new treatments have raised the average life expectancy to seventeen to twenty years of age. Research has demonstrated that chloride ions (Cl⁻) fail to pass through plasma membrane channel proteins in these patients. Ordinarily, after chloride ions have passed through the membrane, water follows. It is believed that lack of water in the lungs is what causes the mucus to be abnormally thick. The cystic fibrosis gene, which is located on chromosome 7, has been isolated and inserted into the lungs of living animals. The hope is that one day it will be possible to use an inhaler to carry copies of the normal gene into the lungs of cystic fibrosis patients.

Phenylketonuria (PKU)

Phenylketonuria (PKU) occurs once in 5,000 births and so it is not as frequent as the disorders previously discussed. However, it is the most commonly inherited metabolic disorder to affect nervous system development. Close relatives are more apt to have a PKU child.

Affected individuals lack an enzyme that is needed for the normal metabolism of the amino acid phenylalanine, and an abnormal breakdown product, a phenylketone, accumulates in the urine. The PKU gene is located on chromosome 12, and there is a prenatal DNA test for the presence of this mutation. Years ago, the urine of newborns was tested at home for phenylketone in order to detect PKU. Presently, newborns are routinely tested in the hospital for elevated levels of phenylalanine in the blood. If necessary, newborns are placed on a diet low in phenylalanine, which must be continued until the brain is fully developed or else severe mental retardation develops.

There are several autosomal recessive disorders in humans. Among these are Tay-Sachs disease, cystic fibrosis, and phenylketonuria (PKU).

Figure 14.11

The mucus in the lungs of a child with cystic fibrosis should be periodically loosened by clapping the back. A new treatment destroys the cells that tend to build up in the lungs. The white blood cells are destroyed by one drug and another drug does away with the DNA the cells leave behind. Judicious use of antibiotics controls pulmonary infection, and aggressive use of other drugs thins mucous secretions.

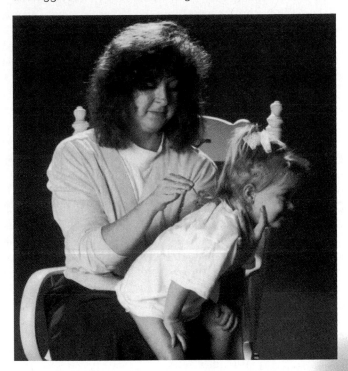

Practice Problems 2*

1. A child has PKU, but neither parent has PKU. What is the genotype of the parents?
2. What is the genotype of a person with sickle-cell trait? Reproductive partners with what genotype would produce a child with sickle-cell disease?
3. Prove that a child does not have to have the blood type of either parent by crossing a person with type A blood (having genotype AO) with a person with type B blood (having genotype BO).

*Answers to Practice Problems appear in appendix D.

CONSIDERING SEX-LINKED TRAITS

The X chromosomes carry many genes unrelated to the sex of the individual. It would be logical to suppose that a sex-linked trait is passed from father to son or from mother to daughter, but this is not the case. A male always receives a sex-linked condition from his mother, from whom he inherited an X chromosome. The Y chromosome from the father does not carry an allele for the trait.

When examining X-linked traits, the allele on the X chromosome is recorded as a letter attached to the X chromosome. For example, the possible genotypes for color blindness are as follows:

$X^B X^B$ = female who has normal color vision
$X^B X^b$ = carrier female who has normal color vision
$X^b X^b$ = female who is color blind
$X^B Y$ = male who has normal vision
$X^b Y$ = male who is color blind

Note that the second genotype is a *carrier* female because although a female with this genotype appears normal, she can pass on an allele for color blindness. Color-blind females are rare because they must receive the allele from both parents; color-blind males are more common since they need only one recessive allele to be color blind. Figure 14.12 shows there is a 50% chance of having a color-blind son when the mother is a carrier and the father has normal vision.

Figure 14.12

Cross involving an X-linked allele. The male parent is normal, but the female parent is a carrier; an allele for color blindness is located on one of her X chromosomes. Therefore, each son stands a 50% chance of being color blind.

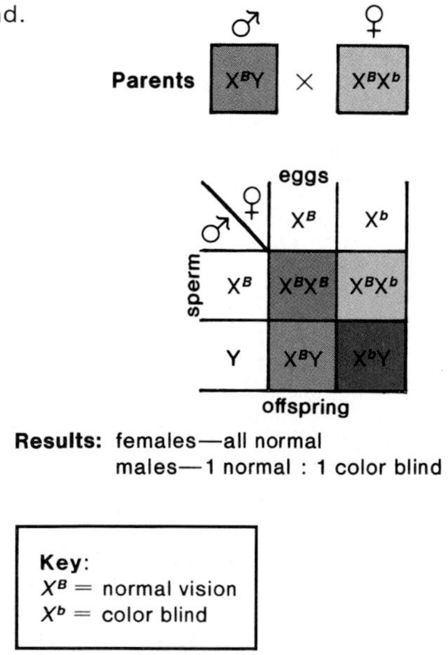

Parents: $X^B Y$ × $X^B X^b$

eggs: X^B, X^b
sperm: X^B, Y

offspring:
$X^B X^B$, $X^B X^b$
$X^B Y$, $X^b Y$

Results: females—all normal
males—1 normal : 1 color blind

Key:
X^B = normal vision
X^b = color blind

Some Disorders Are X-Linked

Figure 14.13 gives a pedigree chart for an X-linked recessive allele. It also lists ways to recognize this pattern of inheritance. Three well-known X-linked recessive disorders with this pattern are color blindness, hemophilia, and Duchenne muscular dystrophy.

Color Blindness

In humans, there are three genes involved in distinguishing color because there are three different types of cones, the receptors for color vision. Two of these are X-linked genes; one affects the green-sensitive cones, whereas the other affects the red-sensitive cones. About 5% of Caucasian men are color blind due to a mutation involving green perception, and about 2% are color blind due to a mutation involving red perception. In either case, the genotype is designated as $X^b Y$.

Hemophilia

Approximately one in 15,000 males are hemophiliacs. The most common type of hemophilia is hemophilia A, which is the absence of a sufficient amount of a clotting factor called factor VIII. *Hemophilia* is called the bleeder's disease because the affected person's blood does not clot. Although hemophiliacs bleed externally after an injury, they also suffer from internal bleeding, particularly around joints. Hemorrhages can be checked with transfusions of fresh blood (or plasma) or with concentrates of the clotting protein. Unfortunately, some hemophiliacs have contracted AIDS but blood donors are now screened more closely.

At the turn of the century, hemophilia was prevalent among the royal families of Europe, and all of the affected males could trace their ancestry to Queen Victoria of England. Because none of Queen Victoria's forebears or relatives were affected, it seems that the gene she carried arose by mutation either in herself or in one of her parents. Her carrier daughters, Alice and Beatrice, introduced the gene into the ruling houses of Russia and Spain, respectively. Alexis, the last heir to the Russian throne before the Russian Revolution, was a hemophiliac. There are no hemophiliacs in the present British royal family because Victoria's eldest son, King Edward VII, did not receive the gene, and therefore he could not pass it on to any of his descendants.

Muscular Dystrophy

Muscular dystrophy, as the name implies, is characterized by a wasting away of the muscles. The most common form, *Duchenne muscular dystrophy,* is X-linked and occurs in about one out of every 5,000 male births. Symptoms, such as waddling gait, toe walking, frequent falls, and difficulty in rising, may appear as soon as the child starts to walk. Muscle weakness intensifies until the individual is confined to a wheelchair. Death usually occurs by age twenty; therefore, affected males are rarely fathers. The recessive allele remains in the population by passage from carrier mother to carrier daughter.

Figure 14.13

X-linked recessive disorders. **a.** Sample pedigree chart. **b.** Ways to recognize X-linked recessive disorders. **c.** Listing of common X-linked recessive disorders.

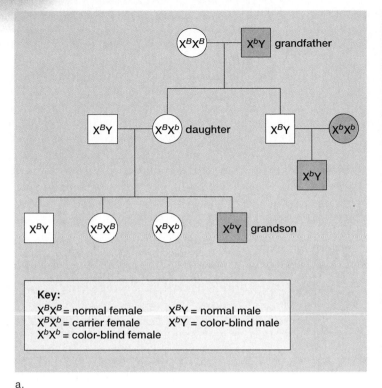

Key:
X^BX^B = normal female X^BY = normal male
X^BX^b = carrier female X^bY = color-blind male
X^bX^b = color-blind female

a.

X-linked Recessive Disorders

- More males than females are affected.
- An affected son can have parents who have the normal phenotype.
- For a female to have the characteristic, her father must also have it. Her mother must have it or be a carrier.
- The characteristic often skips a generation from the grandfather to the grandson.
- If a woman has the characteristic, all of her sons will have it.

b.

Among 205 catalogued X-linked recessive disorders are:

- Agammaglobulinemia—lack of immunity to infections
- Color blindness—inability to distinguish certain colors
- Hemophilia—defect in blood-clotting mechanisms
- Muscular dystrophy (some forms)—progressive wasting of muscles
- Spinal ataxia (some forms)—spinal cord degeneration

c.

Recently, the gene for muscular dystrophy was isolated, and it was discovered that the absence of a protein, now called dystrophin, is the cause of the disorder. Much investigative work determined that dystrophin is involved in the release of calcium from the calcium-storage sacs in muscle fibers. The lack of dystrophin causes calcium to leak into the cell, which promotes the action of an enzyme that dissolves muscle fibers. When the body attempts to repair the tissue, fibrous tissue forms, and this cuts off the blood supply so that more and more cells die.

Some Traits Are Sex-Influenced

Some genes not located on the X or Y chromosomes are expressed differently in the two sexes, and therefore the traits they control are referred to as **sex-influenced traits.** Pattern baldness is caused by an autosomal allele that is dominant in males due to the presence of testosterone, the male sex hormone. Heterozygous women with adrenal tumors develop pattern baldness, but hair returns when the tumor is removed. The adrenal glands normally produce some testosterone, even in women. Therefore the hair loss is due to an abnormally large amount of testosterone being produced by the malfunctioning adrenal gland.

There are sex-linked alleles on the X chromosomes that have nothing to do with sexual characteristics. Males have only one copy of these alleles, and if they inherit a recessive allele, it is expressed.

Practice Problems 3*

1. Both the mother and the father of a hemophilic son appear to be normal. What is the genotype of the mother, the father, and the son? What are the chances any son born to this couple will have hemophilia?

2. A normally-sighted woman has a color-blind daughter. What can you deduce about the girl's father?

*Answers to Practice Problems appear in appendix D.

CONSIDERING POLYGENIC INHERITANCE

Many human traits are not inherited according to dominant/recessive patterns of inheritance. Instead, they are controlled by polygenes, that is, many allelic pairs possibly located on many different chromosomes. Polygenic inheritance is also called quantitative inheritance because each contributing allele adds a certain amount to the phenotype.

Traits such as skin color and height are controlled by polygenes, and it is easy to see that these traits are subject to environmental effects such as exposure to sunlight (skin color) and nutrition (height). The combined effect of control by polygenes and environmental effects produces a continuous variation in phenotypes whose frequency distribution usually resembles a bell-shaped curve:

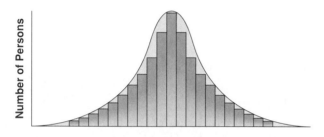

Many human disorders, such as cleft lip and/or palate, clubfoot, congenital dislocations of the hip, hypertension, diabetes, schizophrenia, and even allergies and cancers, are most likely controlled by polygenes and subject to environmental influences. Therefore, many investigators are in the process of considering the *nature versus nurture* question; that is, what percentage of the trait is controlled by genes and what percentage is controlled by the environment? Thus far, it has not been possible to come to precise, generally accepted percentages for any particular trait.

In recent years, reports have surfaced that all sorts of behavioral traits such as alcoholism, homosexuality, phobias, and even suicide can be associated with particular genes. No doubt behavioral traits are to a degree controlled by genes, but again, it is impossible at this time to determine to what degree. And very few scientists would support the idea that these traits are predetermined by our genes.

> Many human traits most likely controlled by polygenes are subject to environmental influences. The frequency of such traits follows a bell-shaped curve.

Summary

1. It is possible to treat and photograph the chromosomes of a cell so that they can be sorted and arranged in pairs. The resulting karyotype can be used to diagnose chromosomal abnormalities.

2. Down syndrome (trisomy 21) is the most common autosomal abnormality. The occurrence of this syndrome, which is often related to the mother's age, can be detected by amniocentesis. Most often, Down syndrome is due to nondisjunction during gamete formation, but in a small percentage of cases, there has been a translocation between chromosomes 14 and 21, in which chromosome 21 is attached to chromosome 14.

3. Turner syndrome (XO) is a monosomy for the X chromosome. There are several trisomies: metafemales, which are XXX; Klinefelter syndrome, which is XXY; and XYY males.

4. When studying human genes, biologists often construct pedigree charts to show the pattern of inheritance of a characteristic within a family. The particular pattern indicates the manner in which a characteristic is inherited. Sample charts are given for autosomal dominant, autosomal recessive, and X-linked recessive patterns.

5. Neurofibromatosis and Huntington disease are autosomal dominant disorders that have been well studied.

6. Sickle-cell disease is a human disorder that is controlled by incompletely dominant alleles.

7. ABO blood type is an example of a human trait controlled by multiple alleles.

8. Tay-Sachs disease, cystic fibrosis, and PKU are autosomal recessive disorders that have been studied in detail.

9. Color blindness, hemophilia, and Duchenne muscular dystrophy are X-linked recessive disorders. Some traits, like pattern baldness, are sex-influenced traits controlled by autosomal genes.

10. Traits controlled by polygenes are subject to environmental effects and show continuous variations whose frequency distribution forms a bell-shaped curve. Many human disorders, including behavior traits, are most likely controlled by polygenes, but the degree of genetic and environmental influence is difficult to determine.

Writing Across the Curriculum

In order to practice writing skills, students should write out the answers to any or all of the study questions and the critical thinking questions. The study questions are sequenced in the same order as the text. Answers to the objective questions, and suggested answers to the critical thinking questions, are in appendix D.

Study Questions

1. What does the normal human karyotype look like? 212

2. What are the characteristics of Down syndrome? What is the most frequent cause of this condition? 213–14

3. What is the only known sex chromosome monosomy in humans? Name and describe three sex chromosome trisomies. 215

4. How might you distinguish an autosomal dominant trait from an autosomal recessive trait when viewing a pedigree chart? 218–19

5. Describe the symptoms of neurofibromatosis and Huntington disease. How does neurofibromatosis illustrate variable expressivity? For most autosomal dominant disorders either of them, what are the chances of a heterozygote and a normal individual having an affected child? 220

6. Explain how sickle-cell disease is inherited. What are the symptoms of sickle-cell trait and sickle-cell disease? If two persons with the sickle-cell trait reproduce, what are the chances of having a child with the sickle-cell trait? with sickle-cell disease? What race of people is more likely to have this condition? Why? 221

7. Why is ABO blood type an example of inheritance by multiple alleles? 224

8. Describe the symptoms of Tay-Sachs disease, cystic fibrosis, and PKU. For any one of these, what are the chances of two carriers having an affected child? 224–25

9. Explain how color blindness, hemophilia and Duchenne muscular dystrophy are inherited. What are the symptoms of these conditions? What are the chances of having an affected male offspring if the mother is a carrier and the father is normal? 226–27

10. What is a sex-influenced trait? Give two examples of such traits. 227

11. What observational data would allow you to hypothesize that a human trait is controlled by polygenes? 228

Objective Questions

For questions 1–3, match the conditions in the key with the descriptions below:

Key:
   a. Down syndrome
   b. Turner syndrome
   c. Klinefelter syndrome
   d. XYY

1. male with underdeveloped testes and some breast development

2. trisomy 21

3. XO female

4. Down syndrome
   a. is always caused by nondisjunction of chromosome 21.
   b. shows no overt abnormalities.
   c. is more often seen in children of mothers past the age of thirty-five.
   d. Both a and c are correct.

5. A person has a genetic disorder. Which of these is inconsistent with autosomal recessive inheritance?
   a. Both parents have the disorder.
   b. Both parents do not have the disorder.
   c. All the children (males and females) have the disorder.
   d. All of these are consistent.
   e. All of these are inconsistent.

6. A male has a genetic disorder. Which one of these is inconsistent with X-linked recessive inheritance?
   a. Both parents do not have the disorder.
   b. Only males in a pedigree chart have the disorder.
   c. Only females in previous generations have the disorder.
   d. Both a and c are inconsistent.

For questions 7–10, match the conditions in the key with the following descriptions:

Key:
   a. cystic fibrosis
   b. Huntington disease
   c. hemophilia
   d. Tay-Sachs disease

7. autosomal dominant

8. most often seen among Jewish people

9. X-linked recessive

10. thick mucus in lungs and digestive system

11. Determine if the characteristic possessed by the darkened squares (males) and circles (females) below is an autosomal dominant, an autosomal recessive, or an X-linked recessive disorder.

Key:

○ normal female

□ normal male

● affected female

■ affected male

Additional Genetics Problems*

1. A hemophilic (X-linked recessive) man reproduces with a homozygous normal woman. What are the chances that their sons will be hemophiliacs? that their daughters will be hemophiliacs? that their daughters will be carriers?

2. A son with cystic fibrosis (autosomal recessive) is born to a couple who appear to be normal. What are the chances that any child born to this couple will have cystic fibrosis?

3. A man has type AB blood. What is his genotype? Could this man be the father of a child with type B blood? If so, what blood types could the child's mother have?

4. What is the genotype of a man who is color blind (X-linked recessive) and has a continuous hairline (autosomal recessive)? If this man has children by a woman who is homozygous dominant for normal color vision and widow's peak, what will be the genotype and phenotype of the children?

5. Determine if the characteristic possessed by the darkened squares (males) is dominant, recessive, or X-linked recessive. Write in the genotypes for the starred individual.

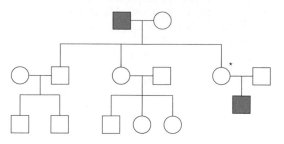

Concepts and Critical Thinking

1. *The principles of genetics are the same for all organisms.*

   What are some similarities and differences between plant genetics and animal genetics? Considering that there are some differences, does this concept still hold?

2. *Inheritance plays a significant role in determining our mental and physical characteristics.*

   Without regard to ethical considerations, design an experiment to solve the nature-nurture question.

3. *Genetic disorders, like other conditions, are sometimes preventable and treatable.*

   What measures, if any, should be taken to prevent genetic diseases in the next generation?

Selected Key Terms

autosome Any chromosome other than a sex chromosome. [Gk. *aut,* self, and *soma,* body]   212

carrier A heterozygous individual who has no apparent abnormality but can pass on an allele for a recessively inherited genetic disorder.   219

karyotype (KAR-ee-uh-typ) Chromosomes arranged by pairs according to their size, shape, and general appearance in mitotic metaphase. [Gk. *kary,* nucleus, and *typos,* mark]   212

multiple allele One form of a gene that has more than several alleles although each individual has only two of these alleles.   224

nondisjunction The failure of homologous chromosomes or daughter chromosomes to separate during meiosis I and meiosis II respectively.   213

sex chromosome A chromosome that determines the sex of an individual; in animals, females have two X chromosomes and males have an X and Y chromosome.   212

sex-influenced trait An autosomal phenotype controlled by an allele that is expressed differently in the two sexes; for example, the possibility of pattern baldness is increased by the presence of testosterone in males.   227

---

*Answers to Additional Genetic Problems appear in appendix D.

15

DNA: THE GENETIC MATERIAL

Learning Objectives

- List the requirements for a substance to serve as the genetic material.   232

Searching for the Genetic Material

- Describe the transformation experiment of Griffith, including his surprising results and conclusion.   232–33

- Tell how Avery and colleagues showed that DNA is the transforming substance.   232–33

- Describe the experiment of Hershey and Chase with T viruses, and tell how it showed that DNA is the genetic material.   234

Finding the Structure of DNA

- Explain Chargaff's rules for DNA and tell why they are significant.   235

- Describe the Watson and Crick model of DNA, and tell how it fits the Chargaff and the Franklin data.   236–37

DNA Can Be Replicated

- Describe the semiconservative manner in which DNA replicates.   238–39

- Tell how Meselson and Stahl demonstrated that DNA replication is semiconservative.   239

- Contrast the process of DNA replication in prokaryotes and eukaryotes.   241

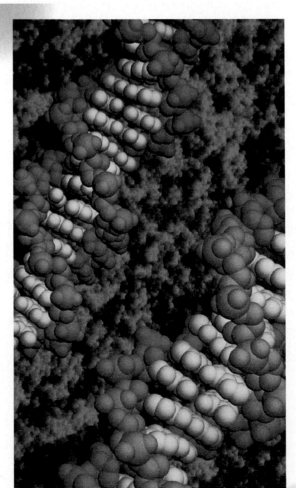

The structure of DNA (brown and tan) resemble a spiral staircase.

ven though previous investigators were able to confirm that the genes are on the chromosomes and were even able to map the *Drosophila* chromosomes, they still didn't know just what genes consisted of. You can well imagine, then, that the search for the genetic material was of utmost importance to biologists at the beginning of the twentieth century. They knew that this material must be:

1. able to *store information* that is used to control both the development and the metabolic activities of the cell or organism;
2. stable so that it *can be replicated* with high fidelity during cell division and be transmitted from generation to generation;
3. able to *undergo rare changes* called **mutations** [L. *muta,* change] that provide the genetic variability required for evolution to occur.

> The genetic material must be able to store information, be replicated, and undergo mutations.

SEARCHING FOR THE GENETIC MATERIAL

Knowledge about the chemistry of DNA was absolutely essential in order to come to the conclusion that DNA is the genetic material. In 1869, the Swiss chemist Friedrich Miescher removed nuclei from pus cells (these cells have little cytoplasm) and found that they contained a chemical he called *nuclein.* Nuclein, he said, was rich in phosphorus and had no sulfur, properties that distinguished it from protein. Later, other chemists did further work with nuclein and said that it contained an acidic substance they called **nucleic acid.** Soon it was realized that there are two types of nucleic acids: **DNA (deoxyribonucleic acid)** and **RNA (ribonucleic acid).**

When it was discovered early in the twentieth century that nucleic acids contain four types of nucleotides, a misguided idea called the *tetranucleotide* (four-nucleotide) *hypothesis* arose. It said that DNA was composed of repeating units, and each unit always had just one of each of the four different nucleotides. In other words, DNA could not vary between species and therefore could not be the genetic material!

Figure 15.1

Griffith's transformation experiment. **a.** Encapsulated S strain is virulent and kills the mouse. **b.** Nonencapsulated R strain is not virulent and does not kill the mouse. **c.** Heat-killed S strain bacteria do not kill the mouse. **d.** If heat-killed S strain bacteria and R strain bacteria are both injected into a mouse, it dies because the R strain bacteria have been transformed into the virulent S strain.

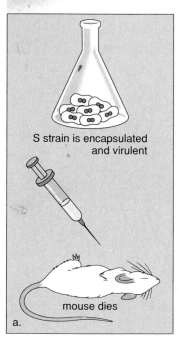

S strain is encapsulated and virulent

mouse dies

a.

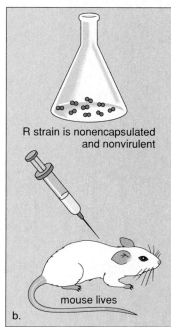

R strain is nonencapsulated and nonvirulent

mouse lives

b.

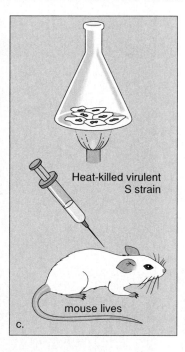

Heat-killed virulent S strain

mouse lives

c.

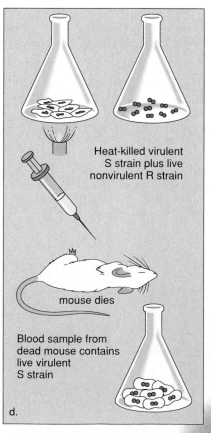

Heat-killed virulent S strain plus live nonvirulent R strain

mouse dies

Blood sample from dead mouse contains live virulent S strain

d.

Bacteria Can Be Transformed

In 1931, the bacteriologist Frederick Griffith performed an experiment with a bacterium (*Streptococcus pneumoniae,* or pneumococcus for short) that causes pneumonia in mammals. He noticed that when these bacteria are grown on culture plates, some, called S strain bacteria, produce shiny, smooth colonies and others, called R strain bacteria, produce colonies that have a rough appearance. Under the microscope, S strain bacteria have a mucous (polysaccharide) coat but R strain bacteria do not. When Griffith injected mice with the S strain of bacteria, the mice died, and when he injected mice with the R strain, the mice did not die (fig. 15.1). In an effort to determine if the smooth coat alone was responsible for the virulence (ability to kill) of the S strain bacteria, he injected mice with heat-killed S strain bacteria. The mice did not die.

Finally, Griffith injected the mice with a mixture of heat-killed S strain and live R strain bacteria. Most unexpectedly, the mice died and living S strain bacteria were recovered from the bodies! Griffith concluded that some substance necessary to the synthesis of a mucous coat and, therefore, virulence must have passed from the dead S strain bacteria to the living R strain bacteria so that the R strain bacteria were *transformed* (fig. 15.1*d*). This change in the phenotype of the R strain bacteria must be due to a change in their genotype. Indeed, couldn't the transforming substance that passed from S strain to R strain be genetic material? Reasoning such as this prompted investigators at the time to begin looking for the transforming substance to determine the chemical nature of the hereditary material.

Finding the Transforming Substance

Obviously, it is not convenient to look for the transforming substance in mice, so it is not surprising that the next group of investigators, led by Oswald Avery, worked in vitro (in laboratory glassware). After sixteen years of research, this group published a paper demonstrating that the transforming substance is DNA. Their evidence included the following observations:

1. DNA from S strain bacteria causes R strain bacteria to be transformed. The DNA they used to transform R strain bacteria was pure—99.98% pure!
2. Enzymes that degrade proteins cannot prevent transformation, nor did RNase, an enzyme that digests RNA.
3. Enzymatic digestion of the transforming substance with DNase, an enzyme that digests DNA, does prevent transformation.
4. The molecular weight of the transforming substance is so great that it must contain about 1,600 nucleotides! Certainly this is enough for some genetic variability.

These experiments showed not only that DNA is the genetic material, but also that DNA controls the biosynthetic properties of a cell. While these experiments seem quite convincing, remember that at the time biologists knew proteins were very complex, but they still were not sure about DNA. Some thought that perhaps these results pertained only to this experiment.

Viruses Also Have Genetic Material

In the twentieth century, many geneticists who were interested in determining the chemical nature of the genetic material began to work with **bacteriophages** [Gk. *bact,* rod, and *phag,* to eat], viruses that attack bacteria (fig. 15.2). The most intensely studied species of bacterium is *Escherichia coli* (*E. coli*), which normally lives within the human gut. Bacteria are unicellular organisms of such a small size that a few thousand of them can be placed in a liquid medium containing only a few salts and an energy source such as the sugar glucose, and within a few hours, there will be as many as 3×10^9 bacteria per ml. Bacteriophages (or phages) consist only of a protein coat surrounding a nucleic acid core. Enormous populations of a phage can be easily obtained—up to 10^{11} per ml or more in an infected bacterial culture is not unusual.

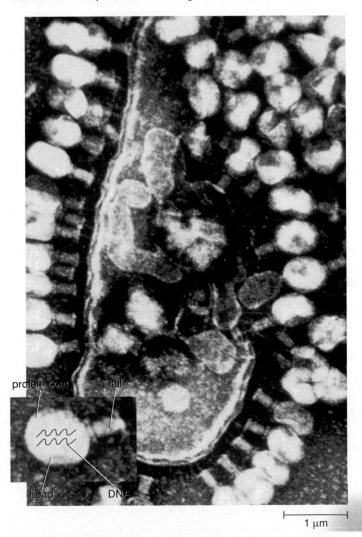

Figure 15.2

Bacteria and bacteriophages. These microbes were the experimental material of choice for determining the physical and chemical characteristics of the genetic material. T viruses are pictured attacking an *E. coli* cell.

protein coat

tail

head

DNA

1 μm

In 1952, two experimenters, Alfred D. Hershey and Martha Chase, chose a bacteriophage known as T2 for their experimental material. They decided to see which of the bacteriophage components—protein or DNA—entered bacterial cells and directed reproduction of the virus. Whichever did this, they reasoned, was the genetic material.

There is a chemical distinction between DNA and protein. Phosphorus is absent, but *sulfur (S) is present in some amino acids* of a protein. On the other hand, sulfur is absent but *phosphorus (P) is present in DNA* in high amounts. Therefore, it was possible for Hershey and Chase to prepare two batches of phages: one that had the DNA labeled with radioactive ^{32}P, and another that had the protein coat labeled with radioactive ^{35}S. Radioactive phages were allowed to attach briefly to *E. coli* bacterial cells; once the infection process had started, most of the adhering phage coats were sheared from the bacterial cells by agitation in a kitchen blender. Centrifugation then caused the bacterial cells to collect as a pellet at the bottom of the tube. In one experiment (fig. 15.3*a*), they found that most of the ^{32}P-labeled DNA remained in the pellet:

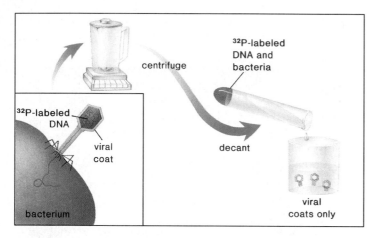

In the other experiment (fig. 15.3*b*), they found that most of the ^{35}S-labeled protein remained in the phage coats. These results indicated that the DNA of the virus (and not the protein) enters the host, where viral replication takes place. Therefore, DNA is the genetic material of bacteriophage T2. It directs protein coat synthesis and allows replication to occur.

Biologists, in general, were persuaded that DNA is the genetic material by this experiment, possibly because recent chemical studies of the composition of DNA had finally shown that the tetranucleotide hypothesis was not true.

The Hershey and Chase experiment showed that DNA and not protein is the genetic material of the T2 bacteriophage.

Figure 15.3

Hershey and Chase experiment. A T virus contains DNA and has a protein coat. It was reasoned that whichever of these enters a bacterium and controls viral replication is the genetic material. **a.** In this experiment, ^{32}P was used to label viral DNA. The coats were removed by agitation in a blender, and the radioactively labeled DNA entered the cell. Because replication proceeded normally, DNA is the genetic material. **b.** In this experiment, ^{35}S was used to label the protein coat. When the cells were agitated in a blender, the radioactively labeled protein coats were removed. Because replication proceeded normally, protein is not the genetic material.

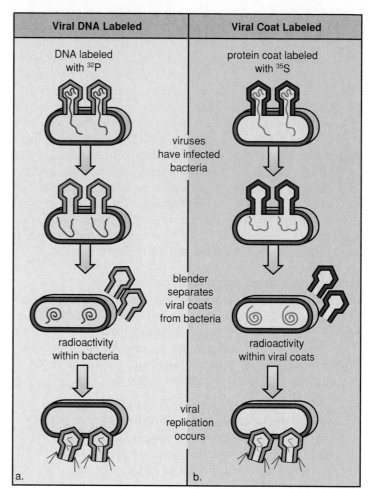

Figure 15.4

Nucleotide composition of DNA. All nucleotides contain phosphate, a five-carbon sugar, and a nitrogen-containing base. (Notice that the numbers count the number of carbons.) In DNA, the sugar is deoxyribose—there is an absence of oxygen in the 2' (read as 2 "prime") position—and the nitrogen-containing bases are **a.** the purines adenine and guanine or **b.** the pyrimidines thymine and cytosine. **c.** Chargaff found that in each species the amount of A = T and the amount of G = C. Between species, however, the A, T, and G, C percentages differ. For example, in humans the A, T percentage is about 31%, but in fruit flies the percentage is about 27%.

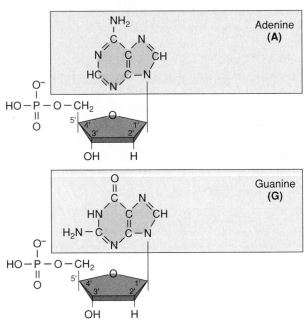

a. **Purine Nucleotides**

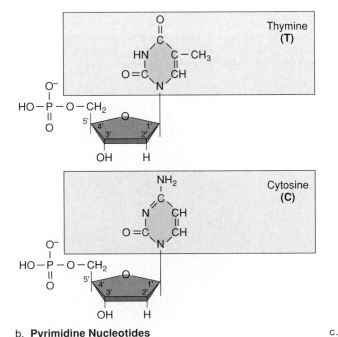

b. **Pyrimidine Nucleotides**

FINDING THE STRUCTURE OF DNA

During the same period of time that biologists were using viruses to show that DNA is the genetic material, biochemists were busy trying to determine its structure. The structure of DNA shows how DNA stores information, as is required of the genetic material.

Making Use of Nucleotide Data

With the development of new chemical techniques in the 1940s, it was possible for Erwin Chargaff to analyze in detail the base content of DNA. It was known that DNA contains four different types of nucleotides: two with **purine** bases, **adenine (A)** and **guanine (G),** and two with **pyrimidine** bases, **thymine (T)** and **cytosine (C)** (fig. 15.4a and b). Did each species contain 25% of each kind of nucleotide, as suggested by the tetranucleotide hypothesis?

A sample of Chargaff's data are seen in figure 15.4c. You can see that while some species—*E. coli* and *Zea mays* (corn), for example—do have approximately 25% of each type of nucleotide as suggested by the tetranucleotide hypothesis, most do not. Further, the percentage of each type of nucleotide differs from species to species. Therefore, DNA does have the *variability* between species required of the genetic material.

Within each species, however, DNA has the *constancy* required of the genetic material. Further, the percentage of A equals the percentage of T and the percentage of G equals the percentage of C. The percentage of A + G equals 50% and the percentage of T + C equals 50%. These relationships are called Chargaff's rules.

Chargaff's rules:

1. The amount of A, T, G, and C in DNA varies from species to species.
2. In each species, the amount of A = T and the amount of G = C.

The tetranucleotide hypothesis, which said that DNA has repeating units, each with one of the four bases, was not supported by these data. Each species had its own constant base composition.

Chargaff's DNA Data Base Composition in Various Species (%)				
Species	**A**	**T**	**G**	**C**
Homo sapiens	31.0	31.5	19.1	18.4
Drosophila melanogaster	27.3	27.6	22.5	22.5
Zea mays	25.6	25.3	24.5	24.6
Neurospora crassa	23.0	23.3	27.1	26.6
Escherichia coli	24.6	24.3	25.5	25.6
Bacillus subtilis	28.4	29.0	21.0	21.6

c.

Base Sequence Varies

Chargaff's data suggest that A is always paired with T and G is always paired with C. The paired bases occur in any order:

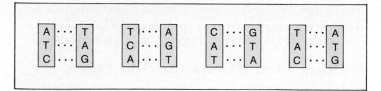

The variability that can be obtained is overwhelming. For example, it has been calculated that the human chromosome contains on the average about 140 million base pairs. Since any of the four possible nucleotides can be present at each nucleotide position, the total number of possible nucleotide sequences is $4^{140} \times 10^6$ or $4^{140,000,000}$. No wonder each species has its own base percentages!

Making Use of Diffraction Data

Rosalind Franklin, a student of M. H. F. Wilkins at King's College in London, studied the structure of DNA using X rays. She found that if a concentrated, viscous solution of DNA is made, it can be separated into fibers. Under the right conditions, the fibers are enough like a crystal (a solid substance whose atoms are arranged in a definite manner) that an X-ray pattern can be formed on a photographic film. Franklin's picture of DNA showed that DNA is a helix (fig. 15.5). The helical shape is indicated by the crossed (X) pattern in the center of the photograph. The dark portions at the top and bottom of the photograph indicate that some portion of the helix is repeated.

Watson and Crick Build a Model

In the early 1950s, James Watson, an American, was on a postdoctoral fellowship at Cavendish Laboratories in Cambridge, England. There he met the biophysicist Francis H.C. Crick. Using the data we have just presented, they constructed a model of DNA (fig. 15.6).

Watson and Crick knew, of course, that DNA is a polymer of nucleotides but they did not know how the nucleotides were arranged within the molecule. This is what they decided.

1. The Watson and Crick model shows that DNA is a double helix with sugar-phosphate backbones on the outside and paired bases on the inside. This arrangement fits the mathematical measurements provided by the X-ray diffraction data for the spacing between the base pairs (.34 nm) and for a complete turn of the double helix (3.4 nm).

2. Chargaff's rules said that A = T and G = C. The model shows that A is hydrogen-bonded to T and G is hydrogen-bonded to C. This so-called **complementary base pairing** means that a purine is always bonded to a pyrimidine. Only in this way will the molecule have the width (2 nm) dictated by its X-ray diffraction pattern, since two pyrimidines together are too narrow and two purines together are too wide.

> The double-helix model of DNA is like a twisted ladder; the sugar-phosphate backbones make up the sides, and the hydrogen-bonded bases make up the rungs, or steps, of the ladder.

Figure 15.5

X-ray diffraction of DNA. **a.** When a crystal is X-rayed, the way in which the beam is diffracted reflects the pattern of the molecules in the crystal. The closer together two repeating structures are in the crystal, the farther from the center the beam is diffracted. **b.** The diffraction pattern of DNA produced by Rosalind Franklin. The crossed (X) pattern in the center told investigators that DNA is a helix, and the dark portions at the top and the bottom told them that some feature is repeated over and over. Watson and Crick determined that this feature was the hydrogen-bonded bases.

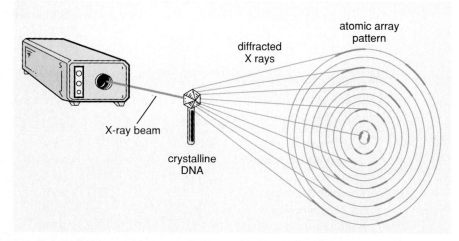

a.

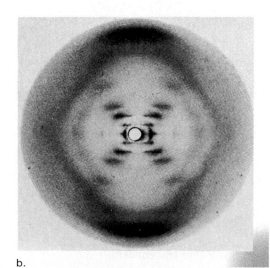

b.

Figure 15.6

Watson and Crick model of DNA. **a.** A space-filling model of DNA. Notice the close stacking of the paired bases, as determined by the X-ray diffraction pattern of DNA. (Color code for atoms: yellow = phosphate, dark blue = carbon, red = oxygen, turquoise = nitrogen, and white = hydrogen.) **b.** Diagram of DNA double helix shows that the molecule resembles a twisted ladder. Sugar-phosphate backbones make up the sides of the ladder, and hydrogen-bonded bases make up the rungs of the ladder. Complementary base pairing dictates that A is bonded to T and G is bonded to C. Notice that the two strands of the molecule are antiparallel; that is, the sugar-phosphate groups are oriented in different directions.

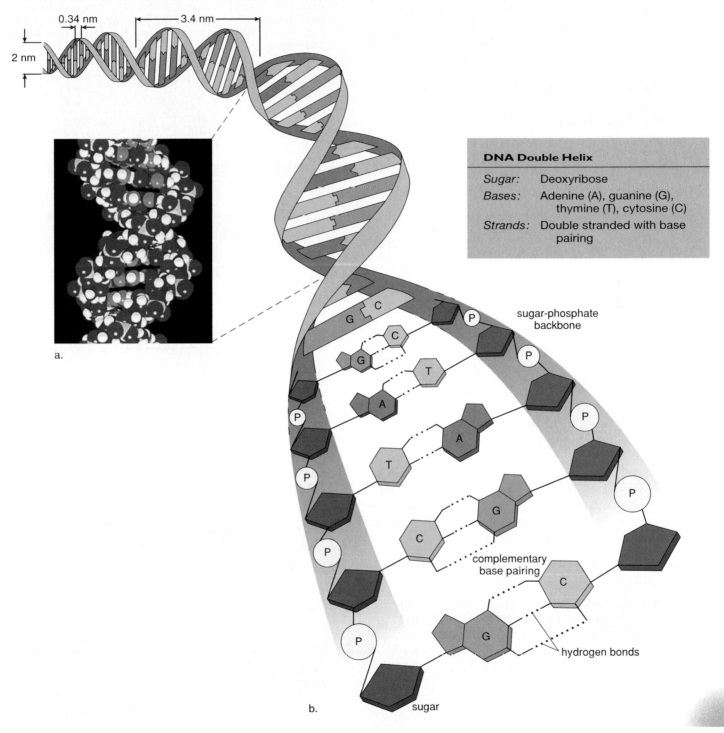

DNA Double Helix	
Sugar:	Deoxyribose
Bases:	Adenine (A), guanine (G), thymine (T), cytosine (C)
Strands:	Double stranded with base pairing

DNA Can Be Replicated

Ability to be replicated is one of the key requirements of a genetic material. As soon as Watson and Crick developed their double-helix model, they commented, "It has not escaped our notice that the specific pairing we have postulated immediately suggests a possible copying mechanism for the genetic material."

It has now been confirmed that DNA is replicated by means of complementary base pairing. During replication, each old DNA strand of the parent molecule serves as a template for a new strand in a daughter molecule (fig. 15.7). A template is most often a mold used to produce a shape complementary to itself. DNA replication is termed **semiconservative replication** because one of the old strands is conserved, or present, in each daughter molecule.

Replication requires the following steps:

1. *Unwinding.* The old strands that make up the parent DNA molecule are unwound and "unzipped" (i.e., the weak hydrogen bonds between the paired bases are broken). There is a special enzyme called helicase that unwinds the molecule.
2. *Complementary base pairing.* New complementary nucleotides, always present in the nucleus, are positioned by the process of complementary base pairing.
3. *Joining.* The complementary nucleotides join to form new strands. Each daughter DNA molecule contains an old strand and a new strand.

Steps 2 and 3 are carried out by a complex called **DNA polymerase.** DNA polymerase works in the test tube as well as in cells. In the so-called polymerase chain reaction (PCR), a small section of DNA is replicated many times, providing many copies of a particular sequence of interest for future testing purposes.

In figure 15.7, the backbones of the parent molecule (original double strand) is bluish and each base is given a particular color. Following replication, the daughter molecules each have a pinkish backbone (new strand) and a bluish backbone (old strand). A daughter DNA double helix has the same sequence of bases as the parent DNA double helix had originally. Although DNA replication can be easily explained in this manner, it is actually a complicated process. Some of the more precise molecular events are discussed in the reading on page 240.

> During DNA replication, the parent DNA molecule unwinds and unzips. Then each old strand serves as a template for a new strand.

Figure 15.7

Semiconservative replication (simplified). After the DNA molecule unwinds, each old strand serves as a template for the formation of the new strand. Complementary nucleotides available in the cell pair with those of the old strand and then are joined together to form a strand. After replication is complete, there are two daughter DNA molecules. Each is composed of an old strand and a new strand. Notice that each daughter molecule has the same sequence of base pairs as the parent molecule had before unwinding occurred.

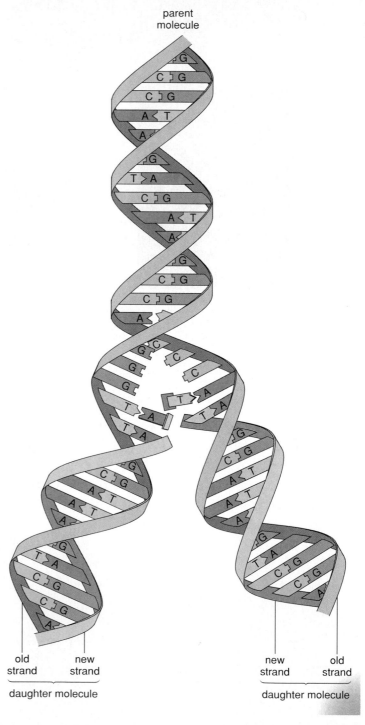

Figure 15.8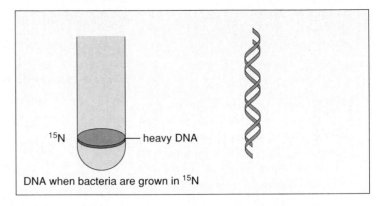

Meselson and Stahl's DNA replication experiment. **a.** When DNA molecules are centrifuged in a CsCl density gradient, they separate on the basis of density. **b.** Cells grown in heavy nitrogen (^{15}N) have dense strands. After one division in light nitrogen (^{14}N), DNA molecules are hybrid and have intermediate density. After two divisions, DNA molecules separate into two bands—one for light DNA and one for hybrid DNA.

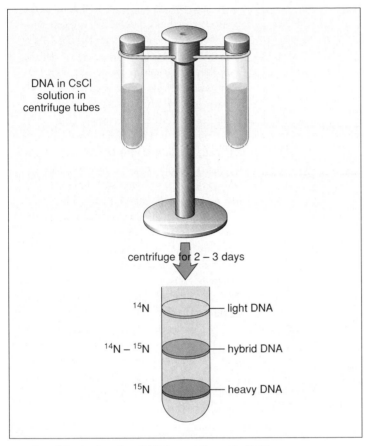

^{15}N — heavy DNA

DNA when bacteria are grown in ^{15}N

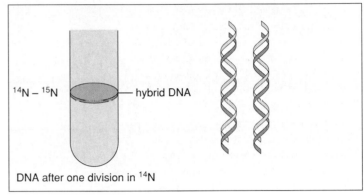

$^{14}N - ^{15}N$ — hybrid DNA

DNA after one division in ^{14}N

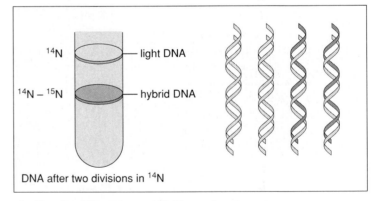

^{14}N — light DNA

$^{14}N - ^{15}N$ — hybrid DNA

DNA after two divisions in ^{14}N

DNA in CsCl solution in centrifuge tubes

centrifuge for 2 – 3 days

^{14}N — light DNA

$^{14}N - ^{15}N$ — hybrid DNA

^{15}N — heavy DNA

a. Possible results when DNA is centrifuged in CsCl

b. Results of Meselson and Stahl experiment

Replication Is Semiconservative

DNA replication is termed semiconservative because each daughter double helix contains an old strand and a new strand. Semiconservative replication was experimentally confirmed by Matthew Meselson and Franklin Stahl in 1958.

These investigators knew that it would be possible to centrifuge DNA molecules in a gradient that can separate them on the basis of density (fig. 15.8*a*). A DNA molecule in which both strands contained heavy nitrogen (^{15}N, with an atomic weight of 15) is most dense. A DNA molecule in which both strands contained light nitrogen (^{14}N, with an atomic weight of 14) is least dense. A hybrid DNA molecule in which one strand is heavy and one is light has an intermediate density.

Meselson and Stahl first grew bacteria in a medium containing ^{15}N so that only heavy DNA molecules were present in the cells. Then they switched the bacteria to a medium containing ^{14}N. After one division, only hybrid DNA molecules were in the cells. After two divisions, half of the DNA molecules were light and half were hybrid. These were exactly the results to be expected if DNA replication is semiconservative.

> DNA replication is semiconservative. Each new strand contains an old and a new strand.

Aspects of DNA Replication

W atson and Crick realized that the strands in DNA had to be antiparallel to allow for complementary base pairing. This opposite polarity of the strands introduces complications for DNA replication, as we will now see. First, it is important to take a look at a deoxyribose molecule in which the carbon atoms are numbered (fig. 15A*a*). Use the structure to see that one of the strands of DNA (fig. 15A*b*) runs in the 5′ → 3′ direction and the other runs in the 3′ → 5′ direction. You can tell the 5′ end because that's the last phosphate.

During replication (fig. 15A*b*), one nucleotide is joined to another. Each new nucleotide already has a phosphate group at the 5′ carbon atom and it is joined to the 3′ carbon atom of a sugar already in place. Therefore it is said that *DNA polymerase synthesizes the replicated strand in the 5′ → 3′ direction.* This presents a problem at the replication fork (fig. 15A*c*), where DNA is unwound and unzipped and where replication is occurring.

At a replication fork, only one of the new (daughter) strands runs in the 5′ → 3′ direction (the template for this strand, of course, runs in the 3′ → 5′ direction). The new strand running in the 5′ → 3′ direction can be synthesized continuously and is called the *leading strand.* But what about the situation when the 5′ → 3′ parental strand is serving as the template? Synthesis of the new strand must also be in the 5′ → 3′ direction, and therefore synthesis has to begin at the fork. (Although

synthesis is in the 5′ → 3′ direction, this new daughter strand in the end runs from 3′ → 5′, opposite to its template. Do you see why?) Because replication of the 5′ → 3′ parental strand must begin repeatedly as the DNA molecule unwinds and unzips, replication is discontinuous; indeed, replication of this strand results in segments called Okazaki fragments , after the Japanese scientist who discovered them. Discontinuous replication takes more time than continuous replication, and therefore the new strand in this case is called the *lagging strand.*

The fact that DNA polymerase can only join a nucleotide to the free 3′ end of another nucleotide presents another problem: *DNA polymerase cannot start the synthesis of a new DNA chain* at the origin of replication. (In the lagging strand there are many origins of replication.) Here, RNA polymerases lay down a short amount of RNA, called an RNA primer, that is complementary to the DNA strand being replicated. Now DNA polymerase can add DNA nucleotides in the 5′ → 3′ direction. Later, while proofreading, DNA polymerase removes the RNA primer and replaces it with complementary DNA nucleotides.

Another enzyme, called DNA ligase, joins the 3′ end of each fragment to the 5′ end of another.

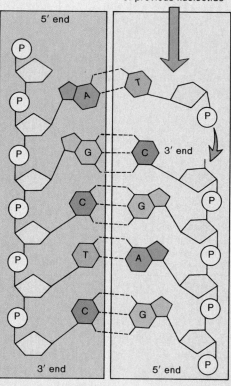

DNA polymerase attaches new nucleotide to the 3′ carbon of previous nucleotide

Figure 15A

DNA replication (in depth). **a.** Structure of deoxyribose, showing where nitrogen base and phosphate groups are attached. **b.** Template strand and replicated strand, the latter of which always grows from the 5′ end toward the 3′ end. **c.** Both parental strands are templates for a daughter strand. Replication is a continuous process for one daughter strand and a discontinuous process for the other daughter strand.

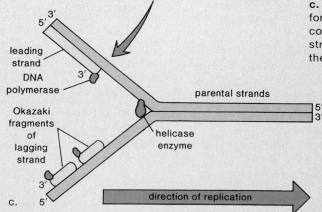

Replication Errors Do Occur

The ability to mutate is one of the requirements for genetic material, and base changes during replication are one way mutations—random changes in genes—can occur. During the replication process, DNA polymerase chooses complementary nucleotide triphosphates from the cellular pool. Then the nucleotide triphosphate is converted to a nucleotide monophosphate and aligned with the template nucleotide.[1]

A mismatched nucleotide slips through this selection process only once per 100,000 base pairs. The mismatched nucleotide causes a pause in replication, during which time it is excised from the daughter strand and replaced with the correct nucleotide. After this so-called proofreading has occurred, the error rate is only one mistake per 10 million base pairs.

The errors that slip through nucleotide selection and proofreading cause a gene mutation to occur. Actually it is of benefit for mutations to occur occasionally because variation is the raw material for the evolutionary process.

> Errors in replication are minimized because DNA polymerase has a "proofreading" function. Mutations occur when a mispairing slips through the proofreading process.

Prokaryotic Versus Eukaryotic Replication

Prokaryotes differ from eukaryotes in a number of ways, including how DNA replication takes place.

DNA Replicates in Prokaryotes

Bacteria have a single circular loop of DNA that must be replicated before the cell divides. In some circular DNA molecules, replication moves around the DNA molecule in one direction only. In others as shown here, replication starts at the origin but moves in opposite directions. The process always occurs in the 5′ to 3′ direction.

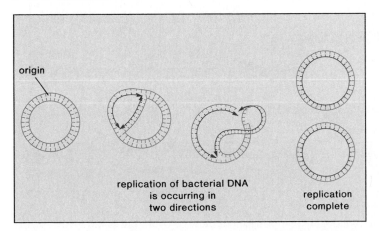

origin

replication of bacterial DNA is occurring in two directions

replication complete

In prokaryotes, the single chromosome is attached to the plasma membrane; after it is replicated the two copies separate as the cell enlarges. Newly formed plasma membrane and cell wall separate the cell into two cells. This process is called binary fission.

Bacterial cells are able to replicate their DNA at a rate of about 10^6 base pairs per minute, and about forty minutes are required to replicate the complete chromosome. Because bacterial cells are able to divide as often as once every twenty minutes, it is possible for a new round of DNA replication to begin even before the previous round is completed!

DNA Replicates in Eukaryotes

In eukaryotes, DNA replication begins at numerous origins of replication along the length of the chromosome, and the so-called replication bubbles spread bidirectionally until they meet. Notice that there is a V shape wherever DNA is being replicated. This is called a *replication fork.*

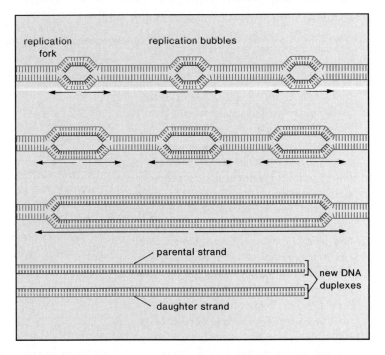

replication fork

replication bubbles

parental strand

new DNA duplexes

daughter strand

Although eukaryotes replicate their DNA at a slower rate—500–5,000 base pairs per minute—there are many individual origins of replication. Therefore, eukaryotic cells complete the replication of the diploid amount of DNA (in humans over 6 billion base pairs) in a matter of hours!

Replication precedes cell division in eukaryotes. The cell cycle contains interphase, during which time replication occurs, and mitosis, during which time the cell divides. A mitotic spindle consisting of microtubules serves to orchestrate the separation of daughter chromosomes into daughter nuclei.

---

1 When nucleotide monophosphates are cleaved from nucleotide triphosphates, energy is provided for DNA synthesis.

Barbara McClintock and the Discovery of Jumping Genes

hen Barbara McClintock (fig. 15B) first began studying inheritance in corn (maize) plants, geneticists believed that each gene had a fixed locus on a chromosome. Just as Morgan and his colleagues mapped the chromosomes of *Drosophila*, so McClintock was busy mapping those of corn. In the course of her studies, she came to the conclusion that "controlling elements" could move from one location to another on the chromosome. If a controlling element landed in the middle of a gene, it prevented the expression of that gene. Today, McClintock's controlling elements are called moveable genetic elements, transposons, or (in slang), "jumping genes."

Based on her experiments with maize, McClintock showed that because transposons are capable of suppressing gene expression, they could account for the pigment pattern of the corn strain popularly known as Indian corn. A colorless corn kernel results when cells are unable to produce a purple pigment due to the presence of a transposon within a particular gene needed to synthesize the pigment. While mutations are usually stable, a transposition is very unstable. When the transposon jumps to another chromosomal location, some cells regain the ability to produce the purple pigment and the result is a corn kernel with a speckled pattern (fig. 15C).

When McClintock first published her results in the 1950s, the scientific community ignored them. Years later, when molecular genetics was well established, transposons were also discovered in bacteria, yeasts, plants, flies, and humans. Geneticists now believe that transposons:

1. can cause localized mutations; that is, mutations that occur in certain cells and not others.
2. can carry a copy of certain host genes with them when they jump. Therefore, they can be a source of chromosomal mutations such as translocations, deletions, and inversions.

3. can leave copies of themselves and certain host genes before jumping. Therefore, they can be a source of a duplication, another type of chromosomal mutation.
4. in bacteria they can contain one or more genes that make a bacterium resistant to antibiotics.

Considering that transposition has a powerful effect on genotype and phenotype (fig. 15D), it most likely has played an important role in evolution. For her discovery of transposons, McClintock was, in 1983, finally awarded the Nobel prize in Physiology or Medicine.

During the years when she received no recognition for her work, McClintock never gave up. She labored alone and often went through the entire day without an opportunity to speak to anyone. She found it difficult to give speeches to those who were unfamiliar with corn genetics, but her closest colleagues said she liked to discuss her work and answer students' questions. Through it all, McClintock was content to communicate with corn. In her Nobel prize acceptance speech, the eighty-one-year-old scientist proclaimed that "it might seem unfair to reward a person for having so much pleasure over the years, asking the maize plant to solve specific problems and then watching its responses."

Figure 15B

Barbara McClintock (1902–92).

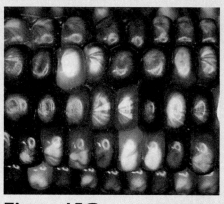

Figure 15C

Some corn kernels are purple, some are colorless, and some are speckled.

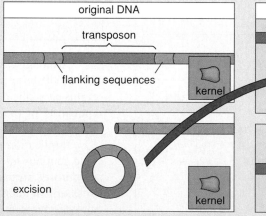
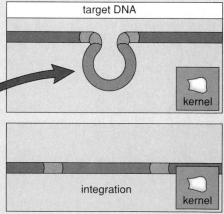

Figure 15D

In its original location, a transposon is interrupting a gene (brown) that is not involved in kernel pigmentation. When the transposon moves, it blocks the action of a gene (blue) required for synthesis of a purple pigment, and the kernel is now colorless.

Summary

1. Early work on the biochemistry of DNA wrongly suggested that it was composed of units each having only one of each of the four different nucleotides—A, T, G, or C. This so-called tetranucleotide hypothesis meant that DNA lacked the variability necessary for the genetic material.

2. Griffith injected strains of pneumococcus into mice and observed that smooth (S) strain bacteria are virulent but rough (R) strain bacteria are not. When heat-killed S strain bacteria were injected along with live R strain bacteria, however, virulent S strain bacteria were recovered from the dead mice. Griffith said that the R strain had been transformed by some substance passing from the dead S strain to the live R strain.

3. Twenty years later, Avery and his colleagues reported that the transforming substance is DNA. They showed that purified DNA (and not protein, for example) is capable of bringing about the transformation.

4. Hershey and Chase turned to bacteriophage T2 as their experimental material. In two separate experiments, they labeled the protein coat with ^{35}S and the DNA with ^{32}P. They then showed that the radioactive P alone is largely taken up by the bacterial host and that reproduction of viruses proceeds normally. This convinced most people that DNA is the genetic material.

5. In the meantime, work on the biochemistry of DNA was progressing. Chargaff did a chemical analysis of the molecule and found that A = T and G = C, and that the amount of purine equals the amount of pyrimidine. These relationships are known as Chargaff's rules.

6. Franklin prepared an X-ray photograph of DNA that showed it is helical, has repeating structural features, and has certain dimensions.

7. Watson and Crick built a model of DNA in which the sugar-phosphate molecules made up the sides of a twisted ladder and the complementary-paired bases were the rungs of the ladder. This model was in keeping with Chargaff's rules and the dimensions provided by the Franklin X-ray diffraction pattern.

8. The Watson and Crick model immediately suggested a method by which DNA could be replicated. The two strands unwind and unzip, and each parental strand acts as a template for a new (daughter) strand. In the end, each new duplex is like the other and like the parental duplex. The actual process is more complicated and involves many enzymes.

9. Replication is semiconservative, since each new duplex contains an old (parental) strand and a new (daughter) strand. Meselson and Stahl demonstrated this by the following experiment: bacteria were grown in heavy nitrogen (^{15}N) and then switched to light nitrogen (^{14}N). The density of the DNA following replication was intermediate between these two, as measured by centrifugation of the molecules through a salt gradient.

10. The enzyme DNA polymerase joins the nucleotides together and proofreads them to make sure the bases have been paired correctly. Incorrect base pairs that survive the process are a mutation.

11. Replication in prokaryotes is sometimes bidirectional from one point of origin and proceeds until there are two copies of the circular chromosome. Replication in eukaryotes is also bidirectional, but there are many points of origin and many bubbles (places where the DNA strands are separating and replication is occurring). Replication occurs at the ends of the bubbles—at replication forks.

Writing Across the Curriculum

In order to practice writing skills, students should write out the answers to any or all of the study questions and the critical thinking questions. The study questions are sequenced in the same order as the text. Answers to the objective questions, and suggested answers to the critical thinking questions, are in appendix D.

Study Questions

1. List and discuss the requirements for genetic material.   232

2. What is the tetranucleotide hypothesis, and why did this hypothesis hinder the acceptance of DNA as the genetic material?   232

3. Describe Griffith's experiments with pneumococcus, his surprising results, and his conclusion.   232–33

4. How did Avery and his colleagues demonstrate that the transforming substance is DNA?   233

5. Describe the experiment of Hershey and Chase, and explain how it shows that DNA is the genetic material.   234

6. What is the difference between a base, a nucleotide, and a nucleic acid? Which of these pertains to Chargaff's rules? What are the rules?   235

7. What is an X-ray diffraction pattern? What information was provided by DNA's diffraction pattern?   236

8. Describe the Watson and Crick model of DNA structure. How did it fit the data provided by Chargaff and the X-ray diffraction pattern?   236–37

9. Explain how DNA replicates semiconservatively. What role does DNA polymerase play? What role does helicase play?   238–39

10. How did Meselson and Stahl demonstrate semiconservative replication?   239

11. Explain how the replication process is a source of mutations.   241

12. List and discuss differences between prokaryotic and eukaryotic replication of DNA.   241

Objective Questions

For questions 1–4, match the names in the key to the statements below:

Key:
  a. Griffith
  b. Chargaff
  c. Meselson and Stahl
  d. Hershey and Chase

1. A = T and G = C.
2. Only the DNA from T2 enters the bacteria.
3. R strain bacteria became an S strain through transformation.
4. DNA replication is semiconservative.
5. If 30% of an organism's DNA is thymine, then
  a. 70% is purine.
  b. 20% is guanine.
  c. 30% is adenine.
  d. Both b and c are correct.

6. If you grew bacteria in heavy nitrogen and then switched them to light nitrogen, how many generations after switching would you have some light/light DNA?
  a. never, because replication is semiconservative
  b. the first generation
  c. the second generation
  d. only the third generation
7. The double-helix model of DNA resembles a twisted ladder in which the rungs of the ladder are
  a. a purine paired with a pyrimidine.
  b. A paired with G and C paired with T.
  c. sugar-phosphate paired with sugar-phosphate.
  d. Both a and b are correct.
8. Cell division requires that the genetic material be able to
  a. store information.
  b. be replicated.
  c. undergo rare mutations.
  d. All of these are correct.

9. In a DNA molecule, the
  a. bases are covalently bonded to the sugars.
  b. sugars are covalently bonded to the phosphates.
  c. bases are hydrogen-bonded to one another.
  d. All of these are correct.
10. In the following diagram, blue stands for heavy DNA (contains ^{15}N) and red stands for light DNA (does not contain ^{15}N). Label each strand of all three DNA molecules as heavy or light DNA, and explain why the diagram is in keeping with the semiconservative replication of DNA.

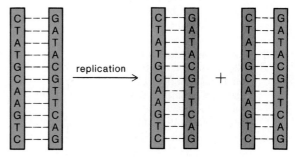

Concepts and Critical Thinking

1. *DNA is the genetic material that dictates the form, the function, and the behavior of organisms.*

   Explain the rationale of the Hershey and Chase experiment.

2. *The genetic material has to be capable of replication.*

   To explain the importance of DNA replication, associate the necessity of replication with the cell cycle and the life cycle.

3. *Evolution is dependent on the ability of the genetic material to mutate.*

   Explain the importance of mutation to the evolutionary process.

Selected Key Terms

adenine (A) (AD-un-een) One of four nitrogen-containing bases in nucleotides composing the structure of DNA and RNA.   235

bacteriophage A virus that infects bacteria. [Gk. *bact,* rod, and *phag,* eat]   233

complementary base pairing Bonding between particular purines and pyrimidines in DNA.   236

cytosine (C) (SYT-uh-seen) One of four nitrogen-containing bases in nucleotides composing the structure of DNA and RNA.   235

DNA (deoxyribonucleic acid) A nucleic acid polymer produced from covalent bonding of nucleotide monomers that contain the sugar deoxyribose; the genetic material of nearly all organisms.   232

DNA polymerase (PAHL-uh-muh-rays) During replication, an enzyme that joins the nucleotides complementary to a DNA template.   238

guanine (G) (GWAHN-een) One of four nitrogen-containing bases in nucleotides composing the structure of DNA and RNA.   235

mutation An alteration in DNA composition and also an alteration in chromosome structure and number. [L. *muta,* change]   232

purine (PYUR-een) A type of nitrogen-containing base, such as adenine and guanine, having a double-ring structure.   235

pyrimidine (py-RIM-uh-deen) A type of nitrogen-containing base, such as cytosine, thymine, and uracil, having a single-ring structure.   235

RNA (ribonucleic acid) A nucleic acid polymer produced from covalent bonding of nucleotide monomers that contain the sugar ribose; RNA helps DNA carry out protein synthesis.   232

semiconservative replication Duplication of DNA resulting in a double helix having one parental and one new strand.   238

thymine (T) (THY-meen) One of four nitrogen-containing bases in nucleotides composing the structure of DNA.   235

16
GENE ACTIVITY

Learning Objectives

What Genes Do
- List and discuss the early studies that led to the recognition of gene activity.   246–47

How Genes Are Expressed
- List the biochemical differences between RNA and DNA.   248
- Draw and explain a diagram that outlines the central dogma of molecular biology.   248

How Genes Code for Amino Acids
- Show that the DNA code is triplet, degenerate, but unambiguous, and almost universal.   249

How Transcription Occurs
- Describe the process by which RNA becomes complementary to DNA.   250–51

- List and discuss two ways that mRNA is processed before it leaves the eukaryotic nucleus.   251

How Translation Occurs
- Describe the roles of ribosomes, mRNA, tRNA, and amino acids during protein synthesis.   252–53
- Determine the mRNA codons, possible tRNA anticodons, and the sequence of amino acids in the resulting protein when given a DNA coding strand and a table of codons.   253

Mutations Are Base Changes
- Discuss the different types of gene mutations, the rate of mutation, and the manner in which DNA is protected from mutation.   256

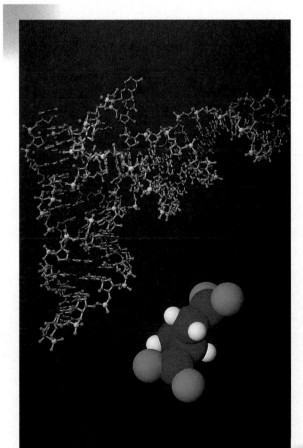

During protein synthesis, amino acids are added in sequence according to DNA's instructions. In this mock-up, a model of the amino acid aspartate (red, white, and blue) will soon be transported to a ribosome by the approaching transfer molecule.

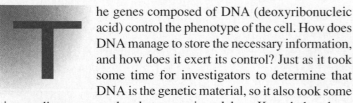

he genes composed of DNA (deoxyribonucleic acid) control the phenotype of the cell. How does DNA manage to store the necessary information, and how does it exert its control? Just as it took some time for investigators to determine that DNA is the genetic material, so it also took some time to discover exactly what a gene is and does. Knowledge about the action of genes preceded that of their makeup.

WHAT GENES DO

In the early 1900s, the English physician Sir Archibald Garrod suggested that there is a relationship between inheritance and metabolic diseases. He introduced the phrase *inborn error of metabolism* to dramatize this relationship. Garrod observed that family members often had the same disorder, and he said this inherited defect could be caused by the lack of a particular enzyme in a metabolic pathway. Since it was known at the time that enzymes are proteins, Garrod was among the first to hypothesize a link between genes and proteins.

Genes Specify Enzymes

Many years later, in 1940, George Beadle and Edward Tatum performed a series of experiments on *Neurospora crassa*, the red

bread mold, which reproduces by means of spores. Normally, the spores become mold capable of growing on minimal medium (containing only a sugar, mineral salts, and the vitamin biotin) because mold can produce all the enzymes it needs. In their experiments, Beadle and Tatum used X rays to induce mutations in asexually produced haploid spores. Some of the X-rayed spores could no longer become mold capable of growing on minimal medium; however, growth was possible on medium enriched by certain metabolites. In the example given in figure 16.1, the mold grows only when supplied with enriched medium that includes all metabolites or C and D alone. Since C and D are a part of this hypothetical pathway

$$A \xrightarrow{\quad 1 \quad} B \xrightarrow{\quad 2 \quad} C \xrightarrow{\quad 3 \quad} D$$

in which the numbers are enzymes and the letters are metabolites, it is concluded that the mold lacks enzyme 2. Beadle and Tatum further found that each of the mutant strains has only one defective gene leading to one defective enzyme and one additional growth requirement. Therefore, they proposed that each gene specifies the synthesis of one enzyme. This is called the *one gene–one enzyme hypothesis.*

Figure 16.1

Beadle and Tatum experiment with *Neurospora crassa.* When haploid spores are X-rayed, some are no longer able to germinate on minimal medium; however, they can germinate on enriched medium. In this example, the mycelia produced do not grow on minimal medium plus metabolite A or B, but they do grow on minimal medium plus metabolite C or D. This shows that enzyme 2 is missing from the hypothetical pathway.

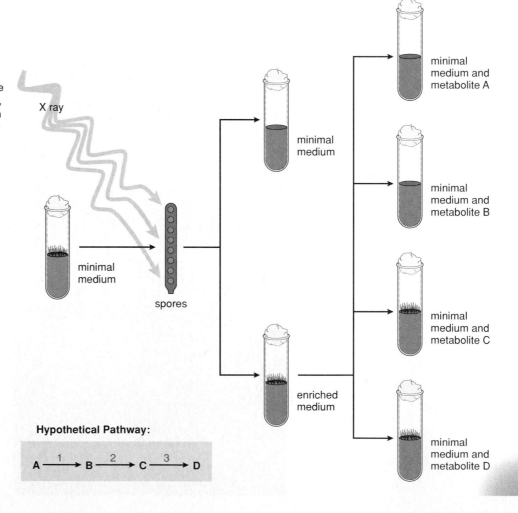

Genes Specify a Polypeptide

The one gene–one enzyme hypothesis suggests that a gene mutation causes a change in the structure of a protein. To test this idea, Linus Pauling and Harvey Itano decided to see if the hemoglobin in the red blood cells of persons with sickle-cell disease has a structure different from that of the red blood cells of normal individuals (fig. 16.2). Recall that proteins are polymers of amino acids, some of which carry a charge. These investigators decided to see if there was a charge difference between normal hemoglobin (Hb^A) and sickle-cell hemoglobin, (Hb^S). To determine this, they subjected hemoglobin collected from normal individuals, sickle-cell trait individuals, and sickle-cell disease individuals to electrophoresis, a procedure that separates molecules according to their size and charge. Here is what they found:

As you can see, there is a difference in migration rate toward the positive pole between normal hemoglobin and sickle-cell hemoglobin. Further, hemoglobin from those with sickle-cell trait separates into two distinct bands, one corresponding to that for Hb^A hemoglobin and the other corresponding to that for Hb^S hemoglobin. Pauling and Itano therefore demonstrated that a mutation leads to a change in the structure of a protein.

Several years later, Vernon Ingram was able to determine the structural difference between Hb^A and Hb^S, where normal hemoglobin Hb^A contains negatively charged glutamate, and sickle-cell hemoglobin contains nonpolar valine (fig. 16.2). This causes Hb^S to be less soluble and to precipitate out of solution, especially when environmental oxygen is low. At these times, the Hb^S molecules stack up into long, semirigid rods that push against the plasma membrane and distort the red blood cell into the sickle shape.

Hemoglobin contains two types of polypeptide chains, designated α (alpha) and β (beta). Only the β chain is affected in persons with sickle-cell trait and sickle-cell disease; therefore, there must be a gene for each type of chain. A refinement of the one gene–one enzyme hypothesis was needed, and it was replaced by the *one gene–one polypeptide hypothesis*.

Each gene specifies one polypeptide of a protein, a molecule that may contain one or more different polypeptides.

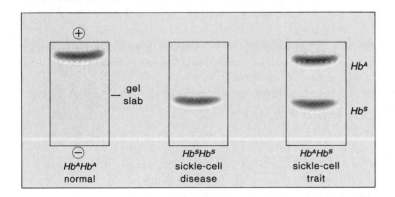

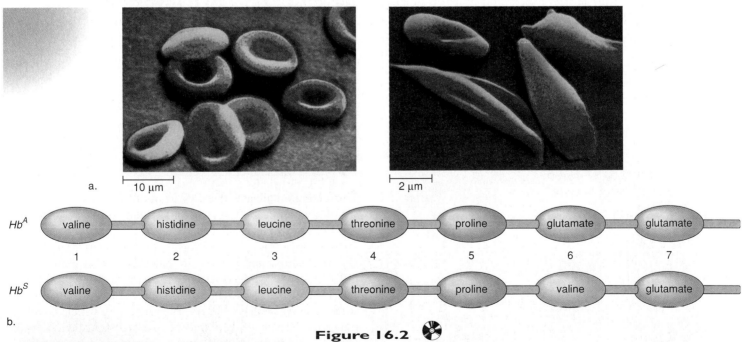

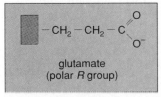 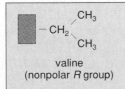

Figure 16.2

Sickle-cell disease in humans. **a.** Scanning electron micrograph of normal (*left*) and sickled (*right*) red blood cells. **b.** Portion of the chain in normal hemoglobin Hb^A and in sickle-cell hemoglobin Hb^S. Although the chain is 146 amino acids long, the one change from glutamate to valine in the sixth position results in sickle-cell disease. **c.** Glutamate has a polar *R* group, while valine has a nonpolar *R* group, and this causes Hb^S to be less soluble and to precipitate out of solution, distorting the red blood cell into the sickle shape.

HOW GENES ARE EXPRESSED

Classical geneticists thought of a gene as a particle on a chromosome. To molecular geneticists, however, a gene is a sequence of DNA nucleotide bases that codes for a product. Most often the gene product is a polypeptide. Therefore, a gene does not affect the phenotype directly; rather, the gene product affects the phenotype. As we have seen, the gene for Hb^S has a product that causes red blood cells to sickle, and this in turn causes sickle-cell disease.

DNA is a linear polymer of nucleotides, and polypeptides are linear polymers of amino acids. This colinearity suggests that the nucleotide sequence of DNA somehow determines the order of amino acids in proteins. A DNA molecule, however, cannot directly control protein synthesis because DNA is found in the nucleus of eukaryotes (or the nucleoid in prokaryotes), and protein synthesis occurs in the cytoplasm. Therefore, there must be a molecule that acts as a go-between, and the most likely candidate is RNA (ribonucleic acid), a nucleic acid found in both the nucleus and the cytoplasm (fig. 16.3).

Figure 16.3

Like DNA, RNA is a polymer of nucleotides. RNA, however, is single stranded, the pentose sugar is ribose, and uracil replaces thymine as one of the pyrimidine bases.

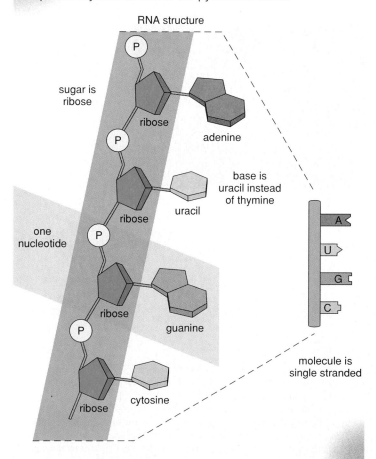

RNA structure

sugar is ribose

ribose

P

adenine

base is uracil instead of thymine

uracil

ribose

one nucleotide

P

ribose

guanine

P

ribose

cytosine

A

U

G

C

molecule is single stranded

Table 16.1

RNA Structure Compared to DNA Structure

	RNA	DNA
Sugar	Ribose	Deoxyribose
Bases	Adenine, guanine, uracil, cytosine	Adenine, guanine, thymine, cytosine
Strands	Single stranded	Double stranded with base pairing
Helix	No	Yes

RNA Is Involved

Like DNA, RNA is a polymer of nucleotides. The nucleotides in RNA, however, contain the sugar ribose and the bases adenine (A), cytosine (C), guanine (G), and uracil (U). In other words, the base uracil replaces the thymine found in DNA (table 16.1). Finally, RNA is single stranded and does not form a double helix in the same manner as DNA.

There are three major classes of RNA, each with specific functions in protein synthesis:

messenger RNA (mRNA): takes a message from DNA in the nucleus to the ribosomes in the cytoplasm.

ribosomal RNA (rRNA): along with proteins, makes up the ribosomes, where proteins are synthesized.

transfer RNA (tRNA): transfers amino acids to the ribosomes.

Several Steps Are Involved

The central dogma of molecular biology explains the manner in which genes are expressed, that is, produce a product:

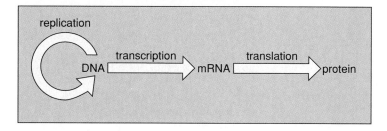

replication

DNA → transcription → mRNA → translation → protein

This diagram indicates that DNA not only serves as a template for its own replication, it is also a template for RNA formation. Most often it is mRNA that is produced. The process by which an mRNA copy is made of a portion of DNA is called **transcription** [L. *trans,* across, and *scribere,* to write]. Following transcription, mRNA moves into the cytoplasm. Photographic data show radioactively labeled RNA moving from the nucleus to the cytoplasm, where protein synthesis occurs. The process by which an mRNA transcript determines the sequence of amino acids in a polypeptide is called **translation** [L. *trans,* across, and *latus,* carried].

During transcription, DNA serves as a template for the formation of RNA. During translation, mRNA is involved in polypeptide synthesis.

HOW GENES CODE FOR AMINO ACIDS

The central dogma of molecular biology suggests that the sequence of nucleotides in DNA and in RNA directs the order of amino acids in a polypeptide. It would seem that there must be a code for each of the 20 amino acids found in proteins. But can four nucleotides provide enough combinations to code for 20 amino acids? If each code word, called a **codon** [L. *cod,* tail], were made up of two bases, such as AG, there could be only 16 codons—not enough to code for 20 amino acids. But if each codon were made up of three bases, such as AGC, there would be 64 codons—more than enough to code for 20 different amino acids:

Number of Bases in Genetic Code	Number of Different Amino Acids That Can Be Specified
1	4
2	16
3	64

It is no surprise, then, to learn that the genetic code is a **triplet code** and that each codon, therefore, consists of three nucleotide bases.

Finding the Genetic Code

In 1961, Marshall Nirenberg and J. Heinrich Matthei performed an experiment that laid the groundwork for cracking the genetic code. First, they found a cellular enzyme could be used to construct a synthetic RNA (one that does not occur in cells), and then they found that the synthetic polymer could be translated in a cell-free system (a test tube that contains "freed" cytoplasmic contents of a cell). Their first synthetic RNA was composed only of uracil, and the protein that resulted was composed only of the amino acid phenylalanine. Therefore, the codon for phenylalanine was known to be UUU. Later, a cell-free system was developed by Nirenberg and Philip Leder in which only three nucleotides at a time were translated; in that way it was possible to assign an amino acid to each of the RNA codons (fig. 16.4).

A number of important properties of the genetic code can be seen by careful inspection of figure 16.4:

1. The genetic code is degenerate. This means that most amino acids have more than one codon; leucine, serine, and arginine have six different codons, for example. The degeneracy of the code is probably a protective device that reduces the potentially harmful effects of mutations.
2. The genetic code is unambiguous. Each triplet codon has only one meaning.
3. The code has start and stop signals. There is only one start signal but three stop signals.

The Code Is Universal

The genetic code in figure 16.4 is just about universally used by living things. This suggests that the code dates back to the very first organisms on earth and that all living things are related. Once the code was established, changes in it would have been very disruptive, and we know that it has remained unchanged over eons.

Exceptions to the universality of the genetic code are found in some prokaryotes and mitochondria. Recall that mitochondria have genes and carry on protein synthesis also. As it turns out, the code in mitochondria is slightly different from that utilized in the nucleus. This is consistent with the endosymbiotic theory that concerns the evolution of the eukaryotic cell. In reference to mitochondria, the theory says these organelles were once independent unicellular organisms that were later taken up by another larger cell.

> The triplet genetic code is made of sixty-four three-base code words called codons. Except for the stop codons, all the codons code for amino acids.

Figure 16.4

Messenger RNA codons. Notice that in this chart, each of the codons (blue squares) is composed of three letters representing the first base, second base, and third base. For example, find the blue square where C for the first base and A for the second base intersect. You will see that U, C, A, or G can be the third base. The three bases CAU and CAC are codons for the histidine; the three bases CAA and CAG are codons for glutamine.

First Base	Second Base				Third Base
	U	C	A	G	
U	UUU phenylalanine	UCU serine	UAU tyrosine	UGU cysteine	U
	UUC phenylalanine	UCC serine	UAC tyrosine	UGC cysteine	C
	UUA leucine	UCA serine	UAA stop	UGA stop	A
	UUG leucine	UCG serine	UAG stop	UGG tryptophan	G
C	CUU leucine	CCU proline	CAU histidine	CGU arginine	U
	CUC leucine	CCC proline	CAC histidine	CGC arginine	C
	CUA leucine	CCA proline	CAA glutamine	CGA arginine	A
	CUG leucine	CCG proline	CAG glutamine	CGG arginine	G
A	AUU isoleucine	ACU threonine	AAU asparagine	AGU serine	U
	AUC isoleucine	ACC threonine	AAC asparagine	AGC serine	C
	AUA isoleucine	ACA threonine	AAA lysine	AGA arginine	A
	AUG (start) methionine	ACG threonine	AAG lysine	AGG arginine	G
G	GUU valine	GCU alanine	GAU aspartate	GGU glycine	U
	GUC valine	GCC alanine	GAC aspartate	GGC glycine	C
	GUA valine	GCA alanine	GAA glutamate	GGA glycine	A
	GUG valine	GCG alanine	GAG glutamate	GGG glycine	G

HOW TRANSCRIPTION OCCURS

Transcription, which takes place in the nucleus of eukaryotic cells, is the first step required for gene expression, the process by which a gene product is made. Most often mRNA formation leads to a polypeptide as the gene product. The molecules tRNA and rRNA are also transcribed from DNA templates, and these are products in and of themselves.

Messenger RNA Is Formed

During transcription, an mRNA molecule is formed that has a sequence of bases complementary to a portion of one DNA strand; wherever A, T, G, or C is present in the DNA template, U, A, C, or G is incorporated into the mRNA molecule (fig. 16.5). A segment of the DNA helix unwinds and unzips, and complementary RNA nucleotides pair with DNA nucleotides of the strand that is to be transcribed. When these RNA nucleotides are joined together by an **RNA polymerase** [Gk. *poly,* many, and *meris,* part], an mRNA molecule results. This molecule now carries a sequence of codons that will be used to order the sequence of amino acids in a polypeptide.

Transcription begins when RNA polymerase attaches to a region of DNA called a promoter. A **promoter** defines the start of a gene, the direction of transcription, and the strand to be copied. Elongation of the mRNA molecule occurs as long as transcription proceeds. The RNA/DNA association is not as stable as the DNA helix. Therefore, only the newest portion of an RNA molecule that is associated with RNA polymerase is bound to the DNA, and the rest dangles off to the side. Finally, RNA polymerase comes to a terminator sequence at the other end of the gene being transcribed. The terminator causes RNA polymerase to stop transcribing the DNA and to release the mRNA molecule, now called an RNA transcript.

Many RNA polymerase molecules can be working to produce mRNA transcripts at the same time (fig. 16.6). This allows the cell to produce many thousands of copies of the same mRNA molecule and eventually many copies of the same protein within a shorter period of time than if the single copy of DNA were used to direct protein synthesis.

> As a result of transcription, there are many mRNA molecules directing protein synthesis. Many more copies of a protein are produced within a given time versus using DNA directly.

Figure 16.5

Transcription. During transcription, complementary RNA is made from a DNA template. At the point of attachment of RNA polymerase, the DNA helix unwinds and unzips, and complementary RNA nucleotides are joined together. After RNA polymerase has passed by, the DNA strands rejoin and the RNA transcript dangles to the side.

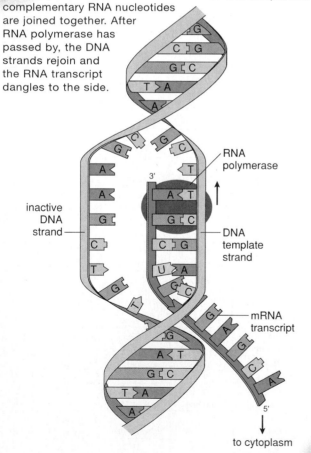

Figure 16.6

RNA polymerase. **a.** Numerous RNA transcripts extend from a horizontal gene in an amphibian egg cell. **b.** The strands get progressively longer because transcription begins to the left. The dark dots along the DNA are RNA polymerase molecules. The dots at the end of the strands are spliceosomes involved in RNA processing (see fig. 16.7).

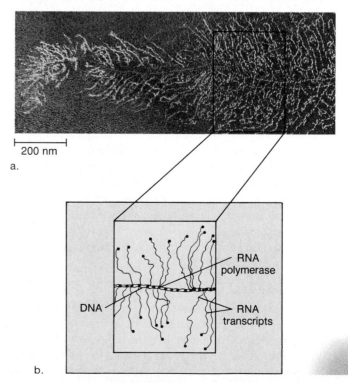

Messenger RNA Is Processed

When investigators first isolated a gene and the corresponding mRNA from eukaryotic cells, they were very surprised to discover that the mRNA was shorter than its template DNA. Only certain portions of the DNA would bind to mRNA, and these portions were called **exons** because they will be eventually expressed. The portions of DNA that did not bind to the mRNA were called intervening sequences or **introns.**

Later, it became clear that both exons and introns are present in the *primary mRNA* transcript, but only exons are present in the *mature mRNA* transcript that leaves the nucleus and enters the cytoplasm. The introns are removed from the primary mRNA transcript during an mRNA processing event called mRNA splicing (fig. 16.7).

Two essential questions are still being asked about these findings. How is mRNA processing carried out? And what is the function of introns in the first place? In most cases mRNA splicing is often done by *spliceosomes,* a complex that contains several kinds of ribonucleoproteins. A spliceosome cuts the primary mRNA and then rejoins the adjacent exons. Just how a spliceosome carries out these functions is still being investigated.

There has been much speculation about the possible role of introns in the eukaryotic genome. It's possible that introns allow crossing-over within a gene during meiosis. It's also possible that introns divide a gene into regions that can be joined in different combinations to produce various products in different cells. For instance, it's been shown that the thyroid gland and pituitary gland process the same primary mRNA transcript differently and therefore produce related but different hormones.

Some researchers are trying to determine whether introns exist in all organisms. They have found that the more simple the eukaryote, the less the likelihood of introns in the genes. An intron has been discovered in the gene for a tRNA molecule in *Anabena,* a cyanobacterium. This particular intron is of interest because it is "self-splicing," that is, it has the capability of splicing itself out of an RNA transcript. RNAs with an enzymatic function, now called **ribozymes,** did away with the belief that only proteins can function as enzymes. Ribozymes, however, are restricted in their function since each one cleaves RNA only at specific locations. Still, the discovery of ribozymes in prokaryotes supports the belief that RNA could have served as both the genetic material and as the first enzymes in the earliest living organisms. This hypothesis does away with the dilemma of what came first, DNA or protein.

> **Particularly in eukaryotes, the primary mRNA transcript is processed before it becomes a mature mRNA transcript.**

Figure 16.7

Messenger RNA (mRNA) processing in eukaryotes. DNA contains both exons (coding sequences) and introns (noncoding sequences). Both of these are transcribed and are present in primary mRNA. During processing, a cap and a poly A tail (a series of adenine nucleotides) are added to the molecule. Also, there is excision of the introns and a splicing together of the exons. This is accomplished by complexes called spliceosomes. Then the mature mRNA molecule is ready to leave the nucleus.

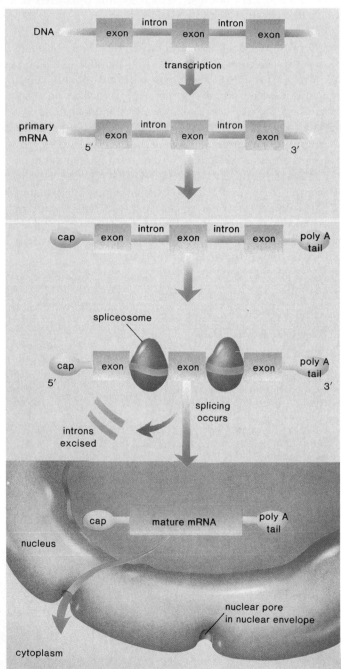

HOW TRANSLATION OCCURS

Translation, which takes place in the cytoplasm of eukaryotic cells, is the second step by which gene expression leads to protein synthesis. During translation, the sequence of codons in mRNA directs the sequence of amino acids in a polypeptide.

Ribosomal RNA Is Structural

Ribosomal RNA (rRNA) molecules, along with a variety of proteins, make up the ribosomes, which are tiny organelles that are attached to endoplasmic reticulum and also exist free within the cytoplasm of eukaryotic cells.

Prokaryotic cells contain about ten thousand ribosomes, but eukaryotic cells contain many times this number. In both types of organisms, ribosomes are composed of two subunits that don't join until protein synthesis begins (fig. 16.8). The small subunit contains one rRNA molecule and many different types of proteins, and the large subunit contains two rRNA molecules and many different types of proteins. Among these proteins is the enzyme that joins amino acids together by means of a peptide bond.

As soon as the initial portion of mRNA has been translated by one ribosome, and the ribosome has begun to move down the mRNA, another ribosome attaches to the mRNA. Therefore, several ribosomes are often attached to and translating the same mRNA. The entire complex is called a **polysome** [Gk. *poly,* many, and *soma,* body] (fig. 16.8).

Transfer RNA Transfers Amino Acids

Transfer RNA (tRNA) molecules transfer amino acids to the ribosomes. A tRNA molecule is a single-stranded nucleic acid that doubles back on itself to create regions where complementary bases are hydrogen-bonded to one another. The structure of a tRNA molecule is generally drawn as a flat cloverleaf, but the space-filling model shows the molecule's three-dimensional shape (fig. 16.9).

There is at least one tRNA molecule for each of the twenty amino acids found in proteins. The amino acid binds to one end of the molecule where there is a ACC sequence. The other end of the molecule contains an **anticodon** [Gk. *anti,* against, and L. *cod,* tail], a group of three bases that is complementary to a specific codon of mRNA. For example, a tRNA that has the anticodon GAA binds to the codon CUU and carries the amino acid leucine. Because the anticodons of tRNA molecules bind to the codons of an mRNA molecule, the amino acids become sequenced in a polypeptide according to the information provided by a gene. In other words, tRNA molecules translate one language (nucleic acids) into another language (protein).

One area of active research is to determine how the correct amino acid becomes attached to the correct tRNA molecule. So far, it is known that the task is carried out by a number of amino acid-activating enzymes, called *tRNA synthetases.* Somehow a tRNA synthetase recognizes which amino acid should be joined

Figure 16.8

Polysome structure. **a.** Several ribosomes, collectively called a polysome, move along a messenger RNA (mRNA) molecule at one time. They function independently of one another; therefore, several polypeptides can be made at the same time. **b.** Electron micrograph of a polysome.

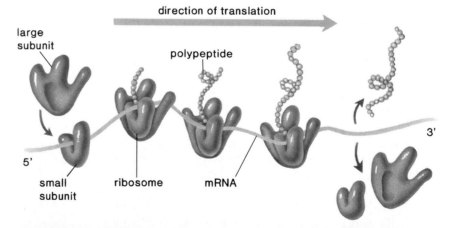

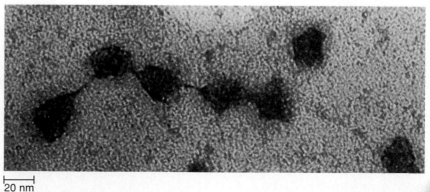

to which tRNA molecule. This is an energy-requiring process that utilizes ATP. Once the amino acid-tRNA complex is formed, it travels through the cytoplasm to a ribosome, where protein synthesis is occurring.

Translation Requires Three Steps

The process of translation must be extremely orderly so that the amino acids of a polypeptide are sequenced correctly. Protein synthesis involves three steps: initiation, elongation, and termination.

1. Initiation of translation: A small ribosomal subunit attaches to the mRNA in the vicinity of the *start codon* (AUG). The first or initiator tRNA pairs with this codon. Then a large ribosomal subunit joins to the small subunit, and translation begins.

2. Chain elongation: Each ribosome contains two sites, the P (for polypeptide) site and the A (for amino acid) site:

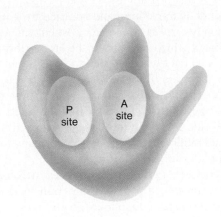

Figure 16.9

Structure of a transfer RNA (tRNA) molecule. **a.** Complementary base pairing indicated by hydrogen bonding occurs between nucleotides of the molecule, and this causes it to form its characteristic loops. The anticodon that base-pairs with a particular messenger RNA (mRNA) codon occurs at one end of the folded molecule; the other two loops help hold the molecule at the ribosome. An appropriate amino acid is attached at the CCA end of the molecule. For this mRNA codon and tRNA anticodon, the appropriate amino acid is leucine. **b.** Space-filling model of tRNA molecule.

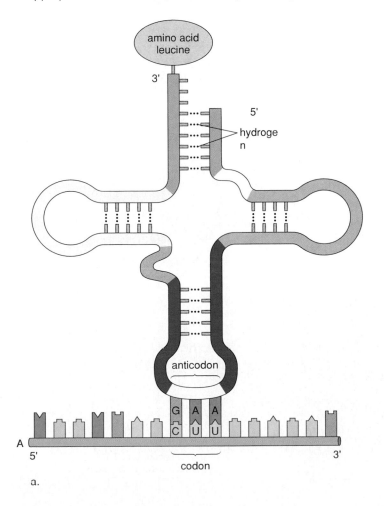

a.

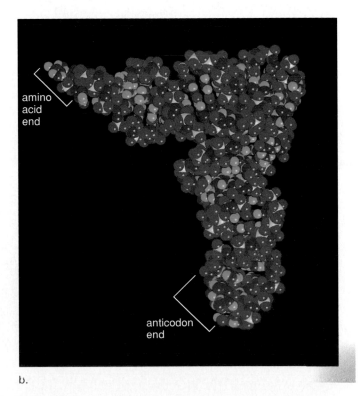

b.

At the start of elongation, a tRNA with an attached polypeptide is at the P site and a tRNA-amino acid complex is just arriving at the A site (fig. 16.10). The polypeptide is transferred and attached by a peptide bond to the newly arrived amino acid. An enzyme (peptidyl transferase), which is a part of the larger ribosomal subunit, and energy are needed to bring about this transfer. Now the tRNA molecule at the P site leaves.

Then *translocation* occurs: the mRNA, along with the peptide-bearing tRNA, moves from the A site to the empty P site. Since the ribosome has moved forward three nucleotides, there is a new codon now located at the empty A site.

The complete cycle—pairing of new tRNA-amino acid complex, transfer of peptide chain, translocation—is repeated at a rapid rate (about fifteen times each second in *Escherichia coli*).

3. Chain termination: Termination of polypeptide synthesis occurs at a *stop codon,* which does not code for an amino acid. The polypeptide is enzymatically cleaved from the last tRNA. The tRNA and polypeptide leave the ribosome, which dissociates into its two subunits (see fig. 16.8).

During translation, the codons of an mRNA base-pair with the anticodons of tRNA molecules carrying specific amino acids. The order of the codons determines the order of the tRNA molecules and the sequence of amino acids in a polypeptide.

Figure 16.10 📼

Translation. Transfer RNA (tRNA)-amino acid molecules arrive at the ribosome, and the sequence of messenger RNA (mRNA) codons dictates the order in which amino acids become incorporated into a polypeptide.

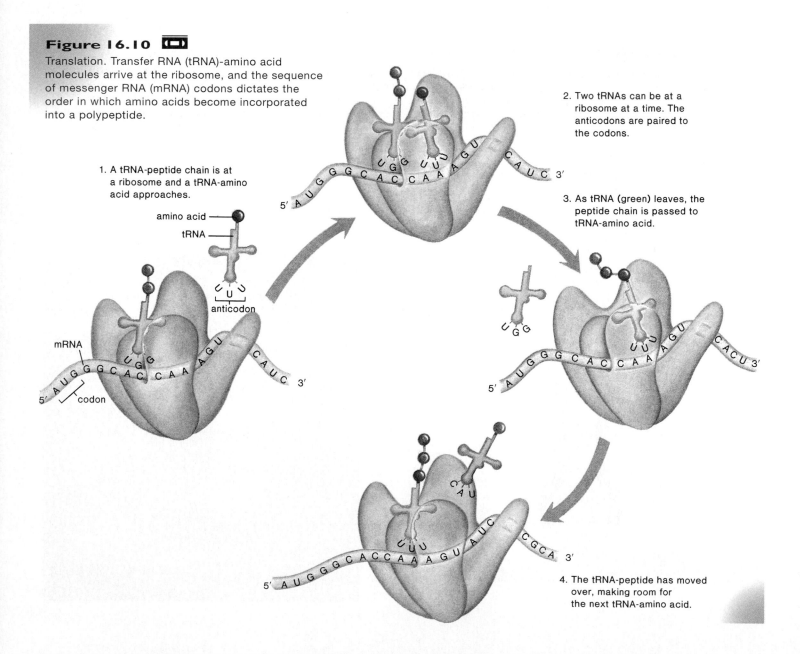

1. A tRNA-peptide chain is at a ribosome and a tRNA-amino acid approaches.

amino acid

tRNA

anticodon

mRNA

codon

2. Two tRNAs can be at a ribosome at a time. The anticodons are paired to the codons.

3. As tRNA (green) leaves, the peptide chain is passed to tRNA-amino acid.

4. The tRNA-peptide has moved over, making room for the next tRNA-amino acid.

The following list, along with table 16.2 and figure 16.11, provides a brief summary of the events involved in gene expression that results in a protein product.

1. DNA contains genetic information. The sequence of its bases determines the sequence of amino acids in a polypeptide.

2. During transcription, one strand of DNA serves as a template for the formation of mRNA. The bases in mRNA are complementary to those in DNA; every three bases is a codon that codes for an amino acid.

3. Messenger RNA (mRNA) is processed before it leaves the nucleus, during which time the introns are removed.

4. Messenger RNA (mRNA) carries a sequence of codons to the ribosomes, which are composed of rRNA and proteins.

5. Transfer RNA (tRNA) molecules, each of which is bonded to a particular amino acid, have anticodons that pair complementarily to the codons in mRNA.

6. During translation, tRNA molecules and their attached amino acids arrive at the ribosomes, and the linear sequence of codons of the mRNA determines the order in which the amino acids become incorporated into a protein.

Table 16.2

Participants in Gene Expression

Name of Molecule	Special Significance	Definition
DNA	Genetic information	Sequence of DNA bases
mRNA	Codons	Sequence of three RNA bases complementary to DNA
tRNA	Anticodon	Sequence of three RNA bases complementary to condon
rRNA	Ribosome	Site of protein synthesis
Amino acid	Building block for protein	Transported to ribosome by tRNA
Protein	Enzyme, structural protein, or secretory product	Amino acids joined in a predetermined order

Figure 16.11

Protein synthesis. Gene expression leads to the formation of a product, most often a protein. Transcription, which occurs in the nucleus, and translation, which occurs in the cytoplasm at the ribosomes, are two steps required for gene expression.

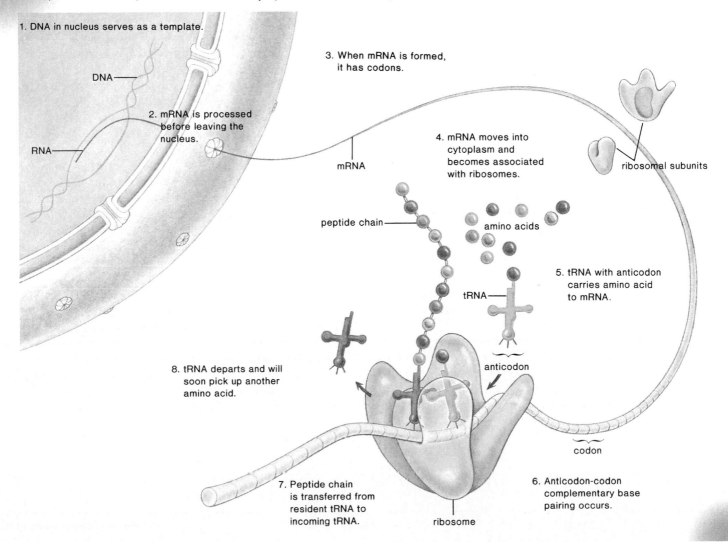

1. DNA in nucleus serves as a template.

DNA

2. mRNA is processed before leaving the nucleus.

RNA

3. When mRNA is formed, it has codons.

mRNA

4. mRNA moves into cytoplasm and becomes associated with ribosomes.

ribosomal subunits

peptide chain

amino acids

5. tRNA with anticodon carries amino acid to mRNA.

tRNA

anticodon

codon

8. tRNA departs and will soon pick up another amino acid.

7. Peptide chain is transferred from resident tRNA to incoming tRNA.

ribosome

6. Anticodon-codon complementary base pairing occurs.

MUTATIONS ARE BASE CHANGES

Early geneticists understood that genes undergo mutations, but they didn't know what causes mutations. It is apparent today that a *gene mutation* is a change in the nucleotide sequence of a gene.

Frameshift Mutations Are Drastic

The term *reading frame* applies to the sequence of codons because they are read from some specific starting point as in this sentence: THE CAT ATE THE RAT. If the letter C is deleted from this sentence and the reading frame is shifted, we read THE ATA TET HER AT—something that doesn't make sense. *Frameshift mutations* occur most often because one or more nucleotides are either inserted or deleted from DNA. The result of a frameshift mutation can be a completely nonfunctional protein because the sequence of codons is altered.

Point Mutations Can Be Drastic

Point mutations involve a change in a single nucleotide and therefore a change in a specific codon. When one base is substituted for another, the results can be variable. For example, in figure 16.12, if UAC is changed to UAU, there is no noticeable effect, because both of these codons code for tyrosine. Therefore, this is called a silent mutation. If UAC is changed to UAG, however, the result could very well be a drastic one because UAG is a stop codon. If this substitution occurs early in the gene, the resulting protein may be too short and may be unable to function. Such an effect is called a nonsense mutation. Finally, if UAC is changed to CAC, then histidine is incorporated into the protein instead of tyrosine. This is a missense mutation. A change in one amino acid may not have an effect if the change occurs in a noncritical area or if the two amino acids have the same chemical properties. In this instance, however, the polarities of tyrosine and histidine differ; therefore, this substitution most likely will have a deleterious effect on the functioning of the protein. Recall that the occurrence of valine instead of glutamate in the ß chain of hemoglobin results in sickle-cell disease (see fig. 16.2).

Cause and Repair of Mutations

Mutations due to DNA replication errors are rare; a frequency of 10^{-8} to 10^{-5} per cell division is often quoted. DNA polymerase, the enzyme that carries out replication, proofreads the new strand against the old strand and detects any mismatched pairs, which are then replaced with the correct nucleotides. In the end, there is usually only one mistake for every one billion nucleotide pairs replicated.

Mutagens [L. *muta,* change], environmental substances that cause mutations, such as radiation (e.g., radioactive elements and X rays) and organic chemicals (e.g., certain pesticides and cigarette smoke), are another source of mutations in organisms, including humans. If these mutagens bring about a mutation in the

Figure 16.12

Point mutation. The effect of a base alteration can vary. Starting at the left, if the base change codes for the same amino acid, there is no noticeable effect; if the base change codes for a stop codon, the resulting protein will be incomplete; and if the base change codes for a different amino acid, a faulty protein is possible.

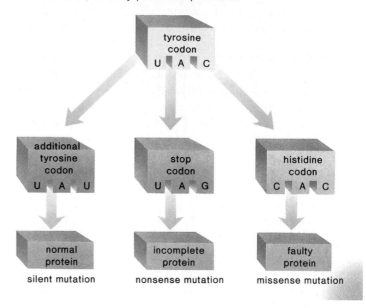

gametes, then the offspring of the individual may be affected. On the other hand, if the mutation occurs in the body cells, then cancer may be the result. Ultraviolet (UV) radiation is a mutagen that everyone is exposed to; it easily penetrates the skin and breaks the DNA of underlying tissues. Wherever there are two thymine molecules next to one another, ultraviolet radiation may cause them to bond together, forming thymine dimers.

Usually, these dimers are removed from damaged DNA by special enzymes called repair enzymes. Repair enzymes constantly monitor DNA and repair any irregularities. One enzyme excises a portion of DNA that contains the dimer; another makes a new section by using the other strand as a template; and still another seals the new section in place. The importance of repair enzymes is exemplified by individuals with the condition known as xeroderma pigmentosum. They lack some of these repair enzymes, and as a consequence these individuals have a high incidence of skin cancer.

A gene mutation is an alteration in the nucleotide sequence of a gene. The usual rate of mutation is low because DNA repair enzymes constantly monitor and repair any irregularities.

Summary

1. Several investigators contributed to recognition of gene activity. Garrod is associated with the phrase "inborn error of metabolism" because he suggested that some of his patients had inherited their inability to carry out certain enzymatic reactions.

2. Beadle and Tatum X-rayed spores of *Neurospora crassa* and found that some of the subsequent cultures lacked a particular enzyme needed for growth on minimal medium. Since they found that the mutation of one gene results in the lack of a single enzyme, they suggested the one gene–one enzyme hypothesis.

3. Pauling and Itano found that the chemical properties of the β (beta) chain of sickle-cell hemoglobin differ from those of normal hemoglobin, and therefore the one gene–one polypeptide hypothesis was formulated. Later, Ingram showed that the biochemical change is due to the substitution of the amino acid valine (nonpolar) for glutamate (polar).

4. RNA differs from DNA in these ways: (1) the pentose sugar is ribose, not deoxyribose; (2) the base uracil replaces thymine; (3) RNA is single stranded.

5. The central dogma of molecular biology says that (1) DNA is a template for its own replication and also for RNA formation during transcription, and (2) the complementary sequence of nucleotides in mRNA orders the correct sequence of amino acids of a polypeptide during translation.

6. The sequence of bases in DNA indicates the proper sequence of amino acids in a polypeptide. The genetic code is a triplet code, and each codon (code word) consists of three bases. The code is degenerate; that is, more than one codon exists for most amino acids. There are also one start and three stop codons.

7. The genetic code is just about universal; one exception is mitochondrial DNA, which has been found to have different codons for certain amino acids.

8. Transcription begins when RNA polymerase attaches to a promoter. Elongation occurs until there is a terminator sequence.

9. Messenger RNA (mRNA) is processed following transcription, and introns are removed. In eukaryotes, introns are excised by spliceosomes.

10. Translation requires mRNA, ribosomal RNA (rRNA), and transfer RNA (tRNA). Each tRNA has an anticodon at one end and an amino acid at the other; there are amino acid-activating enzymes that ensure that the correct amino acid is attached to the correct tRNA. When a tRNA binds with its codon at the ribosome, the correct amino acid is positioned for inclusion in a polypeptide.

11. Many ribosomes move along the same mRNA at a time. Collectively, these are called a polysome.

12. Translation requires these steps. During initiation, mRNA, the first (initiator) tRNA, and the ribosome all come together in the proper orientation at a start codon. During elongation, as the tRNAs recognize their codons, the growing peptide chain is transferred by peptide bonding to the next amino acid in the chain. During termination at a stop codon, the polypeptide is cleaved from the last tRNA. The ribosome now dissociates.

13. In molecular terms, a gene is a sequence of DNA nucleotide bases, and a gene mutation is a change in this sequence. Frameshift mutations result when a base is added or deleted and the result is a nonfunctioning protein. Point mutations can range in effect depending on the particular codon change. Gene mutation rates are rather low because DNA polymerase proofreads the new strand during replication and because there are repair enzymes that constantly monitor the DNA.

Writing Across the Curriculum

In order to practice writing skills, students should write out the answers to any or all of the study questions and the critical thinking questions. The study questions are sequenced in the same order as the text. Answers to the objective questions, and suggested answers to the critical thinking questions, are in appendix D.

Study Questions

1. What made Garrod think there were inborn errors of metabolism?   246

2. Explain Beadle and Tatum's experimental procedure.   246

3. How did Pauling and Itano know that the chemical properties of *Hb*^S differed from those of *Hb*^A? What change does a substitution of valine for glutamate cause in the chemical properties of these molecules?   247

4. What are the biochemical differences between RNA and DNA?   248

5. Draw a diagram for the central dogma of molecular biology and tell where the various events occur in a eukaryotic cell.   248

6. How did investigators reason that the code must be a triplet code, and in what manner was the code cracked? Why is it said that the code is degenerate, unambiguous, and almost universal?   249

7. What are the specific steps that occur during transcription of RNA off a DNA template?   250–51

8. How is messenger RNA (mRNA) processed before leaving the eukaryotic nucleus?   251

9. Compare the functions of mRNA, ribosomal RNA (rRNA), and transfer RNA (tRNA) during protein synthesis. What are the specific events of translation?   252–55

10. Why is a frameshift mutation always expected to result in a faulty protein, while a substitution of one base for another may not always result in a faulty protein?   256

Objective Questions

For questions 1–4, match the investigator to the phrase in the key:

Key:

    a. one gene–one enzyme hypothesis

    b. inborn error of metabolism

    c. one gene–one polypeptide hypothesis

  1. Sir Archibald Garrod

  2. George Beadle and Edward Tatum

  3. Linus Pauling and Harvey Itano

  4. Considering the following pathway, if Beadle and Tatum found that *Neurospora* cannot grow if metabolite A is provided, but can grow if B, C, or D is provided, what enzyme would be missing?

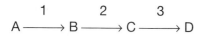

    a. enzyme 1 **c.** enzyme 3

    b. enzyme 2 **d.** All of these are correct.

  5. The central dogma of molecular biology

    a. states that DNA is a template for all RNA production.

    b. states that DNA is a template only for DNA replication.

    c. states that translation precedes transcription.

    d. pertains only to prokaryotes because humans are unique.

  6. If the sequence of bases in DNA is TAGC, then the sequence of bases in RNA will be

    a. ATCG.

    b. TAGC.

    c. AUCG.

    d. Both a and b are correct.

  7. RNA processing is

    a. the same as transcription.

    b. an event that occurs after RNA is transcribed.

    c. the rejection of old, worn-out RNA.

    d. Both b and c are correct.

  8. During protein synthesis, an anticodon on transfer RNA (tRNA) pairs with

    a. DNA nucleotide bases.

    b. ribosomal RNA (rRNA) nucleotide bases.

    c. messenger RNA (mRNA) nucleotide bases.

    d. other tRNA nucleotide bases.

  9. If the DNA codons are CAT CAT CAT, and a guanine base is added at the beginning, then which would result?

    a. G CAT CAT CAT

    b. GCA TCA TCA T

    c. frameshift mutation

    d. Both b and c are correct.

  10. This is a segment of a DNA molecule. (Remember that the template strand only is transcribed.) What are (a) the RNA codons, (b) the tRNA anticodons, and (c) the sequence of amino acids in a protein?

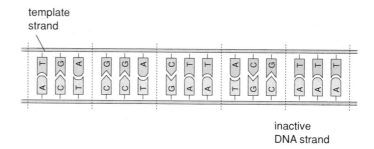

Concepts and Critical Thinking

  1. *DNA stores genetic information.* What is the genetic information stored by DNA, and where is it stored in the molecule?

  2. *The genetic code is almost universal.* What is the evolutionary significance of a universal genetic code?

  3. *There is a flow of information from DNA to RNA to protein.* DNA and a protein are colinear molecules. Explain.

Selected Key Terms

anticodon Three nucleotides on a tRNA molecule attracted to a complementary codon on mRNA. [Gk. *anti,* against, and L. *cod,* tail] 252

codon Three nucleotides of DNA or mRNA; it codes for a particular amino acid or termination of translation. [L. *cod,* tail] 249

exon In a gene, the portion of the DNA code that is expressed as the result of polypeptide formation. [Gk. *exo,* outside] 251

intron Noncoding segments of DNA that are transcribed but removed before mRNA leaves the nucleus. [L. *intra,* within] 251

messenger RNA (mRNA) A type of RNA formed from a DNA template and bearing coded information that directs the amoino acid sequence of a polypeptide. 248

mutagen (MYOOT-uh-jun) An agent, such as radiation or a chemical, that brings about a mutation. [L. *muta,* change] 256

polysome A string of ribosomes, simultaneously translating different regions of the same mRNA strand during protein synthesis. [Gk. *poly,* many, and *soma,* body] 252

ribosomal RNA (rRNA) A type of RNA found in ribosomes that coordinates the coupling of anticodons with codons during polypeptide synthesis. 248

RNA polymerase (PAHL-uh-muh-rays) An enzyme that speeds the formation of RNA from a DNA template. [Gk. *poly,* many, and *meris,* part] 250

transcription The process whereby a DNA strand serves as a template for the formation of mRNA. [L. *trans,* across, and *scribere,* to write] 248

transfer RNA (tRNA) A type of RNA active that transfers a particular amino acid to a ribosome during protein synthesis; at one end it binds to the amino acid and at the other end it has an anticodon that binds to an mRNA codon. 248

translation The process whereby the sequence of codons in mRNA determines (is translated into) the sequence of amino acids in a polypeptide. [L. *trans,* across, and *latus,* carried] 248

17

REGULATION OF GENE ACTIVITY

Learning Objectives

Prokaryotes Utilize Operons

- List and define the components of an operon. Explain why the *lac* operon is an inducible operon and the *trp* operon is a repressible operon.   260

Eukaryotes Utilize Various Methods

- List the levels of control of gene expression in eukaryotic cells.   262

- Provide evidence that genes are regulated at all levels of control in eukaryotes.   263–67

- Using Barr bodies as an example, explain how heterochromatin is genetically inactive.   263

- Using lampbrush chromosomes and giant (polytene) chromosome puffs as examples, explain how euchromatin is genetically active.   265

Cancer Is a Failure in Genetic Control

- Describe cancer as a failure in genetic control.   268

- Discuss the discovery of oncogenes and tumor-suppressor genes and their possible functions.   270–72

- List some recommendations to prevent the development of cancer.   273

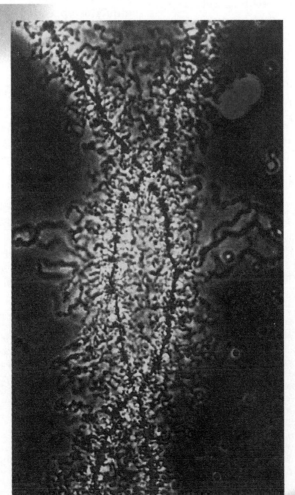

Lampbrush chromosomes have a fuzzy appearance because their DNA is unwound and metabolically active. The activity of DNA is regulated according to the needs of the cell.

ells lining the digestive tract look different and act differently from muscle cells. How did they get to be that way? Numerous experiments indicate that each type of cell contains a full complement of genes. In other words, all human cells have genes for digestive enzymes and muscle proteins, but these genes are expressed only in certain cells. It must be that genes can be switched on or off in each particular type of cell.

Investigators are terribly interested in learning how the expression of genes is regulated. Such knowledge will explain how cells become specialized during development and should also help us understand the occurrence of cancer. Cancer occurs when genes coding for products that promote cell division become overly active and/or when genes coding for products that suppress cell division become inactive.

> Normally, cells are able to regulate the expression of genes so that only certain ones are fully turned on and produce a protein product.

PROKARYOTES UTILIZE OPERONS

Bacteria don't need the same enzymes (and possibly other proteins) all the time. Suppose, for example, the environment is supplying a nutrient—wouldn't it be disadvantageous to produce the enzymes needed to synthesize that nutrient?

In 1961, French microbiologists François Jacob and Jacques Monod showed that *Escherichia coli* (*E. coli*) is capable of regulating the expression of genes necessary for lactose metabolism. They proposed the following **operon** [L. *opera,* work] model to explain gene regulation in prokaryotes and later received a Nobel prize for their investigations.

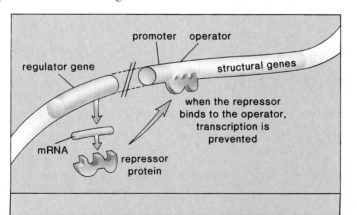

Regulator Gene—a gene that codes for a repressor protein molecule. The repressor molecule binds to the operator and prevents RNA polymerase, an enzyme needed for mRNA synthesis, from binding to the promoter.
Promoter—a short sequence of DNA where RNA polymerase first attaches when a gene is to be transcribed.
Operator—a short sequence of DNA where the repressor binds, preventing RNA polymerase from attaching to the promoter. This often is called the on/off switch of transcription.
Structural Genes—one to several genes for a metabolic pathway that are transcribed as a unit.

Looking at the *Lac* Operon

When *E. coli* is denied glucose and is given the milk sugar lactose instead, it immediately begins to make the three enzymes needed for the metabolism of lactose. These three enzymes are encoded by genes called *lac z, lac y,* and *lac a. Lac z* codes for an enzyme called β-galactosidase, which breaks down the disaccharide lactose to glucose and galactose; *lac y* codes for a permease that facilitates the entry of lactose into the cell; and *lac a* codes for an enzyme called transacetylase, which has an accessory function in lactose metabolism.

The three genes are adjacent to one another on the chromosome and are under the control of a single **promoter** and a single **operator** (fig. 17.1). The regulator gene, located some distance ahead of the promoter, codes for a *lac* operon repressor protein that ordinarily binds to the operator and prevents transcription of the *z, y,* and *a* genes. But when *E. coli* is switched to a medium containing lactose, the lactose binds to the **repressor,** and the repressor undergoes a change in shape that *prevents* it from binding to the operator. Because the repressor is unable to bind to the operator, the promoter is able to bind to RNA polymerase. RNA polymerase carries out transcription, and the three enzymes are produced.[1]

Because the presence of lactose brings about production of enzymes, it is called an **inducer** of the *lac* operon: the enzymes are said to be inducible enzymes, and the entire unit is called an **inducible operon.**

Looking at the *Trp* Operon

Jacob and Monod found that other operons in *E. coli* usually exist in the on rather than off condition. For example, the prokaryotic cell ordinarily produces five enzymes that are needed for the synthesis of the amino acid tryptophan. If tryptophan is present in the medium, however, these enzymes are no longer produced. In this *trp* operon, the regulator codes for a repressor that ordinarily is unable to attach to the operator. The repressor has a binding site for tryptophan, and if tryptophan is present it binds to the repressor. Now, a change in shape allows the repressor to bind to the operator. The enzymes are said to be repressible, and the entire unit is called a **repressible operon.** Tryptophan is called the **corepressor.**

The operon model explains regulation, especially in prokaryotes. It suggests that several genes, located in sequence on a chromosome, are controlled by the same regulatory factors.

> Bacterial DNA contains control regions whose sole purpose is to regulate the transcription of structural genes that code for enzymes or other products.

---

1 Since the 1960s, it's been discovered that matters are a little more complex than originally thought. When glucose is missing, there is a helper complex (cAMP—connected to a protein called catabolite *activator* protein, CAP) which attaches to the promoter and assists the binding of RNA polymerase to the promoter.

Figure 17.1

The *lac* operon. **a.** The regulator gene codes for a repressor protein that is normally active. When active, the repressor protein binds to the operator and prevents RNA polymerase from attaching to the promoter. Therefore, transcription of the three structural genes does not occur. **b.** When lactose (or more correctly, allolactose) is present, it binds to the repressor protein, changing its shape so that it can no longer bind to the operator. Now RNA polymerase binds to the promoter; transcription and translation of the three structural genes follow.

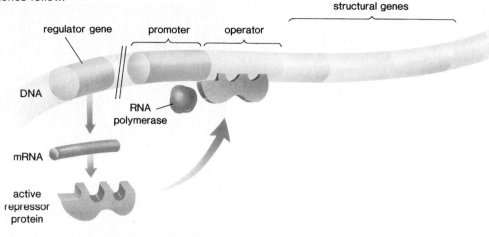

a.

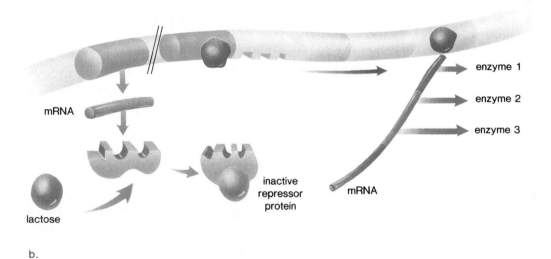

b.

Translational Control

In 1983, Nancy E. Kleckner of Harvard University conducted a series of experiments showing that antisense RNA (ribonucleic acid) can control the expression of a gene in bacteria. Antisense RNA is transcribed from the sense DNA (deoxyribonucleic acid) strand while messenger RNA (mRNA) is transcribed from the template DNA strand. When bacteria transcribe both sense mRNA and antisense RNA, the two bind together by complementary base pairing, forming an RNA duplex. This prevents ribosomes from translating the mRNA into protein.

Later investigators have suggested that inhibition of gene expression with antisense RNA is universal among bacteria. As yet, they have not shown that this is a normal means by which eukaryotic cells regulate gene expression. Laboratory-produced antisense RNA, however, can be injected into eukaryotic cells to control the activity of various sense mRNA molecules. Drug companies are very interested in the possibility of producing this type of product to control the activity of viruses and even cancer genes in humans.

> Bacteria utilize translational control by producing antisense RNA that combines with mRNA, preventing it from being translated into protein.

EUKARYOTES UTILIZE VARIOUS METHODS

In eukaryotes, there is no universal regulatory mechanism to control *gene expression,* which leads to a protein product. Many levels of control are possible, and different genes are regulated in different ways. Regulation at the level of transcription is possible, as is regulation at other stages involved in protein synthesis and protein function. In eukaryotic cells, there are four primary levels of control of gene activity (fig. 17.2).

1. **Transcriptional control:** In the nucleus a number of mechanisms serve to control which structural genes are transcribed and/or the rate at which transcription of the genes occurs. These include the organization of chromatin and the use of transcription factors that initiate transcription, the first step in the process of protein synthesis.

2. **Posttranscriptional control:** Posttranscriptional control occurs in the nucleus after DNA is transcribed and preliminary mRNA (or pre-RNA, as in fig. 17.2) is formed. Differential processing of preliminary mRNA before it leaves the nucleus, and also the speed with which mature mRNA leaves the nucleus, can affect the amount of gene expression.

3. **Translational control:** Translational control occurs in the cytoplasm after mRNA leaves the nucleus and before there is a protein product. The life expectancy of mRNA molecules (how long they exist in the cytoplasm) can vary, as can their ability to bind ribosomes. It is also possible that some mRNAs may need additional changes before they are translated at all.

4. **Posttranslational control:** Posttranslational control, which also occurs in the cytoplasm, occurs after protein synthesis. The polypeptide product may have to undergo additional changes before it is biologically functional. Also, a functional enzyme is subject to feedback control—the binding of an end product can change the shape of an enzyme so that it is no longer able to carry out its reaction.

Control of gene expression occurs at four levels in eukaryotes. In the nucleus there is transcriptional and posttranscriptional control; in the cytoplasm there is translational and posttranslational control.

Figure 17.2

Levels at which control of gene expression occurs in eukaryotic cells. Transcriptional and posttranscriptional control occur in the nucleus. Translational and posttranslational control occur in the cytoplasm.

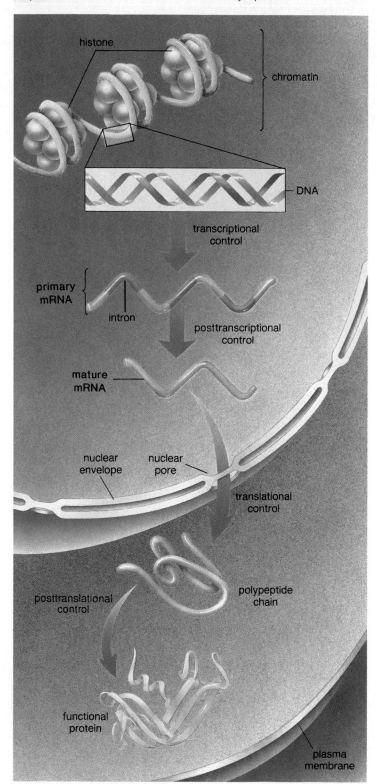

Figure 17.3

Nucleosome structure. **a.** Nucleosome when genes are not being transcribed. **b.** Nucleosome when genes are being transcribed.

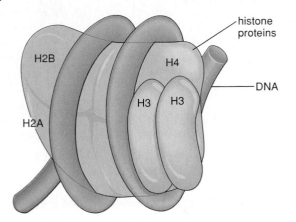

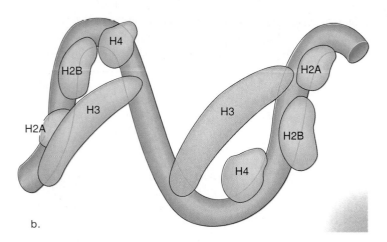

Figure 17.4

Barr body. Each female nucleus contains a Barr body, which is a condensed, inactive X chromosome. Females are mosaics for alleles carried on the X chromosome because chance alone dictates which X chromosome becomes a Barr body. These two females are heterozygous and have inherited one allele for normal sweat glands and another allele for inactive sweat glands. Where in the body the mutant allele expresses itself (purple color) varies from female to female.

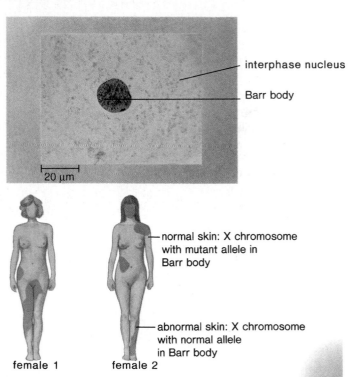

Looking at Transcriptional Control

We might expect transcriptional control in eukaryotes (1) to involve the organization of chromatin and (2) to include regulatory proteins such as those we have just observed in prokaryotes.

Chromatin Plays a Role

In eukaryotes, DNA is associated with proteins. DNA winds around histone proteins that form a spool, and the entire structure is called a nucleosome (fig. 17.3a). The chain of spools coils, loops, and winds to form visible chromosomes during cell division as discussed in the reading on page 264. Chromatin that is highly compacted and visible with the light microscope during interphase is called **heterochromatin.** More diffuse chromatin is called **euchromatin.**

The histone molecules labeled H2-H4 in figure 17.3 may regulate this change in chromosomal structure (fig. 17.3b). Recent studies seem to suggest that histones can both repress and activate genes. Analysis of the amino acid sequences of histones has established that the proteins differ little between species. If folding of DNA were the histone's only job, a variety of

sequences could serve. On the other hand, if histones play a vital role you would expect the original sequence of amino acids to be conserved.

Heterochromatin Is Inactive

To demonstrate that heterochromatin is genetically inactive, we can refer to the **Barr body,** a highly condensed structure. In mammalian females, one of the X chromosomes is found in the Barr body; chance alone determines which of the X chromosomes is condensed. For a given gene, if a female is heterozygous, 50% of her cells have Barr bodies containing one allele and the other 50% have the other allele. This causes the body of heterozygous females to be mosaic, with patches of genetically different cells (fig. 17.4). The mosaic is exhibited in various ways: some females show columns of both normal and abnormal dental enamel; some have patches of pigmented and nonpigmented cells at the back of the eye; some have patches of normal muscle tissue and degenerative muscle tissue. Barr bodies are not found in the cells of the female gonads, where the genes of both X chromosomes appear to be needed for development of the immature egg.

What's in a Chromosome?

By the mid-1900s, it was known that chromosomes are made up of both DNA and protein, largely histones. Much more is now known about histone proteins.

There are five primary types of histone molecules designated H1, H2A, H2B, H3, and H4. Remarkably, the amino acid sequences of H3 and H4 vary little between organisms.

For example, the H4 of peas is only two amino acids different from the H4 of cattle. This similarity suggests that there have been few mutations in the histone proteins during the course of evolution and that the histones therefore have very important functions.

A human cell contains at least 2 meters of DNA. Yet all of this DNA is packed into a nucleus that is about 5 μm in diameter. The histones are responsible for packaging the DNA so that it can fit into such a small space. First the DNA double helix is wound at intervals around a core of eight histone molecules (two copies each of H2A, H2B, H3, and H4), giving the appearance of a string of beads (fig. 17Aa and b).

Each bead is called a nucleosome, and the nucleosomes are said to be joined by "linker" DNA. This string is coiled tightly into a fiber that has six nucleosomes per turn (fig. 17Ac). The H1 histone appears to mediate this coiling process. The fiber loops back and forth (fig. 17Ad and e) and can condense to produce a highly compacted form (fig. 17Af) characteristic of metaphase chromosomes.

An interphase nucleus shows darkly stained chromatin regions called heterochromatin and lightly stained chromatin regions called euchromatin (fig. 17B). Heterochromatin is genetically inactive (fig. 17Ae). The mechanism of inactivation is unknown, but it may involve methylation (adding methyl groups—CH_3—to the bases of DNA). Euchromatin is genetically active (fig. 17Ac). It's believed that in this form, the nucleosomes allow access to the DNA, so that a gene can be turned on and can actively dictate protein synthesis in the cell.

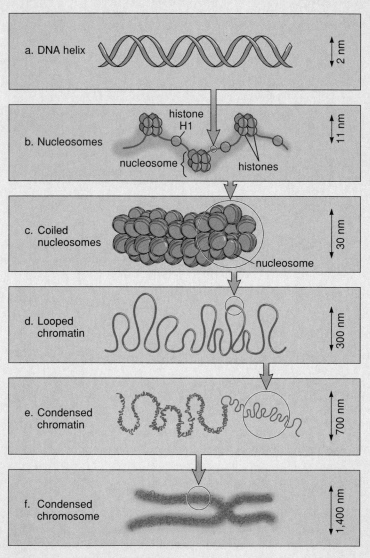

Figure 17A
Levels of chromosomal structure. Each drawing has a scale giving a measurement of length for that drawing. Notice that each measurement represents an ever-increasing length; therefore, it would take a much higher magnification to see the structure in (**a**) compared to that in (**f**).

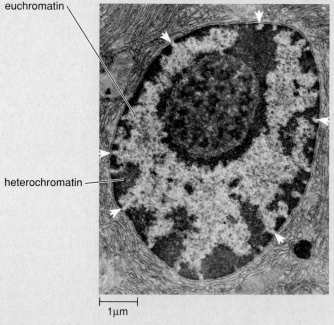

Figure 17B
Eukaryotic nucleus. The nucleus contains chromatin, DNA at two different levels of coiling and condensation. Euchromatin is at the level of coiled nucleosomes (30 nm), and heterochromatin is at the level of condensed chromatin (700 nm) in figure 17A. Arrows indicate nuclear pores.

Likewise, it is clear that the inactivation of one X chromosome in the female zygote lowers the dosage of gene products to that seen in males. Most likely, development has become adjusted to this lower dosage, and a higher dosage would bring about abnormalities. We certainly know that in regard to other chromosomes, any imbalance causes a greatly altered phenotype.

> It appears that transcription is not occurring when chromatin is in the heterochromatin state.

Euchromatin Is Active

In contrast to heterochromatin, euchromatin is genetically active. The chromosomes within the developing egg cells of many vertebrates are called lampbrush chromosomes because they have many loops that appear to be bristles (fig. 17.5). Here mRNA is being synthesized in great quantity; then protein synthesis can be carried out after fertilization, despite rapid cell division. In the salivary glands and other tissues of larval flies, the chromosomes duplicate and reduplicate many times without dividing mitotically. The homologues, each consisting of about 1,000 sister chromatids, synapse together to form giant chromosomes called polytene chromosomes [Gk. *poly,* many, and L. *taenia,* band]. It

is observed that as a larva develops, first one and then another of the chromosomal regions bulge out, forming *chromosome puffs.* The use of radioactive uridine, a label specific for RNA, indicates that DNA is being actively transcribed at these chromosome puffs. It appears that the chromosome is decondensing at the puffs, allowing RNA polymerase to attach to a section of DNA.

Varying the amount of chromatin as in polytene chromosomes is another form of transcriptional control. When the gene product is either transfer RNA (tRNA) or ribosomal RNA (rRNA), only an increased amount of transcription permits an increase in the amount of gene product. In *Xenopus* (a frog) germ cells that are producing eggs, the number of nucleoli and therefore copies of RNA genes actually increases to nearly 1,000. This ensures an immense number of ribosomes in the egg cytoplasm to support protein synthesis during the early stages of development. This form of control is called *gene amplification.*

> Transcriptional control in eukaryotes may involve changes in chromatin structure and in the amount of chromatin for certain genes.

Figure 17.5

Lampbrush chromosomes. These chromosomes, which are present in maturing amphibian egg cells, give evidence that when mRNA is being synthesized, chromosomes most likely decondense. Each chromatid has many loops extended from the axis of the chromosome (white). Many mRNA transcripts are being made off of these DNA loops (red).

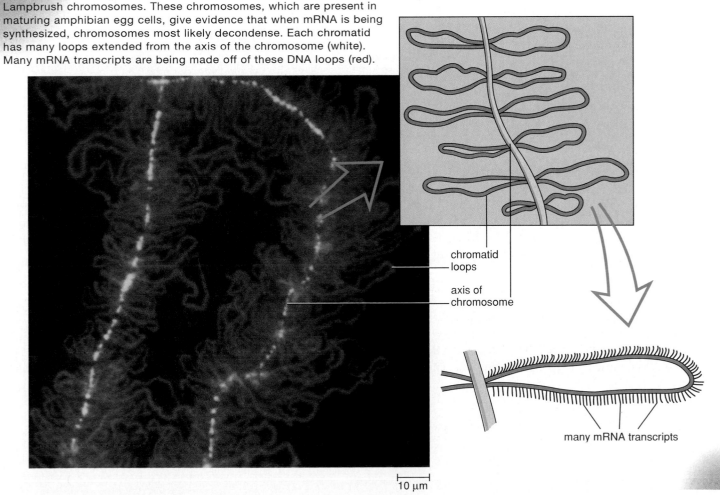

chromatid loops

axis of chromosome

many mRNA transcripts

10 µm

Transcription Factors Are Regulatory Proteins

Although no operons like those of prokaryotic cells have been found in eukaryotic cells, investigations suggest that transcription is controlled by DNA-binding proteins called **transcription factors.** Every cell contains many different types of transcription factors, and a different combination is believed to regulate the activity of any particular gene. A group of transcription factors binds to a promoter adjacent to a gene and then the complex attracts and binds RNA polymerase, but transcription may still not begin. Enhancers are also regions where factors that help regulate transcription of the gene can bind. Enhancers can be quite a distance from the promoter, but a hairpin loop in the DNA can bring the factor attached to the enhancer into contact with the transcription factors and polymerase at the promoter. Now transcription begins (fig. 17.6).

Transcription factors are always present in a cell and most likely they have to be activated in some way before they bind to DNA. The cell has a regulatory pathway that reaches from receptors in the plasma membrane to the nucleus. Kinases, which add a phosphate group to molecules, and phosphatases, which remove a phosphate group, are most likely signaling proteins involved in the regulatory pathway. As we will discuss in the next section, kinases are believed to play a significant role in the development of cancer.

Figure 17.6 🔳

Transcription factors. In this model of how transcription factors in eukaryotic cells work, transcription begins after transcription factors bind to a promoter and to an enhancer. The enhancer is far from the promoter, but physical contact would be possible if the DNA loops bring all factors into contact. Only then does transcription begin.

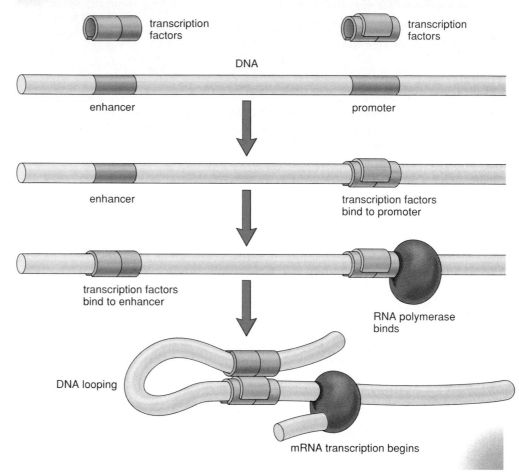

Looking at Posttranscriptional Control

In eukaryotes, genes have both exons (coding regions) and introns (noncoding regions). Messenger RNA (mRNA) molecules (and other RNAs) are processed before they leave the nucleus and pass into the cytoplasm. Differential excision of introns and splicing of mRNA can vary the type of mRNA that leaves the nucleus. For example, both the hypothalamus and the thyroid gland produce a hormone called calcitonin. The mRNA that leaves the nucleus is not the same in both types of cells, however; radioactive labeling studies show that they vary because of a difference in mRNA splicing (fig. 17.7). Evidence of different patterns of mRNA splicing is found in other cells, such as those that produce neurotransmitters, muscle regulatory proteins, and antibodies.

The speed of transport of mRNA from the nucleus into the cytoplasm can ultimately affect the amount of gene product realized per unit time following transcription. There is evidence that there is a difference in the length of time it takes various mRNA molecules to pass through a nuclear pore.

Posttranscriptional control in eukaryotes involves differential mRNA processing and factors that affect the length of time it takes mRNA to travel to the cytoplasm.

Figure 17.7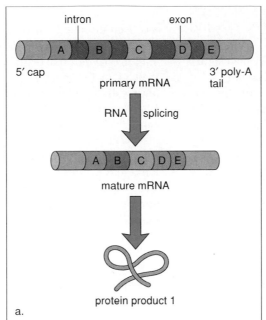

Alternative splicing of identical primary mRNA transcripts. Because the primary mRNAs are processed differently in these two cells, distinct proteins result.

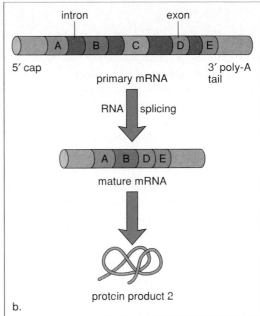

intron   exon

A B C D E

5' cap

primary mRNA

3' poly-A tail

RNA splicing

A B C D E

mature mRNA

protein product 1

a.

intron   exon

A B C D E

5' cap

primary mRNA

3' poly-A tail

RNA splicing

A B D E

mature mRNA

protein product 2

b.

Looking at Translational Control

The eggs of frogs and certain other animals contain mRNA molecules that are not translated at all until fertilization occurs. These mRNAs are called *masked messengers* because apparently the cell is unable to recognize them as available for translation. As soon as fertilization occurs, unmasking takes place, and there is a rapid burst of specific gene product synthesis.

Obviously, the longer an active mRNA molecule remains in the cytoplasm, the more product there will eventually be. During maturation, mammalian red blood cells eject their nucleus, and yet they continue to synthesize hemoglobin for several months thereafter. This means that the necessary mRNAs are able to persist all this time. The agents of mRNA destruction are ribonucleases, enzymes that have been found to be associated with ribosomes. Every mature mRNA has noncoding segments at the 3' and 5' ends; evidently differences in these segments influence how long the mRNA avoids being degraded.

Hormones seem to cause the stabilization of certain mRNA transcripts. For example, the hormone prolactin promotes milk production in mammary glands, but it does so primarily by affecting the length of time the mRNA for casein, a major protein in milk, persists and is translated. Similarly, in estrogen-treated amphibian cells, an mRNA for a protein called vitellogenin persists three weeks, compared to sixteen hours in untreated cells. There is evidence to suggest that estrogen binds to and thereby interferes with the action of a ribonuclease in these cells.

Translational controls directly affect whether an mRNA is translated and the amount of gene product eventually produced.

Looking at Posttranslational Control

Some proteins are not active immediately after translation. For example, bovine proinsulin is at first biologically inactive. After the single long polypeptide folds into a three-dimensional structure, a sequence of about thirty amino acids is enzymatically removed from the middle of the molecule. This leaves two polypeptide chains that are bonded together by disulfide (S—S) bonds and results in an active protein.

Finally, the metabolic activity of genes is often under feedback control (fig. 17.8).

Posttranslational control affects the activity of a protein product, whether or not it is functional, and the length of time it is functional.

Figure 17.8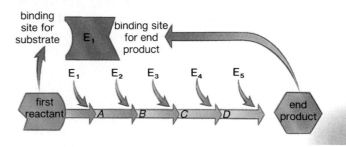

Posttranslational control. The end product of this metabolic pathway can bind to enzyme E₁. When it does, the pathway is shut down because the binding of the end product changes the enzyme's shape so that the substrate cannot bind to the active site.

binding site for substrate

E_1

binding site for end product

E_1 E_2 E_3 E_4 E_5

first reactant   A   B   C   D   end product

CANCER IS A FAILURE IN GENETIC CONTROL

Cancer cells exhibit characteristics that indicate they have experienced a severe failure in the control of gene expression.

Cancer cells lack differentiation. Most cells are specialized; they have a specific form and function that suits them to the role they play in the body. Cancer cells are nonspecialized and do not contribute to the functioning of a body part. A cancer cell does not look like a differentiated epithelial, muscle, nervous, or connective tissue cell and instead has a shape and form that is distinctly abnormal (fig. 17.9). Normal cells can enter the cell cycle for about fifty times, and then they die. Cancer cells can enter the cell cycle repeatedly, and in this way they are immortal. In cell tissue culture, they die only because they run out of nutrients or are killed by their own toxic waste products.

Cancer cells have abnormal nuclei. The nuclei of cancer cells are enlarged, and there may be an abnormal number of chromosomes. The chromosomes have mutated; some parts may be duplicated and some may be deleted. In addition, gene amplification (extra copies of specific genes) is seen much more frequently than in normal cells.

Cancer cells form tumors. Normal cells anchor themselves to a substratum and/or adhere to their neighbors. They exhibit contact inhibition—when they come in contact with a neighbor, they stop dividing. In culture, normal cells form a single layer that covers the bottom of a petri dish. Cancer cells have lost all restraint; they pile on top of one another and grow in multiple layers. They have a reduced need for growth factors, such as epidermal growth factor. Growth factors are hormones needed by normal cells to grow. Epidermal growth factor can stimulate the growth of many types of cells.

In the body, a cancer cell divides to form an abnormal mass of cells called a **tumor** [L. *tumor,* swelling], which invades and destroys neighboring tissue. This new growth, termed *neoplasia,* is made of cells that are disorganized, a condition termed *anaplasia.* A *benign tumor* is a disorganized, usually encapsulated, mass that does not invade adjacent tissue.

Cancer cells undergo angiogenesis and metastasis. *Angiogenesis,* the formation of new blood vessels, is required to bring nutrients and oxygen to a cancerous tumor whose growth is not contained within a capsule. Cancer cells release a growth factor that causes neighboring blood vessels to branch into the cancerous tissue. Some modes of cancer treatment are aimed at preventing angiogenesis from occurring.

Cancer in situ is found in its place of origin; and there has been no invasion of normal tissue. Malignancy is present when **metastasis** [Gk. *meta,* between, and L. *stasis,* standing] establishes new tumors distant from the primary tumor. To accomplish metastasis, cancer cells must first make their way across a basement membrane and into a blood vessel or lymphatic vessel. It has been discovered that cancer cells have receptors that allow them to adhere to basement membranes; they also produce proteinase enzymes that degrade the basement membrane and allow them to invade underlying tissues. Cancer cells tend to be motile, have a disorganized internal cytoskeleton, and lack intact actin filament bundles. After traveling through the blood or lymph, cancer cells may start tumors elsewhere in the body.

The patient's prognosis (probable outcome) is dependent on the degree to which the cancer has progressed: (1) whether the tumor has invaded surrounding tissues, (2) if so, whether there is any lymph node involvement, and (3) whether there are metastatic tumors in distant parts of the body. With each progressive step of the cancerous condition, the prognosis becomes less favorable.

> Cancer cells grow and divide uncontrollably, and then they metastasize, forming new tumors wherever they relocate.

Figure 17.9

Cancer cells differ from normal cells in the ways noted.

Normal Cells

Controlled growth

Contact inhibition

One organized layer

Differentiated cells

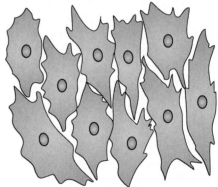

Cancer Cells

Uncontrolled growth

No contact inhibition

Disorganized, multilayered

Nondifferentiated cells

Abnormal nuclei

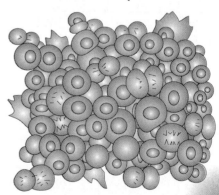

Reflections of a Cancer Researcher

Thomas Gilmore
Boston University

As an undergraduate majoring in English at Princeton University in the early 1970s, I never imagined that I would devote my life to biomedical research. Nevertheless, since 1978, I have been involved in research directed at understanding the molecular events that occur in cells as they progress from a normal to a cancerous state.

One of the most important advances in basic cancer research in the past two decades is the confirmation of the hypothesis that cancer is fundamentally a genetic disease. That is, that progression of a cell to the malignant state is the consequence of the accumulation of mutations in genes involved in cellular growth control.

In human cancers, the most malignant state is likely to involve mutations in at least five genes, but the study of these cancers is often difficult to approach experimentally. Therefore, much basic cancer research, including my own, has involved the use of simple model systems, where expression of one or two mutant genes is sufficient to induce the malignant state. Specifically, I have had a sustained interest in the mechanism by which certain avian retroviruses induce the malignant transformation of chicken cells in tissue culture. These systems have the advantage that expression of a single gene, the retroviral oncogene, causes cells to assume most of the characteristics of a malignantly transformed cell.

I believe I have been very fortunate in my research career. As a graduate student, I happened to be in a lab that was involved in the first characterization of cellular substrates for the tyrosine kinase activity of the *src* oncogene product. This research in the early 1980s led to many other findings that have shown that the phosphorylation of tyrosine residues is a general mechanism used by cells to control cellular growth.

As a post-doctoral fellow working with the late Nobel laureate Howard Temin, I worked on what was, at the time, perhaps the most obscure retroviral oncogene, v-*rel*. Using molecular, biochemical, and cellular approaches, we were able to show that v-*rel* was likely to encode a protein that acted in the nucleus to affect cell growth. It was subsequently found that the v-*rel* gene product has structural and functional homology to proteins that control the expression of genes important for immune cell function in vertebrates and that *rel*-like genes are mutated in many human lymphoid cancers.

My lab and others in the field of cancer research are now increasingly turning to even simpler eukaryotic systems, such as yeast and nematodes, in order to understand cellular pathways that control growth and division. Fortunately, it is becoming evident that such pathways are clearly conserved through evolution.

The selection of appropriate experimental systems to answer important questions is one of the most crucial decisions a scientist can make. It is very easy to get attached to your current system or experimental approach. As a scientist, one must do what is necessary to answer the most important question, even if that means learning new and difficult techniques.

I have chosen this career because I simply enjoy doing, discussing, and arguing science. For me, one of the greatest attractions of science is that it is, for the most part, a field of ideas. Yet I hope there will be a higher goal to my research: that understanding the molecular basis of disease will one day lead to chemical or biological therapeutics.

How Cancer Begins

Certain environmental agents called **carcinogens** [Gk. *carcino,* ulcer, and *gene,* origin] cause mutations that can lead to cancer. These mutations activate oncogenes and/or inactivate tumor-suppressor genes. An **oncogene** [Gk. *onco,* tumor] is a cancer-causing gene. A **tumor-suppressor gene** is so called because it prevents cancer from occurring.

Oncogenes Versus Tumor-Suppressor Genes

Normally, cell growth and differentiation are regulated to meet the needs of the body, and cell division is turned on only when required. A *regulatory pathway* that controls cell division has been discovered. This pathway involves extracellular *growth factors,* plasma membrane *growth factor receptors,* various proteins within the cytoplasm, and various genes within the nucleus.

Figure 17.10

Causes of cancer. Heredity and environmental factors cause mutations of proto-oncogenes and tumor-suppressor genes. A regulatory pathway, which includes plasma membrane receptors for growth factors, intracellular reactions, and the genes, is unbalanced. This leads to uncontrolled growth and a tumor. Cancer still does not develop unless the immune system fails to respond and kill these abnormal cells.

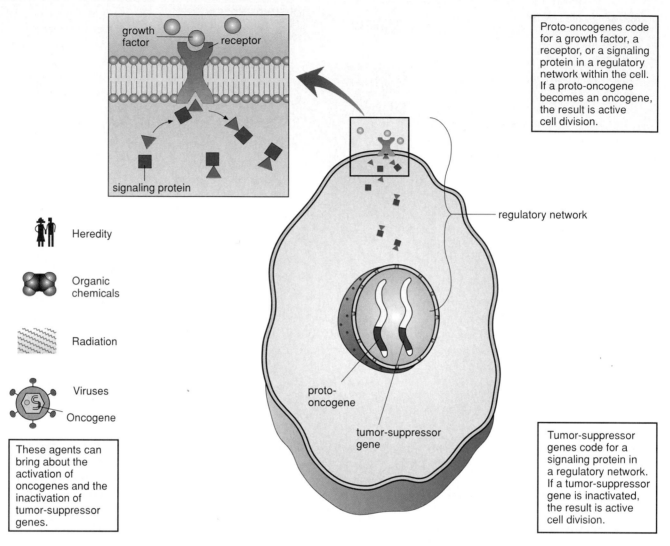

growth factor

receptor

signaling protein

Heredity

Organic chemicals

Radiation

Viruses

Oncogene

These agents can bring about the activation of oncogenes and the inactivation of tumor-suppressor genes.

Proto-oncogenes code for a growth factor, a receptor, or a signaling protein in a regulatory network within the cell. If a proto-oncogene becomes an oncogene, the result is active cell division.

regulatory network

proto-oncogene

tumor-suppressor gene

Tumor-suppressor genes code for a signaling protein in a regulatory network. If a tumor-suppressor gene is inactivated, the result is active cell division.

Oncogenes Promote Cancer

In 1911, Francis Peyton Rous reported that a virus, later named Rous sarcoma virus (RSV), is capable of causing sarcoma, a type of cancer, in chickens. It wasn't until 1966 that the scientific community realized the value of Rous's contribution and awarded him a Nobel prize. In the meantime, it was clear that RSV is an RNA virus. After the virus infects a cell, it inserts a DNA transcript of its RNA genome, which includes a gene known as *src* (for sarcoma gene), into the host chromosome.

Investigators prepared radioactive copies of the *src* gene, knowing that these copies would bind to the host chromosome wherever the *src* gene was located. To their surprise, they found that binding occurred in two locations—one where viral DNA had inserted and another in a normal part of the chromosome! This showed that the *src* gene was a normal gene in chickens, but it had become a cancer-causing gene only because it was being carried by the virus. The *src* gene is now known to be an oncogene. It's possible that the *src* gene is under the control of

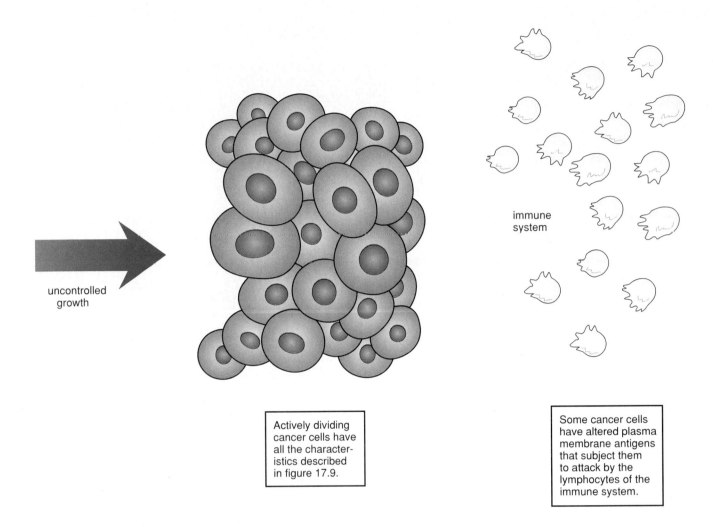

immune system

Actively dividing cancer cells have all the character-istics described in figure 17.9.

Some cancer cells have altered plasma membrane antigens that subject them to attack by the lymphocytes of the immune system.

a viral promoter that has turned it on. In its normal, nonmutated state, it is a **proto-oncogene** [Gk. *proto*, first, *onco*, tumor], a gene that can be transformed into an oncogene (fig. 17.10). Oncogenes are not alien to the cell; they are normal, essential genes that have undergone a mutation.

Research with oncogenes is being done in laboratories as discussed in the reading on page 269. Researchers have identified perhaps one hundred oncogenes that can cause increased growth and lead to a tumor. The oncogenes most frequently in-

volved in human cancers belong to the *ras* gene family. An alteration of only a single nucleotide pair is sufficient to convert a normally functioning *ras* proto-oncogene to an oncogene. The *ras*K oncogene is found in about 25% of lung cancers, 50% of colon cancers, and 90% of pancreatic cancers. The *ras*N oncogene is associated with leukemias (cancer of blood-forming cells) and lymphomas (cancers of lymphoid tissue), and both *ras* oncogenes are frequently found in thyroid cancers.

Figure 17.11 🔘

Regulatory pathway involving the *ras* protein. **a.** Normally, the signaling protein GAP causes an enzyme to inactivate *ras*. **b.** If a growth factor is received, a receptor adds phosphates to GAP and *ras* is always turned on. Inappropriate cell growth can follow.

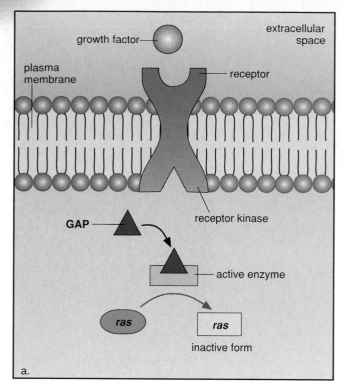

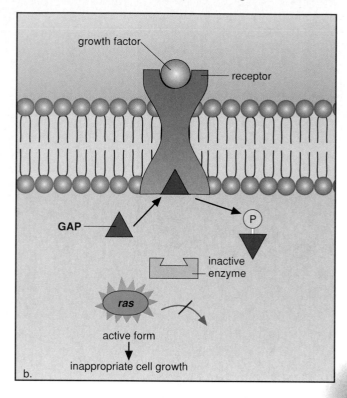

Figure 17.11 illustrates that the *ras* protein (coded for by the *ras* gene) can exist in an active or an inactive form. An active *ras* protein is associated with cell growth, although the precise role of the *ras* protein in the regulatory pathway has not yet been determined. The activity of the *ras* protein is controlled in part by a protein called GAP (GTPase activating protein). Normally, GAP activates an enzyme that inactivates *ras*, and cell growth does not occur. When a growth factor attaches to a receptor that phosphorylates GAP, GAP becomes inactive and *ras* protein becomes active. Phosphorylation (the addition of a phosphate group) is a common way by which *signaling proteins* in the regulatory pathway are turned on or off. Notice in figure 17.11 that a portion of the receptor, called receptor kinase, is an enzyme that phosphorylates GAP. A *kinase* is any enzyme that transfers a phosphate group from one molecule (often ATP, adenosine triphosphate) to another. Many investigators are working to discover other ways in which the *ras* protein is regulated and to determine its precise functions.

Tumor-Suppressor Genes Stop Cancer

Researchers have identified about a half-dozen tumor-suppressor genes. When these genes malfunction, a tumor results. The *RB* tumor-suppressor gene was discovered by Alfred Knudson when he was studying the inherited condition retinoblastoma. When a child receives only one normal *RB* tumor-suppressor gene and that gene mutates, eye tumors develop in the retina by the age of three. *RB* tumor-suppressor gene has now been found to mal-

function in cancers of the breast, prostate, and bladder among others. Loss of *RB* tumor-suppressor gene through chromosomal deletion is particularly frequent in a type of lung cancer called small cell lung carcinoma.

We now know that signaling proteins often regulate the transcription of genes whose products are needed for cell division, and this appears to be true of the *RB* protein. When a particular factor attaches to a receptor, the *RB* protein is activated. An active *RB* protein turns off the expression of a proto-oncogene, whose product initiates cell division.

Another major tumor-suppressor gene is called *p53*, a gene that is more frequently mutated in human cancers than any other known gene. It has been found that the *p53* protein acts as a transcription factor and as such is involved in turning on the expression of a gene called *WAF1* or *Cip1*. The product of this gene is a cell cycle inhibitor. A number of cell proteins combine with the *p53* protein. When a protein combines with *p53*, it is hard to tell whether it is activating *p53* or is being activated by *p53*. This intricate situation is now being unraveled.

Each cell contains a regulatory pathway involving proto-oncogenes and tumor-suppressor genes that code for growth factor receptors, and signaling proteins active in the pathway.

Can Cancer Be Prevented?

There are many who believe that more emphasis should be placed on prevention of cancer. Everyone needs to be aware that despite great effort by the medical and scientific community, the survival rate for all types of cancer is only 53% among Caucasians and 38% among African Americans.[2] Prevention works and saves time and money. Forty thousand fewer individuals will die this year from stomach cancer compared to the 1930s. The drop can be attributed to the reduced need to preserve food by pickling, smoking, or salt-curing because of the universal availability of home refrigerators. On the other hand, there has been a steady rise in lung cancer deaths, which may be associated with an increase in smoking among women since World War II. These behaviors help prevent cancer:

DON'T SMOKE Cigarette smoking accounts for about 30% of all cancer deaths. Smoking is responsible for 90% of lung cancer cases among men and 79% among women— about 87% altogether. Those who smoke two or more packs of cigarettes a day have lung cancer mortality rates fifteen to twenty-five times greater than nonsmokers. Smokeless tobacco (chewing tobacco or snuff) increases the risk of cancers of the mouth, larynx, throat, and esophagus.

DON'T SUNBATHE Almost all cases of basal and squamous cell skin cancers are considered to be sun related. Further sun exposure is a major factor in the development of melanoma, and the incidence of this cancer increases for those living near the equator.

AVOID ALCOHOL Cancers of the mouth, throat, esophagus, larynx, and liver occur more frequently among heavy drinkers, especially when accompanied by tobacco use (cigarettes or chewing tobacco).

AVOID RADIATION Excessive exposure to ionizing radiation can increase cancer risk. Even though most medical and dental X-rays are adjusted to deliver the lowest dose possible, unnecessary X-rays should be avoided. Excessive radon exposure in homes increases the risk of lung cancer, especially in cigarette smokers. It is best to test your home and take the proper remedial actions.

BE TESTED FOR CANCER Do the shower check for breast cancer or testicular cancer. Have other exams done regularly by a physician.

BE AWARE OF OCCUPATIONAL HAZARDS Exposure to several different industrial agents (nickel, chromate, asbestos, vinyl chloride, etc.) and/or radiation increases the risk of various cancers. Risk from asbestos is greatly increased when combined with cigarette smoking.

BE AWARE OF HORMONE THERAPY Estrogen therapy to control menopausal symptoms increases the risk of endometrial cancer. However, including progesterone in estrogen replacement therapy helps to minimize this risk.

The Right Diet Is Helpful

Statistical studies have suggested that persons who follow certain dietary guidelines are less likely to have cancer. The following dietary guidelines greatly reduce your risk of developing cancer:

1. **Avoid obesity.** The risk of cancer (especially colon, breast, and uterine cancers) is 55% greater among obese women and 33% greater among obese men, compared to people of normal weight.

2. **Lower total fat intake.** A high-fat intake has been linked to development of colon, prostate, and possibly breast cancers.

3. **Eat plenty of high-fiber foods.** These include whole-grain cereals, fruits, and vegetables. Studies have indicated that a high-fiber diet protects against colon cancer, a frequent cause of cancer deaths. It is worth noting that foods high in fiber also tend to be low in fat!

4. **Increase consumption of foods that are rich in vitamins A and C.** Beta-carotene, a precursor of vitamin A, is found in dark green leafy vegetables, carrots, and various fruits. Vitamin C is present in citrus fruits. These vitamins are called antioxidants because in cells they prevent the formation of free radicals (organic ions that have an unpaired electron) that can possibly damage DNA. Vitamin C also prevents the conversion of nitrates and nitrites into carcinogenic nitrosamines in the digestive tract.

5. **Cut down on consumption of salt-cured, smoked, or nitrite-cured foods.** Salt-cured or pickled foods may increase the risk of stomach and esophageal cancer. Smoked foods like ham and sausage contain chemical carcinogens similar to those in tobacco smoke. Nitrites are sometimes added to processed meats (e.g., hot dogs and cold cuts) and other foods to protect them from spoilage; as mentioned previously, nitrites are converted to nitrosamines in the digestive tract.

---

2 When cancer patients live five years beyond the time of diagnosis and treatment, it is generally considered that they are cured.

6. **Include vegetables from the cabbage family in the diet.** The cabbage family includes cabbage, broccoli, brussels sprouts, kohlrabi, and cauliflower (fig. 17.12). These vegetables may reduce the risk of gastrointestinal and respiratory tract cancers.

7. **Be moderate in the consumption of alcohol.** People who drink and smoke are at an unusually high risk for cancers of the mouth, larynx, and esophagus.

Increased effort should be placed on preventing cancer. Prevention includes: avoid smoking, sunbathing, alcohol, and radiation; and follow the dietary guidelines provided.

Figure 17.12
Some data suggest that diet can influence the development of cancer. Fresh fruits, especially those high in vitamins A and C, and vegetables, especially those in the cabbage family, are believed to reduce the risk of cancer.

Summary

1. Regulation in prokaryotes usually occurs at the level of transcription. The operon model developed by Jacob and Monod says that a regulator gene codes for a repressor, which sometimes binds to the operator. When it does, RNA polymerase is unable to bind to the promoter and transcription of structural genes cannot take place.

2. The *lac* operon is an example of an inducible operon because when lactose, the inducer, is present it binds to the repressor. The repressor is unable to bind to the operator, and transcription of structural genes takes place.

3. The *trp* operon is an example of a repressible operon because when tryptophan, the corepressor, is present, it binds to the repressor. The repressor is then able to bind to the operator, and transcription of structural genes does not take place.

4. The following levels of control of gene expression are possible in eukaryotes: transcriptional control, posttranscriptional control, translational control, and posttranslational control.

5. Chromatin organization helps regulate transcription. Highly compacted heterochromatin is genetically inactive, as exemplified by Barr bodies. Less compacted euchromatin is genetically active, as exemplified by lampbrush chromosomes in vertebrates and polytene chromosome puffs in insects.

6. Gene amplification is the replication of a gene such that there are more copies of this gene (i.e., ribosomal RNA, [rRNA], genes in the oocyte) than were originally present in the zygotic nucleus.

7. Regulatory proteins called transcription factors, as well as DNA sequences called enhancers, play a role in controlling transcription in eukaryotes.

8. Posttranscriptional control refers to variations in messenger RNA (mRNA) processing and the speed with which a particular mRNA molecule leaves the nucleus.

9. Translational control affects mRNA translation and the length of time it is translated. Posttranslational control affects whether or not an enzyme is active and how long it is active.

10. Cancer cells are nondifferentiated, divide repeatedly, have abnormal nuclei, do not require growth factors, and are not constrained by their neighbors. After forming a tumor, cancer cells metastasize and start new tumors elsewhere in the body.

11. Each cell contains a regulatory network that leads to cell division and growth. When proto-oncogenes mutate, becoming oncogenes, and when tumor-suppressor genes mutate, the regulatory network no longer functions as it should and uncontrolled growth results.

12. Prevention includes these behaviors: avoid smoking, sunbathing, alcohol, and radiation; and be aware of occupational hazards and the danger of taking estrogen without also taking progesterone.

13. Certain dietary guidelines are believed to be helpful in avoiding cancer. High-fiber foods are thought to help reduce the risk of colon cancer, and a diet containing plenty of vegetables and fruits is protective against the development of cancers in general.

Writing Across the Curriculum

In order to practice writing skills, students should write out the answers to any or all of the study questions and the critical thinking questions. The study questions are sequenced in the same order as the text. Answers to the objective questions, and suggested answers to the critical thinking questions, are in appendix D.

Study Questions

1. Name and state the function of the four components of operons. 260
2. Explain the operation of the *lac* operon, and note why it is considered an inducible operon. 260
3. Explain the operation of the *trp* operon, and note why it is considered a repressible operon. 260
4. With regard to transcriptional control in eukaryotes explain how Barr bodies show that heterochromatin is genetically inactive. 263

5. Explain how lampbrush chromosomes in vertebrates and giant (polytene) chromosome puffs in insects show that euchromatin is genetically active. 265
6. What do transcription factors do in eukaryotic cells? What are enhancers? 266
7. Give examples of posttranscriptional, translational, and posttranslational control in eukaryotes. 266–67

8. List and discuss four characteristics of cancer cells that distinguish them from the characteristics of normal cells. 268
9. What are oncogenes and tumor-suppressor genes? What role do they play in a regulatory network that controls cell division and involves plasma membrane receptors and signaling proteins? 269–72
10. List four carcinogens to be avoided to prevent the development of cancer. Give the dietary guidelines that can possibly prevent the development of cancer. 273

Objective Questions

1. Which type of prokaryotic cell would be more successful as judged by its growth potential?
   a. one that is able to express all its genes all the time
   b. one that is unable to express any of its genes any of the time
   c. one that expresses some of its genes some of the time
   d. one that divides only when all types of amino acids and sugars are present in the medium
2. When lactose is present
   a. the repressor is able to bind to the operator.
   b. the repressor is unable to bind to the operator.
   c. transcription of *lac y, lac z,* and *lac a* genes occurs.
   d. Both b and c are correct.
3. When tryptophan is present
   a. the repressor is able to bind to the operator.
   b. the repressor is unable to bind to the operator.
   c. transcription of structural genes occurs.
   d. Both b and c are correct.

4. Which of these is mismatched?
   a. posttranslational control—nucleus
   b. transcriptional control—nucleus
   c. translational control—cytoplasm
   d. posttranscriptional control—nucleus
5. RNA processing varies in different cells. This is an example of _____ control of gene expression.
   a. transcriptional
   b. posttranscriptional
   c. translational
   d. posttranslational
6. A scientist adds radioactive uridine (label for RNA) to a culture of cells and examines an autoradiograph. Which type of chromatin is apt to be labeled?
   a. heterochromatin
   b. euchromatin
   c. Both a and b are correct.
   d. Neither a nor b is correct.
7. If Barr bodies were genetically active, females heterozygous for an X-linked gene would
   a. be mosaics.
   b. not be mosaics.
   c. die.
   d. Both a and c are correct.

8. Which of these might cause a proto-oncogene to become an oncogene?
   a. exposure of cell to radiation
   b. exposure of cell to certain chemicals
   c. viral infection of the cell
   d. All of these are correct.
9. A cell is cancerous. Where might you find an abnormality?
   a. only in the nucleus
   b. only in the plasma membrane receptors
   c. only in cytoplasmic reactions
   d. in any part of the cell concerned with growth and cell division
10. A tumor-suppressor gene
    a. inhibits cell division.
    b. opposes oncogenes.
    c. prevents cancer.
    d. All of these are correct.

11. a. Label the diagram of a *lac* operon. Note that transcription is not occurring.

b. What one change is needed in this drawing to have the diagram represent a *trp* operon when no transcription is occurring?

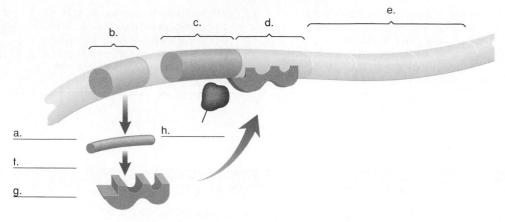

a. _____

f. _____

g. _____

h. _____

b.

c.

d.

e.

Concepts and Critical Thinking

1. *Cells are able to regulate the expression of genes so that only certain ones are expressed at any particular time.*

What firsthand evidence is there that only certain genes are active in certain cells?

2. *Genes are controlled at various levels that involve both transcription and translation.*

Define gene expression, and then explain why it is appropriate to speak of posttranslational control of genes.

3. *Faulty regulation of genes that promote cell division and/or genes that inhibit cell division causes the development of cancer.*

Why would you expect normal cells to have opposing genes and opposing enzymes involved in the regulation of cell division?

Selected Key Terms

Barr body A dark-staining body (discovered by M. Barr) in the nuclei of female mammals that contains a condensed, inactive X chromosome. 263

cancer A malignant tumor whose nondifferentiated cells exhibit loss of contact inhibition, uncontrolled growth, and the ability to invade tissue and metastasize. 268

carcinogen (kar-SIN-uh-jen) An environmental agent that causes mutations leading to the development of cancer. [Gk. *carcino*, ulcer, and *gene*, origin] 269

corepressor A molecule that binds to a repressor, allowing the repressor to bind to an operator in a repressible operon. 260

euchromatin (yoo-KROH-mut-un) Diffuse chromatin, which is being transcribed. 263

heterochromatin (het-uh-roh-KROH-mut-un) Highly compacted chromatin that is not being transcribed 263

inducer A molecule that brings about activity of an operon by joining with a repressor and preventing it from binding to the operator. 263

inducible operon An operon that is normally inactive but is turned on when an inducer is present. 260

metastasis (meh-TAS-tuh-sus) The spread of cancer from the place of origin throughout the body; caused by the ability of cancer cells to migrate and invade tissues. [Gk. *meta*, between, and L. *stasis*, standing] 268

oncogene (ONG-koh-jeen) A cancer-causing gene through mutation. [Gk. *onco*, tumor] 269

operator In an operon the sequence of DNA to which the repressor protein binds. 260

operon (OP-er-on) A group of structural and regulating genes that functions as a single unit. [L. *opera*, work] 260

promoter In an operon a sequence of DNA where RNA polymerase begins transcription. 260

proto-oncogene (PROH-toh-ONG-koh-jeen) A normal gene that can become an oncogene through mutation. [Gk. *proto*, first, *onco*, tumor] 271

regulator gene In an operon, a gene that codes for a repressor. 260

repressible operon (OP-er-on) An operon that is normally active because the repressor must combine with a corepressor before the complex can bind to the operator. 260

repressor In an operon protein molecule that binds to an operator, preventing RNA polymerase from binding to the promoter site of an operon. 260

structural gene Gene that codes for an enzyme in a metabolic pathway. 260

transcription factor In eukaryotes protein required for the initiation of transcription by eukaryotic RNA polymerase. 266

tumor Cells derived from a single mutated cell that has repeatedly undergone cell division; benign tumors remain at the site of origin and malignant tumors metastasize. [L. *tumor*, swelling] 268

tumor-suppressor gene Gene that codes for a protein that ordinarily suppresses cell division. 269

18

RECOMBINANT DNA AND BIOTECHNOLOGY

Learning Objectives

Cloning of a Gene

- Describe the process by which recombinant DNA is prepared and a gene is cloned.   279

Biotechnology Products Are Many

- Categorize and list some of the biotechnology products currently on the market.   280

Replicating Small DNA Segments

- Describe the polymerase chain reaction; note how and for what purpose the DNA segments are analyzed.   281–82

Making Transgenic Organisms

- Describe the services performed by transgenic bacteria.   283
- Discuss some of the ecological concerns surrounding transgenic bacteria.   283

- List some types of transgenic plants presently available and those anticipated in the future.   284
- Discuss the use of animals in regard to gene pharming.   284

Gene Therapy Is a Reality

- Outline current methods employed for gene therapy.   285
- List illnesses that have been or may be corrected by using gene therapy.   285–86

Mapping the Human Chromosomes

- Describe the two goals of the Human Genome Project.   286

DNA can be extracted from a cell and manipulated using available laboratory techniques. This discovery has led to the commercial availability of gene products and to proposed cures for human genetic disorders.

endel's original research was rediscovered in 1900, and since that time geneticists have made startling advances which have led to a new era of biotechnology. Biotechnology, which originally meant the use of a natural biological system to produce a product or to achieve an end desired by humans, is not new. Plants and animals have been bred to express particular phenotypes since the dawn of civilization. The biochemical capabilities of microorganisms have also been exploited for a very long time. For example, the production of both wine and bread is dependent on yeast cells to carry out fermentation reactions.

Genetic engineering is the use of technology to alter the genome of a living cell for medical or industrial use. During the 1980s, biotechnology gave rise to an industry that provides products made by genetic engineering of bacteria. These products include drugs that promote human health and proteins that are useful as vaccines or nucleic acids for laboratory research. Now, a way has been found to alter naturally occurring proteins and indeed to make completely new ones. Someday it may even be possible to bypass bacteria in the production of some human proteins.

Genetically engineered bacteria are currently released into the environment to clean up pollutants, increase the fertility of the soil, or kill insect pests. Biotechnology even extends beyond unicellular organisms; it is now possible to alter the genotype and subsequently the phenotype of plants and animals. Indeed, gene therapy in humans is already undergoing clinical trials.

CLONING OF A GENE

Genetic engineering can produce cells that contain a foreign gene and are capable of producing a new and different protein.

Choosing a Vector

Recombinant DNA (rDNA) contains DNA (deoxyribonucleic acid) from two or more different sources. To make rDNA, a technician often begins by selecting a **vector** [L. *vect,* carried], the means by which rDNA is introduced into a host cell. One common type of vector is a plasmid. **Plasmids** are small accessory rings of DNA found in some bacteria that carry genes not present in the bacterial chromosome. Plasmids were discovered by investigators studying the sex life of the intestinal bacterium *Escherichia coli* (*E. coli*).

Plasmids that are used as vectors have been removed from bacteria and have had a foreign gene inserted into them (fig. 18.1*a*). Treated cells take up plasmids, and then bacteria and plasmids reproduce. Eventually, there are many copies of the plasmid and therefore many copies of the foreign gene. The gene is now said to have been **cloned** [Gk. *clon,* young shoot].

The bacteriophage known as lambda is commonly used as a vector to carry rDNA into bacterial cells (fig. 18.1*b*). Viruses are often the vector of choice for animal cells, also. After a virus has attacked a cell, the DNA is released from the virus and enters the cell proper. Here it may direct the reproduction of many more viruses. Each virus derived from a viral vector contains a copy of the foreign gene. Therefore, viral vectors also allow cloning of a particular gene.

Figure 18.1

Gene cloning using bacteria and viruses. **a.** A plasmid is removed from a bacterium and is used to make recombinant DNA. After the recombined plasmid is taken up by a host cell, replication produces many copies. **b.** Viral DNA is removed from a bacteriophage such as lambda and is used to make recombinant DNA. The virus containing the recombinant DNA infects a host bacterium. Cloning is achieved when the virus reproduces and then leaves the host cell.

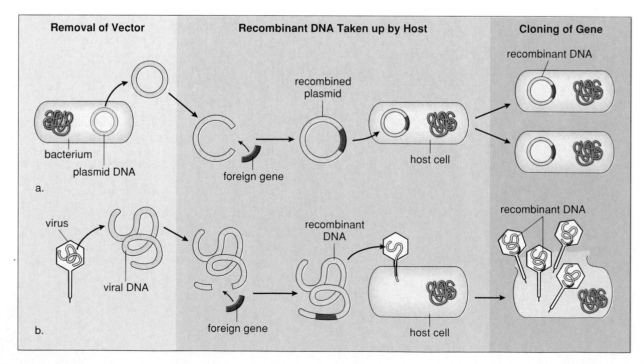

Making Recombinant DNA

The introduction of foreign DNA into vector DNA to produce rDNA requires two enzymes (fig. 18.2). The first enzyme, called a **restriction enzyme,** cleaves plasmid DNA and the second, called **DNA ligase,** seals foreign DNA into the opening created by the restriction enzyme.

Restriction enzymes occur naturally in some bacteria, where they stop viral reproduction by cutting up viral DNA. They are called restriction enzymes because they *restrict* the growth of viruses. In 1970, Hamilton Smith, at Johns Hopkins University, isolated the first restriction enzyme; now hundreds of different restriction enzymes have been isolated and purified. Each one cuts DNA at a specific cleavage site. For example, the restriction enzyme called *Eco*RI always cuts double-stranded DNA when it has this sequence of bases and in this manner:

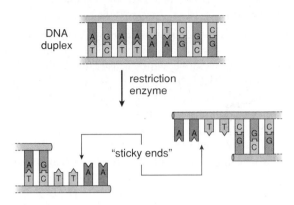

Notice there is now a gap into which a piece of foreign DNA can be placed if it ends in bases complementary to those exposed by the restriction enzyme. To assure this, it is only necessary to cleave the foreign DNA with the same type of restriction enzyme. The single-stranded but complementary ends of the two DNA molecules are called "sticky ends" because they can bind by complementary base pairing. They therefore facilitate the insertion of foreign DNA into vector DNA.

The second enzyme needed for preparation of rDNA, DNA ligase [L. *liga,* tied], is a cellular enzyme that seals any breaks in a DNA molecule. Genetic engineers use this enzyme to seal the foreign piece of DNA into the vector. DNA splicing is now complete; an rDNA molecule has been prepared.

Getting the Product

Bacterial cells take up a recombined plasmid, especially if they are treated with calcium chloride to make them more permeable. Thereafter, if the inserted foreign gene is replicated and actively expressed, the investigator can recover either the cloned gene or a protein product (fig. 18.2).

In order for mammalian gene expression to occur in a bacterium, the gene has to be accompanied by the proper regulatory regions. Also, the gene should not contain introns because bacterial cells do not have the necessary enzymes to process primary messenger mRNA (mRNA; ribonucleic acid). It's possible to make a mammalian gene that lacks introns, however. The enzyme called reverse transcriptase can be used to make a DNA copy of mature mRNA. This DNA molecule, called *complementary DNA (cDNA)*, does not contain introns. Alternatively, it is possible to manufacture small genes in the laboratory. A machine called a DNA synthesizer joins together the correct sequence of nucleotides, and this resulting gene also lacks introns.

Figure 18.2

Cloning of a human gene. Human DNA and plasmid DNA are cleaved by the same type of restriction enzyme and spliced together by the enzyme DNA ligase. Gene cloning is achieved when a host cell takes up the recombined plasmid and the plasmid reproduces. Multiple copies of the gene are now available to an investigator. If the insulin gene functions normally as expected, the product (insulin) may also be retrieved.

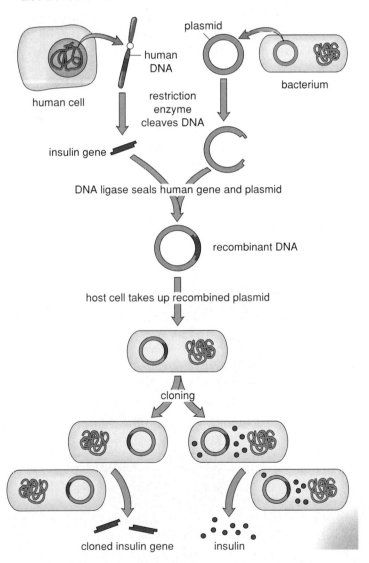

BIOTECHNOLOGY PRODUCTS ARE MANY

Table 18.1 shows at a glance some of the biotechnology products now available. These products include hormones and similar types of proteins or vaccines.

Hormones and Similar Types of Proteins

One impressive advantage of biotechnology is that it allows mass production of proteins that are very difficult to obtain otherwise. The human growth hormone, which is used to treat people who are growing more slowly than normal, was previously extracted from the pituitary glands of cadavers, and it took fifty glands to obtain enough for one dose. Now human growth hormone is produced in quantity by biotechnology. Insulin, to treat diabetics, was previously extracted from the pancreatic glands of slaughtered cattle and pigs; it was expensive and sometimes caused allergic reactions in recipients. And few of us knew of tPA (tissue plasminogen activator), a protein present in the body in minute quantities that activates an enzyme to dissolve blood clots. Now tPA produced by biotechnology is used to treat heart attack victims by dissolving blood clots that are blocking the flow of blood in the coronary arteries of the heart.

The last few entries of table 18.1 lists other troublesome and serious afflictions in humans that may soon be treatable by biotechnology products. Clotting factor VIII treats hemophilia; human lung surfactant treats respiratory distress syndrome in premature infants; atrial natriuretic factor helps control hypertension. And the list will grow, because bacteria (or other cells) can be engineered to produce virtually any protein.

Several hormones produced by biotechnology are for use in animals. Farm animals can now be given growth hormone instead of steroids. Such animals produce a leaner meat that is healthier for humans. When cows are given bovine growth hormone (bGH) they produce 25% more milk than usual, making it possible for dairy farmers to reduce the number of their cows. However, an increased incidence of udder infections can require greater dosages of antibiotic therapy.

Safer Vaccines

Vaccines are used to make people immune to an infectious organism so they do not become ill when exposed to it. In the past, vaccines were made from treated bacteria or viruses and on occasion they caused the illness they were suppose to prevent.

Vaccines produced through biotechnology do not cause illness. Bacteria and viruses have surface proteins, and a gene for just one of these can be used to genetically engineer bacteria. The copies of the surface protein that result can be used as a vaccine. A vaccine for hepatitis B is now available, and potential vaccines for chlamydia, malaria, and AIDS are in experimental stages.

Vaccines are available through biotechnology for the inoculation of farm animals. There are vaccines for such illnesses as hoof-and-mouth disease and scours. These animal ailments were once a severe drain on the time, energy, and resources of farmers because they caused an untold number of animal illnesses and deaths each year.

> Biotechnology products include hormones and similar types of proteins and vaccines. These products are of enormous importance to the fields of medicine and animal husbandry.

Table 18.1

Representative Biotechnology Products

Hormones and Similar Types of Proteins		Potential Vaccines
Treatment of Humans	*For*	*Use in Humans to Prevent*
Insulin	Diabetes	AIDS
Growth hormone	Pituitary dwarfism	Herpes (oral and genital)
tPA (tissue plasminogen activator)	Heart attack	Hepatitis A, B, and C
Interferons	Cancer	Lyme disease
Erythropoietin	Anemia	Whooping cough
Interleukin-2	Cancer	Chlamydia
Clotting factor VIII	Hemophilia	
Human lung surfactant	Respiratory distress syndrome	
Atrial natriuretic factor	High blood pressure	
Tumor necrosis factor	Cancer	
Ceredase	Gaucher disease	

REPLICATING SMALL DNA SEGMENTS

The polymerase chain reaction (PCR) can create millions of copies of a single gene or any specific piece of DNA in a test tube. PCR is very specific—the targeted DNA sequence can be less than one part in a million of the total DNA sample! This means that a single gene among all the human genes can be amplified (copied) using PCR.

PCR takes its name from DNA polymerase, the enzyme that carries out DNA replication in a cell. It is considered a chain reaction because DNA polymerase will carry out replication over and over again, until there are millions of copies of the targeted DNA. PCR does not replace gene cloning; cloning provides many more copies of a gene, and it is still used whenever a large quantity of a gene or a protein product is needed.

Before carrying out PCR, primers—sequences of about twenty bases that are complementary to the bases on either side of the "target DNA"—must be available. The primers are needed because DNA polymerase does not start the replication process; it only continues or extends the process. After the primers bind by complementary base pairing to the DNA strand, DNA polymerase copies the target DNA (fig. 18.3a and b).

PCR has been in use for several years, but now almost every laboratory has automated PCR machines to carry out the procedure. Automation became possible after a temperature-insensitive (thermostable) DNA polymerase was extracted from a bacterium. This enzyme can withstand the high temperature used to separate double-stranded DNA; therefore, replication need not be interrupted by the need to add more enzyme.

Analyzing DNA Segments

Following PCR, the nucleotide sequence of the sample can be determined. There are automated DNA sequences that make use of computers to sequence genes at a fairly rapid rate. Therefore, PCR is carried out in order to:

- Estimate the evolutionary relationship of present-day species by comparing the nucleotide sequences within 16S rRNA, a subunit of ribosomes.

- Determine the nucleotide sequence of human genes. PCR-amplified human chromosome fragments are essential to the Human Genome Project (p. 286).

- Conduct molecular paleontology. Amplified mitochondrial DNA sequences in modern living populations are used to determine the evolutionary history of human populations.

The DNA resulting from PCR amplification can be analyzed by using a **DNA probe,** a single strand of radioactive DNA nucleotides made by a DNA synthesizer. A DNA probe is single-stranded and it will seek out and bind to a complementary DNA strand (fig. 18.3c). Because of the enormous number of probes now available, PCR has a wide range of applications. It is usually needed to:

- Detect viral infections. The probe has a sequence complementary to the viral DNA of interest.

- Diagnose genetic disorders. The probe has a sequence complementary to a particular mutation.

Figure 18.3

Polymerase chain reaction (PCR) amplification and analysis. **a.** DNA is removed from a cell and is placed in a test tube along with appropriate primers, DNA polymerase, and a supply of nucleotides. **b.** Following PCR amplification, many copies of target DNA (pink) are present. **c.** Binding of a labeled DNA probe (blue) enables the scientist to determine that a particular DNA segment was indeed present in the original sample.

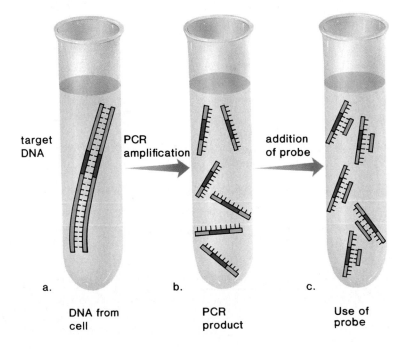

target DNA

PCR amplification

addition of probe

a.

b.

c.

DNA from cell

PCR product

Use of probe

- Diagnose cancer. The probe can identify chromosomal abnormalities, oncogenes, or mutated tumor-suppressor genes.

PCR followed by DNA probe analysis is used during **DNA fingerprinting,** a process described in figure 18.4. The DNA is first treated with restriction enzymes, which cut it into fragments. Each organism's DNA results in a collection of different-sized fragments. Therefore, *restriction fragment length polymorphisms (RFLPs)* exist. During a process called gel electrophoresis, the fragments are separated according to their lengths, and the result is a pattern of bands that is different for each organism. The use of radioactive probes allows specific sequences to be separated from all the other fragments, and the resulting pattern to be recorded on X-ray film.

A DNA fingerprint is inherited and therefore resembles that of one's parents. DNA fingerprinting successfully identified a teenage murder victim from skeletal remains eight years after the death because the skeletal DNA was similar to that obtained from blood samples donated by the victim's parents. DNA from a single sperm is enough to identify a suspected rapist when PCR amplification precedes DNA fingerprinting.

DNA fingerprinting is also helpful to evolutionists. For example, it was used to determine that the quagga, an extinct zebralike animal, was a zebra rather than a horse. The only remains of the quagga consisted of dried skin. In other studies, DNA sequences from a 7,000-year-old mummified human brain and from a 17–20-million-year-old plant fossil were analyzed using PCR amplification followed by DNA fingerprinting.

Figure 18.4

Restriction fragment length polymorphism (RFLP) analysis. DNA samples I and II are from the same individual. DNA sample III is from a different individual. Notice, therefore, that the restriction enzyme cuts are different. Gel electrophoresis separates the DNA fragments according to their length because shorter fragments migrate further in an electrical field than do longer fragments. The fragments are separated (denatured) and transferred to a membrane where a radioactive probe can be applied. The resulting pattern (the DNA fingerprint) can then be detected by autoradiography. In a theoretical rape case, for example, sample I could be from the suspect's white blood cells, sample II could be from sperm in the victim's vagina, and sample III could be from the victim's white blood cells.

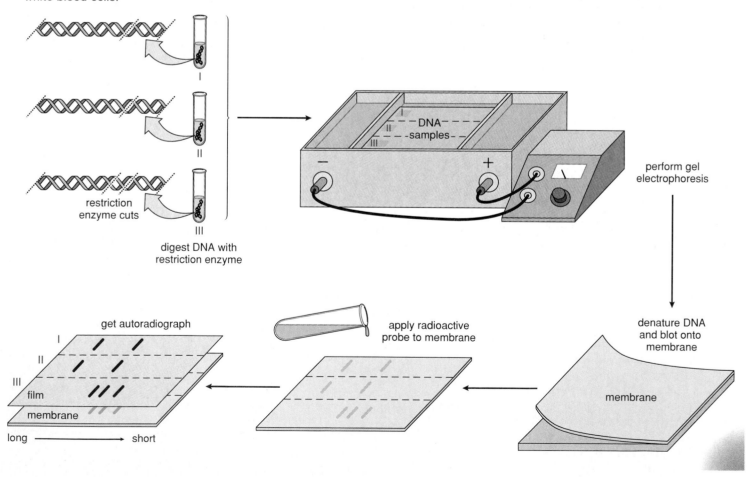

MAKING TRANSGENIC ORGANISMS

Free-living organisms in the environment that have had a foreign gene inserted into them are called **transgenic organisms** [L. *trans*, across, and Gk. *gene*, origin].

Transgenic Bacteria Perform Services

As you know, bacteria are used to clone a gene or to mass-produce a product. They are also genetically engineered to perform other services.

Protection and Enhancement of Plants

Genetically engineered bacteria can be used to promote the health of plants. For example, bacteria that normally live on plants and encourage the formation of ice crystals have been changed from frost-plus to frost-minus bacteria. Field tests showed that these genetically engineered bacteria protect the vegetative parts of plants from frost damage. Also, a bacterium that normally colonizes the roots of corn plants has now been endowed with genes (from another bacterium) that code for an insect toxin. The toxin is expected to protect the roots from insects.

Many other rDNA applications in agriculture are thought to be possible. For example, *Rhizobium* is a bacterium that lives in nodules on the roots of leguminous plants, such as bean plants. Here, the bacteria fix atmospheric nitrogen into a form that can be used by the plant. It might be possible to transfer the necessary genes to other bacteria, which can then infect nonleguminous plants, such as corn, rice, and wheat. This would reduce the amount of fertilizer needed on agricultural fields.

Bioremediation

Bacteria can be selected for their ability to degrade a particular substance, and then this ability can be enhanced by genetic engineering. For instance, naturally occurring bacteria that eat oil can be genetically engineered to do an even better job of cleaning up beaches after oil spills (fig. 18.5). Industry has found that bacteria can be used as biofilters to prevent airborne chemical pollutants from being vented into the air. They can also remove sulfur from coal before it is burned and help clean up toxic dumps.

Chemical Production

Organic chemicals are often synthesized by having catalysts act on precursor molecules or by using bacteria to carry out the synthesis. Today, it is possible to go one step further and to manipulate the genes that code for these enzymes. For instance, biochemists discovered a strain of bacteria that is especially good at producing phenylalanine, an organic chemical needed to make aspartame, the dipeptide sweetener better known as NutraSweet™. They isolated, altered, and formed a vector for the appropriate genes so that various bacteria could be genetically engineered to produce phenylalanine.

Mineral Processing

Many major mining companies already use bacteria to obtain various metals. Genetic engineering may enhance the ability of

Figure 18.5

Bioremediation. Bacteria capable of decomposing oil have been engineered and patented by the investigator, Dr. Chakrabarty. In the inset, the flask toward the rear contains oil and no bacteria; the flask toward the front contains the bacteria and is almost clear of oil. Now that engineered organisms (e.g., bacteria and plants) can be patented, there is an even greater impetus to create them.

1 μm

bacteria to extract copper, uranium, and gold from low-grade sources. At least two mining companies plan to test genetically engineered organisms having improved bioleaching capabilities.

Ecological Considerations

There are those who are very concerned about the deliberate release of genetically engineered microbes (GEMs) into the environment. Ecologists point out that these bacteria might displace those that normally reside in an ecosystem, and the effects could be deleterious. Others rely on past experience with GEMs, primarily in the laboratory, to suggest that these fears are unfounded. Tools are now available to detect, measure, and even disable cell activity in the natural environment. It is hoped that these will eventually pave the way for GEMs to play a significant role in agriculture and in environmental protection. To minimize unforeseen effects, governments worldwide are instituting regulatory programs to ensure that risk assessments are done before the genetically engineered bacteria are released into the environment.

Transgenic bacteria have numerous uses, from protecting plants and the environment to aiding industrial production.

Figure 18.6

Genetically engineered plants. The cotton boll on the right is from a plant that has not been genetically engineered; the boll on the left is from a plant that was genetically engineered to resist cotton bollworm larvae and will go on to produce a normal yield of cotton.

Figure 18.7

Transgenic bull Herman and five of his transgenic offspring. Both parent and offspring possess a gene that codes for human lactoferrin. This protein will be secreted in the milk of transgenic females. Humans who need this medication can drink reconstituted milk powder.

Transgenic Plants Are Here

The only possible plasmid for genetically engineering plant cells belongs to the bacterium *Agrobacterium,* which will infect many but not all plants. Therefore, other techniques have been developed to introduce foreign DNA into plant cells which have had the cell wall removed and are called protoplasts. It is possible to treat protoplasts (plants cells that have had the cell wall removed) with an electric current while they are suspended in a liquid containing foreign DNA. The electric current makes tiny self-sealing holes in the plasma membrane through which genetic material can enter. It is advantageous to use protoplasts for this purpose because each one can develop into a complete plant.

Presently, about fifty types of genetically engineered plants that resist insects, viruses, or herbicides have now entered small-scale field trials (fig. 18.6). The major crops that can be improved in this way are soybean, cotton, alfalfa, and rice; however, even genetically engineered corn may reach the marketplace by the year 2000.

It is hoped that one day genetically engineered plants will have one or more of these attributes: (1) they will be heat-, cold-, drought-, or salt-tolerant; (2) they will be more nutritious; (3) they can be stored and transported without fear of damage; (4) they will require less fertilizer; or (5) they will produce chemicals and drugs that are of interest to humans. Plants have been engineered to produce human proteins, such as hormones, in their seeds. A weed called mouse-eared cress has been engineered to produce a biodegradable plastic (polyhydroxybutyrate, or PHB) in tissue granules.

Transgenic Animals Are Here

Animals, too, are being genetically engineered. Because animal cells will not take up bacterial plasmids, other methods are used to insert genes into their eggs. Previously, the most common method was to microinject foreign genes into eggs before they were fertilized. During vortex mixing, eggs are placed in an agitator with DNA and silicon-carbide needles. The needles make tiny holes through which the DNA can enter the eggs. Using this technique, many types of animal eggs have been injected with bovine growth hormone (bGH). The procedure has been used to produce larger fishes, cows, pigs, rabbits, and sheep. Genetically engineered fishes are now being kept in ponds that offer no escape to the wild because there is much concern that they will upset or destroy natural ecosystems.

Gene pharming, the use of transgenic farm animals to produce pharmaceuticals, is being pursued by a number of firms. It is advantageous to use animals because the product is obtainable from the milk of females.

Genes that code for therapeutic and diagnostic proteins are incorporated into the animal's DNA, and the proteins appear in the animal's milk. There are plans to produce drugs for the treatment of cystic fibrosis, cancer, blood and other disorders. Herman, a bull genetically engineered to carry a gene for human lactoferrin, has sired many offspring that are also transgenic (fig. 18.7). The females will produce lactoferrin in their milk. Lactoferrin is a drug that will protect those at risk for recurrent bacterial gastrointestinal tract infections.

GENE THERAPY IS A REALITY

Gene therapy replaces defective genes with healthy genes. Gene therapy also includes the use of genes to treat genetic disorders and various other human illnesses.

Some Methods Are Ex Vivo

During ex vivo (outside the living organism) therapy, cells are removed from a patient, treated, and returned to the patient. A retrovirus is often used as a vector to carry normal genes into the cells of the patient. A retrovirus has RNA genes; therefore it is equipped with recombinant RNA (viral RNA with an inserted RNA copy of a normal gene) for the purpose of gene therapy. After recombinant RNA enters a human cell, such as a bone marrow stem cell, reverse transcription occurs. During reverse transcription, RNA is used as a template for the formation of DNA. It is the resulting DNA that carries the normal gene into the human genome (fig. 18.8).

Two young girls with severe combined immunodeficiency syndrome (SCID)[1] underwent ex vivo gene therapy several years ago. These girls lack an enzyme that is involved in the maturation of T and B cells, and therefore they were subject to life-threatening infections. White blood cells were removed from their blood and infected with a retrovirus that carried a normal gene for the enzyme. Then the cells were returned to the girls. Recently, one of these girls and two newborn boys received bone marrow stem cells genetically engineered in the same way. Genetically engineered stem cells are preferred because they are long-lived and their use may result in a permanent cure.

Gene therapy is also being used for treatment of familial hypercholesterolemia, a condition that develops when liver cells lack a receptor for removing cholesterol from the blood. The high levels of blood cholesterol make the patient subject to fatal heart attacks at a young age. In a newly developed procedure, a small portion of the liver is surgically excised and infected with a retrovirus containing a normal gene for the receptor. In one gene therapy patient, the cholesterol level dropped from 448 (mg/dl) to 366 (mg/dl). Along the same lines, it may be possible to give patients with failing hearts genetically engineered cardiac muscle cells that carry extra receptors for adrenalin, a heart stimulant. Chemotherapy in cancer patients often kills off healthy cells as well as cancer cells. In upcoming clinical trials, researchers intend to give genes to cancer patients that either will make healthy cells more tolerant of chemotherapy or will make tumors more vulnerable to it. In one trial, bone marrow stem cells from about thirty women with late-stage ovarian cancer are to be infected with a virus carrying a gene for multiple-drug resistance. If successful, this would mean that the women could receive chemotherapy for a longer period of time, possibly improving their chances of survival.

Some Methods Are In Vivo

Other gene therapy procedures use viruses, laboratory-grown cells, or even synthetic carriers to introduce genes directly into patients. If in vivo (inside the living organism) therapy is used, no cells are removed from the patient. For example, an adenovirus that contains a gene to treat cystic fibrosis patients has been placed in an aerosol spray. When the modified virus is inhaled by the patient, the cells of the trachea and bronchi will then have a normal gene for a transmembrane regulator. Without this regulator, cystic fibrosis patients produce a thick, sticky sputum that clogs the respiratory tract.

It's also possible that retroviruses could be used to carry genes for cytokines, soluble hormones of the immune system, directly into the tumors of patients. It has been observed that the presence of cytokines stimulates the immune system to rid the body of cancer cells.

---

1 SCID is often called the "bubble-baby" disease after David, a young person who lived under a plastic dome to prevent infection.

Figure 18.8

Ex vivo gene therapy in humans. Lymphocytes are withdrawn from the body, a normal gene is inserted into them, and they are then returned to the body.

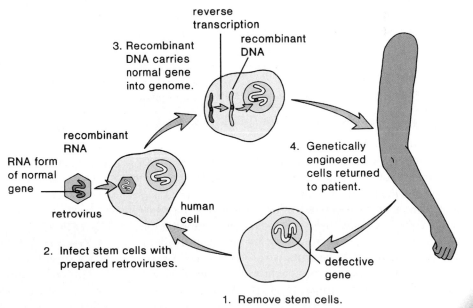

Perhaps it will be possible to also use in vivo therapy to cure hemophilia, diabetes, Parkinson disease, or AIDS. To treat hemophilia, patients could get regular doses of cells that contain normal clotting-factor genes. Or such cells could be placed in organoids, artificial organs that can be implanted in the abdominal cavity. To cure Parkinson disease, dopamine-producing cells could be grafted directly into the brain. These procedures will use laboratory-grown cells that have been stripped of antigens (to decrease the possibility of an immune system attack).

Antisense technology is a new biotechnology tool that has gene therapy applications as well as other applications. *Antisense molecules* are short sequences of DNA or RNA nucleotides complementary to sequences found in genes.

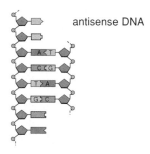

antisense DNA

When an antisense DNA molecule binds to a gene, it turns the gene off. It is possible that someday antisense DNA molecules could be used to turn off the genes of a microbe or an oncogene. An antisense RNA molecule is complementary to the nucleotide sequence of an RNA. When an antisense RNA molecule binds to an mRNA molecule, the mRNA is inactivated. An antisense RNA might be useful to turn off the replication of AIDS viruses, which have RNA genes.

> Gene therapy is now a reality, and researchers are envisioning all sorts of applications aimed at curing human genetic disorders as well as many other types of illnesses.

MAPPING THE HUMAN CHROMOSOMES

If the order and precise location of the genes on the human chromosomes were known, it would facilitate laboratory research and medical diagnosis and treatment. The goals of the Human Genome Project are to map the human chromosomes (fig. 18.9) and to determine the three billion bases in the human genome.

Several methods have been used to attempt mapping the human chromosomes. On occasion, mRNA has been isolated and reverse transcriptase has been used to produce a cDNA copy of a gene. The cDNA copy can be attached to a fluorescent dye and used as a probe to determine to which chromosome, and indeed, to which band of this chromosome, it belongs. Base pairing between probe and chromosome will occur right on a

Figure 18.9

The human X chromosome. Mapping has been done and this is the sequence of some of the more than fifty genes now known to be on the chromosome.

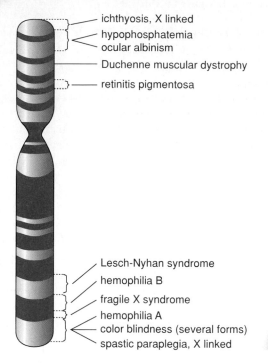

- ichthyosis, X linked
- hypophosphatemia
- ocular albinism
- Duchenne muscular dystrophy
- retinitis pigmentosa

- Lesch-Nyhan syndrome
- hemophilia B
- fragile X syndrome
- hemophilia A
- color blindness (several forms)
- spastic paraplegia, X linked

microscope slide, and the use of fluorescence allows us to see precisely where the gene is located.

A genetic marker is any DNA difference between individuals. Mutations are genetic markers, as are the differences in fragment lengths observed after treatment with restriction enzymes (see fig. 18.4). Genes can sometimes be assigned a location on a chromosome according to their relative relationship to genetic markers on specific chromosomes. Therefore, they have helped scientists develop tests for genetic disorders and to map the human chromosomes. Now that it is known that trinucleotide repeats are associated with genetic disorders, scientists look for these to pinpoint a gene.

Laboratory procedures have been developed to allow sequencing of the DNA bases, and there are now instruments that rapidly carry out this procedure. It has recently been discovered that genetic markers contain unique stretches of DNA called sequence-tagged sites (STSs). It is hoped that these can be used to create links between the genetic map and the known sequence of the bases.

> The goals of the Human Genome Project are to know the sequence of bases of all the chromosomes and to know how this sequence relates to a complete map of each chromosome.

Summary

1. DNA technology has led to the modern field of biotechnology, in which organisms are engineered to produce human proteins or are otherwise given desired characteristics.

2. To achieve a genetically engineered cell, a vector is first prepared. Both plasmids and viruses are used as vectors to carry a foreign gene into a cell. When the plasmid replicates or the virus reproduces, the foreign gene is cloned.

3. The preparation of recombinant DNA (rDNA) requires restriction enzymes, which are used to cleave plasmid DNA and to cleave foreign DNA. The "sticky ends" produced facilitate the insertion of foreign DNA into vector DNA. The foreign gene is sealed into the vector DNA by DNA ligase.

4. Genetically engineered bacteria produce many products of interest to humans, such as hormones and vaccines.

5. The polymerase chain reaction (PCR) uses the enzyme DNA polymerase to carry out multiple replications of target DNA. A suitable radioactive probe can then be used to analyze this DNA for various purposes. The DNA copies can also be subjected to DNA fingerprinting.

6. Transgenic organisms have also been made. Bacteria have been produced to promote the health of plants, perform bioremediation, extract minerals, and produce chemicals.

7. Plant cells genetically engineered while they are protoplasts in tissue culture grow to be transgenic plants.

8. It is hoped that recombinant DNA technology may eventually produce plants that have: a natural resistance to various diseases and pests, an ability to fix atmospheric nitrogen, an increased ability to grow in arid and salty soils, and greater nutritional value.

9. Genetic engineering of animals has made much progress. Many firms are interested in gene pharming, the use of genetically engineered animals to produce pharmaceuticals in milk.

10. The possible applications for human gene therapy are broadening. Sometimes cells are removed from the patient and genetically engineered before being returned to the patient. Other times viruses carry the healthy gene directly to the patient.

11. Mapping the human chromosomes and determining the sequence of bases in DNA are the goals of the Human Genome Project. Special techniques will be needed to relate the genetic map to the known base sequence.

12. The map of a chromosome will give the order of the genes and the markers on that chromosome. Sometimes a variation is linked to a genetic disorder and can be used to tell if a disorder has been inherited.

Writing Across the Curriculum

In order to practice writing skills, students should write out the answers to any or all of the study questions and the critical thinking questions. The study questions are sequenced in the same order as the text. Answers to the objective questions, and suggested answers to the critical thinking questions, are in appendix D.

Study Questions

1. What are the similarities and differences between using a plasmid and using a virus as a vector for gene cloning?   278

2. What is the methodology for producing recombinant DNA to be used in gene cloning?   279

3. Categorize and give examples of the types of biotechnology products available today.   280

4. What is the polymerase chain reaction (PCR), and how is it carried out? How and why is the target DNA analyzed?   281–82

5. Bacteria have been genetically engineered to perform what services? What are the ecological concerns regarding their release into the environment?   283

6. In what ways have plants been genetically engineered, and what type of genetic engineering is expected in the future?   284

7. In what ways have animals been genetically engineered?   284

8. Explain and give examples of gene therapies in humans.   285

9. Explain the two primary goals of the Human Genome Project.   286

Objective Questions

1. Which of these is a true statement?
   a. Both plasmids and viruses can serve as vectors.
   b. Plasmids can carry recombinant DNA but viruses cannot.
   c. Vectors carry only the foreign gene into the host cell.
   d. All of these statements are true.

2. Which of these is a benefit to having insulin produced by biotechnology?
   a. It can be mass-produced.
   b. It is nonallergenic.
   c. It is less expensive.
   d. All of these are correct.

3. Restriction fragment length polymorphisms (RFLPs)
   a. identify individuals genetically.
   b. are the basis for DNA fingerprints.
   c. can be subjected to gel electrophoresis.
   d. All of these are correct.

4. Which of these would you not expect to be a biotechnology product?
   a. modified enzyme
   b. DNA probe
   c. protein hormone
   d. steroid hormone

5. What is the benefit of using a retrovirus as a vector in gene therapy?
   a. It is not able to enter cells.
   b. It incorporates the foreign gene into the host chromosome.
   c. It eliminates a lot of unnecessary steps.
   d. Both b and c are correct.

6. Gel electrophoresis
   a. measures the size of plasmids.
   b. tells whether viruses are infectious.
   c. measures the charge and size of proteins and DNA fragments.
   d. All of these are correct.

7. Using this key, put the steps in the correct order to form a plasmid carrying recombinant DNA.

Key:

Step 1 use restriction enzymes

Step 2 use DNA ligase

Step 3 remove plasmid from parent bacterium

Step 4 introduce plasmid into new host bacterium

   a. 1,2,3,4

   b. 4,3,2,1

   c. 3,1,2,4

   d. 2,3,1,4

8. Which of these is incorrectly matched?

   a. protoplast—plant cell engineering

   b. RFLPs—DNA fingerprinting

   c. DNA polymerase—PCR

   d. DNA ligase—mapping human chromosomes

9. The restriction enzyme called *Eco*RI has cut double-stranded DNA in this manner. The piece of foreign DNA to be inserted ends in what bases (a) to the left? (b) to the right?

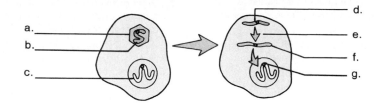

10. Label the following drawings, using these terms: retrovirus, recombinant RNA, defective gene, recombinant DNA (twice), reverse transcription, and human genome.

Concepts and Critical Thinking

I. *Organisms are chemical and physical machines.*

Provide examples to show that DNA can be manipulated, and explain why you think some people would find DNA manipulation disturbing.

2. *DNA is the common genetic material of all organisms.*

How does recombinant DNA technology support our belief in this concept?

Selected Key Terms

cloned The production of identical copies; in genetic engineering, the production of many identical copies of a gene. [Gk. *clon*, young shoot] 278

DNA fingerprinting Using DNA fragment lengths, resulting from restriction enzyme cleavage, to identify particular individuals. 282

DNA ligase (LY-gays) An enzyme that links DNA fragments; used during production of recombinant DNA to join foreign DNA to the vector DNA. [L. *liga*, tied] 279

DNA probe Known sequences of DNA that are used to find complementary DNA strands; can be used diagnostically to determine the presence of particular genes. 281

gene therapy The use of bioengineered cells or other biotechnology techniques to treat human genetic disorders. 285

genetic engineering The use of technology to alter the genome of a living cell for medical or industrial use. 278

plasmid A self-duplicating ring of accessory DNA in the cytoplasm of bacteria. 278

recombinant DNA (rDNA) DNA that contains genes from more than one source. 278

restriction enzyme Bacterial enzyme that stops viral reproduction by cleaving viral DNA; used to cut DNA at specific points during production of recombinant DNA. 279

transgenic organism Free-living organisms in the environment that have had a foreign gene inserted into them. [L. *trans*, across, and Gk. *gene*, origin] 283

vector In genetic engineering, a means to transfer foreign genetic material into a cell—for example, a plasmid. [L. *vect*, carried] 278

Suggested Readings for Part II

Capecchi, M. 1994. Targeted gene replacement. *Scientific American* 270(3):52. Researchers are deciphering DNA segments that control development and immunity.

Cooper, G. 1993. *The cancer book.* Boston: Jones and Bartlett Publishers. This is a non-technical presentation of the basic nature and causes of cancer, and current strategies for its prevention and treatment.

Erikson, D. 1992. Hacking the genome. *Scientific American* 266(4):128. Masses of information written in human DNA are being translated into precise computer codes.

Frederick, R. J., and Egan, M. 1994. Environmentally compatible applications of biotechnology. *BioScience* 44(8):529. Explains the use of living organisms to restore and safeguard the environment.

Gasser, C. S., and Fraley, R. T. 1992. Transgenic crops. *Scientific American* 266(6):62. Genetic engineering helps the world produce better crops.

Grunstein, M. 1992. Histones as regulators of genes. *Scientific American* 267(4):68. Histones participate in the expression and suppression of genes.

Hartl, D. 1994. *Genetics*. 3d ed. Boston: Jones and Bartlett Publishers. Provides a clear, comprehensive, and straightforward introduction to the principles of genetics at the college level.

Mange, E., and Mange, A. 1994. *Basic human genetics*. Sunderland, Mass.: Sinauer Associates. This text for nonmajors presents the general principles of genetics and discusses the implications for individuals and society.

Pääbo, S. 1993. Ancient DNA. *Scientific American* 269(5):86. Evolutionary change can be observed directly from genetic information in fossil remains.

Peters, P. 1994. *Biotechnology: A guide to genetic engineering*. Dubuque, Iowa: Wm. C. Brown Publishers. This understandable text takes the student from a basic understanding of genetic structure and function to an understanding of the basics of biotechnology and genetic engineering.

Rennie, J. 1993. DNA's new twists. *Scientific American* 266(3):122. New genetic discoveries lead to new theories about evolution and the inheritance of disease.

Rennie, J. 1994. Grading the gene tests. *Scientific American* 270(6):88. Raises ethical questions about screening embryos for genetic disease before implantation.

Rennie, J. 1994. Immortal's enzyme. *Scientific American* 271(1):14. An enzyme that maintains telomeres may make tumor cells immortal.

Rhodes, D., and Klug, A. 1993. Zinc fingers. *Scientific American* 268(2):56. Concerns regulation of gene activity in many species.

Rothwell, N. 1993. *Understanding genetics: A molecular approach*. New York: John Wiley & Sons. Focuses on the human genome and provides an insight into approaches that have led to the isolation of genetic regions associated with human afflictions.

Scientific American Medicine. 1993. This special issue covers topics such as heart disease, RU486, the immune system, cancer, and AIDS.

Verma, I. 1993. Gene therapy. *Scientific American Medicine*. Special issue: 78. Concerns the first attempt to treat an inherited human disease by inserting a healthy gene into a patient.

Watson, J., et al, 1992. *Recombinant DNA*. 2d ed. New York: W. H. Freeman and Company. Suitable for undergraduate and graduate students, this book may be useful for those interested in recombinat DNA techniques.

CRITICAL THINKING CASE STUDY

Part II

TRACING HUMAN MIGRATION THROUGH MITOCHONDRIAL DNA ANALYSIS

We have learned that DNA is located in the nucleus as part of the chromosomes. There are also small amounts of DNA localized in the mitochondria. This mitochondrial DNA is a small, two-stranded ring and carries thirty-seven genes compared to about 100,000 genes coded in the chromosomal DNA.

Pedigree charts, which show the pattern of inheritance of a characteristic within a group of people, have told us a great deal about inheritance. Could a study of the mitochondrial DNA (mDNA) give us useful information about inheritance and relationships in humans?

Two unique characteristics of mDNA offer significant advantages in scientific investigations.[1] First, mitochondria (and mDNA) are inherited *only* from the mother. When an egg is fertilized, the sperm contributes only nuclear (chromosomal) DNA, but none of the mitochondria or other cellular organisms. Any changes in mDNA are due only to mutations, not to mixing of genetic information in sexual reproduction.

Second, the mutation rate in mDNA is significantly higher than that in chromosomal DNA. These mutations would be passed on unchanged as "markers" on the mDNA. People whose mDNA share the same "markers" would be related. As mDNA accumulates more mutations, there will be more points of comparison to trace the relations between people.

Geneticists recognized that mDNA offered the possibility for new genetic studies. One group of scientists that was particularly interested in mDNA were those studying the migration of humans to the Americas. Most scientists propose that the first Americans migrated from Siberia to Alaska and then on to North and South America, but other theories have been proposed. Had the first Americans come from Siberia? Was there more than one wave of migration? The possibility of using mDNA allowed new investigations of the following hypothesis:

Hypothesis I The first Americans came from Siberia in more than one wave of migration. (The following prediction can be made based on this hypothesis.)

Prediction I If the first Americans migrated from Siberia, then comparisons of mDNA from Native Americans and native Siberians will indicate similarities.

Result I Analysis of mDNA investigated four "marker" sites resulting from mutations on the mDNA of Native Americans and Siberians. Individuals from twenty-four North and South American tribes were investigated, and in every case the Native Americans shared at least one of the markers with the native Siberian populations. Moreover, such similarities were *not* found with comparisons to European or African populations.[2] These similarities support the hypothesis.

A second prediction was suggested by a study of Native American languages. Two large groups of related Native American languages are the Amerind and the NaDene. Perhaps the tribes speaking these different languages represent descendants of two different and widely separated migrations from Siberia.

Prediction 2 If speakers of the different languages represent different migrations, then mDNA from the two groups should show distinct differences.

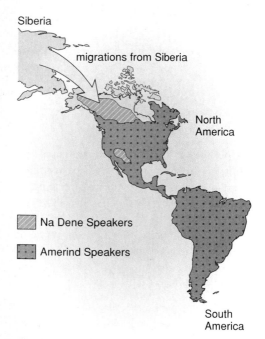

Figure A
Amerind-speaking Native Americans carry four mDNA genetic "markers," NaDene speakers carry only one "marker." These data suggest at least two separate migrations from Siberia.

Result 2 Amerind speakers as a group were found to have all four mDNA "markers" from native Siberians. In contrast, NaDene speakers carried only one of the "markers," and this could be traced back to a single Siberian population that carried only this individual "marker" as indicated in figure A.[2]

While these results are consistent with the hypothesis, it is still possible that the migrations of the different groups occurred at about the same time but from different sources in Siberia, from different peoples who do not have exactly the same mDNA structure.

What we need is a way to estimate the time that might have passed between the two proposed migrations of the Amerind- and NaDene-speaking populations. The rapid mutation rate of mDNA offers just such a possibility. When people migrated from Siberia as the first migration wave, they lost contact with the original Siberian population. As time passed, mutations would accumulate independently in the Siberian and American populations. The longer the separation, the greater the differences in the mDNA between the two populations. The mDNA, then, can act as a "molecular clock" whereby the amount of accumulated genetic mutations can measure the amount of time that has passed since migration.

Based on these concepts, we can make a specific prediction about the possibility of genetic mutations in the mDNA of the different language groups.

Prediction 3 If the Amerind- and NaDene-speaking populations represent different migrations separated by a long period of time, then mDNA from the two populations should have different amounts of genetic variability due to accumulated mutations.

Result 3 Investigations of the variation in mDNA revealed that Amerind speakers show at least three times as much variation as the NaDene speakers.

These results indicate that the Amerinds have been in the Americas much longer and represent the first migration. The NaDene would have migrated much later. Again, these results strongly support the hypothesis of at least two migration waves.

Based on Result 3 and apparent rates of mutation, scientists have estimated that the Amerind migration occurred as much as 42,000 years ago, and the NaDene migration between 12,000 and 6,000 years ago. Along with investigations in archaeology and language studies, these experiments with mDNA are making significant advances in our understanding of the migration of early Americans.

This work with the mDNA is an excellent indication of how investigations can lead to unexpected benefits. Initially, mDNA attracted attention because of the genes that might be carried in the mitochondria and how these genes might be expressed. But as we have seen, knowledge of mDNA has found highly significant application in other areas. It is impressive that disciplines as different as language studies, archaeology, and molecular genetics can work together in their investigations.

References:

1 Wilson, A. C., and Cann, R. L. 1992. The recent African genesis of humans. *Scientific American* 266(4):66.
2 Gibbons, A. 1993. Geneticists trace the DNA trail of the first Americans. *Science* 259(5093):312.

Part III
EVOLUTION

Evolution refers to descent with modification and adaptation to the environment. Descent with modification explains the unity of life—living things share a common chemistry and cellular structure because they are all descended from an original source. Each type of living thing has a history that can be traced by way of the fossil record and discerned from a comparative study of other living things. Human evolution can also be understood by the application of evolutionary principles.

Adaptation to the environment explains the diversity of life as a process that can now be understood in terms of modern genetics. Genetic changes produce the variations that result in the origination of new species (a group that cannot reproduce with other groups no matter how similar in appearance).

Each species is adapted to its environment, reproduces in a particular way, and has unique, evolved solutions to life's problems such as acquiring nutrients. Natural selection is a mechanism that brings about adaptation to the environment.

A moth, *Phalera*, that looks like a twig shows how closely an organism can be adapted through the evolutionary process to avoid predation.

Many of the figures and concepts discussed in *Biology,* fifth edition, are further explored in technology products. The following is a list of figures in part III that correlates to technology products.

A set of five videotapes contains 53 animations of physiological processes integral to the study of biology. These videotapes, entitled *Life Science Animations*, cover such topics as chemistry, genetics, and reproduction. A videotape icon appears in appropriate figure legends to alert the reader to these animations.

Explorations in Human Biology and *Explorations in Cell Biology, Metabolism, and Genetics* by George B. Johnson are interactive CD-ROMs with activities that can be used by an instructor in lecture and/or placed in a lab or resource center for student use. This interactive software consists of modules that cover key topics discussed in a biology course. The CD-ROMs are available for use with Macintosh and IBM Windows computers. A CD-ROM icon appears in appropriate figure legends to alert the reader to these activities.

Corresponding Figures	Videotape Concepts	CD-Rom Modules
21.7 History of continent placement	53. Continental Drift and Plate Tectonics	—
21.8 Plate tectonics	53. Continental Drift and Plate Tectonics	—

19

DARWIN AND EVOLUTION

Learning Objectives

The World Was Ready

- Show that scientific world views were beginning to change during the eighteenth century.   295–96
- Contrast the prevalent pre-Darwinian views with post-Darwinian views.   295
- Describe the catastrophe hypothesis of Cuvier.   296
- Describe Lamarck's theory of evolution, and tell which aspects of his theory were incorrect.   296

Darwin Develops a Theory

- Describe Charles Darwin's background and the path of the voyage of the HMS *Beagle*.   297

- Explain how the study of geology and fossils influenced Darwin's thinking.   297
- Explain how the study of biogeography influenced Darwin's thinking.   298–99
- Describe natural selection as a process that results in adaptation to the environment.   300

Evidences Accumulate

- Explain how the fossil record, biogeography, comparative anatomy, and comparative biochemistry support a hypothesis of common descent.   304–7

Fossils, such as this *Triceratops* skull, give evidence of evolution because they tell us that life forms of the past are not the same as those of today.

harles Darwin was only twenty-two in 1831 when he accepted the position of naturalist aboard the HMS *Beagle*, a British naval ship about to sail around the world (fig. 19.1). The captain was hopeful that Darwin would find evidence of the biblical account of creation. The results of Darwin's observations were just the opposite, however, as we shall examine later in the chapter.

Table 19.1 tells us that prior to Darwin, people had an entirely different way of looking at the world. Their mind-set was determined by deep-seated beliefs held to be intractable truths. To turn from these beliefs and accept the Darwinian view of the world required an intellectual revolution of great magnitude. This revolution was fostered by changes in both the scientific and the social realms. Here, we will only touch on a few of the scientific contributions that helped bring about the new world view.

Figure 19.1

Darwin's trip. **a.** Map shows the journey of the HMS *Beagle* around the world. Notice the encircled colors are keyed to the frames of the photographs, which show us what Darwin may have observed. **b.** As Darwin traveled along the east coast of South America he noted that a bird called a rhea, *Rhea,* looked like the African ostrich. **c.** The sparse vegetation of the Patagonian Desert is in the southern part of the continent. **d.** The Andes Mountains of the west coast, with strata containing fossilized animals. **e.** The lush vegetation of a rain forest. **f.** On the Galápagos Islands, marine iguanas, *Iguana,* have large claws to help them cling to rocks and blunt snouts for eating seaweed. **g.** Galápagos finches are specialized to feed on various foods.

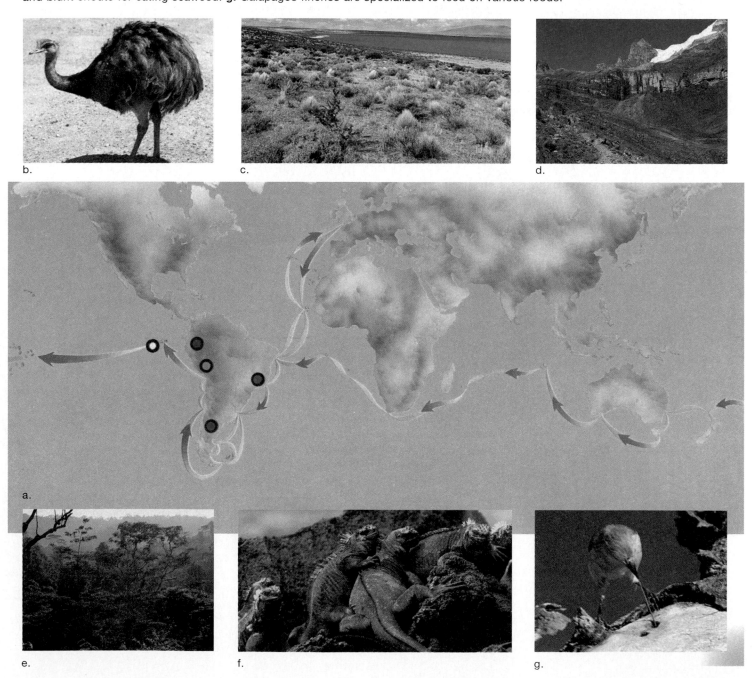

Table 19.1

Contrast of World Views

Pre-Darwinian View	Post-Darwinian View
1. Earth is relatively young—age is measured in thousands of years.	1. Earth is relatively old—age is measured in billions of years.
2. Each species is specially created; species don't change, and the number of species remains the same.	2. Species are related by descent—it is possible to piece together a history of life on earth.
3. Adaptation to the environment is the work of a creator, who decided the structure and function of each type of organism. Any variations are imperfections.	3. Adaptation to the environment is the interplay of random genetic variations and environmental conditions.
4. Observations are supposed to substantiate the prevailing world view.	4. Observation and experimentation are used to test hypotheses, including hypotheses about evolution.

Although it is often believed that Darwin forged this change in world view by himself, biologists during the preceding century had slowly begun to accept the idea of **evolution** [L. *evolut,* an unrolling], that is, that species change with time. As mentioned on page 292, evolution explains the unity and diversity of life. Living things share common charactcristics because they are descended from common ancestors. Living things are diverse because each species is adapted to its habitat and way of life. We will see that the history of evolutionary thought is a history of ideas about descent and adaptation. Darwin himself used the expression "descent with modification," by which he meant that as descent occurs so does diversification. He saw the process of adaptation as the means by which diversification comes about.

THE WORLD WAS READY

Mid-Eighteenth-Century Contributions

Taxonomy, the science of classifying organisms, was an important endeavor during the mid-eighteenth century. Chief among the taxonomists was Carolus Linnaeus (1707–78), who gave us the binomial system of nomenclature (a two-part name for species, such as *Homo sapiens*) and who developed a system of classification for all known plants. Linnaeus, like other taxonomists of his time, believed in the ideas of *special creation* and *fixity of species* (fig. 19.2). He thought each species had an "ideal" structure and function and also a place in the *scala naturae,* a sequential ladder of life. The simplest and most material of beings was on the first rung of the ladder, and the most complex and most spiritual of beings was on the last rung. Human beings occupied the last rung of the ladder.

These ideas were Christian dogma, which can be traced to the works of the famous Greek philosophers Plato and Aristotle. Plato said that every object on earth was an imperfect copy of an ideal form, which can be deduced upon re-

Figure 19.2

Linnaeus. For the most part, Linnaeus believed that each species was created separately and that classification should reveal God's divine plan. Variations were imperfections of no real consequence.

flection and study. To Plato, individual variations were imperfections that only distract the observer. Aristotle saw that organisms were diverse, and some were more complex than others. His belief that all organisms could be arranged in order of increasing complexity became the *scala naturae* just described.

Linnaeus and other taxonomists wanted to describe the ideal characteristics of each species and also wanted to discover the proper place for each species in the *scala naturae.* Therefore, Linnaeus did not even consider the possibility of evolutionary change for most of his working life. Even so, there is evidence he did eventually perform hybridization experiments, which made him think that at least species, if not higher categories of classification, might change with time.

Georges-Louis Leclerc, better known by his title, Comte de Buffon (1707–88), was a French naturalist who devoted many years of his life to writing a forty-four-volume natural history that described all known plants and animals. He provided evidence of descent with modification, and he even speculated on various mechanisms. Throughout his writings, he mentioned that the following factors could influence evolutionary change: direct influences of the environment, migration, geographical isolation, overcrowding, and the struggle for existence. Buffon seemed to vacillate, however, as to whether or not he believed in evolutionary descent, and often he professed to believe in special creation and the fixity of species.

Erasmus Darwin (1731–1802), Charles Darwin's grandfather, was a physician and a naturalist. His writings on both botany and zoology contained many comments, although they were mostly in footnotes and asides, that suggested the possibility of common descent. He based his conclusions on changes undergone by animals during development, artificial selection by humans, and the presence of vestigial organs (organs that are believed to have been functional in an ancestor but are reduced and nonfunctional in a descendant). Like Buffon, Erasmus Darwin offered no mechanism by which evolutionary descent might occur.

Figure 19.3

Artist's re-creation of a *Mastodon,* known only from the fossil record. Cuvier reconstructed the structure of a *Mastodon* when given only a single fossil bone. He said these animals were shorter than modern elephants but had massive, pillarlike legs. The skull was lower and flatter and of generally simpler construction than in modern elephants.

Figure 19.4

Lamarck's contribution. Lamarck is most famous for suggesting that the long neck of the giraffe is due to continual stretching to reach food. Each generation of giraffes stretched a little farther and this was passed to the next generation. With the advent of modern genetics, it became possible to explain why this supposed inheritance of acquired characteristics would not be possible.

Late Eighteenth-Century Contributions

Cuvier and Catastrophism

In addition to taxonomy, comparative anatomy was of interest to biologists prior to Darwin. Explorers and collectors traveled the world and brought back not only currently existing species to be classified but also fossils (remains of once-living organisms), to be studied. Georges Cuvier (1769–1832), a distinguished vertebrate (animals with backbones) zoologist, was the first to use comparative anatomy to develop a system of classifying animals. He also founded the science of **paleontology** [Gk. *paleo,* ancient, and *logy,* study of], the study of fossils, and suggested that a single fossil bone was all he needed to deduce the entire anatomy of an animal (fig. 19.3).

Because Cuvier was a staunch advocate of special creation and fixity of species, he faced a real problem when geological evidence of a particular region showed a succession of life forms in the earth's strata (layers). To explain these observations, he hypothesized that a series of local catastrophes or mass extinctions had occurred whenever a new stratum of that region showed a new mix of fossils. After each catastrophe, the region was repopulated by species from surrounding areas, and this accounted for the appearance of new fossils in the new stratum. The result of all these catastrophes was the appearance of change with time. Some of his followers even suggested that there had been worldwide catastrophes and that after each of these events, God created new sets of species. This explanation of the history of life came to be known as **catastrophism** [Gk. *cata,* downward, and *trop,* change].

Lamarck's Theory of Evolution

Jean-Baptiste de Lamarck (1744–1829) was the first biologist to clearly support common descent and to link diversity with adaptation to the environment. Lamarck's ideas about descent were entirely different from those of Cuvier, perhaps because he was an invertebrate (animals without backbones) zoologist. Lamarck concluded, after studying the succession of life forms in strata, that more complex organisms are descended from less complex organisms. He mistakenly said, however, that increasing complexity was the result of a natural force—a tendency toward perfection—that was inherent in all living things.

To explain the process of adaptation to the environment, Lamarck proposed a hypothesis that was prevalent in his day. He supported the idea of **inheritance of acquired characteristics.** One example that he gave—and for which he is most famous—is that the long neck of a giraffe developed over time because animals stretched their necks to reach food high in trees and then passed on a long neck to their offspring (fig. 19.4). The inheritance of acquired characteristics has never been substantiated by experimentation. The molecular mechanism of inheritance explains why. Phenotypic changes acquired during an organism's lifetime do not result in genetic changes that can be passed to subsequent generations.

Figure 19.5

Formation of sedimentary rock. **a.** This diagram shows how water brings sediments into the sea; the sediments then become compacted to form sedimentary rock. Fossils are often trapped in this rock, and as a result of a later geological upheaval, the rock may be located on what is now land. **b.** Fossil freshwater snails, *Turritella*.

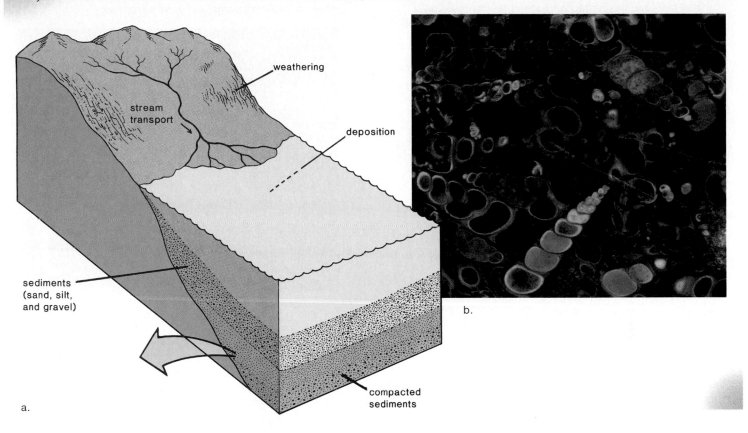

DARWIN DEVELOPS A THEORY

When Darwin signed on as naturalist aboard the HMS *Beagle*, he had a suitable background for the position. He was an ardent student of nature and had long been a collector of insects. His sensitive nature prevented him from studying medicine, and he went to divinity school at Cambridge instead. Even so, he attended many lectures in both biology and geology, and he was also tutored in these subjects by a friend and teacher, the Reverend John Henslow. As a result of arrangements made by Henslow, Darwin spent the summer of 1831 doing field work with Adam Sedgwick, a geologist at Cambridge, and it was Henslow who recommended Darwin for the post aboard the HMS *Beagle*. The trip was to take five years, and the ship was to traverse the Southern Hemisphere (see fig. 19.1), where life is most abundant and varied. Along the way, Darwin encountered forms of life very different from those in his native England.

Descent Does Occur

Although it was not his original intent, Darwin began to gather evidence that common descent does occur and that adaptation to various environments results in diversity.

Geology and Fossils Help Darwin Decide

Darwin took Charles Lyell's *Principles of Geology* on the voyage, which presented arguments to support a theory of geological change proposed by James Hutton. In contrast to the catastrophists, Hutton believed the earth was subject to slow but continuous cycles of erosion and uplift. Weather causes erosion; thereafter dirt and rock debris are washed into the rivers and transported to oceans. These loose sediments are deposited in thick layers, which are converted eventually into sedimentary rocks (fig. 19.5). Then sedimentary rocks, which often contain fossils, are uplifted from below sea level to form land. Hutton concluded that extreme geological changes can be accounted for by slow, natural processes, given enough time. Lyell went on to suggest that these slow changes occurred at a uniform rate. Hutton's general ideas about slow and continual geological change are still accepted today, although modern geologists realize that rates of change have not always been uniform. Darwin was not taken by the idea of uniform change, but he was convinced, as was Lyell, that the earth's massive geological changes are the result of slow processes and that the earth, therefore, must be very old.

Figure 19.6

Glyptodont compared to an armadillo. **a.** A giant armadillo-like glyptodont, *Glyptodon,* known only by the study of its fossil remains. Darwin found such fossils and came to the conclusion that this extinct animal must be related to living armadillos. The glyptodont weighed 2,000 kg. **b.** A modern armadillo, *Dasypus,* weighs about 4.5 kg.

a.

b.

Figure 19.7

The Patagonian hare, *Dolichotis patagonium.* This animal has the face of a guinea pig and is native to South America, which has no native rabbits. The hare has long legs and other adaptations similar to those of rabbits.

On his trip, Darwin observed massive geological changes firsthand. When he explored what is now Argentina, he saw raised beaches for great distances along the coast. When he got to the Andes, he was impressed by their great height. In Chile, he found marine shells inland, well above sea level, and witnessed the effects of an earthquake that caused the land to rise several feet. While Darwin was making geological observations, he also collected fossil specimens. For example, on the east coast of South America, he found the fossil remains of a giant ground sloth and an armadillo-like animal (fig. 19.6). Darwin accepted the supposition that the earth must be very old, and he began to think that there would have been enough time for descent with modification to occur. Therefore, living forms must be descended from extinct forms known only from the fossil record. It would seem that species were not fixed; instead they changed over time.

> Darwin's geological observations were consistent with those of Hutton and Lyell. He began to think that the earth was very old and there would have been enough time for descent with modification to occur.

Biogeography Also Helps

Biogeography [Gk. *bio,* life, *geo,* earth, and *graph,* writing] is the study of the geographic distribution of life forms on earth. Darwin could not help but compare the animals of South America to those with which he was familiar. For example, instead of rabbits he found the Patagonian hare in the grasslands of South America. The Patagonian hare has long legs and ears but the face of a guinea pig, a rodent native to South America (fig. 19.7). Did the Patagonian hare resemble a rabbit because the two types of animals were adapted to the same type of environment? Both animals ate grass, hid in bushes, and moved rapidly using long hind legs. Did the Patagonian hare have the face of a guinea pig because of common descent?

As he sailed southward along the continent of South America, Darwin saw how similar species replaced each other. For example, the greater rhea (an ostrich–like bird) found in the north was replaced by the lesser rhea in the south. Therefore, Darwin reasoned that related species could be modified according to the environment. When he got to the Galápagos Islands he found further evidence of this. The Galápagos Islands are a small group of volcanic islands off the western coast of South America. The few types of plants and animals found there were slightly different from species Darwin had observed on the mainland, and even more important, they also varied from island to island.

Darwin Observes Tortoises

Each of the Galápagos Islands seemed to have its own type of tortoise, and Darwin began to wonder if this could be correlated with a difference in vegetation among islands (fig. 19.8). Long-necked tortoises seemed to inhabit only dry areas, where food was scarce, most likely because the longer neck was helpful in reaching cacti. In moist regions with relatively abundant ground foliage, short-necked tortoises were found. Had an ancestral tortoise given rise to these different types, each adapted to a different environment?

Darwin Observes Finches

Although the finches on the Galápagos Islands seemed to Darwin like mainland finches, there are many more types (fig. 19.9).

Figure 19.8

Galápagos tortoises, *Testudo*. Darwin wondered if all of the tortoises of the various islands were descended from a common ancestor. **a.** The tortoises with dome shells and short necks feed at ground level and are from well-watered islands where grass is available. **b.** Those with shells that flare up in front have long necks and are able to feed on tall treelike cacti. They are from arid islands where prickly pear cactus is the main food source. Only on these islands are the cacti treelike.

a.   b.

Figure 19.9

Galápagos finches. Each of the present-day thirteen species of finches has a bill adapted to a particular way of life. **a.** For example, the large, tree-dwelling finch grinds fruit and insects with a parrotlike bill. **b.** The small, ground-dwelling finch has a pointed bill and eats tiny seeds and ticks picked from iguanas. **c.** The woodpecker-type finch has a stout, straight bill, which chisels through tree bark to uncover insects. But because it lacks the woodpecker's long tongue it uses a tool—usually a cactus spine or a small twig—to ferret out insects.

a. *Camarhychus psittucula*   b. *Geospiza fuliginosa*   c. *Camarhynchus pallidus*

Today, there are ground-dwelling finches with different-sized beaks, depending on the size of the seeds they feed on, and a cactus-eating finch with a more pointed beak. The beak size of the tree-dwelling finches also varies but according to the size of their insect prey. The most unusual of the finches is a woodpecker-type finch. This bird has a sharp beak to chisel through tree bark but lacks the woodpecker's long tongue to probe for insects. To make up for this, the bird carries a twig or cactus thorn in its beak and uses it to poke into crevices. Once an insect emerges, the finch drops this tool and seizes the insect with its beak.

Later, Darwin speculated whether all the different species of finches he saw could have descended from a type of mainland finch. In other words, he wondered if a mainland finch was the common ancestor to all the types on the Galápagos Islands. Had speciation occurred because the islands allowed isolated populations of birds to evolve independently? Could the present-day species have resulted from accumulated changes occurring within each of these isolated populations?

> Biogeography had a powerful influence on Darwin and made him think that adaptation to the environment accounts for diversification; one species can give rise to many species, each adapted differently.

Natural Selection Provides a Mechanism

Once Darwin decided that adaptations develop over time (instead of being the instant work of a creator), he began to think about a mechanism by which adaptations might arise. Both Darwin and Alfred Russel Wallace, who is discussed in the reading on page 301, proposed natural selection as a mechanism for evolutionary change. **Natural selection** brings about adaptation to the environment, but it has no particular goal because environmental conditions are constantly changing. Therefore, perfect adaptation is not a probable outcome of natural selection.

Natural selection is a process in which preconditions (1–3) may result in certain consequences (4–5):

1. The members of a population have heritable variations.
2. In a population, many more individuals are produced each generation than can survive and reproduce.
3. Some individuals have adaptive characteristics that enable them to survive and reproduce better than do other individuals.
4. An increasing proportion of individuals in succeeding generations have the adaptive characteristics.
5. The result of natural selection is a population adapted to its local environment.

Organisms Have Variations

Darwin emphasized that the members of a population vary in their functional, physical, and behavioral characteristics (fig. 19.10). Before Darwin (table 19.1), variations were imperfections that should be ignored since they were not important to the description of a species. For Darwin, variations were essential to the natural selection process. Darwin suspected—but did not have the evidence we have today—that the occurrence of variations is completely random; they arise by accident and for no particular purpose. New variations are just as likely to be harmful as helpful to the organism.

The variations that make adaptation to the environment possible are those that are passed on from generation to generation. The science of genetics was not yet well established, so Darwin was never able to determine the cause of variations or how they are passed on. Today, we realize that genes determine the phenotype of an organism, and that mutations and recombination of alleles during sexual reproduction can cause new variations to arise.

Organisms Struggle to Exist

In Darwin's time, a socioeconomist, Thomas Malthus, stressed the reproductive potential of human beings. He proposed that death and famine were inevitable because the human population tends to increase faster than the supply of food. Darwin applied this concept to all organisms and saw that the available resources were not sufficient for all members of a population to survive. He calculated the reproductive potential of elephants. Assuming a life span of about 100 years and a breeding span of from 30–90 years, a single female probably bears no fewer than six young. If

Figure 19.10
Variations among individuals of a human population. For Darwin, variations were highly significant and were required for natural selection to result in greater adaptation to the environment.

all these young survive and continue to reproduce at the same rate, after only 750 years, the descendants of a single pair of elephants will number about 19 million!

Each generation has the same reproductive potential as the previous generation. Therefore, there is a constant struggle for existence, and only certain members of a population survive and reproduce each generation.

Organisms Differ in Fitness

Fitness is the ability of an organism to survive and reproduce in its local (immediate) environment. The most fit individuals are the ones that survive, that capture a disproportionate amount of resources, and that convert these resources into a larger number of viable offspring. Since organisms vary anatomically and physiologically and the challenges of local environments vary, what determines fitness varies for different populations. For example, among western diamondback rattlesnakes (*Crotalus atrox*) living on lava flows, the most fit are those that are black in color. But among those living on desert soil, the most fit are those with the typical light and dark brown coloring. Background matching helps an animal both capture prey and avoid being captured; therefore, it is expected to lead to survival and increased reproduction.

Alfred Russel Wallace

Alfred Russel Wallace (1823–1913) is best known as the English naturalist who independently proposed natural selection as a process to explain the origin of species (fig. 19A). Like Darwin, Wallace was a collector at home and abroad. Even at age fourteen, while learning the trade of surveying, he became interested in botany and started collecting plants. While he was a school teacher at Leicester in 1844–45, he met Henry Walter Bates, an entomologist, who interested him in insects. Together they went on a collecting trip to the Amazon, which lasted for several years. Wallace's knowledge of the world's extensive flora and fauna was much expanded by a tour he made of the Malay Archipelago from 1854–62. After studying the animals of every important island, he divided the islands into a western group, with animals like those of the Orient, and an eastern group, with animals like those of Australia. The dividing line between the islands of the archipelago is a narrow but deep strait that is now known as the Wallace Line.

Like Darwin, Wallace was a writer of articles and books. As a result of his trip to the Amazon, he wrote two books, entitled *Travels on the Amazon and Rio Negro* and *Palm Trees of the Amazon.* In 1855, during his trip to Malay, he wrote an essay called "On the Law Which Has Regulated the Introduction of New Species." In the essay, he said that "every species has come into existence coincident both in time and space with a preexisting closely allied species." It's clear, then, that by this date he believed in the origin of new species rather than the fixity of species. Later, he said that he had pondered for many years about a mechanism to explain the origin of species. He, too, had read Malthus's treatise on human population increases and, in 1858, while suffering an attack of malaria, the idea of "survival of the fittest" came upon him. He quickly completed an essay discussing a natural selection process, which he chose to send to Darwin for comment. Darwin was stunned upon its receipt. Here before him was the hypothesis he had formulated as

early as 1844 but had never dared to publish. In 1856 he had begun to work on a book that would supply copious data to support natural selection as a mechanism for evolutionary change. He told his friend and colleague Charles Lyell that Wallace's ideas were so similar to his own that even Wallace's "terms now stand as heads of my chapters."

Darwin suggested that Wallace's paper be published immediately, even though he as yet had nothing in print. Lyell and others who knew of Darwin's detailed work substantiating the process of natural selection suggested that a joint paper be read to the Linnean society. The title of Wallace's section was "On the Tendency of Varieties to Depart Indefinitely from the Original Type." Darwin presented an abstract of a paper he had written in 1844 and an abstract of his book *On the Origin of Species,* which was published in 1859.

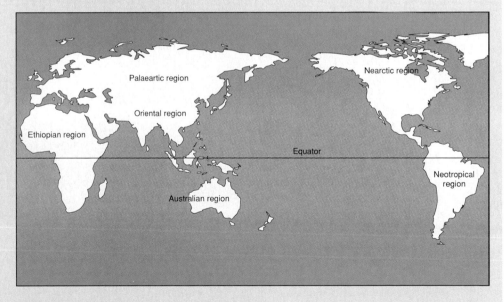

Figure 19A

Alfred Russel Wallace. Wallace was far from England in the Malay Archipelago when he formulated a hypothesis of natural selection to explain the origin of new species. His proposal matched that of Charles Darwin almost exactly, and they jointly presented a paper before the Linnean society in 1858. When Wallace returned home he wrote a book in which he said that the world can be divided into six biogeographical regions separated by impassable barriers. The deep waters between the Oriental and Australian regions are called the Wallace Line.

Figure 19.11

Artificial selection of dogs. All dogs are descended from the wolf, *Canis lupus*, which began to be domesticated about 14,000 years ago. In evolutionary terms, the process of diversification has been exceptionally rapid. Several factors may have contributed: (1) the wolves under domestication were separated from other wolves because human settlements were separate, and (2) humans in each tribe selected for whatever traits appealed to them. Artificial selection of dogs continues even today.

red chow

dalmation

Chihuahua

bloodhound

French bulldog

Shetland sheepdog

beagle

Boston terrier

Darwin noted that when humans help carry out artificial selection, they select the animals that will reproduce. For example, prehistoric humans probably noted desirable variations among wolves and selected particular animals for breeding. Therefore, the desirable traits increased in frequency in the next generation. This same process was repeated many times over. The result today is that there are many varieties of dogs all descended from the wolf (fig. 19.11). In a similar way, several varieties of vegetables can be traced to a single ancestor (fig. 19.12).

In nature, interactions with the environment determine which members of a population reproduce to a greater degree than other members. In contrast to artificial selection, the result of natural selection is not predesired. Natural selection occurs because certain members of a population happen to have a variation that allows them to survive and/or capture resources. For example, any variation that increases the speed of a hoofed animal helps it escape predators and live longer; a variation that reduces water loss helps a desert plant survive; and one that increases the sense of smell helps a wild dog find its prey. Therefore, we expect organisms with these traits to have increased fitness. *Differential reproduction* occurs when the most fit organisms reproduce and leave more offspring than the less fit.

Organisms Become Adapted

An **adaptation** [L. *ad,* toward, and *apt,* adjust] is a trait that helps an organism be more suited to its environment. We can especially recognize an adaptation when unrelated organisms, living in a particular environment, display similar character-istics. For example, manatees, penguins, and sea turtles all have flippers, which help them move through the water. Natural selection results in the adaptation of populations to their specific environments. Because of differential reproduction generation after generation, adaptive traits are disproportionately represented in each succeeding generation. There are other processes of evolution aside from natural selection, but natural selection is the only process that results in adaptation to the environment.

Darwin Writes a Book

After the HMS *Beagle* returned to England in 1836, Darwin waited over twenty years to publish his ideas. During the intervening years, he used the scientific process to test his hypothesis that today's diverse life forms arose by descent from a common ancestor and that natural selection is a mechanism by which species can change and even new species can arise. Darwin was prompted to publish his book after reading a similar hypothesis from Alfred Russel Wallace, as discussed in the reading on page 301.

Darwin became convinced that descent with modification explains the history of life. His theory of natural selection proposes a mechanism by which adaptation to the environment occurs.

Figure 19.12

Vegetables derived from a single species of *Brassica oleracea.* **a.** Chinese cabbage. **b.** Brussels sprouts. **c.** Kohlrabi. Darwin believed that artificial selection provided a model by which to understand natural selection. With natural selection, however, the environment provides the selective force.

a.

b.

c.

EVIDENCE ACCUMULATES

Many different lines of evidence support the hypothesis of common descent. This is significant, because the more varied the evidence supporting a hypothesis, the more certain it becomes. Darwin cited much of the evidence we will discuss, except he had no knowledge, of course, of the biochemical data that became available after his time.

Fossils Tell a Story

The fossil record is the history of life as recorded by remains from the past. Fossils are at least 10,000 years old and include such items as pieces of bone, impressions of plants pressed into shale, and even insects trapped in tree resin (which we know as amber). Over the last two centuries, paleontologists have studied fossils in the earth's strata (layers) all over the world and have pieced together the story of past life.

The fossil record is rich in information. One of its most striking patterns is the succession of life forms over time. Catastrophists offered an explanation for the extinction and subsequent replacement of one group of organisms by another group, but they never could explain successive changes that link groups of organisms historically. Particularly interesting are the fossils that serve as transitional links between groups. For example, the famous fossils of *Archaeopteryx* are intermediate between reptiles and birds (fig. 19.13). The dinosaurlike skeleton of this fossil has reptilian features, including jaws with teeth and a long, jointed tail, but *Archaeopteryx* also had feathers and wings. Other intermediate fossils among the fossil vertebrates include the amphibious fish *Eustheopteron*, the reptile-like amphibian *Seymouria,* and the mammal-like reptiles, or therapsids. These fossils allow us to deduce that fishes preceded amphibians which preceded reptiles which preceded both birds and mammals in the history of life.

Sometimes, the fossil record allows us to trace the history of one particular organism, such as the modern-day horse, *Equus. Equus* evolved originally from *Hyracotherium,* which was about the size of a dog. This fossil animal had cusped, low-crowned molars, four toes on each front foot, and three toes on each hind foot. When grasslands replaced the forest home of *Hyracotherium,* the ancestors of *Equus* were subject to selective pressure for the development of strength, intelligence, speed, and durable grinding teeth. A larger size provided the strength needed for combat, a larger skull made room for a larger brain, elongated legs ending in hooves provided greater speed to escape enemies, and the durable grinding teeth enabled the animals to feed efficiently on grasses. In all cases, living organisms closely resemble the most recent fossils in their line of descent. Underlying similarities, however, allow us to trace a line of descent over vast amounts of time.

The evidence supports the common descent hypothesis. Fossils can be linked over time because they show a similarity in form, despite observed changes.

> The fossil record broadly traces the history of life and more specifically allows us to study the history of particular groups.

Figure 19.13

Transitional fossils. **a.** This is *Archaeopteryx,* a transitional link between reptiles and birds. It had feathers and wing claws. Most likely, it was a poor flier. Perhaps it ran over the ground on strong legs and climbed up into trees with the assistance of these claws. **b.** It also had a feather-covered reptilian-type tail, that shows up well in this artist's representation of the animal.

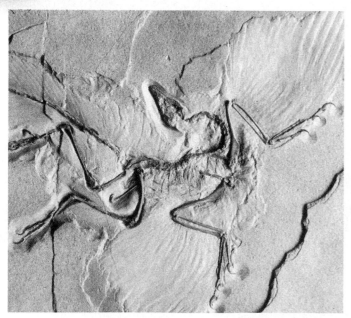

a.

b.

Biogeographical Separations

Biogeography is the study of the distribution of plants and animals throughout the world. Such distributions are consistent with the hypothesis that related forms evolved in one locale and then spread out into other accessible regions. As previously mentioned, Darwin noted that South America lacked rabbits, even though the environment was quite suitable to them. He concluded there are no rabbits in South America because rabbits originated somewhere else and they had no means to reach South America.

The islands of the world have many unique species of animals and plants found no place else, even when the soil and climate are the same as other places. Why are there so many species of finches on the Galápagos Islands when these same species are not on the mainland? The reasonable explanation is that they are all descended from a common ancestor that came to the islands by chance.

Physical factors, such as the location of continents, often determine where a population can spread. Both cacti and euphorbia are plants adapted similarly to a hot, dry environment—they both are succulent, spiny, flowering plants. Why do cacti grow in North American deserts and euphorbia grow in African deserts when each would do well on the other continent? It seems obvious that they just happened to evolve on their respective continents.

At one time in the history of the earth, South America, Antarctica, and Australia were all connected. Marsupials (pouched mammals) arose at this time and today are found in both South America and Australia. When Australia separated and drifted away, the marsupials diversified into many different forms suited to various environments (fig. 19.14). They were free to do so because there were no placental mammals in Australia. In other regions such as South America, where there are placental mammals, marsupials are not as diverse.

> The distribution of organisms on the earth is explainable by assuming that related forms evolved in one locale, where they then diversify and/or spread out into other accessible areas.

Figure 19.14

Marsupials from Australia. Each type of marsupial is adapted to a different way of life. All of the marsupials in Australia presumably evolved from a common ancestor that entered Australia some 60 million years ago.

Course–haired wombat, *Vombatus,* nocturnal and living in burrows

Sugar glider, *Petaurista,* a tree dweller

Kangaroo, *Macropus,* a herbivore of plains and forests

Australian native cat, *Dasyurus,* a carnivore of forests

Tasmanian wolf, *Thylacinus,* a nocturnal carnivore of deserts and plains

Figure 19.15

Bones of the vertebrate forelimbs. Although the specific design details of the limbs are different, the same bones are present (they are color-coded). This unity of plan is evidence of a common ancestor.

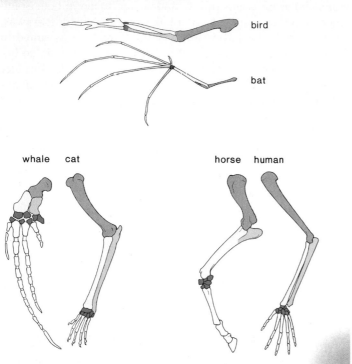

Anatomical Similarities

Darwin was able to show that a common descent hypothesis offers a plausible explanation for anatomical similarities among organisms. Vertebrate forelimbs are used for flight (birds and bats), orientation during swimming (whales and seals), running (horses), climbing (arboreal lizards), or swinging from tree branches (monkeys). Yet all vertebrate forelimbs contain the same sets of bones organized in similar ways, despite their dissimilar functions (fig. 19.15). The most plausible explanation for this unity is that the basic forelimb plan originated with a common ancestor, and then the plan was modified in the succeeding groups as each continued along its own evolutionary pathway. Structures that are similar because they were inherited from a common ancestor are called **homologous structures** [Gk. *homo,* alike].

Vestigial structures [L. *vestig,* trace] are anatomical features that are fully developed in one group of organisms but are reduced and may have no function in similar groups. Most birds, for example, have well-developed wings used for flight. Some bird species (e.g., ostrich), however, have wings that are greatly reduced, and they do not fly. Similarly, snakes have no use for hindlimbs, and yet some have remnants of a pelvic girdle and legs. Humans have a tail bone but no tail. The presence of vestigial structures can be explained by the common descent hypothesis. Vestigial structures occur because organisms inherit their anatomy from their ancestors; they are traces of an organism's evolutionary history.

Figure 19.16

a. A chick embryo. **b.** A pig embryo. At these comparable early developmental stages, the two have many features in common, although eventually they are completely different animals. This is evidence that they evolved from a common ancestor.

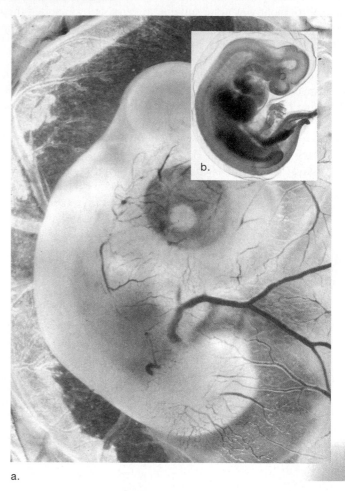

a.

The unity of plan shared by vertebrates extends to their embryological development (fig. 19.16). At some time during development, all vertebrates have a supporting dorsal rod, called a notochord, and exhibit paired pharyngeal pouches. In fishes and amphibian larvae, these pouches develop into functioning gills. In humans, the first pair of pouches becomes the cavity of the middle ear and the eustachian tube. The second pair becomes the tonsils, while the third and fourth pairs become the thymus and parathyroid glands. Why should terrestrial vertebrates develop and then modify structures like pharyngeal pouches that have lost their original function? The most likely explanation is that fishes are ancestral to other vertebrate groups.

> Organisms share a unity of plan when they are closely related because of common descent. This is substantiated by comparative anatomy and embryological development.

Biochemical Differences

Almost all living organisms use the same basic biochemical molecules, including DNA (deoxyribonucleic acid), ATP (adenosine triphosphate), and many identical or nearly identical enzymes. Further, organisms utilize the same DNA triplet code and the same twenty amino acids in their proteins. Organisms even share the same introns and hypervariable regions. There is obviously no functional reason why these elements need be so similar. But their similarity can be explained by descent from a common ancestor.

When the degree of similarity in DNA base sequences or the degree of similarity in amino acid sequences of proteins is examined, the data are as expected assuming common descent. Cytochrome c is a molecule that is used in the electron transport system of all the organisms listed in figure 19.17. Data regarding differences in the amino acid sequence of the cytochrome c show that in a human it differs from that in a monkey by only one amino acid; from that in a duck by eleven, and from that in *Candida*, a yeast, by fifty-one amino acids. These data are consistent with other data regarding the anatomical similarities of these animals and, therefore, their relatedness.

> Darwin discovered that many lines of evidence support the hypothesis of common descent. Since his time, it has been found that biochemical evidence also supports the hypothesis. A hypothesis is strengthened when it is supported by many different lines of evidence.

Evolution is no longer considered a hypothesis. It is one of the great unifying theories of biology. In science, the word *theory* is reserved for those conceptual schemes that are supported by a large number of observations and have not yet been found lacking. The theory of evolution has the same status in biology that the germ theory of disease has in medicine.

Figure 19.17

Cytochrome c diversity. This diagram shows the amino acid differences in cytochrome c among the organisms listed. The number where the two organisms intersect (see listing on bottom and sides) indicates the number of amino acid differences.

	human	monkey	pig, bovine, sheep	horse	dog	rabbit	kangaroo	chicken, turkey	duck	rattlesnake	turtle	tuna fish	moth	Neurospora	typical yeast Saccharomyces	Candida
human	0															
monkey	1	0														
pig, bovine, sheep	10	9	0													
horse	12	11	3	0												
dog	11	10	3	6	0											
rabbit	9	8	4	6	5	0										
kangaroo	10	11	6	7	7	6	0									
chicken, turkey	13	12	9	11	10	8	12	0								
duck	11	10	8	10	8	6	10	3	0							
rattlesnake	14	15	20	22	21	18	21	19	17	0						
turtle	15	14	9	11	9	9	11	8	7	22	0					
tuna fish	21	21	17	19	18	17	18	17	17	26	18	0				
moth	31	30	27	29	25	26	28	28	27	31	28	32	0			
Neurospora	48	47	46	46	46	46	49	47	46	47	49	48	47	0		
typical yeast Saccharomyces	45	45	45	46	45	45	46	46	46	47	49	47	47	41	0	
Candida	51	51	50	51	49	50	51	51	51	51	53	48	47	42	27	0

Summary

1. Charles Darwin formulated hypotheses concerning evolution after taking a trip around the world as naturalist aboard the HMS *Beagle* (1831–36). His hypotheses were that common descent does occur and that natural selection results in adaptation to the environment.

2. In general, the pre-Darwinian world view was different from the post-Darwinian world view (see table 19.1). The scientific community, however, was ready for Darwin's hypothesis, which received widespread acceptance.

3. A century before Darwin's trip, classification of organisms had been a main concern of biology. In keeping with the pre-Darwinian world view, Linnaeus thought that classification should describe the fixed features of species and reveal God's divine plan. Gradually, some naturalists, such as Comte de Buffon and Erasmus Darwin, began to put forth tentative suggestions that species do change over time.

4. Georges Cuvier and Jean-Baptiste de Lamarck, contemporaries in the late eighteenth century, differed sharply on evolution. To explain the fossil record of a region, Cuvier proposed that a whole series of catastrophes (extinctions) and repopulations from other regions had occurred. Lamarck said that descent with modification does occur and that organisms do become adapted to their environments; however, he relied on the commonly held but erroneous beliefs (*scala naturae* and inheritance of acquired characteristics) to substantiate and provide a mechanism for evolutionary change.

5. Darwin's trip involved two primary types of observations. His study of geology and fossils caused him to concur with Lyell that the observed massive geological changes were caused by slow, continuous changes. Therefore, he concluded that the earth is old enough for descent with modification to occur.

6. Darwin's study of biogeography, including the animals of the Galápagos Islands, caused him to conclude that adaptation to the environment can cause diversification, including the origin of new species.

7. Natural selection is the mechanism Darwin proposed for how adaptation comes about. Members of a population exhibit random but inherited variations. (In contrast to the previous world view, variations are highly significant.) Relying on Malthus's ideas regarding overpopulation, Darwin stressed that there was a struggle for existence. The most fit organisms are those possessing characteristics that allow them to acquire more resources, survive, and reproduce more than the less fit. In this way, natural selection results in adaptation to a local environment.

8. The hypothesis that organisms share a common descent is supported by many lines of evidence. The fossil record, biogeography, comparative anatomy, and comparative biochemistry all support the hypothesis. A hypothesis is greatly strengthened when many different lines of evidence support it.

9. Today, the theory of evolution is one of the great unifying theories of biology because it has been supported by so many different lines of evidence.

Writing Across the Curriculum

In order to practice writing skills, students should write out the answers to any or all of the study questions and the critical thinking questions. The study questions are sequenced in the same order as the text. Answers to the objective questions, and suggested answers to the critical thinking questions, are in appendix D.

Study Questions

1. In general, contrast the pre-Darwinian world view with the post-Darwinian world view.   295

2. Cite naturalists who made contributions to biology in the mid-eighteenth century, and state their beliefs about evolutionary descent.   295

3. How did Cuvier explain the succession of life forms in the earth's strata?   296

4. What is meant by the inheritance of acquired characteristics, a hypothesis that Lamarck used to explain adaptation to the environment?   296

5. What reading did Darwin do, and what observations did he make regarding geology?   297

6. What observations did Darwin make regarding biogeography? How did these influence his conclusions about the origin of new species?   298–99

7. What are the essential features of the process of natural selection as proposed by Darwin?   300

8. Distinguish between the concepts of fitness and adaptation to the environment.   300, 303

9. How do data from the fossil record support the concept of common descent? Explain why *Equus* is vastly different from its ancestor *Hyracotherium,* which lived in a forest.   304

10. How do data from biogeography support the concept of common descent? Explain why a diverse assemblage of marsupials evolved in Australia.   305

11. How do data from comparative anatomy support the concept of common descent? Explain why vertebrate forelimbs are similar despite different functions.   306

12. How do data from biochemical studies support the concept of common descent? Explain why the sequence of amino acids in cytochrome *c* differs between two organisms.   307

Objective Questions

1. According to the theory of acquired inheritance,
   a. if a man loses his hand, then his children will also be missing a hand.
   b. changes in phenotype are passed on by way of the genotype to the next generation.
   c. organisms are able to bring about a change in their phenotype.
   d. All of these are correct.

2. Why was it helpful to Darwin to learn that Lyell thought the earth was very old?
   a. An old earth has more fossils than a new earth.
   b. It meant there was enough time for evolution to have occurred slowly.
   c. Evolution doesn't occur without upheavals.
   d. Darwin said that natural selection occurs slowly.

3. All the finches on the Galápagos Islands are
   a. completely unrelated.
   b. descended from a common ancestor.
   c. now in competition with one another because they all feed on seeds.
   d. Both a and c are correct.

4. Organisms
   a. compete with other members of their species.
   b. differ in fitness.
   c. are adapted to their environment.
   d. All of these are correct.

5. DNA nucleotide differences between organisms
   a. indicate how closely related organisms are.
   b. indicate that evolution occurs.
   c. explain why there are phenotypic differences.
   d. All of these are correct.

6. If evolution occurs, we would expect different biogeographical regions with similar environments to
   a. all contain the same mix of plants and animals.
   b. each have its own specific mix of plants and animals.
   c. have plants and animals that have similar adaptations.
   d. Both b and c are correct.

7. The fossil record offers direct evidence for common descent because you can
   a. see that the types of fossils change over time.
   b. sometimes find common ancestors.
   c. trace the ancestry of a particular group.
   d. All of these are correct.

8. Organisms adapted to the same way of life will
   a. have structures that show they share a unity of plan.
   b. have structures that need not indicate a unity of plan.
   c. live in the same biogeographical region.
   d. Both a and c are correct.

For questions 9–12, offer an explanation for each of these observations based on information in the section indicated. Write out your answer.

9. Fossils can be dated according to the strata in which they are located. See *Fossils Tell a Story, p. 304.*

10. Amphibians, reptiles, birds, and mammals all have pharyngeal pouches at some time during development. *See Anatomical Similarities, p. 306.*

11. Cacti and euphorbia exist on different continents, but both have spiny, water-storing, leafless stems. *See Biogeographical Separations, p. 305.*

12. The base sequence of DNA differs from species to species. See *Biochemical Differences, p. 307.*

Concepts and Critical Thinking

1. *All organisms share certain common characteristics because they are descended from a common ancestor.*

   What evidence do you have that organisms as different as bacteria and humans share a common ancestor?

2. *Adaptation to various environments accounts for the diversity of life.*

   The presence of vestigial structures suggests that the process of adaptation is not purposeful. Why?

3. *The scientific method consisting of hypothesis, experimentation, and conclusion has been used to test the unifying theories of biology.*

   Show that the scientific method can be used to test the concept of evolutionary descent.

adaptation An organism's modification in structure, function, or behavior which increases the likelihood of continued existence. [L. *ad,* toward, and *apt,* adjust] 303

biogeography The study of the geographical distribution of organisms. [Gk. *bio,* life, *geo,* earth, and *graph,* writing] 298

catastrophism (ka-TAS-truh-fism) The belief espoused by Cuvier that periods of catastrophic extinctions occurred, after which repopulation of surviving species took place giving the appearance of change through time. [Gk. *cata,* downward, and *trop,* change] 296

evolution The descent of organisms from common ancestors with the development of genetic and phenotypic changes over time that make them more suited to the local environment. 295

fitness The ability of an organism to survive and reproduce in its environment. 300

homologous structure In evolution, a structure that is similar in different organisms because these organisms are derived from a common ancestor. [Gk. *homo,* alike] 306

inheritance of acquired characteristics Lamarckian belief that organisms become adapted to their environment during their lifetime and pass on these adaptations to their offspring. 296

natural selection The guiding force of evolution caused by environmental selection of organisms most fit to reproduce, resulting in adaptation. 300

paleontology (pay-lee-ahn-TAHL-uh-jee) Study of fossils that results in knowledge about the history of life. [Gk. *paleo,* ancient, and *logy,* study of] 296

vestigial structure (ve-STIJ-(ee-)-ul) The remains of a structure that was functional in some ancestor but is no longer functional in the organism in question. [L. *vestig,* trace] 306

20
PROCESS OF EVOLUTION

Learning Objectives

Cheetahs, *Aacinonyx jubatus*, have undergone an evolutionary bottleneck. Their low genetic diversity is evidence that they suffered a severe population reduction in the past, and only those that survived passed on their genes.

With the rise of modern genetics, it became possible to study evolution by examining the genetics of a population. A **population** is all the members of a single species occupying a particular area at the same time. A population could be all the green frogs in a frog pond, all the field mice in a barn, or all the English daisies on a hill. The members of a population reproduce with one another to produce the next generation.

WHAT CAUSES VARIATIONS?

The members of a population vary from one another. Variations, the raw material for evolutionary change, arise by gene mutations, chromosomal mutations, and recombination.

Gene Mutations

Gene mutations provide new alleles, and therefore they are the ultimate source of variation. A gene mutation is an alteration in the DNA (deoxyribonucleic acid) nucleotide sequence of an allele. We have seen that a change in a single DNA base spells the difference between a normal hemoglobin molecule and sickle-cell hemoglobin. Also, a change in a regulatory gene can increase or decrease the expression of a structural gene.

Mutations occur at random. A mutation is like a shot in the dark; any particular gene can mutate at any particular time. This means that the occurrence of a mutation is not tied to its adaptive value, and the chance of a particular mutation is not expected to increase because the mutation is beneficial to the organism. For example, you might think that it is exposure to a drug that causes bacteria to become resistant. However, drug-resistant mutations can occur in bacteria by chance, before they are exposed to the drug.

Rather than being beneficial, a mutation can be neutral in its effect or even harmful to an organism in its present environment. Many times observed mutations seem harmful, such as those that cause human genetic disease. This may be because members of a population are so adapted to their present environment that only nonbeneficial changes are possible. As discussed later, however, some mutations may remain hidden in a diploid organism to become an important source of variation should the environment change. Or the same mutations may arise again when conditions have changed and they are now favorable mutations.

Chromosomal Mutations

Some chromosomal mutations are simply the alteration in the number of chromosomes inherited. As is well known, a person with Down syndrome has inherited three copies of chromosome 21.

Other chromosomal mutations are an alteration in the arrangement of the alleles on the chromosomes. Inversions (a segment of chromosome is inverted) and translocations (exchange of chromosomal segments between nonhomologous chromosomes) can result in altered allelic activity if the allele thereby comes under the control of a different regulatory gene. Duplication of an allele followed by a change in base sequence of one copy introduces a new allele while still retaining the old allele in the human genome. The best studied example of such an event concerns the globin alleles that occur at different loci but have similar DNA sequences. Adult hemoglobin contains two chains of α (alpha) globin and two chains of β (beta) globin. Besides the ones found in hemoglobin, humans have several other versions of both globin alleles. Most of these versions are expressed only during development, but some are expressed in adults.

Recombination

In sexually reproducing organisms, recombination of alleles and chromosomes is an important source of variation. During meiosis, crossing-over between nonsister chromatids and an independent assortment of chromosomes produce unlike gametes. During fertilization, random gamete union occurs, and this also contributes to a genotype that is unlike those of the parents. Altogether, each population has a storehouse of allelic and chromosomal combinations that potentially exceeds the number of individuals in the population.

The entire genotype, and not individual alleles, is subjected to the natural selection process. A new and different combination of alleles may therefore have great selective value. In a population of snails, stripes and brown color combined might make animals less visible in a woodland habitat. If stripes are controlled by one allele and brown color is controlled by another allele, it is a combination of the two alleles that will be selected for. Recombination may at some time bring the two alleles together so that the combined phenotype can be subjected to natural selection.

Along the same line, consider that many traits having to do with structure, function, and behavior are polygenic. Polygenic traits are controlled by more than one gene, each of which exists at a different locus. Certain combinations of the several alleles might be more adaptive than others in a particular environment. The most favorable combination might not occur until just the right alleles are grouped by recombination. Once the improbable but most favorable phenotype occurs, it can become the prevalent phenotype in the population because of a selection process.

> Variations, the raw material for evolutionary change, are controlled by genes. Only gene mutations result in new alleles. Chromosomal mutations and recombination, however, contribute greatly to the production of variant genotypes and phenotypes.

HOW TO DETECT EVOLUTION

Not only are variations created, they are also preserved and passed on from one generation to the next. The various alleles at all the gene loci in all individuals make up the **gene pool** of the population. It is customary to describe the gene pool of a population in terms of gene frequencies. Suppose that in a *Drosophila* population, one-fourth of the flies are homozygous dominant for long wings, one-half are heterozygous, and one-fourth are homozygous recessive for short wings. Therefore, in a population of one hundred individuals, we have

25 *LL*, 50 *Ll*, and 25 *ll*

What is the number of the allele *L* and the allele *l* in the population?

Number of *L* alleles:

LL (2 *L* × 25) = 50
Ll (1 *L* × 50) = 50
ll (0 *L*) = 0
                      100 *L*

Number of *l* alleles:

LL (0 *l*) = 0
Ll (1 *l* × 50) = 50
ll (2 *l* × 25) = 50
                      100 *l*

Figure 20.1

Calculating gene pool frequencies using the Hardy–Weinberg equation.

$$p^2 + 2\,pq + q^2$$

p^2 = % homozygous dominant individuals
p = frequency of dominant allele
q^2 = % homozygous recessive individuals
q = frequency of recessive allele
$2\,pq$ = % heterozygous individuals

Realize that $p + q = 1$ (there are only 2 alleles)
$p^2 + 2\,pq + q^2 = 1$ (these are the only genotypes)

Example

An investigator has determined by inspection that 16% of a human population has a continuous hairline (recessive trait). Using this information, we can complete all the genotypic and allelic frequencies for the population, provided the conditions for Hardy-Weinberg equilibrium are met.

Given: $q^2 = 16\% = 0.16$ are homozygous recessive individuals

Therefore, $q = \sqrt{0.16} = 0.4$ = frequency of recessive allele
$p = 1.0 - 0.4 = 0.6$ = frequency of dominant allele
$p^2 = (0.6)(0.6) = 0.36 = 36\%$ are homozygous dominant individuals
$2\,pq = 2(0.6)(0.4) = 0.48 = 48\%$ are heterozygous individuals

84% have the dominant phenotype

or
$= 1.00 - 0.52 = 0.48$

To determine the frequency of each allele, calculate its percentage from the total number of alleles in the population; in each case, 100/200 = 50% = 0.5. The sperm and eggs produced by this population will also contain these alleles in these frequencies. Assuming random mating (all possible gametes have an equal chance to combine with any other), we can calculate the ratio of genotypes in the next generation by using a Punnett square.

		sperm		Results:
		0.5 *L*	0.5 *l*	0.25*LL* + 0.5*Ll* + 0.25*ll*
eggs	0.5 *L*	0.25 *LL*	0.25 *Ll*	($\frac{1}{4}$ *LL* + $\frac{1}{2}$ *Ll* + $\frac{1}{4}$ *ll*)
	0.5 *l*	0.25 *Ll*	0.25 *ll*	

There is an important difference between this Punnett square and one used for a cross between individuals; here the sperm and eggs are those produced by the members of a population—not those produced by a single male and female. As you can see, the results of the Punnett square indicate that the frequency for each allele in the next generation is still 0.5.

Therefore, sexual reproduction alone cannot bring about a change in allele frequencies. Also, the dominant allele need not increase from one generation to the next. Dominance does not cause an allele to become a common allele. The potential constancy, or equilibrium state, of gene pool frequencies was independently recognized in 1908 by G. H. Hardy, an English mathematician, and W. Weinberg, a German physician. They used the binomial expression ($p^2 + 2pq + q^2$) to calculate the genotypic and allele frequencies of a population. Figure 20.1 shows you how this is done.

Practice Problems 1*

1. Of the members of a population of pea plants, 9% are short (recessive). What are the frequencies of the recessive allele t and the dominant allele T? What are the genotypic frequencies in this population?

2. A student places 600 fruit flies with the genotype *Ll* and 400 with the genotype *ll* in a culture bottle. What will the genotypic frequencies be in the next generation and each generation thereafter, assuming a Hardy-Weinberg equilibrium?

*Answers to Practice Problems appear in appendix D.

The **Hardy-Weinberg law** states that an equilibrium of allele frequencies in a gene pool, calculated by using the expression $p^2 + 2pq + q^2$, will remain in effect in each succeeding generation of a sexually reproducing population as long as five conditions are met.

1. No mutations: allelic changes do not occur, or changes in one direction are balanced by changes in the opposite direction.
2. No gene flow: migration of alleles into or out of the population does not occur.
3. Random mating: individuals pair by chance and not according to their genotypes or phenotypes.
4. No genetic drift: the population is very large, and changes in allele frequencies due to chance alone are insignificant.
5. No selection: no selective force favors one genotype over another.

In real life, these conditions are rarely, if ever, met, and allele frequencies in the gene pool of a population do change from one generation to the next. Therefore, evolution has occurred. *The significance of the Hardy-Weinberg law is that it tells us what factors cause evolution—those that violate the conditions listed.* Evolution can be detected by noting any deviation from a Hardy-Weinberg equilibrium of allele frequencies in the gene pool of a population.

The accumulation of small changes in the gene pool over a relatively short period of two or more generations is called *microevolution.*

In figure 20.2, the original population has only 10% dark-colored moths. When dark-colored moths rest on light trunks, they are seen and eaten by predatory birds. With the advent of pollution, the trunks of trees darken and it is the light-colored moths that stand out and are eaten. The birds are acting as a selective agent and microevolution occurs; the last generation observed has 80% dark-colored moths.

A Hardy-Weinberg equilibrium provides a baseline by which to judge whether evolution has occurred. Any change of allele frequencies in the gene pool of a population signifies that evolution has occurred.

Figure 20.2

Microevolution. Microevolution has occurred when there is a change in gene pool frequencies—in this case, due to natural selection. The percentage of the dark-colored phenotype has increased because predatory birds can see light-colored moths against sooty tree trunks.

Generation 0   Several Generations Later

10% dark-colored phenotype   →   80% dark-colored phenotype

WHAT CAUSES EVOLUTION?

The list of conditions for genetic equilibrium implies that the opposite conditions can cause evolutionary change. The conditions that can cause a deviation from the Hardy-Weinberg equilibrium are mutation, nonrandom mating, gene flow, genetic drift, and natural selection. Only natural selection results in adaptation to the environment.

Genes Mutate

As mentioned, mutations provide new alleles which are the raw material for evolutionary change. Mutations underlie all the other mechanisms that provide variation. Due to elaborate DNA replication and DNA repair mechanisms, the mutation rates of individual genes are low (about 10^{-5} per gene per cell cycle), but each organism has many genes, and a population has many individuals. Therefore, per individual and per population, mutations are common, not rare, events, as we can see from the following calculations:

For an individual human: Since there are about 100,000 genes (200,000 alleles) in humans, the average mutation rate per human gamete is $(2 \times 10^5 \text{ alleles}) \times (10^{-5} \text{ mutation per gene}) = 2$ mutations per human gamete.

For a human population: Since there are about 252 million people in the United States, the mutation rate per generation is $(2.5 \times 10^8 \text{ individuals}) \times (2 \text{ mutations per gamete}) = 5 \times 10^8$ new mutations in each generation.

Therefore, even a modest mutation rate produces a tremendous amount of genetic variation in a population.

In 1966, R. C. Lewontin and J. L. Hubby set out to determine the molecular polymorphism (variation) of eighteen different enzymes in natural populations of *Drosophila pseudoobscura*. They extracted various enzymes and subjected them to electrophoresis, a process that separates proteins according to size and charge. They concluded that a fly population is polymorphic at no less than 30% of all its gene loci and that an individual fly is likely to be heterozygous at about 12% of its loci.

Similar results have been found in studies on many species, demonstrating that high levels of molecular variation are the rule in natural populations. Many of these mutations will not affect the phenotype, and therefore they may not be detected. In a changing environment even a seemingly harmful mutation can be a source of variation that can help a population become adapted to a new environment. For example, the water flea *Daphnia* ordinarily thrives at temperatures around 20° C, but there is a mutation that requires *Daphnia* to live at temperatures between 25° C and 30° C. The adaptive value of this mutation is entirely dependent on environmental conditions.

> Mutations cause a gene pool to have multiple alleles for many genes.

Mating Is Not Always Random

Random mating occurs when individuals pair by chance and not according to their genotypes or phenotypes. Inbreeding, or mating between relatives to a greater extent than by chance, is an example of *nonrandom mating*. This can happen if dispersal is so low that mates are likely to be related. Inbreeding does not change allele frequencies, but it does decrease the proportion of heterozygotes and increase the proportions of both homozygotes at all gene loci. In a human population, inbreeding increases the frequency of recessive abnormalities in the phenotype.

Assortative mating occurs when individuals tend to mate with those that have the same phenotype with respect to some characteristic. For example, in humans tall people seem to prefer to mate with each other. Assortative mating causes the population to subdivide into two phenotypic classes, between which there is reduced gene exchange. Homozygotes for the gene loci that control the trait in question increase in frequency, and heterozygotes for these loci decrease in frequency. Other loci remain in Hardy-Weinberg equilibrium, except for those very closely linked to the loci governing the trait.

> Nonrandom mating involves inbreeding and assortative mating. The former results in increased frequency of homozygotes at all loci, and the latter results in increased frequency of homozygotes at only certain loci.

Gene Flow Brings New Genes

Gene flow, also called gene migration, is the movement of alleles among populations by the migration of breeding individuals. There can be constant gene flow between adjacent animal populations due to the migration of organisms. In order to judge the effect of gene flow, it is necessary to know the difference in gene frequencies between the two populations and the proportion of migrant genes that are introduced.

Gene flow can increase the variation within a population by introducing novel alleles that were produced by mutation in some other population. Continued gene flow among populations makes their gene pools similar and reduces the possibility of allele frequency differences among populations that might be due to natural selection and genetic drift. Indeed, gene flow among populations can prevent speciation from occurring.

> Gene flow tends to decrease the diversity among populations, causing their gene pools to become similar.

Genetic Drift Promotes Changes

Genetic drift refers to changes in allele frequencies of a gene pool due to chance. Although genetic drift occurs in both large and small populations, a larger population is expected to suffer less of a *sampling error* than a smaller population. Suppose you had a large bag containing 1,000 green balls and 1,000 blue balls, and you randomly drew 10%, or 200, of the balls. Because there is a large number of balls of each color in the bag, you can reasonably expect to draw 100 green balls and 100 blue balls or at least a ratio close to this. But suppose you had a bag containing only 10 green balls and 10 blue balls and you drew 10%, or only 2 balls. The chances of drawing one green ball and one blue ball with a single trial are now considerably less.

When a population is small, there is a greater chance that some rare genotype might not participate at all in the production of the next generation. Suppose there is a small population of flowers in which only 5% of individuals carry a rare allele. If by chance these flowers die out, the next generation would certainly have a change in allele frequencies. When genetic drift leads to the loss of one of a pair of alleles, the other allele then becomes *fixed* in the population. The experimental results in figure 20.3 illustrate the occurrence of fixity of one allele or the other in small populations due to genetic drift.

1. The experiment began with 107 *Drosophila* populations, each in its own culture bottle. Each bottle contained eight heterozygous flies of each sex. There were no homozygous recessive or homozygous dominant flies.
2. From the many offspring, the experimenter chose at random eight males and eight females. These were the parents for the next generation, and so forth for nineteen generations.
3. For the first few generations, most populations still contained many heterozygotes. (The exact composition of the population can be calculated by using the Hardy-Weinberg equation, page 313. The recessive characteristic was brown eyes.)
4. By the nineteenth generation, 25% of the populations contained only homozygous recessive flies and 25% contained only homozygous dominant flies.

Figure 20.3

Genetic drift experiment. At the beginning of this experiment, each of 107 *Drosophila* populations had eight heterozygous flies (bw⁷⁵/bw, bw = brown eyes) of each sex. From the many offspring in each generation, only eight females and eight males were chosen at random to be the parents of the next generation. Nineteen generations later, 50% of the populations had fixed alleles.

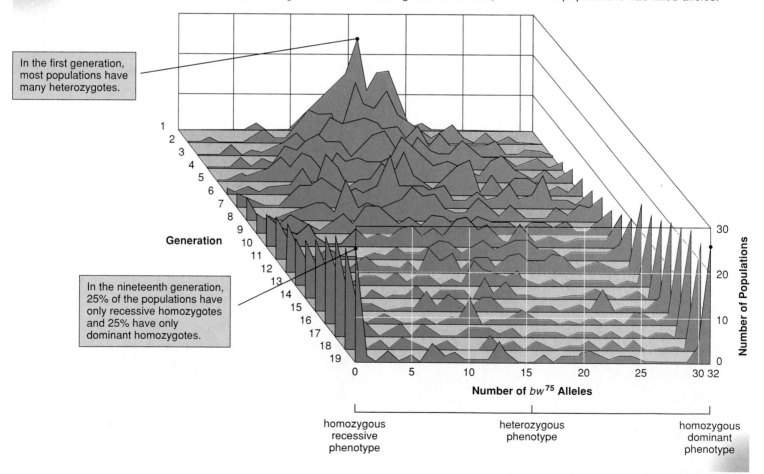

In the first generation, most populations have many heterozygotes.

In the nineteenth generation, 25% of the populations have only recessive homozygotes and 25% have only dominant homozygotes.

In keeping with this experiment, after random genetic drift has continued for a sufficient number of generations, most populations will have become fixed for some alleles.

Simultaneous drift occurring in a number of small, isolated populations causes their gene pools to diverge. The experiment in figure 20.3 considered only one allelic pair. If many pairs had been considered, it is expected that each of the populations would have a different gene pool composition after nineteen generations. Genetic drift is a random process, and therefore it is not likely to produce the same results in several populations. In California, there are a number of cypress groves, each a separate population. All the trees belong to the same species, but the phenotypes within each grove are more similar to one another than they are to the phenotypes in the other groves. Some groves have longitudinally shaped trees, and others have pyramidally shaped trees. The bark is rough in some colonies and smooth in others. The leaves are gray to bright green or bluish, and the cones are small or large. Because the environmental conditions are similar for all groves, and no correlation has been found between phenotype and environment across groves, it is hypothesized that these variations among populations are due to genetic drift.

In nature, two situations, called the founder effect and the bottleneck effect, lead to small populations in which genetic drift affects gene pool frequencies.

Founder Effect

The *founder effect* is an example of genetic drift in which rare alleles, or combinations of alleles, occur at a higher frequency in a population isolated from the general population. After all, founding individuals contain only a fraction of the total genetic diversity of the original gene pool. Which particular alleles are carried by the founders is dictated by chance alone. The Amish of Lancaster County, Pennsylvania, are an isolated group that was begun by German founders. Today, as many as one in fourteen individuals carries a recessive allele that causes an unusual form of dwarfism (affecting only lower arms and legs) and polydactylism (extra fingers) (fig. 20.4). In the population at large, only one in 1,000 individuals has this allele.

All the Amish with this genetic syndrome can trace their ancestry to a single couple (the Kings) who immigrated to Pennsylvania in 1744. They and their offspring had large families, and therefore the rare allele became concentrated in the population.

Bottleneck Effect

Sometimes a population is subjected to near extinction because of a natural disaster (e.g., earthquake or fire) or because of slaughter by humans. Again, chance alone may determine which individuals survive, and these survivors, in effect, create a genetic bottleneck. The *bottleneck effect* prevents the majority of types of genotypes from participating in the production of the next generation.

The large genetic similarity found in cheetahs is believed to be due to a bottleneck. In a study of forty-seven different enzymes, each of which can come in several different forms, all the cheetahs had exactly the same form. This demonstrates that genetic drift can cause certain alleles to be lost from a population.

Exactly what caused the cheetah bottleneck is not known. It is speculated that perhaps cheetahs were slaughtered by nineteenth-century cattle farmers protecting their herds, or were captured by Egyptians as pets 4,000 years ago, or were decimated by a mass extinction tens of thousands of years ago. Today, cheetahs suffer from relative infertility because of the intense inbreeding that occurred after the bottleneck.

Genetic drift is exaggerated when founder effects and bottleneck effects occur. In these instances, only a few types of genotypes contribute to the gene pool of a population, which is much smaller than that in the original population.

Figure 20.4
Founder effect. A member of the founding population of Amish in Pennsylvania had a recessive allele for a rare kind of dwarfism. The percentage of the Amish population now carrying this allele is much higher compared to that of the general population.

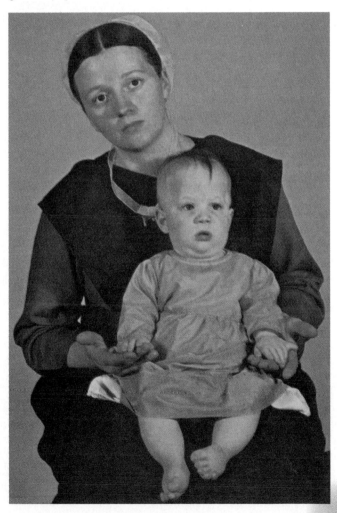

ADAPTATION OCCURS NATURALLY

Natural selection is the process by which populations become adapted to their environment. In the previous century, Charles Darwin, the father of evolution, became convinced that species evolve (change) with time and suggested that natural selection was the process by which they become adapted to their environment. Here, we restate Darwin's hypothesis of natural selection in the context of modern evolutionary theory.

Evolution by natural selection requires:

1. variation. The members of a population differ from one another.

2. inheritance. Many of these differences are heritable genetic differences.

3. differential adaptedness. Some of these differences affect how well an organism is adapted to its environment.

4. differential reproduction. Individuals that are better adapted to their environment are more likely to reproduce, and their fertile offspring will make up a greater proportion of the next generation.

As mentioned previously, random gene mutations are the ultimate source of variation because they provide new alleles. However, in sexually reproducing organisms, recombination of alleles and chromosomes—due to crossing-over during meiosis, independent assortment of chromosomes, and fertilization—contributes greatly to variation. Recombination may at some time produce a more favorable combination of alleles. After all, it is the combined phenotype that is subjected to natural selection.

Fitness

Fitness is the extent to which an individual enjoys reproductive success and contributes fertile offspring to the next generation. Selection, which can be described as a composite of the forces that limit reproductive success of a genotype, opposes fitness. Fitness is a consequence of adaptation to a particular environment and therefore can vary according to the environment in which an individual lives. That is, the same genotype can have a different degree of fitness in different environments. Fitness is relative; it is measured against the reproductive success of other genotypes in the same environment. The more fit an individual, the greater is the genetic contribution of that individual to subsequent generations compared to other members of the same population.

Types of Selection

Most of the traits on which natural selection acts are polygenic and controlled by more than one pair of alleles located at different gene loci. Such traits have a range of phenotypes, the frequency distribution of which usually resembles a bell-shaped curve.

Three types of natural selection have been described for any particular trait. They are directional selection, stabilizing selection, and disruptive selection.

Directional Selection

Directional selection occurs when an extreme phenotype is favored and the distribution curve shifts in that direction (fig. 20.5). Such a shift can occur when a population is adapting to a changing environment. For example, the gradual increase in the size of the modern horse, *Equus*, can be correlated with a change in the environment from forestlike conditions to grassland conditions. Nevertheless, the evolution of the horse should not be viewed as a straight line of descent; we know of many side branches that became extinct.

Industrial Melanism

Before the Industrial Revolution in England, collectors of the peppered moth (*Biston betularia*) noted that most moths were light colored, although occasionally a dark-colored (melanistic) moth was captured. Several decades after the Industrial Revolution, however, black moths made up 99% of the moth population in air-polluted areas.

An experiment by H.B.D. Kettlewell of Oxford University showed that when their coloring matches the trees, moths are more likely to avoid being eaten by predatory birds, which act as a selective agent. Moths rest on the trunks of trees during the day (see fig. 20.2); if they are seen they are eaten by birds. As long as the trees in the environment are light in color, the light-colored moths live to reproduce. But when the trees turn black from industrial pollution, the dark-colored moths survive and reproduce to a greater extent than the light-colored moths. The dark-colored phenotype, then, becomes more prevalent in the population. Thereafter, when pollution is reduced and the trunks of the trees regain their normal color, the light-colored moths increase in number.

Bacteria and Insects

Indiscriminate use of antibiotics and pesticides results in populations of bacteria and insects that are resistant to these chemicals. The mutation that permits resistance is already present before exposure; the chemicals are merely acting as a selective agent. Those organisms that survive exposure have offspring that are resistant, and in this way the population becomes resistant.

Another example of directional selection is the human struggle against malaria, a disease caused by an infection of the liver and the red blood cells. The *Anopheles* mosquito transmits the disease-causing protozoan *Plasmodium vivax* from person to person. In the early 1960s, international health authorities thought that malaria would soon be eradicated. A new drug, chloroquine, was more effective than the quinine that had been used against *Plasmodium*, and DDT (an insecticide) spraying had reduced the mosquito population. But in the mid-1960s, *Plasmodium* showed signs of chloroquine resistance and, worse yet, mosquitoes were becoming resistant to DDT. A few drug-resistant parasites and a few DDT-resistant mosquitoes had survived and multiplied, making the fight against malaria more difficult than ever. Thus, another avenue has now been taken—a vaccine against malaria is being developed.

Figure 20.5

Directional selection. This occurs when natural selection favors one extreme phenotype (see arrows), and there is a shift in the distribution curve. *Equus,* the modern-day horse, evolved from *Hyracotherium,* which was about the size of a dog. This small animal could have hidden among trees and had low-crowned teeth for browsing. When grasslands began to replace forest, the ancestors of *Equus* were subject to selective pressure for the development of strength, intelligence, speed, and durable grinding teeth. A larger size provided the strength needed for combat, a larger skull made room for a larger brain, elongated legs ending in hooves provided greater speed to escape enemies, and the durable grinding teeth enabled the animals to feed efficiently on grasses.

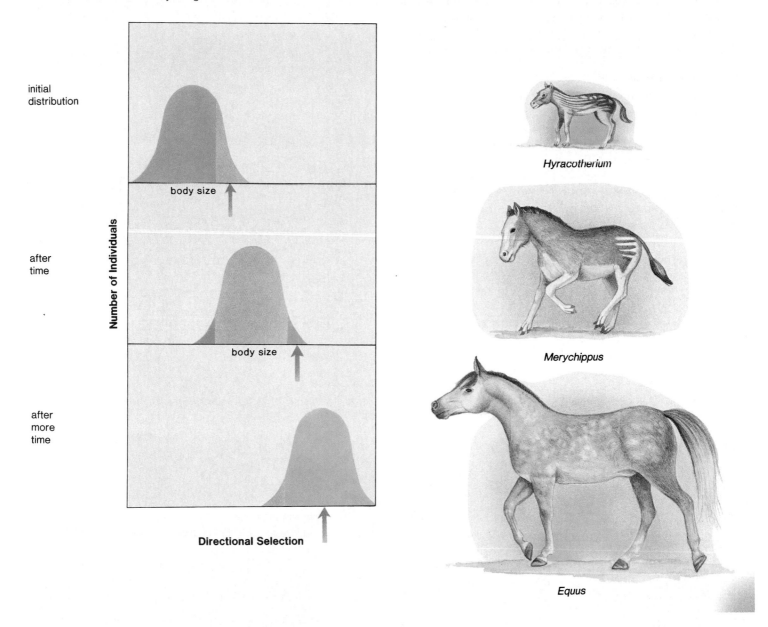

Stabilizing Selection

Stabilizing selection occurs when an intermediate phenotype is favored (fig. 20.6). It can improve adaptation of the population to those aspects of the environment that remain constant. With stabilizing selection, extreme phenotypes are selected against, and individuals near the average are favored. As an example, consider the birth weight of human infants, which ranges from 0.89 kg–4.9 kg (2 lb–10.8 lb). The death rate is higher for infants who are at these extremes and is lowest for babies who have an intermediate birth weight (about 3.2 kg or 7 lb). Most babies have a birth weight within this range, which gives the best chance of survival. Similar results have been found in other animals, also.

Disruptive Selection

In **disruptive selection,** two or more extreme phenotypes are favored over any intermediate phenotype (fig. 20.7). For example, British land snails (*Cepaea nemoralis*) have a wide habitat range that includes low-vegetation areas (grass fields and hedgerows) and forest areas. In low-vegetation areas, thrushes feed mainly on snails with dark shells that lack light bands, and in forest areas, they feed mainly on snails with light-banded shells. Therefore, these two distinctly different phenotypes are found in the population.

> Directional selection favors one of the extreme phenotypes; stabilizing selection favors the intermediate phenotype; disruptive selection favors more than one extreme phenotype.

Figure 20.6

Stabilizing selection. Natural selection favors the intermediate phenotype (see arrows) over the extremes. Today, it is observed that most human babies are of intermediate weight (about 3.2 kg, or 7 lb), and very few babies are either very small or very large.

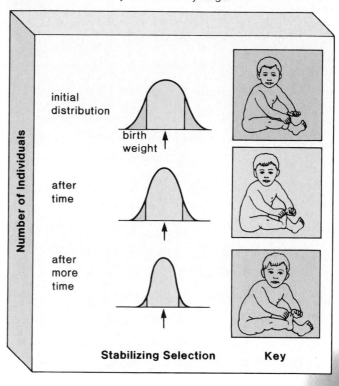

Figure 20.7

Disruptive selection. Natural selection favors two extreme phenotypes (see arrows). Today, it is observed that British land snails comprise mainly two different phenotypes, each adapted to a particular habitat.

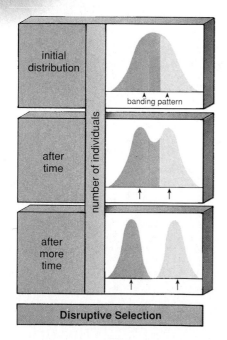

Variations Are Maintained

A population always shows some genotypic variation. The maintenance of variation is beneficial because populations that lack variation may not be able to adapt to new conditions and may become extinct. How can variation be maintained in spite of selection constantly working to reduce it?

First, we must remember that the forces that promote variation are still at work: mutation still creates new alleles, and recombination still recombines these alleles during gametogenesis and fertilization. Second, gene flow might still occur. If the receiving population is small and is mostly homozygous, gene flow can be a significant source of new alleles. Finally, we have seen that natural selection reduces, but does not eliminate, the range of phenotypes. And disruptive selection even promotes polymorphism in a population. There are also other ways variation is maintained.

Diploidy and the Heterozygote

Only alleles that are exposed (cause a phenotypic difference) are subject to natural selection. In diploid organisms, this makes the heterozygote a potential protector of recessive alleles that otherwise would be weeded out of the gene pool. Consider these gene pool frequency distributions:

Genotypic Frequencies

Frequency of Allele *a* in Gene Pool	AA	Aa	aa
0.9	0.01	0.18	0.81
0.1	0.81	0.18	0.01

Notice that even when selection reduces the recessive allele from a frequency of 0.9 to 0.1, the frequency of the heterozygote remains the same. The heterozygote remains a source of the recessive allele for future generations. In a changing environment the recessive allele may then be favored by natural selection.

Sickle-Cell Disease

In certain regions of Africa, the importance of the heterozygote in maintaining variation is exemplified by sickle-cell disease. The phenotype of heterozygotes is more fit than either of the phenotypes of the homozygotes and all three genotypes are maintained in the population. The relative fitness of the heterozygote and the two homozygotes will determine their percentages in the population. The optimum ratio will be the one that correlates with the survival of the most offspring. When the ratio of two or more phenotypes remains the same in each generation, it is called *balanced polymorphism.*

Individuals with sickle-cell disease have the genotype $Hb^S Hb^S$ and tend to die at an early age due to hemorrhaging and organ destruction. Those who are heterozygous and have sickle-cell trait ($Hb^A Hb^S$) are better off; their red blood cells become sickle shaped only when the oxygen content of the environment is low. Geneticists studying the distribution of sickle-cell disease in Africa have found that the recessive allele (Hb^S) has a higher frequency (0.2 to as high as 0.4 in a few areas) in regions

Figure 20.8

The pink color shows the areas where malaria was prevalent in Africa, the Middle East, and southern Europe in 1920, before eradication programs began; the blue color shows the areas where sickle-cell disease most often occurred. The overlap of these two distributions (purple) suggested that there might be a causal connection.

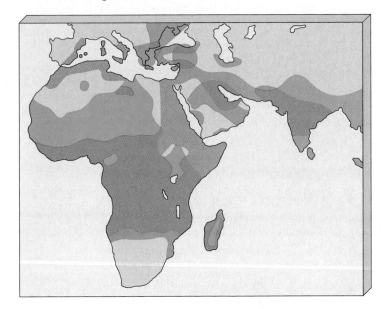

with malaria (fig. 20.8). Malaria is caused by a parasite that lives in and destroys red blood cells. Further research has confirmed that the frequency of the genotype $Hb^S Hb^S$ is maintained because the heterozygote has an advantage over the normal phenotype in these regions.

Genotype	Phenotype	Result
$Hb^A Hb^A$	Normal	Dies due to malarial infection
$Hb^A Hb^S$	Sickle-cell trait	Lives due to protection from both
$Hb^S Hb^S$	Sickle-cell disease	Dies due to sickle-cell disease

The malarial parasite flourishes in normal homozygotes but dies in heterozygotes because potassium ions leak out of the red blood cells when they become sickle shaped. For this reason more heterozygotes survive than do the normal homozygotes in regions with malaria.

Even after populations become adapted to their environments, variation is promoted and maintained by various mechanisms. In diploid organisms, the heterozygote genotype can help maintain variation.

Figure 20.9

Three closely related flycatcher species. Although the three species are nearly identical, we would still expect to find some structural feature that distinguishes them. We know they are separate species because they are reproductively isolated—the members of each species reproduce only with one another. Each species has a characteristic song and has its own particular habitat during the mating season as well.

least flycatcher, *Empidonax minimus*

Acadian flycatcher, *Empidonax virescens*

Traill's flycatcher, *Empidonax trailli*

Speciation is the splitting of one species into two or more species or the transformation of one species into a new species over time. Speciation is the final result of changes in gene pool allelic and genotypic frequencies.

What Is a Species?

Sometimes it is very difficult to tell one **species** [L. *speci,* a kind] from another. Before we consider the origin of species, then, it is first necessary to define a species. For Linnaeus, the father of taxonomy, one species was separated from another by morphology; that is, their physical traits differed. Darwin saw that similar species, such as the three flycatcher species in figure 20.9, are related by common descent. The field of population genetics has produced the *biological definition of a species:* the members of one species interbreed and have a shared gene pool, and each species is reproductively isolated from every other species. The flycatchers in figure 20.9 are members of separate species because they do not interbreed in nature.

Gene flow occurs between the populations of a species but not between populations of different species. For example, the human species has many populations that certainly differ in physical appearance. We know, however, that all humans belong to one species because the members of these populations can produce fertile offspring. On the other hand, the red maple and the sugar maple are separate species. Each species is found over a wide geographical range in the eastern half of the United States and is made up of many populations. The members of each species' populations, however, rarely hybridize in nature. Therefore, these two plants are related but separate species.

Reproductive Isolating Mechanisms

For two species to be separate, they must be reproductively isolated; that is, gene flow must not occur between them. A *reproductive isolating mechanism* is any structural, functional, or behavioral characteristic that prevents successful reproduction from occurring. Table 20.1 lists the mechanisms by which reproductive isolation is maintained.

Premating isolating mechanisms are those that prevent reproduction attempts. Habitat isolation, temporal isolation, behavioral isolation, and mechanical isolation make it highly unlikely that particular genotypes will contribute to the gene pool of a population.

Habitat Isolation. When two species occupy different habitats, even within the same geographic range, they are less likely to meet and to attempt to reproduce. This is one of the reasons the flycatchers in figure 20.9 do not mate and the red maple and sugar maple already mentioned do not exchange pollen. In tropical rain forests, many animal species are restricted to a particular level of the forest canopy, and in this way they are isolated from similar species.

Table 20.1

Reproductive Isolating Mechanisms

Isolating Mechanism	Example
Premating	
Habitat isolation	Species at same locale occupy different habitats
Temporal isolation	Species reproduce at different seasons or different times of day
Behavioral isolation	In animals, courtship behavior differs or they respond to different songs, calls, pheromones, or other signals
Mechanical isolation	Genitalia unsuitable for one another
Postmating	
Gamete isolation	Sperm cannot reach or fertilize egg
Zygote mortality	Fertilization occurs, but zygote does not survive
Hybrid sterility	Hybrid survives but is sterile and cannot reproduce
F_2 fitness	Hybrid is fertile but F_2 hybrid has reduced fitness

Figure 20.10

Temporal isolation. Five species of frogs of the genus *Rana* are all found at Ithaca, New York. The species remain separate because the period of most active mating is different for each and because whenever there is an overlap, different breeding sites are used. For example, pickerel frogs are found in streams and ponds on high ground, leopard frogs in lowland swamps, and wood frogs in woodland ponds or shallow water.

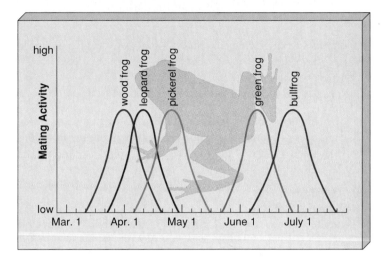

Temporal Isolation. Two species can live in the same locale, but if each reproduces at a different time of year, they do not attempt to mate. For example, *Reticulitermes hageni* and *R. virginicus* are two species of termites. The former has mating flights in March through May, whereas the latter mates in the fall and winter months. Similarly, the frogs featured in figure 20.10 have different periods of most active mating.

Behavioral Isolation. Many animal species have courtship patterns that allow males and females to recognize one another. Male fireflies are recognized by females of their species by the pattern of their flashings; similarly, male crickets are recognized by females of their species by their chirping. Many males recognize females of their species by sensing chemical signals called pheromones. For example, female gypsy moths secrete chemicals from special abdominal glands. These chemicals are detected downwind by receptors on antennae of males.

Mechanical Isolation. When animal genitalia or plant floral structures are incompatible, reproduction cannot occur. Inaccessibility of pollen to certain pollinators can prevent cross-fertilization in plants, and the sexes of many insect species have genitalia that do not match or other characteristics that make mating impossible. For example, male dragonflies have claspers that are suitable for holding only the females of their own species.

Postmating isolating mechanisms prevent hybrid offspring from developing or breeding, even if reproduction attempts have been successful. Gamete isolation, zygote mortality, hybrid ste-

rility, and reduced F_2 fitness all make it unlikely that particular genotypes will contribute to the gene pool of a population.

Gamete Isolation. Even if the gametes of two different species meet, they may not fuse to become a zygote. In animals, the sperm of one species may not be able to survive in the reproductive tract of another species, or the egg may have receptors only for sperm of its species. In plants, the stigma controls which pollen grains can successfully complete pollination.

Zygote Mortality, Hybrid Sterility, and F_2 Fitness. If by chance the two of the frog species in figure 20.10 do form hybrid zygotes, the zygotes fail to complete development or else the offspring are frail. As is well known, a cross between a horse and a donkey produces a mule, which is usually sterile—it cannot reproduce. In some cases, mules are fertile, but the F_2 generation is not. This has also been observed in both evening primrose and cotton plants.

> The members of a biological species are able to breed and produce fertile offspring only among themselves. There are several mechanisms that keep species reproductively isolated from one another.

How Do Species Arise?

Whenever reproductive isolation develops, speciation has occurred. Ernst Mayr, at Harvard University, proposed one model of speciation after observing that when a population is geographically isolated from other populations, gene flow stops. Different variations due to mutations, drift, and selection build up, causing first postmating and then premating reproductive isolation to occur. Mayr called this model **allopatric speciation** [Gk. *allo,* different, and *patri,* fatherland] (fig. 20.11).

> Allopatric speciation occurs when populations are separated by a geographical barrier that prevents them from reproducing with each other.

With **sympatric speciation** [Gk. *sym,* together, and *patri,* fatherland], a population develops into two or more reproductively isolated groups without prior geographic isolation. The best evidence for this type of speciation is found among plants, where it can occur by means of polyploidy. In this case there would be a multiplication of the chromosomal number in certain plants of a single species. Sympatric speciation can also occur due to hybridization between two species, followed by a doubling of the chromosomal number. Polyploid plants are reproductively isolated by a postmating mechanism; they can reproduce successfully only with other like polyploids, and backcrosses with diploid parents are sterile.

> Sympatric speciation occurs when members of a single population develop a genetic difference that prevents them from reproducing with the parent type.

Figure 20.11 contrasts allopatric speciation with sympatric speciation. Allopatric speciation is by far the more common means of speciation.

Figure 20.11

Allopatric versus sympatric speciation. **a.** Allopatric speciation occurs after a geographic barrier prevents gene flow between populations that originally belonged to a single species. **b.** Sympatric speciation occurs when members of a population achieve immediate reproductive isolation without any prior geographic barrier.

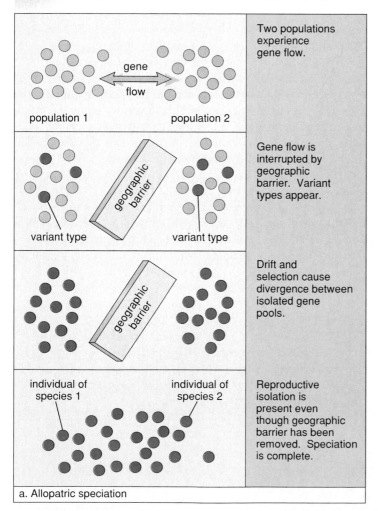

a. Allopatric speciation

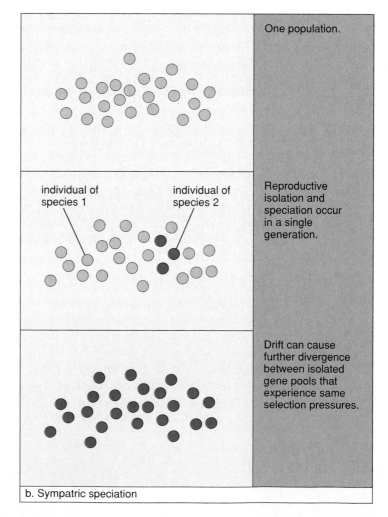

b. Sympatric speciation

Figure 20.12

Adaptive radiation in Hawaiian honeycreepers. More than twenty species evolved from a single species of a finchlike bird that colonized the Hawaiian Islands. This illustration shows only six of the more extreme adaptive forms.

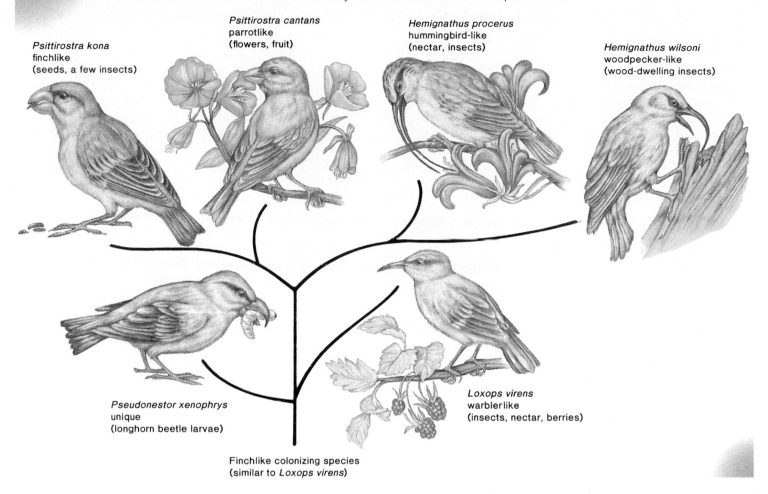

Psittirostra kona
finchlike
(seeds, a few insects)

Psittirostra cantans
parrotlike
(flowers, fruit)

Hemignathus procerus
hummingbird-like
(nectar, insects)

Hemignathus wilsoni
woodpecker-like
(wood-dwelling insects)

Pseudonestor xenophrys
unique
(longhorn beetle larvae)

Loxops virens
warblerlike
(insects, nectar, berries)

Finchlike colonizing species
(similar to *Loxops virens*)

Adaptive Radiation Produces Many Species

Adaptive radiation is the rapid development from a single ancestral species of many new species, which have spread out and become adapted to various ways of life. The thirteen species of finches that live on the Galápagos Islands are believed to be descended from a type of mainland finch that invaded the islands. As the parent population increased in size, daughter populations were established on the various islands. These daughter populations were subjected to the founder effect and the process of natural selection. Because of natural selection, each population became adapted to a particular habitat on its island. In time, the various populations became so genotypically different that now, when they by chance reside on the same island, they do not interbreed and are therefore separate species. There is evidence that the finches use beak shape to recognize members of the same species during courtship. Rejection of suitors with the wrong type of beak is a behavioral type of premating isolating mechanism.

Similarly, on the Hawaiian Islands, there is a wide variety of honeycreepers that are descended from a common goldfinchlike ancestor that arrived from Asia or North America about 5 million years ago. Today, honeycreepers have a range of beak sizes and shapes for feeding on various food sources, including seeds, fruits, flowers, and insects (fig. 20.12). Adaptive radiation has also been observed in plants on the Hawaiian Islands, as discussed in the reading on pages 326–327.

> After a species undergoes adaptive radiation, there are many new species adapted to living in different habitats.

Origin and Adaptive Radiation of the Hawaiian Silversword Alliance

When I was a graduate student at the University of California at Davis, I studied a genus of plants (*Calycadenia*) that belongs to a largely Californian group of plants called tarweeds. I knew that the tarweeds and plants belonging to the silversword alliance (an alliance is an assemblage of closely related species) are in the same large family of plants called Asteraceae (Compositae). But Sherwin Carlquist's anatomical research had suggested that the silversword plants and the tarweeds are even more closely related. The silverswords are found only in Hawaii, so when I took a faculty position at the University of Hawaii, I decided to gather evidence to possibly support Carlquist's interpretation.

There are twenty-eight species of plants in the silversword alliance: five species of *Argyroxiphium,* two species of *Wilkesia*, and twenty-one species of *Dubautia*. This alliance constitutes one of the most spectacular examples of adaptive radiation among plants. Adaptive radiation characterizes many insular groups that have evolved in isolation away from related and nonrelated organisms. Members of the silversword alliance range in form from matlike subshrubs and rosette shrubs to large trees and climbing vines (lianas). They grow in habitats as diverse as exposed lava, dry scrub, dry woodland, moist forest, wet forest, and bogs. These habitats have a range in elevation from 75 to 3,800 meters (250–12,500 feet), and in annual precipitation from 38 to 1,230 cm (15–485 inches).

Gerald D. Carr
University of Hawaii at Manoa

Members of the alliance found in moist to wet forest habitats typically exhibit modifications that are adaptive in competition for light, such as increased height, vining habit, and thin leaves with a comparatively large surface area (fig. 20A). Members of the alliance from open, more arid sites typically show features associated with conservation of water, such as decreased height, thickened leaves with comparatively low surface area, and compact internal tissues (fig. 20B). Species of *Argyroxiphium* have more or less succulent leaves with compact tissue and channels filled with a water-binding gelatinous matrix of pectin (fig. 20C). These adaptions help this species survive under the conditions of extreme water stress in its habitats—i.e., largely in oxygen-deficient, acid bogs or dry alpine cinder habitats.

I have done cytogenetic analyses of meiotic chromosome pairing in hybrids to determine relationships among the silversword plants and between these plants and the tarweeds. I have sought and found many natural interspecific and intergeneric hybrids among the diverse species of the silversword alliance. Many such hybrids also were produced artificially. Each newly discovered or created hybrid potentially provided information to fill in a missing piece of an intriguing and mysterious natural puzzle of evolution—or sometimes these findings complicated the picture further. Nearly twenty years later, the picture is still not complete. Perhaps the most exciting and personally gratifying result of my involvement with this group is the series of hybrids that have been produced between Hawaiian species and the tarweeds. These hybrids, and also a growing body of molecular data provided by one of my collaborators, Bruce Baldwin, clearly establish the origin of the Hawaiian silversword alliance from the tarweeds.

I like working with others who are innately curious about their natural surroundings and who do research for pure personal satisfaction. My scientific research helps provide insight into the mystery and meaning of the wonderful diversity of nature. An added element of excitement comes in sharing with others a discovery of one of nature's secrets that perhaps no other human has witnessed. Therefore, for me, teaching and research are naturally complementary and rewarding activities.

▶ **Biological Relationships**

Evolution accounts for both the unity and diversity of life. Because of common descent, all organisms use DNA as the genetic material, use ATP (adenosine triphosphate) as the energy molecule, and have the same twenty amino acids in their proteins. Closely related organisms share a more recent ancestor and therefore share a unity of plan easily recognizable in their anatomy and embryological development.

Diversity is due to adaptation to the environment that enables organisms to play a particular role in an ecosystem. Because evolution builds on what has gone before and because the environment is constantly changing, an organism can never be perfectly suited to its present environment. This has its benefits because an organism too closely adapted to the present environment may not be able to adapt to a new environment. Change, not constancy, is the overriding quality of the earth and the biosphere.

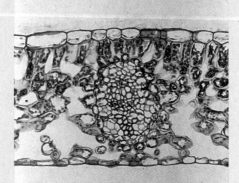

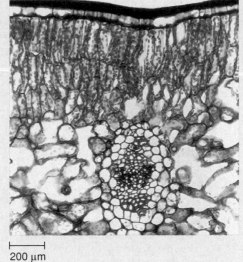

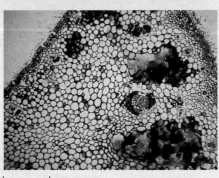

200 μm

200 μm

1 mm

Figure 20A

Dubautia knudsenii is adapted to living in a moist habitat. In the cross section of the leaf, note the loose organization of tissue and thin cuticle on the upper and lower epidermis.

Figure 20B

Dubautia menziesii is adapted to living in open, more arid sites. In cross section, note the thick leaf with compact organization of tissue and very highly developed cuticle on upper and lower epidermis (lower epidermis not shown).

Figure 20C

Argyroxiphium kauense is adapted to living under conditions of water stress. In cross section, note the compact tissue and large channels of water-binding extracellular pectin that alternate with the major vascular bundles.

Population genetics, as exemplified by the Hardy-Weinberg law, shows us how to make the study of evolution objective rather than subjective. A change in gene pool frequencies signifies evolution. We can identify various agents of evolutionary change; natural selection is only one of many agents.

Population genetics has also given us the biological definition of a species: the members of a species reproduce with each other, resulting in fertile offspring. Now we know when new species arise—when populations no longer reproduce with each other, they are separate species. A change in gene pool frequencies, even to the point of speciation, is sometimes called microevolution. The term macroevolution is used to refer to evolutionary relationships between groups of organisms above the species level.

Summary

1. The members of a population vary from one another. Primary sources of variation are gene mutations, which produce new alleles; chromosomal mutations, which can rearrange alleles on a chromosome; and recombination, which can bring certain alleles together into the same genotype. Most traits of evolutionary significance are polygenic.

2. All the various genes of a population make up its gene pool. The Hardy-Weinberg equilibrium is a constancy of gene pool frequencies that remains from generation to generation if certain conditions are met. The conditions are no mutation, no gene flow, random mating, no genetic drift, and no selection.

3. Since these conditions are rarely met, a change in gene pool frequencies is likely. When gene pool frequencies change, evolution has occurred. Deviations from a Hardy-Weinberg equilibrium allow us to determine when evolution has taken place.

4. The agents of evolutionary change are mutation, nonrandom mating, gene flow, genetic drift, and natural selection.

5. The rate of mutation per gene per generation is low, but since individuals have many genes and a population has many individuals, the mutation rate in a population is an adequate source of new alleles. Genotypic variations may be of evolutionary significance only should the environment change.

6. Nonrandom mating occurs when relatives mate (inbreeding) and assortative mating occurs. Both of these cause an increase in homozygotes.

7. Gene flow occurs when a breeding individual (animals) migrates to another population or when gametes and seeds (plants) are carried into another population. Constant gene flow between two populations causes their gene pools to become similar.

8. Genetic drift occurs when allele frequencies are altered by chance—that is, by sampling error. Genetic drift can cause the gene pools of two isolated populations to become dissimilar as some alleles are lost and others are fixed. Genetic drift is particularly evident when founders start a new population, or after a bottleneck, when severe inbreeding occurs.

9. The process of natural selection can now be restated in terms of population genetics (p. 318). A change in gene pool frequencies results in adaptation to the environment.

10. Three types of selection occur: directional (dark-colored peppered moths are prevalent in polluted areas and light-colored peppered moths are prevalent in nonpolluted areas); stabilizing (the average human birth weight is near the optimum birth weight for survival); and disruptive (*Cepaea* snails vary because a wide geographic range causes selection to vary).

11. Despite constant natural selection, variation is maintained. Mutation and recombination still occur; gene flow among small populations can introduce new alleles; and natural selection itself sometimes results in variation. In sexually reproducing diploid organisms, the heterozygote acts as a repository for recessive alleles whose frequency is low. In regard to sickle-cell disease, the heterozygote is more fit in areas with malaria and, therefore, the homozygotes are maintained in the population.

12. The biological definition of a species recognizes that populations of the same species breed only among themselves and are reproductively isolated from other species.

13. Reproductive isolating mechanisms prevent gene flow among species. Premating isolating mechanisms (habitat, temporal, behavioral, and mechanical isolation) prevent mating from being attempted. Postmating isolating mechanisms (gamete isolation, zygote mortality, hybrid sterility, and F_2 fitness) prevent hybrid offspring from surviving and/or reproducing.

14. Allopatric speciation requires geographic isolation before reproductive isolation occurs.

15. Sympatric speciation does not require geographic isolation for reproductive isolation to develop. The occurrence of polyploidy in plants is an example of this other type of speciation.

16. Adaptive radiation, as exemplified by the Galápagos finches, is a form of allopatric speciation. It occurs because the opportunity exists for new species to adapt to new habitats.

Writing Across the Curriculum

In order to practice writing skills, students should write out the answers to any or all of the study questions and the critical thinking questions. The study questions are sequenced in the same order as the text. Answers to the objective questions, and suggested answers to the critical thinking questions, are in appendix D.

Study Questions

1. What are the sources of variation in a population of sexually reproducing diploid organisms?   312

2. What is the Hardy-Weinberg law?   314

3. Name and discuss the five agents of evolutionary change.   315

4. What is the founder effect, and what is a bottleneck?   317

5. State the steps required for adaptation by natural selection in modern terms.   318

6. Distinguish among directional, stabilizing, and disruptive selection by giving examples.   318–20

7. State ways in which variation is maintained in a population.   321

8. What is the biological definition of a species?   322

9. What is a reproductive isolating mechanism? Give examples of both premating and postmating isolating mechanisms.   322–23

10. How does allopatric speciation occur? sympatric speciation?   324

11. What is adaptive radiation and how is it exemplified by the Galápagos finches and the Hawiian honey creepers?   325

1. Assuming a Hardy-Weinberg equilibrium, 21% of a population is homozygous dominant, 50% is heterozygous, and 29% is homozygous recessive. What percentage of the next generation is predicted to be homozygous recessive?
   a. 21%
   b. 50%
   c. 29%
   d. 25%

2. A human population has a higher-than-usual percentage of individuals with a genetic disease. The most likely explanation is
   a. gene flow.
   b. natural selection.
   c. genetic drift.
   d. All of these are correct.

3. The offspring of better-adapted individuals are expected to make up a larger proportion of the next generation. The most likely explanation is
   a. mutation.
   b. gene flow.
   c. natural selection.
   d. genetic drift.

4. The continued occurrence of sickle-cell disease in parts of Africa with malaria is due to
   a. continual mutation.
   b. gene flow between populations.
   c. fitness of the heterozygote.
   d. disruptive selection.

5. Which of these is/are necessary to natural selection?
   a. variations
   b. differential reproduction
   c. inheritance of differences
   d. All of these are correct.

6. When a population is small, there is a greater chance of
   a. gene flow.
   b. genetic drift.
   c. natural selection.
   d. mutations occurring.

7. The biological definition of a species depends on
   a. anatomical and developmental differences between two groups of organisms.
   b. the geographic distribution of two groups of organisms.
   c. differences in the adaptations of two groups of organisms.
   d. reproductive isolation of two groups of organisms.

8. Which of these is a premating isolating mechanism?
   a. habitat isolation
   b. temporal isolation
   c. gamete isolation
   d. Both a and b are correct.

9. Male moths recognize females of their species by sensing chemical signals called pheromones. This is an example of
   a. gamete isolation.
   b. habitat isolation.
   c. behavioral isolation.
   d. mechanical isolation.

10. Allopatric but not sympatric speciation requires
    a. reproductive isolation.
    b. geographic isolation.
    c. prior hybridization.
    d. spontaneous differences in males and females.

11. The many species of Galápagos finches were each adapted to eating different foods. This is an example of
    a. gene flow.
    b. adaptive radiation.
    c. sympatric speciation.
    d. All of these are correct.

12. The following diagrams represent a distribution of genotypes (phenotypes) in a population. Draw another diagram under (*a*) to show that directional selection has occurred, under (*b*) to show that stabilizing selection has occurred, and under (*c*) to show that disruptive selection has occurred.

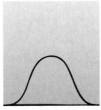

a. Disruptive selection

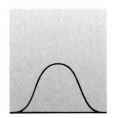

b. Stabilizing selection

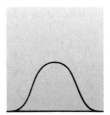

c. Directional selection

13. The following diagram represents one species. (a) Use the labels *population* and *gene flow* where appropriate. (b) What changes would you make to this diagram in order to symbolize two species?

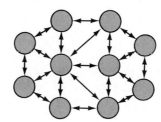

Additional Genetics Problems*

1. If $p^2 = 0.36$, what percentage of the population has the recessive phenotype?

2. If 1% of a human population has the recessive phenotype, what percentage has the dominant phenotype, assuming a Hardy-Weinberg equilibrium?

3. Four percent of the members of a population of pea plants are short (recessive characteristic). What are the frequencies of both the recessive allele and the dominant allele? What are the genotypic frequencies in this population, assuming a Hardy-Weinberg equilibrium?

Concepts and Critical Thinking

1. *The process of evolution has a genetic basis.*

   Why is the process of evolution consistent with a particulate theory of inheritance rather than a blending theory of inheritance?

2. *Selection is the process by which populations accumulate adaptive traits.*

   Reconcile this statement with your knowledge that selection acts at the level of the individual.

3. *The diversity of life is dependent upon the process of speciation.*

   If only new species evolve, then of what use are the higher taxa (classification categories)?

Selected Key Terms

adaptive radiation The formation of a large number of species from a common ancestor.   325

allopatric speciation (al-uh-PA-trik) The origin of new species in populations that are separated geographically. [Gk. *allo,* different, and *patri,* fatherland]   324

directional selection An outcome of natural selection in which an extreme phenotype is favored, usually in a changing environment.   318

disruptive selection An outcome of natural selection in which extreme phenotypes are favored over the average phenotype and can lead to more than one distinct form.   320

fitness The ability of an organism to survive and reproduce in its environment.   318

gene flow The sharing of genes between two populations through interbreeding.   315

gene pool The total of all the genes of all the individuals in a population.   313

genetic drift A change in the genetic makeup of a population due to chance (random) events; important in small populations or when only a few individuals mate.   316

Hardy-Weinberg law A law stating that the frequency of an allele in a population remains stable under certain assumptions, such as random mating; therefore, no change or evolution occurs.   314

population A group of organisms of the same species occupying a certain area and sharing a common gene pool.   312

postmating isolating mechanism An anatomical or physiological difference between two species that prevents successful reproduction after mating has taken place.   323

premating isolating mechanism An anatomical or behavioral difference between two species that prevents the possibility of mating.   322

speciation The process whereby a new species originates or is produced.   322

species A taxonomic category whose members can only breed successfully with each other. [L. *speci,* a kind]   322

stabilizing selection An outcome of natural selection in which extreme phenotypes are eliminated and the average phenotype is conserved.   320

sympatric speciation (sim-PA-trik) The origin of new species in populations that overlap geographically. [Gk. *sym,* together, and *patri,* fatherland]   324

*Answers to Additional Genetic Problems appear in appendix D.

21

ORIGIN AND HISTORY OF LIFE

Learning Objectives

Origin of Life

- Trace the steps by which a chemical evolution may have produced the protocell.   333–34

- Describe the experiments and/or data that support the occurrence of a chemical evolution.   333–34

- Describe differences between the protocell and a true cell.   333–34

- Explain why the protocell likely was a heterotrophic fermenter.   335

- Describe how a self-replication system may have evolved.   335

History of Life

- Describe how the fossil record developed and how fossils are dated.   336–37

- Give evidence for continental drift and explain how and why it occurs.   338–39

- Outline the main events of the Precambrian, the Paleozoic era, the Mesozoic era, and the Cenozoic era.   340–47

- Give reasons for the five significant mass extinctions in the history of life.   348–49

- State and discuss two models of evolutionary change in relation to the fossil record.   351

Outgassing from volcanoes contributed to the primitive atmosphere so necessary to the origin of life.

Figure 21.1

A possible scenario to describe the origin of life.

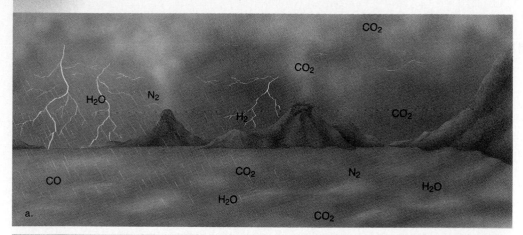

a.

a. The primitive atmosphere contained gases, including water vapor, that escaped from volcanoes; as the water vapor cooled, some gases were washed into the ocean by rain.

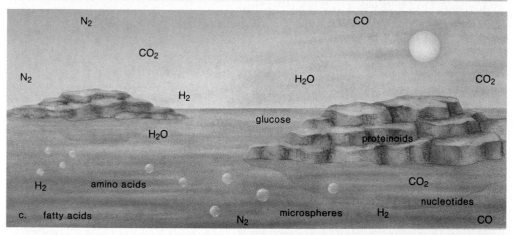

b.

b. The availability of energy from volcanic eruption and lightning allowed gases to form simple organic molecules.

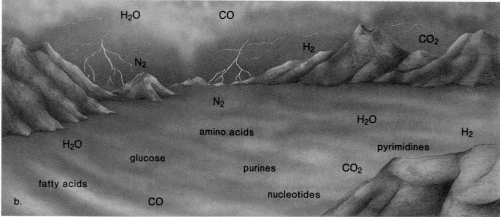

c.

c. Amino acids that splashed up onto rocky coasts could have polymerized into polypeptides (proteinoids) that became microspheres when they reentered the water.

d.

d. Eventually, various types of prokaryotes and then eukaryotes evolved. Some of the prokaryotes were oxygen-producing photosynthesizers.

ife has a history. It began with the evolution of the first cell or cells and continues even today. The fossil record provides information regarding the history and patterns of life's evolution.

ORIGIN OF LIFE

Today we do not believe that life arises spontaneously from non-life, and we say that "life comes only from life." But if this is so, how did the first form of life come about? Since it was the very first living thing, it had to come from nonliving chemicals. Could there have been an increase in the complexity of the chemicals—could a **chemical evolution** as depicted in figure 21.1 have produced the first cell(s) on the primitive earth?

The sun and the planets, including earth, probably formed over a 10-billion-year period from aggregates of dust particles and debris. At 4.6 billion years ago, the solar system was in place. Intense heat produced by gravitational energy and radioactivity caused the earth to become stratified into several layers. Heavier atoms of iron and nickel became the molten liquid core, and dense silicate minerals became the semiliquid mantle. Upwellings of volcanic lava produced the first crust.

The Atmosphere Forms

The size of the earth is such that the gravitational field is strong enough to have an atmosphere. If the earth were smaller and lighter, atmospheric gases would escape into outer space. The earth's *primitive atmosphere* was not the same as today's atmosphere. It is now thought that the primitive atmosphere was produced by outgassing from the interior, particularly by volcanic action. In that case, the primitive atmosphere would have consisted mostly of water vapor (H_2O), nitrogen (N_2), and carbon dioxide (CO_2), with only small amounts of hydrogen (H_2) and carbon monoxide (CO). The primitive atmosphere, with little if any free oxygen, was a *reducing atmosphere* as opposed to the *oxidizing atmosphere* of today. This was fortuitous because oxygen (O_2) attaches to organic molecules, preventing them from joining to form larger molecules.

At first the earth was so hot that water was present only as a vapor that formed dense, thick clouds. Then as the earth cooled, water vapor condensed to liquid water, and rain began to fall (fig. 21.1*a*). It rained in such enormous quantity over hundreds of millions of years that the oceans of the world were produced. The earth is an appropriate distance from the sun: any closer, water would have evaporated; any further, water would have frozen.

Small Organic Molecules Evolve

The atmospheric gases, dissolved in rain, were carried down into newly forming oceans. Aleksandr Oparin, a Soviet biochemist, suggested as early as 1938 that organic molecules could have been produced from the gases of the primitive atmosphere in the presence of strong outside *energy sources*. The energy sources on the primitive earth included heat from volcanoes and meteorites, radioactivity from isotopes in the earth's crust, powerful electric discharges in lightning, and solar radiation, especially ultraviolet radiation (fig. 21.1*b*).

Figure 21.2

In Miller's experiment, gases were admitted to the apparatus, circulated past an energy source (electric spark), and cooled to produce a liquid that could be withdrawn. Upon chemical analysis, the liquid was found to contain various small organic molecules.

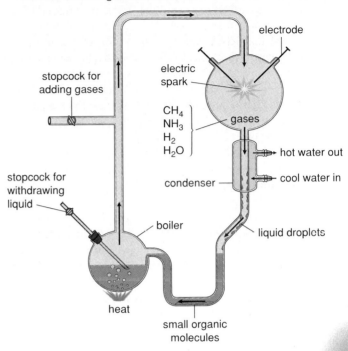

In 1953, Stanley Miller provided support for Oparin's ideas through an ingenious experiment (fig. 21.2). Miller placed a mixture resembling a strongly reducing atmosphere (methane [CH_4], ammonia [NH_3], hydrogen [H_2], and water [H_2O]) in a closed system, heated the mixture, and circulated it past an electric spark (simulating lightning). After a week's run, Miller discovered that a variety of amino acids and organic acids had been produced. Since that time, other investigators have achieved similar results by utilizing other, less-reducing combinations of gases dissolved in water.

These experiments support the hypothesis that the primitive gases could have reacted with one another to produce small organic compounds. Neither oxidation (there was no free oxygen) nor decay (there were no bacteria) would have destroyed these molecules, and they would have accumulated in the oceans for hundreds of millions of years. With the accumulation of these small organic compounds, the oceans became a thick, warm organic soup containing a variety of organic molecules.

> Atmospheric gases dissolved in the ocean may have reacted with one another to produce simple organic molecules.

Macromolecules Evolve and Interact

The newly formed organic molecules likely polymerized to produce still larger molecules and then macromolecules. There are three primary hypotheses concerning this stage in the origin of life. One is the *RNA-first hypothesis,* which suggests that only the macromolecule RNA (ribonucleic acid) was needed at this time to progress toward formation of the first cell or cells. Thomas Cech and Sidney Altman shared a Nobel prize in 1989 because they discovered that RNA can be both a substrate and an enzyme. Other types of ribozymes (RNA enzymes) have since been discovered. It would seem, then, that RNA could have carried out the processes of life commonly associated today with DNA (deoxyribonucleic acid, the genetic material) and proteins (enzymes). Some viruses today have RNA genes; therefore, the first genes could have been RNA. And the first enzymes also could have been RNA molecules, since we now know that ribozymes exist. Those who support this hypothesis say that it was an "RNA world" some 4 billion years ago.

Another hypothesis is termed the *protein-first hypothesis.* Sidney Fox, has shown that amino acids polymerize abiotically when exposed to dry heat (see fig. 21.1*c*). He suggests that amino acids collected in shallow puddles along the rocky shore and the heat of the sun caused them to form **proteinoids,** small polypeptides that have some catalytic properties. When proteinoids are returned to water, they form **microspheres** [Gk. *micr,* small, and *spher,* ball], structures composed only of protein that have many properties of a cell. Its possible that the first polypeptides had enzymatic properties and some proved to be more capable than others. Those that led to the first cell or cells had a selective advantage. This hypothesis assumes that DNA genes came after protein enzymes arose. After all, it is protein enzymes that are needed for DNA replication.

The third hypothesis is put forth by Graham Cairns-Smith. He believes that clay was especially helpful in causing polymerization of both proteins and nucleic acids at the same time. Clay attracts small organic molecules and contains iron and zinc, which may have served as inorganic catalysts for polypeptide formation. In addition, clay has a tendency to collect energy from radioactive decay and to discharge it when the temperature and/or humidity changes. This could have been a source of energy for polymerization to take place. Cairns-Smith suggests that RNA nucleotides and amino acids became associated in such a way that polypeptides were ordered by and helped synthesize RNA. It is clear that this hypothesis suggests that both polypeptides and RNA arose at the same time.

> Small organic molecules polymerized to produce macromolecules. This could have occurred on heated rocks or in clay.

A Protocell Evolves

Before the first true cell arose, there would have been a **protocell** [Gk. *proto,* first], a structure that has a lipid-protein membrane and carries on energy metabolism (fig. 21.3). Fox

Figure 21.3

Protocell anatomy. **a.** Microspheres, which are composed only of protein, have a number of cellular characteristics and could have evolved into the protocell. **b.** Liposomes form automatically when phospholipid molecules are put into water. Cellular membrane may have evolved similarly.

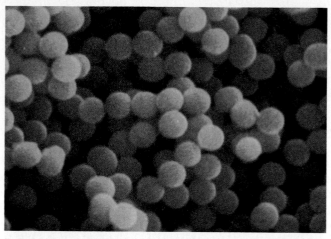

a.

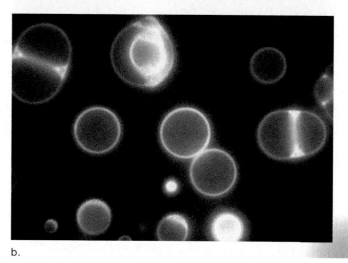

b.

has shown that if lipids are made available to microspheres, lipids tend to become associated with microspheres producing a lipid-protein membrane.

Some researchers support the work of Oparin, who was mentioned previously. Oparin showed that under appropriate conditions of temperature, ionic composition, and pH, concentrated mixtures of macromolecules tend to give rise to complex units called *coacervate droplets.* Coacervate droplets have a tendency to absorb and incorporate various substances from the surrounding solution. Eventually, a semipermeable-type boundary may form about the droplet. In a liquid environment, phospholipid molecules automatically form droplets called **liposomes** [Gk. *lipo,* fat, and *soma,* body]. Perhaps the first membrane formed in this manner. In that case, the protocell could have contained only RNA, which functioned as both genetic material and enzymes.

Protocells Were Heterotrophs

The protocell would have had to carry on nutrition so that it could grow. Nutrition was no problem because the protocell existed in the ocean, which at that time contained simple organic molecules that could have served as food. Therefore, the protocell likely was a **heterotroph** [Gk. *heter,* different, and *troph,* feeder], an organism that takes in preformed food. Notice that this suggests that heterotrophs are believed to have preceded **autotrophs** [Gk. *auto,* self, and *troph,* feeder], organisms that make their own food.

At first, the protocell may have used preformed ATP (adenosine triphosphate), but as this supply dwindled, natural selection favored any cells that could extract energy from carbohydrates in order to transform ADP (adenosine diphosphate) to ATP. Glycolysis is a common metabolic pathway in living things, and this testifies to its early evolution in the history of life. Since there was no free oxygen, we can assume that the protocell carried on a form of fermentation.

It seems logical that the protocell at first had limited ability to break down organic molecules and that it took millions of years for glycolysis to evolve completely. It is of interest that Fox has shown that a microsphere from which the protocell may have evolved has some catalytic ability and that Oparin found that coacervates do incorporate enzymes if they are available in the medium.

> The protocell is hypothesized to have had a membrane boundary and to have been a heterotrophic fermenter with some degree of enzymatic ability.

A Self-Replication System Evolves

A true cell is a membrane-bounded structure that can carry on protein synthesis needed to produce the enzymes that allow DNA to replicate (fig. 21.4). The central dogma of genetics states that DNA directs protein synthesis and that there is a flow of information from DNA → RNA → protein. It is possible that this sequence developed in stages.

According to the RNA-first hypothesis, RNA would have been the first to evolve, and the first true cell would have had RNA genes. These genes would have directed and enzymatically carried out protein synthesis. As mentioned, RNA enzymes called ribozymes have been discovered. Also, today we know there are viruses that have RNA genes. These viruses have a protein enzyme called reverse transcriptase that uses RNA as a template to form DNA. Perhaps with time, reverse transcription occurred within the protocell, and this is how DNA genes arose. Once there were DNA genes, then protein synthesis would have been carried out in the manner dictated by the central dogma of genetics.

According to the protein-first hypothesis, proteins, or at least polypeptides, were the first of the three (i.e., DNA, RNA, and protein) to arise. Only after the protocell developed sophisticated enzymes did it have the ability to synthesize DNA and RNA from small molecules provided by the ocean. Researchers

Figure 21.4

A chemical evolution produced the protocell. There was an increase in the complexity of macromolecules, leading to a self-replicating system (DNA → RNA → protein) enclosed by a plasma membrane. The protocell, a heterotrophic fermenter, underwent biological evolution, becoming a true cell, which then diversified.

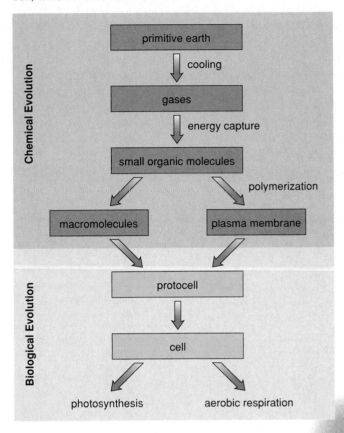

point out that a nucleic acid is a very complicated molecule, and the likelihood that RNA arose *de novo* (on its own) is minimal. It seems more likely that enzymes were needed to guide the synthesis of nucleotides and then nucleic acids.

Cairns-Smith proposes that polypeptides and RNA evolved simultaneously. Therefore, the first true cell would have contained RNA genes that could have replicated because of the presence of proteins. This eliminates the baffling chicken-and-egg paradox: which came first, proteins or RNA? But it does mean, however, that two unlikely events would have to happen at the same time.

Once the protocells acquired genes that could replicate, they became cells capable of reproducing, and biological evolution began. The history of life began!

> Once the protocell was capable of reproduction, it became a true cell and biological evolution began.

HISTORY OF LIFE

Figure 21.5 shows the history of the earth as if it had occurred during a twenty-four-hour time span that starts at midnight. (The actual years are shown on an inner ring of the diagram.) This figure illustrates dramatically that only unicellular organisms were present during most (about 80%) of the history of the earth.

If the earth formed at midnight, prokaryotes do not appear until about 5 A.M., eukaryotes are present at approximately 4 P.M., and multicellular forms do not appear until around 8 P.M. Invasion of the land doesn't occur until about 10 P.M. and humans don't appear until thirty seconds before the end of the day. This timetable has been worked out by studying the fossil record.

Fossils Tell a Story

Fossils [L. *fossil,* dug up] are the remains and traces of past life or any other direct evidence of past life. Traces include trails, footprints, burrows, worm casts, or even preserved droppings. Usually when an organism dies, the soft parts are either consumed by scavengers or undergo bacterial decomposition. Occasionally, the organism is buried quickly and in such a way that decomposition is never completed or is completed so slowly that the soft parts leave an imprint of their structure. Most fossils, however, consist only of hard parts such as shells, bones, or teeth, because these are usually not consumed or destroyed.

The great majority of fossils are found embedded in or recently eroded from sedimentary rock. **Sedimentation** [L.

Figure 21.5

The outer ring of this diagram shows the history of the earth as it would be measured on a twenty-four-hour time scale starting at midnight. (The inner ring shows the actual years starting at 4.5 billion years ago.) When the history of the earth is measured as if it had all happened in a day, the Cambrian period does not start until 8 P.M.! This means that a very large portion of life's history was devoted to the evolution of unicellular organisms. The first multicellular organisms probably did not appear until just before 8 P.M., and humans were not on the scene until less than a minute before midnight.

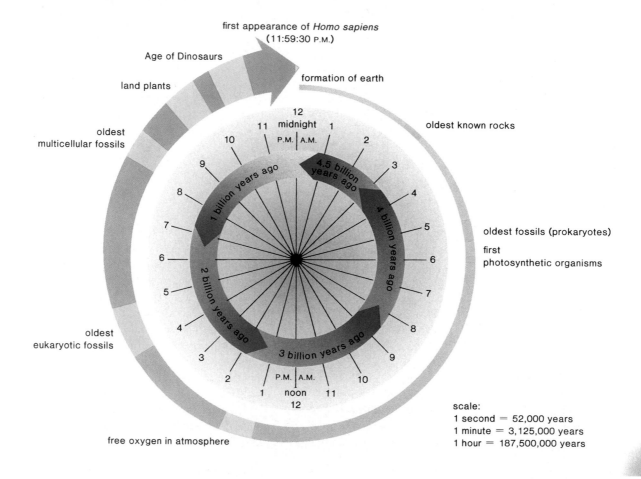

scale:
1 second = 52,000 years
1 minute = 3,125,000 years
1 hour = 187,500,000 years

Figure 21.6

The Grand Canyon. No other place on earth displays such an extensive record of the earth's events for analysis, dating, and study. Even so, it does not have a stratigraphic sequence for the whole of geological time. This was determined by correlating the strata of the canyon to that of other parts of the world.

sedimentum, a settling], a process that has been going on since the earth was formed, can take place on land or in bodies of water. Weathering and erosion of rocks produces an accumulation of particles that vary in size and nature and are called sediment. Sediment becomes a *stratum* (pl., strata), a recognizable layer in a stratigraphic sequence (fig. 21.6). Any given stratum is older than the one above it and younger than the one immediately below it.

The fossils trapped in strata are the fossil record that tells us about the history of life. **Paleontology** [Gk. *paleo,* ancient, and *logy,* study of] is the science of discovering and studying the fossil record and, from it, making decisions about the history of life. Paleontologists not only want to know the structure and adaptations of an organism, they are also interested in how the organism interacted with others and with the physical environment.

Dating Fossils Relatively

In the early nineteenth century, even before the theory of evolution was formulated, geologists sought to correlate the strata worldwide. The problem was that strata change their character over great distances, and therefore a stratum in England might contain different sediments than one of the same age in Russia. Geologists discovered, however, that a stratum of the same age might contain the same fossil, and therefore, fossils could be used for the purpose of *relative dating* of the strata. For example, a particular species of fossil ammonite (an animal related to the chambered nautilus) has been found over a wide range and for a limited time period. Therefore, all strata around the world that contain this fossil must be of the same age.

This approach helped geologists determine the relative dates of the strata despite upheavals, but it was not particularly helpful to biologists who wanted to know the absolute age of fossils in years.

Dating Fossils Absolutely

The absolute dating method that relies on radioactive dating techniques assigns an actual date to a fossil. All radioactive isotopes have a particular half-life, the length of time it takes for half of the radioative isotope to change into another stable element. If the fossil has organic matter, half of the carbon-14, ^{14}C, will have changed to nitrogen-14, 14_N, in 5,730 years. In order to know how much ^{14}C was in the organism to begin with, it is reasoned that organic matter always begins with the same amount of ^{14}C. (In reality, it is known that the ^{14}C levels in the air—and therefore the amount in organisms—can vary from time to time.) Now we need only compare the ^{14}C radioactivity of the fossil to that of a modern sample of organic matter. The amount of radiation left can be converted to the age of the fossil. After 50,000 years, however, the amount of ^{14}C radioactivity is so low it cannot be used to measure the age of a fossil accurately.

^{14}C is the only radioactive isotope contained within organic matter, but it is possible to use others to date rocks and from that infer the age of a fossil contained in the rock. For instance, the ratio of potassium-40 (^{40}K) to argon-40 trapped in rock is often used. If the ratio happens to be 1:1, then half of the ^{40}K has decayed and the rock is 1.3 billion years old. The ratio of isotope uranium-238 to lead-207 can be used only for rocks older than 100 million years. This isotope has such a long half-life that no perceptible decay will have occurred in a shorter length of time.

> Fossils, which can be dated relatively according to their location in strata and absolutely according to their content of radioactive isotopes, give us information about the history of life.

Earth's Crust Is Dynamic

It used to be thought that the earth's crust was immobile, that the continents had always been in their present positions, and that the ocean floors were only a catch basin for the debris that washed off the land. In 1920 Alfred Wegener, a German meteorologist, presented data from a number of disciplines to support his hypothesis of **continental drift.** This hypothesis, which was finally confirmed in the 1960s, states that the continents are not fixed; instead, their positions and the position of the oceans have changed over time (fig. 21.7). About 225 million years ago (MYA) the continents joined to form one supercontinent that Wegener called Pangaea. First, Pangaea divided into two large subcontinents, called Gondwanaland and Laurasia, and then these also split to form the continents of today. Presently, the continents are still drifting in relation to one another.

Continental drift explains why the coastlines of several continents are mirror images of each other—the outline of the west coast of Africa matches that of the east coast of South America. The same geological structures are also found in many of the areas where the continents touched. A single mountain range runs through South America, Antarctica, and Australia. Continental drift also explains the unique distribution patterns of several fossils. Fossils of the same species of seed fern (*Glossopteris*) have been found on all the southern continents. No suitable explanation was possible previously, but now it seems plausible that the plant evolved on one continent and spread to the others when they were joined as one. Similarly, the fossil reptile *Cynognathus* is found in Africa and South America and *Lystrosaurus,* a mammal-like reptile, has now been found in Antarctica, far from Africa and southeast Asia, where it is also found. With mammalian fossils, the situation is different: Australia, South America, and Africa all have their own distinctive mammals because mammals evolved after the continents separated. The mammalian biological diversity of today's world is the result of isolated evolution on separate continents.

> The relationship of the continents to one another has affected the biogeography of the earth.

Figure 21.7

History of the placement of today's continents. **a.** About 200–250 million years ago, all the continents were joined into a supercontinent called Pangaea. **b.** When the joined continents of Pangaea first began moving apart, there were two large continents called Laurasia and Gondwanaland. **c.** By 65 million years ago, all the continents had begun to separate. This process is continuing today. **d.** North America and Europe are presently drifting apart at a rate of about 2 cm per year.

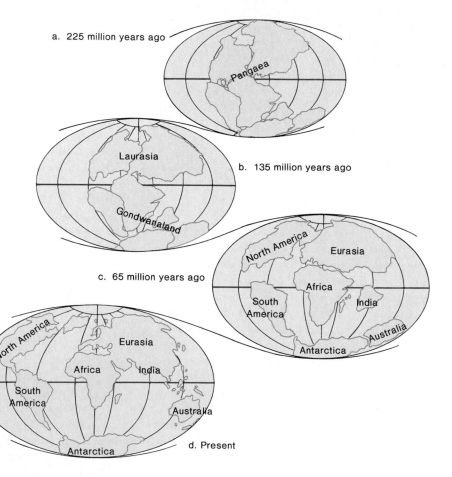

a. 225 million years ago

b. 135 million years ago

c. 65 million years ago

d. Present

Why do the continents drift? According to a branch of geology known as **plate tectonics** [Gk. *tect,* a covering] (tectonics refers to movements of the earth's crust), the earth's crust is fragmented into slablike plates that float on a lower hot mantle layer. The continents and the ocean basins are a part of these rigid plates, which move like conveyor belts (fig. 21.8). At **ocean ridges,** seafloor spreading occurs as molten mantle rock rises and material is added to the ocean floor. Seafloor spreading causes the continents to move a few centimeters a year on the average. At *subduction zones* the forward edge of a moving plate sinks into the mantle and is destroyed. When an ocean floor is at the leading edge of a plate, a deep trench forms that is bordered by volcanoes or volcanic island chains. When two continents collide, the result is often a mountain range; for example, the Himalayas resulted when India collided with Eurasia. Two plates also meet along a *transform fault* where two plates scrape past one another. The San Andreas fault in southern California is at a transform boundary, and the movement of the two plates is responsible for the many earthquakes in that region.

> The earth's crust is divided into plates that move because of seafloor spreading at ocean ridges.

Figure 21.8

Plate tectonics. **a.** Plates form and move away from ocean ridges toward subduction zones, where they are carried into the mantle and are destroyed. **b.** A transform fault, such as the San Andreas fault in southern California, occurs where two plates scrape past each other during their movement. Earthquakes are apt to occur here. **c.** Iceland is one of the few places in the world where an ocean ridge reaches the surface of the sea. The entire island is volcanic in origin.

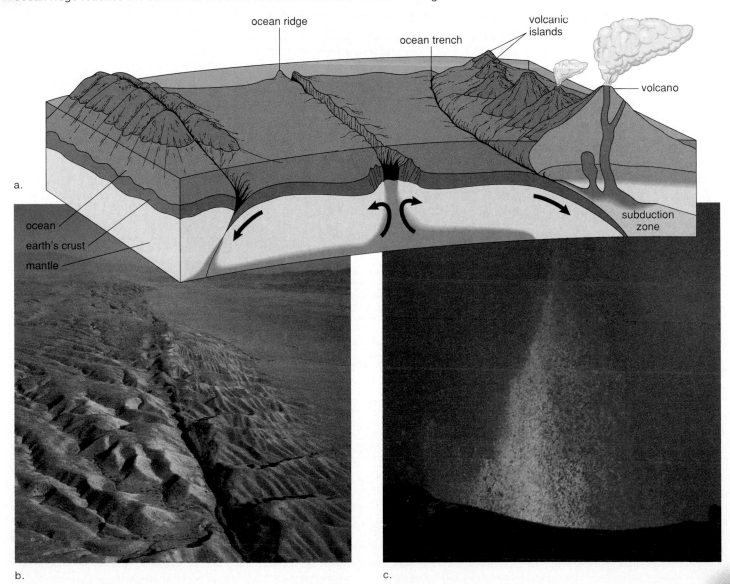

How the Story Unfolds

As a result of their study of strata, geologists have divided the history of the earth into eras, then periods and epochs (table 21.1). We will follow the biologist's tradition of first discussing the Precambrian, a period of time that encompasses the first two eras: the Archean eon and the Proterozoic eon.

Life Begins in the Precambrian

The Precambrian is a very long period of time—it comprises about 87% of the geologic time scale. It is during this period of time that life arose and the first cells came into existence. The first cells must have been prokaryotes. Prokaryotes are bacteria that do not have a nucleus or any membranous organelles. Of the

Table 21.1

The Geological Time Scale: Major Divisions of Geological Time with Some of the Major Evolutionary Events of Each Geological Period

Era	Period	Epoch	Millions of Years Ago	Plant Life	Animal Life
Cenozoic* (from the present to 66.4 million years ago)	Neogene	Holocene	0–0.01	Destruction of tropical rain forests by humans accelerates extinctions	AGE OF HUMAN CIVILIZATION
				Significant Mammalian Extinction	
		Pleistocene	0.01–2	Herbaceous plants spread and diversify	Modern humans appear
		Pliocene	2–6	Herbaceous angiosperms flourish	First hominids appear
		Miocene	6–24	Grasslands spread as forests contract	Apelike mammals and grazing mammals flourish; insects flourish
	Paleogene	Oligocene	24–37	Many modern families of flowering plants evolve	Browsing mammals and monkeylike primates appear
				Significant Mammalian Extinction	
				Significant Mammalian Extinction	
		Eocene	37–58	Subtropical forests with heavy rainfall thrive	All modern orders of mammals are represented
		Paleocene	58–66	Angiosperms diversify	Primitive primates, herbivores, carnivores, and insectivores appear
Mesozoic (from 66.4 to 245 million years ago)				**Mass Extinction: Dinosaurs and Most Reptiles**	
	Cretaceous		66–144	Flowering plants spread; coniferous trees decline	Placental mammals appear; modern insect groups appear
	Jurassic		144–208	Cycads and other gymnosperms flourish	Dinosaurs flourish; birds appear
				Mass Extinction	
	Triassic		208–245	Cycads and ginkgos appear; forests of gymnosperms and ferns dominate	First mammals appear; first dinosaurs appear; corals and mollusks dominate seas
Paleozoic (from 245 to 570 million years ago)				**Mass Extinction**	
	Permian		245–286	Conifers appear	Reptiles diversify; amphibians decline
	Carboniferous		286–360	Age of great coal-forming forests: club mosses, horsetails, and ferns flourish	Amphibians diversify; first reptiles appear; first great radiation of insects
				Mass Extinction	
	Devonian		360–408	First seed ferns appear	Jawed fishes diversify and dominate the seas; first insects and first amphibians appear
	Silurian		408–438	Low-lying primitive vascular plants appear on land	First jawed fishes appear
				Mass Extinction	
	Ordovician		438–505	Marine algae flourish	Invertebrates spread and diversify; jawless fishes, first vertebrates, appear
	Cambrian		505–570	Marine algae flourish	Invertebrates with skeletons are dominant
Precambrian time (from 570 to 4,600 million years ago)			700 1,500 3,100–3,500 4,600	Multicellular organisms appear First complex (eukaryotic) cells appear First prokaryotic cells in stromatolites appear Earth forms	

*Many authorities divide the Cenozoic era into the Tertiary period (contains Paleocene, Eocene, Oligocene, Miocene, and Pliocene) and the Quaternary period (contains Pleistocene and Holocene).

living prokaryotes today (i.e., bacteria), there is a type called archaebacteria that live in the most inhospitable of environments such as hot springs, very salty lakes, and airless swamps—all of which may typify habitats on the primitive earth. The cell wall, plasma membrane, RNA polymerase, and ribosomes of archaebacteria are more like those of eukaryotes than those of other bacteria.

As discussed, the first cell or cells must have been anaerobic heterotrophs (there was no oxygen in the primitive atmosphere). Also, the first photosynthesizers most likely did not give off oxygen. By 2 billion years ago (BYA), however, oxygen-releasing photosynthesis began. Some of the earliest cells, dated about 3.5 BYA, are found in fossilized stromatolites, which are pillarlike structures composed of sedimentary layers containing communities of prokaryotic organisms (fig. 21.9). Stromatolites containing cyanobacteria, which carry on oxygen-releasing photosynthesis, exist even today in shallow waters off the west coast of Australia.

Due to the action of photosynthesizers, the atmosphere became an oxidizing one instead of a reducing one. Oxygen in the upper atmosphere forms ozone (O_3), which filters out the ultraviolet (UV) rays of the sun. Before the formation of the **ozone shield,** the amount of ultraviolet radiation reaching the earth could have helped create organic molecules, but it would have destroyed any land-dwelling organisms. Once the ozone shield was in place, it meant that living things would be sufficiently protected and would be able to live on land. Life on land is threatened if the ozone shield is reduced. This is why there is such concern today about pollutants, which act to break down the ozone shield.

> **The evolution of photosynthesizing organisms caused oxygen to enter the atmosphere.**

The presence of oxygen in the atmosphere meant that most environments were no longer suitable for anaerobic prokaryotes, and they began to decline in importance. Photosynthetic cyanobacteria and aerobic bacteria proliferated as new metabolic pathways evolved.

Figure 21.9

Fossils of prokaryotes dated from about 3.5 billion years ago. **a.** This prokaryotic microorganism, *Primaevifilum,* (with interpretive drawing), was found in a fossilized stromatolite. **b.** Living stromatolites are located in shallow waters off the shores of western Australia and also in other tropical seas.

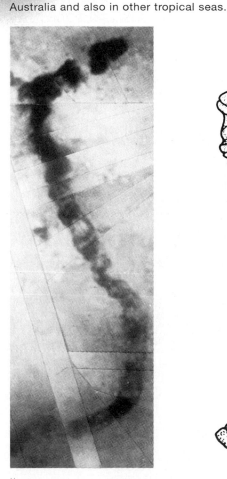
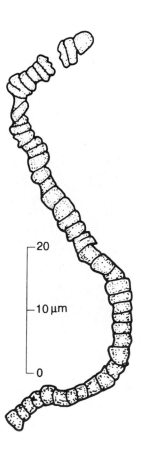

a.

b.

Eukaryotic Cells Arise

The eukaryotic cell, which originated about 2.1 BYA, is nearly always aerobic and contains a nucleus as well as other membranous organelles. Most likely the eukaryotic cell acquired its organelles gradually. It may be that the nucleus developed by an invagination of the plasma membrane. The mitochondria of the eukaryotic cell probably were once free-living aerobic prokaryotes, and the chloroplasts probably were free-living photosynthetic prokaryotes. The theory of endosymbiosis says that the nucleated cell engulfed these prokaryotes, which then became organelles. Its been suggested that flagella (and cilia) also arose by endosymbiosis. First, slender undulating prokaryotes could have attached themselves to a host cell in order to take advantage of food leaking from the host's outer membrane. Eventually, these prokaryotes were drawn inside the host cell and became the flagella and cilia we know today. The first eukaryotes were unicellular, as are prokaryotes.

> Only unicellular organisms existed on earth during most of its history. During this time many biochemical pathways evolved.

It is not known when multicellularity began but the very first multicellular forms were most likely microscopic. Its possible that the first multicellular organisms practiced sexual reproduction. Among protoctists (eukaryotes classified in the kingdom Protoctista) today, we find colonial forms in which some cells are specialized to produce gametes needed for sexual reproduction. Separation of germ cells, which produce gametes from somatic cells, may have been an important first step toward the development of complex macroscopic animals that appeared about 600 million years ago (MYA). In 1947, fossils of soft-bodied invertebrates of this date were found in the Ediacara Hills in South Australia. Since then, similar fossils have been discovered on a number of other continents. They represent a community of animals that most likely lived on mud flats in shallow marine waters (fig. 21.10). Many biologists interpret the fossils as being like jellyfish, sea pens (relatives of corals), and segmented worms. Other fossils seem unrelated to the types of animals alive today.

> Diverse, complex organisms appear in the fossil record about 600 MYA, perhaps as a result of the evolution of multicellularity in association with sexual reproduction.

Figure 21.10

Late Precambrian animals. **a.** Artist's representation of a community of animals, based on Ediacaran fossils. The large frondlike organisms are interpreted here as soft corals, known today as sea pens. Silvery jellyfish swim about and an elongate, wormlike creature is on the seafloor.
b. *Dickinsonia costata,* a fossil that is interpreted to be a segmented worm.

a.

b.

Complexity Increases in Paleozoic

The Paleozoic era lasted over 300 million years. Many events occurred during this time, which is quite short compared to the length of the Precambrian. For one thing, there were three major mass extinctions. An **extinction** is the total disappearance of all the members of a species or a higher taxonomic group. A **mass extinction** is the disappearance of a large number of species or higher taxonomic groups within an interval of just a few million years. After a mass extinction, remaining groups are apt to undergo adaptive radiations (new groups arise from a single ancestral group) as they spread out into the empty habitats.

Explosion in the Cambrian

Figure 21.11 shows that the seas teemed with invertebrate life during the Cambrian period. *Invertebrates* are animals without a vertebral column. All of today's animals can undoubtedly trace their ancestry to this time, which is called the Cambrian explosion because the strata are suddenly filled with fossils. Why are fossils from this time period easier to find? Because the animals had protective outer skeletons, and skeletons are capable of surviving the forces that are apt to destroy fossils. For example, Cambrian seafloors were dominated by now-extinct trilobites, which had thick, jointed armor covering them from head to tail. Trilobites are classified as arthropods, a major phylum of animals today. (Some Cambrian species, with most unusual eating and locomotor appendages, have been classified in phyla that no longer exist today.)

Paleontologists have sought an explanation for the Cambrian explosion. They have noted that not only are fossils more abundant, they are also more diverse. The richness of the fossil record may have also been due to the evolution of skeletons. What might have caused the evolution of skeletons?

By this time, not only cyanobacteria but also various algae, which are floating photosynthetic organisms, were pumping oxygen into the atmosphere. Perhaps the oxygen supply became great enough to permit aquatic animals to acquire oxygen even though they had outer skeletons. The presence of a skeleton cuts down on possible access to oxygen in seawater.

Studies of present-day ecosystems suggest that the presence of predators maintains the diversity of a community. Steven Stanley of Johns Hopkins University has gone one step further to suggest that predators, which first appear in the Cambrian period, may have caused an increase in diversity at that time. Skeletons may have been an evolved solution to predation because outer skeletons help protect animals from predation.

> **The Cambrian period saw an abundance of life not observed before in the fossil record. This increase in diversity is associated with the presence of outer skeletons.**

Figure 21.11

Artist's interpretation of the shallow seas of the Cambrian period. All major phyla of animals arose during a short few tens of millions of years. The animals depicted here are found as fossils in the Burgess Shale, a formation of the Rocky Mountains of British Columbia. Some lineages represented by these animals are still evolving today; others have become extinct.

Figure 21.12

Vast swamp forests of treelike club mosses and horsetails dominated the land during the Carboniferous period. The air contained insects with wide wingspans, such as the dragonfly shown here, and amphibians lumbered from pool to pool.

Later, Land Is Invaded

Sometime during the Paleozoic era, algae, which were common in the seas, most likely began to take up residence in bodies of freshwater; from there, they may have invaded damp areas on land. An association of plant roots with fungi called mycorrhizae is credited with allowing plants to live on bare rocks. The fungi are able to absorb minerals, which they pass to the plant, and the plant in turn passes carbohydrates, the product of photosynthesis, to the fungi.

The most successful land plants have vascular tissue for water transport, but there are no fossils of vascular plants until the Silurian period. The first vascular plants flourished in the warm swamps of the *Carboniferous period* (fig. 21.12). Club mosses, horsetails, and seed ferns were the trees of that time, and they grew to enormous size. A wide variety of smaller ferns and fernlike plants formed an underbrush.

The first animals to live on land were scorpions, carnivorous relatives of spiders with a poisonous stinger at the end of their tail and two large pincers on their front legs. Insects enter the fossil record in the Carboniferous period. The outer skeleton and jointed appendages of insects were suitable to a land existence. An outer skeleton prevents drying out, and jointed appendages provide a suitable means of locomotion on land. These traits, plus the evolution of wings, provided advantages that allowed insects to radiate into the most diverse and abundant group of animals today. Flying provides a way to escape enemies and find food.

Vertebrates are animals with a vertebral column. The vertebrate line of descent began in the early Ordovician period with the evolution of fishes. First there were jawless fishes and then fishes with jaws. *Fishes* are ectothermic (cold-blooded), aquatic vertebrates that have gills, scales, and fins. The ray-finned fishes, which include today's most familiar fish, make their appearance in the Devonian period, which is called the Age of Fishes. Amphibians are more directly related to lobed-finned fishes, which may have ventured onto shore to avoid predators. The only vertebrates in the wet Carboniferous forests were *amphibians*, thin-skinned vertebrates that are not fully adapted to life on land, particularly because they must return to water to reproduce. The swamp forests provided the water they needed and amphibians radiated into many different sizes and shapes. Some superficially resembled alligators and were covered with protective scales, others were small and snakelike, and a few were larger plant eaters. The largest measured 6 meters (20 feet) from snout to tail. The Carboniferous period is called the Age of the Amphibians.

There was a change of climate at the end of the Carboniferous period as Gondwanaland wandered over the south pole. Cold and dry weather brought an end to the Age of the Amphibians and began the process that turned the great Carboniferous forests into the coal we use today to fuel our modern society.

> **Primitive vascular plants and amphibians were larger and more abundant during the Carboniferous period. Insects appeared and flourished to become the largest animal group today.**

Figure 21.13

Dinosaurs. **a.** The dinosaurs of the Jurassic period included *Apatosaurus,* which fed on cycads and conifers. **b.** *Tyrannosaurus rex* was a dinosaur of the Cretaceous period, when flowering plants were increasing in dominance.

a.

b.

Dinosaurs Rule in the Mesozoic

Although there was a mass extinction at the end of the Paleozoic era, the evolution of certain types of plants and animals continued into the Triassic, the first period of the Mesozoic era. Nonflowering seed plants (collectively called *Gymnosperms*), which had been present in the fossil record of the Permian period, became dominant. Among these largely cone-bearing plants were cycads and conifers. Cycads are short and stout with palmlike leaves; the female plant produces very large cones. Cycads were so prevalent during the Jurassic period that it is sometimes called the Age of the Cycads. By the Cretaceous period of the Mesozoic era, flowering plants (collectively called *angiosperms*) had begun to radiate and cone-bearing plants declined in importance.

Reptiles, too, can be traced back to the Permian period of the Paleozoic era. Unlike amphibians, *reptiles* can thrive in a dry climate because they have scaly skin and lay a shelled egg that hatches on land. Reptiles underwent an adaptive radiation during the Mesozoic to produce forms that lived in the air, in the sea, and on the land. At the beginning of the Mesozoic era, mammal-like reptiles called therapsids were prevalent. *Therapsids* had vertically positioned limbs that held the body off the ground. During the Jurassic period, large flying reptiles called *pterosaurs* ruled the air and giant marine reptiles with paddlelike limbs ate fishes in the sea, but on land it was the *dinosaurs* (fig. 21.13) that prevented the evolving mammals from taking center stage.

The dinosaurs were reptiles, some of an enormous size. During the Jurassic period, the gargantuan *Apatosaurus* and the armored tractor-sized *Stegosaurus* fed on cycad seeds and conifer trees. During the Cretaceous period, great herds of rhinolike *Triceratops* roamed the plains, as did the infamous *Tyrannosaurus rex,* which was carnivorous and played the same ecological role as lions do today. The size of a dinosaur such as *Apatosaurus* is hard for us to imagine. It was as tall as a four-story office building, and its weight was as much as that of a thousand people! How might dinosaurs have benefited from being so large? One theory is that being ectothermic, the volume-to-surface ratio was favorable for retaining heat. Others present evidence, based largely on bone construction, that at least some of the dinosaurs were endothermic (warm-blooded). Newly found evidence, as discussed in the reading on page 346, suggests that dinosaurs should not be classified as reptiles at all!

During the Jurassic period, one group of dinosaurs called theropods were bipedal and had an elongate, mobile S-shaped neck. The fossil *Archaeopteryx* is a transitional link, which shows that theropods are related to birds. Despite this animal's feathers, its jaw bore teeth and it had a long lizardlike tail. The fossil record for birds begins at this time and continues on into the next era.

By the end of the Cretaceous period, the dinosaurs were extinct. They were victims of a mass extinction brought about by causes that are still being debated.

During the Mesozoic era, the dinosaurs achieved an enormous size while mammals remained small and insignificant. Flowering plants replaced cone-bearing plants as the dominant vegetation.

Real Dinosaurs, Stand Up!

Today's paleontologists are setting the record straight about dinosaurs. Because dinosaurs are classified as reptiles, it is assumed that they must have had the characteristics of today's reptiles. They must have been ectothermic, slow moving, and antisocial, right? Wrong!

First of all, not all dinosaurs were great lumbering beasts. Many dinosaurs were less than 1 meter (3 feet) long and their tracks indicate they moved right along. These dinosaurs stood on two legs that were positioned directly under the body. Perhaps they were as agile as ostriches, which are famous for their great speed.

Dinosaurs may have been endothermic. Could they have competed successfully with the pre-evolving mammals otherwise? They must have been able to hunt prey and escape from predators as well as mammals, which are known to be active because of their high rate of metabolism. Some argue that ectothermic animals have little endurance and cannot keep up. They also believe that the bone structure of dinosaurs also indicates they were endothermic.

Dinosaurs cared for their young much like birds do today. In Montana, paleontologist Jack Horner has studied fossilized nests complete with eggs, embryos, and nestlings (fig. 21A). The nests are about 7.5 meters (24.6 feet) apart, the space needed for the length of an adult parent. About twenty eggs are laid in neatly arranged circles and may have been covered with decaying vegetation to keep them warm. Many contain the bones of juveniles as much as a meter long. It would seem then that baby dinosaurs remained in the nest to be fed by their parents. They must have obtained this size within a relatively short period of time, again indicating that dinosaurs were endothermic. Ectothermic animals grow slowly and take a long time to reach this size.

Dinosaurs were also social! An enormous herd of dinosaurs found by Horner and colleagues is estimated to have nearly 30 million bones, representing 10,000 animals in one area measuring about 1.6 square miles. Most likely, the herd kept on the move in order to be assured of an adequate food supply, which consisted of flowering plants that could be stripped one season and grow back the next season. The fossilized herd is covered by volcanic ash, suggesting that the dinosaurs died following a volcanic eruption.

Some dinosaurs, such as the duck-billed dinosaurs and horned dinosaurs, have a skull crest. How might it have functioned? Perhaps it was a resonating chamber, used when dinosaurs communicated with one another. Or, as with modern horned animals that live in large groups, the males could have used the skull crest in combat to establish dominance.

If dinosaurs were endothermic, fast-moving, and social animals, should they be classified as reptiles? Some say no!

Figure 21A

Nesting habits of dinosaurs. **a.** Nest of fossil dinosaur eggs found in Montana, dating from the Cretaceous period. **b.** Bones of a hatchling (about 50 cm [20 inches]) found in the nest. These dinosaurs have been named *Maiosaura,* which means "good mother lizard" in Greek.

a.

b.

Figure 21.14

Mammals from the Oligocene epoch. The artist's representation of these mammals is based on skeletal remains, and the vegetation is also based on fossils.

Mammals Take Over in the Cenozoic

According to a new system of dividing the Cenozoic era, there is a Paleogene period and a Neogene period. We are living in the Neogene period.

Mammals Diversify in the Paleogene

At the end of the Mesozoic era, mammals began an adaptive radiation into the many habitats now left vacant by the demise of the dinosaurs. Mammals are endothermic and they have hair, which helps keep body heat from escaping. Their name refers to the presence of mammary glands, which produce milk to feed their young. At the start of the Paleocene epoch, mammals were small and resembled a mouse. By the end of the Eocene epoch, mammals had diversified to the point that most of the modern orders were in existence. Bats are mammals that have conquered the air. Whales, dolphins, and other marine mammals live in the sea where vertebrates began their evolution in the first place. Hoofed mammals populate forests and grasslands and are fed upon by diverse carnivores. Many of the types of herbivores and carnivores of the late Paleogene period, however, are extinct today (fig. 21.14).

Primates Evolve in the Neogene

Primates are a type of mammal adapted to living in flowering trees where there is protection from predators and where food in the form of fruit is plentiful. The first primates were small squirrel-like animals, but from them evolved the first monkeys and then apes. During the Miocene epoch, there was a change in the weather such that grasslands replaced many of the African forests. It was then that hominids began to walk on two legs and the human line of descent began.

The world's climate was progressively cooler during the Neogene period, so much so that the latter two epochs are known as the Ice Age. During periods of glaciation, snow and ice covered about one-third of the land surface of the earth. The Pleistocene

Figure 21.15

The woolly mammoth, *Mammuthus*. These magnificent animals lived along the borders of continental glaciers during the late Pleistocene epoch.

epoch was an age of not only humans, but also giant ground sloths, beavers, wolves, bison, woolly rhinoceroses, mastodons, and mammoths (fig. 21.15). Humans have survived, but what happened to the oversized mammals just mentioned? Some think that humans became such skilled hunters they are at least partially responsible for the extinction of these awe-inspiring animals.

> The Cenozoic era is the present era.
> Only during this time did mammals diversify
> and human evolution begin.

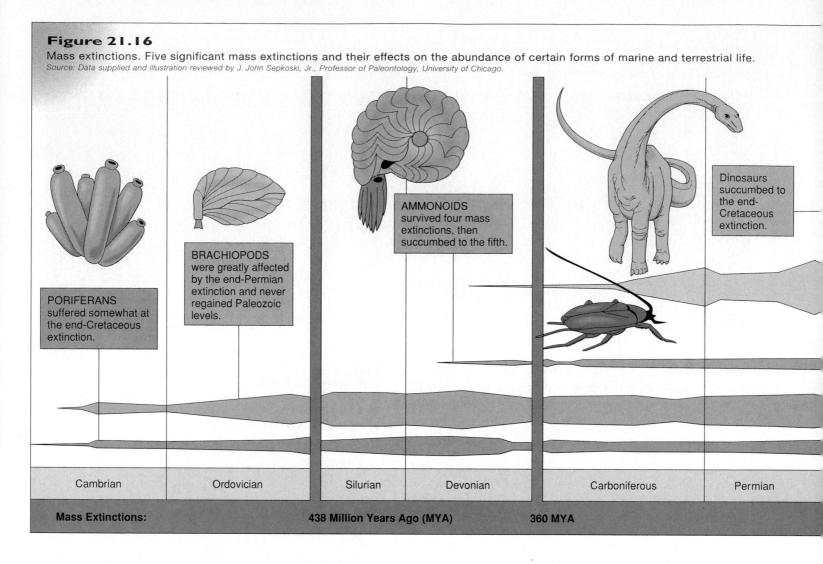

Figure 21.16

Mass extinctions. Five significant mass extinctions and their effects on the abundance of certain forms of marine and terrestrial life.
Source: Data supplied and illustration reviewed by J. John Sepkoski, Jr., Professor of Paleontology, University of Chicago.

AMMONOIDS survived four mass extinctions, then succumbed to the fifth.

Dinosaurs succumbed to the end-Cretaceous extinction.

BRACHIOPODS were greatly affected by the end-Permian extinction and never regained Paleozoic levels.

PORIFERANS suffered somewhat at the end-Cretaceous extinction.

| Cambrian | Ordovician | Silurian | Devonian | Carboniferous | Permian |

Mass Extinctions: 438 Million Years Ago (MYA)   360 MYA

Exploring Mass Extinctions

Mass extinctions are times when a large percentage of existing species becomes extinct within a relatively short period of time. There have been at least five mass extinctions throughout history: at the ends of the Ordovician, Devonian, Permian, Triassic, and Cretaceous periods (fig. 21.16). Mass extinctions are usually followed by at least partial evolutionary recovery in which the remaining groups of organisms undergo adaptive radiations and fill the habitats vacated by those that have become extinct.

Is a mass extinction due to some cataclysmic event, or is it a more gradual process brought on by environmental changes including tectonic, oceanic, and climatic fluctuations? This question was brought to the fore when Walter and Luis Alvarez proposed in 1977 that the Cretaceous extinction was due to a bolide. A *bolide* is an asteroid that explodes, producing meteorites that fall to earth. They found that Cretaceous clay contains an abnormally high level of iridium, an element that is rare in the earth's crust but more common in asteroids (or their fragments, meteorites). The result of a large meteorite striking the earth could have been similar to that from a worldwide atomic bomb explosion: a cloud of dust would have mushroomed into the atmosphere, blocking out the sun and causing plants to freeze and die. Recently, a

layer of soot has also been identified in the strata alongside the iridium, and a huge crater that could have been caused by a meteorite was found a few years ago in the Caribbean-Gulf of Mexico region on the Yucatán peninsula.

In 1984, paleontologists David Raup and John Sepkoski suggested that the fossil record of marine animals shows that mass extinctions have occurred every 26 million years and, surprisingly, astronomers can offer an explanation. Our solar system is in the Milky Way, a starry galaxy that is 1,000,000 light-years[1] in diameter and 1,500 or so light-years thick. Our sun moves up and down as it orbits in the Milky Way. Astronomers predict that this vertical movement will cause our solar system to approach certain other members of the Milky Way every 26–33 million years, producing an unstable situation that could lead to the occurrence of a bolide. This evidence suggests that mass extinctions are very often associated with extraterrestrial events, but they are not necessarily the total cause.

Certainly continental drift contributed to the Ordovician extinction. This extinction occurred after Gondwanaland arrived

---

1 One light-year, which is the distance light travels in a year, is about 6 trillion miles.

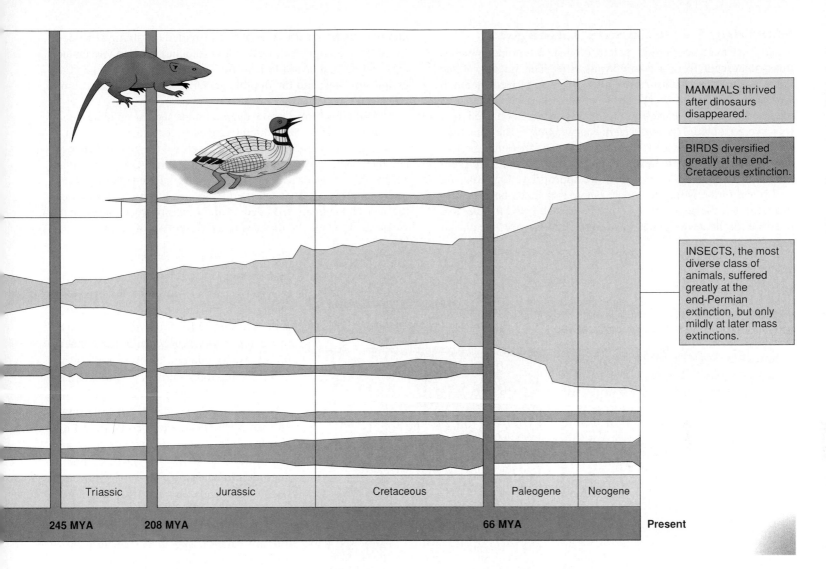

MAMMALS thrived after dinosaurs disappeared.

BIRDS diversified greatly at the end-Cretaceous extinction.

INSECTS, the most diverse class of animals, suffered greatly at the end-Permian extinction, but only mildly at later mass extinctions.

| Triassic | Jurassic | Cretaceous | Paleogene | Neogene |

245 MYA   **208 MYA**   **66 MYA**   **Present**

at the south pole. Immense glaciers, which drew water from the oceans, chilled even the once-tropical land. Marine invertebrates and coral reefs, which were especially hard hit, didn't recover until Gondwanaland drifted away from the pole and warmth returned. The mass extinction at the end of the Devonian saw an end to 70% of marine invertebrates. Helmont Geldsetzer of Canada's Geological Survey notes that iridium has also been found in Devonian rocks in Australia, suggesting that a bolide event was also involved in the Devonian extinction. Other scientists believe that this mass extinction could have occurred when Gondwanaland headed back over the south pole.

At the end of the Permian period, all land masses joined to form the supercontinent Pangaea. The amount of shallow offshore water shrank dramatically and marine life was greatly affected. The trilobites became extinct and the crinoids (sea lilies) barely hung on. Glaciers originating at either pole poured periodically over the land, and the inland weather grew drier and colder. The swamp forests that had originated in the Carboniferous period proliferated. These trees and their amphibian inhabitants were particularly affected. The Permian extinction is the worst by far, with nearly 96% of species disappearing. But the mammal-like reptiles that had evolved by now made it through to the Triassic period.

The extinction at the end of the Triassic period is another that has been attributed to the environmental effects of a meteorite collision with earth. Central Quebec has a crater half the size of Connecticut that some believe is the impact site. The dinosaurs may have benefited from this event because this is the time when the first of the gigantic dinosaurs took charge of the land. The second wave occurred in the Cretaceous period.

Whether a bolide caused or contributed to the Cretaceous extinction is still being investigated. This extinction—which doomed the dinosaurs, pterosaurs, ammonoids, and over 75% of the known species of marine plankton—did not happen overnight. Terrestrial events such as tectonic, oceanic, and climatic fluctuations contributed to sporadic periods of extinction over a period of 0.5 to 5 million years. It could be that an extraterrestrial event dealt the final blow.

> **Mass extinctions have been attributed to tectonic, oceanic, and climatic changes, as well as the aftereffects of a meteorite striking the earth.**

Studying Evolutionary Lineages

When fossil evidence permits, paleontologists determine **lineages**, lines of descent from a common ancestor. The lineage of the horse *Equus* begins with *Hyracotherium,* a dog-sized mammal with a small head and small low-crowned molars with cusps. The feet, with four toes on each forefoot and three toes on each hind foot, were padded. *Hyracotherium* was adapted to the forestlike environment of the Eocene epoch during the Paleogene period. This small animal could have hidden among the trees for protection, and the low-crowned teeth were appropriate for browsing on leaves. In the Miocene epoch, when grasslands began to replace forests, the ancestors of *Equus* were subjected to selective pressure for the development of strength, intelligence, speed, and durable grinding teeth. A large size provided the strength needed for combat, a large skull made room for a larger brain, elongated legs ending in a hoof (derived from a single toe) gave speed to escape enemies, and the durable grinding teeth enabled the animals to feed efficiently on grasses.

Does this history show overall trends such as an increase in size, an increase in the grinding surface of the molar teeth, and a reduction in the number of toes? It does only if we pick and choose among the many fossils available. Closer examination reveals that as *Hyracotherium* evolved into *Equus,* the evolution of every character varied greatly and there were even times of reversal. If one of the ancestral animals had lived on and *Equus* had become extinct, we no doubt would be discussing a different set of "trends."

Progress Versus Stasis

In the history of life there are a few fossils that can be used to link one major group of organisms to another. But the expression "missing link" points to the fact that few such *transitional links* have been found. *Archaeopteryx,* the most famous of these fossils, links reptiles to birds. Other transitional links include the amphibious fish *Eustheopteron,* the reptile-like amphibian *Seymouria,* and the mammal-like reptiles, or therapsids. To explain the scarcity of transitional links, some paleontologists mention the slim chance of organisms becoming fossils and the subsequent incompleteness of the fossil record.

There are also examples of organisms that are called *living fossils* because they are so similar to an ancestor known from the fossil record. Recently, investigators found exquisitely preserved specimens of cyanobacteria that have the same sizes, shapes, and organization as living forms. These findings suggest that the cyanobacteria of today have not changed at all in over 3 billion years. Among plants, the dawn redwood was thought to be extinct; then a living specimen was discovered in a small area of China. Horseshoe crabs, crocodiles, and coelacanth fish are animals that still resemble their earliest ancestors. Pangolins are also called scaly anteaters. A recently found pangolin fossil from the Eocene epoch shows that these animals have changed minimally in 60 million years (fig. 21.17). A time of limited evolutionary change in a lineage is called *stasis.*

Figure 21.17

Pangolin evolution. This Eocene fossil found in a mine at Messel in Germany is the oldest one known for this group of animals. It shows that pangolins, *Manis,* have changed little since the time they evolved.

a.

b.

Phyletic Gradualism Versus Punctuated Equilibrium

Evolutionists who support **phyletic gradualism** [Gk. *phyl,* tribe] suggest that evolutionary change is rather slow and steady within a lineage and is not necessarily dependent upon speciation—that is, the origination of a new species (fig. 21.18*a*). In other words, fossils of the same species designation can show a trend over time, say from shorter to longer leg length. Indeed the fossil record, even if complete, is unlikely to indicate when speciation has occurred. A species is defined on the basis of reproductive isolation, and reproductive isolation cannot be detected in the fossil record! Since evolution occurs gradually, the expectation is that more transitional links will eventually be found in the fossil record.

Contrary to this evolutionary model, certain paleontologists—Stephen J. Gould, Nile Eldredge, and Steven Stanley in particular—propose that the fossil record demonstrates a model they call **punctuated equilibrium** (fig. 21.18*b*). Stasis, a period of equilibrium, is due to the failure of a lineage to convert variation into the origination of new species. Living fossils indicate that stasis can persist even for millions of years. In most lineages, however, a period of equilibrium is punctuated by evolutionary change—that is, speciation occurs. With reference to the length of the fossil record (about 3.5 billion years), speciation occurs relatively rapidly. Therefore, transitional links are not likely to become fossils, nor to be found! Indeed, speciation most likely involves only an isolated population at one locale. When a new species evolves and displaces the existing species, then it is likely to show up in the fossil record.

> Aside from finding fossils, paleontologists try to determine lineages and develop models of evolutionary change.

Figure 21.18

Phyletic gradualism (a) versus punctuated equilibrium (b). The differences between these two models for evolutionary change is reflected in these patterns of time versus structure.

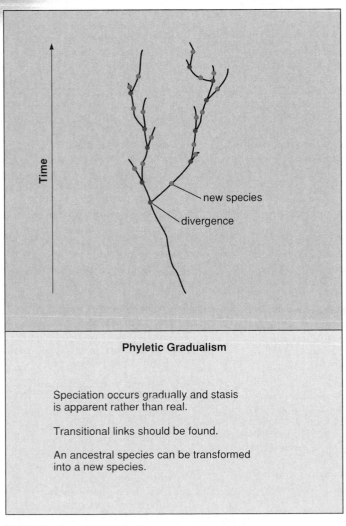

Phyletic Gradualism

Speciation occurs gradually and stasis is apparent rather than real.

Transitional links should be found.

An ancestral species can be transformed into a new species.

a.

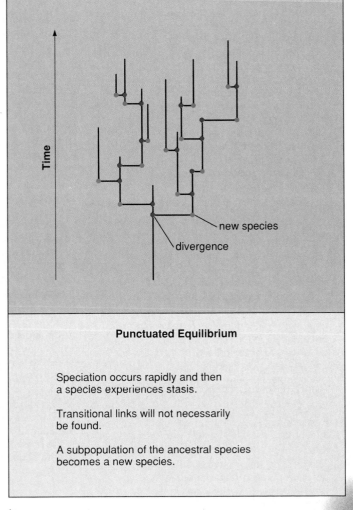

Punctuated Equilibrium

Speciation occurs rapidly and then a species experiences stasis.

Transitional links will not necessarily be found.

A subpopulation of the ancestral species becomes a new species.

b.

Summary

1. The unique conditions of the primitive earth allowed a chemical evolution to occur.

2. The gases of the primitive atmosphere probably escaped from volcanoes and included water vapor, nitrogen, and carbon dioxide, with small amounts of hydrogen and carbon monoxide.

3. The primitive atmosphere was a reducing atmosphere with no free oxygen gas.

4. At first the earth was very hot, but when it cooled, the water vapor condensed and the rains began to fall. The rains carried the gases into the newly formed oceans.

5. In the presence of an outside energy source, such as ultraviolet radiation, lightning, or radioactivity, the gases reacted with one another to produce small organic molecules such as amino acids and glucose. This scenario is supported by experiments performed by Stanley Miller and others.

6. The next step was the formation of macromolecules by polymerization. The RNA-first hypothesis is supported by the discovery of ribozymes, RNA molecules that are present in today's cells and are both substrate and enzyme. The protein-first hypothesis is supported by the observation that amino acids will polymerize in a preferred fashion when heated to drying. Cairns-Smith has suggested that amino acid polymerization and nucleotide polymerization could have occurred in clay, where radioactivity would have supplied the necessary energy.

7. Polymerized amino acids, called proteinoids, become microspheres when placed in water. Microspheres have many properties similar to cells and may have evolved into protocells, structures that carry on energy metabolism and can have a lipid-protein boundary if lipids are added to the medium.

8. On the other hand, the protocell could have developed from coacervate droplets that automatically form when concentrated mixtures of macromolecules are held at the right temperature, ionic composition, and pH.

9. Phospholipids readily form spherical liposomes, and perhaps this was the origin of the plasma membrane.

10. The protocell must have been a heterotrophic fermenter living on the preformed organic molecules in the organic soup.

11. The protocell was not a true cell until it contained genes. The RNA-first hypothesis suggests that the first genes and enzymes were RNA molecules. The protein-first hypothesis suggests that protein enzymes were needed before nucleic acids could form. Cairns-Smith suggests that polypeptides and RNA became associated in clay in such a way that the polypeptides catalyzed RNA formation. So the first cell would have contained both genes and protein enzymes at the same time.

12. The fossil record set in sedimentary strata tells the history of life. The stratigraphic sequence indicates the relative date of fossils. Radioactive dating is used to determine the absolute date of fossils in years.

13. The continents are on massive plates that move, carrying the continents with them. The study of the movement of the plates, called plate tectonics, is a branch of geology. Continental drift has affected biogeography and helps explain the distribution pattern of today's land organisms.

14. The Precambrian encompasses the first two eras of the geological time scale. The first cell or cells evolved about 3.5 billion years ago during the Precambrian. Prokaryotes existed alone on the surface of the earth for at least 1.5 billion years. During this time all the metabolic pathways found in modern cells developed. Photosynthetic cyanobacteria added oxygen to the atmosphere.

15. The presence of oxygen in the atmosphere allowed the formation of the ozone shield, which filters out ultraviolet rays. This, along with the fact that oxygen attaches to small organic molecules, accounts for the inability of organisms to originate by chemical evolution today.

16. Eukaryotes evolved about 2.0 billion years ago, probably by endosymbiosis. Multicellularity and sexual reproduction arose about 600 million years ago, which may account for the first evidence of marine animals before the Paleozoic era began.

17. The fossil record is so rich at the start of the Cambrian period that it is called the Cambrian explosion. Perhaps the evolution of external skeletons was due to the presence of plentiful oxygen in the atmosphere or perhaps it was due to predation.

18. Plants, and then insects, invaded land during the Silurian period. The swamp forests of the Carboniferous period contained primitive vascular plants, insects, and amphibians. This period is sometimes called the Age of Amphibians.

19. The Mesozoic era was the Age of Cycads and Reptiles. Twice during this era, dinosaurs of enormous size evolved. By the end of the Cretaceous period the dinosaurs were extinct.

20. The Cenozoic era is divided into the Paleogene period and the Neogene period. The Paleogene is associated with the evolution of mammals and flowering plants that formed vast tropical forests. The Neogene is associated with the evolution of primates into monkeys, apes, and then humans. Grasslands were replacing forests and this put pressure on primates, who were adapted to living in trees. The result was evolution of humans—primates who left the trees.

21. Mass extinctions are topics of intense discussion and research. Since it was suggested that the extinction at the end of the Cretaceous period was due to a large meteorite impact, evidence has been gathered that other extinctions are due to a similar cause as well. Others look to terrestrial events such as tectonic, oceanic, and climatic fluctuations, particularly due to continental drift, to explain mass extinctions.

22. The study of evolutionary lineages has also sparked the interest of many. Two models are proposed to explain evolutionary change in reference to the fossil record. Those who support phyletic gradualism believe that slow, gradual change leads to speciation, an event that is not necessarily required for evolutionary change to be noted in the fossil record. Those who support punctuated equilibrium present evidence that a long period of equilibrium (stasis) is punctuated by speciation, which is most likely required for evolutionary change.

Writing Across the Curriculum

In order to practice writing skills, students should write out the answers to any or all of the study questions and the critical thinking questions. The study questions are sequenced in the same order as the text. Answers to the objective questions, and suggested answers to the critical thinking questions, are in appendix D.

Study Questions

1. Trace the steps by which a chemical evolution may have produced a protocell. 333–34
2. Describe Stanley Miller's experiment, and discuss its significance. 333
3. Contrast the RNA-first hypothesis and the protein-first hypothesis. If polymerization occurred in clay, what macromolecules would have been present at the same time? 334
4. What is a protocell? How might a plasma membrane have evolved? 334–35
5. Why is it likely the protocell was a heterotrophic fermenter? 335
6. What is a true cell? How might the first replication system have come about? 335
7. Explain how the fossil record develops and how fossils are dated relatively and absolutely. 336–37
8. What is continental drift, and how is it related to plate tectonics? Give examples to show how biogeography supports the occurrence of continental drift. 338–39
9. Describe the history of life on earth by stating some of the main events of the Precambrian, and the Paleozoic, Mesozoic, and Cenozoic eras. 347
10. When did five significant mass extinctions occur? Note which type of organisms were most affected for each one, and give causes for each of these mass extinctions. 348–49
11. Give an example of an evolutionary lineage. What is a transitional link and a living fossil? How do these pertain to the phyletic gradualism and the punctuated equilibrium models of evolutionary change? 350–51

Objective Questions

1. Which of these gives a possible sequence of organic chemicals prior to the protocell?
   a. inorganic gases, amino acids, polypeptide, microsphere
   b. inorganic gases, nucleotides, nucleic acids, genes
   c. water, salts, protein, oxygen
   d. Both a and b are correct.
2. Which of these did Stanley Miller place in his experimental system to show that organic molecules could have arisen from inorganic molecules on the primitive earth?
   a. microspheres
   b. purines and pyrimidines
   c. the primitive gases
   d. All of these are correct.
3. Which of these is the chief reason the protocell was probably a fermenter?
   a. It didn't have any enzymes.
   b. The atmosphere didn't have any oxygen.
   c. Fermentation provides the most amount of energy.
   d. All of these are correct.
4. Which of these is a true statement?
   a. The primitive atmosphere was an oxidizing one and today's is a reducing one, making photosynthesis possible.
   b. The primitive atmosphere was 20% oxygen, just like it is today.
   c. The reducing primitive atmosphere contributed to the origin of life, and the oxidizing one of today would hinder it.
   d. It took so long for prokaryote evolution because the primitive atmosphere screened out the ultraviolet radiation from the sun.

5. The significance of liposomes, phospholipid droplets, is that they show that
   a. the first plasma membrane contained protein.
   b. a plasma membrane could have easily evolved.
   c. a biological evolution produced the first cell.
   d. there was water on the primitive earth.
6. Evolution of the DNA→RNA→protein system was a milestone because the protocell
   a. was a heterotrophic fermenter.
   b. could now reproduce.
   c. needed energy to grow.
   d. All of these are correct.
7. Which of these is a true statement?
   a. Eukaryotes evolved before prokaryotes.
   b. Prokaryotes evolved before eukaryotes.
   c. The true cell evolved before the protocell.
   d. Prokaryotes didn't evolve until 1.5 billion years ago.
8. Most of the history of life concerns the evolution of
   a. prokaryotes.
   b. eukaryotes.
   c. photosynthesizers.
   d. plants and animals.
9. Which best describes strata?
   a. sedimentary rock layers that contain fossils
   b. sedimentary rock layers that all date from the same historical time
   c. molten rock that contains radioactive material and is dangerous to the health of humans
   d. All of these are correct.

10. Continental drift helps explain the occurrence of
    a. mass extinctions.
    b. distribution of fossils on earth.
    c. geological upheavals like earthquakes.
    d. All of these are correct.
11. Which of these is mismatched?
    a. Mesozoic—cycads and dinosaurs
    b. Cenozoic—grasses and humans
    c. Paleozoic—prokaryotes and unicellular eukaryotes
    d. Cambrian—marine organisms with external skeletons
12. Place these terms in the diagram in the proper order:
    formation of earth, multicellularity, oxidizing atmosphere, oldest known fossils, origin of eukaryotic cells, Cambrian period begins.

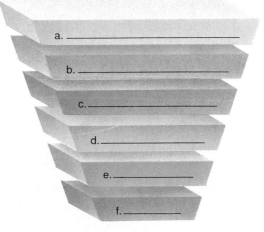

a. _____
b. _____
c. _____
d. _____
e. _____
f. _____

Concepts and Critical Thinking

1. *Life is a physical and chemical phenomenon.*

How do all three hypotheses about the origin of life support this concept?

2. *Cells come only from preexisting cells.* Reconcile this concept with the belief that a chemical evolution produced the first cells.

3. *Speciation accounts for the diversity of life.*

Would this statement be supported by both the phyletic gradualism and the punctuated equilibrium models of evolutionary change? Why or why not?

Selected Key Terms

autotroph An organism that can make organic molecules from inorganic nutrients. [Gk. *aut,* self, and *troph,* feeder] 335

chemical evolution An increase in the complexity of chemicals that could have led to the first cells. 333

continental drift The movement of continents with respect to one another over the earth's surfaces. 338

extinction The total disappearance of a species or higher group. 343

fossil The remains or tangible traces of an ancient organism preserved in sediment or rock. [L. *fossil,* dug up] 336

heterotroph An organism that cannot synthesize organic compounds from inorganic substances and therefore must take in preformed food. [Gk. *heter,* different, and *troph,* feeder] 335

lineage A line of evolutionary descent from a common ancestor. 350

liposome Droplet of phospholipid molecules formed in a liquid environment. [Gk. *lipos,* fat, and *soma,* body] 334

mass extinction An episode of large-scale extinction in which large numbers of species disappear in a few million years or less. 343

microsphere Formed from proteinoids exposed to water; has properties similar to today's cells. [Gk. *micr,* small, and *spher,* ball] 334

ocean ridge The ridge on the ocean floor where oceanic crust forms and from which it moves laterally in each direction. 339

ozone shield Formed from oxygen in the upper atmosphere, it protects the earth from ultraviolet radiation. 341

paleontology (pay-lee-ahn-TAHL-uh-jee) Study of fossils that results in knowledge about the history of life. [Gk. *paleo,* ancient, and *logy,* study of] 337

phyletic gradualism (fy-LET-ik) An evolutionary model that proposes evolutionary change resulting in a new species can occur gradually in an unbranched lineage. [Gk. *phyl,* tribe] 351

plate tectonics (tek-TAHN-iks) The study of the behavior of the earth's crust in terms of moving plates that are formed at ocean ridges and destroyed at subduction zones. [Gk. *tect,* a covering] 339

proteinoid (PROHT-en-oyd) Abiotically polymerized amino acids that are joined in a preferred manner; possible early step in cell evolution. 334

protocell A cell forerunner developed from cell-like microspheres. [Gk. *proto,* first] 334

punctuated equilibrium An evolutionary model that proposes there are periods of rapid change dependent on speciation followed by long periods of stasis. 351

sedimentation The process by which particulate material accumulates and forms a stratum. [L. *sedimentum,* a settling] 336

22

HUMAN EVOLUTION

Learning Objectives

A modern human seeking evidence that might pertain to the evolutionary history of *Homo sapiens.*

HUMANS

Phylum Chordata
Subphylum Vertebrata
Class Mammalia
Order Primates
Suborder Anthropoidea
Superfamily Hominoidea
Family Hominidae
Genus *Homo*
Species *H. sapiens*

To specifiy an organism, you must use the full binomial name (e.g., *Homo sapiens*).

he evolutionary principle of descent with modification applies to any group of organisms, including human beings. It could be argued that the evolution of humans, like that of all living things, begins with the very first cell (or cells). But specifically, as animals our evolutionary history begins in the Cambrian period of the Paleozoic era (fig. 22.1). Vertebrates (animals with a backbone) arose soon after invertebrates (animals without a backbone) during this era. Fishes, the first vertebrates to evolve, have had a long and successful history. They still dominate the seas today.

The insects (invertebrates) were among the first animals to live on land, and their variety outstrips all living things known. Among vertebrates, the amphibians and then the reptiles held sway on land. **Mammals** [L. *mammil*, teat] (animals that have hair and mammary glands) evolved from the mammal-like reptiles by the Triassic period of the Mesozoic era. Mammals remained small and insignificant while the dinosaurs dominated the land for over 150 million years. Extinction of the dinosaurs marked the end of the Mesozoic era, and then mammals diversified into many groups during the Cenozoic era. Today, there are mammals adapted to living on land, in the water, and in the air.

The dependence of animals upon plants is consistent with the observation that plants invaded land before any group of animals. Angiosperms, which include most trees, evolved at the same time as mammals. Angiosperms are the flowering plants that produce fruits, and primates—mammals adapted to living in trees—often used fruits as a central part of their diet. Many human characteristics are explainable on the basis of adaptation to an arboreal (tree-dwelling) life.

> **Human beings are related to all living things, especially to other primates, which are mammals adapted to living in trees.**

Figure 22.1

An abbreviated geological time scale showing some major evolutionary events of animals.

Era	Period	MYA*	Major Biological Events—Animals
Cenozoic	Neogene		Age of Human Civilization
Cenozoic	Paleogene	24	First hominids appear
Cenozoic			Dominance of land by mammals and insects — Age of Mammals
Mesozoic	Cretaceous	66	Dinosaurs become extinct
Mesozoic	Jurassic	144	First mammals and birds appear
Mesozoic	Triassic	208	First dinosaurs appear — Age of Dinosaurs
Paleozoic	Permian	245	Reptiles appear and expand
Paleozoic		286	Decline of amphibians
Paleozoic	Carboniferous	360	Insects appear
Paleozoic	Devonian		First amphibians move onto land — Age of Amphibians
Paleozoic	Silurian	408	Age of Fishes
Paleozoic	Ordovician	438	First fishes (jawless) appear
Paleozoic		500	Invertebrates dominate the seas
Paleozoic	Cambrian	570	Trilobites abundant — Age of Invertebrates

* MYA = millions of years ago.

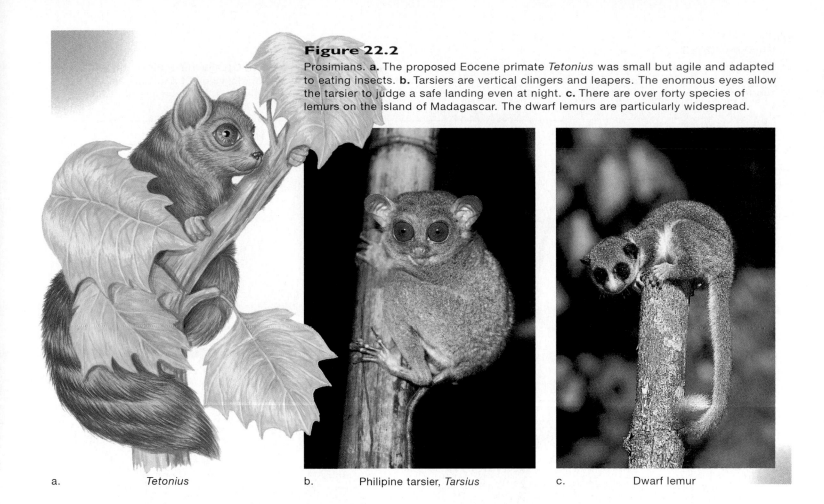

Figure 22.2

Prosimians. **a.** The proposed Eocene primate *Tetonius* was small but agile and adapted to eating insects. **b.** Tarsiers are vertical clingers and leapers. The enormous eyes allow the tarsier to judge a safe landing even at night. **c.** There are over forty species of lemurs on the island of Madagascar. The dwarf lemurs are particularly widespread.

a. *Tetonius*

b. Philipine tarsier, *Tarsius*

c. Dwarf lemur

PRIMATES LIVE IN TREES

Primates [Gk. *prima*, first] are a mammalian order in which the animals are adapted to living in trees.

What Are Primate Characteristics?

Primate limbs are mobile, as are the hands, because the thumb (and in nonhuman primates, the big toe as well) is opposable; that is, the thumb can touch each of the other fingers. Therefore, a primate can easily reach out and bring food such as fruit to the mouth. When locomoting, tree limbs can be grasped and released freely because nails have replaced claws.

The sense of smell is of primary importance in animals with a snout. In primates, the snout is shortened considerably, allowing the eyes to move to the front of the head. The stereoscopic vision (or depth perception) that results permits primates to make accurate judgments about the distance and position of adjoining tree limbs.

Gestation is lengthy, allowing time for good forebrain development; the visual portion of the brain is proportionately large, as are those centers responsible for hearing and touch. One birth at a time is the norm in primates; it is difficult to care for several offspring while moving from limb to limb. The juvenile period of dependency is extended, and there is an emphasis on learned behavior and complex social interactions.

> These characteristics especially distinguish primates from other mammals:
>
> opposable thumb (and in some cases, big toe)
> nails (not claws)
> single birth
>
> expanded forebrain
> emphasis on learned behavior
> extended period of parental care

PRIMATES ARE DIVERSE

The primate order contains two suborders: prosimians and anthropoids.

Prosimians Came First

Among living primates, the **prosimians** (suborder Prosimii) [Gk. *pro*, before, and *simos*, monkey, ape] best resemble the first primates (fig. 22.2). Tarsiers, which are found in the Philippines and East Indies, are curious, mouse-sized creatures with enormous eyes suitable to their nocturnal way of life. Tarsiers are insectivorous, and it's believed that primates may have evolved from mammals that first climbed into the trees to feed on insects. Lemurs, which have a squirrellike appearance, are confined largely to the island of Madagascar. They feed on plant material, including fruits. Lorises, which are prosimians living in both Africa and Asia, resemble lemurs.

Figure 22.3

Evolutionary tree of the primate order began in the late Cretaceous period when a small insect-eating mammal climbed into the spreading angiosperm forests. The descendants of this mammal adapted to a new way of life and developed traits such as a shortened snout and nails instead of claws. Note the epoch in which each type of primate diverged from the main line of descent.

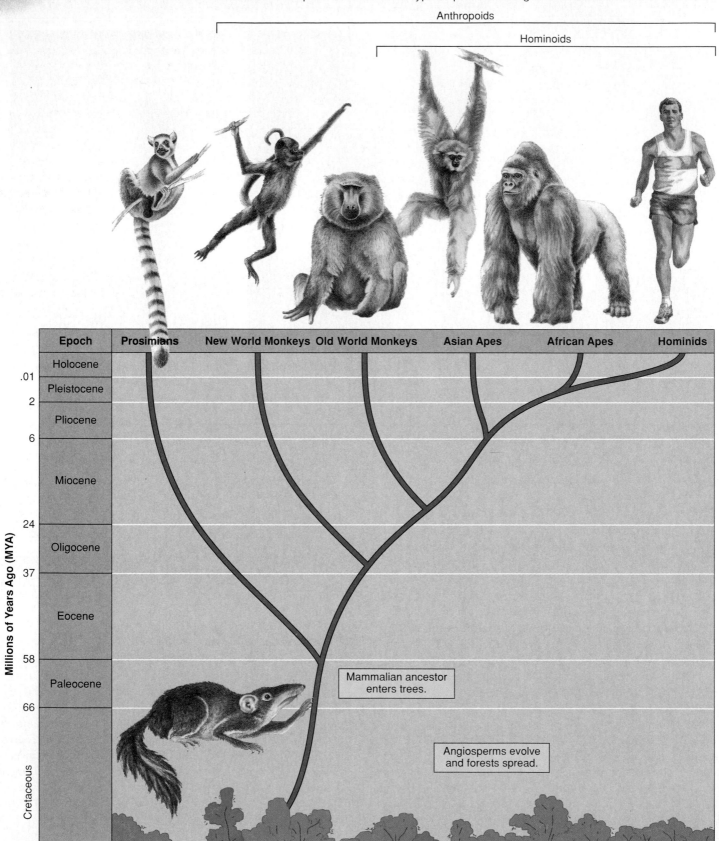

Anthropoids Followed

Figure 22.3 shows the sequence of anthropoid evolution during the Cenozoic era. The surviving **anthropoids** (suborder Anthropoidea) [Gk. *anthrop,* man, and *oid,* like] are classified into three superfamilies: New World monkeys (Ceboidea), Old World monkeys (Cercopithecoidea), and the hominoids (Hominoidea). The New World monkeys often have long prehensile (grasping) tails and flat noses, and Old World monkeys, which lack such tails, have protruding noses. Two of the well-known New World monkeys are the spider monkey and the capuchin, the "organ grinder's" monkey. Some of the better-known Old World monkeys are now ground dwellers, such as the baboon and the rhesus monkey, which has been used in medical research. The **hominoids** [L. *hom,* man, and Gk. *oid,* like] include all the apes and humans.

Primates flourished in the forests of northern continents during the Paleocene and Eocene epochs of the Cenozoic era (fig. 22.3). But as these continents drifted slowly northward, the weather cooled and primates migrated southward. A group of early primates reached South America possibly by crossing the then-narrow Atlantic and evolved there into the New World monkeys. This means that New World monkeys are not more closely related to Old World monkeys than they are to apes.

In Africa, the ancestors of Old World monkeys and of hominoids were most likely four-limbed tree-climbers who fed on fruit. Sometime in the Miocene epoch, the monkeys adapted a more fibrous diet of leaves and diverged from the main line of descent. The hominoids, the more abundant group which fed on fruit, are well represented by apelike forms of that time. The anatomy of **Proconsul,** is sufficiently primitive to be ancestral to all apes and humans (fig. 22.4). These hominoids were about the size of a baboon, and the brain was a comparable size at about 165 cc. Their general anatomy seems similar to an Old World monkey also. Although primarily tree-dwellers, *Proconsul* may have also spent time exploring nearby grasslands for food.

At the end of the Miocene epoch, Africarabia (Africa plus the Arabian Peninsula) joined with Asia and the hominoids migrated into Europe and Asia. Two groups can be distinguished: dryomorphs and ramamorphs. While at one time it was believed that ramamorphs were ancestral to the later-appearing hominids, a group that contains humans, ramamorphs are now classified within an ancestral organgutan group.

> The apelike *Proconsul,* which was prevalent in Africa during the Miocene epoch, is believed to be ancestral to today's hominoids—apes and humans.

Figure 22.4

Comparison of monkey skeleton (*a*) and *Proconsul heseloni* (*b*), a hominoid of the Miocene epoch. **c.** Skull of *P. heseloni.*

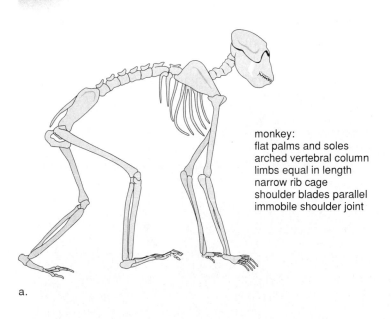

monkey:
flat palms and soles
arched vertebral column
limbs equal in length
narrow rib cage
shoulder blades parallel
immobile shoulder joint

a.

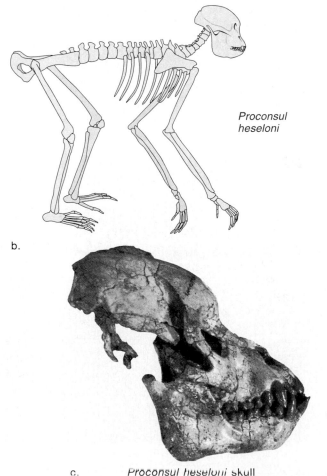

Proconsul heseloni

b.

c.   *Proconsul heseloni* skull

Figure 22.5

Ape diversity. **a.** Of the apes, gibbons are the most distantly related to humans. They dislike coming down from trees, even at watering holes. They will extend a long arm into the water and then drink collected moisture from the back of the hand. **b.** Orangutans are solitary except when they come together to reproduce. Their name means "forest man"; early Malayans believed that they were intelligent and could speak but did not because they were afraid of being put to work. **c.** Gorillas are terrestrial and live in groups in which a silver-backed male, such as this one, is always dominant. **d.** Of the apes, chimpanzees sometimes seem the most humanlike.

a.　　　white-handed gibbon, *Hylobates*

b.　　　orangutan, *Pengo*

c.　　　mountain gorilla, *Gorilla*

d.　　　common chimpanzee, *Pan*

Learning from Living Hominoids

The close relationship between humans and apes is signified by their placement in the same superfamily, Hominoidea. Four types of apes have survived until today: the gibbon and the orangutan are found in Asia; the gorilla and the chimpanzee inhabit Africa (fig. 22.5). The *gibbon* is the smallest of the apes, with a body weight of about 5.5–11 kg. Gibbons have extremely long arms that are specialized for swinging between tree limbs. The *orangutan* is large (75 kg) but nevertheless spends a great deal of time in trees. The *gorilla,* the largest of the apes (180 kg), spends most of its time on the ground. *Chimpanzees,* which are at home both in trees and on the ground, are the most humanlike of the apes in appearance and are frequently used in psychological experiments.

Molecular biologists have studied our relationship to the apes by comparing the similarity of our proteins and DNA to that of apes. Certain amino acid and DNA base-pair differences are not tied to natural selection and instead occur randomly at a fixed rate. Such differences can be used as a type of **molecular clock** by which we can judge when any two groups of organisms diverged (separated) from one another. The DNA of two species can be compared in the following manner: DNA strands are first separated into single strands. Then a strand from each species is allowed to pair complementarily. The degree of fit is judged by the thermal stability of the hybrid DNA. A molecular study of this sort suggests that monkeys most likely diverged from the primate line of descent about 33 million years ago (MYA), the orangutan diverged 10 MYA, and African apes and humans did not split until around 6 MYA. Therefore, it is believed that the last common ancestor between the African apes and **hominids** (family Hominidae) lived during the Pliocene epoch. Unfortunately, this common ancestor has not yet been found.

The geography of Africa holds a clue as to why the ape and the hominid lines of descent split from each other. A great furrow called the *rift valley* runs north and south in eastern Africa. Tectonic forces which began 12.5 MYA are slowly causing eastern Africa to separate from the rest of the continent. Here, huge mountainous volcanoes and lakes form a geographic barrier that is difficult to cross. Winds that have swept across the African continent for millions of years have deposited rain to the west of the mountains, and the east has become ever more dry. Forests and woodlands have remained in the west but the east is a grassland called a savanna.

The changing environment to the east may have influenced the evolution of hominids, who differ from the apes in the ways noted in figure 22.6. Anatomical differences of prime importance concern: type of locomotion, which is dependent on skeletal features involving the spine, the pelvis, and the bones of the appendages; jaw shape, which is related to the size and the shape of the teeth; and brain size, which is related to the shape of the head and the brow. The hominid features promoted survival in a grassland as opposed to a forest ecosystem. We can imagine that it was beneficial to be able to stand tall to look over grasses while searching for food or avoiding predators, that jaw and teeth changes were adaptive to a new (perhaps omnivorous), diet, and that an erect posture left the hands free to throw rocks or even manipulate tools as the brain grew larger.

The ape line of descent and the hominid line of descent split about 6 MYA; differences regarding mode of locomotion, shape of jaw, and brain size became distinctive.

Figure 22.6

Comparison of human skeletal features with those of a gorilla.

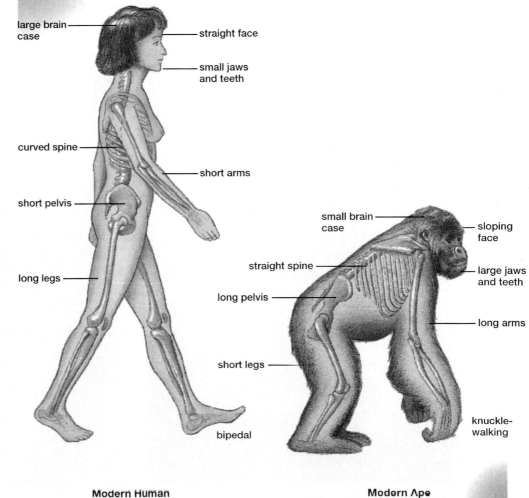

large brain case

straight face

small jaws and teeth

curved spine

short arms

short pelvis

long legs

small brain case

sloping face

straight spine

large jaws and teeth

long pelvis

long arms

short legs

bipedal

knuckle-walking

Modern Human

Modern Ape

THE HOMINIDS BREAK AWAY

The hominid line of descent begins with the australopithecines, which evolved and diversified in eastern Africa.

First Hominids Walked Erect

It wasn't until the 1960s that paleontologists, following the lead of the renowned couple Louis and Mary Leakey, began to concentrate their efforts in eastern Africa. It has proven to be worth their while. One 1994 find consisting of skull fragments, teeth, arm bones, and a part of a child's lower jaw has been dated at 4.4 MYA. Called *Australopithecus ramidus* [L. *austr,* southern, Gk. *pithec,* ape, and L. *rami,* branch] it is believed to represent a transitional stage between apes and humans. In comparison to later **australopithecines,** the cheek teeth are smaller, the canine teeth (eye teeth) are larger, and the skull is more like that of a chimpanzee. It seems that even though this hominid may have lived in a woodland environment, it could have walked erect. Apparently, the use of the forelimbs for gathering food and the hind limbs for locomotion is a general characteristic for all hominids. An estimate of body size and the degree of bipedal locomotion must await the discovery of foot, leg, and hip fossils, however.

More than twenty years ago, a team led by Donald Johanson unearthed nearly 250 fossils of a hominid called *A. afarensis.* A now-famous female skeleton dated at about 3.4 MYA is known worldwide by its field name, Lucy. (The name derives from the Beatles' song "Lucy in the Sky with Diamonds.") Although her brain was quite small (400 cc), the shapes and relative proportions of her limbs indicate that Lucy did stand upright and walk bipedally (fig. 22.7). Even better evidence of bipedal locomotion comes from a trail of footprints in Laetoli dated about 3.5 MYA. The larger prints are double—a smaller-sized being was stepping in the footfalls of another—and there are small prints off to the side, within hand-holding distance. Since the australopithecines were apelike above the waist and humanlike below the waist, it seems that human characteristics did not evolve all at one time. The term *mosaic evolution* is applied when different body parts change at different rates and therefore at different times.

The australopithecines were sexually dimorphic. Lucy was about four feet tall and weighed about 30 kg. In contrast, the males of the species were five feet tall and weighed up to 45 kg. Some have speculated that such size differences may indicate two separate species, but in 1994 new finds, including a more complete skull (dubbed the son of Lucy and dated at just about 3 MYA),

Figure 22.7

Australopithecus afarensis. **a.** A reconstruction on display at the St. Louis Zoo. **b.** Fossilized footprints made by three members of the species as they walked across wet ash from a volcanic eruption some 3.75 million years ago. The footprints suggest that this species walked bipedally.

a.

b.

confirmed the opinion that the fossils belong to one species (fig. 22.8). Taking into account their smaller body size, the relative brain size is about half of ours and the jaw is heavy. The cheek teeth are enormous, and in males large canine teeth project forward.

It's interesting to speculate that the daily lives of australopithecines may have been comparable to those of baboons. In baboons, as in australopithecines, males are much larger than females. Baboons travel in a troop rather than forming permanent family groups. The troop has a home range, which it constantly travels foraging for food. At night the troop climbs trees to remain safe from predators. Australopithecines had long, curved fingers and toes, and the legs were short in comparison to the mobile arms. This suggests that they, too, still climbed trees on occasion.

A. afarensis had descendants. After a period of stasis that may have lasted a million years (from 3 to 2 MYA), branching speciation occurred. Therefore, instead of thinking about hominid descent in terms of a straight line, it is far better to envision a bush. Some think there may have been as many as ten species of hominids about 2 MYA in Africa, but we will discuss only four of them; three of which are australopithecines. *A. africanus,* which was first named in southern Africa by Raymond Dart in the 1920s, is a gracile (slender) type. *A. boisei* is a robust form from eastern Africa, and *A. robustus* is a similar form from southern Africa. Both gracile and robust forms have a brain size of about 500 cc; their skull differences are essentially due to dental and facial adaptations for different diets. The robust forms have stronger jaws, larger attachments for larger chewing muscles, and bigger grinding teeth because they most likely fed on tougher foods than the gracile form. The robust forms lived in drier habitats where soft fruits and leaves would be harder to come by. In both forms, the pelvis resembles that of Lucy but the hands were more humanlike; possibly they were capable of making tools. Both forms, which are believed to have eaten meat at least occasionally, may have used the tools to process animal carcasses. Of interest is a recent report that the thumb anatomy of *A. robustus* is similar to our own. Modern human hands are adapted to handling tools because of their strong, well-muscled, and opposable thumb.

At one time it was believed that the gracile australopithecine form gave rise to the robust forms. However, in 1985, Alan Walker discovered a robust skull, called the black skull, which was old enough (2.5 MYA) to be ancestral to the robust forms we have been discussing. It has been given the name *A. aethiopicus.* As discussed in the reading on page 364, the earliest *Homo* species also evolved from the *Australopithecus* line of descent.

> **Several species of australopithecines have been identified. After a period of stasis, during which only *A. afarensis* existed, branching speciation occurred.**

Figure 22.8

Australopithecus afarensis skull and dentition. **a.** *A. afarensis* had an apelike face with prominent brow ridges and a projecting jaw. **b.** Dentition of an ape, *A. afarensis,* and a modern human. Note the size of the canine teeth, the gap between canine teeth and adjacent incisor (arrow), and the size of the cheek teeth.

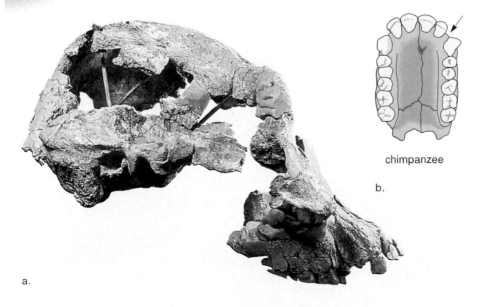
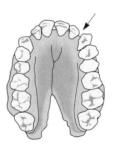
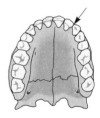

chimpanzee   *Australopithecus afarensis*   modern human

b.

a.

Origin of the Genus Homo

F ossil evidence shows that the earliest *Homo* species evolved in Africa from the *Australopithecus* line of descent about 2.4 MYA. Remains of australopithecines indicate that they spent part of their time climbing trees and that they retained many apelike traits. Australopithecine arms, like those of an ape, were long compared to the length of the legs. *A. afarensis* also had strong wrists and long, curved fingers and toes. These traits would have served well for climbing, and the australopithecines probably climbed trees for the same reason that chimpanzees do today: to gather fruits and nuts in trees and to sleep above ground at night so as to avoid predatory animals, such as lions and hyenas.

Whereas our brain is about the size of a grapefruit, that of the australopithecines was about the size of an orange. Their brain was only slightly larger than that of a chimpanzee. There is no evidence that the australopithecines manufactured stone tools; presumably, they were not smart enough to do so.

We know that the genus *Homo* evolved from the genus *Australopithecus,* but several years ago I concluded that this could not have happened as long as the australopithecines climbed trees every day. The obstacle relates to the way in which we, members of *Homo,* develop our large brain. Unlike other primates, we retain the high rate of fetal brain growth through the first year after birth. (That is why a one-year-old child has a very large head.) The brain of other primates, including monkeys and apes, grows rapidly before birth, but immediately after birth their brain grows more slowly. An adult human brain is more than three times as large as that of an adult chimpanzee.

A continuation of the high rate of fetal brain growth eventually allowed the genus *Homo* to evolve from the genus *Australopithecus*. But there was a problem in that continued brain growth is linked to under development of the entire body. Although the human brain becomes much larger, human babies are remarkably weak and uncoordinated. Such helpless infants

Steven Stanley
The Johns Hopkins University

must be carried about and tended. Human babies are unable to cling to their mothers the way chimpanzee babies can (fig. 22A).

How, then, did the evolutionary transition from *Australopithecus* to *Homo* take place? Fossilized pollen and other geological evidence reveal that at the time the *Homo* genus evolved, the climate was becoming cooler and drier. This caused forests to shrink and grasslands to expand across broad areas of Africa. The australopithecine line of descent became extinct

just as did many African antelope species that depended on forests for food and shelter. Before extinction occurred, however, humans—who walk erect, rarely climb trees, and have large brains—evolved.

The origin of the *Homo* genus entailed a great evolutionary compromise. Humans gained a large brain, but they were saddled with the largest interval of infantile helplessness in the entire class Mammalia. The positive value of a large brain must have outweighed the negative aspects of infantile helplessness, however, or natural selection would not have produced the *Homo* genus. Having a larger brain meant that humans were able to outsmart or ward off predators with weapons they were clever enough to manufacture.

Probably very few genetic changes were required to delay the maturation of *Australopithecus* and produce the large brain of *Homo*. The mutation of a regulatory gene that controls one or more other genes most likely could have delayed early maturation. As we learn more about the human genome, we will eventually uncover the particular gene or gene combinations that cause us to have a large brain, and this will be a very exciting discovery.

Figure 22A

A human infant is often cradled and has no means to cling to its mother when she goes about her daily routine.

Homo habilis Made Tools

The oldest fossils to be classified in the genus *Homo* are known as ***Homo habilis*** [L. *hom,* man, and *habilis,* handy]. This appellation seems appropriate because the remains are often accompanied by stone tools. Dated as early as 2 MYA, this hominid lived at a time when the earth was cooling and tropical regions in general were becoming more dry due to the formation of glaciers at the North and South Poles. Many animals, including the robust forms of *Australopithecus,* show dentition that indicates a shift to a more fibrous diet. It is, perhaps, significant that the modern horse appears at this time.

What is distinctive about these hominid fossils that they should be classified within our own genus? *H. habilis* was small—about the size of Lucy—but the brain at 700 cc is about 45% larger. Not only that, certain portions of the brain thought to be associated with speech areas are enlarged. The skull is positioned to be in line with a more upright vertebral column, and the cheek teeth are smaller than those of even the gracile australopithecines. Apparently, *H. habilis* had a different way of life than the other hominids of this time.

Cut marks on bones that could have been made by stone flakes have been found at many sites throughout eastern Africa that date from 2 MYA. *H. habilis* could have made and used tools in order to strip meat off these bones and, in keeping with the size of the teeth, could have eaten meat to satisfy protein demands. As a scavenger, *H. habilis* may have depended simply on the kills of other animals; or as a predator, may have killed small- to medium-sized prey. This new way of life became available to hominids when they had the ability to make and use tools intelligently.

The stone tools made by *H. habilis* are called Oldowan tools because they were first identified as tools by the Leakeys in Olduvai Gorge (see fig. 22.14). Oldowan tools are simple and look rather clumsy, but perhaps we are looking at the core that remains after flakes have been removed. The flakes would have been sharp and able to scrape away hide and cut tendons to easily remove meat from a carcass.

H. habilis most likely still ate fruits, berries, seeds, and other plant materials. Perhaps a division of labor arose with certain members of a group serving as hunters and others as gatherers. Speech would have facilitated their cooperative efforts, and later they most likely shared their food and ate together. In this way, society and culture could have begun. *Culture,* which encompasses human behavior and products (such as technology and the arts) is dependent upon the capacity to learn and transmit knowledge through the ability to speak and think abstractly.

Prior to the development of culture, adaptation to the environment necessitated a biological change. The acquisition of culture provided an additional way by which adaptation was possible. And the possession of culture by *H. habilis* may have hastened the extinction of the australopithecines during the early Pleistocene epoch (fig. 22.9).

> *H. habilis* warrants classification as a *Homo* because of brain size, posture, and dentition. Circumstantial evidence suggests the use of tools to prepare meat and also the development of culture.

Figure 22.9

Recently constructed hominoid evolutionary tree. African apes and hominids split about 6 million years ago (MYA), *Australopithecus ramidus* is the oldest of the hominids; *A. afarensis* lasted about a million years before branching speciation occurred. In particular, there were gracile and robust australopithecine forms and also the first human form, *Homo habilis.*

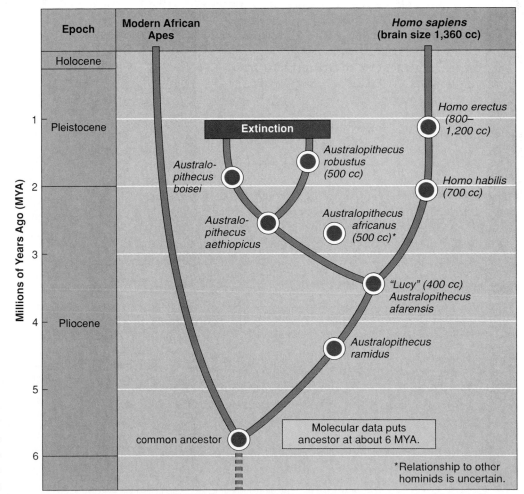

Homo erectus Traveled

Homo erectus [L. *hom*, man, and *erect*, upright] is the name assigned to hominid fossils found in Africa, Asia, and Europe and dated between 1.9 and 0.5 MYA. A Dutch anatomist named Eugene Dubois was the first to unearth *H. erectus* bones in Java in 1891, and since that time many other fossils have been found in the same area. Although all fossils assigned the name *H. erectus* are similar in appearance, there is enough discrepancy to suggest that several different species have been included in this group. In particular, some experts believe that the African and Asian forms are two different species.

Compared to *H. habilis*, *H. erectus* had a larger brain (about 1,000 cc), more pronounced brow ridges, a flatter face, and a nose that projects like ours. This type of nose is adaptive for a hot, dry climate because it permits water to be removed before air leaves the body. The recovery of an almost complete skeleton of a ten-year-old boy indicates that *H. erectus* was much taller than the hominids discussed thus far (fig. 22.10). Males were 1.8 meters (about 6 feet) and females were 1.55 meters (approaching 5 feet) tall. Indeed, these hominids were erect and most likely had a striding gait like ours. But the robust and most likely heavily muscled skeleton still retains some australopithecine features. Even so, the size of the birth canal indicates that infants were born in an immature state that required an extended period of care.

It's believed that *H. erectus* first appeared in Africa and then migrated into Asia and Europe. At one time, the migration was thought to have occurred about 1 MYA, but recently *H. erectus* fossil remains in Java and the Republic of Georgia have been dated at 1.9 and 1.6 MYA, respectively. Therefore, it seems that *H. erectus* either left Africa soon after it evolved, or perhaps an earlier, related form has to be credited with the migration. In any case, such an extensive population movement is a first in the history of humankind and a tribute to the intellectual and physical skills of the species.

H. erectus was the first hominid to use fire, and it also fashioned more advanced tools called Acheulean tools after a site in France (see fig. 22.14). They used heavy teardrop-shaped axes and cleavers as well as flakes, which were probably used for cutting and scraping. Some believe that *H. erectus* was a systematic hunter and brought kills to the same site over and over again. In one location paleontologists have found over 40,000 bones and 2,647 stones. These sites could have been "home bases" where social interaction occurred and a prolonged childhood allowed time for much learning. Perhaps a language evolved and a culture more like our own developed.

H. erectus, which evolved from *H. habilis*, had a striding gate, made well-fashioned tools (perhaps for hunting), and could control fire. This hominid migrated into Europe and Asia from Africa about 1 MYA.

Figure 22.10

Homo erectus. Skeleton of a ten-year-old boy who lived 1.6 MYA in eastern Africa. The femurs are angled and the neck are much longer than that of a modern human.

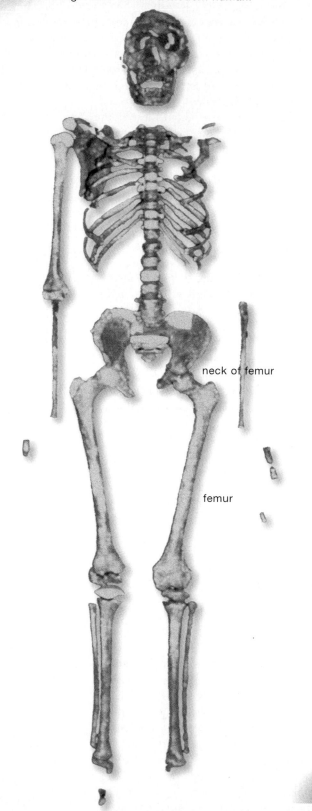

neck of femur

femur

Modern Humans Originated How?

It is generally recognized that modern humans originated from *H. erectus,* but where did this occur? About 300,000 years BP (before present) so-called "archaic *Homo sapiens*" had evolved in Europe, Asia, and Africa. (Neanderthal is a well-known archaic *H. sapiens.*) The hypothesis that each of these individual populations went on to evolve into modern humans is called the *multiregional continuity hypothesis* (fig. 22.11*a*). This hypothesis, which proposes no migrations, requires that evolution be essentially similar in several different places. Each region would show a continuity of its own anatomical characteristics from about a million years ago, when *H. erectus* first arrived in Eurasia. Opponents argue that it seems highly unlikely that evolution would have produced essentially the same result in these different places. They suggest, instead, the *out-of-Africa hypothesis,* which proposes that archaic *H. sapiens* became fully modern only in Africa, and thereafter they migrated to Europe and Asia just about 100,000 years BP. If so, there would be no continuity of characteristics between fossils of 300,000 years BP and fossils of 100,000 years BP. Modern humans may have interbred to a degree with archaic populations but in effect they supplanted them (fig. 22.11*b*).

According to which hypothesis would modern humans be most genetically alike? With the multiregional hypothesis, human populations have been evolving separately for a long time and therefore genetic differences are expected. With the out-of-Africa hypothesis, we are all descended from a few individuals from about 100,000 years BP. Therefore, the out-of-Africa hypothesis suggests that we are more genetically similar. A few years ago, a study attempted to show that all the people of Europe (and the world for that matter) have essentially the same mitochondrial DNA. Called the mitochondrial Eve hypothesis by the press (note this is a misnomer because no single ancestor is proposed), the statistics that calculated the date of the African migration were found to be flawed. Still, the raw data—which indicate a close genetic relationship among all Europeans—support the out-of-Africa hypothesis.

These opposing hypotheses have sparked many other innovative studies to test them. The final conclusions are still being determined.

> Investigators are currently testing two hypotheses: that modern humans (1) evolved separately in Europe, Africa, and Asia, and (2) evolved in Africa and then migrated.

Figure 22.11

Two hypotheses concerning the origins of modern humans. **a.** The multiregional continuity hypothesis proposes that modern humans evolved separately in at least three different places: Asia, Africa, and Europe. Therefore, continuity of genotypes and phenotypes is expected in these regions. **b.** The out-of-Africa hypothesis proposes that modern humans originated only in Africa; then they migrated and supplanted populations of *Homo* in Asia and Europe about 100,000 years ago.

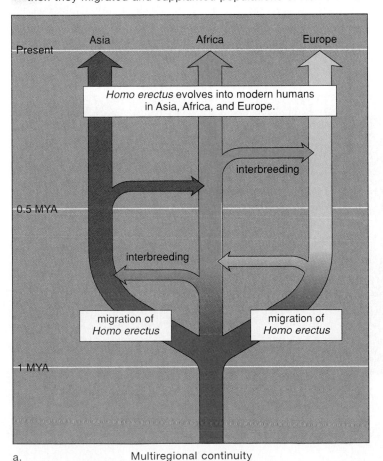

a. Multiregional continuity

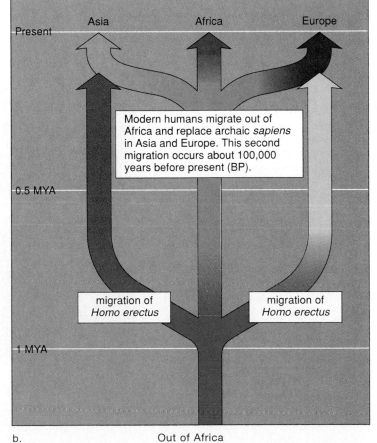

b. Out of Africa

Neanderthals Were Archaic

The **Neanderthals** (*H. sapiens neanderthalensis*) take their name from Germany's Neander Valley, where one of the first Neanderthal skeletons was discovered. Their roots can be traced back to 250,000 years BP, but the classic Neanderthal anatomy became well established about 125,000 years BP. The Neanderthals had massive brow ridges, and the nose, the jaws, and the teeth protruded far forward. The forehead was low and sloping, and the lower jaw sloped back without a chin. New fossils show that the pubic bone is long compared to ours. At this time, the Neanderthals are thought to be an archaic *H. sapiens* and most likely not in the main line of *Homo* descent. Surprisingly, however, the Neanderthal brain was, on the average, slightly larger than that of modern humans (1,400 cc, compared to 1,360 cc in most modern humans).

The Neanderthals were heavily muscled, especially in the shoulders and the neck (fig. 22.12). The bones of the limbs were shorter and thicker than those of modern humans. It is hypothesized that a larger brain than that of modern humans was required to control the extra musculature. Their sturdy build was probably an adaptation to a cold climate because they lived in Eurasia during the last Ice Age.

The Neanderthals give evidence of being culturally advanced. Most lived in caves, but those in the open may have built houses. They manufactured a variety of stone tools, including spear points, which could have been used for hunting, and scrapers and knives that would have helped in food preparation. They most likely successfully hunted bears, mammoths, woolly rhinoceroses, reindeer, and other contemporary animals. They used and could control fire, which probably helped in cooking frozen meat and in keeping warm. They even buried their dead with flowers and tools and may have had a religion.

Cro-Magnon Were Modern Humans

The out-of-Africa hypothesis discussed on page 367 is currently receiving much support by both anatomists and molecular biologists. It is increasingly believed that modern humans, by custom called **Cro-Magnon** after a fossil location in France, entered Eurasia 100,000 years ago or even earlier. New finds more in keeping with this date have recently been made.

Figure 22.12

Neanderthals. This drawing shows that the nose and the mouth of these people protruded from the face, and their muscles were massive. They made stone tools and were most likely excellent hunters.

Figure 22.13

Cro-Magnon people are the first to be designated *Homo sapiens sapiens*. Their toolmaking ability and other cultural attributes, such as their artistic talents, are legendary.

Everyone agrees that the Cro-Magnons (*H. sapiens sapiens*) had a thoroughly modern appearance (fig. 22.13). They made advanced stone tools called Aurignacian tools (fig. 22.14). Included were compound tools, as when stone flakes were fitted to a wooden handle. They may have been the first to throw spears, enabling them to kill animals from a distance, or to have made knifelike blades. They were such accomplished hunters that some researchers believe they were responsible for the extinction of many larger mammals, such as the giant sloth, the mammoth, the saber-toothed tiger, and the giant ox during the late Pleistocene epoch.

Cro-Magnons hunted cooperatively, and perhaps they were the first to have had a language. They are believed to have lived in small groups, with the men hunting by day while the women remained at home with the children. Its quite possible that a hunting way of life among prehistoric people influenced our behavior even until today.

The Cro-Magnon culture included art. They sculpted small figurines out of reindeer bones and antlers. They also painted beautiful drawings of animals on cave walls in Spain and France (see fig. 22.13).

> **The main line of hominid descent is now believed to include *A. ramidus*, *A. afarensis*, *H. habilis*, *H. erectus*, and Cro-Magnon.**

Figure 22.14

Comparative hominid skull anatomy and tools. Oldowan tools are crude. Acheulean tools are better made and more varied, and Aurignacian tools are well designed for specific purposes.

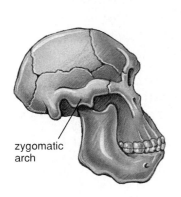

zygomatic arch

Australopithecus
low forehead
projecting face
large brow ridge
small brain case
large zygomatic arch

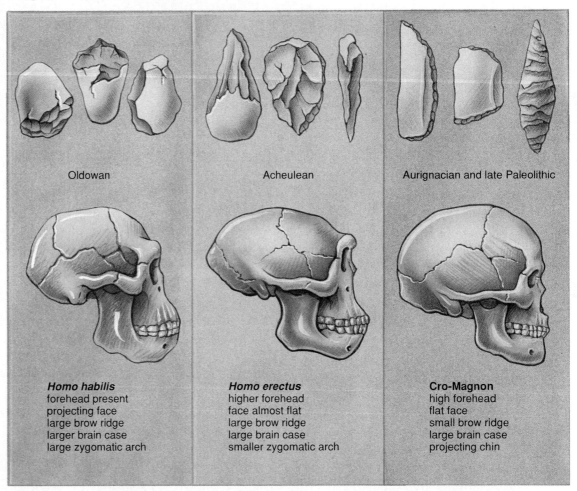

Oldowan

Acheulean

Aurignacian and late Paleolithic

Homo habilis
forehead present
projecting face
large brow ridge
larger brain case
large zygomatic arch

Homo erectus
higher forehead
face almost flat
large brow ridge
large brain case
smaller zygomatic arch

Cro-Magnon
high forehead
flat face
small brow ridge
large brain case
projecting chin

We Are One Species

Human beings are diverse but even so we are all classified as *H. sapiens sapiens* (fig. 22.15). This is consistent with the biological definition of species because it is possible for all types of humans to interbreed and to bear fertile offspring. While it may appear that there are various "races," molecular data shows that the DNA base sequence varies as much between individuals of the same ethnicity as between individuals of different ethnicity.

It is generally accepted that the phenotype is adapted to the climate of a region. Although it might seem as if dark skin is a protection against the hot rays of the sun, it has been suggested that it is actually a protection against ultraviolet ray absorption. Dark-skinned persons living in southern regions and white-skinned persons living in northern regions absorb the same amount of radiation. (Some absorption is required for vitamin D production.) Other features that correlate with skin color, such as hair type and eye color, may simply be side effects of genes that control skin color.

Differences in body shape represent adaptations to temperature. A squat body with short limbs and a short nose retains more heat than an elongated body with long limbs and a long nose. Also, almond-shaped eyes, a flat nose and forehead, and broad cheeks are believed to be adaptations to the last Ice Age.

While it always has seemed to some that physical differences warrant assigning humans to different "races," this contention is not borne out by the molecular data mentioned previously.

Figure 22.15
All human beings belong to one species. There is as much molecular diversity between individuals of the same ethnicity as between individuals of different ethnicity.

a.

b.

c.

d.

e.

Biological Relationships

The evolutionary principles of descent with modification and adaptation to the environment apply to humans as they do to all living things. During the evolution of modern humans four trends can be distinguished: walking upright, reduction in frontal teeth and enlargement of cheek teeth, notable increase in brain size, and an elaborate culture. Do these trends indicate an adaptation to the environment?

The first hominids originated in eastern Africa, which is separated from the rest of the continent by the rift valley. During the Pliocene epoch when the rift valley developed, savannah was replacing forests because of an increasingly dry environment. Most likely, the first hominids (australopithecines) already had an upright posture because this posture is adaptive for life in trees. Walking upright promoted the ability to move about and find food among the tall grasses of the savannah. The glaciations of the Pleistocene epoch accentuated the drying conditions, and it is then that the descendants of *A. afarensis* took two different adaptive directions. The robust forms developed massive jaws and teeth suitable to a more fibrous diet. They became extinct perhaps because they were outcompeted by the ungulates (e.g., horses) of that day. The gracile forms of *A. afarensis* are ancestral to humans.

A study of the *Homo* line of descent shows that they took another approach to solving dietary problems. In the *Homo* line, the eyeteeth are reduced in size and the molars are not massive. Their dentition is suitable to an omnivorous diet that includes the eating of meat. An increase in brain size and the making of tools facilitated first the scavenging and later the hunting of game to acquire meat. Standing upright frees the hands for tool use; so does an opposable thumb, which is a basic primate characteristic. It is clear, then, that humans were preadapted for tool use.

Culture begins with the making and using of tools. Language facilitated cooperative efforts to acquire a diverse diet that still included plant materials. Human evolution was no longer dependent upon biological changes; instead technological advancements have allowed humans to adapt to many diverse environments throughout the world. In general, the hunting way of life gave way to an agricultural economy about 12,000 to 15,000 years ago, perhaps because we became too efficient at the killing of big game. The agricultural period extended from that time to about 200 years ago when the Industrial Revolution began. Since then many people have lived in cities, in large part divorced from nature but endowed with the philosophy of exploitation and control of nature. Only recently have we begun to realize that if the human population continues to work against rather than with nature, our species will also become extinct.

Summary

1. The evolution of human beings can be traced from the Cambrian period when animals originated. Among vertebrates, fishes dominated (and still dominate) the seas; on land, amphibians gave way to reptiles as the dominant land group during the Mesozoic era. Mammals evolved from reptiles but did not diversify until the Cenozoic era, after the dinosaurs became extinct. Human beings are primates, animals adapted to living in trees.

2. Primates have opposable thumbs, and nails replace claws. The forebrain in particular is enlarged, and there is an emphasis on learned behavior during an extended period of parental care.

3. During the evolution of primates, various groups diverged in a particular sequence from the main line of descent. Prosimians (tarsiers and lemurs), which diverged first, are most distantly related to us and most closely related to the original primate.

4. Anthropoids include New-World monkeys, Old-World monkeys, and hominoids. New-World monkeys took up residence in South America and diverged before Old-World monkeys. These two groups are not any more related to each other than to the apes.

5. The first hominoid ancestor may have been *Proconsul,* whose apelike fossils date from the Miocene epoch.

6. Among living apes, two are Asian (gibbon and orangutan) and two are African (gorilla and chimpanzee). Molecular biologists tell us we are most closely related to the African apes whose ancestry split from ours about 6 MYA (during the Pliocene epoch).

7. Hominid evolution continued in eastern Africa, which is isolated from the rest of the continent by the rift valley where tectonic forces are causing eastern Africa to separate from the continent. Eastern Africa became dry and the forests began to disappear.

8. The oldest hominid is classified as an australopithecine. *Australopithecus ramidus* is dated at 4.4 MYA; *A. afarensis* (Lucy) at 3.4 MYA; and the son of Lucy at just about 3 MYA. Although the brain was small, these hominids walked erect. After a period of stasis, branching speciation occurred.

9. Both gracile australopithecines (*A. africanus*) and robust forms (*A. boisei* and *A. robustus*) existed. Both forms have a brain of about 500 cc and may have made tools and eaten meat. However, the robust forms had a more fibrous grass diet.

10. *Homo habilis*, also present about 2 MYA, is certain to have made tools. Most likely this species killed small- to-medium-sized prey. The larger brain (700 cc) indicates that this hominid may have had speech; if so, culture could have begun. From then on, hunting and culture were inseparable.

11. *H. erectus*—with a brain capacity of 1,000 cc and a striding gait—was the first to migrate out of Africa, to have fire, to be a big game hunter, and, possibly, to use home bases.

12. Two contradicting hypotheses have been suggested about the origination of modern humans. The multiregional continuity hypothesis says that modern humans originated separately in Asia, Europe, and Africa. If so, a distinctive continuity in anatomy and genes is expected in each location. The out-of-Africa hypothesis says that modern humans originated only in Africa and, after migrating into Europe and Asia, they replaced the archaic *Homo* species found there. Many studies are being done to determine the possible validity of these hypotheses.

13. The Neanderthals may have been an archaic *Homo* species of Europe. Their chinless face, squat frame, and heavy muscles are apparently adaptations to the cold. Cro-Magnon is a name often given to modern humans. Their tools were sophisticated, and they definitely had a culture, as witnessed by the paintings on the walls of caves.

14. The human phenotype can adapt to the climate but such adaptations do not signify any great differences in genotype. There is as much DNA base sequence variation between individuals of the same ethnicity as between individuals of a different ethnicity. While it may seem that humans are divided into "races" this is not borne out by molecular data.

Writing Across the Curriculum

In order to practice writing skills, students should write out the answers to any or all of the study questions and the critical thinking questions. The study questions are sequenced in the same order as the text. Answers to the objective questions, and suggested answers to the critical thinking questions, are in appendix D.

Study Questions

1. In general terms, trace the evolution of humans from the time that animals arose. Mention sequential eras and periods and their significant events.   356

2. In what ways are primates adapted to an arboreal life?   357

3. What are the groups of living prosimians, and what is their significance regarding human evolution?   357

4. What are the two groups of living monkeys and how are they related? What is the significance of the fossils classified as *Proconsul*?   359

5. What are the four groups of living apes and how are they related? What is their degree of relatedness to modern humans as determined by molecular biology?   360–61

6. How did geographical changes in Africa affect the evolution of hominids?   361

7. Name the various species of *Australopithecus* and explain how they are believed to be related to one another and to humans.   362–64

8. Why is *Homo habilis* classified as a *Homo*? If this hominid did make tools, what does this say about its possible way of life?   365

9. What role(s) might *H. erectus* have played in the evolution of modern humans according to the multiregional theory? the out-of-Africa theory? What was this hominid's possible way of life?   367

10. Who were the Neanderthals and the Cro-Magnons, and what is their place in the evolution of humans according to the two hypotheses mentioned in question 9?   368–69

11. Why are all human beings classified as *H. sapiens sapiens*? What do molecular data tell us about peoples of different ethnicity or "race"?   370

Objective Questions

1. Which of these gives the correct order of divergence from the main line of descent leading to humans?
   a. prosimians, monkeys, gibbons, orangutans, African apes, humans
   b. gibbons, orangutans, prosimians, monkeys, African apes, humans
   c. monkeys, gibbons, prosimians, African apes, orangutans, humans
   d. African apes, gibbons, monkeys, orangutans, prosimians, humans

2. Lucy is a member of what species?
   a. *Homo erectus*
   b. *Australopithecus afarensis*
   c. *H. habilis*
   d. *A. robustus*

3. Hominids did not evolve until
   a. South Africa became hot and tropical.
   b. a rift valley separated eastern Africa.
   c. the climate became drier.
   d. Both b and c are correct.

4. The son of Lucy lived
   a. about 3 MYA.
   b. about 3.5 MYA.
   c. in the same epoch as Lucy.
   d. Both a and c are correct.

5. *H. erectus* could have been the first to
   a. use and control fire.
   b. migrate out of Africa.
   c. make tools.
   d. All of these are correct.

6. Which of these characteristics is not consistent with the others?
   a. large brow ridge
   b. large zygomatic arch
   c. high forehead
   d. projecting face

7. Which of these is true? The last common ancestor for apes and hominids
   a. has been found and it resembles a gibbon.
   b. has not been found but it is expected to be from the Pliocene epoch.
   c. has been found and it has been dated at 30 MYA.
   d. is not expected to be found because there was no such common ancestor.

8. Which of these is incorrectly matched?
   a. gibbon—hominoid
   b. *A. africanus*—hominid
   c. tarsier—anthropoid
   d. *H. erectus*—Homo

9. If the multiregional continuity hypothesis is correct, then hominid fossils in China after 100,000 BP
   a. are not expected to resemble earlier fossils.
   b. are expected to resemble earlier fossils.
   c. Either one is consistent with the hypothesis.

10. Which of these is incorrectly matched?
   a. *H. erectus* —made tools
   b. Neanderthal—good hunter
   c. *H. habilis*—controlled fire
   d. Cro-Magnon—good artist

11. Classify humans by filling in the missing lines.
   Kingdom Animalia
   Phylum **a.** _____
   Subphylum **b.** _____
   c. _____ Mammalia
   d. _____ Primates
   Suborder **e.** _____
   Superfamily **f.** _____
   Family **g.** _____
   h. _____ *Homo*
   Species **i.** _____

Concepts and Critical Thinking

1. *Humans have an evolutionary history as do all living things.*

   List ways in which you would show that we are closely related to the African apes.

2. *Geographic isolation promotes speciation.*

   Show how this concept pertains to the evolution of humans.

3. *Molecular biology can contribute to our understanding of human evolution.*

   Explain why DNA similarities show relatedness, and give at least two examples of the application of molecular biology to the evolution of humans.

Selected Key Terms

anthropoid (AN-thruh-poyd) A group of primates that includes only monkeys, apes, and humans. [Gk. *anthrop,* man, and *oid,* like]   359

australopithecine (aw-stray-loh-PITH-uh-syn) One of several species of *Australopithecus,* a genus that contains the first generally recognized hominids. [L. *austr,* southern, and Gk. *pithec,* ape]   362

Cro-Magnon Hominid who lived 40,000 years ago; these people were accomplished hunters, made compound stone tools, and possibly had a language.   368

hominid A member of the family hominid containing humans and their direct ancestors known only by the fossil record. [L. *hom,* man, and *id,* a condition of]   361

hominoid A member of a superfamily containing humans and the great apes. [L. *hom,* man, and Gk. *oid,* like]   359

Homo erectus Hominid who lived during the Pleistocene epoch; had a posture and locomotion similar to modern humans. [L. *hom,* man, and *erect,* upright]   366

Homo habilis Hominid of 2 million years ago; possibly a direct ancestor of modern humans. [L. *hom,* man, and *habilis,* handy]   365

mammal Member of a class of vertebrates characterized especially by the presence of hair and mammary glands. [L. *mammil,* teat]   356

molecular clock The idea that the rate at which mutation changes accumulate in certain types of genes is constant over time and is not involved in adaptation to the environment.   361

Neanderthal Hominid who lived during the last Ice Age in Europe and the Middle East; these people made stone tools, hunted large game, and lived together in a kind of society.   368

primate Animal that belongs to the order Primates, the order of mammals that includes prosimians, monkeys, apes, and humans.   357

Proconsul A possible hominoid ancestor; a forest-dwelling primate with some characteristics of living apes.   359

prosimian (proh-SIM-ee-un) A group of primates that includes lemurs and tarsiers and may resemble the first primates to have evolved. [Gk. *pro,* before, and *simos,* mokey, ape]   357

Suggested Readings for Part III

Bar-Yosef, O., and Vandermeersch, B. 1993. Modern humans in the Levant. *Scientific American* 268(4):94. Findings in Israel raise questions about the emergence of *Homo sapiens.*

Blumenschine, R. J., and Cavallo, J. A. 1992. Scavenging and human evolution. *Scientific American* 267(4):90. Early humans may have developed their hunting skills by competing with scavengers for food.

Carroll, R. 1988. *Vertebrate paleontology and evolution.* New York: W. J. Freeman and Company. Vertebrate history is analyzed in depth through 600 million years.

Coffin, M. F., and Eldholm, O. October 1993. Large ingenous provinces. *Scientific American.* The effect of ancient lava flows on global climate and evolution is discussed.

Coppens, Y. 1994. East side story: The origin of humankind. *Scientific American* 270(5):88. Explores and provides a theory for why hominids branched off from chimpanzees.

Cowen, R. 1995. *History of life,* 2d ed. Boston: Blackwell Scientific Publications. From the origin of life through human evolution, this is an introduction to paleontology and paleobiology.

Dalziel, I. W. D. 1995. Earth before Pangaea. *Scientific American* 272(1):58. Geologists search for clues to early continental drift.

deWaal, F. B. M. 1995. Bonobo sex and society. *Scientific American* 272(3):82. Discusses the Bonobo great ape and its resemblance to humans in behavior, appearance, and intelligence.

Doolittle, R. F., and Bork, P. 1993. Evolutionary mobile modules in proteins. *Scientific American* 269(4):50. This article discusses the role of proteins in evolution.

Grant, P. R. 1991. Natural selection and Darwin's finches. *Scientific American* 265(4):82. Uses the Galápagos finches as an example of recent evolution and natural selection.

Horgan, J. February 1991. In the beginning . . . *Scientific American.* Questions about the origin of life are discussed.

Kent, G. 1992. *Comparative anatomy of the vertebrates.* 7th ed. St. Louis: Mosby-Year Book, Inc. The basics of vertebrate comparative structure and function from an evolutionary perspective.

Klein, J., et al. 1993. MHC polymorphism and human origins. *Scientific American* 269(6):78. Explains that human tissue diversity developed long before *Homo sapiens* emerged.

Knecht, H. July 1994. Late Ice Age hunting technology. *Scientific American.* Early humans developed skills for crafting hunting implements.

Knoll, A. H. October 1991. End of the Proterozoic eon. *Scientific American.* The change from single to unicellular organisms may have resulted from rapid increases in atmospheric oxygen.

Laureates' Anthology. 1952. The origin of the earth. *Scientific American.* The theory that the solar system arose from a cloud of dust has led to a new inquiry into the chemical history of Earth.

Levin, H. L. 1994. *The earth through time.* 4th ed. Philadelphia: Saunders College Publishing. Provides an in-depth study of evolutionary and geological eras and events.

Levinton, J. S. 1992. The big bang of animal evolution. *Scientific American* 267(5):84. An evolutionary burst gave rise to the basic body plans of modern multicellular animals.

Lewin, R. 1993. *The origin of modern humans.* New York: Scientific American Library. This colorfully illustrated book describes discoveries and controversaries surrounding human origins.

Li, W. H., and Graver, D. 1991. *Fundamentals of molecular evolution.* Sunderland, Mass.: Sinaur Associates. Evolutionary history can be studied from molecular data.

Macdonald, K. C., and Fox, P. J. 1990. The mid-ocean ridge. *Scientific American* 262(6):72. New maps reveal details of mid-ocean ridge formation.

Marshall, L. February 1994. The terror birds of South America. *Scientific American.* These animals were at the top of the food chain 65 million years ago.

Milner, R. 1990. *The encyclopedia of evolution: Humanity's search for its origins.* New York: Henry Holt and Company. A discussion of persons, events, and ideas associated with the theory of evolution.

Milton, K. 1993. Diet and primate evolution. *Scientific American* 269(2):86. Presents the role of diet in primate evolution.

Novacek, M. J., et al. 1994. Fossils of the flaming cliffs. *Scientific American* 271(6):60. Describes recent discoveries of dinosaur and other fossils in the Gobi desert.

Pääbo, S. 1993. Ancient DNA. *Scientific American* 269(5):86. Evolutionary change can be observed directly from genetic information in fossil remains.

Pollack, H., and Chapman, D. 1993. Underground records of changing climate. *Scientific American* 268(6):44. More is being learned about global climate through geological studies.

Ross, P. E. 1992. Eloquent remains. *Scientific American* 266(5):114. Describes new biotechnology techniques that are being used to study residues of nucleic acids and proteins in fossils.

Ross, R., and Allmon, W. 1990. *Causes of evolution.* Chicago: The University of Chicago Press. Presents a paleontological perspective of evolution.

Rudwick, M. 1976. *The meaning of fossils.* 2d ed. Chicago: The University of Chicago Press. Presents a study of natural science and geology for undergraduates.

Schopf, J. W. 1992. *Major events in the history of life.* Boston: Jones and Bartlett Publishers. Summarizes crucial events shaping the earth's development and evolution over time.

Scientific American. 1994. 271(4). This special issue is devoted to evolution.

Storch, G. 1992. The mammals of island Europe. *Scientific American* 266(2):64. This interesting article describes mammalian fossils found in German shale beds.

Strickberger, M. 1990. *Evolution.* Boston: Jones and Bartlett Publishers. Presents the basics of evolutionary theories.

Tattersall, I. 1992. Evolution comes to life. *Scientific American* 267(2):80. Describes how lifelike figures of early humans are created for museum displays.

Tattersall, I. 1993. Madagascar's lemurs. *Scientific American* 268(1):110. The lemur, which closely resembles human ancestors, is becoming extinct.

Thorne, A. G., and Wolpoff, M. H. 1992. The multiregional evolution of humans. *Scientific American* 266(4):76. Fossil remains show interconnected lineages that gave rise to modern humans.

Toth, N., et al. July 1992. The last stone ax makers. *Scientific American.* Craftsmen in an isolated area of New Guinea still make stone axes that resemble those of early humans.

Vickers-Rich, P., and Hewitt-Rich, T. 1993. Australia's polar dinosaurs. *Scientific American* 269(1):50. Antarctic dinosaurs have been discovered.

Wellnhofer, P. May 1990. Archaeopteryx. *Scientific American.* Archaeopteryx is a source of information about the evolution of flight in birds.

Wenke, R. 1990. *Patterns in prehistory: Humankind's first three million years.* 3d ed. New York: Oxford University Press. A comprehensive review of world prehistory.

Wilson, A. C., and Cann, R. L. 1992. The recent African genesis of humans. *Scientific American* 266(4):66. Modern humans may have moved outward from Africa to populate other continents.

York, D. 1993. Earliest history of the earth. *Scientific American* 268(1):90. New dating techniques allow geologists to determine early earth history.

Part III
GENETIC VARIATION AND EVOLUTION

Both natural selection and genetic variation in populations are essential components of the modern theory of evolution. Genetic variation presents a diversity of characteristics on which natural selection can act to favor the survival of those characteristics that are advantageous to a population. In this way, gradual change over many generations results in adaptations that uniquely suit organisms to their environment.

While this generalized scheme provides an overview of the mechanism of evolution, several critical questions can be immediately raised. How much genetic variation exists in populations? Is there a relation between genetic variation and the rate of evolutionary change?

Such questions serve to generate testable hypotheses on the relationship between genetic variation and the process of evolution. One such hypothesis can be stated as follows: *Natural populations contain a large amount of genetic variation. Selection acts on this large pool of genetic variation to produce adaptive change.*

In an initial test of this hypothesis, two populations of fruit flies were subjected to intense selection pressure. One population (Y) was a single pure strain, while the other population (Z) was produced by crossbreeding two single strains.

Due to the crossbreeding, population Z contained about twice as much genetic variation as population Y. Equal numbers of flies from both populations were then placed in separate large culture bottles, where the flies would be subjected to intense competition for food and space. After 500 days (about twenty-five generations), the number of flies in each bottle was counted. What result would you predict?

Prediction 1 The greater genetic variation due to crossbreeding to initially produce population Z should permit more rapid adaptation to the environment. Therefore, more flies should be found in population Z than in Y after twenty-five generations of selection.

Result 1 The results of this experiment are shown in figure 22A. Although both populations increased in number, population Z (with more genetic variability) increased more rapidly. This result suggests that population Z adapted to the environmental conditions more rapidly. Thus, selection pressure leads to adaptive change and supports the hypothesis. Moreover, the greater the genetic variability, the more rapid the adaptation.

Question 1. **(a)** Why does this experiment indicate adaptive change rather than just the growth of the population?

(b) If flies from population Y were bred with flies from population Z, would the offspring be more or less able to survive in the culture bottles?

(c) What were the selection pressures in this experiment?

While this experiment does show adaptation, it does not indicate selection of specific traits or show how selection occurred. Can highly focused selection lead to specific changes?

In another experiment, selection was artificially controlled and changes in specific traits was observed. Corn kernels were artificially selected for either high or low oil content (i.e., experimenters selected those corn kernels in each generation that were highest in oil content and, also, those that were lowest in oil content). High oil and low oil kernels were planted in separate plots. The resulting plants in the separate plots were not allowed to interbreed. This procedure was continued for fifty generations. Would this highly directed selection for a specific trait lead to genetic change?

Prediction 2 If the genetic variation for oil content is sufficiently large, changes in oil content should continue in response to selection for many generations.

Result 2 The results of this experiment indicated that oil content increased from 5% to 14% and was still increasing even after fifty generations of intense selection for the group with high oil content. In the group selected for low oil content, no significant change was observed in the later generations, but oil content had decreased from 5% to less than 2% in the early stages. These results provide further support for the hypothesis by showing selection can lead to highly significant change in specific traits.

Figure A

Increase in number of flies maintained in separate culture bottles over 500 days (about twenty-five generations). Population Y is a single pure strain. Population Z was produced by crossbreeding two single strains and contains about twice as much genetic variability as population Y.

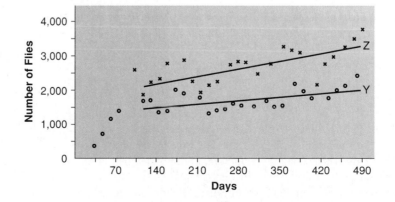

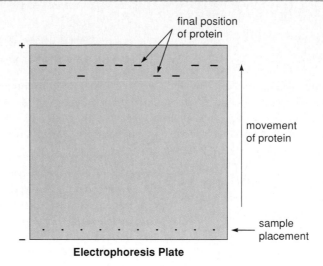

Electrophoresis Plate

Figure B

Electrophoresis of proteins from ten fruit flies. Tissue samples were placed at the bottom of the plate, and an electric field was applied between the top and the bottom of the plate for a period of time. The final position of two forms of a specific enzyme are indicated by applying a stain specific for the enzyme being investigated. Three of the flies have one form of the enzyme and seven have the other form.

The evidence from these experiments suggests that natural populations *do* contain a large amount of genetic variation but provides no measure of how much variation exists. New techniques in molecular biology, however, have produced much more precise measurements. A particularly useful technique is the electrophoresis of proteins.

In electrophoresis, an electrical field is applied across a gel plate composed of starch or synthetic polymer, with material, such as a protein, placed on the gel. If the molecules of the material have an electrical charge, the molecules will move across the plate in response to the electrical field. The distance of movement in a specified time period is related to the charge on the molecule. The greater the charge, the further the movement.

Since the amino acids composing the proteins in an organism are coded by the sequence of nucleotides in DNA (deoxyribonucleic acid), any change in the DNA should be reflected by a change in the amino acid sequence of the protein. Such changes can be detected by electrophoresis of proteins because different amino acids carry a different electric charge. Proteins with different electrical charges will travel different distances when subjected to electrophoresis. These different distances of travel will separate proteins on the electrophoresis plate and indicate very slight genetic changes in proteins (i.e., changes in the DNA).

This technique is especially useful in detecting slight differences existing in proteins that are synthesized from the same gene on homologous chromosomes. Each diploid cell contains homologous pairs of chromosomes. The pair of homologues contain the same genes, but mutation may have led to differences between the DNA of the same gene on the two homologues.

For example, suppose the gene for a specific enzyme is carried on both homologues. It is the same gene but the amino acid sequence may differ slightly in the enzyme produced by each homologue, even though both forms are still functional and catalyze the same reaction. If these differences are reflected by differences in the electrical charge, the two enzyme forms can be separated by electrophoresis.

What would you predict would happen if a specific enzyme were examined in several individual organisms of the same species?

Prediction 3 Genetic variability existing in the DNA coding for the enzyme will be detected in the electrophoretic movement of the enzyme in tissue from separate organisms.

Result 3 Figure B shows the electrophoretic separation of a specific enzyme from ten fruit flies of the same species. Three have one form of the enzyme, while seven possess a second form. Obviously, the different forms of this enzyme represent a high degree of genetic variability.

Electrophoretic analysis of a great many proteins from numerous species of animals has indicated that for vertebrates, the average percentage heterozygosity (the percentage of genes that are dissimilar) is 6.6% for each individual. In other words, the average individual is heterozygous for 6.6% of their genes. Investigators consider such figures a large

amount of genetic variability. Indeed, these figures were much higher than many geneticists thought existed before the application of new experimental techniques.

Diverse studies involving both natural and artificial selection and investigations of the molecular structure of proteins have been used to study genetic variability and the process of evolution.

Scientists investigating evolution and genetic variability consider these experiments strong support for the hypothesis that populations contain large amounts of genetic variation and that selection acts on this variation to bring about adaptive change.

Sources:

Ayala, F. J., ed. 1976. *Molecular Evolution.* Sunderland, Mass.: Sinauer Associates.
___. September 1978. The mechanisms of evolution. *Scientific American* 239(3):56.

Part IV

DIVERSITY OF LIFE

Using fossil, molecular, and other types of evidence, biologists have determined the evolutionary relationships between major groups of organisms and know in general the history of life's diversity. Evolutionary trees help us see these relationships, but it is important to realize that there is no direction to the evolutionary process and that life does not progress from the simple to the complex. Each lineage is but a tiny twig on a sprawling bush that has no main trunk.

Adaptation to a particular way of life accounts for life's diversity. Unicellular protozoa and green algae are suited to living in a pond, mushrooms feed on organic matter in your lawn, and insects utilize flight as a way to escape enemies and to seek food. These organisms are just as well adapted to their way of life as are the more complex flowering plants and the vertebrate animals to theirs. The study of biology is the study of the many ways that living organisms have evolved various solutions to the same fundamental problems. All organisms must acquire materials and energy, protect themselves, and reproduce.

A sea horse, *Hippo campus*, exemplifies how diverse the jawed fishes and therefore life can be.

Many of the figures and concepts discussed in *Biology*, fifth edition, are further explored in technology products. The following is a list of figures in part IV that correlates to technology products.

A set of five videotapes contains 53 animations of physiological processes integral to the study of biology. These videotapes, entitled *Life Science Animations*, cover such topics as chemistry, genetics, and reproduction. A videotape icon appears in appropriate figure legends to alert the reader to these animations.

Explorations in Human Biology and *Explorations in Cell Biology, Metabolism, and Genetics* by George B. Johnson are interactive CD-ROMs with activities that can be used by an instructor in lecture and/or placed in a lab or resource center for student use. This interactive software consists of modules that cover key topics discussed in a biology course. The CD-ROMs are available for use with Macintosh and IBM Windows computers. A CD-ROM icon appears in appropriate figure legends to alert the reader to these activities.

Corresponding Figures	Videotape Concepts	CD-Rom Modules
25.13 Life cycle of *Plasmodium vivax*	45. Life Cycle of Malaria	—

23

CLASSIFICATION OF LIVING THINGS

Learning Objectives

Naming and Classifying Organisms

- Describe and explain an organism's scientific name. 380–81
- Discuss how species are classified, and note the problems involved in designating species. 382
- State the classification categories and the significance of classification. 383
- Name the five kingdoms recognized by this text and give examples of organisms in these kingdoms. 384

Constructing Phylogenetic Trees

- Describe the field of systematics as it relates to phylogeny and the construction of phylogenetic trees. 387
- Describe the types of data used to construct phylogenetic trees. 388–89
- Contrast three schools of systematics and describe how to construct a cladogram. 390–92

Giant tube worms, *Rifta pachyptila*, first discovered in deep-sea dredgings during 1900 were later assigned to a new phylum in the Animal Kingdom called Pogonophora.

Figure 23.1
How would you classify these organisms? An artificial system would not take into account how they might be related. A natural
system would take this into account.

NAMING AND CLASSIFYING ORGANISMS

Suppose you were asked to classify the living things you know about (fig. 23.1). Most likely you would begin by making a list, and naturally this would require that you give each one a name. Then you would start assigning the organisms on your list to particular groups. But what criteria would you use—color, size, how the organisms relate to you? Deciding on the number, types, and arrangement of the groups would not be easy, and periodically you might change your mind or even start over. Biologists, too, have not had an easy time of deciding how living things should be classified, and changes have been made throughout the history of this field.

Taxonomy [Gk. *taxis,* arrangement, and *nomy,* science of], the branch of biology concerned with identifying and naming organisms, began with the ancient Greeks and Romans. Some of the scientific names we use today were chosen by the Romans and the scientific name of all species is still given in Latin or Greek. The famous Greek philosopher Aristotle was the first to be interested in taxonomy. Much later, John Ray, a British naturalist, also believed that each organism should have a set name. He said, "When men do not know the name and properties of natural objects—they cannot see and record accurately."

Assigning a Two-Part Name

The number of known types of organisms expanded greatly in the mid-eighteenth century due to European travel to distant parts of the world. It was during this time that Carolus Linnaeus (1707–78), developed the *binomial system* of naming species (fig. 23.2). The name is a binomial because it has two parts. For example, *Rosa odorata* and *Rosa damascena* are two different species of roses. The first word, *Rosa,* is the genus (pl., genera), a classification category that can contain many species. The second word is the specific epithet of the species within that genus. The *specific epithet* sometimes tells us something descriptive about the organism. In this case, *odorata* suggests a strong fragrance while *damascena* suggests a certain petal texture. Notice that the scientific name is in italics; the genus is capitalized while the specific epithet is not. The species is designated by the full name; in this case either *Rosa odorata* or

Figure 23.2

Taxonomy. **a.** Linnaeus was the father of taxonomy and gave us the binomial system of classifying organisms. He was particularly interested in classifying plants such as these two roses. **b.** *Rosa odorata.* **c.** *Rosa damascena.*

b.

a.

c.

Rosa damascena. The specific epithet alone gives no clue as to species—just as the house number alone without the street name gives no clue as to which house is specified. The genus name can be used alone, however, to refer to a group of related species.

Why do organisms need to be given a scientific name in Latin? Why can't we just use common names for organisms? A common name will vary from country to country just because different countries use different languages. Hence the need for a universal language such as Latin, which used to be well known by most scholars. Even those who speak the same language sometimes use different common names for the same organism. The Louisiana heron and the tricolored heron are the same bird found in southern United States. Between countries, the same common name is sometimes given to different organisms. A "robin" in England is very different from a "robin" in the United States, for example. When scientists use the same scientific name, they know they are speaking of the same organism.

The job of identifying and naming the species of the world is a daunting task. Of the estimated 3 to 20 million species now living on earth, we have named a million species of animals and a half million species of plants and microorganisms. We are further along on some groups than others; it's possible we have just about finished the birds, but there may yet be hundreds of thousands of unnamed insects.

The scientific name of an organism consists of its genus and a specific epithet. The complete binomial name indicates the species.

Figure 23.3

Identifying the members of a species can be difficult—especially when the male and female members do not look alike, as in these mallards, *Anas platyrhynchos*.

Figure 23.4

Zebroids. Zebroids are horse-zebra hybrids. Like mules, zebroids are generally infertile, due to differences in the chromosomes of their parents.

What Is a Species?

There are several ways to distinguish species and each way has its advantages and disadvantages. For Linnaeus, every species has its own distinctive structural characteristics that are not shared by members of a similar species. In birds, the structural differences can involve the shape, size, and color of the body, feet, bill, or wings. We know very well, however, that variations do occur among members of a species. Differences between males and females or between juveniles and adults may even make it difficult to tell which organism belongs to what species (fig. 23.3).

The *biological definition* of a species rests on the recognition that distinctive characteristics are passed on from parents to offspring. This definition, which states that members of a species interbreed and share the same gene pool, applies only to sexually reproducing organisms and cannot apply to asexually reproducing organisms. Sexually reproducing organisms are not always as reproductively isolated as we would like them to be. When a species has a wide geographic range there may be variant types that tend to interbreed where their populations overlap. This observation has led to calling these populations subspecies, designated by a three part name. For example, *Elaphe obsoleta bairdi* and *Elaphe obsoleta obsoleta* are two subspecies within the same snake species *Elaphe obsoleta*. It could be that these subspecies are actually distinct species. Even species that seem to be obviously distinct interbreed on occasion (fig. 23.4). Therefore, the presence or absence of hybridization may not be informative as to what constitutes a species.

This chapter concerns **classification,** the assignment of organisms to categories on the basis of their evolutionary relationship to other organisms. In this context, a species is a taxonomic category below the rank of genus. Species in the same genus share a more recent common ancestor than do species in other taxa. **Taxa** [Gk. *taxis,* arrangement] are groups of organisms that fill a particular category of classification; the *Rosa* and *Felis* are taxa in the category genus. A **common ancestor** is one that produced at least two lines of descent; there is one ancestor for all the types of roses, for example.

Now Let's Classify

Classification of an organism begins when it is named, since genus and species are two classification categories. Since taxonomy and classification go hand in hand, it is to be expected that the individuals we have so far mentioned contributed to classification. Aristotle divided living things into fourteen groups—mammals, birds, fish, and so on. Then he went on to subdivide the groups according to the size of the organisms. Ray used a more natural system, since he grouped animals and plants according to how he thought they were related; but Linnaeus simply used flower part differences to assign plants to these categories, which are still in use today: species, genus, order, and class. His studies were published in a book called *Systema Naturae*.

Figure 23.5

Levels of classification. Each level of classification is more inclusive than the next.
There can be several species in a genus, several genera in each family, and so forth.

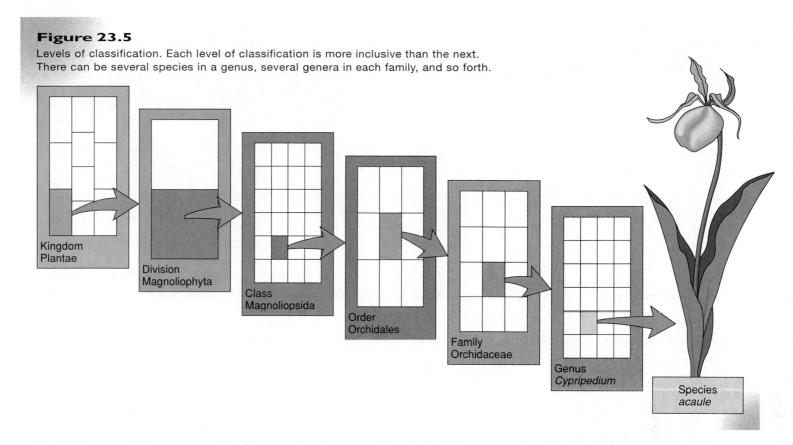

Kingdom Plantae
Division Magnoliophyta
Class Magnoliopsida
Order Orchidales
Family Orchidaceae
Genus *Cypripedium*
Species *acaule*

Table 23.1

Classification of Humans

Kingdom Animalia	Eukaryotic, usually motile, multicellular organisms, without cell walls or chlorophyll; usually, internal cavity for digestion of nutrients
Phylum Chordata	Organisms that at one time in their life history have a dorsal hollow nerve cord, a notochord, and pharyngeal pouches
Class Mammalia	Warm-blooded vertebrates possessing mammary glands; body more or less covered with hair; well-developed brain
Order Primates	Good brain development, opposable thumb and sometimes big toe; lacking claws, scales, horns, and hoofs
Family Hominidae	Limb anatomy suitable for upright stance and bipedal locomotion
Genus *Homo*	Maximum brain development, especially in regard to particular portions; hand anatomy suitable to the making of tools
Species *sapiens**	Body proportions of modern humans; speech centers of brain well developed

To specify an organism, you must use the full name, such as Homo sapiens.

Today, we make use of at least seven obligatory categories: **species, genus, family, order, class, phylum,** and **kingdom.** (The plant kingdom uses the category *division* instead of *phylum*.) There can be several species within a genus, several genera within a family, and so forth—the higher the category the more inclusive it is (fig. 23.5). Therefore, there is a *hierarchy* of categories. The organisms that fill a particular classification category are distinguishable from other organisms by having certain characteristics, or simply characters. A *character* is any structural,

chromosomal, or molecular feature that distinguishes one group from another. Organisms in the same kingdom have *general* characters in common; those in the same species have quite *specific* characters in common. Table 23.1 lists some of the characters that help classify humans into major categories.

Each of the seven obligatory categories of classification can be subdivided into three additional categories as in superorder, order, suborder, and infraorder. Considering this, there are more than thirty categories of classification.

How Many Kingdoms?

From Aristotle's time to the middle of the twentieth century, biologists recognized only two kingdoms, **kingdom Plantae** (plants) and **kingdom Animalia** (animals). Plants were literally organisms that were planted and immobile, while animals were animated and moved about. After the microscope revealed many single-celled creatures that didn't fit neatly into these two kingdoms, Ernst Haeckel, a German, proposed a third kingdom. He suggested the name Protista, in order to separate these unicellular organisms from multicellular ones. During the last two decades, however, it has become evident that certain multicellular forms are closely related to unicellular forms and should be classified with them. As suggested by H. F. Copeland in 1956, we will call this third kingdom **kingdom Protoctista** [Gk. *proto,* first, and *ktistos,* to establish]. Kingdom Protoctista (protoctists) contains the algae, including multicellular forms; protozoa, including multicellular forms; water molds; and slime molds. The organisms in this kingdom lack tissue differentiation. When Haeckel was classifying organisms, he also put bacteria and cyanobacteria in a major group called Monera (within the kingdom Protista), because they lacked a cell nucleus. In 1969, R. H. Whittaker suggested a five-kingdom system that has become widely accepted. In a modification of Whittaker's system, we will put bacteria and cyanobacteria, formerly called blue-green algae, in the **kingdom Prokaryotae** [Gk. *pro,* before, and *kary,* nucleus] (prokaryotes) because of their prokaryotic status. It can be noted that the prokaryotes and protoctists are grouped according to characters they do *not* have rather than characters they do have. Prokaryotes lack a true nucleus and protoctists lack tissue differentiation.

According to the Whittaker system, the fungi (mushrooms and molds) are in a separate kingdom, appropriately called **kingdom Fungi.** Fungi are eukaryotes that form spores and lack flagella throughout their life cycle. Whittaker argued for a separate kingdom for fungi because they are multicellular saprotrophs, organisms that absorb nutrients from dead organic matter after secreting digestive enzymes. He pointed out that plants, animals, and fungi are all multicellular and that each has a unique mode of nutrition: plants are photosynthetic; animals are ingestive; and fungi are saprotrophic. The five-kingdom system used by this text is depicted in figures 23.6 and 23.7. Figure 23.6, which shows their possible evolutionary relationships, also lists their characters in regard to type of cell, nutrition, reproduction, and motility. Figure 23.7 is a pictorial display.

Just now there is some discussion about the need for a sixth kingdom for the archaebacteria, organisms able to live under the extreme conditions that may have dominated the primitive earth—hot springs, salty waters, and anaerobic muds. Archaebacteria are structurally similar to other bacteria, called eubacteria, but a significant molecular difference has been found. Cells cannot function properly without ribosomes; therefore, ribosomes have probably changed little since the first cells. Yet, the sequence of ribosomal nucleotides is different in archaebacteria and eubacteria. This is interpreted to mean that the archaebacteria and eubacteria separated early in the history of the earth.

> **T**his text recognizes five kingdoms: kingdoms Prokaryotae, Protoctista, Fungi, Plantae, and Animalia. The kingdoms are distinguished on the basis of type of cell, type of nutrition, type of reproduction, and motility.

Figure 23.6

The five-kingdom system of classification. Representatives of each kingdom are depicted in the ovals, and a phylogenetic tree roughly indicates the lines of descent. The characteristics for each kingdom are listed inside the ovals.

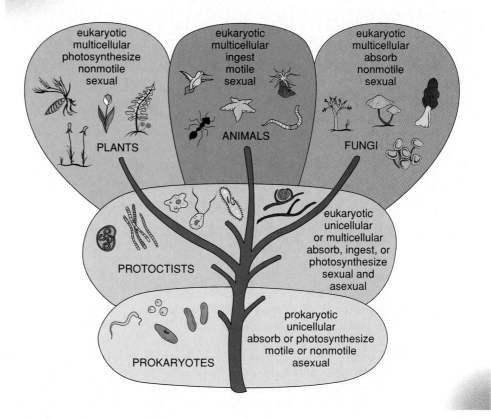

Figure 23.7
The five kingdoms—a pictorial representation.

Grey wolf, *Canis*
Kingdom Animalia

Black-eyed Susan, *Rudbeckia*
Kingdom Plantae

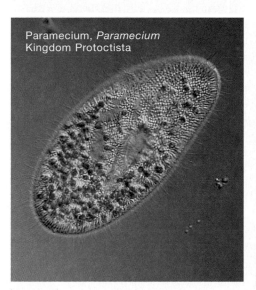

Paramecium, *Paramecium*
Kingdom Protoctista

100 µm

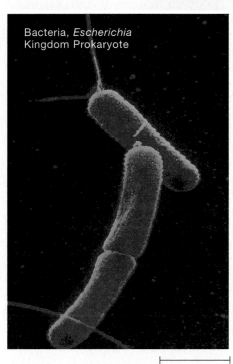

Bacteria, *Escherichia*
Kingdom Prokaryote

500 nm

Mushroom, *Hygrocybe*
Kingdom Fungi

Spider Webs And Spider Classification

By using information from many sources, the evolution, and thus the classification, of an animal group can be clarified. A good example comes from the spiders, members of the class Arachnida, order Araneae. Spiders are distinguished from other similar animals by their ability to weave webs of silk. The silk is produced from glands in their abdomens, and it emerges from modified appendages called spinnerets.

Arachnologists (scientists who study spiders) are largely convinced that spider webs were originally used to line a cavity or a burrow in which an early spider hid. Many spiders that still live in such burrows extend threads or a collar of silk over their burrow entrances to detect prey over a wider area than they could otherwise easily search. From this array of threads evolved the basic sheet web, made by a wide variety of spider families. The sheet of closely woven threads is useful not only in signaling the presence of prey, but also in slowing the prey as the insect's legs tangle in the matted silk. However, the appearance of the sheet web in many clearly unrelated families of spiders suggests that it evolved numerous times and cannot be used to answer questions about the true relationships of spider families. Only if some advanced (apomorphic) feature of a sheet web is shared by two or more families does it indicate a common ancestry.

The geometric orb web probably evolved from a sheet web. The orb web, which has threads placed in a regular fashion, uses less silk and thus "costs" less. However, it is possible that the orb web itself also evolved more than once. In fact, this was the predominant theory until recently. The orb web was thought to have arisen at least twice because it is made by two groups of spiders that look very different. The **superfamily Dinopoidea** includes spiders with a *special spinning apparatus, the cribellum,* which produces extremely fine fibers. The **superfamily Araneoidea,** which also makes orb webs, lacks the cribellum, and thus are called ecribellates. If the

William A. Shear
Hampden-Sydney College

cribellum is a specialization that arose only in the dinopoid lineage, then it seems most logical (as arachnologists have thought for most of this century) that the araneoids and dinopoids are not closely related and their orb webs are quite separate developments: a case of convergent evolution (see p. 388).

The similarities of the orbs made by the two families are so detailed—even extending to the specific movements made by the spiders' legs while weaving them—that the two families seem closely related.

A sweeping study of spider classification carried out in 1967 by Finnish biologist Pekka Lehtinen revealed that the cribellum was not, in fact, a specialization, but was part of the original equipment of all spiders except the tarantulas. Since its first appearance, probably in the Permian period some 260 million years

ago, the cribellum has been lost many times in many phylogenetic lines of spiders. Lehtinen found numerous examples of spiders that were nearly identical except for the presence or absence of the cribellum, and the mass of evidence he accumulated convinced arachnologists that the cribellum could be easily lost.

By considering this new view of the cribellum, along with the extensive data on orb-web building behavior, we now think that the orb originated only once, in a cribellate common ancestor of both the cribellate dinopoids and the ecribellate araneoids (fig. 23A).

Thus, it would seem that despite differences the dinopoids and the araneoids are close relatives—and that the character defining them is the orb web. One difficulty remains. The araneoids include two large families that do not make orb webs, but we know from studying the behavior of dinopoids that many peculiar-looking webs are, in fact, orbs or are derived from them. At this time, the behavior of araneoids has not been studied closely enough to determine if their webs are also extreme derivatives of orb webs. If they are derived from orb webs, then, like the cribellum, the orb web has been lost by some spiders whose ancestors possessed it. But if they are not derived from orb webs, then it would appear that the orb web cannot be used to show that the dinopoids and araneoids are closely related, and the convergent evolution hypothesis could be revived.

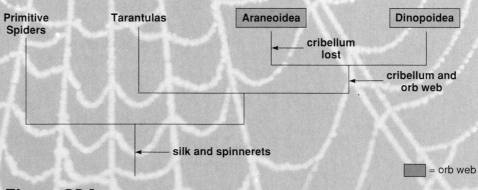

Figure 23A
Phylogenetic tree of spiders.

CONSTRUCTING PHYLOGENETIC TREES

Taxonomy and classification are a part of the broader field of **systematics** [Gk. *sys,* together] which is the study of the diversity of organisms at all levels of organization. One goal of systematics is to determine **phylogeny** [Gk. *phyl,* tribe], or the evolutionary history of a group of organisms. Classification is a part of systematics because it lists the unique characters of each taxon and ideally is designed to reflect phylogeny. A species is most closely related to other species in the same genus, then to genera in the same family, and so forth, from order to class to phylum to kingdom. When we say that two species (or genera, families, etc.) are closely related, we mean they share a recent common ancestor.

Figure 23.8 shows how the classification of groups of organisms allows one to construct a **phylogenetic tree,** a diagram that indicates common ancestors and lines of descent (lineages). In order to classify organisms and to construct a phylogenetic tree, it is necessary to determine the characters of the various taxa. A **primitive character** is one that is present in the common ancestor and all members of a group. A **derived character** is one that is found only in a particular line of descent. Different lineages diverging from a common ancestor may have different derived characters. For example, all the animals in the family Cervidae have antlers, but they are highly branched in red deer and palmate in reindeer.

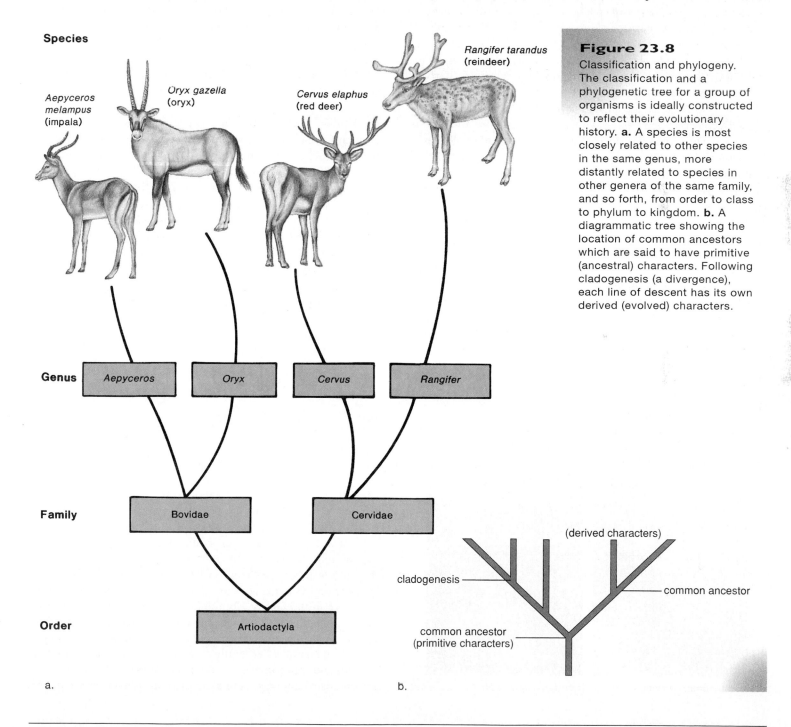

Figure 23.8
Classification and phylogeny. The classification and a phylogenetic tree for a group of organisms is ideally constructed to reflect their evolutionary history. **a.** A species is most closely related to other species in the same genus, more distantly related to species in other genera of the same family, and so forth, from order to class to phylum to kingdom. **b.** A diagrammatic tree showing the location of common ancestors which are said to have primitive (ancestral) characters. Following cladogenesis (a divergence), each line of descent has its own derived (evolved) characters.

What Are Our Data?

Systematists gather all sorts of data in order to discover the evolutionary relationship between species. Species placed in one group should have a common ancestry—that is, they should form a monophyletic [Gk. *mono,* one, and *phyl,* tribe] group. Systematists rely heavily on homology, molecular data, and the fossil record in order to determine monophyletic groups.

When Parts Are Similar

Homology [Gk. *homo,* alike, and *logy,* study of] is character similarity that stems from having a common ancestry. Comparative anatomy, including embryological evidence, provides information regarding homology. The forelimbs of vertebrates are homologous because they contain the same bones organized in the same general way as in a common ancestor. *Homologous structures* are related to each other through common descent, although they may now differ in their structure and function. In contrast, *analogous structures* have the same function in different groups but are not derived from the same organ in a common ancestor. The wings of an insect and the wings of a bat are analogous structures.

Deciphering homology is sometimes difficult because of convergent evolution and parallel evolution. **Convergent evolution** is the acquisition of the same or similar characters in distantly related lines of descent. Convergence occurs when organisms have similar structural and functional traits, not because of a common ancestor but because they are adapted to the same type of environment. Both euphorbia and cacti are adapted similarly to a hot, dry environment, and they both are succulent, spiny, flowering plants (fig. 23.9). However, the details of their flower structure indicate that these plants are not closely related. **Parallel evolution** is the acquisition of the same or similar characters in two or more related lineages without it being present in a common ancestor. A similar banding pattern is found in several species of moths, for example. It is sometimes difficult to tell if features are parallel, primitive, or derived.

Figure 23.9

Cacti and spurges evolved on different continents, and yet they are both succulent flowering plants with spines. Cacti are adapted to living in African deserts, whereas spurges are adapted to living in tropical habitats of Africa and America. This is an example of convergent evolution.

prickly pear, *Opuntia*

Spurge, *Euphorbia*

When Genes Are Similar

When two lineages first diverge from a common ancestor, the genes and proteins of the lineages are nearly identical. But as time goes by, each lineage accumulates its own changes in gene and protein structure. Many changes are neutral (not tied to adaptation) and accumulate at a fairly constant rate; such changes can be used as a kind of *molecular clock* to indicate evolutionary time.

The genetic difference between two species is determined in a number of ways. Immunological techniques can roughly judge the similarity of two species. In one procedure, antibodies are produced by transfusing a rabbit with the cells of one species. Cells of the second species are exposed to these antibodies, and the degree of the reaction is observed. The stronger the reaction, the more similar the cells from the two species. DNA (deoxyribonucleic acid) differences can be determined more directly. The DNA double helix of each species is separated into single strands. Then strands from both species are allowed to combine. The more closely related the two species, the better the strands of the hybrid DNA will stick together.

Some long-standing questions in systematics have been resolved by doing molecular analyses. The giant panda, which lives in China, was at one time considered to be a bear, but its bones and teeth resemble those of a raccoon. The giant panda eats only bamboo and has a false thumb by which it grasps bamboo stalks. The red panda, which lives in the same area and has the same raccoonlike features, also feeds on bamboo but lacks the false thumb. The results of DNA hybridization studies suggest that after raccoons and bears diverged from a common lineage 50 million years ago, the giant panda diverged from the bear line and the red panda diverged from the raccoon line:

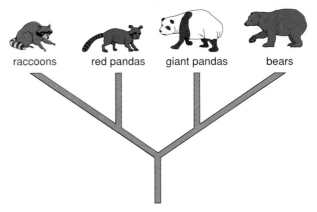
raccoons   red pandas   giant pandas   bears

Therefore it can be seen that some of the characters of the giant panda and the red panda are primitive (present in a common ancestor), and some are due to parallel evolution.

The results of another study involving DNA differences suggest that chimpanzees are more closely related to humans than they are to other apes (fig. 23.10). Yet in most classifications, humans and chimpanzees are placed in different families; humans are in the family Hominidae and chimpanzees are in the family Pongidae. In contrast, the rhesus monkey and the green monkey, which have more numerous DNA differences, are placed in the same family (Cerocpithecidae). To be consistent, shouldn't humans and chimpanzees also be in the same family? While some systematists believe so, others argue that humans are markedly different from chimpanzees (because of adaptation to a different environment) and, therefore, it is justifiable to place humans in a separate family than chimpanzees.

Of late, systematists have begun to doubt the usefulness of DNA hybridization studies because they do not produce data regarding a particular character that pertains to the phylogeny of a species. Many researchers now prefer to compare data regarding the base sequence of a particular gene or restriction site. Restriction enzymes digest DNA at particular sites, and the location of such sites (as in DNA fingerprinting) can reveal a possible similarity that indicates relatedness.

When Fossils Are Available

The fossil record shows the history of life in broad terms. However, the fossil record in regard to individual lineages is incomplete for several reasons. First, soft-bodied organisms do not fossilize. The chances of any organism becoming a fossil are not too good; most organisms decay before they have a chance to be buried. Second, fossils tend to exist for only harder body parts, such as bones and teeth. Even then, fossils must survive powerful geological processes and yet be positioned so that someone will find them.

Fossils can be dated, and therefore an available fossil can establish the antiquity of a species. In some instances, the fossil record can trace a lineage through time. Even so, the fossil record does not necessarily provide evidence of whether a feature is primitive or derived. The only objective method for distinguishing primitive from derived characters is discussed in the reading on page 392.

> Homology, molecular data, and the fossil record help researchers decipher phylogeny and construct phylogenetic trees.

Figure 23.10

The relationship of certain primate species based on a molecular study of their genomes. The length of the branches indicates the relative number of nucleotide pair differences that were found among groups. With the help of the fossil record, it is possible to suggest a date at which each group diverged from the other.

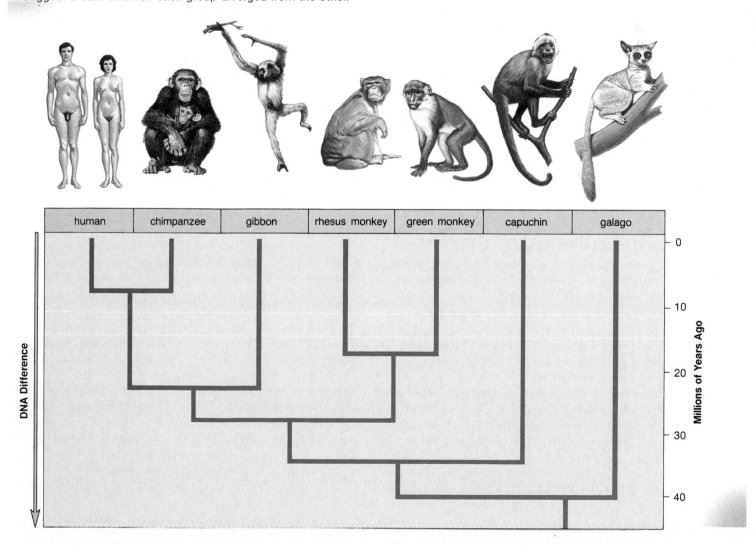

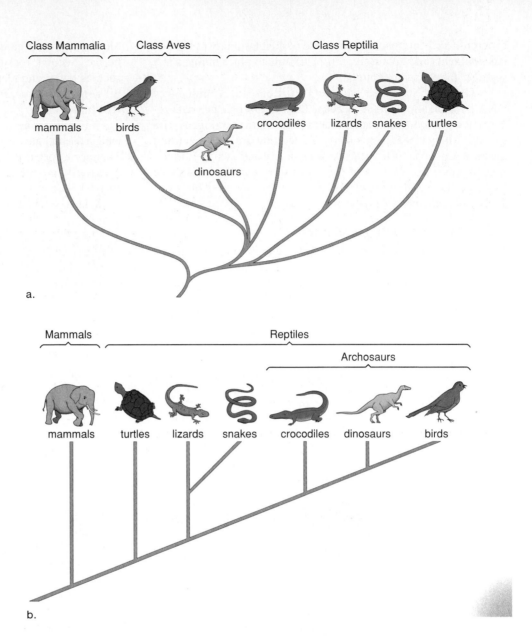

Figure 23.11
Traditional versus cladistic view of
reptilian phylogeny. **a.** According to
traditionalists, mammals and birds
are in separate classes. **b.** According
to the cladists, crocodiles, dinosaurs,
and birds all share a recent common
ancestor and should be in the
same subclass.

Who Constructs Phylogenetic Trees?

There are three main schools of systematics: traditional, cladistics, and numerical phenetics. The traditional school stresses both common ancestry *and* the degree of structural difference among divergent groups. Therefore, a group that has adapted to a new environment and shows a high degree of evolutionary change is not always classified with the common ancestor from which it evolved. For example, in figure 23.11*a* birds and mammals are shown as separate lines of descent because it is quite obvious to the most casual observer that mammals (having hair and mammary glands) and birds (having feathers) are quite different in appearance from reptiles (having scaly skin). The traditionalist goes on to say that birds and mammals evolved from reptiles.

To the cladists, the traditional method of determining phylogeny is arbitrary and results in a nonevolutionary way of classifying organisms. In the sample cited, birds are more similar to dinosaurs and crocodiles than they are different from them. It is doubtful that "reptiles" should even be considered a taxon because the only thing dinosaurs, crocodiles, snakes, lizards, and turtles have in common is that they are not birds or mammals.

Cladists believe that species should be grouped solely on the basis of shared derived characters. All the animals in figure 23.11*b* evolved from a common ancestor, which was an egg-laying creature, but the direct ancestor for mammals must be considered a mammal. A mammal can be recognized by the presence of hair, mammary glands, and three middle ear bones. Since crocodiles, dinosaurs, and birds all share common derived characters, they should all be in the same subclass, called archosaurs. The traditionalist asks, "So does this mean that crocodiles and dinosaurs are birds?" Cladists reply that their method is objective and not subjective like that of the traditionalist.

Figure 23.12

Alternate, simplified cladograms. **a.** X, Y Z share the same characters, designated by the first arrow, and are judged to form a monophyletic group. Y and Z are grouped together because they share the same derived character, designated by the second arrow and symbolized by the colored box. **b, c.** These cladograms are rejected because in each you would have to assume that the same charter (colored boxes) evolved in different groups. Since this seems unlikely, the first branching pattern is chosen as the hypothesis.

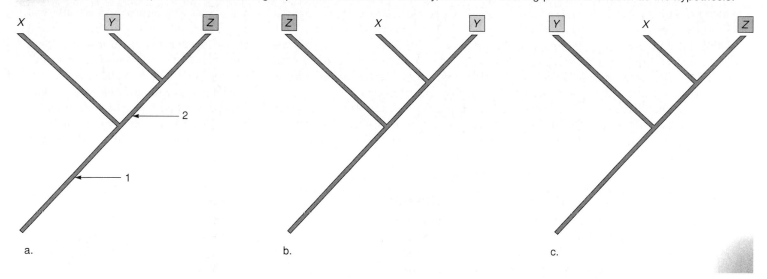

a.

b.

c.

Cladistics Is Objective

This school of **cladistics** is based on the work of Willi Hennig, who sought a more objective way of establishing relationships and classifying organisms. He felt that the present traditional system, which was based on general similarities, was subjective and did not produce testable hypotheses. Instead, he suggested that species be grouped according to their *shared, derived characters*. All mammals have characters that they share and that distinguish them from other taxa. But the different types of mammals have their own derived characters. For example, all bats have forelimbs modified as wings, and all whales have forelimbs modified as flippers. However, bat's wings and whale's flippers are homologous, and the presence of homologous structures indicates that taxa share a common ancestry.

Once cladists have assembled their data regarding shared characters, they construct **cladograms** [Gk. *klados,* having branches] to show the branching (cladistic) relationships among species in regard to the distribution of shared derived characters. A cladogram should be regarded as a hypothesis that can be tested and either corroborated or refuted on the basis of additional data. A cladogram differs from a traditional phylogenetic tree, particularly because (1) only data (not subjective evaluations) are used in its construction and (2) the data are presented as a part of the cladogram. Figure 23.12 shows a simple cladogram that involves only three species; construction of a more complex cladogram is discussed in the reading on page 392. A cladogram is not considered a phylogenetic tree, but its branching pattern does resemble a true phylogenetic tree.

Figure 23.12 shows a cladogram in which all three species represented by *x, y,* and *z* belong to the same monophyletic group, since they all share the derived characters designated by the first arrow. Species *y* and *z* are placed in the same subgroup because they share the derived characters designated by the second arrow. How do you know you have done the cladogram correctly, and that the other two patterns shown in figure 23.12 are not likely? In the other two arrangements, the characters represented by the colored box would have had to evolve twice. Cladists are always guided by the principle of *parsimony*—the minimum number of assumptions is the most logical. That is, they construct the cladogram that minimizes the number of assumed evolutionary changes. However, they must be on the lookout for the possibility that convergent evolution has produced what appears to be common ancestry. Then, too, there is the realization that the reliability of a cladogram is dependent on the knowledge and skill of the particular investigator gathering the data and doing the character analysis.

Phenetics Is Numerical

In numerical phenetics, species are clustered according to the number of their similarities. Systematists of this school believe that you cannot construct a classification that actually reflects phylogeny, and that it is better to rely strictly on a method that does away with personal prejudices. They measure as many traits as possible, count the number the two species share, and then estimate the degree of relatedness. They simply ignore the possibility that some of the shared characters are probably the result of convergence or parallelism, or that some of the characters might depend on one another. For example, a large animal is bound to have larger parts. The results of their analysis are depicted in a phenogram. (Phenograms have been known to vary for the same group of organisms, depending on how the data are collected and handled.) Figure 23.10 is an example of a phenogram that is based solely on the number of DNA differences among the species shown.

How to Construct a Cladogram

hoosing the characters for analysis requires knowledge of the organisms in question. A cladogram (as a scientific hypothesis) is only as reliable as the evidence that produced it. When constructing a cladogram, the first step is to draw up a table that summarizes the characters of the taxa being compared. At least one but preferably several species are studied as outgroups; an outgroup is a taxon outside the study groups. Any character found both in the study groups and the outgroup is considered to be primitive (ancestral) for the study groups. Any character found in all taxa or in only one taxon is excluded from the cladogram. The other characters are considered shared derived characters and are used to construct the cladogram.

Figure 23B is an example of a cladogram. A common ancestor, together with all its descendant species, is a **clade** [Gk. *klados,* having branches]; this cladogram has three clades that differ in size because the first includes the other two, and so forth. All the study groups belong to the first clade because they all have vertebrae; newts, snakes, and lizards are in the clade that has lungs and a three-chambered heart, and only snakes and lizards have an amniote egg and internal fertilization. In the event that there is more than one possible cladogram consistent with the evidence, the one that leaves the fewest shared derived characters unexplained or has the fewest evolutionary changes in derived characters is selected.

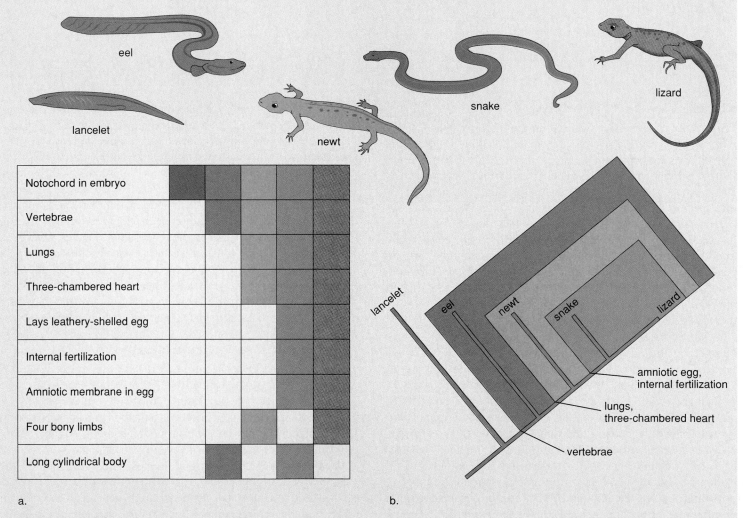

a.

b.

Figure 23B

Steps in producing a cladogram. **a.** Construction of a table. The table shown here is simplified; a real table would have many more characters. **b.** Notice that this cladogram does not include the presence of four bony limbs versus a long, cylindrical body. Evidence is needed that snakes have lost their limbs through evolution; otherwise, it appears that eels and snakes share a derived character.

Summary

1. Taxonomy deals with the naming of organisms; each species is given a binomial name consisting of the genus and specific epithet.

2. Distinguishing species on the basis of structure can be difficult because members of a species can vary in structure.

3. Distinguishing species on the basis of reproductive isolation runs into problems because some species hybridize and because reproductive isolation is very difficult to observe.

4. In this chapter, species is a taxon occurring below the level of genus. Species in the same genus share a more recent common ancestor than species in related genera, etc.

5. Classification involves the assignment of species to categories. When an organism is named, a species has been assigned to a particular genus.

6. There are seven obligatory categories of classification: species, genus, family, order, class, phylum, and kingdom. Each higher category is more inclusive; members of the same kingdom share general characters and members of a species share quite specific characters.

7. This text recognizes five kingdoms on the basis of type of cell, type of nutrition, type of reproduction, and motility. Kingdoms Plantae, Animalia, and Fungi (mushrooms and molds) are believed to have evolved from members of the kingdom Protoctista (algae, protozoa, water molds, slime molds) which in turn evolved from members of the kingdom Prokaryotae (bacteria and cyanobacteria).

8. Ribosomal RNA analysis has revealed differences between bacteria, suggesting that archaebacteria should be in their own separate kingdom.

9. Systematics, a very broad field, encompasses both taxonomy and classification. Classification should reflect phylogeny, and one goal of systematics is to create phylogenetic trees, based on primitive and derived characters.

10. Homology, molecular data, and the fossil record are used to help decipher phylogenies.

11. Homology helps indicate when species belong to a monophyletic group; however, convergent evolution and parallel evolution sometimes make it difficult to distinguish homologous structures from analogous structures.

12. Molecular data are used to indicate relatedness, but DNA base sequence and restriction site data may pertain more directly to phylogenetic characters.

13. Because fossils can be dated, available fossils can establish the antiquity of a species. If the fossil record is complete enough, we can sometimes trace a lineage through time.

14. Today there are three main schools of systematics: the traditional, the cladistic, and the numerical phenetic school. The traditional school stresses common ancestry and the degree of structural difference among divergent groups in order to construct phylogenetic trees.

15. The cladistic school analyzes primitive and derived characters and constructs cladograms on the basis of shared derived characters. A clade is a common ancestor and all the species derived from that common ancestor. Cladograms are diagrams based on objective data.

16. The numerical phenetic school clusters species on the basis of the number of shared similarities regardless of whether they might be convergent, parallel, or depend on one another.

Writing Across the Curriculum

In order to practice writing skills, students should write out the answers to any or all of the study questions and the critical thinking questions. The study questions are sequenced in the same order as the text. Answers to the objective questions, and suggested answers to the critical thinking questions, are in appendix D.

Study Questions

1. Explain the binomial system of naming organisms. Why must the species be designated by the complete name?   380–81

2. Why is it necessary to give organisms scientific names?   381

3. Discuss three ways to define a species. Which way relates to classification?   382

4. What are the seven obligatory classification categories? In what way are they a hierarchy?   383

5. Name the five kingdoms recognized by this text and give examples of each kingdom.   384

6. State the characters of each kingdom and explain how the kingdoms might be related.   384

7. Why might a sixth kingdom be necessary, and for what type organism?   384

8. How is it that taxonomy and classification are a part of systematics? What three types of data help systematists construct phylogenetic trees?   387–89

9. In what ways do the traditional school, the cladistic school, and the numerical phenetic school of systematics differ?   390

10. Discuss the principles of cladistics and explain how to construct a cladogram.   391–92

Objective Questions

1. Which is the scientific name of an organism?
   a. *Rosa rugosa*
   b. *Rosa*
   c. *rugosa*
   d. All of these are correct.

2. Which of these best pertains to taxonomy? Species
   a. have three-part names such as *Homo sapiens sapiens*.
   b. are reproductively isolated from other species.
   c. share the most recent common ancestor.
   d. have only primitive characters.

3. The classification category below the level of family is
   a. class.
   b. species.
   c. phylum.
   d. genus.

4. Which kingdom is mismatched?
   a. Prokaryotae—fungi
   b. Protoctista—multicellular algae
   c. Plantae—flowers and mosses
   d. Animalia—arthropods and humans

5. Which kingdom is mismatched?
   a. Fungi—usually saprotrophic
   b. Plantae—usually photosynthetic
   c. Animalia—rarely ingestive
   d. Protoctista—various modes of nutrition

6. In a phylogenetic tree, which is incorrect?
   a. Dates of divergence are always given.
   b. Common ancestors occur at the notches.
   c. The more recently evolved are at the top of the tree.
   d. Ancestors have primitive characters.

7. Which is mismatched?
   a. homology—character similarity due to a common ancestor.
   b. molecular data—DNA strands match
   c. fossil record—bones and teeth
   d. homology—functions always differ

8. One benefit of the fossil record is
   a. that hard parts are more likely to fossilize.
   b. fossils can be dated.
   c. its completeness.
   d. All of these are correct.

9. In the traditional school of systematics, birds are assigned to a different group from reptiles because
   a. they evolved from reptiles.
   b. they are quite different from reptiles.
   c. feathers came from scales.
   d. All of these are correct.

10. In cladistics
    a. a clade must contain the common ancestor plus all its descendants.
    b. derived characters help construct cladograms.
    c. data for the cladogram is presented.
    d. All of these are correct.

11. Answer the following questions about this cladogram.

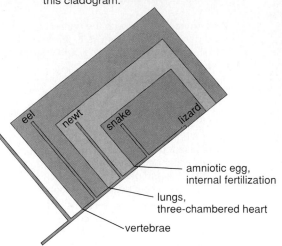

lancelet   eel   newt   snake   lizard

amniotic egg, internal fertilization

lungs, three-chambered heart

vertebrae

a. This cladogram contains how many clades? How are they designated in the diagram?
b. What character is shared by all the study groups? What characters are shared by only snakes and lizards?
c. Which groups share a common ancestry? How do you know?

Concepts and Critical Thinking

1. *Classification reflects phylogeny.*
   What does the classification of humans tell you about their evolutionary history?

2. *Organisms exist only at the species level.*
   Discuss the difficulties of defining a species.

3. *Classification is based on data.*
   Why do cladists believe that traditionalists are being subjective when they construct phylogenetic trees?

Selected Key Terms

clade In cladistics, a common ancestor and all the species descended from this common ancestor. [Gk. *klados,* having branches]   392

cladistics (kluh-DIS-tiks) A school of systematics that determines the degree of relatedness by analyzing primitive and derived characters and constructing cladograms.   391

cladogram (KLAD-uh-gram) In cladistics, a branching diagram that shows the relationship among species in regard to their shared, derived characters. [Gk. *klados,* having branches]   391

classification A set of categories to which species are assigned on the basis of their relationship to other species.   382

common ancestor An ancestor held in common by at least two lines of descent.   382

convergent evolution Similarity in structure in distantly related groups due to adaptation to the environment.   388

derived character A structural, physiological, or behavioral trait that is present in a specific lineage and is not present in the common ancestor for several lineages.   387

homology Similarity in structure due to having a common ancestor. [Gk. *homo,* alike, and *logy,* study of]   388

parallel evolution Similarity in structure in related groups that cannot be traced to a common ancestor.   388

phylogenetic tree (fy-loh-jen-ET-ik) A diagram that indicates common ancestors and lines of descent.   387

phylogeny (fy-LAHJ-uh-nee) The evolutionary history of a group of organisms. [Gk. *phyl,* tribe]   387

primitive character A structural, physiological, or behavioral trait that is present in a common ancestor and all members of a group.   387

systematics The study of the diversity of organisms at all levels of organization, from the cellular level to the population level. [Gk. *sys,* together]   387

taxon (pl., taxa) Group of organisms that fills a particular classification category. [Gk. *taxis,* arrangement]   382

taxonomy The branch of biology concerned with identifying and naming organisms. [Gk. *taxis,* arrangement, and *nomy,* science of]   380

24

VIRUSES AND KINGDOM PROKARYOTAE

Learning Objectives

Viruses Are Particles

- Contrast the characteristics of viruses and bacteria to show that viruses are nonliving and bacteria are living organisms.   396
- Describe the structure of viruses and how they replicate.   397–99
- Describe how bacteriophages and animal viruses, including retroviruses, reproduce.   398–400
- Discuss how viral infections can be controlled and how antiviral drugs work.   400–401

Prokaryotes Are Cellular

- Describe the structure of a prokaryotic cell.   401–2
- Describe how bacteria reproduce, how variations are generated, and how genetic recombination occurs.   403
- Explain how bacteria differ in their tolerance and need for oxygen.   404

- List the different types of autotrophic bacteria, and specifically explain why some photosynthesizers give off oxygen and others do not.   404
- Describe the nutrition of most heterotrophic bacteria, and give examples of different types of symbiotic bacteria.   404–5

How Prokaryotes Are Classified

- Describe the two subkingdoms of kingdom Prokaryotae and describe the common criteria used to divide eubacteria into groups.   405–6
- Describe the anatomy and physiology of the cyanobacteria and discuss their historical significance.   406–7
- Discuss how bacterial infections can be controlled and how antibiotics work.   407

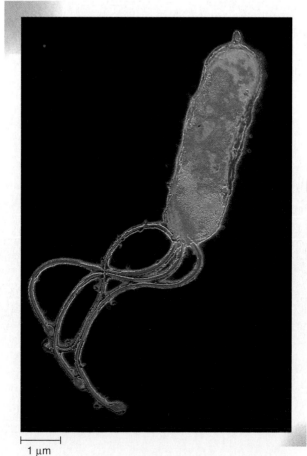

Colored transmission electron micrograph of a bacterium, *Helicobacter pylori,* whose flagella make it highly motile.

1 μm

iruses and prokaryotes (bacteria) are so tiny that you cannot see them without a microscope. While most bacteria can be seen with a light microscope using the highest magnification, viruses require electron microscopy. Sometimes these organisms are grouped with other disease-causing agents and called microbes. But there is a vast difference between viruses and bacteria. Viruses are not included in the classification table found in appendix A because they are noncellular and cannot be classified with cellular organisms. Bacteria are cellular and are often fully functioning organisms that can live independently; indeed, bacteria perform many functions that benefit all living things. Table 24.1 compares the general characteristics of viruses and bacteria.

> **Viruses and bacteria are conveniently called microbes. Viruses are noncellular; bacteria are cellular and many perform useful functions.**

VIRUSES ARE PARTICLES

Viruses [L. *viro*, poison] are nonliving particles with varied appearance, but even so they share certain common characteristics (fig. 24.1). They are all infectious. In 1884, French chemist Louis Pasteur suggested that something smaller than a bacterium was the cause of rabies, and it was he who chose the word *virus* from a Latin word meaning poison. In 1892, Dimitri Ivanowsky, a Russian biologist, was studying a disease of tobacco leaves, called tobacco mosaic disease because of the leaves' mottled appearance. He noticed that an infective extract could be filtered through a fine-pore porcelain filter and it still caused disease. This substantiated Pasteur's belief because it meant that the disease-causing agent was smaller than any known bacterium. In the next century electron microscopy was born and viruses were seen for the first time. By the 1950s, virology was an active field of research; the study of viruses has contributed much to our understanding of disease, genetics, and even the characteristics of living things.

Figure 24.1

Viruses (micrographs below, drawings above). Despite their diversity, all viruses have an outer capsid composed of protein subunits and a nucleic acid core—either DNA or RNA, but not both. Some types of viruses also have a membranous envelope.

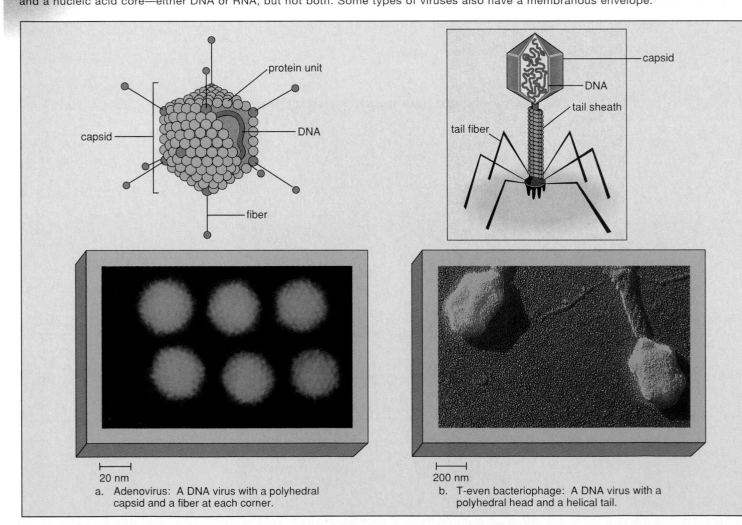

a. Adenovirus: A DNA virus with a polyhedral capsid and a fiber at each corner.

b. T-even bacteriophage: A DNA virus with a polyhedral head and a helical tail.

Table 24.1

Comparison of Viruses and Bacteria

Characteristic of Life	Viruses	Bacteria
Consist of cell	No	Yes
Metabolize	No	Yes
Respond to stimuli	No	Yes
Multiply	Yes (inside living cell)	Yes (independently)
Evolve	Yes	Yes

Viruses Are Noncellular

The size of a virus is comparable to that of a large protein macromolecule; they are generally smaller than 200 nm in diameter. Many viruses can be purified and crystallized, and the crystals can be stored just as chemicals are stored. Still, viral crystals will become infectious when the viral particles they contain are given the opportunity to invade a host cell.

Each type of virus always has at least two parts: an outer *capsid* composed of protein subunits and an inner core of nucleic acid—either DNA (deoxyribonucleic acid) or RNA (ribonucleic

acid), but not both. The viral genome at most has several hundred genes; a human cell contains thousands of genes. The capsid is often surrounded by an outer membranous envelope; if not, the virus is said to be naked. The envelope is actually a piece of the host's plasma membrane that also contains viral glycoprotein spikes. A viral particle may also contain various proteins, especially enzymes such as the polymerases, needed to produce viral DNA and/or RNA. The following diagram summarizes viral structure:

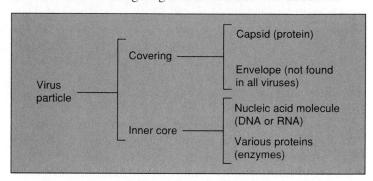

The classification of viruses is based on (1) their type of nucleic acid, including whether it is single stranded or double stranded, (2) their size and shape, and (3) the presence or absence of an outer envelope.

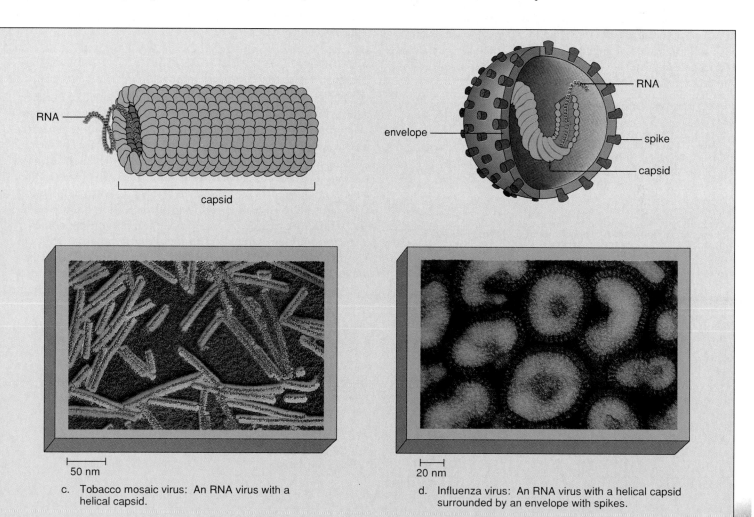

c. Tobacco mosaic virus: An RNA virus with a helical capsid.

d. Influenza virus: An RNA virus with a helical capsid surrounded by an envelope with spikes.

Viruses Are Parasites

Viruses are *obligate intracellular parasites,* which means they cannot multiply outside a living cell. To maintain animal viruses in the laboratory, they are sometimes injected into live chick embryos (fig. 24.2). Today, host cells are often maintained in tissue (cell) culture by simply placing a few cells in a glass or plastic container with appropriate medium. The cells can then be infected with the animal virus to be studied. Viruses infect all sorts of cells—from bacterial cells to human cells—but they are very specific. Bacteriophages infect only bacteria, the tobacco mosaic virus infects only plants, and the rabies virus infects only mammals, for example. We know that human viruses even specialize in a particular tissue. Human immunodeficiency virus (HIV) will enter only certain blood cells, the polio virus reproduces in spinal nerve cells, the hepatitis viruses infect only liver cells. What could cause this remarkable parasite-host cell correlation? It is now believed that viruses are derived from the very cell they infect; the nucleic acid of viruses came from their host cell genomes! Therefore, viruses must have evolved after cells came into existence, and new viruses are probably evolving even now.

Viruses can also mutate; therefore, it is correct to say that they evolve. Those that mutate often can be quite troublesome because a vaccine that is effective today may not be effective tomorrow. Flu viruses are well known for mutating, and this is why you have to have a flu shot every year—antibodies generated from last year's shot are not expected to be effective this year.

It is important to remember that even though viruses can reproduce and evolve, they do not fulfill all the characteristics of life and therefore are not considered living.

> Viruses evolve and reproduce but they are obligate intracellular parasites. They only grow inside their specific host cells.

Figure 24.2

Inoculation of live chick eggs with viral particles. A virus reproduces only inside a living cell, not because it uses the cell as nutrients, but rather because it takes over the machinery of the cell.

Viruses Replicate

Viruses gain entry into and are specific to a particular host cell because portions of the capsid (or the spikes of the envelope) adhere in a lock-and-key manner with a receptor on the host cell plasma membrane. Their nucleic acid then takes up residence inside the cell. Once inside, the nucleic acid codes for the protein units in the capsid. In addition, the virus may have genes for a few special enzymes needed for the virus to reproduce and exit from the host cell. In large measure, however, a virus relies on the host's enzymes, ribosomes, transfer RNA (tRNA), and ATP (adenosine triphosphate) for its own reproduction. In other words, a virus *takes over the metabolic machinery of the host cell* when it reproduces.

Bacteriophages Have Two Cycles

Bacteriophages [Gk. *bact,* rod, and *phag,* eat], or simply phages, are viruses that parasitize bacteria; the bacterium in figure 24.3 could be *Escherichia coli,* which lives in our intestines, for example. Two types of bacteriophage life cycles, termed the lytic cycle and the lysogenic cycle, have been carefully studied. In the lytic cycle, viral replication occurs and the host cell undergoes *lysis,* a breaking open of the cell to release viral particles. In the lysogenic cycle, viral replication does not immediately occur, but replication may take place sometime in the future. The bacteriophage, termed lambda, is capable of carrying out either cycle.

Lytic Cycle

The **lytic cycle** [Gk. *ly,* loose] may be divided into five stages: attachment, penetration, biosynthesis, maturation, and release. During *attachment,* portions of the capsid combine with a receptor on the rigid bacterial cell wall in a lock-and-key manner. During *penetration,* a viral enzyme digests away part of the cell wall, and viral DNA is injected into the bacterial cell. *Biosynthesis* of viral components begins after the virus brings about inactivation of host genes not necessary to viral replication. The virus takes over the machinery of the cell in order to carry out viral DNA replication and production of multiple copies of the capsid protein subunits. During *maturation,* viral DNA and capsids are assembled to produce several hundred viral particles. Lysozyme, an enzyme coded for by a viral gene, is produced; this disrupts the cell wall, and the *release* of phage particles occurs. The bacterial cell dies as a result.

> During the lytic cycle, a bacteriophage takes over the machinery of the cell so that viral replication and release occur.

Lysogenic Cycle

With the **lysogenic cycle** [Gk. *ly,* loose, and *genos,* descent], the infected bacterium does not immediately produce phage but may do so sometime in the future. In the meantime the phage is *latent*—not actively replicating. Following attachment and penetration, viral DNA becomes integrated into bacterial DNA with no destruction of host DNA. While latent, the viral DNA is called a *prophage.* The prophage is replicated along with the host DNA, and all subsequent cells, called lysogenic cells, carry a copy of the prophage. Certain environmental factors, such as ultraviolet radiation, can induce the prophage to enter the lytic stage of biosynthesis, followed by maturation and release.

> During the lysogenic cycle, the phage becomes a prophage that is integrated into the host genome. At a later time, the phage may reenter the lytic cycle and replicate itself.

Animal Viruses Also Cycle

Animal viruses replicate in a manner similar to bacteriophages but there are modifications. If the virus has an envelope, its glycoprotein spikes allow the virus to adhere to plasma membrane receptors. Then the entire virus (not just the nucleic acid) penetrates a host cell by endocytosis. Once inside, the virus is uncoated as the envelope and capsid are removed. The viral genome, either DNA or RNA, is now free of its coverings and biosynthesis proceeds. Another difference among enveloped viruses is that viral release occurs by budding. During budding, the virus picks up its envelope consisting of lipids, proteins, and carbohydrates that are present in the plasma membrane of the host cell. Other envelope markers, such as the glycoproteins that allow the virus to enter a host cell, are coded for by viral genes. Budding does not necessarily result in the death of the host cell.

Some animal viruses are specific to human cells. Of special concern are those such as the papillomavirus, the herpes viruses, the hepatitis viruses, and the adenoviruses, which can cause specific types of cancer. These viruses undergo a period of latency and their presence so alters the genotype of the cell that the

Figure 24.3
Comparison of the lytic and lysogenic cycles. **a.** In the lytic cycle, viral particles escape when the cell is lysed (broken open). **b.** In the lysogenic cycle, viral DNA is integrated into host DNA. At some time in the future, the lysogenic cycle can be followed by the lytic cycle.

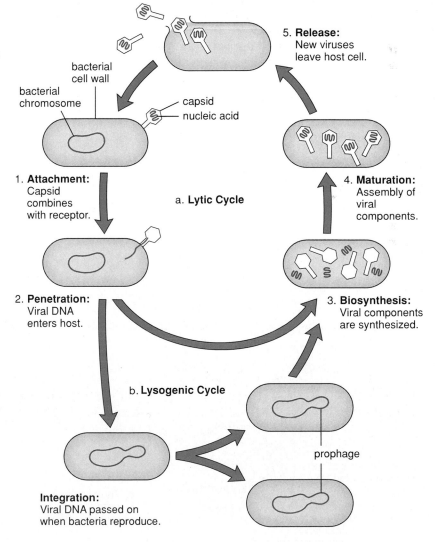

bacterial cell wall

bacterial chromosome

capsid
nucleic acid

1. **Attachment:**
Capsid combines with receptor.

2. **Penetration:**
Viral DNA enters host.

a. **Lytic Cycle**

5. **Release:**
New viruses leave host cell.

4. **Maturation:**
Assembly of viral components.

3. **Biosynthesis:**
Viral components are synthesized.

b. **Lysogenic Cycle**

prophage

Integration:
Viral DNA passed on when bacteria reproduce.

cells become cancerous. Some viruses are cancer-producing because they bring with them *oncogenes,* normal genes that have been transformed and that now can cause the cell to undergo repeated cell division.

> After animal viruses enter the host cell, uncoating releases viral DNA or RNA and replication occurs. If release is by budding, the viral particle acquires a membranous envelope.

Retroviruses Have RNA Genes

Retroviruses are RNA animal viruses that have a DNA stage. Figure 24.4 illustrates the reproduction of a retrovirus. A **retrovirus** [L. *retro,* backward, and *viro,* poison] contains a special enzyme called reverse transcriptase, which carries out RNA→cDNA transcription. The DNA is called cDNA because it is a DNA copy of the viral genome. Following replication, the resulting double-stranded DNA is integrated into the host genome. The viral DNA remains in the host genome and is repli-

cated when host DNA is replicated. When and if this DNA is transcribed, new viruses are produced by the steps we have already cited: biosynthesis, maturation, and release—not by destruction of the cell, but by budding.

Retroviruses are of interest because human immunodeficiency viruses (HIV), which cause AIDS, are retroviruses. Retroviruses also cause certain forms of cancer.

Viruses Cause Infections

Viruses are best known for causing infectious diseases in plants and animals, including humans. In plants, infectious diseases can be controlled only by burning those plants that show symptoms of disease. In humans, viral diseases are controlled by preventing transmission, administering vaccines, and only recently by the administration of antiviral drugs. Knowing how viral diseases are transmitted can help prevent their spread. Use of a condom will help prevent the transmission of HIV; frequent hand washing during cold season can help prevent a cold. **Vaccines** [L. *vacci,* of a cow], which are drugs administered to stimulate immunity to a microbe so that it cannot later cause disease, are available for some viral diseases such as polio, measles, and

Figure 24.4

Reproduction of a retrovirus. Notice that the mode of entry requires uncoating, that the virus integrates into the host genome, and that the virus acquires an envelope when it buds from the host cell.

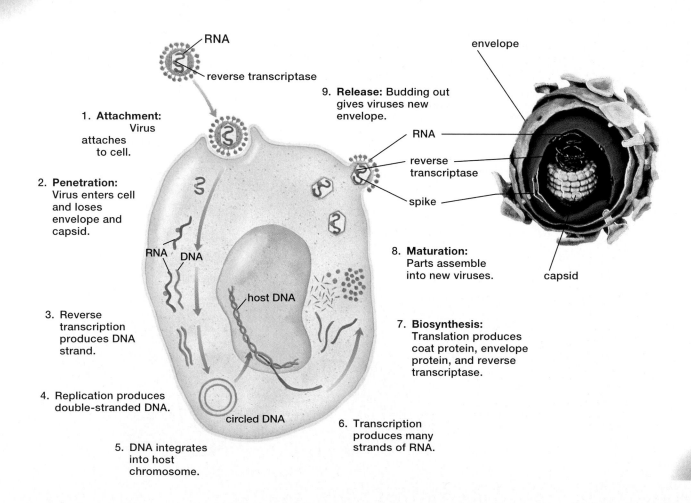

RNA

reverse transcriptase

9. **Release:** Budding out gives viruses new envelope.

envelope

RNA

reverse transcriptase

spike

capsid

1. **Attachment:** Virus attaches to cell.

2. **Penetration:** Virus enters cell and loses envelope and capsid.

RNA DNA

host DNA

3. Reverse transcription produces DNA strand.

4. Replication produces double-stranded DNA.

circled DNA

5. DNA integrates into host chromosome.

6. Transcription produces many strands of RNA.

7. **Biosynthesis:** Translation produces coat protein, envelope protein, and reverse transcriptase.

8. **Maturation:** Parts assemble into new viruses.

mumps. Our study of viral replication should allow you to readily see why *antibiotics,* which are designed to interfere with bacterial metabolism, have no effect on viral illnesses. Viruses lack most enzymes and instead utilize the enzymes of the host cell. Rarely has it been possible to find a drug that successfully interferes with viral reproduction without also interfering with host metabolism in cells free of the virus. The drugs acyclovir for herpes infections and azidothymidine (AZT) for AIDS prevent viruses from reproducing by interfering with DNA replication. They are analogues of normal nucleotides, which, when incorporated into a DNA strand, prevent replication from proceeding. These drugs are expected to do minimal damage to the body because most mature cells are not synthesizing DNA.

Antibiotics do not cure viral infections because viruses use host cell enzymes, not their own enzymes. Only antiviral drugs interfere with viral replication.

PROKARYOTES ARE CELLULAR

Kingdom Prokaryotae [Gk. *pro,* before, and *kary,* nucleus] (formerly Kingdom Monera) includes only **bacteria** [Gk. *bact,* rod], which were not discovered until Dutch naturalist Antonie van Leeuwenhoek invented the first microscope in the seventeenth century and examined all sorts of specimens, including scrapings from his own teeth. Leeuwenhoek and others after him believed that the "little animals" he saw could arise spontaneously from inanimate matter. For about 200 years scientists carried out various experiments to determine the origination of microorganisms, including bacteria. Finally, in about 1850, Louis Pasteur devised an experiment for the French Academy of Sciences that is described in figure 24.5. It showed that previously sterilized fluid medium cannot become cloudy with bacterial growth unless it is exposed directly to the air. Today we know that bacteria are abundant in air, water, and soil, and on most objects. A single spoonful of earth can contain 10^{10} of bacteria. Clearly, the combined number of all bacteria exceeds that of any other type of organism on earth.

Figure 24.5
Pasteur's experiment.

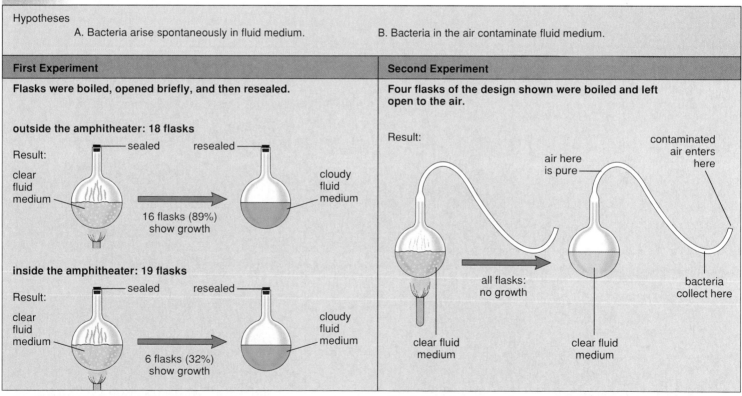

Hypotheses
  A. Bacteria arise spontaneously in fluid medium.
  B. Bacteria in the air contaminate fluid medium.

First Experiment

Flasks were boiled, opened briefly, and then resealed.

outside the amphitheater: 18 flasks

Result:
clear fluid medium — sealed — resealed — cloudy fluid medium
16 flasks (89%) show growth

inside the amphitheater: 19 flasks

Result:
clear fluid medium — sealed — resealed — cloudy fluid medium
6 flasks (32%) show growth

Conclusion:
With hypothesis A, all flasks would be cloudy. Relative concentrations of bacteria in the air explain the results; therefore, hypothesis B is supported.

Second Experiment

Four flasks of the design shown were boiled and left open to the air.

Result:
air here is pure
contaminated air enters here
all flasks: no growth
bacteria collect here
clear fluid medium — clear fluid medium

Conclusion:
When air reaching the medium contains no bacteria, the medium remains free of growth; therefore, hypothesis B is further supported.

Prokaryotic Structure Is Simple

Bacteria generally range in size from 1 μm to 10 μm in length and from 0.7 μm to 1.5 μm in width. The term prokaryotic means "before a nucleus" and these organisms, which lack a eukaryotic nucleus (fig. 24.6), are the first to have evolved. There are prokaryotic fossils dated as long ago as 3.5 billion years, and the fossil record indicates that the prokaryotes were alone on earth for at least 2 billion years. During that length of time they became extremely diverse, not in structure but in metabolic capabilities. Bacteria are adapted to living in most environments because types differ in the ways they acquire and utilize energy.

Outside the plasma membrane of most prokaryotic cells is a rigid cell wall, which keeps the cell from bursting or collapsing due to osmotic changes. In eubacteria, the cell wall is composed of *peptidoglycan*, a molecule that contains chains of a unique amino disaccharide joined by peptide chains. The cell wall may be surrounded by an attached *capsule* and/or by a loose gelatinous *sheath* called a slime layer. In parasite forms, these outer coverings protect the cell from host defenses.

Some bacteria move by means of *flagella*. The flagellum has a filament composed of three strands of the protein flagellin wound in a helix. The filament is inserted into a hook that is anchored by a basal body (fig. 24.6*b*). The 360° rotation of the flagellum causes the cell to spin and move forward. Many bacteria adhere to surfaces by means of fimbriae, short hairlike filaments extending from the surface. The fimbriae of *Neisseria gonorrhoeae* allow it to attach to host cells and cause gonorrhea.

The prokaryotic cell lacks the membranous organelles of the eukaryotic cell. However, the plasma membrane folds up into fingerlike projections called *mesosomes,* which may help compartmentalize the cell. Both anabolic and catabolic metabolic pathways are located on the plasma membrane. Although bacteria do not have a nucleus, they do have a dense area called a *nucleoid* where a single circular strand of DNA, designated the *bacterial chromosome,* is found. Many bacteria also have accessory rings of DNA called plasmids. Plasmids can be extracted and used as vectors to carry foreign DNA into host bacteria during genetic engineering processes. Protein synthesis in a bacterial cell is carried out by thousands of ribosomes, which are smaller than eukaryotic ribosomes. In recent years, an analysis of ribosomal RNA (rRNA) has led to new knowledge of bacterial relationships. In particular, the unique sequence of RNA nucleotides in archaebacterial ribosomes has shown that they should at least be in their own subkingdom. The following diagram summarizes bacterial cell structure:

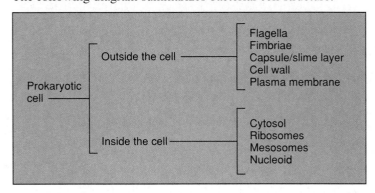

Figure 24.6

Generalized structure of a bacterium. **a.** The cell. **b.** The flagellum contains a basal body, a hook, and a filament. The arrow indicates that the hook (and filament) turn 360°.

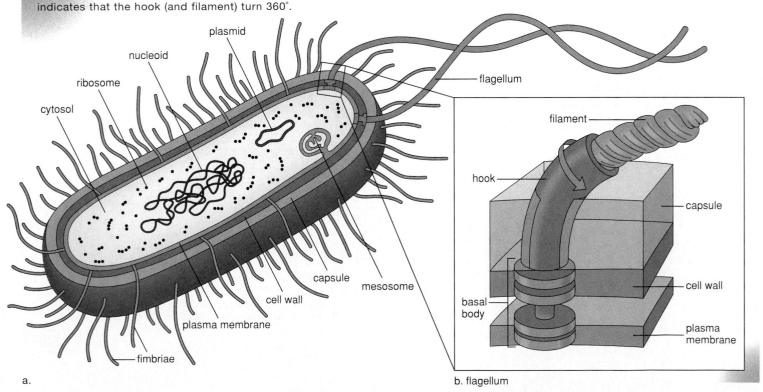

a.

b. flagellum

Prokaryotes Reproduce Asexually

Prokaryotes reproduce asexually by means of **binary fission** [L. *bi,* two, and *fiss,* cleft], a process that can be diagrammed as follows:

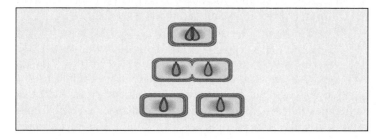

The single circular chromosome replicates, and then two copies separate as the cell enlarges. Newly formed plasma membrane and cell wall separate the cell into two cells. Mitosis, which requires the formation of a spindle apparatus, does not occur in prokaryotes.

In eukaryotes, genetic recombination occurs as a result of sexual reproduction. In prokaryotes, genetic recombination can occur in three ways. *Conjugation* has been observed between bacteria when the so-called male cell passes DNA to the female by way of a sex pilus which temporarily joins the two cells. Conjugation takes place only between bacteria in the same or closely related species. *Transformation* occurs when a bacterium picks up (from the medium) free pieces of DNA secreted by live bacteria or released by dead bacteria. During *transduction,* bacteriophages carry portions of bacterial DNA from one cell to another. Plasmids, which sometimes carry genes for resistance to antibiotics, can be transferred between bacteria by any of these ways.

Because genetic recombination does not occur routinely, mutation becomes a most important avenue for evolutionary change. With a generation time as short as twelve minutes under favorable conditions, mutations are generated and distributed throughout a population more quickly than in eukaryotes. Also, prokaryotes are haploid, and so mutations are immediately subjected to natural selection to assess any possible benefit.

> **Prokaryotes reproduce asexually by binary fission. Mutations are the chief means of achieving genetic variation.**

When faced with unfavorable environmental conditions, some bacteria form **endospores** [Gk. *endo,* within, and *spor,* seed] (fig. 24.7). A portion of the cytoplasm and a copy of the chromosome dehydrate and are then encased by three heavy, protective spore coats. The rest of the bacterial cell deteriorates and the endospore is released. Spores survive in the harshest of environments—desert heat and dehydration, boiling temperatures, polar ice, and extreme ultraviolet radiation. They also survive for very long periods. When anthrax spores 1,300 years old are activated, they can still cause a severe infection (usually seen in cattle and sheep). When environmental conditions are again suitable for growth, the endospore absorbs water and grows out of the spore coat. In a few hours' time, it becomes a typical bacterial cell, capable of reproducing once again by binary fission. Humans particularly fear a deadly but uncommon type of food poisoning called botulism that is caused by the germination of endospores inside cans of food. Spore formation is not a means of reproduction, but it does allow survival and dispersal to new places.

Figure 24.7

Clostridium botulinum containing an endospore. This organism causes the type of food poisoning known as botulism. Sterilization, a process that kills all living things, even endospores, is used whenever all bacteria must be killed. Sterilization can be achieved using an autoclave, a container that maintains steam under pressure.

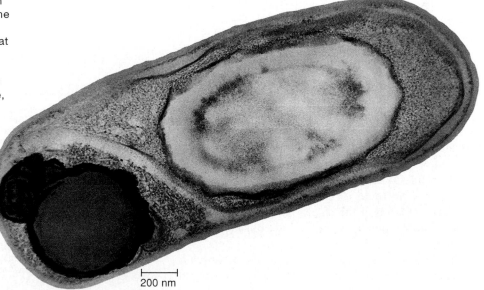

200 nm

Prokaryotic Nutrition Is Diverse

With respect to nutrient requirements, bacteria are not much different from other organisms. Bacteria adapted to living in hot, salty, or dry environments still have the same requirements of carbon, hydrogen, and nitrogen as other organisms. One difference, however, concerns the need for oxygen. Some bacteria are *obligate anaerobes* and are unable to grow in the presence of oxygen. A few serious illnesses—such as botulism, gas gangrene, and tetanus—are caused by anaerobic bacteria. Other bacteria, called *facultative anaerobes,* are able to grow in either the presence or the absence of gaseous oxygen. Most bacteria, however, are *aerobic* and, like animals, require a constant supply of oxygen to carry out cellular respiration.

Every type of nutrition is found among bacteria except for the ingestion of whole food. There are both autotrophic and heterotrophic bacteria.

Autotrophic Bacteria

Most autotrophic bacteria are photosynthetic; they use light as a source of energy to produce their own food. These photosynthetic bacteria can be divided into two types—those that evolved first and do not give off oxygen (O_2) and those that evolved later and do give off oxygen.

Do not give off O_2	Do give off O_2
Photosystem I only	Photosystems I and II
Unique type of chlorophyll called bacteriochlorophyll	Type of chlorophyll found in plants

The green sulfur bacteria and purple sulfur bacteria carry on the first type of photosynthesis. These bacteria do not give off oxygen because they do not use water as an electron donor; instead, they use hydrogen sulfide (H_2S):

$$CO_2 + 2H_2S \longrightarrow (CH_2O)_n + 2S$$

These bacteria usually live in anaerobic conditions such as the muddy bottom of marshes and cannot photosynthesize in the presence of oxygen.

In contrast, the cyanobacteria (see fig. 24.10) contain chlorophyll *a* and carry on photosynthesis in the same manner as algae and plants:

$$CO_2 + H_2O \longrightarrow (CH_2O)_n + O_2$$

Some autotrophic bacteria carry out **chemosynthesis** [Gk. *chemo,* chemistry, *syn,* together, and *thesis,* an arranging]. They oxidize inorganic compounds such as nitrites, hydrogen gas, and hydrogen sulfide to obtain the necessary energy to produce their own organic food. *Chemosynthetic* bacteria (also called chemoautotrophs) trap the small amount of energy released from these oxidations to use in the reactions that synthesize carbohydrates.

There are three groups of chemosynthesizers of particular interest. First, at the mid-oceanic ridge system, 2.5 km below sea level, hot minerals spew out of the earth, providing hydrogen sulfide to chemosynthetic bacteria, which live both freely and within the bodies of giant tube worms. The organic molecules produced by the bacteria support the growth of the worms, as well as clams and crabs. The methanogens are a second and very unusual group of chemosynthetic bacteria that produce methane (CH_4) from hydrogen gas and carbon dioxide:

$$CO_2 + 4H_2 \longrightarrow CH_4 + 2H_2O$$

ATP synthesis and carbon dioxide reduction are linked to this reaction in ways that vary among the methanogens. Methane, sometimes called "swamp gas," is produced under anaerobic conditions in soil, swamps, mud, and even the intestines of some animals. After adding methanogens to a mixture of decomposers and animal wastes, it is possible to use the resultant "biogas" to run a generator that produces electricity. This is an ecologically sound procedure; otherwise methane is a pollutant that contributes to the greenhouse effect and global warming. Finally, chemosynthetic bacteria carry out reactions that help keep nitrogen cycling within ecosystems. The nitrifying bacteria oxidize ammonia (NH_3) to nitrites (NO_2^-), and nitrites to nitrates (NO_3^-).

Heterotrophic Bacteria

The majority of bacteria are aerobic **saprotrophs** [Gk. *sapro,* putrid, and *troph,* feeder]. They break down dead organic matter by secreting digestive enzymes and then they absorb the nutrient molecules. These so-called **decomposers** can break down such a large variety of molecules that there probably is no natural organic molecule that cannot be digested by at least one bacterial species. The decomposing bacteria play a critical role in recycling matter in ecosystems and in making inorganic molecules available to photosynthesizers. The metabolic capabilities of various heterotrophic bacteria have long been exploited by human beings.

Heterotrophs may be free-living or **symbiotic** [Gk. *symbio,* living together], meaning that they form mutualistic, commensalistic, or parasitic relationships.

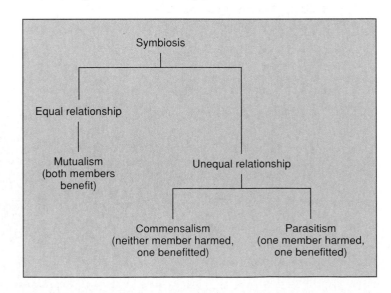

Some *mutualistic* bacteria are involved in nitrogen cycling. They live in the root nodules of soybean, clover, and alfalfa plants where they reduce atmospheric nitrogen (N_2) to ammonia, a process called **nitrogen fixation** (fig. 24.8). Plants are unable to fix atmospheric nitrogen and those without nodules take up nitrate and ammonia from the soil. Other mutualistic bacteria that live in human intestines release vitamins K and B_{12}, which we can use to help produce blood components. In the stomachs of cows and goats, special mutualistic bacteria digest cellulose, enabling these animals to feed on grass. *Commensalistic* bacteria live on organisms and cause them no harm, but *parasitic* bacteria are responsible for a wide variety of plant and animal diseases.

Bacteria are used commercially to produce chemicals, such as ethyl alcohol, acetic acid, butyl alcohol, and acetones. Bacterial action is also involved in the production of butter, cheese, sauerkraut, rubber, cotton, silk, coffee, and cocoa. Even antibiotics, discussed later, are produced by some bacteria.

> Most bacteria are free-living heterotrophs (saprotrophic decomposers) that recycle matter through ecosystems. Others are symbiotic heterotrophs, as are those that cause disease.

Figure 24.8
While there are some free-living bacteria that carry on nitrogen fixation, those of the genus *Rhizobium* invade the roots of legumes with the resultant formation of nodules. Here the bacteria convert atmospheric nitrogen to an organic nitrogen that the plant can use. These are nodules on the roots of a soybean plant, *Glycine*.

HOW PROKARYOTES ARE CLASSIFIED

All prokaryotes lack a nucleus and the membranous organelles of the eukaryotic cell. On the basis of rRNA nucleotide sequences and other biochemical data, the prokaryotes are divided into two subkingdoms, the **archaebacteria** and the **eubacteria.** The eubacteria have a cell wall that contains peptidoglycan. In some archaebacteria, the cell wall is largely composed of polysaccharides, and in others, the wall is pure protein. In a few others there is no cell wall. The plasma membrane lipids of archaebacteria contain glycerol linked to branched hydrocarbon chains rather than to fatty acids, as in eubacteria.

Archaebacteria Came First

The archaebacteria [Gk. *archae,* ancient, and *bact,* rod] are well known for living in the most extreme of environments, perhaps representing the kinds of habitats that were available when the earth first formed.

There are three types of archaebacteria. The *methanogens* produce the gas methane and live anaerobically in swamps, marshes, and the guts of animals. Their nutrition was described on page 404. As mentioned previously, humans use methanogens to help decompose sewage. And the biogas produced can be collected and used to run generators that produce electricity.

The *halophiles* live where it is salty, such as the Great Salt Lake in Utah, the Dead Sea, and the edge of the ocean. Curiously, a type of rhodopsin pigment (related to the one found in our own eyes) allows halophiles to carry on ATP production by chemiosmosis. The *thermoacidophiles* live where it is both hot and acidic. Those that live in the hot sulfur springs of Yellowstone National Park are chemosynthetic and obtain energy by oxidizing sulfur.

> Biochemical data are used to place archaebacteria in a separate subkingdom. Methanogens, halophiles, and thermoacidophiles all live in extreme habitats.

CLASSIFICATION

KINGDOM PROKARYOTAE

Prokaryotic, unicellular organisms; heterotrophic by absorption, autotrophic by chemosynthesis or by photosynthesis. Primarily asexual reproduction by binary fission but genetic exchange occurs by conjugation, transformation, and transduction; motile forms move by flagella

Subkingdom Archaebacteria
  bacteria that lack peptidoglycan walls

Subkingdom Eubacteria
  bacteria that have peptidoglycan walls:
    gram-positive bacteria have thick walls,
    gram-negative bacteria have thin walls
  bacteria that lack cell walls

Figure 24.9

Diversity of bacteria. **a.** Spirillum (spiral-shaped) bacterium. **b.** Bacillus (rod-shaped) bacterium. **c.** Coccus (round) bacterium in chains.

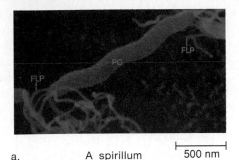

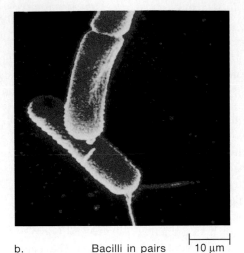

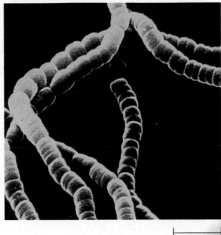

a.   A spirillum |— 500 nm —|

b.   Bacilli in pairs |— 10 µm —|

c.   Cocci in chains |— 250 nm —|

Eubacteria Are Prevalent

All of the discussion on the previous pages pertains particularly to eubacteria [Gk. *eu,* good, and *bact,* rod], which are adapted to most habitats and exhibit both autotrophic and heterotrophic forms of nutrition. They are among the most numerous of organisms, play critical roles in ecosystems, and are of great practical importance to humans. Our knowledge of bacterial biochemistry and bacterial genetics is applicable to all living things, including humans.

Classification of eubacteria is still being developed, but it is common to divide them into three groups:

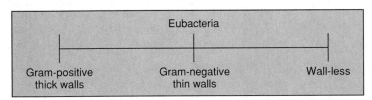

The Gram stain procedure (developed by Hans Christian Gram, a Danish bacteriologist) differentiates bacteria. Gram-positive bacteria stain purple and gram-negative bacteria stain red when the procedure is carried out. This difference is dependent on the construction of the cell wall; namely, the gram-positive bacteria have a thick layer of peptidoglycan in their cell wall, whereas gram-negative bacteria have only a thin layer.

The eubacteria are found in three basic shapes (fig. 24.9): rod (bacillus), round or spherical (coccus), and spiral. The cocci and bacilli may form clusters or chains of a length typical of the particular bacterium. Among the bacteria that are spiral shaped, a spirillum is a rigid helix while a spirochete is more flexible. *Staphylococcus aureus,* which can cause skin infections, is a gram-positive coccus, while *Treponema pallidum,* which causes the sexually transmitted disease syphilis, is a gram-negative spirochete.

Cyanobacteria

Cyanobacteria [Gk. *cyano,* blue, and *bact,* rod] are gram-negative rods with a number of unusual traits. They photosynthesize in the same manner as plants and are believed to be responsible for first introducing oxygen into the primitive atmosphere. Formerly, the cyanobacteria were called blue-green algae and were classified with eukaryotic algae, but now we know that they are prokaryotes. They can have other pigments that mask the color of chlorophyll, so that they appear, for example, not only blue-green but also red, yellow, brown, or black.

Cyanobacterial cells are rather large and range in size from 1 µm to 50 µm in width. They can be unicellular, colonial, or filamentous (fig. 24.10). Cyanobacteria lack any visible means of locomotion, although some glide when in contact with a solid surface and others oscillate (sway back and forth). Some cyanobacteria have a special advantage because they possess heterocysts, which are thick-walled cells without nuclei, where nitrogen fixation occurs. The ability to photosynthesize and also to fix atmospheric nitrogen (N_2) means that their nutritional requirements are minimal. They can serve as food for heterotrophs in ecosystems.

Cyanobacteria are common in fresh water, in soil, and on moist surfaces, but they are also found in harsh habitats, such as hot springs. They are symbiotic with a number of organisms, such as liverworts, ferns, and even at times invertebrates like corals. In association with fungi, they form **lichens** that can grow on rocks. A lichen is a symbiotic relationship in which the cyanobacterium provides organic nutrients to the fungus, while the fungus possibly protects and furnishes inorganic nutrients to its partner. It is also possible that the fungus is parasitic on the algal component. Lichens help transform rocks into soil; other forms of life then may follow. It is presumed that cyanobacteria were the first colonizers of land during the course of evolution.

Figure 24.10

Diversity among the cyanobacteria. **a.** In *Gloeocapsa,* single cells are grouped in a common gelatinous sheath. **b.** Filaments of cells occur in *Oscillatoria.* **c.** One cell of *Oscillatoria* as it appears through the electron microscope.

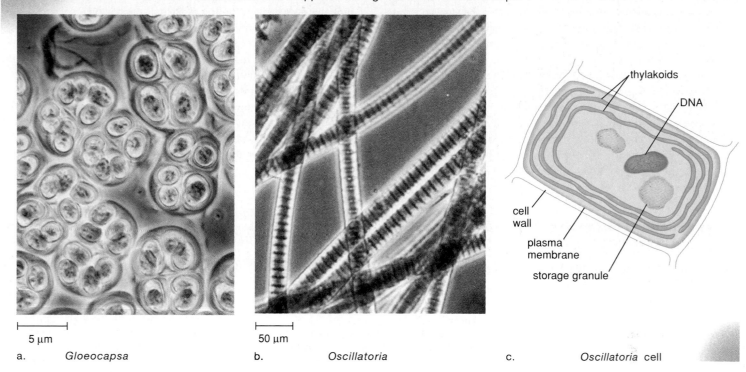

5 µm

a. *Gloeocapsa*

50 µm

b. *Oscillatoria*

c. *Oscillatoria* cell

thylakoids
DNA
cell wall
plasma membrane
storage granule

Cyanobacteria are ecologically important in still another way. If care is not taken in the disposal of industrial, agricultural, and human wastes, phosphates and nitrates drain into lakes and ponds, resulting in a "bloom" of these organisms. The surface of the water becomes turbid, and light cannot penetrate to lower levels. When a portion of the cyanobacteria die off, the decomposing bacteria use up the available oxygen, causing fishes to die from lack of oxygen.

> Cyanobacteria are photosynthesizers that sometimes can also fix atmospheric nitrogen. In association with fungi, they form lichens, which are important soil formers.

Some Bacteria Cause Infections

General cleanliness is the first step toward preventing the spread of diseases caused by bacteria. Disinfectants and antiseptics also help reduce the number of infectious bacteria. Typhoid fever is kept in check by adding chlorine to water; diphtheria, typhoid, and tuberculosis are partially controlled by pasteurization of milk (heating to 65° C for thirty minutes). Sterilization, which requires a temperature of 121° C for ten to forty minutes, kills all living things, even endospores. Sterilization can be achieved by use of an autoclave, a container that maintains steam under pressure.

Vaccines are available to prevent some bacterial infections; children are immunized for diphtheria, tetanus, and whooping

cough. And **antibiotics** [Gk. *anti*, against, and *bio*, life], which selectively kill bacteria, have been available since the 1940s. Penicillin is made by the fungus *Penicillium;* streptomycin, tetracycline, and erythromycin are all produced by the bacterium *Streptomyces.* Sulfa, a synthetic chemical agent rather than an antibiotic, is an analogue of a bacterial growth factor. Antibiotics are metabolic inhibitors, specific for bacterial enzymes. This means that they inactivate bacterial enzymes without harming host enzymes. Penicillin blocks the synthesis of the bacterial cell wall; streptomycin, tetracycline, and erythromycin block protein synthesis; and sulfa prevents the production of a coenzyme.

There are problems associated with antibiotic therapy, however. Some patients are allergic to antibiotics, and the reactions can be fatal. In addition, antibiotics not only kill off disease-causing bacteria, they also reduce the number of beneficial bacteria in the intestinal tract and other locations. These beneficial bacteria hold in check the growth of certain microbes that now begin to flourish. Diarrhea can result, as can a vaginal yeast infection. The use of antibiotics can also prevent natural immunity from occurring, leading to a need for recurrent antibiotic therapy. Most important, perhaps, is the growing resistance of certain strains of bacteria to antibiotics. While penicillin used to be 100% effective against hospital strains of *Staphylococcus aureus,* today it is almost useless. Tetracycline and penicillin, long used to cure gonorrhea, now have a failure rate of more than 20%. Until recently, antibiotics brought tuberculosis under control. Now there are new strains that are resistant to the usual antibiotic therapy.

Biological Relationships

We began our study of diversity with viruses, not because they were the first to appear in the history of life, but because they fulfill only one characteristic of life—they do have a mechanism to reproduce (see table 24.1). It now appears that viruses are covered bits of their hosts' genomes, so they must have originated after life came into being.

Only bacteria have a prokaryotic cell in which there are no individual organelles to perform specialized functions. In prokaryotes, the DNA is located in a central region, and certain metabolic pathways are associated with the plasma membrane. The structure of bacteria may not be diverse but their metabolic pathways are diverse. Every type of nutrition is seen except holozoism, the eating of whole food. Their success is witnessed by a wide distribution in all sorts of habitats, both ordinary and extreme.

The archaebacteria, which live in the harshest of environments, probably evolved first. They have rRNA nucleotide differences not seen in other organisms, and many biologists believe they should be in a separate kingdom. Modern biochemical methods of analysis have brought to the fore many such taxonomic questions, and generally accepted classification changes are expected soon.

Did the eukaryotes evolve from the prokaryotes? The answer is not clear-cut right now; uncertainty and the need for more research are common in biology. The current hypothesis is that a prokaryote evolved a nucleus and then acquired other organelles by taking up prokaryotes smaller than itself. This is called the endosymbiotic hypothesis.

Summary

1. Viruses are noncellular, while bacteria are fully functioning organisms. Viruses are noncellular and they are unable to replicate independently.

2. Before the advent of the electron microscope, viruses were known to be infectious agents smaller than bacteria, but nothing was known about their structure.

3. All viruses have at least two parts: an outer capsid composed of protein subunits and an inner core of nucleic acid, either DNA or RNA but not both. Some also have an outer membranous envelope.

4. Viruses are obligate intracellular parasites that can be maintained only inside living cells such as those of a chick egg or those propagated in cell (tissue) culture.

5. The lytic cycle of a bacteriophage consists of attachment, penetration, biosynthesis, maturation, and release.

6. In the lysogenic cycle of a bacteriophage, viral DNA is integrated into bacterial DNA for an indefinite period of time, but it can undergo the lytic cycle when stimulated.

7. The reproductive cycle differs for animal viruses with a membranous envelope. Uncoating is needed to free the genome, and budding releases the viral particles from the cell.

8. RNA retroviruses have an enzyme, reverse transcriptase, that carries out reverse transcription. This produces cDNA, which becomes integrated into host DNA. The AIDS virus is a retrovirus.

9. A viral infection can be controlled by administering vaccines and antiviral drugs. Antiviral drugs prevent DNA replication.

10. Kingdom Prokaryotae contains unicellular prokaryotes—that is, the bacteria including cyanobacteria. Bacteria are microscopic, and it was once thought they could arise spontaneously. Pasteur devised an experiment around 1850 which showed that they are present in the air and can contaminate suitable growth media.

11. Prokaryotic cells lack a nucleus and most other cytoplasmic organelles found in eukaryotic cells. In eubacteria, the cell wall contains peptidoglycan.

12. Bacteria reproduce asexually by binary fission; genetic recombination occurs by means of conjugation, transformation, and transduction, but their chief method for achieving genetic variation is mutation.

13. Some bacteria form endospores which are extremely resistant to destruction; the genetic material can thereby survive unfavorable conditions.

14. Bacteria differ in their need (and tolerance) for oxygen. There are obligate anaerobes, facultative anaerobes, and aerobic bacteria.

15. Some bacteria are autotrophic and are either photosynthetic or chemosynthetic. Some photosynthetic bacteria (cyanobacteria) give off oxygen and some (purple and green sulfur bacteria) do not. Chemosynthetic bacteria oxidize inorganic compounds, such as hydrogen sulfide, to acquire energy to make their own food. Surprisingly, these bacteria support communities at mid-oceanic ridges.

16. Most bacteria are aerobic heterotrophs and are saprotrophic decomposers that are absolutely essential to the cycling of nutrients in ecosystems. Their metabolic capabilities are so vast that they are used by humans both to dispose of and to produce substances.

17. Many heterotrophic bacteria are symbiotic. The mutualistic nitrogen-fixing bacteria live in nodules on the roots of legumes. Some symbiotes, however, are parasitic and cause plant and animal diseases.

18. There are two subkingdoms in the kingdom Prokaryotae: the archaebacteria and the eubacteria. They differ in terms of cell wall components, the sequence of nucleotides in rRNA, and other biochemical characteristics.

19. The archaebacteria live under harsh conditions such as anaerobic marshes (methanogens), salty lakes (halophiles), and hot sulfur springs (thermoacidophiles).

20. The classification of eubacteria is still being developed. Of primary importance at this time is the shape of the cell and the structure of the cell wall, which affects gram staining. There are three basic shapes: rod shaped (bacillus), round (coccus), and spiral shaped (spirillum).

21. Of special interest are the cyanobacteria, which were the first organisms to photosynthesize in the same manner as plants. When symbionts with fungi, they form lichens.

Writing Across the Curriculum

In order to practice writing skills, students should write out the answers to any or all of the study questions and the critical thinking questions. The study questions are sequenced in the same order as the text. Answers to the objective questions, and suggested answers to the critical thinking questions, are in appendix D.

Study Questions

1. Contrast viruses with bacteria as per the characteristics of life.   396

2. Describe the general structure of viruses and tell why they are obligate parasites.   397–98

3. How are viruses specific, and how can they be cultured in the laboratory?   398

4. Describe both the lytic cycle and the lysogenic cycle of bacteriophages. 398–99

5. How do animal viruses differ in structure and reproductive cycle from bacteriophages?   399–400

6. How do retroviruses differ from other animal viruses? Describe the reproductive cycle of retroviruses in detail.   400

7. How are viral infections controlled, and why don't antibiotics work against viruses?   400–401

8. Explain Pasteur's experiment which shows that bacteria do not arise spontaneously.   401

9. Describe the general structure of bacteria, and tell how they reproduce.   402–3

10. How does genetic recombination occur in bacteria, and what is the more common source of variation?   403

11. How do some bacteria survive the severest of unfavorable environments?   403

12. How do bacteria differ in their tolerance of and need for oxygen?   404

13. How does photosynthesis differ between the green and purple sulfur bacteria and the cyanobacteria?   404

14. What are chemosynthetic bacteria, and where have they been found to support whole communities? What reaction allows methanogens to give off methane?   404

15. Discuss the nutrition of heterotrophic bacteria, note their importance in ecosystems, and give examples of their symbiotic relationships with other types of organisms.   404–5

16. On what basis are there two subkingdoms in kingdom Prokaryotae? What two characteristics are used to divide eubacteria into groups?   406

17. Discuss the importance of cyanobacteria in ecosystems and in the history of the earth.   406–7

18. List and discuss at least four ways bacterial infections are controlled. Discuss the dangers of antibiotic overuse.   407

Objective Questions

1. Viruses are considered nonliving because
   a. they don't mutate and therefore don't adapt.
   b. they do not locomote.
   c. they cannot reproduce independently.
   d. their nucleic acid does not code for protein.

2. Which of these are found in all viruses?
   a. envelope, nucleic acid, capsid
   b. DNA, RNA, and proteins
   c. proteins and a nucleic acid
   d. proteins, nucleic acids, carbohydrates, and lipids

3. Which step in the lytic cycle follows attachment of virus and release of DNA into the cell?
   a. production of lysozyme
   b. disintegration of host DNA
   c. assemblage
   d. DNA replication

4. Which of these is a true statement?
   a. Viruses carry with them their own ribosomes for protein formation.
   b. New viral ribosomes form after viral DNA enters the cell.
   c. Viruses use the host ribosomes for their own ends.
   d. Viruses do not need ribosomes for protein formation.

5. Which part of an animal virus is not reproduced in multiple copies?
   a. envelope
   b. proteins
   c. capsid
   d. ribosomes

6. RNA retroviruses have a special enzyme that
   a. disintegrates host DNA.
   b. polymerizes host DNA.
   c. transcribes viral RNA to cDNA.
   d. translates host DNA.

7. Which is not true of prokaryotes? They
   a. are living cells.
   b. lack a nucleus.
   c. all are parasitic.
   d. are either archaebacteria or eubacteria.

8. Facultative anaerobes
   a. require a constant supply of oxygen.
   b. are killed in an oxygenated environment.
   c. do not always need oxygen.
   d. are photosynthetic.

9. Cyanobacteria, unlike other types of bacteria that photosynthesize, do
   a. not give off oxygen.
   b. give off oxygen.
   c. not have chlorophyll.
   d. not have a cell wall.

10. Chemosynthetic bacteria
   a. are autotrophic.
   b. use the rays of the sun to acquire energy.
   c. oxidize inorganic compounds to acquire energy.
   d. Both a and c are correct.

11. Label this condensed version of bacteriophage reproductive cycles using these terms: bacterial chromosome, penetration, maturation, release, prophage, attachment, and integration.

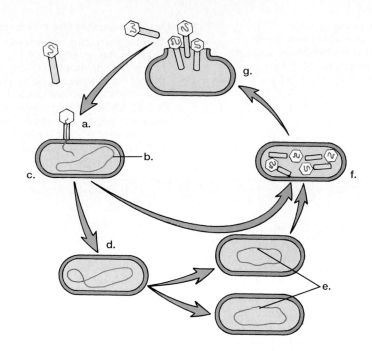

Concepts and Critical Thinking

1. *Viruses are obligate parasites.*
   Explain the meaning of this statement.

2. *Prokaryotes are a diverse group of organisms.*
   What evidence do you have that prokaryotes are diverse?

3. *Life evolved from the simple to the complex.*
   How can you reconcile this concept with the former concept?

Selected Key Terms

archaebacterium (ar-kee-bak-TEE-ree-um) Probably the earliest prokaryote; the cell wall and ribosomal RNA differ from those in other bacteria, and many live in extreme environments. [Gk. *archae,* ancient, and *bact,* rod]   405

bacteriophage (bak-TEER-ee-uh-fayj) A virus that parasitizes a bacterial cell as its host, destroying it by lytic action. [Gk. *bact,* rod, and *phag,* eat]   398

bacterium (pl., bacteria) A unicellular organism that lacks a nucleus and cytoplasmic organelles other than ribosomes; reproduces by binary fission and occurs in one of three shapes (rod, sphere, spiral). [Gk. *bact,* rod]   401

binary fission A splitting of a parent cell into two daughter cells; serves as an asexual form of reproduction in prokaryotes. [L. *bi,* two, and *fiss,* cleft]   403

chemosynthesis The process of making food by using energy derived from the oxidation of inorganic compounds in the environment. [Gk. *chemo,* chemistry, *syn,* together, and *thesis,* an arranging]   404

cyanobacterium (sy-ah-noh-bak-TEE-ree-um) A photosynthetic eubacterium that contains chlorophyll and releases oxygen; formerly called a blue-green alga. [Gk. *cyano,* blue, and *bact,* rod]   406

decomposer An organism, usually a bacterial or fungal species, that breaks down large organic molecules into elements that can be recycled in the environment.   404

endospore A bacterium that has shrunk its cell, rounded up within the former plasma membrane, and secreted a new and thicker cell wall in the face of unfavorable environmental conditions. [Gk. *endo,* within, and *spor,* seed]   403

eubacterium (yoo-bak-TEE-ree-um) Most common type of bacteria, including the cyanobacteria. [Gk. *eu,* good, and *bact,* rod]   405

lysogenic cycle A bacteriophage life cycle in which the virus incorporates its DNA into that of the bacterium; only later does it begin a lytic cycle, which ends with the destruction of the bacterium. [Gk. *ly,* loose and *genos,* descent]   399

lytic cycle One of the bacteriophage life cycles in which the virus takes over the operation of the bacterium immediately upon entering it and subsequently destroys the bacterium. [Gk. *ly,* loose]   398

retrovirus RNA virus containing the enzyme reverse transcriptase that carries out RNA/DNA transcription; retroviruses include oncogenes and the AIDS viruses. [L. *retro,* backward, and *viro,* poison]   400

saprotroph (SAP-roh-trohf) An organism that secretes digestive enzymes and absorbs the resulting nutrients back across the plasma membrane. [Gk. *sapro,* putrid, and *troph,* feeder]   404

vaccine A substance that stimulates the immune response without causing illness. [L. *vacci,* of a cow]   400

virus A nonliving, obligate, intracellular parasite consisting of an outer capsid and an inner core of nucleic acid. [L. *viro,* poison]   396

25

KINGDOM PROTOCTISTA

Learning Objectives

How the Eukaryotic Cell Evolved

- Tell how the eukaryotic cell may have arisen, including the nucleus, the mitochondria, and the chloroplasts. 412

- Give data to substantiate the endosymbiotic hypothesis. 412

Algae Are Plantlike

- List and give the phylum name for the different types of algae. Note why algae are not classified as plants. 413

- Tell how the green algae are grouped, and give an example of each type. Contrast the manner in which these organisms reproduce. 413–16

- Describe several forms of brown algae. Note what characteristics they share with diatoms, where they live, and how they are economically important. 417

- Describe the structure and discuss the importance of diatoms and dinoflagellates. 418

- Describe the characteristics of euglenoids, and tell how they typify the problem of classifying protoctists. 418–19

- Describe the characteristics of red algae. Note where they live, and discuss their economic importance. 419

Protozoa Are Animal-like

- List and give the phylum name for the different types of protozoa, and tell why they are not considered animals. 413, 420

- Compare and contrast the characteristics of amoeboids and ciliates; discuss their diversity. 420–22

- Describe illnesses caused by zooflagellates and sporozoa, and describe the life cycle of *Plasmodium vivax*, a cause of malaria. 422–23

Slime Molds and Water Molds Are Funguslike

- Compare and contrast plasmodial slime molds and cellular slime molds. Explain how slime molds differ from fungi. 425–26

- Describe the characteristics of water molds. Explain how water molds differ from fungi. 426

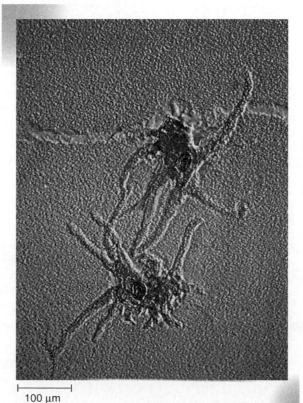

Two amoeba, *Amoeba*, are meeting and touching by using cytoplasmic extensions called pseudopods.

100 µm

he protoctists are a diverse group of organisms whose ancestry goes back to the evolution of the eukaryotic cell about 1.5 billion years ago. Over millions of years they diversified, and today they include not only unicellular forms but also colonial and even a few multicellular forms. This chapter will discuss the evolution of the eukaryotic cell, survey protoctist diversity, and examine their various life cycles.

HOW THE EUKARYOTIC CELL EVOLVED

Invagination of the plasma membrane might explain the origination of the nuclear envelope and organelles such as the endoplasmic reticulum and the Golgi apparatus. Some believe that the other organelles could also have arisen in this manner. But another hypothesis has been put forth. It has been observed that in the laboratory an amoeba infected with bacteria can become dependent upon them. Some investigators, especially Lynn Margulis, believe that mitochondria and chloroplasts are derived from prokaryotes that were taken up by a much larger cell (fig. 25.1). Perhaps mitochondria were originally aerobic heterotrophic bacteria and chloroplasts were originally cyanobacteria. The host cell would have benefited from an ability to utilize oxygen or synthesize organic food when by chance the prokaryote was not destroyed. Therefore, after these prokaryotes entered by *endocytosis,* a *symbiotic* relationship was established. The evidence for the endosymbiotic hypothesis is as follows:

1. Mitochondria and chloroplasts are similar to bacteria in size and in structure.
2. Both organelles are bounded by a double membrane—the outer membrane may be derived from the engulfing vesicle, and the inner one may be derived from the plasma membrane of the original prokaryote.
3. Mitochondria and chloroplasts contain a limited amount of genetic material and divide by splitting. Their DNA (deoxyribonucleic acid) is a circular loop like that of bacteria.
4. Although most of the proteins within mitochondria and chloroplasts are now produced by the eukaryotic host, they do have their own ribosomes and they do produce some proteins. Their ribosomes resemble those of bacteria.
5. The RNA (ribonucleic acid) base sequence of their ribosomes suggests a eubacterial origin for chloroplasts and mitochondria.

Margulis even suggests that the flagella of eukaryotes are derived from a spirochete prokaryote which became attached to a host cell (fig. 25.1). However, it is important to remember that the flagella of eukaryotes but not prokaryotes have the 9 + 2 patterns of microtubules. In any case, the acquisition of basal bodies, which could have become centrioles, may have led to the ability to form a spindle during mitosis and meiosis. The process of meiosis, of course, is associated with sexual reproduction of eukaryotes. Genetic recombination due to crossing-over, independent assortment of chromosomes, and random recombination during fertilization contributes to variation among members of a population and the evolution of new species.

> According to the endosymbiotic hypothesis, heterotrophic bacteria became mitochondria and cyanobacteria became chloroplasts after being taken up by a eukaryotic cell.

Figure 25.1

Evolution of the eukaryotic cell. Invagination of the plasma membrane could account for the formation of the nucleus and certain other organelles. The endosymbiotic hypothesis suggests that mitochondria, chloroplasts, and flagella are derived from prokaryotes that were taken up by a much larger eukaryotic cell.

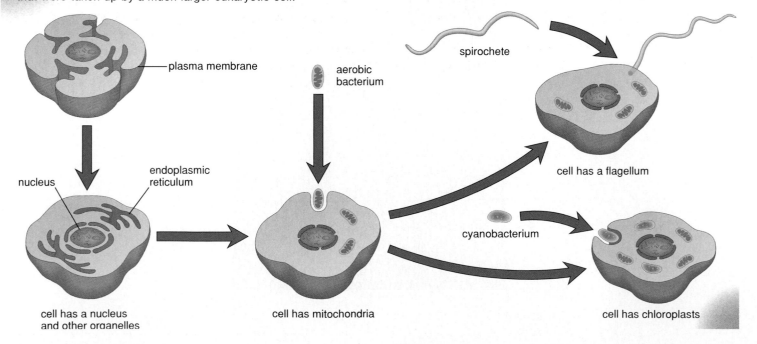

Classification of Protoctists

Kingdom Protoctista [Gk. *proto,* first, and *ktistos,* to establish] is also known as kingdom Protista. The name **protoctist,** instead of protist, is used because the kingdom includes multicellular forms; protist is a term that connotes unicellular forms to some. Just how the multicellular forms in this kingdom should be classified is a matter of debate, as is classification of the protoctists in general. Since this kingdom includes groups that are as distantly related as plants are from animals, it might one day be split into several separate kingdoms.

It has long been the custom to informally divide the protoctists into the plantlike algae, the animal-like protozoa, and the funguslike slime molds and water molds. We continue to use these groupings with the recognition that placing particular phyla in one group or another is artificial—it does not reflect true evolutionary relationships.

CLASSIFICATION

KINGDOM PROTOCTISTA

Eukaryotic; unicellular organisms and their immediate multicellular descendants; sexual reproduction; flagella and cilia with 9 + 2 microtubules

The Algae*
Phylum Chlorophyta: green algae
Phylum Phaeophyta: brown algae
Phylum Chrysophyta: diatoms and allies
Phylum Dinoflagella: dinoflagellates
Phylum Euglenophyta: euglenoids
Phylum Rhodophyta: red algae

The Protozoa*
Phylum Sarcodina: amoebas and allies
Phylum Ciliophora: ciliates
Phylum Zoomastigophora: zooflagellates
Phylum Sporozoa: sporozoa

The Slime Molds*
Phylum Gymnomycota: slime molds

The Water Molds*
Phylum Oomycota: water molds

---

* Not in the classification of organisms, but added here for clarity

ALGAE ARE PLANTLIKE

There is no taxonomic category called **algae** [L. *alg,* seaweed]; this term has long been used in biology as a matter of convenience to mean aquatic organisms that carry on photosynthesis. In the ocean and freshwater lakes and ponds, algae are a part of **plankton** [Gk. *plankt,* wandering], organisms that largely drift along with the current or float near the surface. Algae are a part of the **phytoplankton** [Gk. *phyt,* plant, and *plankt,* wandering], which photosynthesize and produce the food that maintains an entire community of organisms. They also produce much of the oxygen in the atmosphere.

Like plants, algae have chloroplasts and the cell is usually strengthened by the presence of a cell wall. Some algae are colonial; a **colony** is a loose association of independent cells in which there may be cells specialized for reproduction. Some algae are actually multicellular and even have specialized tissues. Why aren't multicellular algae considered plants? In this text, all plants have modifications that protect the gametes and zygote from drying out. Obviously these are adaptations to the land environment. Algae, which are adapted to a water environment, do not have these modifications.

For many years it has been customary to classify algae according to their color; therefore, we speak of green, brown, golden brown, and red algae. For the most part, recent biochemical analyses also support these designations. All algae contain at least one type of chlorophyll, but they also contain other types of pigments and these may mask the color of the chlorophyll. The type of cell wall and the way they store reserve food also help distinguish algae.

Green Algae Are Most Plantlike

Green algae (**phylum Chlorophyta,** 7,000 species) live in the ocean but are more likely found in fresh water and can even be found on land, especially if moisture is available. Some, however, have modifications that allow them to live on tree trunks even in bright sun. Green algae are believed to be closely related to the first plants because both of these groups (1) have a cell wall that contains cellulose, (2) possess chlorophylls *a* and *b,* and (3) store reserve food as starch inside the chloroplast. (Other types of algae store reserve food outside the chloroplast.) Green algae are not always green because some have pigments that give them an orange, red, or rust color.

Green Algae That Have Flagella

Chlamydomonas is a unicellular green alga usually less than 25 µm long that has been studied in detail using the electron microscope (fig. 25.2). It has a definite cell wall and a single, large, cup-shaped chloroplast that contains a *pyrenoid,* a dense body where starch is synthesized. The chloroplast also contains a red-pigmented *eyespot* (stigma), which is sensitive to light and helps bring the organism into the light, where photosynthesis can occur. Two long whiplash flagella project from the anterior end of this alga and curl backward to propel the cell freely toward the light.

As discussed in the accompanying reading, when growth conditions are favorable, *Chlamydomonas* reproduces asexually. The adult divides, forming *zoospores* (flagellated spores) that resemble the parent cell. A **spore** [Gk. *spor,* seed] is a haploid body that develops into a mature adult when conditions are favorable.

When growth conditions are unfavorable, *Chlamydomonas* reproduces sexually. Gametes of two different mating types come into contact and join to form a zygote. A heavy wall forms around the zygote, and it becomes a resistant zygospore able to survive until conditions are favorable for germination. When a zygospore germinates, it produces four zoospores by meiosis. In most species, the gametes are identical, a condition known as **isogamy** [Gk. *iso,* equal, and *gamy,* reproduction]. The gametes are called *isogametes.* In other species, there is a nonmotile egg specialized for storing food, and the motile sperm are specialized for seeking out an egg. This condition is known as **oogamy** [Gk. *oo,* egg, and *gamy,* reproduction] and the gametes are *heterogametes.*

Green Algae That Are Colonial

A number of *colonial* (loose association of cells) forms occur among the flagellated green algae. A *Volvox* colony is a hollow sphere with thousands of cells arranged in a single layer surrounding a watery interior. Each cell of a *Volvox* colony resembles a *Chlamydomonas* cell—perhaps it is derived from daughter cells that fail to separate following zoospore formation. In *Volvox,* the cells cooperate in that the flagella beat in a coordinated fashion. Some cells are specialized for reproduction, and each of these can divide asexually to form a new daughter colony (fig. 25.3). This daughter colony resides for a time within the parental colony, but then it leaves by releasing an enzyme that dissolves away a portion of the parental colony, allowing it to escape. Sexual reproduction among these algae involves oogamy.

Figure 25.2

The structure and life cycle of *Chlamydomonas*, a motile green alga. During asexual reproduction, all structures are haploid; during sexual reproduction, meiosis follows the zygote stage, which is the diploid part of the cycle.

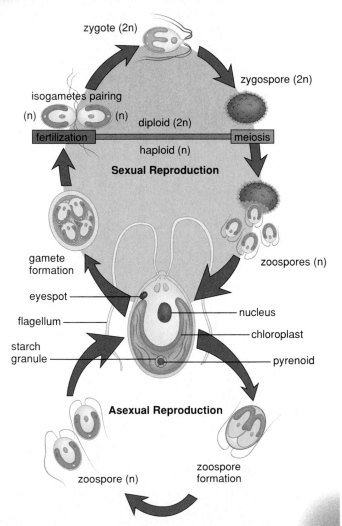

Figure 25.3

Volvox, a colonial green alga. The adult *Volvox* colony often contains daughter colonies, which are asexually produced by special cells. During sexual reproduction, colonies produce a definite sperm and egg.

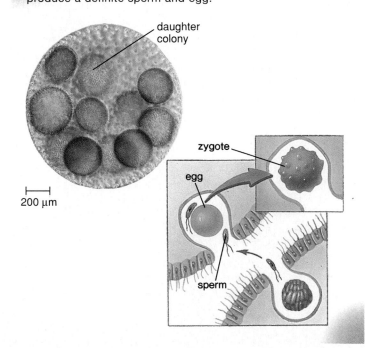

Behavior In a Unicellular Alga

I have been studying the unicellular, eukaryotic alga *Chlamydomonas reinhardtii* for the last eleven years. *Chlamydomonas,* an organism that is only about 10 micrometers (µm) in length, lives in soil and puddles. Most of the cytoplasm is occupied by a large cup-shaped chloroplast that is used for photosynthesis. At the anterior end of the cell are the organelles that attracted me to work on *Chlamydomonas*. These organelles are the two flagella, which are used to propel the cell at velocities of 200 µm per minute. These flagella, like all eukaryotic flagella, have at least 250 different polypeptides assembled into the classic structure of nine doublet microtubules in a circle around two singlet microtubules. The motors of flagella are dyneins, proteins that convert the chemical energy of ATP (adenosine triphosphate) into the bending action of flagella.

Chlamydomonas uses its flagella for swimming and for several complicated behaviors, including recognition of a mating partner. Generally, a *Chlamydomonas* cell swims with a whiplike motion accompanied by a rolling movement. It can be likened to a swimmer crossing a swimming pool by using the breaststroke but at the same time turning from the stomach, to the side, to the back, and then to the stomach again. Then, too, *Chlamydomonas* can change direction by regulating the strength by which each flagellum beats. When *Chlamydomonas* swims, it orients itself toward a source of light—a behavior known as phototaxis.

Phototaxis most likely helps the organism find light at the correct intensity for photosynthesis. How does *Chlamydomonas* detect light? Like many other algae, *Chlamydomonas* contains a structure known as an eyespot. Its single eyespot appears to utilize a molecule like rhodopsin, which is found in the mammalian eye. The rotation used by *Chlamydomonas* as it swims allows the eyespot to scan the environment. If the light intensity remains the same throughout the rotation, the cell continues to swim straight. If the light intensity is dif-

Susan Dutcher
University of Colorado at Boulder

ferent, the cell adjusts its direction by changing the relative degree of flagellar bending.

Why does one want to study a unicellular green alga instead of a fly, a mouse, or a human? One of the main reasons is the ease of finding mutations that disrupt the biological process being studied. As a geneticist, I dissect a process by removing one piece of the genetic machinery at a time, and then I observe what happens to the structure and function of the cell or organism. Genetic dissection has been used to learn a great deal about the cell cycle, development, and many

other processes. Mutations that affect flagella functions have even been identified in humans. There is a class of genetic diseases known as Kartagener's syndrome, in which the flagella and cilia are paralyzed. The symptoms include infertility (due to immotile sperm or immotile cilia in the oviduct) and bronchitis (from the failure of immotile cilia in bronchial tubes to clear away mucus). We hope that our studies will help to understand the causes of this particular class of human diseases.

In order to study the role of flagella in phototaxis, my laboratory and others study a variety of mutations that affect the assembly and function of flagella. When *Chlamydomonas* fails to orient toward light, it could be that the organism is unable to detect light or is unable to signal that light is present. Or it could be that a mutation has affected the assembly of flagella so that they cannot respond to the signal. We are interested in understanding this latter class of mutations, as we believe that they will allow us to understand how flagella construction can affect response to a signal. We hope that this type of study in a model genetic organism like *Chlamydomonas* will help to clarify similar processes in other organisms.

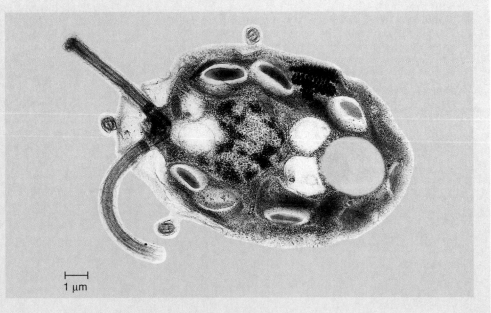

1 µm

Green Algae That Are Filamentous

Filaments [L. *fil*, thread] are end-to-end chains of cells that form after cell division occurs in only one plane. *Spirogyra*, a filamentous green alga, is found in green masses on the surfaces of ponds and streams. It has chloroplasts that are ribbonlike and are arranged in a spiral within the cell (fig. 25.4). **Conjugation** [L. *conjug*, joined together], the temporary union of two individuals during which there is an exchange of genetic material, occurs during sexual reproduction. The two filaments line up next to each other, and the cell contents of one filament move into the cells of the other filament, forming diploid zygotes. These zygotes survive the winter, and in the spring they undergo meiosis to produce new haploid filaments.

Oogamy does occur among the filamentous green algae. The genus *Oedogonium* contains filamentous algae in which the cells are cylindrical with netlike chloroplasts; during sexual reproduction there is a definite egg and sperm.

Green Algae That Are Multicellular

Multicellular *Ulva* is commonly called sea lettuce because of its leafy appearance (fig. 25.5). The thallus is two cells thick and can be a meter long. *Ulva* has an alternation of generations like that of plants except that both generations look exactly alike, the gametes look alike (isogamy), and the spores are flagellated. In plants one generation is typically dominant over (lasts longer than) the other, egg and sperm are produced (oogamy), and the spores are not flagellated.

> Green algae occur in unicellular, colonial, and multicellular forms. During sexual reproduction, the zygote usually undergoes meiosis and the only adult is haploid. *Ulva* has an alternation of generations like plants do.

Figure 25.4

Spirogyra, a filamentous green alga, in which each cell has a ribbonlike chloroplast. During conjugation the cell contents of one filament enter the cells of another filament. Zygote formation follows.

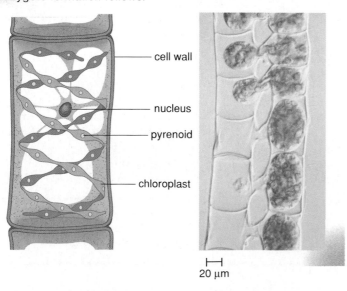

- cell wall
- nucleus
- pyrenoid
- chloroplast

├─┤
20 μm

Figure 25.5

Ulva, a multicellular green alga. *Ulva* has an alternation of generations life cycle, as do plants. Notice that the sporophyte and gametophyte have the same appearance and that the gametophyte produces isogametes. These features are unlike plants.

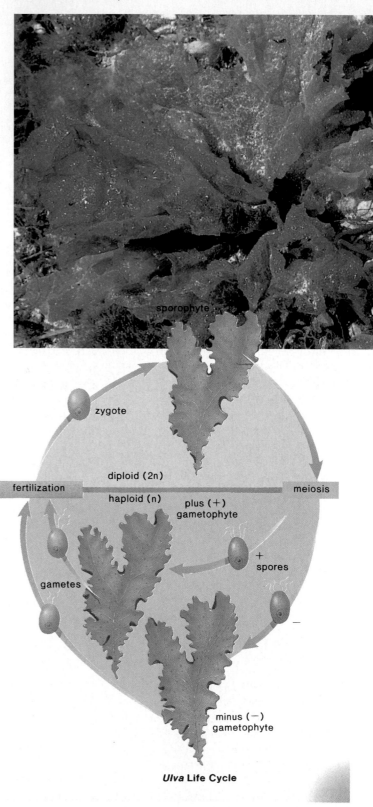

sporophyte

zygote

diploid (2n)

fertilization   meiosis

haploid (n)

plus (+) gametophyte

gametes

+ spores

minus (−) gametophyte

Ulva Life Cycle

Figure 25.6

Diversification among the brown algae. *Laminaria* and *Fucus* are seaweeds known as kelps. They live along rocky coasts of the north temperate zone. The other brown algae featured live at sea.

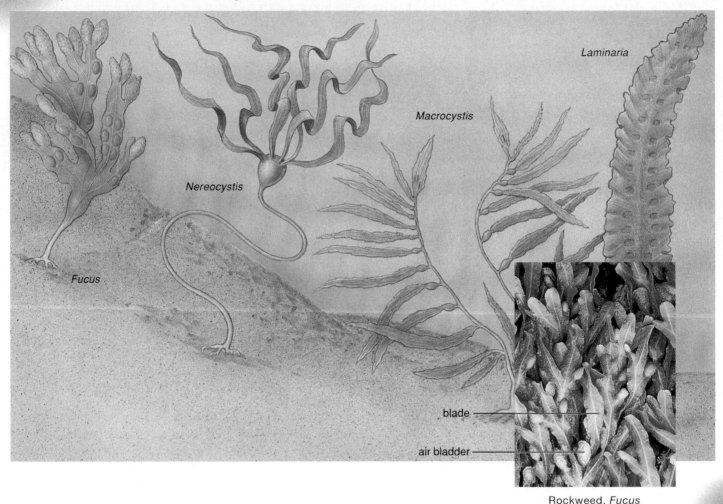

Rockweed, *Fucus*

Brown Algae and Golden Brown Algae Are Biochemically Alike

The brown algae and the golden brown algae have chlorophylls *a* and *c* in their chloroplasts and a type of carotenoid pigment (fucoxanthin) that gives them their color. The reserve food is a carbohydrate called laminarin.

Brown Algae Are Seaweeds

Brown algae (phylum Phaeophyta, 1,500 species) range from small forms with simple filaments to large multicellular forms (50–100 μm long) (fig. 25.6). The multicellular forms are a type of **seaweed,** a common term for any large, complex alga. Brown algae are often observed along the rocky coasts in the north temperate zone, where they are pounded by waves as the tide comes in and are exposed to dry air as the tide goes out. They do not dry out, however, because their cell walls contain a mucilaginous, water-retaining material.

Both *Laminaria,* commonly called a *kelp,* and *Fucus,* known as rockweed, are examples of brown algae that grow along the shoreline. In deeper waters, the giant kelps (*Nereocystis* and *Macrocystis*) often form spectacular underwater forests. Individuals of the genus *Sargassum* sometimes break off from their holdfasts and form floating masses, where life forms congregate in the ocean. Brown algae not only provide food and habitat for marine organisms, they are harvested for human food and for fertilizer in several parts of the world. They are also a source of algin, a pectinlike material that is added to ice cream, sherbet, cream cheese, and other products to give them a stable, smooth consistency.

Laminaria is unique among the protoctists because members of this genus show tissue differentiation—they transport organic nutrients by way of a tissue that resembles phloem in land plants. Most brown algae have the alternation of generations life cycle, but some species of *Fucus* are unique in that meiosis produces gametes and the adult is always diploid, as in animals.

Figure 25.7

Two extremely numerous marine protoctists. **a.** Diatoms may be variously colored, but their chloroplasts contain a unique golden brown pigment in addition to chlorophylls *a* and *c*. The beautiful pattern results from markings on the silica-embedded wall. **b.** Dinoflagellates have cellulose plates; these belong to *Gonyaulax,* the dinoflagellate that contains a red pigment and is responsible for occasional "red tides."

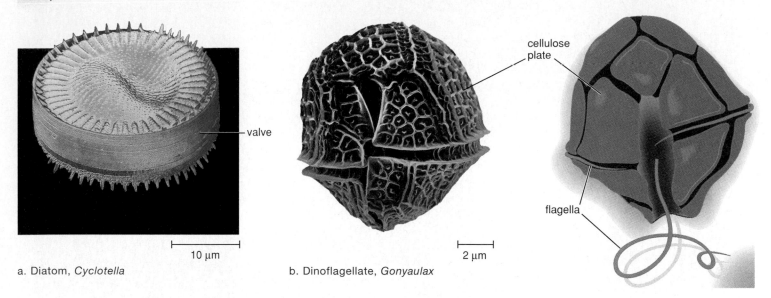

a. Diatom, *Cyclotella*

b. Dinoflagellate, *Gonyaulax*

Golden Brown Algae Include Diatoms

The **golden brown algae** (**phylum Chrysophyta,** 11,000 species) are distinctive from one another, and some authorities place diatoms in their own phylum called phylum Bacillariophyta. **Diatoms** [Gk. *dia,* through, and *tom,* cut] are the most numerous unicellular algae in the oceans (fig. 25.7*a*). They are also plentiful in fresh water. Because of their small size, thousands can live in a single millimeter of water. Therefore, they are an important source of food and oxygen for heterotrophs in both freshwater and marine ecosystems.

The structure of a diatom is often compared to a box because the cell wall has two halves or valves, with the larger valve acting as a "lid" for the smaller valve. When diatoms reproduce asexually, each receives one old valve. The new valve fits inside the old one; therefore, the new diatom is smaller than the original one. This continues until diatoms are about 30% of their original size. Then they reproduce sexually. The zygote becomes a structure that grows and then divides mitotically to produce diatoms of normal size.

The cell wall has an outer layer of silica, a common ingredient of glass. The valves are covered with a great variety of striations and markings that form beautiful patterns when observed under the microscope. These are actually depressions or pores through which the organism makes contact with the outside environment. The remains of diatoms, called diatomaceous earth, accumulate on the ocean floor and are mined for use as filtering agents, soundproofing materials, and scouring powders.

Dinoflagellates Have Two Flagella

Many **dinoflagellates** [Gk. *din,* whirling, and L. *flagell,* whip] (**phylum Dinoflagella,** 1,000 species) are bounded by protective cellulose plates (fig. 25.7*b*). Most have two flagella; one lies in a longitudinal groove with its distal end free, and the other, which is flat and ribbonlike, lies in a transverse groove that encircles the organism. The longitudinal flagellum acts as a rudder and the beating of the transverse one causes the cell to spin as it moves forward.

The chloroplasts of a dinoflagellate, which contain chlorophylls *a* and *c* as do those of golden brown algae, are probably derived from an endosymbiotic event. They vary in color from yellow-green to brown. Some species of dinoflagellates are heterotrophic, and it has been suggested that they are really protozoa.

Like the diatoms, dinoflagellates are extremely numerous in the oceans; their density can equal 30,000 in a single millimeter. Under certain conditions, those in the genus *Gymnodinium* and *Gonyaulax* increase in number and cause a "red tide" in the ocean. At these times, they produce a neurotoxin that causes paralytic shellfish poisoning—humans who eat shellfish that have fed on these dinoflagellates suffer paralysis of the respiratory muscles.

Usually the dinoflagellates are an important source of food for small animals in the ocean. They also live as symbionts within the bodies of some invertebrates. For example, corals usually contain large numbers of these organisms, and this allows corals to grow much faster than would otherwise be possible.

Euglenoids Are Flexible

Euglenoids (**phylum Euglenophyta,** 1,000 species) are small (10–500 μm) freshwater unicellular organisms which typify the problem of classifying protoctists. One-third of all genera have chloroplasts; the rest do not. Those that lack chloroplasts ingest or absorb their food. In addition, euglenoids grown in the absence of light have been known to lose their chloroplasts and become heterotrophic. This may not be surprising when one knows that their chloroplasts are like those of green algae and are probably derived from a green alga through endosymbiosis. The chloroplasts are surrounded by three rather than two membranes. The pyrenoid produces an unusual type of carbohydrate polymer (paramylon) not seen in green algae, however.

Euglenoids have two flagella, one of which typically is much longer than the other and projects out of an anterior vase-shaped invagination (fig. 25.8). It is called a tinsel flagellum because it has hairs on it. Near the base of this flagellum is an eyespot, which shades a photoreceptor for detecting light. Because euglenoids are bounded by a flexible *pellicle* composed of protein strips lying side by side, they can assume different shapes as the underlying cytoplasm undulates and contracts. As in certain protozoa, there is a contractile vacuole for ridding the body of excess water. Euglenoids reproduce by longitudinal cell division, and sexual reproduction is not known to occur.

> **Euglenoids have both plant- and animal-like characteristics. They have chloroplasts but lack a cell wall and swim by flagella.**

Figure 25.8

Euglena, a flagellated green alga with both animal-like and plantlike characteristics. A very long flagellum propels the body, which is enveloped by a flexible pellicle. A photoreceptor shaded by an eyespot allows *Euglena* to find light, after which photosynthesis can occur in the numerous chloroplasts. Pyrenoids synthesize a reserve carbohydrate, which is stored in the chloroplasts and also in the cytoplasm.

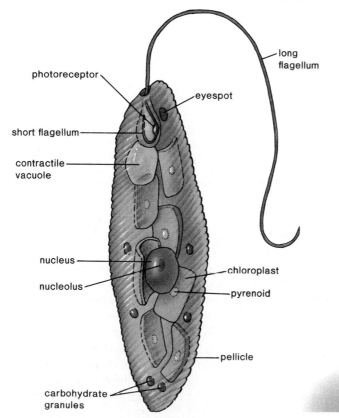

Red Algae Are Source of Agar

Like the brown algae, **red algae (phylum Rhodophyta,** 4,000 species) are multicellular, but they live chiefly in warmer seawater, growing in both shallow and deep waters. Red algae are usually much smaller and more delicate than the brown algae, although they can be up to a meter long. Some forms of red algae are simple filaments, but more often they are complexly branched, with the branches having a feathery, flat, or expanded ribbonlike appearance (fig. 25.9). Coralline algae are red algae that have cell walls impregnated with calcium carbonate. In some instances, they contribute as much to the growth of coral reefs as do coral animals.

Despite their macroscopic size, red algae show little tissue differentiation. Oogamy is seen during sexual reproduction but the sperm are nonflagellated, an unusual feature in a water environment. Their chloroplasts resemble cyanobacteria in that they contain chlorophyll *a* and a type of pigment called phycobilin. The reserve food resembles glycogen and is called floridean starch.

Like brown algae, red algae are economically important. The mucilaginous material in the cell walls of certain genera of red algae is a source of agar used commercially to make capsules for vitamins and drugs, as a material for making dental impressions, and as a base for cosmetics. In the laboratory, agar is a culture medium for bacteria. When purified, it becomes the gel for electrophoresis, a procedure that separates proteins and nucleotides. Agar is also used in food preparation—as an antidrying agent for baked goods and to make jellies and desserts set rapidly.

> **Many red algae have filamentous branches or are multicellular.**

Figure 25.9

Representative red alga, *Microcladia*, magnified to reveal detail. Red algae are smaller and more delicate than brown algae.

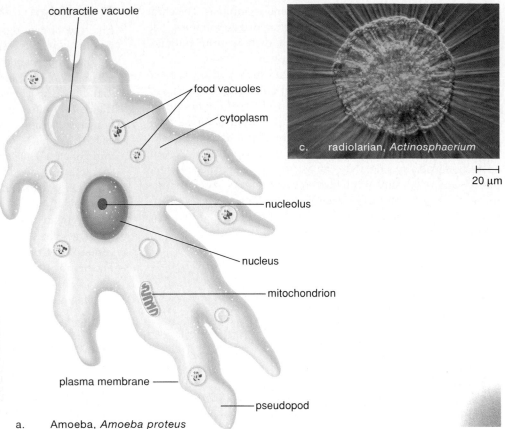

Figure 25.10

Amoeboid protozoa. **a.** Structure of *Amoeba proteus*, an amoeboid common in freshwater ponds. Bacteria and other microorganisms are digested in food vacuoles, and contractile vacuoles rid the body of excess water. **b.** Pseudopods of a live foraminiferan project through holes in the calcium carbonate shell. These shells were so numerous they became a large part of the White Cliffs of Dover when a geological upheaval occurred. **c.** Pseudopods of a live radiolarian extend outward through openings in a siliceous shell.

contractile vacuole

food vacuoles

cytoplasm

c. radiolarian, *Actinosphaerium*

20 μm

nucleolus

nucleus

mitochondrion

b. Foraminiferan, *Globigerina*

plasma membrane

pseudopod

a. Amoeba, *Amoeba proteus*

PROTOZOA ARE ANIMAL-LIKE

The term protozoa, which is used for convenience, is not a taxonomic category. **Protozoa** [Gk. *proto,* first, and *zoa,* animal] are typically heterotrophic, motile, unicellular organisms of small size (2–1,000 μm). They are not animals because animals in the classification used by this text are multicellular and have more than one kind of nonreproductive cell and undergo embryonic development.

Protozoa usually live in water, but they can also be found in moist soil or inside other organisms. In oceans and freshwater lakes and ponds, they are a part of plankton. Specifically, they are **zooplankton** that feed on phytoplankton. Some protozoa engulf whole food and are termed *holozoic;* others are saprotrophic, and they absorb nutrient molecules across the plasma membrane. Still others are parasitic and are responsible for several significant human infections.

Most protozoa are unicellular but there are also colonial and even multicellular forms. Even the unicellular ones should not be considered simple organisms. Each cell alone must carry out all the functions performed by specialized tissues and organs in more complex organisms. They have organelles for purposes we have not seen before. Their food is digested inside food vacuoles, and freshwater protozoa have "contractile" vacuoles for the elimination of water.

Although asexual reproduction involving binary fission and mitosis is the rule, many protozoa also reproduce sexually during some part of their life cycle. During times of unfavorable growth, some of them form cysts which have a protective coat and are metabolically inactive. Once favorable growth conditions return, cysts are sites for nuclear reorganization and cell division. Therefore, they are sometimes called reproductive cysts.

The protozoa we will study can be placed in four groups according to their type of locomotor organelle:

NAME	LOCOMOTION	EXAMPLE
Amoeboids	Pseudopods	*Amoeba*
Ciliates	Cilia	*Paramecium*
Zooflagellates	Flagella	*Trypanosoma*
Sporozoa	No locomotion	*Plasmodium*

Amoeboids and Relatives Move by Pseudopods

The **amoeboids (phylum Sarcodina,** 40,000 species) are protoctists that move and engulf their prey with **pseudopods** [Gk. *pseudo,* false, and *pod,* foot]. Pseudopods form when the cytoplasm streams forward in a particular direction. Many amoebas have shells, as do the foraminifera and radiolaria.

Amoeba proteus is a commonly studied freshwater member of this group (fig. 25.10). When amoeboids feed, they **phagocytize** [Gk. *phag,* eat, and *cyt,* cell]; the pseudopods surround and engulf the prey, which may be algae, bacteria, or other protozoa.

Figure 25.11

Ciliated protozoa. **a.** *Stentor*, a large, vase-shaped, freshwater protozoan. **b.** Two *Stylonychia* conjugating. **c.** Structure of *Paramecium*, adjacent to an electron micrograph. Ciliates are the most complex of the protozoa. Note the oral groove and the gullet and anal pore.

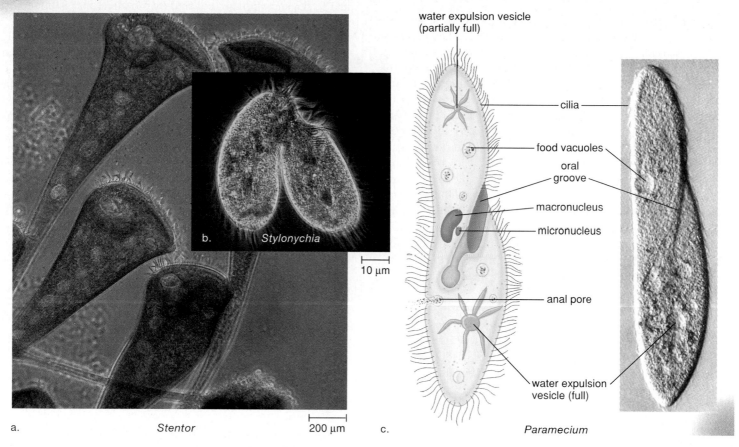

a.   *Stentor*   200 μm

b.   *Stylonychia*   10 μm

water expulsion vesicle (partially full)

cilia

food vacuoles

oral groove

macronucleus

micronucleus

anal pore

water expulsion vesicle (full)

c.   *Paramecium*

Digestion then occurs within a food vacuole. Some white blood cells in humans are amoeboid and they phagocytize debris, parasites, and worn out cells. Freshwater amoeboids, including *Amoeba proteus*, have contractile vacuoles where excess water from the cytoplasm collects before the vacuole appears to "contract," releasing the water through a temporary opening in the plasma membrane.

Entamoeba histolytica is a parasite that lives in the human intestine and causes amoebic dysentery. Complications arise when this parasite invades the intestinal lining and reproduces there. If the parasites enter the body proper, liver and brain involvement can be fatal.

The *foraminifera*, which are largely marine, have an external calcareous shell (made up of calcium carbonate) with foramina, holes through which long, thin pseudopods extend. The pseudopods branch and join to form a net where the prey is digested. Foraminifera live in the sediment of the ocean floor in incredible numbers—there may be as many as 50,000 shells in a single gram of sediment. Deposits for millions of years, followed by a geological upheaval, formed the White Cliffs of Dover along the southern coast of England. Also, the great Egyptian pyramids are built of foraminiferan limestone.

The *radiolaria*, which have an internal skeleton composed of silica or strontium sulfate, float near the ocean surface. Their exquisite skeletons are found in almost infinite variety. They extend spikelike pseudopods strengthened by microtubules through openings in their shells for feeding purposes.

> The amoeboids have pseudopods for locomotion and feeding. *Amoeba proteus* lives in fresh water, but the shelled foraminifera and radiolaria are very abundant in the ocean.

Ciliates Move by Cilia

The **ciliates (phylum Ciliophora,** 8,000 species) such as those in the genus *Paramecium* are the most complex of the protozoa (fig. 25.11). Hundreds of cilia, which beat in a coordinated rhythmic manner, project through tiny holes in a semirigid outer covering, or pellicle. Numerous oval capsules lying in the cytoplasm just beneath the pellicle contain *trichocysts*. Upon mechanical or chemical stimulation, trichocysts discharge long, barbed threads, useful for defense and for capturing prey. *Toxicysts* are similar but they release a poison that paralyzes prey.

Most ciliates are holozoic. For example, when a paramecium feeds, food is swept down a gullet, below which food vacuoles form. Following digestion, the soluble nutrients are absorbed by the cytoplasm, and the indigestible residue is eliminated at the anal pore.

During asexual reproduction ciliates divide by transverse binary fission. Ciliates have two types of nuclei: a large *macronucleus* and one or more small *micronuclei*. The macronucleus controls the normal metabolism of the cell, while the micronuclei are concerned with reproduction. Sexual reproduction involves conjugation. The macronucleus disintegrates and, after the micronuclei undergo meiosis, two ciliates exchange a haploid micronucleus. Then the micronuclei give rise to a new macronucleus, which contains copies of only certain housekeeping genes.

The diversity of ciliates is quite remarkable. The barrel-shaped didinia expand to consume paramecia much larger than themselves. Suctoria have an even more dramatic way of getting food. They rest quietly on a stalk until a hapless victim comes along. Then they promptly paralyze it and use their tentacles like straws to suck it dry. *Stentor* may be the prettiest ciliate. It resembles a giant blue vase decorated with stripes.

Ciliates, which move by cilia, are diverse and very complex. The single cell has specialized regions to carry out various functions.

Zooflagellates Move by Flagella

Protozoa that move by means of flagella are called **zooflagellates (phylum Zoomastigophora)** to distinguish them from unicellular algae that also have flagella. Zooflagellates [Gk. *zoo,* animal, and L. *flagell,* whip] are covered by a pellicle that is often reinforced by underlying microtubules.

Many zooflagellates enter into symbiotic relationships (fig. 25.12). *Trichonympha collaris* lives in the gut of termites; it contains a bacterium that enzymatically converts the cellulose of wood to soluble carbohydrates that are easily digested by the insect. *Giardia lamblia,* whose cysts are transmitted through contaminated water, causes severe diarrhea. *Trichomonas vaginalis,* a sexually transmitted organism, infects the vagina and urethra of women and the prostate, seminal vesicles, and urethra of men. A **trypanosome,** *Trypanosoma gambiense,* transmitted by the bite of the tsetse fly, is the cause of African sleeping sickness. The white blood cells in an infected animal accumulate around the blood vessels leading to the brain and cut off circulation. The lethargy characteristic of the disease is caused by an inadequate supply of oxygen to the brain.

Flagellates usually reproduce by transverse binary fission.

Zooflagellates, which move by flagella, are often symbiotic. The various diseases they cause in humans range from being annoying to being extremely serious.

Figure 25.12

Zooflagellates. **a.** *Trichonympha collaris* lives in the gut of termites and helps digest cellulose. **b.** Photograph of *Trypanosoma brucei,* the cause of African sleeping sickness, among red blood cells. **c.** The drawing shows its general structure.

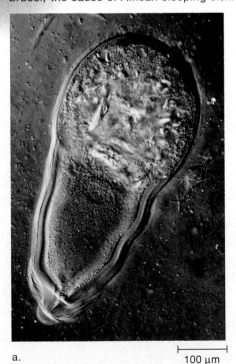

a.   100 μm

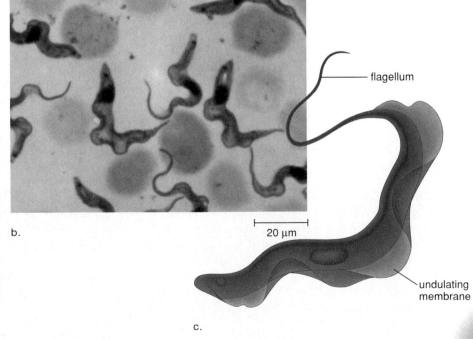

b.

20 μm

flagellum

undulating
membrane

c.

Sporozoa Form Spores

Sporozoa (phylum Sporozoa, 3,600 species) are nonmotile parasites. They contain a complex of organelles that may help the organism invade host cells or tissues. Their name recognizes that these organisms form spores at some point in their life cycle. Their complicated life cycle alternates between a sexual and an asexual phase, often with two or more hosts.

Pneumocystis carinii causes the type of pneumonia seen primarily in AIDS patients. During sexual reproduction, thick-walled cysts form in the lining of pulmonary air sacs. The cysts contain spores that successively divide until the cyst bursts and the spores are released. Each spore becomes a new mature organism that can reproduce asexually but may also enter the encysted sexual stage.

The most widespread human parasite is *Plasmodium vivax,* the cause of one type of malaria. When a human is bitten by an infected female *Anopheles* mosquito, the parasite eventually invades the red blood cells. The chills and fever of malaria appear when the infected cells burst and release toxic substances into the blood (fig. 25.13). Malaria is still a major killer of humans, despite extensive efforts to control it. A resurgence of the disease was caused primarily by the development of insecticide-resistant strains of mosquitoes and by parasites resistant to current antimalarial drugs.

Toxoplasma gondii, another sporozoan, causes toxoplasmosis, particularly in cats but also in people. In pregnant women the parasite can infect the fetus and cause birth defects; in AIDS patients it can infect the brain and cause neurological symptoms.

Figure 25.13

Life cycle of *Plasmodium vivax*. Asexual reproduction occurs in humans, while sexual reproduction takes place within the *Anopheles* mosquito.

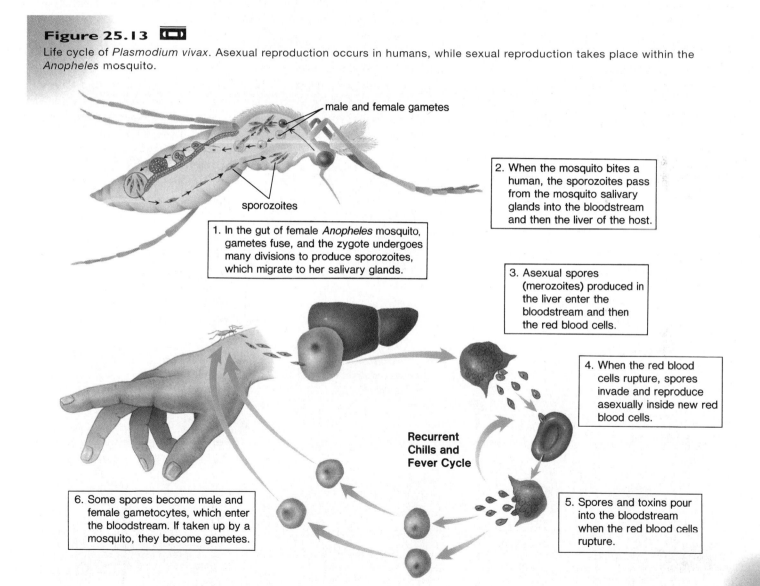

male and female gametes

sporozoites

2. When the mosquito bites a human, the sporozoites pass from the mosquito salivary glands into the bloodstream and then the liver of the host.

1. In the gut of female *Anopheles* mosquito, gametes fuse, and the zygote undergoes many divisions to produce sporozoites, which migrate to her salivary glands.

3. Asexual spores (merozoites) produced in the liver enter the bloodstream and then the red blood cells.

4. When the red blood cells rupture, spores invade and reproduce asexually inside new red blood cells.

Recurrent Chills and Fever Cycle

6. Some spores become male and female gametocytes, which enter the bloodstream. If taken up by a mosquito, they become gametes.

5. Spores and toxins pour into the bloodstream when the red blood cells rupture.

Life Cycles Among the Protoctists

Organisms reproduce asexually and sexually. Asexual reproduction requires only one parent. The offspring are identical to this parent because the offspring receive a copy of only this parent's genes. There are various modes of asexual reproduction. Single cells such as amoeboids, flagellates, and diatoms simply split in two; Chlamydomonas and water molds produce zoospores. In any case, growth alone produces a new adult. Asexual reproduction is the frequent mode of reproduction among protoctists when the environment is favorable to growth. Individuals identical to the parent are likely to survive and flourish. Sexual reproduction, with its genetic recombination due to fertilization and independent assortment of chromosomes, is more likely to occur among protoctists when the environment is changing and is unfavorable to growth. Recombination of genes might produce individuals that are more likely to survive extremes in the environment—such as high or low temperatures, acidic or basic pH, or a lack of some particular nutrient.

Sexual reproduction requires two parents, each of which contributes chromosomes (genes) to the offspring by way of gametes. The gametes fuse to produce a diploid zygote. Meiosis occurs during sexual reproduction—just *when* it occurs makes the sexual life cycles diagrammed below differ from one another. In these diagrams, the diploid phase is above and the haploid phase is below the line. In the haplontic cycle (fig. 25A), the zygote divides by meiosis to form haploid spores that develop into a haploid adult. In aquatic protoctists, the spores are typically zoospores. The zygote is only the diploid stage in this life cycle, and the haploid adult gives rise to gametes. This sexual cycle is seen in *Chlamydomonas,* a number of algae, protozoa, and fungi.

In alternation of generations (sporic meiosis), the sporophyte (2n) produces haploid spores by meiosis (fig. 25B). A spore develops into a haploid gametophyte that produces gametes. The gametes fuse to form a diploid zygote, and the zygote develops into the sporophyte. This life cycle is characteristic of some algae (for example, *Ulva* and *Laminaria*) and all plants. In *Ulva,* the haploid and diploid generations have the same appearance. In plants, they are noticeably different from each other.

In the diplontic cycle, a diploid adult produces gametes by meiosis (fig. 25C). Gametes are the only haploid stage in this cycle. They fuse to form a zygote that develops into the diploid adult. This life cycle is characteristic of a few protoctists (for example, *Oomycota* and *Fucus*) and all animals. The cycle is isogamous when the gametes look alike—called isogametes—and the cycle is oogamous when the gametes are dissimilar—called heterogametes, usually a small flagellated sperm and a large egg with plentiful cytoplasm.

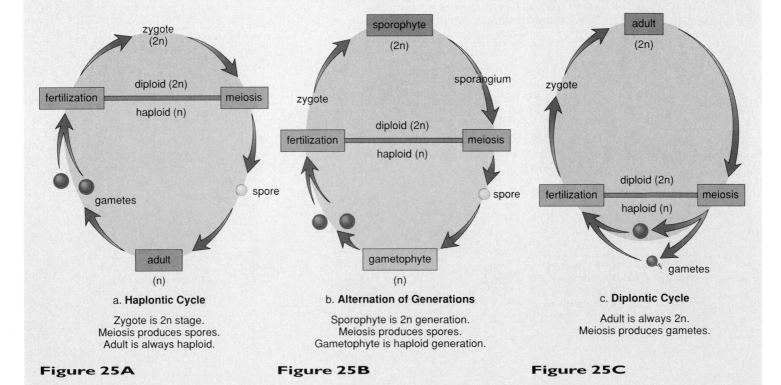

a. Haplontic Cycle

Zygote is 2n stage.
Meiosis produces spores.
Adult is always haploid.

Figure 25A

b. Alternation of Generations

Sporophyte is 2n generation.
Meiosis produces spores.
Gametophyte is haploid generation.

Figure 25B

c. Diplontic Cycle

Adult is always 2n.
Meiosis produces gametes.

Figure 25C

SLIME MOLDS AND WATER MOLDS ARE FUNGUSLIKE

Both slime molds and water molds are similar in some respects to fungi. Fungi have a filamentous body and are saprotrophic. A **saprotroph** [Gk. *sapro,* putrid, and *troph,* feeder] carries on external digestion and absorbs the resulting nutrients across the plasma membrane. In fungi, meiosis typically follows formation of the zygote, and there are nonmotile spores during both sexual and asexual reproduction. Slime molds and water molds also differ from fungi, as discussed in the following.

Slime Molds Are Amoeboid

Upon a cursory examination, **slime molds** (**phylum Gymnomycota,** 560 species) might look like molds but their vegetative state is mobile and amoeboid! At this time they seem more like an amoeboid protozoan than a fungus. Indeed they are heterotrophic by ingestion—they engulf organic material and bacteria. When conditions are unfavorable to growth they produce and release spores that are resistant to environmental extremes. When the spores germinate, they release cells that begin the life cycle again.

Plasmodial Slime Molds Are a Multinucleated Mass

Usually *plasmodial slime molds* exist as a plasmodium, a diploid multinucleated cytoplasmic mass enveloped by a slime sheath that creeps along, phagocytizing decaying plant material in a forest or agricultural field (fig. 25.14). The fan-shaped mass contains tubules formed by concentrated cytoplasm in which more liquefied cytoplasm streams. At times unfavorable to growth, such as during a drought, the plasmodium develops many sporangia. A **sporangium** [Gk. *spor,* seed, *ang,* vessel, and *ium,* small] is a reproductive structure that produces spores by meiosis. The spores can survive until moisture is sufficient for them to germinate. In plasmodial slime molds, spores release a haploid flagellated cell or an amoeboid cell. Eventually, two of them fuse to form a zygote that feeds and grows, producing a multinucleated plasmodium once again.

Cellular Slime Molds Are Single Cells

Cellular slime molds, as you might expect, exist as individual amoeboid cells. Each lives by phagocytizing bacteria and yeast. As the food supply runs out, the cells release a chemical that causes them to aggregate into a pseudoplasmodium. The

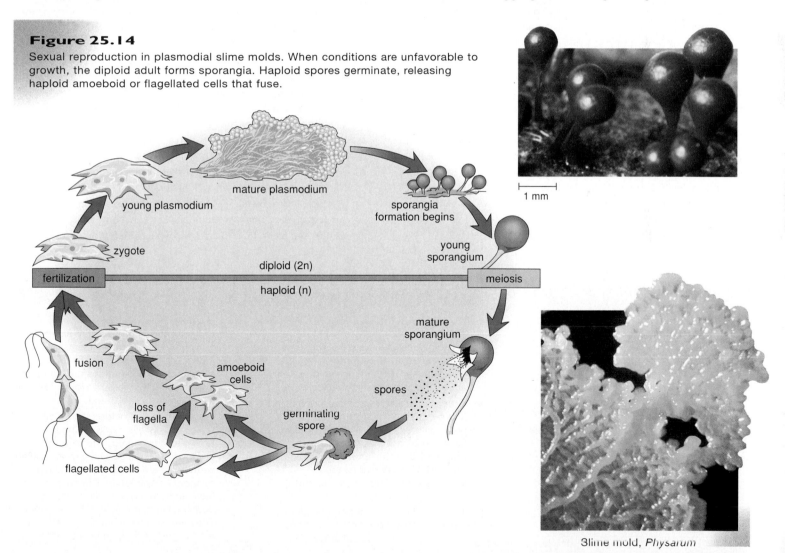

Figure 25.14

Sexual reproduction in plasmodial slime molds. When conditions are unfavorable to growth, the diploid adult forms sporangia. Haploid spores germinate, releasing haploid amoeboid or flagellated cells that fuse.

young plasmodium
mature plasmodium
sporangia formation begins
zygote
young sporangium
fertilization
diploid (2n)
haploid (n)
meiosis
mature sporangium
fusion
amoeboid cells
spores
loss of flagella
germinating spore
flagellated cells

1 mm

Slime mold, *Physarum*

pseudoplasmodium stage is temporary and eventually gives rise to a sporangium that produces spores. When favorable conditions return, the spores germinate, releasing haploid amoeboid cells, and this asexual cycle begins again. A sexual cycle is known to occur under very moist conditions.

> Slime molds, which produce nonmotile spores, are unlike fungi in that they have an amoeboid stage and are heterotrophic by ingestion.

Water Molds Are Filamentous

The **water molds** (**phylum Oomycota,** 580 species) live in the water, where they parasitize fishes, forming furry growths on their gills. In spite of their common name, others live on land and parasitize insects and plants. A water mold was responsible for the 1840s potato famine in Ireland. Most water molds are saprotrophic and live off dead organic matter, however.

Water molds have a filamentous body as do fungi, but their cell walls are largely composed of cellulose whereas fungi have cell walls of chitin. The life cycle of water molds differs from that of fungi. During asexual reproduction water molds produce motile spores (2n zoospores), which are flagellated. The adult is diploid (not haploid as in the fungi), and meiosis produces the gametes. Their phylum name refers to the enlarged tips (called oogonia) where eggs are produced.

> Water molds have a filamentous body and are saprotrophic. The adult is diploid and meiosis produces gametes; during asexual reproduction there are motile zoospores.

Biological Relationships

Several firsts are seen among the protoctists. They were the first organisms to be eukaryotes, the first to show signs of multicellularity, and the first to engage in sexual reproduction utilizing gametes. The eukaryotic cell is larger than the prokaryotic cell and it is compartmentalized. Specific regions have a specific structure and function: cellular respiration occurs in mitochondria and photosynthesis occurs in chloroplasts, for example. As cells increase in size, efficiency is maintained as long as there is compartmentalization. As an analogy, consider that as a business grows larger, various departments handle specific tasks.

Colonies most likely evolved before multicellularity. We can imagine that by chance *Chlamydomonas* zoospores failed to separate and a colony such as a *Volvox* was the result. Now, the stage would have been set for cells to become specialized. In *Volvox,* there are cells specialized for reproduction, and in multicellular brown algae there are specialized regions: holdfast, stipe, blade, and reproductive tips. Both plants and animals have specialized organs.

The life cycle of many protoctists includes both asexual and sexual reproduction. Asexual reproduction allows mass production during times of plenty, and mutation alone produces variations. In sexual reproduction, which involves meiosis and fertilization, the offspring always varies from the parent. When members of a species vary, the species is more likely to survive in a changing environment. It is significant, then, that sexual reproduction is seen among protoctists when the environment is unfavorable in some way. Sexual reproduction is routinely utilized in plants and animals, which are diploid. In most protoctists and fungi, the zygote undergoes meiosis and the adult is haploid. A diploid adult could have arisen, if the zygote by chance divided by mitosis instead of meiosis. A diploid adult has two sets of chromosomes and genes. If one allele is faulty, the other one may function properly.

Protoctists are diverse and it is uncertain if any particular one evolved into fungi, plants, or animals. But it is clear that many of the basic biological features of plants and animals began with the protoctists.

Summary

1. Protoctists are eukaryotes. The nuclear envelope most likely evolved through invagination of the plasma membrane, but mitochondria and chloroplasts may have arisen through endosymbiotic events.

2. Kingdom Protoctista contains (1) algae, which carry on photosynthesis in the same manner as plants, (2) protozoa, which, like multicellular animals, are heterotrophic and ingest food, and (3) slime molds and water molds, which have some of the characteristics of fungi.

3. Algae are a part of phytoplankton, which serves as a source of food in both marine and freshwater ecosystems. They are grouped according to their pigments (color).

4. Green algae possess chlorophylls *a* and *b,* store reserve food as starch, and have cell walls of cellulose as do plants. Green algae are divided into those that are flagellated (*Chlamydomonas*), colonial (*Volvox*), filamentous (*Spirogyra* and *Oedogonium*), and multicellular (*Ulva*).

5. The life cycle varies among the green algae. In most the zygote undergoes meiosis and the adult is haploid. Both isogamy and oogamy are seen. *Ulva* has alternation of generations like plants but the sporophyte and gametophyte generations are similar in appearance; the gametes look alike and the spores are flagellated.

6. Brown algae and golden brown algae have chlorophylls *a* and *c* plus a brownish carotenoid. The large, complex brown algae, commonly called seaweeds, are well known and have economic importance. Diatoms, which have an outer layer of silica, are the best known of the golden brown algae. They are extremely numerous in both marine and freshwater ecosystems.

7. Dinoflagellates have cellulose plates and two flagella, one at a right angle to the other. Their chloroplasts are probably derived from golden brown algae by endosymbiosis. They are extremely numerous in the ocean and on occasion produce a neurotoxin when they form red tides.

8. Euglenoids are flagellated cells with a pellicle instead of a cell wall. Their chloroplasts are most likely derived from a green alga through endosymbiosis.

9. Red algae are filamentous or multicellular seaweeds more delicate than brown algae and usually growing in warmer waters. Like brown algae, red algae have economic importance.

10. Protozoa are part of zooplankton and serve as food for animals in marine and freshwater ecosystems. Protozoa are grouped according to the type of locomotor organelle.

11. Amoeboids move and feed by forming pseudopods. Whereas *Amoeba proteus* is usually studied, the radiolaria and the shelled foraminifera responsible for limestone deposits are more significant.

12. Ciliates, which move by means of cilia, are the most complex protozoa and show great diversity.

13. Zooflagellates, which have flagella, are often symbiotic; *Trypanosoma* causes African sleeping sickness in humans. Sporozoa are nonmotile parasites that form spores; *Plasmodium* causes malaria.

14. Slime molds, which produce nonmotile spores, are unlike fungi in that they have an amoeboid stage and are heterotrophic by ingestion. Water molds, which are filamentous and saprotrophic, are unlike fungi in that they produce 2n zoospores. Meiosis produces the gametes.

Writing Across the Curriculum

In order to practice writing skills, students should write out the answers to any or all of the study questions and the critical thinking questions. The study questions are sequenced in the same order as the text. Answers to the objective questions, and suggested answers to the critical thinking questions, are in appendix D.

Study Questions

1. How might the eukaryotic cell have evolved, and what evidence is there to support your description?   412

2. What are the three types of protoctists, and what are their distinguishing characteristics?   413

3. In general what is the role of algae in aquatic ecosystems? What primary characteristic is used to group algae?   413

4. Describe the structure of *Chlamydomonas* and *Volvox;* contrast how they reproduce.   413–15

5. Describe the structure of *Spirogyra* and *Oedogonium;* contrast how they reproduce.   416

6. Describe the structure of *Ulva* and explain how its life cycle differs from that of plants.   416

7. Describe the structure of brown algae and diatoms. Discuss their ecological and economic importance.   417–18

8. Describe the structure of dinoflagellates. What feature do they share with diatoms? What is a red tide?   418

9. Describe the structure of euglenoids. What feature do they share with green algae?   418–19

10. Describe the structure of red algae and contrast their structure with that of brown algae. Why are both called seaweeds?   419

11. What is the general role of protozoa in aquatic ecosystems, and what primary characteristic is used to group protozoa? Give an example from each group.   420–23

12. Describe the life cycle of *Plasmodium vivax,* the causative agent of malaria.   423

13. What features do slime molds and water molds share with fungi? Describe the life cycle of a plasmodial slime mold.   425–26

Objective Questions

1. Which organelle would not have originated by endosymbiosis?
   a. mitochondria
   b. flagella
   c. nucleus
   d. chloroplasts

2. Which of these is not a green alga?
   a. *Volvox*
   b. *Fucus*
   c. *Spirogyra*
   d. *Chlamydomonas*

3. Which is not a characteristic of brown algae?
   a. multicellular
   b. chlorophylls *a* and *b*
   c. lives along rocky coast
   d. harvested for commercial reasons

4. In *Chlamydomonas*
   a. the adult is haploid.
   b. spores survive times of stress.
   c. sexual reproduction occurs.
   d. All of these are correct.

5. Which is found in *Ulva* but not in plants?
   a. alternation of generations
   b. generations look alike
   c. sperm and egg are produced
   d. Both b and c are correct.

6. Which of these algae are not flagellated?
   a. *Volvox*
   b. *Spirogyra*
   c. dinoflagellates
   d. *Chlamydomonas*

7. Which is mismatched?
   a. diatoms—silica shell, boxlike, golden brown
   b. euglenoids—flagella, pellicle, eyespot
   c. *Fucus*—adult is diploid, seaweed, chlorophylls *a* and *c*
   d. *Paramecium*—cilia, calcium carbonate shell, gullet

8. Which is a false statement?
   a. There are flagellated algae and flagellated protozoa.
   b. Among protozoa, both flagellates and sporozoa are symbiotic.
   c. Among the protoctists, only green algae have a sexual life cycle.
   d. Ciliates exchange genetic material during conjugation.

9. Which is mismatched?
   a. trypanosome—African sleeping sickness
   b. *Plasmodium vivax*—malaria
   c. amoeboid—severe diarrhea
   d. AIDS—*Giardia lamblia*

10. Which is found in slime molds but not fungi?
    a. nonmotile spores
    b. amoeboid adult
    c. zygote formation
    d. photosynthesis

11. Label this diagram of the *Chlamydomonas* life cycle.

12. Name two features that distinguish the asexual from the sexual portion of the cycle shown in the diagram.

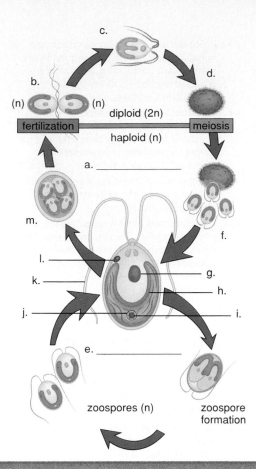

diploid (2n)

haploid (n)

a. _____

m.

l.

k.

j.

e. _____

g.

h.

i.

zoospores (n)

zoospore formation

f.

Concepts and Critical Thinking

1. *Endosymbiosis can account for the presence of certain organelles in eukaryotic cells.*

   How does endosymbiosis make it difficult to determine evolutionary relationships among the algae?

2. *Protoctists are a diverse group of organisms.*

   The manner in which protoctists are currently divided is artificial. Explain.

3. *Protozoa are the animal-like protoctists.*

   Argue that sporozoa should not be considered protozoa on the basis of this concept.

Selected Key Terms

alga (pl., algae) Aquatic, plantlike organism carrying out photosynthesis and belonging to the kingdom Protoctista. [L. *alg*, seaweed] 413

amoeboid Protoctist that moves and engulfs prey with pseudopods; amoebalike in movement. 420

conjugation The transfer of genetic material from one cell to another. [L. *conjug*, joined together] 416

diatom A freshwater or marine unicellular golden-brown alga, with a cell wall consisting of two silica-impregnated valves, which is extremely numerous in phytoplankton. [Gk. *dia*, through, and *tom*, cut] 416

dinoflagellate (dy-noh-FLAJ-uh-layt) A unicellular alga, with two flagella, one whiplash and the other located within a groove between protective cellulose plates, whose numbers periodically explode to cause a toxic "red tide" in ocean waters. [Gk. *din*, whirling, and L. *flagell*, whip] 418

euglenoid (yuu-GLEE-noyd) A flagellated and flexible freshwater unicellular organism which usually contains chloroplasts and is often characterized as having both animal-like and plantlike characteristics. 418

phytoplankton (fyt-oh-PLANGK-tun) The part of plankton containing organisms that (1) photosynthesize and produce much of the oxygen in the atmosphere and (2) serve as food producers in aquatic ecosystems. [Gk. *phyt*, plant, and *plankt*, wandering] 413

plankton Freshwater and marine organisms that are suspended on or near the surface of the water. [Gk. *plankt*, wandering] 413

protozoan (pl., protozoa) Animal-like, heterotrophic, unicellular organism. [Gk. *proto*, first, and *zoa*, animal] 420

pseudopod Cytoplasmic extension of amoeboid protoctists; used for locomotion and engulfing food. [Gk. *pseudo*, false, and *pod*, foot] 420

spore An asexual reproductive structure that is resistant to unfavorable environmental conditions and develops into a haploid generation. [Gk. *spor*, seed] 414

trypanosome (trip-AN-uh-sohm) A member of a genus of parasitic zooflagellates that cause severe disease in human beings and domestic animals, including a condition called sleeping sickness. [Gk. *tryp*, hole, and *soma*, body] 422

zooflagellate (zoh-uh-FLAJ-uh-layt) Protozoan that moves by means of flagella. [Gk. *zoo*, animal, and L. *flagell*, whip] 422

zooplankton (zoh-uh-PLANGK-tun) The part of plankton containing protozoa and microscopic animals. [Gk. *zoo*, animal, and *plankt*, wandering] 420

KINGDOM FUNGI

Learning Objectives

What Fungi Are Like
- List and discuss the characteristics of fungi, stressing their ecological importance.   430-31

How Fungi Are Classified
- Explain why fungi are classified in their own kingdom, and tell how fungi differ from organisms in the other four kingdoms.   432
- Give examples of the zygospore fungi.   432-33
- Give examples of the sac fungi. Explain how sac fungi asexually reproduce and describe the structure of an ascocarp.   434-35

- Give examples of the club fungi. Draw and explain a diagram of the life cycle of a typical mushroom.   436-37
- Give examples of the imperfect fungi. Explain the significance of the name imperfect fungi, and give examples of their importance to human beings.   439

Fungi Form Symbiotic Relationships
- Describe the structure of a lichen, the different types of lichens, and the nature of this fungal association. 439 40
- Describe the structure and function of mycorrhizae and note their importance to plants.   440

Golden trumpet mushrooms, *Mycena,* are fungi that acquire nutrients by decomposing organic material.

ost people know that mushrooms are fungi, and some might know that mildew, molds, and morels are fungi, too. From this litany you would think a fungus couldn't be very large. But researchers claim to have found one that spreads over 1,500 acres in Washington State. Since the body of the fungus is partially underground it's difficult to tell exactly how large it really is. What's this huge fungus doing there? As fungi spread, they feed off the organic remains of plants and animals. Dead leaves, tree trunks, and even carcasses of animals are their daily fare. They, along with bacteria, are the decomposers that enrich the immediate environs with inorganic nutrients and thereby keep chemicals cycling in ecosystems. Trees grow, grass turns green, and flowers appear all because fungi, while digesting for themselves, have also digested for others. Perhaps we should think of them as being mutualistic with the entire world of nature.

We humans are quite interested in the fungi that perform services for us, spoil our stored foods, or cause disease. But even so, we should never lose sight of the major contribution fungi make to the continued existence of all living things.

WHAT FUNGI ARE LIKE

Fungi are mostly multicellular eukaryotes of varied structure that share a common mode of nutrition. Like animals, they are heterotrophic and consume preformed organic matter. Animals, however, are heterotrophic by ingestion; fungi are heterotrophic by absorption. Their cells send out digestive enzymes into the immediate environment and then, when organic matter is broken down, the cells absorb the resulting nutrient molecules.

Most fungi are *saprotrophic decomposers* that break down the waste products and dead remains of plants and animals. Some fungi are parasitic; they live off the tissues of living plants and animals. Fungi can enter leaves through the stomates and this makes plants especially subject to fungal diseases. Fungal diseases account for millions of dollars in crop losses each year, and they have greatly reduced the numbers of various types of trees. They also cause human diseases such as ringworm, athlete's foot, and yeast infections.

Several types of fungi have a mutualistic relationship with the roots of seed plants; they acquire inorganic nutrients for plants and in return they are given organic nutrients. Others form an association with a green alga or cyanobacterium within a lichen. Lichens can live on rocks and are important soil formers.

> Fungi carry on external digestion and are heterotrophic by absorption. They are saprotrophic or parasitic, and form symbiotic relationships.

Figure 26.1

Mycelium. **a.** On a corn tortilla each mycelium grown from a different spore is quite symmetrical. **b.** Hyphae are either septate (have cross walls) or nonseptate (do not have cross walls). **c.** Scanning electron micrograph showing fungal hyphae.

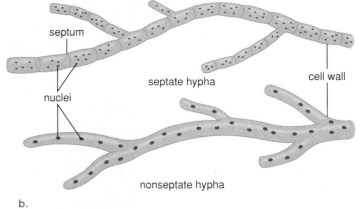

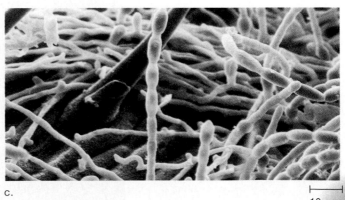

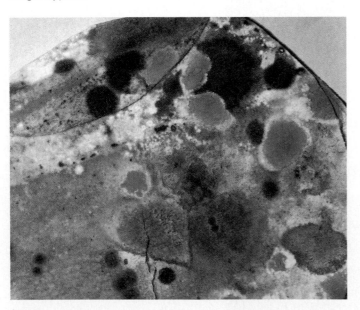

a.

b.

c.

Most Fungi Are Filamentous

Fungi can be unicellular—yeast are the best known example. But the thallus (body) of most fungi is a multicellular structure known as a mycelium (fig. 26.1). A **mycelium** [Gk. *myc*, fungus, and *ium*, small] is a network of filaments called **hyphae** [Gk. *hyph*, web]. Hyphae give the mycelium quite a large surface area per volume of cytoplasm, and this facilitates absorption of nutrients into the body of a fungus. Hyphae grow at their tips and the mycelium absorbs and then passes nutrients on to the growing tips. When a fungus reproduces, a specific portion of the mycelium becomes a reproductive structure which is then nourished by the rest of the mycelium.

Fungal cells are quite different from plant cells not only by lacking chloroplasts but also by having a cell wall that contains *chitin* and not cellulose. Chitin, like cellulose, is a polymer of glucose organized into microfibrils. In chitin, however, each glucose molecule has an amino group attached to it. Chitin is also found in the external skeleton of insects and all arthropods. The energy reserve of fungi is not starch but glycogen, as in animals. Fungi are nonmotile; they lack basal bodies and do not have flagella at any stage in their life cycle. They move toward a food source by growing toward it. Hyphae can cover as much as a kilometer a day!

Some fungi have no cross walls in their hyphae. These hyphae are called **nonseptate**—septum (pl., septa) is the term used for cross walls in fungi. Nonseptate fungi are multinucleated; they have many nuclei in the cytoplasm of a hypha. **Septate** [L. *sept*, fence] fungi have cross walls, but actually the presence of septa makes little difference because pores allow cytoplasm and even sometimes organelles to pass freely from one cell to the other. The septa that separate reproductive cells, however, are complete in all fungal groups.

> The nonmotile body of a fungus is made up of hyphae that form a mycelium.

Most Fungi Produce Spores

In general, fungal sexual reproduction involves these stages:

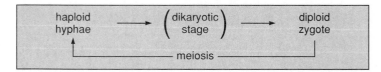

The relative length of time of each phase varies with the species.

During sexual reproduction, hyphae (or a portion thereof) from two different mating types make contact and fuse. You would expect the nuclei from the two mating types to also fuse immediately, and they do in some species. In other species the nuclei pair but do not fuse for days, months, or even years. The nuclei continue to divide in such a way that every cell (in septate hyphae) has at least one of each type. A hypha that contains paired haploid nuclei is said to be n + n or **dikaryotic** [Gk. *di*, two, and *kary*, nucleus]. When the nuclei do eventually fuse, the zygote

undergoes meiosis prior to spore formation. Fungal spores germinate directly into haploid hyphae without any noticeable embryological development.

How can a terrestrial and nonmotile organism ensure that the species will be dispersed to new locations? As an adaptation to life on land, fungi produce nonmotile, but usually windblown, spores during both sexual and asexual reproduction (fig. 26.2). A **spore** is a reproductive cell that can grow directly into a new organism.

Asexual reproduction usually involves the production of spores by a single mycelium. Alternately, asexual reproduction can occur by fragmentation—a portion of a mycelium begins a life of its own. Also, unicellular yeast reproduce asexually by **budding;** a small cell forms and gets pinched off as it grows to full size (see fig. 26.6).

Figure 26.2

Fungal strategy for dispersal of the species. **a.** Electron micrograph shows the external appearance of spores discharged by **b.** Earth star, *Geastrum,* which releases hordes of spores into the air.

a.   ⊢——⊣ 20 µm

b.

HOW FUNGI ARE CLASSIFIED

The ancestry of fungi, which evolved about 570 million years ago, has not been determined. It is possible that the organisms now classified in the **Kingdom Fungi** do not share a recent common ancestor. In that case, they probably evolved separately from different protoctists. It's been suggested, though, that fungi evolved from red algae because both fungi and red algae lack flagella in all stages of the life cycle.

In the past, fungi have been classified in other kingdoms. Originally they were considered a part of the plant kingdom, and then they were placed in the kingdom Protoctista. But in 1969, R. H. Whittaker argued that their multicellular nature and mode of nutrition (extracellular digestion and absorption of nutrients) meant they should be in their own kingdom. Table 26.1 contrasts the features of fungi with the features of certain other organisms now included in kingdom Protoctista by this text. In the absence of knowing their evolutionary relations, fungal groups are classified according to differences in the life cycle and the type of structure that produces spores. Recently scientists have been using comparative DNA (deoxyribonucleic acid) data and analysis of enzymes and other proteins to decipher evolutionary relationships, but as yet this has not changed the classification of fungi.

Zygospore Fungi Form Zygospores

The **zygospore fungi** (**division Zygomycota**, 600 species) are mainly saprotrophs living off plant and animal remains in the soil or bakery goods in your own pantry. Some are parasites of small soil protoctists or worms, and even insects such as the housefly.

The black bread mold, *Rhizopus stolonifer,* is commonly used as an example of this phylum. The body of this fungus, which is composed of nonseptate hyphae, demonstrates that although there is little cellular differentiation among fungi, the hyphae may be specialized for various purposes. In *Rhizopus, stolons* are horizontal hyphae that exist on the surface of the bread; *rhizoids* grow into the bread, anchor the mycelium and carry out digestion; and *sporangiophores* are stalks that bear sporangia. A **sporangium** is a capsule that produces spores called sporangiospores. During asexual reproduction all structures involved are haploid (fig. 26.3).

The phylum name refers to the zygospore, which is seen during sexual reproduction. The hyphae of opposite mating types, termed plus (+) and minus (−), are chemically attracted, and they grow toward each other until they touch. The ends of the hyphae swell as nuclei enter; then cross walls develop a short distance behind each end, forming *gametangia*. The gametangia merge and the result is a large multinucleate cell in which nuclei of the two mating types pair and then fuse. A thick wall develops around the cell, which is now called a **zygospore.** The zygospore undergoes a period of dormancy before meiosis, and germination takes place. One or more sporangiophores with sporangia at their tips develop, and many spores are released. The spores, dispersed by air currents, give rise to new haploid mycelia.

Zygospore fungi produce spores within sporangia. During sexual reproduction, a zygospore forms prior to meiosis and production of spores.

Table 26.1

Certain Protoctists Compared to Fungi

Feature	Fungi	Red Algae	Plasmodial Slime Molds	Water Molds
Body form	Filamentous	Filamentous	Multinucleate plasmodium	Filamentous
Mode of nutrition	Heterotrophic by absorption	Autotrophic by photosynthesis	Heterotrophic by absorption	Heterotrophic by absorption
Basal bodies/flagella	In no stages	In no stages	In one stage	Flagellated zoospores
Cell wall	Contains chitin	Contains cellulose	None	Contains cellulose
Life cycle	Zygotic meiosis (haplontic cycle)	Sporic meiosis (alternation of generations)	Unique	Gametic meiosis (diplontic cycle)

Sac Fungi Form Ascospores

Most **sac fungi** (**division Ascomycota,** 30,000 species) are saprotrophs that play an essential ecological role by digesting resistant (not easily decomposed) materials containing cellulose, lignin, or collagen. Red bread molds (e.g., *Neurospora*) are ascomycetes, as are cup fungi, morels, and truffles. Morels and truffles are highly prized as gourmet delicacies. A large number of ascomycetes are parasitic on plants; powdery mildews grow on leaves, as do leaf curl fungi; chestnut blight and Dutch elm disease destroy the trees named. Ergot, a parasitic sac fungus that infects rye and (less commonly) other grains, is discussed in the reading on page 438.

Yeasts are unicellular but most ascomycetes are composed of septate hyphae. Their phylum name refers to the **ascus** [Gk. *asc,* bag], a fingerlike sac that develops during sexual reproduction. Ascus-producing hyphae remain dikaryotic (fig. 26.5) except in the walled-off portion that becomes the ascus where nuclear fusion, meiosis, and ascospore formation take place. Each ascus contains eight haploid nuclei and produces eight ascospores.

The asci are usually surrounded and protected by sterile hyphae within a fruiting body called an *ascocarp*. A **fruiting body** is a reproductive structure where spores are produced and released. Ascocarps can have different shapes; in cup fungi they are cup shaped, in molds they are flask shaped and in morels they are stalked and crowned by bell-shaped convoluted tissue that bears the asci. In most ascomycetes, the asci become swollen as they mature and then they burst, expelling the ascospores. If released into the air, the spores are then windblown.

Asexual reproduction, which is the norm among ascomycetes, involves the production of spores called **conidiospores** [Gk. *coni,* dust, and *spor,* seed], or conidia, which vary in size and shape and may be multicellular. There are no sporangia in ascomycetes, and the conidiospores develop directly on the tips of modified aerial hyphae called conidiophores (see fig. 26.9). When released, they are windblown.

> Sac fungi usually produce asexual conidiospores. During sexual reproduction, asci within a fruiting body produce spores.

Yeasts Are Single Cells

Yeasts are unicellular organisms that reproduce asexually either by mitosis or by budding. *Saccharomyces cerevisiae,* brewer's yeast, is representative of budding yeasts: a small cell forms and gets pinched off as it grows to full size (fig. 26.6). Sexual reproduction, which occurs when the food supply runs out, results in

Figure 26.6

Yeast cells. *Saccharomyces cerevisiae,* brewer's yeast, reproduces asexually by budding.

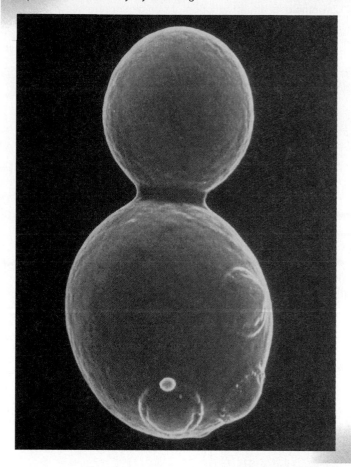

the formation of asci and ascospores. Ascospores from two different mating types can fuse, and the result is a diploid cell that will reproduce asexually before meiosis occurs and ascospores are produced again. The haploid ascospores function directly as new yeast cells.

When yeasts ferment, they produce ethanol and carbon dioxide. In the wild, yeasts grow on fruits, and historically the yeasts already present on grapes were used to produce wine. Today selected yeasts are added to relatively sterile grape juice in order to make wine. Also, yeasts are added to prepared grains to make beer. Both the ethanol and the carbon dioxide are retained for beers and sparkling wines; it is released for still wines. In baking, the carbon dioxide given off by yeast is the leavening agent that causes bread to rise.

Yeasts are serviceable to humans in another way. They have become the material of choice in genetic engineering experiments requiring a eukaryote. *Escherichia coli,* the usual experimental material, is a prokaryote and does not function during protein synthesis as a eukaryote would.

Figure 26.7

Club fungi. **a.** Life cycle of a mushroom. Sexual reproduction is the norm. After hyphae from two compatible mating types fuse, the dikaryotic mycelium is long-lasting. Nuclear fusion results in zygotes within basidia on the gills of the fruiting body shown. Zygomeiosis and production of basidiospores follow. Germination of a spore results in a haploid mycelium. **b.** Fairy ring. Mushrooms develop in a ring on the outer living fringes of a dikaryotic mycelium. The center has used up its nutrients and is no longer living. **c.** Fruiting bodies of *Boletus*. This mushroom is not gilled; instead it has basidia-lined tubes that open on the undersurface of the cap. **d.** Puffballs grow to be quite large. It is estimated that the mature one shown contains 7 trillion spores.

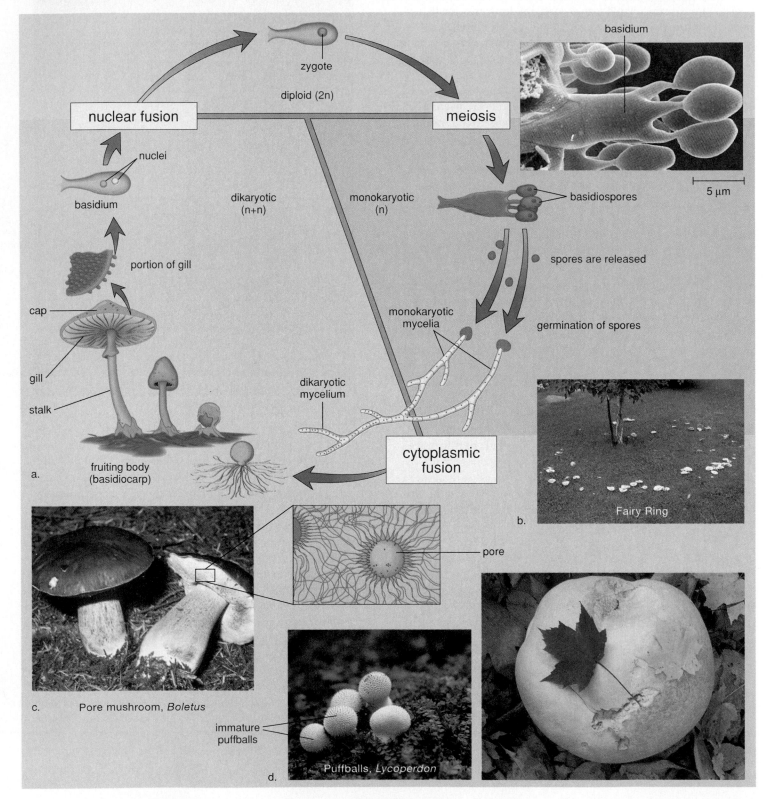

Club Fungi Have Basidiospores

Club fungi (division **Basidiomycota**, 16,000 species), which have septate hyphae, include the familiar mushrooms growing on lawns and the shelf or bracket fungi found on dead trees. Less well known are puffballs, bird's nest fungi, and stinkhorns. These structures are all fruiting bodies called basidiocarps. Basidiocarps contain the **basidia** [L. *basidi*, small pedestal], club-shaped structures which produce basidiospores and from which this phylum takes its name.

Although club fungi on occasion do produce conidiospores asexually, they usually reproduce sexually. When monokaryotic hyphae of two different mating types meet, they fuse and a dikaryotic (n + n) mycelium results (fig. 26.7). The dikaryotic mycelium continues its existence year after year, even hundreds of years on occasion. In mushrooms, the dikaryotic mycelium often radiates out and produces basidiocarps in an ever larger so-called fairy ring. Basidiocarps are composed of nothing but tightly packed hyphae whose walled-off ends become the club-shaped basidia. In the gilled mushrooms, the hyphae terminate in radiating lamellae, and in pore mushrooms and shelf fungi the hyphae terminate in tubes. In any case, the extensive surface area is lined by basidia where nuclear fusion, meiosis, and spore production occur. A basidium has four projections into which cytoplasm and a haploid nucleus enter as the basidiospore forms.

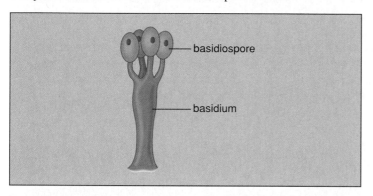

Basidiospores are often windblown; when they germinate, a new haploid mycelium forms.

In puffballs, spores are produced inside parchmentlike membranes, and the spores are released through a pore or when the membrane breaks down. In bird's nest fungi, falling raindrops provide the force that causes the nest's basidiospore-containing "eggs" to fly through the air and land on vegetation that may be eaten by an animal. If so, the spores pass unharmed through the digestive tract. Stinkhorns resemble a mushroom with a spongy stalk and a compact, slimy cap. The long stalk bears the elongated basidiocarp. Stinkhorns emit an incredibly disagreeable odor; flies are attracted by the odor, and when they linger to feed on a sweet jelly, the flies pick up spores which they later distribute.

> Club fungi usually reproduce sexually. The dikaryotic stage is prolonged and periodically produces fruiting bodies where spores are produced in basidia.

Figure 26.8
Rusts and smuts. **a.** Corn smut. **b.** Wheat rust.

a.   Corn smut, *Ustilago*

b.   Wheat rust, *Puccinia*

Rusts and Smuts Are Parasites

Rusts and *smuts* are club fungi that parasitize cereal crops such as corn, wheat, oats, and rye. They are of great economic importance because of the crop losses they cause every year. Rusts and smuts don't form basidiocarps, and their spores are small and numerous, resembling soot. Some smuts enter seeds and exist inside the plant, becoming visible only near maturity. Other smuts externally infect plants. In corn smut, the mycelium grows between the corn kernels and secretes substances that cause the development of tumors on the ears of corn (fig. 26.8*a*).

The life cycle of rusts, which may be particularly complex, often requires two different plant host species to complete the cycle. Black stem rust of wheat uses barberry bushes as an alternate host, and blister rust of white pine uses currant and gooseberry bushes. Campaigns to eradicate these bushes help keep these rusts in check. Wheat rust (fig. 26.8*b*) is also controlled by producing new and resistant strains of wheat. The process is continuous, because rust can mutate to cause infection once again.

Deadly Fungi

t is unwise for amateurs to collect mushrooms in the wild because certain mushroom species are poisonous. The red and yellow *Amanita muscaria* is especially dangerous. This species is also known as fly agaric because it was formerly used to kill flies (it was grown and then sprinkled with sugar to attract flies). Its toxins include muscarine and muscaridine, which produce symptoms similar to acute alcoholic intoxication. In one to six hours, the victim staggers, loses consciousness, and becomes delirious, sometimes suffering from hallucinations, manic conditions, and stupor. Luckily it also causes vomiting, which rids the system of the poison, so death occurs in less than 1% of cases. Death Angel (*Amanita phalloides*, fig. 26A) causes 90% of the fatalities attributed to mushroom poisoning. When this mushroom is eaten, symptoms don't begin until ten to twelve hours later. Abdominal pain, vomiting, delirium, and hallucinations are not the real problem; rather, a poison interferes with RNA (ribonucleic acid) transcription by inhibiting RNA polymerase, and the victim dies from liver and kidney damage.

Some hallucinogenic mushrooms are used in religious ceremonies, particularly among Mexican Indians. *Psilocybe mexicana* contains a chemical called psilocybin that is a structural analogue of LSD and mescaline. It produces a dreamlike state in which visions of colorful patterns and objects seem to fill up space and dance past in endless succession. Other senses are also sharpened to produce a feeling of intense reality.

The only reliable way to tell a nonpoisonous mushroom from a poisonous one is to be able to correctly identify the species. Poisonous mushrooms cannot be identified with simple tests, such as whether they peel easily, have a bad odor, or blacken a silver coin during cooking.

In addition to club fungi, some sac fungi also contain chemicals that can be dangerous to people. *Claviceps purpurea*, the ergot fungus, infects rye and replaces the grain with ergot—hard, purple-black bodies consisting of tightly cemented hyphae (fig. 26B). When ground with the rye and made into bread, the fungus releases toxic alkaloids that cause the disease ergotism. In humans, vomiting, feel-

ings of intense heat or cold, muscle pain, a yellow face, and hand and feet lesions are accompanied by hysteria and hallucinations. We now know that ergot contains lysergic acid, from which LSD is easily synthesized. From recorded symptoms, historians believe that those who accused their neighbors of witchcraft in Salem, Massachusetts, in the seventeenth century could very well have been suffering from ergotism. As recently as 1951 an epidemic of ergotism occurred in Pont-Saint-Esprit, France. Over 150 persons became hysterical and four died.

Because the alkaloids that cause ergotism stimulate smooth muscle and selectively block the sympathetic nervous system, they can be used in medicine to cause uterine contractions and to treat certain circulatory disorders, including migraine headaches. Although the ergot fungus can be cultured in petri dishes, no one has succeeded in inducing it to form ergot in the laboratory. So far, the only way to obtain ergot, even for medical purposes, is to collect it in an infected field of rye.

Figure 26A
Poisonous mushrooms, *Amanita phalloides*.

Figure 26B
Ergot infection of rye, caused by *Claviceps purpurea*.

Figure 26.9

Conidiospores. Sac fungi and imperfect fungi reproduce asexually by producing spores called conidiospores at the ends of certain hyphae. The organism shown here is *Penicillium,* an imperfect fungus.

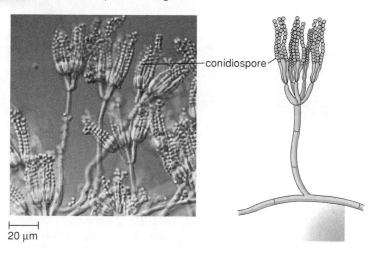

conidiospore

20 µm

Imperfect Fungi Reproduce Asexually Only

The **imperfect fungi** (**division Deuteromycota,** 25,000 species) always reproduce asexually by forming conidiospores (fig. 26.9). These fungi are "imperfect" in the sense that no sexual stage has yet been observed and may not exist. Without knowing the sexual stage, it is often difficult to classify a fungus as belonging to one of the other phyla. Usually, cellular morphology and biochemistry indicate these fungi are sac fungi that have lost the ability to reproduce sexually. Even so, genetic recombination does occur; hyphae fuse, and crossing-over between chromosomes results in haploid nuclei with varied genetic content.

Several imperfect fungi are serviceable to humans. Some species of the mold *Penicillium* are sources of the antibiotic penicillin, while other species give the characteristic flavor and aroma to cheeses such as Roquefort and Camembert. The bluish streaks in blue cheese are patches of conidiospores. The drug cyclosporine, which is administered to suppress the immune system following an organ transplant operation, is derived from an imperfect fungus found in soil. Another mold, *Aspergillus,* as well as other fungi, are used to produce soy sauce by fermentation of soybeans. In this country *Aspergillus* is used to produce citric and gallic acids, which serve as additives during the manufacture of different products—from inks to chewing gum.

Unfortunately, some imperfect fungi cause disease in humans. Certain dust-borne spores can cause infections of the respiratory tract, while athlete's foot and ringworm are spread by direct contact. *Candida albicans* is a yeastlike organism that causes infections of the vagina, especially in women on the birth-control pill. This organism also causes thrush, an inflammation of the mouth and throat.

> The imperfect fungi cannot be classified into one of the other phyla because their mode of sexual reproduction is unknown.

FUNGI FORM SYMBIOTIC RELATIONSHIPS

We have already mentioned several instances in which fungi are parasites of plants and animals. Two other associations are of interest.

Lichens Are Soil Formers

Lichens are an association between a fungus and a cyanobacterium or a green alga. The body of a lichen has three layers: the fungus forms a thin, tough upper layer and a loosely packed lower layer that shield the photosynthetic cells in the middle layer (fig. 26.10). Specialized fungal hyphae, which penetrate or envelop the photosynthetic cells, transfer nutrients directly to the rest of the fungus. Lichens can reproduce asexually by releasing fragments that contain hyphae and an algal cell.

Figure 26.10

Lichen morphology. **a.** A section of a lichen shows the placement of the algal cells and the fungal hyphae, which encircle and penetrate the algal cells. **b.** Crustose lichens are compact. **c.** Foliose lichens are leaflike. **d.** Fruticose lichens are shrublike.

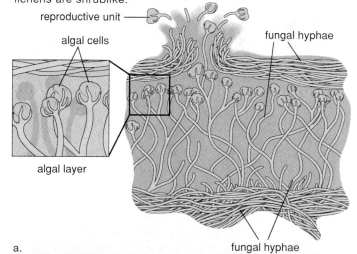

reproductive unit

algal cells

fungal hyphae

algal layer

a.

fungal hyphae

b.   Mixture of crustose lichens

c. fruticose lichen, *Cladonia*   d.   Foliose lichen, *Xanthoparmelia*

In the past, lichens were assumed to be mutualistic relationships in which the fungus received nutrients from the algal cells, and the algal cells were protected from desiccation by the fungus. Actually, lichens might involve a controlled form of parasitism of the algal cells by the fungus. Algae may not benefit at all from these associations. This is supported by experiments in which the fungal and algal components are removed and grown separately. The algae grow faster when they are alone rather than when they are part of a lichen. On the other hand, it is difficult to cultivate the fungus, which does not naturally grow alone. The different lichen species are, therefore, identified according to the fungal partner.

Three types of lichens are recognized. Compact crustose lichens are often seen on bare rocks or on tree bark; foliose lichens are leaflike; and fruticose lichens are shrublike (fig. 26.10). Lichens are efficient at acquiring nutrients, and therefore they can survive in areas of low moisture and low temperature as well as areas with poor or no soil. They produce and improve the soil, thus making it suitable for plants to invade the area. Unfortunately, lichens also take up pollutants and cannot survive where the air is polluted. Therefore, their presence is an indication that the air is healthy for humans to breathe.

> Lichens, an association between fungal hyphae and algal cells, can live in areas of extreme conditions and are important soil formers.

Mycorrhizae Are "Fungus Roots"

Mycorrhizae [Gk. *myc,* fungus, and *rhiz,* root] are mutualistic relationships between soil fungi and the roots of most plants (fig. 26.11). Plants whose roots are infected with mycorrhizae grow more successfully in poor soils—particularly soils deficient in phosphates—than do plants without mycorrhizae. The fungal partner may enter the cortex of roots but does not enter plant cells. Ectomycorrhizae form a mantle that is exterior to the root, and they grow between cell walls. Endomycorrhizae can penetrate cell walls. In any case, the presence of the fungus gives the plant a greater absorptive surface for the intake of minerals. The

Figure 26.11
Plant growth experiment. Soybean plant, *Glycine,* without mycorrhizae grows poorly compared to two other plants infected with different strains of mycorrhizae.

fungus also benefits from the association by receiving carbohydrates from the plant.

It is of interest to know that the truffle, a gourmet delight whose ascocarp is somewhat prunelike in appearance, is a mycorrhizal fungus living in association with oak and beech tree roots. It used to be that the French used pigs to sniff out and dig up truffles, but now they have succeeded in cultivating truffles by inoculating the roots of seedlings with the proper mycelium.

Even the earliest fossil plants have mycorrhizae associated with them. It would appear, then, that mycorrhizae helped plants adapt to and flourish on land.

> Mycorrhizae (fungus roots), a mutualistic association between a fungus and plant roots, help plants acquire mineral nutrients.

Summary

1. Fungi are multicellular eukaryotes which are heterotrophic by absorption. After external digestion, they absorb the resulting nutrient molecules.

2. Most fungi act as saprotrophic decomposers that aid the cycling of chemicals in ecosystems. Some fungi are parasitic, especially on plants, and others are symbiotic with plant roots and algae.

3. The body of a fungus is composed of thin filaments called hyphae, which collectively are termed a mycelium. The cell wall contains chitin, and the energy reserve is glycogen. Fungi do not have flagella at any stage in their life cycle.

4. Nonseptate hyphae have no cross walls; septate hyphae have cross walls, but there are pores that allow the cytoplasm and even organelles to pass through.

5. Fungi produce nonmotile and often windblown spores during both asexual and sexual reproduction. During sexual reproduction hyphae tips fuse so that dikaryotic (n + n) hyphae sometimes result depending on the type of fungus. Following nuclear fusion, zygotic meiosis occurs during the production of the sexual spores.

6. There are four divisions of fungi: division Zygomycota (zygospore fungi), division Ascomycota (sac fungi), division Basidiomycota (club fungi), and division Deuteromycota (imperfect fungi).

7. The evolutionary history of fungi is not known; the different groups may have evolved separately from protoctist ancestors. Red algae are sometimes mentioned as a possible ancestor. Slime molds are not composed of hyphae, and they are heterotrophic by absorption. Water molds absorb nutrients, have flagellated zoospores, and during sexual reproduction they have gametic meiosis.

8. The zygospore fungi are nonseptate, and during sexual reproduction they have a dormant stage consisting of a thick-walled zygospore. When the zygospore germinates, sporangia produce windblown spores. Asexual reproduction occurs when nutrients are plentiful and again sporangia produce spores.

9. The sac fungi are septate, and during sexual reproduction saclike cells called asci produce spores. Asci are located in fruiting bodies called ascocarps. Asexual reproduction, which is dependent on the production of conidiospores, is more common.

10. Yeasts are unicellular sac fungi that usually reproduce by budding. Yeast fermentation is important in the production of wine and beer. Carbon dioxide given off by yeast causes bread to rise.

11. The club fungi are septate, and during sexual reproduction club-shaped structures called basidia produce spores. Basidia are located in fruiting bodies called basidiocarps. Club fungi have a prolonged dikaryotic stage, and asexual reproduction by conidiospores is rare. A dikaryotic mycelium periodically produces fruiting bodies.

12. Rusts and smuts are club fungi that are parasitic on cereal crops. They have a life cycle that may be complicated and that may involve more than one host; control has centered on eradicating the alternate hosts.

13. The imperfect fungi always reproduce asexually by conidiospores; they have not been observed to reproduce sexually. Therefore, they cannot be placed in one of the other divisions.

Several imperfect fungi are of interest; for example, *Penicillium* is the source of penicillin, and *Candida* causes yeast infections.

14. Lichens are an association between a fungus and a cyanobacterium or a green alga. Traditionally, this association was considered to be mutualistic, but experimentation suggests a controlled parasitism by the fungus on the alga. Lichens may live in extreme environments and on bare rocks; they are soil formers.

15. Mycorrhizae refers to an association between a fungus and the roots of a plant. The fungus helps the plant absorb more minerals and the plant passes on carbohydrates to the fungus.

Writing Across the Curriculum

In order to practice writing skills, students should write out the answers to any or all of the study questions and the critical thinking questions. The study questions are sequenced in the same order as the text. Answers to the objective questions, and suggested answers to the critical thinking questions, are in appendix D.

Study Questions

1. Which characteristics best define a fungus? Describe the body of fungi and how they reproduce.   430–31

2. On what basis are fungi classified?   432

3. Explain the term zygospore fungi. How does black bread mold reproduce asexually? sexually?   432–33

4. Explain the term sac fungi. How do sac fungi reproduce asexually? Describe the structure of an ascocarp.   435

5. Describe the structure of yeasts and explain how they reproduce. How are yeasts useful to humans?   435

6. Explain the term club fungi. Draw and explain a diagram of the life cycle of a typical mushroom.   436–37

7. What is the economic importance of rusts and smuts? How can their numbers be controlled?   437

8. Explain the term imperfect fungi. Give examples of imperfect fungi that serve humans and examples of those that cause disease.   439

9. Describe the structure of a lichen and name the three different types. What is the nature of this fungal association?   439–40

10. Describe the association known as mycorrhizae and explain how each partner benefits.   440

Objective Questions

1. A decomposer is most likely to utilize which mode of nutrition?
   a. parasitic
   b. saprotrophic
   c. ingestion
   d. Both a and b are correct.

2. Which feature is best associated with hyphae?
   a. strong impermeable walls
   b. rapid growth
   c. large surface area
   d. Both b and c are correct.

3. A spore
   a. contains an embryonic organism.
   b. germinates directly into an organism.
   c. is always windblown.
   d. Both b and c are correct.

4. The taxonomy of fungi is based on
   a. sexual reproductive structures.
   b. shape of the sporocarp.
   c. mode of nutrition.
   d. type of cell wall.

5. In the life cycle of black bread mold, the zygospore
   a. undergoes meiosis and produces zoospores.
   b. produces spores as a part of asexual reproduction.
   c. is a thick-walled dormant stage.
   d. is equivalent to asci and basidia.

6. In an ascocarp
   a. there are fertile and sterile hyphae.
   b. hyphae fuse, forming the dikaryotic stage.
   c. a sperm fertilizes an egg.
   d. hyphae do not have chitinous walls.

7. In which fungus is the dikaryotic stage longer lasting?

   a. zygospore fungi

   b. imperfect fungi

   c. sac fungi

   d. club fungi

8. Conidiospores are formed

   a. by sporangia.

   b. during sexual reproduction.

   c. by sac, club, and imperfect fungi only.

   d. when nutrients are in short supply.

9. Imperfect fungi are called imperfect because

   a. they have no zygospore.

   b. they cause diseases.

   c. they form conidiospores.

   d. sexual reproduction has not been observed.

10. Lichens

   a. cannot reproduce.

   b. need a nitrogen source to live.

   c. are parasitic on trees.

   d. are able to live in extreme environments.

11. Label this diagram of the life cycle of a mushroom.

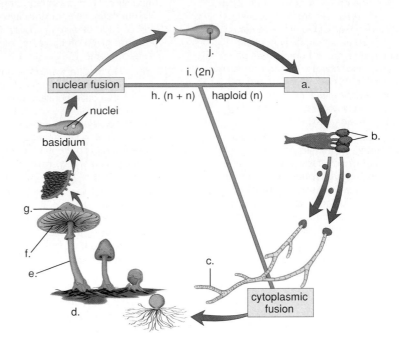

Concepts and Critical Thinking

1. *Organisms are adapted to a way of life.*
How are the structure and reproductive strategy of fungi related to their way of life?

2. *Living things are diverse.*
All fungi have the same mode of nutrition; in what ways are they diverse?

3. *Classification systems (do not always reflect evolutionary relationships).*
What basic difficulties do you have when trying to draw a phylogenetic tree for fungi?

Selected Key Terms

ascus (pl., asci) A fingerlike sac in which nuclear fusion, meiosis, and ascospore formation occur during sexual reproduction of the sac fungi. [Gk. *asc,* bag]   435

basidium (pl., basidia) (buh-SID-ee-um) A club-like structure in which nuclear fusion, meiosis and basidiospore production occur during sexual reproduction of club fungi. [L. *basidi,* small pedestal]   437

conidiospore (kuh-NID-ee-uh-spohr) Spore produced by sac and club fungi during asexual reproduction   435

fruiting body A spore-producing and spore-disseminating structure found in sac and club fungi.   435

fungus (pl., fungi) A saprotrophic decomposer; the body is made up of filaments called hyphae that form a mass called a mycelium.   430

hypha (pl., hyphae) A filament of the vegetative body of a fungus. [Gk. *hyph,* web]   431

lichen (LY-kun) A symbiotic relationship between certain fungi and algae, which has long been thought to be mutualistic, in which the fungi provide inorganic food and the algae provide organic food.   439

mycelium (my-SEE-lee-um) A tangled mass of hyphal filaments composing the vegetative body of a fungus. [Gk. *myc,* fungus, and *ium,* small]   431

mycorrhiza (my-kuh-RY-zuh) A symbiotic relationship between fungal hyphae and roots of vascular plants. The fungus allows the plant to absorb more mineral ions and obtains carbohydrates from the plant. [Gk. *myc,* fungus, and *rhiz,* root]   440

sporangium (pl., sporangia) (spuh-RAN-jee-um) A capsule that produces sporangiospores. [Gk. *spor,* seed, *ang,* vessel, and *ium,* small]   432

zygospore (ZY-guh-spohr) A thick-walled, resting cell formed during sexual reproduction of zygospore fungi.   432

KINGDOM PLANTAE

Learning Objectives

- List the characteristics shared by all plants. 444

Bryophytes Are Diverse
- Describe the bryophytes and give the most significant stages of the moss life cycle. 445–47
- Discuss the human uses and the adaptations of bryophytes. 448

Vascular Plants Include Seedless and Seed Plants
- Describe the general characteristics of vascular plants and contrast the life cycle of seedless vascular plants with seed vascular plants. 448

Ferns and Allies Are the Seedless Vascular Plants
- Describe the rhyniophytes and list the seedless vascular plants alive today. 450–52
- Discuss the human uses and the adaptations of ferns. 452
- Describe the life cycle of the fern and discuss its adaptation to a terrestrial environment. 453

Gymnosperms Have Naked Seeds
- Describe the life cycle of seed plants, and tell how their life cycle is adapted to a terrestrial environment. 454
- List and describe the four divisions of gymnosperms, and describe the life cycle of the pine tree. 454–57
- Discuss the human uses and the adaptations of gymnosperms. 457

Angiosperms Have Covered Seeds
- Contrast dicots with monocots, and describe the life cycle of flowering plants. 458
- Compare the various plant life cycles, and explain why angiosperms are more diverse and widespread than the other plant groups. 459
- Discuss the human uses and the adaptations of flowering plants. 461

Plants dominate the terrestrial environment and provide services for all living things.

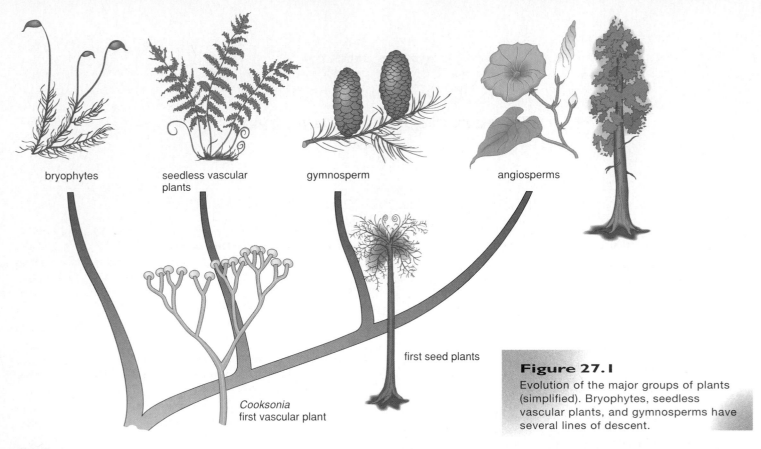

bryophytes

seedless vascular plants

gymnosperm

angiosperms

first seed plants

Cooksonia
first vascular plant

Figure 27.1

Evolution of the major groups of plants (simplified). Bryophytes, seedless vascular plants, and gymnosperms have several lines of descent.

Plants (**Kingdom Plantae**) are multicellular eukaryotes with well-developed tissues (fig. 27.1). Plants, which are autotrophic by photosynthesis, live in a wide variety of terrestrial environments, from lush forest to dry desert or frozen tundra. A land existence offers some advantages to plants. One advantage is the great availability of light for photosynthesis—water, even if clear, filters light. Also, carbon dioxide and oxygen are present in higher concentrations and diffuse more readily in air than in water.

The land environment, however, requires adaptations to deal with the constant threat of desiccation (drying out). Most plants can obtain water from the substratum by means of roots. And to conserve water, leaves and stems are, at the very least, covered by a waxy cuticle that is impervious to water. The surface of leaves is interrupted by pores which can open and close to regulate gas exchange and water loss. Some plants have a vascular system that transports water up to and nutrients down from the leaves. In conjunction with this system, trees have a strong internal skeleton that opposes the force of gravity and lifts the leaves toward the sun. All plants protect the embryo from desiccation and some protect their entire gametophyte generations. In these plants, sperm-containing pollen grains are transported by wind or motile animal to the egg, and the subsequent embryo becomes a seed.

Plants are adapted to living on land. In general, they tend to have features that allow them to ... and reproduce on land.

CLASSIFICATION

KINGDOM PLANTAE

Multicellular; primarily terrestrial eukaryotes with well-developed tissues; autotrophic by photosynthesis; alternation of generations life cycle. Like green algae, plants contain chlorophylls *a* and *b* and carotenoids; store starch in chloroplasts; cell wall contains cellulose.

Bryophytes
Division Hepatophyta: liverworts
Division Bryophyta: mosses
Division Anthocerotophyta: hornworts

Seedless Vascular Plants
Division Psilotophyta: whisk ferns
Division Lycopodophyta: club mosses
Division Equisetophyta: horsetails
Division Pteridophyta: ferns

Gymnosperms
Division Pinophyta: conifers
Division Cycadophyta: cycads
Division Ginkgophyta: maidenhair tree
Division Gnetophyta: gnetophytes

Angiosperms
Division Magnoliophyta: flowering plants
  Class Magnoliopsida: dicots
  Class Liliopsida: monocots

Plants are believed to be closely related to green algae because these two groups have several characteristics in common. Both utilize chlorophylls *a* and *b* as well as carotenoid pigments during photosynthesis. The primary food reserve is starch, which is stored inside the chloroplast. Their cell walls contain cellulose, and both types of organisms form a cell plate during cell division.

Why aren't multicellular green algae like *Ulva* considered plants? Plants, but not green algae, have multicellular gametangia and sporangia in which reproductive cells are protected by several layers of nonreproductive cells. Later, the zygote and then the embryo are protected within the body of the plant. In algae fertilization is external and the embryo is not protected from the environment.

Plants and some algae have a two-generation life cycle called alternation of generations that involves sporic meiosis:

1. The **sporophyte** [Gk. *spor*, seed, and *phyt*, plant], the diploid generation, produces haploid spores by meiosis. Spores develop into a haploid generation.
2. The **gametophyte** [Gk. *gamet*, wife or husband, and *phyt*, plant] the haploid generation, produces gametes that unite to form a diploid zygote.

The two generations are dissimilar and one is dominant over the other. The dominant generation is larger and exists for a longer period of time. In addition, plants are oogamous; the gametes are eggs and sperm. The characteristics of plants are listed in table 27.1.

> Plants, unlike green algae, protect the embryo from drying out. During an alternation of generations life cycle, one generation is dominant over the other.

BRYOPHYTES ARE DIVERSE

Plants are currently divided into two main groups: bryophytes and vascular plants. The **bryophytes** [Gk. *bryo*, moss, and *phyt*, plant] consist of three groups: hornworts (division Anthocerotophyta), liverworts (division Hepatophyta), and mosses (division Bryophyta). Bryophytes lack vascular plants' specialized means of transporting water and organic nutrients. Although they often have a "leafy" appearance, these plants do not have true roots, stems, and leaves—which by definition must contain true vascular tissue. Therefore, bryophytes are said to have rootlike, stemlike, and leaflike structures.

The gametophyte is the dominant generation in bryophytes—it is the generation we recognize as the plant. Flagellated sperm swim to the vicinity of the egg in a continuous film of water. The sporophyte, when present, is attached to and derives its nourishment from the photosynthetic gametophyte.

Bryophytes are quite small; the largest is no more than 20 cm tall. This characteristic is linked to the lack of an efficient means to transport water to any height. And because sexual reproduction involves flagellated sperm, bryophytes are usually found in moist habitats. Nevertheless, mosses compete well in harsh environments because the gametophyte can reproduce asexually, allowing mosses to spread into stressful and even dry habitats. If need be mosses can dry up and later, when water is available, begin to photosynthesize again.

It is not known how closely related the various bryophytes are. The current thinking is that these plants have individual lines of descent, so this text classifies the bryophytes into three separate divisions. Some mosses have a rudimentary form of vascular tissue, and therefore mosses are believed to be more closely related to vascular plants than are liverworts and hornworts. We will be discussing the liverworts and mosses, the more familiar plants.

> In bryophytes, the dominant gametophyte is water dependent because it lacks vascular tissue and produces flagellated sperm.

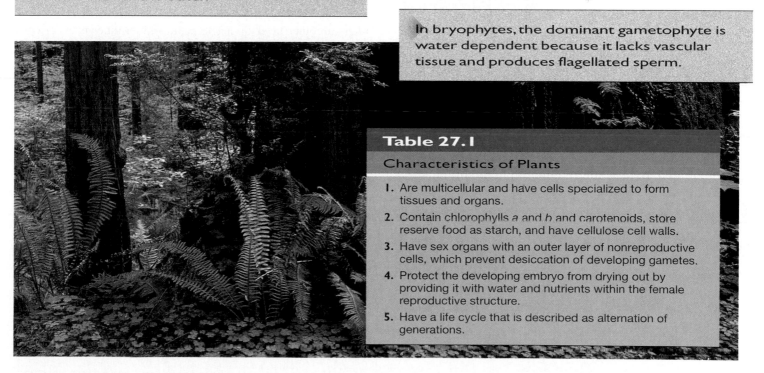

Table 27.1

Characteristics of Plants

1. Are multicellular and have cells specialized to form tissues and organs.
2. Contain chlorophylls *a* and *b* and carotenoids, store reserve food as starch, and have cellulose cell walls.
3. Have sex organs with an outer layer of nonreproductive cells, which prevent desiccation of developing gametes.
4. Protect the developing embryo from drying out by providing it with water and nutrients within the female reproductive structure.
5. Have a life cycle that is described as alternation of generations.

Liverworts Are Bryophytes

Liverworts (division Hepatophyta, 10,000 species) that have a flat, lobed thallus (body) are more familiar than the more numerous leafy liverworts. The name "liverwort" arose in the ninth century when it seemed to some that the plant had lobes like the liver. They thought the plant might therefore be beneficial in treating liver ailments, a hypothesis that has never been supported.

Marchantia is most often used as an example of this group of plants (fig. 27.2). Each lobe of the thallus is perhaps a centimeter or so in length; the upper surface is smooth and the lower surface bears numerous **rhizoids** [Gk. *rhiz,* root, and *oid,* like] (rootlike hairs) projecting into the soil. *Marchantia* reproduces both asexually and sexually. Gemmae cups on the upper surface of the thallus contain *gemmae,* groups of cells that detach from the thallus and can start a new plant. Sexual reproduction depends on disk-headed stalks that bear **antheridia** [Gk. *anth,* flower, and *idia,* small], where flagellated sperm are produced and umbrella-headed stalks that bear **archegonia** [Gk. *archeg,* first], where eggs are produced. Following fertilization a tiny sporophyte no more than a few millimeters in length is composed of a foot, a short stalk, and a capsule. Windblown spores are produced within the capsule.

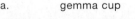

gemma

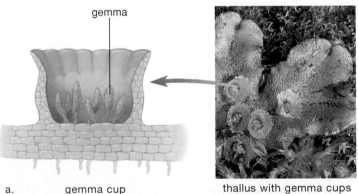

a.   gemma cup   thallus with gemma cups

b.   structures that bear   structures that bear
      antheridia   archegonia

Mosses Are Bryophytes

Mosses (division Bryophyta, 12,000 species) can be found from the Arctic through the tropics to parts of the Antarctic. Although most prefer damp, shaded locations in the temperate zone, some survive in deserts and others inhabit bogs and streams. In forests, they frequently form a mat that covers the ground and rotting logs. Mosses can store large quantities of water in their cells, but if a dry spell continues for long, they become dormant. The whole plant shrivels, turns brown, and looks completely dead. As soon as it rains, however, the plant becomes green and resumes metabolic activity.

Some mosses are adapted to unusual conditions. The so-called copper mosses live only in the vicinity of copper and can serve as an indicator plant for copper deposits. Luminous moss, which glows with a golden green light, is found in caves, under the roots of trees, and other dimly lit places. Its cells, which are shaped like tiny lenses, focus what little light there is on the grana of chloroplasts.

The common name of several plants implies they are mosses when they are not. Irish moss is an edible alga that grows in leathery tufts along northern seacoasts. Reindeer moss, a lichen, is the dietary mainstay of reindeer and caribou in northern lands. Club mosses, discussed later in this chapter, are vascular plants; and Spanish moss, which hangs in grayish clusters from trees in the southeastern United States, is a flowering plant of the pineapple family.

Most mosses can reproduce asexually by fragmentation. Just about any part of the plant is able to grow and eventually produce leafy shoots. Figures 27.3 and 27B (see page 459) describe the life cycle of a typical temperate-zone moss. The gametophyte of mosses has two stages. First, there is the algalike *protonema,* a branching filament of cells. After about three days of favorable growing conditions, upright leafy shoots are seen at intervals along the protonema. Rhizoids anchor the shoots, which bear antheridia and archegonia. An antheridium consists of a short stalk, an outer layer of sterile cells, and an inner mass of cells that become the flagellated sperm. An archegonium, which looks like a vase with a long neck, has a single egg located at the base.

The dependent sporophyte consists of a *foot,* which grows down into the gametophyte tissue, a *stalk,* and an upper *capsule,* or *sporangium,* where spores are produced. At first the sporophyte is green and photosynthetic; at maturity it is brown and nonphotosynthetic.

Figure 27.2

Liverwort, *Marchantia* **a.** The thallus can reproduce asexually by forming gemmae, cells that detach from the thallus and are present in gemmae cups. **b.** During sexual reproduction, the antheridia are present in disk-shaped structures and the archegonia are present in umbrella-shaped structures.

Figure 27.3

Moss Life Cycle.

The gametophyte is dominant in bryophytes, such as mosses. ① The leafy shoots bear separate male and female gametangia: the antheridia and archegonia. ② Flagellated sperm are produced in antheridia, and these swim in external water to an archegonium that contains a single egg. ③ When the egg is fertilized, the developing embryo is retained within the archegonium. In some species of mosses, a hoodlike covering (calyptra) derived from the archegonium is carried upward by the growing sporophyte. ④ The mature sporophyte growing atop a gametophyte shoot consists of a foot that grows down into the gametophyte tissue, a stalk, and an upper capsule, or sporangium, where meiosis occurs and spores are produced. ⑤ When the covering and capsule lid (operculum) fall off, the spores are mature and are ready to escape. The release of spores is controlled by one or two rings of "teeth" that project inward from the margin of the capsule. The teeth close the opening when the weather is wet but curl up and free the spores when the weather is dry. ⑥ Spores are released at times when they are most likely to be dispersed by air currents. ⑦ When a spore lands on an appropriate site, it germinates into a protonema, the first stage of the gametophyte.

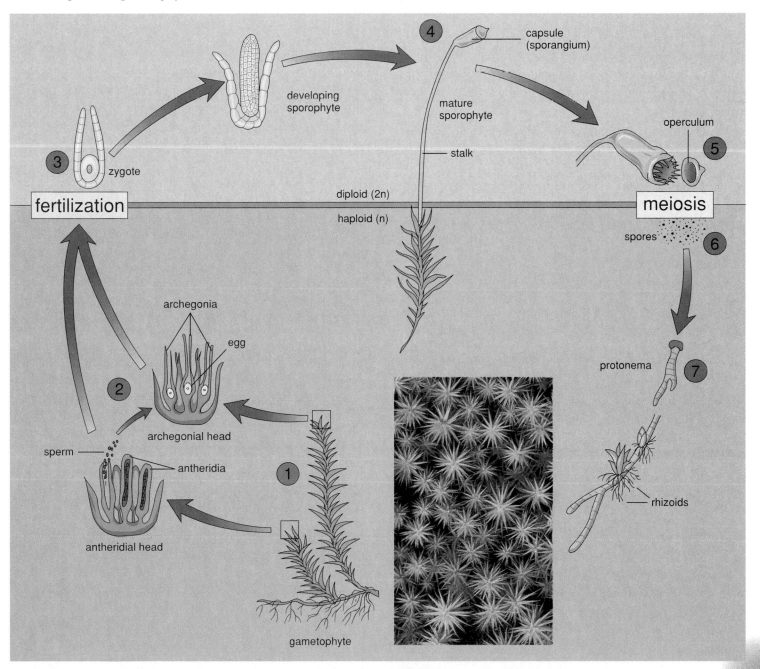

Uses of Bryophytes

Sphagnum, also called bog or peat moss, has commercial importance. This moss has special nonliving cells that can absorb moisture, which is why peat moss is often used in gardening to improve the water-holding capacity of the soil. In some areas where the ground is wet and acidic, such as bogs, dead mosses, especially sphagnum, accumulate and do not decay. This accumulated moss, called peat, can be used as fuel.

Adaptation of Bryophytes

Bryophytes are small and simple plants generally found in moist habitats for two reasons: they lack vascular tissue and their sexual reproduction involves flagellated sperm. Bryophytes do not have the complexity of, nor are they found in the variety of habitats occupied by, the vascular plants. Nevertheless, mosses are better than flowering plants at living on stone walls and on fences and even in the shady cracks of hot exposed rocks. They slowly convert rocks to soil that can be used for the growth of other organisms. For these particular microhabitats, there seems to be a selective advantage to being small and simple (fig. 27.4).

Bryophytes (liverworts and mosses) lack specialized vascular tissue and have a dominant gametophyte. Fertilization requires an outside source of moisture, and they are often found in moist locations.

Figure 27.4

Moss growing on rocks. The mosses that are adapted to growing on rocks contribute to the formation of soil so that other plants can enter the area.

VASCULAR PLANTS INCLUDE SEEDLESS AND SEED PLANTS

Vascular plants [L. *vascul,* little vessel] include ferns and their allies, gymnosperms, and angiosperms. Vascular tissue in these plants consists of **xylem** [Gk. *xyl,* wood, and L. *em,* in], which conducts water and minerals up from the soil, and **phloem** [Gk. *phloe,* tree bark, and L. *em,* in], which transports organic nutrients from one part of the plant to another. The vascular plants have true roots, stems, and leaves. The roots absorb water from the soil and the stem conducts water to the leaves. Xylem, with its strong-walled cells, supports the body of the plant against the pull of gravity. The leaves are fully covered by a waxy cuticle except where it is interrupted by **stomates,** little pores whose size can be regulated to control water loss.

The sporophyte generation is dominant in vascular plants. This is the generation that has vascular tissue and the other features just discussed. Another advantage of having a dominant sporophyte relates to its being diploid. If a faulty gene is present, it can be masked by a functional gene. Then, too, the greater the amount of genetic material, the greater the possibility of mutations that will lead to increased variety and complexity. Indeed, the vascular plants are complex, extremely varied, and widely distributed.

The seedless vascular plants (ferns and their allies) disperse the species by producing windblown spores. When the spores germinate, a relatively large gametophyte is independent of the sporophyte for its nutrition. In these plants flagellated sperm are released by antheridia and swim in a film of external water to the archegonia, where fertilization occurs. Because the water-dependent gametophyte is independent of the sporophyte, these plants cannot wholly benefit from the adaptations of the sporophyte to a terrestrial environment. As discussed in the reading on the following page, the seedless vascular plants formed the great swamp forest of the Carboniferous period.

In seed plants microgametophytes (male) and megagametophytes (female) are dependent on the sporophyte, which is fully adapted to a dry environment. The mature microgametophyte is the pollen grain. The megagametophye and subsequent embryo, which is retained within the body of the sporophyte, becomes a seed. The life cycle of seed plants is discussed further on pages 454, 460.

The seedless vascular plants are dispersed by windblown spores; those that produce seeds are dispersed by seeds.

The First Forests

ur industrial society runs on fossil fuels such as coal. The term "fossil fuel" might seem odd at first until one realizes that it refers to the remains of organic material from ancient times. During the Carboniferous period more than 300 million years ago, a great swamp forest (fig. 27A) encompassed what is now the Appalachian mountains, northern Europe, and the Ukraine. The weather was warm and humid and the trees grew very tall. These are not the trees we know today; instead they are related to today's seedless vascular plants: the club mosses, horsetails, and ferns! Club mosses today might stand as high as 30 cm; their ancient relatives were 30.5 meters

(over 100 feet) tall and 1 meter wide. The spore-bearing cones were up to 30 cm long and some had leaves more than 1 meter long. Horsetails too—at 15 meters tall—were giants compared to today's specimens. The tree ferns were also taller than today's tree ferns found in the tropics, and there were two other types of trees: seed ferns and ancient gymnosperms. "Seed fern" is a misnomer because it has been shown that these plants, which only resemble ferns, were actually a type of gymnosperm.

The amount of biomass was enormous and occasionally the swampy water rose and the trees fell. Trees under water do not decompose well, and their partially decayed remains became covered by sediment that

sometimes changed to sedimentary rock. Sedimentary rock applied pressure and the organic material then became coal, a fossil fuel. This process continued for millions of years, resulting in immense deposits of coal. Geological upheavals raised the deposits to the level they are today, where they can be mined.

With a change of climate, the trees of the Carboniferous period became extinct and only their herbaceous relatives survived to our time. Without these ancient forests, our life today would be far different than it is because they helped bring about our industrialized society.

Figure 27A
Swamp forest of Carboniferous period.

Table 27.2

The Geological Time Scale: Some Major Evolutionary Events of Plants

Era	Period	MYA*	Major Biological Events—Plants
Cenozoic	Neogene	2	Number of herbaceous plants increases
Cenozoic	Paleogene		Land dominated by angiosperms **Age of angiosperms**
		66	
Mesozoic	Cretaceous	144	Angiosperms spread
Mesozoic	Jurassic		First angiosperms appear **Age of gymnosperms**
		208	
Mesozoic	Triassic		Land dominated by gymnosperms and ferns
		245	
Paleozoic	Permian	286	Land covered by forests of seedless vascular plants
Paleozoic	Carboniferous		Age of great coal-forming forests, including club mosses, horsetails, and ferns
		360	
Paleozoic	Devonian		Expansion of seedless vascular plants on land **Swamp Forest**
		408	
Paleozoic	Silurian		Seedless vascular plants appear on land
		438	
Paleozoic	Ordovician		First plant fossils
		505	
Paleozoic	Cambrian	570	Unicellular marine algae abundant **Age of algae**

* MYA = millions of years ago

FERNS AND ALLIES ARE THE SEEDLESS VASCULAR PLANTS

Because the seedless vascular plants are not closely related, each type is placed in its own division. The seedless vascular plants include whisk ferns (division Psilotophyta), club mosses (division Lycopodophyta), horsetails (division Equisetophyta), and ferns (division Pteridophyta).

Table 27.2 shows the evolutionary history of plants. Among the first vascular plants were the rhyniophytes, which were dominant from the mid-Silurian period until the mid-Devonian period. *Cooksonia* may have been the very first vascular plant, but *Rhynia,* which is also a rhyniophyte, is better known. In *Rhynia,* the erect stems fork repeatedly (are dichotomous). They are attached to a *rhizome,* a horizontal, underground stem that bears rhizoids below. The stem does have vascular tissue, but the plant has no true roots or leaves. Sporangia are at the ends of some of the branches. Ferns and their allies are believed to trace their ancestry back to the rhyniophytes or closely related forms.

Psilotophytes Are Whisk Ferns

The **psilotophytes (division Psilotophyta),** are represented by *Psilotum,* a plant that closely resembles *Rhynia* (fig. 27.5). Whisk ferns, named for their resemblance to whisk brooms, are found in Arizona, Texas, Louisiana, and Florida, as well as Hawaii and Puerto Rico. The whisk ferns have *no leaves or roots.* A branched rhizome has rhizoids and a mycorrhizal fungus helps gather nutrients. Aerial stems with tiny scales fork repeatedly and carry on photosynthesis. Sporangia are located at the ends of short branches. The independent gametophyte, which is found underground and is penetrated by a mycorrhizal fungus, produces flagellated sperm.

Figure 27.5

Whisk fern, *Psilotum.* Whisk ferns have no roots or leaves—the branches carry on photosynthesis. The sporangia are yellow.

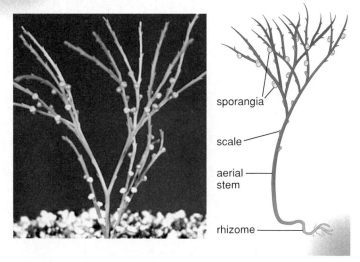

sporangia

scale

aerial stem

rhizome

Figure 27.6

Club moss, *Lycopodium*. Green photosynthetic stems are covered by scalelike leaves, and sporangia are found on leaves arranged as strobili.

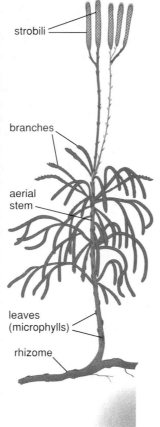

strobili

branches

aerial stem

leaves (microphylls)

rhizome

Figure 27.7

Horsetail, *Equisetum*. There are whorls of branches and tiny leaves at the joints of the stem. The sporangia are borne in strobili.

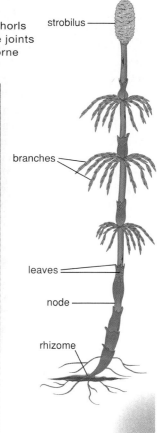

strobilus

branches

leaves

node

rhizome

Club Mosses Have Club-Shaped Strobili

The **club mosses** (**division Lycopodophyta,** 1,000 species) are common in moist woodlands of the temperate zone where they are known as ground pines. Typically, a branching rhizome sends up aerial stems less than 30 cm tall. Tightly packed, scalelike leaves cover stems and branches, giving the plant a mossy look (fig. 27.6). The leaves are *microphylls,* so called because they have only one strand of vascular tissue. Such a leaf may have evolved from a scale:

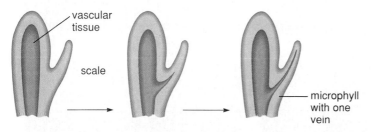

vascular tissue

scale

microphyll with one vein

In club mosses, the sporangia are borne on terminal clusters of leaves, called *strobili* (sing., strobilus), which are club shaped. The spores germinate into inconspicuous and independent gametophytes. The majority of club mosses live in the tropics and subtropics where many of them are epiphytes—plants that live on, but are not parasitic on, trees. The closely related spike mosses

(*Selaginella*) are extremely varied and include the resurrection plant, which curls up into a tight ball when dry but unfurls as if by magic when moistened.

Club mosses trace their ancestry to the Devonian period (table 27.2). They are the only living plants to have microphylls, and it would appear that they are indirectly (rather than directly) related to the ferns and their allies.

Horsetails Resemble Horses' Tails

Horsetails (**division Equisetophyta,** 15 species), which thrive in waste places around the globe, are represented by *Equisetum*, the only genus in existence today (fig. 27.7). A rhizome produces aerial stems that stand about 1.3 meters. The whorls of slender green side branches at the joints (nodes) of the stem make the plant bear a fanciful resemblance to a horse's tail. The small, scalelike leaves also form whorls at the nodes. Although the leaves have only a single strand of vascular tissue, they are reduced megaphylls (with many strands of vascular tissue), not microphylls. Many horsetails have strobili at the tips of the stems; others send up special buff-colored stems that bear the strobili. The spores germinate into inconspicuous and independent gametophytes.

The stems are tough and rigid because of silica deposited in cell walls. Early Americans, in particular, used horsetails for scouring pots and called them "scouring rushes." Today they are still used as ingredients in a few abrasive powders.

Ferns Are Leafy

Ferns (division Pteridophyta, 12,000 species) are a widespread group of plants. They are most abundant in warm, moist tropical regions but they are also found in northern regions and in dry, rocky places. They range in size from those that are low growing and resemble mosses to those that are tall trees. The fronds (leaves) in particular can vary. The royal fern has fronds that stand 6 feet tall; those of the Venus maidenhair fern are branched with broad leaflets. And those of the hart's tongue fern are straplike and leathery. In nearly all ferns, the leaves first appear in a curled-up form called a fiddlehead, which unrolls as it grows. Figure 27.8 shows the usual habitats of ferns and gives examples of their diversity. The life cycle of a typical temperate fern is shown in figures 27.9 and 27C on page 459.

The fronds are megaphylls secondarily subdivided into leaflets. Megaphylls may have evolved in the following way:

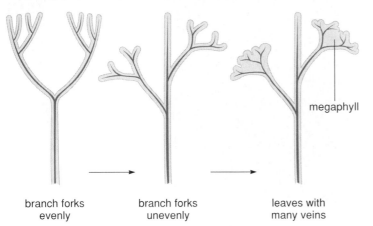

branch forks evenly   branch forks unevenly   leaves with many veins

megaphyll

Uses of Ferns

At first it may seem that ferns do not have much economic value, but they are much used by florists in decorative bouquets and as ornamental plants in the home and garden. Wood from tropical tree ferns is often used as a building material because it resists decay, particularly by termites. Ferns have medicinal value; many Indians use ferns as an astringent during childbirth to stop bleeding, and the maidenhair fern is the source of an expectorant.

Adaptation of Ferns

Ferns have true roots, stems, and leaves. The well-developed leaves fan out, capture solar energy, and photosynthesize. The water-dependent gametophyte, which lacks vascular tissue, is separate from the sporophyte. Flagellated sperm require an outside source of water in which to swim to the eggs in the archegonia. Once established, some ferns, like the bracken fern *Pteridium aquilinum,* can spread into drier areas by means of vegetative (asexual) reproduction. Ferns also spread by means of the rhizomes growing horizontally in the soil, producing the fiddleheads that grow up as new fronds.

> The seedless vascular plants include ferns and their allies. The sporophyte is dominant and the species is dispersed by spores. The independent, nonvascular gametophyte produces flagellated sperm.

Figure 27.8
Diversity of ferns.

maidenhair fern, *Adiantum pedatum*

hart's tongue fern, *Campyloneurum scolopendrium*

royal fern, *Osmunda regalis*

Figure 27.9
Fern Life Cycle.

① The sporophyte is dominant in ferns. ② In the fern shown here, the sori, protected by an indusium, are on the underside of the leaflets. Within the sporangia, meiosis occurs and spores are produced. ③ As a band of thickened cells on the rim of a sporangium (the annulus) dries out, it moves backward, pulling the sporangium open, and the spores are released. ④ A spore germinates into a prothallus, which bears antheridia and archegonia on the underside. Typically, the archegonia are at the notch and antheridia are toward the tip, between the rhizoids. ⑤ Fertilization takes place when moisture is present, because the flagellated sperm must swim in a film of water from the antheridia to the egg within the archegonium. ⑥ The resulting zygote begins its development inside an archegonium, but the embryo soon outgrows the available space. As a distinctive first leaf appears above the prothallus and as the roots develop below it, the sporophyte becomes visible. Often the sporophyte tissues and the gametophyte tissues are distinctly different shades of green. ⑦ The young sporophyte develops a root-bearing rhizome from which the fronds project.

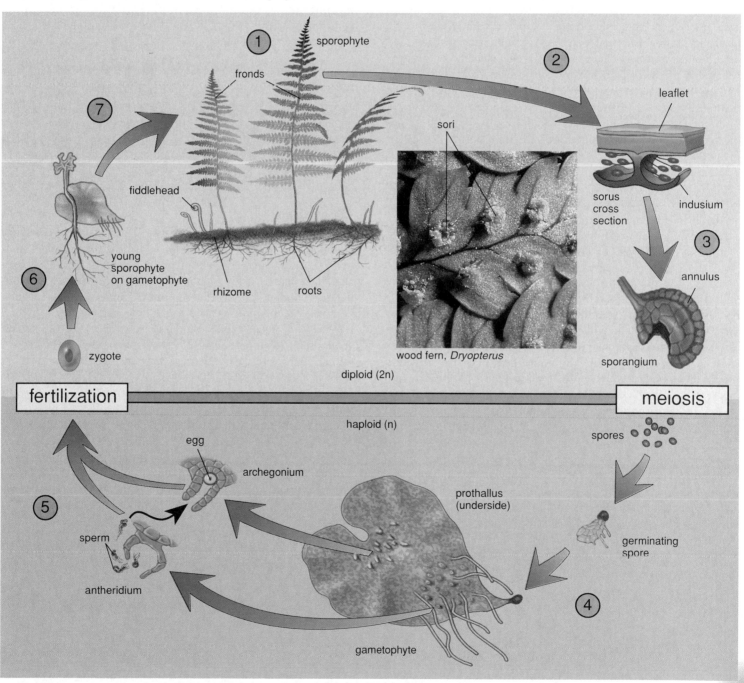

GYMNOSPERMS HAVE NAKED SEEDS

There are four groups of **gymnosperms** [Gk. *gymn*, naked, and *sperm*, seed]: conifers (division Pinophyta), cycads (division Cycadophyta), ginkgo (division Ginkgophyta), and gnetophytes (division Gnetophyta).

In gymnosperms, the seeds are not covered. Instead, they are exposed on the surface of sporophylls, leaves that bear sporangia. (In flowering plants, seeds are enclosed within a fruit.) Reproductive organs are usually borne in cones on which the sporophylls are spirally arranged. Other than these features, the four divisions of gymnosperms have little in common.

The gymnosperms didn't begin to flourish until the Mesozoic era. When the supercontinent Pangaea formed during the later part of the former Paleozoic era, mountain ranges arose and deserts appeared on their leeward side. Land that had been swampy became much drier. A mass extinction occurred, and among those that all but vanished were the seedless vascular plants that had made up the great swamp forests of the Carboniferous period. Then the first seed plants, many which are now extinct (such as the tree ferns), and also modern-day gymnosperms, with their many adaptations to life on land, came into their own.

> The gymnosperms didn't begin to flourish until the Mesozoic era, when geological upheavals brought about a change in the climate that fostered their dominance.

A generalized life cycle for seed plants is shown in figure 27D on page 459. Seed plants, like a few of their predecessors, produce *heterospores* called microspores and megaspores. There are also separate microgametophyes (male) and megagametophytes (female). A microspore develops into **grain,** is the immature microgametophyte, which is the **pollen grain** [L. *pollen*, fine dust], still retained within a microsporangium. After they are released, pollen grains develop into mature, sperm-bearing microgametophytes. **Pollination** is the transfer of pollen to the vicinity of the megagametophyte. The sperm is delivered to the egg through a pollen tube; therefore, no external water is required for fertilization. Independence from external water when reproducing is a major evolutionary trend in the plant kingdom.

A megaspore develops into an egg-bearing megagametophyte while still retained within an ovule. An **ovule** is the sporophyte structure that holds the megasporangium and then the megagametophyte. After fertilization, the zygote becomes an embryonic plant enclosed within the ovule, which then becomes the seed. Notice that megagametophytes and microgametophytes are dependent to a degree upon the diploid sporophyte. This means that the sporophyte can evolve into diverse forms without any corresponding changes in the gametophyte. The seed disperses the sporophyte among seed plants.

In seed plants, seeds disperse the sporophyte, which is the diploid generation. A **seed** is the mature ovule; it contains an embryonic sporophyte and stored food enclosed by a protective seed coat derived from the integuments (coverings) of the ovule. Seeds are resistant to adverse conditions, such as dryness or temperature extremes. They contain an embryo that is already partially developed and a food reserve that supports the emerging seedling until it can exist on its own. The survival value of seeds contributed greatly to the success of seed plants and their present dominance among plants.

> Seed plants produce micro- and megagametophytes. This has led to two evolutionary events: replacement of flagellated sperm by pollen grains, and the production of seeds for dispersal of the sporophyte and the species.

Conifers

Conifers [Gk. *con*, pine cone, and L. *fer*, bear, carry] (**division Pinophyta,** 550 species) are cone-bearing trees such as pines, hemlocks, and spruces. Conifers, which usually have evergreen needlelike leaves, are well adapted to withstand extremes of temperature, humidity, and wind strength. The leaves have a thick cuticle, sunken stomates, and a reduced surface area. Conifers are found in windswept mountaintops, swampy lowlands, and semideserts—from the equator to the frigid far north. The taiga is a coniferous forest extending in a broad belt across northern Eurasia and North America.

Conifers set records for their size and longevity. A giant sequoia named the General Sherman tree, located in California's Sequoia National Park, is 84 meters tall, 10 meters in diameter, and weighs an estimated 1,385 tons. Douglas firs are quite tall and sometimes reach heights of 75 meters, but redwood trees commonly grow more than 90 meters high. Some redwood trees are 2,000 years old, but the gnarled and twisted bristlecone pines in the Nevada mountains are known to be more than 4,500 years old.

The life cycle of pines, outlined in figure 27.10, is typical of conifers.

Figure 27.10

Pine Life Cycle.

① The sporophyte is dominant and its sporangia are borne in cones. ② There are two types of cones: pollen cones and seed cones. Typically, the pollen cones are quite small and develop near the tips of lower branches. ③ Each scale of a pollen cone has two or more microsporangia on the underside. ④ Within these sporangia, each microsporocyte (microspore mother cell) undergoes meiosis and produces four microspores. ⑤ Each microspore develops into a microgametophyte, which is the pollen grain. The microgametophyte has two wings and is carried by the wind to the seed cone during pollination. The seed cones are larger than the pollen cones and are located near the branch tips. ③ Each scale of the seed cone has two ovules that lie on the upper surface. Each ovule is surrounded by a thick, layered integument, having an opening at one end. ④ The megasporangium is within the ovule, where a megasporocyte (megaspore mother cell) undergoes meiosis, producing four megaspores. ⑤ Only one of these spores develops into a megagametophyte, with two to six archegonia, each containing a single large egg lying near the ovule opening. ⑥ Once a pollen grain is enclosed within the seed cone, it develops a pollen tube that digests its way slowly toward a megagametophyte. The pollen tube discharges two nonflagellated sperm. One of these fertilizes an egg in an archegonium and the other degenerates. Fertilization, which takes place one year after pollination, is an entirely separate event from pollination. ⑦ After fertilization, the ovule matures and becomes the seed, composed of the embryo, the reserve food, and the seed coat. Finally, in the fall of the second season, the seed cone, by now woody and hard, opens to release winged seeds. When a seed germinates, the sporophyte embryo develops into a new pine tree, and the cycle is complete.

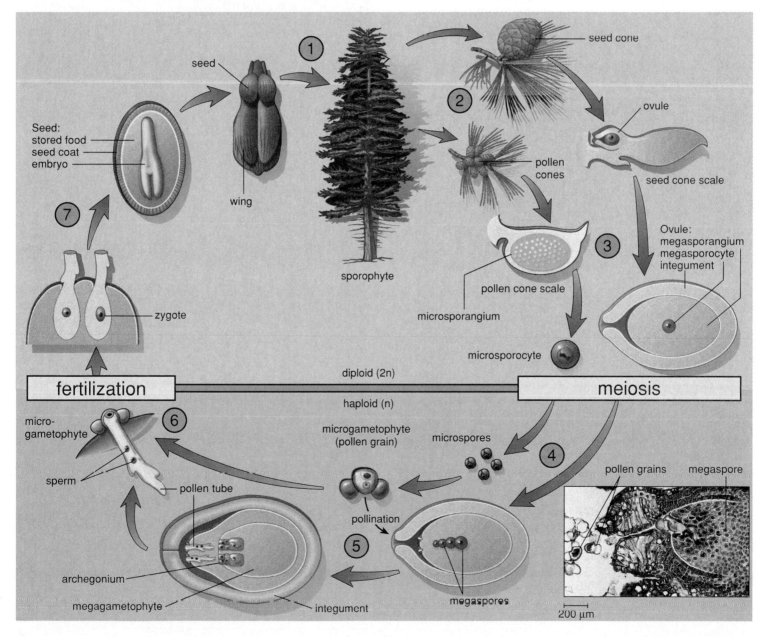

Cycads Fed Dinosaurs

The trunk of **cycads** (**division Cycadophyta,** 100 species) is stout and unbranched, and the large leaves are compound. This combination of features gives the plant a palmlike appearance. Cycads flourished during the Mesozoic era (see table 27.2) and they were so numerous that this era is sometimes referred to as the Age of Cycads and Dinosaurs. Dinosaurs most likely fed on cycad seeds and foliage. Today, cycads are found mainly in tropical and subtropical regions (fig. 27.11*a*). One species grows as tall as 20 meters and has meter-long cones that weigh almost 90 pounds.

Ginkgo Trees Adorn Parks

Only one species of **ginkgo** (**division Ginkgophyta**), known as the maidenhair tree (fig. 27.11*b*), survives today. Growing up to 70 feet, it is covered with forked-veined, fan-shaped leaves that are shed in autumn. Microsporangia are in cones but the ovules are stalked. In modern times, the maidenhair tree was largely restricted to ornamental gardens in China until it was discovered that it does quite well in polluted areas. Because female trees produce seeds with a fleshy covering that falls and makes a foul-smelling mess, it is the custom to use only male trees, propagated vegetatively, in city parks.

Figure 27.11

Representatives of the lesser known gymnosperm divisions. **a.** Cycads resemble palm trees but are gymnosperms that produce cones. Male plants have pollen cones and female plants have seed cones. **b.** Ginkgoes exist only as a single species, the maidenhair tree. This photograph of a female plant features the seeds. Male plants have pollen cones. **c.** There are three genera of gnetophytes—this is *Welwitschia mirabilis,* a very unusual African plant. In this photograph, we see seed cones at the ends of the two enormous, straplike leaves.

a.   Kaffir bread cycad, *Encephalartos altensteinii*

b.   Maidenhair tree, *Ginkgo biloba*

c.   Gnetophyte, *Welwitschia mirabilis*

Gnetophytes

The **gnetophytes** (**division Gnetophyta,** 70 species), which also live mainly in the tropics, contain only three genera of plants. They look quite different from one another, though they share certain anatomical features (related to their gametophytes and vascular tissue) that make them seem more related to angiosperms than other gymnosperms. Only one genus is found in the United States: *Ephedra* is a many-branched shrub with small, scalelike leaves that is found largely in desert regions. *Welwitschia* belongs to a genus of very unusual plants found in Africa. Most of the plant exists underground. Only a few centimeters of trunk grow above ground, but the trunk can be over a meter wide! There are only two enormous, straplike leaves, which grow for hundreds of years. These may cover most of the exposed portion of the trunk (fig. 27.11*c*).

> Gymnosperms share a common characteristic: the seeds are naked (not covered). Conifers, with their ability to live under extreme conditions, are still a very prevalent and successful group.

Uses of Gymnosperms

Conifers grow on large areas of the earth's surface and are economically important. They supply much of the wood used for building construction and paper production. They also produce many valuable chemicals, such as those extracted from resin, a viscous liquid substance that protects the conifers from attack by fungi and insects.

Adaptation of Gymnosperms

Gymnosperms have well-developed roots and stems. Many are tall trees that can withstand heat, dryness, and cold. The reproductive pattern of conifers has several important innovations not found in the plants we have considered so far. There is no need of external water for fertilization to occur. Pollen grains are transferred by wind, and the growth of the pollen tube delivers sperm to an egg. Enclosure of the dependent megagametophyte in an ovule protects it during its development and shelters the developing zygote as well. Finally, the embryo is protected by the seed and is provided with a store of nutrients that supports development for the first period of its growth following germination. All of these factors increase the chance for reproductive success on land.

> Conifers are the most prevalent of the gymnosperms. In the conifer life cycle, windblown pollen grains replace flagellated sperm. Following fertilization, the seed develops from the ovule, a structure that is on a cone. The seeds are uncovered and dispersed by the wind.

ANGIOSPERMS HAVE COVERED SEEDS

Angiosperms [Gk. *ang,* vessel, and *sperm,* seed] (**division Magnoliophyta**) are the flowering plants; their seeds are enclosed by fruits. With 235,000 species, they are an exceptionally large and successful group of plants. This is six times the number of species of all other plant groups combined. Angiosperms live in all sorts of habitats, from fresh water to desert and from the frigid north to the torrid tropics. They range in size from the tiny, almost microscopic, duckweed to *Eucalyptus* that are over 100 meters tall. It would be impossible to exaggerate the importance of angiosperms in our everyday lives. They provide us with clothing, food, medicines, and commercially valuable products.

Origin and Evolution of Angiosperms

Angiosperms evolved from ancient gymosperms. By the Jurassic period in the middle of the Mesozoic era, many of the gymnosperms had features similar to those we associate with angiosperms. Some had vascular tissue resembling that of angiosperms and some had sporophylls that were beginning to look like parts of flowers. The flowers were visited by beetles—many flowering plants today depend on animals for pollination. Most of these transitional gymnosperms became extinct; only a few lines are in existence today, notably the gnetophytes and the angiosperms. Among today's gymnosperms, the gnetophyte *Ephedra* is believed to be most closely related to angiosperms.

The oldest fossils definitely considered to be angiosperms come from the Cretaceous period (see table 27.2) of the Mesozoic era, but flowering plants didn't diversify until the Cenozoic era. The continents drifted to their present locations during the Cenozoic era, and the climate grew colder. Perhaps the angiosperms were better able to diversify during these changing times, and this led to their present dominance. Perhaps also helpful was the prevalence of insects to assist in pollination.

Rather than being tall trees, the first angiosperms may have been fast-growing woody shrubs that took on the appearance of weeds in open places. Both tall trees and herbaceous plants could have evolved from such an ancestor. Today many angiosperms are nonwoody **herbaceous plants** [L. *herb,* grass] rather than being woody shrubs or trees. **Woody plants** have an internal skeleton composed of the xylem of previous seasons. Herbs are able to colonize disturbed places and exist in areas that woody plants cannot tolerate. Angiosperms that are adapted to the temperate, subarctic, and arctic zones are perennials or annuals. *Perennials* are plants that live two or more years; they die back seasonally in herbaceous plants and become dormant in woody plants. Trees that lose their leaves in autumn are called deciduous trees. *Annuals* are plants that live for only one growing season.

How Flowering Plants Are Classified

Angiosperms are divided into two groups: dicotyledons (class Magnoliopsida) and monocotyledons (class Liliopsida). The **dicotyledons** [Gk, *di,* two, and *kotyl,* cavity] (or dicots) are either woody or herbaceous and they have flower parts usually in fours and fives, net-veined leaves, vascular bundles arranged in a circle within the stem, and two cotyledons, or seed leaves. Dicot families include many familiar plant groups, such as the buttercup, mustard, maple, cactus, pea, and rose families. The rose family includes roses, apples, plums, pears, cherries, peaches, strawberries, raspberries, and a number of other shrubs. The **monocotyledons** (or monocots) are almost always herbaceous and have flower parts in threes, parallel-veined leaves, scattered vascular bundles in the stem, and one cotyledon, or seed leaf. Monocot families include the lily, palm, orchid, iris, and grass families. The grass family includes wheat, rice, corn (maize), and other agriculturally important plants.

The Flower Contains Modified Leaves

The flower consists of several kinds of highly modified leaves that are arranged in concentric rings and attached to a modified stem tip, the receptacle (fig. 27.12). The sepals, which form the outermost ring, are frequently green and are quite similar to ordinary foliage leaves. They enclose the flower before it opens. Next are the petals, which are often large and colorful. Their color often helps attract pollinators. Within the petals, the stamens form a whorl around the pistil. **Stamens** are the pollen-producing portion of the flower. Each stamen has a slender filament with an anther at the tip. The **anthers** are modified sporophylls containing microsporangia where microspores (pollen grains) are produced. An anther could have evolved by the following stages involving a reduction in its leaflike portion:

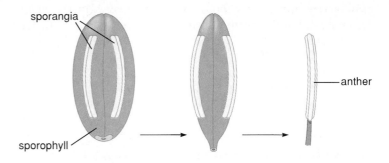

The pollen grains are either blown by the wind or carried by pollinators (most often insects) to the **pistil,** the portion of the flower that contains one or more fused carpels. *Carpels* are also modified sporophylls; they contain ovules in which megasporangia are located. A carpel could have evolved by the following stages:

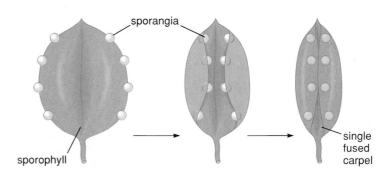

Eventually the pistil came to have its three parts: **stigma, style,** and **ovary.** The ovary contains from one to many ovules, depending on the species of plant. The ovule becomes a seed and the ovary becomes a fruit; therefore, the seeds are enclosed by fruit. A **fruit** is a mature ovary and possible accessory part of a flower that provides a fleshy or dry covering for seeds. Fruits are sometimes specialized to aid in dispersal of seeds. Fleshy fruits may be eaten by animals, which transport the seeds to a new location and then deposit them when they defecate.

The life cycle of flowering plants is given in figure 27.13.

Figure 27.12

Flower structure and diversity of flowering plants.

Comparing Plant Life Cycles

Three groups of plants are found in the fossil record. The nonvascular plants, represented today by the bryophytes, appear first. These are followed by the nonseed vascular plants and finally the seed plants. All three groups of plants have a life cycle described as alternation of generations: a diploid (2n) generation, the sporophyte, which produces haploid (n) spores by meiosis, alternates with a haploid generation, the gametophyte, which produces the gametes. Following fertilization, the diploid zygote develops into the sporophyte generation.

In mosses, a type of bryophyte, the haploid gametophyte is the long-lasting generation and the generation we recognize as the plant. Therefore, the gametophyte is dominant and more space is allotted to this generation in figure 27B.

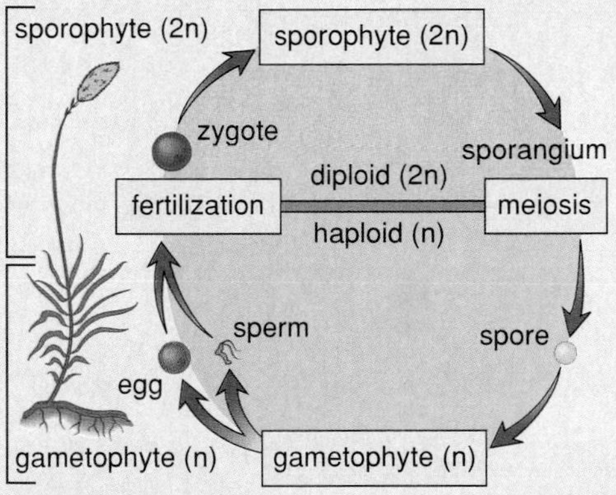

generation is the dominant one. How might this have happened? The sporophyte is attached to the almost microscopic gametophyte but, since it has vascular tissue, it becomes the larger and the longer lasting of the two generations. In figure 27C more space is allotted to the sporophyte. The sporophyte generation produces usually windblown homospores following germination. The spore gives rise to a gametophyte, which produces both male and female gametes. Sperm are flagellated and swim to the egg in a film of water. These nonvascular plants were dominant and grew to enormous sizes during the Carboniferous period (p. 454), when the weather was warm and wet. Many of these plants became extinct when the weather turned dryer and colder over much of the earth. Today's seedless vascular plants that live in the temperate zone use asexual propagation to spread into environments that are not favorable for a water-dependent gametophyte generation.

Seed plants also have an alternation of generations life cycle, but it is much modified (fig. 27D). The spores are retained within the sporophyte; there are heterosporangia and heterospores, termed microspores and megaspores. The gametophytes are so reduced that the megagametophyte is also retained within the structure (ovule) that held the megasporangium! Microspores become the windblown or animal-transported microgametophytes—the pollen grains. Following fertilization, the ovule becomes the seed. A seed contains a sporophyte embryo, and therefore seeds disperse the sporophyte generation. Notice that the flagellated sperm have been replaced by pollen grains and that the gametophyte, which lacks vascular tissue, is now completely dependent upon the vascular sporophyte. Fertilization no longer utilizes external water, and sexual reproduction is fully adapted to the terrestrial environment.

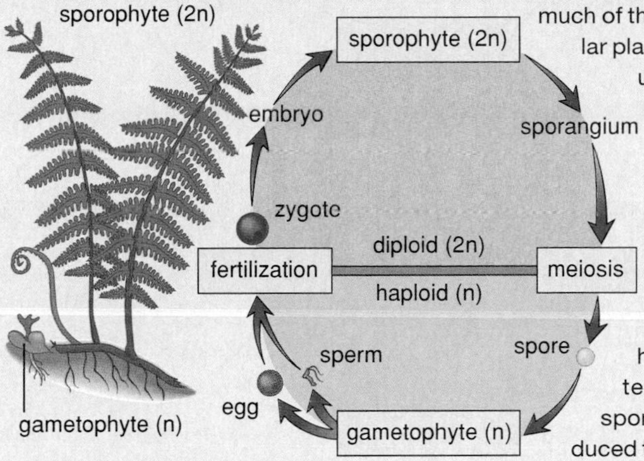

Figure 27C

Seedless Vascular Plants
- Dominant sporophyte
- Homospores disperse the species
- Independent gametophyte
- Flagellated sperm

Figure 27D

Seed Vascular Plants
- Dominant sporophyte
- Heterosporous
- Dependent micro-, macrogametophytes
- Pollen grains
- Seeds disperse the species

Figure 27B

Nonvascular Plants
- Dominant gametophyte
- Flagellated sperm
- Dependent sporophyte
- Homospores disperse the species

In bryophytes, the sperm are flagellated and swim in a film of water to the egg. The zygote is retained in the female gametangium, and the sporophyte is dependent upon the gametophyte—it is only temporarily present and photosynthesizes to a very limited extent. The sporophyte produces a single type of spore that is usually windblown and disperses the gametophyte generation.

In the ferns, a seedless vascular plant, both generations are independent but the sporophyte

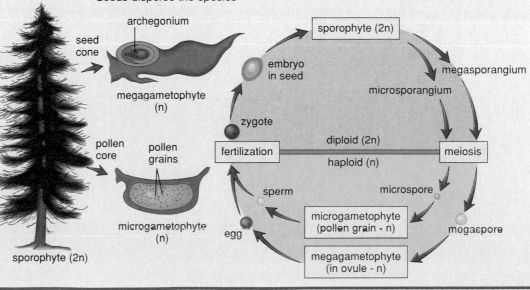

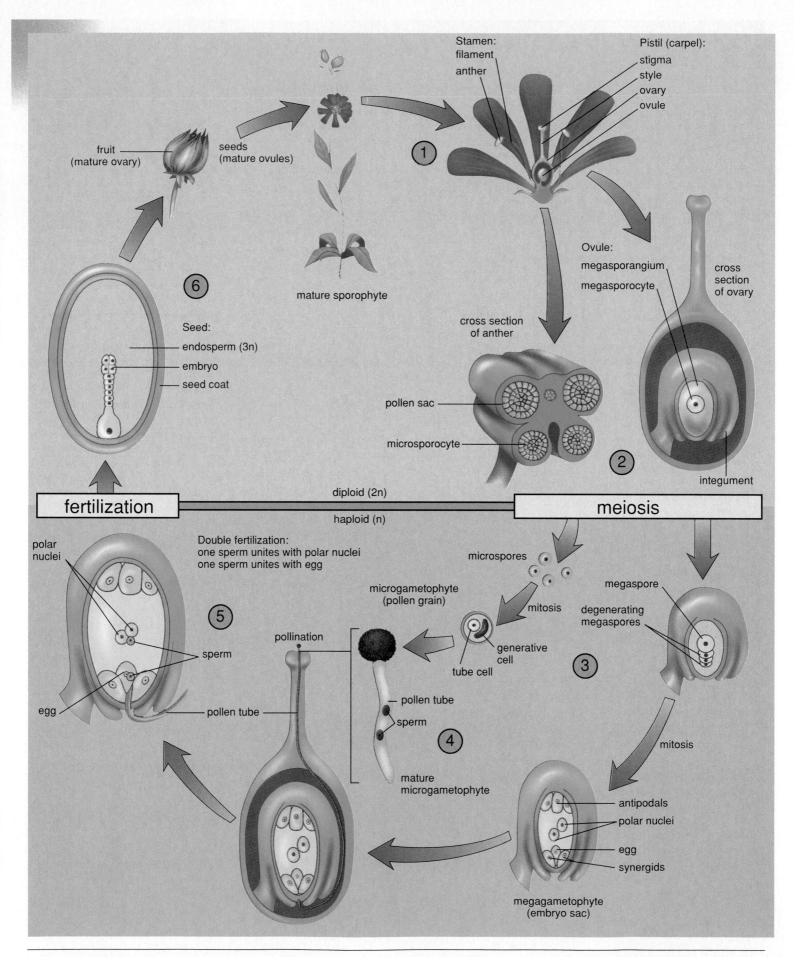

Stamen:
filament
anther

Pistil (carpel):
stigma
style
ovary
ovule

①

fruit (mature ovary)

seeds (mature ovules)

mature sporophyte

Ovule:
megasporangium
megasporocyte

cross section of ovary

cross section of anther

pollen sac

microsporocyte

②

integument

⑥

Seed:
endosperm (3n)
embryo
seed coat

fertilization

diploid (2n)

haploid (n)

meiosis

Double fertilization:
one sperm unites with polar nuclei
one sperm unites with egg

microspores

megaspore

degenerating megaspores

polar nuclei

microgametophyte
(pollen grain)

mitosis

⑤

pollination

generative cell

tube cell

③

mitosis

sperm

egg

pollen tube

pollen tube

sperm

④

mature microgametophyte

antipodals

polar nuclei

egg

synergids

megagametophyte
(embryo sac)

Figure 27.13

Flowering Plant Life Cycle.

① The parts of the flower involved in reproduction are the stamens and the pistil. Reproduction has been divided into development of the megagametophyte, development of the microgametophyte, double fertilization, and the seed. *Development of the megagametophyte.* The ovary at the base of the pistil contains one or more ovules. ② Within an ovule, a megasporocyte (megaspore mother cell) undergoes meiosis to produce four haploid megaspores. ③ Three of these megaspores disintegrate, leaving one functional megaspore, which divides mitotically. ④ The result is the megagametophyte, or embryo sac, which typically consists of eight haploid nuclei embedded in a mass of cytoplasm. The cytoplasm differentiates into cells, one of which is an egg and another of which is the endosperm cell with two nuclei (called the polar nuclei). *Development of the microgametophyte.* ① The anther at the top of the stamen has pollen sacs, which contain numerous microsporocytes (microspore mother cells). ② Each microsporocyte undergoes meiosis to produce four haploid cells called microspores. When the microspores separate, each one becomes a microgametophyte or pollen grain. ③ At this point, the young microgametophyte contains two nuclei: the generative cell and the tube cell. Pollination occurs when pollen is windblown or carried by insects, birds, or bats to the stigma of the same type of plant. ④ Only then does a pollen grain germinate and produce a long pollen tube. This pollen tube grows within the style until it reaches an ovule in the ovary. Before fertilization occurs, the generative nucleus divides, producing two sperm, which have no flagella. This germinated pollen grain with its pollen tube and two sperm is the mature microgametophyte. *Double fertilization.* ⑤ On reaching the ovule, the pollen tube discharges the sperm. One of the two sperm migrates to and fertilizes the egg, forming a zygote; the other unites with the two polar nuclei, producing a 3n (triploid) endosperm nucleus. The endosperm nucleus divides to form endosperm, food for the developing plant. This so-called double fertilization is unique to angiosperms. *The seed.* ⑥ The ovule now develops into the seed, which contains an embryo and food enclosed by a protective seed coat. The wall of the ovary and sometimes adjacent parts develop into a fruit that surrounds the seeds. Therefore, angiosperms are said to have *covered seeds.*

Flowers Aid Diversification

We have seen that flowers are involved in the production and development of spores, gametophytes, gametes, and embryos enclosed within seeds. The successful completion of these processes requires the effective dispersal of pollen and then seeds. The various ways in which pollen and fruits can be dispersed has resulted in many different types of flowers.

Although some flowers disperse their pollen by wind, many are adapted to attract specific pollinators such as bees, wasps, flies, butterflies, moths, and even bats, which carry only a particular pollen from flower to flower. For example, bee-pollinated flowers are usually blue or yellow and have ultraviolet shadings that lead the pollinator to the location of nectar at the base of the flower. The mouthparts of bees are fused into a long tube that is able to obtain nectar from this location.

Not only do flowers lend themselves to efficient cross-pollination, they also aid in the dispersal of seeds through the production of fruits. There are fruits that utilize wind, gravity, water, and animals for dispersal. Because animals live in particular habitats and/or have particular migration patterns, they are apt to deliver the fruit enclosed seeds to a suitable location for seed germination (when the embryo begins to grow again) and development of the adult sporophyte plant.

> Flower diversification may be associated with the numerous means by which flowers are pollinated and fruits are dispersed.

Uses of Angiosperms

Angiosperms provide the food that sustains most animals on land, including humans. Humans also use plant fibers to produce cloth, to provide firewood, and to supply construction materials. Plant oils, spices, and drugs are derived from different parts of various angiosperm plants. The uses of angiosperms are discussed further on pages 457–58.

Adaptation of Angiosperms

Angiosperms have true roots, stems, and leaves. The vascular tissue is well developed, and the leaves are generally broad. Angiosperms are found in all sorts of habitats; some have even returned to the water.

The reproductive organs are in the flowers, which often attract animal pollinators; their ovules are located in ovaries that develop into fruits. Therefore, angiosperms produce covered seeds. Fruits often help with dispersal of seeds.

> Angiosperms are the flowering plants. The flower both attracts animals (e.g., insects) that aid in pollination and produces seeds enclosed by fruit, which aid dispersal.

Biological Relationships

In any particular environment, selective pressures favor a successful reproductive strategy, which is essential to the continuation of the species. Bryophytes and ferns produce flagellated sperm and are dependent on external water to complete their life cycle. In these plants, windblown spores disperse the species, reducing competition for the same resources between the generations. The seed plants have a reproductive strategy that protects against desiccation of gametes, gametophytes, the zygote, and the embryo. Pollen grains protect sperm, the sporophyte protects the megagametophye and the zygote, and the seed protects the embryo as it is dispersed to a new location. Today seed plants are more widely distributed than are bryophytes and ferns.

The reproductive strategy of seed plants can be compared to the reproductive strategy of mammals. Mammals produce flagellated sperm and engage in sexual intercourse, which deposits the sperm in the female and, thereby protects the sperm from drying out. The egg, the zygote, and the embryo are all retained within the body of the female where they are protected from drying out. Aquatic animals are apt to deposit their gametes in the water where fertilization, zygote formation, and external development occurs. The reproductive strategy of plants and animals is therefore adapted to the environment.

Summary

1. Plants are photosynthetic organisms adapted to a land existence. Among the various adaptations, all plants protect the developing embryo from desiccation.

2. All plants have the alternation of generations life cycle. Some types of plants have a dominant gametophyte; others have a dominant sporophyte.

3. The bryophytes, which include the liverworts and mosses, are nonvascular plants and therefore lack true roots, stems, and leaves.

4. In the moss life cycle, the gametophyte is dominant. Antheridia produce swimming sperm that need external water to reach the eggs in the archegonia. Following fertilization, the dependent sporophyte consists of a foot, a stalk, and a capsule within which windblown spores are produced by meiosis. Each spore germinates to produce a gametophyte.

5. Vascular plants arose during the Silurian period of the Paleozoic era. The extinct rhyniophytes may be ancestral vascular plants. These plants had photosynthetic stems (no leaves or roots) with sporangia at their tips. Most likely, the life cycle was similar to today's ferns. The sporophyte, which is diploid and has vascular tissue, is the dominant generation in vascular plants.

6. The seedless vascular plants include whisk ferns, club mosses, horsetails, and ferns. While the first three are rather small and limited in diversity today, lycopods, horsetails, and ferns were also trees during the Carboniferous period. Seedless vascular plants have a life cycle like that of the ferns.

7. In ferns, the separate and water-dependent gametophyte (the heart-shaped prothallus) produces swimming sperm in antheridia and eggs in archegonia. Following fertilization, the zygote develops into the sporophyte, which has large fronds. On the underside of the fronds are sori, each containing several sporangia. Here meiosis produces windblown spores, each of which develops into a prothallus.

8. The Mesozoic era saw many geological changes as Pangaea formed and then broke apart. A mass extinction occurred that paved the way for the diversification of the seed plants. Seed plants that are trees have especially well-developed roots and stems due to secondary growth of vascular tissue. Seed plants produce heterospores, microgametophytes, and megagametophytes. The pollen grain replaces external swimming sperm, and the megagametophyte is retained within the ovule that develops into the seed.

9. There are four divisions of gymnosperms (meaning naked seeds): the familiar conifers and the little-known cycads, ginkgo, and gnetophytes.

10. In conifers, pollen and seed cones are produced by the sporophyte plant. On the underside of a male cone scale, there are two sporangia that produce microspores; each becomes the microgametophyte, or pollen grain. On the upper surface of a female cone scale, there are two ovules, where meiosis produces one megaspore that develops into the megagametophyte.

After windblown pollination, the pollen grain develops a tube through which sperm reach the egg. After fertilization, the ovule matures to be the seed.

11. Angiosperms (meaning seeds within a vessel) are more diverse than the other types of plants. Their success may be associated with climatic changes in the Cenozoic era.

12. In a flower, the microsporangia develop within the anther portion of a stamen, and the megasporangia develop within ovules located in the ovary of the pistil. Pollination brings the mature microgametophyte (pollen grain) to the pistil and the pollen tube brings the sperm to the ovule within the ovary. Angiosperms exhibit double fertilization: one sperm fertilizes the egg, and the other unites with the polar nuclei to form the endosperm, which is food for the embryo. The ovule develops into the seed, and the ovary becomes the fruit.

13. Angiosperms have complex vascular tissue and are found in various habitats. Their reproductive organs are found in flowers. Animal pollination increases the chance of appropriate fertilization, and fruit production helps with the dispersal of seeds.

Writing Across the Curriculum

In order to practice writing skills, students should write out the answers to any or all of the study questions and the critical thinking questions. The study questions are sequenced in the same order as the text. Answers to the objective questions, and suggested answers to the critical thinking questions, are in appendix D.

1. What are the characteristics that define plants?   445

2. What are the general characteristics of bryophytes and what are the three main types?   446

3. Draw a diagram to describe the life cycle of the moss, pointing out significant features.   447

4. What are the human uses of bryophytes and what are their adaptations?   448

5. What are the general characteristics of vascular plants and how do features of the seedless plant life cycle differ from that of the seed plant life cycle?   448, 454

6. What is the significance of rhyniophytes in the history of plants? What are the living seedless vascular plants and describe the period of time in the earth's history when they were larger and more abundant than today.   450–51

7. Draw a diagram to describe the life cycle of the fern pointing out significant features. What are the human uses of ferns and what are their adaptations?   453

8. List and describe the four divisions of gymnosperms.   454–57

9. Use a diagram of the pine life cycle to point out significant features including those that distinguish a seed plant's life cycle from that of a seedless vascular plant.   454

10. What are the human uses of gymnosperms and what are their adaptations?   457

11. What role may have been played by beetles and insects in the evolution of flowering plants?   457

12. What are the parts of a flower? Use a diagram to explain and point out significant features of the flowering plant life cycle.   460–61

13. Offer an explanation as to why flowering plants are the dominant plants today. What are the human uses of angiosperms and what are their adaptations?   461

Objective Questions

1. Which of these are characteristics of plants?
   a. multicellular with specialized tissues and organs
   b. photosynthetic and contain chlorophylls *a* and *b*
   c. protect the developing embryo from desiccation
   d. All of these are correct.

2. In the moss life cycle, the sporophyte
   a. consists of leafy green shoots.
   b. is the heart-shaped prothallus.
   c. consists of a foot, a stalk, and a capsule.
   d. is the dominant generation.

3. The rhyniophytes
   a. are a flourishing group of plants today.
   b. had large leaves like today's ferns.
   c. had sporangia at the tips of their branches.
   d. All of these are correct.

4. You are apt to find ferns in a moist location because they have
   a. a water-dependent sporophyte generation.
   b. flagellated spores.
   c. swimming sperm.
   d. All of these are correct.

5. Which of these is mismatched?
   a. pollen grain—microgametophyte
   b. ovule—megagametophyte
   c. seed—immature sporophyte
   d. pollen tube—spores

6. In the life cycle of the pine tree, the ovules are found on the
   a. needlelike leaves.
   b. seed cones.
   c. pollen cones.
   d. All of these are correct.

7. Which of these is mismatched?
   a. anther—produces microsporangia
   b. pistil—produces pollen
   c. ovule—becomes seed
   d. ovary—becomes fruit

8. Which of these plants contributed the most to our present-day supply of coal?
   a. bryophytes
   b. seedless vascular plants
   c. conifers
   d. angiosperms

9. Which of these is found in seed plants?
   a. complex vascular tissue
   b. pollen grains replace swimming sperm
   c. retention of megagametophyte within the ovule
   d. All of these are correct.

10. Label the following diagram of alternation of generations.

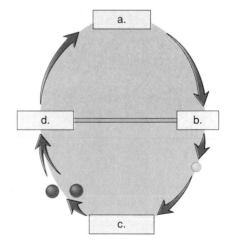

Concepts and Critical Thinking

I. *Plants are one of the major groups of organisms alive today.*

Should all organisms that photosynthesize be placed in the same kingdom? Why or why not?

2. *Plants are adapted to living on land.*

Vascular plants have roots, stems, and leaves. How does each organ contribute to a plant's adaptation to life on land?

3. *Plants have an alternation of generations life cycle.*

List several advantages of having a dominant sporophyte, and discuss each one.

Selected Key Terms

angiosperm A flowering plant; the seeds are borne within a fruit. [Gk. *ang,* vessel, and *sperm,* seed]   457

antheridium A reproductive organ found in bryophytes and some vascular plants which produces flagellated sperm. [Gk. *anth,* flower, and *idia,* small]   446

archegonium A reproductive organ found in bryophytes and some vascular plants which produce an egg. [Gk. *archeg,* first]   446

conifer One of the four groups of gymnosperm plants; cone-bearing trees that include pine, cedar, and spruce. [Gk. *con,* pine cone, and L. *fer,* bear, carry]   454

dicotyledon (dy-KAHT-ul-eed-un) A flowering plant group; members show two embryonic leaves, net-veined leaves, cylindrical arrangement of vascular bundles, and other characteristics. [Gk. *di,* two, and *kotyl,* cavity]   458

fruit A flowering plant structure consisting of one or more ripened ovaries that usually contains seeds.   458

gametophyte (guh-MEET-uh-fyt) The haploid generation of the alternation of generations life cycle of a plant; it produces gametes that unite to form a diploid zygote. [Gk. *gamet,* wife or husband, and *phyt,* plant]   445

gymnosperm (JIM-nuh-sperm) A vascular plant producing naked seeds, as in conifers. [Gk. *gymn,* naked, and *sperm,* seed]   454

herbaceous plant A plant that lacks persistent woody tissue. [L. *herb,* grass]   457

monocotyledon (mahn-uh-KAHT-ul-eed-un) A flowering plant group; members show one embryonic leaf, parallel-veined leaves, scattered vascular bundles, and other characteristics. [Gk. *mono,* one, and *kotyl,* cavity]   458

ovule In seed plants, a structure that contains the megasporangium, where meiosis occurs and the gametophyte is produced; develops into the seed.   454

phloem (FLOH-um) The vascular tissue that conducts organic solutes in plants; it contains sieve-tube cells and companion cells. [Gk. *phloe,* tree bark, and L. *em,* in]   448

pollen grain A microgametophyte in seed plants. [L. *pollen,* fine dust]   454

pollination In seed plants, the transfer of pollen from microsporangium to the ovule, which by this time contains a megagametophyte. [L. *pollen,* fine dust]   454

rhizoid A rootlike hair that anchors a plant and absorbs minerals and water from the soil. [Gk. *rhiz,* root, and *oid,* like]   446

sporophyte (SPOR-uh-fyt) The diploid generation of the alternation of generations life cycle of a plant; meiosis produces haploid spores that develop into the haploid generation. [Gk. *spor,* seed, and *phyt,* plant]   445

woody plant A plant that contains wood; usually trees such as evergreen trees (gymnosperms) and flowering trees (angiosperms). Alternative is a herbaceous plant.   457

xylem (ZY-lum) The vascular tissue that transports water and mineral solutes upward through the plant body; it contains vessel elements and tracheids. [Gk. *xyl,* wood, and L. *em,* in]   448

28

KINGDOM ANIMALIA:
INTRODUCTION TO INVERTEBRATES

Learning Objectives

How Animals Evolved and Are Classified

- List the characteristics of animals.   466
- Draw a phylogenetic tree that shows the nine major animal phyla.   467

Multicellularity Evolves

- Describe the way of life and the anatomical features of sponges.   468–69

Two Tissue Layers Evolve

- Describe comb jellies in general and cnidaria in particular, including their body forms and other anatomical features.   470

Bilateral Symmetry Evolves

- Describe ribbon worms in general and flatworms in particular, using a free-living planarian as an example.   474–75
- Describe the life cycle of flukes and tapeworms, emphasizing anatomical changes that accompany the parasitic way of life.   476–77

A Pseudocoelom Evolves

- Describe rotifers in general and roundworms in particular, including their way of life and anatomical features.   478–79
- Compare the phyla in terms of body plan, type of symmetry, number of tissue layers, level of organization, and presence of coelom.   480

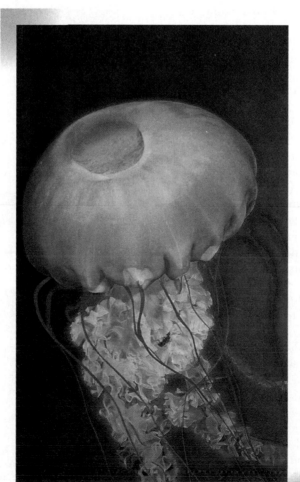

The sea nettle, *Chrysaora*, with its stinging cells, is sometimes an unwelcomed swimming companion to humans.

Whereas plants are multicellular photosynthetic organisms, animals are multicellular eukaryotes that are heterotrophic by ingesting food (fig. 28.1). Unlike the fungi that rely on external digestion, animals usually digest their food in a central cavity. Animals produce heterogametes (eggs and sperm), and they follow the diplontic life cycle in which the adult is always diploid. In this cycle, meiosis produces haploid gametes, which join to form a zygote that develops into an adult. Table 28.1 reviews the characteristics of animals.

HOW ANIMALS EVOLVED AND ARE CLASSIFIED

All animals are believed to have evolved from a protoctistan ancestor, most likely a protozoan (fig. 28.2). There are approximately thirty-four animal phyla, but we will consider in depth only the nine phyla illustrated in the tree. These are the ones recognized as the major animal phyla. All nine phyla contain **invertebrates** [L.*in,* without, and *vertebr,* vertebra], which are animals without backbones. The phylum Chordata also contains the vertebrates, which are animals with backbones. Many invertebrates live in the sea, where early animal evolution occurred. All major animal phyla are represented by Cambrian fossils, but it has been very difficult to trace the complete evolutionary history because the fossil record is so much better for hard-shelled animals. In large part, the possible evolutionary relationship of living invertebrates has been worked out by using the anatomical criteria noted in the tree.

One criterion used to classify animals is type of symmetry. **Asymmetry** means that the animal has no particular symmetry. **Radial symmetry** means that the animal is organized circularly and, just as with a wheel, two identical halves are obtained no matter how the animal is sliced longitudinally. **Bilateral symmetry** means that the animal has definite right and left halves; only one longitudinal cut down the center of the animal will produce two equal halves. Radially symmetrical animals tend to be attached to a substrate; that is, they are **sessile**. This type of symmetry is useful to these animals since it allows them to reach out in all directions from one center. Bilaterally symmetrical animals tend to be active and to move forward at an anterior end.

One of the main events during the development of animals is the establishment of *germ layers* from which all other structures are derived. Although a total of three germ layers is seen in most animal embryos, some animals only have two germ layers: ectoderm and endoderm. Such animals have the *tissue level of organization.* Animals with three germ layers—ectoderm, mesoderm, and endoderm—have an *organ level of organization.*

The four animal phyla in the lower half of the phylogenetic tree in figure 28.2 lack a true **coelom** [Gk. *coel,* hollow], an internal body cavity completely lined by mesoderm, where internal organs are found. Some are acoelomates—they have no coelom at all. One phylum contains pseudocoelomates, animals that have a cavity, though it is incompletely lined with mesoderm. There is a layer of mesoderm beneath the body wall but not around the gut. All the animal phyla in the two top branches of the tree

Figure 28.1

The animal kingdom is diverse. Both a hydra and a toad are multicellular heterotrophic organisms that must take in preformed food.

Hydra, *Hydra*

American toad, *Bufo*

Table 28.1

Characteristics of Animals

1. Are heterotrophic and usually acquire food by ingestion followed by digestion.
2. Typically have the power of motion or locomotion by means of muscle fibers.
3. Are multicellular, and most have cells specialized to form tissues and organs.
4. Have a life cycle in which the adult is always diploid.
5. Usually practice sexual reproduction and produce an embryo that undergoes specific stages of development.

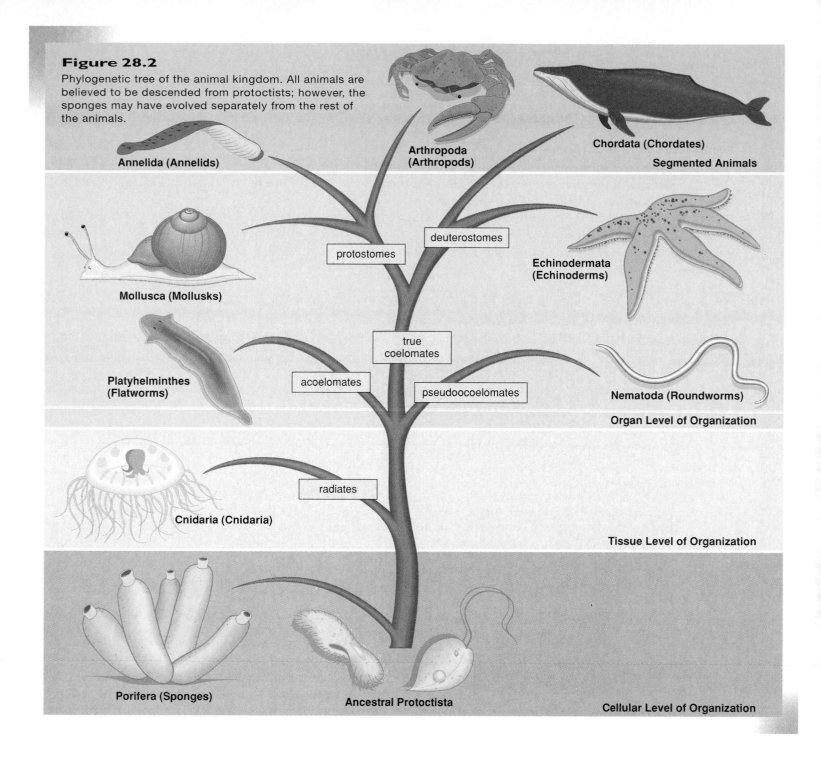

Figure 28.2

Phylogenetic tree of the animal kingdom. All animals are believed to be descended from protoctists; however, the sponges may have evolved separately from the rest of the animals.

Arthropoda (Arthropods)

Chordata (Chordates)

Annelida (Annelids)

Segmented Animals

deuterostomes

protostomes

Echinodermata (Echinoderms)

Mollusca (Mollusks)

true coelomates

acoelomates

pseudoocoelomates

Platyhelminthes (Flatworms)

Nematoda (Roundworms)

Organ Level of Organization

radiates

Cnidaria (Cnidaria)

Tissue Level of Organization

Porifera (Sponges)

Ancestral Protoctista

Cellular Level of Organization

are true coelomates—they have a coelom that is completely lined with mesoderm. Coelomates are either protostomes or deuterostomes. When the blastopore (the site of invagination of endoderm during development) is associated with the mouth, the animal is a protostome. When the blastopore is associated with the anus and a second opening becomes the mouth, the animal is a deuterostome.

Coelomates are also divided into those that are nonsegmented and those that are segmented. Segmented animals have repeating units. *Segmentation* leads to specialization of parts because the various segments can become differentiated for specific purposes.

> **C**lassification of animals is based on type of symmetry, number of tissue layers, type of coelom, and presence of segmentation.

KINGDOM ANIMALIA

Multicellular organisms with well-developed tissues; usually motile; heterotrophic by ingestion, generally in a digestive cavity; diplontic life cycle. Protostomes include phyla Mollusca, Annelida, and Arthropoda. Deuterostomes include phyla Echinodermata, Hemichordata, and Chordata.

Invertebrates*

Phylum Porifera: sponges

Phylum Cnidaria: jellyfishes, sea anemones, corals, e.g., *Hydra, Obelia*

Phylum Ctenophora: comb jellies, sea walnuts

Phylum Platyhelminthes: flatworms, e.g., planaria, flukes, tapeworms

Phylum Nemertea: ribbon worms

Phylum Nematoda: roundworms, e.g., *Ascaris*

Phylum Rotifera: rotifers

Phylum Mollusca: chitons, snails, slugs, clams, mussels, squids, octopuses

Phylum Annelida: segmented worms, e.g., clam worms, earthworms, leeches

Phylum Arthropoda: spiders, scorpions, horseshoe crabs, lobsters, crayfish, shrimps, crabs, millipedes, centipedes, insects

Phylum Echinodermata: sea lilies, sea stars, brittle stars, sea urchins, sand dollars, sea cucumbers, sea daisies

Phylum Hemichordata: acorn worms

Phylum Chordata
Subphylum Urochordata: tunicates
Subphylum Cephalochordata: lancelets

Vertebrates*

Subphylum Vertebrata
Superclass Agnatha: jawless fishes, e.g., lampreys, hagfishes
Superclass Gnathostomata: jawed fishes, all tetrapods
Class Chondrichthyes: cartilaginous fishes, e.g., sharks, skates, rays
Class Osteichthyes: bony fishes, e.g., herring, salmon, cod, eel, flounder
Class Amphibia: frogs, toads, salamanders
Class Reptilia: snakes, lizards, turtles
Class Aves: birds, e.g., sparrows, penguins, ostriches
Class Mammalia: mammals, e.g., cats, dogs, horses, rats, humans

* Not in the classification of organisms, but added here for clarity

MULTICELLULARITY EVOLVES

All animals are multicellular, but sponges are the only animals to have the *cellular level of organization*. Sponges, which have no symmetry and no tissues, are believed to be out of the mainstream of animal evolution. Most likely they evolved separately from protozoan ancestors and represent a dead-end branch of the evolutionary tree.

Sponges Have Pores

Sponges (phylum Porifera, 5,000 species) are aquatic, largely marine animals, that vary greatly in size, shape, and color. Their saclike bodies are perforated by many pores; the phylum name, Porifera, means pore bearing.

The cellular organization of sponges is demonstrated by experimentation. After a sponge is broken into separate cells, the cells will exist individually until they spontaneously reorganize into a sponge once again. What types of cells are found in a sponge? The outer layer of the wall contains flattened epidermal cells, some of which have contractile fibers; the middle layer is a semifluid matrix with wandering amoeboid cells; and the inner layer is composed of flagellated cells called *collar cells* (or choanocytes) that look like protozoa (fig. 28.3). There are no nerve cells or other means of coordination between the cells. To some, a sponge is best thought of as a colony of protozoa.

The beating of the flagella of collar cells produces water currents that flow through the pores into the central cavity and out through the osculum, the upper opening of the body. Although

Figure 28.3

Generalized sponge anatomy. The wall contains two layers of cells: the outer epidermal cells and the inner collar cells. The collar cells (enlarged) have flagella that beat, moving the water through pores as indicated by the arrows. Food particles in the water are trapped by the collar cells and digested within their food vacuoles. Amoeboid cells transport nutrients from cell to cell; spicules compose an internal skeleton of some sponges.

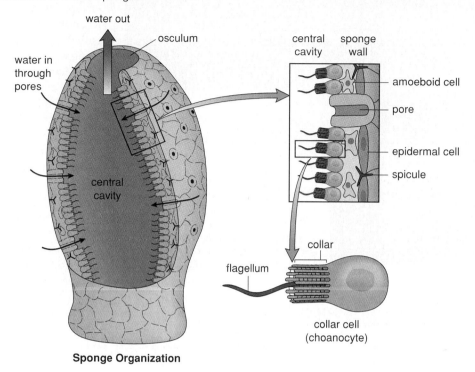

Sponge Organization

it may seem that sponges can't do much, even a simple one only 10 cm tall is estimated to filter as much as 100 liters of water each day. It takes this much water to supply the needs of the organism. Simple sponges have pores leading directly from the outside into the central cavity. Larger and more complex sponges have canals leading from external to internal pores.

A sponge is a **sessile filter feeder,** an organism that stays in one place and filters its food from the water. Oxygen is also supplied to the sponge and waste products are taken away by the constant stream of water through the organism. Microscopic food particles brought by the water are engulfed by the collar cells and digested by them in food vacuoles or are passed to the amoeboid cells for digestion. The amoeboid cells also act as a circulatory device to transport nutrients from cell to cell, and they produce the sex cells (the egg and the sperm) and spicules.

Sponges can reproduce asexually by fragmentation or by budding. During budding, a small protuberance appears and gradually increases in size until a complete organism forms. Budding produces colonies of sponges that can become quite large. During sexual reproduction, eggs and sperm are released into the central cavity. Fertilization results in a zygote that develops into a ciliated larva that may swim to a new location. Such a larva

assures dispersal of the species for the sessile animal. Like all less specialized organisms, sponges are capable of regeneration, or growth of a whole from a small part. Thus, if a sponge is removed, chopped up, and returned to the water, each piece may grow into a complete sponge.

Sponges are classified on the basis of the type of skeleton they have. Some sponges also have an internal skeleton composed of **spicules** [L. *spic,* spike, and *ule,* little], little needle-shaped structures with one to six rays. Chalk sponges have spicules made of calcium carbonate; glass sponges have spicules that contain silica. Most sponges have fibers of spongin, a modified collagen. But some sponges contain only spongin fibers; a bath sponge is the dried spongin skeleton from which all living tissue has been removed. Today, however, commercial "sponges" are usually synthetic.

Sponges have a cellular level of organization and most likely evolved independently from protozoa. They are classified according to the type of skeleton they have.

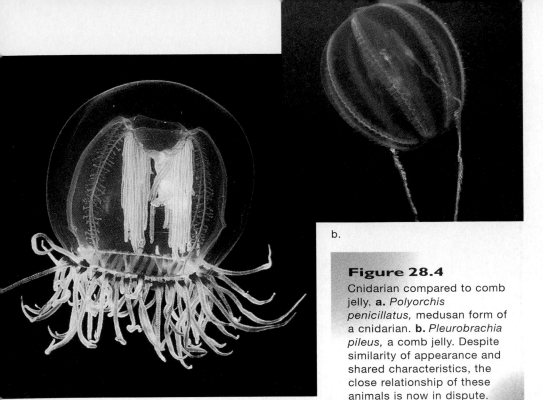

b.

Cnidaria Have Radial Symmetry

Cnidaria (**phylum Cnidaria,** 9,000 species) are tubular or bell-shaped animals that reside mainly in shallow coastal waters, except for the oceanic jellyfishes. Unique to cnidaria are specialized stinging cells, called cnidocytes, which give the phylum its name. Each cnidocyte has a fluid-filled capsule called a **nematocyst** [Gk. *nem,* thread, and *cyst,* bag], which contains a long, spirally coiled hollow thread. When the trigger of the cnidocyte is touched, the nematocyst is discharged. Some threads merely trap a prey or predator; others have spines that penetrate and inject paralyzing toxins.

Figure 28.4
Cnidarian compared to comb jelly. **a.** *Polyorchis penicillatus,* medusan form of a cnidarian. **b.** *Pleurobrachia pileus,* a comb jelly. Despite similarity of appearance and shared characteristics, the close relationship of these animals is now in dispute.

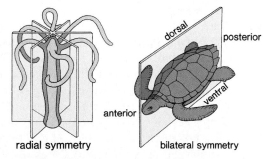

The body of a cnidarian is a two-layered sac. The outer tissue layer is a protective epidermis derived from ectoderm. The inner tissue layer, which is derived from endoderm, secretes digestive juices into the internal cavity, called the **gastrovascular cavity** [Gk. *gastro,* stomach, and L. *vascul,* little vessel] because it serves for digestion of food and circulation of nutrients. The two tissue layers are separated by mesoglea. There are muscle fibers at the base of the epidermal and gastrodermal cells. Nerve cells located below the epidermis near the mesoglea interconnect and form a nerve net throughout the body. In contrast to highly organized nervous systems, the nerve net allows transmission of impulses in several directions at once—multiple firings of nematocysts in parts of the body not directly stimulated have been observed. Having both muscle fibers and nerve fibers, these animals are capable of directional movement; the body can contract or extend, and the tentacles that ring the mouth can reach out and grasp prey.

Two basic body forms are seen among cnidaria. The mouth of a hydroid or *polyp* is directed upward, while the mouth of a jellyfish or *medusa* is directed downward. A medusa has more mesoglea than a polyp and the tentacles are concentrated on the margin of the bell. At one time, both body forms may have been a part of the life cycle of all cnidaria, since in certain cnidaria today we see an alternation of generations of these two forms (fig. 28.5*a*). When this alternation of generations does exist, the polypoid stage is sessile and produces medusae. The medusan stage is motile and produces egg and sperm, thereby dispersing the species. In some cnidaria, one stage is dominant and the other is reduced; in other species one form is absent altogether.

a.

TWO TISSUE LAYERS EVOLVE

As mentioned, during animal development there are a total of three possible germ layers: ectoderm, endoderm, and mesoderm. Animals in two phyla—comb jellies in **phylum Ctenophora** and cnidaria in phylum Cnidaria—develop only ectoderm and are said to be diploblasts (fig. 28.4). Animals in these phyla are radially *symmetrical,* meaning that any longitudinal cut, such as those shown, produces two identical halves. If an animal is *bilaterally symmetrical,* only the longitudinal cut shown yields two roughly identical halves.

dorsal

posterior

anterior

ventral

radial symmetry

bilateral symmetry

Comb jellies are small (a few cm), transparent often luminescent animals that take their name from their eight plates of fused cilia that resemble long combs. Most of their body is a jellylike packing material called **mesoglea** [Gk. *meso,* middle, and *gle,* glue]. They are the largest animals to be propelled by the beating of cilia. They capture prey either by means of long tentacles, covered with sticky filaments, or by using the entire body, which is covered with a sticky mucus.

> Cnidaria have a tissue level of organization and are radially symmetrical. They have a sac body plan and exist as polyps or medusae.

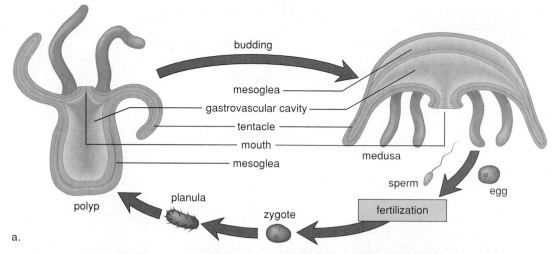

Figure 28.5

Cnidarian diversity. **a.** The alternation of generations life cycle of a cnidarian; in some cnidaria, one generation is dominant, and in others, one generation is absent altogether. **b.** The anemone, which is sometimes called the flower of the sea, is a solitary polyp. **c.** Corals. **d.** Portuguese man-of-war are both colonial polyps. **e.** True jellyfish that undergoes the complete life cycle; this is the medusan stage.

budding

mesoglea

gastrovascular cavity

tentacle

mouth

mesoglea

medusa

sperm

egg

fertilization

zygote

planula

polyp

a.

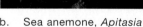

b.   Sea anemone, *Apitasia*

c.   Coral, *Tubastrea*

d.   Portuguese man-of-war, *Physalia*

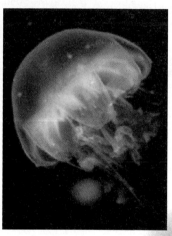
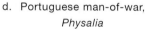

e.   jellyfish, *Aurelia*

Cnidarian Diversity

Among the cnidarian classes, class Anthozoa contains the sea anemones and corals (fig. 28.5*b, c*). Sea anemones are solitary polyps that become larger and heavier than hydrozoan polyps. Most sea anemones are 5–100 mm in height and 5–200 mm in diameter; some are much larger. They may be brightly colored and look like beautiful flowers.

A large part of the sea anemone body is a heavy, thick column, which rests on a pedal disk at the lower end. The oral disk that bears a mouth is surrounded by large number of hollow tentacles. Sea anemones feed on various invertebrates, and large species can capture fish. Sea anemones live attached to a submerged rock, timber, or shell. A number of species form mutualistic relationships (in which both species benefit) with hermit crabs and live attached to the shell of the crab. The anemone provides protection and camouflage for the crab, and the crab provides locomotion and perhaps some food for the sea anemone.

Corals, which are also anthozoa, resemble sea anemones in appearance. Some corals are solitary, but most are colonial with flat, rounded, or upright and branching colonies. Corals are usually found in shallow waters; this is particularly true of reef-building stony corals whose walls contain mutualistic algae. When

threatened, stony corals can retract inside their calcium-carbonate skeletons. The slow accumulation of coral skeletal remains can result in massive structures such as the Great Barrier Reef along the eastern coast of Australia. Several thousand different types of animals interact in coral reefs, areas of biological abundance in tropical seas.

In class Hydrozoa, the polypoid stage is dominant. One of the most unusual hydrozoa is the Portuguese man-of-war, Physalia, which is a colony of polyps, although it looks as if it might be an odd-shaped medusa (fig. 28.5*d*). The original polyp becomes a gas-filled float that provides buoyancy—it keeps the colony afloat. Other polyps, which bud from this one, are specialized for feeding or for reproduction. A long single tentacle armed with numerous nematocysts arises from the base of each feeding polyp. Swimmers who accidently come upon a Portuguese man-of-war can receive painful, even serious, injuries from these stinging tentacles.

Class Scyphozoa includes the true jellyfishes, such as *Aurelia* (fig. 28.5*e*). In jellyfishes, the medusa is the primary stage and the polyp remains quite small and insignificant. Jellyfishes are a part of the zooplankton of the ocean and as such serve as food for larger animals.

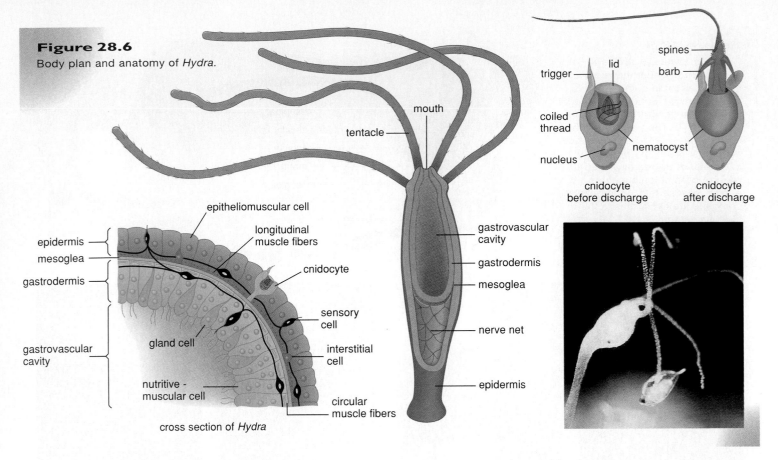

Figure 28.6
Body plan and anatomy of *Hydra*.

trigger
lid
spines
barb
coiled thread
nematocyst
nucleus
cnidocyte before discharge
cnidocyte after discharge

mouth
tentacle

epitheliomuscular cell
longitudinal muscle fibers
epidermis
mesoglea
gastrodermis
cnidocyte
sensory cell
gland cell
interstitial cell
gastrovascular cavity
nutritive - muscular cell
circular muscle fibers

cross section of *Hydra*

gastrovascular cavity
gastrodermis
mesoglea
nerve net
epidermis

Hydra and *Obelia* in Depth

Hydra and *Obelia* in class Hydrozoa are two hydrozoa of particular interest. *Hydra* is a solitary polyp and *Obelia* is a colonial form, which does undergo alternation of generations.

Hydra Is a Solitary Polyp

Hydras [Gk. *hydr,* water] are freshwater cnidaria. Hydras are likely to be found attached to underwater plants or rocks in most lakes and ponds. The body is a small tubular polyp about one-quarter inch in length. The only opening (the mouth) is in a slight elevation that is surrounded by four to six tentacles that contain a large number of nematocysts. The central cavity of the animal is the gastrovascular cavity.

Although a hydra usually remains in one location, it can glide along on its base or even move rapidly by means of somersaulting.

Hydras can respond to stimuli, and if a tentacle is touched with a needle, all the tentacles and the body contract, only to extend later. It is apparent, then, that like other animals capable of locomotion, hydras have both muscular and nerve fibers.

Figure 28.6 shows the microscopic anatomy of *Hydra*. The cells of the epidermis are termed *epitheliomuscular cells* because they contain muscle fibers. Also present in the epidermis are cnidocytes and sensory cells. The latter have long extensions that make contact with the nerve cells within the nerve net. The interstitial, or embryonic, cells also seen in this layer are capable of becoming other types of cells. For example, they can produce an ovary and/or a testis and probably also account for the animal's great regenerative powers. Like the sponges, cnidaria can grow whole from a small piece.

Gland cells of the gastrodermis secrete digestive juices that pour into the gastrovascular cavity. Hydras feed on small prey that are captured when they trigger the release of nematocysts. The tentacles capture and stuff the prey into the gastrovascular cavity, which distends to accommodate the food. The enzymes released by the gland cells begin the digestive process, which is completed within food vacuoles of *nutritive-muscular cells,* the main type of gastrodermal cell. Nutrient molecules are passed by diffusion to the rest of the cells of the body. Nutritive-muscular cells also contain contractile fibers that run circularly about the body; when these contract, the animal lengthens.

Hydras can reproduce both asexually and sexually. They reproduce asexually by forming buds, small outgrowths that develop into a complete animal and then detach. When hydras reproduce sexually, sperm from a testis swim to an egg within an ovary. Fertilization and early development occur within the ovary, after which the embryo is encased within a hard, protective shell that allows it to survive until conditions are optimum for it to emerge and develop into a new polyp.

Figure 28.7

Obelia structure and life cycle. *Obelia,* a colony of feeding polyps and reproductive polyps, undergoes an alternation of generations life cycle.

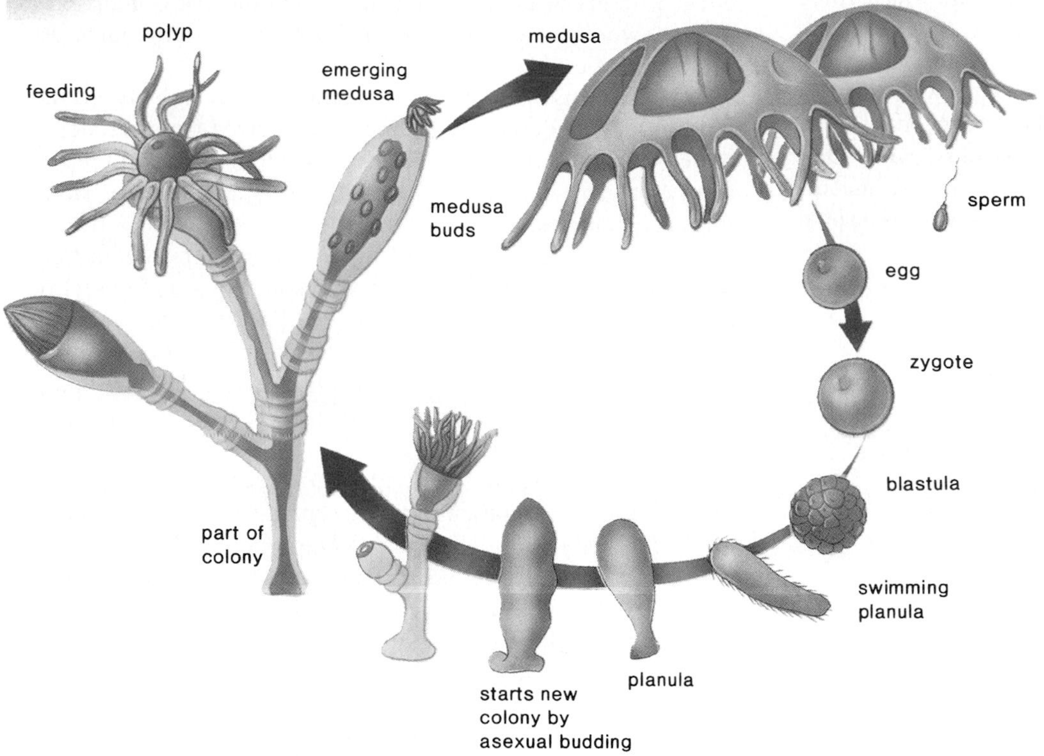

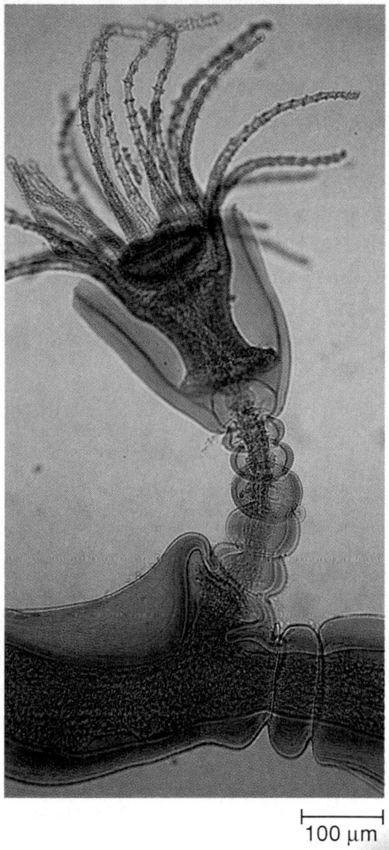

100 μm

Obelia Is a Colonial Form

Obelia (fig. 28.7) is a colony of polyps that is enclosed by a hard, chitinous covering. There are two types of polyps. The *feeding polyps* extend beyond the covering and can withdraw into it for protection. They have nematocyst-bearing tentacles that can capture and bring prey—such as tiny crustacea, worms, and larvae—into the gastrovascular cavity. The polyps are connected and the partially digested food is distributed to the rest of the colony.

The colony increases in size asexually by the budding of new polyps. Sexual reproduction involves the production of medusae, which bud from the second type of polyp called *reproductive polyps*. Hydroid *medusae* tend to be smaller than those of the true jellyfishes. The tentacles attached to the bell margin have nematocysts and they bring food into a gastrovascular cavity that extends even into the tentacles. The nerve net is concentrated into two nerve rings; the bell margin is supplied with sensory cells, such as statocysts, organs of equilibrium, and ocelli, light-sensitive organs.

While some species produce free-swimming medusae, in other species the medusae remain attached to the colony and shed only their gametes. The resulting zygote develops into a ciliated planula larva. The planula larva settles down and develops into a polyp colony.

> *Obelia* is an example of a colonial hydroid consisting of feeding and reproductive polyps. Alternation of generations involving free-swimming medusae is typical.

The relationship of radially symmetrical cnidaria to the rest of the animal groups, which at some time during their life history are bilaterally symmetrical, has not been easy to determine. However, there are those who believe that a planuloid-type organism could have given rise to both the cnidaria and the flatworms, which are discussed next. The cnidaria have a two-tissue level of organization and radial symmetry. The flatworms have three germ layers and bilateral symmetry.

BILATERAL SYMMETRY EVOLVES

All other animals to be studied are bilaterally symmetrical, at least in some stage of development. As embryos, they have three germ layers and are, therefore, called *triploblasts*. As adults, they have the *organ level of organization*. Flatworms in the phylum Platyhelminthes have these features, as do ribbon worms in the phylum Nemertea. Flatworms, however, like cnidaria, have a **sac body plan,** while ribbon worms have a **tube-within-a-tube body plan.** Animals with a sac body plan are said to have an incomplete digestive tract, while those with the tube-within-a-tube plan have a complete digestive tract.

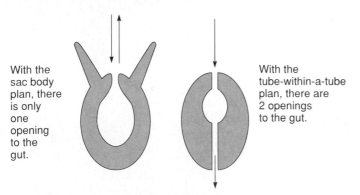

With the sac body plan, there is only one opening to the gut.

With the tube-within-a-tube plan, there are 2 openings to the gut.

In the tube-within-a-tube body plan, there is the possibility of specialization of parts along the length of the tube.

Ribbon worms (**phylum Nemertea,** 650 species), which are mainly marine, have a distinctive proboscis apparatus—a long, hollow tube lying in a cavity called the rhynchocoel (fig. 28.8). Contraction of the rhynchocoel wall causes the proboscis to evert and shoot outward through a pore located just above the mouth. The proboscis is used primarily for prey capture but also for defense, locomotion, and burrowing. Like flatworms, ribbon worms are acoelomates.

Figure 28.8

Ribbon worm, *Amphiporus,* with proboscis partially extended. Ribbon worms, like flatworms, are bilaterally symmetrical, have three germ layers, and demonstrate the organ level of organization. They also have a complete digestive tract.

Flatworms Are Flat

Flatworms (**phylum Platyhelminthes,** 13,000 species), planaria, and their relatives are freshwater animals in the class Turbellaria. The majority of flatworms are parasites. The flukes, which are either external or internal parasites, are in the class Trematoda. The tapeworms, which are intestinal parasites of vertebrates, are in the class Cestoda.

Flatworms are complex. In addition to an endodermis derived from endoderm and an epidermis derived from ectoderm, there is a mesoderm layer that gives rise to muscles and reproductive organs. There is no coelom; these animals are, therefore, acoelomates.

Although flatworms have the organ level of organization, there are no specialized circulatory or respiratory structures. How are nutrients distributed about the body? The gastrovascular cavity, which is sometimes highly branched, serves this function. Gas exchange can occur by diffusion because of the animal's flat, thin body. Often, there is an excretory system that functions as an osmotic-regulating system.

Flatworms are *bilaterally symmetrical,* and free-living forms have undergone **cephalization** [Gk. *cephal,* head]—the development of a head region. There is a *ladder-type nervous system,* so called because the two lateral nerve cords plus the connecting nerves look like a ladder. Paired ganglia (collection of nerve cells) function as a brain; sensory cells are located in the body wall and the animal is able to respond to various stimuli.

> **Flatworms have a sac body plan but three germ layers and the organ level of organization. They are bilaterally symmetrical, and cephalization is present.**

Planaria Are Free Living

The turbellaria include freshwater planaria such as *Dugesia,* which are small (several mm to several cm) literally flat worms, with brown or black pigmentation (fig. 28.9). They live in lakes, ponds, and streams, where they feed on small living or dead organisms.

The head is bluntly arrow shaped, with lateral extensions called auricles that function as sense organs to detect potential food sources and enemies. There are two light-sensitive eyespots whose pigmentation causes the worm to look cross-eyed. Inside, the brain is connected to a ladder-type nervous system. There are three kinds of muscle layers—an outer circular layer, an inner longitudinal layer, and a diagonal layer—that allow for quite varied movement. In larger forms, locomotion is accomplished by the movement of cilia on the ventral and lateral surfaces. Numerous gland cells secrete a mucous material upon which the animal moves.

Figure 28.9

Planarian anatomy. **a.** The photograph shows that flatworms, *Dugesia,* are bilaterally symmetrical and have a head region with eyespots. **b.** When the pharynx is extended as shown, food is sucked up into a digestive organ that branches throughout the body. **c.** The excretory system with flame cells is shown in detail. **d.** The reproductive system has both male and female organs, and the digestive system has a single opening. **e.** The nervous system has a ladderlike appearance.

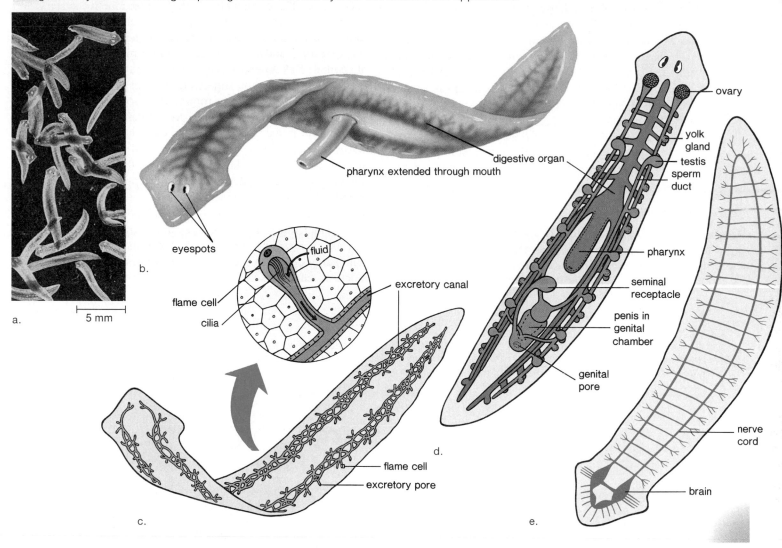

The animal captures food by wrapping itself around the prey, entangling it in slime, and pinning it down. Then a muscular pharynx is extended and by a sucking motion the food is torn up and swallowed. The pharynx leads into a three-branched gastrovascular cavity in which digestion is both extracellular and intracellular.

Why is it to be expected that planaria would have a well-developed excretory organ system? They live in fresh water, and their excretory organ functions in osmotic regulation as well as excreting water. The organ consists of a series of interconnecting canals that run the length of the body on each side. Bulblike structures containing cilia are at the ends of the side branches of the canals. The cilia move back and forth, bringing water into the canals that empty at pores. The beating of the cilia reminded some early investigator of the flickering of a flame, and so the excretory organ of the flatworm is called a *flame-cell system.*

Planaria reproduce both asexually and sexually. They constrict beneath the pharynx and each part grows into a whole animal again. Many experiments in development have utilized planaria because of their marked ability to regenerate. Planaria are **hermaphroditic,** which means that they possess both male and female sex organs. The worms practice cross-fertilization when the penis of one is inserted into the genital pore of the other. The fertilized eggs are enclosed in a cocoon and hatch in two or three weeks as tiny worms.

> Free-living planaria best exhibit the bilateral symmetry and organ development—including the nervous system and muscles—of a flatworm.

Parasitic Flatworms Cause Serious Illnesses

Among the *parasitic* flatworms are flukes (trematodes) and tapeworms (cestodes). The structure of both of these worms illustrates the modifications that occur in parasitic animals. Concomitant with the loss of predation, there is an absence of cephalization; the anterior end notably carries hooks and/or suckers for attachment to the host. There is an extensive development of the reproductive system at the expense of the other organs. Well-developed nerves and a gastrovascular cavity are not needed because the animal no longer seeks out and digests prey; instead, it acquires nutrients from its host. Flukes and tapeworms are covered by a *tegument,* a specialized body wall resistant to host digestive juices.

Both flukes and tapeworms utilize a secondary, or intermediate, host to transport the species from primary host to primary host. The primary host is infected with the sexually mature adult; the secondary host contains the larval stage or stages.

Flukes Invade Organs

Trematodes (class Trematoda) include the flukes, which are usually named for the type of vertebrate organ they inhabit; for example, there are blood, liver, and lung flukes. While the structure may vary slightly, in general the fluke body tends to be oval to elongate. There is no definite head, but the oral sucker (surrounded by sensory papillae) is at the anterior end. Usually there is at least one other sucker for attachment to the host. Inside, there is a reduced digestive system, a reduced nervous system, and a modified excretory system with a reduction in the number of excretory canals. There is a well-developed reproductive system, and the adult fluke is usually hermaphroditic, as are planaria. An exception is the blood fluke, which causes **schistosomiasis** and is seen predominantly in Africa and South America. In this disease, the female flukes deposit their eggs in small blood vessels close to the lumen of the intestine, and the eggs make their way into the digestive tract by a slow migratory process (fig. 28.10). After the eggs pass out with the feces, they hatch into tiny larvae that swim about in the rice paddies and elsewhere until they enter a particular species of snail. Within the snail asexual reproduction occurs, and these new larval forms leave the snail. If they enter the body of a human, they mature and implant themselves in the small intestinal blood vessels. Those infected usually die of secondary diseases brought on by their weakened condition.

The Chinese liver fluke requires two hosts: the snail and the fish. Humans become infected when they eat uncooked fish. The adults reside in the liver and deposit their eggs in the bile duct, which carries the eggs to the intestine.

Figure 28.10

Schistosomiasis. This infection of humans, caused by blood flukes, *Schistosoma,* is an extremely prevalent disease in Egypt—especially since the building of the Aswan High Dam. Standing water in irrigation ditches, combined with unsanitary practices, has created the conditions for widespread infection.

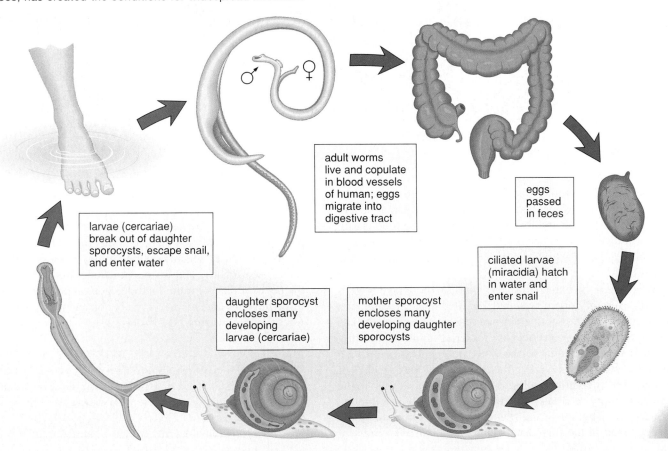

adult worms live and copulate in blood vessels of human; eggs migrate into digestive tract

eggs passed in feces

ciliated larvae (miracidia) hatch in water and enter snail

larvae (cercariae) break out of daughter sporocysts, escape snail, and enter water

daughter sporocyst encloses many developing larvae (cercariae)

mother sporocyst encloses many developing daughter sporocysts

Tapeworms Live in the Gut

A tapeworm has a head region (fig. 28.11), containing hooks and suckers for attachment to the intestinal wall of the host. Behind the head region, called a **scolex,** there is a short neck and then a long series of proglottids. **Proglottids** are segments, each of which contains a full set of both male and female sex organs and little else. There are excretory canals but no digestive system and only the rudiments of nerves.

After fertilization, the organs disintegrate and the proglottids become nothing but a bag filled with maturing eggs. Mature proglottids such as these break off and, as they pass out with the feces, the eggs are released.

If feces-contaminated food is fed to pigs or cattle, larvae escape when the covering of the eggs is digested away. They burrow through the intestinal wall and travel in the bloodstream to finally lodge and encyst in muscle. Here a **cyst** means a small, hard-walled structure that contains a larval worm. When humans eat infected meat that has not been thoroughly cooked, the larvae break out of the cyst, attach themselves to the intestinal wall, and grow to adulthood. Then the cycle begins again.

> **Flukes and tapeworms illustrate the modifications that occur when animals take up the parasitic way of life.**

Table 28.2 contrasts features of planaria, tapeworms, and flukes to illustrate the anatomical changes to be associated with the parasitic way of life.

Figure 28.11

Life cycle of a tapeworm, *Taenia*. The life cycle includes a human (primary host) and a pig (secondary host). The adult worm is modified for its parasitic way of life. It consists of a scolex and many proglottids, which, when mature, are simply bags of eggs.

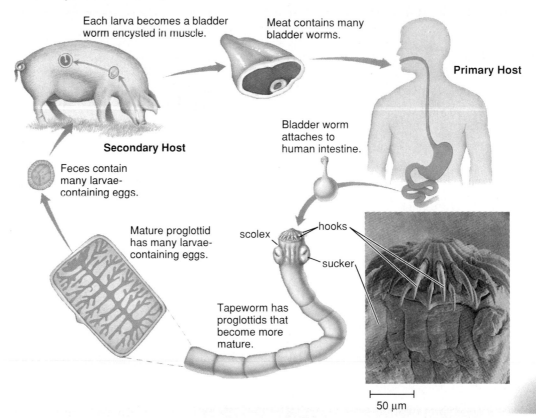

Each larva becomes a bladder worm encysted in muscle.

Meat contains many bladder worms.

Primary Host

Secondary Host

Bladder worm attaches to human intestine.

Feces contain many larvae-containing eggs.

Mature proglottid has many larvae-containing eggs.

scolex

hooks

sucker

Tapeworm has proglottids that become more mature.

50 μm

Table 28.2

Free-Living Flatworms Versus Parasitic Flatworms

	Free Living	Parasitic	
	Planaria	*Flukes*	*Tapeworms*
Body wall	Ciliated epidermis	Tegument	Glycocalyx covers tegument
Cephalization	Yes—eyespots and auricles	No—oral suckers	No—scolex with hooks and suckers
Nervous system	Nerves and brain	Reduced	Reduced
Digestive organ	Branched	Reduced	Absent
Reproductive organs	Hermaphroditic	Increased in volume	Extensively developed
Larva	Absent	Present	Present

Presence of a Coelom

A coelom is a body cavity surrounding the digestive organ or system. Flatworms are acoelomates (fig. 28A). They have no body cavity, and the mesoderm is packed solidly between the ectoderm and endoderm. The roundworms are pseudocoelomate. They have a body cavity in which the organs lie loose. Apparently, this is disadvantageous to an increase in size, because most of these worms are small. In coelomates, the coelom develops as a cavity within the mesoderm; therefore, it is completely lined with mesoderm. Such a coelom is often called a "true coelom."

The organs in a true coelom are held in place by mesenteries, assuring a more stable arrangement with less crowding. Further, the gut is muscular (muscles are derived from mesoderm) and shows specialization of parts not seen in the pseudocoelomates. In the true coelomates (all the other animals we will study), the internal organs are more complex.

The coelom also serves other functions. It allows the organs and the body wall to move independently. This means an animal can stretch and bend without putting a strain on the internal organs. The coelom is fluid filled, and this fluid protects and cushions the inter-

nal organs. In some animals, the fluid aids in the movement of materials, such as metabolic wastes; in others, this function is taken over by blood vessels. Not only metabolic wastes but also sex cells may be deposited into the coelomic cavity before they are transported away by ducts. The gastrovascular cavity of acoelomates (cnidarians and flatworms) and the fluid-filled coelom of soft-bodied coelomates can act as a hydrostatic skeleton. It offers some resistance to the contraction of muscles and yet permits flexibility, so that the animal can change shape and perform a variety of movements.

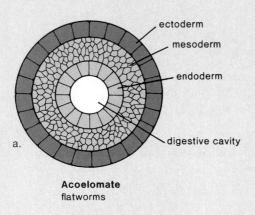

a.

Acoelomate
flatworms

- ectoderm
- mesoderm
- endoderm
- digestive cavity

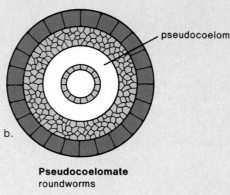

b.

Pseudocoelomate
roundworms

- pseudocoelom

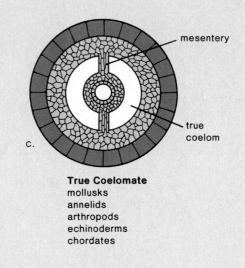

c.

True Coelomate
mollusks
annelids
arthropods
echinoderms
chordates

- mesentery
- true coelom

Figure 28A
Body cavities.

A PSEUDOCOELOM EVOLVES

The accompanying reading compares animals on the basis of coelom type and describes how a coelom can serve as a *hydrostatic skeleton*. A **pseudocoelom** [Gk. *pseudo,* false, and *coel,* hollow] is a body cavity that is *incompletely lined by mesoderm;* a true coelom is completely lined by mesoderm. In other words, mesoderm does not form a complete layer next to the body wall or around the gut. Two animal phyla consist of pseudocoelomates: roundworms (phylum Nematoda) and **rotifers (phylum Rotifera,** 2,000 species). These animals also have the tube-within-a-tube body plan. The digestive tract is the inner tube within the rest of the animal, which is the outer tube.

Rotifers, which are abundant in fresh water, are microscopic. Although rotifers are limited in size, they are multicellular, with internal organs. They are named for a crown of cilia (corona) that resembles a rotating wheel and serves both as an organ of locomotion and as an aid in bringing food to the mouth.

> Pseudocoelomate animals (e.g., roundworms and rotifers) have a coelom that is incompletely lined by mesoderm. A coelom provides a space for internal organs and can serve as a hydrostatic skeleton.

Roundworms Are Nonsegmented

Roundworms (phylum Nematoda, 500,000 species), as their name implies, have a smooth outside wall, indicating that they are nonsegmented. These worms, which are generally colorless and 2.5–30 cm in length, are found almost anywhere—in the sea, in fresh water, and in the soil—in such numbers that thousands of them can be found in a small area. Some are predators with teeth and other mouthparts, but many are scavengers or parasites. Among the latter, the pinworms, the hookworms, and *Trichinella* are small worms that are not easily examined. *Ascaris,* a large parasitic roundworm, is often studied as an example of this phylum.

Ascaris Infects Humans

Ascaris (fig. 28.12) females (20–35 cm) tend to be larger than males, which have an incurved tail. Both sexes move by means of a characteristic whiplike motion because only longitudinal muscles lie next to the body wall.

The internal organs, including the tubular reproductive organs, lie within the pseudocoelom. Because mating produces eggs that mature in the soil, the parasite is limited to warmer environments. When these eggs are swallowed, larvae escape and burrow through the intestinal wall. Making their way through the organs of the host, they move from the intestine to the liver, the heart, and then the lungs. Within the lungs, molting takes place and, after about ten days, the larvae migrate up the windpipe to the throat where they are swallowed, once again reaching the intestine. Then the mature worms mate and the female deposits eggs that pass out with the feces. In this life cycle, as with that of other roundworms, feces must reach the mouth of the next host; therefore, proper sanitation is the best means to prevent infection with such worms as *Ascaris* and pinworms.

Other Roundworm Parasites

Trichinosis (fig. 28.12) is a serious infection that humans can contract when they eat rare pork containing encysted larvae. After maturation, the female adult burrows into the wall of the small intestine and produces living offspring that are carried by the bloodstream to the skeletal muscles, where they encyst.

Figure 28.12

Roundworm anatomy. Note that roundworms such as *Ascaris* have a pseudocoelom and a complete digestive tract with a mouth and an anus. Therefore, roundworms have a tube-within-a-tube body plan. The sexes are separate; this is a male roundworm. Some roundworms, such as *Trichinella,* are parasites that encyst in muscle. This infection in humans is called trichinosis.

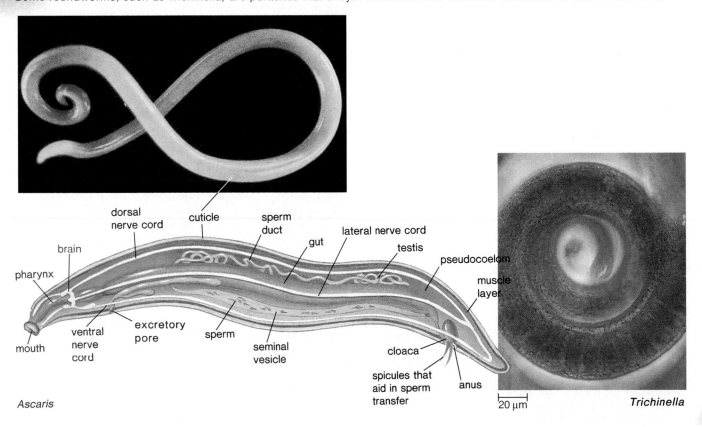

Filarial worms, a type of roundworm, cause various diseases. *Dirofilaria,* the heartworm of dogs, is a common filarial worm of temperate zones. The cause of **elephantiasis,** a disease restricted to tropical areas of Africa, is caused by a filarial worm that utilizes the mosquito as a secondary host. Because the adult worms reside in lymphatic vessels, collection of fluid is impeded and the limbs of an infected person may swell to a monstrous size (fig. 28.13). Elephantiasis is treatable in its early stages but not after scar tissue has blocked lymphatic vessels.

Roundworms can be free living or parasitic. Free-living forms live in the soil; parasitic ones cause some common infections such as pinworm and hookworm infections of humans and heartworm infection of dogs.

Figure 28.13

An infection from a filarial worm, *Wuchereria,* causes elephantiasis, a condition in which the individual experiences extreme swelling in regions where the worms have blocked the lymphatic vessels.

Table 28.3

Comparison of Animals Without a True Coelom

	Sponges	Cnidaria	Flatworms	Roundworms
Symmetry	Radial or none	Radial	Bilateral	Bilateral
Type of body plan	—	Sac	Sac	Tube-within-a-tube
Tissue layers	—	Two	Three	Three
Level of organization	Cell	Tissue	Organ	Organ
Body cavity	—	—	Acoelomate	Pseudocoelomate

Summary

1. Animals are multicellular organisms that are heterotrophic and ingest their food. They follow the diplontic life cycle. Typically, they have the power of motion by means of contracting fibers.

2. It's possible to construct a phylogenetic tree for animals, but this is largely based on a study of today's forms. All the major phyla studied today are represented by Cambrian fossils.

3. Type of symmetry, number of tissue layers, type of coelom, and presence or absence of segmentation are criteria that are used in classification. Table 28.3 compares these criteria among the animals studied in this chapter.

4. Sponges may have evolved separately from other animals, since they have features that set them apart. They have the cellular level of organization and lack tissues and symmetry. Sponges are sessile and depend on a flow of water through the body to acquire food, which is digested in vacuoles within collar cells that line a central cavity.

5. Cnidaria and comb jellies have two tissue layers derived from the germ layers ectoderm and endoderm. They are radially symmetrical.

6. Cnidaria have a sac body plan. They exist as either polyps or medusae, or they can alternate between the two. Hydras and relatives—sea anemones and corals—are polyps; in jellyfishes the medusan stage is dominant.

7. In *Hydra* and other cnidaria, an outer epidermis is separated from an inner gastrodermis by mesoglea. They possess tentacles to capture prey and nematocysts to stun it. A nerve net coordinates movements. Digestion of prey begins in the gastrovascular cavity and is finished within gastrodermal cells.

8. Flatworms and ribbon worms have bilateral symmetry and the organ level of organization, including organs derived from mesoderm, a third germ layer, as do all the other phyla of animals to be studied.

9. Flatworms may be free living or parasitic. Freshwater planaria exemplify the features of flatworms in general and free-living forms in particular. They have muscles and a ladder-type nervous system, and they show cephalization. They take in food through an extended pharynx leading to a gastrovascular cavity, which extends throughout the body. There is an osmotic-regulating organ that contains flame cells.

10. Flukes and tapeworms are parasitic. Flukes have two suckers by which they attach to and feed from their hosts. Tapeworms have a scolex with hooks and suckers for attaching to the host. The body is made up of proglottids, which, when mature, contain thousands of eggs. If these eggs are taken up by pigs or cattle, the larvae become encysted in their muscles. If humans eat this meat, they too may become infected.

11. Roundworms and rotifers are pseudocoelomate. A coelom provides a space for internal organs and can serve as a hydrostatic skeleton.

12. Roundworms are mostly small and very diverse; they are present almost everywhere in great numbers. The parasite *Ascaris* is representative of the group. Infections can also be caused by *Trichinella,* whose larval stage encysts in the muscles of humans. Elephantiasis is caused by a filarial worm that blocks lymphatic vessels.

Writing Across the Curriculum

In order to practice writing skills, students should write out the answers to any or all of the study questions and the critical thinking questions. The study questions are sequenced in the same order as the text. Answers to the objective questions, and suggested answers to the critical thinking questions, are in appendix D.

Study Questions

1. What are the characteristics that separate animals from plants? from fungi?   466

2. What does the phylogenetic tree (see fig. 28.2) tell you about the evolution of the animals studied in this chapter?   467

3. List the types of cells found in a sponge, and describe their functions.   468–69

4. What features make sponges different from the other organisms placed in the animal kingdom?   469

5. What features do comb jellies and cnidaria have in common? How are they different?   470

6. What are the two body forms found in cnidaria? Explain how they function in the life cycle of various types of cnidaria.   470

7. Describe the anatomy of *Hydra,* pointing out those features that typify cnidaria.   472

8. What features do flatworms and ribbon worms have in common? How are they different?   474

9. Describe the anatomy of a free-living planarian, pointing out those features that typify nonparasitic flatworms.   474–75

10. Describe the parasitic flatworms, and give the life cycle of both the pork tapeworm and the blood fluke that causes schistosomiasis.   476–77

11. What is a pseudocoelom? What are the advantages of having a coelom? What two groups of animals have a pseudocoelom?   478

12. Describe the anatomy of *Ascaris,* pointing out those features that typify roundworms.   479

13. Compare the animals studied in this chapter in terms of symmetry, tissue layers, level of organization, body plan, and type of coelom.   480

Objective Questions

1. Which of these is not a characteristic of animals?
   a. heterotrophic
   b. diplontic life cycle
   c. have contracting fibers
   d. single cells or colonial

2. The phylogenetic tree of animals shows that
   a. cnidaria evolved from sponges.
   b. flatworms evolved from roundworms.
   c. both sponges and cnidaria evolved from protoctista.
   d. All of these are correct.

3. Which of these sponge characteristics is not typical of animals?
   a. They practice sexual reproduction.
   b. They have the cellular level of organization.
   c. They are asymmetrical.
   d. Both b and c are correct.

4. Which of these is mismatched?
   a. sponges—spicules
   b. tapeworms—proglottids
   c. cnidaria—nematocysts
   d. roundworms—cilia

5. Flukes and tapeworms
   a. show cephalization.
   b. have well-developed reproductive systems.
   c. have well-developed nervous systems.
   d. are plant parasites.

6. The presence of mesoderm
   a. restricts the development of a coelom.
   b. is associated with the organ level of organization.
   c. is associated with the development of muscles.
   d. Both b and c are correct.

7. *Ascaris* is a parasitic
   a. roundworm.   **c.** hydra.
   b. flatworm.   **d.** sponge.

8. Label the following diagram of the cnidarian life cycle:

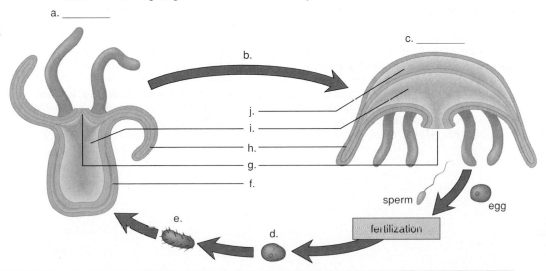

a. _____

b.

c. _____

j. _____

i. _____

h. _____

g. _____

f. _____

e.

d.

sperm

egg

fertilization

9. Under the phyla headings given, write which of these terms apply:

Terms:	Sponges	Cnidaria	Flatworms	Roundworms
radial symmetry				
pseudocoelom				
tissue level of organization				
three tissue layers				
tube-within-a-tube body plan				

10. Under the names of the animals given, write which of these features apply:

Terms:	Sponges	Planaria	Tapeworms	Roundworms
proglottids				
uterus				
eyespots				
collar cells				
cnidocytes				
gastrovascular cavity				

Concepts and Critical Thinking

1. *Animals are one of the major groups of organisms alive today.*

    What features might you expect animals to have in common because they are heterotrophic by ingesting food? How might this common trait cause them to be differently adapted between the digestive tract and body wall?

2. *Animals have a phylogenetic history.*

    A common ancestor for flatworms and roundworms might have had what anatomical features?

3. *Parasites are adapted to their way of life.*

    What types of adaptations are helpful to an internal parasite?

Selected Key Terms

asymmetry A body plan having no particular symmetry.   466

bilateral symmetry Body plan having two corresponding or complementary halves.   466

cephalization (sef-uh-luh-ZAY-shun) Development of a well-recognized anterior head with concentrated nerve masses and receptors. [Gk. *cephal,* head]   447

coelom A body cavity lying between the digestive tract and body wall that is completely lined by mesoderm. [Gk. *coel,* hollow]   466

gastrovascular cavity A blind digestive cavity that also serves a circulatory (transport) function in animals that lack a circulatory system. [Gk. *gastro,* stomach, and L. *vascul,* little vessel]   470

hermaphroditic (hur-maf-ruh-DIT-ik) Characterizes an animal having both male and female sex organs.   475

invertebrate Referring to an animal without a serial arrangement of vertebrae, or a backbone. [L. *in,* without, and *vertebr,* vertebra]   466

mesoglea (mez-uh-GLEE-uh) A jellylike layer between the epidermis and the gastrodermis of cnidaria. [Gk. *meso,* middle, and *gle,* glue]   470

nematocyst (NEM-ut-uh-sist) In cnidaria, a capsule that contains a threadlike fiber whose release aids in the capture of prey. [Gk. *nem,* thread, and *cyst,* bag]   470

pseudocoelom A body cavity lying between the digestive tract and body wall that is incompletely lined by mesoderm. [Gk. *pseudo,* false, and *coel,* hollow]   478

radial symmetry Body plan in which similar parts are arranged around a central axis, like spokes of a wheel.   466

sac body plan A body with a digestive cavity that has only one opening, as in cnidaria and flatworms.   474

sessile filter feeder An organism that stays in one place and filters its food from the water.   469

spicule (SPIK-yool) A skeletal structure of sponges composed of calcium carbonate or silicate. [L. *spic,* spike, and *ule,* little]   469

tube-within-a-tube body plan A body with a digestive tract that has both a mouth and an anus.   474

KINGDOM ANIMALIA: PROTOSTOMES

Learning Objectives

- List and discuss several advantages of having a coelom.   484
- List the embryological differences between protostomes and deuterostomes, and tell which animal phyla belong to each group.   484–85

Three-Part Body Plan

- Describe the general characteristics of mollusks and the specific features of selected classes.   486–489
- Contrast the anatomy of the clam, the squid, and the snail, indicating how each is adapted to its way of life.   487–89

Segmentation Evolves

- Describe the general characteristics of annelids and the specific features of the three major classes.   490–92
- Contrast the anatomy of the clam worm and the earthworm, indicating how each is adapted to its way of life.   490–91

Jointed Appendages Evolve

- Describe the general characteristics of arthropods and the specific features of the three major subphyla.   493–96
- Describe the general characteristics of insects, using the grasshopper as an example.   498–99
- Contrast the anatomy of the crayfish and the grasshopper, indicating how each is adapted to its way of life.   499

An exoskeleton, jointed appendages, and wings are all adaptations that make insects like this grasshopper well suited for life on land.

he Cambrian period began with an explosion of life that included all the major animal phyla. In particular, arthropods, with their hard outer skeleton, diversified. This chapter will consider not only arthropods but also annelids and mollusks. These animals are bilaterally symmetrical, have three germ layers, the organ level of organization, and the tube-within-a-tube body plan. In addition they have a true **coelom** [Gk. *coel,* hollow], a body cavity completely lined by mesoderm.

The presence of a coelom has many advantages. Body movements are freer because the outer wall can move independently of the enclosed organs. The ample space of a coelom allows complex organs and organ systems to develop. For example, the digestive tract can coil and provide a greater surface area for absorption of nutrients. And the coelomic cavity can serve as a storage area for eggs and sperm before they are released into the environment. Coelomic fluid protects internal organs against damage and against marked temperature changes. It can also assist in respiration and circulation by providing oxygen and nutrients to nearby cells. Metabolic wastes can accumulate in the cavity prior to being taken away by the excretory system. Also fluid within the cavity protects internal organs and can provide a *hydrostatic skeleton*—muscular contraction pushes against the fluid and allows the animal to move.

> When a coelom is present, the digestive system and the body wall can move independently, and internal organs can become more complex. Coelomic fluid can assist respiration, circulation, and excretion. It also serves as a hydrostatic skeleton.

Phyla that have a true coelom are divided into the **protostomes** and **deuterostomes.** There are three major differences in the embryological development of protostomes and deuterostomes (fig. 29.1). **Cleavage,** the first event of development, is cell division without an increase in size of the cells. In protostomes, *spiral cleavage* occurs, and daughter cells sit in grooves formed by the previous cleavages. It can also be noted that the fate of these cells is fixed and determinate in protostomes; each can contribute to development in only one particular way. In deuterostomes, *radial cleavage* occurs, and the daughter cells sit right on top of the previous cells. The fate of these cells is indeterminate; that is, if they are separated from one another, each cell can go on to become a complete organism.

As development proceeds, a hollow sphere forms, and the indentation that follows produces an opening called the blastopore. In protostomes [Gk. *proto,* first, and *stom,* mouth], the *mouth* appears at or near the blastopore, hence the origin of their name; in deuterostomes [Gk. *deutero,* second, and

Figure 29.1

Protostomes versus deuterostomes. In the embryo of protostomes (mollusks, annelids, arthropods), cleavage is spiral—new cells are at an angle to old cells—and each cell has limited potential and cannot develop into a complete embryo; the blastopore is associated with the mouth and the coelom is a schizocoelom. In deuterostomes (echinoderms and chordates), cleavage is radial—new cells sit on top of old cells—and each one can develop into a complete embryo; the blastopore is associated with the anus, and the coelom is an enterocoelom.

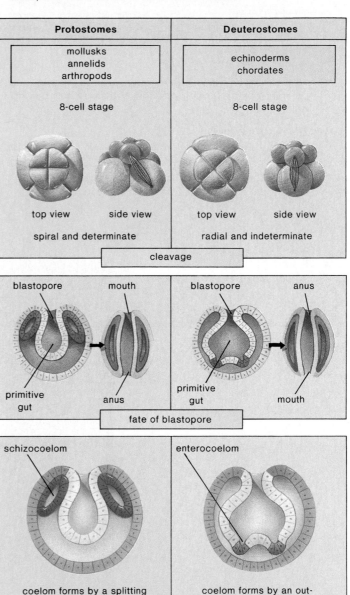

stoma, mouth], the *anus* appears at or near the blastopore and only later does a new opening form the mouth, hence the origin of their name.

KINGDOM ANIMALIA

Multicellular organisms with well-developed tissues; usually motile; heterotrophic by ingestion, generally in a digestive cavity; diplontic life cycle. Protostomes include phyla Mollusca, Annelida, and Arthropoda. Deuterostomes include phyla Echinodermata, Hemichordata, and Chordata.

Invertebrates*

    Phylum Porifera: sponges

    Phylum Cnidaria: jellyfishes, sea anemones, corals, e.g., *Hydra, Obelia*

    Phylum Ctenophora: comb jellies, sea walnuts

    Phylum Platyhelminthes: flatworms, e.g., planaria, flukes, tapeworms

    Phylum Nemertea: ribbon worms

    Phylum Nematoda: roundworms, e.g., *Ascaris*

    Phylum Rotifera: rotifers

    Phylum Mollusca: chitons, snails, slugs, clams, mussels, squids, octopuses

    Phylum Annelida: segmented worms, e.g., clam worms, earthworms, leeches

    Phylum Arthropoda: spiders, scorpions, horseshoe crabs, lobsters, crayfish, shrimps, crabs, millipedes, centipedes, insects

    Phylum Echinodermata: sea lilies, sea stars, brittle stars, sea urchins, sand dollars, sea cucumbers, sea daisies

    Phylum Hemichordata: acorn worms

    Phylum Chordata
        Subphylum Urochordata: tunicates
        Subphylum Cephalochordata: lancelets

Vertebrates*

    Subphylum Vertebrata
        Superclass Agnatha: jawless fishes, e.g., lampreys, hagfishes
        Superclass Gnathostomata: jawed fishes, all tetrapods
            Class Chondrichthyes: cartilaginous fishes, e.g., sharks, skates, rays
            Class Osteichthyes: bony fishes, e.g., herring, salmon, cod, eel, flounder
            Class Amphibia: frogs, toads, salamanders
            Class Reptilia: snakes, lizards, turtles
            Class Aves: birds, e.g., sparrows, penguins, ostriches
            Class Mammalia: mammals, e.g., cats, dogs, horses, rats, humans

CLASSIFICATION

*Not in the classification of organisms, but added here for clarity

The coelom develops differently in the two groups. In protostomes, the mesoderm arises from cells located near the embryonic blastopore, and a splitting occurs that produces the coelom, called a *schizocoelom*. In deuterostomes, the coelom arises as a pair of mesodermal pouches from the wall of the primitive gut. The pouches enlarge until they meet and fuse, forming an *enterocoelom*.

> All complex animals have a true coelom. They are divided into the protostomes (spiral cleavage, blastopore associated with mouth, schizocoelom) and the deuterostomes (radial cleavage, blastopore associated with anus, enterocoelom).

This chapter will discuss the protostomes and the next chapter will discuss the deuterostomes:

PROTOSTOMES	**DEUTEROSTOMES**
mollusks	echinoderms
annelids	chordates
arthropods	

Protostomes, like other animals, evolved in the sea but some ventured onto land and became very successful there. In this chapter, we will have an opportunity to contrast animal adaptations suitable to living in water with adaptations suitable to living on land. Terrestrial existence requires breathing air, preventing desiccation, and having a means of locomotion and reproduction that are not dependent on external water. The excretory system may be modified for the excretion of a solid nitrogenous waste to help conserve water.

THREE-PART BODY PLAN

Mollusks have a three-part body plan—visceral mass, mantle, and foot—which distinguishes this phylum from others. The success of this body plan is seen in mollusk diversity, with modifications in methods of feeding and locomotion.

Mollusks Have Soft Bodies

There are over 110,000 living species of **mollusks (phylum Mollusca)**—more than twice the number of vertebrate species! Most are marine but there are also freshwater and terrestrial mollusks (fig. 29.2). All mollusks share three common features: a visceral mass, a mantle, and a foot.

The *visceral mass* contains the internal organs, including a highly specialized digestive tract, paired kidneys, and reproductive organs. The phylum name comes from the Latin word *mollusc,* meaning soft, which refers to the visceral mass. The *mantle* is a covering that lies to either side of but does not completely enclose the visceral mass. It may secrete a shell and/or contribute to the development of gills or lungs. The space between the folds of the mantle is called the mantle cavity. The *foot* is a muscular organ that may be adapted for locomotion, attachment, food capture, or a combination of functions. Another feature often present is a *radula,* an organ that bears many rows of teeth and is used to obtain food.

The nervous system of a mollusk consists of several ganglia connected by nerve cords. The *coelom is reduced* and is largely limited to the region around the heart. Most mollusks have an *open circulatory system.* The heart pumps blood, more properly called hemolymph, through vessels into sinuses (cavities) collectively called a hemocoel. Blue hemocyanin, rather than red hemoglobin, is the respiratory pigment.

Some mollusks are slow moving and have no head; many others undergo marked cephalization, having both a head and sense organs, and are active predators. Chitons, class Polyplacophora, have a shell that consists of a row of eight overlapping plates. Their flat foot is used for creeping along or clinging to rocks. The chiton scrapes algae and other plant food from rocks with its well-developed radula.

> All mollusks have a visceral mass, mantle, and foot. Many also have a shell and/or radula. A reduced coelom and an open circulatory system are also present.

Figure 29.2

Molluscan diversity. **a.** A chiton has a flattened foot and a shell that consists of eight articulating valves. **b.** A scallop, with sensory tentacles extended between the valves. **c.** A chambered nautilus achieves buoyancy by regulating the amount of air in the chambers of its shell. **d.** A nudibranch (sea slug) lacks a shell, gills, and a mantle cavity. Dorsal projections function in gas exchange.

a.　　　　　　　　　Chiton, *Tonicella*

b.　　Scallop, *Pecten*

c.　　Chambered nautilus, *Nautilus*

d. Spanish shawl nudibranch, *Flabellina*

Bivalves Have a Double Shell

Clams, oysters, mussels, and scallops are all **bivalves** (class Bivalvia) with a two-part shell that is hinged and closed by powerful muscles. They have no head, no radula, and very little cephalization. Clams use their *hatchet-shaped foot* for burrowing in sandy or muddy soil, and mussels use their foot for production of threads, which attach them to nearby objects. Scallops both burrow and swim; rapid clapping of the valves releases water in spurts and causes the animal to move forward in jerklike fashion for a few feet.

In freshwater clams such as *Anodonta* (fig. 29.3), the shell, secreted by the mantle, is composed of protein and calcium carbonate with an inner layer of pearl. If a foreign body is placed between the mantle and the shell, pearls form as concentric layers of shell are deposited about the particle. The compressed muscular foot projects ventrally from the shell; by expanding the tip of the foot and pulling the body after it, the clam moves forward.

Within the mantle cavity, the ciliated gills hang down on either side of the visceral mass. The beating of the cilia causes water to enter the mantle cavity by way of the incurrent siphon and to exit by way of the excurrent siphon. The clam is a filter feeder; small particles in this constant stream of water adhere to the gills and ciliary action sweeps them toward the mouth.

The mouth leads to a stomach and then to an intestine, which coils about in the visceral mass before going right through the heart and ending in an anus. The anus empties at the excurrent siphon. There is also an accessory organ of digestion called a digestive gland. The heart lies just below the hump of the shell within the pericardial cavity, the only remains of the coelom. The circulatory system is open; the heart pumps hemolymph into vessels that open into the hemocoel. The nervous system is composed of three pairs of ganglia (located anteriorly, posteriorly, and in the foot), which are connected by nerves.

There are two excretory kidneys, which lie just below the heart and remove waste from the pericardial cavity for excretion into the mantle cavity. The clam excretes ammonia (NH_3), a toxic substance that requires the concomitant excretion of water.

The sexes are separate. The gonad is located about the coils of the intestine. Certain clams have a trochophore larva which indicates a relationship to the annelids, some of which also have this type of larva.

> In clams, which are bivalves, the body is protected by a heavy shell. They are filter feeders with a hatchet foot that allows them to burrow slowly in sand and mud.

Figure 29.3

Anatomy of a clam, *Anodonta*. The shell and the mantle have been removed from one side. Trace the path of food from the incurrent siphon to the gills, to the mouth, the stomach, the intestine, the anus, and the excurrent siphon. Locate the three ganglia: anterior, foot, and posterior. The heart lies in the reduced coelom.

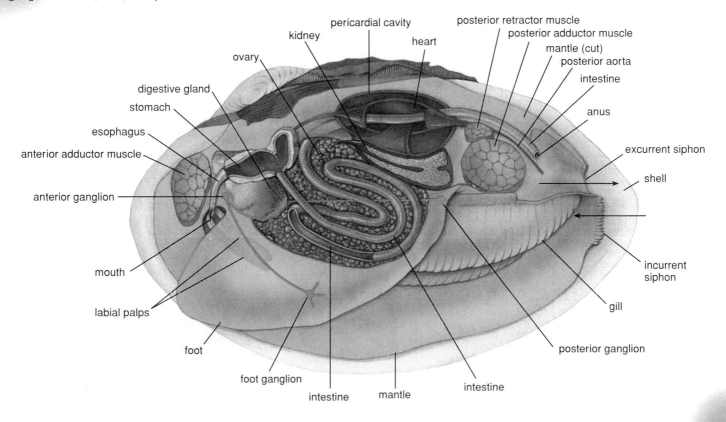

Cephalopods Have Heads

Cephalopods [Gk. *cephal*, head, and *pod*, foot] (class Cephalopoda) include squids, cuttlefish, octopuses, and nautiluses, all of which are fast-swimming predators in the open ocean. Cephalopod means head footed; both squids and octopuses can squeeze their mantle cavity so that water is forced out through a funnel, propelling them by a sort of *jet propulsion*. Also, there are tentacles around the head that capture prey by adhesive secretions or by suckers. A powerful, parrotlike beak is used to tear prey apart. They have well-developed sense organs, including focusing *camera-type eyes* that are very similar to those of vertebrates. Cephalopods, particularly octopuses, have well-developed brains and show a remarkable capacity for learning. Nautiluses are enclosed in shells, but squids have a shell that is reduced and internal. Octopuses lack shells entirely. For protection, squids and octopuses possess *ink sacs*, from which they can squirt a cloud of brown or black ink. This action often leaves a potential predator completely confused.

In squids, such as *Loligo* (fig. 29.4), a tough, muscular mantle contains a vestigial skeleton called the pen and surrounds the visceral mass. It is elongated and lies vertically. Jet propulsion is accomplished in this manner: water freely enters the mantle cavity by way of a space that circles the head. When the cavity is closed off and constricted tightly against the head, water exits the funnel, propelling the squid in the opposite direction. The funnel can be directed anteriorly or posteriorly, resulting in either forward or backward movement. A squid has an effective means of seizing and eating food. For example, *Loligo* darts backward rapidly into a school of young mackerel, seizes a fish with its tentacles, quickly biting the neck and severing the nerve cord with its jaws.

Unlike other mollusks and in keeping with its active life, the squid has a closed circulatory system, meaning that blood is always enclosed within blood vessels or a heart. The squid has three hearts—one of which pumps blood to all the internal organs while the other two pump blood to the gills located in the mantle cavity. This efficient closed system effectively circulates oxygen and nutrients to body parts. The brain is formed from a fusion of the three molluscan ganglia. Nerves leave the brain and supply various parts of the body, including an especially large pair that control the rapid contraction of the mantle. The gonads take up a large part of the visceral mass, and the sexes are separate. Packets called spermatophores contain sperm, which the male passes to the female mantle cavity by means of a specialized tentacle. After the eggs are fertilized, they are attached to the substratum in elongated string each containing as many as 100 eggs.

> Squids, which are cephalopods, have a closed circulatory system and a well-developed nervous system with cephalization. They are active predators in the deep ocean.

Table 29.1 compares the anatomy and behavior of a clam, whic is a filter feeder, and a squid, which is an active predator.

Table 29.1
Comparison of Clam and Squid

	Clam	Squid
Food-intake	Filter feeder	Active predator
Skeleton	Heavy shell for protection	No external skeleton
Circulation	Open	Closed
Cephalization	None	Marked
Locomotion	Hatchet foot	Jet propulsion
Nervous system	Three separate ganglia	Brain and nerves

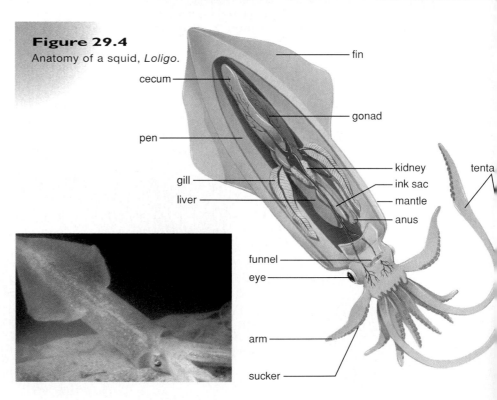

Figure 29.4
Anatomy of a squid, *Loligo*.

cecum
pen
gill
liver
fin
gonad
kidney
ink sac
mantle
anus
tenta
funnel
eye
arm
sucker

Gastropods Undergo Torsion

Gastropods [Gk. *gastro,* stomach, and *pod,* foot] (class Gastropoda)—including snails, whelks, conchs, periwinkles, and sea slugs—are usually found in marine habitats, although they sometimes inhabit freshwater environments. In addition, garden snails and slugs are adapted to terrestrial habitats. Many gastropods are herbivores that use their radula to scrape food from surfaces. Others are carnivores, using their radula to bore through surfaces such as bivalve shells to obtain food.

Gastropods have an elongated, flattened foot. In most, a well-developed head region with eyes and tentacles projects from a coiled shell that protects the visceral mass. Nudibranchs (sea slugs) and terrestrial slugs, however, lack a shell. During development, gastropods undergo a *torsion,* or twisting, that brings the anus and mantle cavity downward, then forward and around to a position above the head. Torsion positions the visceral mass squarely above the foot.

In aquatic gastropods, gills are found in the mantle cavity, but in those adapted to land, the mantle is richly supplied with blood vessels and functions as a lung when air is moved in and out through respiratory pores. As another adaptation to life out of water, terrestrial gastropod development does not include the swimming larval stage found in aquatic species.

Land snails, such as *Helix aspersa,* have three obvious divisions of the body: a head with two pairs of *tentacles,* one pair of which bears *eyes* at the tips; a flat, long, muscular foot; and a visceral mass surrounded by a shell (fig. 29.5). The shell not only offers protection but also prevents desiccation (drying out). The foot contracts in such a way that waves of contraction run from anterior to posterior, and a lubricating mucus is secreted to facilitate movement.

Land snails are hermaphroditic; when two snails meet, they shoot calcareous darts into each other's body wall as a part of premating behavior. Then each inserts a *penis* into the vagina of the other to provide sperm for the future fertilization of eggs that are deposited in the soil. Development proceeds directly without the formation of larvae.

The presence of a copulatory organ such as the penis, and even hermaphroditism, are adaptations to life on land. The penis allows easy transfer of sperm from one animal to another; hermaphroditism assures that any two animals can mate. This is especially useful in slow-moving animals that have limited ranges.

Table 29.2 compares adaptations of the clam and squid to water with adaptations of the snail to land.

Table 29.2

Comparison of Clam and Squid to Snail

	Clam and Squid	Snail
Skeleton	Protection in clam	Protection and prevention of desiccation
Locomotion	Suitable to beach (clam), water (squid)	Suitable to dry surface
Respiration	Gills that are kept moist by external water	Mantle serves as lungs
Excretion	Ammonia diluted in water	Uric acid as a solid
Reproduction	No penis, separate sexes, larval stage in clam	Penis, hermaphroditism, no larval stage

Figure 29.5
Anatomy of a land snail, *Helix.*

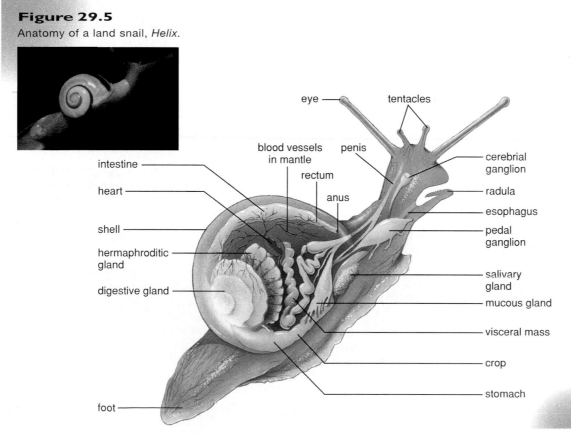

eye — tentacles

blood vessels in mantle — penis

intestine

rectum

heart

anus

shell

hermaphroditic gland

digestive gland

foot

cerebrial ganglion

radula

esophagus

pedal ganglion

salivary gland

mucous gland

visceral mass

crop

stomach

Land snails are gastropods, which are adapted to a terrestrial environment. All snails have a coiled shell, a large, flat, muscular foot, and a head region. In addition, the mantle in a garden snail becomes a lung.

SEGMENTATION EVOLVES

Segmentation is a subdivision of the body along its length into repeating units, called segments. Segmentation may have evolved in conjunction with a hydrostatic skeleton. When an animal utilizes a hydrostatic skeleton, partitioning of the coelom permits each body segment independence of movement. Now instead of just burrowing in the mud, an animal can crawl on a surface. Once segmentation appeared it became significant for another reason. Each segment or group of segments can become specialized to perform a particular function.

Annelids Are Segmented Worms

Annelids [L. *annelus*, little ring] (**phylum Annelida,** 12,000 species) are *segmented,* as is externally evidenced by the rings that encircle the body. Internally, *partitions called septa* (sing., septum) *divide the well-developed, fluid-filled coelom,* which acts as a hydrostatic skeleton.

In annelids, the tube-within-a-tube body plan has led to *specialization of the digestive tract.* For example, the digestive system may include a pharynx, a stomach, and accessory glands. They have an extensive *closed circulatory system* with blood vessels that run the length of the body and branch to every segment. The nervous system consists of a *brain connected to a ventral solid nerve cord, with a ganglion in each segment.* The excretory system consists of *paired* **nephridia** [Gk. *nephri,* kidney], which are coiled tubules in each segment that collect waste material from the coelom and excrete it through openings in the body wall.

> Annelids are segmented worms. The coelom is divided by septa, and organ systems have repeating parts. There is a closed circulatory system and a ventral solid nerve cord.

Marine Worms Have Parapodia

Most annelids (class Polychaeta) are marine; their class name refers to the presence of many setae. **Setae** [Gk. *set,* a bristle] are bristles that anchor the worm or help it move. In *polychaetes* [Gk. *poly,* many, and *chaet,* bristle], the setae are in bundles on *parapodia* [Gk. *para,* beside, and *pod,* foot], which are paddlelike appendages found on most segments. These are used not only in swimming but also as respiratory organs where the expanded surface area allows for exchange of gases. Clam worms (fig. 29.6) such as *Nereis* are predators. They prey on crustacea and other small animals, which are captured by a pair of strong chitinous jaws that extend with a part of the pharynx when the animal is feeding. Associated with its way of life, *Nereis* undergoes *cephalization* and has a head region with eyes and other sense organs.

Other polychaetes are sedentary (sessile) tube worms, with tentacles that form a funnel-shaped fan. Water currents, created by the action of cilia, trap food particles that are directed toward the mouth. They are *sessile filter feeders;* a sorting mechanism rejects large particles and only the smaller ones are accepted for consumption.

Polychaetes have breeding seasons, and only during these times do the worms have sex organs. In *Nereis,* many worms concurrently shed a portion of their bodies containing either eggs or sperm, and these float to the surface where fertilization takes place. The zygote rapidly develops into a *trochophore larva,* just as in marine clams. The existence of this larva in both the annelids and mollusks shows that these two groups of animals are related.

> Polychaetes are marine worms with bundles of setae attached to parapodia.

Figure 29.6

Polychaete diversity. **a.** *Nereis* is a predaceous polychaete that undergoes cephalization. Note the parapodia, which are used for swimming and as respiratory organs. **b.** Fan worms (a type of tube worm) are sessile filter feeders whose tentacles form a funnel-shaped fan.

jaw
pharynx (extended)
sensory projections
eyes
parapodia

a.   Clam worm, *Nereis*

b.   Fan worm, *Spirobranchus*

Earthworms Hide Underground

The **oligochaetes** [Gk. *olig,* few, and *chaet,* bristle] (class Oligochaeta), which include earthworms, have few setae. Earthworms (e.g., *Lumbricus*) do not have a well-developed head or parapodia (fig. 29.7). Their setae protrude in clusters directly from the surface of their body. Locomotion, which is accomplished section by section, utilizes muscle contraction and the setae. When longitudinal muscles contract, segments bulge and their setae protrude into the dirt; then when circular muscles contract, the setae are withdrawn and these segments move forward.

Earthworms reside in soil where there is adequate moisture because the body wall must remain moist for gas exchange purposes. They are scavengers that lack obvious cephalization and feed on leaves or any other organic matter, living or dead, which can conveniently be taken into the mouth along with dirt. Food drawn into the mouth by the action of the muscular pharynx is stored in a crop and ground up in a thick, muscular gizzard. Digestion and absorption occur in a long intestine whose dorsal surface is expanded by a *typhlosole* that allows additional surface for absorption.

Earthworm segmentation, which is so obvious externally, is also internally evidenced by septa. The long ventral solid nerve cord leading from the brain has ganglionic swellings and lateral nerves in each segment. The paired nephridia, or coiled tubules, in each segment have two openings: one is a ciliated funnel that collects coelomic fluid and the other is an exit in the body wall. Between the two openings is a convoluted region where waste material is removed from the blood vessels about the tubule. Red blood moves anteriorly in a dorsal blood vessel and then is pumped by five pairs of hearts into a ventral vessel. As the ventral vessel takes the blood toward the posterior regions of the worm's body, it gives off branches in every segment. Altogether, segmentation is evidenced by

- body rings
- coelom divided by septa
- setae on each segment
- ganglia and lateral nerves in each segment
- nephridia in each segment
- branch blood vessels in each segment

The worms are *hermaphroditic;* the male organs are the testes, the seminal vesicles, and the sperm ducts, and the female organs are the ovaries, the oviducts, and the seminal receptacles. Two worms lie parallel to each other facing in opposite directions. The fused mid-body segment, called a *clitellum,* secretes mucus, protecting the sperm from drying out as they pass between the worms. After the worms separate, the clitellum of each

Figure 29.7

Anatomy and behavior of an earthworm, *Lumbricus.*
a. Internal anatomy of the anterior part of an earthworm. Notice that each body segment bears a pair of setae and that internal septa divide the coelom into compartments.
b. When earthworms mate, they are held in place by a mucus secreted by the clitellum. The worms are hermaphroditic and sperm pass from the seminal vesicles of each to the seminal receptacles of the other.

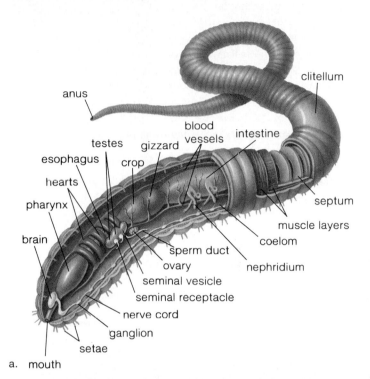

a.

b.

Bloodsuckers

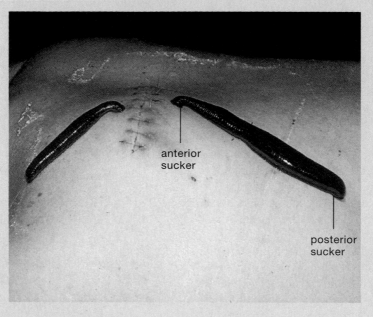

Parasitic leeches attach themselves to the body of their hosts and suck blood or other body fluids from fishes, turtles, snails, or mammals. The European species of *Hirudo medicinalis* was used in the 1700s and 1800s to "let blood" in feverish patients in order to withdraw any poisons and "excess" blood. This procedure, which is most debilitating for the patient, is no longer practiced, but leeches are still used on occasion to remove blood from bruised skin. The anterior sucker of the medicinal leech has three jaws that saw through the skin, producing a Y-shaped incision through which blood is drawn up by the sucking action of the muscular pharynx (fig. 29A). The

anterior sucker

posterior sucker

salivary glands secrete an anticoagulant called hirudin which keeps the blood flowing while the leech is feeding. Other salivary ingredients dilate the host's blood vessels and act as an anesthetic. A medicinal leech can take up to five times its body weight in blood because the crop has pouches where the blood can be stored as the animal expands in size. When it has taken its fill, the leech drops off and digests its meal. Complete digestion takes a long time, and it's been suggested that a leech needs to feed only once a year.

Not all leeches suck blood or fluids; some are even predaceous and eat a variety of small invertebrates.

Figure 29A

Medicinal leeches, *Hirudo*. They are sometimes used medically to remove blood that has accumulated in damaged tissues.

---

produces a slime tube, which is moved along over the head by muscular contractions. As it passes, eggs and the sperm received earlier are deposited and fertilization occurs. The slime tube then forms a cocoon to protect the worms as they develop. There is no larval stage.

It is interesting to compare the anatomy of clam worms with earthworms because it highlights the manner in which earthworms are adapted to life on land. Cephalization is not needed by the nonpredatory earthworms that extract organic remains from the soil they eat. The lack of parapodia helps reduce the possibility of water loss and facilitates burrowing in soil. The clam worm makes use of external water while the earthworm provides a mucous secretion to aid fertilization. It is the water form that has the swimming, or trochophore, larva and not the land form.

Leeches Are Parasites

Leeches (class Hirudinea) are usually found in fresh water, but some are marine or even terrestrial. They have the same body plan as other annelids but they have no setae, and each body ring has several transverse grooves. Most leeches are only 2–6 cm in length but some, including the medicinal leech, are as long as 20 cm.

Among their modifications are two *suckers,* a small oral one around the mouth and a large posterior one. While some leeches are free-living predators, most are fluid feeders that attach themselves to open wounds. Some bloodsuckers, such as the medicinal leech, are able to cut through tissue. Leeches are able to keep blood flowing and prevent clotting by means of a substance in their saliva known as *hirudin,* a powerful anticoagulant. This has added to their potential usefulness in the field of medicine today, as discussed in the accompanying reading.

Earthworms, which burrow in the soil, lack cephalization and parapodia. They are hermaphroditic, and there is no larval stage.

Leeches are modified in a way that lends itself to the parasitic way of life. Some are external parasites known as bloodsuckers.

JOINTED APPENDAGES EVOLVE

Arthropods are related to annelids, as discussed in the reading on page 499. Arthropods are segmented, but they also have a rigid, but jointed, **exoskeleton** [Gk. *exo*, outside, and *skelet*, dried body]. Arthropod literally means "jointed foot," but actually they have freely movable **jointed appendages.** Segmentation and jointed appendages are seen both in arthropods and vertebrates, two groups that are quite successful on land.

Arthropods Have Jointed Appendages

Arthropods [Gk. *arthron*, joint, and *pod*, foot] (**phylum Arthropoda,** over 6 million species) show such diversity and are adapted to so many different habitats that they are often said to be the most successful of all animals. Some claim the modern era should be called the age of arthropods, not the age of mammals!

What characteristics account for the success of arthropods? First, there is the strong but flexible *exoskeleton*. The exoskeleton of arthropods is composed primarily of **chitin** [Gk. *chit*, a tunic], a strong, flexible, nitrogenous polysaccharide. The *exoskeleton* serves many functions such as protection, attachment for muscles, locomotion, and prevention of desiccation. However, because it is hard and nonexpandable, arthropods must **molt,** or shed, the exoskeleton as they grow larger. Before molting, the body secretes a new, larger exoskeleton, which is soft and wrinkled, underneath the old one. After enzymes partially dissolve and weaken the old exoskeleton, the animal breaks it open and wriggles out. The new exoskeleton then quickly expands and hardens.

Arthropods are segmented but some *segments are fused into regions*, such as a head, a thorax, and an abdomen. In trilobites (subphylum Trilobitomorpha), which flourished during the Cambrian period, there was a pair of appendages on each body segment (see fig. 29B). In modern arthropods, *appendages are specialized* for such functions as walking, swimming, reproducing, eating, and sensory reception. These modifications account for much of the diversity of arthropods. Several arthropod groups, such as insects, arachnids, centipedes, and millipedes, contain species that are adapted to terrestrial life.

Arthropods have a *well-developed nervous system*. There is a brain and a ventral solid nerve cord. The head bears various types of sense organs, including eyes of two types—compound and simple (fig. 29.8). The compound eye is composed of many complete visual units, each of which operates independently. The lens of each visual unit focuses an image on the light-sensitive membranes of a small number of photoreceptors within that unit. The simple eye has a single lens that brings the image to focus into many receptors, each of which receives only a portion of the image.

Arthropods have a *variety of respiratory organs*. Marine forms utilize gills, which are vascularized, highly convoluted, thin-walled tissue specialized for gas exchange. Terrestrial forms have book lungs (e.g., spiders) or air tubes called **tracheae** [L. *trache*, windpipe]. Tracheae serve as a rapid way to transport oxygen directly to the cells.

Finally, the occurrence of *metamorphosis* has contributed to the success of arthropods. **Metamorphosis** [Gk. *met*, change, and *morph*, form] is a drastic change in form and physiology that occurs as an immature stage, called a larva, becomes an adult. Among arthropods, the larva eats different food and lives in a different environment than the adult. This reduces competition and allows more members of a species to exist at one time. For example, larval crabs live among and feed on plankton, while adult crabs are bottom dwellers that catch live prey or scavenge dead organic matter. Among insects, such as butterflies, the caterpillar feeds on leafy vegetation while the adult feeds on nectar.

> The success of arthropods is largely attributable to a flexible exoskeleton, specialization of body regions, and jointed appendages. Also important are a high degree of cephalization, a variety of respiratory organs, and reduced competition through metamorphosis.

Figure 29.8

Compound eye of arthropods versus simple eye of cephalopods. **a.** The compound eye contains many individual units, each of which has its own lens. The lens focuses the image onto a rhabdom consisting of the light-sensitive membranes of a small number of photoreceptor. **b.** The simple eye of cephalopods has a single lens, which focuses the image onto a double layer of receptor cells.

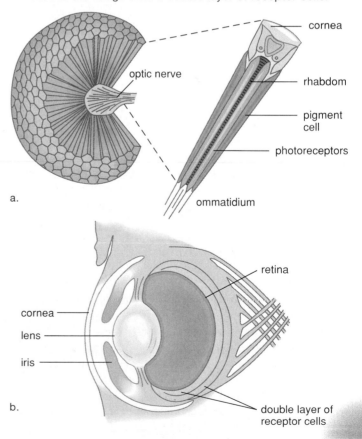

Figure 29.9

Chelicerate diversity. **a.** Scorpions are more common in tropical areas. **b.** Horseshoe crabs are common along the east coast. **c.** The black widow spider is   a poisonous spider found in the United States. **d.** Terrestrial chelicerates breathe by means of book lungs.

a.   Kenyan giant scorpion, *Pandinus*

c.   Black widow spider, *Latrodectus*

b.   Horseshoe crab, *Limulus*

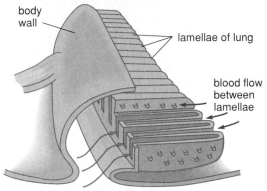

d.   air flowing in through spiracle

Chelicerates Have Pincerlike Appendages

The **chelicerates (subphylum Chelicerata)** include terrestrial spiders, scorpions, ticks, mites, and the less familiar marine horseshoe crabs and sea spiders (fig. 29.9). In this group, the first pair of appendages—the pincerlike *chelicerae*— are feeding organs. The second pair—*pedipalps*—are feeding or sensory in function. The pedipalps are followed by four pairs of walking legs. All of these appendages are attached to a **cephalothorax** [Gk. *cephal,* head, and *thora,* thorax] (fused head and thorax) which is followed by an abdomen that contains internal organs. (There are no antennae, mandibles, or maxillae appendages found on the head of the animals as in the other subphyla.)

Horseshoe crabs of the genus *Limulus* are familiar along the east coast of North America. They scavenge sandy and muddy substrates for annelids, small mollusks, and other invertebrates. The body is covered by exoskeletal shields. The anterior shield is a horseshoe-shaped *carapace* which bears two prominent compound eyes. A long, unsegmented telson projects to the rear. These marine animals have book gills, named for their resemblance to the pages of a closed book.

Scorpions, which are arachnids, are the oldest terrestrial arthropods. Today, they occur in the tropics, subtropics, and temperate regions of North America. They are nocturnal and spend most of the day hidden under a log or a rock. In these animals, the pedipalps are large pincers and the long abdomen ends with a stinger that contains venom. Ticks and mites, with 25,000 species, may outnumber all other kinds of arachnids. They are often parasites. Ticks suck the blood of vertebrates and are sometimes transmitters of diseases, such as Rocky Mountain spotted fever or Lyme disease. Chiggers, the larvae of certain mites, feed on the skin of vertebrates.

Spiders, the most familiar arachnids, have a narrow waist that separates the cephalothorax from the abdomen. Spiders don't have compound eyes; instead, they have numerous simple eyes that perform a similar function. The chelicerae are modified as fangs, with ducts from poison glands, and the pedipalps are used to hold, taste, and chew food. The abdomen often contains silk glands, and they spin a web in which to trap their prey. Invaginations of the body wall form lamellae ("pages") of their so-called book lungs. Air flowing into the folded lamellae on one side exchanges gases with blood flowing in the opposite direction on the other side.

> The chelicerates include horseshoe crabs, spiders, and scorpions. These animals have pincerlike appendages called chelicerae, which are modified as fangs in spiders.

Crustacea Have a Calcified Exoskeleton

Crustacea (**subphylum Crustacea,** 40,000 species) are successful, largely marine, arthropods. Crustacea are named for their hard shells; the exoskeleton is calcified. Although their anatomies are extremely diverse, the head usually bears a pair of compound eyes and *five pairs of appendages*. The first two pairs, called antennae and antennules, lie in front of the mouth and have sensory functions. The other three pairs (mandibles, first and second maxillae) lie behind the mouth and are usually used in feeding as mouth parts. *Biramous* [L. *bi,* two, and *ram,* a branch] *appendages* on the thorax and abdomen are segmentally arranged; one branch is the gill branch and the other is the leg branch:

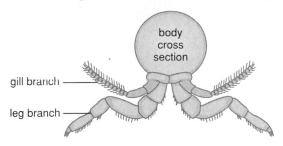

Copepods and krill are small crustacea (less than 2 mm long) that live in the water, where they feed on algae. In the marine environment, they serve as food for fishes, sharks, and whales. They are so numerous that despite their small size, some believe that they are harvestable as food. Barnacles are also crustacea but they have a thick, heavy shell as befits their inactive life-style. Stalked (goose) barnacles are attached by a stalk, and stalkless (acorn) barnacles are attached directly by their shells. You see barnacles on wharf pilings, ship hulls, seaside rocks, and even the bodies of whales. They begin life as free-swimming larvae, but they undergo a metamorphosis that transforms their swimming appendages to cirri, feathery structures that are extended and allow them to filter feed when they are submerged.

Decapods are the most familiar and numerous of the crustacea. They include shrimps, lobsters, and crabs, in which the thorax bears five pairs of walking legs. The first pair may be modified as claws. Typically, there are gills situated above the walking legs. Figure 29.10 gives a view of the external anatomy of the crayfish. The head and thorax are fused into a *cephalothorax,* which is covered on the top and sides by a nonsegmented carapace. The abdominal segments are equipped with *swimmerets,* small paddlelike structures. The first pair of swimmerets in the male are quite strong and are used to pass sperm to the female, somewhat like the way in which squid pass sperm by means of specialized tentacles.

The last two segments bear the uropods and the telson, which make up a fan-shaped tail. Ordinarily, a crayfish lies in wait for prey. It faces out from an enclosed spot with the claws extended and the antennae moving about. The claws seize any small animal, dead or alive, that happens by and carry it to the mouth. When a crayfish moves about, it generally crawls slowly but may swim rapidly by using its heavy abdominal muscles and tail.

The respiratory system consists of gills that lie above the walking legs protected by the carapace. The digestive system includes a stomach, which is divided into two main regions: an anterior portion called the *gastric mill,* equipped with chitinous teeth to grind coarse food, and a posterior region, which acts as a filter to prevent coarse particles from entering the digestive glands where absorption takes place. *Green glands* lying in the head region, anterior to the esophagus, excrete metabolic wastes through a duct that opens externally at the base of the antennae. The *coelom,* which

Figure 29.10

Anatomy of a crayfish, *Homarus.* **a.** Externally, it is possible to observe the jointed appendages, including the swimmerets, the walking legs, and the claws. These appendages, plus a portion of the carapace, have been removed from theright side so that the gills are visible. **b.** Internally, the parts of the digestive system are particularly visible. The circulatory system can also be clearly seen. Note the ventral solid nerve cord.

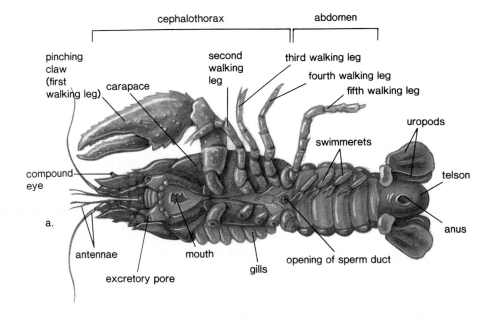

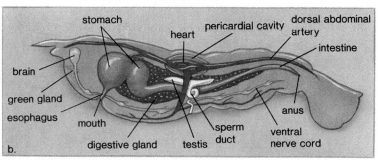

is so well developed in the annelids, *is reduced* in the arthropods and is composed chiefly of the space about the reproductive system. A heart pumps blood containing the respiratory pigment hemocyanin into a **hemocoel** [Gk. *hem*, blood, and *coel*, hollow] consisting of sinuses (open spaces) where the hemolymph flows about the organs. (Whereas hemoglobin is a red pigment, hemocyanin is a blue pigment.) This is an open circulatory system because blood is not contained within blood vessels. This type of circulatory system can be associated with a relatively inactive animal that does not need an inefficient means of transporting blood throughout the body.

The nervous system is quite similar to that of the earthworm. There is a brain, as well as a *ventral nerve cord* that passes posteriorly. Along the length of the nerve cord, periodic ganglia give off lateral nerves.

The sexes are separate in the crayfish, and the gonads are located just ventral to the pericardial cavity. In the male, a coiled sperm duct opens to the outside at the base of the fifth walking leg. Sperm transfer is accomplished by the modified first two swimmerets of the abdomen. In the female, the ovaries open at the bases of the third walking legs. A stiff fold between the bases of the fourth and fifth pairs serves as a seminal receptacle. Following fertilization, the eggs are attached to the swimmerets of the female.

> **Crustacea are mainly marine arthropods in which the head bears five pairs of appendages, including mandibles and maxillae. Typically, there are biramous appendages.**

Uniramia Breathe with Tracheae

Uniramia (subphylum Uniramia) include millipedes, centipedes (superclass Myriapoda), and insects (superclass Insecta) whose *uniramous appendages* attached to the thorax and abdomen have only one branch—the leg branch. The head appendages include only *one pair of antennae*, one pair of mandibles, and one or two pairs of maxillae. The uniramia live on land and breathe by means of a system of air tubes called tracheae.

Centipedes and Millipedes

Centipedes (class Chilopoda) have a body composed of a head and trunk. The body has many segments, and each segment has a pair of walking legs. They are carnivorous animals, and the head bears antennae and mouthparts with jaws.

Millipedes (class Diplopoda) have the same segmented organization as centipedes, but the body is cylindrical and some segments are fused. Therefore they appear to have two pairs of walking legs on each segment. Millipedes dwell in the soil, feeding on dead organic matter.

The term centipede means one hundred legs and millipede means one thousand legs. Although these arthropods do not have this many legs, a millipede does have more legs than a centipede (fig. 29.11).

Figure 29.11
Anatomy of a centipede and a millipede. **a.** A centipede is a carnivorous animal, with a pair of appendages on every segment. **b.** A millipede is a scavenger that appears to have two pairs of appendages on each segment because every two segments are fused.

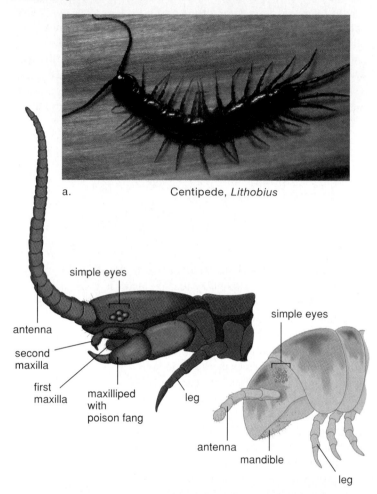

a.　　　Centipede, *Lithobius*

b.　　　Millipede, *Sigmoria*

Figure 29.12

Insect (superclass Insecta) diversity.

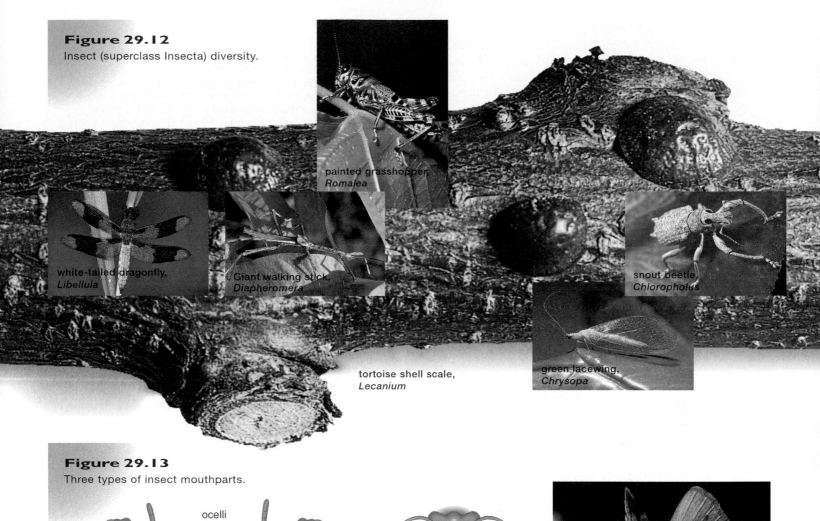

painted grasshopper
Romalea

white-tailed dragonfly,
Libellula

Giant walking stick,
Diapheromera

snout beetle,
Chloropholus

tortoise shell scale,
Lecanium

green lacewing,
Chrysopa

Figure 29.13

Three types of insect mouthparts.

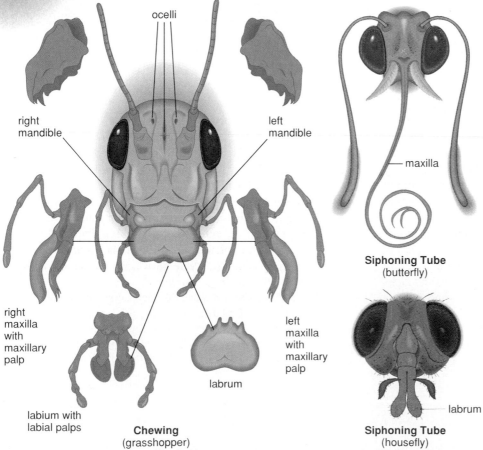

ocelli

right
mandible

left
mandible

maxilla

Siphoning Tube
(butterfly)

right
maxilla
with
maxillary
palp

left
maxilla
with
maxillary
palp

labrum

labium with
labial palps

Chewing
(grasshopper)

labrum

Siphoning Tube
(housefly)

American copper butterfly, *Lycaena*

Housefly, *Musca*

Most Insects Have Wings

Insects (900,000 species) include more known species than all other animal species combined. Only a few types can be represented in figure 29.12. Insects are adapted for an active life on land, although some have secondarily invaded aquatic habitats. The body of an insect is divided into a head, a thorax, and an abdomen. The head bears the sense organs and mouthparts (fig. 29.13); the thorax bears three pairs of legs and one or two pairs of wings; and the abdomen contains most of the internal organs. Wings enhance an insect's ability to survive by providing a way of escaping enemies, finding food, facilitating mating, and dispersing the species. The exoskeleton of an insect is lighter and contains less chitin than that of many other arthropods.

In the grasshopper (fig. 29.14), the third pair of legs is suited to jumping. There are two pairs of wings. The forewings are tough and leathery, and when folded back at rest they protect the broad, thin hindwings. On the lateral surface, the first abdominal segment bears a large tympanum on each side for the reception of sound waves. The posterior region of the exoskeleton in the female has two pairs of projections that form an ovipositor, which is used to dig a hole in which eggs are laid.

The digestive system is suitable for a herbivorous diet. In the mouth, food is broken down mechanically by mouthparts and enzymatically by salivary secretions. Food is temporarily stored in the crop before passing into the gizzard, where it is finely ground. Digestion is completed in the stomach, and nutrients are absorbed into the hemocoel from outpockets called gastric ceca. A *cecum* is a cavity open at one end only. The excretory system consists of **Malpighian tubules,** which extend into the hemocoel and collect nitrogenous wastes that are concentrated and excreted into the digestive tract. The formation of a solid nitrogenous waste, namely uric acid, conserves water.

The respiratory system begins with openings in the exoskeleton called spiracles. From here, the air enters small tubules called tracheae (fig. 29.14*a*). The tracheae branch and rebranch, finally ending in moist areas where the actual exchange of gases takes place. The movement of air through this complex of tubules is not a passive process; air is pumped through by a series of several bladderlike structures (air sacs), which are attached to the tracheae near the spiracles. Air enters the anterior four spiracles and exits by the posterior six spiracles. Breathing by tracheae may account for the small size of insects (most are less than 60 mm in length) since the tracheae are so tiny and fragile that they would be crushed by any amount of weight.

The circulatory system contains a slender, tubular heart that lies against the dorsal wall of the abdominal exoskeleton and pumps hemolymph into the hemocoel where it circulates before returning to the heart again. The hemolymph is colorless and lacks a respiratory pigment, and the tracheal system transports gases.

Reproduction is adapted to life on land. The male has a penis, which passes sperm to the female. Internal fertilization protects both gametes and zygotes from drying out. The female deposits the fertilized eggs in the ground with her ovipositor.

Figure 29.14

Anatomy of a female grasshopper *Romalea*. **a.** Externally, the tympanum uses air waves for sound reception, and the hopping legs and the wings are for locomotion. **b.** Internally, the digestive system is specialized. The Malpighian tubules excrete a solid nitrogenous waste (uric acid). A seminal receptacle receives sperm from the male, which has a penis.

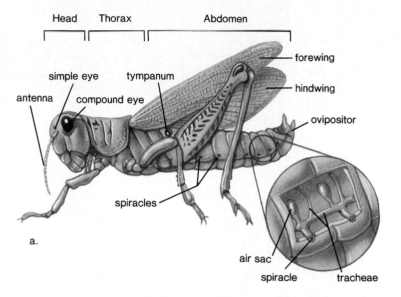

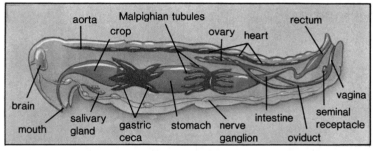

Grasshoppers undergo *incomplete metamorphosis,* a gradual change in form as the animal matures. The immature grasshopper, called a nymph, is recognizable as a grasshopper, even though it differs somewhat in shape and form from the adult. Other insects, such as butterflies, undergo *complete metamorphosis,* involving drastic changes in form. At first, the animal is a wormlike larva (caterpillar) with chewing mouthparts. It then forms a case, or cocoon, about itself and becomes a *pupa.* During this stage, the body parts are completely reorganized; the *adult* then emerges from the cocoon. This life cycle allows the larvae and adults to make use of different food sources.

Insects also show remarkable behavior adaptations, exemplified by the social systems of bees, ants, termites, and other colonial insects. Insects are so numerous and so diverse that the study of this one group is a major specialty in biology called entomology.

Evolutionary Relationships Among the Protostomes

The protostomes (annelids, arthropods, and mollusks) share embryological features that indicate they are related, but how they are related is not known. A possible direct relationship between arthropods and annelids can be found, however. *Peripatus* (phylum Onychophora) (fig. 29B) is called the walking worm because it has 14 to 400 pairs of short, stumpy legs and possesses organs with annelid or arthropod characteristics. Its excretory organs and musculature are more like those of annelids, but its respiratory and circulatory systems are more like those of arthropods. It has a cuticle of chitin and modified appendages that serve as jaws. Although the appendages of *Peripatus* are not jointed, the fossil record does contain wormlike animals with jointed appendages. It's possible that arthropods and annelids share a common ancestor, or perhaps arthropods are descended directly from annelids.

Mollusks are not segmented except for *Neopilina gelatheae* (fig. 29C). This animal was presumed to be extinct for the past 500 million years, but ten living specimens were dredged up from a depth of more than 3,500 meters in the Pacific Ocean near Costa Rica in 1952. There is a segmental arrangement of gills, nephridia, and muscles, which could indicate the animal is similar to a possible common ancestor of both mollusks and annelids. On the other hand, it is possible that the segmentation seen in *Neopilina* arose independently in the molluskan line and that both mollusks and annelids are descended from nonsegmented flatworms.

Figure 29B
Walking worm, *Peripatus*.

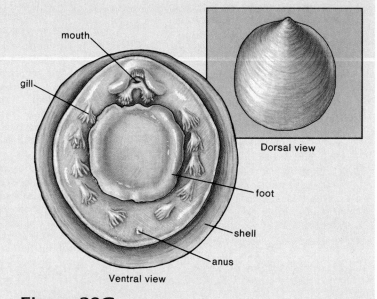

Figure 29C
Mollusk, *Neopilina*.

Uniramia—in which the legs have only one branch—include centipedes, millipedes, and insects. Insects, which are adapted to life on land, comprise more species than any other group of animals.

The grasshopper is adapted to a terrestrial environment while the crayfish is adapted to an aquatic environment. In crayfish, gills take up oxygen from water, while in the grasshopper, tracheae allow oxygen-laden air to enter the body. Appropriately, the crayfish has an oxygen-carrying pigment and a grasshopper has no such pigment in its blood. A liquid waste (ammonia) is excreted by a crayfish, while a solid waste (uric acid) is excreted by a grasshopper. Only in grasshoppers (1) is there a tympanum for the reception of sound waves and (2) do males have a penis and females an ovipositor. Crayfish utilize their uropod when they swim; a grasshopper has legs for hopping and wings for flying.

Summary

1. Annelids, arthropods, and mollusks are all protostomial coelomates. As adults they all have bilateral symmetry, the tube-within-a-tube body plan, and organs derived from three germ layers.

2. The presence of a coelom has many advantages. The digestive system and body wall can move independently and internal organs can become more complex. Coelomic fluids can assist respiration, circulation, and excretion, and can serve as a hydrostatic skeleton.

3. There are two groups of coelomate animals. In the protostomes, the mouth appears at or near the blastopore, and in the deuterostomes, the anus appears at or near the blastopore. Other differences between the two are spiral cleavage and a schizocoelom in protostomes versus radial cleavage and an enterocoelom in deuterostomes.

4. The body of a mollusk typically contains a visceral mass, a mantle, and a foot. Many also have a head and a radula. The nervous system consists of several ganglia connected by nerve cords. There is a reduced coelom and an open circulatory system. Snails are adapted to life on land, squids to an active life in the sea, and clams to a sedentary coastal life.

5. Bivalves are filter feeders. Water enters and exits by siphons and food trapped on the gills is swept toward the mouth. The nervous system has three major ganglia.

6. Predaceous squids undergo cephalization, move rapidly by jet propulsion, and have a closed circulatory system.

7. Annelids are segmented worms. They have a well-developed coelom divided by septa, a closed circulatory system, a ventral solid nerve cord, and paired nephridia. Polychaetes ("many bristles") are marine worms that have parapodia. They may be predators, with a defined head region, or they may be filter feeders, with ciliated tentacles to filter food from the water. Earthworms are oligochaetes ("few bristles") that use the body wall for gas exchange. Leeches (class Hirudinea) are also part of this phylum.

8. Arthropods are the most varied and numerous of animals. Their success is largely attributable to a flexible exoskeleton, specialization of body regions, and jointed appendages. Also important are a high degree of cephalization, a variety of respiratory organs, and reduced competition through metamorphosis.

9. The arthropods are classified into four subphyla. Subphylum Trilobitomorpha includes animals that have been extinct for some 200 million years. The subphylum Chelicerata (horseshoe crabs, spiders, scorpions, ticks, and mites) have chelicerae, pedipalps, and four pairs of walking legs attached to a cephalothorax.

10. Arthropods classified in the subphylum Crustacea (crayfish, lobsters, shrimps, copepods, krill, and barnacles) have a head that bears compound eyes, antennae, antennules, mandibles, and maxillae. There are biramous (two-branched) appendages on the thorax and abdomen. The crayfish illustrates other features such as an open circulatory system, respiration by gills, and a ventral solid nerve cord.

11. Arthropods classified in the subphylum Uniramia (centipedes, millipedes, and insects) have uniramous (one-branched) appendages on thorax and abdomen. The head has one pair of antennae, one pair of mandibles, and one or two pairs of maxillae. These terrestrial animals breathe by means of tracheae.

12. Insects include butterflies, grasshoppers, bees, and beetles. The anatomy of the grasshopper illustrates insect anatomy and ways they are adapted to life on land. Like other insects, grasshoppers have wings and three pairs of legs attached to the thorax. Grasshoppers have a tympanum for sound reception, a specialized digestive system for a grass diet, excretion of solid, nitrogenous waste by Malpighian tubules, tracheae for respiration, internal fertilization, and incomplete metamorphosis.

Writing Across the Curriculum

In order to practice writing skills, students should write out the answers to any or all of the study questions and the critical thinking questions. The study questions are sequenced in the same order as the text. Answers to the objective questions, and suggested answers to the critical thinking questions, are in appendix D.

Study Questions

1. List and discuss several advantages of the coelom.   484

2. Contrast the development of protostomes and deuterostomes in three ways. Tell which phyla belong to each group.   484

3. Name at least three members of each phylum studied in this chapter.   485

4. What are the general characteristics of mollusks and the specific features of bivalves, cephalopods, and gastropods?   486–89

5. Contrast the anatomy of the clam, the squid, and the snail, indicating how each is adapted to its way of life.   487–89

6. What are the general characteristics of annelids and the specific features of the three major classes?   490–92

7. Contrast the anatomy of the clam worm and the earthworm, indicating how each is adapted to its way of life.   490–91

8. What are the general characteristics of arthropods and the specific features of the three major subphyla?   493–96

9. Describe the specific features of insects, using the grasshopper as an example.   498–99

10. Contrast the anatomy of the crayfish and the grasshopper, indicating how each is adapted to its way of life.   499

1. Which of these does not pertain to a protostome?
   a. spiral cleavage
   b. blastopore is associated with the anus
   c. schizocoelom
   d. annelids, arthropods, and mollusks

2. Which of these best shows that annelids and arthropods are closely related? Both
   a. have a complete digestive tract.
   b. have a ventral solid nerve cord.
   c. are segmented.
   d. All of these are correct.

3. Which of these best shows that snails are not closely related to crayfish?
   a. Snails are terrestrial and crayfish are aquatic.
   b. Snails have a broad foot and crayfish have jointed appendages.
   c. Snails are hermaphroditic and crayfish have separate sexes.
   d. Snails are insects but crayfish are fishes.

4. Which of these is mismatched?
   a. clam—gills
   b. lobster—gills
   c. grasshopper—book lungs
   d. polychaete—parapodia

5. Which of these is an incorrect statement?
   a. Spiders are carnivores in the phylum Arthropoda.
   b. Clams are filter feeders in the phylum Mollusca.
   c. Earthworms are scavengers in the phylum Arthropoda.
   d. Squids are predators in the phylum Mollusca.

6. A radula is a unique organ for feeding found in
   a. mollusks.
   b. annelids.
   c. arthropods.
   d. All of these are correct.

7. Which of these is mismatched?
   a. crayfish—walking legs
   b. clam—hatchet foot
   c. grasshopper—wings
   d. earthworm—many cilia

8. Which of these is mismatched?
   a. mollusk—schizocoelom
   b. insects—hemocoel
   c. crayfish— coelom divided by septa
   d. clam worm—true coelom

9. Which of these is an adaptation to a terrestrial way of life in the snail?
   a. using the mantle instead of gills for respiration
   b. cephalization with antennae and eyes
   c. hatchet foot for crawling
   d. torsion so that anus is above the head

10. Which of these terms apply to annelids, to arthropods, and/or to mollusks?

Terms:
   ____ a. organ system level of organization
   ____ b. segmentation
   ____ c. true coelom
   ____ d. cephalization in some representatives
   ____ e. bilateral symmetry
   ____ f. complete gut
   ____ g. jointed appendages
   ____ h. three-part body plan

11. Which of these terms apply to clams and/or to earthworms?

Terms:
   ____ a. annelid
   ____ b. mollusk
   ____ c. three ganglia
   ____ d. gills
   ____ e. closed circulatory system
   ____ f. setae
   ____ g. open circulatory system
   ____ h. hatchet foot
   ____ i. hydrostatic skeleton
   ____ j. ventral solid nerve cord

12. Label this diagram.

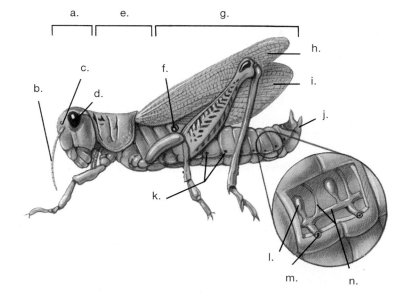

Concepts and Critical Thinking

1. *Segmentation leads to specialization of parts.*

Compare external features of the earthworm to those of the grasshopper to demonstrate this concept.

2. *Animals are adapted to the manner they acquire food.*

Support this concept in regard to one animal from each of the phyla studied in the chapter.

3. *Insects are very well adapted to a land environment.*

List and discuss grasshopper features that adapt it to a life on land.

Selected Key Terms

annelid A member of the phylum Annelida, which includes clam worms, tubeworms, earthworms, and leeches; characterized by a segmented body. [L. *annelus,* little ring]   490

arthropod (AR-throh-pahd) A member of the phylum Arthropoda, which includes lobsters, insects, and spiders; characterized by jointed appendages. [Gk. *arthron,* joint, and *pod,* foot]   493

chitin (KYT-un) A strong but flexible nitrogenous polysaccharide found in the exoskeleton of arthropods. [Gk. *chit,* a tunic]   493

cleavage Cell division without cytoplasmic addition or enlargement; occurs during the first stage of animal development.   484

deuterostome (DOOT-uh-ruh-stohm) A group of coelomate animals in which the second embryonic opening is associated with the mouth; the first embryonic opening, the blastopore, is associated with the anus. [Gk. *deutero,* second, and *stoma,* mouth]   484

exoskeleton (ek-soh-SKEL-ut-un) A protective external skeleton, as in arthropods. [Gk. *exo,* outside, and *skelet,* dried body]   493

jointed appendage A freely moveable appendage of arthropods.   493

Malpighian tubule (mal-PIG-ee-un) Blind, threadlike excretory tubule near the anterior end of an insect hindgut.   498

metamorphosis A change in shape and form that some animals, such as insects, undergo during development. [Gk. *met,* change, and *morph,* form]   493

mollusk Member of the phylum Mollusca that includes squids, clams, snails, and chitons; characterized by a visceral mass, a mantle, and a foot.   486

molt Periodic shedding of the exoskeleton in arthropods.   493

nephridium (pl., nephridia) (nih-FRID-ee-um) Segmentally arranged, paired excretory tubules of many invertebrates, as in the earthworm, where the contents are released through a nephridiopore. [Gk. *nephri,* kidney]   490

protostome (PROH-toh-stohm) A group of coelomate animals in which the first embryonic opening (the blastopore) is associated with the mouth. [Gk. *proto,* first, and *stom,* mouth]   484

segmentation Repetition of body units as is seen in the earthworm.   490

trachea (pl., tracheae) (TRAY-kee-uh) An air tube in insects. [L. *trache,* windpipe]   493

30

KINGDOM ANIMALIA: DEUTEROSTOMES

Learning Objectives

Radial Symmetry, Again?

- Name several echinoderms and describe the characteristics they have in common. 504–6
- Describe the anatomy and the way of life of the sea star. 505–6

Chordate Characteristics Evolve

- List the three chordate characteristics, and note which animals are the invertebrate chordates. 506
- Show that the hemichordates may be related to the echinoderms and to the chordates. 506

Vertebrate Body Plan Evolves

- List and describe the characteristics of vertebrates. 509
- Describe the supposed appearance of the first vertebrate, and describe the jawless fishes of today. 509

Jaws Evolve

- List at least three ways in which the cartilaginous fishes differ from the major group of bony fishes. 510
- Account for the success of bony fishes today. 510–11

Limbs Evolve

- Tell how amphibians may have evolved from bony fishes. 512

(continued)

- Give examples of modern-day amphibians and discuss their adaptations to life on land. 512–13

Amniote Egg Evolves

- Describe the amniote egg and its importance in the evolution of vertebrates. 514
- Give examples of modern-day reptiles and describe other ways in which they are adapted to life on land. 514–15
- Trace the evolution of birds and mammals from reptiles. 515

Wings and Feathers Evolve

- Give examples of modern-day birds, and tell how birds are adapted for flight. 519

Homeothermy Pays Off

- Give the two main characteristics of mammals, and contrast the way in which the three types of modern-day mammals reproduce. 519
- Name and describe several types of modern-day mammals to show that they are adapted to land, water, or aerial existence. 519–20

The skin of this aqua-colored chameleon, *Chamaeleo,* protects the animal from drying out and allows it to blend in with its surroundings.

The phyla discussed in this chapter contain the **deuterostomes** [Gk. *deutero*, second, and *stom*, mouth], animals in which the second embryonic opening is associated with the mouth (the first opening is associated with the anus). *Cleavage*, the first series of embryonic cell divisions, is radial in deuterostomes, and the daughter cells sit on top of the previous cells. The cells are *indeterminate;* if separated, each one can develop into a complete organism. Finally, the coelom develops as outpockets from the primitive gut; it is an *enterocoelom*.

The deuterostomes include two major phyla, phylum Echinodermata and phylum Chordata. At first it might seem that the animals in these two phyla could not possibly be related. However, all these animals show evidence of being related to the hemichordates, which are members of a third, minor phylum.

Vertebrates such as ourselves are chordates. Even though we have a strong interest in vertebrate animals, we should keep in mind that most animal species are invertebrates and that it is our bias that makes us see a world populated mostly by vertebrates.

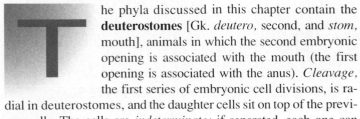

RADIAL SYMMETRY, AGAIN?

Echinoderms are *radially symmetrical as adults,* as are cnidaria. However, their larva (called a bipinnaria) is a free-swimming planktonic filter feeder with bilateral symmetry. Metamorphosis results in the radially symmetrical adult.

Echinoderms Have a Spiny Skin

Echinoderms [L. *echinatus,* set with prickles, and *derm,* skin] **(phylum Echinodermata,** 6,000 species), a diverse group of marine animals, have an *endoskeleton* (internal skeleton) consisting of spine-bearing, calcium-rich plates. The *spines,* which stick out through the delicate skin, account for their name. Class Crinoidea (600 species) includes the stalked sea lilies and the motile feather stars. Their branched arms, used for filter feeding, give them a flowerlike appearance. Class Holothuroidea (1,500 species) are the sea cucumbers with a long leathery body that resembles a cucumber, except that there are feeding tentacles about the mouth.

CLASSIFICATION

KINGDOM ANIMALIA

Multicellular organisms with well-developed tissues; usually motile, heterotrophic by ingestion, generally in a digestive cavity; diplontic life cycle. Protostomes include phyla Mollusca, Annelida, and Arthropoda. Deuterostomes include phyla Echinodermata, Hemichordata, and Chordata.

Invertebrates*

Phylum Porifera: sponges

Phylum Cnidaria: jellyfishes, sea anemones, corals, e.g., *Hydra, Obelia*

Phylum Ctenophora: comb jellies, sea walnuts

Phylum Platyhelminthes: flatworms, e.g., planaria, flukes, tapeworms

Phylum Nemertea: ribbon worms

Phylum Nematoda: roundworms, e.g., *Ascaris*

Phylum Rotifera: rotifers

Phylum Mollusca: chitons, snails, slugs, clams, mussels, squids, octopuses

Phylum Annelida: segmented worms, e.g., clam worms, earthworms, leeches

Phylum Arthropoda: spiders, scorpions, horseshoe crabs, lobsters, crayfish, shrimps, crabs, millipedes, centipedes, insects

Phylum Echinodermata: sea lilies, sea stars, brittle stars, sea urchins, sand   dollars, sea cucumbers, sea daisies

Phylum Hemichordata: acorn worms

Phylum Chordata
    Subphylum Urochordata: tunicates
    Subphylum Cephalochordata: lancelets

Vertebrates*

Subphylum Vertebrata
    Superclass Agnatha: jawless fishes, e.g., lampreys, hagfishes
    Superclass Gnathostomata: jawed fishes, all tetrapods
        Class Chondrichthyes: cartilaginous fishes, e.g., sharks, skates, rays
        Class Osteichthyes: bony fishes, e.g., herring, salmon, cod, eel, flounder
        Class Amphibia: frogs, toads, salamanders
        Class Reptilia: snakes, lizards, turtles
        Class Aves: birds, e.g., sparrows, penguins, ostriches
        Class Mammalia: mammals, e.g., cats, dogs, horses, rats, humans

*Not in the classification of organisms, but added here for clarity

---

Class Echinoidea (950 species) includes sea urchins and sand dollars, both of which use their spines for locomotion, defense, and burrowing. Sea urchins are well known for their long, blunt spines, and the flattened, somewhat circular skeleton of a sand dollar has a familiar five-part flowerlike pattern. Actually the pattern is due to pores for skin projections in the living animal. Class Ophiuroidea (2,000 species) contains the brittle stars, which have a central disk from which long, flexible arms radiate. They move quickly by using their arms to push themselves along.

Class Asteroidea (1,500 species) consists of the sea stars, also called the starfishes. The somewhat flattened body of most sea stars has a central disk from which five, or a multiple of five, sturdy arms (rays) extend.

Sea Stars Have Arms

Sea stars are commonly found along rocky coasts where they feed on clams, oysters, and other bivalve mollusks. The *five-rayed body* has an oral, or mouth, side (the underside) and an aboral, or anus, side (the upper side) (fig. 30.1). Various structures project through the body wall: (1) spines from the endoskeletal plates offer some protection; (2) pincerlike structures called pedicellarie keep the surface free of small particles; and (3) skin gills, tiny fingerlike extensions of the skin, are used for respiration. On the oral surface, each arm has a groove lined by little *tube feet*.

To feed, a sea star positions itself over a bivalve and attaches some of its tube feet to each side of the shell. By working its tube feet in alternation, it pulls the shell open. A very small crack is enough for the sea star to evert its cardiac stomach and push it through the crack, so that it contacts the soft parts of the bivalve. The stomach secretes enzymes, and digestion begins even while the bivalve is attempting to close its shell. Later, partly digested food is taken into the sea star's body, where digestion continues in the pyloric stomach using enzymes from the digestive glands found in each arm. A short intestine opens at the anus on the aboral side.

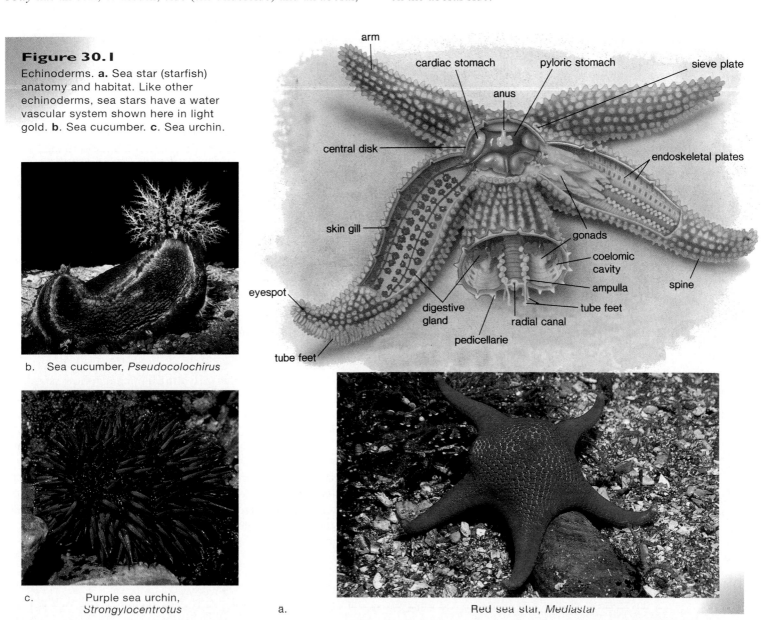

Figure 30.1
Echinoderms. **a.** Sea star (starfish) anatomy and habitat. Like other echinoderms, sea stars have a water vascular system shown here in light gold. **b.** Sea cucumber. **c.** Sea urchin.

b. Sea cucumber, *Pseudocolochirus*

c. Purple sea urchin, *Strongylocentrotus*

a.

Red sea star, *Mediaster*

In each arm the well-developed coelom contains a pair of digestive glands and gonads (either male or female) which open on the aboral surface by very small pores. The nervous system consists of a central nerve ring that gives off radial nerves in each arm. A light-sensitive eyespot is at the tip of each arm. Sea stars are capable of coordinated but slow responses and body movements.

Locomotion depends on the **water vascular system.** Water enters this system through a structure on the aboral side called the sieve plate, or madreporite. From there it passes through a stone canal to a ring canal, which surrounds the mouth, and then to a radial canal in each arm. From the radial canals, many lateral canals extend into the tube feet, each of which has an ampulla. Contraction of the ampulla forces water into the tube foot, expanding it. When the foot touches a surface, the center is withdrawn, giving it suction so that it can adhere to the surface. By alternating the expansion and contraction of the tube feet, a starfish moves slowly along.

Echinoderms don't have a respiratory, excretory, or circulatory system. Fluids within the coelomic cavity and the water vascular system carry out many of these functions. For example, gas exchange occurs across the skin gills and the tube feet. Nitrogenous wastes diffuse through the coelomic fluid and the body wall. Cilia on the peritoneum lining the coelom keep the coelomic fluid moving.

Sea stars reproduce asexually and sexually. If the body is fragmented, each fragment can regenerate a whole animal. Fishermen who try to get rid of sea stars by cutting them up and tossing them overboard are merely propagating more sea stars! Sea stars spawn and release either eggs or sperm at the same time. The bilateral larva undergoes a metamorphosis to become the radially symmetrical adult.

> **Echinoderms have a well-developed coelom and internal organs despite being radially symmetrical. Spines project from their internal skeleton, and there is a unique water vascular system.**

Figure 30.2

Hemichordates. Longitudinal section of acorn worm, *Glossobalanus,* showing the proboscis, the collar, the pharyngeal regions, and the internal structures.

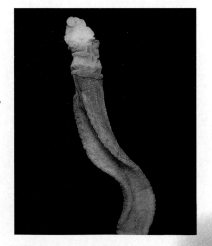

CHORDATE CHARACTERISTICS EVOLVE

To be considered a **chordate** (**phylum Chordata**, 45,000 species), an animal must have the three basic characteristics listed below at some time during its life history:

1. A dorsal supporting rod called a **notochord** [Gk. *noto,* back, and *chord,* string]. The notochord is located just below the nerve cord. Vertebrates have an embryonic notochord that is replaced by the vertebral column during development.

2. A *dorsal hollow nerve cord.* By hollow, it is meant that the cord contains a canal filled with fluid. In vertebrates, the nerve cord, more often called the spinal cord, is protected by the vertebrae.

3. *Pharyngeal pouches.* These are seen only during embryonic development in most vertebrates. In the invertebrate chordates, the fishes, and amphibian larvae, the pharyngeal pouches become functioning gills. Water passing into the mouth and the pharynx goes through the gill slits, which are supported by gill arches. In terrestrial vertebrates, the pouches are modified for various purposes. In humans, the first pair of pouches become the eustachian tubes. The second pair become the tonsils, while the third and fourth pairs become the thymus gland and the parathyroids.

Other features also distinguish chordates. Most have an internal skeleton against which muscles work and—as embryos if not as adults—they have a *post-anal tail,* a tail that extends beyond the anus.

The **hemichordates** (**phylum Hemichordata,** 90 species), are not considered chordates but they have features that resemble those of chordates. Acorn worms, which are hemichordates living in or on tidal mud flats, have a *proboscis,* a *collar,* and a *trunk* (fig. 30.2). There is a dorsal nerve cord in the collar and trunk that resembles the nerve cord of chordates, and the pharynx just below the collar has gill slits. Most interesting, *the larva of hemichordates resembles that of echinoderms.* Is it possible then that echinoderms and hemichordates share a common ancestor and that the hemichordates and chordates are related by way of a common ancestor? Some think so.

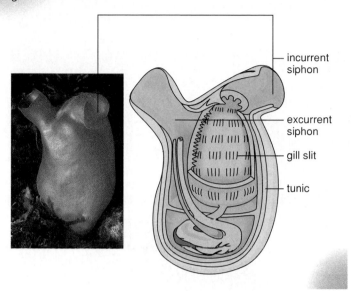

Figure 30.3

Anatomy of the tunicate sea peach, *Halocynthia*. Note that the only chordate characteristic remaining in the adult is gill slits.

incurrent siphon

excurrent siphon

gill slit

tunic

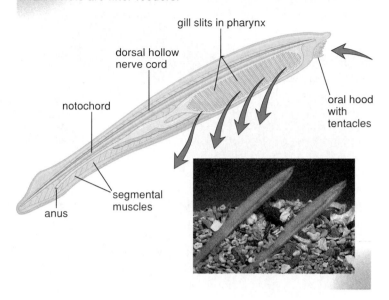

Figure 30.4

Habitat and anatomy of the lancelet *Branchiostoma*. The arrows show the path of water through the gill slits. Lancelets are filter feeders.

gill slits in pharynx

dorsal hollow nerve cord

notochord

oral hood with tentacles

anus

segmental muscles

Invertebrate Chordates

There are a few *invertebrate chordates* in which the notochord persists and is never replaced by the vertebral column.

Tunicates Have Gill Slits

Tunicates (subphylum Urochordata, 1,250 species) live on the ocean floor and take their name from a tunic that makes them look like thick-walled, squat sacs. They are also called sea squirts because they squirt out water from one of their siphons when disturbed. The tunicate larva is bilaterally symmetrical and has the three chordate characteristics. Metamorphosis produces the sessile adult with an incurrent and excurrent siphon (fig. 30.3).

The pharynx is lined by numerous cilia whose beating creates a current of water that moves into the pharynx and out the numerous *gill slits,* the only chordate characteristic that remains in the adult. Microscopic particles adhere to a mucous secretion and are eaten.

Is it possible that the tunicates are directly related to the vertebrates? It has been suggested that a larva with the three chordate characteristics may have become sexually mature without developing the other adult tunicate characteristics. Then it may have evolved into a fishlike vertebrate. Or perhaps it was a cephalochordate larva that became a vertebrate.

Lancelets Have Three Chordate Characteristics

Lancelets (subphylum Cephalochordata, 23 species) are in the genus *Branchiostoma,* formerly called Amphioxus. These marine chordates, which are only a few centimeters long, are named for their resemblance to a lancet—a small, two-edged surgical knife (fig. 30.4). Lancelets are found in the shallow water along most coasts where they usually lie partly buried in sandy or muddy substrates with only their anterior mouth and gill apparatus exposed. They feed on microscopic particles filtered out of the constant stream of water that enters the mouth and exits through the gill slits.

Lancelets retain the three chordate characteristics as an adult. In addition, segmentation is present, as witnessed by the fact that the muscles are segmentally arranged and the dorsal hollow nerve cord has periodic branches.

The invertebrate chordates include the tunicates and the lancelets. A lancelet is the best example of a chordate that possesses the three chordate characteristics as an adult.

Figure 30.5

Phylogenetic tree of the deuterostomes—from ancestors to modern-day groups. The geological time scale tells when each modern-day group evolved.

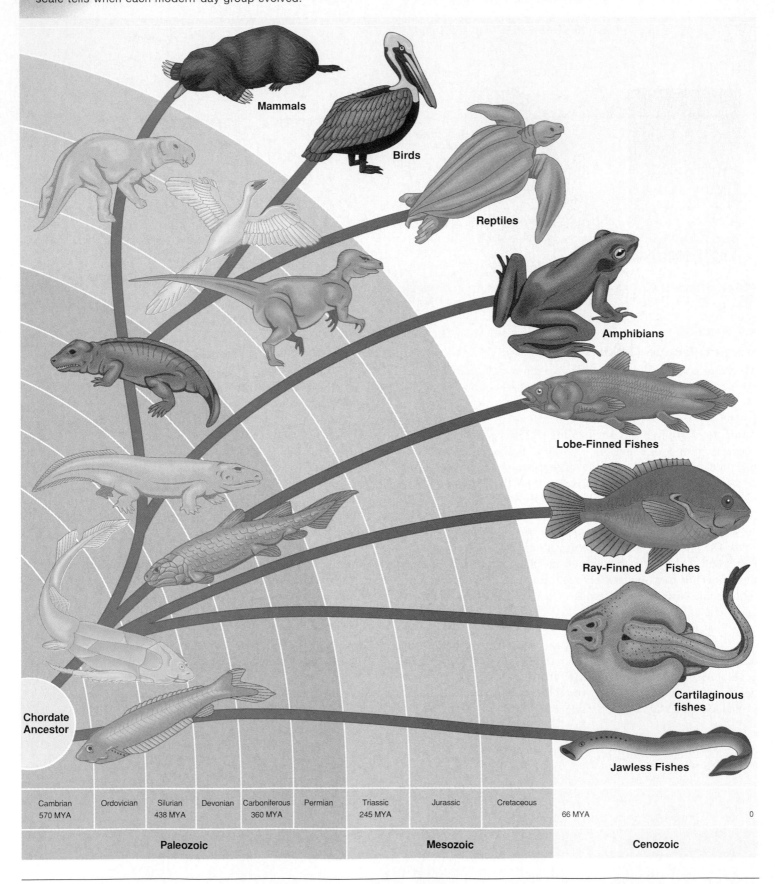

Mammals

Birds

Reptiles

Amphibians

Lobe-Finned Fishes

Ray-Finned Fishes

Cartilaginous fishes

Chordate Ancestor

Jawless Fishes

Cambrian 570 MYA	Ordovician	Silurian 438 MYA	Devonian	Carboniferous 360 MYA	Permian	Triassic 245 MYA	Jurassic	Cretaceous	66 MYA	0
		Paleozoic					Mesozoic		Cenozoic	

VERTEBRATE BODY PLAN EVOLVES

At some time in their life history, **vertebrates (subphylum Vertebrata,** 43,700 species) have all three chordate characteristics (notochord, dorsal hollow nerve cord, and pharyngeal pouches). The embryonic notochord, however, is generally replaced by a *vertebral column* composed of individual vertebrae. The vertebral column, which is a part of the flexible but strong endoskeleton, gives evidence that vertebrates are segmented. In contrast to the arthropod skeleton, the vertebrate skeleton (either cartilage or bone) is a living tissue that grows with the animal. It also protects internal organs and serves as a place of attachment for muscles. Together the skeleton and muscles form a system that permits rapid and efficient movement. *Two pairs of appendages* are characteristic. The pectoral and pelvic fins of fish evolved into the jointed appendages that allowed vertebrates to move onto land.

The main axis of the internal jointed skeleton consists of not only the vertebral column, but also a skull that encloses and protects the brain. During vertebrate evolution the brain increased in complexity, and specialized regions developed to carry out specific functions. The high degree of cephalization is accompanied by complex sense organs. The eyes develop as outgrowths of the brain. The ears are primarily equilibrium devices in aquatic vertebrates, but they also function as sound-wave receivers in land vertebrates.

Vertebrates have a complete digestive tract and a large coelom. The circulatory system is closed (the blood is contained entirely within blood vessels). Vertebrates have an efficient means of extracting oxygen from water or air, as appropriate. The kidneys are important excretory and water-regulating organs that conserve or rid the body of water as necessary. The sexes are generally separate, and reproduction is usually sexual.

Figure 30.5 shows the evolutionary history of vertebrates and their relationship to echinoderms, hemichordates, and the invertebrate chordates. Vertebrates include fishes, amphibians, reptiles, birds, and mammals.

Vertebrates are distinguished in particular by:

living endoskeleton	closed circulatory system
paired appendages	efficient respiration and
high degree of	excretion
cephalization	

In short, vertebrates are adapted to an active life-style.

Fishes are aquatic, gill-breathing vertebrates that usually have fins and skin covered with scales. The first vertebrates were fishlike. The larval form of a modern-day lamprey, which looks like a lancelet, may resemble the first vertebrates. It not only has the three chordate characteristics like the tunicate larva, it also has a two-chambered heart, a three-part brain, and other internal organs that are like those of vertebrates. The small, jawless, and finless ostracoderms are the earliest vertebrate fossils. They were filter feeders, but most likely they were capable of moving water through their gills by muscular action. Ostracoderm fossils have been dated from the Cambrian and as late as the Devonian period, but then they apparently became extinct. Although none of the living jawless fishes has any external protection, large defensive head-shields were not uncommon in the early jawless fishes.

Lampreys and Hagfishes

All the jawless fishes are called **agnathans** [Gk. *a,* without, and *gnath,* jaw] (superclass Agnatha, 63 species). Lampreys and hagfishes are modern-day jawless fishes which lack a bony skeleton. They are cylindrical, up to a meter long, and have *smooth, nonscaly* skin (fig. 30.6). The hagfishes are scavengers feeding on soft-bodied invertebrates and dead fishes they suck into their mouths. Many lampreys are filter feeders like their ancestors. Parasitic lampreys have a round, muscular mouth to attach themselves to another fish and suck nutrients from the host's circulatory system. Marine parasitic lampreys gained entrance to the Great Lakes when a canal from the St. Lawrence River was deepened. The lamprey population grew quickly and caused extensive reduction in the trout population of the Great Lakes in the early 1950s.

Figure 30.6

Lamprey, *Petromyzon.* Note its toothed oral disk attached to aquarium glass. Lampreys, which are members of the vertebrate superclass Agnatha, have an elongated, rounded body and nonscaly skin.

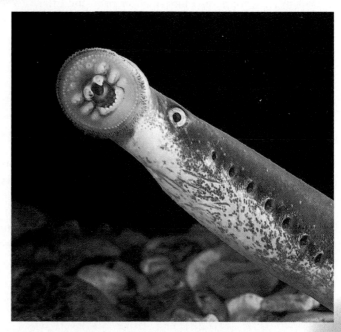

JAWS EVOLVE

All the other animals to be studied are **gnathostomates** [Gk. *gnath*, jaw, and *stom*, mouth]; they have **jaws**, tooth-bearing bones of the head. Jaws are believed to have evolved from the first pair of gill arches of agnathans.

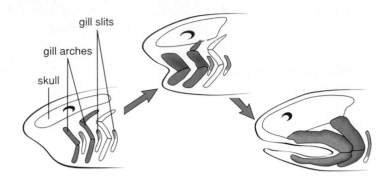

gill slits
gill arches
skull

The placoderms are well-known extinct jawed fishes of the Devonian period. Placoderms were armored with heavy, bony plates and had strong jaws. Like modern-day fishes, they had paired pectoral and pelvic fins (fig. 30.7). *Paired fins,* which allow a fish to balance and to maneuver well in the water, are also an asset for predation.

The jawed fishes of today include the cartilaginous fishes and the bony fishes.

Cartilaginous Fishes Include Sharks

Sharks, rays, and skates (class Chondrichthyes, 850 species) are the largely marine **cartilaginous fishes;** they have a skeleton of cartilage instead of bone. There are five to seven gill slits on both sides of the pharynx, and they lack the gill cover of bony fishes. Their body is covered with epidermal *placoid* (toothlike) *scales* that project posteriorly, which is why a shark's skin feels like sandpaper. The menacing teeth of sharks and their relatives are simply larger, specialized versions of these scales. At any one time, a shark such as the great white shark may have up to 3,000 teeth in its mouth, arranged in six to twenty rows. Only the first row or two are actively used for feeding; the other rows are replacement teeth.

Three well-developed senses enable sharks and rays to detect their prey. They have the ability to sense electric currents in water—even those generated by the muscle movements of animals. They have a *lateral line system,* a series of pressure-sensitive cells that lie within canals along both sides of the body, which can sense pressure caused by a fish or other animal swimming nearby. They also have a very keen sense of smell; the part of the brain associated with this sense is twice as large as the other parts. Sharks can detect about one drop of blood in 115 liters (25 gallons) of water.

The largest sharks are filter feeders, not predators. The basking sharks and whale sharks ingest tons of small crustacea, collectively called krill. Many sharks are fast-swimming predators in the open sea. The great white shark, about 7 meters (23 feet) in length, feeds regularly on dolphins, sea lions, and other seals. Humans are normally not attacked except when mistaken for sharks' usual prey. Tiger sharks, so named because the young have dark bands, reach 6 meters (18 feet) in length and are unquestionably one of the most dangerous sharks. As it swims through the water, a tiger shark will swallow anything it can—including rolls of tar paper, shoes, gasoline cans, paint cans, and even human parts.

In rays and skates, which live on the ocean floor, the pectoral fins are greatly enlarged into a pair of large, winglike fins. They usually swim slowly along the sea bottom and feed on animals that they dredge up. Stingrays of the genus *Raja* have a tail modified into a defensive lash—the dorsal fin persists as a venomous spine. Members of the electric ray family are slow swimmers that feed on fishes they capture after stunning them with electric shocks. Their large electric organs, located at the bases of their pectoral fins, can discharge over 300 volts. Sawfish rays are named for their large, protruding anterior "saw." Swimming into a school of fishes, they rapidly move their saw back and forth, stunning or killing fish which they later eat.

Bony Fishes Are Most Numerous of Vertebrates

Bony fishes (class Osteichthyes, 20,000 species) have a skeleton of bone. Most bony fishes are ray-finned fishes in which fan-shaped fins are supported by thin, bony rays. The lobe-finned fishes, a very small group of bony fishes, are important because lobe-finned fishes of the Devonian period are ancestral to amphibians.

Ray-Finned Fishes Include Familiar Fishes

The **ray-finned fishes** are the most successful and diverse of all the vertebrates. Some, like herrings, are filter feeders; others, like trout, are insectivorous; and still others are predaceous carnivores, like the piranhas and barracudas. Often the common names of fishes reflect their appearance. Zebra fish are striped, stone fish resemble stones, sea horses look like tiny upright horses, and porcupine fish (when inflated) are protected by lateral spikes.

Despite their diversity, bony fishes have features in common (fig. 30.7). The skeleton is of bone and they are covered by *scales* formed *of bone.* The gills do not open separately and instead are covered by an *operculum.* They have a *swim bladder,* a gas-filled sac whose pressure can be altered to change buoyancy and, therefore, their depth in the water. Some fishes (trout, salmon, eels) can move from fresh water to salt water. When in fresh water, their kidneys excrete very dilute urine and their gills absorb salts from the water by active transport.

Figure 30.7

External and internal anatomy of a ray-finned fish called a soldierfish, *Myripristis*.

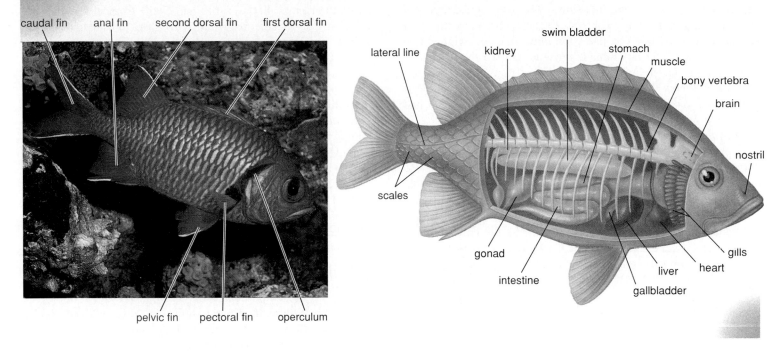

caudal fin   anal fin   second dorsal fin   first dorsal fin

pelvic fin   pectoral fin   operculum

lateral line   kidney   swim bladder   stomach   muscle   bony vertebra   brain   nostril

scales

gonad   intestine   gallbladder   liver   heart   gills

Bony fishes depend on color vision to detect both rivals and mates. Usually eggs and sperm are shed in the water or into a nest constructed by the parents. In almost all bony fishes, fertilization and embryo development occur outside the female's body.

Lobe-Finned Fishes

In **lobe-finned fishes,** the fleshy fins are supported by central bones. They include six species of lungfishes with lungs and one species of coelacanth with especially noticeable lobes (fig. 30.8). *Lungfishes* live in Africa, South America, and Australia either in stagnant fresh water or in ponds that dry up annually. *Coelacanths,* in contrast, inhabit deep ocean environments. Because only Mesozoic fossils had been found, it was once thought that coelacanths were extinct. Then one was captured off the eastern coast of South Africa in 1938, and now about 200 more have been captured. Comparisons of mitochondrial DNA (deoxyribonucleic acid) suggest that lungfishes, and not coelacanths, are the closest living relatives of modern amphibians.

The cartilaginous and bony fishes are characterized by:

- jaws
- paired appendages
- scales

Figure 30.8

Lobe-finned fishes. The coelacanth, *Latimeria*, is a living fossil—the only survivor of a line once thought extinct.

LIMBS EVOLVE

All the other animals to be studied are **tetrapods** [Gk. *tetra,* four, and *pod,* foot]—they have four limbs. The lobe-finned fishes of the Devonian period are ancestral to the amphibians, the first tetrapods. Figure 30.9 compares the limbs of a lobe-finned fish to those of an early amphibian, and you can see that the same bones are present in both animals. Animals that live on land use limbs to support the body, especially since air is less buoyant than water. Lobe-finned fishes and early amphibians also had lungs and internal nares as a means to respire air.

Two hypotheses have been suggested to account for the evolution of amphibians from lobe-finned fishes. Perhaps lobe-finned fishes, which were capable of using their limbs to move from pond to pond, had an advantage over those who could not do so. Or perhaps the supply of food on land in the form of plants and insects—and the absence of predators—promoted further adaptations to the land environment. In any case, the first amphibians diversified during the Carboniferous period, which is known as the Age of Amphibians.

Amphibians

Aside from presence of limbs and appropriate modifications of the girdles, amphibians have other features not seen in bony fishes. **Amphibians** [Gk. *amph,* on both sides] (class Amphibia, 3,900 species) have a tongue for catching prey, eyelids for keeping eyes moist, ears adapted to picking up sound waves, and a voice-producing larynx. The brain is larger than that of a fish and the cerebral cortex is more developed.

The *smooth, nonscaly skin* of an amphibian is kept moist by numerous mucous glands. It plays an active role in water balance and respiration and can also help in temperature regulation when on land, through evaporative cooling. A thin, moist skin does mean, however, that most amphibians stay close to water or else they risk drying out. Glands in the skin secrete poisons which make the animal distasteful to eat. Some tropical species with brilliant fluorescent green and red coloration are particularly poisonous. Colombian Indians dip their darts in the deadly secretions of these frogs, aptly called dart-poison frogs.

Amphibians usually have *lungs,* but they are relatively small and must be supplemented by exchange of gases across the porous skin. The single-loop circulatory path of the fish has been replaced by a double loop (fig. 30.10); a *three-chambered heart* pumps blood before and after it has gone to the lungs. Oxygenated blood is partially mixed with deoxygenated blood, however, in the single ventricle (lower chamber of the heart).

The class name, Amphibia, means "on both sides," a reference to the fact that most amphibians return to water for the purpose of reproduction. They shed their eggs and sperm into the water, where external fertilization takes place (fig. 30.11). Generally, the eggs are protected only by a jelly coat and not by a shell. When the young hatch, they are tadpoles (aquatic larvae with gills) that feed and grow in the water. After they undergo a metamorphosis, amphibians emerge from the water as adults that breathe air. Some amphibians, however, have evolved mechanisms that allow them to reproduce on land.

Amphibians are **ectothermic** [Gk. *ecto,* outer, and *therm,* heat]; they depend on environmental sources of heat to regulate their body temperature. During winters in the temperate zone, they become inactive and enter *torpor.* The European common frog can survive even if the temperature drops to −6° C.

Among the amphibians are frogs, toads, salamanders, and newts. The salamanders and newts have an elongated body, with a long tail and usually two pairs of legs. Because their legs are set

Figure 30.9

Comparison of the appendages of a lobe-finned fish and an ancestral amphibian. The drawings show similarities in skeletal structure.

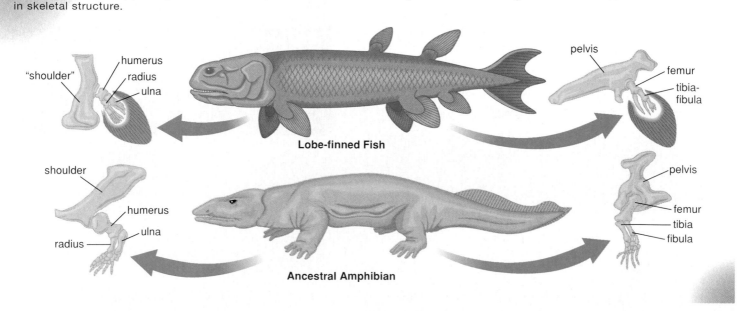

Figure 30.10

Vertebrate circulatory systems. **a.** The single-loop system of fishes utilizes a two-chambered heart. **b.** The double-loop system of amphibians sends blood to the lungs and to the body. There is some mixture of oxygenated and deoxygenated blood in the three-chambered heart. **c.** The four-chambered heart of birds and mammals sends only deoxygenated blood to the lungs and oxygenated blood to the body.

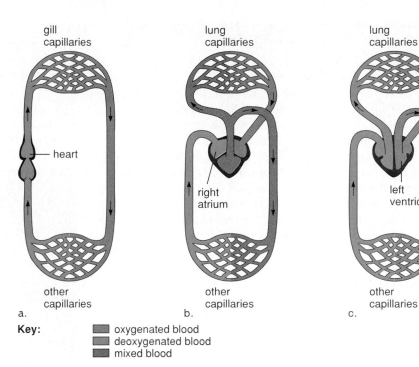

gill capillaries

lung capillaries

lung capillaries

heart

right atrium

left ventricle

other capillaries

other capillaries

other capillaries

a.

b.

c.

Key:
- ■ oxygenated blood
- ■ deoxygenated blood
- ■ mixed blood

Figure 30.11

Frog metamorphosis, during which the animal changes from an aquatic to a terrestrial organism.

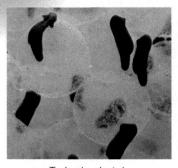

a. Tadpoles hatch

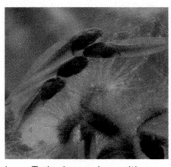

b. Tadpole respires with external gills

c. Front and hindlegs are present

d. Frog, *Rana*, respires with lungs, tail resorbed

at right angles to the body, they resemble more closely the earliest fossil amphibians. They locomote like a fish, with side to side sinusoidal (S-shaped) movements:

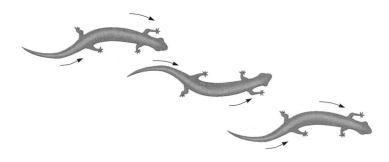

Both salamanders and newts are carnivorous, feeding on small invertebrates such as insects, slugs, snails, and worms. Salamanders practice internal fertilization; in most, males produce a sperm-containing *spermatophore* that females pick up with the **cloaca** (the common receptacle for the urinary, genital, and digestive canals). Then the eggs are laid in water or on land, depending on the species. Some newts, such as the mudpuppy of eastern North America, remain in the water and retain the gills of the larva.

Frogs and toads are the tailless amphibians. In these animals, the head and trunk are fused and the hindlimbs are specialized for jumping. Numerous muscles are located in the limbs as well as the trunk. Frogs have smooth skin and long legs, and they live in or near fresh water; toads have stout bodies and warty skin, and they live in dark, damp places away from the water.

These features in particular distinguish amphibians:		
usually tetrapods	usually lungs in adult	metamorphosis
smooth and moist skin	three-chambered heart	

AMNIOTE EGG EVOLVES

It is adaptive for land animals to have a means of reproduction that is not dependent on external water. The reptiles were the first animals to practice internal fertilization and lay eggs that are protected by a *leathery shell* (fig. 30.12). The **amniote egg** contains *extraembryonic membranes,* which protect the embryo, remove nitrogenous wastes, and provide the embryo with oxygen, food, and water. These membranes are not part of the embryo itself and are disposed of after development is complete. One of the membranes, the *amnion,* is a sac that fills with fluid and provides a "private pond," within which the embryo develops.

Reptiles are believed to have evolved from amphibian ancestors sometime during the Carboniferous period when amphibians were already diversifying and living on land (fig. 30.13). The first reptiles, known as the stem reptiles, gave rise to several other lineages, each adapted to a different way of life. Of interest to us are the pelycosaurs, or sail lizards, so named because of a sail-like web of skin held above the body by slender spines. They are related to the therapsids, mammal-like reptiles that came later. Other lines of descent returned to the aquatic environment; one marine reptile (ichthyosaurs) of the Mesozoic era was fishlike while another (plesiosaurs) had a long neck and large rowing paddles for limbs. Reptiles known as thecodonts gave rise to most of the reptiles, living and extinct. The flying reptiles (pterosaurs) of the Mesozoic era had a keel for the attachment of large flight muscles and air spaces in their bones to reduce weight. Their wings were membranous and supported by elongated bones of the fourth finger. Then there were the "ruling reptiles," as the dinosaurs are sometimes called. The dinosaurs were varied in size and behavior but are well remembered for the great size of some. *Brachiosaurus,* a herbivore, was about 23 meters (75 feet) long and about 17 meters (56 feet) tall. *Tyrannosaurus rex,* a carnivore, was 5 meters (16 feet) tall when standing on its hind legs. A bipedal stance frees the forelimbs for seizing prey or fighting off predators. It is also preadaptive for the evolution of wings: birds are descended from dinosaurs—in fact some say birds are actually living dinosaurs.

The dinosaurs and mammal-like reptiles did not sprawl; the limbs supported the body from underneath, providing increased agility and swiftness that otherwise would not be possible. The amniote egg and improved locomotion were both adaptive for surviving on land.

Reptiles dominated the earth for about 170 million years during the Mesozoic era and then most died out. What could have caused the mass extinction that occurred at the end of the Cretaceous period? The answer is not known, but recently a layer of the mineral iridium, which is rare on earth but common in meteorites, has been found in rocks of that age. The impact of a large meteorite could have set off earthquakes and fires, raising enough dust to block out the sun. Death of most plants and animals would have followed. Such a scenario has been proposed by Luis and Walter Alvarez and several others who are still gathering evidence to support their hypothesis.

Figure 30.12

The reptilian egg allows reproduction on land. **a.** Baby American crocodile, *Crocodylus,* hatching out of its shell. Note that the shell is leathery and flexible, not brittle like birds' eggs. **b.** Inside the egg, the embryo is surrounded by membranes. The chorion aids gas exchange, the yolk sac provides nutrients, the allantois stores waste, and the amnion encloses a fluid that prevents drying out and provides protection.

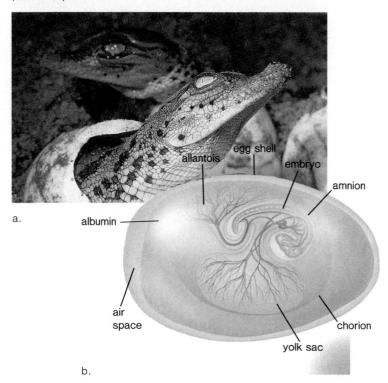

Reptiles

Most **reptiles** [L. *reptil,* creep, crawl] (class Reptilia, 6,000 species) today live in the tropics or subtropics. Among reptiles are lizards and snakes that usually live on or in the soil, and turtles, crocodiles, and alligators that live in the water.

Reptiles have a thick, *scaly skin* that is keratinized and impermeable to water. Keratin is the protein found in hair, fingernails, and feathers. The protective skin prevents water loss but requires several *molts* a year. The reptilian lung is more developed, and air rhythmically moves in and out due to the presence of an expandable rib cage, except in turtles. The heart is nearly four chambered in most and is completely four chambered in crocodiles; therefore, deoxygenated blood is completely separate from oxygenated blood. The well-developed kidneys excrete uric acid and, therefore, less water is required to rid the body of nitrogenous waste.

Reptiles, like amphibians, are *ectothermic.* This feature allows them to survive on a fraction of the food input required by birds and mammals. Still, they are adapted behaviorally to maintain a warm body temperature by warming themselves in the sun.

Figure 30.13

Phylogenetic tree showing the relationship among reptiles (including the dinosaurs), birds, and mammals.

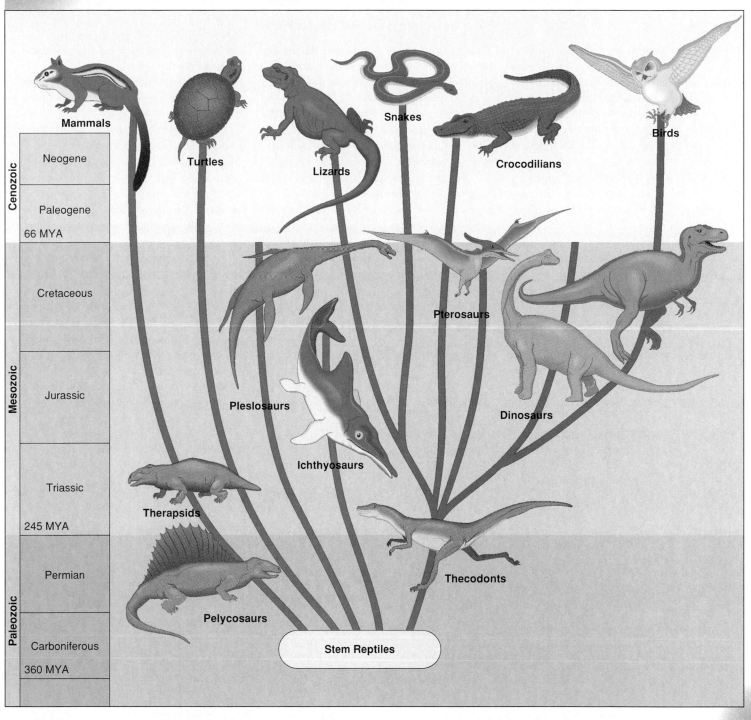

There are about 6,000 species of snakes and lizards which live mainly in the tropics and deserts. Lizards have four clawed legs and resemble their prehistoric ancestor in appearance. They are carnivorous and feed on insects and small animals, including other lizards. Marine iguanas of the Galápagos Islands are adapted to spend long periods of time at sea where they feed on sea let-tuce. Chameleons are adapted to live in trees and have long, sticky tongues for catching insects some distance away. They can change color in order to blend in with their background. Other lizards use different means to avoid being eaten. An Australian frilled lizard erects a collar of skin about its neck which greatly in-creases its apparent size and makes it look frightening. Worm

Venomous Snakes Are Few

Modern snakes and lizards make up 95% of living reptiles. Snakes evolved from lizards during the Cretaceous period and became adapted to burrowing. They lack limbs, so their prey must be subdued and swallowed without the benefit of appendages for manipulating food. Most snakes, like the boas and pythons, are powerful constrictors, suffocating their struggling prey with strong coils. Smaller snakes, such as the familiar garter snakes and water snakes, frequently swallow their food while it is still alive. Still others use toxic saliva to subdue their prey, usually lizards. It is likely that snake venom evolved as a way to obtain food and is used only secondarily in defense.

There are two major groups of venomous snakes. Elapids are represented in the United States by the coral snakes, *Micrurus fulvius* and *Micruroides euryxanthus*, which inhabit the southern states and display bright bands of red, yellow (or white), and black that completely encircle the body (fig. 30A). In these snakes, the fangs, which are modified teeth, are short and permanently erect. The venom is a powerful neurotoxin that usually paralyzes the nervous system. Actually, coral snakes are responsible for very few bites—probably because of their secretive nature, small size, and relatively mild manner.

Vipers, represented in the United States by pitvipers such as the copperhead and cottonmouth, (both *Agkistrodon*) and about 15 species of rattlesnakes *(Sistrurus* and *Crotalus)*, make up the remaining venomous snakes of the United States. They have a sophisticated venom delivery system terminating in two large, hollow, needle-like fangs that can be folded against the roof of the mouth when not in use. The venom destroys the victim's red blood cells and causes extensive local tissue damage. These snakes are readily identified by the combination of heat-sensing facial pits, elliptical pupils in the eyes, and a single row of scales on the underside of the tail (fig. 30B). None of our harmless snakes has any combination of these characteristics.

First aid for snakebite is not advised if medical attention is less than a few hours away; application of a tourniquet, incising the wound to promote bleeding, and other radical treatments often cause more harm than good. The best method of treating snakebite is through the use of prescribed antivenin, a serum containing antibodies to the venom. A hospital stay is required because some people are allergic to the serum.

Most people are not aware that snakes are perhaps the greatest controllers of disease-carrying, crop-destroying rodents because they are well adapted to following such prey into their hiding places. Also, snakes are important food items in the diets of many other carnivores, particularly birds of prey such as hawks and owls. Their presence in an ecosystem demonstrates the overall health of the environment.

Figure 30A

Coral snake, *Micrurus fulvius*. This is a front-fanged snake, one of the major groups of venomous snakes.

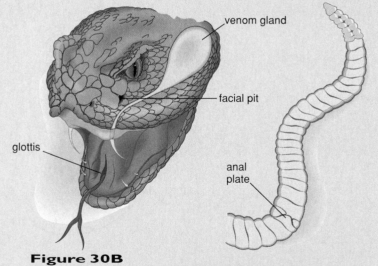

venom gland

facial pit

glottis

anal plate

Figure 30B

Viper characteristics. Vipers, the other major group of venomous snakes, can be identified by these characteristics.

lizards have adapted a subterranean life and look somewhat like an earthworm, since they lack legs and are blind.

Snakes evolved from lizards and have also lost their legs as an adaptation to burrowing. They are carnivorous and have a jaw that is only loosely attached to the skull; therefore, they can eat prey, such as a mouse, that is much larger than their head size. When a snake flicks out its tongue, it is collecting airborne molecules and transferring them to a Jacobson's organ for analysis. *Jacobson's organ,* which opens at the roof of the mouth, is a sensory structure for the analysis of airborne chemicals. Though most snakes are not poisonous, the poisonous rattlesnakes, coral snakes, copperheads, and cobras have fangs for puncturing the skin.

Turtles have a heavy shell to which the ribs and thoracic vertebrae are fused. They lack teeth but have a sharp beak. Most turtles spend some time in water. Sea turtles leave the ocean only to lay their eggs. Their legs are flattened and paddlelike, while tortoises, which are usually terrestrial, have strong legs for walking. Crocodiles and alligators lead a largely aquatic life, feeding on fishes, turtles, and terrestrial animals that venture close enough to be caught (fig. 30.14).

They have long, powerful jaws with numerous teeth and a muscular tail that serves as both a weapon and a paddle. Although other reptiles are voiceless, male crocodiles and alligators bellow to attract mates. In some species, the male protects the eggs and cares for the young.

These features in particular distinguish reptiles:
- usually tetrapods
- shelled egg
- lungs with expandable rib cage
- dry, scaly skin

Figure 30.14

Anatomy and habitat of the American alligator, *Alligator*.

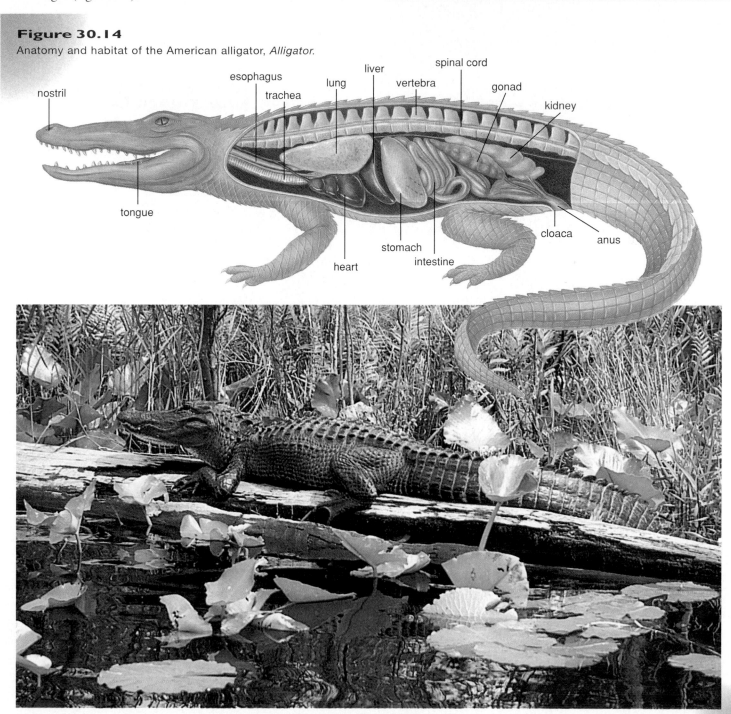

Figure 30.15

Anatomy of the bird. **a.** Birds have a large, keeled breastbone (sternum) to which flight muscles attach. Bird bones are strong but weigh very little because of the air cavities they contain. In feathers, a hollow central shaft gives off barbs and barbules, which interlock in a latticelike array. **b.** Among living vertebrates, only birds and bats rely on true flight—they fly by flapping their wings. Bird flight requires an airstream and a powerful wing downstroke for lift, a force at right angles to the airstream.

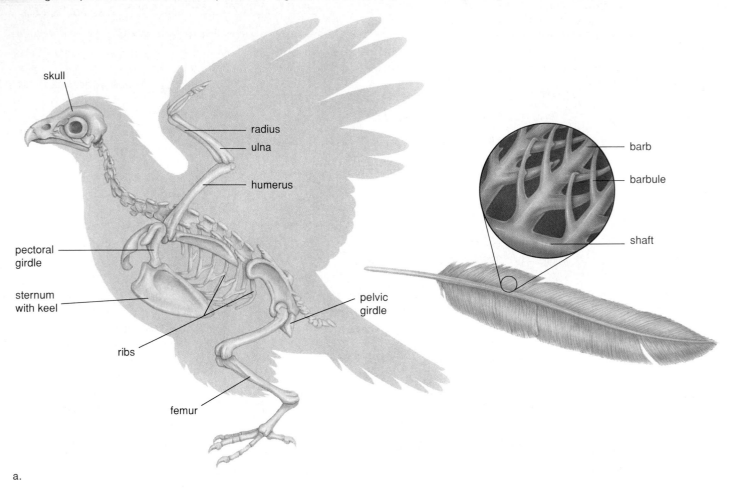

a.

upstroke

Bald eagle, *Haliaetus*

b.

downstroke

WINGS AND FEATHERS EVOLVE

Today's birds lack teeth and have only a vestigial tail, but they still retain many reptilian features such as the shape of the body, scales on their legs, claws on their toes, and a horny beak. They also lay amniotic eggs, although the *shell is hard* rather than leathery. The exact ancestry of birds is in dispute, but there are those who contend that birds are closely related to bipedal dinosaurs and that they should be classified as such.

Birds Have Feathers

Birds (class Aves, 9,000 species) are the only modern animals that have *feathers,* which are actually modified reptilian scales. Bird feathers are of two types. *Contour feathers* are attached to the wings in such a way that they overlap to produce a broad, flat surface beneficial for flight. *Down feathers* provide excellent insulation against body heat loss. This is important because birds arc **endothermic** [Gk. *endo,* within, and *therm,* hcat]; they maintain a constant, relatively high body temperature, which permits them to be continuously active even in cold weather. It's possible that feathers evolved for insulation and secondarily became adapted for flight.

Nearly every anatomical feature of birds can be related to their ability to fly (fig. 30.15). Their forelimbs are modified as *wings.* They have hollow, very light bones laced with air cavities. A horny *beak* has replaced jaws equipped with teeth and a slender neck connects the head to a rounded, compact torso. The breastbone is enlarged and has a *keel,* to which the strong muscles are attached for flying. Oxygen delivery to these muscles is efficient; there is no dead space in the lungs because air flows one way through the air sacs and the lungs, and the double-loop circulation is improved because the *four-chambered heart* keeps oxygenated blood separated from deoxygenated blood.

Flight requires well-developed sense organs and nervous system. Birds have particularly acute vision and excellent muscle reflexes. Flight has other advantages in seeking food; birds migrate and exploit food sources in widely separated habitats. Complex hormonal regulation and behavior responses are involved in bird behavior, which also includes caring for newly hatched birds before they are able to fly away and seek food for themselves.

Classification of birds is particularly based on beak and foot types, and to some extent on habitat and behavior. The various orders include birds of prey with notched beaks and sharp talons; shorebirds with long, slender, probing bills and long, stiltlike legs; woodpeckers with sharp, chisel-like bills and grasping feet; waterfowl with webbed toes and broad bills; penguins with wings modified as paddles; and songbirds with perching feet.

These features, in particular, distinguish birds:

- feathers
- hard-shelled egg
- four-chambered heart
- usually wings for flying
- air sacs
- endothermic

HOMEOTHERMY PAYS OFF

Mammals evolved during the Mesozoic era from therapsids, the mammal-like reptiles. The mammalian skull accommodates a larger brain relative to body size than does the reptilian skull; mammalian cheek teeth are differentiated as premolars and molars; their vertebrae are highly differentiated and the middle region of the backbone is arched, providing more effective movement on land. True mammals appeared during the Jurassic period, about the same time as the first dinosaurs. These first mammals were small, about the size of mice. All the time the dinosaurs flourished (165 million years), mammals were a minor group that changed little. Some of the earliest mammalian groups, represented today by the monotremes and marsupials, are not abundant today. The placental mammals that evolved later went on to occupy the many habitats previously occupied by the dinosaurs.

Mammals Have Hair and Mammary Glands

The chief characteristics of **mammals** [L. *mammil,* teat] (class Mammalia, 4,500 species) are hair and milk-producing mammary glands. Mammals are not only endothermic, they are also **homeothermic** [Gk. *homeo,* like, and *therm,* heat]—they produce heat metabolically and maintain a constant internal temperature. Many of the adaptations of mammals are related to temperature control. *Hair,* for example, provides insulation against heat loss and allows mammals to be active even in cold weather. Like birds, mammals have efficient respiratory and circulatory systems, which assure a ready oxygen supply to muscles whose contraction produces body heat. Like birds, mammals have a double-loop circulation and a *four-chambered heart.*

Mammary glands enable females to feed (nurse) their young without deserting them to find food. Nursing also creates a bond between mother and offspring that helps ensure parental care while the young are helpless. In most mammals, the young are born alive after a period of development in the uterus, a part of the female reproductive tract. Internal development shelters the young and allows the female to move actively about while the young are maturing. Mammals are classified according to means of reproduction.

Mammals That Lay Eggs

Monotremes [Gk. *mono,* one, and *trema,* hole], mammals that have a cloaca and lay hard-shelled amniote eggs, are represented by the duckbill platypus and the spiny anteater, both of which are found in Australia (fig. 30.16). The female duckbill platypus lays her eggs in a burrow in the ground. She incubates the eggs and, after hatching, the young lick up milk that seeps from modified sweat glands on the abdomen of both males and females. The spiny anteater has a pouch on the belly side formed by swollen mammary glands and longitudinal muscle. The egg moves from the cloaca to this pouch where hatching takes place, and the young remain for about fifty-three days. Then they stay in a burrow, where the mother periodically visits and nurses them.

Figure 30.16

Three types of mammals. **a.** The duckbill platypus is a monotreme, which lays shelled eggs. **b.** The koala is a marsupial, whose young are born immature and complete their development within the mother's pouch. **c.** The white-tailed deer is a placental mammal, whose young develop within a uterus.

a.   Duckbill platypus, *Ornithorhynchus*

b.   Koala, *Phascolarctos*

Mammals That Have Pouches

The young of **marsupials** [Gk. *marsupi,* bag] begin their development inside the female's body, but they are born in a very immature condition. Newborns crawl up into a *pouch* on their mother's abdomen. Inside the pouch, they attach to nipples of mammary glands and continue to develop. Frequently, more are born than can be accommodated by the number of nipples, and it's "first come, first served."

Today, marsupial mammals are found mainly in Australia; only a few marsupials, such as the American opossum, are found outside that continent. In Australia, marsupials underwent adaptive radiation for several million years without competition from placental mammals, which arrived there only recently. Among the herbivorous marsupials, koalas are tree-climbing browsers (fig. 30.16) and kangaroos are grazers. The Tasmanian wolf or tiger, thought to be extinct, was a carnivorous marsupial about the size of a collie dog.

Mammals That Have Placentas

Developing **placental mammals** are dependent on the *placenta,* an organ of exchange between maternal blood and fetal blood. Nutrients are supplied to the growing offspring, and wastes are passed to the mother for excretion. While the fetus is clearly parasitic on the female, in exchange, she is free to move about as she chooses while the fetus develops. The young are born at a relatively advanced stage of development.

Placental mammals lead an active life. The senses are acute and the brain is enlarged due to the expansion of the foremost part—the cerebral hemispheres. These have become convoluted

and have expanded to such a degree that they hide many other parts of the brain from view. The brain is not fully developed for some time after birth, and there is a *long period of dependency* on the parents, during which the young learn to take care of themselves.

Placental mammals populate all continents except Antarctica. Most mammals live on land, but some (e.g., whales, dolphins, seals, sea lions, manatees) are secondarily adapted to live in water, and bats are able to fly. Classification is primarily based on mode of locomotion and methods of obtaining food. The following are some of the major orders of mammals:

Order Chiroptera (925 species) includes the nocturnal bats whose wings consist of two layers of skin and connective tissue stretched between the elongated bones of all fingers but the first. Many species use echolocation to locate their usual insect prey. But there are also bird-, fish-, frog-, and plant-eating bats.

Order Rodentia (1,760 species), the largest order, includes mice, rats, squirrels, beavers, and porcupines. Rodents have incisors that grow continuously. They usually feed on seeds but some are omnivorous and some eat mainly insects.

The hoofed mammals include the orders Perissodactyla (e.g., horses, zebras, tapirs, rhinoceroses, 17 species) and the Artiodactyla (e.g., pigs, cattle, deer, buffaloes, giraffes, 185 species) whose elongated limbs are adapted for running across open grasslands. Both groups of animals are herbivorous and have large grinding teeth.

c.   White-tailed deer, *Odocoileus*

Order Carnivora (270 species) includes dogs, cats, bears, raccoons, and skunks. All these animals have limbs adapted for running and have a well-developed sense of smell. The canines of meat eaters are large and conical. There are some aquatic carnivores—namely seals, sea lions, and walruses—which must return to land to reproduce.

Order Proboscidea (2 species) includes the elephants, the largest living land mammals. The upper lip and nose have become elongated and muscularized to form a trunk.

Order Cetacea (80 species) includes the whales and dolphins, which are mammals despite their lack of hair or fur. Blue whales, the largest animal ever to have lived on this planet, are baleen whales which feed by straining large quantities of water containing plankton. Toothed whales feed mainly on fish and squid.

Order Primates (180 species) includes lemurs, monkeys, gibbons, chimpanzees, gorillas, and humans. Typically, primates are tree-dwelling fruit eaters although some, like humans, are ground dwellers. They all have a freely movable head, they have five digits with nails (not claws), and the thumb in many (sometimes the large toe) is opposable. Primates, especially humans, are well known for their well-developed brains.

Order Lagomorpha (65 species) includes the herbivorous rabbits, hares, and pikas—animals that superficially resemble rodents. They also have two pairs of continually growing incisors, and their hind legs are longer than their front legs.

These features in particular distinguish placental mammals:

- body hair
- differentiated teeth
- constant internal temperature
- internal development
- mammary glands
- well-developed brain
- infant dependency

Biological Relationships

Plants are multicellular organisms that stay in one place and make their own organic food; animals are multicellular organisms that locomote in order to acquire food. Even in sponges, flagella beat to move water and potential food through the central cavity of the animal. During the evolution of animals, bilateral symmetry, three germ layers, an organ level of organization, the tube-within-a-tube body plan, and a coelom developed. In soft-bodied animals such as roundworms, coelomic fluid acted upon by muscular contraction serves as a hydrostatic skeleton, allowing the animal to move.

All the features mentioned contributed to the adaptive potential of protostomes and deuterostomes, animals that have a true coelom. A coelom provides space for complex organs and can be subdivided to make the body even more flexible. Coordinated muscle contraction of segments produces both swimming and crawling movements. Segmentation, which also leads to specialization of parts, has contributed to the diversity of both arthropods and vertebrates. Arthropods and vertebrates also have a strong skeleton with jointed appendages. On land, a skeleton supports the body of the animal while the jointed appendages allow it to move. The exoskeleton of arthropods is pro-

tective, but it limits overall size more than an endoskeleton does. Still, the environment offers many more habitats for small animals, and this helps account for the fantastically huge number of arthropod species. The exoskeleton of arthropods even lends itself to wing construction—wing diversity is a major factor in the classification of insects, which are more numerous than any other type of animal. On the other hand, land vertebrates whose skeletons grow with them may be smaller in number, but they are the largest animals on land and in the sea.

Animals have various ways of obtaining food. Animals adapted to filter feeding and burrowing generally lack cephalization and other characteristics of predators. Among mollusks, the squid (not the clam) has well-developed muscular and nervous systems, including sense organs. On land, the available plant material serves as food for vertebrate herbivores, which then are preyed upon by ever-larger predators. In such a situation, it is adaptive for herbivores to be able to escape predators and they, like carnivores, have well-developed sense organs. Both predation and adaptation to the land environment have strongly influenced animal evolution.

Summary

1. In the dueterostomes, the blastopore is associated with the anus, radial cleavage produces indeterminate cells, and there is an enterocoelom. Echinoderms and chordates are deuterostomes.

2. Echinoderms (e.g., sea stars, sea urchins, sea cucumbers and sea lilies) have radial symmetry as adults (not as larvae) and internal calcium-rich plates with spines.

3. Typical of echinoderms, sea stars have tiny skin gills, a central nerve ring with branches, and a water vascular system for locomotion. Each arm of a sea star contains branches from the nervous, digestive, and reproductive systems.

4. Hemichordates indicate that the echinoderms are related to the chordates. Their larva resembles the larva of echinoderms, and they have two chordate features (a dorsal hollow nerve cord and gill slits).

5. Chordates (tunicates, lancelets, and vertebrates) have a notochord, a dorsal hollow nerve cord, and pharyngeal pouches at one time in their life history. Also, there is a post-anal tail.

6. Tunicates and lancelets are the invertebrate chordates. Tunicates lack chordate characteristics (except gill slits) as adults, but they have a larva that could be ancestral for the vertebrates. Lancelets are the only chordate to have the three characteristics in the adult stage.

7. Vertebrates are in the phylum Chordata and have the three chordate characteristics as embryos. As adults, the notochord is replaced by the vertebral column. Vertebrates, which undergo cephalization, have an endoskeleton, paired appendages, and well-developed internal organs.

8. The first vertebrates lacked jaws and paired appendages. They are represented today by the hagfishes and lampreys. Ancestral bony fishes, which have jaws and paired appendages, gave rise during the Devonian period to two groups: today's cartilaginous fishes (skates, rays, and sharks) and the bony fishes, including the ray-finned fishes and the lobe-finned fishes. The ray-finned fishes became the most diverse group among the vertebrates. The lobe-finned fishes, represented today by three species of lungfishes and the coelacanth, gave rise to the amphibians.

9. Ancestral amphibians were tetrapods that diversified during the Carboniferous period. They are represented primarily today by frogs and salamanders, which usually return to the water to reproduce and then metamorphose into terrestrial adults.

10. Reptiles (today's snakes, lizards, turtles, and crocodiles) lay a shelled egg, which allows them to reproduce on land.

11. One main group of ancient reptiles, the stem reptiles that presumably evolved from amphibian ancestors, produced a line of descent that evolved into both dinosaurs and birds during the Mesozoic era. A different line of descent from stem reptiles evolved into mammals.

12. Birds are feathered, which helps them maintain a constant body temperature. They are adapted for flight: their bones are hollow, their shape is compact, their breastbone is keeled, and they have well-developed sense organs.

13. Mammals remained small and insignificant while the dinosaurs existed, but when the latter became extinct at the end of the Cretaceous period, mammals became dominant land organisms.

14. Mammals are vertebrates with hair and mammary glands. The former helps them maintain a constant body temperature, and the latter allows them to nurse their young. Monotremes lay eggs; marsupials have a pouch in which the newborn matures; and the placental mammals, which are far more varied and numerous, retain offspring inside the uterus until birth.

Writing Across the Curriculum

In order to practice writing skills, students should write out the answers to any or all of the study questions and the critical thinking questions. The study questions are sequenced in the same order as the text. Answers to the objective questions, and suggested answers to the critical thinking questions, are in appendix D.

Study Questions

1. What are the general characteristics of deuterostomes? 504

2. What are the general characteristics of echinoderms? Explain how the water vascular system works in sea stars. 504–6

3. What three characteristics do all chordates have at some time in their life history? How do hemichordates show that echinoderms are related to the chordates? 506

4. Describe the two groups of invertebrate chordates, and explain how the tunicates might be ancestral to vertebrates. 507

5. What is the vertebrate body plan? Discuss the distinguishing characteristics of vertebrates. 509

6. Describe the jawless fishes, including ancient ostracoderms. 509

7. What is the significance of having jaws? Describe the ancient placoderms and today's cartilaginous and bony fishes. The amphibians evolved from what type of fish? 510–12

8. What is the significance of being a tetrapod? Discuss the characteristics of amphibians, stating which ones are especially adaptive to a land existence. Explain how their class name (Amphibia) chacterizes these animals. 512–13

9. What is the significance of the amniote egg? What other characteristics make reptiles less dependent on a source of external water? 514

10. Draw a simplified phylogenetic tree for reptiles showing their relationship to birds and mammals. Your tree should also include stem reptiles and dinosaurs. 515

11. What is the significance of wings? In what other ways are birds adapted to flying? 519

12. What is the significance of homeothermy? What are the three subclasses of mammals, and what are their primary characteristics? 519–21

Objective Questions

1. Which of these does not pertain to a deuterostome?
   a. blastopore is associated with the anus
   b. spiral cleavage
   c. enterocoelom
   d. echinoderms and chordates

2. The tube feet of echinoderms
   a. are their head.
   b. are a part of the water vascular system.
   c. help pass sperm to females during reproduction.
   d. All of these are correct.

3. Which of these is not a chordate characteristic?
   a. dorsal supporting rod, the notochord
   b. dorsal hollow nerve cord
   c. pharyngeal pouches
   d. vertebral column

4. Adult tunicates
   a. do not have all three chordate characteristics.
   b. have a larva that resembles that of hemichordates.
   c. are fishlike in appearance.
   d. All of these are correct.

5. Sharks and bony fishes are different in that only
   a. bony fishes have paired fins.
   b. bony fishes have an operculum.
   c. sharks have a bony skeleton.
   d. sharks are predaceous.

6. Amphibians arose from
   a. cartilaginous fishes.
   b. jawless fishes.
   c. ray-finned fishes.
   d. bony fishes with lungs.

7. Which of these is not a feature of amphibians?
   a. dry skin that resists desiccation
   b. metamorphosis from a swimming form to a land form
   c. small lungs and a supplemental way of gas exchange
   d. reproduction in the water

8. How are frogs different from snakes?
   a. The ancestors of snakes but not salamanders were tetrapods.
   b. Salamanders reproduce on land but snakes do not.
   c. Snakes but not salamanders lay a shelled egg.
   d. Salamanders are carnivores and snakes are herbivores.

9. Dinosaurs
   a. were dominant during the Mesozoic era.
   b. are closely related to the birds.
   c. lay shelled eggs.
   d. All of these are correct.

10. Which of these is a true statement?
    a. In all mammals, offspring develop within the female.
    b. All mammals have hair and mammary glands.
    c. All mammals are land-dwelling forms.
    d. All of these are true.

11. Complete the following diagram.

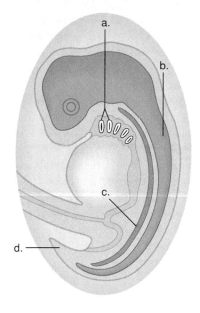

Concepts and Critical Thinking

1. *Protostomes and deuterostomes both evolved similar features.*

   Support this statement by referring to common features of arthropods and chordates.

2. *Arthropods and vertebrates are highly successful groups of animals on land.*

   What characteristics shared by arthropods and vertebrates are adaptive to a land existence?

3. *Reptiles are adapted to reproduce on land.*

   Compare the adaptations of reptiles and angiosperms for reproduction on land.

Selected Key Terms

amniote egg An egg that has an amnion, as seen during the development of reptiles, birds, and mammals.   514

amphibian A member of a class of terrestrial vertebrates that includes frogs, toads, and salamanders; they are still tied to a watery environment for reproduction. [Gk. *amph,* on both sides]   512

echinoderm (ih-KY-nuh-durm) A member of a phylum of marine animals that includes sea stars, sea urchins, and sand dollars; characterized by radial symmetry and a water vascular system. [L. *echinatus,* set with prickles, and *derm,* skin]   504

ectothermic Having a body temperature that varies according to the environmental temperature. [Gk. *ecto,* outer, and *therm,* heat]   512

endothermic Having a body temperature that is derived from the oxidative metabolism of the organism. [Gk. *endo,* inner, and *therm,* heat]   519

homeotherm An animal (bird or mammal) that maintains a uniform body temperature independent of the environmental temperature. [Gk. *homeo,* like, and *therm,* heat]   519

mammal A member of a class of vertebrates characterized especially by the presence of hair and mammary glands. [Gk. *mammil,* teat] 519

marsupial (mar- SOO-pee-ul) A mammal bearing immature young nursed in a marsupium, or pouch—for example, kangaroo and opossum. [Gk. *marsupi,* bag] 520

monotreme (MAHN-uh-treem) An egg-laying mammal—for example, duckbill platypus and spiny anteater. [Gk. *mono,* one, and *trema,* hole] 519

placental mammal A member of a mammalian subclass characterized by a placenta, an organ of exchange between maternal and fetal blood that supplies nutrients to the growing offspring. 520

reptile A member of a class of terrestrial vertebrates with internal fertilization, scaly skin, and an egg with a leathery shell; includes snakes, lizards, turtles, and crocodiles. [L. *reptil,* creep, crawl] 514

Suggested Readings for Part IV

Anderson, D. M. 1994. Red tides. *Scientific American* 271(2):62. Red tide algal blooms release toxins into oceans, killing whales and fish, and causing illness to humans.

Brusca, R. C., and Brusca, G. J. 1990. *Invertebrates.* Sunderland, Mass.: Sinauer Associates. Discusses invertebrate zoology using the Bauplan concept of body design, development, evolution, and phylogenetics.

Carmichael, W. 1994. The toxins of cyanobacteria. *Scientific American* 270(1):78. Cyanobacteria can be hazardous or beneficial, depending on the approach taken.

Castro, P., and Huber, M. 1992. *Marine biology.* St. Louis: Mosby-Year Book, Inc. This introductory text is designed to provide a stimulating overview of marine biology.

Cowen, R. 1995. *History of life.* 2d ed. Boston: Blackwell Scientific Publications. A readable account for the undergraduate of the history of life based on the fossil record.

DeRobertis, E. M., et al. 1990. Homeobox genes and the vertebrate body plan. *Scientific American* 263(1):46. A group of genes with the homeobox feature tells identical-appearing embryonic cells to differentiate.

Duellman, W. E. 1992. Reproductive strategies of frogs. *Scientific American* 267(1):80. Frogs have managed to colonize niches throughout the terrestrial environment.

Eigen, M. 1993. Viral quasispecies. *Scientific American* 269(1):42. A more dynamic view of viral populations holds clues to understanding and defeating them.

Hickman, C. J., et al. 1993. *Integrated principles of zoology.* 9th ed. St. Louis: Mosby-Year Book, Inc. This introductory text provides the basics for understanding the animal kingdom.

Kantor, F. S. 1994. Disarming Lyme disease. *Scientific American* 271(3):34. Discusses the progress being made in understanding and treating Lyme disease.

Kardong, K. V. 1995. *Vertebrates: Comparative anatomy, function, evolution.* Dubuque, Iowa: Wm. C. Brown Publishers. An understanding of function and evolution is integrated with discussion of vertebrate morphology.

Levin, H. L. 1994. *The earth through time.* 4th ed. Philadelphia: Saunders College Publishing. Provides an in-depth study of evolutionary and geological eras and events.

Margulis, L., et al. 1994. *The illustrated five kingdoms: A guide to the diversity of life on earth.* New York: HarperCollins College Publishers. Presents a catalog of the world's living diversity.

Mauseth, J. 1991. *Botany: An introduction to plant biology.* Philadelphia: Saunders College Publishing. The text emphasizes evolution and diversity in botany, as well as general principles of plant physiology and anatomy.

May, R. M. 1992. How many species inhabit the earth? *Scientific American* 267(4):42. After more than 250 years, fewer than 2 million species have been catalogued.

McClanahan, L., et al. 1994. Frogs and toads in deserts. *Scientific American* 270(3):82. Certain amphibians reveal diverse and unusual adaptations to extreme environments.

Miller, S. A., and Harley, J. P. 1992. *Zoology.* Dubuque, Iowa: Wm. C. Brown Publishers. This introductory zoology text emphasizes the interrelationships of all life forms.

Morello, J., et al. 1994. *Microbiology in patient care.* 5th ed. Dubuque, Iowa: Wm. C. Brown Publishers. Provides a basic knowledge of the principles of microbiology and epidemiology.

Pechenik, J. A. 1991. *Biology of invertebrates.* 2d ed. Dubuque, Iowa: Wm. C. Brown Publishers. Written for the beginning college student, this is a readable, authoritative introduction to the biology of the invertebrates.

Prescott, L., et al. 1993. *Microbiology.* 2d ed. Dubuque, Iowa: Wm. C. Brown Publishers. This introductory text covers all major areas of microbiology.

Raven, P., et al. 1992. *Biology of plants.* 5th ed. New York: Worth Publishers. This book introduces viruses, bacteria, photosynthetic protoctists, fungi, and plants.

Rinderer, T. E., et al. 1993. Africanized bees in the U. S. *Scientific American* 269(6):84. Africanized honeybees have reached the United States from points south.

Rismiller, P. D., and Seymour, R. S. 1991. The echida. *Scientific American* 264(2):96. The reclusive Australian spiny anteater is featured.

Schopf, J. W. 1992. *Major events in the history of life.* Boston: Jones and Bartlett Publishers. Summarizes crucial events shaping the earth's development and evolution over time.

Stern, K. 1994. 6th ed. *Introductory plant biology.* Dubuque, Iowa: Wm. C. Brown Publishers. Presents basic botany in a clear, informative manner.

Talaro, K., and Talaro, A. 1993. *Foundations in microbiology.* Dubuque, Iowa: Wm. C. Brown Publishers. Surveys general topics for students entering health careers.

Vollrath, F. 1992. Spider webs and silks. *Scientific American* 266(3):70. Presents the marvels of spider web engineering.

Walters, D., and Keil, D. 1988. *Vascular plant taxonomy.* 3d ed. Dubuque, Iowa: Kendall/Hunt Publishing. Introduces plant families and experimental aspects of taxonomy.

PART IV
THE CAMBRIAN EXPLOSION

The first single-celled organisms appeared on earth about 3.5 billion years ago. Fossil evidence of these first cells and later organisms indicates that evolution proceeded very slowly for another 3 billion years, until about 530 million years ago. At that time in the early seas of the Cambrian period, the evolution of new life forms experienced the most spectacular leap ever recorded in the fossil record. Many new and highly unusual animals appeared (fig. A). As one scientist has stated, "The lid was off; evolution was going full tilt. Never again in the history of marine life do we see so many phyla, classes or orders appearing so rapidly."[1]

During this Cambrian explosion, all the body forms arose that are used to classify animals. These are the radially symmetric cnidaria such as jellyfish that have a body composed of two layers of tissue, the flatworms with three layers of tissue, and the coelomates (almost all other animals) that have three tissue layers with a cavity in the middle layer.

Why did this explosion occur? What caused this sudden proliferation in animal diversity, and why have no other fundamental body plans evolved since the Cambrian period? Several hypotheses have been proposed by scientists. One of these is that atmospheric oxygen played a crucial role.[1]

Hypothesis I Rising atmospheric oxygen concentration supported more complex, multicellular animals that could evolve into a much greater variety of organisms during the Cambrian period. Atmospheric oxygen began rising rapidly about 2.1 billion years ago and reached present levels about 1.5 billion years ago.[2]

Prediction I Before the Cambrian period, when the atmospheric oxygen was lower, there should be few, if any, multicellular animals.

Result I Careful examination of the fossil record indicates that sizable multicellular animals appeared 575 million years ago. Since this clearly precedes any "explosion" of diversity, the result does not agree with the prediction, and Hypothesis 1 is contradicted.

> **Question I.** Suppose fossils of multicellular animals had not been found before the Cambrian period. Would this observation have proved that Hypothesis 1 was true? How could you argue that the hypothesis was invalid even if multicellular animals had not been found before the Cambrian period?

This incredibly rapid rate of evolution has led some scientists to suggest that evolution was much more rapid during the Cambrian period than at other periods of time. This possibility leads to the hypothesis that the rate of evolution has varied.

Figure A

Cambrian animals. The fossil record indicates an "explosion" of animal diversity at the beginning of the Cambrian period. Some of these animals had basic body plans similar to today's animals, but other species represented new and unusual animals. Hard body parts and appendages, which appear to indicate predatory behavior, are apparent.

Hypothesis 2 The rate of evolution was much more rapid in the Cambrian period than at later times (i.e., the rate of evolution today is much slower than in the Cambrian period). The hypothesis does not indicate *why* or *how* the evolutionary rates might vary. Perhaps it might be due to intense selection acting in the Cambrian period or to some other unknown factor. This leads to the following prediction.

> **Question 2.** **(a)** Skeletons and other hard body parts are much more likely to form fossils than are soft-bodied animals. How could this fact lead to misleading conclusions about the kinds of animals present at any specific time period?

Prediction 2 If the rate of evolution is measured today, relatively little change should be observed.

Result 2 One test of this prediction was made by examining the toxic metal tolerance of invertebrates in the Hudson River in New York.[2] In one particular area, named Foundry Cove, battery factories had dumped tons of nickel-cadmium wastes into the area since 1953. Nickel and cadmium are extremely poisonous to animals and accumulate in high concentrations in the river bottom sediments. As a consequence, we would expect that no organisms should be found living in the cove. Surveys of the cove environment, however, revealed a healthy population of water- and bottom-dwelling organisms. When the same species of organisms from nearby unpolluted parts of the river were moved to Foundry Cove, they quickly died or showed signs of obvious distress. The native Foundry Cove organisms had apparently developed an effective resistance to the toxic wastes.

> **Question 2.** **(b)** Why was it necessary to move bottom-dwelling organisms from unpolluted areas to Foundry Cove and observe their response to the polluted environment?

In another experiment to investigate the response of the Foundry Cove organisms, the investigators moved bottom-dwelling worms from the cove to the laboratory, where they were raised in unpolluted sediments for several generations. When these offspring were tested for cadmium resistance, they had retained the ability to survive in the polluted environment.

> **Question 2.** **(c)** What did this experiment show about cadmium resistance? Why was this experiment done? Suppose a bottom-dwelling organism from Foundry Cove was bred with the same species from an unpolluted area. What would you predict about the cadmium tolerance of the offspring?

The bottom-dwelling organisms developed resistance to cadmium in only the thirty years since they were first exposed to high cadmium concentrations. This is an incredibly rapid rate of change, contrary to Prediction 2. It appears that modern organisms do have a remarkable capacity for rapid evolution. Such evidence of rapid change contradicts Hypothesis 2 and we must again search for an acceptable hypothesis.

A third hypothesis proposed by scientists is based on the simplicity of the organisms.

Hypothesis 3 Only after animals reached some critical level of complexity could they evolve into a great diversity of life forms and into the three basic body plans of multicellular animals.

Prediction 3 As soon as animals began to evolve into complex, multicellular forms, then an explosion of diversity should be observed.

Result 3 Actually, the observations reported in Result 1 can also be used to evaluate this hypothesis. As indicated earlier, multicellular animals arose as early as 575 million years ago, well before the start of the Cambrian explosion 530 million years ago. Of course, it can always be argued that the first multicellular animals were not complex enough to initiate the explosion. However, it would seem that the origin of multicellular body forms should be the

critical event allowing evolution to rapidly enter a new phase. Again, the hypothesis is not supported.

The appearance of a body skeleton and other hard body parts just before the Cambrian period has led to a fourth hypothesis.[1,2]

Hypothesis 4 The evolution of predation was a strong selection pressure, giving rise to the evolution of a much greater diversity of animals.

Prediction 4 Skeletons and hard body parts appear in the Cambrian explosion. These structures provide a greater survival advantage because these animals would be more likely to survive predation.

Result 4 Many fossils have revealed that animals with skeletons and hard body parts appeared during the Cambrian explosion, as shown in figure A. Such structures, however, begin to appear well before the explosion—as much as 580 million years ago. It is also highly likely that predation was common well before the Cambrian period. Many soft-bodied animals prey on other soft-bodied animals. While predation is no doubt a strong selection pressure, it does not appear to support Hypothesis 4.

The cause of the Cambrian explosion and the stability of the basic body plans remain an intriguing mystery. Even though several reasonable hypotheses have been proposed and tested, none of these alone has proven to be an acceptable explanation. This is a situation often found in science and, indeed, every successful hypothesis was preceded by several others that were tested and discarded. Perhaps a successful explanation will be a combination of these and other, as yet, undiscovered hypotheses.

References

1 Kerr, R. A. 1993. Evolution's big bang gets even more explosive. *Science* 261:1274–1275.

2 Levinton, J. S. 1992. The Big Bang of animal evolution. *Scientific American* 267(5):84.

Part V

PLANT STRUCTURE AND FUNCTION

31
PLANT STRUCTURE

32
NUTRITION AND TRANSPORT IN PLANTS

33
GROWTH AND DEVELOPMENT IN PLANTS

34
REPRODUCTION IN PLANTS

Organisms are adapted to how they acquire energy and where they live. Plants photosynthesize and live on land. Their leaves are lifted toward the sun and capture solar energy, while the roots are anchored in the soil where they absorb water. A vascular system transports water up the stem to the leaves and transports the products of photosynthesis down to the roots. The physical properties of water aid transport, and the physical process of diffusion allows carbon dioxide to enter leaves.

The immobility of plants does not interfere with their ability to make their own food by

photosynthesis. And just like animals, plants are able to respond to environmental stimuli—they bend and grow toward light, for example. A complex network of hormones controls their responses and indeed all aspects of their physiology. Embryonic tissues allow plants to grow their entire lives; their ability to produce new body parts is distinctly different from animals. In addition, their life span can differ from that of animals—some trees live for thousands of years! The complexity of plants is due to the metabolic functioning of their cells, which carry on many additional chemical reactions not found in animal cells.

We will study the structure and the physiology of flowering plants. Their adaptation to the land environment is especially evident when one considers the manner in which they carry on reproduction. Gametes, zygotes, and embryos are all protected from desiccation. And though plants themselves are nonmobile, many utilize the mobility of wind and animals to accomplish gamete and seed distribution.

Velvet banana, *Musa velutina*, is a representative of flowering plants that are adapted to grow and reproduce on land.

Many of the figures and concepts discussed in *Biology*, fifth edition, are further explored in technology products. The following is a list of figures in part V that correlates to technology products.

A set of five videotapes contains 53 animations of physiological processes integral to the study of biology. These videotapes, entitled *Life Science Animations*, cover such topics as chemistry, genetics, and reproduction. A videotape icon appears in appropriate figure legends to alert the reader to these animations.

Explorations in Human Biology and *Explorations in Cell Biology, Metabolism, and Genetics* by George B. Johnson are interactive CD-ROMs with activities that can be used by an instructor in lecture and/or placed in a lab or resource center for student use. This interactive software consists of modules that cover key topics discussed in a biology course. The CD-ROMs are available for use with Macintosh and IBM Windows computers. A CD-ROM icon appears in appropriate figure legends to alert the reader to these activities.

Corresponding Figures		Videotape Concepts	CD-Rom Modules
31.2	Vegetative organs	47. How Water Moves Through a Plant; 48. How Food Moves from a Source to a Sink	—
31.4b	Leaf epidermis	46. Journey into a Leaf	—
31.6	Xylem structure	47. How Water Moves Through a Plant	—
31.7	Phloem structure	48. How Food Moves from a Source to a Sink	—
31.18	Leaf structure	46. Journey into a Leaf	—
31.19	Leaf classification	46. Journey into a Leaf	—
32.1	Plant transport system	47. How Water Moves Through a Plant; 48. How Food Moves from a Source to a Sink	—
32.2	Water potential and turgor pressure	47. How Water Moves Through a Plant	—
32.3	Pathways across cortex to xylem	47. How Water Moves Through a Plant	—
32.5	Cohesion-tension model of xylem transport	47. How Water Moves Through a Plant	—
32.12	Pressure-flow model of phloem transport	48. How Food Moves from a Source to a Sink	—
33.11	Interaction of hormones	50. Mitosis and Cell Division in Plants	—

31
PLANT STRUCTURE

Learning Objectives

Plants Have Organs

- Describe the location and the function of three vegetative organs of a plant.   530–31

Monocot Versus Dicot Plants

- Contrast dicot and monocot plants in at least five ways.   532

Plant Organs Have Tissues

- Describe the structure and the function of epidermis (epidermal tissue) in vegetative plant organs.   533

- Describe the structure and the function of the parenchyma, collenchyma, and sclerenchyma cells in ground tissue.   534

- Describe the structure and the function of xylem and phloem in vascular tissue.   534–35

How Dicot Roots Are Organized

- Describe the primary growth of a root tip; describe the organization of herbaceous dicot and monocot roots.   536

- Discuss how roots differ in various types of plants.   537

How Stems Are Organized

- Describe the primary growth of a stem; describe the organization of a herbaceous dicot stem and a monocot stem.   540–41

- Describe the secondary growth of stems; describe the organization of a woody stem.   542–43

- Describe several ways in which stems are modified in various types of plants.   544

How Leaves Are Organized

- Describe the organization of a typical leaf.   546

- Describe several leaf modifications in various types of plants.   546–47

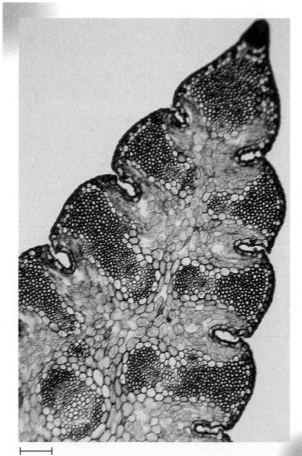

Leaf of a Spanish bayonet, *Yucca glauca,* displays an intricate microscopic organization.

200 μm

ver 80% of all living plants are flowering plants, or angiosperms. Therefore, it is fitting that we set aside one part of the text to examine the structure and the function of flowering plants in particular. The organization of a flowering plant is suitable to photosynthesizing on land. During photosynthesis, carbon dioxide from the air and water from the soil are joined in the presence of sunlight to produce carbohydrate.

PLANTS HAVE ORGANS

Flowering plants are extremely diverse because they have adapted to living in varied environments. There are even flowering plants that live in water! Despite their great diversity in size and shape, flowering plants all have three vegetative organs. An organ contains different types of tissues and performs one or more specific functions. The vegetative organs of a flowering plant—the root, the stem, and the leaf (fig. 31.1)—allow a plant to live and grow. The flower, which functions during reproduction, contains a number of organs.

Roots Anchor

Although we are accustomed to speaking of the root, it is more appropriate to refer to the root system. The **root system** of a plant is the main root, together with any and all of its lateral (side) branches (fig. 31.2*a*). As a rule of thumb, the root system is at least equivalent in size and extent to the shoot system (the part of the plant above ground). An apple tree, then, has a much larger root system than, say, a corn plant. A single corn plant may have roots as deep as 2.5 meters and spread out over 1.5 meters, but a mesquite tree that lives in the desert may have roots that penetrate to a depth of 20 meters. The extensive root system of a plant anchors it in the soil and gives it support.

The root system also absorbs water and minerals from the soil, and then these are distributed to the rest of the plant. Root hairs, which are projections from root hair cells, are especially responsible for this function. Root hair cells are found in a special zone located near the root tip. Root hairs are so numerous that they increase the absorptive surface of a root tremendously. It's been estimated that a single rye plant has about 14 billion hair cells and, if placed end to end, the root hairs would stretch 10,626 km. Root hair cells are constantly being replaced. So this same rye plant most likely forms about 100 million new root hair cells every day. You are probably familiar with the fact that a plant yanked out of the soil will not fare well when transplanted; this is because the root hairs are torn off. Transplantation is more apt to be successful if you take a part of the surrounding soil along with the plant.

Figure 31.1

Organization of plant body. Roots, stems, and leaves are vegetative organs. A flower is a reproductive structure.

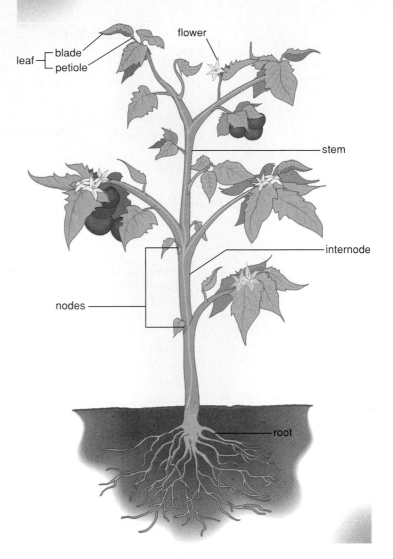

Roots have still another function. In particular, perennial plants, which die back and then regrow the next season, store the products of photosynthesis in their roots. Carrots and sweet potatoes come from the roots of such plants, for example.

Stems Support

A **stem** is the main axis of a plant along with its lateral branches (fig. 31.2*b*). The stem of a flowering plant produces leaves and, if upright as most are, supports leaves in such a way that each one

Figure 31.2 🎞

Vegetative organs. **a.** The root, which is extensive, anchors the plant and absorbs water and minerals. **b.** The stem supports the leaves and transports water and organic nutrients. **c.** The leaf, which is often broad and thin, carries on photosynthesis.

a.

b.

c.

is exposed to as much sunlight as possible. A *node* occurs where leaves are attached to the stem and an *internode* is the region between the nodes. The presence of nodes and internodes is used to identify a stem even if it happens to be an underground stem.

Aside from supporting the leaves, a stem has vascular tissue that transports water and minerals from the roots to the leaves and transports the products of photosynthesis in the opposite direction.

Some stems also function in storage. The stem stores water in cactuses and in other plants. Tubers are horizontal stems that store nutrients.

Leaves Photosynthesize

A **leaf** is that part of a plant that usually carries on photosynthesis, a process that requires water, carbon dioxide, and sunlight (fig. 31.2c). Leaves receive water from the root system by way of the stem. Broad, thin leaves have a maximum surface area for the absorption of carbon dioxide and the collection of solar energy. The wide portion of a leaf is called the *blade;* the *petiole* is a stalk that attaches the blade to the stem. The upper and acute angle between the petiole and stem is designated the leaf axil, and this is where an *axillary* (lateral) *bud* originates, which may become a branch or a flower.

A flowering plant has three vegetative organs: the root absorbs water and minerals, the stem supports and services leaves, and the leaf carries on photosynthesis.

Figure 31.3

Flowering plants are either monocots or dicots. Three features used to distinguish monocots from dicots are the number of cotyledons, the arrangement of vascular bundles, and the pattern of leaf veins. (Not discussed in this chapter are the number of flower parts; monocots have flower parts in threes, dicots have them in fours or fives.)

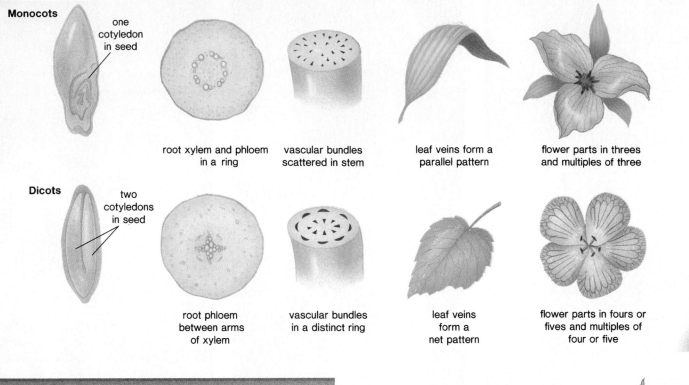

Monocots

one cotyledon in seed

root xylem and phloem in a ring

vascular bundles scattered in stem

leaf veins form a parallel pattern

flower parts in threes and multiples of three

Dicots

two cotyledons in seed

root phloem between arms of xylem

vascular bundles in a distinct ring

leaf veins form a net pattern

flower parts in fours or fives and multiples of four or five

MONOCOT VERSUS DICOT PLANTS

Flowering plants are divided into the *monocots* and *dicots,* depending on the number of cotyledons or seed leaves in the embryonic plant (fig. 31.3). **Cotyledons** [Gk. *cotyl,* cup-shaped cavity] provide nutrient molecules either by storing or absorbing food for growing embryos before the true leaves begin photosynthesizing. Some embryos have one cotyledon, and these plants are known as monocotyledons, or monocots. Other embryos have two cotyledons, and these plants are known as dicotyledons, or dicots.

There is a different arrangement of vascular (transport) tissue in monocot and dicot roots. In the monocot root, *xylem,* the vascular tissue that transports water, occurs in a ring, and in the dicot, xylem has a star shape. *Vascular bundles* contain vascular tissue surrounded by a bundle sheath. In a monocot stem, the vascular bundles are scattered; in a dicot stem, they occur in a ring. Figure 31.3 shows cross sections of stems, but keep in mind that vascular bundles extend lengthwise in the stem. Leaf veins are vascular bundles within a leaf. Monocots exhibit parallel venation and dicots exhibit netted venation which may be either pinnate or palmate. Pinnate venation means that branch veins originate from points along the centrally placed main vein and palmate venation means that the branch veins all originate at the point of attachment of the blade to the petiole:

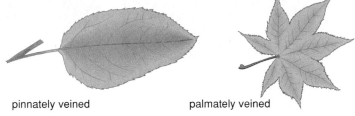

pinnately veined   palmately veined

Adult monocots and dicots have other structural differences such as differences in the usual number of flower parts and the number of apertures (thin areas in the wall) of pollen grains. Dicot pollen grains usually have three apertures and monocot pollen grains usually have one aperture.

Although the division between monocots and dicots may seem arbitrary, it does in fact represent a separation that most likely dates back to the origin of flowering plants. The dicots are the larger group and include some of our most familiar flowering plants—from dandelions to oak trees. The monocots include grasses, lilies, orchids, and palm trees, among others. Some of our most significant food sources are monocots, including rice, wheat, and corn.

> **Flowering plants are divided into monocots and dicots on the basis of structural differences.**

Figure 31.4 📷

Epidermis is modified in different parts of a plant. **a.** Root epidermis has root hairs to absorb water. **b.** Leaf epidermis contains stomates for gas exchange. **c.** Cork replaces epidermis in older, woody stems.

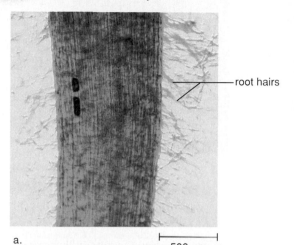

a.

500 μm

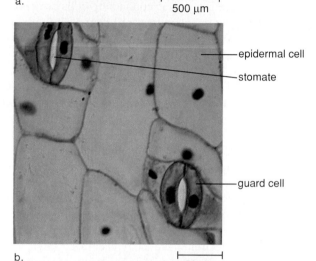

— epidermal cell

— stomate

— guard cell

b.

50 μm

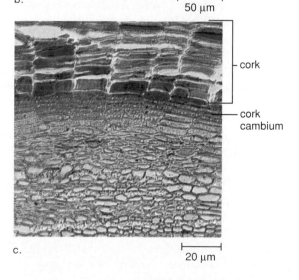

cork

cork cambium

c.

20 μm

PLANT ORGANS HAVE TISSUES

A plant grows its entire life because it has **meristem** (embryonic tissue) located in the stem and root apexes. Three types of meristem continually produce the three types of specialized tissue in the body of a plant: protoderm, the outer most primary meristem, gives rise to epidermis; ground meristem produces ground tissue; and procambium produces vascular tissue.

We will be discussing these three specialized tissues:

1. *Epidermal tissue*—forms the outer protective covering of a plant.
2. *Ground tissue*—fills the interior of a plant.
3. *Vascular tissue*—transports water and nutrients in a plant and provides support.

Epidermal Tissue Protects

The entire bodies of nonwoody (herbaceous) and young woody plants are covered by a layer of **epidermis** [Gk. *epi,* upon, and *derm,* skin], which contains closely packed epidermal cells. The walls of epidermal cells that are exposed to air are covered with a waxy cuticle to minimize water loss. The cuticle also protects against bacteria and other organisms that might cause disease.

In roots, certain epidermal cells have long, slender projections called **root hairs** (fig. 31.4*a*). As mentioned, the hairs increase the surface area of the root for absorption of water and minerals; they also help to anchor the plant firmly in place.

Protective hairs of a different nature are produced by epidermal cells of stems and leaves. Epidermal cells may also be modified as glands that secrete protective substances of various types.

In leaves, the lower epidermis in particular contains specialized cells, such as guard cells (fig. 31.4*b*). The guard cells surround microscopic pores called stomates (also called stomata). When the stomates are open, gas exchange can occur. During the day, carbon dioxide diffuses in and oxygen diffuses out.

In older woody plants, the epidermis of the stem is replaced by cork tissue. **Cork,** the outer covering of the bark of trees, is made up of dead cork cells that may be sloughed off (fig. 31.4*c*). New cork cells are made by a meristem called cork cambium. As the new cork cells mature, they increase slightly in volume and their walls become encrusted with *suberin,* a lipid material, so that they are waterproof and chemically inert. These nonliving cells protect the plant and make it resistant to attack by fungi, bacteria, and animals.

Epidermal tissue forms the outer protective covering of a herbaceous plant. It is modified in roots, stems, and leaves.

Figure 31.5

Ground tissue cells. **a.** Parenchyma cells are the least specialized of the plant cells. **b.** Collenchyma cells. Notice how much thicker the walls are compared to those of parenchyma cells. **c.** Sclerenchyma cells have very thick walls and are nonliving—their only function is to give strong support.

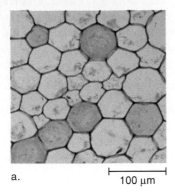

a.   100 μm

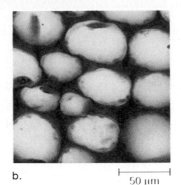

b.   50 μm

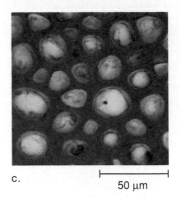

c.   50 μm

Ground Tissue Fills

Ground tissue forms the bulk of a plant and contains parenchyma, collenchyma, and sclerenchyma cells (fig. 31.5). **Parenchyma** [Gk. *para,* beside, and *enchyma,* infusion] cells correspond best to the typical plant cell. These are the least specialized of the cell types and are found in all the organs of a plant. They may contain chloroplasts and carry on photosynthesis, or they may contain colorless plastids that store the products of photosynthesis. Parenchyma cells can divide and give rise to more specialized cells, such as when roots develop from stem cuttings placed in water.

Collenchyma cells are like parenchyma cells except they have thicker primary walls. The thickness is uneven and usually involves the corners of the cell. Collenchyma cells often form bundles just beneath the epidermis and give flexible support to immature regions of a plant body. The familiar strands of celery stalks are composed mostly of collenchyma cells.

Sclerenchyma cells have thick secondary cell walls, usually impregnated with *lignin,* which is an organic substance that makes the walls tough and hard. Most sclerenchyma cells are nonliving; their primary function is to support mature regions of a plant. Two types of sclerenchyma cells are fibers and sclereids. Although fibers are occasionally found in ground tissue, most are found in vascular tissue, which is discussed next. Fibers are long and slender and may be found in bundles that are sometimes commercially important. Hemp fibers can be used to make rope, and flax fibers can be woven into linen. Flax fibers, however, are not lignified, which is why linen is soft. Sclereids, which are shorter than fibers and more varied in shape, are found in seed coats and nut shells. They also give pears their characteristic gritty texture.

Vascular Tissue Transports

There are two types of vascular (transport) tissue. **Xylem** transports water and minerals from the roots to the leaves, and **phloem** transports organic nutrients, usually from the leaves to the roots. Xylem contains two types of conducting cells: *tracheids* and *vessel elements* (fig. 31.6). Both types of conducting cells are hollow and nonliving, but the vessel elements are larger, lack transverse end walls, and are arranged to form a continuous pipeline for water and mineral transport. The elongated tracheids, with tapered ends, form a less obvious means of transport, but water can move across the end walls and sidewalls because there are pits, or depressions, where the secondary wall does not form. In addition to vessel elements and tracheids, xylem contains parenchyma cells that store various substances. Vascular rays, which are flat ribbons or sheets of parenchyma cells located between rows of tracheids, conduct water and minerals laterally. Xylem also contains fibers, sclerenchyma cells that lend support.

The conducting cells of phloem are sieve-tube cells, each of which has a companion cell (fig. 31.7). *Sieve-tube cells* contain cytoplasm but no nuclei. These cells have channels in their end walls that in cross section make them resemble a sieve. Plasmodesmata (sing., plasmodesma), which are strands of cytoplasm, extend from one cell to another through this so-called *sieve plate.* The smaller *companion cells* are more generalized cells in that they do have a nucleus in addition to cytoplasm. Companion cells are closely connected to sieve-tube cells by numerous plasmodesmata, and the nucleus of the companion cell may control and maintain the life of both cells. The companion cells are also believed to be involved in the transport function of phloem.

It is important to realize that vascular tissue (xylem and phloem) extends from the root to the leaves and vice versa. In the roots, the vascular tissue is located in the vascular cylinder; in the stem, it forms vascular bundles; and in the leaves, it is found in leaf veins.

The vascular tissues are xylem and phloem. Xylem transports water and minerals and phloem transports organic nutrients.

Figure 31.6

Xylem structure. **a.** General organization of xylem (*far left*) followed by an external view of vessel elements (stacked on top of each other) and a longitudinal view of several tracheids. **b.** Photomicrograph of xylem vessels.

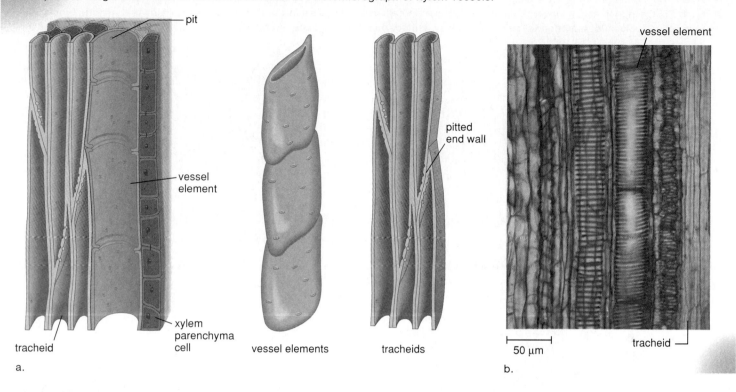

pit

vessel element

vessel element

pitted end wall

xylem parenchyma cell

tracheid

vessel elements

tracheids

50 µm

tracheid

a.

b.

Figure 31.7

Phloem structure. **a.** General organization of phloem (*far left*) followed by external view of two sieve-tube cells and their companion cells. **b.** Photomicrograph of phloem sieve tubes.

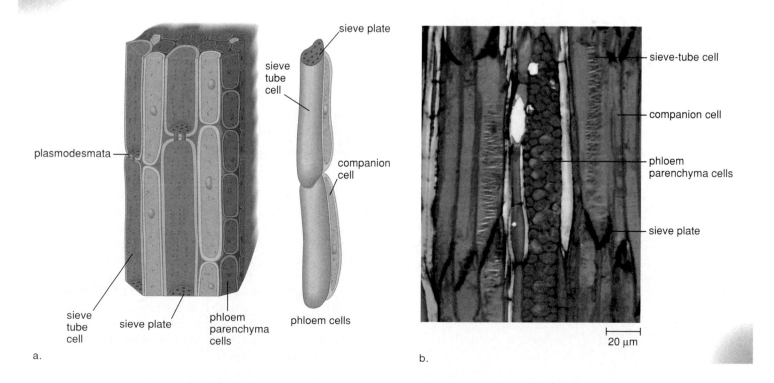

plasmodesmata

sieve plate

sieve tube cell

companion cell

sieve-tube cell

companion cell

phloem parenchyma cells

sieve plate

sieve tube cell

sieve plate

phloem parenchyma cells

phloem cells

20 µm

a.

b.

Figure 31.8

Dicot root tip. **a.** The root tip is divided into four zones, best seen in a longitudinal section such as this. **b.** The vascular cylinder of a dicot root contains the vascular tissue. Xylem is typically star shaped, and phloem lies between the points of the star. **c.** Endodermis showing the Casparian strip, a layer of lignin and suberin in cell walls. Because of the Casparian strip, water and minerals must pass through the cytoplasm of endodermal cells. In this way, endodermal cells regulate the passage of minerals into the vascular cylinder.

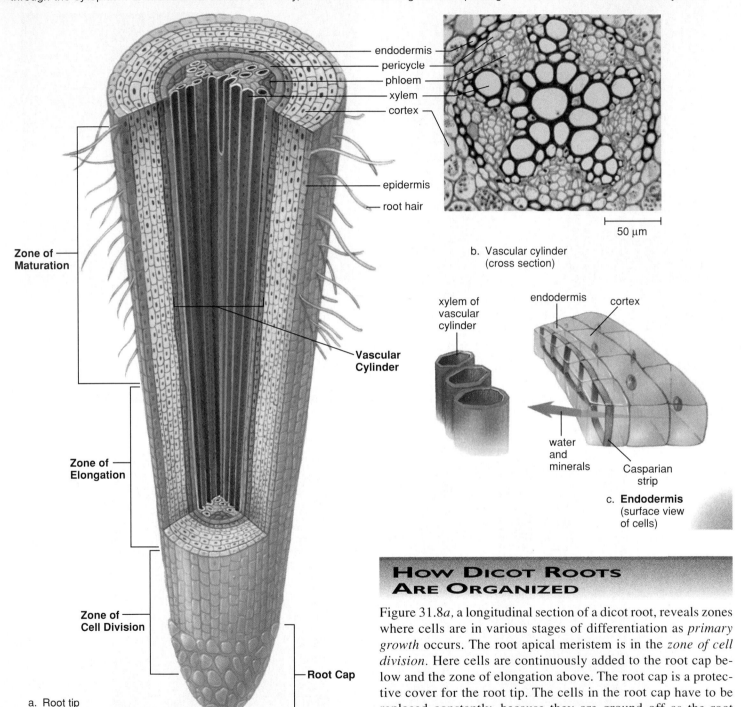

endodermis
pericycle
phloem
xylem
cortex

epidermis
root hair

50 μm

b. Vascular cylinder
(cross section)

xylem of vascular cylinder

endodermis   cortex

water and minerals

Casparian strip

c. **Endodermis**
(surface view of cells)

Zone of Maturation

Vascular Cylinder

Zone of Elongation

Zone of Cell Division

Root Cap

a. Root tip
(longititudinal section)

HOW DICOT ROOTS ARE ORGANIZED

Figure 31.8*a*, a longitudinal section of a dicot root, reveals zones where cells are in various stages of differentiation as *primary growth* occurs. The root apical meristem is in the *zone of cell division*. Here cells are continuously added to the root cap below and the zone of elongation above. The root cap is a protective cover for the root tip. The cells in the root cap have to be replaced constantly, because they are ground off as the root pushes through rough soil particles. In the *zone of elongation*, the cells become longer as they become specialized. In the *zone of maturation*, the cells are mature and fully differentiated. This zone is recognizable even in a whole root because root hairs are borne by many of the epidermal cells.

Tissues of a Dicot Root

Figure 31.8*a* also shows a cross section of a root at the region of maturation. These specialized tissues are identifiable:

Epidermis The epidermis, which forms the outer layer of the root, consists of only a single layer of cells. The majority of epidermal cells are thin walled and rectangular, but in the zone of maturation, many epidermal cells have root hairs. These project as far as 5–8 mm into the soil particles.

Cortex Moving inward, next to the epidermis, large, thin-walled parenchyma cells make up the *cortex* of the root. These irregularly-shaped cells are loosely packed, and it is possible for water and minerals to move through the cortex without entering the cells. The cells contain starch granules, and the cortex functions in food storage.

Endodermis The **endodermis** [Gk. *endo*, within, and *derm*, skin] is a single layer of rectangular endodermal cells that forms a boundary between the cortex and the inner vascular cylinder. The endodermal cells fit snugly together and are bordered on four sides (but not the two sides that contact the cortex and the vascular cylinder) by a layer of impermeable lignin and suberin known as the **Casparian strip** (fig. 31.8*c*). This strip does not permit water and mineral ions to pass between adjacent cell walls. Therefore, the only access to the vascular cylinder is through the endodermal cells themselves, as shown by the arrow in figure 31.8*c*. It is said that the endodermis regulates the entrance of minerals into the vascular cylinder.

Vascular Tissue The **pericycle,** the first layer of cells within the *vascular cylinder,* has retained its capacity to divide and can start the development of branch or secondary roots (fig. 31.9). The main portion of the vascular cylinder, though, contains vascular tissue. The xylem appears star shaped in dicots because several arms of tissue radiate from a common center (fig. 31.8*b*). The phloem is found in separate regions between the arms of the xylem.

How Monocot Roots Are Organized

Monocot roots often have pith, which is centrally located ground tissue. In a monocot root, pith is surrounded by a vascular ring composed of alternating xylem and phloem bundles (fig. 31.10). They also have pericycle, endodermis, cortex, and epidermis. Typically, monocot roots do not undergo secondary growth.

Figure 31.9
Cross section of dicot root. This cross section of a willow, *Salix,* shows the origination of a branch root from the pericycle.

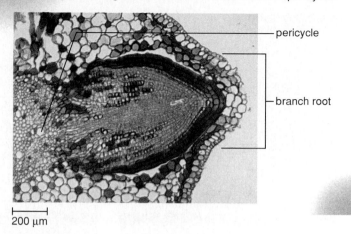

pericycle

branch root

200 µm

Figure 31.10
Cross section of monocot root. **a.** In the overall micrograph, it is possible to observe that a vascular ring surrounds a central pith. **b.** The enlargement shows the exact placement of various tissues.

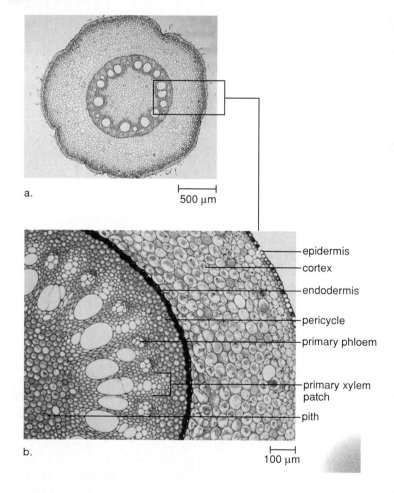

a.

500 µm

epidermis
cortex
endodermis
pericycle
primary phloem
primary xylem patch
pith

b.

100 µm

Figure 31.11

Three types of roots. **a.** A taproot may have secondary roots in addition to a main root. **b.** A fibrous root has many secondary roots with no main root. **c.** Adventitious roots, such as prop roots, extend from the stem.

a.

b.

c.

How Roots Differ

Roots have various adaptations and associations to better perform their functions: anchorage, absorption of water and minerals, and storage of carbohydrates.

In some plants, notably dicots, the first or primary root grows straight down and remains the dominant root of the plant. This so-called *taproot* is often fleshy and stores food (fig. 31.11*a*). Carrots, beets, turnips, and radishes have taproots that we consume as vegetables. Sweet potato plants don't have taproots but they do have roots with special storage areas for starch. We call these storage areas sweet potatoes.

In other plants, notably monocots, there is no single, main root; instead there are a large number of slender roots. These slender roots and their lateral branches make up a *fibrous root* system (fig. 31.11*b*). Everyone has observed the fibrous root systems of grasses and has noted how these roots can hold the soil.

Sometimes a root system develops from an underground stem or from the base of an aboveground stem. These are *adventitious roots,* whose main function may be to help anchor the plant. If so, they are called *prop roots.* Mangrove plants have large prop roots that spread away from the plant to help anchor it in marshy soil, where mangroves are typically found. Corn plants also develop prop roots for support (fig. 31.11*c*).

Plants such as black mangrove grow with their roots in the water. Water contains less oxygen than air and so the roots have difficulty acquiring enough oxygen to carry on aerobic cellular respiration. An adaptation is the growth of root projections called *pneumatophores* that rise above the surface of the water.

Some plants such as dodders and broomrapes are parasitic on other plants. Their stems have rootlike projections called *haustoria* that grow into the host plant and make contact with vascular tissue from which they extract water and nutrients.

Mycorrhizae are fungus roots—an association between roots and fungi—which can extract water and minerals from the soil better than roots that lack a fungus partner. This is called a mutualistic relationship because the fungus receives sugars and amino acids from the plant, which receives water and minerals via the fungus.

Peas, beans, and other legumes have root nodules where nitrogen-fixing bacteria live. Plants cannot extract nitrogen from the air, but the bacteria within the nodules can take up and reduce atmospheric nitrogen. This means that the plant is no longer dependent upon a supply of nitrogen (i.e., nitrate or ammonium) in the soil, and indeed these plants are often planted just to bolster the nitrogen supply of the soil.

> Roots have various adaptations and associations to enhance their ability to anchor a plant, absorb water and minerals, and store the products of photosynthesis.

Tree Rings Tell a Story

Each year a tree adds a new growth ring to its trunk. In the spring, growth is fast and the wood is light in color; in the summer, growth is slower and the wood is dark in color. Counting the dark rings tells you the age of the tree, but studying tree rings to determine their shape, thickness, color, and evenness lets you know what a tree has been through (fig. 31A). Rings can reveal the years in which there were forest fires, smog damage, and leaf damage from caterpillars.

A great deal can also be learned from tree rings about past climatic conditions. For many years, A. E. Douglass, Harold C. Fritts, and others associated with the Laboratory of Tree-Ring Research at the University of Arizona studied ring widths in trees from arid sites. They discovered that very significant statistical relationships exist between growth of trees and climatic data. With the aid of computers and statistical analyses, they developed techniques that take into account subtle climatic and other environmental variables. They were able to reconstruct relatively precise histories of climatic fluctuations and changes dating back hundreds of years. Today, tree ring data are analyzed to try to determine climates dating back to prehistoric times.

Trees do not have to be cut down to examine the rings. A simple instrument called an *increment borer*, which consists primarily of a rigid metal cylinder, is driven into the trunk of a tree, and a core of wood is removed. The hole is then plugged to prevent disease-causing organisms from entering the tree, and the rings revealed by the core are then examined and analyzed.

Figure 31A

Life history of a tree planted in 1908 and cut down in 1970. The anatomy of the tree rings correlates to the events listed by date.

Source: Data from St. Regis Paper Company, New York, NY., 1966.

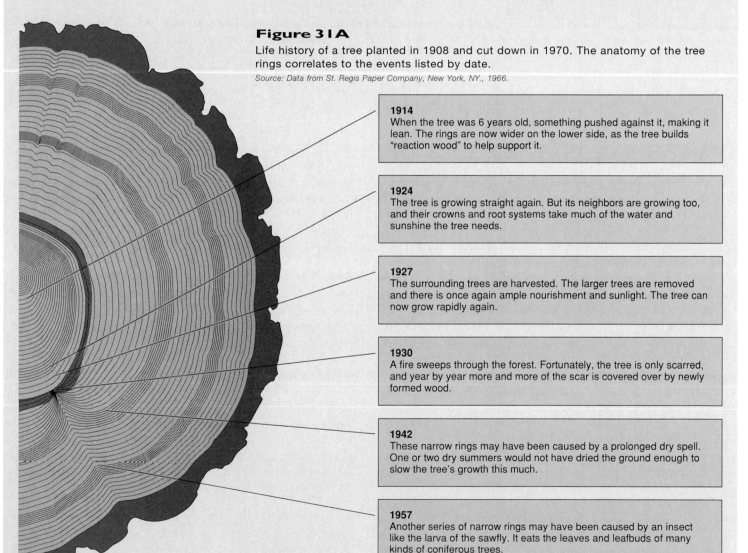

1914
When the tree was 6 years old, something pushed against it, making it lean. The rings are now wider on the lower side, as the tree builds "reaction wood" to help support it.

1924
The tree is growing straight again. But its neighbors are growing too, and their crowns and root systems take much of the water and sunshine the tree needs.

1927
The surrounding trees are harvested. The larger trees are removed and there is once again ample nourishment and sunlight. The tree can now grow rapidly again.

1930
A fire sweeps through the forest. Fortunately, the tree is only scarred, and year by year more and more of the scar is covered over by newly formed wood.

1942
These narrow rings may have been caused by a prolonged dry spell. One or two dry summers would not have dried the ground enough to slow the tree's growth this much.

1957
Another series of narrow rings may have been caused by an insect like the larva of the sawfly. It eats the leaves and leafbuds of many kinds of coniferous trees.

Figure 31.12

Stem tip and primary meristems. **a.** The shoot apical meristem within a terminal bud is surrounded by leaf primordia. **b.** The shoot apical meristem produces the primary meristems: protoderm gives rise to epidermis, ground meristem gives rise to pith and cortex, and procambium gives rise to xylem and phloem.

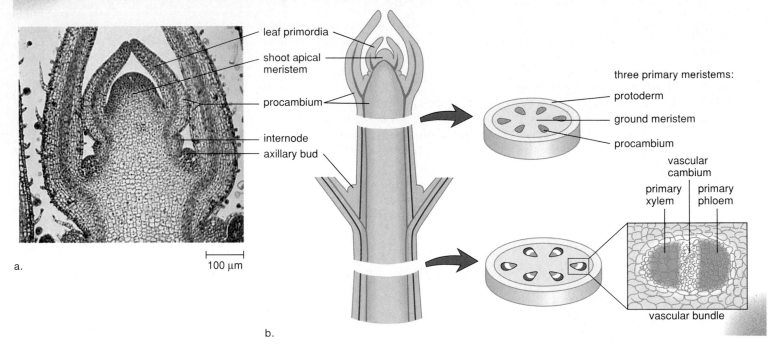

HOW STEMS ARE ORGANIZED

Growth of a stem can be compared to the growth of a root. During *primary growth,* apical meristem at the stem tip called **shoot apical meristem** produces new cells that elongate and thereby increase the length of the stem. The shoot apical meristem, however, is protected within a terminal bud where *leaf primordia* (immature leaves) envelop it (fig. 31.12*a*). In the temperate zone, a terminal bud stops growing in the winter and is then protected by bud scales. In the spring, when growth resumes, these scales fall off and leave a scar. You can tell the age of a stem by counting these bud scale scars.

Leaf primordia are produced by the apical meristem at regular intervals called nodes. The portion of a stem between two sequential nodes is called an internode. As a stem grows, the internodes increase in length. **Axillary buds,** which are usually dormant but may develop into branch shoots or flowers, are seen at the axes of the leaf primordia.

A shoot is a developing structure in which tissues are continually becoming differentiated. In addition to leaf primordia, three specialized types of primary meristem develop from shoot apical meristem (fig. 31.12*b*). These primary meristems contribute to the length of a shoot. As mentioned, the *protoderm,* the outermost primary meristem, gives rise to epidermis. The *ground meristem* produces two tissues composed of parenchyma cells. The parenchyma tissue in the center of the stem is the pith and the parenchyma tissue inside the epidermis is the cortex.

The *procambium,* seen as an obvious strand of tissue in figure 31.12*a,* produces the first xylem cells, called primary xylem, and the first phloem cells, called primary phloem. Differen-

tiation continues as certain cells become the first tracheids or vessel elements of the xylem within a vascular bundle. The first sieve-tube cells of the phloem do not have companion cells and are short lived (some live only a day before being replaced). Mature phloem develops later, when all surrounding cells have stopped expanding and **vascular cambium** [L. *vascul,* little vessel, and *cambi,* exchange] occurs between xylem and phloem.

Herbaceous Stems Are Nonwoody

Mature nonwoody stems, called **herbaceous stems** [L. *herb,* grass], exhibit only primary growth. The outermost tissue of herbaceous stems is the epidermis, which is covered by a waxy cuticle to prevent water loss. These stems have distinctive *vascular bundles,* where xylem and phloem are found. In each bundle, xylem is typically found toward the inside of the stem and phloem is found toward the outside.

In the dicot herbaceous stem, the bundles are arranged in a distinct ring that separates the cortex from the central pith, which stores water and products of photosynthesis (fig. 31.13). The cortex is sometimes green and carries on photosynthesis, and the pith may function as a storage site. In the monocot stem, the vascular bundles are scattered throughout the stem, and there is no well-defined cortex or well-defined pith (fig. 31.14).

As a stem grows, the shoot apical meristem produces new leaves and primary meristems. The primary meristems produce the other tissues found in herbaceous stems.

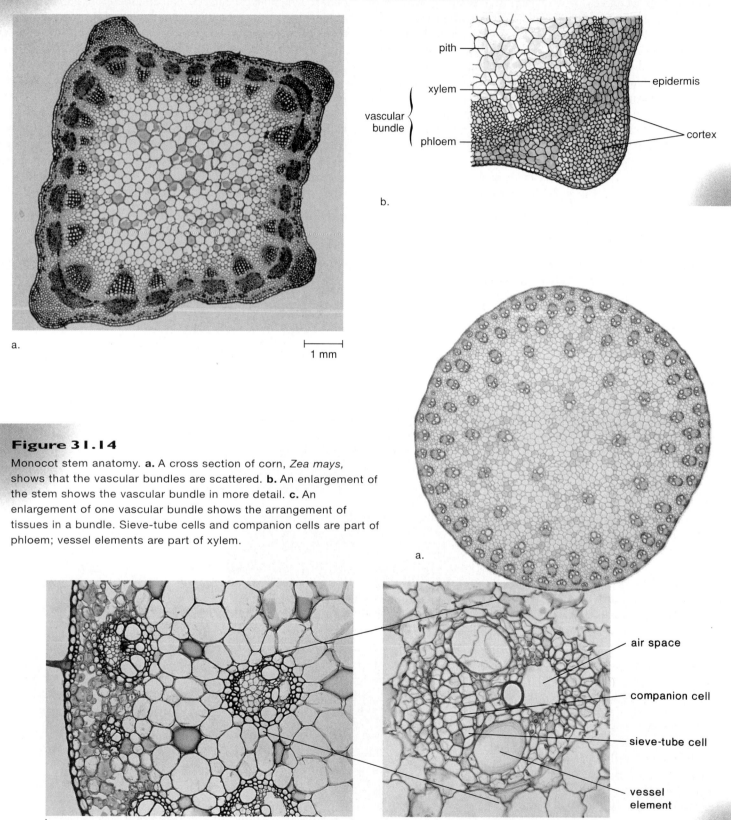

Figure 31.13

Dicot herbaceous stem anatomy. **a.** A cross section of an alfalfa stem, *Medicago,* shows that the vascular bundles are in a ring. **b.** The drawing of a section of the stem indentifies the tissues in the vascular bundle and the stem.

pith

xylem

vascular bundle

phloem

epidermis

cortex

b.

a.

1 mm

Figure 31.14

Monocot stem anatomy. **a.** A cross section of corn, *Zea mays,* shows that the vascular bundles are scattered. **b.** An enlargement of the stem shows the vascular bundle in more detail. **c.** An enlargement of one vascular bundle shows the arrangement of tissues in a bundle. Sieve-tube cells and companion cells are part of phloem; vessel elements are part of xylem.

a.

air space

companion cell

sieve-tube cell

vessel element

b.

100 µm

c.

20 µm

How Stems Become Woody

A woody plant has both primary and secondary tissues. Primary growth continues for only a short distance behind apical meristem; then secondary growth begins. Primary growth increases the length of a plant and secondary growth increases its girth. Trees and some shrubs are woody. Shrubs, and almost all trees other than conifers, are dicot flowering plants. As a result of secondary growth, a woody dicot stem has an entirely different type of organization than that of a herbaceous dicot stem. After secondary growth has continued for a time, it is no longer possible to make out individual vascular bundles. Instead, a woody stem has three distinct areas: the bark, the wood, and the pith (fig. 31.15a).

Trees undergo secondary growth because of a change in vascular cambium. Recall that vascular cambium begins as a meristem between the xylem and phloem of each vascular bundle.

In woody plants, the vascular cambium develops to form a ring of meristem that divides parallel to the surface of the plant. The secondary tissues produced by the vascular cambium, called secondary xylem and secondary phloem, therefore add to the girth of the stem instead of to its length (fig. 31.16). Another change is the presence of rays—both phloem rays and vascular rays—that store materials and conduct them radially for a short distance.

In trees that have a growing season, vascular cambium is dormant during the winter. In the spring, when moisture is plentiful and leaves require much water for growth, the xylem [Gk. *xyl,* wood, and L. *em,* in] contains wide vessel elements with thin walls. In this so-called spring wood, wide vessels transport sufficient water to the growing leaves. Later in the season, moisture is scarce and the wood at this time, called summer wood, has a lower proportion of vessels. Strength is required because the tree is growing larger and summer wood contains numerous fibers and thick-walled

Figure 31.15

Dicot woody stem. **a.** A three-year-old stem showing bark, vascular cambium, wood, and pith. The wood consists of secondary xylem, which accumulates and becomes the annual rings. **b.** A cross section of a 39-year-old larch, *Larix decidua.* The xylem within the darker heartwood is now inactive; the xylem within the lighter sapwood is active. **c.** The relationship of bark, vascular cambium, and wood is retained in a mature stem. The pith has disappeared.

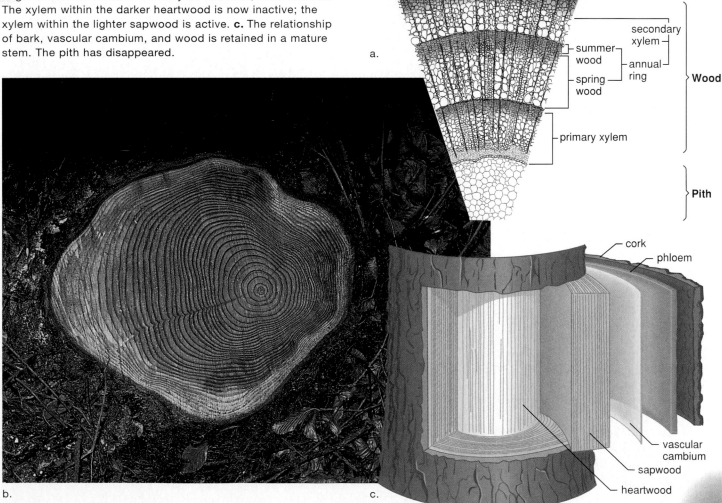

Figure 31.16

Secondary growth in a stem. **a.** A dicot herbaceous stem before secondary growth begins. **b.** Secondary growth has begun. Cork has replaced the epidermis. Vascular cambium produces secondary xylem and secondary phloem. **c.** A three-year-old stem. Cork cambium produces new cork. The primary phloem and cortex will eventually disappear and only the secondary phloem (within the bark), produced by vascular cambium, will be active that year. The secondary xylem, also produced by vascular cambium, builds up to become the annual rings.

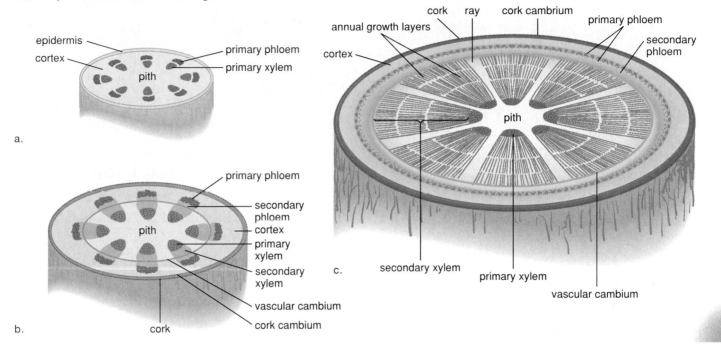

tracheids. At the end of the growing season, just before the cambium becomes dormant again, only heavy fibers with especially thick secondary walls may develop. When the trunk of a tree has spring wood followed by summer wood, the two together make up one year's growth, or annual ring. You can tell the age of a tree by counting the annual rings. The outer annual rings, where transport occurs, is called sapwood (fig. 31.15b, c).

In older trees, the inner annual rings, called the heartwood, no longer function in water transport. The cells become plugged with deposits, such as resins, gums, and other substances that inhibit the growth of bacteria and fungi. Heartwood may help support a tree, although some trees stand erect and live for many years after the heartwood has rotted away.

The bark of a tree contains cork, cork cambium, and phloem [Gk. *phloe,* tree bark, and L. *em,* in]. Although secondary phloem is produced each year by vascular cambium, phloem does not build up for many seasons. The phloem tissue is soft, making it possible to remove the bark of a tree; however, this is very harmful because without phloem there is no conduction of organic nutrients.

Cork cambium [L. *cambi,* exchange] is meristem located beneath the epidermis. When cork cambium begins to divide, it produces tissue that disrupts the epidermis and replaces it with cork cells. Cork cells are impregnated with suberin, a lipid material that makes them waterproof but also causes them to die. This is protective because now there is nothing nutritious for an ani-

mal to eat. But an impervious barrier means that gas exchange is impeded except at *lenticels,* which are pockets of loosely arranged cork cells not impregnated with suberin.

The first flowering plants to evolve may have been woody shrubs; herbaceous plants evolved later. Is it advantageous to be woody? If there is adequate rainfall, woody plants can grow taller and have more growth because they have adequate vascular tissue to support and service leaves. However, it takes energy to produce secondary growth and prepare the body for winter if the plant lives in the temperate zone. Also, there is a greater need for defense mechanisms because a long-lasting plant that stays in one spot is likely to be attacked by herbivores and parasites. Then, too, trees don't usually reproduce until they have grown several seasons, by which time they may have succumbed to an accident or disease. Perhaps it is more advantageous for a plant to put most of its energy into simply reproducing rather than being woody.

> Woody plants grow in girth due to the presence of vascular cambium and cork cambium. Their bodies have three main parts: bark (which contains cork, cork cambium, and phloem), wood (which contains xylem), and pith.

Figure 31.17

Stem modifications. **a.** A strawberry plant has aboveground, horizontal stems called stolons. Every other node produces a new shoot system. **b.** The underground horizontal stem of an iris is a fleshy rhizome. **c.** The underground stem of a potato plant has enlargements called tubers. We call the tubers potatoes. **d.** The corm of a gladiolus is a stem covered by papery leaves.

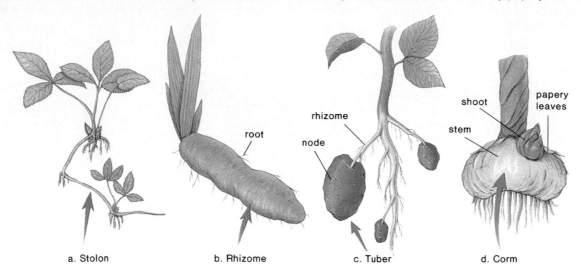

a. Stolon   b. Rhizome   c. Tuber   d. Corm

How Stems Differ

Stem modifications are illustrated in figure 31.17. Aboveground horizontal stems, called **stolons** [L. *stolo,* shoot] or runners, produce new plants where nodes touch the ground. The strawberry plant is a common example of this type of stem.

Underground horizontal stems, **rhizomes** [Gk. *rhizo,* root], may be long and thin, as in sod-forming grasses, or thick and fleshy, as in iris. Rhizomes survive the winter and contribute to asexual reproduction because each node bears a bud. Some rhizomes have enlarged portions called *tubers,* which function in food storage. For example, potatoes are tubers. The eyes of potatoes are buds that mark the nodes.

Corms are bulbous underground stems that lie dormant during the winter, just as rhizomes do. They also produce new plants the next growing season. Gladiolus corms are referred to as bulbs by laypersons, but the botanist reserves the term *bulb* for a structure composed of modified leaves.

Aboveground, vertical stems can also be modified. For example, cacti have succulent stems modified for water storage. The tendrils of grape plants that twine around a support structure are modified stems.

Humans make use of stems in many ways. The stem of the sugarcane plant is a primary source of table sugar. The spice cinnamon and the drug quinine are derived from the bark of different plants. And wood is especially helpful to humans, as discussed next.

Humans Utilize Wood

Humans have used wood for various purposes since antiquity. Much of the wood harvested in the United States is used to produce lumber. There is much waste in lumber production but the waste can be used for pulp, fiberboard, and particleboard. Paper is made from pulp, as is discussed in the reading on the next page.

A veneer is a thin layer or sheet of wood that is uniform in thickness. Many times the last step in furniture making occurs when an expensive veneer is glued to a piece made from cheaper wood. Plywoods and laminated woods are made by gluing together several layers of veneers in such a way as to give added strength. One advantage of these products is that they can be curved and used for boats, furniture, and other products. Aircraft decking and helicopter blades are made from laminated wood as well.

Particleboard, which is manufactured by gluing particles of wood together, and fiberboard, which is made from fibers, also have many uses. They are used for construction of cabinets, refrigeration cars, toys, concrete forms, and even parts of automobiles.

Poles, posts, and certain mine timbers are wood products in round form. Poles are used to support telephone and electric wires. They are also used as pilings for wharves and building foundations, and are used in fences.

Wood is also important for recreational purposes. Hard maple, which makes fine croquet balls or bowling pins, is also used as the flooring of bowling alleys. White ash is perfect for baseball bats, rackets, and oars. Red spruce is a favorite wood for the making of violins.

In nonindustrialized countries, much wood is still used as fuel. Indeed, coal itself was once wood.

Paper Comes From Plants

T he word *paper* takes it origin from papyrus, the plant Egyptians used to make the first form of paper. The Egyptians manually made sheets from the treated stems of papyrus grass and then strung together into scrolls. From that beginning some 5,500 years ago, the production of paper is now a world-wide industry of major importance. The process is fairly simple. Plant material is ground up mechanically, and chemically treated to form a pulp that contains "fibers" which biologists know are the tracheids and vessel elements of a plant. The fibers automatically form a sheet when they are screened from the pulp. Today a revolving wire-screen belt is used to deliver a continuous wet sheet of paper to heavy rollers and heated cylinders which remove most of the remaining moisture and press the paper flat.

There are, of course, different types of paper dependent upon the plant material used and the way it is treated. Among the major plants used to make paper are

Eucalyptus trees. In recent years Brazil has devoted huge areas in the Amazon to the growing of cloned eucalyptus seedlings, specially selected and engineered to be ready for harvest after about seven years.

Temperate hardwood trees. Plantation cultivation in Canada provides birch, beech, chestnut, poplar and particularly aspen wood for paper making. Tropical hardwoods usually coming from Southeast Asia are also used.

Softwood trees. In the United States, several species of pine trees have been genetically improved to have a higher wood density and to be harvestable five years earlier than ordinary pines. Southern Africa, Chile, New Zealand, and Australia also devote thousands of acres to growing pines for paper pulp production.

Bamboo. Several Asian countries, especially India, provide vast quantities of bamboo pulp for the making of paper. Because bamboo is harvested without destroying the roots, and the growing cycle is favorable, this plant, which is actually a grass, is expected to be a significant source of paper pulp despite high processing costs to remove impurities.

Flax and cotton plants. Linen and cotton cloth from textile and garment mills are used to produce *rag paper* whose flexibility and durability are desirable in legal documents, high-grade bond paper and high-grade stationery.

It has been known for sometime that paper largely consists of the cellulose within plant cell walls. It seems reasonable to suppose, then, that paper could be made from synthetic polymers (e.g. rayon). Indeed, synthetic polymers produce a paper that has qualities superior to those of paper made from natural sources, but the cost thus far is prohibitive. Another consideration, however, is the ecological effects of making paper from trees. Plantations containing stands of uniform trees replace natural ecosystems and when the trees are clear-cut, the land is laid bare. Paper mill wastes, which include caustic chemicals, add significantly to the pollution of rivers and streams.

The use of paper for packaging and to make all sorts of products has increased dramatically in this century. Each person in the United States consumes about 318 kilograms (699 pounds) of paper products per year, and this compares to only 2.3 kilograms (5 pounds) of paper per person in India. It is clear, then, we should take the initiative in recycling paper. When newspaper, office paper, and photocopies are soaked in water, the fibers are released and they can be used to make a new batch of paper. It's estimated that recycling the Sunday newspapers alone would save an estimated number of 500,000 trees each week!

Figure 31B

Machine No. 35 at Champion International's Courtland, Alabama, mill produces a 29-foot-wide roll of office paper every 60 minutes.

HOW LEAVES ARE ORGANIZED

Leaves are the organs of photosynthesis in vascular plants. As mentioned earlier, a leaf usually consists of a flattened *blade* and a *petiole* connecting the blade to the stem. The blade may be single or composed of several leaflets. Externally, it is possible to see the pattern of the *leaf veins,* which contain vascular tissue. Leaf veins have a net pattern in dicot leaves and a parallel pattern in monocot leaves (see fig. 31.3).

Figure 31.18 shows a cross section of a typical dicot leaf of a temperate zone plant. At the top and bottom is a layer of epidermal tissue that often bears protective hairs and/or glands that produce irritating substances. These features may prevent the leaf from being eaten by insects. The epidermis characteristically has an outer, waxy **cuticle** [L. *cut,* skin] that keeps the leaf from drying out. Unfortunately, the cuticle also prevents gas exchange because it is not gas permeable. However, the epidermis, particularly the lower epidermis, contains stomates that allow gases to move into and out of the leaf. Each stomate has two guard cells that regulate its opening and closing.

The body of a leaf is composed of **mesophyll** [Gk. *meso,* middle, and *phyll,* leaf] tissue, which has two distinct regions: **palisade mesophyll,** containing elongated cells, and **spongy mesophyll,** containing irregular cells bounded by air spaces. The parenchyma cells of these layers have many chloroplasts and carry on most of the photosynthesis for the plant. The loosely packed arrangement of the cells in the spongy layer increases the amount of surface area for gas exchange.

How Leaves Differ

The blade of a leaf can be simple or compound, with two or more separate leaflets making up the blade (fig. 31.19). There are also various vascular arrangements in leaves and innumerable combinations of overall leaf shape, margin, and base modifications.

Leaves are adapted to environmental conditions. Shade plants tend to have broad, wide leaves, and desert plants tend to have reduced leaves with sunken stomates. The leaves of a cactus are the spines attached to the succulent stem (fig. 31.20*a*). Other succulents have leaves adapted to hold moisture.

An onion *bulb* is made up of leaves surrounding a short stem. In a head of cabbage, large leaves overlap one another. The petiole of a leaf can be thick and fleshy, as in celery and rhubarb. Climbing leaves, such as those of peas and cucumbers, are modified into tendrils that can attach to nearby objects (fig. 31.20*b*). The leaves of a few plants are specialized for catching insects. The leaves of a sundew have sticky epidermal hairs that trap insects and then secrete digestive enzymes. The Venus's-flytrap has hinged leaves that snap shut and interlock when an insect triggers sensitive hairs (fig. 31.20*c*). The leaves of a pitcher plant resemble a pitcher and have downward-pointing hairs that lead insects into a pool of digestive enzymes. Insectivorous plants commonly grow in marshy regions, where the supply of soil nitrogen is severely limited. The digested insects provide the plants with a source of organic nitrogen.

Figure 31.18

Leaf structure. Photosynthesis takes place in the mesophyll tissue. The veins contain xylem and phloem for the transport of water and solutes. The leaf is enclosed by epidermal cells covered with a waxy layer, the cuticle. The leaf hairs are also protective. A stomate is an opening in the epidermis that permits the exchange of gases.

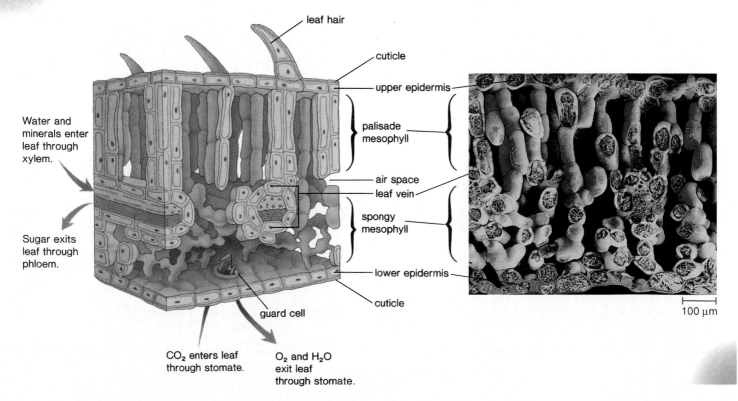

leaf hair

cuticle

upper epidermis

Water and minerals enter leaf through xylem.

palisade mesophyll

air space

leaf vein

Sugar exits leaf through phloem.

spongy mesophyll

lower epidermis

cuticle

guard cell

CO_2 enters leaf through stomate.

O_2 and H_2O exit leaf through stomate.

100 µm

Figure 31.19

Classification of leaves. **a.** The cottonwood tree has a simple leaf.
b. The shagbark hickory has a pinnately compound leaf.
c. The honey locust has a twice pinnately
compound leaf. **d.** The buckeye has
a palmately compound leaf.

a. Simple leaf

b. Pinnately compound
leaf

c. Twice pinnately
compound leaf

d. Palmately compound
leaf

Figure 31.20

Leaf modifications. **a.** The spines of a cactus, *Optunia,* plant are leaves modified to protect the fleshy stem from animal consumption. **b.** The tendrils of a cucumber, *Cucumis,* are leaves modified to attach the plant to a physical support. **c.** The leaves of the Venus's-flytrap, *Dionaea,* are modified to serve as a trap for insect prey. When triggered by an insect, the leaf snaps shut. Once shut, the leaf secretes digestive juices, which break down the soft parts of the insect's body.

Venus's-flytrap,
Dionaea

a.   Cactus, *Optunia*

b.   Cucumber, *Cucumis*

Table 31.1

Vegetative Organs and Major Tissues

	Roots	Stems	Leaves
Function	Absorb water and minerals Anchor plant Store materials	Transport water and nutrients Support leaves Help store materials	Carry on photosynthesis
Tissue			
Epidermis*	Protect inner tissues Root hairs absorb water and minerals	Protect inner tissues	Protect inner tissues Stomates carry on gas exchange
Cortex†	Store water and products of photosynthesis	Carry on photosynthesis, if green Some storage of products of photosynthesis	—
Endodermis†	Regulate passage of minerals in vascular tissue	Regulate passage of minerals in vascular tissue if present	—
Vascular‡	Transport water and nutrients	Transport water and nutrients	Transport water and nutrients
Pith†	Store products of photosynthesis and water	Store products of photosynthesis	—
Mesophyll†	—	—	Primary site of photosynthesis

Note: *Plant tissues belong to one of three tissue systems:*

* *Dermal tissue system*

† *Ground tissue system*

‡ *Vascular tissue system*

▶ Summary

1. A flowering plant has three vegetative organs. A root anchors a plant, absorbs water and minerals, and stores the products of photosynthesis (table 31.1). Stems support leaves, conduct materials to and from roots and leaves, and help store plant products. Leaves carry on photosynthesis.

2. Flowering plants are divided into the dicots and monocots according to the number of cotyledons in the seed, the arrangement of vascular tissue in root, stems, and leaves, and the number of flower parts.

3. Three types of meristem continually divide and produce specialized tissues. Protoderm produces epidermis tissue, ground meristem produces ground tissue, and procambium produces primary vascular tissue.

4. Epidermal tissue contains the epidermis, which is modified in different organs of the plant. In the roots, epidermal cells bear root hairs; in the leaves, the epidermis contains guard cells. Cork replaces epidermis in woody plants.

5. Ground tissue contains parenchyma cells, which are thin walled and capable of photosynthesis when they contain chloroplasts. If they contain only colorless plastids, they serve as storage cells. Collenchyma cells have thicker walls for flexible support. Sclerenchyma cells are hollow, nonliving support cells with secondary walls.

6. Vascular tissue consists of xylem and phloem. Xylem contains vessel elements and tracheids, which are elongated and tapered with pitted end walls. Xylem transports water and minerals. Phloem contains sieve-tube cells, each of which has a companion cell. Phloem transports organic nutrients.

7. A root tip shows three zones: the zone of cell division (apical meristem) protected by the root cap, the zone of elongation, and the zone of maturation.

8. A cross section of a herbaceous dicot root reveals the epidermis (protects), the cortex (stores food), the endodermis (regulates the movement of minerals), and the vascular cylinder (vascular tissue). In the vascular cylinder of a dicot, the xylem appears star shaped and the phloem is found in separate regions, between the arms of the xylem. In contrast, a monocot root has a ring of vascular tissue with alternating bundles of xylem and phloem surrounding pith.

9. Three types of roots are taproots, fibrous roots, and adventitious roots.

10. Primary growth of a stem is due to the activity of the shoot apical meristem, which is protected within a terminal bud. A terminal bud contains leaf primordia at nodes, and internodes between the nodes. When stems grow, the internodes lengthen.

11. In cross section, a nonwoody dicot has epidermis, cortex tissue, vascular bundles in a ring, and an inner pith. Monocot stems have scattered vascular bundles, and the cortex and pith are not well defined.

12. Secondary growth of a woody stem is due to vascular cambium, which produces new xylem and phloem every year, and cork cambium, which produces new cork cells when needed. Cork replaces epidermis in woody plants. The cross section of a woody stem shows bark, wood, and pith. The bark contains cork and phloem. Wood contains annual rings of xylem.

13. Stems are modified in various ways, such as horizontal aboveground and underground stems. Corms and some tendrils are also modified stems. Humans use wood for many purposes.

14. A cross section of a leaf shows the epidermis, with stomates mostly below. Vascular tissue is present within leaf veins.

15. One way to classify leaves is to note whether they are simple or compound. If compound, they may be either pinnately or palmately compound. Leaves are variously modified. The spines of a cactus are leaves. Other succulents have fleshy leaves. An onion is a bulb with fleshy leaves, and the tendrils of peas are leaves. The Venus's-flytrap has leaves that trap and digest insects.

Writing Across the Curriculum

In order to practice writing skills, students should write out the answers to any or all of the study questions and the critical thinking questions. The study questions are sequenced in the same order as the text. Answers to the objective questions, and suggested answers to the critical thinking questions, are in appendix D.

Study Questions

1. Name and discuss the vegetative organs of a plant. 530–31

2. List five differences between monocots and dicots. 532

3. Contrast an epidermal cell with a cork cell. These cells are found in what type of plant tissue? Explain how epidermis is modified in various organs of a plant. 533

4. Contrast the structure and function of parenchyma, collenchyma, and sclerenchyma cells. These cells occur in what type of plant tissue? 534

5. Contrast the structure and function of xylem and phloem. Xylem and phloem occur in what type of plant tissue? 534–35

6. Name and discuss the zones of a root tip. Trace the path of water and minerals from the root hairs to xylem. Be sure to mention the Casparian strip. 536–37

7. Describe three basic types of roots, and give examples of other root modifications. 538

8. Describe the primary and secondary growth of a stem. 540–43

9. Describe the cross section of a monocot, a herbaceous dicot, and a woody stem. 540–43

10. Discuss the adaptation of stems by giving several examples. 544

11. Describe the structure and organization of a typical dicot leaf. 546

12. Note several ways in which leaves are specialized. 547

13. Name and state the function of the main tissues within each plant organ. 548

Objective Questions

1. Which of these is an incorrect contrast between monocots and dicots?
   monocots—dicots
   a. one cotyledon—two cotyledons
   b. leaf veins parallel—net veined
   c. vascular bundles in a ring—vascular bundles scattered
   d. All of these are incorrect.

2. Which of these types of cells is most likely to divide?
   a. parenchyma
   b. meristem
   c. epidermis
   d. xylem

3. Which of these cells in a plant is apt to be nonliving?
   a. parenchyma
   b. collenchyma
   c. sclerenchyma
   d. epidermal

4. Root hairs are found in the zone of
   a. cell division.
   b. elongation.
   c. maturation.
   d. All of these are correct.

5. Cortex is found in
   a. roots, stems, and leaves.
   b. roots and stems.
   c. roots only.
   d. stems only.

6. Between the bark and the wood in a woody stem, there is a layer of meristem called
   a. cork cambium.
   b. vascular cambium.
   c. apical meristem.
   d. the zone of cell division.

7. Which part of a leaf carries on most of the photosynthesis of a plant?
   a. epidermis
   b. mesophyll
   c. epidermal layer
   d. guard cells

8. Annual rings are the number of
   a. internodes in a stem.
   b. rings of vascular bundles in a monocot stem.
   c. layers of secondary xylem in a stem.
   d. Both b and c are correct.

9. The Casparian strip is found
   a. between all epidermal cells.
   b. between xylem and phloem cells.
   c. on four sides of endodermal cells.
   d. within the secondary wall of parenchyma cells.

10. Which of these is a stem?
    a. taproot of carrots
    b. stolon of strawberry plants
    c. spine of cacti
    d. Both b and c are correct.

11. Label this root using the terms endodermis, phloem, xylem, cortex, and epidermis:

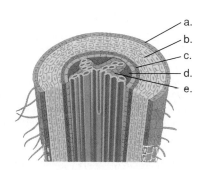

a.
b.
c.
d.
e.

12. Label this woody stem using the terms annual ring, bark, cork, phloem, pith, vascular cambium, and xylem (wood):

13. Label this leaf using the terms leaf vein, lower epidermis, palisade mesophyll, spongy mesophyll, and upper epidermis:

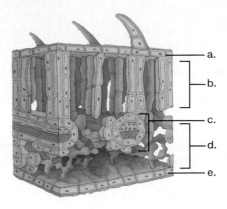

Concepts and Critical Thinking

1. *Structure suits the function.*

How does the structure of a dicot leaf suit its function of carrying on photosynthesis?

2. *Living things are organized.*

Show that a plant is organized on all levels of its structure.

3. *Organisms are adapted to the environment.*

In what ways do xylem rings (wood) help a plant live on land?

Selected Key Terms

Casparian strip (kas-PAIR-ee-un) A layer of impermeable lignin and suberin bordering four sides of root endodermal cells; prevents water and solute transport between adjacent cells. 537

cork Outer covering of bark of trees; made of dead cells that may be sloughed off. 533

cork cambium A lateral meristem that produces cork. [L. *cambi*, exchange] 543

cotyledon (kaht-ul-EED-un) Seed leaf for embryonic plant, providing nutrient molecules for the developing plant before its mature leaves begin to photosynthesize. [Gk. *cotyl*, cup-shaped cavity] 532

cuticle A waxy layer covering the epidermis of plants that protects the plant against water loss and disease-causing organisms. [L. *cut*, skin] 546

endodermis Internal plant root tissue forming a boundary between the cortex and the vascular cylinder. [Gk. *endo*, within, and *derm*, skin] 537

epidermis Covering tissue of plant roots and leaves and also stems of nonwoody organisms. [Gk. *epi*, upon, and *derm*, skin] 533

herbaceous stem A nonwoody stem. [L. *herb*, grass] 540

leaf Usually broad, flat structure of a plant shoot system, containing cells that carry out photosynthesis. 531

meristem Undifferentiated embryonic tissue in the active growth regions of plants. [Gk. *meristo*, divided] 531

mesophyll Inner, thickest layer of a leaf consisting of palisade and spongy mesophyll; the site of most of photosynthesis. [Gk. *meso*, middle, and *phyll*, leaf] 546

palisade mesophyll In a plant leaf, the layer of mesophyll containing elongated cells with many chloroplasts. 546

parenchyma (puh-REN-kuh-muh) The least specialized of all plant cell or tissue types; contains plastids and is found in all organs of a plant. [Gk. *para*, beside, and *enchyma*, infusion] 534

phloem (FLOH-um) The vascular tissue that conducts organic solutes in plants; contains sieve-tube cells and companion cells. [Gk. *phloe*, tree bark, and L. *em*, in] 534

rhizome A rootlike, underground stem. [Gk. *rhizo*, root] 534

root hair An extension of a root epidermal cell that collectively increases the surface area for the absorption of water and minerals. 533

spongy mesophyll In a plant leaf, the layer of mesophyll containing loosely packed, irregularly spaced cells that increase the amount of surface area for gas exchange. 546

stem Usually upright, vertical portion of a plant, which transports substances to and from the leaves. 530

stolon A stem that grows horizontally along the ground and establishes plantlets periodically when it contacts the soil (e.g., the runners of a strawberry plant). [L. *stolo*, shoot] 544

vascular cambium A lateral meristem that produces secondary phloem and secondary xylem. [L. *vascul*, little vessel, and *cambi*, exchange] 540

xylem (ZY-lum) A vascular tissue that transports water and mineral solutes upward through the plant body. [Gk. *xyl*, wood, and L. *em*, in] 534

32

NUTRITION AND TRANSPORT IN PLANTS

Learning Objectives

- Explain the composition of vascular tissue, and note why plants need a vascular system.   552

How Water Moves Through a Plant

- Explain the concept of water potential in relation to the development of turgor pressure within a plant cell.   553
- Trace two pathways of water from the soil to the vascular cylinder of a dicot root.   554
- Explain why root pressure cannot account for movement of water in xylem.   554
- Relate water availability to soil type, and contrast field capacity with permanent wilting point.   554
- Explain the mechanism of water transport according to the cohesion-tension model.   555
- Explain the mechanism by which stomates open and close.   556

Plants Require Inorganic Nutrients

- Distinguish between essential and beneficial inorganic nutrients needed by a plant, and describe how mineral requirements are determined.   558
- Explain how acid deposition affects availability of minerals to a plant.   559
- Describe the mechanism by which mineral ions cross plasma membranes.   560
- Describe some adaptations of roots for nutrient uptake.   560–61

How Organic Nutrients Are Transported

- Explain how phloem is suited to the transport of organic nutrients in a plant.   562
- Explain the mechanism of phloem transport according to the pressure-flow model.   562–63

The roots of a plant, *Impatiens,* absorb water and minerals that are sent to the leaves where photosynthesis takes place.

Plants are adapted to living on land. The land environment offers many advantages such as the greater availability of light for photosynthesis (water, even if clear, filters out light). In addition, carbon dioxide and oxygen are present in higher concentrations and diffuse more readily in air than in water.

Still there is a problem that is best solved by developing a transport system (fig. 32.1). Water and minerals are primarily available from the soil, and it is advantageous to lift the leaves toward the sun. Vascular plants have evolved a water and mineral transport system that allows them to reach great heights. Xylem, the vascular tissue that transports water and minerals, contains two types of conduction cells: tracheids and vessel elements. Tracheids have end walls that are pitted, but the vessel elements have no end walls at all. The vessel elements placed end to end form a completely hollow pipeline from the roots to the leaves. These strong-walled nonliving cells also give trees much-needed internal support.

Similarly, a transport system is needed for organic nutrients, which are produced primarily by leaves but are needed throughout the plant. Roots buried in the soil cannot possibly carry on photosynthesis, but they still require a source of energy in order to carry on cellular metabolism. Vascular plants are able to transport the products of photosynthesis to regions that require them and/or where they will be stored for future use. The conducting cells in phloem are sieve-tube cells, each of which typically has a companion cell. Companion cells can provide energy to sieve-tube cells, which contain cytoplasm but have no nucleus. Their end walls are called sieve plates because they contain numerous pores. The sieve-tube cells are aligned end to end, and strands of cytoplasm called plasmodesmata extend from one cell to the other through the sieve plates. Therefore, there is a continuous pathway for organic nutrient transport throughout the plant.

> **Vascular plants have transport tissues; xylem transports water and minerals from the roots to the leaves, and phloem transports organic nutrients to various parts, particularly from the leaves to the roots.**

Knowing that vascular plants are structured in a way that allows materials to move from one part to another part does not tell us the mechanisms involved. Plant physiologists have performed numerous experiments to determine how water and minerals rise to the top of very tall trees in xylem and how organic nutrients move in the opposite direction in phloem.

We would expect these mechanisms to be mechanical in nature and based on the properties of water because water is a large part of both xylem sap and phloem sap. Keep in mind, therefore, that

Figure 32.1 🎞

Plant transport system. Vascular tissue in plants includes xylem, which transports water and minerals from the roots to the leaves, and phloem, which transports organic nutrients particularly in the opposite direction. Notice that the xylem and the pholem are in the roots, the stem, and the leaves, which are the vegetative organs of a plant.

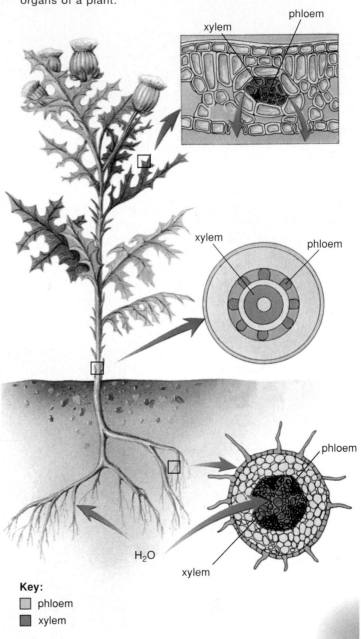

Key:
☐ phloem
■ xylem

water molecules diffuse freely across plasma membranes, and that because water molecules are polar, hydrogen bonding occurs between water molecules themselves and between water molecules and other molecules.

Figure 32.2 ▭

Water potential and turgor pressure. **a.** The cells of a wilted plant have a lower water potential due to a lower osmotic potential. When available, water therefore enters the cells. **b.** Equilibrium is achieved when the pressure potential rises in the cells. Cells are now turgid, and the plant is no longer wilted.

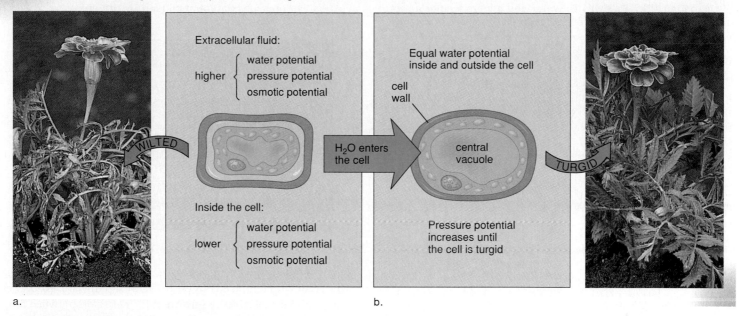

a.   b.

HOW WATER MOVES THROUGH A PLANT

In order for water to move from the roots to the leaves, it must cross plasma membranes. Let's now examine a conceptual model of this movement, developed by plant physiologists.

Water Potential Is Critical

As you may know, potential energy is stored energy due to the position of an object. A boulder placed at the top of a hill has potential energy. When pushed, the boulder moves down the hill as potential energy is converted into kinetic (motion) energy. The boulder at the bottom of the hill has lost much of its potential energy.

Let us define **water potential** as the potential energy of water. Just like the boulder, water at the top of a waterfall has a higher water potential than water at the bottom of the waterfall. As illustrated by this example, water moves from a region of higher water potential to a region of lower water potential.

In terms of cells, two factors usually determine water potential, which in turn determines the direction in which water will move across a plasma membrane (fig. 32.2). These factors concern differences in:

1. water pressure across a membrane
2. solute concentration across a membrane

In regard to pressure, it is obvious to us that water will move across a membrane from the area of greater pressure potential to the area of lower pressure potential. We also know that water will move across a membrane from the area of lesser solute concen-

tration to the area of greater solute concentration. The area of greater solute concentration, therefore, has the lower osmotic potential![1] Water moves from the area of greater osmotic potential to the area of lesser osmotic potential.

Let us consider a common situation in regard to plant cells. Water will flow by osmosis into a plant cell that has a greater solute concentration than the surrounding solution. As water enters the cell, water pressure will increase inside the cell; a plant cell has a strong cell wall that allows water pressure to build up. When will water stop entering the cell? When the pressure potential inside the cell increases and balances the osmotic potential outside the cell. In this way pressure potential and osmotic potential both help determine water potential and the movement of water between plant cells.

Pressure potential that increases due to the process of osmosis is often called *turgor pressure*. Turgor pressure is critical, since plants depend on it to maintain the turgidity of their bodies (fig. 32.2). The cells of a wilted plant have lost water due to a reversal in the usual pressure potential difference across plasma membranes.

> **Water moves across plasma membranes from the area of higher water potential to the area of lower water potential.**

---

1 Osmotic potential is not the same as osmotic pressure. Osmotic pressure is defined as the buildup of pressure due to water coming into a cell.

Figure 32.3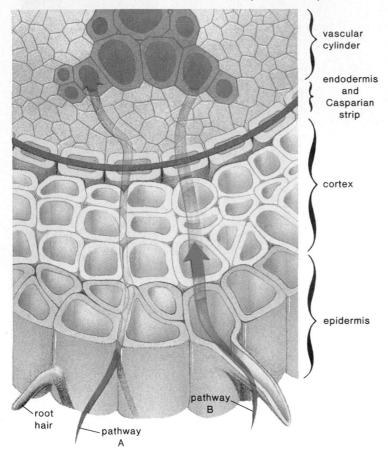

Pathways across the cortex to the xylem of the vascular cylinder. Pathway A: water and minerals travel via porous cell walls and then enter endodermal cells because of the Casparian strip. Pathway B: water and minerals enter a root hair cell and move from cell to cell to finally enter the xylem.

vascular cylinder

endodermis and Casparian strip

cortex

epidermis

pathway B

root hair

pathway A

Xylem Transports Water

The movement of water and minerals in a plant involves passage through a root, then in the xylem (particularly the vessels), and finally through the leaves. Special problems dealing with mineral transport are discussed in the next section.

From the Roots

In order for water to reach the xylem, it must pass through the root. As figure 32.3 shows, water can enter the root of a flowering plant from the soil simply by diffusing *between* the cells. Eventually, however, the *Casparian strip,* a band of suberin and lignin bordering four sides of root endodermal cells, forces water to enter endodermal cells. Alternatively, water can enter root hair cells and then progress from cell to cell across the cortex and endodermis. Regardless of the pathway, water enters root cells when they have a lower osmotic potential, and therefore lower water potential, than does soil solution. Water entering root cells creates a positive pres-

Figure 32.4

Guttation. Drops of guttation water on the edges of a strawberry leaf. Guttation, which occurs at night, is thought to be due to root pressure. Root pressure is a positive pressure potential caused by the entrance of water into root cells.

sure potential called **root pressure.** Root pressure, which primarily occurs at night, tends to push xylem sap upward. Root pressure is also responsible for **guttation** [L. *gutt,* a drop], when drops of water are forced out of vein endings along the edges of leaves (fig. 32.4). Although root pressure may contribute to the upward movement of water in some instances, it is not believed to be the mechanism by which water can rise to the tops of very tall trees.

When Is Water Available?

After a rain or irrigation, gravity causes water in the soil to drain away. The speed with which this happens can be correlated with the permeability of the soil. Sandy soil, which is very permeable, drains rapidly while clay soil, which is much less permeable, drains slowly. The water remaining in the soil after drainage is referred to as its *field capacity.*

Just because water is in the soil does not mean it is available to the plant. The point at which water is no longer available to the roots is called the *permanent wilting point* of the soil. At this point, the soil, especially clay soil, still contains water, but it is held tightly on tiny particles. The soil and root water potentials have become the same or have reversed, and the roots can no longer remove water from the soil.

The ideal soil holds water, has air spaces (roots need oxygen for cellular respiration), and is easily penetrated by roots. The best agricultural soils turn out to be loams that are 10–25% clay, with the rest being equal parts of sand and silt.

> Water and minerals must enter root cells before they reach the xylem. Water enters root cells because the water potential within root cells is less than that of the soil solution.

To the Leaves

Once water enters xylem it must be transported upward the entire height of a tree. This can be a daunting task, given that redwood trees can exceed 110 meters in height.

The **cohesion-tension model** of xylem transport outlined in figure 32.5 suggests a mechanism for xylem transport. The term *cohesion* refers to the tendency of water molecules to cling together. Because of hydrogen bonding, water molecules interact with one another, and there is a continuous water column in xylem from the leaves to the roots that is not easily broken. Adhesion is a property of water that gives the water column extra strength and prevents its from slipping back. *Adhesion* refers to the ability of water, a polar molecule, to interact with the molecules making up the walls of the vessels in xylem.

Why does the continuous water column move upward? It does so because it is under *tension*—it is pulled up by a *negative pressure potential*. Consider the structure of a leaf. When the sun rises, it is appropriate for the stomates (stomata) to open to allow carbon dioxide to enter. Within the leaf the mesophyll cells—particularly the spongy layer—are exposed to the air, which can be quite dry. Water now evaporates from mesophyll cells. Evaporation of water from leaf cells is called **transpiration.** At least 90% of the water taken up by the roots is eventually lost by transpiration. This means that the total amount of water lost by a plant over a long period of time is surprisingly large. A single *Zea mays* (corn) plant loses somewhere between 135 and 200 liters of water through transpiration during a growing season.

As transpiration occurs, the water column is pulled upward—first within the leaf, then from the stem, and finally from the roots. During the day, root cells have a more negative water potential than that of the soil due to transpiration at the leaves! For the negative water potential to reach from the leaves to the root, the water column must be continuous.

What happens if the water column within xylem is broken, as by cutting a stem? The water column "snaps back" down the xylem vessel away from the site of breakage, making it more difficult for conduction to occur. This is why it is best to maximize water conduction by cutting flower stems under water. This effect has also allowed investigators to measure the tension in stems. A device called the pressure bomb measures how much pressure it takes to push the xylem sap back to the cut surface of the stem.

> The driving force for the ascent of water in xylem is a negative pressure potential brought about by transpiration at the leaves.

There is an important consequence to the way water is transported in plants; when a plant is under water stress, the stomates close. Now the plant loses little water because the leaves are protected against water loss by the waxy cuticle of the upper and lower

Figure 32.5

Cohesion-tension model of xylem transport. A negative pressure potential created by evaporation (transpiration) at the leaves pulls water along the length of the plant—even down to the root hairs.

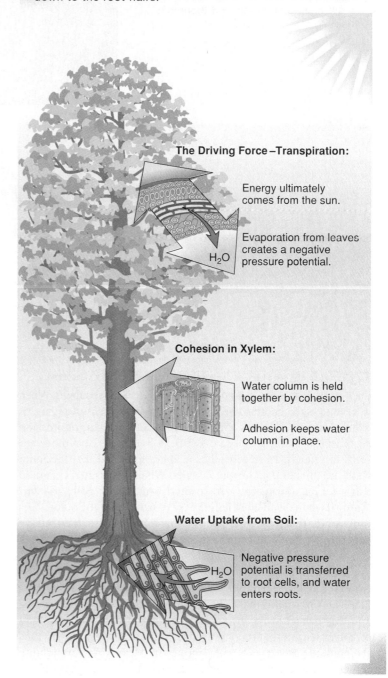

The Driving Force –Transpiration:

Energy ultimately comes from the sun.

Evaporation from leaves creates a negative pressure potential.

H_2O

Cohesion in Xylem:

Water column is held together by cohesion.

Adhesion keeps water column in place.

Water Uptake from Soil:

Negative pressure potential is transferred to root cells, and water enters roots.

H_2O

epidermis. When the stomates are closed, however, carbon dioxide cannot enter the leaves and plants are unable to photosynthesize. Photosynthesis, therefore, requires an abundant supply of water so that the stomates can remain open and allow carbon dioxide to enter.

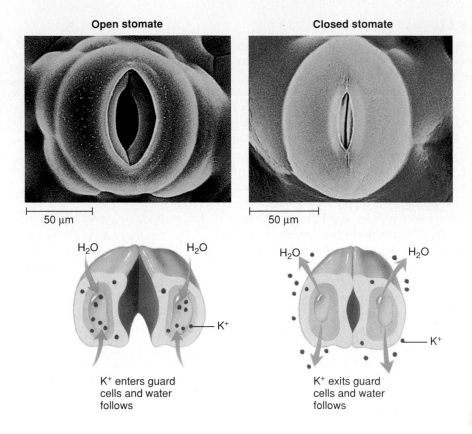

Figure 32.6

Opening and closing of stomates. Stomates open when water enters guard cells and turgor pressure increases. Stomates close when water exits guard cells and there is a loss of turgor pressure.

Open stomate

Closed stomate

50 μm

50 μm

H_2O H_2O

H_2O H_2O

K^+

K^+

K^+ enters guard cells and water follows

K^+ exits guard cells and water follows

Opening and Closing of Stomates

Each stomate has two **guard cells** with a pore between them. When water enters the guard cells and *turgor pressure increases,* the stomate opens; when water exits the guard cells and turgor pressure decreases, the stomate closes. Notice in figure 32.6 that the guard cells are attached to each other at their ends and that the inner walls are thicker than the outer walls. When water enters, a guard cell's radial expansion is restricted because of cellulose microfibrils in the walls, but lengthwise expansion of the outer walls is possible. When the guard cells expand lengthwise, they buckle out from the region of their attachment and the stomate opens.

Since about 1968 it has been clear that there is an accumulation of potassium ions (K^+) within guard cells when stomates open. In other words, active transport of K^+ results in a water potential that is lower than that of surrounding cells, and this causes water to enter guard cells. Also interesting is the observation that there is an accumulation of hydrogen ions (H^+) outside guard cells as K^+ moves into them. A proton pump run by the breakdown of ATP to ADP + ⓟ transports H^+ to the outside of the cell. This establishes an electrochemical gradient that allows K^+ to enter by way of a channel protein (see fig. 32.8).

What regulates the opening and closing of stomates? It appears that the blue-light component of sunlight is a signal that can cause stomates to open. There is evidence to suggest that a flavin pigment absorbs blue light, and then this pigment sets in motion the cytoplasmic response that leads to activation of the proton pump. Similarly, there could be a receptor in the plasma membrane of guard cells that brings about inactivation of the pump when carbon dioxide (CO_2) concentration rises, as might happen when photosynthesis ceases. Abscisic acid (ABA), which is produced by cells in wilting leaves, can also cause stomates to close. Although photosynthesis cannot occur, water is conserved.

If plants are kept in the dark, the stomates open and close on a twenty-four-hour basis just as if they were responding to the presence of sunlight in the daytime and the absence of sunlight at night. This means that there must be some sort of internal *biological clock* that is keeping time. Circadian rhythms (a behavior that occurs every twenty-four hours) and biological clocks are areas of intense investigation at this time.

When stomates open, first K^+ and then water enters guard cells. Stomates open and close in response to environmental signals, and the exact mechanism is being investigated.

Competition for Resources and Biodiversity

From my earliest years in school, I have loved both mathematics and biology. In college, the biological issues that intrigued me most were those concerned with the relationship of species to their environment, including the effects of interactions such as competition or predation. It seemed to me that biodiversity might relate to these interactions and, if so, it might be possible to develop a theory, expressed mathematically, to explain biodiversity. The first step toward this goal is to establish that competition and/or predation do relate to biodiversity.

The Minnesota grasslands in which I work often have more than 100 plant species coexisting in an area the size of a few hectares. Long-term experiments have shown that all these plant species are held in check by (limited by) competition for the same resource, namely soil nitrogen. Mathematical models predict that the number of coexisting species can never be more than the number of resources that limit them. Is there an answer to this seeming paradox? There is if these species are competing with one another on some other basis besides soil nitrogen.

To find out what this basis might be, we did a series of experiments. We found that the factor limiting these species was not insect or mammalian herbivores, light availability, or fire. However, the plant species did differ in their

G. David Tilman
University of Minnesota

ability to disperse to new sites. We discovered this by planting over fifty different plant species in several plots and finding how well they could germinate, grow, and reproduce there. The best competitors for nitrogen were native bunchgrasses that allocated 85% of their biomass to root but only 0.5% of their biomass to seed. Little bluestem (*Schizachyrium scoparium*) is an example of a bunchgrass (fig. 32A). The best dispersers allocated 30% of their biomass to seed, but only 40% of their biomass to root. Bent grass (*Agrostis scabra*) is an example of a poor competitor for soil nitrogen but a good disperser (fig. 32B).

A mathematical model showed that such allocation-based tradeoffs could explain the stable coexistence of a whole range of plant species that differ according to their ability to compete for nitrogen and to disperse to new areas. Coexistence occurs because better competitors for soil nitrogen are poorer dispersers, and therefore they do not occupy all sites. Better dispersers are also better at finding and occupying all sites. Because their ability to compete and disperse vary, a number of species can coexist.

Figure 32C

During drought, plots with higher plant species richness attained plant biomasses that were a larger proportion of their predrought plant biomass. This graph compares biomass in 1988, a drought year, with that in 1986, a year before the drought. The numbers placed at the means indicate the number of plots used to calculate that mean. The high and low values for each biomass ratio are also indicated.

Another issue of interest to me is the relationship between biodiversity and the stability of an ecosystem. My colleagues and I were annually sampling 207 permanent plots when there was a drought in 1987–88. The 1988 drought was the third worst in the past 150 years. We found that plots that contained only one to four species had their productivity (total mass of living plants) fall to between $1/8$ and $1/16$ of the predrought level. But plots that contained sixteen to twenty-six species were able to maintain their productivity at about $1/2$ the predrought level (fig. 32C). This suggests that high biodiversity does buffer ecosystems against a disturbance and that it is wise to conserve the biodiversity of ecosystems in all areas—whether in Minnesota, New Jersey, Oregon, or the tropics.

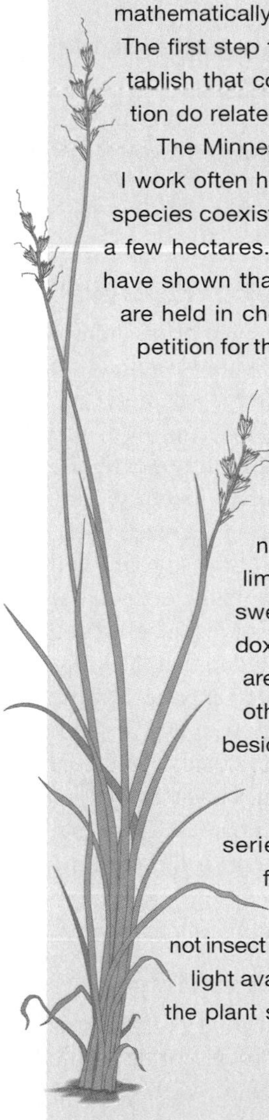

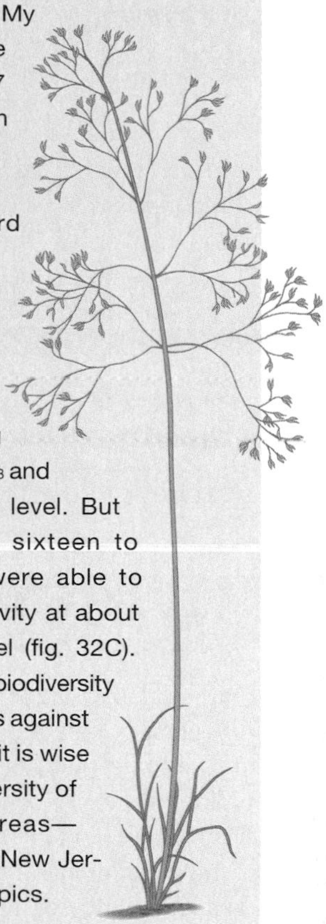

Figure 32B

Bent grass (*Agrostis scabra*) is a native North American prairie grass that is a poor competitor for soil nitrogen. It disperses rapidly into disturbed areas because of its high allocation of seed.

Figure 32A

Little bluestem (*Schizachyrium scoparium*) is a North American bunchgrass that prefers sandy or rocky habitats. It is an excellent competitor for soil nitrogen because of its high allocation of roots.

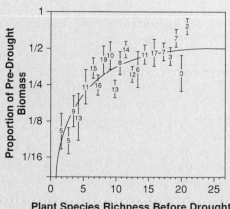

Plant Species Richness Before Drought

Table 32.1

Some Essential Nutrients in Plants

Elements	Chemical Symbol	Form Available to Plant	Major Functions
Macronutrients			
Nitrogen	N	NO_3^-, NH_4^+	Part of nucleic acids, proteins, chlorophyll, and coenzymes
Potassium	K	K^+	Cofactor for enzymes; involved in water balance and movement of stomates
Calcium	Ca	Ca^{++}	Regulates responses to stimuli and movement of substances through plasma membrane; involved in formation and stability of cell walls
Phosphorus	P	$H_2PO_4^-$, $HPO_4^=$	Part of nucleic acids, ATP, and phospholipids
Magnesium	Mg	Mg^{++}	Part of chlorophyll; activates a number of enzymes
Sulphur	S	$SO_4^=$	Part of amino acids, some coenzymes
Micronutrients			
Iron	Fe	Fe^{++}, Fe^{+++}	Part of cytochrome needed for cellular respiration
Manganese	Mn	Mn^{++}	Activates some enzymes such as those of the Krebs cycle
Boron	B	$BO_3^=$, $B_4O_7^=$	Participates in nucleic acid synthesis, hormone responses, and membrane function

PLANTS REQUIRE INORGANIC NUTRIENTS

Table 32.1 lists the mineral nutrients that are considered *essential nutrients* for plants. These elements are divided into macronutrients and micronutrients according to their relative concentration in plant tissue. To be considered essential, an element must fulfill these criteria: (1) it must have an identifiable nutritional role, (2) no other element can substitute and fulfill the same role, and (3) a deficiency of the element causes the plant to die without completing its life cycle.

Carbon, hydrogen, and oxygen make up 96% of a plant's dry weight and are essential inorganic nutrients. Carbon dioxide (CO_2) is the source of carbon for a plant, and water is the source of hydrogen. Oxygen can come from atmospheric oxygen, carbon dioxide, or water. The essential inorganic nutrients listed in table 32.1 are minerals that come from the soil. Nitrogen (N) is a common atmospheric gas, but plants are unable to make use of it. Instead, plants take up either ammonium (NH_4^+) or nitrate (NO_3^-) from the soil. Usually, soil bacteria have converted ammonium to nitrate, and therefore plants take up nitrate. As discussed on pages 560-61, some plants have root nodules containing mutualistic bacteria that fix atmospheric nitrogen and make nitrogen compounds available to their host.

Beneficial nutrients are another category of elements taken up by plants. Beneficial nutrients either are required or enhance the growth of a particular plant. Plants such as *Equisetum* (horsetails) require silicon as a mineral nutrient, and halophytes such as sugar beets show enhanced growth in the presence of sodium. Nickel is a beneficial mineral nutrient in soybeans when root nodules are present.

How Are Requirements Determined?

If you burn a plant, its nitrogen component is given off as ammonia and other gases, but most other mineral elements remain in the ash. The presence of a particular element in the ash, however, does not necessarily mean that the plant normally requires it. The preferred method for determining the mineral requirements of a plant was developed at the end of the nineteenth century. This method is called water culture, or **hydroponics** [Gk. *hydr,* water, and *pono,* toil] (fig. 32.7). Hydroponics allows plants to grow well if they are supplied with all the mineral nutrients they need. The investigator omits a particular mineral and observes the effect on plant growth. If growth suffers, it can be concluded that the omitted mineral is a required nutrient. This method has been more successful for macronutrients than for micronutrients. For studies involving the latter, the water and the mineral salts used must be absolutely pure; purity is difficult to attain, because even instruments and glassware can introduce micronutrients. Then, too, the element in question may already be present in the seedling used in the experiment. These factors complicate the determination of essential plant micronutrients by means of hydroponics.

What Affects Mineral Availability?

As mentioned previously, the essential minerals that a plant needs are normally taken from the soil. Location of minerals in the soil is critical, because if a root does not come within a few millimeters of an ion, no uptake occurs. The downward movement of minerals through soil is influenced by the quantity and the pH of water. Sometimes water makes mineral ions available to roots, but often it leaches, or removes, mineral ions from the soil zone in which roots grow. The lower the pH, the greater the leaching power of water.

Figure 32.7

Plant nutrition. The cause of plant nutrient deficiencies is easily diagnosed when plants are grown in a series of complete nutrient solutions except for the elimination of just one nutrient at a time. Sunflower plants respond rapidly to a deficiency of the following: **a.** Nitrogen. **b.** Phosphorus. **c.** Calcium. Nutrient-deficient plants are shown on the left in each photograph; healthy plants with a complete nutrient solution are shown on the right.

b.

a.

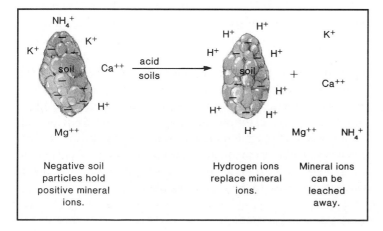

c.

Soil particles, particularly clay and any organic matter in soil, contain negative charges that attract positively charged ions, such as calcium (Ca^{++}), potassium (K^+), and magnesium (Mg^{++}). This attraction keeps these ions at a soil level where they are available to plants. In acidic soils, however, hydrogen ions (H^+) replace these other positive ions so that the useful ions float free and are easily leached by water:

| Negative soil particles hold positive mineral ions. | Hydrogen ions replace mineral ions. | Mineral ions can be leached away. |

On the other hand, in very acidic soils, aluminum (Al^{+++}) and iron (Fe^{+++}) ions become available to plants. These mineral ions are insoluble above a pH of 4, but they become soluble at a more acidic pH. They displace calcium, potassium, and magnesium on soil particles in the same way as hydrogen does. High levels of aluminum and iron in soils are toxic to plants.

It is clear, then, that acid deposition has two effects that are deleterious to plants: it causes the removal of the mineral ions that plants need for proper nutrition, and it makes available other mineral ions that are toxic at high levels. The death of trees in certain portions of the United States is, in part, the result of acid deposition (from acid rain/snow).

> Certain elements are required by plants for good nutrition. Lack of an essential nutrient causes plants to die. Beneficial nutrients serve particular purposes in certain plants.

How Minerals Are Taken in and Distributed

The pathway for mineral transport in a plant is the same as that for water. Like water, minerals can move past the epidermis and through the cortex by way of porous cell walls (see fig. 32.3). Eventually, however, because of the Casparian strip, minerals must enter the cytoplasm of endodermal cells if they are to proceed any farther. In addition, minerals often move directly into the cytoplasm of epidermal cells at the root hair region. Plants possess an astonishing ability to concentrate minerals—that is, to take up minerals until they are many times more concentrated in the plant than in the surrounding medium. The concentration of certain minerals in roots is as much as 10,000 times greater than in the surrounding soil.

Following their uptake by root cells, minerals are secreted into xylem and are transported toward the leaves by the upward movement of water. Along the way, minerals can exit xylem and enter those cells that require them. Some eventually reach leaf cells. In any case, minerals must again cross a selectively permeable plasma membrane when they exit xylem and enter living cells. By what mechanism do minerals cross plasma membranes?

Table 32.1 shows that plant cells absorb minerals in the ionic form: nitrogen is absorbed as nitrate (NO_3^-) or ammonium (NH_4^+) ions, phosphorus as phosphate ($HPO_4^=$), potassium as potassium ions (K^+), and so forth. Since the plasma membrane is charged, ions are likely to have difficulty crossing it. It has long been known that plant cells expend energy to actively take up and concentrate mineral ions. If roots are deprived of oxygen or are poisoned so that cellular respiration cannot occur, mineral ion uptake is diminished. The energy of ATP is required for mineral ion transport, but not directly (fig. 32.8). A plasma membrane pump, called a proton pump, hydrolyzes ATP and uses the energy released to transport hydrogen ions (H^+) out of the cell. This sets up an electrochemical gradient that drives positively charged ions like K^+ through a channel protein into the cell. Negatively charged mineral ions are transported, along with H^+, by carrier proteins. Since H^+ is moving down its concentration gradient, no energy is required. Notice that this model of mineral ion transport in plant cells is based on chemiosmosis, the establishment of an electrochemical gradient to perform work.

> Minerals follow the same path as water. When minerals cross plasma membranes, energy is expended to establish an electrochemical gradient that promotes mineral uptake.

How Roots Are Adapted for Uptake

Two symbiotic relationships are known to assist roots in supplying mineral nutrients to a plant. In the first type, plants are unable to make use of atmospheric nitrogen (N_2) because they do not

Figure 32.8

Transport of minerals across the plasma membrane. First, an ATP-driven pump removes hydrogen ions from the cell. This establishes an electrochemical gradient that allows potassium (K^+) and other positively charged ions to cross the membrane via a channel protein. Negatively charged mineral ions (I^-) can cross the membrane by way of a carrier when they hitch a ride with hydrogen ions (H^+), which are diffusing down their concentration gradient.

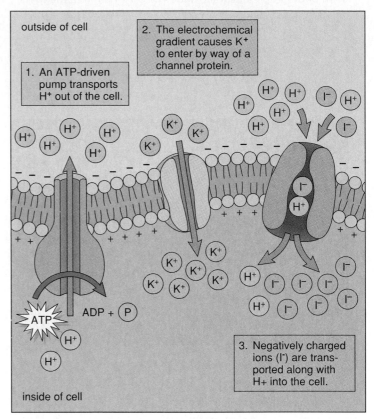

outside of cell

1. An ATP-driven pump transports H^+ out of the cell.

2. The electrochemical gradient causes K^+ to enter by way of a channel protein.

ATP   ADP + P

3. Negatively charged ions (I^-) are transported along with $H+$ into the cell.

inside of cell

have the cellular enzymes to break the $N \equiv N$ bond. Some plants remove nitrate (NO_3^-) or ammonium (NH_4^+) from the soil. But others—such as legumes, soybeans, and alfalfa—have roots infected by *Rhizobium* bacteria, which can break the $N \equiv N$ bond and reduce nitrogen to NH_4^+ for incorporation into organic compounds. (The reduction of N_2 to NH_4^+ is called nitrogen fixation.) The bacteria live in root **nodules** [L. *nodul*, little knot] and are supplied with carbohydrates by the host plant (fig. 32.9). The bacteria, in turn, furnish their host with nitrogen compounds. Many other plants are now known to have a semi-symbiotic relationship with free-living, nitrogen-fixing microorganisms in the soil. In some grasses these microorganisms live on the surface of roots and receive carbon compounds exuded by the roots. They use the energy derived from these compounds to fix nitrogen, some of which they release to the root of the plant.

Figure 32.9

Root nodules. Nitrogen-fixing bacteria infect and live in nodules on the roots of plants, particularly legumes. They make reduced nitrogen available to a plant and the plant passes carbohydrates to the bacteria. The insert shows the inner composition of a nodule.

nodule
vascular
tissue

infected
zone

Figure 32.10

Mycorrhizae. Fungal hyphae form an association with many plant roots, including trees. The fungus passes minerals to the plant and the plant provides the fungus with carbohydrates. Plants that don't have mycorrhizae are quite restricted in terms of their habitat.

The second type of symbiotic relationship, called a mycorrhizal association, involves fungi and almost all plant roots (fig. 32.10). Only a small minority of plants do not have **mycorrhizae** [Gk. *myc,* fungus, and *rhiz,* root], and these plants are most often limited as to the environment in which they can grow. The fungal hyphae may enter the cortex of roots but do not enter plant cells. Ectomycorrhizae form a mantle that is exterior to the root, and they grow between cell walls. Ectomycorrhizae can penetrate cell walls. In any case, the fungus increases the surface area available for mineral and water uptake and breaks down organic matter, releasing nutrients that the plant can use. In return, the root furnishes the fungus with sugars and amino acids. Plants are extremely dependent on mycorrhizae. Orchid seeds, which are quite small and contain limited nutrients, do not germinate until a my-

corrhizal fungus has invaded their cells. Nonphotosynthetic plants, such as Indian pipe, use their mycorrhizae to extract nutrients from nearby trees.

As a special adaptation, some plants have poorly developed roots or no roots at all because minerals and water are supplied by other mechanisms. Carnivorous plants such as the Venus's-flytrap and sundews obtain some nitrogen and minerals when their leaves capture and digest insects. **Epiphytes** [Gk. *epi,* upon, and *phyt,* plant] are "air plants"; they do not grow in soil but on larger plants, which give them support. They do not receive nutrients from their host, however. Some epiphytes have roots that absorb moisture from the atmosphere, and many catch rain and minerals in special pockets at the base of their leaves. Parasitic plants such as dodders, broomrapes, and pinedrops send out rootlike projections called haustoria that grow into the host stem and tap into the xylem and phloem of the host.

Most plants are assisted in acquiring minerals by a symbiotic relationship with microorganisms and/or fungi. Some, such as predaceous or parasitic plants, have special adaptations for mineral acquisition.

HOW ORGANIC NUTRIENTS ARE TRANSPORTED

Not only must plants transport water and minerals from the roots to the leaves, they must also transport organic nutrients to the parts of plants that have need of them. This includes young leaves that have not yet reached their full photosynthetic potential, flowers that are in the process of making seeds and fruits, and the roots whose location in the soil prohibits them from carrying on photosynthesis.

Phloem Transports Organic Nutrients

As long ago as 1679, Marcello Malpighi suggested that bark is involved in translocating sugars from leaves to roots. He observed the results of removing a strip of bark from around a tree, a procedure called **girdling.** If a tree is girdled below the level of the majority of leaves, the bark swells just above the cut and sugar accumulates in the swollen tissue. We know today that when a tree is girdled, the phloem is removed but the xylem is left intact. Therefore, the results of girdling suggest that phloem is the tissue that transports sugars.

Radioactive tracer studies with ^{14}C have confirmed that phloem transports organic nutrients. When ^{14}C-labeled carbon dioxide (CO_2) is supplied to mature leaves, radioactively labeled sugar is soon found moving down the stem into the roots. This labeled sugar is found mainly in the phloem, not in the xylem. Radioactive tracer studies have also confirmed the role of phloem in transporting other substances, such as amino acids, hormones, and even mineral ions. Hormones are transported from their production sites to target areas, where they exert their regulatory influences. In the autumn, before leaves fall, mineral ions are removed from the leaves and are taken to other locations in the plant.

Chemical analysis of phloem sap has shown that its main component is sucrose, and the concentration of nutrients is usually 10–13% by volume. It is difficult to take samples of sap from the phloem without injuring the phloem, but this problem is solved by using aphids (fig. 32.11), small insects that are phloem feeders. The aphid drives its stylet, which is a sharp mouthpart that functions like a hypodermic needle, between the epidermal cells and withdraws sap from a sieve-tube cell. If the aphid is anesthetized using ether, its body can be carefully cut away, leaving the stylet. Phloem can then be collected and analyzed by the researcher.

Phloem Transport Uses Positive Pressure

As mentioned, the conducting cells of phloem are sieve-tube cells lined up end to end with their sieve plates abutting. Cytoplasm extends through the sieve plates of adjoining cells to form a continuous sieve-tube system that extends from the roots to the leaves and vice versa. An explanation of phloem transport must account for the movement of fairly large amounts of organic material for long distances in a relatively short period of time. The movement rate of radioactively labeled ^{14}C sugar has been determined by analysis of sap withdrawn from two areas of the stem. Materials appear to move through the phloem at a rate of 60–100 cm per hour and possibly up to 300 cm per hour.

The **pressure-flow model** is a current explanation for the movement of organic materials in phloem (fig. 32.12). During the growing season, the leaves are photosynthesizing and producing sugar. Sucrose is actively transported into phloem. Again, this is dependent upon an electrochemical gradient established by a proton pump. Sucrose is carried across the membrane in conjunction with hydrogen ions (H^+), which are moving down

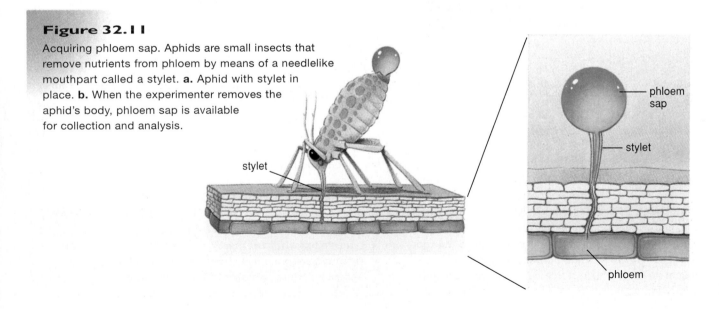

Figure 32.11

Acquiring phloem sap. Aphids are small insects that remove nutrients from phloem by means of a needlelike mouthpart called a stylet. **a.** Aphid with stylet in place. **b.** When the experimenter removes the aphid's body, phloem sap is available for collection and analysis.

stylet

phloem sap

stylet

phloem

their concentration gradient (see fig. 32.8). Water now flows into sieve tubes because of their lower osmotic potential. Transport across sieve-tube membranes is possible because sieve-tube cells have a living plasma membrane. Also, the energy needed for sucrose transport is provided by the companion cells. The buildup of water creates a *positive pressure potential* within the sieve tubes of the leaves compared to the roots.

A positive pressure potential gradient exists from the leaves to the roots because at the roots sucrose is transported out of phloem and water follows. This being the case, the positive pressure potential gradient causes a *flow* of water from the leaves to the roots. As water flows within phloem, it brings sucrose with it.

The pressure-flow model is supported by the following experiment: two bulbs are connected by a glass tube. The first bulb contains solute at a higher concentration than the second bulb. Each bulb is bounded by a differentially permeable membrane, and the entire apparatus is submerged in distilled water:

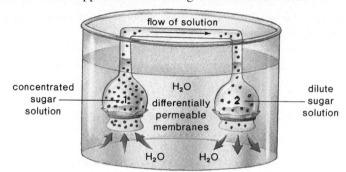

Distilled water flows into the first bulb because it has the lower water potential due to a higher concentration of solute. The entrance of water raises the water potential due to an increase in *pressure potential,* and water *flows* toward the second bulb. This flow not only drives water toward the second bulb, it also provides enough drive to force water out through the membrane of the second bulb—even though the second bulb contains a higher concentration of solute than the distilled water.

The pressure-flow model of phloem transport can account for any direction of flow in sieve tubes if we consider that the direction of flow is always from *source to sink*. In young seedlings, the cotyledons, containing reserve food, are a major source of sucrose and roots are a sink. Therefore, the flow is from the cotyledons to the roots. In older plants, the most recently formed leaves can be a sink and they will receive sucrose from other leaves until they begin to maximally photosynthesize. When a plant is in fruit, phloem flow is monopolized by the fruits, little goes to the rest of the plant, and vegetative growth is slow.

Because phloem sap flows from a source to a sink, situations arise in which there is a bidirectional flow within phloem—not just at different times in the life cycle but even at the same time! It is not known at this time if bidirectional flow is occurring within a single sieve tube or if different sieve tubes are conducting phloem sap in opposite directions.

Figure 32.12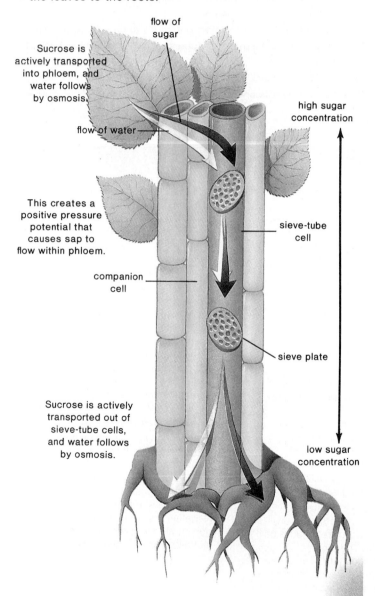

Pressure-flow model of phloem transport. Phloem sap flows from a source (often leaves) to a sink (often roots) because of a positive pressure potential gradient from the leaves to the roots.

> The pressure-flow model of phloem transport suggests that phloem sap can move either up or down as appropriate for the plant at a particular time in its life cycle.

Biological Relationships

Biologists seek to discover the chemical and physical basis of life. They have found that vascular transport is always dependent on physical forces. In the human body, the heart pumps the blood and creates blood pressure, just as a mechanical pump brings water under pressure from the ground. In plants, the evaporation of water at the leaves (transpiration) creates a negative pressure potential that pulls water from the roots to the leaves in xylem because of the cohesive and adhesive properties of water. Active transport of sugar into phloem causes water to enter sieve tubes by osmosis so that a positive pressure potential pushes phloem sap to the roots.

Vascular transport requires energy. In the human body, muscular contraction fueled by the breakdown of ATP supplies the energy for arterial transport. In plants, the sun supplies the energy for transpiration and xylem transport. And active transport, dependent upon ATP, is required for phloem transport. A new discovery is that chemiosmosis is involved in the transport of minerals across the plasma membrane of plant cells. Although we sometimes prefer to think in terms of the organism or whole organ, we are reminded once again that life first and foremost has a cellular basis.

An internal clock called a biological clock sometimes controls the behavior of organisms. Human beings living inside an enclosed chamber with no outside contact still tend to have daily waking and sleeping periods. The clock, however, gets out of sync and is normally reset by environmental stimuli. In a similar manner, guard cells within the epidermis of plants tend to open and close regularly but usually respond to the presence or absence of sunlight. How plants, which lack a nervous system, respond to environmental stimuli is currently an active field of research. It requires that a signal (1) be received, (2) be transduced, or changed into a form that affects metabolism, so that (3) a response will occur. In the same way, the retina of our eyes changes light signals into nerve impulses for interpretation by the brain so that we might respond appropriately.

Although plants and animals outwardly appear to be entirely different types of organisms, it is apparent that on a cellular basis, the same types of mechanisms are at work. The unity of life is, of course, explained by descent from a common ancestor. Sometime during the Paleozoic era, plants and animals shared a common ancestor.

Summary

1. Life on land requires a vascular system because plants must transport water and minerals from the roots to the leaves and must also transport the products of photosynthesis in the opposite direction. Vascular tissue includes xylem and phloem.

2. Water flows from a region of higher water potential to a region of lower water potential. In regard to cells, water potential includes pressure potential and osmotic potential.

3. Water can enter the root by moving between the cells until it reaches the Casparian strip, after which it passes through an endodermal cell before entering xylem. Water can also enter root hairs, then pass through the cells of the cortex and endodermis to reach xylem.

4. Water is drawn into root cells because they have the lower water potential. Particularly at night, a pressure potential called root pressure can build in the root. However, this does not contribute significantly to xylem transport.

5. Much of the water in soil is not available to plants. In sandy soils, it drains quickly, and in clay, it adheres to the tiny particles. Field capacity is the amount of water in a soil after drainage. At the permanent wilting point, no more water is available to the plant.

6. The cohesion-tension model of xylem transport states that transpiration creates a tension—a negative pressure potential—that pulls water upward in xylem. This means of transport works only because water molecules are cohesive with one another and adhesive with xylem walls.

7. Most of the water taken in by a plant is lost through stomates by transpiration. Only when there is plenty of water do stomates remain open, allowing carbon dioxide to enter the leaf and photosynthesis to occur.

8. Stomates open when guard cells take up water. They stretch lengthwise, and this causes them to buckle out. Water enters the guard cells after potassium ions (K^+) have entered. Light signals stomates to open, and high carbon dioxide (CO_2) signals stomates to close. Abscisic acid produced by wilting leaves also signals for closure.

9. Plants need both essential and beneficial inorganic nutrients. Carbon, hydrogen, and oxygen make up 96% of a plant's dry weight. The other necessary elements are taken up by the roots as mineral ions. Even nitrogen (N), which is present in the atmosphere, is most often taken up as NO_3^-.

10. You can determine mineral requirements by hydroponics, which is growing plants in a solution. The solution is varied by the omission of one mineral. If the plant grows poorly, then the missing mineral is required for growth.

11. Roots can only take up the minerals that are available in soil. Acid deposition reduces the availability of some minerals and increases the availability of other minerals. Ions such as calcium (Ca^{++}), potassium (K^+), and magnesium (Mg^{++}) are displaced from soil particles by hydrogen ions (H^+) and are leached from the soil. Acid deposition increases the solubility of aluminum (Al^{+++}) and iron (Fe^{+++}) and makes them available in toxic amounts.

12. Mineral ions cross plasma membranes by a chemiosmotic mechanism. A proton pump transports H^+ out of the cell. This establishes an electrochemical gradient that causes positive ions to flow into the cells. Negative ions are carried across in conjunction with H^+, which is moving along its concentration gradient.

13. Plants have various adaptations that assist them in acquiring nutrients. Legumes have nodules infected with the bacterium *Rhizobium,* which makes nitrogen compounds available to these plants. Many other plants have mycorrhizae, or fungus roots. The fungus gathers nutrients from the soil, and the root provides the fungus with sugars and amino acids. Some plants have poorly developed roots. Most epiphytes live on, but do not parasitize, trees, whereas mistletoe and some other plants parasitize their host.

14. The pressure-flow model of phloem transport proposes that a positive pressure potential drives phloem sap from the leaves in any direction. Sucrose is actively transported into phloem—also by a chemiosmotic mechanism—at a source, and water follows because of the lower osmotic potential. The resulting increase in pressure potential creates a flow that moves water and sucrose to a sink. A sink can be at the roots or any other part of the plant that requires nutrients.

Writing Across the Curriculum

In order to practice writing skills, students should write out the answers to any or all of the study questions and the critical thinking questions. The study questions are sequenced in the same order as the text. Answers to the objective questions, and suggested answers to the critical thinking questions, are in appendix D.

Study Questions

1. Why does a land existence cause plants to need a vascular system? What is their vascular system? 552

2. What is water potential? In regard to cells, what two components determine water potential? When cells are turgid, water potential is equal on both sides of the membrane. Why? 553

3. Give two pathways by which water and minerals can cross the epidermis and cortex of a root. What feature allows endodermal cells to regulate the entrance of molecules into the vascular cylinder? 554

4. What is root pressure, and why can't it account for transport of water in xylem? 554

5. Explain how field capacity and permanent wilting point relate to water availability in soils. Why do soils differ as to water availability? 554

6. Describe and give evidence for the cohesion-tension theory of water transport. 555

7. Describe the structure of stomates and explain how they can open and close. By what mechanism do guard cells take up potassium (K^+) ions? 556

8. Name the elements that make up most of a plant's body. What are essential mineral nutrients and beneficial mineral nutrients? 558

9. Briefly describe two methods used to determine the mineral nutrients of a plant. 558

10. Explain how acid deposition affects availability of minerals to a plant and why this can lead to plant death. 000

11. Describe the chemiosmotic mechanism by which mineral ions cross plasma membranes. 558-59

12. Name two symbiotic relationships that assist plants in taking up minerals and two types of plants that tend not to take up minerals by roots from soil. 560-61

13. What data are available to show that phloem transports organic compounds? Explain the pressure-flow model of phloem transport. 562–63

Objective Questions

1. Which of these is not a nutrient for plants?
   a. water
   b. carbon dioxide gas
   c. mineral ions
   d. nitrogen gas

2. The Casparian strip affects
   a. how water and minerals move into the vascular cylinder.
   b. how water but not minerals move.
   c. how minerals but not water move.
   d. neither the flow of water nor the flow of minerals into a plant.

3. Field capacity is
   a. the same as permanent wilting point.
   b. the amount of water in soil available to plants.
   c. the amount of water in soil after drainage takes place.
   d. higher for sandy soils than clay soils.

4. Stomates are usually open
   a. at night, when the plant requires a supply of oxygen.
   b. during the day, when the plant requires a supply of carbon dioxide.
   c. whenever there is excess water in the soil.
   d. All of these are correct.

5. Which of these is not a mineral ion?
   a. NO^-
   b. Mg^+
   c. CO_2
   d. Al^{+++}

6. Water flows from the
   a. higher water potential to the lower water potential.
   b. more positive water potential to the more negative water potential.
   c. more positive osmotic potential to the more negative water potential.
   d. All of these are correct.

7. The pressure-flow model of phloem transport states that
   a. phloem sap always flows from the leaves to the root.
   b. phloem sap always flows from the root to the leaves.
   c. water flow brings sucrose from a source to a sink.
   d. Both a and c are correct.

8. Root hairs do not play a role in
   a. oxygen uptake.
   b. mineral uptake.
   c. water uptake.
   d. carbon dioxide uptake.

9. Explain why this experiment supports the hypothesis that transpiration can cause water to rise to the top of tall trees.

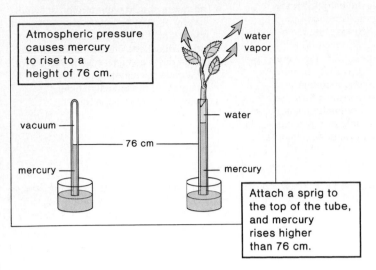

Atmospheric pressure causes mercury to rise to a height of 76 cm.

vacuum

76 cm

mercury

water vapor

water

mercury

Attach a sprig to the top of the tube, and mercury rises higher than 76 cm.

10. Label water (H_2O) and potassium (K^+) ions in these diagrams. What is the role of K^+ in the opening of stomates?

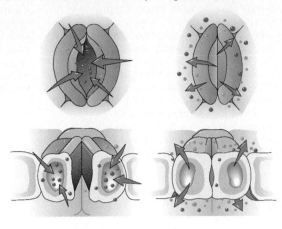

11. Explain why there is a flow of solution from the left bulb to the right bulb.

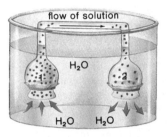

flow of solution

H_2O

H_2O H_2O

▶ Concepts and Critical Thinking

1. *Living things are physical and chemical machines.*

How does transport of water in xylem support this concept? How does the opening and closing of a stomate support this concept? How does transport of organic substances in phloem support this concept?

2. *Plants, like other living things, are highly organized.*

How does the structure of xylem contribute to the coordination of plant processes and parts?

▶ Selected Key Terms

cohesion-tension model An explanation for the transport of water to great heights in a plant due to a negative water potential (compared to the roots). This movement is brought about by transpiration and is dependent upon the ability of water molecules to cohere and to adhere to cell walls. 555

epiphyte (EP-uh-fyt) A plant that takes its nourishment from the air because its attachment to other plants gives it an aerial position. [Gk. *epi*, upon, and *phyt*, plant] 561

girdling Removing a strip of bark from around a tree. 562

guard cell A type of plant cell that is found in pairs, with one on each side of a leaf stomate; changes in the turgor pressure of these cells regulate the size and passage of gases through the stomate. 556

guttation (guh-TAY-shun) The liberation of water droplets from the edges and tips of leaves. [L. *gutt*, a drop] 554

hydroponics (hy-druh-PAHN-iks) A water culture method of growing plants that allows an experimenter to vary the nutrients and minerals provided so as to determine the essential nutrients. [Gk. *hydr*, water, and *pono*, toil] 558

mycorrhiza (my-kuh-RY-zuh) A symbiotic relationship in which a fungus grows around and into a plant root; it assists in the uptake of minerals by the plant and receives organic nutrients from the plant. [Gk. *myc*, fungus, and *rhiz*, root] 561

nodule A structure on plant roots that contains nitrogen-fixing bacteria. [L. *nodul*, little knot] 560

pressure-flow model Model explaining transport through sieve tubes of phloem by a positive pressure potential (compared to a sink) due to the active transport of sucrose and the passive transport of water. 562

root pressure A force generated by an osmotic gradient that serves to elevate sap through xylem for a short distance. 554

transpiration A plant's loss of water to the atmosphere, mainly through evaporation at leaf stomates. [L. *trans*, across, and *spir*, breathe] 555

water potential The potential energy of water; it is a measure of the capability to release or take up water. 553

33

GROWTH AND DEVELOPMENT IN PLANTS

Learning Objectives

- Describe response to a stimulus in terms of a reception (or perception)-transduction-response pathway.   568

How Plants Respond to Stimuli

- Describe three types of tropisms and ways that plants respond to stimuli; indicate any involvement of plant hormones in these responses.   568–70
- Describe nastic movements as requiring turgor pressure changes.   570
- Provide evidence that a biological clock functions in plants.   570–71

Plant Hormones Coordinate Responses

- Name three types of hormones that promote growth, and describe their primary functions.   572–77
- Describe early experiments showing that a hormone is involved in phototropism.   572–73

- Describe how auxin is believed to bring about cell elongation.   572–73
- Indicate the manner in which plant hormones function according to gibberellin research.   574
- Describe a tissue culture experiment demonstrating that plant hormones interact.   577
- Name two types of hormones that inhibit growth, and describe their functions.   579

The Photoperiod Controls Seasonal Changes

- Discuss the relationship of photoperiodism to flowering in certain plants.   580
- Explain the phytochrome conversion cycle, and suggest possible functions of phytochrome in plants.   580–81

Upon germination of a bean seed, growth and development result in a seedling that emerges from the soil.

rganisms are capable of responding to environmental stimuli, as when you withdraw your hand from a hot stove. It is adaptive for organisms to respond to environmental stimuli because it leads to their longevity and ultimately to the survival of the species.

Animals often respond to external stimuli by an appropriate motion. Presented with a nipple, a newborn instinctively begins sucking. Sometimes plants, too, respond rapidly, as when the stomates (also called stomata) open at sunrise. While animals can change their location in response to a stimulus, plants, which are rooted in one place, change their growth pattern. This is why we can determine what a tree has been through— or even the history of the earth's climate—by studying tree rings!

What mechanism permits organisms to respond to stimuli? When humans respond to light, the stimulus is first received by a pigment in the retina at the back of the eyes, and then nerve impulses are generated which go to the brain. Thereafter, humans respond appropriately. In other words, the first step is *reception* (or perception) of the stimulus. The next step is *transduction*, meaning that the stimulus has been changed into a form that is meaningful to the organism. (In our example, the light stimulus was changed to nerve impulses.) Finally, there is the *response* by the organism. As discussed in the reading on page 575, investigators are beginning to study on a cellular basis how a signal is coupled to a response in plants. But let us begin by examining various ways in which a whole plant responds to stimuli.

HOW PLANTS RESPOND TO STIMULI

Tropisms, nastic movements, and thigmomorphogenesis are all ways in which plants respond to stimuli by a change of growth pattern.

Plants Respond by Growing

Plant growth toward or away from a directional stimulus is called a **tropism** [Gk. *trop,* turn]. The term directional means that the stimulus is coming from only one direction instead of multiple directions. Three well-known tropisms, each named for the stimulus that causes the response, are:

Phototropism: a movement in response to a light stimulus
Gravitropism: a movement in response to gravity
Thigmotropism: a movement in response to touch

Growth toward a stimulus is called a positive tropism and growth away from a stimulus is called a negative tropism. Tropisms are due to differential growth—one side of an organ elongates faster than the other, and the result is a curving toward or away from the stimulus (fig. 33.1).

Figure 33.1

Time-lapse photograph of a buttercup, *Ranunculus ficaria*, curving toward and tracking a source of light.

tracking light

curving of stem

Plants Respond to Light

Early researchers, including Charles Darwin and his son Francis, observed that plants curve toward the light. The positive **phototropism** [Gk. *photo,* light, and *trop,* turn] of stems occurs because the cells on the shady side of the stem elongate. Curving away from light is called negative phototropism. Roots, depending on the species examined, are either insensitive to light or they exhibit negative phototropism.

Because blue light in particular causes phototropism to occur, it's believed that a yellow pigment related to the vitamin riboflavin acts as a photoreceptor for light. Following reception, the plant hormone auxin migrates from the bright side to the shady side of a stem. The cells on that side elongate faster than those on the bright side, causing the stem to curve toward the light. It's not yet known how reception of the stimulus (light) is coupled to the production of auxin. That is, it is not known how transduction occurs.

As discussed in the next sections, auxin is also involved in gravitropism, apical dominance, root development, and seed development.

Plants Respond to Gravity

When an upright plant is placed on its side, the stem displays negative **gravitropism** [Gk. *grav,* heavy, and *trop,* turn] because it grows upward, opposite the pull of gravity (fig. 33.2*a*). Again, Charles Darwin and his son were among the first to say that roots, in contrast to stems, show positive gravitropism (fig. 33.2*b*). Further, they discovered that if the root cap is removed, roots no longer respond to gravity. Later investigators came up with an explanation. Root cap cells contain sensors called statoliths, which are believed by some to be starch grains located within amyloplasts, a type of plastid. (Chloroplasts are a different type of plastid.) Due to gravity, the amyloplasts settle to the lowest part of the cell (fig. 33.2*c*).

Again, the hormone auxin brings about the positive gravitropism of roots and the negative gravitropism of stems. The two types of tissues respond differently to auxin, which moves to the lower side of both stems and root after gravity has been perceived. Auxin inhibits the growth of root cells; therefore the cells of the upper surface elongate and the root curves downward. Auxin stimulates the growth of stem cells; therefore, the cells of the lower surface elongate and the stem curves upward.

Figure 33.2

Gravitropism. **a.** Negative gravitropism of the stem of a *Coleus* plant twenty-four hours after the plant was placed on its side. **b.** Positive gravitropism of a root emerging from a corn kernel. **c.** Sedimentation of statoliths (see arrows), which are amyloplasts containing starch granules, is thought to explain how roots perceive gravity.

a.

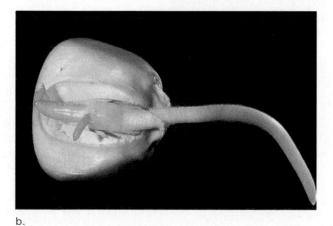

b.

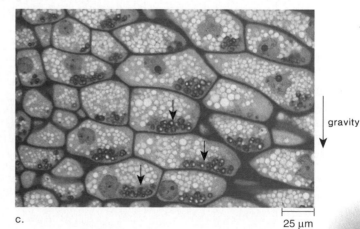

c.

gravity

25 μm

Figure 33.3
Coiling response of a morning glory plant, *Ipomoea*.

can bring about a response that lasts for several days. The response can also be delayed; tendrils touched in the dark will respond once they are illuminated. ATP (adenosine triphosphate) rather than light can cause the response; therefore the need for light may simply be a need for ATP. Also, the hormones auxin and ethylene may be involved since they can induce curvature of tendrils even in the absence of touch.

Thigmomorphogenesis is a touch response related to thigmotropism. In this case, however, the entire plant responds to the presence of environmental stimuli like wind or rain. The same type of tree growing in a windy location often has a shorter, thicker trunk than one growing in a more protected location. Even simple mechanical stimulation like rubbing a plant with a stick can inhibit cellular elongation and produce a sturdier plant with increased amounts of support tissue.

Plants Respond by Turgor Pressure Changes

In contrast to tropisms, *nastic movements* are independent of the direction of the stimulus. *Seismonastic movements* result from touch, shaking, or thermal stimulation. If you touch a *Mimosa pudica* leaf, the leaflets fold because the petiole droops (fig. 33.4). This response, which takes only a second or two, is due to a loss of turgor pressure within cells located in a thickening, called a pulvinus at the base of each leaflet. Investigation shows that potassium ions (K^+) move out of the cells and then water follows by osmosis. A single stimulus such as a hot needle is enough to cause all the leaves to respond. There must be some means of communication in order for this to occur, and in fact a nerve impulse-type stimulus has been recorded in these plants!

A Venus's-flytrap has three sensitive hairs at the base of the trap, and if these are touched by an insect, a nerve impulse-type stimulus brings about a closing of the trap. This, too, is due to turgor pressure changes in the leaf cells that form the trap.

Some Plants Have Sleep Movements

A *sleep movement* is a nastic response that occurs daily in response to light and dark changes. One of the most common examples occurs in a houseplant called the prayer plant because at night the leaves fold upward into a shape resembling that of hands at prayer (fig. 33.5). This movement is also due to changes in the turgor pressure of motor cells in a pulvinus located at the base of each leaf.

An Internal Clock Tells Time

Organisms exhibit periodic fluctuations that correspond to environmental changes. For example, your temperature and blood pressure tend to change with the time of day, and you become sleepy at a certain time of night. The prayer plant just mentioned displays rhythmic "sleep" behavior (fig. 33.5). A biological rhythm with a twenty-four-hour cycle is called a **circadian rhythm** [L. *circa,* about, and *dies,* day].

Plants Respond to Contact

Unequal growth due to contact with solid objects is called **thigmotropism** [Gk. *thigm,* touch, and *trop,* turn]. An example of this response is the coiling of tendrils or the stems of plants such as morning glory (fig. 33.3).

The plant grows straight until it touches something. Then the cells in contact with an object, such as a pole, grow less while those on the opposite side elongate. Thigmotropism can be quite rapid; a tendril has been observed to encircle an object within ten minutes. The response endures; a couple of minutes of stroking

Figure 33.4
Seismonastic movement. A leaf of the sensitive plant, *Mimosa pudica,* before and after it is touched.

before

after

Figure 33.5
Sleep movement. Prayer plant, *Maranta leuconeura,* before dark and after dark when the leaves fold up.

before

after

Circadian rhythms tend to persist, even if the appropriate environmental cues are no longer present. For example, on a transcontinental flight, you will likely suffer jet lag, and it will take several days to adjust to the time change because your body will still be attuned to the day-night pattern of your previous environment. The internal mechanism by which a biological rhythm is maintained in the absence of appropriate environmental stimuli is termed a **biological clock.** Typically, if organisms are sheltered from environmental stimuli, their circadian rhythms continue, but the cycle extends. In prayer plants, for example, the sleep cycle changes to twenty-six hours.

Therefore, it is believed that biological clocks are synchronized by external stimuli to twenty-four-hour rhythms. The length of daylight compared to the length of darkness, called the photoperiod, sets the clock. Temperature has little or no effect. This is adaptive because the photoperiod indicates seasonal changes better than temperature changes. Spring and fall, in particular, can have both warm and cold days.

There are other examples of circadian rhythms in plants. Stomates and certain flowers usually open in the morning and close at night, and some plants secrete nectar at the same time of the day or night.

PLANT HORMONES COORDINATE RESPONSES

In order for plants to respond to stimuli, the activities of plant cells and structures have to be coordinated. Almost all communication in a plant is done by **hormones** [Gk. *hormon,* excite], chemical messengers produced in very low concentrations and active in another part of the organism. A particular response is probably influenced by several hormones and most likely requires a specific ratio of two or more hormones. Hormones are synthesized or stored in regions of transduction; they travel within phloem or from cell to cell after reception of the appropriate stimulus.

Each naturally occurring hormone has a specific chemical structure. Other chemicals, some of which differ only slightly from the natural hormones, also affect the growth of plants. These and the naturally occurring hormones are sometimes grouped together and called plant growth regulators. The various uses of plant growth regulators are discussed in the reading on page 576.

Figure 33.6

Apical dominance. If the terminal bud is removed, a plant becomes fuller because apical dominance has been removed and axillary buds are free to develop into branches.

Auxin and Its Many Effects

The most common naturally occurring **auxin** [Gk. *aux,* grow] is indoleacetic acid (IAA). It is produced in shoot apical meristem and is found in young leaves and in flowers and fruits. Therefore, you would expect that auxin would affect many aspects of plant growth and development. Apically produced auxin prevents the growth of axillary buds, a phenomenon called apical dominance. When a terminal bud is removed deliberately or accidentally, the nearest axillary buds begin to grow, and the plant branches. To achieve a fuller look, one generally prunes the top (apical meristem) of the plant. This removes apical dominance and causes more branching of the main body of the plant (fig. 33.6).

The application of a weak solution of auxin to a woody cutting causes roots to develop. Auxin production by seeds also promotes the growth of fruit. As long as auxin is concentrated in leaves or fruits rather than in the stem, leaves and fruits do not fall off. Therefore, trees can be sprayed with auxin to keep mature fruit from falling to the ground.

As discussed earlier, auxin is also involved in gravitropism and phototropism. After gravity has been perceived, auxin moves to the lower surface of roots and stems. Thereafter, roots curve downward and stems curve upward (see fig. 33.2). The role of auxin in the positive phototropism of stems has been studied for quite some time. The experimental material of choice has been oat seedlings with coleoptile intact. A coleoptile is a protective sheath for the young leaves of the seedling. In 1881, the Darwins found that phototropism will not occur if the tip of the seedling is cut off or is covered by a black cap. They concluded that some influence that causes curvature is transmitted from the coleoptile tip to the rest of the shoot.

In 1926 Frits W. Went cut off the tips of coleoptiles and placed them on agar (a gelatinlike material). Then he placed an agar block to one side of a tipless coleoptile and found that the shoot would curve away from that side. The bending occurred even though the seedlings were not exposed to light (fig. 33.7). Went concluded that the agar blocks contained a chemical that had been produced by the coleoptile tips. It was this chemical, he decided, that had caused the shoots to curve. He named the chemical substance auxin after the Greek word aux, which means to grow.

How Auxin Works

When a plant is exposed to unidirectional light, auxin moves to the shady side where it binds to receptors and activates the ATP-driven proton pump (fig. 33.8). As hydrogen ions (H$^+$) are being pumped out of the cell, the cell wall becomes acidic, breaking hydrogen bonds. Cellulose fibrils are weakened, and activated enzymes further degrade the cell wall. The electrochemical gradient established by the proton pump causes solutes to enter the cell and water follows by osmosis. The turgid cell presses against the cell wall, stretching it so that elongation occurs. Auxin-mediated elongation is observed in younger, as opposed to more mature, cells. Perhaps older cells lack auxin receptors.

Figure 33.7

Demonstrating phototropism. Oat seedlings are protected by a hollow sheath called a coleoptile. After a tip is removed and placed on agar, an agar block placed on one side of the coleoptile can cause it to curve.

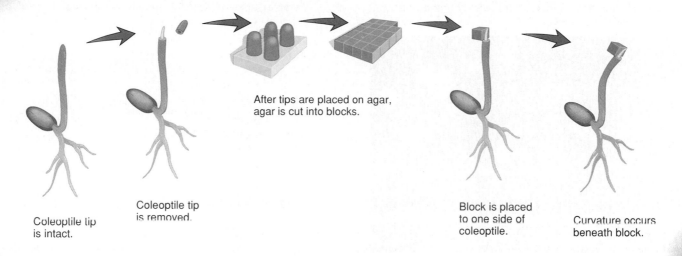

After tips are placed on agar, agar is cut into blocks.

Coleoptile tip is intact.

Coleoptile tip is removed.

Block is placed to one side of coleoptile.

Curvature occurs beneath block.

Figure 33.8

Auxin mode of action. After auxin binds to a receptor, the combination stimulates the proton pump so that hydrogen ions (H^+) are transported out of the cell. The resulting acidity causes the cell wall to weaken, and the electrochemical gradient causes solutes to enter the cell. Water follows by osmosis and the cell elongates.

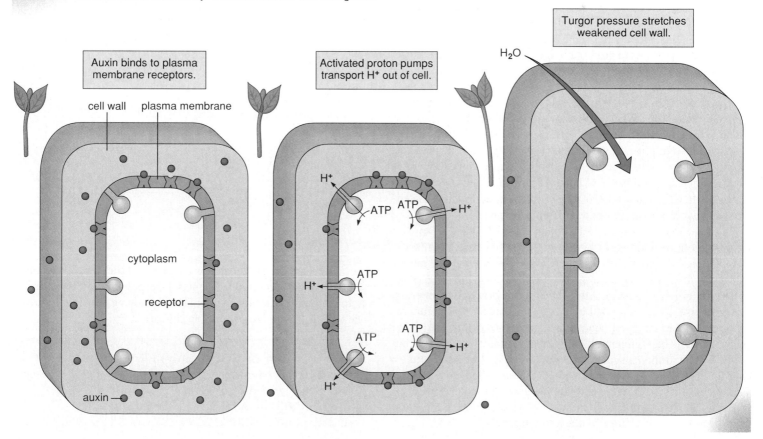

Auxin binds to plasma membrane receptors.

Activated proton pumps transport H^+ out of cell.

Turgor pressure stretches weakened cell wall.

H_2O

cell wall   plasma membrane

cytoplasm

receptor

auxin

Figure 33.9

Gibberellins. The *Cyclamen* plant on the right was treated with gibberellins; the plant on the left was not treated. Gibberellins are often used to promote stem elongation in economically important plants, but the exact mode of action still remains unclear.

Figure 33.10

Possible gibberellin mode of action. The hormone (gibberellin) binds to a receptor, and a second messenger (Ca++) inside the cell activates a protein (*calmodulin*) and the complex binds to DNA. Thereafter, an enzyme is produced.

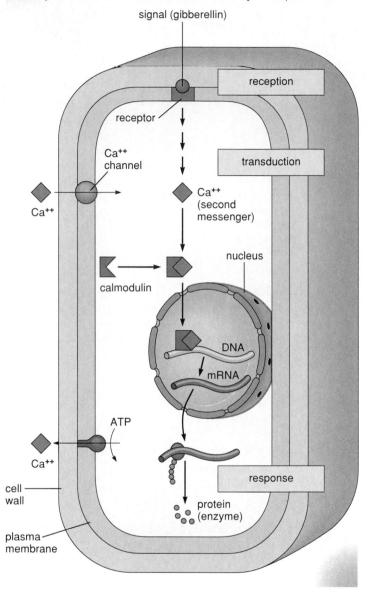

Gibberellins and Stem Elongation

We know of about seventy gibberellins that chemically differ only slightly. The most common of these is GA_3 (the subscript designation distinguishes it from other gibberellins). **Gibberellins** [L. *gibb*, humped] are growth promoters that bring about elongation of the resulting cells. When gibberellins are applied externally to plants, the most obvious effect is *stem elongation* (fig. 33.9). Gibberellins can cause dwarf plants to grow, cabbage plants to become 2 meters tall, and bush beans to become pole beans.

Gibberellins were discovered in 1926, the same year that Went performed his classic experiments with auxin. Ewiti Kurosawa, a Japanese scientist, was investigating a fungal disease of rice plants called "foolish seedling disease." The plants elongated too quickly, causing the stem to weaken and the plant to collapse. Kurosawa found that the fungus infecting the plants produced an excess of a chemical he called gibberellin, named after the fungus *Gibberella fujikuroi*. It wasn't until 1956 that gibberellic acid was isolated from a flowering plant rather than from a fungus.

The dormancy of seeds and buds can be broken by applying gibberellins, and research with barley seeds has shown how GA_3 acts as a chemical messenger. Barley seeds have a large, starchy endosperm, which must be broken down into sugars to provide energy for growth. After the embryo produces gibberellins, amylase, an enzyme that breaks down the starch, appears in cells just inside the seed coat. It is hypothesized that GA_3 (the first chemical messenger) attaches to a receptor in the plasma membrane, and then a second messenger inside the cell, namely calcium ions (Ca^{++}), combines with a protein called calmodulin. This complex is believed to activate the gene that codes for amylase (fig. 33.10). Amylase then acts on starch to release sugars used as a source of energy by the growing embryo.

The action of hormones on the cellular level is another example of the reception-transduction-response pathway described at the beginning of this chapter. The following reading describes the work of two investigators in this area.

Gibberellins promote cell division and elongation of cells. They increase the formation of hydrolytic enzymes that release energy needed for growth.

Husband and Wife Team Explores Signal Transduction in Plants

P lants perceive and react to a variety of environmental stimuli. Some examples include light intensity and quality, gravity, carbon dioxide levels, pathogen infection, drought, and touch. Plant responses may be short term, such as the rapid localized cell death that occurs at the site of infection by a pathogen. This rapid cell death, termed the hypersensitive response, serves to limit the further progression of infection. Another form of short-term response is the opening or closing of leaf stomates in response to light levels. High light causes the stomates to open, while low light or darkness causes them to close. In this way, the supply of carbon dioxide to the leaves via the stomates is coordinated with light-driven photosynthetic reactions occurring in leaf cells. On the other hand, plant responses to environmental stimuli may be more long term and involve actual plant growth. An example is the plant response to gravity (gravitropism), which results in the downward growth of the root and the upward growth of the stem. In each of these situations, the coupling of a stimulus to an appropriate response represents signal transduction.

Although we know that plants do not have a nervous system and a brain, some system or process must be present in these organisms to allow the perception of a stimulus and its conversion to an appropriate response. While we are both interested in attempting to understand this process, we approach this complex research area from different perspectives related to our training, expertise, and interests.

As a plant biochemist, Donald focuses on how membrane transport processes are involved in signal transduction. Here, research has shown that membrane transport of calcium ions (Ca^{++}) can play a fundamental role in the signal transduction process. When a stimulus is perceived by a plant cell, a transient increase in cytoplas-

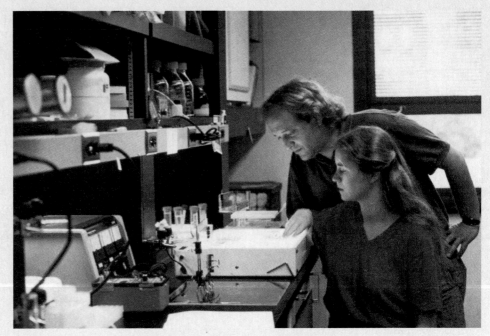

Donald Briskin and Margaret Gawienowski
University of Illinois at Urbana-Champaign

mic Ca^{++} concentration occurs due to the rapid opening of Ca^{++} channels at plant membranes, which operate not unlike Ca^{++} channels present in animal membranes. This transient increase in cytoplasmic Ca^{++} acts as a sort of message linking the stimulus to a response at the biochemical level. In particular, Donald studies how Ca^{++}-transporting enzymes (called Ca^{++}-ATPases) and Ca^{++} channels are coordinated after a stimulus is received.

Just how a single type of message—such as a rapid change in cytoplasmic Ca^{++}—can elicit so many different types of specific plant responses is Margaret's interest. As a plant molecular biologist, Margaret focuses on how proteins in the plant cytoplasm that bind Ca^{++} might impart specificity to the response. Of particular interest to her is a Ca^{++}-binding protein called calmodulin, which controls the activity of a number of other proteins once it binds to Ca^{++}. Her work has shown that calmodulin in plants is encoded by multiple genes that produce variants of the protein called isoforms.

The isoforms are present to a different extent in different plant tissues, have different properties (Ca^{++} binding, target protein regulation), and may play a role in determining which responses are coupled to transient cytoplasmic Ca^{++} changes. Margaret is also interested in using a molecular approach to find more calmodulin-binding proteins that may be associated with various plant membranes.

Although our approaches towards understanding plant signal transduction are very different, the work of each of us tends to complement the other's. We view each other's work from a slightly different perspective, and this helps generate ideas for new experiments and strategies. Furthermore, we work together in the same laboratory at the University of Illinois at Urbana-Champaign, and this leads to much discussion and exchange of opinions. For us, research is not only challenging and exciting, but it keeps us wondering what the next day will bring.

Plant Growth Regulators

Now that the formulas for many plant hormones are known, it is possible to synthesize them, as well as related chemicals, in the laboratory. Collectively, these substances are known as plant growth regulators. Many scientists hope plant growth regulators will bring about an increase in crop yield, just as fertilizers, irrigation, and pesticides have done in the past.

Since auxin was first discovered, researchers have found many agricultural and commercial uses for it. Auxins cause the base of stems to form new roots quickly, so that new plants are easily started from cuttings. When sprayed on apples, pears, and citrus fruits shortly before harvest, auxins prevent fruit from dropping too soon. Because auxins inhibit the growth of lateral buds, potatoes sprayed with an auxin do not sprout and thus have a longer storage life.

In high concentrations, some auxins are used widely in agriculture as herbicides to prevent the growth of broad-leaved plants. In addition to their use in weed control, the synthetic auxins known as 2,4D and 2,4,5T were used as defoliants during the Vietnam War. Even though 2,4D has been used for over thirty-five years, we do not yet know how it works. Apparently, it is structurally different enough from natural auxin that a plant's own enzymes cannot break it down. Its concentration rises until metabolism is disrupted, cellular order is lost, and the cells die.

The other plant hormones studied in this chapter also have agricultural and commercial uses. Gibberellins are used to stimulate seed germination and seedling growth of some grains, beans, and fruits. They also increase the size of some mature plants. Treatment of sugarcane with as little as 2 oz per acre increases the cane yield by more than 5 metric tons. The application of either auxins or gibberellins can cause an

Figure 33A

Effect of gibberellin (GA$_3$) on Thompson seedless grapes, *Vitis vinifera*. Control grapes (*left*). GA$_3$ was sprayed at bloom and at fruit set (*right*). Almost all grapes sold in stores are now treated with gibberellin.

ovary and accessory flower parts to develop into fruit, even though pollination and fertilization have not taken place. In this way, it is sometimes possible to produce seedless fruits and vegetables or bigger, more uniform bunches with larger fruit, as shown in figure 33A.

Because cytokinins retard the aging of leaves and other organs, they are sprayed on vegetables to keep them fresh during shipping and storage. Such treatment of holly, for example, allows it to be harvested many weeks prior to a holiday.

Plant growth regulators are used in tissue culture when seedlings are grown from a few cells in laboratory glassware. New varieties of food crops with particular characteristics—such as tolerance to herbicides and insects—are being developed by genetically engineering the original cells. It may one day be possible to endow most crops with the ability to utilize atmospheric nitrogen and/or make a wider range of proteins.

Several synthetic inhibitors are used to oppose the action of auxins, gibberellins, and cytokinins normally present in plants. Some of

these can cause leaf and fruit drop at a time convenient to the farmer. Removing leaves from cotton plants aids in their harvest, and thinning the fruit of young fruit trees results in larger fruit as the trees mature. Retarding the growth of other plants sometimes increases their hardiness. For example, an inhibitor has been used to reduce stem length in wheat plants, so that the plants do not fall over in heavy winds and rain.

The commercial uses of ethylene were greatly increased with the development of ethylene-releasing compounds. Ethylene gas is injected into airtight storage rooms to ripen bananas, honeydew melons, and tomatoes. It will also degreen oranges, lemons, and grapefruit when the rind would otherwise remain green because of a high chlorophyll level. When sprayed on certain fruit and nut crops, ethylene increases the chances that the fruit will detach when the trees are shaken at harvest time.

Today, fields and orchards are often sprayed with synthetic growth regulators.

Figure 33.11 🔲

Interaction of hormones. Tissue culture experiments have revealed that auxin and cytokinin interact to affect differentiation during development. **a.** In tissue culture that has the usual amounts of these two hormones, tobacco strips develop into a callus of undifferentiated tissue. **b.** If the ratio of auxin to cytokinin is appropriate, the callus produces roots. **c.** Change the ratio, and vegetative shoots and leaves are produced. **d.** Yet another ratio causes floral shoots. It is now clear that plant hormones rarely act alone; it is the relative concentrations of these hormones that produce an effect. The modern emphasis is to look for an interplay of hormones when a growth response is studied.

a.

b.

c.

d.

Cytokinins and Cell Division

The **cytokinins** [Gk. *cyt*, cell, and *kine*, movement] are a class of plant hormones that promote cell division; *cytokinesis means cell division*. These substances are derivatives of the purine adenine, one of the bases in DNA (deoxyribonucleic acid) and RNA (ribonucleic acid). A naturally occurring cytokinin called *zeatin* has been extracted from corn kernels. Kinetin, a synthetic cytokinin, also promotes cell division.

The cytokinins were discovered as a result of attempts to grow plant tissue and organs in culture vessels in the 1940s (fig. 33.11). It was found that cell division occurs when coconut milk (a liquid endosperm) and yeast extract are added to the culture medium. Although the effective agent or agents could not be isolated, they were collectively called cytokinins. Not until 1967 was the naturally occurring cytokinin zeatin isolated from coconut milk. Cytokinins have been isolated from various seed plants, where they occur in the actively dividing tissues of roots and also in seeds and fruits.

Plant tissue culturing is now common practice, and researchers are well aware that the ratio of auxin to cytokinin and the acidity of the culture medium determine whether the plant tissue forms an undifferentiated mass, called a callus, or differentiates to form roots, vegetative shoots, leaves, or floral shoots (fig. 33.11). Researchers have reported that chemicals they called oligosaccharins (chemical fragments released from the cell wall) are also effective in directing differentiation. They hypothesize that auxin and cytokinins are a part of a reception-transduction-response pathway (see fig. 33.10), which leads to the activation of enzymes that release these fragments from the cell wall. Perhaps all plant hormones have a similar effect.

Cytokinins Affect Leaves

When a plant organ, such as a leaf, loses its natural color, it is most likely undergoing an aging process called *senescence*. During senescence, large molecules within the leaf are broken down and transported to other parts of the plant. Senescence does not always affect the entire plant at once; for example, as some plants grow taller, they naturally lose their lower leaves. It has been found that senescence of leaves can be prevented by the application of cytokinins. Not only can cytokinins prevent death of leaves, they can also initiate leaf growth. Lateral buds begin to grow despite apical dominance when cytokinin is applied to them.

> Cytokinins promote cell division, prevent senescence, and initiate growth. The interaction of hormones is well exemplified by the effect of varying ratios of auxin and cytokinins on differentiation of plant tissues.

Arabidopsis thaliana, *the Valuable Weed*

powerful new tool is available for the study of plant growth and development. *Arabidopsis thaliana* is a weed that few people knew of fifteen years ago. But now it is being studied in hundreds of laboratories all over the world because it lends itself to genetic manipulation (fig. 33B). Adult plants can be grown from a few cells in tissue culture and, after a short generation time, adult plants will produce 10,000 seeds each in only four to six weeks. Because of its small size, dozens of plants can grow in a single pot. *A. thaliana* has a small genome; there are only five pairs of chromosomes and a 100 million nucleotides total. In contrast, tobacco plants, which often were used as experimental material in the past, probably have the same number of genes but fifteen times the number of nucleotides. This excess noncoding DNA makes it difficult to find the genes and determine what they do.

There are many natural mutants of *Arabidopsis,* and much can be determined by studying them. In one instance, a dwarf plant was found to be deficient in the amount of gibberellin-producing enzymes. Since the plant showed a lack of internodal elongation but showed normal development of leaves and flowers, it was known that gibberellins were affecting only internodal elongation. Many additional mutants can be produced because these plants are susceptible to infection by *Agrobacterium tumefaciens*, the bacterium with a plasmid that inserts into plant genomes. On occasion the plasmid inserts itself into the middle of a normal gene, disrupting it and preventing it from functioning as it should. Researchers have used this method to determine that there are three classes of genes essential to normal floral pattern formation. Triple mutants that lack all types of genetic activities have flowers that consist entirely of leaves arranged in whorls (compare fig. 33C and D). These floral organ identity genes appear to be transcriptional regulators that are expressed and required for extended periods.

An international collaborative effort is under way to map the *Arabidopsis* genome and sequence each of its genes. Once the genes of *Arabidopsis* are known, they can be used to identify the same genes in crop plants. It is reasonable to expect that plant cells function similarly; therefore it is likely we will learn how to improve crops by studying *Arabidopsis*.

Figure 33B

Arabidopsis thaliana. Many investigators have turned to this weed as an experimental material to study the actions of genes, including those that control growth and development.

Figure 33C

The structure of the normal flower of *Arabidopsis thaliana* is determined in part by three classes of floral organ identity genes.

Figure 33D

Mutations affecting all three classes of floral organ identity genes result in flowers that contain leaves arranged in whorls.

Figure 33.12

Stomates are opened and closed by guard cells. The hormone abscisic acid (ABA) is believed to bring about the closing of the stomates when water stress occurs. First potassium ions (K⁺) exit and then water (H_2O) also leaves guard cells.

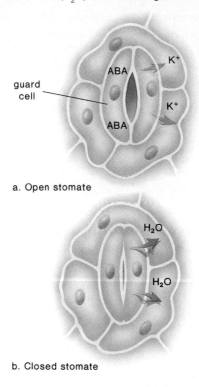

a. Open stomate

b. Closed stomate

Figure 33.13

Abscission layer. Before a leaf falls, a special band of cells called the abscission layer develops at the base of the petiole, the leaf stem. Here the hormone ethylene promotes the breakdown of plant cell walls so that the leaf finally falls. Here also, a layer forms a leaf scar, which protects the plant from possible invasion by microorganisms.

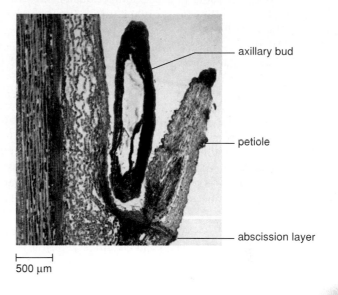

— axillary bud

— petiole

— abscission layer

500 μm

Plant Hormones That Inhibit

In contrast to the hormones discussed so far, the plant hormones abscisic acid and ethylene inhibit growth.

Abscisic Acid Is the Stress Hormone

Abscisic acid (ABA) is sometimes called the stress hormone because it initiates and maintains seed and bud dormancy and brings about the closure of stomates. *Dormancy* occurs when a plant organ readies itself for adverse conditions by stopping growth (even though conditions at the time are favorable for growth). For example, it is believed that abscisic acid moves from leaves to vegetative buds in the fall, and thereafter these buds are converted to winter buds. A winter bud is covered by thick and hardened scales. A reduction in the level of abscisic acid and an increase in the level of gibberellins are believed to break seed and bud dormancy. Then seeds germinate and buds send forth leaves.

Abscisic acid brings about the closing of stomates when a plant is under water stress (fig. 33.12). In some unknown way, abscisic acid causes potassium ions (K⁺) to leave guard cells. Thereafter, the guard cells lose water and the stomates close. Although the external application of abscisic acid promotes abscission, this hormone is no longer believed to function naturally in this process. Instead, the hormone ethylene is believed to bring about abscission (fig. 33.13).

Ethylene Is for Fruit Ripening

In the early 1900s, it was common practice to prepare citrus fruits for market by placing them in a room with a kerosene stove; only later did researchers realize that an incomplete combustion product of kerosene, namely **ethylene,** ripens fruit. It does so by increasing the activity of enzymes that soften fruits. For example, it stimulates the production of *cellulase,* an enzyme that hydrolyzes cellulose in plant cell walls. Because it is a gas, ethylene moves freely through the air—a barrel of ripening apples can induce ripening of a bunch of bananas even some distance away. Ethylene is released at the site of a wound due to physical damage or infection (which is why one rotten apple spoils the whole bunch).

The presence of ethylene in the air inhibits the growth of plants in general; homeowners who use natural gas to heat their homes sometimes report difficulties in growing houseplants. Ethylene is also present in automobile exhaust, and it's possible that plant growth is inhibited by the exhaust that enters the atmosphere. It only takes one part of ethylene per 10 million parts of air to bring about inhibition of plant growth.

Ethylene is also involved in **abscission** [L. *ab,* away, and *sciss,* cut], the dropping of leaves, fruits, and flowers from a plant. Lower levels of auxin and perhaps gibberellin in these areas of the plant (compared to the stem) probably initiate abscission (fig. 33.13). But once the process of abscission has begun, ethylene stimulates such enzymes as cellulase, which cause leaf, fruit, or flower drop.

THE PHOTOPERIOD CONTROLS SEASONAL CHANGES

Many physiological changes in plants are related to a seasonal change in day length. Such changes include seed germination, the breaking of bud dormancy, and the onset of senescence. A physiological response prompted by changes in the length of day or night is called **photoperiodism** [Gk. *photo,* light, and *perio,* on the other side]. In some plants, photoperiodism influences flowering: violets and tulips flower in the spring, and asters and goldenrods flower in the fall.

In the 1920s, when U.S. Department of Agriculture scientists began to study photoperiodism in more detail, they decided to grow plants in a greenhouse, where they could artificially alter the photoperiod. This work led them to conclude that plants can be divided into three groups:

1. **Short-day plants**—flower when the day length is shorter than a critical length (examples are cocklebur, poinsettia, and chrysanthemum).
2. **Long-day plants**—flower when the day length is longer than a critical length (examples are wheat, barley, clover, and spinach).
3. **Day-neutral plants**—flowering is not dependent on day length (examples are tomato and cucumber).

Further, we should note that both a long-day plant and a short-day plant can have the same critical length (fig. 33.14). Spinach is a long-day plant that has a critical length of fourteen hours; ragweed is a short-day plant with the same critical length. Spinach, however, flowers in the summer when the day length increases to fourteen hours or more, and ragweed flowers in the fall, when the day length shortens to fourteen hours or less. We now know that some plants may require a specific sequence of day lengths in order to flower.

In 1938, K. C. Hammer and J. Bonner began to experiment with artificial lengths of light and dark that did not necessarily correspond to a normal twenty-four-hour day. They discovered that the cocklebur, a short-day plant, flowers as long as the dark period is continuous for 8.5 hours, regardless of the length of the light period. Further, if this dark period is interrupted by a brief flash of white light, the cocklebur does not flower. (Interrupting the light period with darkness has no effect.) Similar results have also been found for long-day plants. They require a dark period that is shorter than a critical length, regardless of the length of the light period. If a slightly longer-than-critical-length night is inter-rupted by a brief flash of light, however, long-day plants flower. We must conclude, then, that the length of the dark period controls flowering, not the length of the light period. Of course, in nature, short days always go with long nights and vice versa.

> **Short-day plants require a period of darkness that is longer, and long-day plants require a period of darkness that is shorter, than a critical length to flower.**

Phytochrome and Plant Flowering

If flowering is dependent on day and night length, plants must have some way to detect these periods. Many years of research by U.S. Department of Agriculture scientists led to the discovery of a plant pigment called phytochrome. **Phytochrome** [Gk. *phyt,* plant, and *chrom,* color] is a blue-green leaf pigment that alternately exists in two forms. As figure 33.15 indicates:

P_r (phytochrome red) absorbs red light (of 660 nm wavelength) and is converted to P_{fr}.

P_{fr} (phytochrome far-red) absorbs far-red light (of 730 nm wavelength) and is converted to P_r.

Direct sunlight contains more red light than far-red light; therefore, P_{fr} is apt to be present in plant leaves during the day. In

Figure 33.14

Day length effect on two types of plants. **a.** Short-day plant. (1) When the day is shorter than a critical length, this type of plant flowers. (2) The plant does not flower when the day is longer than the critical length. (3) It also does not flower if the longer-than-critical-length night is interrupted by a flash of light. **b.** Long-day plant. (1) When the day is shorter than a critical length, this type plant does not flower. (2) The plant flowers when the day is longer than a critical length. (3) It also flowers if the slightly longer-than-critical-length night is interrupted by a flash of light.

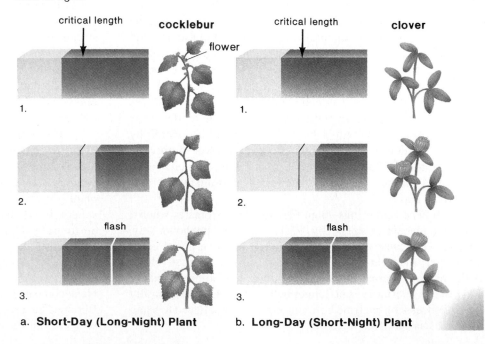

a. Short-Day (Long-Night) Plant **b. Long-Day (Short-Night) Plant**

Figure 33.15

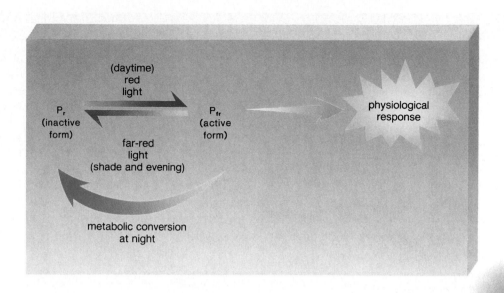

$P_r \rightarrow P_{fr}$ conversion cycle. The inactive form P_r is prevalent during the night. At sunset or in the shade, when there is more far-red light, P_{fr} is converted to P_r. Also during the night, metabolic processes cause P_{fr} to be converted into P_r. P_{fr}, the active form of phytochrome, is prevalent during the day because at that time there is more red light than far-red light.

the shade and at sunset, there is more far-red light than red light; therefore, P_{fr} is converted to P_r as night approaches. There is also a slow metabolic replacement of P_{fr} by P_r during the night.

It is possible that phytochrome conversion is the first step in a reception-transduction-response pathway that results in flowering. At one time, researchers hypothesized that there was a special flowering hormone called florigen, but such a hormone has never been discovered.

> Phytochrome alternates between two forms (P_{fr} during the day and P_r during the night), and this conversion allows a plant to detect photoperiod changes.

Phytochrome Has Other Functions

The $P_r \rightarrow P_{fr}$ conversion cycle is now known to control other growth functions in plants. It promotes seed germination and inhibits stem elongation, for example. The presence of P_{fr} indicates to some seeds that sunlight is present and conditions are favorable for germination. This is why some seeds must be partly covered with soil when planted. Germination of other seeds is inhibited by light, so they must be planted deeper. Following germination, the presence of P_r indicates that stem elongation may be needed to reach sunlight. Seedlings that are grown in the dark etiolate; that is, the stem increases in length and the leaves remain small (fig. 33.16). Once the seedling is exposed to sunlight and P_r is converted to P_{fr}, the seedling begins to grow normally—the leaves expand and the stem branches. It has now been shown that phytochrome in the P_{fr} form leads to the activation of one or more regulatory proteins in the cytosol. These proteins migrate to the nucleus where they bind to so-called "light-stimulated" genes that code for proteins found in chloroplasts.

Figure 33.16

Phytochrome control of growth pattern. If far-red light is prevalent, as it is in the shade, the stem of a seedling elongates but the leaves remain small (*left*). However, if red light is prevalent, as it is in bright sunlight, the stem does not elongate but the leaves expand (*right*). These effects are due to phytochrome.

Biological Relationships

The chemical and physical basis of life is exemplified by both plants and animals. Biologists have discovered, for example, that vascular transport in both plants and animals is dependent on physical forces. In the human body, the heart pumps the blood and creates blood pressure, just as a mechanical pump brings water from the ground under pressure. In plants, the evaporation of water at the leaves (called transpiration) pulls water from the roots. And active transport of sugar into phloem is followed by an osmotic pressure that sends phloem sap to the roots.

Vascular transport requires energy. In the human body, muscle contraction fueled by the breakdown of ATP (adenosine triphosphate) supplies the energy for arterial transport. In plants, the sun supplies the energy for transpiration and xylem transport. And active transport, dependent upon ATP energy, supplies the energy for phloem transport.

The movement of ions across the plasma membrane utilizes similar mechanisms in both plants and animals. Such movements are critical not only to nutrition in plants but also to muscle contraction and nerve conduction in animals. Plants respond to stimuli, and the plant life cycle of growth, flowering, and seed and fruit production is regulated by hormones alone. In plants these processes are controlled by hormones alone. The similarity of hormonal action between plants and animals is only now becoming apparent. It should not come as a surprise that plants and animals and their cells share common mechanisms since at one time they also shared a common ancestor.

Summary

1. Like animals, plants utilize a reception (or perception)-transduction-response pathway when they respond to a stimulus.

2. When plants respond to stimuli, growth and/or movement occurs.

3. Tropisms are growth responses toward or away from unidirectional stimuli. The positive phototropism of stems results in a bending toward light and the negative gravitropism of stems results in a bending away from the direction of gravity. Roots that bend toward the direction of gravity show positive gravitropism. Thigmotropism occurs when a plant part makes contact with an object, as when tendrils coil about a pole.

4. Nastic movements are not directional. Due to turgor pressure changes, some plants respond to touch and some perform sleep movements.

5. Plants exhibit circadian rhythms, which are believed to be controlled by a biological clock. The sleep movements of prayer plants, the closing of stomates, and the daily opening of certain flowers have a twenty-four-hour cycle.

6. Both stimulatory and inhibitory hormones help control certain growth patterns of plants. There are hormones that stimulate growth (auxins, gibberellins, and cytokinins) and hormones that inhibit growth (abscisic acid and ethylene) (table 33.1).

7. Auxin-controlled cell elongation is involved in phototropism and gravitropism. When a plant is exposed to light, auxin moves laterally from the bright to the shady side of a stem. There it activates the proton (H$^+$) pump, leading to the uptake of solutes and an increase in turgor pressure, and the result is elongation of cells on that side.

8. Gibberellin research indicates that after a hormone attaches to a plasma membrane receptor, a second chemical messenger inside the cell leads to transcription and protein synthesis.

9. Cytokinins cause cell division, the effects of which are especially obvious when plant tissues are grown in culture.

10. Abscisic acid (ABA) and ethylene are two plant growth inhibitors. ABA is well known for causing stomates to close, and ethylene is known for causing fruits to ripen.

11. Photoperiodism is seen in some plants. For example, short-day plants flower only when the days are shorter than a critical length, and long-day plants flower only when the days are longer than a critical length. Actually, research has shown that it is the length of darkness that is critical. Interrupting the dark period with a flash of white light prevents flowering in a short-day plant and induces flowering in a long-day plant.

12. Phytochrome is a pigment that responds to both red and far-red light and is involved in flowering. Daylight causes phytochrome to exist as P$_{fr}$, but during the night, it is reconverted to P$_r$ by metabolic processes. Phytochrome in the P$_{fr}$ form leads to activation of regulatory proteins that bind to genes.

13. In addition to being involved in the flowering process, P$_{fr}$ promotes seed germination, leaf expansion, and stem branching. When P$_r$ dominates, the stem elongates and grows toward sunlight.

Writing Across the Curriculum

In order to practice writing skills, students should write out the answers to any or all of the study questions and the critical thinking questions. The study questions are sequenced in the same order as the text. Answers to the objective questions, and suggested answers to the critical thinking questions, are in appendix D.

Table 33.1

Plant Hormones

Type	Primary Example	Notable Function
Growth Promoters		
Auxin	Indoleacetic acid (IAA)	Promotes cell elongation in stems; phototropism, gravitropism; apical dominance; formation of roots, development of fruit
Gibberellins	Gibberellic acid (GA)	Promote stem elongation; release some buds and seeds from dormancy
Cytokinins	Zeatin	Promote cell division and embryo development; prevent leaf senescence and promote bud activation
Growth Inhibitors		
Abscisic acid	Abscisic acid (ABA)	Resistance to stress conditions; causes stomatal closure; maintains dormancy
Ethylene	Ethylene	Promotes fruit ripening; promotes abscission and fruit drop; inhibits growth

Study Questions

1. List and describe three tropisms and indicate the involvement of any hormones in these responses.   568–70

2. What are nastic responses, and how do turgor pressure changes bring about movements of plants?   570

3. What is a biological clock, how does it function, and what is its primary usefulness in plants?   570–71

4. Name three types of hormones that promote growth processes, and give several specific functions for each.   572–77

5. Why does removing a terminal bud cause a plant to get bushier? What experiments led to knowledge that a hormone is involved in phototropism?   572

6. Explain the mechanism by which auxin brings about elongation of cells.   572-73

7. What is the hypothesized mode of hormone action according to gibberellin research?   574

8. Give experimental evidence to suggest that hormones interact when they bring about an effect.   577

9. Name two types of hormones that inhibit growth processes, and give several specific functions for each.   579

10. Define photoperiodism, and discuss its relationship to flowering in certain plants.   580

11. What is the phytochrome conversion cycle, and what are some possible functions of phytochrome in plants?   580–81

Objective Questions

For questions 1–5, match the items below with the hormones in the key.

Key:
   a. auxin
   b. gibberellin
   c. cytokinin
   d. ethylene
   e. abscisic acid

1. One rotten apple can spoil the barrel.
2. Cabbage plants bolt (grow tall).
3. Stomata close when a plant is water stressed.
4. Sunflower plants all point toward the sun.
5. Coconut milk causes plant tissues to undergo cell division.

6. After unidirectional light is received, auxin moves to the shady side of a stem and then the stem bends toward the light. Which step in this sequence represents transduction?
   a. sensitivity of a receptor to light
   b. auxin movement toward the shady side
   c. curving of stem toward light
   d. All of these are correct.

7. Which of these is a correct statement?
   a. Both stems and roots show positive gravitropism.
   b. Both stems and roots show negative gravitropism.
   c. Only stems show positive gravitropism.
   d. Only roots show positive gravitropism.

8. Short-day plants
   a. are the same as long-day plants.
   b. are apt to flower in the fall.
   c. do not have a critical photoperiod.
   d. All of these are correct.

9. A plant requiring a dark period of at least fourteen hours will
   a. flower if a fourteen-hour night is interrupted by a flash of light.
   b. not flower if a fourteen-hour night is interrupted by a flash of light.
   c. not flower if the days are fourteen hours long.
   d. Both b and c are correct.

10. Phytochrome
   a. is a plant pigment.
   b. is present as P_{fr} during the day.
   c. activates regulatory proteins.
   d. All of these are correct.

11. Circadian rhythms
   a. require a biological clock.
   b. do not exist in plants.
   c. are involved in the tropisms.
   d. All of these are correct.

12. Label the following diagram. Explain what causes stomates to close when a plant is water stressed.

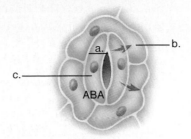

Concepts and Critical Thinking

1. *Physiological processes are coordinated in organisms.*

Give an example to show that plant hormones are involved in coordinating physiological processes.

2. *Biological clocks help organisms maintain adaptive behaviors.*

(a) Give examples to show that circadian rhythmic behavior in plants is adaptive. (b) How might flowering be controlled by a biological clock system?

3. *Reception-transduction-response pathways operate in all organisms.*

Relate the elongation of cells brought about by auxin to this pathway, using figure 33.10 as a guide.

Selected Key Terms

abscisic acid (ABA) (ab-SIZ-ik) A plant hormone that causes stomates to close and that initiates and maintains dormancy.   579

abscission (ab-SIZH-un) The dropping of leaves, fruits, or flowers from a plant. [L. *ab,* away, and *sciss,* cut]   579

auxin (AHK-sun) A plant hormone regulating growth, particularly cell elongation; also called indoleacetic acid (IAA). [Gk. *aux,* grow]   572

biological clock Internal mechanism that maintains a biological rhythm in the absence of environmental stimuli.   571

circadian rhythm A biological rhythm with a twenty-four-hour cycle. [L. *circa,* about, and *dies,* day]   570

cytokinin (syt-uh-KY-nun) A plant hormone that promotes cell division; often works in combination with auxin during organ development in plant embryos.   577

ethylene (ETH-uh-leen) A plant hormone that causes ripening of fruit and is also involved in abscission.   579

gibberellin (jib-uh-REL-un) A plant hormone producing increased stem growth; also involved in flowering and seed germination. [L. *gibb,* humped]   574

gravitropism (grav-ih-TRUH-piz-um) Directional growth of plants in response to the earth's gravity; roots demonstrate positive gravitropism, and stems demonstrate negative gravitropism. [Gk. *grav,* heavy, and *trop,* turn]   569

hormone A chemical messenger produced in one part of the body that controls the activity of other parts. [Gk. *hormon,* excite]   572

photoperiodism (foht-oh-PIR-ee-ud-iz-um) The relative lengths of daylight and darkness that affect the physiology and behavior of an organism. [Gk. *photo,* light, and *perio,* on the other side]   580

phototropism (foh-TAH-truh-piz-um) Directional growth of plants in response to light; stems demonstrate positive phototropism. [Gk. *photo,* light, and *trop,* turn]   569

phytochrome (FYT-uh-krohm) A photoreversible plant pigment whose active form seems to be involved in regulating transcription of certain genes. [Gk. *phyt,* plant, and *chrom,* color]   580

thigmotropism (thig-MAH-truh-piz-um) In plants, unequal growth due to contact with solid objects, as the coiling of tendrils around a pole. [Gk. *thigm,* touch, and *trop,* turn]   570

tropism In plants, a growth response toward or away from a directional stimulus. [Gk. *trop,* turn]   568

34

REPRODUCTION IN PLANTS

Learning Objectives

Flowering Plants Undergo Alternation of Generations

- Draw and explain a diagram that shows the life cycle of flowering plants.   586
- State and describe the parts of a flower.   587
- Describe the development of a megagametophyte in flowering plants from the megasporocyte to the production of an egg.   588–89
- Describe the development of the microgametophyte in flowering plants from the microsporocyte to the production of sperm.   588–89
- Distinguish between pollination and fertilization, and explain the events of double fertilization in flowering plants.   592

The Embryo Develops in Stages

- Describe the development of a dicot embryo in terms of a sequence of stages.   593

The Seeds Are Enclosed by Fruit

- Give a classification of fruits, and list examples of different types of fruits.   595
- Describe different means of dispersing seeds and fruits.   596
- Contrast the structure and the germination of a bean seed with those of a corn kernel.   596–97

Plants Can Reproduce Asexually

- Give examples of routine vegetative propagation in plants.   600
- Describe the process and the advantages of micropropagation utilizing tissue culture.   600
- Discuss the possible benefits of somatic embryos, anther culture, cell suspension culture, and protoplast culture.   600–602
- Discuss the status of genetic engineering of plants.   602–3

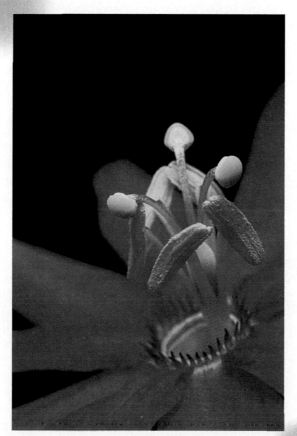

The reproductive parts of a passion, *Passiflora,* flower rise above the petals.

The flowering plants, or angiosperms, are the most diverse and widespread of all the plants. The structure of the flower allows them to produce seeds within fruits. The evolution of the flower has no doubt contributed heavily to the enormous success of angiosperms in another way. It permits pollination to take place not only by wind, but also by animals. Flowering plants that rely on animals for pollination have a mutualistic relationship with them. The flower provides nutrients for the pollinator such as a bee, a fly, a beetle, a bird, or even a bat. The animals in turn inadvertently carry pollen from one flower to another, allowing pollination to occur.

Figure 34.1

Alternation of generations in a flowering plant (overview). The diploid zygote develops into an embryo enclosed within a seed. The embryo becomes the sporophyte which bears flowers. The flower produces microspores and megaspores by meiosis. A megaspore becomes a megagametophyte, which produces an egg, and a microspore becomes a microgametophyte (pollen grain), which produces sperm. Fertilization results in a zygote once more.

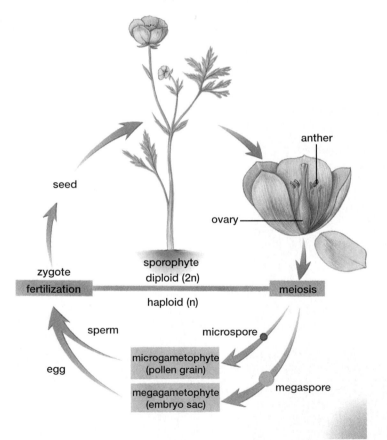

FLOWERING PLANTS UNDERGO ALTERNATION OF GENERATIONS

A *life cycle* is the entire sequence of events from the time of fertilization and formation of the zygote to gamete formation once again. In contrast to animals, which have only one type of adult generation in their life cycle, plants have two types—a diploid generation and a haploid generation—that alternate with each other. The diploid generation is called the *sporophyte* because it produces spores. The spores are haploid, and they divide to become the haploid generation, which is called the *gametophyte* because it produces gametes. In flowering plants, the diploid sporophyte is said to be dominant. It is larger, longer lasting, and the generation we generally recognize as the plant. This is the generation that flowers (fig. 34.1).

A flower produces two types of spores, microspores and megaspores. A **microspore** [Gk. *micr,* small, and *spor,* seed] develops into a microgametophyte; **megaspore** develops into a megagametophyte. The microgametophyte is the pollen grain, which is either windblown or carried by an animal to the vicinity of the megagametophtye. When a pollen grain matures, it contains nonflagellated sperm cells, which travel by way of a pollen tube to the megagametophyte, which is called an embryo sac. Once a sperm fertilizes an egg in the embryo sac, the life cycle begins again.

Notice that the sporophyte is dominant in flowering plants. It is the generation that contains vascular tissue and has other adaptations suitable to living on land. The life cycle of a flowering plant is also adapted to a land existence. The gametophytes which produce the gametes are microscopic and dependent upon the sporophyte. Since the microgametophyte (pollen grain) is transported to the megagametophtye by wind or an animal, water is not needed for transport. The pollen tube carries a sperm to an egg, and again no outside water is needed. (This may be compared to the manner in which fertilization is accomplished in human beings. At the time of sexual intercourse, the penis deposits sperm into the vagina of the female.) Following fertilization, the diploid zygote develops into an embryo protected within a seed enclosed by a fruit.

Unlike flowering plants, some plants produce only one kind of spore and this develops into a separate, but water-dependent, gametophyte. The evolution of two separate and dependent gametophytes in flowering plants led to the production of pollen and a means to carry on pollination and fertilization without need of external water.

> Flowering plants undergo an alternation of generations life cycle that is modified in such a way that a sperm does not require an outside source of water to reach an egg.

A Flower Is a Sporophyte Structure

A **flower,** the reproductive structure of angiosperms, develops within a bud. In many plants, the same shoot apical meristem that previously formed leaves suddenly stops producing leaves and starts producing a flower. In other plants, axillary buds develop directly into flowers. Flower structures are modified leaves attached to a short stem tip called a *receptacle* (fig. 34.2). In monocots, flower parts occur in threes and multiples of three. In dicots, flower parts are in fours or fives and multiples of four or five. The **sepals,** which are the most leaflike of all the flower parts, are usually green, and they protect the bud as the flower develops within. When the flower opens, there is an outer whorl of sepals and an inner whorl of **petals,** whose color accounts for the attractiveness of many flowers. The size, the shape, and the color of a flower are attractive to a specific pollinator. Wind-pollinated flowers often have no petals at all.

At the very center of a flower is the **pistil** [L. *pistill,* pestle], which is often vaselike in appearance. A pistil may be simple or compound. A simple pistil contains a single reproductive unit called a **carpel** [Gk. *carpus,* fruit]. A carpel usually has three parts: the **stigma,** an enlarged sticky knob, the **style,** a slender stalk, and the **ovary,** an enlarged base. A compound pistil has multiple carpels, which are often fused:

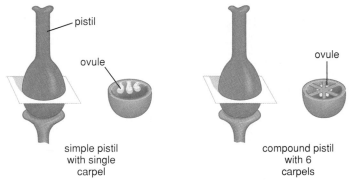

simple pistil
with single
carpel

compound pistil
with 6
carpels

The ovary of a pistil contains a number of **ovules** [L. *ovul,* little egg], which play a significant role in the production of megaspores and therefore megagametophytes. Grouped about the pistil are a number of **stamens,** each of which has two parts: the **anther,** a saclike container, and the **filament** [L. *fil,* thread], a slender stalk. Pollen grains develop in the anther.

Not all flowers have sepals, petals, stamens, and a pistil. Those that do are said to be complete and those that do not are said to be incomplete. Flowers that have both stamens and a pistil are called perfect flowers: those with only stamens are staminate flowers and those with only pistils are pistillate flowers. If staminate flowers and pistillate flowers are on one plant, as in corn, the plant is monoecious [Gk. *monos,* single, and *oikos,* house]. If staminate and pistillate flowers are on separate plants, the plant is dioecious. Holly trees are dioecious and, if red berries are a priority, it is necessary to acquire a plant with staminate flowers and another with pistillate flowers.

Sometimes the pistil is called the female part of the flower and the stamens are called the male part of the flower, but this is not strictly correct. The pistil and stamens do not produce gametes; they produce megaspores and microspores, respectively. A microspore matures into a microgametophyte, which produces sperm, and a megaspore matures into a megagametophyte, which produces an egg.

> **A flower contains four basic parts: sepals, petals, stamens, and a pistil.**

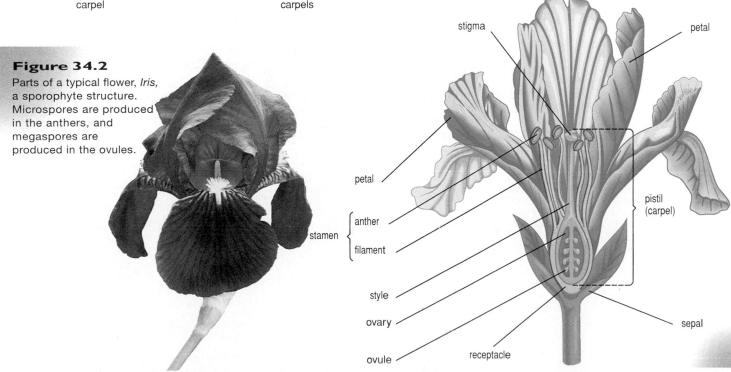

Figure 34.2
Parts of a typical flower, *Iris,* a sporophyte structure. Microspores are produced in the anthers, and megaspores are produced in the ovules.

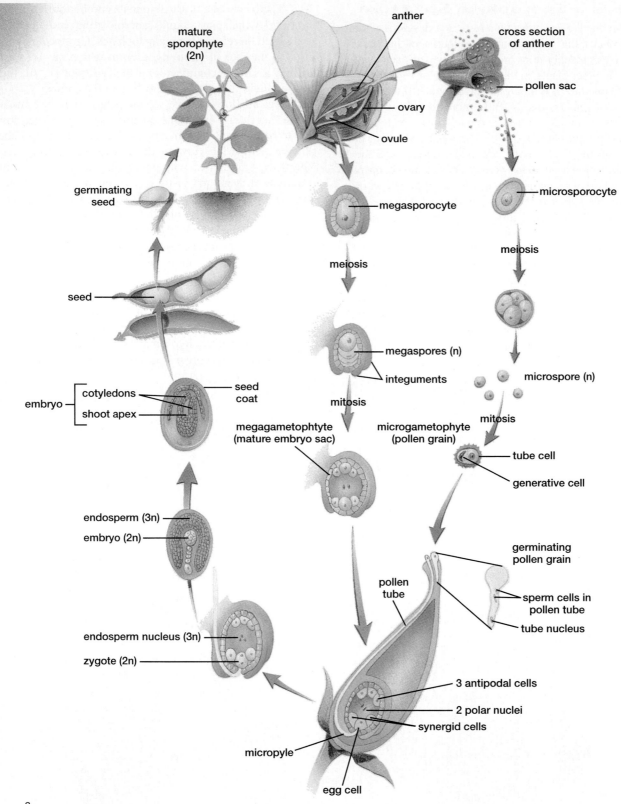

anther

cross section of anther

mature
sporophyte
(2n)

pollen sac

ovary

ovule

germinating
seed

microsporocyte

megasporocyte

meiosis

seed

meiosis

megaspores (n)

integuments

microspore (n)

embryo

cotyledons

shoot apex

seed
coat

mitosis

megagametophtyte
(mature embryo sac)

microgametophyte
(pollen grain)

mitosis

tube cell

generative cell

endosperm (3n)

embryo (2n)

germinating
pollen grain

pollen
tube

sperm cells in
pollen tube

tube nucleus

endosperm nucleus (3n)

zygote (2n)

3 antipodal cells

2 polar nuclei

synergid cells

micropyle

egg cell

a.

Figure 34.3

Life cycle of a flowering plant (in detail). **a.** An ovary in the carpel contains an ovule where a megasporocyte produces a megaspore by meiosis. A megaspore develops into an embryo sac containing seven cells, one of which is an egg. A pollen sac in the anther contains microsporocytes, which produce microspores by meiosis. A microspore develops into a pollen grain which contains sperm cells by the time it germinates. The sperm cells travel down a pollen tube; one sperm fertilizes the egg to form a diploid zygote and the other fuses with the polar nuclei of the central cell to form a triploid endosperm nucleus. A seed contains the developing embryo plus stored food. Germination and growth of a seed results in a new sporophyte plant. **b.** Flow diagram.

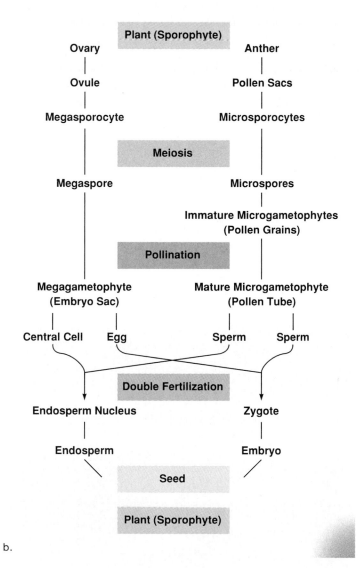

b.

The Gametophytes Are Separate

The ovary of a carpel contains one or more ovules (fig. 34.3*a*, middle). Ovules have a central mass of parenchyma cells almost completely covered by integuments except where there is an opening, the micropyle. One parenchyma cell enlarges to become a **megasporocyte** (megaspore mother cell) which undergoes meiosis, producing four haploid megaspores. Three of these disintegrate, leaving one functional megaspore, whose nucleus divides mitotically until there are eight nuclei of the embryo sac or **megagametophyte** [Gk. *mega*, large, *gamet*, wife, and *phyt*, plant]. When cell walls form later there are seven cells, one of which is binucleate. The megagametophyte called the **embryo sac** consists of these seven cells:

> one egg cell associated with
> two synergid cells
> one central cell with two polar nuclei
> three antipodal cells

Microgametophytes are produced in the stamens (fig. 34.3*a*, far right). An anther has four pollen sacs, each containing many **microsporocytes** (microspore mother cells). A microsporocyte undergoes meiosis to produce four haploid microspores. A microspore divides mitotically, forming two cells enclosed by a finely sculptured wall. This structure, called the **pollen grain,** is the immature **microgametophyte** [Gk. *micr*, small, *gamet*, husband, and *phyt*, plant] and contains a *tube cell* and a *generative cell*. Either now or later, the generative cell divides mitotically to produce two sperm cells. The walls separating the pollen sacs in the anther break down when the pollen grains are ready to be released.

Look back at figure 34.1 and realize that the sporophyte, the flowering diploid generation, has now produced a haploid megaspore and haploid microspores. The megaspore has developed into an embryo sac, the egg-producing megagametophyte generation. Each microspore has developed into a pollen grain, the sperm-producing microgametophyte generation. The haploid generation in flowering plants is represented by the megagametophyte and the microgametophyte, which are microscopic. The megagametophyte is retained within the body of the sporophyte. As discussed in the reading on pages 590–91, microgametophytes (pollen grains) are windblown or carried by various kinds of animals to the stigma of a pistil.

> In flowering plants, the megagametophyte within the ovule produces an egg. The microgametophyte (pollen grain) produces two sperm.

Plants and Their Pollinators

A plant and its pollinator(s) are adapted to one another. They have a mutualistic relationship in which each benefits—the plant uses its pollinator to ensure that cross-pollination takes place, and the pollinator uses the plant as a source of food. This mutualistic relationship came about through the process of coevolution; that is, the codependency of the plant and the pollinator is the result of suitable changes in structure and function in each. The evidence for coevolution is observational. For example, floral coloring and odor are suited to the sense perceptions of the pollinator, the mouthparts of the pollinator are suited to the structure of the flower, the type of food provided is suited to the nutritional needs of the pollinator, and the pollinator forages at the time of day that specific plants are open. The following are examples of such coevolution.

Bee-Pollinated Flowers

There are now 20,000 different species of bees that pollinate flowers. The best-known pollinators are the honeybees (fig. 34Aa). Bee eyes see a spectrum of light that is different from the spectrum seen by humans. The bee's visible spectrum is shifted so that they do not see red wavelengths but do see ultraviolet wavelengths. Bee-pollinated flowers are usually brightly colored and are predominantly blue or yellow; they are not entirely red. They may also have ultraviolet shadings called honey guides, which highlight the portion of the flower that contains the reproductive structures. The mouthparts of bees are fused into a long tube that contains a tongue. This tube is an adaptation for sucking up nectar provided by the plant, usually at the base of the flower.

Bee flowers are delicately sweet and fragrant to advertise that nectar is present. The honey guides often point to a narrow floral tube large enough for the bee's feeding apparatus but too small for other insects to reach the nectar. Bees also collect pollen as food for their larvae. Pollen clings to the hairy body of a bee, and the bees also gather it by means of bristles on their legs. They then store the pollen in pollen baskets on the third pair of legs. Bee-pollinated flowers are sturdy and irregular in shape because they often have a landing platform where the bee can alight. The landing platform requires the bee to brush up against the anther and stigma as it moves toward the floral tube to feed. One type of orchid, *Ophrys,* has evolved a unique adaptation. The flower resembles a female bee, and when the male of that species attempts to copulate with the flower, the bee receives pollen.

Figure 34A

Flowers have adaptations that make them attractive to their pollinators. **a.** A bee-pollinated flower is a color other than red (bees cannot detect this color) and has a landing platform where the reproductive structures of the flower brush up against the bee's body. **b.** A butterfly-pollinated flower is often a composite, containing many individual flowers. The broad expanse provides room for the butterfly to land, after which it lowers its proboscis into each flower in turn. **c.** Hummingbird-pollinated flowers are curved back, allowing the bird to insert its beak to reach the rich supply of nectar. While doing this, the bird's forehead and other body parts touch the reproductive structures. **d.** Bat-pollinated flowers are large, sturdy flowers that can take rough treatment. Here the head of the bat is positioned so that its bristly tongue can lap up nectar.

a.

b.

Moth- and Butterfly-Pollinated Flowers

Contrasting moth- and butterfly-pollinated flowers emphasizes the close adaptation between pollinator and flower. Both moths and butterflies have a long, thin, hollow proboscis, but they differ in other characteristics. Moths usually feed at night and have a well-developed sense of smell. The flowers they visit are visible at night because they are lightly shaded (white, pale yellow, or pink), and they have strong, sweet perfume, which helps attract moths. Moths hover when they feed, and their flowers have deep tubes with open margins that allow the hovering moths to reach the nectar with their long proboscis. Butterflies are active in the daytime and have good vision but a weak sense of smell. Their flowers have bright colors—even red because butterflies can see the color red—but the flowers tend to be odorless. Unable to hover, butterflies need a place to land. Flowers that are visited by butterflies often have flat landing platforms (fig. 34A*b*). The flowers also tend to be composites, with many individual flowers clustered in a head. Each flower has a long, slender floral tube, accessible to the long, thin butterfly proboscis.

Bird- and Bat-Pollinated Flowers

In North America, the most well-known bird pollinators are the hummingbirds. These tiny animals have good eyesight but do not have a well-developed sense of smell. Like moths, they hover when they feed. Typical flowers pollinated by hummingbirds are red, with a slender floral tube and margins that are curved back and out of the way. And although they produce copious amounts of nectar, the flowers have little odor. As a hummingbird feeds on nectar with its long, thin beak, its head comes into contact with the stamens and pistil (fig. 34A*c*).

Bats are adapted to gathering food in various ways, including feeding on the nectar and pollen of plants. Bats are nocturnal and have an acute sense of smell. Those that are pollinators also have keen vision and a long, extensible, bristly tongue. Typically, bat-pollinated flowers open only at night and are light-colored or white. They have a strong, musty smell similar to the odor that bats produce to attract one another. The flowers are generally large and sturdy and are able to hold up when a bat inserts part of its head to reach the nectar. While the bat is at the flower, its head is dusted with pollen (fig. 34A*d*).

Coevolution

These examples are evidence of coevolution, but how did coevolution come about? Some 200 million years ago, when seed plants were just beginning to evolve and insects were not as diverse as they are today, wind alone was used to carry pollen. Wind pollination, however, is a hit-or-miss affair. Perhaps beetles feeding on vegetative leaves were the first insects to carry pollen directly from plant to plant by chance. This use of animal motility to achieve cross-fertilization no doubt resulted in the evolution of flowers, which have features, such as the production of nectar, to attract pollinators. Then, if beetles developed the habit of feeding on flowers, other features, such as the protection of ovules within ovaries, may have evolved.

As cross-fertilization continued, more and more flower variations likely developed, and pollinators became increasingly adapted to specific angiosperm species. Today, there are some 235,000 species of flowering plants and over 700,000 species of insects. This diversity suggests that the success of angiosperms has contributed to the success of insects, and vice versa.

c.

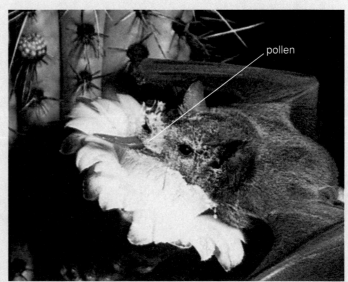

pollen

d.

Pollination Precedes Fertilization

Pollination and fertilization are two separate events. **Pollination** is simply the transfer of pollen (fig. 34.4) from the anther to the stigma of a pistil. **Fertilization** [L. *fertil,* fruitful] is the fusion of nuclei, as when the sperm nucleus and the egg nucleus fuse.

Pollination Transfers Pollen

As mentioned previously, pollination is brought about by the wind or with the assistance of a particular pollinator. Self-pollination occurs if the pollen is from the same plant, and cross-pollination occurs if the pollen is from a different plant. Cross-pollination is preferred because it fosters genetic recombination resulting in new and varied plants.

Fertilization Is Double

When a pollen grain lands on the stigma of the same species, it germinates, forming a pollen tube (fig. 34.5). The germinated pollen grain, containing a tube cell and two sperm cells, is the mature microgametophyte. As it grows, the pollen tube passes between the cells of the stigma and the style to reach the micropyle of the ovule. Now *double fertilization* occurs. One sperm nucleus unites with the egg nucleus, forming a 2n zygote, and the other sperm nucleus migrates and unites with the polar nuclei of the central cell, forming a 3n endosperm nucleus. The zygote divides mitotically to become the **embryo,** a young sporophyte, and the endosperm nucleus divides mitotically to become the endosperm. **Endosperm** [Gk. *endo,* within, and *sperm,* seed] is the tissue that will nourish the embryo and seedling as they undergo development.

> Flowering plants practice double fertilization. One sperm nucleus unites with the egg nucleus, producing a zygote, and the other unites with the polar nuclei, forming a 3n endosperm cell.

Figure 34.4

Development of pollen grains. **a.** A mature anther showing that the walls between the pollen sacs have opened, allowing the pollen grains to be released. **b.** Germinating pollen grains of *goosegrass, Galium aparine,* are colored yellow in this false-colored scanning electron micrograph.

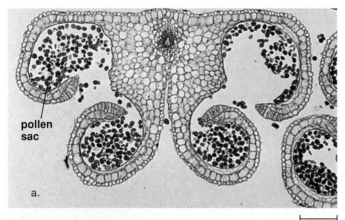

pollen sac

a.

100 µm

b.

100 µm

Figure 34.5

Fertilization. **a.** The pollen tube grows down the style carrying with it two sperm cells. The pollen tube grows through the micropyle and releases both sperm. **b.** One of these migrates to the egg; this sperm nucleus fuses with the egg nucleus, forming a zygote. The second sperm migrates into the central cell; this sperm nucleus fuses with the polar nuclei, forming a large triploid endosperm nucleus within a central cell.

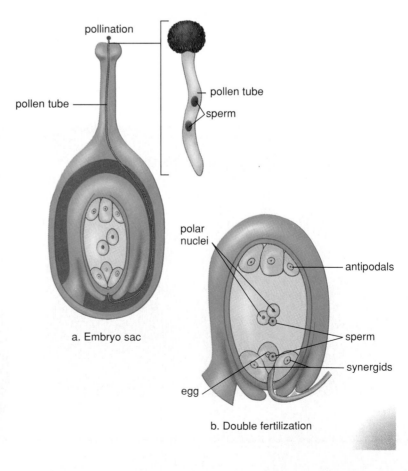

pollination

pollen tube

pollen tube

sperm

a. Embryo sac

polar nuclei

antipodals

sperm

synergids

egg

b. Double fertilization

THE EMBRYO DEVELOPS IN STAGES

Stages in the development of a dicot embryo are shown in figure 34.6. After double fertilization has taken place, the single-celled zygote lies beneath the endosperm nucleus. The endosperm nucleus divides to produce a mass of endosperm tissue surrounding the embryo. The zygote also divides, forming two parts: the upper part is the embryo, and the lower part is the suspensor, which anchors the embryo and transfers nutrients to it from the sporophyte plant. Soon the **cotyledons** [Gk. *cotyl,* cup-shaped cavity], or seed leaves, can be seen. At this point, the dicot embryo is heart-shaped. Later, when it becomes torpedo-shaped, it is possible to distinguish the shoot apex and the root apex. These contain apical meristems, the tissues that bring about primary growth in a plant; the shoot apical meristem is responsible for aboveground growth, and the root apical meristem is responsible for underground growth.

Monocots, unlike dicots, have only one cotyledon. Another important difference between monocots and dicots is the manner in which nutrient molecules are stored in the seed. In a monocot, the cotyledon rarely stores food; rather, it absorbs food molecules from the endosperm and passes them to the embryo. During the development of a dicot embryo, the cotyledons usually store the nutrient molecules that the embryo uses. Therefore, in figure 34.6 we can see that the endosperm seemingly disappears. Actually, it has been taken up by the two cotyledons. In a plant embryo, the epicotyl is above the cotyledon and contributes to shoot development; the hypocotyl is that portion below the cotyledon that contributes to stem development; and the radicle contributes to root development. The embryo plus stored food is now contained within a seed.

> The plant embryo (which has gone through a set series of stages), plus its stored food, is contained within a seed.

Figure 34.6

Stages in the development of a dicot embryo. **a.** The single-celled zygote lies beneath the endosperm nucleus. **b, c.** The endosperm is a mass of tissue surrounding the embryo. The embryo is located above the suspensor. **d.** The embryo becomes heart-shaped as the cotyledons begin to appear. **e.** There is progressively less endosperm as the embryo differentiates and enlarges. As the cotyledons bend, the embryo takes on a torpedo shape. **f.** The embryo consists of the epicotyl (represented here by the shoot apex), the hypocotyl, and the radicle (the latter of which contains the root apex).

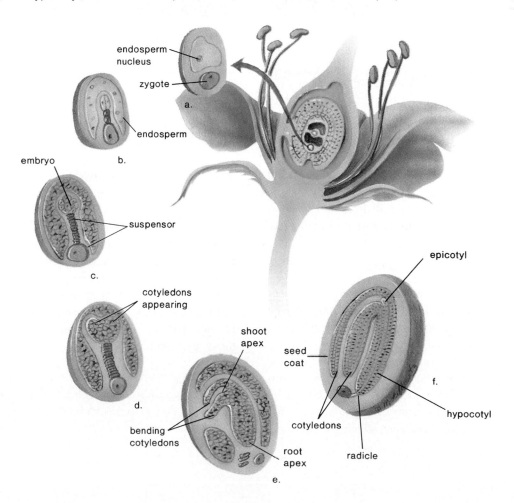

Figure 34.7

Fruit diversity. **a.** The almond, *Prunus*, fruit is fleshy, with a single seed enclosed by a hard covering. **b.** The tomato, *Lycopersicon*, is derived from a compound ovary. **c.** Dry fruit of the pea, *Pisum*, plant develops from a simple ovary. **d.** Blackberry, *Rubus*, flowers contain several separate ovaries; each cluster is a berry from a single flower.

a.   Almond, *Prunus*

one portion
of ovary

b.   Tomato, *Lycopersicon*

THE SEEDS ARE ENCLOSED BY FRUIT

As the zygote develops into an embryo, the integuments of the ovule harden and become the seed coat. A **seed** is a structure formed by the maturation of the ovule; it contains a sporophyte embryo plus stored food. The ovary, and sometimes other floral parts, develops into a fruit. Although peas and beans in their shell, tomatoes, and cucumbers are commonly called vegetables, botanists categorize them as fruits. A **fruit** is a mature ovary that usually contains seeds.

Fruits Are Varied

As fruit develops from an ovary, the ovary wall thickens to become the *pericarp*. Most fruits are *simple fruits;* they are derived from an individual ovary, either simple or compound. In simple fleshy fruits, the pericarp is at least somewhat fleshy. Peaches and plums are good examples of simple fleshy fruits. In almonds, the fleshy part of the pericarp is a husk removed before marketing. We crack the remaining portion of the pericarp to obtain the seed (fig. 34.7*a*). An apple develops from a compound ovary, but much of the flesh comes from the receptacle, which grows around the ovary. It's more obvious that a tomato comes from a compound ovary, because in cross section, you can see several seed-filled cavities (fig. 34.7*b*).

Dry fruits have a dry pericarp (table 34.1). Legumes, such as peas (fig. 34.7*c*) and beans, produce a fruit that splits along two sides, or seams. Not all dry fruits split at maturity. The pericarp of a grain is tightly fused to the seed and cannot be separated from it. A corn kernel is actually a grain, as are the fruits of wheat, rice, and barley plants.

Some fruits are compound fruits; they develop from several individual ovaries. A blackberry is an aggregate fruit in which each berry is derived from a separate ovary of a single flower (fig. 34.7*d*). The strawberry is also an aggregate fruit, but each ovary becomes a one-seeded fruit called an achene. The flesh of a strawberry is from the receptacle. In contrast, a pineapple comes from the fruit of many individual flowers attached to the same fleshy stalk. As the ovaries mature, they fuse to form a large, multiple fruit.

In flowering plants, the seed develops from the ovule and the fruit develops from the ovary.

developing
fruit

seed

c.   Pea, *Pisum*

many ovaries

d.   Blackberry, *Rubus*

Table 34.1

Kinds of Fruit

Name	Description	Example
Simple Fruits	*Develop from an individual ovary*	
Fleshy	Pericarp is usually fleshy	
Drupe	From simple ovary with one seed (pit) and soft "skin"	Peach, plum, olive
Berry	From compound ovary with many seeds	Grape, tomato
Pome	From compound ovary; flesh is from accessory flower parts	Apple, pear
Dry	Pericarp is dry	
Follicle	From simple ovary that splits open down one side	Milkweed, peony
Legume	From simple ovary that splits open down both sides	Pea, bean, lentil
Capsule	From compound ovary with capsules that split in various ways	Poppy
Achene	From simple ovary with one-seeded small fruit; pericarp easily removed	Sunflower
Nut	From simple ovary with one-seeded fruit; hard pericarp	Acorn, hickory nut, chestnut
Grain	From simple ovary with one-seeded small fruit; pericarp completely united with seed coat	Rice, oat, barley
Compound Fruits	*Develop from a group of individual ovaries*	
Aggregate fruits	Ovaries are from a single flower	Blackberry, raspberry, strawberry
Multiple fruits	Ovaries are from separate flowers clustered together	Pineapple

How Seeds Disperse and Germinate

For plants to be widely distributed, their seeds have to be dispersed—that is, distributed preferably long distances from the parent plant. Following dispersal, the seeds germinate: they begin to grow so that a seedling appears.

Dispersal Requires Help

Plants have various means to ensure that dispersal takes place. The hooks and spines of clover, bur, and cocklebur attach to the fur of animals and the clothing of humans. Birds and mammals sometimes eat fruits, including the seeds, which are then defecated (passed out of the digestive tract with the feces) some distance from the parent plant. Squirrels and other animals gather seeds and fruits, which they bury some distance away.

The fruit of the coconut palm, which can be dispersed by ocean currents, may land many hundreds of kilometers away from the parent plant. Some plants have fruits with trapped air or seeds with inflated sacs that help them float in water. Many seeds are dispersed by wind. Woolly hairs, plumes, and wings are all adaptations for this type of dispersal. The seeds of an orchid are so small and light that they need no special adapta-

tion to carry them far away. The somewhat heavier dandelion fruit uses a tiny "parachute" for dispersal. The winged fruit of a maple tree, which contains two seeds, has been known to travel up to 10 km from its parent. A touch-me-not plant has seed pods that swell as they mature. When the pods finally burst, the ripe seeds are hurled out.

> Animals, water, and wind help plants disperse their seeds.

Germination of Seeds

Some seeds do not **germinate** until they have been dormant for a period of time. For seeds, *dormancy* is the time during which no growth occurs, even though conditions may be favorable for growth. In the temperate zone, seeds often have to be exposed to a period of cold weather before dormancy is broken. In deserts, germination does not occur until there is adequate moisture. This requirement helps ensure that seeds do not germinate until the most favorable growing season has arrived. Germination—an

Figure 34.8
Common garden bean. **a.** Seed structure. **b.** Germination and development of the seedling.

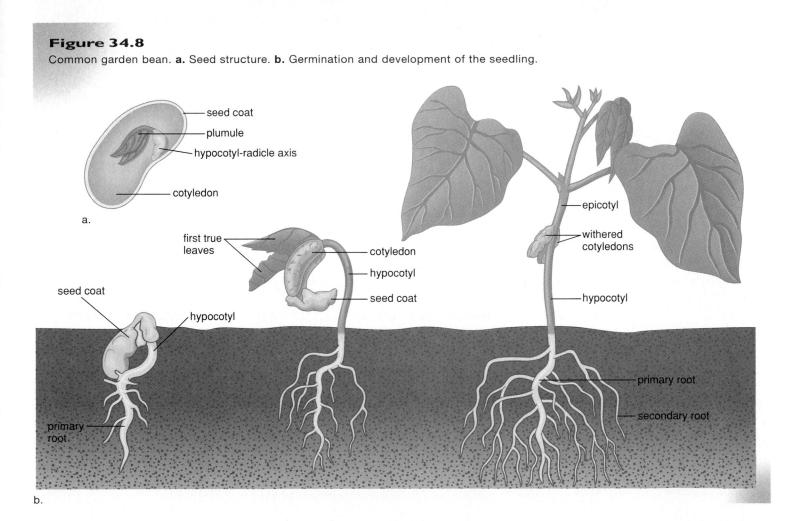

event that takes place if there is sufficient water, warmth, and oxygen to sustain growth—requires regulation, and both inhibitors and stimulators are known to exist. It is known that fleshy fruits (e.g., apples, pears, oranges, and tomatoes) contain inhibitors so that germination does not occur until the seeds are removed and washed. In contrast, stimulators are present in the seeds of some temperate zone woody plants. Mechanical action may also be required. Water, bacterial action, and even fire can act on the seed coat, allowing it to become permeable to water. The uptake of water causes the seed coat to burst.

Germination in Dicots and Monocots

As mentioned, the embryo of a dicot, such as a bean plant, has two seed leaves, called cotyledons. The cotyledons, which supply nutrients to the embryo and seedling, eventually shrivel and disappear. If the two cotyledons of a bean seed are parted, you can see a rudimentary plant (fig. 34.8). The epicotyl bears young leaves and is called a **plumule** [L. *plum,* feather]. As the dicot seedling emerges from the soil, the shoot is hook-shaped to protect the delicate plumule. The hypocotyl becomes the stem and the radicle develops into the roots. When a seed germinates

in darkness, it etiolates—the stem is elongated, the roots and leaves are small, and the plant lacks color and appears spindly. Phytochrome, a pigment that is sensitive to red and far-red light, regulates this response and induces normal growth once proper lighting is available.

A corn plant is a monocot that contains a single cotyledon. Actually, the endosperm is the food-storage tissue in monocots and the cotyledon does not have a storage role. Corn kernels are actually fruits, and therefore the outer covering is the pericarp (fig. 34.9). The plumule and radicle are enclosed in protective sheaths called the coleoptile and the coleorhiza, respectively. The plumule and the radicle burst through these coverings when germination occurs.

Germination is a complex event regulated by many factors. The embryo breaks out of the seed coat and becomes a seedling with leaves, stem, and roots.

Figure 34.9

Corn. **a.** Grain structure. **b.** Germination and development of the seedling.

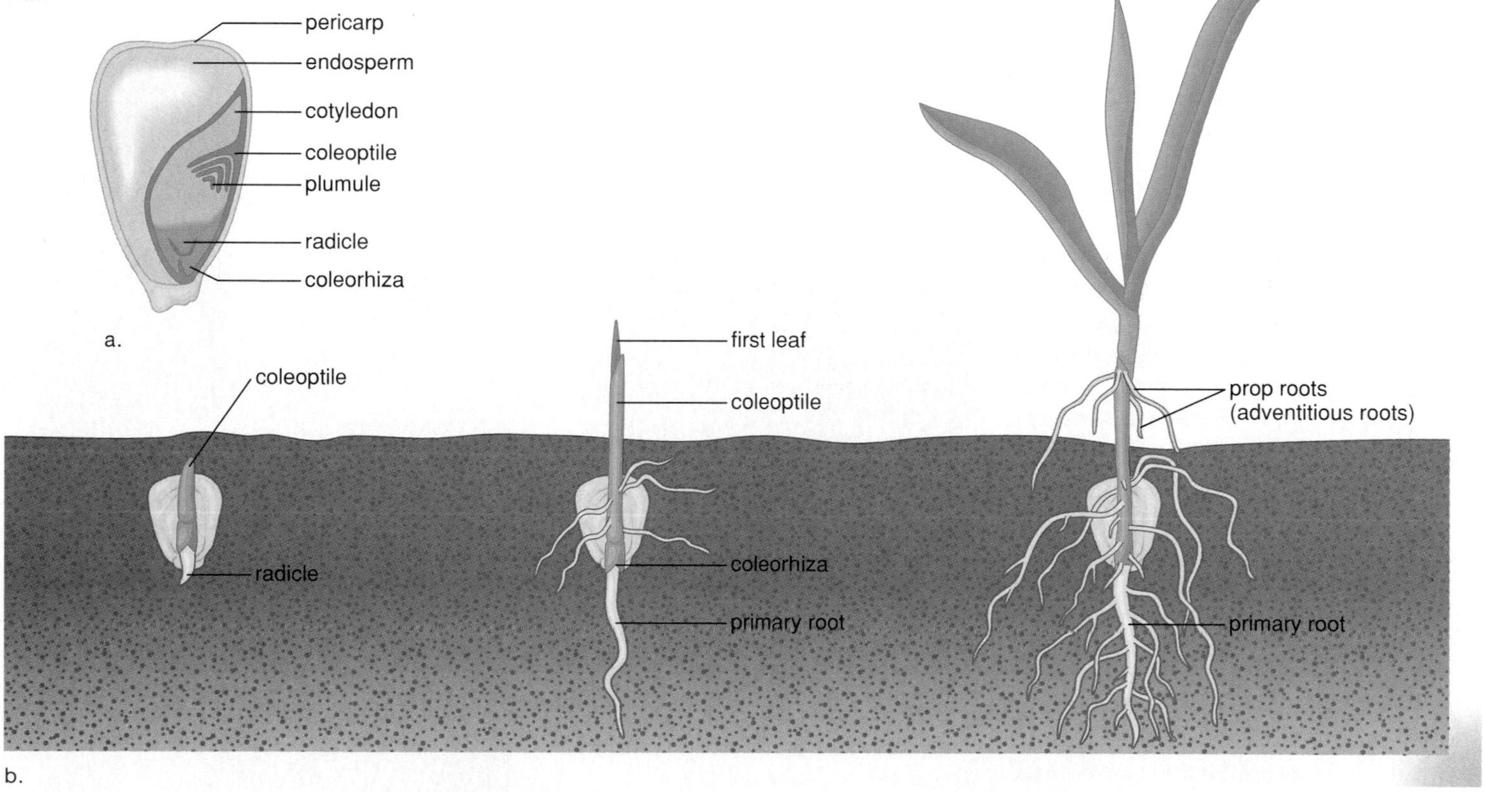

Economic Importance of Plants

Stop a minute to think about how important plants are in everyday life. Essentially everywhere you look, the many materials you use are directly produced from plants or their production was modeled after a plant product.

We derive most of our sustenance from three plants: wheat, corn, and rice. All three of these plants are of the grass family and are collectively, along with other species, called grains. Most of the earth's 5.6 billion people live a simple way of life, growing their food on family plots. The continued growth of these plants is essential to human existence. A virus or other disease could hit any one of these three plants and could cause massive loss of life from starvation.

Corn, wheat, and rice originated and were first cultivated in different parts of the globe. Corn, or what is properly called maize, was first cultivated in Central America about 7,000 years ago. Disagreement still exists as to exactly what the wild plant looks like and where it originally grew. A most recent theory is that maize was developed from a plant called teosinte, which grows in the highlands of central Mexico. By the time Europeans were exploring Central America, over 300 varieties were already in existence—growing from Canada to Chile. We now commonly grow six major varieties of corn: sweet, pop, flour, dent, pod, and flint. Rice has its origin in southeastern Asia several thousand years ago, where it grew in swamps. Today we are familiar with white and brown rice which differ in the extent of processing. The initially harvested rice is thrashed to remove the hulls, creating brown rice. After polishing to remove the seed coat and embryo, the starchy, endosperm, or white rice, is left. Unfortunately, it is the seed coat and embryo that contain the greatest nutritional value. Today rice is grown throughout the tropics and subtropics where water is abundant. Wheat is commonly used in the United States to produce flour and bread. It was first cultivated in the Near East (Iran, Iraq, and neighboring countries) about 8,000 B.C.; hence, it is thought to be one of the earliest cultivated plants. Wheat was brought to North America in 1520 with early settlers; now the United States is one of the world's largest producers of wheat.

Many of us have an "addiction" to sugar. This nifty carbohydrate comes almost exclusively from two plants—sugarcane (grown in South America, Africa, Asia, and the Caribbean) and sugar beets (grown mostly in Europe). Each provides about 50% of the world's sugar.

Numerous other foods are bland or tasteless without spices. In the Middle Ages, wealthy Europeans spared no cost to obtain spices from the Near and Far East. In the fifteenth and sixteenth centuries, major expeditions were launched in an attempt to find better and cheaper routes for spice importation. The queen of Portugal became convinced that Columbus would actually find a shorter route to the Far East by traveling west by ocean rather than east by land. Columbus's idea was sound, but he encountered a little barrier, the New World. This later provided Europe with a wealth of new crops, including corn, potatoes, peppers, and tobacco.

Our most popular drinks—coffee, tea, and cola—also come from plants. Coffee has its origin in Ethiopia, where it was first used (along with animal fat) during long trips for sustenance and to relieve fatigue. Coffee as a drink was not developed until the thirteenth century in Arabia and Turkey, and it did not catch on in Europe until the seventeenth century. Tea is thought to have been developed somewhere in central Asia. Its earlier uses were almost exclusively medicinal, especially among the Chinese. The drink as we now know, was not developed until the fourth century. By the mid-seventeenth century it became popular in Europe. Cola is a common ingredient in tropical drinks and was used around the turn of the century, along with the drug coca (used to make cocaine), in the "original" Coca-Cola.

Until a few decades ago cotton and other natural fibers were our only source of clothing. China is now the largest producer of cotton. Over thirty species of native cotton grow around the world. In the United States, cotton grows as an annual, but in the tropics shrubs over six feet tall are not uncommon. The cotton fiber

Figure 34B
These cereal grains are the principle source of calories and protein for our civilization.

itself comes from hair that grows on the seed. In sixteenth-century Europe, cotton was a little understood fiber known only from stories brought back from Asia. Columbus and other explorers were amazed to see the elaborately woven cotton fabrics in the New World. But by 1800 Liverpool was the world's center of cotton trade. Interestingly, when Levi Strauss wanted to make a tough pair of jeans, he needed a stronger fiber than cotton, so he used hemp. No longer used for clothes, hemp (marijuana) is now known primarily as a hallucinogenic drug.

Rubber is another plant that has many uses today. The product had its origins in Brazil from the thick, white sap of the rubber tree. Once collected, the sap is placed in a large vat where acid is added to coagulate the latex. When the water is pressed out, the product is formed into sheets or crumbled and placed into bales. Much stronger rubber, such as that in tires, was made by adding sulfur and heating in a process called vulcanization; this produces a flexible material less sensitive to temperature changes. Today though, much rubber is synthetically produced.

Beyond these uses, plants have been used for centuries for a number of important household items, including the house itself. We are most familiar with lumber being used as the major structural portion in buildings. This wood comes mostly from a variety of trees: pine, fir, and spruce, among others. In the tropics, trees and even herbs provide important components for houses. In Central and South America, palm leaves are preferable to tin for roofs, since they last as long as ten years and are quieter during a rain storm. In the Near East, numerous houses along rivers are made entirely of reeds.

An actively researched area of plant use today is that of medicinal plants. Currently about 50% of all pharmaceutical drugs have their origin from plants. The treatment of cancers and AIDS appears to rest in the discovery of miracle plants. Indeed, the National Cancer Institute (NCI) and most pharmaceutical companies have spent millions (or, more likely, billions) of dollars to send botanists out to collect and test plant samples from around the world. Tribal medicine men, or shamen, of South America and Africa have already been of great importance in developing numerous drugs.

One of the most amazing stories is of the development of quinine to treat malaria. Over the centuries, malaria has caused far more human deaths than any other disease. Yet it was not until the 1630s that word of a cure reached Europe. The cure came from the bark of the cinchona tree, common to northeastern South America. In the 1940s a synthetic form of the drug was developed, chloroquine. By the late 1960s it was found that some of the malaria parasites, which live in red blood cells, had become resistant to the synthetically produced drug, especially in Africa. More recently, resistant parasites are showing up in Asia and the Amazon. Today the only 100% effective drug for malaria treatment must come directly from the cinchona tree.

Obviously numerous plant extracts continue to be misused for their hallucinogenic or other effects on the human body; coca for cocaine and crack, opium poppy for morphine, and yam for steroids.

In the end, however, who can neglect the simple beauty of plants in their natural setting? Shade trees are so inviting during the summer, ornamental plants accent an architectural setting, and flowers brighten any yard. We should remember, then, that plants are good for much, much more than producing oxygen for us to breathe.

a. dwarf fan palms, *Chamaerops,* can be used to make baskets

c. rubber, *Hevea,* is used to make tires

b. cotton, *Gossypium,* is used to make clothing

Figure 34C

Plants have various uses. **a.** Dwarf fan palms can be used to make baskets. **b.** Cotton becomes clothing worn by all. **c.** A rubber plant provides latex for making tires.

PLANTS CAN REPRODUCE ASEXUALLY

Because plants contain nondifferentiated meristem tissue, they routinely reproduce asexually by *vegetative propagation.* In asexual reproduction there is only one parent, instead of two as in sexual reproduction. Complete strawberry plants will grow from the nodes of stolons (aboveground horizontal stems) and violets will grow from the nodes of rhizomes (underground horizontal stems) (fig. 34.10). White potatoes are actually portions of underground stems, and each eye is a bud that will produce a new potato plant if it is planted with a portion of the swollen tuber. Sweet potatoes are modified roots; they can be propagated by planting sections of the root. You may have noticed that the roots of some fruit trees, such as cherry and apple trees, produce "suckers," small plants that can be used to grow new trees.

In addition to plants already mentioned, sugarcane, pineapple, cassava, and many ornamental plants have been propagated from stem cuttings for some time. In these plants, pieces of stem will automatically produce roots. The discovery that auxin will cause roots to develop has expanded the list of plants that can be propagated from stem cuttings.

Plants Propagate in Tissue Culture

Hydroponics, the growth of plants in aqueous solutions, had begun by the 1860s. This practice, along with the ability of plants to reproduce asexually, led the German botanist Gottleib Haberlandt to speculate in 1902 that entire plants could be produced by tissue culture. **Tissue culture** is the growth of a *tissue* in an artificial liquid *culture* medium. Haberlandt said that plant cells are **totipotent** [L. *tot,* all, and *poten,* powerful]—each cell has the full genetic potential of the organism—and therefore a single cell could become a complete plant. But it wasn't until 1958 that Cornell botanist F. C. Steward grew a complete carrot plant from a tiny piece of phloem (fig. 34.11). Like former investigators, he provided the cells with sugars, minerals, and vitamins, but he also added coconut milk. (Later, it was discovered that coconut milk contains the hormone cytokinin.) When the cultured cells began dividing they produced a *callus,* an undifferentiated group of cells. Then the callus differentiated into shoot and roots and developed into complete plants.

Hybridization [L. *hybrid,* mongrel], the crossing of different varieties of plants or even species, is routinely done to produce plants with desirable traits. Hybridization, followed by vegetative propagation of the mature plants, will generate a large number of identical plants with these traits. But tissue culture has led to *micropropagation,* a commercial method of producing thousands, even millions, of identical seedlings in a limited amount of space. One favorite method to accomplish micropropagation is by *meristem culture.* If the correct proportions of auxin and cytokinin are added to a liquid medium, many new shoots will develop from a single shoot apex. When these are removed, more shoots form. Since the shoots are genetically identical, the adult plants that develop from them, called *clonal plants,* all have the same traits. Another advantage to meristem culture is that meristem, unlike other portions of a plant, is virus-free; therefore the plants produced are also virus-free. (The presence of plant viruses weakens plants and makes them less productive.)

When flower meristem is used to clone plants, embryolike structures called *somatic embryos* form at the top of the callus.

Figure 34.10
Meristematic tissue at nodes can generate new plants, as when the "runners" of strawberry plants, *Fragaria,* give rise to new plants.

Somatic (asexually produced) embryos that are encapsulated in a protective hydrated gel (and sometimes called artificial seeds), can be shipped anywhere. It's possible to produce millions of somatic embryos at once in large tanks called bioreactors. This is done for certain vegetables like tomato, celery, and asparagus and for ornamental plants like lilies, begonias, and African violets. *Anther culture* is a new technique in which mature anthers are cultured in a medium containing vitamins and growth regulators. The haploid tube cells within the pollen grains divide, producing proembryos consisting of as many as twenty to forty cells. Finally the pollen grains rupture, releasing haploid embryos. The experimenter can now generate a haploid plant, or chemical agents can be added that encourage chromosomal doubling. After chromosomal doubling, the resulting plants are diploid but homozygous for all their alleles. Anther culture is a direct way to produce plants that express recessive alleles. If the recessive alleles govern desirable traits, the plants have these traits. In contrast to anther culture, it would probably take several generations of hybridized plants to bring out desirable recessive traits.

The culturing of leaf, stem, or root tissues has led to a technique called *cell suspension culture*. Rapidly growing calluses are cut into small pieces and shaken in a liquid nutrient medium so that single cells or small clumps of cells break off and form a suspension. These cells will produce the same chemicals as the entire plant. For example, cell suspension cultures of *Cinchona ledgeriana* produce quinine and those of *Digitalis lanata* produce digitoxin. Scientists envision that it will also be possible to maintain cell suspension cultures in bioreactors for the purpose of producing chemicals used in the production of drugs, cosmetics, and agricultural chemicals. If so, it will no longer be necessary to farm plants simply for the purpose of acquiring the chemicals they produce.

Figure 34.11

Cloning of entire carrot plants from tissue cells. **a.** Sections of carrot root are cored, and thin slices are placed in a liquid nutrient medium. **b.** After a few days, the cells form a nondifferentiated callus. **c.** After several weeks, the callus begins sprouting cloned carrot plants. **d.** Eventually the carrot plants can be moved from culture to medium to pots.

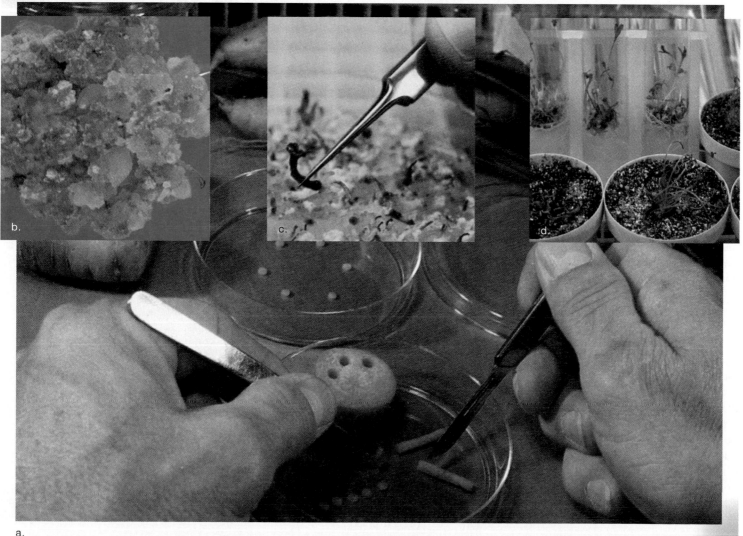

Figure 34.12

Plant protoplasts. **a.** When plant cell walls are removed by digestive enzyme action, the result is a naked cell, the protoplast. **b.** Photomicrograph of protoplasts. **c.** Protoplasts from two different species will sometimes fuse to produce hybrid plants. This pomato plant resulted from the fusion of a potato protoplast and a tomato protoplast. The white flowers are like those of a potato plant and the yellow flowers are like those of a tomato plant.

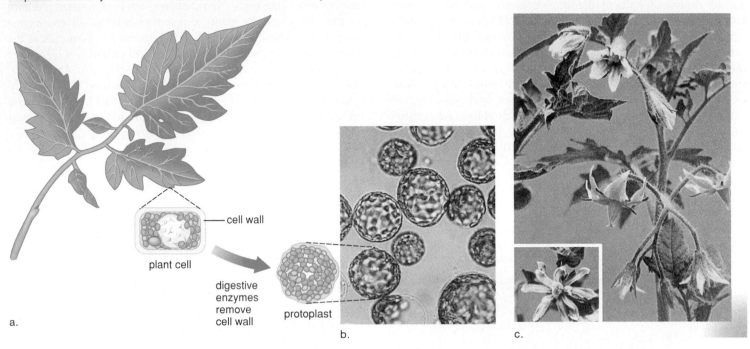

cell wall

plant cell

digestive
enzymes
remove
cell wall

protoplast

a.

b.

c.

Because plant cells are totipotent, it should be possible to grow an entire plant from a single cell. This, too, has been done. Enzymes are used to digest the cell walls of a small piece of tissue, usually mesophyll tissue, from a leaf, and the result is naked cells without walls, called **protoplasts** [Gk. *proto,* first, and *plast,* formed, molded] (fig. 34.12). The protoplasts regenerate a new cell wall and begin to divide. These clumps of cells can be manipulated to produce somatic embryos or entire plants. Plants generated from the somatic embryos vary somewhat because of mutations that arise during the production process. These so-called *somaclonal variation*s are another way to produce new plants with desirable traits.

Genetic Engineering of Plants

It is possible today to alter the genes of organisms so that they have new and different traits. *Transgenic plants* carry a foreign gene that has been introduced into their cells. Since a whole plant will grow from a protoplast, it is necessary only to place the foreign gene into a living protoplast. A foreign gene isolated from any other type organism is placed in the tissue culture medium. High-voltage electric pulses can then be used to create pores in the plasma membrane so that the DNA (deoxyribonucleic acid) enters. For example, after genes for the production of the firefly enzyme luciferase were inserted into tobacco protoplasts, the adult plants glowed when sprayed with the substrate luciferin (fig. 34.13).

Figure 34.13

Genetically engineered plant. This transgenic plant glows when sprayed with luciferin because its cells contain the protein luciferase, a firefly enzyme that acts on the chemical luciferin, which emits light.

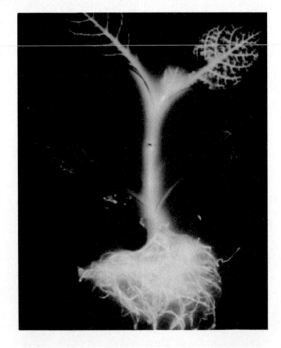

Figure 34.14

Transgenic crops. **a.** Herbicide-tolerant soybeans thrive despite being sprayed with the dame herbicide as nontolerant soybeans. **b.** potato plant which received a gene from *Bacillus thurigiensis* (B.t.) is protected from the Colorado potato beetle, whereas the control plant is not. **c.** Tomatos that have been engineered to resist the spoilage as seen in fruits that have not been improved. **d.** A list of crops that have been genetically engineered.

a.

b.

c.

d.

Genetically Engineered Plants

Cereals	Fiber Crops	Food Legumes and Oilseeds	Horticultural Crops		Pastures	Trees
Rice	Cotton	Flax	Carrot	Petunia	Alfalfa	Poplar
Corn		Canola	Cauliflower	Potato	White clover	Apple
Wheat		Soybean	Celery	Sugar beet	Orchard grass	Walnut
Barley		Sunflower	Cucumber	Tobacco		
Rye		Bean	Lettuce	Tomato		
		Pea	Melon			

Unfortunately, the regeneration of cereal grains from protoplasts has been difficult. Corn and wheat protoplasts produce infertile plants. As a result, other methods are used to introduce DNA into plant cells that still have their cell walls. In one technique, foreign DNA is inserted into the plasmid of the bacterium *Agrobacterium,* which normally infects plant cells. A plasmid, which is a circular fragment of DNA separated from the bacterial chromosome, can be used to produce recombinant DNA. Recombinant DNA contains genes from different sources, namely those of the plasmid and the foreign genes of interest. When the bacterium infects the plant cells, the plasmid and its DNA are introduced into the plant cells. In 1987, John C. Sanford and Theodore M. Klein of Cornell University developed another method of introducing DNA into intact plant cells. They constructed a device, called a *particle gun,* that bombards plant cells with DNA-coated microscopic metal particles. Many types of plant cells in tissue culture, including corn and wheat, have been genetically engineered using a particle gun. Later, adult plants are generated.

Various crops have been engineered to be resistant to viral infections, insect predation, and herbicides that are judged to be environmentally safe (fig. 34.14). If crops are resistant to a broad-spectrum herbicide and weeds are not, then the herbicide can be used to kill the weeds. The hope is that in the future it will be possible to produce plants that have a higher protein content and that require less water and fertilizer.

> The ability of plants to reproduce asexually has led to the generation of plants in tissue culture. This, in turn, has promoted the genetic engineering of plants.

1. Flowering plants produce flowers and often have a mutualistic relationship with an animal pollinator. They also produce seeds that are covered by fruits.

2. Flowering plants exhibit an alternation of generations life cycle that includes the microgametophyte and megagametophyte. The pollen grain is the microgametophyte. The megagametophyte is called the embryo sac, and it remains within the body of the sporophyte plant.

3. Typical parts of a flower are: sepals, which are usually green in color and form an outer whorl; petals, often colored, which form an inner whorl; the pistil, which is in the center and contains the carpels, each consisting of stigma, style, and ovary; and the stamens, each having a filament and anther, which are around the base of the carpels. The ovary contains ovules.

4. Each ovule within the ovary contains a megasporocyte, which divides meiotically to produce four haploid megaspores, only one of which survives. This megaspore divides mitotically to produce the megagametophyte (embryo sac), which usually has eight nuclei. The central cell contains two polar nuclei, and one of the three cells next to the micropyle is an egg cell.

5. The anthers contain microsporocytes, each of which divides meiotically to produce four haploid microspores. Each of these divides mitotically to produce a two-celled pollen grain. One cell is the tube cell, and the other is the generative cell. The generative cell later divides to produce two sperm cells. The pollen grain is the microgametophyte. After pollination, the pollen grain germinates, and as the pollen tube grows, the sperm cells travel to the embryo sac. Pollination is simply the transfer of pollen from anther to stigma.

6. Flowering plants practice double fertilization. One sperm nucleus unites with the egg nucleus, forming a 2n zygote, and the other unites with the polar nuclei of the central cell, forming a 3n endosperm cell.

7. After fertilization, the endosperm cell divides to form the endosperm. The zygote becomes the sporophyte embryo. The ovule matures into the seed (its integuments become the seed coat). The ovary becomes the fruit.

8. As the ovule is becoming a seed, the zygote is becoming an embryo. After the first several divisions, it is possible to discern the embryo and the suspensor. The suspensor attaches the embryo to the ovule and supplies it with nutrients. The dicot embryo becomes first heart-shaped and then torpedo-shaped. Once you can see the two cotyledons, it is possible to distinguish the shoot apex and the root apex, which contain the apical meristems. In dicot seeds, the cotyledons frequently take up the endosperm.

9. The seeds of flowering plants are enclosed by fruits. There are different types of fruits. Simple fruits are derived from a single ovary (which can be simple or compound). Some simple fruits are fleshy, such as a peach or an apple. Others are dry, such as peas, nuts, and grains. Aggregate fruits develop from a number of ovaries of a single flower, and compound fruits develop from multiple ovaries of separate flowers.

10. Flowering plants have several ways to disperse seeds. Seeds may be blown by the wind, attached to animals that carry them away, eaten by animals that defecate them some distance away, or adapted to water transport.

11. Prior to germination, you can distinguish a bean (dicot) seed's two cotyledons and plumule, which is the shoot that bears leaves. Also present are the epicotyl, the hypocotyl, and the radicle. In a corn kernel (monocot), the endosperm, the cotyledon, the plumule, and the radicle are visible.

12. Many flowering plants reproduce asexually, as when the nodes of stems (either aboveground or underground) give rise to entire plants, or when roots produce new shoots.

13. The practice of hydroponics—and the recognition that plant cells can be totipotent—led to plant tissue culture, a technique that now has many applications.

14. Micropropagation, the production of clonal plants as a result of meristem culture in particular, is now a commercial venture. Flower meristem culture results in somatic embryos that can be packaged in gel for worldwide distribution. Anther culture results in homozygous plants that express recessive genes. Leaf, stem, and root culture can result in cell suspensions that may eventually allow the production of plant chemicals in large tanks. Development of adult plants from protoplasts results in somaclonal variations, a new source of plant varieties.

15. Protoplasts in particular lend themselves to direct genetic engineering in tissue culture. Otherwise, the *Agrobacterium* technique or the particle-gun technique allow foreign genes to be introduced into plant cells, which then develop into adult plants with particular traits.

Writing Across the Curriculum

In order to practice writing skills, students should write out the answers to any or all of the study questions and the critical thinking questions. The study questions are sequenced in the same order as the text. Answers to the objective questions, and suggested answers to the critical thinking questions, are in appendix D.

Study Questions

1. Name two unique features regarding the reproduction of flowering plants. 586

2. Draw a diagram of a flower and name the parts. 587

3. Draw a diagram that illustrates the life cycle of flowering plants. Why don't flowering plants require a source of outside water for pollination? 588–89

4. Describe the development of a megagametophyte, from the megasporocyte to the production of an egg. 588–89

5. Describe the development of the microgametophyte, from the microsporocyte to the production of sperm. 588–89

6. What is the difference between pollination and fertilization? 592

7. Describe the sequence of events as a dicot zygote becomes an embryo enclosed within a seed. 593

8. Distinguish between simple fleshy fruits and simple dry fruits. Give an example of each type. What is an aggregate fruit? a multiple fruit? 594–95

9. Name several mechanisms of seed and/or fruit dispersal. Contrast the germination of a bean seed with that of a corn kernel. 596–97

10. In what ways do plants ordinarily reproduce asexually? What is the importance of totipotency in regard to tissue culture? 600

11. What are the benefits of: meristem culture to achieve micropropagation; flower meristem culture to produce somatic embryos; anther culture to produce homozygous plants; leaf, stem, or root culture to produce cell suspension cultures; and the maintenance of protoplasts in tissue culture? 600–602

12. How are transgenic plants produced? What types of plants have been produced, and for what purpose have they been genetically engineered? 602–3

Objective Questions

1. In plants,
   a. gametes become the gametophyte generation.
   b. spores become the sporophyte generation.
   c. sporophyte organisms produce spores.
   d. Both a and b are correct.

2. The flower part that contains ovules is the
   a. carpel.
   b. stamen.
   c. sepal.
   d. petal.

3. The megasporocyte and the microsporocyte
   a. both produce pollen grains.
   b. both divide meiotically.
   c. both divide mitotically.
   d. produce pollen grains and embryo sacs, respectively.

4. A pollen grain is
   a. a haploid structure.
   b. a diploid structure.
   c. first a diploid and then a haploid structure.
   d. first a haploid and then a diploid structure.

5. Which of these is mismatched?
   a. polar nuclei—plumule
   b. egg and sperm—zygote
   c. ovule—seed
   d. ovary—fruit

6. Which of these is not a fruit?
   a. walnut
   b. pea
   c. green bean
   d. peach

7. Animals assist with
   a. both pollination and seed dispersal.
   b. only pollination.
   c. only seed dispersal.
   d. only asexual propagation of plants.

8. A seed contains
   a. a zygote.
   b. an embryo.
   c. stored food.
   d. Both b and c are correct.

9. Which of these is mismatched?
   a. plumule—leaves
   b. cotyledon—seed leaf
   c. epicotyl—root
   d. pericarp—corn kernel

10. Which of these best shows that plant cells are totipotent?
   a. shoot apex culture for the purpose of micropropagation
   b. flower meristem culture for the purpose of somatic embryos
   c. leaf, stem, and root culture for the purpose of cell suspension cultures
   d. protoplast culture for the purpose of genetic engineering of plants

11. Label the following diagram of alternation of generations in flowering plants.

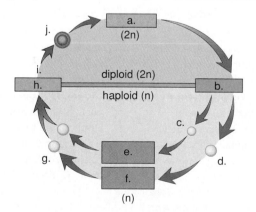

Concepts and Critical Thinking

I. *Living things have a reproductive strategy.*

What is the reproductive strategy of flowering plants?

2. *Living things have life cycles that promote survival of the species.*

How does the life cycle of flowering plants promote the possibility of gametophyte and sporophyte survival?

3. *Coevolution increases the fitness of both parties.*

How does coevolution between plants and their pollinators increase the fitness of the pollinators?

Selected Key Terms

carpel (KAHR-pul) In flowering plants, a reproductive unit of a pistil; consisting of three parts—the stigma, the style, and the ovary. [Gk. *carpus,* fruit]   587

cotyledon (kaht-ul-EED-un) Seed leaf for embryo of a flowering plant; provides nutrient molecules for the developing plant before begins to photosynthesize. [Gk. *cotyl,* cup-shaped cavity]   593

embryo sac The megagametophyte of flowering plants that contains an egg cell.   589

flower The reproductive organ of a flowering plant, consisting of several kinds of modified leaves arranged in concentric rings and attached to a modified stem called the receptacle.   587

fruit A flowering plant structure consisting of one or more ripened ovaries that usually contain seeds.   594

hybridization The crossing of different varieties or species. [L. *hybrid,* mongrel]   600

megagametophyte In seed plants, the gametophyte that produces an egg; in flowering plants, an embryo sac. [Gk. *mega,* large, *gamet,* wife, and *phyt,* plant]   589

megaspore The spore produced by the megasporocyte of a seed plant; of the four produced, one develops into a megagametophyte (embryo sac).   586

microgametophyte In seed plants, the gametophyte that produces sperm; a pollen grain. [Gk. *micr,* small, *gamet,* husband, and *phyt,* plant]   589

microspore The spore produced by a microsporocyte of a seed plant; it develops into a microgametophyte (pollen grain).   586

pistil A flower structure consisting of an ovary, a style, and a stigma. [L. *pistill,* pestle]   587

plumule (PLOO-myool) In flowering plants, the embryonic plant shoot that bears young leaves. [L. *plum,* feather]   597

pollen grain A microgametophyte in seed plants such as flowering plants.   589

pollination In flowering plants, the transfer of pollen from the anther of the stamen to the stigma of the pistil. [L. *pollen,* fine dust]   592

protoplast A plant cell from which the cell wall has been removed. [Gk. *proto,* first, and *plast,* formed, molded]   602

seed A mature ovule that contains an embryo, with stored food enclosed in a protective coat.   594

tissue culture The process of growing tissue artificially in a usually liquid medium in laboratory glassware.   600

Suggested Readings for Part V

Bazzaz, F. A., and Fajer, E. D. 1992. Plant life in a CO_2-rich world. *Scientific American* 266(1):68. Experiments with plants grown in a CO_2-enriched atmosphere show that the risks to ecosystems outweigh the gains in productivity.

Chrispeels, M., and Sadava, D. 1994. *Plants, genes and agriculture*. Boston: Jones and Bartlett Publishers. Teaches plant biology in an agricultural context.

Cox, P. A. 1993. Water-pollinated plants. *Scientific American*. 269(4):68. Some flowering aquatic species provide evidence for evolutionary convergence toward efficient pollination strategies.

Lea, P., and Leegood, R. 1993. *Plant biochemistry and molecular biology*. Chichester, England: John Wiley & Sons. Gives an overview of plant metabolism.

Lewington, A. 1990. *Plants for people*. New York: Oxford University Press. This is a full-color account of the ways in which people make use of plant products.

Mauseth, J. 1991. *Botany: An introduction to plant biology*. Philadelphia: Saunders College Publishing. Emphasizes evolution and diversity in botany and general principles of plant physiology and anatomy.

Meyerowitz, E. M. 1994. The genetics of flower development. *Scientific American* 271(5):56. Shows how flower design is determined by genetic signals.

Moore, R., and Clark, W. D. 1995. *Botany, plant form & function*. Dubuque, Iowa: Wm. C. Brown Publishers. This is a comprehensive discussion of general botany that captures the excitement of new developments.

Niklas, K. 1992. *Plant biomechanics*. Chicago: The University of Chicago Press. The book explores how plants function, grow, reproduce, and evolve within limits set by their physical environment.

Northington, D., and Goodin, J. R. 1984. *The botanical world*. St. Louis: Times-Mirror/ Mosby College Publishing. This is an account of plant interactions and basic physiology.

Raven, P., et al. 1992. *Biology of plants*. 5th ed. New York: Worth Publishers. Written for the undergraduate, this book covers viruses, bacteria, photosynthetic protists, fungi, and plants.

Redington, C. 1994. *Plants in wetlands.* Dubuque, Iowa: Kendall/Hunt Publishing Company. Explains how specific plants interact within the wetlands ecosystem.

Salisbury, F., and Ross, C. 1992. *Plant physiology.* 4th ed. Belmont, Calif.: Wadsworth Publishers. This text for botany majors emphasizes seed plant physiology.

Steeves, T., and Sussex, I. 1990. *Patterns in plant development.* 2d ed. Cambridge: Cambridge University Press. Details plant development, from embryo through secondary growth.

Stern, K. 1994. 6th ed. *Introductory plant biology.* Dubuque, Iowa: Wm. C. Brown Publishers. Presents basic botany in a clear, informative manner.

Taiz, L., and Zeiger, E. 1991. *Plant physiology.* Redwood City, Calif.: The Benjamin/Cummings Publishing Company, Inc. Presents the dynamic processes of growth, metabolism, and reproduction in plants.

Tedeschi, H. 1993. *Cell physiology.* 2d ed. Dubuque, Iowa: Wm. C. Brown Publishers. This text emphasizes the need to study original articles as the physiology of the cell is studied from the prospective of the cell as an energy converter.

CRITICAL THINKING CASE STUDY

Part V
LEAF SENESCENCE

The senescence (aging) and death of older leaves is a part of a plant's life cycle. It is hypothesized that *senescence of leaves is controlled by hormones and is accompanied by the breakdown of organic macromolecules.*

To test the hypothesis, researchers determined if the amount of macromolecules decreased in *attached* leaves as a function of age. Do you predict that macromolecules decrease in attached leaves as they age?

Prediction I   In keeping with the hypothesis, it is predicted that macromolecules decrease in attached leaves as they age.

Result I   As shown in figure A, RNA (ribonucleic acid) and protein decrease in attached leaves as a function of age.

> **Question I.   (a)** Why does it seem logical that the amount of RNA (fig. A*a*) would decrease in leaves as they age before the amount of protein (fig. A*b*) decreases?
>
>   **(b)** Is protein synthesis outstripping protein breakdown before or after age forty-seven days? How do you know? Is this consistent with the hypothesis?

In other experiments, researchers investigated whether the amino acid content within *detached* leaves increases. Following detachment, the petiole of the leaf is placed in water. Even so, the characteristics of senescence, such as a yellowing of the leaves, become evident quickly. In keeping with the hypothesis, do you predict that amino acid content will increase in detached leaves?

Prediction 2   Yes, it is predicted that the amino acid content of detached leaves will increase.

Result 2   The amino acid content of detached leaves does increase in detached leaves.

> **Question 2.   (a)** Add a curve to figure A*b* to indicate amino acid content of the leaf. Is your curve consistent with the observation that protein synthesis at first increases and only later decreases?
>
>   **(b)** If amino acids are being translocated out of the leaf, how would the shape of your curve change?

Roots sometimes develop at the base of the petiole in detached leaves. In these instances, senescence is immediately reversed; that is, protein synthesis begins again. Cytokinins are known to be hormones that are synthesized and released by roots. Do you predict that the application of cytokinins to detached leaves will prevent senescence from occurring?

Prediction 3   If cytokinins are applied to detached leaves, senescence will be prevented.

Result 3   Application of kinetin (a synthetic cytokinin) causes detached leaves to remain green.

> **Question 3.   (a)** In intact plants, older, larger leaves undergo senescence before younger, smaller leaves. Which of these leaves do you predict are receiving more cytokinins from the root by way of xylem?
>
>   **(b)** Application of cytokinin to one part of a leaf causes metabolites to accumulate in that part. In intact plants, cytokinins may be causing young leaves or older leaves to act as sinks for phloem transport?
>
>   **(c)** In intact plants, could the older leaves be a source of metabolites to the younger leaves? Why do you say so?

Figure A

Decrease in RNA content and leaf protein with senescence. **a.** Changes in RNA content of attached leaves of pea, *Pisum sativum*. **b.** Changes in protein content of attached leaves of *Perilla frutescens*.

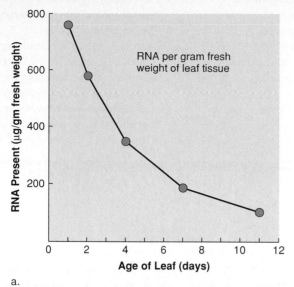

a.

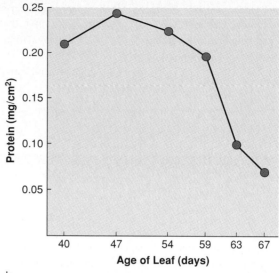

b.

Other investigations have indicated that senescence of detached leaves is markedly decreased in the light when photosynthesis is occurring. Researchers decided to test if glucose, a product of photosynthesis, delays senescence. If glucose delays senescence, will the application of DCMU, an inhibitor of glucose production, delay or promote senescence of detached leaves in the light?

Prediction 4 If glucose production in the light delays senescence, the application of an inhibitor of sugar production will promote senescence.

Result 4 When the inhibitor DCMU is applied to detached leaves in the light, senescence is unaffected.

Question 4. **(a)** What do these results indicate about the effect of light on senescence? about the effect of glucose production in the light on senescence? about the effect of some other product of photosynthesis, such as ATP, on senescence? **(b)** How could you test whether ATP production in the light affects senescence?

These results support the hypothesis that senescence of leaves is controlled by hormones and is accompanied by the breakdown of organic macromolecules. Further investigation is needed to determine if cytokinins cause the translocation of nutrient molecules from aging leaves into young leaves.

Reference

Street, H. E., and Opik, H. 1976. *The physiology of flowering plants*. 2d ed. London: Edward Arnold Publishers Ltd.

Part VI
ANIMAL STRUCTURE AND FUNCTION

In contrast to plants, animals are heterotrophic. Their mobility, which is dependent upon nerve fibers and muscle fibers, is essential in finding food. Then the food must be digested and the nutrients distributed to cells. Finally, wastes are expelled.

We will observe a progressive modification from simple to more complex structures to carry out these functions. Genes permit the retention of suitable anatomical and physiological solutions to environmental requirements, and evolution results in modifications of these solutions. Complexity has arisen through the evolutionary process as a way to adapt to the environment, especially the biotic (living) environment.

In this part, we will map out the various lines of animal descent and, in so doing, will trace the evolution of the major types of animals. We will observe the many modifications that allow animals to utilize resources, extract energy, protect themselves, and reproduce.

Invertebrates in a tidal pool whose structure and function is suitable to living in sea water.

Many of the figures and concepts discussed in *Biology*, fifth edition, are further explored in technology products. The following is a list of figures in part VI that correlates to technology products.

A set of five videotapes contains 53 animations of physiological processes integral to the study of biology. These videotapes, entitled *Life Science Animations*, cover such topics as chemistry, genetics, and reproduction. A videotape icon appears in appropriate figure legends to alert the reader to these animations.

Explorations in Human Biology and *Explorations in Cell Biology, Metabolism, and Genetics* by George B. Johnson are interactive CD-ROMs with activities that can be used by an instructor in lecture and/or placed in a lab or resource center for student use. This interactive software consists of modules that cover key topics discussed in a biology course. The CD-ROMs are available for use with Macintosh and IBM Windows computers. A CD-ROM icon appears in appropriate figure legends to alert the reader to these activities.

Corresponding Figures		Videotape Concepts	CD-Rom Modules
36.2	Open and closed circulatory systems	37. Blood Circulation	How Proteins Function: Hemoglobin
36.3	Circulation in birds and mammals	37. Blood Circulation	—
36.4	Comparison of vertebrate circulatory systems	37. Blood Circulation	—
36.5	External heart anatomy	—	Evolution of the Heart
36.6	Internal view of the heart	37. Blood Circulation	Evolution of the Heart
36.7	Control of the cardiac cycle	32. The Cardiac Cycle & Production of Sounds; 38. Production of Electrocardiogram	Evolution of the Heart
36.8	Blood vessels in the pulmonary and systemic circuit	37. Blood Circulation	Evolution of the Heart
36.9	Blood pressure diagram	38. Production of Electrocardiogram	Life Span and Lifestyle
36.10	Valve cross section	38. Production of Electrocardiogram	—
36B	Plaque	—	Life Span and Lifestyle
36.12	Blood clotting	40. Common Congenital Defects of the Heart	—
36.15	Blood typing	40. A, B, O Blood Types	—
36.16	Development of hemolytic disease of the newborn	39. A, B, O Blood Types	—
37.3	White blood cells	—	Immune Response
37.4	Inflammatory reaction	—	Immune Response
37.5	Complement system	—	Immune Response
37.6	Clonal selection theory	41. B-Cell Immune Response	Immune Response
37.7	Antigen-antibody reaction	42. Structure and Function of Antibodies	Immune Response
37.8	Cell-mediated immunity	43. Types of T-cells; 44. Relationship of Helper T-cells & Killer T-cells	Immune Response
37.9	Activation and diversity of T-cells	43. Types of T-cells; 44. Relationship of Helper T-cells & Killer T-cells	Immune Response
37B	HIV-1 attachment to CD4 receptors	—	AIDS
37.10	Development of active immunity due to immunization	—	AIDS
38.7	Peristalsis	33. Peristalsis	
38.11	Ideal American diet	—	Diet and Weight Loss
39.8	External and internal respiration	—	How Proteins Function: Hemoglobin
39.9	Properties of hemoglobin	—	How Proteins Function: Hemoglobin
39.10	Common lung disorders	—	Life Span and Lifestyle; Smoking and Cancer
41.2	Human nervous system	—	Nerve Conduction
41.3	Neuron anatomy	22. Formation of Myelin Sheath	Nerve Conduction
41.4	Action potential (voltage changes)	24. Signal Integration	Nerve Conduction
41.5	Action potential and resting potential	24. Signal Integration	Nerve Conduction
41.6	Saltatory conduction	23. Saltatory Nerve Conduction	Nerve Conduction
41.7	Synapse structure and function	24. Signal Integration	Synaptic Transmission
41.9	Reflex arc	25. Reflex Arcs	Nerve Conduction
41.10	Autonomic system structure and function	—	Synaptic Transmission
42.11	Inner ear anatomy	26. Organ of Static Equilibrium	—
42.12	Statocysts in mollusks and crustacea	26. Organ of Static Equilibrium	—
42.13	Sense of hearing	26. Organ of Static Equilibrium; 27. The Organ of Corti	—
43.11	Antagonistic muscle pairs	—	Muscle Contraction
43.12	Muscle fiber vs. whole muscle contraction	30. Sliding Filament Model of Muscle Contraction	Muscle Contraction
43.13	Muscle fiber anatomy	29. Levels of Muscle Structure	Muscle Contraction
43.14	Sliding filament theory	30. Sliding Filament Model of Muscle Contraction	Muscle Contraction
43.15	Neuromuscular junction	31. Regulation of Muscle Contraction	Synaptic Transmission; Muscle Contraction
44.1	Cellular activity of steroid hormones	—	Hormone Action
44.2	Cellular activity of peptide hormones	28. Peptide Hormone Action (cAMP)	Hormone Action
44.3	Human endocrine system	—	Hormone Action
44.8	Insulin and glucagon homeostatic system	—	Hormone Action
45.7	Testis and sperm	19. Spermatogenesis	—
45.10	Anatomy of ovary and follicle	20. Oogenesis	—
46.9	Extraembryonic membranes	21. Human Embryonic Development	—
46.10	Human development before implantation	21. Human Embryonic Development	—
46.11	Early development of humans	21. Human Embryonic Development	—
46.12	Human embryo at fifth week	21. Human Embryonic Development	—

ANIMAL ORGANIZATION AND HOMEOSTASIS

Learning Objectives

Tissues Have Structure and Functions

- Name the four types of tissues in animals, and give a general function for each.   612
- Describe the structure and the function of three types of epithelium, along with their possible modifications.   612–13
- Describe the structure and the function of the various types of connective tissue.   614–15
- Describe the structure and the function of three types of muscular tissue.   616–17
- Describe the structure and the function of two types of cells found in nervous tissue.   617

Organs Have Structure and Functions

- Describe the structure of human skin, and explain how this illustrates the composition of an organ.   618–19
- Name the various organ systems in humans, associate each with a particular life process, and note the specific functions of each system.   620
- Name the body cavities in a human, and name the organ systems in each cavity.   620

Homeostasis Is Necessary

- Define homeostasis, and explain how control by negative feedback works.   622
- Describe how body temperature is controlled in humans, and explain why body temperature fluctuates above and below a mean.   623

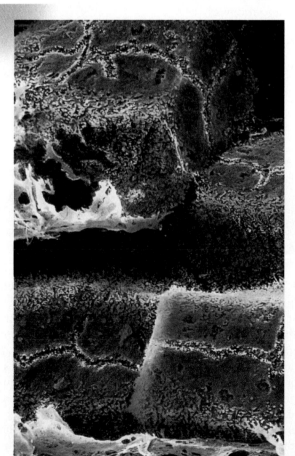

Cells organized into tissues result in the much convoluted wall of the duodenum as revealed by this false-colored scanning electron micrograph.

5 μm

nimals have levels of organization (fig. 35.1). In this chapter we begin at the tissue level, but we also consider the organ and system levels of organization. A tissue is a group of similar cells performing a similar function. Different types of tissues make up organs, and several organs are found within an organ system. The organ systems make up the organism.

The structure and functions of an organ system are dependent upon the structure and functions of the organ, tissue, and cell type contained therein. For instance, the columnar epithelial cells of the intestine, which absorb nutrients, have microvilli. Skeletal muscle cells are tubular and contain elements that contract to a shorter length. Nerve cells have long, slender projections that carry nerve impulses to distant body parts.

TISSUES HAVE STRUCTURE AND FUNCTIONS

There are four major types of **tissue** in animals: *epithelial tissue* covers body surfaces and lines body cavities; *connective tissue* binds and supports body parts; *muscular tissue* causes body parts to move; and *nervous tissue* responds to stimuli and transmits impulses from one body part to another.

At an early stage in the embryological development of an animal there are three fundamental layers called the germ layers. These four types of tissues arise from the germ layers. The relationship between tissues and germ layers is as follows:

Embryonic Germ Layer	Vertebrate Adult Structures
Ectoderm (outer layer)	Epidermis of skin; epithelial lining of mouth and rectum; nervous system
Mesoderm (middle layer)	Skeleton; muscular system; dermis of skin; circulatory system; excretory system; reproductive system, including most epithelial linings; outer layers of respiratory and digestive systems
Endoderm (inner layer)	Epithelial lining of digestive tract and respiratory tract; associated glands of these systems; epithelial lining of the urinary bladder

Epithelial Tissue Covers

Epithelial tissue [Gk. *epi*, upon, and *thec*, a case], also called epithelium, forms a continuous layer, or sheet, over body surfaces and the inner cavities. There are three types of epithelial tissue. *Squamous epithelium* is composed of flat cells; *cuboidal epithelium* contains cube-shaped cells; and in *columnar epithelium*, the oblong cells resemble pillars or columns. Figure 35.2 describes the structure and function of epithelium in vertebrates. Any epithelium can be simple or stratified. *Simple* means that the tissue has a single layer of cells, and *stratified* means that the tissue has layers piled one on top of the other. One type of epithe-

Figure 35.1

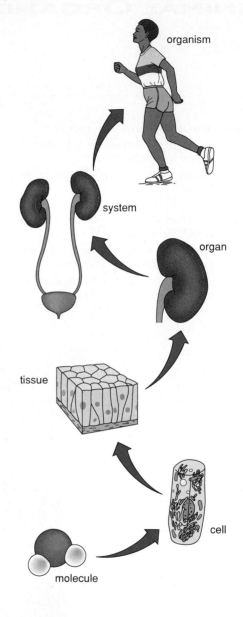

Levels of organization in the human body. A cell is composed of molecules, a tissue is made up of cells, an organ is composed of tissues, and the organism contains organ systems.

lium is pseudostratified—it appears to be layered, but actually true layers do not exist because each cell touches a basement membrane. Epithelium is usually attached to a basement membrane, which is glycoprotein reinforced by fibers supplied by an underlying connective tissue.

Epithelial tissues have various functions. Epithelial cells can have hairlike extensions called cilia, which bend and move materials in a particular direction. In the human body, the ciliated epithelium lining the respiratory tract sweeps impurities toward the throat so they do not enter the lungs. An epithelium sometimes secretes a product and is described as glandular. A

Figure 35.2

Types of epithelial tissues in vertebrates. Epithelial tissues are classified according to shape of cell, whether they are simple or stratified, and whether they have cilia. Epithelial tissues have functions associated with protection, absorption, and secretion.

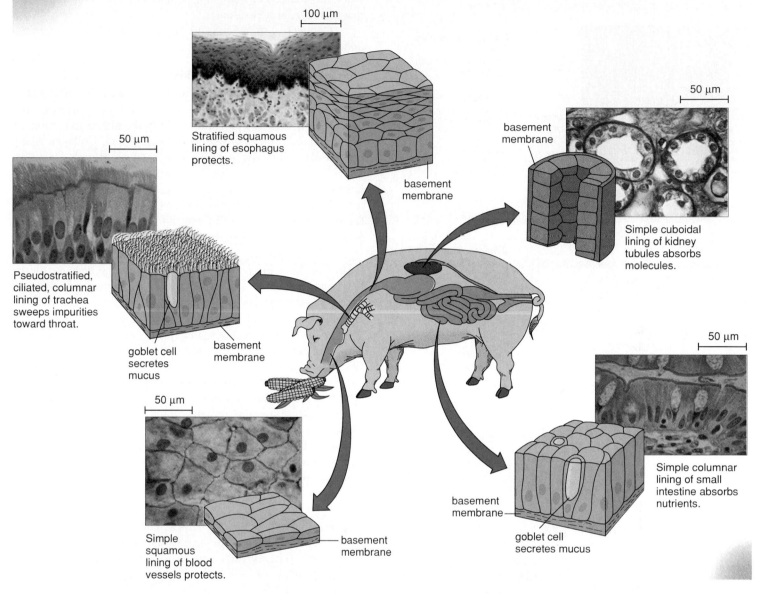

100 μm

Stratified squamous lining of esophagus protects.

basement membrane

50 μm

basement membrane

Simple cuboidal lining of kidney tubules absorbs molecules.

50 μm

Pseudostratified, ciliated, columnar lining of trachea sweeps impurities toward throat.

goblet cell secretes mucus

basement membrane

basement membrane

50 μm

50 μm

Simple squamous lining of blood vessels protects.

basement membrane

basement membrane

goblet cell secretes mucus

Simple columnar lining of small intestine absorbs nutrients.

gland can be a single epithelial cell, such as the mucus-secreting goblet cells in the lining of the human intestine, or a gland can contain numerous cells. *Exocrine glands* secrete their product into ducts, and *endocrine glands* secrete their product directly into the bloodstream.

Epithelium forms the outer layer of skin of most animals. The skin of earthworms and snails is glandular and produces mucus that lubricates the body, helping to ease movement through a dry environment. In roundworms, annelids, and arthropods, an outer nonliving and protective cuticle is produced by epithelium. In terrestrial vertebrates, skin cells contain keratin, a substance that protects the skin from the possible loss of water.

Epithelial tissue cells are packed tightly and joined to one another in one of three ways: tight junctions, adhesion junctions (desmosomes), and gap junctions. In *tight junctions*, plasma mem-

brane proteins extending between neighboring cells bind them tightly. For example, they prevent digestive juices from passing between the epithelial cells lining the lumen (cavity). In *adhesion junctions*, cytoskeletal elements join internal plaques present in both cells. They allow the skin to withstand considerable stretching and mechanical stress. *Gap junctions* form when two identical plasma membrane channels join. They allow ions and small molecules to pass between the cells.

Epithelial tissue is classified according to cell shape. There can be one or many layers of cells, and the epithelium can be ciliated and/or glandular.

Figure 35.3

Examples of connective tissue. **a.** Loose connective tissue. **b.** Adipose tissue cells. Nuclei (arrow) are pushed to one side because the cells are filled with fat. **c.** Hyaline cartilage. **d.** Compact bone.

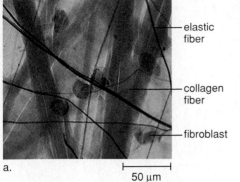

a.

50 μm

Loose Connective Tissue
has space between components.

Located:
under skin and most epithelial layers

Function:
supports and binds organs

- elastic fiber
- collagen fiber
- fibroblast

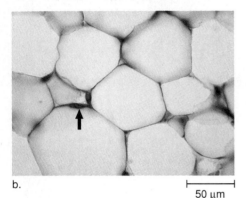

b.

50 μm

Adipose Tissue
cells are filled with fat.

Located:
under skin, around organs

Function:
insulates, stores fat

Hyaline Cartilage
has cells in a lacuna.

Located:
in ends of bones, nose, walls of respiratory passages

Function:
supports, protects

c.

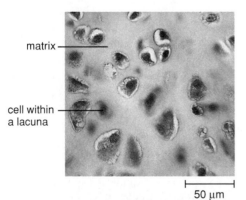

- matrix
- cell within a lacuna

50 μm

Compact Bone
has cells in concentric rings

Located:
in bones of skeleton

Function:
supports, protects

d.

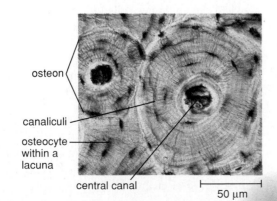

- osteon
- canaliculi
- osteocyte within a lacuna
- central canal

50 μm

Connective Tissue Connects

Connective tissue binds structures together, provides support and protection, fills spaces, stores fat, and forms blood cells. It provides the source cells for muscle and skeletal cells in animals that can regenerate lost parts.

Connective tissue cells are separated widely by a *matrix,* a noncellular material found between cells.

Loose and Fibrous Give

The cells of loose and fibrous connective tissues, called **fibroblasts** [L. *fibr,* fiber, and Gk. *blast,* bud], are located some distance from one another and are separated by a jellylike matrix that contains white collagen fibers and yellow elastic fibers. Collagen fibers provide flexibility and strength; elastic fibers provide elasticity.

Loose connective tissue supports epithelium and also many internal vertebrate organs (fig. 35.3*a*). Its presence in lungs, arteries, and the urinary bladder allows these organs to expand. It forms a protective covering encasing many internal organs, such as muscles, blood vessels, and nerves.

Adipose tissue [L. *adeps,* fat], a type of loose connective tissue, insulates the body and provides padding because the fibroblasts enlarge and store fat (fig. 35.3*b*). In mammals, adipose tissue is found particularly beneath the skin, around the kidneys, and on the surface of the heart. **Reticular connective tissue** is present in the lymph nodes, the spleen, and the bone marrow. Here, reticular fibers, associated with reticular cells resembling fibroblasts, support many free blood cells.

Fibrous connective tissue contains many collagenous fibers that are packed closely together. This type of tissue has more specific functions in vertebrates than does loose connective tissue. For example, fibrous connective tissue is found in **tendons** [L. *tend,* stretch], which connect muscles to bones, and in **ligaments** [L. *liga,* bound], which connect bones to other bones at joints.

> Loose connective tissue and fibrous connective tissue contain fibroblasts separated by a matrix, which contains collagen and elastic fibers.

Cartilage and Bone Are Solid

Cartilage and bone are rigid connective tissues in which structural proteins (cartilage) or calcium salts (bone) are deposited in the intercellular matrix.

In **cartilage** [L. *cartilago,* gristle], the cells lie in small chambers called **lacunae** (sing., lacuna), separated by a matrix that is strong yet flexible (fig. 35.3*c*). There are various types of cartilage, which are classified according to type of collagen and elastic fiber found in the matrix. In some vertebrates, notably sharks and rays, the entire skeleton is made of cartilage. In humans, the fetal skeleton is cartilage, but it is later replaced by bone. Cartilage is retained at the ends of long bones, at the end of the nose, in the framework of the ear, in the walls of respiratory ducts, and within intervertebral disks.

In **bone,** the matrix of calcium salts is deposited around protein fibers. The minerals give bone rigidity, and the protein fibers provide elasticity and strength, much as steel rods do in reinforced concrete.

In *compact bone,* bone cells (e.g., osteocytes) are located in lacunae that are arranged in concentric circles within osteons (Haversian systems) around tiny tubes called central canals (fig. 35.3*d*). Nerve fibers and blood vessels are in these canals. The latter bring the nutrients that allow bone to renew itself. The nutrients can reach all of the cells because there are minute canals (canaliculi) containing thin processes of the osteocytes that connect them with one another and with the central canals.

The ends of a long bone contain spongy bone, which has an entirely different structure. *Spongy bone* contains numerous bony bars and plates separated by irregular spaces. Although lighter than compact bone, spongy bone still is designed for strength. Just as braces are used for support in buildings, the solid portions of spongy bone follow lines of stress.

Cartilage and bone are support tissues. Cartilage is more flexible than bone because the matrix is rich in protein; bone is rich in calcium salts.

Blood Is a Liquid

Blood is a connective tissue in which the cells are separated by a liquid called plasma. In vertebrates, blood cells are primarily two types: red blood cells (erythrocytes), which carry oxygen, and white blood cells (leukocytes), which aid in fighting infection (fig. 35.4). Also present in plasma are platelets, which are important to the initiation of blood clotting. Platelets are not complete cells; rather, they are fragments of giant cells found in the bone marrow.

Blood is unlike other types of connective tissue in that the intercellular matrix (i.e., plasma) is not made by the cells. Plasma is a mixture of different types of molecules that enter the blood at various locations.

Blood is a connective tissue in which the matrix is plasma.

Figure 35.4

Blood, a liquid tissue. **a.** Blood is classified as connective tissue because the cells are separated by a matrix—plasma. Plasma, the liquid portion of blood, usually contains several types of cells. This shows the cells in human blood (red blood cells, white blood cells, and platelets, which are actually fragments of a larger cell). **b.** Drawing of the components of blood.

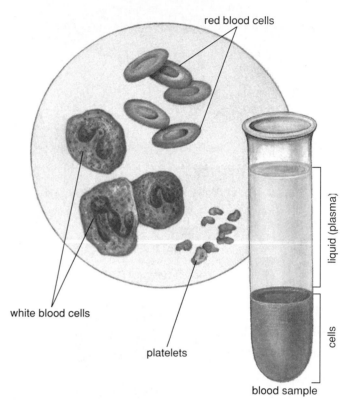

red blood cells

white blood cells

platelets

liquid (plasma)

cells

blood sample

a.

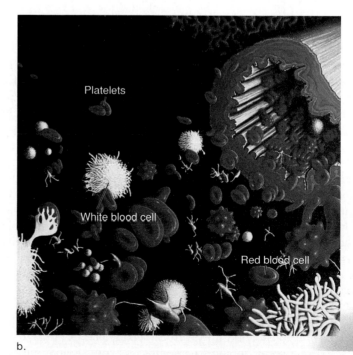

Platelets

White blood cell

Red blood cell

b.

Figure 35.5

Components of muscle. **a.** A whole muscle. **b.** Muscle cells, or fibers. **c.** Myofibrils within muscle fibers account for the striations observed when skeletal muscle is viewed under the microscope (see fig. 35.6a).

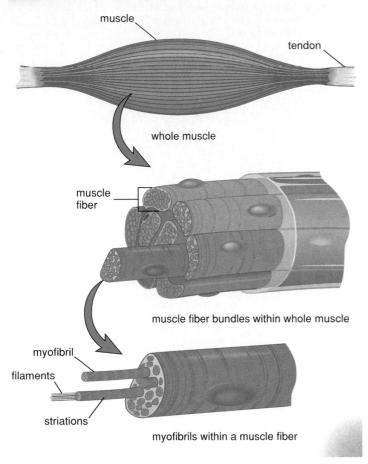

muscle

tendon

whole muscle

muscle fiber

muscle fiber bundles within whole muscle

myofibril

filaments

striations

myofibrils within a muscle fiber

Figure 35.6

Muscular tissue. **a.** Skeletal muscle is striated and attached to the bones. **b.** Cardiac muscle is striated and pumps blood. Note the branching of the fibers and the presence of intercalated disks. **c.** Smooth muscle is nonstriated, and the fibers have a single nucleus.

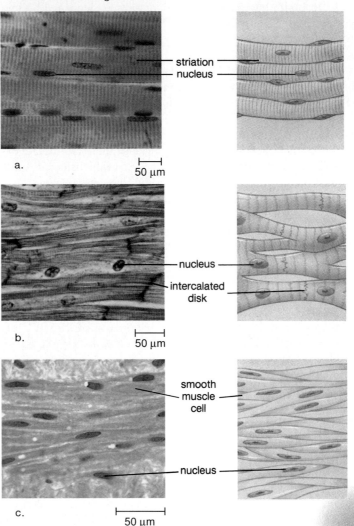

a.

striation

nucleus

50 μm

b.

nucleus

intercalated disk

50 μm

c.

smooth muscle cell

nucleus

50 μm

Muscular Tissue Contracts

Muscular (contractile) tissue is composed of cells called *muscle fibers*. Muscle fibers contain actin filaments and myosin filaments, whose interaction accounts for the movements we associate with animals. There are three types of vertebrate muscle tissue: skeletal, cardiac, and smooth.

Skeletal muscle is attached via tendons to the bones of the skeleton; it moves body parts. It is under voluntary control and contracts faster than all the other muscle types. Skeletal muscle fibers are cylindrical and quite long—sometimes they run the length of the muscle (fig. 35.5). They arise during development when several cells fuse, producing one muscle fiber with multiple nuclei. The nuclei are located at the periphery of the fiber, just inside the plasma membrane. Skeletal muscle fibers are **striated** [L. *stria,* streaked]. Light and dark bands run perpendicular to the length of the fiber. These bands are due to the placement of actin filaments and myosin filaments in the cell (fig. 35.6a).

Cardiac muscle, which is found only in the wall of the heart, is responsible for the heartbeat, which pumps blood. Cardiac muscle seems to combine features of both smooth muscle

and skeletal muscle (fig. 35.6b). Its fibers have striations like skeletal muscle, but the contraction of the heart is involuntary for the most part. Cardiac muscle fibers also differ from skeletal muscle fibers in that they have a single, centrally placed nucleus. These fibers are branched and seemingly fused one with the other, and the heart appears to be composed of one large interconnecting mass of muscle fibers. Actually, cardiac muscle fibers are separate and individual, but they are bound end to end at intercalated disks, areas where folded plasma membranes between two fibers contain desmosomes and gap junctions. Intercalated disks allow impulses to move from cell to cell so that the beat of the heart is coordinated.

Smooth (visceral) muscle is so named because its fibers lack striations. The spindle-shaped fibers form layers in which the thick middle portion of one fiber is opposite the thin ends of adjacent fibers. Consequently, the nuclei form an irregular pat-

Figure 35.7

Neuron. **a.** Conduction of the nerve impulse is dependent on neurons, each of which has the parts indicated. A dendrite takes nerve impulses to the cell body, and an axon takes them away from the cell body. **b.** Photomicrograph of a neuron.

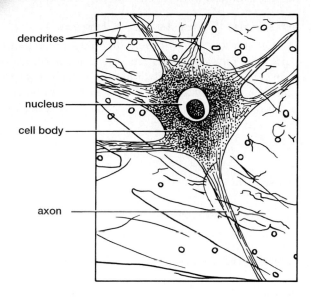

dendrites

nucleus

cell body

axon

a.

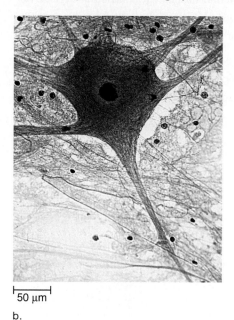

50 μm

b.

tern in the tissue (fig. 35.6c). Smooth muscle is not under voluntary control and therefore is said to be involuntary. Smooth muscle, found in walls of viscera (intestine, stomach, and other internal organs) and blood vessels, contracts more slowly than skeletal muscle but can remain contracted for a longer time. When the smooth muscle of the intestine contracts, it moves the food along, and when the smooth muscle of the blood vessels contracts, it constricts the blood vessels, helping to raise the blood pressure.

> All muscle tissue contains actin and myosin filaments; these overlap, forming striations in skeletal and cardiac muscle but not in smooth muscle.

Nervous Tissue Conducts

Nervous tissue which contains nerve cells called **neurons** [Gk. *neuro,* nerve] (fig. 35.7) is present in the brain and spinal cord. A neuron is a specialized cell that has three parts: (1) dendrites conduct impulses (send messages) to the cell body; (2) the cell body contains the major concentration of the cytoplasm and the nucleus of the neuron; and (3) the axon conducts impulses away from the cell body.

Long axons and dendrites are called nerve fibers, and they are bound together by connective tissue to form nerves which extend from the brain and spinal cord. Neurons are specialized to detect environmental stimuli and then to conduct signals to the brain and spinal cord, which then signal muscle or glands to react via other neurons. In this way, a coordinated response to the stimulus is achieved.

In addition to neurons, nervous tissue contains neuroglial cells. These cells do not conduct impulses, but they maintain the tissue by supporting and protecting neurons. They also provide nutrients to neurons and help to keep the tissue free of debris.

> Nerve cells, called neurons, have fibers (processes) called axons and dendrites. Long fibers are found in nerves.

How Tissues Are Examined

The micrographs in this chapter were obtained by viewing prepared slides with the light microscope. Preparation required these sequential steps:

Fixation occurs when the tissue is immersed in a preservative solution in order to maintain the tissue's existing structure.

During *embedding,* water is removed with alcohol and the tissue is impregnated with paraffin wax.

During *sectioning,* the tissue is cut into extremely thin slices by an instrument called a microtome.

During *staining,* the tissue is immersed in dyes that stain different structures. The most common dyes are hematoxylin and eosin stains (H & E). They give a differential blue and red color to the basic and acidic structures within the tissue. Other dyes are available for staining specific structures.

Many other procedures are also available for light microscopy. One new procedure utilizes an antibody labeled with a fluorescent dye to detect specific structures such as the plasma membrane of cells.

ORGANS HAVE STRUCTURE AND FUNCTIONS

We tend to associate particular tissues with particular organs. For example, we associate muscular tissue with muscles and nervous tissue with the brain. In actuality, however, an **organ** is a structure that is composed of two or more types of tissues working together to perform particular functions. An **organ system** contains many different organs that cooperate to carry out a process such as digestion of food. We are going to examine human skin as an example of an organ. Some authorities even call skin the *integumentary system* (especially since it cannot be placed in one of the other systems). They maintain that the hair follicles, the oil and sweat glands, the receptors, and the skin are separate organs, and these organs work together to perform various functions.

Human Skin Is an Organ

Human skin (fig. 35.8) covers the body, protecting underlying parts from physical trauma, microbial invasion, and water loss. Skin cells contain a precursor molecule that is converted to vitamin D in the body after it is exposed to ultraviolet (UV) light. Since only a small amount of UV radiation is needed to change

Figure 35.8

Human skin anatomy. Skin contains three layers: epidermis, dermis, and subcutaneous.

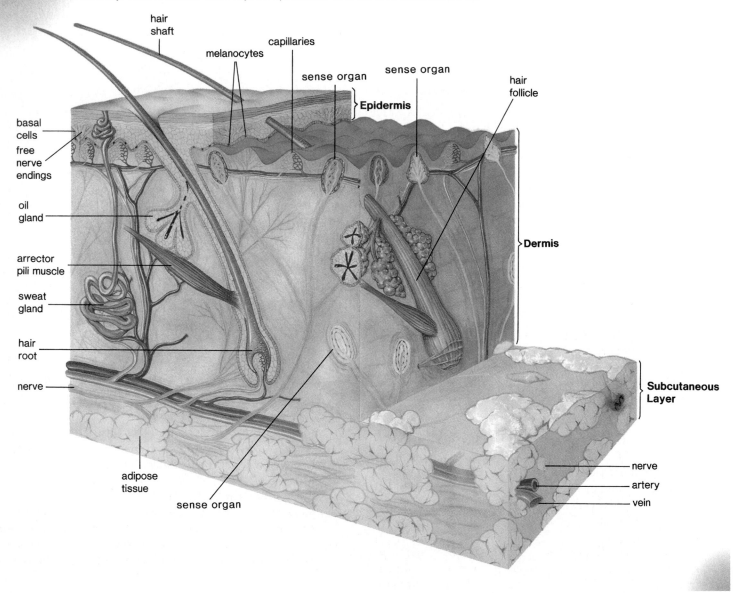

the precursor to vitamin D, the skin should not be exposed unnecessarily. The skin also helps regulate body temperature, and because it contains receptors (sense organs), the skin helps us to be aware of our surroundings and to know when to communicate with others.

Skin has an outer epidermal layer (the epidermis) and an inner layer (the dermis). Beneath the dermis, a subcutaneous layer binds the skin to underlying organs.

Skin Has Layers

The **epidermis** [Gk. *epi,* upon, and *derm,* skin] is the outer, thinner layer of the skin. It is a stratified squamous epithelium, and its cells are derived from the basal cells, which undergo continuous cell division. As newly formed cells are pushed to the surface away from their blood supply, they gradually flatten and harden. Eventually, they die and are sloughed off. Hardening is caused by cellular production of a waterproof protein called keratin. Over much of the body, keratinization is minimal, but the palm of the hand and the sole of the foot have a particularly thick outer layer of dead keratinized cells arranged in spiral and concentric patterns. We call these patterns fingerprints and footprints.

Specialized cells in the dividing layer of epidermis, called melanocytes, produce melanin, the pigment responsible for skin color in dark-skinned persons. When you sunbathe, the melanocytes become more active, producing melanin in an attempt to protect the skin from the damaging effects of the ultraviolet (UV) radiation in sunlight.

Nails grow from special epidermal cells at the base of the nail in the region called the nail root. These cells become keratinized as they grow out over the nail bed. The visible portion of the nail is called the nail body. The pink color of nails is due to the vascularized dermal tissue beneath the nail. The whitish color of the half-moon-shaped base results from the thicker germinal layer in this area. Ordinarily, nails grow only about one millimeter a week.

> The epidermis of skin is made up of stratified squamous epithelium. In this layer, new cells are pushed outward, become keratinized, die, and are sloughed off.

The **dermis** [Gk. *derm,* skin] is a layer of fibrous connective tissue that is deeper and thicker than the epidermis. It contains elastic fibers and collagen fibers. The collagen fibers form bundles that interlace and run, for the most part, parallel to the skin surface. There are several types of structures in the dermis. A hair, except for the root, is formed of dead, hardened epidermal cells; the root is alive and resides in a hair follicle found in the dermis. Each follicle has one or more oil (sebaceous) glands that secrete sebum, an oily substance that lubricates the hair and the skin. A smooth muscle called the arrector pili muscle is attached to the hair follicle in such a way that when contracted, the muscle causes the hair to stand on end. When you are frightened or cold, goose bumps appear due to a mounding up of the skin from the contraction of these muscles.

Many sweat (sudoriferous) glands are present in all regions of the skin. A sweat gland begins as a coiled tubule within the dermis, but then it straightens out near its opening. Some sweat glands open into hair follicles, but most open onto the surface of the skin.

Small receptors are present in the dermis. There are different receptors for pressure, touch, temperature, and pain. Pressure receptors are in onion-shaped sense organs that lie deep inside the dermis and around joints and tendons. They are also believed to provide instant information about how and where we move. In cats, Pacinian corpuscles are concentrated on the paws, the leg joints, and the connective tissue of the abdomen. Those close to the ground may provide information about the location of prey. Closely related sensors on the tongues of woodpeckers help them find insects in tree bark.

Touch receptors, which are flat and oval shaped, are concentrated in the fingertips, the palms, the lips, the tongue, the nipples, the penis, and the clitoris. Their prevalence is thought to provide these regions with special sensitivity. Heat and cold sense organs are encapsulated by sheaths of connective tissue and contain lacy networks of nerve fibers. Nerve fibers branch out through all skin, and free nerve endings are believed to be the receptors for pain.

The dermis also contains blood vessels. When blood rushes into these vessels, a person blushes, and when blood volume is reduced in them, a person turns ashen or white.

> The dermis, composed of fibrous connective tissue, lies beneath the epidermis. It contains hair follicles, sebaceous glands, and sweat glands. It also contains receptors, blood vessels, and nerve fibers.

The subcutaneous layer, which lies below the dermis, is composed of loose connective tissue, including adipose tissue. Adipose tissue helps to insulate the body by minimizing both heat gain and heat loss. A well-developed subcutaneous layer gives a rounded appearance to the body. Excessive development of this layer accompanies obesity.

Skin Cancer Can Develop

In recent years, there has been a great increase in the number of persons with skin cancer, and physicians believe this is due to sunbathing or even to the use of tanning machines. Protecting your skin from the sun's damaging rays is discussed in the reading on page 621.

Figure 35.9

Mammalian body cavities. **a.** Side view. There is a dorsal cavity, which contains the cranial cavity and the vertebral canal. The brain is in the cranial cavity, and the spinal cord is in the vertebral canal. There is a well-developed ventral cavity, which is divided by the diaphragm into the thoracic cavity and the abdominal cavity. The heart and lungs are in the thoracic cavity, and most other internal organs are in the abdominal cavity. **b.** Frontal view of the thoracic cavity.

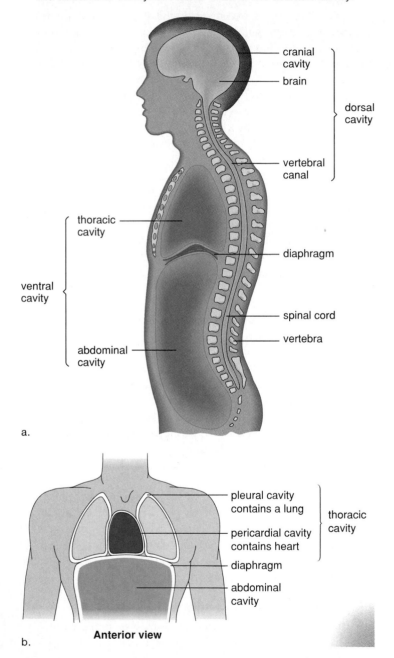

a.

b. **Anterior view**

Organs Form Systems

In most animals, individual organs function as part of an *organ system,* the next higher level of animal organization (see fig. 35.1). These same systems are found in all vertebrate animals. The organ systems carry out the life processes that are common to all animals, and indeed to all organisms:

Life Processes	Human Systems
Coordinate body activities	Nervous system
Acquire materials and energy (food)	Skeletal system Muscular system Digestive system
Maintain body shape	Muscular system Skeletal system
Exchange gases	Respiratory system
Transport materials	Circulatory system
Excrete wastes	Excretory system
Protect the body from disease	Lymphatic system
Coordinate body activities	Endocrine system
Produce offspring	Reproductive system

Bodies Have Cavities

Each organ system has a particular location within the human body. There are two main body cavities: the smaller dorsal body cavity and the larger ventral body cavity (fig. 35.9). The brain and the spinal cord are in the dorsal body cavity.

During development, the ventral body cavity develops from the *coelom.* In humans and other mammals, the coelom is divided by a muscular diaphragm that assists breathing. The heart (a pump for the closed circulatory system) and the lungs are located in the upper (thoracic or chest) cavity. The major portions of the digestive system, the excretory system, and much of the reproductive system are located in the lower (abdominal) cavity. The major organs of the excretory system are the paired kidneys. The accessory organs of the digestive system are the liver and pancreas. Each sex has characteristic sex organs.

> The animal body is organized; the organs have a specific structure, function, and location. The performance of the organs of each system are coordinated.

Skin Cancer on the Rise

I n Victorian days, Caucasian women carried parasols to keep their skin fair. But early in this century, some fair-skinned people began to prefer the golden-brown look, and they took up sunbathing as a way to achieve a tan. A few hours after exposure to the sun, pain and redness due to dilation of blood vessels occur. Tanning occurs when melanin granules increase and melanocytes rise to the surface of the skin as a way to prevent any further damage by ultraviolet (UV) rays. The sun gives off two types of UV rays: UV-A rays and UV-B rays. UV-A rays penetrate the skin deeply, affect connective tissue, and cause the skin to sag and wrinkle. UV-A rays are also believed to increase the effects of the UV-B rays, which are the cancer-causing rays. UV-B rays are more prevalent at midday.

Skin cancer is categorized as either nonmelanoma or melanoma. Nonmelanoma cancers are of two types. Basal cell carcinoma, the most common type, begins when UV radiation causes epidermal basal cells to form a tumor, while at the same time suppressing the immune system's ability to detect the tumor. The signs of a tumor are varied. They include an open sore that will not heal, a recurring reddish patch, a smooth, circular growth with a raised edge, a shiny bump, or a pale mark. About 95% of patients are easily cured, but reoccurrence is common.

Squamous cell carcinoma begins in the epidermis proper. Squamous cell carcinoma is five times less common than basal cell carcinoma, but it is more likely to spread to nearby organs, and the death rate is about 1% of cases. The signs of squamous cell carcinoma are the same as that for basal cell carcinoma, except that it may also show itself as a wart that bleeds and scabs.

Melanoma that starts in the melanocytes has the appearance of an unusual mole. Unlike a dark mole that is circular and confined, melanoma moles look like spilled ink spots. A variety of shades can be seen in the same mole, and they can itch, hurt, or feel numb. The skin around the mole turns grey, white, or red. Melanoma is most apt

a.

Figure 35A

Sunbathing is even more dangerous today because of ozone depletion. **a.** Sunbathing on the beach. **b.** The UV index measures the relative amount of solar UV radiation for cities. An ozone hole will increase each city's index by about 20%; as the index rises, so does the incidence of skin cancer.

City	UV Index
Anchorage	100
Seattle	477
Minneapolis	570
Boston	591
Chicago	637
New York City	639
Philadelphia	656
Washington, D.C.	683
Columbus	698
St. Louis	714
San Francisco	715
Boise	715
Los Angeles	824
Dallas	871
Atlanta	875
Las Vegas	876
Phoenix	889
Denver	951
Houston	999
Miami	1028
Honolulu	1147

b.

to appear in persons who have fair skin, particularly if they have suffered occasional severe burns as children. The chance of melanoma increases with the number of moles a person has. Most moles appear before the age of fourteen, and their appearance is linked to sun exposure. Melanoma rates have risen since the turn of the century, but the incidence has doubled in the last decade. Now about 32,000 cases of melanoma are diagnosed each year, and one in five persons diagnosed dies within five years.

Since the incidence of skin cancer is related to UV exposure, scientists have developed a UV index to determine how powerful the solar rays are in different U.S. cities (fig. 35A*b*). The index assigns a baseline level of 100 to Anchorage, Alaska. In general, the more southern the city, the higher the UV index, and the greater the risk of skin cancer.

Looking ahead, we should note that for every 10% decrease in the ozone layer, the UV index per city rises by 13–20%, and the chance of skin cancer rises as well. Even if you live in Anchorage, you should take the following steps to protect yourself from the sun.

To prevent the possible occurrence of skin cancer, observe the following:

- Use a broad-spectrum sunscreen, which protects you from both UV-A and UV-B radiation, with an SPF (sun protection factor) of at least 15. (This means, for example, that if you usually burn after a twenty-minute exposure, it will take fifteen times that long before you will burn.)
- Wear protective clothing. Choose fabrics with a tight weave and wear a wide-brimmed hat. A baseball cap does not protect the rims of the ears.
- Stay out of the sun altogether between the hours of 10 A.M. and 3 P.M. This will reduce your annual exposure by as much as 60%.
- Wear sunglasses that have been treated to absorb both UV-A and UV-B radiation. Otherwise, sunglasses can expose your eyes to more damage than usual because pupils dilate in the shade.
- Avoid tanning machines. Although most tanning devices use high levels of only UV-A, the deep layers of the skin become more vulnerable to UV-B radiation when you are later exposed to the sun.

Figure 35.10

Homeostasis and physiological negative feedback mechanism. A receptor signals a regulator center that directs a response. Once normalcy is achieved, the receptor is no longer stimulated.

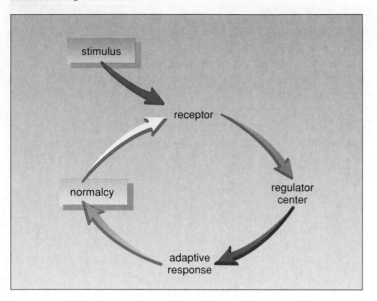

Figure 35.11

Homeostasis and a mechanical negative feedback example. A thermostat that can signal a furnace to turn on or off helps to maintain a relatively stable room temperature.

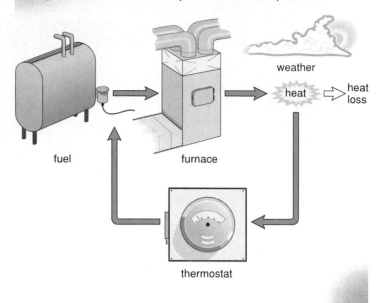

HOMEOSTASIS IS NECESSARY

Claude Bernard, a famous French physiologist, pointed out in 1859 that while an animal lives in an external environment, the cells of the body lie within an internal environment. The *internal environment* is a fluid, called tissue fluid, that bathes the cells of the body. Bernard said that the relative stability of the internal environment allows animals to live in an external environment that can vary considerably. Later, Walter Cannon, an American physiologist, introduced the term **homeostasis** [Gk. *homeo,* same, and *stasis,* standing]. He said there is a dynamic interplay between events that tend to change the internal environment and those that act against this possibility. To achieve homeostasis, the composition of blood and tissue fluid, the body temperature, and the blood pressure, for example, must stay within a normal range.

> The internal environment of an animal's body consists of tissue fluid, which bathes the cells.

Most organ systems of the human body contribute to homeostasis. The digestive system takes in and digests food, providing nutrient molecules that enter the blood and replace the nutrients that are constantly being used by the body cells. The respiratory system adds oxygen to the blood and removes carbon dioxide. The amount of oxygen taken in and carbon dioxide given off can be increased to meet body needs. The liver and the kidneys contribute greatly to homeostasis. For example, immedi-ately after glucose enters the blood, it can be removed by the liver and stored as glycogen. Later, glycogen is broken down to replace the glucose used by the body cells; in this way, the glucose composition of the blood remains constant. The hormone insulin, secreted by the pancreas, regulates glycogen storage. The kidneys are also under hormonal control as they excrete wastes and salts, substances that can affect the pH level of the blood.

Although homeostasis is, to a degree, controlled by hormones, it is ultimately controlled by the nervous system. In humans, the brain contains centers that regulate such factors as temperature and blood pressure. Maintaining the proper temperature and blood pressure levels requires a receptor that detects unacceptable levels and signals a regulator center. If a correction is required, the center then directs an adaptive response (fig. 35.10). Once normalcy is obtained, the receptor is no longer stimulated. This is called control by **negative feedback** because the regulator centers bring about a response that is opposite to present conditions. A useful analogy that helps illustrate how such a negative feedback mechanism works is the control of the heating system of a house by a thermostat (fig. 35.11). Through negative feedback control, indoor temperature can be maintained within a relatively narrow range. In a similar way, temperature in humans is controlled by a portion of the brain that functions much like a thermostat, allowing slight fluctuations within narrow limits (fig. 35.12). **Positive feedback** also occurs on occasion. In these instances, certain events increase the likelihood of a particular response. For example, once the childbirth process begins, each succeeding event makes it more likely that the process will continue until completion.

Figure 35.12

Homeostasis and temperature control. When the body temperature rises, the regulator center directs the blood vessels to dilate and the sweat glands to be active. Now, the body temperature lowers. The regulator center then directs the blood vessels to constrict, causing the hairs to stand on end, and shivering to occur if needed. The body temperature rises again. Because the receptors are sensitive only to a change in the internal environment, the body temperature fluctuates above and below normal.

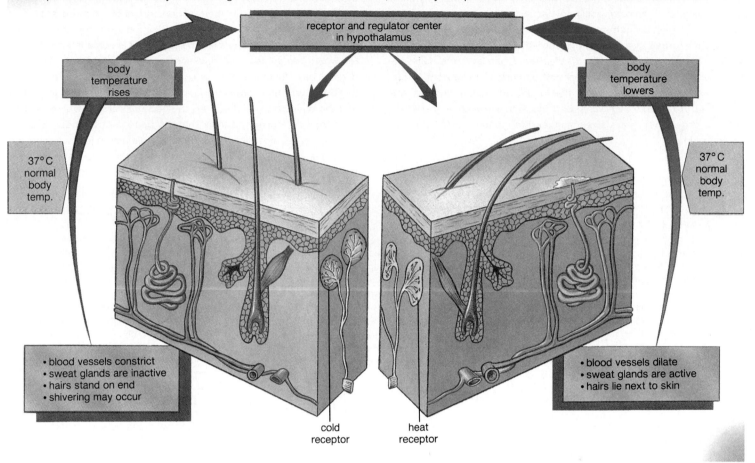

receptor and regulator center
in hypothalamus

body temperature rises

body temperature lowers

37°C normal body temp.

37°C normal body temp.

- blood vessels constrict
- sweat glands are inactive
- hairs stand on end
- shivering may occur

- blood vessels dilate
- sweat glands are active
- hairs lie next to skin

cold receptor

heat receptor

How the Body Controls Temperature

The receptor and the regulator center for body temperature are located in the hypothalamus, a part of the brain. The receptor is sensitive to the temperature of the blood, and when the temperature falls below normal, the receptor signals the regulator center, which directs (via nerve impulses) the muscles (the effectors) of blood vessels in the skin to constrict. This conserves heat. In more hairy animals, the arrector pili muscles also pull hairs erect, and a layer of insulating air is trapped next to the skin. If body temperature falls even lower, the regulator center sends nerve impulses to the skeletal muscles, and shivering occurs. Shivering generates heat, and gradually body temperature rises to 37° C and perhaps higher.

During the period of time the body temperature is normal, the receptor and the regulator center are not active, but once body temperature is higher than normal, they are activated. Now the regulator center directs the blood vessels of the skin to dilate. This allows more blood to flow near the surface of the body, where heat can be lost to the environment. The regulator center also activates the sweat glands, and the evaporation of sweat also helps lower body temperature. Gradually, body temperature decreases to 37° C and perhaps lower. Once body temperature is below normal, the cycle begins again.

Homeostasis of internal conditions is a self-regulating mechanism that results in slight fluctuations above and below a mean.

Biological Relationships

The cells of an animal's body are bathed in tissue fluid. In animals with a circulatory system, this fluid is refreshed by internal exchanges between the capillaries (the smallest vessels in the circulatory system) and tissue fluid. If the composition of tissue fluid is to remain relatively constant, so must the composition of blood remain relatively constant. The various organ systems function to keep the composition of the blood within certain limits. Some of these organ systems have exchange surfaces with the external environment. For example, in humans gas exchange occurs in the lungs, nutrient molecules are absorbed in the small intestine, and the kidneys excrete metabolic wastes. The sense organ also exchanges information with the external environment.

The functions of the various organs are regulated by the nervous system and by the hormones of the endocrine system. The nervous system allows a speedy response to external and internal stimuli, while hormones are slower in their action but allow a more sustained response. There is an intimate connection between the nervous system and the endocrine system such that it is sometimes difficult to tell where the influence of one ends and the influence of the other begins. Many functions of the nervous system and the endocrine system are to maintain homeostasis. We are indeed multicellular animals, and the entire body is designed to keep the cells alive and healthy. You might be inclined to think that the beating of the heart is absolutely essential without considering that this action leads to capillary exchange with tissue fluid. This exchange is the essential purpose of the circulatory system.

Summary

1. Tissues arise from the embryonic germ layers: ectoderm, mesoderm, and endoderm. Ectoderm produces nervous tissue; mesoderm produces muscle and certain systems (circulatory, excretory, reproductive); endoderm produces the linings of the digestive and respiratory tracts and associated organs. Epithelial tissue comes from all three layers.

2. Epithelial tissue covers the body and lines cavities. There is squamous, cuboidal, and columnar epithelium. Each type can be simple or stratified; it can also be glandular, or have modifications like cilia. Epithelial tissue protects, absorbs, secretes, and excretes.

3. Connective tissue has a matrix between cells. Loose connective tissue and fibrous connective tissue contain fibroblasts and fibers (collagen and elastic). Adipose tissue is a type of loose connective tissue; tendons and ligaments are fibrous connective tissue.

4. Cartilage (protein matrix) and bone (calcium matrix) are rigid connective tissues. Blood is connective tissue in which plasma is the matrix.

5. Muscular (contractile) tissue can be smooth or striated (both skeletal and cardiac). In humans, smooth muscle is in the wall of internal organs, skeletal muscle is attached to bone, and cardiac muscle is in the heart.

6. Nervous tissue contains neurons having three parts: dendrites, a cell body, and an axon. Neuroglial cells support and protect neurons.

7. Organs contain various tissues. Skin is an organ that has tissue layers. Epidermis (stratified squamous epithelium) overlies the dermis (fibrous connective tissue containing receptors, hair follicles, blood vessels, and nerves). The subcutaneous layer is composed of loose connective tissue.

8. Organ systems contain several organs. Organ systems of humans carry out the life processes that are common to all organisms and also have specific functions.

9. The human body contains two main cavities. The dorsal cavity contains the brain and spinal cord. The ventral cavity is divided into the thoracic cavity (heart and lungs) and the abdominal cavity (most other internal organs).

10. Homeostasis refers to the relative constancy of the internal environment, which is very often maintained by a negative feedback mechanism in which the response negates the stimulus. As an example, consider body temperature control in humans. When the body is cold, receptors signal a regulator center that directs the muscles of the blood vessels (effectors) to constrict. When the body is warm, receptors signal the regulator center that directs the blood vessels to dilate. Also, sweat glands are activated. It can be seen that this type of regulation causes fluctuations above and below a mean.

Writing Across the Curriculum

In order to practice writing skills, students should write out the answers to any or all of the study questions and the critical thinking questions. The study questions are sequenced in the same order as the text. Answers to the objective questions, and suggested answers to the critical thinking questions, are in appendix D.

Study Questions

1. Name the four major types of tissues.   612

2. Describe the structure and the functions of three types of epithelial tissue.   612–13

3. Describe the structure and the functions of six types of connective tissue.   614–15

4. Describe the structure and the functions of three types of muscular tissue.   616–17

5. Nervous tissue contains what types of cells?   617

6. Describe the structure of skin, and state at least two functions of this organ.   617

7. In general terms, describe the location of the human organ systems.   620

8. Tell how the various systems of the body contribute to homeostasis.   622

9. What is the function of receptors, the regulator center, and effectors in a negative feedback mechanism? Why is it called negative feedback?   622

Objective Questions

1. Which of these is mismatched?
   a. epithelial tissue—protection and absorption
   b. muscular tissue—contraction and conduction
   c. connective tissue—binding and support
   d. nervous tissue—conduction and message sending

2. Which of these is not epithelial tissue?
   a. simple cuboidal and stratified columnar
   b. bone and cartilage
   c. stratified squamous and simple squamous
   d. All of these are epithelial tissue.

3. Which tissue is more apt to line a lumen?
   a. epithelial tissue
   b. connective tissue
   c. nervous tissue
   d. muscular tissue

4. Tendons and ligaments are
   a. connective tissue.
   b. associated with the bones.
   c. found in vertebrates.
   d. All of these are correct.

5. Which tissue has cells in lacunae?
   a. epithelial tissue
   b. cartilage
   c. bone
   d. Both b and c are correct.

6. Cardiac muscle is
   a. striated.
   b. involuntary.
   c. smooth.
   d. Both a and b are correct.

7. Which of these components of blood fights infection?
   a. red blood cells
   b. white blood cells
   c. platelets
   d. All of these are correct.

8. Which of these body systems contribute to homeostasis?
   a. digestive and excretory systems
   b. respiratory and nervous systems
   c. nervous and endocrine systems
   d. All of these are correct.

9. With negative feedback,
   a. the output cancels the input.
   b. there is a fluctuation above and below the average.
   c. there is self-regulation.
   d. All of these are correct.

10. When a person is cold, the blood vessels
    a. dilate, and the sweat glands are inactive.
    b. dilate, and the sweat glands are active.
    c. constrict, and the sweat glands are inactive.
    d. constrict, and the sweat glands are active.

11. Identify each of these tissues, and tell whether the tissue is a type of epithelial tissue, muscular tissue, nervous tissue, or connective tissue.

a.

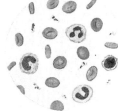

b.

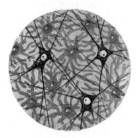

c.

d.

Concepts and Critical Thinking

1. *An animal's body has levels of organization.*

How is each level of organization more than the sum of its parts?

2. *All organisms carry out certain life processes.*

Review the chart on page 620 and explain the associations listed.

3. *The internal environment of organisms stays relatively constant.*

How does each of the life processes (except produce offspring) help keep the internal environment relatively constant?

Selected Key Terms

adipose tissue A connective tissue in which fat is stored. [L. *adeps*, fat]   614

blood A type of connective tissue in which cells are separated by a liquid called plasma.   615

bone Connective tissue in which the cells lie within lacunae embedded in a hard matrix of calcium salts deposited around protein fibers.   615

cardiac muscle Striated, involuntary muscle tissue found only in the heart. [Gk. *card*, heart]   616

cartilage A connective tissue in which the cells lie within lacunae embedded in a flexible proteinaceous matrix. [L. *cartilago*, gristle]   614

connective tissue A type of animal tissue that binds structures together, provides support and protection, fills spaces, stores fat, and forms blood cells; adipose tissue, cartilage, bone, and blood are types of connective tissue.   614

dermis The deeper, thicker layer of the skin that consists of fibrous connective tissue and contains various structures such as sense organs. [Gk. *derm*, skin]   619

epidermis The outer, protective layer of the skin. [Gk. *epi*, upon, and *derm*, skin]   619

epithelial tissue A type of animal tissue forming a continuous layer over most body surfaces (i.e., skin) and inner cavities; squamous, cuboidal, and columnar are the three types of epithelial tissue. [Gk. *epi*, upon, and *thec*, a case]   612

fibroblast Cell type of loose and fibrous connective tissue with cells at some distance from one another and separated by a jellylike matrix containing collagen and elastin fibers. [L. *fibr*, fiber, and Gk. *blast*, bud]   614

homeostasis The maintenance of internal conditions in a cell or an organism by means of a self-regulating mechanism. [Gk. *homeo*, same, and *stasis*, standing]   622

muscular (contractile) tissue A type of animal tissue composed of fibers that shorten and lengthen to produce movements; skeletal, cardiac, and smooth (visceral) are the three types of vertebrate muscles.   616

negative feedback A mechanism of homeostatic response in which the output is counter to and cancels the input.   622

nervous tissue A type of animal tissue; contains nerve cells (neurons), which conduct impulses, and neuroglial cells, which support, protect, and provide nutrients to neurons.   617

neuron Nerve cell that characteristically has three parts: dendrites, cell body, and axon. [Gk. *neuro*, nerve]   617

organ A combination of two or more different tissues performing a common function.   618

organ system A group of related organs working together.   618

positive feedback A mechanism of homeostatic response in which the output intensifies and increases the likelihood of response, instead of countering it and canceling it.   622

skeletal muscle Striated, voluntary muscle tissue that comprises skeletal muscles; also called striated muscle.   616

smooth (visceral) muscle Nonstriated, involuntary muscles found in the walls of internal organs.   616

striated Having bands; cardiac and skeletal muscle are striated with bands of light and dark. [L. *stria*, streaked]   616

tendon Strap of fibrous connective tissue that joins skeletal muscle to bone. [L. *tend*, stretch]   614

tissue A group of similar cells combined to perform a common function.   612

36

CIRCULATORY SYSTEM

Learning Objectives

Transporting in Invertebrates
- Describe how transport is carried out in invertebrates. 628–29

Transporting in Vertebrates
- Compare the structure and the function of the three types of blood vessels. 630–31
- Compare the circulatory pathways of vertebrate animals. 631

Transporting in Humans
- Trace the path of blood through the heart and about the body. 633
- Describe how the heart beats, and tell how the heartbeat is controlled. 634–35
- List the factors that control the pressure and velocity of blood in the vessels. 637

Cardiovascular Disorders Occur
- Explain how strokes and heart attacks can occur. 638–39

Blood Is Transport Medium
- List the components of human blood plasma, and describe the function and the source of each. 641
- Describe the structure and function of human blood cells. 641–42
- List the three steps necessary for the clotting of blood. 642
- Draw and explain a diagram depicting capillary exchange within tissues. 642–43
- List the ABO blood types and describe a laboratory procedure for typing blood. 644

When blood clots, red blood cells are caught in fibrin threads.

10 µm

Every animal cell requires a supply of oxygen and of nutrient molecules and must rid itself of waste molecules. Unicellular animal-like protozoa make these exchanges directly with the external environment that surrounds their body. Even some small multicellular animals do not have an internal transport system because their cells can be serviced without one (fig. 36.1). Larger invertebrates and vertebrates usually have a circulatory system that transports oxygen and nutrient molecules to cells and transports waste molecules away from cells.

TRANSPORTING IN INVERTEBRATES

Some invertebrates are organized in a way that does not require a circulatory system. Others utilize either an open or a closed circulatory system.

With a Cavity

Sea anemones, which are cnidaria, and planaria, which are flatworms, have a sac body plan (fig. 36.1*b,* and *c*). This body plan makes a circulatory system unnecessary. In a sea anemone, cells are either part of an external layer or they line the gastrovascular cavity. In either case, each cell is exposed to water and can independently exchange gases and rid itself of wastes. The cells that line the gastrovascular cavity are specialized to carry out digestion. They pass nutrient molecules to other cells by diffusion. In a planarian, a trilobed gastrovascular cavity ramifies throughout the small and flattened body. No cell is very far from one of the three digestive branches, so nutrient molecules can diffuse from cell to cell. Similarly, diffusion meets the respiratory and excretory needs of the cells.

With an Open or a Closed System

Certain arthropods and mollusks have an *open circulatory system* in which fluid is not always contained within vessels (fig. 36.2*a*). A heart pumps the circulatory fluid into vessels, and then these vessels empty either into body cavities, where interstitial fluid bathes the internal organs, or into sinuses located within the organs themselves. Eventually this combined fluid drains back to the heart. Because the circulatory fluid mixes with interstitial fluid, the term *hemolymph* is used instead of blood.

Figure 36.1

Aquatic organisms without a circulatory system. **a.** A paramecium is a unicellular organism that carries on gas exchange across its cell surface. Food particles that flow into a specialized region called a gullet are enclosed within food vacuoles (green), where digestion occurs. Molecules leave these vacuoles as they are distributed about the cell by a movement of the cytoplasm. **b.** In a sea anemone, a cnidarian, digestion takes place inside the gastrovascular cavity, so named because it (like a vascular system) makes digested material available to the cells that line the cavity. These cells can also acquire oxygen from the watery contents of the cavity and discharge their wastes there. **c.** In a planarian, a flatworm, the gastrovascular cavity ramifies throughout the body, bringing nutrients to body cells. Diffusion is sufficient to pass molecules to every cell from either the cavity or the exterior surface.

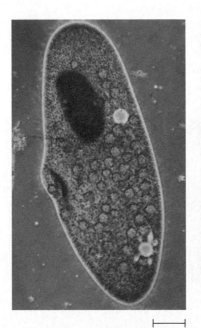
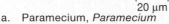
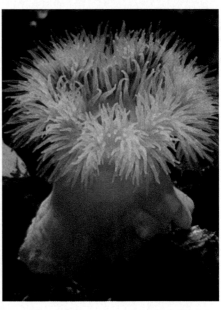

a. Paramecium, *Paramecium*   b.   Sea anemone, *Apitasia*

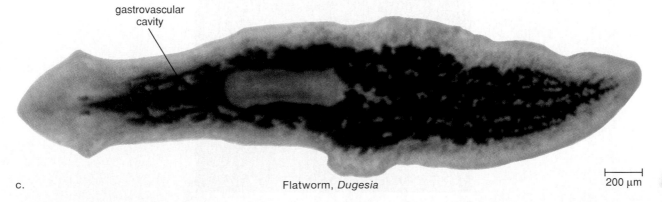

gastrovascular cavity

c.   Flatworm, *Dugesia*   200 µm

In the grasshopper, the dorsal heart pumps hemolymph into a dorsal aorta, which empties into a body cavity termed a *hemocoel*. When the heart contracts, openings called ostia (sing., ostium) are closed; when the heart relaxes, the hemolymph is sucked back into the heart by way of the ostia. The hemolymph of a grasshopper is colorless because it does not contain hemoglobin or any other respiratory pigment. It does not carry oxygen but only nutrients. Oxygen is taken to cells and carbon dioxide is removed from them by way of air tubes, called tracheae, which are found throughout the body. Flight muscles require a very efficient means of receiving oxygen, and the tracheae do a more efficient job than an open circulatory system would do.

All vertebrates and several types of invertebrates, including earthworms, which are annelids, and squids and octopuses, which are mollusks, have a *closed circulatory system*. Blood, which usually consists of cells and plasma, is pumped by the heart into a system of blood vessels (fig. 36.2b). There are valves that prevent the backward flow of blood.

In the segmented earthworm, five pairs of anterior lateral vessels pump blood into the ventral blood vessel, which has a branch in every segment of the worm's body. Blood moves through these branches into capillaries, where exchanges with tissue fluid take place. Blood then moves into veins that return it to the dorsal blood vessel. This dorsal blood vessel returns blood to the heart for repumping.

The earthworm has red blood that contains the respiratory pigment hemoglobin. Hemoglobin is dissolved in the blood and is not contained within cells. The earthworm has no specialized boundary for gas exchange with the external environment. Gas exchange takes place across the body wall, which must always remain moist for this purpose.

> Animals with a gastrovascular cavity do not have a circulatory system. Other animals have an open or a closed circulatory system.

Figure 36.2 💿 📼

Open versus closed circulatory system. **a.** The grasshopper has an open circulatory system. A hemocoel is a body cavity filled with, hemolymph which freely bathes the internal organs. The heart keeps the hemolymph moving, but this open system probably could not supply oxygen to wing muscles rapidly enough. These muscles receive oxygen directly from trachea (air tubes). **b.** The earthworm has a closed circulatory system. The dorsal and ventral blood vessels are joined by five pairs of anterior hearts and by branch vessels in the rest of the worm.

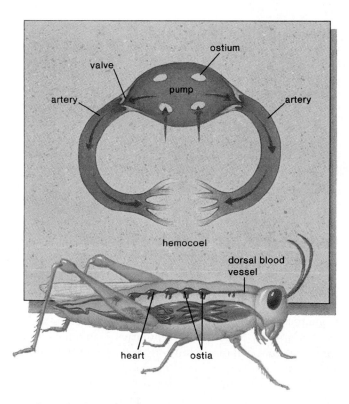

a. Open circulatory system

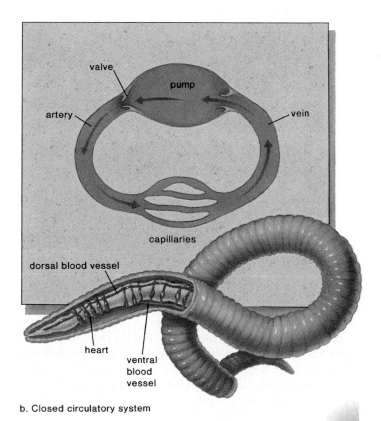

b. Closed circulatory system

Figure 36.3 🔲

Circulation in birds and mammals. **a.** Blood leaving the heart moves from an artery to arterioles to capillaries to venules and then returns to the heart by way of a vein. **b.** Arteries have well-developed walls with a thick middle layer of elastic tissue and smooth muscle. **c.** Capillary walls are only one cell thick. **d.** Veins have flabby walls, particularly because the middle layer is not as thick as in arteries. Veins have valves, which point toward the heart.

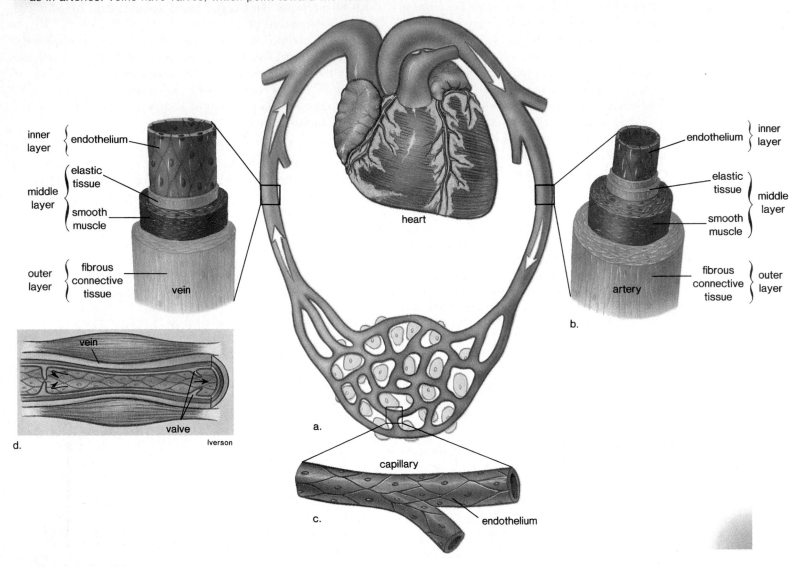

TRANSPORTING IN VERTEBRATES

All vertebrate animals have a closed circulatory system called a **cardiovascular system** [Gk. *card,* heart, and L. *vascul,* little vessel]. It consists of a strong, muscular heart, in which the *atria* (sing., atrium) primarily receive blood and the muscular *ventricles* pump blood out through the blood vessels. There are three kinds of blood vessels: **arteries,** which carry blood away from the heart; **capillaries** [L. *capilla,* hair], which exchange materials with tissue fluid; and **veins** [L. *ven,* vein], which return blood to the heart (fig. 36.3).

Arteries have thick walls and are resilient; therefore, they are able to expand and accommodate the sudden increase in blood volume that results after each heartbeat. **Arterioles** are small arteries whose constriction can be regulated by the nervous system. Arteriole constriction and dilation affect blood pressure in general. The greater the number of vessels dilated, the lower the blood pressure.

Arterioles branch into capillaries, which are extremely narrow, microscopic tubes with a wall composed of only one layer of cells. Capillary beds (many capillaries interconnected) are so prevalent that, in humans, all cells are within 60–80 μm of a capillary. But only about 5% of the capillary beds are open at the same time. After an animal has eaten, the capillary beds in the digestive tract are usually open, and during muscular exercise, the capillary beds of the muscles are open. Capillaries, which are usually so narrow that red blood cells pass through in single file, allow exchange of nutrient and waste molecules across their thin walls.

Figure 36.4 📼

Comparison of circulatory systems in vertebrates. **a.** In a fish, the blood moves in a single loop. The heart has a single atrium and ventricle and pumps the blood into the gill region, where gas exchange takes place. Blood pressure created by the pumping of the heart is dissipated after the blood passes through the gill capillaries. This is a disadvantage of this single-loop system. **b.** Amphibians have a double-loop system in which the heart pumps blood to both the lungs and the body itself. Although there is a single ventricle, there is little mixing of oxygenated and deoxygenated blood. **c.** The pulmonary and systemic systems are completely separate in birds and mammals, since the heart is divided by a septum into a right and left half. The right side pumps blood to the lungs, and the left side pumps blood to the body proper.

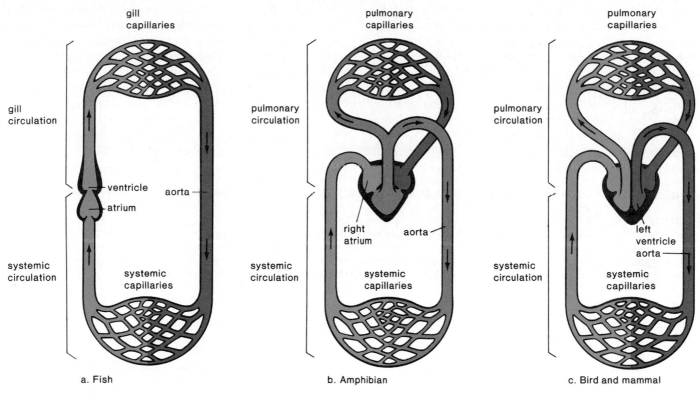

Key:

- ■ oxygenated blood
- ☐ deoxygenated blood
- ▨ mixed blood

Venules and veins collect blood from the capillary beds and take it to the heart. First the venules drain the blood from the capillaries, and then they join to form a vein. The wall of a vein is much thinner than that of an artery and this may be associated with a lower blood pressure in the veins. Valves within the veins point, or open, toward the heart, preventing a backflow of blood when they close (fig. 36.3d).

Comparing Circulatory Pathways

Among vertebrate animals, there are three different types of circulatory pathways. In fishes, blood follows a one-circuit (single-loop circulatory) pathway through the body. The heart has a single atrium and a single ventricle (fig. 36.4a). The pumping action of the ventricle sends blood under pressure to the gills, where it is oxygenated. After passing through the gills, blood is under reduced pressure and flow.

As a result of evolutionary changes, the other vertebrates have a two-circuit (double-loop circulatory) pathway. The heart pumps blood to the tissues, called *systemic circulation,* and also pumps blood to the lungs, called *pulmonary circulation.* This double pumping action is an adaptation to breathing air on land.

In amphibians and most reptiles, the heart has two atria, but there is only a single ventricle (fig. 36.4b). The hearts of some reptiles, all birds, and all mammals are divided into right and left halves (fig. 36.4c). The right ventricle pumps blood to the lungs, and the left ventricle pumps blood to the rest of the body. This arrangement provides adequate blood pressure for both the pulmonary and systemic circulations.

> In mammals, birds, and some reptiles, the heart is divided into a right side and a left side; this ensures adequate blood pressure for both the pulmonary and systemic circulations.

TRANSPORTING IN HUMANS

The functions of the circulatory system include (1) transporting gases, nutrients, and wastes about the body, (2) clotting to prevent loss of blood from injured blood vessels, and (3) fighting infection or invasion of the body by microbes.

The Heart Pumps Blood

The **heart** is a cone-shaped, muscular organ about the size of a fist (fig. 36.5). It is located between the lungs directly behind the sternum (breastbone) and is tilted so that the apex is directed to the left. The major portion of the heart, called the **myocardium** [Gk. *myo,* muscle, and *card,* heart], consists largely of cardiac muscle tissue. The muscle fibers of the myocardium are branched and tightly joined to one another. The heart lies within the pericardium, a thick, membranous sac that contains pericardial fluid, which has a cushioning effect. The inner surface of the heart is lined with endocardium, which consists of connective tissue and endothelial tissue.

Internally, a wall called the septum separates the heart into a right side and a left side (fig. 36.6). The heart has four chambers: two upper, thin-walled **atria,** sometimes called auricles, and two lower, thick-walled **ventricles.** The atria are much smaller and weaker than the muscular ventricles, but they hold the same volume of blood.

The heart also has **valves,** which direct the flow of blood and prevent its backward movement. These valves are supported by strong fibrous strings called chordae tendineae. The chordae, which are attached to muscular projections of the ventricular walls, support the valves and prevent them from inverting when the heart contracts. The **atrioventricular valve** on the right side is called the *tricuspid valve* because it has three cusps, or flaps. The valve on the left side is called the *bicuspid* (or the *mitral*) because it has two flaps. There are also *semilunar valves,* which resemble half moons, between the ventricles and their attached vessels. The pulmonary semilunar valve lies between the right ventricle and the pulmonary trunk. The aortic semilunar valve lies between the left ventricle and the aorta.

Figure 36.5

External heart anatomy. **a.** The venae cavae bring deoxygenated blood to the right side of the heart from the body, and the pulmonary arteries take this blood to the lungs. The pulmonary veins bring oxygenated blood from the lungs to the left side of the heart, and the aorta takes this blood to the body. **b.** The coronary arteries and cardiac veins pervade cardiac muscle. They bring oxygen and nutrients to cardiac cells, which derive no benefit from blood coursing through the heart.

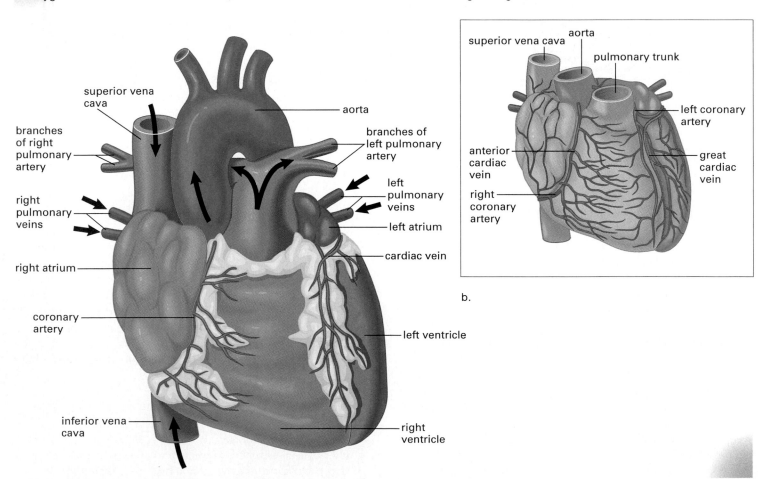

How the Blood Moves

We can trace the path of blood through the heart (fig. 36.6) in the following manner:

The superior vena cava and the inferior vena cava, both carrying deoxygenated blood, enter the right atrium.

The right atrium sends blood through an atrioventricular valve (the tricuspid valve) to the right ventricle.

The right ventricle sends blood through the pulmonary semilunar valve into the pulmonary trunk and the pulmonary arteries to the lungs.

The pulmonary veins, carrying oxygenated blood from the lungs, enter the left atrium.

The left atrium sends blood through an atrioventricular valve (the bicuspid or mitral valve) to the left ventricle.

The left ventricle sends blood through the aortic semilunar valve into the aorta and to the body proper.

From this description, you can see that blood must go through the lungs in order to pass from the right side to the left side of the heart. The heart is a double pump because the right side of the heart sends blood through the lungs, and the left side sends blood throughout the body. Since the left ventricle has the harder job of pumping blood to the entire body, its walls are thicker than those of the right ventricle.

Figure 36.6

Internal view of the heart. **a.** The right side of the heart contains deoxygenated blood and the left side of the heart contains oxygenated blood. **b.** This diagrammatic representation of the heart allows you to trace the path of the blood. On the right side of the heart: venae cavae, right atrium, right ventricle, pulmonary arteries to lungs. On the left side of the heart: pulmonary veins, left atrium, left ventricle, aorta to body. Restate this and write in the names of the valves where appropriate.

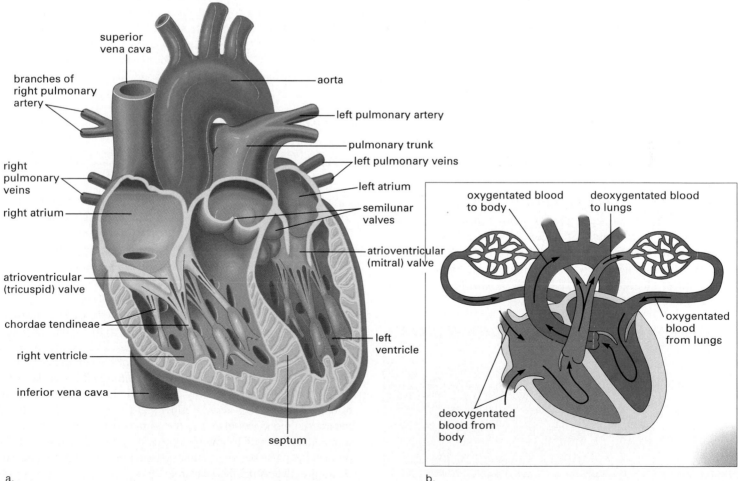

William Harvey and Circulation of the Blood

illiam Harvey (1578–1657) was the first to offer proof that the blood circulates in the body of humans and other animals. Harvey was an English scientist of the seventeenth century, a time of renewed interest in the collection of facts, the use of the hypothesis, the use of experimentation, and the respect for mathematics. This time period is known as the scientific revolution.

After many years of research and study, Harvey hypothesized that the heart is a pump for the entire circulatory system and that blood flows in a circuit. In contrast to former anatomists, Harvey dissected not only dead but also live organisms and observed that when the heart beats, it contracts, forcing blood into the aorta. Had this blood come from the right side of the heart? To do away with the complication of the lungs (pulmonary circulation), Harvey turned to fishes and noticed that the heart first receives and then pumps the blood forward. He observed that blood in the mammalian fetus passes directly from the right side of the heart through the septum to the left side. He felt confident that in mature higher organisms, all blood moves from the right to the left side of the heart by way of the lungs.

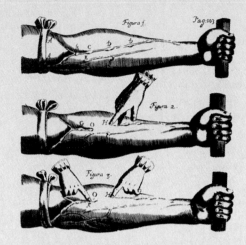

Figure 36A

Harvey's drawings showing how he concluded that the veins return blood to the heart. Harvey tied a ligature (*Figure 1*) above the elbow to observe the accumulation of blood in the veins. Blood can be forced past a valve from H to O (*Figure 2*), but not in the opposite direction (*Figure 3*). Therefore, it can be deduced that blood ordinarily moves toward the heart in the veins.

Harvey then wanted to show an intimate connection between the arteries and veins in the tissues of the body. Again using live organisms, he demonstrated that if an artery is slit, the whole blood system empties, includ-

ing arteries and veins. He measured the capacity of the left ventricle in humans and found it to be 2 oz. Since the heart beats seventy times a minute, in one hour the left ventricle forces into the aorta no less than $70 \times 60 \times 2 = 8,400$ oz = 525 lb, or about three times a man's weight! Could so much blood be created and consumed every hour? The same blood must return again and again to the heart.

Harvey also studied the valves in the veins and suggested their true purpose. By the use of ligatures, he demonstrated that a tight ligature on the arm causes the artery to swell on the side of the heart, and a slack ligature causes the vein to swell on the opposite side (fig. 36A). He said "This is an obvious indication the blood passes from the arteries into the veins . . . . and there is an anastomosis of the two orders of vessels."

Harvey's methods showed how fruitful research might be done. He established that physical and mechanical evidence could provide data for a theory of circulation. He erred, however, when he speculated that the heart heated the blood, and the lung served to cool it or control the degree of heat. His basic method, however, contributed to the scientific revolution and set an example for others to follow.

How the Heartbeat Occurs

The heart contracts, or beats, about seventy times a minute, and each heartbeat lasts about 0.85 seconds. The term **systole** [Gk. *systol,* contraction] refers to contraction of heart chambers and the word **diastole** [Gk. *diastol,* standing apart] refers to relaxation of these chambers. Each heartbeat, or *cardiac cycle,* consists of the following phases:

Cardiac Cycle		
Time	Atria	Ventricles
0.15 sec	Systole	Diastole
0.30 sec	Diastole	Systole
0.40 sec	Diastole	Diastole

First the atria contract (while the ventricles relax), then the ventricles contract (while the atria relax), and then all chambers rest. The short systole of the atria is appropriate since the atria send blood only into the ventricles. It is the muscular ventricles that actually pump blood out into the circulatory system proper. When the word *systole* is used alone, it usually refers to the left ventricular systole.

When the heart beats, the familiar lub-dub sound is heard as the valves of the heart close. The *lub* is caused by vibrations of the heart when the atrioventricular valves close, and the *dub* is heard when vibrations occur due to the closing of the semilunar valves. These valves aid circulation of the blood through the heart because they permit only one-way flow and do not allow a backward flow of blood. The *pulse* is a wave effect that passes down the walls of the arterial blood vessels when the aorta expands and then almost immediately recoils following ventricle systole. Because there is one arterial pulse per ventricular systole, the arterial pulse rate can be used to determine the heart rate.

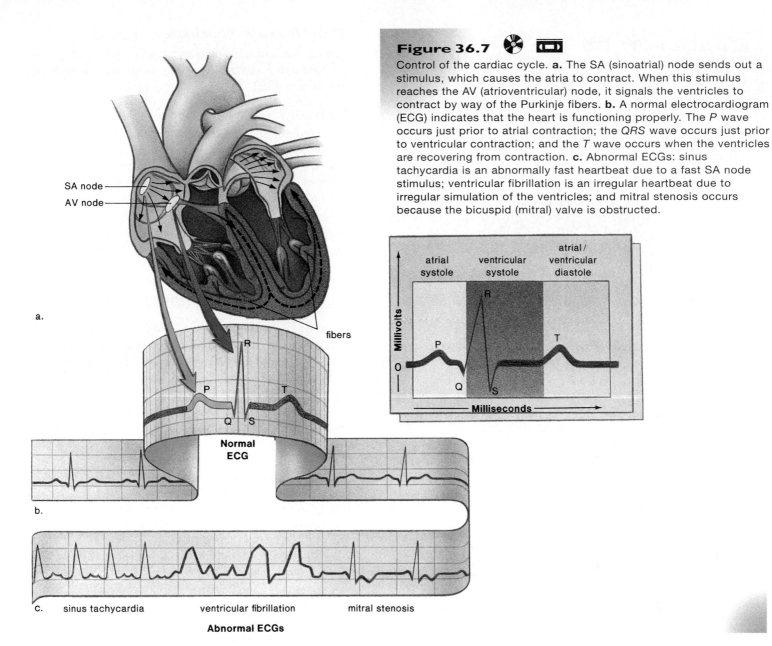

Figure 36.7

Control of the cardiac cycle. **a.** The SA (sinoatrial) node sends out a stimulus, which causes the atria to contract. When this stimulus reaches the AV (atrioventricular) node, it signals the ventricles to contract by way of the Purkinje fibers. **b.** A normal electrocardiogram (ECG) indicates that the heart is functioning properly. The *P* wave occurs just prior to atrial contraction; the *QRS* wave occurs just prior to ventricular contraction; and the *T* wave occurs when the ventricles are recovering from contraction. **c.** Abnormal ECGs: sinus tachycardia is an abnormally fast heartbeat due to a fast SA node stimulus; ventricular fibrillation is an irregular heartbeat due to irregular simulation of the ventricles; and mitral stenosis occurs because the bicuspid (mitral) valve is obstructed.

SA node

AV node

a.

fibers

Normal ECG

b.

c.   sinus tachycardia   ventricular fibrillation   mitral stenosis

Abnormal ECGs

atrial systole   ventricular systole   atrial / ventricular diastole

Millivolts

P   R   Q   S   T

Milliseconds

The contraction of the heart is intrinsic, meaning that the heart will beat independent of any nervous stimulation. In fact, it is possible to dissect out a small heart, such as a frog's heart, and watch it undergo contraction in a petri dish. This is due to a unique type of tissue called nodal tissue, with both muscular and nervous characteristics, located in two regions of the heart. The first of these, the *SA (sinoatrial) node*, is found in the upper dorsal wall of the right atrium; the other, the *AV (atrioventricular) node*, is found in the base of the right atrium very near the septum (fig. 36.7a). The SA node initiates the heartbeat and automatically sends out an excitation impulse every 0.85 seconds to cause the atria to contract. Therefore the SA node is called the pacemaker

because it usually keeps the heartbeat regular. When the impulse reaches the AV node, it signals the ventricles to contract by way of specialized fibers. Although the beat of the heart is intrinsic, it is regulated by the nervous system which can increase or decrease the heartbeat rate.

With the contraction of any muscle, including the myocardium, ionic changes occur; these can be detected with electrical recording devices. The pattern that results, called an electrocardiogram (ECG or EKG), is associated with the cardiac cycle as indicated (fig. 36.7b, c). An examination of the electrocardiogram indicates whether the heartbeat has a normal or an irregular pattern.

Figure 36.8

Blood vessels in the pulmonary and systemic circuits. The blue-colored vessels carry deoxygenated blood, and the red-colored vessels carry oxygenated blood; the arrows indicate the flow of blood. In order to trace blood from the right to the left side of the heart, you must begin at the lung capillaries. In order to trace blood from the capillaries of the digestive tract to the right atrium, you must consider the hepatic portal vein and the hepatic vein.

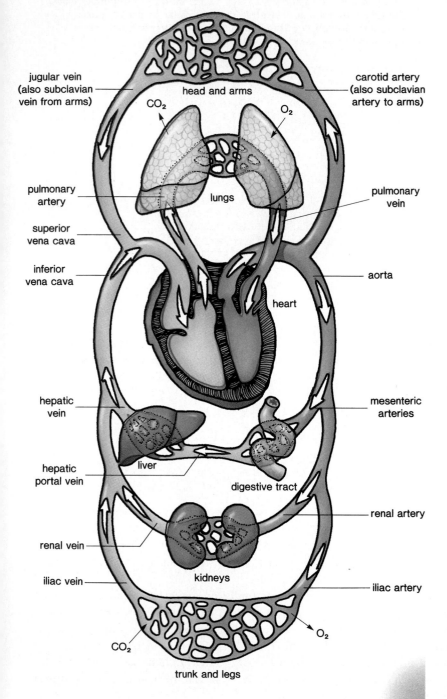

The Vessels Conduct Blood

Human circulation includes two major circular pathways, the **pulmonary circuit** [L. *pulmo,* lung] and the **systemic circuit** (fig. 36.8).

To the Lungs

In the pulmonary circuit, the path of blood can be traced as follows. Deoxygenated blood from all regions of the body collects in the right atrium and then passes into the right ventricle, which pumps it into the pulmonary trunk. The pulmonary trunk divides into the right and left pulmonary arteries, which carry blood to the lungs. As blood passes through the pulmonary capillaries, carbon dioxide is given off and oxygen is picked up. Blood returns through pulmonary venules and veins to the left atrium of the heart.

To the Body

The **aorta** [L. *aorta,* great artery] and the **venae cavae** (sing., vena cava) [L. *ven,* vein, and *cav,* hollow] serve as the major pathways for blood in the systemic circuit. To trace the path of blood to any organ in the body, you need only mention the aorta, the proper branch of the aorta, the organ, and the vein returning blood to the vena cava. In the systemic circuit, arteries contain oxygenated blood and have a bright red color, but veins contain deoxygenated blood and appear dull red or, when viewed through the skin, blue.

The *coronary arteries* are extremely important because they serve the heart muscle itself (see fig. 36.5). (The heart is not nourished by the blood in its chambers.) The coronary arteries arise from the aorta just above the aortic semilunar valve. They lie on the exterior surface of the heart, where they branch into arterioles and then capillaries. The capillary beds enter venules, which join to form the cardiac veins, and these empty into the right atrium.

A **portal system** [L. *porta,* door] is one that begins and ends in capillaries. One place in the human body where a portal system is found is between the small intestine and the liver. Blood passes from the capillaries of intestinal villi into venules that join to form the hepatic portal vein, a vessel that connects the intestine with the liver. The hepatic vein leaves the liver and enters the inferior vena cava.

> The pulmonary circuit takes deoxygenated blood to the lungs and oxygenated blood to the heart. The systemic circuit takes blood throughout the body from the aorta to the venae cavae.

Figure 36.9

Diagram illustrating how velocity and blood pressure are related to the total cross-sectional area of blood vessels. Capillaries have the greatest cross-sectional area, and blood in capillaries is under the least pressure and has the least velocity. Skeletal muscle contraction, not blood pressure, accounts for the velocity of blood in the veins.

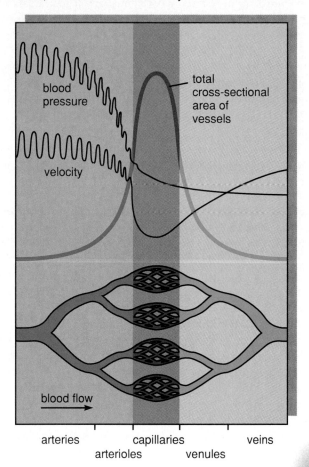

Figure 36.10

Cross section of a valve. **a.** When a valve is open—a result of pressure on the veins exerted by skeletal muscle contraction—the blood flows toward the heart in veins. **b.** Valves close when external pressure is no longer applied to the veins. Closure of the valves prevents the blood from flowing in the opposite direction.

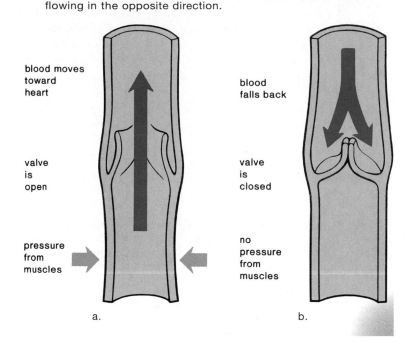

Blood Pressure Drops Off

When the left ventricle contracts, blood is forced into the arteries under pressure. *Systolic pressure* results from blood being forced into the arteries during ventricular systole, and *diastolic pressure* is the pressure in the arteries during ventricular diastole. Human **blood pressure** is measured with a sphygmomanometer, which has a pressure cuff that measures the amount of pressure required to stop the flow of blood through an artery. Blood pressure is normally measured on the brachial artery, which is in the upper arm, and is stated in millimeters of mercury (mm Hg). A blood pressure reading consists of two numbers, for example, 120/80—which represents systolic and diastolic pressures, respectively.

As blood flows from the aorta into the various arteries and arterioles, blood pressure falls. Also, the difference in pressure between systolic and diastolic gradually diminishes. In the capil-

laries, there is a slow, fairly even, flow of blood. This may be related to the very high total cross-sectional area of the capillaries (fig. 36.9). It's even been suggested that if all the blood vessels in a human were connected end to end, the total distance would reach around the earth two times at the equator, or about 50,000 miles. A large portion of this distance would be due to the quantity of capillaries.

Blood pressure in the veins is low and cannot move blood back to the heart, especially from the limbs of the body. When skeletal muscles near veins contract, they put pressure on the collapsible walls of the veins and on blood contained in these vessels. Veins, however, have *valves* that prevent the backward flow of blood, and therefore pressure from muscle contraction is sufficient to move blood through veins toward the heart (fig. 36.10). *Varicose veins,* abnormal dilations in superficial veins, develop when the valves of the veins become weak and ineffective due to a backward pressure of the blood.

The beat of the heart supplies the pressure that keeps blood moving in the arteries, and skeletal muscle contraction pushes blood in the veins back to the heart.

Cardiovascular Disease

Because sudden cardiac death happens once every seventy-two seconds in the United States, we will examine the factors that predispose an individual to cardiovascular disease. The risk factors for cardiovascular disease include the following:

- Male sex
- Family history of heart attack under age fifty-five
- Smoking more than ten cigarettes a day
- Severe obesity (30% or more overweight)
- Hypertension
- Unfavorable HDL (high-density lipoprotein) and LDL (low-density lipoprotein) cholesterol blood levels
- Impaired circulation to the brain or the legs
- Diabetes mellitus

Hypertension is well recognized as a major factor in cardiovascular disease, and two controllable behaviors contribute to hypertension. Smoking cigarettes—including filtered cigarettes—causes hypertension, as does obesity. When a person smokes, the drug nicotine, present in cigarette smoke, enters the bloodstream. Nicotine causes the arterioles to constrict and the blood pressure to rise. More dangerous is the need for the heart to pump harder to propel blood through the lungs at a time when the oxygen-carrying capacity of the blood is reduced due to intake of carbon monoxide.

A person who is more than 20% above recommended weight is considered obese. More tissues require servicing, and the heart sends the extra blood out under greater pressure. Since it is very difficult for obese individuals to lose weight, it is recommended that weight control be a lifelong endeavor.

Another behavior that is much in the news of late is the adoption of a diet low in saturated fats and cholesterol. Many believe that such a diet protects against the development of cardiovascular disease. Cholesterol is ferried in the blood by two types of plasma proteins—LDL and HDL. LDL (called "bad" lipoprotein) transports cholesterol to the tissues from the liver, and HDL (called "good" lipoprotein) transports cholesterol out of the tissues to the liver. When the LDL level in blood is abnormally high or the HDL level is abnormally low, cholesterol accumulates in the cells. When cholesterol-laden cells line the arteries, plaque develops, which interferes with circulation (fig. 36B).

The National Heart, Lung, and Blood Institute recommends that everyone know his or her blood cholesterol level. Individuals with a high level (240 mg/100 ml) should always be further tested to determine what their LDL blood cholesterol level is. If the LDL level is 160 mg/100 ml or higher, and/or if the total cholesterol-to-HDL cholesterol ratio is higher than 4.5, the person is considered at risk. Individuals with a normal total cholesterol level, but with an unfavorable total cholesterol-to-HDL cholesterol ratio, have had heart attacks.

A diet low in saturated fat and cholesterol has been found to lower the total blood cholesterol and the LDL level in some patients, but until recently drugs were not very helpful. This is expected to change. In a recent study of 4,444 patients in Norway, those who received a drug called simvastatin had a 30% lower risk of dying from any cause and a 43% reduced chance of dying from coronary heart disease. New regimens involving this type of drug—or even hormonal therapies in women—are expected soon.

Exercise can also be helpful. One study found that moderately active men who spent on the average of forty-eight minutes a day on a leisure-time activity such as gardening, bowling, or dancing had one-third fewer heart attacks than peers who spent an average of only sixteen minutes each day in these activities. Exercise helps control weight, reduces hypertension, and may help minimize stress. One physician recommends that his cardiovascular patients walk for one hour, three times a week, and in addition they are to practice meditation and yogalike stretching and breathing exercises to reduce stress.

CARDIOVASCULAR DISORDERS OCCUR

More than 50% of all deaths in the United States are attributable to cardiovascular disease. The number of deaths due to hypertension, stroke, and heart attack is greater than the number due to cancer and accidents combined.

Hypertension Is a Concern

Hypertension is present when the systolic and diastolic pressures are significantly higher than 120/80 mm Hg. Hypertension is sometimes called a silent killer because it may not be detected until a stroke or heart attack occurs. Therefore, it is important to have regular blood pressure checks and to adopt a life-style that protects against the development of hypertension, as discussed in the reading above. Hypertension is seen in individuals with kidney disease and also in individuals who have atherosclerosis, which is an accumulation of soft masses of fatty materials, particularly cholesterol, beneath the inner linings of arteries. Such deposits are called plaque, and as it develops, it tends to protrude into the vessel, interfering with blood flow. Plaque can cause a blood clot to form on the irregular aterial wall. As long as the blood clot remains stationary, it is called a *thrombus,* but when and if it dislodges and moves along with blood, it is called an *embolus.* If thromboembolism is not treated, complications can arise.

Stroke and Heart Attack Kill

A stroke occurs when a portion of the brain dies due to a lack of oxygen. A stroke that results in paralysis or death often occurs

Figure 36B

Plaque. **a.** Plaque (yellow) in the coronary artery of a heart patient. **b.** Cross section of plaque shows its composition and indicates how it bulges out into the lumen of an artery, obstructing blood flow.

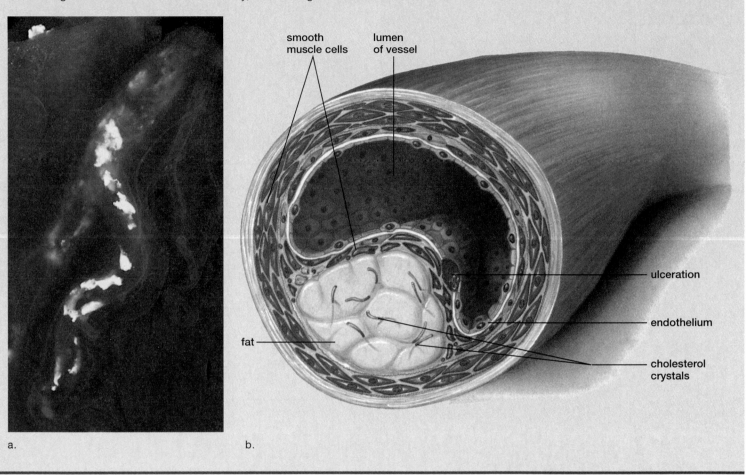

a.

b.

when a small arteriole bursts or is blocked by an embolus. A heart attack occurs when a portion of the heart muscle dies because of a lack of oxygen. If the coronary artery is partially blocked due to plaque, the individual may suffer from *angina pectoris,* characterized by a radiating pain in the left arm. When a coronary artery is completely blocked, perhaps because of thromboembolism, a heart attack occurs.

Medical treatment for thromboembolism includes two drugs that can be given intravenously to dissolve a clot: streptokinase, normally produced by bacteria, and tPA, which is genetically engineered. Both drugs convert plasminogen, a molecule found in blood, into plasmin, an enzyme that dissolves blood clots. In fact, tPA, which stands for tissue plasminogen activator, is the body's own way of converting plasminogen to plasmin. If a person has symptoms of angina or a thrombolytic stroke, then an

anticoagulant drug such as aspirin may be given. Aspirin reduces the stickiness of platelets and therefore lowers the probability that a clot will form.

Surgical procedures are also available to clear clogged arteries. In angioplasty, a cardiologist threads a plastic tube into an artery of an arm or a leg and guides it through a major blood vessel toward the heart. When the tube reaches the region clogged by plaque in a coronary artery, the balloon attached to the end of the tube is inflated, forcing the vessel open. Another alternative is coronary artery bypass surgery. During this operation, surgeons take a segment of another blood vessel from the patient's body and stitch one end to the aorta and the other end to a coronary artery past the point of obstruction. Once the heart is exposed, some physicians also use lasers to open clogged coronary vessels.

Figure 36.11

Composition of blood. When blood is transferred to a test tube and is prevented from clotting, it forms two layers. The transparent yellow top layer is plasma, the liquid portion of blood. The formed elements are in the bottom layer. The tables describe these components in detail.

Formed Elements	Function and Description	Source
Red Blood Cells (erythrocytes)  4 million–6 million per mm³ blood	Transport O_2 and help transport CO_2 7–8 μm in diameter Bright-red to dark-purple biconcave disks without nuclei	Bone marrow
White Blood Cells (leukocytes)	Fight infection	Bone marrow
Granular leukocytes* Basophil 20–50 per mm³ blood	10–12 μm in diameter Spherical cells with lobed nuclei; large, irregularly shaped, deep-blue granules in cytoplasm	
 Eosinophil 100–400 per mm³ blood	10–14 μm in diameter Spherical cells with bilobed nuclei; coarse, deep-red, uniformly sized granules in cytoplasm	
 Neutrophil 3,000–7,000 per mm³ blood	10–14 μm in diameter Spherical cells with multilobed nuclei; fine, pink granules in cytoplasm	
Agranular leukocytes* Lymphocyte 1,500–3,000 per mm³ blood	5–17 μm in diameter (average 9–10 μm) Spherical cells with large, round nuclei	
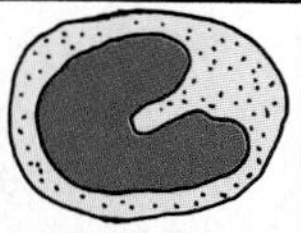 Monocyte 100–700 per mm³ blood	14–24 μm in diameter Large spherical cells with kidney-shaped, round, or lobed nuclei	
Platelets (thrombocytes)  250,000–500,000 per mm³ blood	Initiate clotting 2–4 μm in diameter Disk-shaped cell fragments with no nuclei; purple granules in cytoplasm	Bone marrow

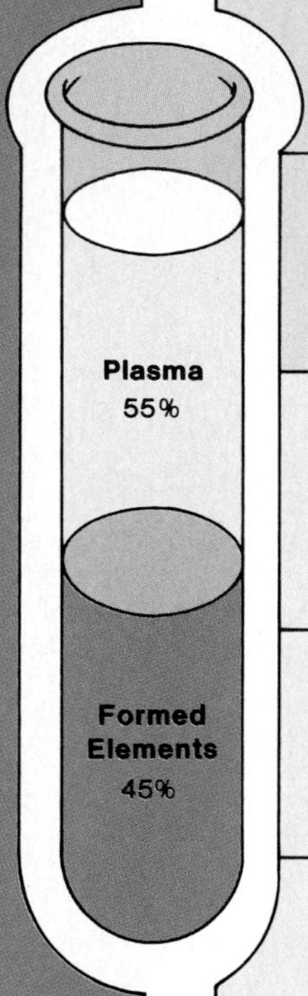

Plasma 55%

Formed Elements 45%

Plasma	Function	Source
Water (90–92% of plasma)	Maintains blood volume; transports molecules	Absorbed from intestine
Plasma proteins (7–8% of plasma) Albumin Fibrinogen Globulins	Maintain blood osmotic pressure and pH Maintains blood volume and pressure Clotting Transport; fight infection	Liver
Salts (less than 1% of plasma)	Maintain blood osmotic pressure and pH; aid metabolism	Absorbed from intestinal villi
Gases Oxygen Carbon dioxide	 Cellular respiration End product of metabolism	 Lungs Tissues
Nutrients Fats Glucose Amino acids	Food for cells	Absorbed from intestinal villi
Urea	Nitrogenous waste	Liver
Hormones, vitamins, etc.	Aid metabolism	Varied

*with Wright's stain

BLOOD IS TRANSPORT MEDIUM

Blood has two main portions: the liquid portion, called plasma, and the formed elements consisting of various cells and platelets (fig. 36.11). **Plasma** [Gk. *plasm,* something molded] contains many types of molecules, including nutrients, wastes, salts, and proteins. The salts and proteins buffer the blood, effectively keeping the pH near 7.4. They also maintain blood's osmotic pressure so that water has an automatic tendency to enter blood capillaries. The plasma proteins assist in transporting large organic molecules in blood. Lipoproteins that transport cholesterol are globulins, and bilirubin, a breakdown product of hemoglobin, is transported by albumin. They also aid in blood clotting.

Blood Cells Are Varied

Blood cells are of three types: red blood cells (RBCs), or **erythrocytes** [Gk. *erythr,* red]; white blood cells (WBCs), or **leukocytes** [Gk. *leuko,* white]; and platelets, or **thrombocytes** [Gk. *thrombo,* blood clot].

RBCs Transport Oxygen

Red blood cells are small biconcave disks that at maturity lack a nucleus and contain the respiratory pigment hemoglobin. There are 4 million to 6 million red blood cells per mm³ of whole blood, and each one of these cells contains about 250 million hemoglobin molecules. **Hemoglobin** [Gk. *hem,* blood, and L. *glob,* ball] contains four globin protein chains, each associated with heme, an iron-containing group. Iron combines loosely with oxygen, and in this way oxygen is carried in the blood. If there is an insufficient number of red blood cells or if the cells do not have enough hemoglobin, the individual suffers from anemia and has a tired, run-down feeling.

Red blood cells are manufactured continuously in the red bone marrow of the skull, the ribs, the vertebrae, and the ends of the long bones. The growth factor erythropoietin, which is produced when an enzyme from the kidneys acts on a precursor made by the liver, stimulates the production of red blood cells. Now available as a drug, erythropoietin is helpful to persons with anemia and is also sometimes abused by athletes who want to increase performance.

Before they are released from the bone marrow into blood, red blood cells lose their nucleus and synthesize hemoglobin. After living about 120 days, they are destroyed chiefly in the liver and the spleen, where they are engulfed by large phagocytic cells. When red blood cells are destroyed, hemoglobin is released. The iron is recovered and is returned to the red bone marrow for reuse. The heme portions of the molecules undergo chemical degradation and are excreted by the liver as bile pigments in the bile. The bile pigments are primarily responsible for the color of feces.

WBCs Fight Infection

White blood cells differ from red blood cells in that they are usually larger and have a nucleus, they lack hemoglobin, and, without staining, they appear translucent. With staining, white blood cells appear light blue unless they have granules that bind with certain stains. The *granular leukocytes* have a lobed nucleus and may be: neutrophils, which have granules that do not take up a dye; eosinophils, which have granules that take up the red dye eosin; and basophils, which have granules that take up a basic dye, staining them a deep blue. *Agranular leukocytes* (with no granules) have a circular or indented nucleus. There are two types—the larger monocytes and the smaller lymphocytes. The newly discovered stem cell growth factor (SGF) can be used to increase the production of all white blood cells, and there are also various specific stimulating factors that can be used to stimulate the production of specific stem cells. These growth factors should be helpful to patients with low immunity, such as AIDS patients.

When microorganisms enter the body due to an injury, the response is called an *inflammatory reaction* because there is swelling and reddening at the injured site. The damaged tissue has released kinins, which cause vasodilation, and histamines, which cause increased capillary permeability. **Neutrophils** [L. *neutro,* neither, and *phil,* loving], which are amoeboid, squeeze through the capillary wall and enter the tissue fluid, where they phagocytize foreign material. Monocytes appear and are transformed into **macrophages** [Gk. *macr,* large, and *phag,* eat], which are large phagocytizing cells that release white blood cell growth factors. Soon there is an explosive increase in the number of leukocytes. The thick, yellowish fluid called pus contains a larger proportion of dead white blood cells that have fought the infection.

Lymphocytes [L. *lymph,* water, and *cyt,* cell] also play an important role in fighting infection. Certain lymphocytes called T cells attack cells that contain viruses. Other lymphocytes called B cells produce antibodies. Each B cell produces just one type of antibody, which is specific for one type of antigen. An **antigen** [Gk. *anti,* against, and *gene,* origin], which is most often a protein but is sometimes a polysaccharide, causes the body to produce an antibody because the antigen doesn't belong to the body. Antigens are found in the outer covering of parasites or are present in their toxins. When **antibodies** [Gk. *anti,* against] combine with antigens, the complex is often phagocytized by a macrophage. An individual is actively immune when a large number of B cells are all producing the specific antibody needed for a particular infection.

Figure 36.12 📼

Blood clotting. **a.** Platelets and damaged tissue cells release prothrombin activator, which acts on prothrombin in the presence of calcium ions (Ca^{++}) to produce thrombin, which acts on fibrinogen to form fibrin. **b.** A scanning electron micrograph shows a red blood cell caught in the fibrin threads of a clot.

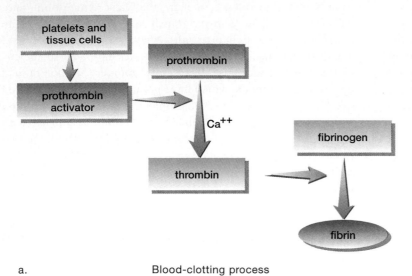

a.   Blood-clotting process

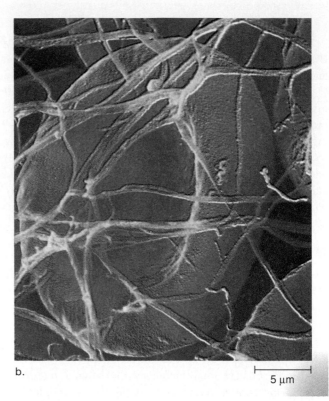

b.

5 μm

Platelets Assist Blood Clotting

Platelets (thrombocytes) result from fragmentation of certain large cells, called megakaryocytes, in the bone marrow. **Platelets** [Gk. *plate*, flat] are involved in the process of blood clotting, or coagulation. Also necessary to the process are fibrinogen and prothrombin, proteins manufactured and deposited in blood by the liver. If clotting occurs in a test tube, a fluid called *serum* collects above the clot. Serum has the same composition as plasma except that it lacks prothrombin and fibrinogen.

Blood Clotting Has Steps

When a blood vessel in the body is damaged, platelets clump at the site of the puncture and partially seal the leak. They and the injured tissues release a clotting factor called *prothrombin activator* that converts prothrombin to thrombin. This reaction requires calcium ions (Ca^{++}). Thrombin, in turn, acts as an enzyme that severs two short amino acid chains from each fibrinogen molecule. These activated fragments then join end to end, forming long threads of *fibrin*. Fibrin threads wind around the platelet plug in the damaged area of the blood vessel and provide the framework for the clot. Red blood cells also are trapped within the fibrin threads; these cells make a clot appear red (fig. 36.12). A fibrin clot is present only temporarily. As soon as blood vessel repair is initiated, an enzyme called plasmin destroys the fibrin network and restores the fluidity of plasma.

> A blood clot consists of platelets and red blood cells entangled within fibrin threads.

Servicing the Cells

No cell is far away from one or more capillaries because capillaries are found throughout every tissue in the body. The cross-sectional area of capillaries is so large that blood flows very slowly through them (see fig. 36.9). This slow rate allows adequate time for exchange of materials between blood and tissue fluid. **Tissue fluid** surrounds cells, and the circulatory system performs an important homeostatic function by providing nutrients to and removing wastes from tissue fluid.

Much of the exchange between blood and tissue fluid occurs by diffusion through the one-cell-thick capillary walls. While lipid-soluble substances can pass freely through the plasma membrane of cells, water-soluble substances usually diffuse through pores present in junctions between the cells of the capillary walls. Two forces control movement of fluid through the capillary wall: osmotic pressure, which tends to cause water to move from tissue fluid to blood, and blood pressure, which tends to cause water to move in the opposite direction.

Figure 36.13

Exchanges between blood and tissue fluid across a capillary wall.

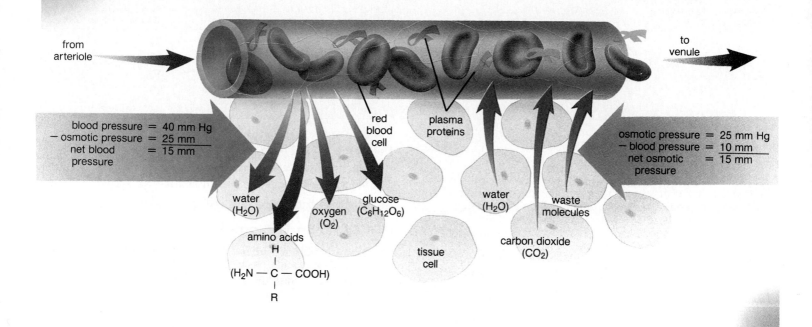

blood pressure = 40 mm Hg
− osmotic pressure = 25 mm
net blood = 15 mm
pressure

osmotic pressure = 25 mm Hg
− blood pressure = 10 mm
net osmotic = 15 mm
pressure

red blood cell

plasma proteins

water (H₂O)

oxygen (O₂)

glucose (C₆H₁₂O₆)

water (H₂O)

waste molecules

amino acids

H
|
(H₂N — C — COOH)
|
R

carbon dioxide (CO₂)

tissue cell

As figure 36.13 illustrates, blood pressure is higher than osmotic pressure at the arterial end of a capillary. This tends to force fluid out through the pores in the capillary wall. Midway along the capillary, where blood pressure is lower, the two forces essentially cancel each other, and there is no net movement of water. Solutes now diffuse according to their concentration gradient—nutrients (glucose and oxygen) diffuse out of the capillary, and wastes (carbon dioxide) diffuse into the capillary. Since proteins are too large to pass out of the capillary, tissue fluid tends to contain all components of plasma except proteins. At the venule end of a capillary, where blood pressure has fallen, osmotic pressure is greater than blood pressure, and water tends to move into the capillary. Almost the same amount of fluid that left the capillary returns to it, although there is always some excess tissue fluid collected by the lymphatic capillaries (fig. 36.14).

Oxygen and nutrient molecules exit a capillary near the arterial end; carbon dioxide and waste molecules enter a capillary near the venous end.

Figure 36.14

Lymphatic vessels. Arrows indicate that lymph is formed when lymphatic capillaries take up excess tissue fluid. Lymphatic capillaries lie near blood capillaries.

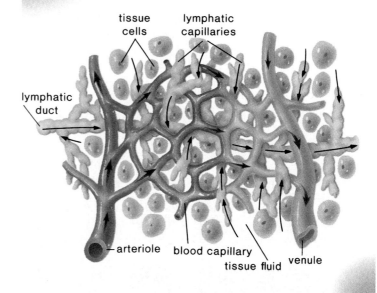

tissue cells

lymphatic capillaries

lymphatic duct

arteriole

blood capillary

tissue fluid

venule

Table 36.1

The ABO System

Blood Type	Antigen on Red Blood Cells	Antibody in Plasma	% U.S. African American	% U.S. Caucasian	% U.S. Asian	% North American Indians	% Americans of Chinese Descent
A	A	Anti-B	27	41	28	8	25
B	B	Anti-A	20	9	27	1	35
AB	A, B	None	4	3	5	0	10
O	None	Anti-A and anti-B	49	47	40	92	30

Figure 36.15

Blood typing. The standard test to determine ABO and Rh blood type consists of putting a drop of anti-A antibodies, anti-B antibodies, and anti-Rh antibodies on a slide. To each of these, a drop of the person's blood is added. **a.** If agglutination occurs, as seen in the photo on the right, the person has this antigen on red blood cells. **b.** Several possible results. The blood type reveals the antigens that are present on the red blood cells (represented by dots).

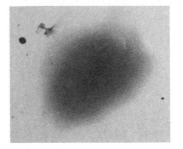

Antigen not present and agglutination does not occur.

Antigen present and agglutination occurs.

a.

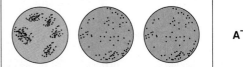

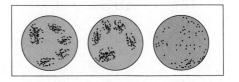

b.

Know Your Blood Type

Although there are at least twelve well-known blood type identification systems, the ABO system and the Rh system are most often used to determine blood type.

ABO System Is Common

Before the twentieth century, blood transfusions sometimes resulted in adverse reactions or even death. A concerned Viennese physician, Karl Lansteiner, began to study the matter by mixing different samples of blood and examining the effect under the microscope. In the end, he and his associates determined that there are four major blood groups among humans. They designated the types of blood as A, B, AB, and O (table 36.1). The types of blood are dependent on whether A antigen and/or B antigen is present on red blood cells. Type O blood has neither the A antigen nor the B antigen on red blood cells; the other types of blood have one or both of the antigen(s) present. A (or B) is not an antigen to an individual with blood type A, but it can be an antigen to a recipient with a different blood type.

Within the plasma of the individual, there are antibodies to the antigens that are not present on the red blood cells. Therefore, for example, type A has an antibody called anti-B in the plasma. Type AB blood has neither anti-A nor anti-B antibodies because both antigens are on the red blood cells. This is reasonable because if these antibodies were present, **agglutination** [L. *agglutin, glued together*], or clumping of red blood cells, would occur.

For a recipient to receive blood from a donor, the recipient's plasma must not have an antibody that causes the donor's cells to agglutinate. For this reason it is important to determine each person's blood type. Figure 36.15 demonstrates a way to use the antibodies derived from plasma to determine blood type. If clumping occurs after a sample of blood is exposed to anti-A or anti-B antibody, the person has that antigen on the red blood cells. In the first example given, the individual's blood sample does not react to either anti-A or anti-B antibody; therefore, the blood type is O. The + and − are discussed in the next section.

Figure 36.16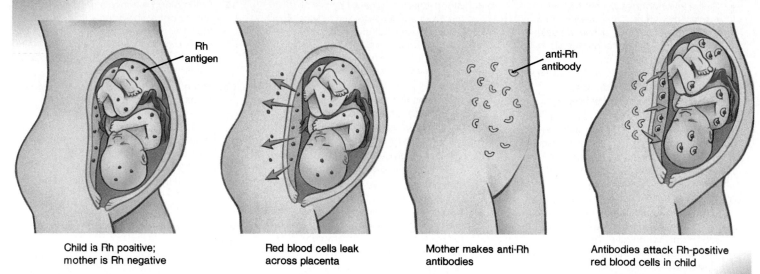

Development of hemolytic disease of the newborn (HDN).

| Child is Rh positive; mother is Rh negative | Red blood cells leak across placenta | Mother makes anti-Rh antibodies | Antibodies attack Rh-positive red blood cells in child |

In the figure: **Rh antigen**, **anti-Rh antibody**

In the ABO system, there are four blood types (A, B, AB, and O) designated by the antigens present on red blood cells.

Rh System Also

Another important antigen in matching blood types is the Rh (for rhesus monkey) factor. About 85% of the U.S. population has the Rh factor on the red blood cells and are Rh positive (Rh^+). About 15% percent do not have the antigen and are Rh negative (Rh^-). Rh-negative individuals do not normally make antibodies to the Rh factor, but they will make them when exposed to the Rh factor.

When Rh positive blood is mixed with anti-Rh antibodies, agglutination occurs (fig. 36.15). The designation of blood type usually also includes whether the person has or does not have the Rh factor on the red blood cells.

The Rh factor is particularly important during pregnancy. Rh positive is dominant over Rh negative. If the mother is Rh negative and the father is heterozygous, the child has a 50% chance of being Rh positive (fig. 36.16). The child's Rh positive red blood cells begin leaking across the placenta into the mother's circulatory system because placental tissues normally break down before and at birth. The presence of these Rh antigens causes the mother to produce anti-Rh antibodies. In this or a subsequent pregnancy with an Rh positive baby, anti-Rh antibodies produced by the mother may cross the placenta and destroy this child's red blood cells. This is called *hemolytic disease of the newborn,* (HDN), because hemolysis continues after the baby is born. Due to red blood cell destruction followed by heme breakdown, bilirubin rises in the blood. Excess bilirubin can lead to brain damage, mental retardation, or even death.

The Rh problem has been solved by giving Rh-negative women an Rh immunoglobulin injection either midway through the first pregnancy or no later than seventy-two hours after giving birth to an Rh-positive child. This injection contains anti-Rh antibodies that attack any of the baby's red blood cells in the mother's blood before these cells stimulate her immune system to produce her own antibodies. This injection is not beneficial if the woman has already begun to produce antibodies; therefore, the timing of the injection is most important.

The possibility of hemolytic disease of the newborn exists when the mother is Rh negative and the father is Rh positive.

Summary

1. Some invertebrates do not have a transport system. The presence of a gastrovascular cavity allows diffusion alone to supply the needs of cells in cnidaria and flatworms.

2. Other invertebrates do have a transport system. Insects have an open circulatory system and earthworms have a closed one.

3. Vertebrates have a closed system in which arteries carry blood away from the heart to capillaries, where exchange takes place, and veins carry blood to the heart.

4. Fishes have a single-loop circulatory pathway because the heart, with the single atrium and ventricle, pumps blood only to the gills. The other vertebrates have both pulmonary and systemic circulation. Amphibians have two atria but a single ventricle. Birds and mammals, including humans, have a heart with two atria and two ventricles, in which oxygenated blood is always separate from deoxygenated blood.

5. The heartbeat in humans begins when the SA node (pacemaker) causes the two atria to contract, sending blood through the atrioventricular valves to the two ventricles. The AV (atrioventricular) node causes the two ventricles to contract, sending blood through the semilunar valves to the pulmonary trunk and the aorta. Now all chambers rest. The heart sounds, lub-dub, are caused by the closing of the valves.

6. Blood pressure created by the beat of the heart accounts for the flow of blood in the arteries, but skeletal muscle contraction is largely responsible for the flow of blood in the veins, which have valves preventing a backward flow.

7. Blood has two main parts: plasma and cells. Plasma contains mostly water (90–92%) and proteins (7–8%) but also nutrients and wastes.

8. The red blood cells contain hemoglobin and function in oxygen transport.

9. Defense against disease depends on the various types of leukocytes. Neutrophils and monocytes are phagocytic and are especially responsible for the inflammatory reaction. Lymphocytes are involved in the development of immunity to disease.

10. The platelets and two plasma proteins, prothrombin and fibrinogen, function in blood clotting, an enzymatic process that results in fibrin threads.

11. Blood clotting is a complex process that includes three major events: platelets and injured tissue release prothrombin activator, which enzymatically changes prothrombin to thrombin; thrombin is an enzyme that causes fibrinogen to be converted to fibrin threads.

12. When blood reaches a capillary, water moves out at the arterial end, due to blood pressure. At the venule end, water moves in, due to osmotic pressure. In between, nutrients diffuse out and wastes diffuse in.

13. In the ABO blood system there are four types of blood: A, B, AB, and O, depending on the type of antigen present on red blood cells. If the red blood cells have a particular antigen, they clump when exposed to the corresponding antibody. Table 36.1 tells which types of antibodies are present in the plasma for the various ABO blood groups.

Writing Across the Curriculum

In order to practice writing skills, students should write out the answers to any or all of the study questions and the critical thinking questions. The study questions are sequenced in the same order as the text. Answers to the objective questions, and suggested answers to the critical thinking questions, are in appendix D.

Study Questions

1. Describe transport in those invertebrates that have no circulatory system; in those that have an open circulatory system; and in those that have a closed circulatory system. 628–29

2. Compare the circulatory systems of a fish, an amphibian, and a mammal. 631

3. Trace the path of blood in humans from the right ventricle to the left atrium; from the left ventricle to the kidneys and to the right atrium; from the left ventricle to the small intestine and to the right atrium. 633

4. Describe the beat of the heart, mentioning all the factors that account for this repetitive process. Describe how the heartbeat affects blood flow. What other factors are involved in blood flow? 634

5. Define these terms: pulmonary circuit, systemic circuit, and portal system. 636

6. Discuss the life cycle and function of red blood cells. 641

7. How are white blood cells classified? What are the functions of neutrophils, monocytes, and lymphocytes? 642

8. Name the steps that take place when blood clots. Which substances are present in blood at all times, and which appear during the clotting process? 642

9. What forces facilitate exchange of molecules across the capillary wall? 642–43

10. What are the four ABO blood types? For each, state the antigen(s) on red blood cells and the antibody(ies) in the plasma. 644

11. Problems can arise during childbearing if the mother is which Rh type and the father is which Rh type? Explain why. 645

1. Which one of these would you expect to be part of a closed, but not an open, circulatory system?
   a. ostia
   b. capillary beds
   c. hemocoel
   d. heart

2. In a one-circuit circulatory system, blood pressure
   a. is constant throughout the system.
   b. drops significantly after gas exchange has taken place.
   c. is higher at the intestinal capillaries than at the gill capillaries.
   d. cannot be determined.

3. In which of the following animals is the blood entering the aorta incompletely oxygenated?
   a. frog
   b. chicken
   c. monkey
   d. fish

4. Which of these factors has little effect on blood flow in arteries?
   a. heartbeat
   b. blood pressure
   c. total cross-sectional area of vessels
   d. skeletal muscle contraction

5. In humans, blood returning to the heart from the lungs returns to the
   a. right ventricle.
   b. right atrium.
   c. left ventricle.
   d. left atrium.

6. Systole refers to the contraction of the
   a. major arteries.
   b. SA node.
   c. atria and ventricles.
   d. All of these are correct.

7. Which of these associations is incorrect?
   a. white blood cells—infection fighting
   b. red blood cells—blood clotting
   c. plasma—water, nutrients, and wastes
   d. platelets—blood clotting

8. Water enters capillaries on the venule side as a result of
   a. active transport from tissue fluid.
   b. an osmotic pressure gradient.
   c. increased blood pressure on this side.
   d. higher red blood cell concentration on this side.

9. The last step in blood clotting
   a. requires calcium ions.
   b. occurs outside the bloodstream.
   c. converts prothrombin to thrombin.
   d. converts fibrinogen to fibrin.

10. During blood typing, agglutination indicates that the
    a. plasma contains certain antibodies.
    b. red blood cells carry certain antigens.
    c. plasma contains certain antigens.
    d. red blood cells carry certain antibodies.

11. A baby born to which of these couples is most likely to suffer from hemolytic disease of the newborn?
    a. Rh^+ mother and Rh^- father
    b. Rh^- mother and Rh^- father
    c. Rh^+ mother and Rh^+ father
    d. Rh^- mother and Rh^+ father

12. Label this diagram of the heart:

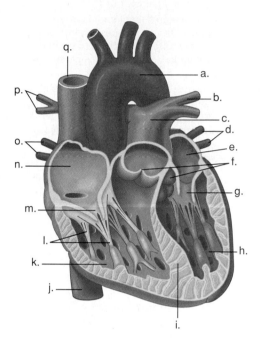

1. *The internal environment of most animals remains relatively constant.*

   How does the composition of tissue fluid stay relatively constant in vertebrates?

2. *A circulatory system is necessary to the life of a complex animal.*

   Why is a circulatory system imperative for complex animals?

3. *Animals are physical and chemical machines; for example, energy must be exerted in order to keep the blood circulating.*

   What type of energy keeps the blood circulating? How do animals acquire the necessary energy?

Selected Key Terms

agglutination (uh-gloot-un-AY-shun) Clumping of red blood cells due to a reaction between antigens on red blood cell membranes and antibodies in the plasma. [L. *agglutin,* glued together]   644

antibody A protein produced by the body in response to the presence of an antigen; it destroys or inactivates the antigen. [Gk. *anti,* against]   641

antigen A foreign substance, usually a protein, that stimulates the immune system to react, such as to produce antibodies. [Gk. *anti,* against, and *gene,* origin]   641

aorta Major systemic artery that takes blood from the heart to the tissues. [L. *aorta,* great artery]   636

arteriole Vessel that takes blood from an artery to capillaries.   630

artery A blood vessel that transports blood away from the heart.   630

atrioventricular valve A heart valve located between an atrium and a ventricle.   632

atrium (sing., atria) Chamber; particularly an upper chamber of the heart lying above the ventricle(s).   632

blood pressure Force of blood pushing against the inside wall of an artery.   637

capillary A microscopic blood vessel; gas and nutrient exchange occurs across the walls of a capillary. [L. *capilla,* hair]   630

cardiovascular system Organ system consisting of the blood, heart, and a series of blood vessels that distribute blood under the pumping action of the heart. [Gk. *card,* heart, and L. *vascul,* little vessel]   630

diastole (dy-AS-tuh-lee) The relaxation period of a heart during the cardiac cycle. [Gk. *diastol,* standing apart]   634

erythrocyte A red blood cell that contains hemoglobin and carries oxygen from the lungs or gills to the tissues in vertebrates. [Gk. *erythr,* red, and *cyt,* cell]   641

heart A muscular organ located in the thoracic cavity that is responsible for maintenance of blood circulation.   632

hemoglobin Red respiratory pigment of erythrocytes used for transport of oxygen. [Gk. *hem,* blood, and L. *glob,* ball]   641

leukocyte White blood cell of which there are several types, each having a specific function in protecting the body from invasion by foreign substances and organisms. [Gk. *leuko,* white, and *cyt,* cell]   641

lymphocyte Specialized white blood cell; occurs in two forms—T lymphocyte and B lymphocyte. [L. *lympho,* water, and *cyt,* cell]   641

macrophage A large phagocytic cell derived from a monocyte that ingests microbes and debris. [Gk. *macr,* large, and *phag,* eat]   641

myocardium Muscle of the heart. [Gk. *myo,* muscle, and *card,* heart]   632

neutrophil Granular leukocyte that is the most abundant of the white blood cells; first to respond to infection. [L. *neutro,* neither, and *phil,* loving]   641

plasma The liquid portion of blood; contains nutrients, wastes, salts, and proteins. [Gk. *plasm,* something molded]   641

platelet A component of blood that is necessary to blood clotting. [Gk. *plate,* flat]   642

portal system A pathway of blood flow that begins and ends in capillaries, such as the one found between the small intestine and liver. [L. *porta,* door]   636

pulmonary circuit A circulatory pathway between the lungs and the heart. [L. *pulmo,* lung]   636

systemic circuit A circulatory pathway of blood flow between the tissues and the heart.   636

systole (SIS-tuh-lee) The contraction period of a heart during the cardiac cycle. [Gk. *systol,* contraction]   634

thrombocyte Platelet; cell fragment in the blood that initiates the process of blood clotting. [Gk. *thrombo,* blood clot, and *cyt,* cell]   641

tissue fluid A filtrate, containing all the small molecules of blood plasma, that bathes all the cells of the body.   642

valve Membranous extension of a vessel or the heart wall that opens and closes, ensuring one-way flow; common to the systemic veins, the lymphatic veins, and the heart.   632

vein A blood vessel that arises from venules and transports blood toward the heart. [L. *ven,* vein]   630

vena cava A large systemic vein that returns blood to the right atrium of the heart in tetrapods; either the superior or inferior vena cava. [L. *ven,* vein, and *cav,* hollow]   636

ventricle Cavity in an organ, such as a lower chamber of the heart; or the ventricles of the brain.   632

venule Vessel that takes blood from capillaries to a vein.   631

37

LYMPHATIC SYSTEM AND IMMUNITY

Learning Objectives

Lymphatic System Helps Circulatory System

- Name three functions of the lymphatic system.   650
- Describe the structure and the function of the lymphatic vessels and the lymphoid organs.   650–52

Some Defenses Are Nonspecific

- Name three nonspecific ways the body defends itself against infections, and give examples of each.   652–54

Other Defenses Are Specific

- Contrast the maturation, the structure, and the function of B and T lymphocytes.   654
- Explain the clonal selection theory as it pertains to B cells and T cells.   655

- Describe the structure and the function of an antibody.   656
- Describe the different types of T cells, and describe the function of each type.   658–59

Immunity Can Be Induced

- Contrast active immunity with passive immunity, and tell why the former lasts longer.   661–62
- Tell how monoclonal antibodies are produced, and list ways in which they are used today.   663

Immunity Has Side Effects

- Name and discuss three types of immunological side effects.   663–64

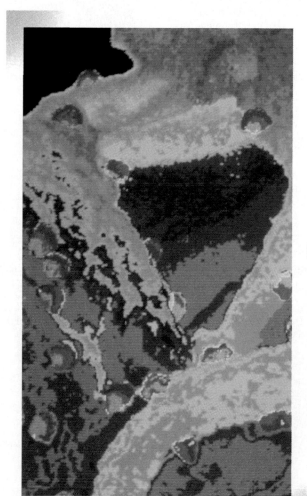

Human immunodeficiency viruses (HIV) attacking a lymphocyte, the very type of cell that ordinarily protects us from disease.

500 nm

We spend our lives surrounded by viruses, bacteria, and other possible parasitic invaders of our bodies. Homeostasis would be impossible without a way to deal with this constant threat, and several mechanisms have evolved to resist a possible takeover. Immunity includes all the possible means to defend ourselves, including assistance from the lymphatic system.

LYMPHATIC SYSTEM HELPS CIRCULATORY SYSTEM

The mammalian **lymphatic system** [L. *lymph,* water] consists of lymphatic vessels and the lymphoid organs. This system, which is closely associated with the cardiovascular system, has three main functions: (1) lymphatic vessels take up excess tissue fluid and return it to the bloodstream; (2) lymphatic capillaries absorb fats at the intestinal villi and transport them to the bloodstream; and (3) the lymphatic system helps to defend the body against disease.

Lymphatic Vessels Transport One Way

Lymphatic vessels are quite extensive; most regions of the body are richly supplied with lymphatic capillaries (fig. 37.1). The construction of the larger lymphatic vessels is similar to that of cardiovascular veins, including the presence of valves. Also, the movement of lymph within these vessels is dependent upon skeletal muscle contraction. When the muscles contract, the lymph is squeezed past a valve that closes, preventing the lymph from flowing backwards.

   The lymphatic system is a one-way system that begins with lymphatic capillaries. These capillaries take up fluid that has diffused from and has not been reabsorbed by the blood capillaries. **Edema** [Gk. *edema,* swelling] is localized swelling caused by the accumulation of tissue fluid. This can happen if too much tissue fluid is made and/or not enough of it is drained away. Once tissue fluid enters the lymphatic vessels, it is called **lymph** [L. *lymph,* water]. The lymphatic capillaries join to form lymphatic vessels that merge before entering one of two ducts: the thoracic duct or the right lymphatic duct. The *thoracic duct* is much larger than the right lymphatic duct. It serves the lower extremities, the abdomen, the left arm, and the left side of both the head and the neck. The *right lymphatic duct* serves the right arm, the right side of both the head and the neck, and the right thoracic area. The lymphatic ducts enter the subclavian veins, which are cardiovascular veins in the thoracic region.

> Lymph flows one way from a capillary to ever-larger lymphatic vessels and finally to a lymphatic duct, which enters a subclavian vein.

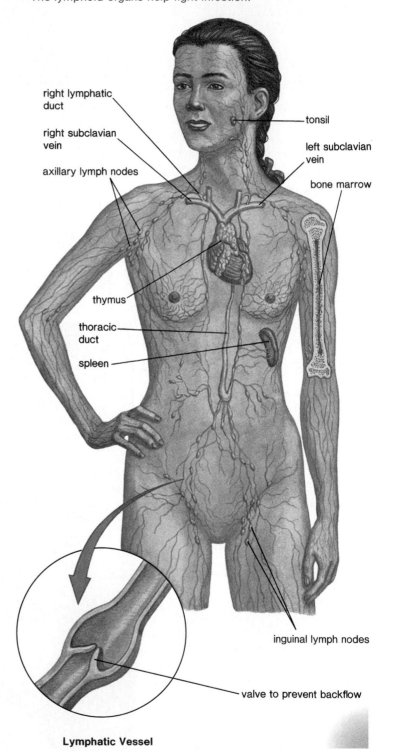

right lymphatic duct
right subclavian vein
axillary lymph nodes
thymus
thoracic duct
spleen
tonsil
left subclavian vein
bone marrow
inguinal lymph nodes
valve to prevent backflow

Lymphatic Vessel

Figure 37.2

The lymphoid organs. The lymphoid organs include the lymph nodes, the thymus gland, the spleen, and the bone marrow, which all contain lymphocytes.

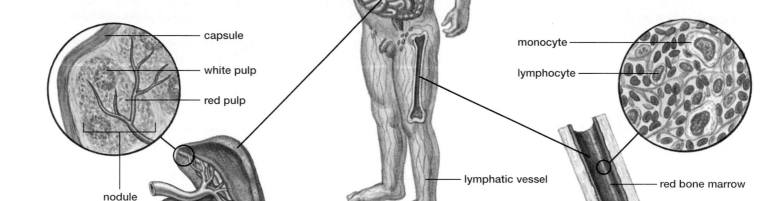

Thymus Gland

cortex
medulla
lobule

tonsil

capsule
sinus
lymph nodule

Lymph Node

capsule
white pulp
red pulp
nodule

Spleen

monocyte
lymphocyte

lymphatic vessel
red bone marrow

Bone Marrow

Lymphoid Organs Assist Immunity

The lymphoid organs of special interest are the lymph nodes, the spleen, the thymus gland, and the bone marrow (fig. 37.2).

Lymph nodes, which are small (about 1–25 mm) ovoid or round structures, are found at certain points along lymphatic vessels. A lymph node has a fibrous connective tissue capsule penetrated by incoming and outgoing lymphatic vessels. Connective tissue also divides a node into nodules. Each nodule contains a sinus (open space) filled with many lymphocytes and macrophages. As lymph passes through the sinuses, the macrophages purify it of infectious organisms and any other debris.

Nodules can occur singly or in groups. The *tonsils,* located in back of the mouth on either side of the tongue, and the *adenoids,* located on the posterior wall above the border of the soft palate, are composed of partly encapsulated lymph nodules. Also, nodules called *Peyer's patches* are found within the intestinal wall.

The lymph nodes are found in groups in certain regions of the body. For example, the inguinal nodes are in the groin and the axillary nodes are in the armpits.

The **spleen** is located in the upper left abdominal cavity just beneath the diaphragm. The construction of the spleen is similar to that of a lymph node. Outer connective tissue divides the organ into lobules, which contain sinuses. In the spleen, however, the sinuses are filled with blood instead of lymph. The blood vessels of the spleen can expand, and this enhances the carrying capacity of this organ to serve as a blood reservoir and to make blood available in times of low pressure or when the body needs extra oxygen carrying capacity.

A spleen nodule contains red pulp and white pulp. The white pulp contains mostly lymphocytes. Red pulp contains red blood cells, lymphocytes, and macrophages. The red pulp helps to purify blood that passes through the spleen by removing bacteria and worn-out or damaged red blood cells. If the spleen ruptures due to injury, it can be removed. Although its functions are replaced by other organs, the individual is often slightly more susceptible to infections and may have to receive antibiotic therapy indefinitely.

The **thymus gland** is located along the trachea behind the sternum in the upper thoracic cavity. This gland varies in size, but it

Figure 37.3

Leukocytes. There are five types of white blood cells, which differ according to structure and function. The frequency of each type of cell is given as a percentage of the total.

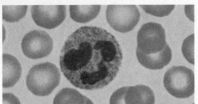

Neutrophil
40–70%
Phagocytizes
primarily bacteria

├── 20 µm ──┤

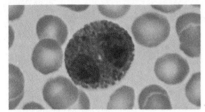

Eosinophil
1–4%
Phagocytizes and destroys
antigen-antibody
complexes

├── 20 µm ──┤

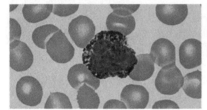

Basophil
0–1%
Congregates in tissues;
releases histamine
when stimulated

├── 20 µm ──┤

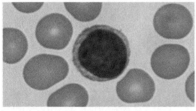

Lymphocyte
20–45%
B type produces antibodies
in blood and lymph;
T type kills virus-
containing cells

├── 20 µm ──┤

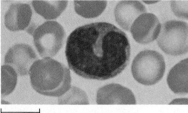

Monocyte
4–8%
Becomes macrophage—
phagocytizes bacteria and
viruses

├── 20 µm ──┤

is larger in children than in adults and may disappear completely in old age. The thymus is divided into lobules by connective tissue. The T lymphocytes mature in these lobules. The interior (medulla) of the lobule, which consists mostly of epithelial cells, stains lighter. It produces thymic hormones, such as thymosin, that are thought to aid in maturation of T lymphocytes. Thymosin may also have other functions in immunity.

Red bone marrow is the site of origination for all types of blood cells, including the five types of white blood cells that function in immunity (fig. 37.3). The marrow contains stem cells that are ever capable of dividing and producing cells that go on to differentiate into the various types of blood cells. In a child, most bones have red bone marrow, but in an adult it is present only in the bones of the skull, the sternum (breastbone), the ribs, the clavicle, the pelvic bones, and the vertebral column. The red bone marrow consists of a network of connective tissue fibers, called reticular fibers, which are produced by cells called reticular cells. These and the stem cells and their progeny are packed about thin-walled sinuses filled with venous blood. Differentiated blood cells enter the bloodstream at these sinuses.

The lymphoid organs have specific functions that assist immunity. Lymph is cleansed in lymph nodes; blood is cleansed in the spleen; T lymphocytes mature in the thymus; and white blood cells are made in the bone marrow.

SOME DEFENSES ARE NONSPECIFIC

Immunity [L. *immun*, safe, free] is the ability of the body to defend itself against infectious agents, foreign cells, and even abnormal body cells, such as cancer cells. Natural immunity ordinarily keeps us free of diseases, including those caused by **microbes** [Gk. *micr*, small] and also cancer.

Immunity includes nonspecific and specific defenses. The three nonspecific defenses—barriers to entry, the inflammatory reaction, and protective proteins—are effective against many types of infectious agents.

Barring Entry

Skin and the mucous membranes lining the respiratory, digestive, and urinary tracts serve as mechanical barriers to entry by microbes. Oil gland secretions contain chemicals that weaken or kill bacteria on skin. The respiratory tract is lined by ciliated cells that sweep mucus and trapped particles up into the throat, where they can be swallowed, or expectorated (coughed out). The stomach has an acidic pH, which inhibits the growth of many types of bacteria. The various bacteria that normally reside in the intestine and other areas, such as the vagina, prevent pathogens from taking up residence.

Phagocytizing the Enemy

Whenever the skin is broken due to a minor injury, a series of events occurs that is known as the **inflammatory reaction** [L. *in*, into, and *flamm*, burn]. The inflamed area has four symptoms: redness, pain, swelling, and heat. Figure 37.4 illustrates the participants in the inflammatory reaction. The mast cells, one type of participant, are derived from basophils (see fig. 37.3), which take up residence in the tissues.

When an injury occurs, a capillary and several tissue cells are apt to rupture and to release **bradykinin** [Gk. *brad*, slow, and

Figure 37.4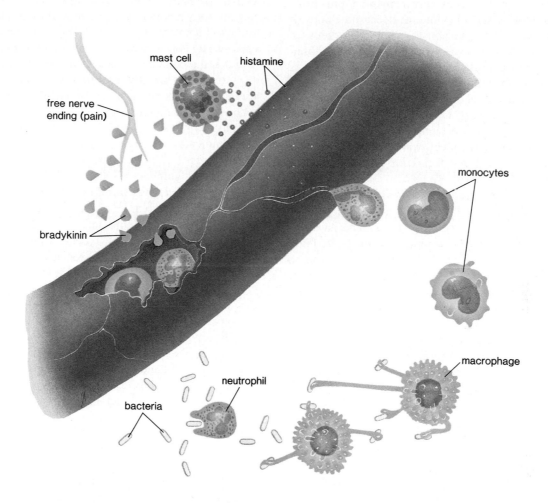

Inflammatory reaction. When a blood vessel is injured, mast cells release histamine, which dilates blood vessels, and bradykinin, which promotes vasodilation and stimulates the pain nerve endings. Neutrophils and monocytes congregate at the injured site and squeeze through the capillary wall. The neutrophils begin to phagocytize bacteria. The monocytes become macrophages, large cells that are especially good at phagocytosis and that also stimulate other white blood cells to action.

kine, movement]. This molecule initiates nerve impulses, resulting in the sensation of pain, and stimulates mast cells to release **histamine** [Gk. *hist,* tissue] which, together with bradykinin, causes the capillaries to dilate and become more permeable. The enlarged capillaries cause the skin to redden, and the increased permeability allows proteins and fluids to escape so swelling results. A rise in temperature reduces the number of invading microbes and increases phagocytosis by white blood cells.

Any break in the skin allows microbes to enter the body and triggers a migration of neutrophils and monocytes to the site of injury. Neutrophils and monocytes are amoeboid; they can change shape and squeeze through capillary walls to enter tissue fluid. Neutrophils phagocytize bacteria and when phagocytosis occurs, an endocytic vesicle forms. The engulfed bacteria are destroyed by hydrolytic enzymes when the vesicle combines with a lysosome, one of the cellular organelles.

Monocytes differentiate into **macrophages** [Gk. *macr,* large, and *phag,* eat], large phagocytic cells that are able to devour a

hundred bacteria or viruses and still survive. Some tissues, particularly connective tissue, have resident macrophages, which routinely act as scavengers, devouring old blood cells, bits of dead tissue, and other debris. Macrophages can also bring about an explosive increase in the number of leukocytes by liberating a growth factor; this passes by way of blood to the red bone marrow, where it stimulates the production and the release of white blood cells, usually neutrophils.

As the infection is being overcome, some neutrophils die. These—along with dead tissue, cells, bacteria, and living white blood cells—form **pus** [L. *pus,* inflammation], a whitish material. Pus indicates that the body is trying to overcome the infection.

> The inflammatory reaction is a "call to arms"—it marshals phagocytic white blood cells to the site of bacterial invasion.

Chemo Warfare

The **complement system,** often simply called complement, is a number of plasma proteins designated by the letter *C* and a subscript. Once a complement protein is activated, it activates another protein, and the result is a set series of reactions. A limited amount of activated protein is needed because a domino effect occurs: each protein in the series is capable of activating many other proteins.

Complement is activated when microbes enter the body. It "complements" certain immune responses, and this accounts for its name. For example, it is involved in and amplifies the inflammatory response because complement proteins attract phagocytes to the scene. Some complement proteins bind to the surface of microbes already coated with antibodies, which ensures that the microbes will be phagocytized by a neutrophil or macrophage.

Another series of reactions is complete when complement proteins produce holes in bacterial cell walls and plasma membranes. When potassium ions leave, fluids and salt enter the bacterial cell to the point that it bursts (fig. 37.5).

Interferon [L. *inter,* between, and *fero,* fierce] is a protein produced by virus-infected cells. Interferon binds to receptors of noninfected cells, causing the cells to prepare for possible attack by producing substances that interfere with viral replication. Interferon is specific to the species; therefore, only human interferon can be used in humans. Although it once was a problem to collect enough interferon for clinical and research purposes, interferon is now made by recombinant DNA (deoxyribonucleic acid) technology.

> **Immunity includes these nonspecific defenses: barriers to entry, the inflammatory reaction, and protective proteins.**

Figure 37.5

Action of the complement system against a bacterium. When complement proteins in the plasma are activated by an immune reaction, they form holes in bacterial cell walls and plasma membranes, allowing fluids and salts to enter until the cell eventually bursts.

OTHER DEFENSES ARE SPECIFIC

Sometimes, it is necessary to rely on a specific defense rather than a nonspecific defense against a particular antigen. An **antigen** [Gk. *anti,* against, and *gene,* origin] is a protein or carbohydrate chain of a glycoprotein within the plasma membrane that the body recognizes as nonself. Microbes have antigens, but antigens can also be part of a foreign cell or a cancer cell. Because we do not ordinarily become immune to our own cells, it is said that the immune system is able to tell self from nonself.

Immunity usually lasts for some time. For example, once we recover from the measles, we usually do not get the illness a second time. Immunity is primarily the result of the action of the **B lymphocytes** [L. *lymph,* water, and *cyt,* cell] and the **T lymphocytes.** B (for bone marrow) lymphocytes mature in the bone marrow, and T (for thymus) lymphocytes mature in the thymus gland. B lymphocytes, also called B cells, give rise to plasma cells, which produce **antibodies** [Gk. *anti,* against], proteins that are capable of combining with and neutralizing antigens. These antibodies are secreted into the blood and the lymph. In contrast, T lymphocytes, also called T cells, do not produce antibodies. Instead, certain T cells directly attack cells that bear antigens. Other T cells regulate the immune response.

Lymphocytes are capable of recognizing an antigen because they have receptor molecules on their surface. The shape of the receptors on any particular lymphocyte is complementary to a specific antigen. It is often said that the receptor and the antigen fit together like *a lock and a key.* It is estimated that during our lifetime, we encounter a million different antigens, so we need the same number of different lymphocytes for protection against those antigens. It is remarkable that diversification occurs to such an extent during the maturation process that there is a different lymphocyte type for each possible antigen. Just how this occurs is discussed in the reading on page 657. Despite this great diversity, none of the lymphocytes ordinarily attacks the body's own cells. It is believed that if by chance a lymphocyte arises that is equipped to respond to the body's own proteins, it is normally suppressed and develops no further.

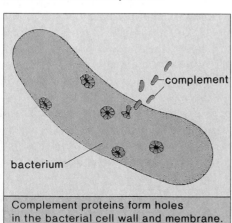

Complement proteins form holes in the bacterial cell wall and membrane.

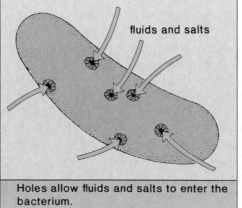

Holes allow fluids and salts to enter the bacterium.

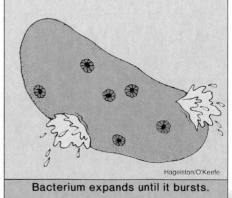

Bacterium expands until it bursts.

B Cells Make Plasma and Memory Cells

Each type of B cell carries its specific antibody, as a membrane-bound receptor, on its surface. When a B cell in a lymph node of the spleen encounters a bacterial cell or a toxin bearing an appropriate antigen, it becomes activated to divide many times. Most of the resulting cells are plasma cells, which secrete antibodies against this antigen. A **plasma cell** is a mature B cell that mass-produces antibodies in the blood or lymph.

The *clonal selection theory* states that the antigen selects which B cell will produce a clone of plasma cells (fig. 37.6). Notice that a B cell does not clone until its antigen is present and that it can recognize the antigen directly without assistance from another immune cell. However, B cells are stimulated to clone by helper T cells, as is discussed in the next section.

Once antibody production is sufficient to agglutinate and/or neutralize the amount of antigen present in the system, the development of plasma cells ceases. Those members of a clone that do not participate in antibody production remain in the bloodstream as memory B cells. **Memory B cells** are the means by which long-term immunity is possible. If the same antigen enters the system again, memory B cells quickly divide and give rise to new antibody-producing plasma cells.

Defense by B cells is called **antibody-mediated immunity** because the various types of B cells produce antibodies. It is also called *humoral immunity* because these antibodies are present in the bloodstream. A *humor* is any fluid normally occurring in the body.

Characteristics of B Cells:

- Antibody-mediated immunity
- Produced and mature in bone marrow
- Undergo clonal selection in spleen and lymph nodes
- Direct recognition of antigen
- Clonal expansion produces antibody-secreting plasma cells as well as memory B cells

Figure 37.6

Clonal selection theory as it applies to B cells. In this diagram, color is used to signify that the membrane-bound antibody differs on three B cells. An antigen activates only the B cell with the brown receptors, then it undergoes clonal expansion. During the process many plasma cells, which produce specific antibodies against this antigen, are produced. Memory cells, which retain the ability to recognize this antigen are produced also.

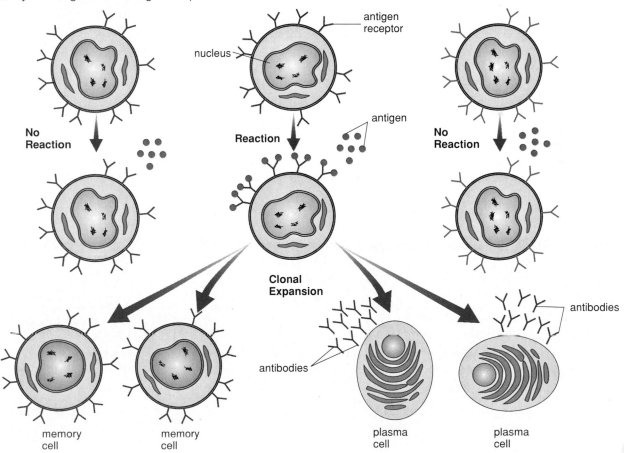

How Antibodies Work

The most common type of antibody (IgG) is a Y-shaped protein molecule with two arms. Each arm has a "heavy" (long) polypeptide chain and a "light" (short) polypeptide chain of amino acids. These chains have *constant regions,* where the sequence of amino acids is set, and *variable regions,* where the sequence of amino acids varies (fig. 37.7). The constant regions are not identical among all the antibodies. Instead, they are the same within different classes of antibodies. The variable regions form an antigen-binding site, and their shape is specific to a particular antigen, as discussed in the reading on the next page. The antigen combines with the antibody at the antigen-binding site in a lock-and-key manner.

The antigen-antibody reaction can take several forms, but quite often the reaction produces complexes of antigens combined with antibodies. Such an antigen-antibody complex, sometimes called the immune complex, marks the antigen for destruction by other forces. For example, the complex may be engulfed by neutrophils or macrophages, or it may activate complement. Complement makes microbes more susceptible to phagocytosis, as discussed previously.

How Antibodies Differ

There are five different classes of circulating antibodies (table 37.1). IgG antibodies are the major type in blood, and lesser amounts are also found in lymph and tissue fluid. IgG antibodies attack microbes and their toxins. A toxin is a specific chemical (produced by bacteria, for example) that is poisonous to other living things. IgM antibodies are pentamers, meaning that they contain five of the Y-shaped structures shown in figure 37.7*a*. These antibodies appear in blood soon after an infection begins and disappear before it is over. They are good activators of the complement system. IgA antibodies are dimers and contain two Y-shaped structures. They are the main type of antibody found in bodily secretions. They attack microbes and their toxins before they reach the bloodstream. The role of IgD antibodies in immunity is uncertain, but a very limited number is present in blood. IgE antibodies, which are responsible for allergic reactions, are discussed on page 663.

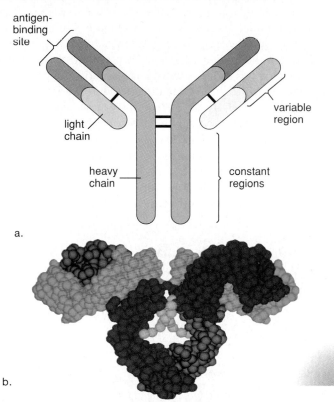

Figure 37.7

Antigen-antibody reaction. **a.** An IgG antibody contains two heavy (long) amino acid chains and two light (short) amino acid chains arranged in two variable regions, where a particular antigen is capable of binding with the antibody. **b.** Quite often, the antigen-antibody reaction produces complexes of antigens combined with antibodies.

antigen-binding site

light chain

heavy chain

variable region

constant regions

a.

b.

An antigen combines with an antibody at the antigen-binding site in a lock-and-key manner. The reaction can produce antigen-antibody complexes, which contain several molecules of antibody and antigen.

Table 37.1

Antibodies

Classes	Presence	Function
IgG	Main antibody type in circulation	Attacks microbes* and bacterial toxins; enhances phagocytosis
IgM	Antibody type found in circulation; largest antibody	Activates complement; clumps cells
IgA	Main antibody type in secretions such as saliva and milk	Attacks microbes and bacterial toxins
IgD	Antibody type found in circulation in extremely low quantity	Presence signifies maturity of B cell
IgE	Antibody type found as membrane-bound receptor on basophils in blood and on mast cells in tissues	Responsible for allergic reactions

* Viruses and bacteria

Susumu Tonegawa and Antibody Diversity

In 1987, Susumu Tonegawa became the first Japanese scientist to win the Nobel prize in Physiology or Medicine. Described by his colleagues as a creative genius who intuitively knows how to design experiments, Dr. Tonegawa had dedicated himself to finding the solution to an engrossing puzzle. Immunologists and geneticists knew that each B cell makes an antibody especially equipped to recognize the specific shape of a particular antigen. But how could the human genome contain enough genetic information to permit the production of up to a billion different antibody types needed to combat all of the microbes we are likely to encounter during the course of our lives?

As you know, an antibody is composed of two light and two heavy polypeptide chains which are divided into constant and variable regions. The constant region determines the antibody class and the variable region determines the specificity of the antibody, because this is where an antigen binds to a specific antibody (see fig. 37.7). Each B cell must make use of a unique gene to code for the variable region of the light chain and another for the variable region of the heavy chain.

Working with embryonic and mature mice, Tonegawa found that the DNA sequences coding for the variable and constant regions were scattered throughout the genome in embryonic B cells and that only certain DNA segments had come together in mature antibody-secreting B cells. He said that as a B cell matures, it randomly selects certain DNA segments, which collectively code for a specific variable region, and then these are joined to another segment coding for a constant region (fig. 37A). As an analogy, consider that each person entering a supermarket chooses various items for purchase, and that the possible combination of items in any particular grocery bag is astronomical. Tonegawa also found that mutations occur as the variable segments are undergoing rearrangements. Such mutations are another source of antibody diversity.

Tonegawa received his B.S. in chemistry in 1963 at Kyoto University and earned his Ph.D. in biology from the University of California at San Diego (UCSD) in 1969. After that he worked as a research fellow at UCSD and the Salk Institute. In 1971, he moved to the Basel Institute for Immunology and began the experiments that eventually led to his Nobel prize-winning discovery. Since the 1970s, Tonegawa has been doing experiments to isolate the receptors of T cells. This is an even more challenging area of research than the diversity of antibodies produced by B cells. Since 1981, he has been a full professor at the Massachusetts Institute of Technology (MIT), where he has a reputation for being an "aggressive, determined researcher" who often works late into the night.

Figure 37A

Antibody diversity. **a.** Susumu Tonegawa, who received a Nobel prize for his findings. **b.** Immature B cells have V (for variable) genes, J (for junction) genes, and C (for constant) genes. During maturation, any V gene can join with any C gene to produce a sequence for an antibody chain. Each B cell has its own sequence and therefore produces its own unique antibody.

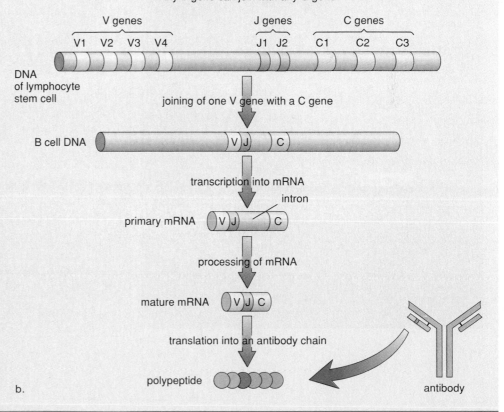

T Cells Become Cytotoxic, Helper, Memory, or Suppressor Cells

There are different types of T cells: cytotoxic T cells, helper T cells, memory T cells, and suppressor T cells. (Some doubt the existence of suppressor T cells and believe instead that suppression may depend upon the mixture of cytokines released by T cells.) Cytotoxic and helper T cells differentiate in the thymus; memory T cells and suppressor T cells arise at a later time. All types of T cells look alike but can be distinguished by their functions.

Cytotoxic T cells [Gk. *cyt,* cell, and L. *toxic,* poison] sometimes are called killer T cells. They attack and destroy antigen-bearing cells, such as virus-infected or cancer cells. Cytotoxic T cells have storage vacuoles containing perforin molecules.

Perforin molecules perforate a plasma membrane, forming a hole that allows water and salts to enter. The cell under attack then swells and eventually bursts (fig. 37.8). It often is said that T cells are responsible for **cell-mediated immunity,** characterized by destruction of antigen-bearing cells. Of all the T cells, only cytotoxic T cells are involved in this type of immunity.

Helper T cells regulate immunity by enhancing the response of other immune cells. When exposed to an antigen, they enlarge and secrete **lymphokines** [L. *lymph,* water, and *kine,* movement], stimulatory molecules that cause helper T cells to clone and other immune cells to perform their functions. For example, lymphokines stimulate macrophages to phagocytize and stimulate B cells to become antibody-producing plasma cells. Because the HIV

Figure 37.8

Cell-mediated immunity. **a.** The scanning electron microscope shows cytotoxic T cells attacking and destroying a cancer cell. **b.** During the killing process, the vacuoles in a cytotoxic T cell fuse with the cancer cell's plasma membrane and release units of the protein perforin. These units combine to form holes in the target plasma membrane. Thereafter, fluid and salts enter so that the target cell eventually bursts.

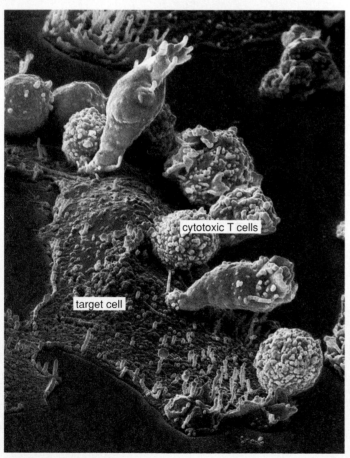

a.

1 µm

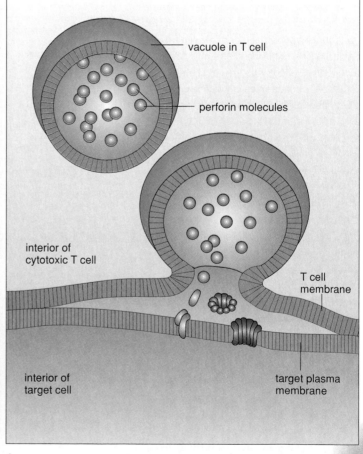

b.

vacuole in T cell

perforin molecules

interior of cytotoxic T cell

T cell membrane

interior of target cell

target plasma membrane

cytotoxic T cells

target cell

Figure 37.9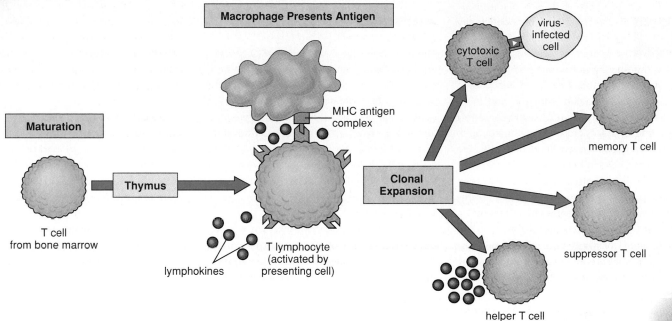

Activation and diversity of T cells. T cells mature in the thymus and are activated when presented with an antigen by a macrophage. Clonal expansion follows with the production of the four types of T cells. Cytotoxic T cells are responsible for cell-mediated immunity.

virus that causes AIDS attacks helper T cells and certain other cells of the immune system, it inactivates the immune response. AIDS is discussed in the reading on page 660.

Suppressor T cells also regulate the immune response by suppressing further development of helper T cells. Since helper T cells also stimulate antibody production by B cells, the suppressor T cells help to prevent both the B cell and T cell immune response from getting out of hand. Following suppression, a population of **memory T cells** persists, perhaps for life. These cells are able to secrete lymphokines and to stimulate macrophages and B cells whenever the same antigen reenters the body. In this way they contribute to active immunity.

Activating Cytotoxic and Helper T Cells

T cells have receptors just as B cells do. Unlike B cells, however, cytotoxic T cells and helper T cells are unable to recognize an antigen that simply is present in lymph or blood. Instead, the antigen must be presented to them by an *antigen-presenting cell* (*APC*). When an APC, usually a macrophage, engulfs a microbe, it is enclosed within an endocytic vesicle, where it is broken down to release peptide fragments. These fragments are antigenic (have the properties of an antigen). The antigenic peptide fragment is linked to an **MHC** (major histocompatibility complex) **protein,** and together they are displayed at the plasma membrane and are presented to a T cell.

The importance of MHC proteins in plasma membranes was first recognized when it was discovered that they contribute to the specificity of tissues and make it difficult to transplant tissue from one person to another. In other words, when the donor and the recipient are histo-(tissue) compatible (the same or nearly so), a transplant is more likely to be successful.

Figure 37.9 shows a macrophage presenting an antigen to a helper T cell. Once a helper T cell recognizes an antigen, it undergoes clonal expansion, producing memory T cells, which can also recognize this same antigen. Once a cytotoxic T cell recognizes an antigen, it attacks and destroys any cell that is infected with the same virus. In this way T cells contribute to active immunity.

Characteristics of T Cells:

- Cell-mediated immunity
- Produced in bone marrow, mature in thymus
- Antigen must be presented, usually by macrophage
- Cytotoxic T cells search and destroy antigen-bearing cells
- Helper T cells secrete lymphokines and stimulate other immune cells

The AIDS Epidemic

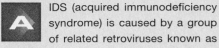IDS (acquired immunodeficiency syndrome) is caused by a group of related retroviruses known as HIV (human immunodeficiency viruses). Worldwide, as many as 20 million people may now be infected with HIV, and there could be as many as 100 million infected by the end of the century. A new infection is believed to occur every fifteen seconds, the majority between heterosexuals.

In this country, AIDS was first seen among those male homosexuals who frequently sought new partners, and therefore passed the virus from one to the other. The number of HIV infections in male homosexuals now appears to have peaked, as many of these men have adopted a more conservative life-style. In 1988, male homosexuals accounted for 61% of U.S. AIDS cases; now they account for 58%. In contrast, the percentage of heterosexuals infected is rising, and one in five new infections is now a woman. The tragedy of female infection is magnified when the virus or the infected lymphocytes pass to a fetus via the placenta or to an infant via mother's milk. About 29% of total AIDS cases are intravenous drug users who pass the virus directly from one to the other by sharing needles.

Symptoms of AIDS

A person has AIDS after HIV enters the blood and infects certain helper T lymphocytes known as T4 cells. It is possible to relate the progression of an HIV infection to a decline in the number of T4 cells. There are three stages of the disease, which are discussed as follows.

Asymptomatic Carrier

Only 1–2% of recently infected individuals experience fever, chills, and swollen lymph nodes. After these symptoms disappear, the individual exhibits no symptoms and yet is highly infectious. The standard HIV blood test for the presence of antibody becomes positive during this stage.

AIDS-Related Complex (ARC)

The most common symptom of ARC is swelling of the lymph nodes in the neck, the armpits, or the groin that persists for three months or more. Also common are fatigue, fevers, a cough, diarrhea, and numerous nervous system impairments. When the individual develops non-life-threatening and recurrent infections such as thrush or herpes simplex, it is a signal that full-blown AIDS will occur shortly.

Full-Blown AIDS

The majority of people with ARC eventually develop full-blown AIDS. A blood count of 200 T4 cells per mm^3 signal that the person has AIDS. The patient suffers severe weight loss and weakness due to persistent diarrhea and coughing. Most likely, death will be due to opportunistic infections, so called because they arise in the presence of the severely impaired immune system. These infections can include *Pneumocystis carinii* pneumonia, Kaposi's sarcoma, *Mycobacterium* tuberculosis, and invasive cervical cancer.

Treatment for AIDS

The three drugs now approved for treatment of AIDS (AZT, ddI, and ddC) all work by interfering with reverse transcription because they are analogues (chemically altered forms) of normal nucleotides. Many investigators are working on a vaccine for AIDS. Jonas Salk, who developed the first polio vaccine, has weakened the AIDS virus and is using it as a vaccine. Other vaccines consist of individual capsid and membrane proteins attached to a carrier that can be recognized by the immune system (fig. 37B).

Figure 37B

HIV-1, the most common cause of AIDS in the United States, has an envelope molecule called gp120, which allows it to attach to CD4 receptors that project from a T4 cell. Infection of the T4 cell follows, and HIV eventually buds from the infected T4 cell. If the immune system can be trained by the use of a vaccine to attack and destroy all cells that bear gp120, a person could not be infected with HIV-1.

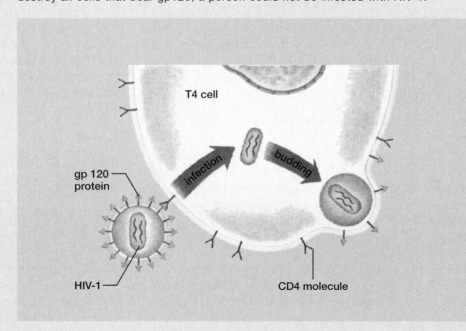

IMMUNITY CAN BE INDUCED

Immunity occurs naturally through infection or is brought about artificially by medical intervention. There are two types of induced immunity: active and passive. In active immunity, the individual alone produces antibodies against an antigen; in passive immunity, the individual is given prepared antibodies.

Active Immunity Is Long-Lived

Active immunity sometimes develops naturally after a person is infected with a microbe. However, active immunity is often induced when a person is well so that possible future infection will not take place. To prevent infections, people can be artificially immunized against them.

Immunization involves the use of **vaccines** [L. *vaccin,* of a cow], substances that contain an antigen to which the immune system responds. The use of vaccines dates back to the late eighteenth century when the English physician Edward Jenner used matter from cowpox pustules to protect individuals from smallpox. At the end of the nineteenth century, the renowned French researcher, Louis Pasteur, succeeded in producing vaccines for cholera, anthrax, and rabies, which are bacterial diseases. To prepare these vaccines, the microbes themselves were treated so they were no longer virulent (able to cause disease). Only recently has an entirely different method of producing vaccines been developed. Today, it is possible to genetically engineer bacteria to mass-produce a protein from microbes, and this protein can be used as vaccine. This method now is being used to prepare a vaccine against malaria, a protozoan disease, and hepatitis B, a viral disease.

After a vaccine is given, it is possible to follow an immune response by determining the amount of antibody present in a sample of serum—this is called the *antibody titer*. After the first exposure to a vaccine, a primary response occurs. For a period of several days, no antibodies are present; then, there is a slow rise in the titer, followed by first a plateau and then a gradual decline as the antibodies bind to the antigen or simply break down (fig. 37.10). After a second exposure, a secondary response is expected. The titer rises rapidly to a plateau level much greater than before. The second exposure is called a "booster" because it boosts the antibody titer to a high level. The high antibody titer now is expected to help prevent disease symptoms even if the individual is exposed to the disease-causing microbe. Immunological memory causes an individual to be actively immune.

Memory Cells Provide a State of Readiness

Immunological memory is dependent upon the number of memory B and memory T cells capable of responding to a particular antigen. The receptors of memory B cells usually have a higher affinity for the antigen due to the selection process that occurred during the first exposure to the antigen, and therefore they are prone to make IgG earlier. Both memory B cells and memory T

Figure 37.10

Development of active immunity due to immunization. The primary response, after the first exposure to a vaccine, is minimal, but the secondary response, which may occur after the second exposure, shows a dramatic rise in the amount of antibody present in serum.

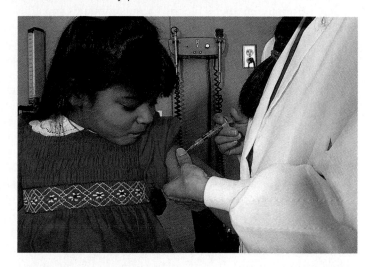

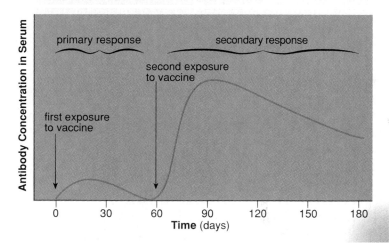

cells can respond to lower doses of antigen. Good active immunity lasts as long as clones of memory B and memory T cells are present in blood. Active immunity is usually long-lived.

> Active (long-lived) immunity can be induced by the use of vaccines when a person is well and in no immediate danger of contracting an infectious disease. Active immunity is dependent upon the presence of memory B cells and memory T cells in the body.

Passive Immunity Is Short-Lived

Passive immunity occurs when an individual is given prepared antibodies (immunoglobulins) to combat a disease. Since these antibodies are not produced by the individual's B cells, passive immunity is short-lived. For example, newborn infants are passively immune to disease because antibodies have crossed the placenta from the mother's blood. These antibodies soon disappear, however, so that within a few months, infants become more susceptible to infections. Breast-feeding prolongs the natural passive immunity an infant receives from the mother because antibodies are present in the mother's milk (fig. 37.11).

Even though passive immunity does not last, it sometimes is used to prevent illness in a patient who has been unexpectedly exposed to an infectious disease. Usually, the patient receives a gamma globulin injection (serum that contains antibodies), perhaps taken from individuals who have recovered from the illness. In the past, horses were immunized, and serum was taken from them to provide the needed antibodies against such diseases as diphtheria, botulism, and tetanus. In the past, a patient who received these antibodies occasionally became ill because the serum contained proteins that the individual's immune system recognized as foreign. This was called serum sickness. But problems can still occur; more recently, an immunoglobulin intravenous product, called Gammagard, was withdrawn from the market because of possible implication in the transmission of hepatitis.

> **Passive immunity is needed when an individual is in immediate danger of succumbing to an infectious disease. Passive immunity is short-lived because the antibodies are administered to and not made by the individual.**

Lymphokines Boost White Blood Cells

Lymphokines—the messenger proteins made by lymphocytes—are being investigated as possible adjunct therapy for cancer and AIDS because they stimulate white blood cell formation and/or function. Both interferon and various other types of lymphokines called interleukins have been used as immunotherapeutic drugs, particularly to potentiate the ability of the individual's own T cells (and possibly B cells) to fight cancer.

Interferon, discussed previously on page 654, is a substance produced by leukocytes, fibroblasts, and probably most cells in response to a viral infection. When it is produced by T cells, interferon is called a lymphokine. Interferon still is being investigated as a possible cancer drug, but so far it has proven to be effective only in certain patients, and the exact reasons for this as yet cannot be discerned.

When and if cancer cells carry an altered protein on their cell surface, they should be attacked and destroyed by cytotoxic T cells. Whenever cancer does develop, it is possible that the cytotoxic T cells have not been activated. In that case, lymphokines might awaken the immune system and lead to the destruc-

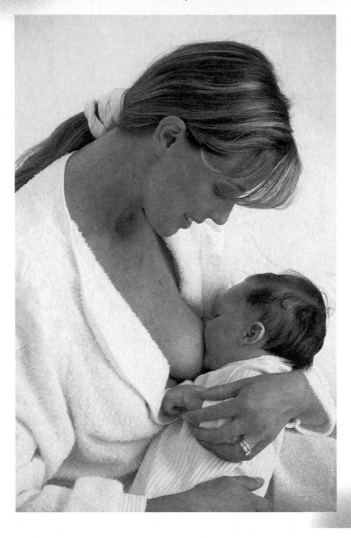

Figure 37.11
Example of passive immunity. Breast-feeding is believed to prolong the passive immunity an infant receives from the mother because antibodies are present in the mother's milk.

tion of the cancer. In one technique being investigated, researchers first withdraw T cells from the patient and activate the cells by culturing them in the presence of an interleukin. The cells then are reinjected into the patient, who is given doses of interleukin to maintain the killer activity of the T cells.

Those who are actively engaged in interleukin research believe that interleukins soon will be used as adjuncts for vaccines, for the treatment of chronic infectious diseases, and perhaps for the treatment of cancer. Interleukin antagonists also may prove helpful in preventing skin and organ rejection, autoimmune diseases, and allergies.

> **The interleukins and other lymphokines show some promise of potentiating the individual's own immune system.**

Monoclonal Antibodies Have Same Specificity

As previously discussed, every plasma cell derived from the same B cell secretes antibodies against a specific antigen. These are **monoclonal antibodies** [Gk. *mono,* one, and *clon,* branch, and *anti,* against] because all of them are the same type and because they are produced by plasma cells derived from the same B cell.

One method of producing monoclonal antibodies in vitro (outside the body in glassware) is depicted in figure 37.12. B lymphocytes are removed from the body (today, usually mice are used) and are exposed to a particular antigen. The activated B lymphocytes are fused with myeloma cells (malignant plasma cells that live and divide indefinitely). The fused cells are called hybridomas; *hybrid* because they result from the fusion of two different cells, and *oma* because one of the cells is a cancer cell.

At present, monoclonal antibodies are being used for quick and certain diagnosis of various conditions. For example, a particular hormone is present in the urine of a pregnant woman. A monoclonal antibody can be used to detect the hormone and so indicate that the woman is pregnant. Monoclonal antibodies also are used to identify infections. They are so accurate they can even sort out the different types of T cells in a blood sample. And because they can distinguish between cancer and normal tissue cells, they are used to carry radioactive isotopes or toxic drugs to tumors so that they can be selectively destroyed.

Monoclonal antibodies are considered to be a biotechnology product because the production process makes use of a living system to mass-produce the product.

> Monoclonal antibodies are produced in pure batches—they all react to just one type of molecule (antigen). Therefore, they can distinguish one cell, or even one molecule, from another.

IMMUNITY HAS SIDE EFFECTS

The immune system protects us from disease because it can tell self from nonself. Sometimes, however, the immune system is underprotective, as when an individual develops cancer, or is overprotective, as when individuals have allergies.

Allergies: Overactive Immune System

Allergies are caused by an overactive immune system, which forms antibodies to substances that usually are not recognized as foreign substances. Unfortunately, allergies usually are accompanied by coldlike symptoms or, at times, by severe systemic reactions such as anaphylactic shock, which is a sudden drop in blood pressure.

Of the five varieties of antibodies—IgG, IgM, IgA, IgD, and IgE (see table 37.1)—IgE antibodies are involved in allergic reaction. IgE antibodies are found in the bloodstream; but they, unlike the other types of antibodies, also reside in the membrane

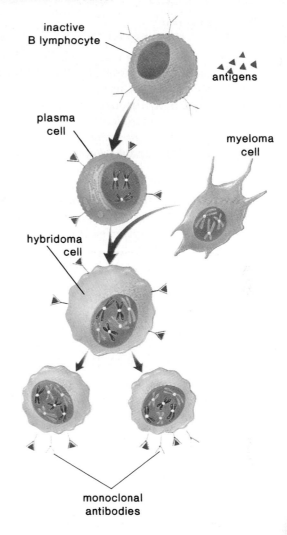

Figure 37.12

Production of monoclonal antibodies. Inactive lymphocytes are exposed to an antigen so that they become plasma cells that can produce antibodies. The plasma cells are fused with myeloma (cancer cells), producing hybridoma cells that are "immortal." Hybridoma cells divide and continue to produce the same type of antibody, called monoclonal antibodies.

inactive B lymphocyte

antigens

plasma cell

myeloma cell

hybridoma cell

monoclonal antibodies

of mast cells found in the tissues. As mentioned, *mast cells* are basophils that have left the bloodstream and taken up residence in the tissues. In any case, when the *allergen,* an antigen that provokes an allergic reaction, attaches to the IgE antibodies on mast cells, these cells release histamine and other substances, which cause mucus secretion and airway constriction. This results in the characteristic allergy symptoms. On occasion, basophils and other white blood cells release these substances into the bloodstream. The increased capillary permeability that results from this can lead to fluid loss and shock.

Allergy shots sometimes prevent the onset of allergic symptoms. Injections of the allergen cause the body to build up high quantities of IgG antibodies, and these combine with allergens received from the environment before they have a chance to reach the IgE antibodies located in the membrane of mast cells.

> Histamine and other substances released by mast cells cause allergic symptoms.

Tissue Rejection: Foreign MHC Proteins

Certain organs, such as skin, the heart, and the kidneys, could be transplanted easily from one person to another if the body did not attempt to *reject* them. Rejection occurs because cytotoxic T cells bring about disintegration of foreign tissue in the body.

Organ rejection can be controlled by careful selection of the organ to be transplanted and the administration of immunosuppressive drugs. It is best if the transplanted organ has the same type of MHC proteins as those of the recipient, because cytotoxic T cells recognize foreign MHC proteins. The immunosuppressive drug cyclosporine has been used for many years. A new drug, tacrolimus (formerly known as FK-506), shows some promise, especially in liver transplant patients. However both drugs, which act by inhibiting the production of interleukin-2, are known to adversely affect the kidneys.

> When an organ is rejected, the immune system is attacking cells that bear different MHC proteins from those of the individual.

Autoimmune Diseases: The Body Attacks Itself

Certain human illnesses are referred to as **autoimmune diseases** [Gk. *aut,* self, and L. *immun,* safe, free] because they are due to an attack on tissues by the body's own antibodies and T cells. Exactly what causes autoimmune diseases is not known, but they seem to appear after the individual has recovered from an infection. Some bacteria have been observed to produce toxic products that can cause T cells to bind prematurely to macrophages. Perhaps at that time the T cell learns to recognize the body's own tissues. This might be the cause of at least some autoimmune diseases. In myasthenia gravis, neuromuscular junctions do not work properly and muscular weakness results. In multiple sclerosis (MS), the myelin sheath of nerve fibers is attacked, and this causes various neuromuscular disorders. A person with systemic lupus erythematosus (SLE) has various symptoms prior to death due to kidney damage. In rheumatoid arthritis, the joints are affected. It is suspected that heart damage following rheumatic fever and type I diabetes are also autoimmune illnesses. There are no cures for autoimmune diseases.

> Autoimmune diseases seem to be preceded by an infection that results in cytotoxic T cells or antibodies attacking the body's own organs.

> ## Biological Relationships

The circulatory system of birds and mammals is most efficient because the blood is pumped by the heart simultaneously into two circuits. The pulmonary circuit takes blood through the lungs and the systemic circuit transports blood to and away from capillaries where exchange with tissue fluid and cells take place. Nutrient molecules leave the capillaries to be taken up by the cells, and waste molecules given off by the cells are received by the capillaries and transported away. Homeostasis, the relative constancy of the internal environment is dependent upon the constancy of the blood and tissue fluid. The composition of blood and therefore tissue fluid remains within normal limits because the vertebrate body has exchange surfaces with the external environment. Oxygen is exchanged for carbon dioxide in the lungs; nutrients are received at the intestinal tract and metabolic wastes are excreted in the kidneys. The liver is also involved in maintaining the composition of the blood; as an example, the liver stores glucose as glycogen after eating and breaks down glycogen to provide glucose in between eating.

The body is threatened daily by viruses and disease-causing organisms and even its own cells can become cancerous. The immune system which encompasses all sorts of defense mechanisms contributes greatly to homeostasis. There are barriers to entry such as the skin and mucous membranes and there are nonspecific defenses such as those performed by complement and the neutrophils, a type of white blood cell.

The lymphatic system which is an accessory to the circulatory system is also a part of the immune system. Lymphatic capillaries collect excess tissue fluid and return it to the systemic veins. Along the way, lymph is purified by passing through lymph nodes. White blood cells called lymphocytes are responsible for specific defenses: the B lymphocytes produce antibodies and the T lymphocytes kill virus-infected cells and cancer cells directly. The medical profession has discovered ways to induce immunity; vaccines stimulate the body to produce antibodies and the interleukins are chemicals produced by helper T cells that are now available for cancer therapy.

Summary

1. The lymphatic system consists of lymphatic vessels and lymphoid organs.

2. The lymphatic vessels collect fat molecules at intestinal villi, collect excess tissue fluid, and carry these to the bloodstream.

3. Lymphocytes are produced and accumulate in the lymphoid organs (lymph nodes, spleen, thymus gland, and red bone marrow).

4. Immunity involves nonspecific and specific defenses. Nonspecific defenses include barriers to entry, the inflammatory reaction, and protective proteins.

5. Specific defenses require lymphocytes, which are produced in the bone marrow. B cells mature in the bone marrow and undergo clonal selection in the lymph nodes and the spleen. T cells mature in the thymus.

6. B cells are responsible for antibody-mediated immunity. They directly recognize an antigen and give rise to antibody-secreting plasma cells and memory B cells. Memory B cells respond if the same antigen enters the body at a later date.

7. An antibody is a Y-shaped molecule that has two binding sites. Each antibody is specific for a particular antigen.

8. There are four types of T cells. Cytotoxic T cells kill cells on contact; helper T cells stimulate other immune cells and produce lymphokines; suppressor T cells suppress the immune response; and memory T cells remain in the body to provide long-lasting immunity.

9. For the T cell to recognize an antigen, the antigen must be presented by an antigen-presenting cell (APC), usually a macrophage, along with an MHC (major histocompatibility complex) protein. Cytotoxic T cells are responsible for cell-mediated immunity.

10. AIDS is an HIV infection of helper T cells, primarily, and therefore it destroys the cells that are needed to mount an immune response.

11. Immunity can be induced in various ways. Vaccines are available to promote long-lived active immunity, and antibodies sometimes are available to provide an individual with short-lived passive immunity.

12. Lymphokines, notably interferon and interleukins, are used in an attempt to promote the body's ability to recover from cancer and to treat AIDS.

13. Immunity has certain side effects. Allergies result when an overactive immune system forms antibodies to substances not normally recognized as foreign.

14. Cytotoxic T cells attack transplanted organs as nonself; therefore immunosuppressive drugs must be administered.

15. Autoimmune illnesses occur when antibodies and T cells attack the body's own tissues.

Writing Across the Curriculum

In order to practice writing skills, students should write out the answers to any or all of the study questions and the critical thinking questions. The study questions are sequenced in the same order as the text. Answers to the objective questions, and suggested answers to the critical thinking questions, are in appendix D.

Study Questions

1. What is the lymphatic system, and what are its three functions?   650

2. Describe the structure and the function of the lymph nodes, the spleen, the thymus, and bone marrow.   651–52

3. What are the body's nonspecific defense mechanisms?   652–53

4. Describe the inflammatory reaction, and give a role for each type of cell and molecule that participates in the reaction.   652–53

5. What is the clonal selection theory? B cells are responsible for which type of immunity?   655

6. Describe the structure of an antibody, and define the terms variable regions and constant regions.   656

7. Name the four types of T cells, and state their functions.   658–59

8. Explain the process by which a T cell is able to recognize an antigen.   659

9. How is active immunity achieved? How is passive immunity achieved?   661–62

10. What are lymphokines, and how are they used in immunotherapy?   662

11. How are monoclonal antibodies produced, and what are their applications?   663

12. Discuss allergies, tissue rejection, and autoimmune diseases as they relate to the immune system.   663–64

Objective Questions

1. Complement
   a. is a general defense mechanism.
   b. is a series of proteins present in the plasma.
   c. plays a role in destroying bacteria.
   d. All of these are correct.

2. Which of these pertain(s) to T cells?
   a. have specific receptors
   b. have cell-mediated immunity
   c. stimulate antibody production by B cells
   d. All of these are correct.

3. Which one of these does not pertain to B cells?
   a. have passed through the thymus
   b. specific receptors
   c. antibody-mediated immunity
   d. synthesize and liberate antibodies

4. The clonal selection theory says that
   a. an antigen selects certain B cells and suppresses them.
   b. an antigen stimulates the multiplication of B cells that produce antibodies against it.
   c. T cells select those B cells that should produce antibodies, regardless of antigens.
   d. T cells suppress all B cells except the ones that should multiply and divide.

5. Plasma cells are
   a. the same as memory cells.
   b. formed from blood plasma.
   c. B cells that are actively secreting antibody.
   d. inactive T cells carried in the plasma.

6. For a T cell to recognize an antigen, it must interact with
   a. complement.
   b. a macrophage.
   c. a B cell.
   d. All of these are correct.

7. Antibodies combine with antigens
   a. at variable regions.
   b. at constant regions.
   c. only if macrophages are present.
   d. Both a and c are correct.

8. Which one of these is mismatched?
   a. helper T cells—help complement react
   b. cytotoxic T cells—active in tissue rejection
   c. suppressor T cells—shut down the immune response
   d. memory T cells—long-living line of T cells

9. Vaccines are
   a. the same as monoclonal antibodies.
   b. treated bacteria or viruses or one of their proteins.
   c. MHC proteins.
   d. All of these are correct.

10. The theory behind the use of lymphokines in cancer therapy is that
    a. if cancer develops, the immune system has been ineffective.
    b. lymphokines stimulate the immune system.
    c. cancer cells bear antigens that should be recognizable by cytotoxic T cells.
    d. All of these are correct.

11. Give the function of the four types of T cells shown.

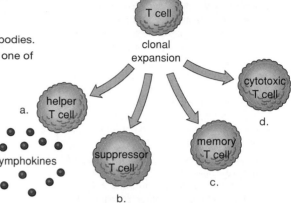

Concepts and Critical Thinking

1. *The body defends its integrity.*
   How does your study of immunity support this concept?

2. *Multitiered mechanisms maintain homeostasis.*
   How does your study of immunity support this concept?

3. *Organs belong to organ systems.*
   Argue that red bone marrow is a part of the skeletal, circulatory, and lymphatic systems.

Selected Key Terms

antibody A protein produced in response to the presence of an antigen; each antibody combines with a specific antigen. [Gk. *anti,* against]   654

antigen A foreign substance, usually a protein or a polysaccharide, that stimulates the immune system to react, such as to produce antibodies. [Gk. *anti,* against, and *gene,* origin]   654

B lymphocyte (LIM-fuh-syt) A lymphocyte that matures in the bone marrow and, when stimulated by the presence of a specific antigen, gives rise to antibody-producing plasma cells. [L. *lymph,* water, and *cyt,* cell]   654

complement system A series of proteins in plasma that form a nonspecific defense mechanism against a microbe invasion; it complements the antigen-antibody reaction.   654

immunity The ability of the body to protect itself from foreign substances and cells, including infectious microbes. [L. *immun,* safe, free]   652

inflammatory reaction A tissue response to injury that is characterized by redness, swelling, pain, and heat. [L. *in,* into, and *flamm,* burn]   652

lymph Fluid, derived from tissue fluid, that is carried in lymphatic vessels. [L. *lymph,* water]   650

lymphatic system Mammalian organ system consisting of lymphatic vessels and lymphoid organs. [L. *lymph,* water]   650

lymph nodes A mass of lymphoid tissue located along the course of a lymphatic vessel. [L. *lymph,* water]   651

lymphokine (LIM-fuh-kyn) A molecule secreted by T lymphocytes that has the ability to affect the activity of all types of immune cells. [L. *lymph,* water, and *kine,* movement]   658

macrophage A large phagocytic cell derived from a monocyte that ingests microbes and debris. [Gk. *macr,* large, and *phag,* eat]   653

MHC (major histocompatibility complex) protein A membrane protein that serves to identify the cells of a particular individual.   659

T lymphocyte (LIM-fuh-syt) A lymphocyte that matures in the thymus and exists in four varieties, one of which kills antigen-bearing cells outright. [L. *lymph,* water, and *cyt,* cell]   654

vaccine Antigens prepared in such a way that they can promote active immunity without causing disease. [L. *vaccin,* of a cow]   661

38

DIGESTIVE SYSTEM AND NUTRITION

Learning Objectives

Comparing Digestive Tracts

- Contrast the characteristics of an incomplete and a complete digestive tract.   668
- Contrast the characteristics of a continuous and a discontinuous feeder.   669
- Contrast the dentition and digestive tracts of mammalian herbivores and mammalian carnivores.   670

Humans Have a Complete Tract

- Name the parts of the human digestive system and describe, in general, their structure and function.   671
- Outline the digestion of carbohydrates (e.g., starch), proteins, and fats in humans by listing the names and the functions of the appropriate digestive enzymes; note where in the human digestive tract these enzymes function.   671–75

- List the contributions of the liver and the pancreas to the digestive process in humans.   676–77
- Name six functions of the liver.   676
- Give the names and the functions of hormones that affect the flow of digestive juices.   676

Nutrition Affects Health

- Describe in detail the recommended food pyramid.   678
- Discuss the various roles played by vitamins and minerals in the body.   678–80

Galápagos land iguana, *conolphus.* By feeding on cactus, *opuntia,* this animal acquires the nutrient it needs to maintain its organization.

nimals are heterotrophic organisms that must take in preformed food. Animals' many adaptations to acquire and digest food are extremely varied and can be related to a wide variety of available food; we will be able to discuss only a few examples. When animals take in food, they acquire both the energy needed to carry on daily activities and the building blocks needed to grow and/or repair tissues.

COMPARING DIGESTIVE TRACTS

Generally, animals have some sort of digestive tract or gut. The gut can be simple or complex. A simple gut has few, if any, specialized parts, and a complex gut has one or more specialized parts.

Gut Is Complete or Incomplete

An *incomplete gut* has a single opening, usually called a mouth. The planarian is an example of an animal with an incomplete gut (fig. 38.1). It is carnivorous and feeds largely on smaller aquatic animals. Its digestive system contains only a mouth, a pharynx, and an intestine. When the worm is feeding, the pharynx actually extends beyond the mouth. It wraps its body about the prey and uses its muscular pharynx to suck up minute quantities at a time. Digestive enzymes present in the *gastrovascular cavity* allow some extracellular ("outside the cells") digestion to occur. Digestion is finished intracellularly by the cells that line the cavity,

which branches throughout the body. No cell in the body is far from the intestine, and therefore diffusion alone is sufficient to distribute nutrient molecules.

The digestive system of a planarian is notable for its lack of specialized parts. It is saclike because the pharynx serves not only as an entrance for food but also as an exit for nondigestible material. Specialization of parts does not occur under these circumstances.

A planarian has some parasitic relatives. A tapeworm, for example, has no digestive system at all—it simply absorbs nutrient molecules from the intestinal juices that surround its body. The body wall is highly modified for this purpose: it has millions of microscopic fingerlike projections that increase the surface area for absorption.

In contrast to the planarian, an earthworm has a *complete gut,* meaning that it has a mouth and an anus. Earthworms feed mainly on decayed organic matter in soil (fig. 38.2). The muscular *pharynx* draws in food with a sucking action. The *crop* is a storage area that has thin expansive walls. The *gizzard* has thick muscular walls for churning and grinding the food. Digestion is extracellular—in the intestine. The surface area of digestive tracts is often increased for absorption of nutrient molecules, and in the earthworm there is an intestinal fold called the typhlosole. Undigested remains pass out of the body at the anus.

Specialization of parts is obvious in the earthworm because the pharynx, the crop, the gizzard, and the intestine each has a particular function in the digestive process.

> In contrast to the incomplete, saclike gut, the complete gut, with both a mouth and an anus, has many specialized parts.

Figure 38.1

Incomplete digestive tract of a planarian. **a.** Planaria have a gastrovascular cavity with a single opening that acts as both an entrance and an exit. Planaria rely on intracellular digestion to complete the digestive process. **b.** Phagocytosis produces a vacuole, which joins with an enzyme-containing lysosome. The digested products pass from the vacuole into the cytoplasm before any nondigestible material is eliminated at the plasma membrane.

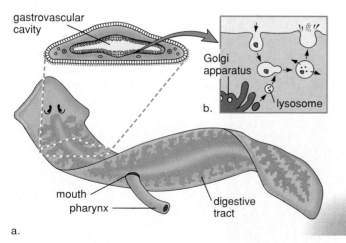

Figure 38.2

Complete digestive tract of an earthworm. Complete digestive tracts have both a mouth and an anus and usually have many specialized parts. In earthworms, the absorptive surface of the intestine is increased by an internal fold called the typhlosole.

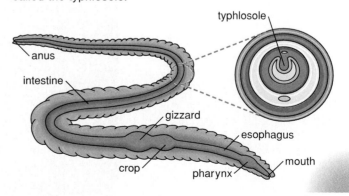

Figure 38.3

Nutritional mode of a clam compared to a squid. A clam burrows in the sand or mud, where it filter feeds, whereas the squid swims freely in open waters. **a.** A flow of water (see arrows) brings debris (food particles) into and carries waste out of a clam's mantle cavity. **b.** In contrast, a squid captures other aquatic animals with its tentacles and bites off pieces with its jaws. A strong contraction of the mantle forces water (see arrows), which has entered the mantle cavity, out the funnel, resulting in a type of "jet propulsion."

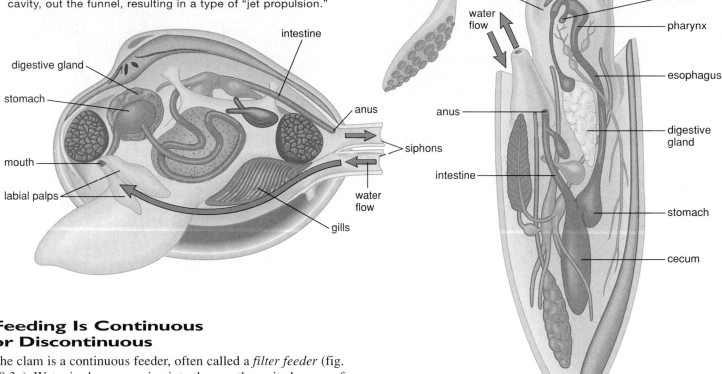

a.

b.

Feeding Is Continuous or Discontinuous

The clam is a continuous feeder, often called a *filter feeder* (fig. 38.3*a*). Water is always moving into the mantle cavity by way of the incurrent siphon (slitlike opening) and depositing particles on the gills. The size of the incurrent siphon permits the entrance of only small particles, which adhere to the gills. Ciliary action moves suitably sized particles to the labial palps, which force them through the mouth into the stomach. Digestive enzymes are secreted by a large digestive gland, but amoeboid cells present throughout the tract are believed to complete the digestive process by intracellular digestion.

Marine fanworms are sessile filter feeders that live in a tube and extend feathery tentacles to capture food. The baleen whale is an active filter feeder. The baleen, a curtainlike fringe, hangs from the roof of the mouth and filters small shrimp called krill from the water. The baleen whale filters up to a ton of krill every few minutes.

The squid is an example of a discontinuous feeder (fig. 38.3*b*). The body of a squid is streamlined, and the animal moves rapidly through the water using jet propulsion (forceful expulsion of water from a tubular funnel). The head of a squid is surrounded by ten arms, two of which have developed into long, slender tentacles whose suckers have toothed, horny rings. These tentacles seize prey (fishes, shrimps, and worms) and bring it to the squid's bearlike jaws, which bite off pieces pulled into the mouth by the action of a radula, a toothy tongue. An esophagus leads to a stomach and a cecum (blind sac) where digestion occurs. The stomach, supplemented by the cecum, holds food until digestion is complete. Discontinuous feeders, whether they are carnivores or herbivores, require such a storage area.

> Continuous feeders, such as sessile filter feeders, do not need a storage region for food; discontinuous feeders, such as herbivores and carnivores, do need a storage region for food.

Dentition Is Suitable

Some animals are omnivores; they eat both plants and animals. Others are herbivores; they feed only on plants. Still others are carnivores; they eat only other animals. Among invertebrates, filter feeders like clams and tube worms are omnivores. Molluscs, such as land snails and some insects like grasshoppers and locusts, are herbivores. Spiders are carnivores, as are sea stars that feed on clams. A sea star positions itself above a clam and uses its tube feet to pull the valves of the shell apart. Then, it everts a part of its stomach to start the digestive process, even while the clam is trying to close its shell. Some invertebrates are cannibalistic. The female praying mantis is famous for feeding on her mate as the reproductive act is taking place!

Among mammals, the dentition differs according to mode of nutrition (fig. 38.4). Humans, as well as raccoons, rats, and brown bears, are omnivores. Therefore, the dentition is nonspecialized to accommodate both a vegetable diet and a meat diet. An adult human has thirty-two teeth. One-half of each jaw has teeth of four different types: two chisel-shaped *incisors* for biting; one pointed *canine* for tearing; two fairly flat *premolars* for grinding; and three *molars,* well-flattened for crushing.

Among herbivores, the koala of Australia is famous for its diet of only eucalyptus leaves, and likewise many other mammals are browsers, feeding off bushes and trees. Grazers, like the horse, feed off grasses. The horse has sharp, even incisors for neatly clipping off blades of grass and large, flat premolars and molars for grinding and crushing the grass. Extensive grinding and crushing disrupts plant cell walls, allowing bacteria located in the cecum to get at and digest cellulose. Other mammalian grazers, like the cow and deer, are ruminants. In contrast to horses, they graze quickly and swallow partially chewed grasses into a special part of the stomach called a rumen. Here, microorganisms start the digestive process and the result, called cud, is regurgitated at a later and more convenient time. The cud is chewed again before being swallowed for complete digestion.

Many mammals, including dogs, toothed whales, and polar bears, are carnivores. A carnivore, like a lion, uses pointed incisors and enlarged canine teeth to tear off pieces small enough to be quickly swallowed. Meat is rich in protein and fat and is easier to digest than plant material. Therefore, the digestive system of carnivores is shorter and doesn't have the specialization seen in herbivores.

Omnivores have nonspecialized teeth. Herbivores have large, flat molars that grind food; carnivores have incisors and canines to tear off chunks of meat.

Figure 38.4

Dentition. **a.** Horses are herbivores that graze on grasses. Note the sharp incisors, reduced canines, and large, flat premolars and molars. **b.** Lions are carnivores that prey on other animals. Note the pointed incisors, enlarged canines, and jagged premolars and molars. **c.** Humans are omnivores that have nonspecialized teeth.

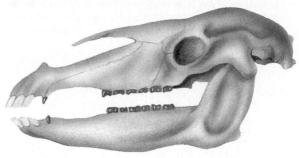

a. Horse

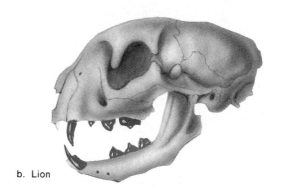

b. Lion

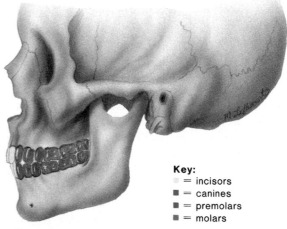

c. Human

Key:
▫ = incisors
■ = canines
■ = premolars
■ = molars

HUMANS HAVE A COMPLETE TRACT

The human gut is complete, and there is a complex digestive system (fig. 38.5). The functions of the digestive system are to ingest the food, to digest it to small molecules that can cross plasma membranes, to absorb these nutrient molecules, and to eliminate nondigestible wastes. Each part of the system has a specific function (table 38.1).

Digestion of food in humans is an extracellular process, and digestive enzymes are secreted by the digestive tract or by glands that lie nearby. Food is never found within these accessory glands, only within the tract itself. Digestion requires a cooperative effort between different parts of the body. The production of hormones and the performance of the nervous system achieve the cooperation of body parts.

Mouth Receives Food

Food is chewed in the mouth, where it is mixed with saliva. We have already mentioned that human dentition is nonspecialized because humans are omnivores (see fig. 38.4c). There are three pairs of **salivary glands** that send their juices by way of ducts to the mouth. Saliva contains the enzyme **salivary amylase,** which begins the process of starch digestion. The disaccharide maltose is a typical end product of salivary amylase digestion:

salivary
amylase

starch + H$_2$O $\longrightarrow$ maltose

While in the mouth, food is manipulated by a muscular tongue, which has touch and pressure receptors similar to those in the skin. *Taste buds,* chemical receptors that are stimulated by the chemical composition of food, are also found primarily on the tongue as well as on the surface of the mouth and the wall of the pharynx. After the food has been thoroughly chewed and mixed with saliva, the tongue starts the process of swallowing by pushing the food (bolus) back to the pharynx.

Table 38.1

Path of Food

Organ	Special Feature	Function
Mouth	Teeth, tongue	Chewing of food; digestion of starch
Esophagus		Movement of food by peristalsis
Stomach	Gastric glands	Storage of food; acidity kills some bacteria; digestion of protein
Small intestine	Villi	Digestion of all foods; absorption of nutrients
Large intestine		Absorption of water; storage of nondigestible remains
Anus		Defecation

Figure 38.5

Human digestive tract. The large intestine consists of three parts: the transverse colon, the ascending colon, and the descending colon plus the rectum and the anal canal. Note the placement of the accessory organs of digestion—the liver and the pancreas.

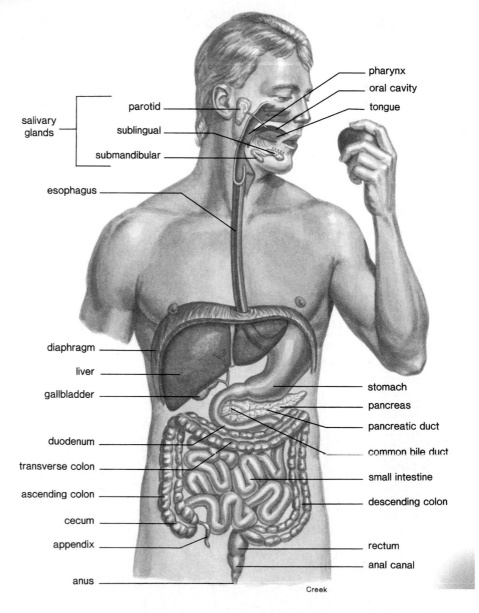

Figure 38.6

Swallowing. Respiratory and digestive passages converge and diverge in the pharynx. During swallowing, the epiglottis covers the opening to the trachea and prevents food from entering this airway.

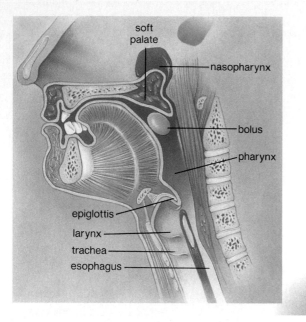

soft palate

nasopharynx

bolus

pharynx

epiglottis

larynx

trachea

esophagus

Figure 38.7

Peristalsis in the digestive tract. Rhythmic waves of muscle contraction move material along the digestive tract. The three drawings show how a peristaltic wave moves through a single section of intestine over time.

Esophagus Conducts Food

The digestive and respiratory passages cross in the pharynx (fig. 38.6). Therefore, during swallowing, the path of air to the lungs could be blocked if food entered the trachea (windpipe). Normally, however, a flap of tissue called the **epiglottis** [Gk. *epi,* upon, and *glotti,* tongue] covers the opening into the **trachea** [L. *trache,* windpipe] as muscles move the bolus through the pharynx into the esophagus, a tubular structure that takes food to the stomach. When food enters the **esophagus** [Gk. *eso,* within, and *phag,* eat], the rhythmic contraction of the gut wall, **peristalsis** [Gk. *peristole,* contraction], begins (fig. 38.7). Peristalsis pushes the bolus down the esophagus to the stomach.

Stomach Stores Food

Usually, the stomach stores up to two liters of partially digested food. Therefore, humans can periodically eat relatively large meals and spend the rest of their time at other activities. But the stomach is much more than a mere storage organ, as was discovered by William Beaumont in the mid-nineteenth century. Beaumont, an American doctor, had a French Canadian patient, Alexis St. Martin. St. Martin had been shot in the stomach, and when the wound healed, he was left with a fistula, or opening, that allowed Beaumont to look inside the stomach and to collect gastric (stomach) juices produced by *gastric glands.* Beaumont was able to determine that the muscular walls of the stomach contract vigorously and mix food with juices that are secreted whenever food enters the stomach (fig. 38.8). He found that *gastric juice* contains *hydrochloric acid* (HCl) and a substance active in digestion. (This substance was later identified as pepsin.) He also found that the gastric juices are produced independently of the protective mucus secretions of the stomach. Beaumont's work, which was very carefully and painstakingly done, pioneered the study of the physiology of digestion.

So much hydrochloric acid is secreted by the stomach that it routinely has a pH of about 2. Such a high acidity usually is sufficient to kill bacteria and other microorganisms that might be in food. This low pH also stops the activity of salivary amylase, which functions optimally at the near-neutral pH of saliva, but it promotes the activity of pepsin. **Pepsin** is a hydrolytic enzyme that acts on protein to produce peptides:

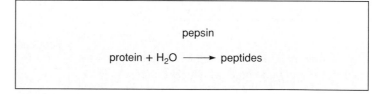

$$\text{protein} + H_2O \xrightarrow{\text{pepsin}} \text{peptides}$$

By now the stomach contents have a thick, soupy consistency and are called *chyme.* At the base of the stomach is a narrow opening controlled by a *sphincter.* Whenever the sphincter relaxes, a small quantity of chyme passes through the opening into the **duodenum,** the first part of the *small intestine* (see fig. 38.5). When chyme enters the duodenum, it sets off a neural reflex that causes the muscles of the sphincter to contract vigorously and to close the opening temporarily. Then the sphincter relaxes again and allows more chyme to enter. The slow manner in which chyme enters the small intestine allows for thorough digestion.

As with the rest of the digestive tract, a thick layer of mucus protects the wall of the stomach and the first part of the duodenum. But if by chance gastric juice does penetrate the mucus, pepsin starts to digest the stomach or duodenal lining and an *ulcer* results. An ulcer is an open sore in the wall caused by the gradual disintegration of tissues. For a long time it was believed that the most frequent cause of an ulcer was over-secretion of gastric juice due to too much nervous stimulation, but now there is strong evidence that a bacterial infection is involved.

Prior to entering the small intestine, food passes through the mouth, pharynx, esophagus, and stomach. In the mouth, salivary amylase digests starch to maltose; in the stomach, pepsin digests protein to peptides.

Figure 38.8

Anatomy of the stomach. The stomach, which has thick walls, expands as it fills with food. The mucous membrane layer of its walls secretes mucus and contains gastric glands, which secrete a gastric juice active in the digestion of protein. A peptic ulcer is an opening in the digestive tract that is acted upon by acidic gastric juice.

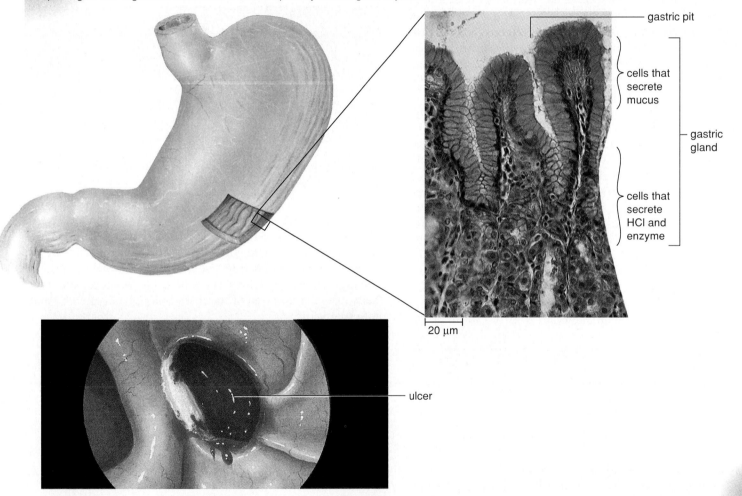

gastric pit

cells that secrete mucus

gastric gland

cells that secrete HCl and enzyme

20 μm

ulcer

Table 38.2
Digestive Enzymes

Reaction	Enzyme	Produced by	Site of Occurrence
Starch + H_2O → maltose	Salivary amylase Pancreatic amylase	Salivary glands Pancreas	Mouth Small intestine
Maltose + H_2O → glucose*	Maltase	Intestinal cells	Small intestine
Protein + H_2O → peptides	Pepsin Trypsin	Gastric glands Pancreas	Stomach Small intestine
Peptides + H_2O → amino acids*	Peptidases	Intestinal cells	Small intestine
Fat + H_2O → glycerol + fatty acids*	Lipase	Pancreas	Small intestine

Absorbed by villi.

Small Intestine Absorbs Nutrients

The human *small intestine* is a coiled tube about 7 meters long. The mucous membrane layer has ridges and furrows that give it an almost corrugated appearance. On the surface of these ridges and furrows are small, fingerlike projections called **villi** [L. *vill, shaggy hair*]. Cells on the surfaces of the villi have minute projections called microvilli. The villi and microvilli greatly increase the effective surface area of the small intestine. If the small intestine were simply a smooth tube, it would have to be 500–600 meters long to have a comparable surface area.

When chyme enters the duodenum, proteins and carbohydrates are only partly digested, and fat digestion still needs to be carried out. Considerably more digestive activity is required before these nutrients can be absorbed through the intestinal wall. Two important accessory glands, the liver and the pancreas, send secretions to the duodenum (see fig. 38.5). The liver produces **bile,** which is stored in the **gallbladder** and is sent to the duodenum by way of a duct. Bile looks green because it contains pigments that are products of hemoglobin breakdown. This green color is familiar to anyone who has observed how bruised tissue changes color. Hemoglobin within the bruise is breaking down into the same types of pigments found in bile. Bile also contains bile salts, which are *emulsifying* agents that break up fat into fat droplets so that they mix with the water:

$$\text{fat} \xrightarrow{\text{bile salts}} \text{fat droplets}$$

Emulsified fat is more easily acted on by enzymes.

The pancreas sends pancreatic juice into the duodenum, also by way of a duct. Pancreatic juice contains sodium bicarbonate ($NaHCO_3$), which neutralizes the chyme and makes the pH of the small intestine slightly basic. Pancreatic juice also contains digestive enzymes that act on every major component of food (table 38.2). **Pancreatic amylase** digests starch to maltose; **trypsin** and other enzymes digest protein to peptides; and **lipase** digests fat droplets to glycerol and fatty acids:

$$\text{starch} + H_2O \xrightarrow{\text{pancreatic amylase}} \text{maltose}$$

$$\text{protein} + H_2O \xrightarrow{\text{trypsin}} \text{peptides}$$

$$\text{fat droplets} + H_2O \xrightarrow{\text{lipase}} \text{glycerol + fatty acids}$$

The epithelial cells of the villi produce *intestinal enzymes,* which remain attached to the plasma membrane of microvilli. These enzymes complete the digestion of peptides and sugars. Peptides, which result from the first step in protein digestion, are digested by peptidases to amino acids. Maltose, which results from the first step in starch digestion, is digested by maltase to glucose:

$$\text{peptides} + H_2O \xrightarrow{\text{peptidases}} \text{amino acids}$$

$$\text{maltose} + H_2O \xrightarrow{\text{maltase}} \text{glucose}$$

Other disaccharides, each of which is acted upon by a specific enzyme, are digested in the small intestine. Table 38.2 reviews both the reactions required for the digestion of food and the various digestive enzymes discussed in this chapter.

Figure 38.9

Anatomy of intestinal lining. The products of digestion are absorbed by villi, fingerlike projections of the intestinal wall that contain blood vessels and a lacteal.

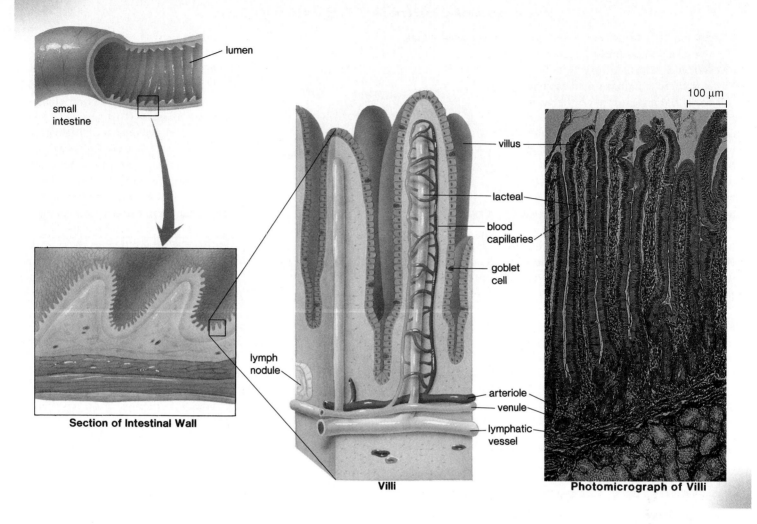

Section of Intestinal Wall

Villi

Photomicrograph of Villi

lumen

small intestine

villus

lacteal

blood capillaries

goblet cell

lymph nodule

arteriole

venule

lymphatic vessel

100 µm

Into the Villi

The small intestine is specialized for absorption. Molecules are absorbed by the huge number of villi that line the intestinal wall (fig. 38.9). Each villus contains blood vessels and a lymphatic vessel called a **lacteal.** Sugars and amino acids enter villi cells and then are absorbed into the bloodstream. Glycerol and fatty acids enter villi cells and are reassembled into fat molecules, which move into the lacteals.

Absorption continues until almost all products of digestion have been absorbed. Absorption involves active transport and requires an expenditure of cellular energy.

Food is largely made up of carbohydrate (starch), protein, and fat. These very large macromolecules are broken down by digestive enzymes to small molecules that can be absorbed by intestinal villi.

> The wall of the small intestine is lined by villi. Sugars and amino acids enter blood vessels, and reformed fats enter the lacteals of the villi.

Hormonal Control of Digestive Juices

The study of the control of digestive gland secretion began in the late 1800s. At that time, Ivan Pavlov showed that dogs would begin to salivate at the ringing of a bell because they had learned to associate the sound of the bell with being fed. Pavlov's experiments demonstrated that even the thought of food can cause the nervous system to order the secretion of digestive juices. If food is present in the mouth, the stomach, and the small intestine, digestive secretion occurs because of simple reflex action. The presence of food sets off nerve impulses that travel to the brain. Thereafter, the brain stimulates the digestive glands to secrete.

In this century, investigators discovered that specific control of digestive secretions is achieved by hormones. A *hormone* is a substance produced by one set of cells that affects a different set of cells, the so-called target cells. Hormones are transported by the bloodstream. For example, when a person has eaten a meal

Figure 38A
Hormonal control of digestive gland secretions.

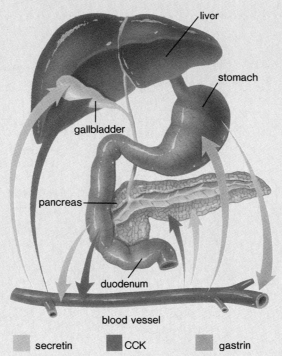

secretin   CCK   gastrin

particularly rich in protein, the gastric glands of the stomach wall produce the hormone gastrin (fig. 38A). Gastrin enters the bloodstream, and soon stomach churning and the secretory activity of gastric glands increase.

Cells of the duodenal wall also produce hormones, two of which are of particular interest—secretin and CCK (cholecystokinin). Acid, especially hydrochloric acid (HCl) present in chyme, stimulates the release of secretin, while partially digested protein and fat stimulate the release of CCK. Soon after these hormones enter the bloodstream, the pancreas increases its output of pancreatic juice and the liver increases its output of bile. The gallbladder contracts to release bile.

Another hormone produced by the duodenal wall, GIP (gastric inhibitory peptide), works opposite to gastrin—it inhibits gastric gland secretion and stomach motility. This is not surprising, because the body's hormones often have opposite effects.

Two Accessory Organs Help Out

The pancreas and the liver are the accessory organs of digestion. Figure 38.5 shows how ducts conduct pancreatic juice from the pancreas, and bile from the liver, to the duodenum.

Pancreas Secretes Juices

The pancreas lies deep in the abdominal cavity, resting on the posterior abdominal wall. It is an elongated and somewhat flattened organ that is an endocrine gland when it produces and secretes insulin into the bloodstream, and is an exocrine gland when it produces and secretes pancreatic juice into the duodenum. Just now we are interested in its exocrine function—most of its cells produce pancreatic juice, which contains enzymes for digestion of all types of food (see table 38.2). The enzymes travel by way of ducts to the duodenum of the small intestine. Regulation of pancreatic secretion is discussed in the reading on this page.

Liver Secretes Bile

Blood vessels from the large and small intestines merge to form the hepatic portal vein, which leads to the liver (fig. 38.10). The liver has numerous functions, including the following:

1. Detoxifies the blood by removing and metabolizing poisonous substances.
2. Makes the blood proteins.
3. Destroys old red blood cells and converts hemoglobin to the breakdown products in bile (bilirubin and biliverdin).
4. Produces bile, which is stored in the gallbladder before entering the small intestine, where it emulsifies fats.
5. Stores glucose as glycogen and breaks down glycogen to glucose between meals to maintain a constant glucose concentration in the blood.
6. Produces urea from amino groups and ammonia.

Here we are interested in the last two functions listed. The liver helps maintain the glucose concentration in blood at about 0.1% by removing excess glucose from the hepatic portal vein and storing it as glycogen. Between meals, glycogen is broken down and glucose enters the hepatic vein. Glycogen is sometimes called *animal starch* because both starch and glycogen are made up of glucose molecules. If by chance the supply of glycogen and glucose runs short, the liver converts amino acids to glucose molecules. Amino acids contain nitrogen in the form of amino groups, whereas glucose contains only carbon, oxygen,

Figure 38.10

Hepatic portal system. The hepatic portal vein takes the products of digestion from the digestive system to the liver, where they are processed before entering the circulatory system proper.

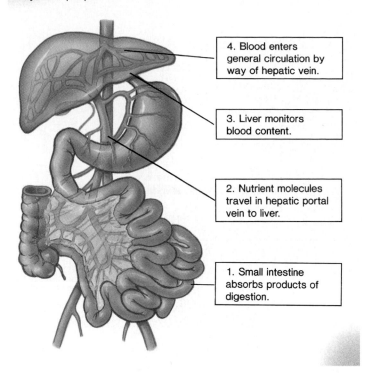

4. Blood enters general circulation by way of hepatic vein.

3. Liver monitors blood content.

2. Nutrient molecules travel in hepatic portal vein to liver.

1. Small intestine absorbs products of digestion.

and hydrogen. Therefore, before amino acids can be converted to glucose molecules, *deamination,* or the removal of amino groups from the amino acids, must take place. By an involved metabolic pathway, the liver converts these amino groups to urea, the most common nitrogenous waste product of humans. After urea is formed in the liver, it is transported by the bloodstream to the kidneys, and eventually it is excreted.

> Blood from the small intestine enters the hepatic portal vein, which goes to the liver, a vital organ that has numerous important functions.

Liver Disorders

Jaundice, hepatitis, and cirrhosis are three serious diseases that affect the entire liver and hinder its ability to repair itself. When a person is jaundiced, there is a yellowish tint to the skin due to an abnormally large amount of bilirubin in the blood. In *hemolytic jaundice,* red blood cells are broken down in abnormally large amounts; in *obstructive jaundice,* there is an obstruction of the bile duct or damage to the liver cells. Obstructive jaundice often occurs when crystals of cholesterol precipitate out of bile and form gallstones.

Jaundice can also result from *viral hepatitis,* a term that includes hepatitis A, hepatitis B, and hepatitis C. Hepatitis A is most often caused by eating contaminated food. Hepatitis B and C are commonly spread by blood transfusions, kidney dialysis, and injection with unsterilized needles. All three types of hepatitis can be spread by sexual contact.

Cirrhosis is a chronic liver disease in which the organ first becomes fatty. Liver tissue is then replaced by inactive fibrous scar tissue. In alcoholics, who often get cirrhosis, the condition most likely is caused by the excessive amounts of alcohol the liver is forced to break down.

Large Intestine Absorbs Water

About 1.5 liters of water enter the digestive tract daily as a result of eating and drinking. An additional 8.5 liters enter the digestive tract each day carrying the various substances secreted by the digestive glands. About 95% of this water is absorbed by the small intestine, and much of the remaining portion is absorbed into cells of the *large intestine,* or **colon.** If this water is not reabsorbed, then *diarrhea* will result, which can lead to serious dehydration and ion loss, especially in children.

The large intestine also functions in ion regulation. Notably, the large intestine absorbs some salts from the material passing through it. *Vitamin K,* produced by intestinal bacteria, is also absorbed in the colon.

The last 20 cm of the large intestine is the rectum, which terminates in the anus, an external opening. Digestive wastes (feces) eventually leave the body through the rectum and anus. Feces are about 75% water and 25% solid matter. Almost one-third of this solid matter is made up of intestinal bacteria. The remainder is undigested plant material, fats, waste products (such as bile pigments), inorganic material, mucus, and dead cells from the intestinal lining.

Two serious medical conditions are associated with the large intestine. The small intestine joins the large intestine in such a way that there is a blind end on one side (see fig. 38.5). This blind sac, or cecum, has a small projection about the size of the little finger, called the appendix. In the case of *appendicitis,* the appendix becomes infected and so filled with fluid that it may burst. If an infected appendix bursts before it can be removed, it can lead to a serious, generalized infection of the abdominal lining, called peritonitis.

The colon is subject to the development of polyps, which are small growths arising from the epithelial lining. Polyps, whether they are benign or cancerous, can be removed individually. A low-fat, high-fiber diet, which promotes regularity, is recommended as a protective measure against colon cancer because mutagenic agents, which might promote cancer, are quickly eliminated.

> The large intestine does not produce digestive enzymes; it absorbs water and salts.

Figure 38.11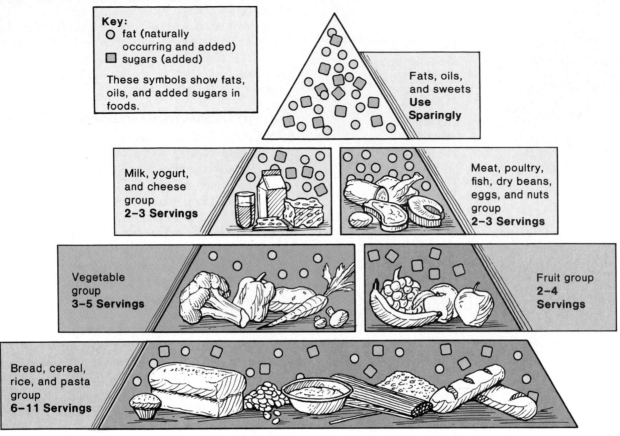

Ideal American diet. The U.S. Department of Agriculture uses a pyramid to show the ideal American diet because it emphasizes the importance of grains in the diet and the undesirability of fats, oils, and sweets.

Source: U.S. Department of Agriculture.

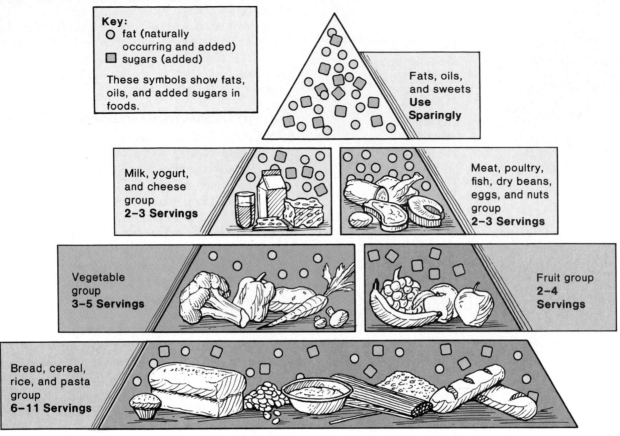

Key:
○ fat (naturally occurring and added)
□ sugars (added)

These symbols show fats, oils, and added sugars in foods.

Fats, oils, and sweets
Use Sparingly

Milk, yogurt, and cheese group
2–3 Servings

Meat, poultry, fish, dry beans, eggs, and nuts group
2–3 Servings

Vegetable group
3–5 Servings

Fruit group
2–4 Servings

Bread, cereal, rice, and pasta group
6–11 Servings

Food Guide Pyramid: A Guide to Daily Food Choices

NUTRITION AFFECTS HEALTH

To be sure that the essential nutrients are included in the diet, it is necessary to eat a balanced diet. A balanced diet includes a variety of foods proportioned as shown in figure 38.11.

Vitamins Activate Metabolism

Vitamins [L. *vita,* life] are organic compounds (other than carbohydrates, fats, and proteins) that the body needs for metabolic purposes but is unable to produce. They yield no calories. Many vitamins are portions of coenzymes; niacin is part of the coenzyme NAD^+, and riboflavin is a part of FAD. These two enzymes are essential for cellular respiration. Coenzymes are needed in only small amounts because each one can be used repeatedly.

If vitamins are lacking in the diet, various symptoms develop. Many substances are advertised as vitamins, but in reality there are only thirteen vitamins (table 38.3). In general, carrots, squash, turnip greens, and collards are good sources for vitamin A. Citrus fruits, other fresh fruits, and vegetables are natural sources

of vitamin C. Fortified milk is the primary source of vitamin D, and whole grains are a good source of B vitamins.

The National Academy of Sciences suggests that we eat more fruits and vegetables to acquire a good supply of vitamins C and A because these two vitamins may help guard against the development of cancer. Nevertheless, the intake of excess vitamins by way of pills is discouraged because this practice can possibly lead to illness. Excess vitamin C can cause kidney stones and can also be converted to oxalic acid, a molecule that is toxic to the body. Vitamin A taken in excess can cause peeling of the skin, bone and joint pains, and liver damage. Excess vitamin D can cause vomiting, diarrhea, and kidney damage. Megavitamin therapy, therefore, should always be supervised by a physician.

A properly balanced diet includes all the vitamins and minerals needed by most individuals to maintain health.

Table 38.3

Vitamins: Their Role in the Body and Their Food Sources

Vitamin	Major Role in Body	Good Food Sources
Fat Soluble		
Vitamin A	Vision, health of skin, hair, bones, and sex organs	Deep green or yellow vegetables, dairy products
Vitamin D	Health of bones and teeth	Dairy products, tuna, eggs
Vitamin E	Strengthening of red blood cell membrane	Green leafy vegetables, whole grains
Vitamin K	Clotting of blood, bone metabolism	Green leafy vegetables, cabbage, cauliflower
Water Soluble		
Thiamine (B$_1$)	Carbohydrate metabolism	Pork, whole grains
Riboflavin (B$_2$)	Energy metabolism	Whole grains, milk, green vegetables
Niacin (B$_3$)	Energy metabolism	Organ meats, whole grains
Pyridoxine (B$_6$)	Amino acid metabolism	Meats, fish, whole grains
Vitamin B$_{12}$	Red blood cell formation	Meats, dairy foods
Biotin	Carbohydrate metabolism	Eggs, most foods
Folic acid	Formation of red blood cells, DNA and RNA	Green leafy vegetables, nuts, whole grains
Pantothenic acid	Energy metabolism	Most foods
Vitamin C	Collagen formation	Citrus fruits, tomatoes

Table 38.4

Minerals: Their Role in the Body and Their Food Sources

Mineral	Major Role in Body	Good Food Sources
Macrominerals		
Calcium (Ca)	Strong bones and teeth, nerve conduction	Dairy products, green leafy vegetables
Phosphorus (P)	Strong bones and teeth	Meat, dairy products, whole grains
Potassium (K)	Nerve conduction, muscle contraction	Many fruits and vegetables
Sodium (Na)	Nerve conduction, pH balance	Table salt
Chlorine (Cl)	Water balance	Table salt
Magnesium (Mg)	Protein synthesis	Whole grains, green leafy vegetables
Microminerals		
Zinc (Zn)	Wound healing, tissue growth	Whole grains, legumes, meats
Iron (Fe)	Hemoglobin synthesis	Whole grains, legumes, eggs
Fluorine (F)	Strong bones and teeth	Fluoridated drinking water, tea
Copper (Cu)	Hemoglobin synthesis	Seafood, whole grains, legumes
Iodine (I)	Thyroid hormone synthesis	Iodized table salt, seafood

Minerals Are for Structure and Function

In addition to vitamins, various minerals are also required by the body (table 38.4). Some minerals (calcium, phosphorus, potassium, sulfur, sodium, chlorine, and magnesium) are recommended in amounts more than 100 mg per day. These macrominerals serve as constituents of cells and body fluids, and as structural components of tissues. Calcium is needed for the construction of bones and teeth and also for nerve conduction and muscle contraction. Other minerals (iron, manganese, copper, iodine, cobalt, and zinc) are recommended in amounts of less than 20 mg per day.

These microminerals are more likely to have very specific functions. Iron is needed for the production of hemoglobin, and iodine is used in the production of thyroxin, a hormone produced by the thyroid glands. As research continues, more and more elements have been added to the list of those considered essential. During the past three decades, very small amounts of molybdenum, selenium, chromium, nickel, vanadium, silicon, and even arsenic have been found to be essential to good health.

Some individuals do not receive enough iron (especially women), calcium, magnesium, or zinc in their diets. Adult females need more iron in their diet than males (18 mg compared to 10 mg) because they lose hemoglobin each month during menstruation. Stress can bring on a magnesium deficiency, and a vegetarian diet may lack zinc, which is usually obtained from meat. A varied and complete diet, however, usually supplies the recommended daily allowances for minerals.

Calcium Builds Bones

There is much interest in calcium supplements to counteract the development of *osteoporosis,* a degenerative bone disease that afflicts an estimated 25% of older men and 50% of older women in the United States. These individuals have porous bones that tend to break easily because they lack sufficient calcium. Studies have shown, however, that calcium supplements cannot prevent osteoporosis after menopause, even when the dosage is 3,000 mg per day. In postmenopausal women, bone-eating cells called osteoclasts are known to be more active than bone-forming cells called osteoblasts. Until now, the most effective defense against osteoporosis in older women has been estrogen replacement and exercise, which encourages the work of osteoblasts. Recently, however, studies have shown that the drug etidronate disodium, which inhibits osteoclast activity, is effective in osteoporotic women when administered at the proper dosage.

Women can guard against the possibility of developing osteoporosis when they grow older by forming strong, dense bones when they are young. Eighteen-year-old women are apt to get only 679 mg of calcium a day, when they require at least 800 mg. They should consume more calcium-rich foods, such as milk and dairy products. Calcium supplements may not be as effective; a cup of milk supplies 270 mg of calcium, while a 500 mg tablet of calcium carbonate provides only 200 mg. The rest is just not taken up by the body; it is not in a form that is *bioavailable.* Futhermore, an excess of bioavailable calcium can lead to kidney stones.

> Dietary calcium and exercise, plus estrogen therapy if needed, are the best safeguards against osteoporosis.

Sodium Causes Water Retention

The recommended amount of sodium intake per day is 400–3,300 mg, and the average American intake is 4,000–4,700 mg, mostly as salt (sodium chloride). In recent years, this imbalance has caused concern because high-sodium intake has been linked to hypertension in some people. About one-third of the sodium we consume occurs naturally in foods; another third is added during commercial processing; and we add the last third either during home cooking or at the table in the form of table salt.

Clearly, it is possible for us to cut down on the amount of sodium in the diet by reducing the amount of salt we eat.

> Excess sodium in the diet can lead to hypertension; therefore, we should reduce sodium intake.

Summary

1. Some animals (e.g., planaria) have an incomplete digestive tract, which shows little specialization of parts. Other animals (e.g., earthworms) have a complete digestive tract, which does show specialization of parts.

2. Some animals are continuous feeders (e.g., clams, which are sessile filter feeders); others are discontinuous feeders (e.g., squid). Discontinuous feeders need a storage area for food.

3. All mammals have teeth. Herbivores need teeth that can clip off plant material and grind it up. Also, the herbivore's stomach contains bacteria that can digest cellulose.

4. Carnivores need teeth that can tear and rip meat into pieces. Meat is easier to assimilate, so the digestive system of carnivores has less specialization of parts and a shorter intestine than that of herbivores.

5. In the human digestive tract, food is chewed and manipulated in the mouth, where salivary glands secrete saliva. Saliva contains salivary amylase, which begins carbohydrate digestion.

6. Food then passes down the esophagus to the stomach. The stomach stores and mixes food with mucus and gastric juice to produce chyme. Pepsin begins protein digestion here.

7. Chyme gradually enters the duodenum where bile, pancreatic juice, and the intestinal secretions are found. Enzymes in the small intestine hydrolyze all of the organic nutrients. Table 38.2 summarizes the enzymes involved in digesting food.

8. There are three hormones that regulate digestive-tract secretions: gastrin, which stimulates acid- and enzyme-secreting cells in the stomach; secretin, which stimulates the pancreas to release sodium bicarbonate; and CCK (cholecystokinin), which stimulates the gallbladder to release bile and the pancreas to release digestive enzymes.

9. The pancreas produces digestive enzymes for every major component of food.

10. The liver produces bile, which is stored in the gallbladder. The liver is also involved in the processing of absorbed nutrient molecules and in maintaining the blood concentration of nutrient molecules, such as glucose. The liver converts ammonia to urea and breaks down toxins.

11. Most nutrient absorption takes place in the small intestine, but some water and minerals are absorbed in the colon. Digestive wastes leave the colon by way of the anus.

12. A balanced diet is required for good health. Food should provide us with all the necessary vitamins, minerals, amino acids, fatty acids, and an adequate amount of energy.

Writing Across the Curriculum

In order to practice writing skills, students should write out the answers to any or all of the study questions and the critical thinking questions. The study questions are sequenced in the same order as the text. Answers to the objective questions, and suggested answers to the critical thinking questions, are in appendix D.

1. Contrast the incomplete gut with the complete gut, using the planarian and earthworm as examples. 668

2. Contrast a continuous feeder with a discontinuous feeder, using the clam and squid as examples. 669

3. Contrast the dentition of the mammalian herbivore with that of the mammalian carnivore, using the horse and lion as examples. 670

4. List the parts of the human digestive tract, anatomically describe them, and state the contribution of each to the digestive process. 671–75

5. Assume that you have just eaten a ham sandwich. Discuss the digestion of the contents of the sandwich. 671–75

6. State the location and describe the functions of both the liver and the pancreas. 676–77

7. Discuss the absorption of the products of digestion into the circulatory system. 675

8. What are gastrin, secretin, and CCK (cholecystokinin)? Where are they produced and what are their functions? 676

9. Explain why carbohydrates, fats, proteins, vitamins, and minerals are all necessary to good nutrition. 678–80

> **Objective Questions**

1. Animals that feed discontinuously
   a. must have digestive tracts that permit storage.
   b. are able to avoid predators by limiting their feeding time.
   c. exhibit extremely rapid digestion.
   d. Both a and b are correct.

2. In which of the following types of animals would you expect the digestive system to be more complex?
   a. those with a single opening for the entrance of food and exit of wastes
   b. those with two openings, one serving as an entrance and the other as an exit
   c. only those complex animals that also have a respiratory system
   d. Both b and c are correct.

3. The typhlosole within the gut of an earthworm compares best to which of these organs in humans?
   a. teeth in the mouth
   b. esophagus in the thoracic cavity
   c. folds in the stomach
   d. villi in the small intestine

4. Which of these animals is a continuous feeder with a complete gut?
   a. planarian   c. squid
   b. clam   d. lion

5. The products of digestion are
   a. large macromolecules needed by the body.
   b. enzymes needed to digest food.
   c. small nutrient molecules that can be absorbed.
   d. regulatory hormones of various kinds.

6. The most common food digested in the human stomach is
   a. carbohydrate.
   b. fat.
   c. protein.
   d. nucleic acid.

7. Which association is incorrect?
   a. protein—trypsin
   b. fat—lipase
   c. maltose—pepsin
   d. starch—amylase

8. Most of the absorption of the products of digestion takes place in humans across the
   a. squamous epithelium of the esophagus.
   b. convoluted walls of the stomach.
   c. fingerlike villi of the small intestine.
   d. smooth wall of the large intestine.

9. The hepatic portal vein is located between the
   a. hepatic vein and the vena cava.
   b. mouth and the stomach.
   c. pancreas and the small intestine.
   d. small intestine and the liver.

10. Bile in humans
    a. is an important enzyme for the digestion of fats.
    b. is made by the gallbladder.
    c. emulsifies fat.
    d. All of these are correct.

11. Which of these is not a function of the liver in adults?
    a. produce bile
    b. store glucose
    c. produce urea
    d. make red blood cells

12. The large intestine in humans
    a. digests all types of food.
    b. is the longest part of the intestinal tract.
    c. absorbs water.
    d. is connected to the stomach.

13. Predict and explain the digestive results per test tube for this experiment.

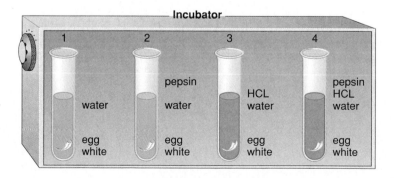

Concepts and Critical Thinking

1. *All systems of the animal's body contribute to homeostasis.*

   List several ways in which the human digestive system contributes to homeostasis.

2. *Organisms are adapted to obtaining a share of available resources.*

   Animals vary according to how they obtain and process food. Use the grasshopper, the earthworm, the clam, or the squid to support this concept.

3. *Forms of life depend on each other for materials and energy.*

   Explain how you are dependent on plants as a source of materials and energy.

Selected Key Terms

amylase A starch-digesting enzyme secreted by salivary glands and pancreas.   671

bile A secretion of the liver that is temporarily stored in the gallbladder before being released into the small intestine, where it emulsifies fat.   674

colon The large intestine.   677

duodenum (doo-uh-DEE-num) The first part of the small intestine where chyme enters from the stomach.   672

epiglottis (ep-uh-GLAHT-us) A structure that covers the glottis, the air-tract opening, during the process of swallowing. [Gk. *epi,* upon, and *glotti,* tongue]   672

esophagus (i-SAHF-uh-gus) A muscular tube for moving swallowed food from the pharynx to the stomach. [Gk. *eso,* within, and *phag,* eat]   672

gallbladder An organ attached to the liver that serves as a storage organ for bile.   674

lacteal (LAK-tee-ul) A lymphatic vessel in an intestinal villus, it aids in the absorption of fats. [L. *lac,* milk]   675

lipase A fat-digesting enzyme secreted by the pancreas.   674

pepsin A protein-digesting enzyme secreted by gastric glands.   672

salivary gland A gland associated with the mouth that secretes saliva.   671

trypsin A protein-digesting enzyme secreted by the pancreas.   674

peristalsis (per-uh-STAWL-sus) The rhythmic, wavelike contraction that moves food through the digestive tract. [Gk. *peristole,* contraction]   672

villus (pl., villi) (VIL-us) A small, fingerlike projection of the inner small intestinal wall. [L. *vill,* shaggy hair]   674

vitamin Essential requirement in the diet, needed in small amounts. They are often part of coenzymes. [L. *vita,* life]   678

39

RESPIRATORY SYSTEM

Learning Objectives

- Distinguish among breathing, external respiration, and internal respiration. 684

How Animals Exchange Gases

- Describe the mechanism of gas exchange in a hydra and a planarian. 684
- Compare the respiratory organs of aquatic and terrestrial animals. 685–87
- Compare the various methods for ventilating the lungs among terrestrial vertebrates. 686–87
- Compare the incomplete method of ventilation used by amphibians, reptiles, and mammals with the complete method used by birds. 687

How Humans Exchange Gases

- Describe the path of air in humans, and describe in general the structure and the function of all organs mentioned. 688
- Describe the breathing process and how the breathing rate is controlled in humans. 689
- Give the equations applicable to the exchange of gases in the lungs and tissues, and tell how the gases are transported in the blood. 691

Keeping the Respiratory Tract Healthy

- List two common infections of the respiratory tract, and discuss five disorders of the lungs. 692–93

Both the bottle-nosed dolphin, *Tursiops,* and boy, *Homo,* are mammals that breathe air to acquire oxygen for aerobic respiration.

A nimals do not have a storage area for gases and must continually acquire oxygen and rid the body of carbon dioxide. Without a constant supply of oxygen, an animal dies. Eighteenth-century Frenchman Antoine Lavoisier, correctly deduced that both combustion by a lit candle and breathing by an animal remove oxygen from the air. This was one of the first times that a physiological process was explained with reference to a nonliving mechanism.

Breathing is only the first step of respiration, which can be said to include the following steps:

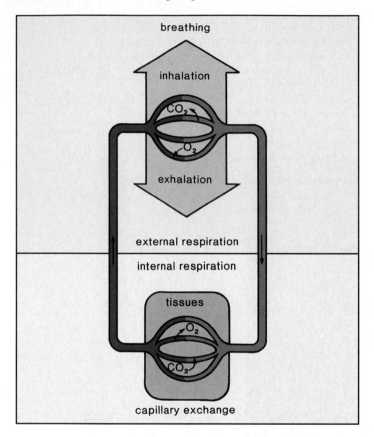

- Breathing: includes inspiration (breathing air in) and expiration (breathing air out).
- External respiration: gas exchange with the environment at a respiratory surface; in more complex animals, gas exchange between air and blood.
- Internal respiration: in more complex animals, gas exchange between blood and tissue fluid.
- Aerobic cellular respiration: production of ATP (adenosine triphosphate) in cells.

HOW ANIMALS EXCHANGE GASES

Gas exchange takes place by the physical process of diffusion. For diffusion to be effective, the gas-exchange region must be (1) moist, (2) thin, and (3) large in relation to the size of the body. Some animals are small and shaped in a way that allows the surface of the animal to be the gas-exchange surface. Other ani-

mals are complex and have a specialized gas-exchange surface. The effectiveness of diffusion is enhanced by vascularization, and delivery to cells is promoted when the blood contains a respiratory pigment such as hemoglobin.

In the Water

It is more difficult for animals to obtain oxygen from water than from air. Water fully saturated with air contains only a fraction of the amount of oxygen in the same volume of air. Also, water is more dense than air. Therefore, aquatic animals expend more energy to breathe than do terrestrial animals. Fishes use up to 25% of their energy output to breathe, while terrestrial mammals use only 1–2% of their energy output.

Hydras and planaria have a large surface area in comparison to their size (fig. 39.1). This makes it possible for most of their cells to exchange gases directly with the environment. In hydras, the outer layer of cells is in contact with the external environment, and the inner layer can exchange gases with the water in the gastrovascular cavity. In planaria, the flattened body permits cells to exchange gases with the external environment.

Figure 39.1

Animal shapes and gas exchange. Some small aquatic animals use the body surface for gas exchange. This works because the body surface is large compared to the size of the animal. **a.** In hydras, every cell is near a source of oxygen. **b.** The flattened body of planaria allows most cells to carry out gas exchange with the external environment.

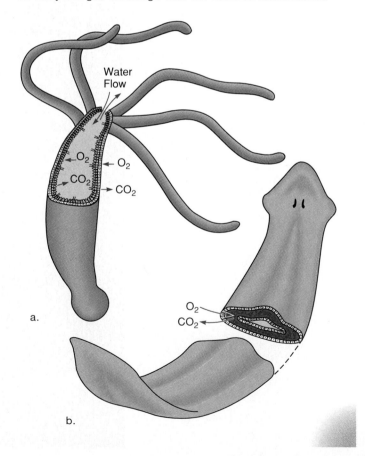

A tubular shape also provides a surface area adequate for gas-exchange purposes. In addition to a tubular shape, polychaete worms have extensions of the body wall called parapodia, which are vascularized. Quite often, aquatic animals have **gills,** which are finely divided and vascularized outgrowths of either the outer or the inner body surface. Among mollusks, such as clams and many snails, water is drawn into the mantle cavity, where it passes through the gills. In decapod crustacea, the gills are located in brachial chambers covered by the exoskeleton. Water is kept moving by the action of specialized appendages located near the mouth.

Among vertebrates, the gills of fishes are outward extensions of the pharynx (fig. 39.2). Ventilation is brought about by the combined action of the mouth and gill covers, or opercula (sing., operculum). When the mouth is open, the opercula are closed and water is drawn in. Then the mouth closes and the opercula open, drawing the water from the pharynx through the gill slits located between the gill arches. On the outside of the gill arches, the gills are composed of *filaments* that are folded into platelike *lamellae*. In the capillaries of each lamella, the blood flows in a direction opposite to the movement of water across the gills. This *countercurrent flow* increases the amount of oxygen that can be taken up; as the blood in each lamella gains oxygen, it encounters water having a still higher oxygen content. The countercurrent mechanism allows about 80–90% of the initial dissolved oxygen in water to be extracted.

> Small aquatic animals sometimes use the body surface for gas exchange, but many larger ones have localized gas-exchange surfaces known as gills.

Figure 39.2

Anatomy of gills in detail. **a.** The operculum (folded back) covers and protects several layers of delicate gills. **b.** Each layer of gills has two rows of gill filaments. **c.** Each filament has many thin, platelike lamellae. Gases are exchanged between the capillaries inside the lamellae and the water that flows between the lamellae. **d.** Blood in the capillaries flows in the direction opposite to that of the water. Blood takes up almost all of the oxygen in the water as a result of this countercurrent flow.

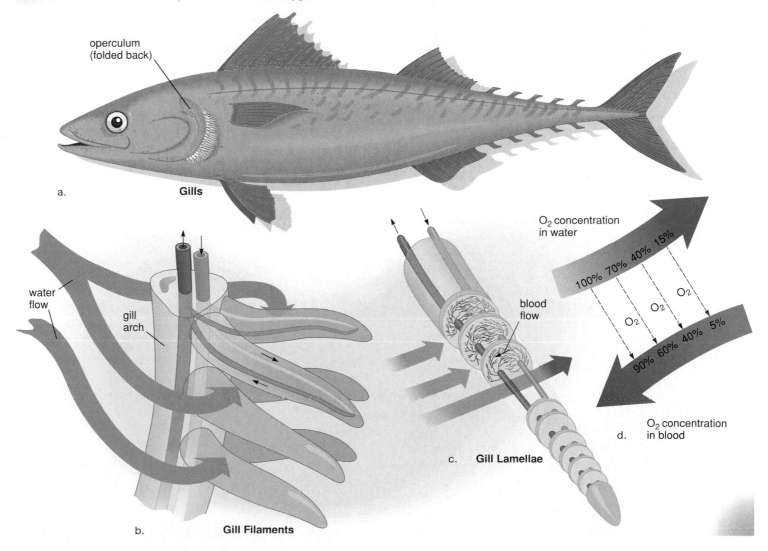

Figure 39.3

Tracheal system of insects. **a.** A system of air tubes extends throughout the body of an insect and they, rather than blood, carry oxygen to the cells. **b.** Air enters the tracheae at openings called spiracles. From here, the air moves to the smaller tracheoles, which take it to the cells, where gas exchange takes place.

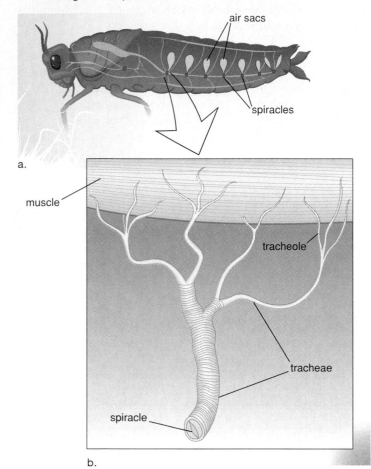

a.

b.

On the Land

Air is a rich source of oxygen compared to water; however, it does have a drying effect on respiratory surfaces. A human loses about 350 ml of water per day when the air has a relative humidity of only 50%.

The earthworm is an example of an invertebrate terrestrial animal that uses its body surface for respiration. An earthworm expends much energy to keep its body surface moist by secreting mucus and by releasing fluids from excretory pores. Further, the worm is behaviorally adapted to remain in damp soil during the day, when the air is driest.

Insects and certain other terrestrial arthropods have a respiratory system known as a tracheal system (fig. 39.3). Oxygen enters the tracheae at spiracles, which are valvelike openings on each side of the body. The tracheae branch and then rebranch, ending in tiny channels, the tracheoles, that are in direct contact with the body cells. Larger insects have a ventilation system to keep the air moving in and out of the trachea. Many have air sacs located near major muscles; contraction of these muscles causes the air sacs to empty, and relaxation causes the air sacs to expand and draw air in. The tracheal system of insects is very effective in delivering oxygen to the cells so that the circulatory system plays no role in gas transport.

Terrestrial vertebrates, in particular, have evolved **lungs,** which are vascularized outgrowths from the lower pharyngeal region. The lungs of amphibians are simple, saclike structures (fig. 39.4*a*). Many amphibians possess a short trachea, which divides into two bronchi that open into the lungs. Most amphib-

Figure 39.4

Respiration in amphibians compared to reptiles.
a. Amphibians use positive pressure to push air into small and saclike lungs. The moist, thin skin of amphibians is often used as an auxiliary gas-exchange surface. **b.** Reptiles use negative pressure to draw air into lungs which are more convoluted. The tough, scaly skin protects the animal from drying

a.

b.

ians breathe to some extent through the skin, which is kept moist by the presence of mucus produced by numerous glands on the surface of the body. During the winter in temperate climates, amphibians burrow in the mud, and all gas exchange occurs by way of the skin.

The inner lining of the lungs is more finely divided in reptiles than in amphibians (fig. 39.4b). The lungs of birds and mammals are elaborately subdivided into small passageways and spaces. It has been estimated that human lungs have a total surface area that is at least fifty times the skin's surface area. To keep the lungs from drying out, air is moistened as it moves through passageways leading to the lungs.

Terrestrial vertebrates ventilate the lungs by moving air in and out of the respiratory tract. Frogs use positive pressure to force air into the respiratory tract. With the nostrils firmly shut, the floor of the mouth rises and pushes the air into the lungs. Reptiles, birds, and mammals use negative pressure to move air into the lungs. Reptiles have jointed ribs that can be raised to expand the lungs. Mammals have a **rib cage** that is lifted up and out and a muscular **diaphragm** [Gk. *dia,* separate, and *phragm,* partition] that is flattened. As the **thoracic cavity** (chest cavity) expands and lung volume increases, air will flow into the lungs due to differences in air pressure. Following **inhalation** (or in-

spiration), **exhalation** (or expiration) occurs. In reptiles, lowering the ribs exerts a pressure that forces air out. In mammals, when the rib cage is lowered and the diaphragm rises, the thoracic pressure increases, forcing air out of the lungs.

The lungs of amphibians, reptiles, and mammals are not completely emptied and refilled during each breathing cycle. Because of this *incomplete ventilation* method, the air entering mixes with used air remaining in the lungs. While this does help conserve water, it also decreases gas-exchange efficiency. The high oxygen requirement of flying birds, however, requires a method of *complete ventilation* (fig. 39.5). Incoming air is carried past the lungs by a bronchus that takes it to a set of posterior air sacs. The air then passes forward through the lungs into a set of anterior air sacs. From here, it is finally expelled. Fresh, oxygen-rich air passes through the lungs in one direction only and does not mix with used air.

> Most terrestrial animals have a specialized gas exchange region. Insects have a tracheal system, while terrestrial vertebrates depend on lungs, which are ventilated variously.

Figure 39.5

Respiratory system in birds. Because of the presence of air sacs, there is a one-way flow of air through the lungs. Upon inhalation, air moves into the air sacs; upon exhalation, air moves through the lungs.

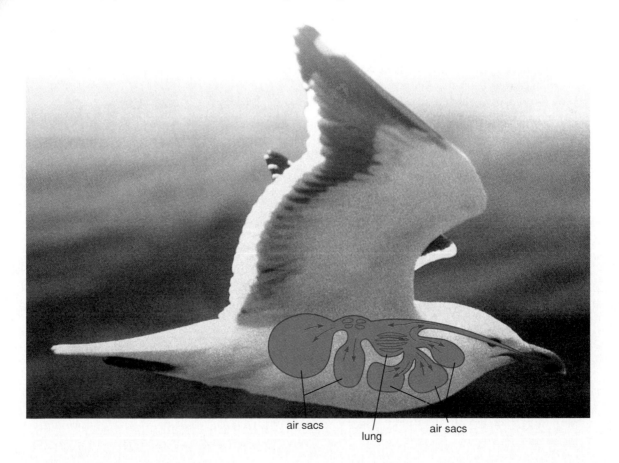

air sacs   lung   air sacs

HOW HUMANS EXCHANGE GASES

The human respiratory system includes all structures that conduct air to and from the lungs (fig. 39.6 and table 39.1). The lungs lie deep within the thoracic cavity, where they are protected from drying out. As air moves through the nose, the pharynx, the trachea, and the bronchi to the lungs, it is filtered so that it is free of debris, warmed, and humidified. By the time the air reaches the lungs, it is at body temperature and is saturated with water. In the nose, hairs and cilia act as a screening device. In the trachea and the bronchi, cilia beat upward, carrying mucus, dust, and occasional bits of food that "went down the wrong way" into the throat, where the accumulation may be swallowed or expectorated.

The hard and soft palates separate the nasal cavities from the mouth, but the air and food passages cross in the **pharynx** [Gk. *pharyn,* throat]. This may seem inefficient, and there is danger of choking if food accidentally enters the trachea, but this arrangement does have the advantage of letting you breathe through your mouth in case your nose is plugged up. In addition, it permits greater intake of air during heavy exercise, when greater gas exchange is required.

Air passes from the pharynx through the **glottis** [Gk. *glotti,* tongue], an opening into the **larynx** [Gk. *laryn,* gullet], or voice box. At the edges of the glottis, embedded in mucous membrane, are the **vocal cords.** These flexible and pliable bands of connective tissue vibrate and produce sound when air is expelled past them through the glottis from the larynx.

The larynx and the **trachea** [L. *trache,* windpipe] are permanently held open to receive air. The larynx is held open by the complex of cartilages that form the Adam's apple. The trachea is held open by a series of C-shaped, cartilaginous rings that do not completely meet in the rear. When food is being swallowed, the larynx rises, and the glottis is closed by a flap of tissue called the **epiglottis** [Gk. *epi,* upon, and *glotti,* tongue]. A backward movement of the soft palate covers the entrance of the nasal passages into the pharynx. The food then enters the esophagus, which lies behind the larynx.

Table 39.1

Path of Air

Structure	Function
Nasal cavities	Filter, warm, and moisten
Pharynx (throat)	Connection to larynx
Glottis	Permits passage of air
Larynx (voice box)	Sound production
Trachea (windpipe)	Passage of air to bronchi
Bronchi	Passage of air to lung
Bronchioles	Passage of air to alveoli
Alveoli	Air sacs for gas exchange

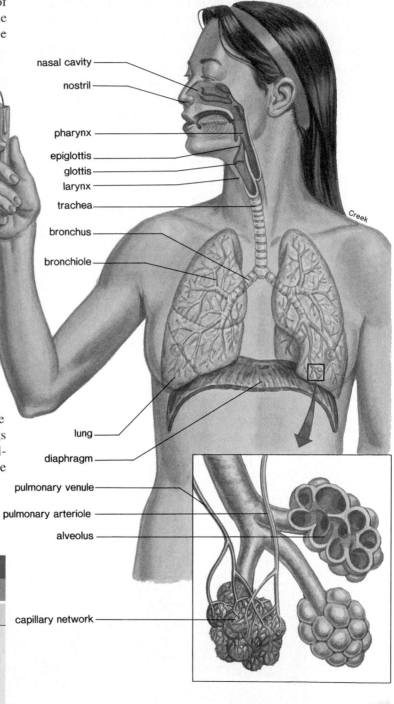

Figure 39.6

The human respiratory tract, with an enlargement showing the internal structure of a lung portion. Gas exchange occurs between the alveoli and the blood within the surrounding capillary network. Notice that the pulmonary arteriole carries deoxygenated blood (colored blue) and the pulmonary venule carries oxygenated blood (colored red).

nasal cavity

nostril

pharynx

epiglottis

glottis

larynx

trachea

bronchus

bronchiole

lung

diaphragm

pulmonary venule

pulmonary arteriole

alveolus

capillary network

Creek

The trachea divides into two **bronchi** [Gk. *bronch,* windpipe], which enter the right and left lungs; each then branches into a great number of smaller passages called **bronchioles** [Gk. *bronch,* windpipe, and *iol,* little]. The two bronchi resemble the trachea in structure, but as the bronchial tubes divide and subdivide, their walls become thinner, and rings of cartilage are no longer present. Each bronchiole terminates in an elongated space enclosed by a multitude of air pockets, or sacs, called **alveoli** [L. *alve,* cavity], which make up the lungs.

Breathing In and Out

Humans breathe using the same mechanism employed by all other mammals. The volume of the thoracic cavity and lungs is increased by muscle contractions that lower the diaphragm and raise the ribs (fig. 39.7). These movements create a negative pressure in the thoracic cavity and lungs, and air then flows into the lungs. When rib and diaphragm muscles relax, air is exhaled as a result of increased pressure in the thoracic cavity and lungs.

Increased carbon dioxide (CO_2) and hydrogen ion (H^+) concentrations in the blood are the primary stimuli that increase breathing rate. The chemical content of the blood is monitored by *chemoreceptors* called the *aortic* and *carotid bodies,* which are specialized structures located in the walls of the aorta and the carotid arteries. These receptors are very sensitive to changes in carbon dioxide and hydrogen ion concentrations, but they are only minimally sensitive to a lower oxygen (O_2) concentration. Information from the chemoreceptors goes to the respiratory center in the medulla oblongata of the brain, which then increases the breathing rate when carbon dioxide or hydrogen ion concentration increases. This respiratory center is itself sensitive to the chemical content of the blood reaching the brain.

Figure 39.7

Inhalation versus exhalation. During inhalation, the rib cage lifts up and out, the diaphragm lowers, the lungs expand, and air flows in. This sequence of events is possible only because the pressure within the intrapleural space, containing a thin film of fluid, is less than atmospheric pressure. During exhalation, the rib cage lowers, the diaphragm rises, the lungs recoil, and air is forced out.

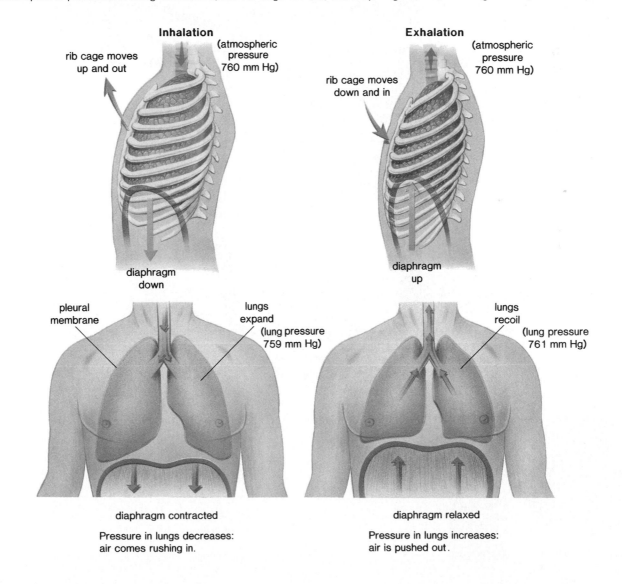

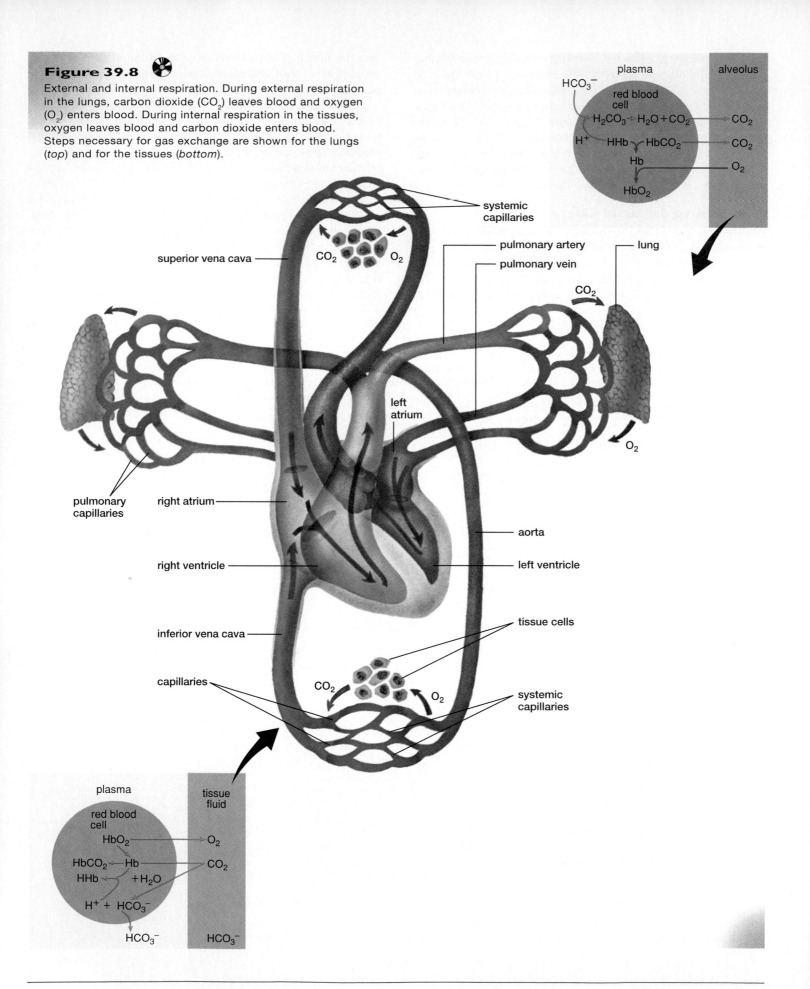

Figure 39.8

External and internal respiration. During external respiration in the lungs, carbon dioxide (CO_2) leaves blood and oxygen (O_2) enters blood. During internal respiration in the tissues, oxygen leaves blood and carbon dioxide enters blood. Steps necessary for gas exchange are shown for the lungs (*top*) and for the tissues (*bottom*).

systemic capillaries

superior vena cava

CO_2

O_2

pulmonary artery

pulmonary vein

lung

CO_2

left atrium

O_2

pulmonary capillaries

right atrium

aorta

right ventricle

left ventricle

inferior vena cava

tissue cells

capillaries

CO_2

O_2

systemic capillaries

plasma

alveolus

HCO_3^-

red blood cell

$H_2CO_3 \rightleftharpoons H_2O + CO_2$

CO_2

H^+

HHb $\searrow$ $HbCO_2$

CO_2

Hb

O_2

HbO_2

plasma

tissue fluid

red blood cell

HbO_2

O_2

$HbCO_2 \leftarrow Hb$

CO_2

HHb $\leftarrow$

$+ H_2O$

$H^+ +$ HCO_3^-

HCO_3^-

HCO_3^-

Exchanging and Transporting Gases

Diffusion primarily accounts for the exchange of gases between the air in the alveoli and the blood in the pulmonary capillaries (fig. 39.8). Atmospheric air contains little carbon dioxide (CO_2), but blood flowing into the pulmonary capillaries is almost saturated with the gas. Therefore, carbon dioxide diffuses out of the blood and into the alveoli. The pattern is the reverse for oxygen: blood coming into the pulmonary capillaries is oxygen poor and the alveolar air is oxygen (O_2) rich; therefore, oxygen diffuses into the capillaries.

Transporting O_2 and CO_2

Most oxygen entering the blood combines with **hemoglobin** (Hb) [Gk. *hem,* blood, and L. *glob,* ball] in red blood cells to form oxyhemoglobin (HbO_2):

$$Hb + O_2 \longrightarrow \underset{\text{oxyhemoglobin}}{HbO_2}$$

Each hemoglobin molecule contains four polypeptide chains, and each chain is folded around an iron-containing group called heme. It is actually the iron that forms a loose association with oxygen. Since there are about 250 million hemoglobin molecules in each red blood cell, each cell is capable of carrying more than one billion molecules of oxygen.

Carbon monoxide, present in automobile exhaust, combines with hemoglobin more readily than oxygen, and it stays combined for several hours regardless of the environmental conditions. Accidental death or suicide from carbon monoxide poisoning occurs because the hemoglobin of the blood is not available for oxygen transport.

Oxygen-binding characteristics of hemoglobin can be studied by examining oxyhemoglobin dissociation curves (fig. 39.9). These curves show the percentage of oxygen-binding sites of hemoglobin that are carrying oxygen at various oxygen partial pressures (PO_2). A partial pressure of a gas is simply the amount of pressure exerted by that gas among all the gases present. At the normal partial pressures of oxygen in the lungs, hemoglobin becomes practically saturated with oxygen, but at the partial pressures in the tissues, oxyhemoglobin quickly gives up much of its oxygen:

$$HbO_2 \longrightarrow Hb + O_2$$

The acid pH and warmer temperature of the tissues also promote this dissociation (breakdown).

In the tissues, some hemoglobin combines with carbon dioxide to form *carbaminohemoglobin.* Most of the carbon dioxide, however, is transported in the form of the **bicarbonate ion.** First carbon dioxide combines with water, forming *carbonic acid,* and then this dissociates to a hydrogen ion and the bicarbonate ion:

$$CO_2 + H_2O \longrightarrow \underset{\substack{\text{carbonic} \\ \text{acid}}}{H_2CO_3} \longrightarrow \underset{\substack{\text{bicarbonate} \\ \text{ion}}}{H^+ + HCO_3^-}$$

Carbonic anhydrase [Gk. *an,* without, and *hydr,* water], an enzyme in red blood cells, speeds this reaction. The released hydrogen ions, which could drastically change the pH of the blood, are absorbed by the globin portions of hemoglobin, and the bicarbonate ions diffuse out of the red blood cells to be carried in the plasma. Hemoglobin that combines with a hydrogen ion is called reduced hemoglobin and can be symbolized as HHb. HHb plays a vital role in maintaining the pH of the blood.

As blood enters the pulmonary capillaries, most of the carbon dioxide is present in plasma as the bicarbonate ion. The little free carbon dioxide remaining begins to diffuse out, and the following reaction occurs:

$$H^+ + HCO_3^- \longrightarrow H_2CO_3 \longrightarrow H_2O + CO_2$$

Carbonic anhydrase also speeds this reaction, during which time hemoglobin gives up the hydrogen ions it has been carrying, and HHb becomes Hb.

> **Oxygen is transported in the blood by hemoglobin, and carbon dioxide is largely carried in plasma as the bicarbonate ion.**

Figure 39.9

Properties of hemoglobin as revealed by hemoglobin dissociation curves. These curves show that as the partial pressure of oxygen (PO_2) decreases, hemoglobin gives up its oxygen more readily. Both (a) higher temperature and (b) higher acidity promote this effect. These are the very conditions of the tissues compared to the lungs.

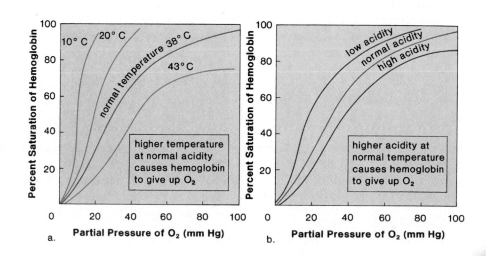

a.

b.

We have seen that the entire respiratory tract has a warm, wet, mucous membrane lining, which is constantly exposed to environmental air. The quality of this air, determined by the pollutants and the microbes therein, can affect our health.

The Tract Gets Infected

Microbes frequently spread from one individual to another by way of the respiratory tract. Droplets from a single sneeze can carry billions of bacteria or viruses. The mucous membranes are protected by mucus and by the constant beating of the cilia, but if the number of infectious agents is large and/or our resistance is reduced, respiratory infections such as colds and influenza (flu) can result. Other more serious infections and disorders are discussed here.

Viral infections can spread from the nasal cavities to the sinuses (sinusitis), to the middle ears (otitis media), to the larynx (laryngitis), and to the bronchi (bronchitis). Acute bronchitis (fig. 39.10) usually is caused by a secondary bacterial infection of the bronchi, resulting in a heavy mucus discharge with much coughing. Acute bronchitis usually responds to antibiotic therapy. Chronic bronchitis, on the other hand, is not necessarily due to infection. It is often caused by constant irritation of the lining of the bronchi, which consequently undergo degenerative changes, including the loss of cilia and their accompanying cleansing action. There is frequent coughing, and the individual is more susceptible to respiratory infections. Chronic bronchitis is most often seen in cigarette smokers or those exposed to secondhand smoke or other types of polluted air.

Strep throat is a very severe throat infection caused by the bacterium *Streptococcus pyogenes*. Swallowing may be difficult, and there is fever. Unlike a viral infection, strep throat should be treated with antibiotics. If not treated, it can lead to complications such as rheumatic fever, which can permanently damage the heart valves.

The Lungs Have Disorders

Pneumonia and tuberculosis are two serious infections of the lungs ordinarily controlled by antibiotics. Two other illnesses discussed, emphysema and lung cancer, are not due to infections; in most instances, they are due to cigarette smoking.

Pneumonia Can Kill

Most forms of pneumonia (fig. 39.10) are caused by either a bacterium or a virus that has infected the lungs. AIDS patients are subject to a particularly rare form of pneumonia caused by the protozoan *Pneumocystis carinii*. Sometimes, pneumonia is localized in specific lobules of the lungs. These lobules become nonfunctional as they fill with mucus and pus. Obviously, the more lobules involved, the more serious the infection.

Figure 39.10

Common bronchial and pulmonary infectious diseases and disorders. Exposure to infectious microbes and/or polluted air, including tobacco smoke, causes the diseases and disorders shown here.

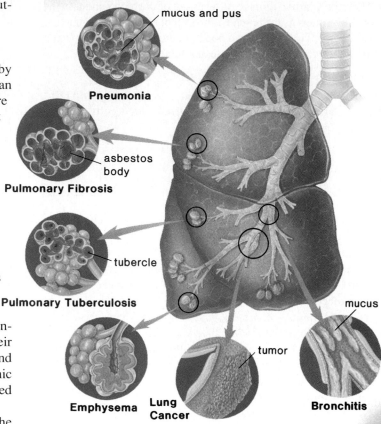

mucus and pus

Pneumonia

asbestos body

Pulmonary Fibrosis

tubercle

Pulmonary Tuberculosis

Emphysema

Lung Cancer

tumor

mucus

Bronchitis

Tuberculosis Is Back

Pulmonary tuberculosis (fig. 39.10) is caused by the tubercle bacillus, a type of bacterium. When a person has tuberculosis, the alveoli burst and are replaced by inelastic connective tissue. It is possible to tell if a person has ever been exposed to tuberculosis with a skin test, in which a highly diluted extract of the bacilli is injected into the skin of the patient. A person who has never been in contact with the bacillus shows no reaction, but one who has developed immunity to the organism shows an area of inflammation that peaks in about two days. If these bacilli invade the lung tissue, the cells build a protective capsule about the foreigners and isolate them from the rest of the body. This tiny capsule is called a *tubercle*. If the resistance of the body is high, the imprisoned organisms die, but if the resistance is low, the organisms eventually can be liberated. If a chest X ray detects active tubercles, the individual is put on appropriate drug therapy to ensure the localization of the disease and the eventual destruction of any live bacterial organisms.

Tuberculosis killed about 100,000 people in the United States annually before the middle of this century, when antibiotic therapy brought it largely under control. In recent years, however, the incidence of tuberculosis is on the rise, particularly among AIDS patients, the homeless, and the rural poor. Worse, the new strains are resistant to the usual antibiotic therapy. Therefore, some physicians would like to again use sanitoriums to quarantine patients needing treatment.

Emphysema Reduces Capacity

Emphysema (fig. 39.10) refers to the destruction of lung tissue, with accompanying ballooning or inflation of the lungs due to trapped air. The trouble stems from the damage and the collapse of the bronchioles. When this occurs, the alveoli are cut off from renewed oxygen supply and the air within them is trapped. The trapped air very often causes the alveolar walls to rupture, and a loss of elasticity makes breathing difficult. The victim is breathless and may have a cough. Since the surface area for gas exchange is reduced, not enough oxygen reaches the heart and the brain. Even so, the heart works furiously to force more blood through the lungs, and this can lead to a heart condition. Lack of oxygen to the brain can make the person feel depressed, sluggish, and irritable.

Pulmonary Fibrosis Is Dangerous

Inhaling particles such as silica (sand), coal dust, and asbestos (fig. 39.11) can lead to pulmonary fibrosis (fig. 39.10), a condition in which fibrous connective tissue builds up in the lungs. Breathing capacity can be seriously impaired, and the development of cancer is common. Since asbestos has been used so widely as a fireproofing and insulating agent, unwarranted exposure has occurred. It is projected that 2 million deaths could be caused by asbestos exposure—mostly in the workplace—between 1990 and 2020.

Lung Cancer Due to Smoking

Lung cancer (fig. 39.10) used to be more prevalent in men than in women, but recently it has surpassed breast cancer as a cause of death in women. This can be linked to an increase in the number of women who smoke today. Autopsies on smokers have revealed the progressive steps by which the most common form of lung cancer develops. The first event appears to be thickening and callusing of the cells lining the bronchi. (Callusing occurs whenever cells are exposed to irritants.) Then there is a loss of cilia so that it is impossible to prevent dust and dirt from settling in the lungs. Following this, cells with atypical nuclei appear in the callused lining. A tumor, consisting of disordered cells with atypical nuclei, is considered to be cancer in situ (at one location). When some of these cells finally break loose and penetrate other tissues—a process called metastasis—the cancer spreads. The tumor may grow until the bronchus is blocked, cutting off the supply of air to that lung. The entire lung then collapses, the secretions trapped in the lung spaces become infected, and pneu-

Figure 39.11
Asbestos fibers. A scanning electron micrograph of macrophages reveals an "asbestos body" in the lung tissue of a person exposed to asbestos for some time. Asbestos bodies are fibers that have been coated with iron, plasma proteins, and other materials.

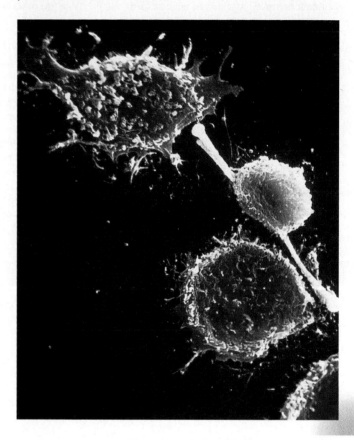

monia or a lung abscess (localized area of pus) results. The only treatment that offers a possibility of cure is to remove a lobe or the lung completely before secondary growths have had time to form. This operation is called *pneumonectomy*.

> The incidence of lung cancer is over twenty times higher in individuals who smoke than in those who do not.

Current research indicates that *passive smoking*—simply breathing in air filled with cigarette smoke—can also cause lung cancer and a number of other illnesses associated with smoking. If a person stops both voluntary and involuntary smoking, and if the body tissues are not already cancerous, the tissues usually return to normal over time.

Summary

1. Some aquatic animals like hydras and planarians use their entire body surface for gas exchange.

2. Most animals have a special, localized gas-exchange area. Most large aquatic animals pass water over gills. On land, insects utilize tracheal systems and vertebrates have lungs.

3. Lungs are found inside the body, where water loss is reduced. To ventilate the lungs, some vertebrates use positive pressure, but most inhale, using muscular contraction to produce a negative pressure that causes air to rush into the lungs. When the breathing muscles relax, air is exhaled.

4. Birds have a series of air sacs that allow a one-way flow of air over the gas-exchange area. This is called a complete ventilation system.

5. Table 39.1 lists the structures found in the human respiratory system.

6. Humans breathe by negative pressure, as do other mammals. During inhalation, the rib cage goes up and out, and the diaphragm lowers. The lungs expand and air comes rushing in.

7. During exhalation, the rib cage goes down and in, and the diaphragm rises. Therefore, air rushes out.

8. The rate of breathing is dependent upon the amount of carbon dioxide in the blood, as detected by chemoreceptors such as the aortic and carotid bodies.

9. Gas exchange in the lungs and tissues is brought about by diffusion. Hemoglobin transports oxygen in the blood; carbon dioxide is mainly transported in plasma as the bicarbonate ion. The enzyme carbonic anhydrase found in red blood cells speeds the formation of the bicarbonate ion.

10. The respiratory tract is subject to infections. Two disorders of the lungs, emphysema and cancer, are usually due to cigarette smoking.

Writing Across the Curriculum

In order to practice writing skills, students should write out the answers to any or all of the study questions and the critical thinking questions. The study questions are sequenced in the same order as the text. Answers to the objective questions, and suggested answers to the critical thinking questions, are in appendix D.

Study Questions

1. Compare the respiratory organs of aquatic animals to those of terrestrial animals.   685–87

2. How does the countercurrent flow of blood within gill capillaries and water passing across the gills assist respiration in fishes?   685

3. Why don't insects require circulatory system involvement in air transport? Why is it beneficial for the body wall of earthworms to be moist?   686

4. Explain the phrase, "breathing by using negative pressure."   687

5. Contrast incomplete ventilation in humans with complete ventilation in birds.   687

6. Name the parts of the human respiratory system, and list a function for each part.   688

7. The concentration of what gas in the blood controls the breathing rate in humans? Explain.   689–91

8. Which conditions depicted in figure 39.10 are due to infection? Which are due to behavioral or environmental factors? Explain.   692–93

Objective Questions

1. One problem faced by terrestrial animals with lungs, but not by freshwater aquatic animals with gills, is that
   a. gas exchange involves water loss.
   b. breathing requires considerable energy.
   c. oxygen diffuses very slowly in air.
   d. All of these are correct.

2. In which animal is the circulatory system not involved in gas transport?
   a. mouse
   b. dragonfly
   c. trout
   d. sparrow

3. Birds have a more efficient lung than humans because the flow of air
   a. is the same during both inhalation and exhalation.
   b. travels in only one direction through the lungs.
   c. never backs up like in human lungs.
   d. is not hindered by a larynx.

4. Which animal breathes by positive pressure?
   a. fish
   b. human
   c. bird
   d. frog

5. Which of these is a true statement?
   a. In lung capillaries, carbon dioxide combines with water to produce carbonic acid.
   b. In tissue capillaries, carbonic acid breaks down to carbon dioxide and water.
   c. In lung capillaries, carbonic acid breaks down to carbon dioxide and water.
   d. In tissue capillaries, carbonic acid combines with hydrogen ions to form the carbonate ion.

6. Air enters the human lungs because
   a. atmospheric pressure is less than the pressure inside the lungs.
   b. atmospheric pressure is greater than the pressure inside the lungs.
   c. although the pressures are the same inside and outside, the partial pressure of oxygen is lower within the lungs.
   d. the residual air in the lungs causes the partial pressure of oxygen to be less than it is outside.

7. If the digestive and respiratory tracts were completely separate in humans, there would be no need for
   a. swallowing.
   b. a nose.
   c. an epiglottis.
   d. a diaphragm.

8. To trace the path of air in humans you would place the trachea
   a. directly after the nose.
   b. directly before the bronchi.
   c. before the pharynx.
   d. Both a and c are correct.

9. In humans, the respiratory center
   a. is stimulated by carbon dioxide.
   b. is located in the medulla oblongata.
   c. controls the rate of breathing.
   d. All of these are correct.

10. Carbon dioxide is carried in the plasma
    a. in combination with hemoglobin.
    b. as the bicarbonate ion.
    c. combined with carbonic anhydrase.
    d. All of these are correct.

11. Label this diagram of the human respiratory system:

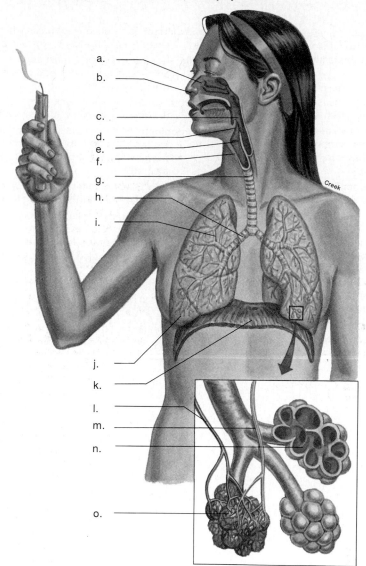

a.
b.
c.
d.
e.
f.
g.
h.
i.
j.
k.
l.
m.
n.
o.

Creek

Concepts and Critical Thinking

1. *All systems of the animal's body contribute to homeostasis.*

   Describe two ways in which the human respiratory system contributes to homeostasis.

2. *Organisms have localized boundaries for exchanging materials with the environment.*

   Compare the similarities and differences between gills and lungs and the obvious localized boundaries with the environment.

3. *The structure of an organ suits its function.*

   How does the structure of the lungs suit their function?

alveolus (pl., alveoli) (al-VEE-uh-lus) Terminal, microscopic, grapelike air sac found in vertebrate lungs. [L. *alve,* cavity]   689

bicarbonate ion The form in which most of the carbon dioxide is transported in the bloodstream.   691

bronchiole (BRAHNG-kee-ohl) A small tube that conducts air from a bronchus to the alveoli. [Gk. *bronch,* windpipe, and *iol,* little]   689

bronchus (pl., bronchi) (BRAHNG-kus) One of two main branches of the trachea in vertebrates that have lungs. [Gk. *bronch,* windpipe]   689

carbonic anhydrase An enzyme in red blood cells that speeds the formation of carbonic acid from water and carbon dioxide. [Gk. *an,* without, and *hydr,* water]   691

diaphragm A dome-shaped muscularized sheet separating the thoracic cavity from the abdominal cavity in mammals. [Gk. *dia,* separate, and *phragm,* partition]   687

exhalation Stage during respiration when air is pushed out of the lungs; expiration.   687

gills Respiratory organ in most aquatic animals; in fish an outward extension of the pharynx.   685

glottis (GLAHT-us) An opening for airflow in the larynx. [Gk. *glotti,* tongue]   688

hemoglobin Red respiratory pigment of erythrocytes used for transport of oxygen. [Gk. *hem,* blood, and L. *glob,* ball]   691

inhalation Stage during respiration when air is drawn into the lungs; inspiration.   687

larynx (LAR-ingks) Cartilaginous organ located between the pharynx and the trachea in tetrapods which contains the vocal cords; voice box. [Gk. *laryn,* gullet]   688

lung An internal respiratory organ containing moist surfaces for gas exchange.   686

pharynx (FAR-ingks) A common passageway for both food intake and air movement, located between the mouth and the esophagus. [Gk. *pharyn,* throat]   688

rib cage The top and side of the thoracic cavity in vertebrates; contains ribs and intercostal muscles.   687

thoracic cavity The internal body space of some animals that contains the lungs, protecting them from desiccation; the chest.   687

trachea (TRAY-kee-uh) An air tube (windpipe) in tetrapod vertebrates that runs between the larynx and the bronchi; also an air tube in insects that is located between the spiracles and the tracheoles. [L. *trache,* windpipe]   688

vocal cord Fold of tissue within the larynx; creates vocal sounds when it vibrates.   688

40
EXCRETORY SYSTEM

Learning Objectives

Excretion Is for Homeostasis

- Relate the excretion of ammonia, urea, and uric acid to an animal's environment.   698–99

- Give examples of how various animals regulate the water and salt balance of the body.   700

- Contrast the manner in which marine bony fishes and freshwater bony fishes regulate the water and salt content of the blood.   700

Animals Have Organs of Excretion

- Compare the operation of planarian flame cells, earthworm nephridia, insect Malpighian tubules, and human kidneys.   701–2

Humans Have a Urinary System

- Trace the path of urine in humans, and describe in general the structure and the function of each organ mentioned.   702

- List the parts of the kidney nephron, and relate these to the macroscopic anatomy of the kidney.   702–3

- Describe the three steps in urine formation, and relate these to the parts of the nephron.   704–5

- Explain the countercurrent mechanism by which water is reabsorbed by the nephron.   706

- Describe how water excretion is regulated and how the pH of the blood is adjusted by the kidneys.   706–7

- Explain, in general, how an artificial kidney machine works.   707

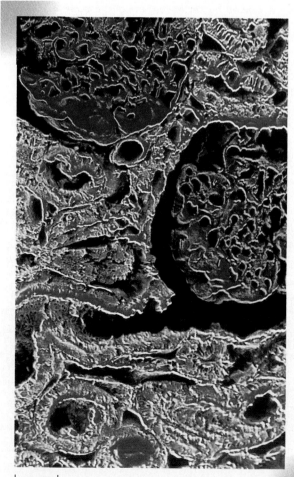

Two tiny knots of blood capillaries (red and green in this false-colored scanning electron micrograph) are cupped by kidney tubules that receive metabolic wastes.

100 μm

like the digestive and respiratory systems, the excretory system plays a major role in maintaining homeostasis. Excretion is the elimination of molecules that have taken part in metabolic reactions and should not be confused with defecation, which is the elimination of nondigested material from the gut.

Homeostasis includes not only getting oxygen and nutrients to cells but also ridding the body of wastes, which is just as important. Wastes tend to be toxic, and if they were to accumulate in the body, illness and finally death would result. Another important regulatory function performed by excretory organs is water and salt balance. Since the body is more than two-thirds water, it is of paramount importance that the body stay hydrated, despite the fact that some water is typically used to excrete wastes.

EXCRETION IS FOR HOMEOSTASIS

All animals, including humans, excrete metabolic wastes such as carbon dioxide and nitrogenous wastes. Humans have several organs of excretion, as illustrated in figure 40.1, to free the body of these wastes. Wastes move from the cells to tissue fluid to the blood and finally to these organs, which pass them to the external environment. Other animals eliminate waste in a similar or more direct manner.

Eliminating Nitrogenous Wastes

The breakdown of various molecules, including nucleic acids and amino acids, results in nitrogenous wastes. For simplicity's sake, however, we will limit our discussion to amino acid metabolism. Amino acids, derived from protein in food, can be used by cells for synthesis of new body protein or other nitrogen-containing molecules. The amino acids not used for synthesis are oxidized to generate energy or are converted to fats or carbohydrates that can be stored. In either case, the *amino groups* ($—NH_2$) must be removed because they are not needed when amino acids are converted to these forms of energy storage (fig. 40.2). Once the amino groups have been removed from amino acids, they may be excreted from the body in the form of ammonia, urea, or uric acid, depending on the species (table 40.1). Removal of amino groups from amino acids requires a fairly constant amount of energy. The energy requirement for the conversion of amino groups to ammonia, urea, or uric acid, however, differs, as indicated in figure 40.2.

Figure 40.1

Excretory organs in humans. The internal environment of cells (blood and tissue fluid) in humans and other animals stays relatively constant because the blood is continually refreshed by certain organs of the body. **a.** These organs are involved in excretion—ridding the body of metabolic wastes. In particular, the gut (large intestine) excretes heavy metals, the lungs excrete carbon dioxide, and the kidneys and skin excrete nitrogenous wastes. The liver removes toxic substances from the blood and converts them to molecules that are excreted by the kidneys. **b.** Diagrammatic representation of exchanges that occur in the body and with the external environment. The arrows that point toward the external environment represent pathways of excretion.

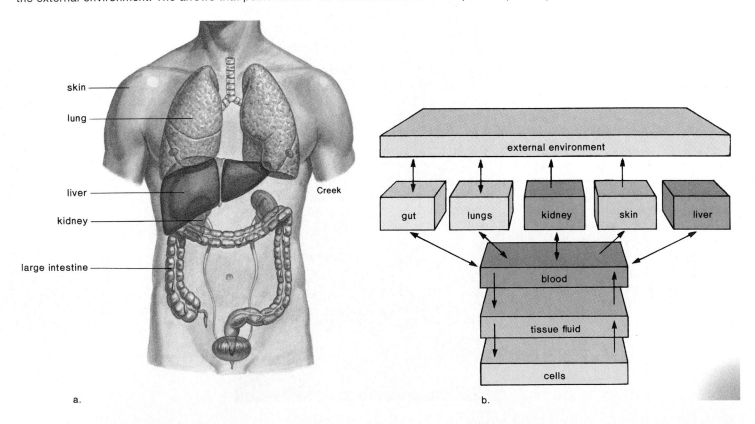

Table 40.1

Nitrogenous Waste Excretion

Product	Habitat	Animals
Ammonia	Water	Aquatic invertebrates Bony fishes Amphibian larvae
Urea	Land	Adult amphibians Mammals
Uric acid	Land	Insects Birds Reptiles

Excreting Ammonia

Amino groups removed from amino acids immediately form *ammonia* (NH_3) by addition of a third hydrogen ion. Little or no energy is required to convert an amino group to ammonia by the addition of a hydrogen ion. Ammonia is quite toxic and can be used as a nitrogenous excretory product only if a good deal of water is available to wash it from the body. The high solubility of ammonia permits this means of excretion in bony fishes, aquatic invertebrates, and amphibians whose gills and skin surfaces are in direct contact with the water of the environment.

Excreting Urea

Terrestrial amphibians and mammals usually excrete **urea** [Gk. *ure,* urine] as their main nitrogenous waste. Urea is much less toxic than ammonia and can be excreted in a moderately concentrated solution. This allows body water to be conserved, an important advantage for terrestrial animals with limited access to water.

Production of urea, however, requires the expenditure of energy. Urea is produced in the liver by a set of energy-requiring enzymatic reactions known as the *urea cycle.* In the cycle, carrier molecules take up carbon dioxide and two molecules of ammonia, finally releasing urea.

Excreting Uric Acid

Uric acid is excreted by insects, reptiles, birds, and some dogs (e.g., Dalmatians). Uric acid is not very toxic and is poorly soluble in water. Poor solubility is an advantage if water conservation is needed because uric acid can be concentrated even more readily than can urea. In reptiles and birds, a dilute solution of uric acid passes from the kidneys to the *cloaca,* a common reservoir for the products of the digestive, urinary, and reproductive systems. After water is absorbed by the cloaca, the uric acid passes out with the feces.

In humans, purine metabolism results in uric acid which, if present to excess, produces the symptoms of gout. Uric acid tends to accumulate in the joints, particularly that of the big toe. With accompanying swelling, redness and severe pain result.

Figure 40.2

Nitrogenous wastes from protein breakdown. Proteins are hydrolyzed to amino acids, whose breakdown results in a carbon skeleton and amino groups. The carbon skeleton can be used as an energy source, but the amino groups must be excreted as ammonia, urea, or uric acid.

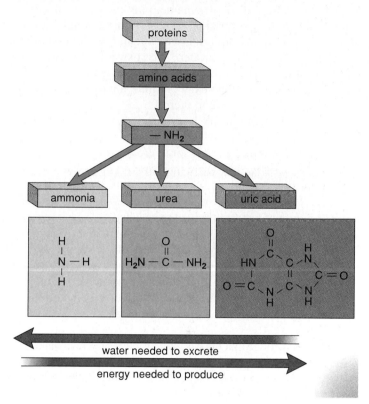

Embryos of reptiles and birds develop inside completely enclosed, shelled eggs. The production of insoluble, relatively nontoxic uric acid is advantageous for shelled embryos because all nitrogenous wastes are stored inside the shell until hatching takes place.

Uric acid is synthesized by a long, complex series of enzymatic reactions that require expenditure of even more ATP (adenosine triphosphate) than does urea synthesis. Here again, there seems to be a trade-off between the advantage of water conservation and the disadvantage of energy expenditure for synthesis of an excretory molecule.

Animals excrete nitrogenous wastes as ammonia, urea, or uric acid. Ammonia requires the most water to excrete; uric acid requires the most energy to produce.

Maintaining Osmotic Balance

In addition to their role in excretion of nitrogenous wastes, excretory organs also have the important function of regulating the water and salt balance of the body. Among animals, only marine invertebrates and cartilaginous fishes, such as sharks and rays, have body fluids that are nearly isotonic to seawater. These organisms have little difficulty maintaining their normal salt and water balance. It is surprising, though, that while they are isotonic, the body fluids of cartilaginous fishes do not contain the same amount of salt as seawater. The answer to this paradox is that their blood contains a concentration of urea high enough to match the tonicity of the sea! For some unknown reason, this amount of urea is not toxic to them.

The body fluids of all bony fishes have only a moderate amount of salt. Apparently their common ancestor evolved in fresh water, and only later did some groups invade the sea. Marine bony fishes (fig. 40.3*a*) are therefore prone to water loss and could become dehydrated. To counteract this, they drink seawater almost constantly. On the average, marine bony fishes swallow an amount of water estimated to be equal to 1% of their body weight every hour. This is equivalent to a human drinking about 700 ml of water every hour around the clock. While they get water by drinking, this habit also causes these fishes to acquire salt. Instead of forming a hypertonic urine, however, they actively transport sodium (Na^+) and chloride (Cl^-) ions into the surrounding seawater at the gills. There is also a passive loss of water through gills.

It is easy to see that the osmotic problems of freshwater bony fishes are exactly opposite to those of marine bony fishes (fig. 40.3*b*). The body fluids of freshwater bony fishes are hypertonic to fresh water, and they are prone to passively gain water. These fishes never drink water but instead eliminate excess water through production of large quantities of dilute (hypotonic) urine. They discharge a quantity of urine equal to one-third their body weight each day. Because they tend to lose salts, they actively transport salts into the blood across the membranes of their gills.

> To regulate water and salt balance, marine bony fishes drink water constantly and excrete salt from the gills. Freshwater bony fishes never drink water; they excrete a dilute urine.

The difference in adaptation between marine and freshwater bony fishes makes it remarkable that some fishes actually can move between the two environments during their life cycle. Salmon, for example, begin their lives in freshwater streams and rivers, move to the ocean for a period of time, and finally return to fresh water to breed. These fishes alter their behavior and their gill and kidney functions in response to the osmotic changes they encounter when moving from one environment to the other.

Like marine bony fishes, some animals that evolved on land are also able to drink seawater despite its high toxicity. Birds and reptiles that live near the sea have a nasal salt gland that can excrete large volumes of concentrated salt solution. Mammals that live at sea, like whales, porpoises, and seals, most likely can concentrate their urine enough to drink seawater. Humans cannot do this, and they die if they drink only seawater.

Most terrestrial animals need to drink water occasionally, but the kangaroo rat manages to get along without drinking water at all. It forms a very concentrated urine, and its fecal material is almost completely dry. These abilities allow it to survive using metabolic water derived from the breakdown of nutrient molecules alone.

Figure 40.3

Water and salt balances in bony fishes. The black arrows represent passive transport from the environment, and the blue arrows represent active transport by the fishes to counteract environmental pressures. **a.** Marine bony fish. **b.** Freshwater bony fish.

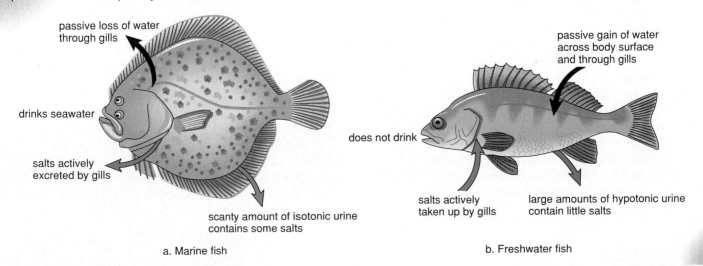

passive loss of water through gills

drinks seawater

salts actively excreted by gills

scanty amount of isotonic urine contains some salts

a. Marine fish

passive gain of water across body surface and through gills

does not drink

salts actively taken up by gills

large amounts of hypotonic urine contain little salts

b. Freshwater fish

ANIMALS HAVE ORGANS OF EXCRETION

Most animals have tubular organs that function in the excretion of nitrogenous wastes and osmotic regulation. Sometimes the primary function of these organs is osmotic regulation.

Planaria Have Flame Cells

Planaria have two strands of branching excretory tubules that open to the outside of the body through excretory pores (fig. 40.4*a*). Located along the tubules are bulblike *flame cells,* each of which contains a cluster of beating cilia that looks like a flickering flame under the microscope. The beating of flame-cell cilia propels fluid through the excretory canals and out of the body. The system is believed to function in osmotic regulation and also in excreting wastes.

Earthworms Have Nephridia

The earthworm's body is divided into segments, and nearly every body segment has a pair of excretory structures called **nephridia** [Gk. *nephri,* kidney]. Each nephridium is a tubule with a ciliated opening (the nephridiostome) and an excretory pore (the nephridiopore) (fig. 40.4*b*). As fluid from the body cavity is propelled through the tubule by beating cilia, certain substances are reabsorbed and carried away by a network of capillaries surrounding the tubule. This process results in the formation of urine that contains only metabolic wastes, salts, and water.

Each day, an earthworm excretes a lot of water and may produce a volume of urine equal to 60% of its body weight. Its excretion of ammonia is consistent with this finding.

Insects Have Malpighian Tubules

Insects have a unique excretory system consisting of long, thin tubules, **Malpighian tubules,** attached to the gut. Water and uric acid simply flow from the surrounding hemolymph into these tubules before moving into the gut. Here, water and other useful substances are reabsorbed, but the uric acid eventually passes out of the gut. Insects that live in water or that eat large quantities of moist food reabsorb little water. But insects in dry environments reabsorb most of the water and excrete a dry, semisolid mass of uric acid.

> Most animals have a primary excretory organ. Planaria have flame cells, earthworms have nephridia, and insects have Malpighian tubules.

Figure 40.4

Excretory organs in animals. **a.** The flame cell excretory system in planaria. Two or more tracts of branching tubules run the length of the body and open to the outside by pores. At the ends of side branches there are small flame cells, bulblike cells whose beating cilia cause fluid to enter the tubules that remove excess fluid from the body. **b.** The earthworm nephridium. The nephridium has a ciliated opening, the nephridiostome, that leads to a coiled tubule surrounded by a capillary network. Urine can be temporarily stored in the bladder before being released to the outside via a pore termed a nephridiopore. Most segments contain a pair of nephridia, one on each side.

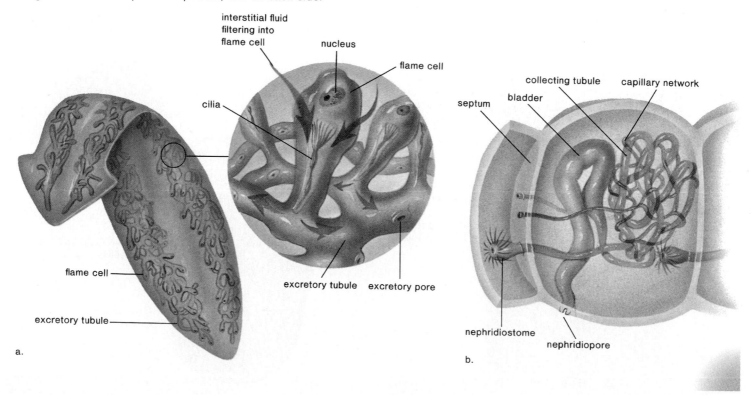

The human urinary system consists of the organs shown in figure 40.5. The human **kidneys** are bean-shaped, reddish brown organs, each about the size of a fist. They are located on either side of the vertebral column just below the diaphragm, where they are partially protected by the lower rib cage. **Urine** [Gk. *ure*, urine] made by the kidneys is carried from the body by the other organs in the urinary system. Each kidney is connected to a **ureter**, a duct that carries urine from the kidney to the **urinary bladder**, where it is stored until it is voided from the body through the single **urethra**. In males, the urethra passes through the penis, and in females, it opens ventral to the opening of the vagina. There is no connection between the genital (reproductive) and urinary systems in females, but there is a connection in males. In males, the urethra also carries sperm during ejaculation.

Kidneys Have Three Regions

If a kidney is sectioned longitudinally, three major parts can be distinguished (fig. 40.6). The outer region is the *renal cortex,* which has a somewhat granular appearance. The *renal medulla* consists of striped, pyramid-shaped regions that lie on the inner side of the cortex. The innermost part of the kidney is a hollow chamber called the *renal pelvis.* Urine formed in the kidney collects in the renal pelvis before entering the ureter. Microscopically, each kidney is composed of about one million tiny tubules called **nephrons** [Gk. *nephri,* kidney]. Some nephrons are located primarily in the cortex, but others dip down into the medulla, as shown in figure 40.6*b*.

Nephrons Are Numerous

Each nephron is made of several parts (fig. 40.7). The blind end of a nephron is pushed in on itself to form a cuplike structure called the **glomerular capsule** [L. *glomer,* ball, and *ula,* little] (formerly called Bowman's capsule). The outer layer of the glomerular capsule is composed of squamous epithelial cells; the inner layer is composed of specialized cells that allow easy passage of molecules. Near the glomerular capsule is a region known as the **proximal convoluted tubule** [L. *proxim,* nearest], which is lined by cells with many mitochondria and an inner brush border (tightly packed microvilli). Then simple squamous epithelium appears in a portion called the **loop of the nephron** (formerly called the loop of Henle). This is followed by the **distal convoluted tubule** [L. *dista,* distant]. Several distal convoluted tubules enter one **collecting duct.** The collecting duct transports urine down through the medulla and delivers it to the pelvis. The loop of the nephron and the collecting duct give the pyramids of the medulla their striped appearance (fig. 40.6).

Each nephron has its own blood supply (fig. 40.7). The renal artery branches into numerous small arteries, which branch into arterioles, one for each nephron. Each arteriole, called an *afferent arteriole,* divides to form a capillary tuft, the **glomerulus** [L. *glomer,* ball, and *ula,* little], which is surrounded by the glo-

Figure 40.6

Macroscopic and microscopic anatomy of the kidney.
a. Longitudinal section of kidney showing the location of the renal cortex, the renal medulla, and the renal pelvis.
b. An enlargement of one renal lobe showing the placement of nephrons.

Figure 40.5

The urinary system. Urine is found only within the kidneys, the ureters, the urinary bladder, and the urethra.

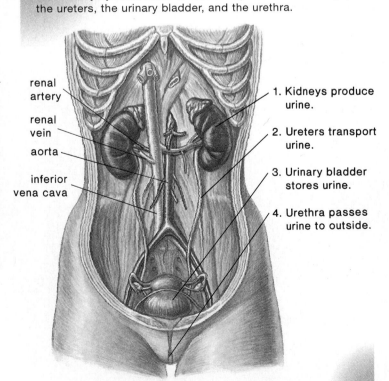

renal artery

renal vein

aorta

inferior vena cava

1. Kidneys produce urine.

2. Ureters transport urine.

3. Urinary bladder stores urine.

4. Urethra passes urine to outside.

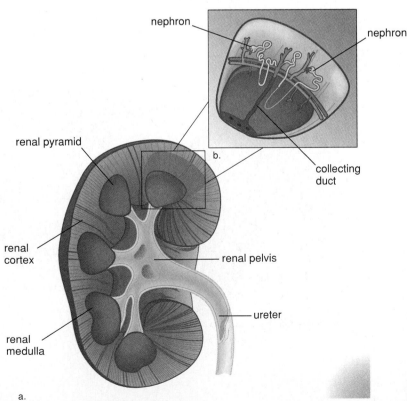

nephron

nephron

renal pyramid

renal cortex

renal medulla

renal pelvis

collecting duct

ureter

b.

a.

merular capsule. The glomerular capillaries drain into an *efferent arteriole*, which subsequently branches into a second capillary network around the tubular parts of the nephron. These capillaries, called *peritubular capillaries*, lead to venules that join the renal vein, a vessel that enters the inferior vena cava.

Microscopically, the human kidney is composed of nephrons, tubules with specific parts that are richly supplied with capillaries.

Figure 40.7

Nephron anatomy. The enlargements show types of tissue at the locations noted. Trace the path of blood about the nephron by following the arrows.

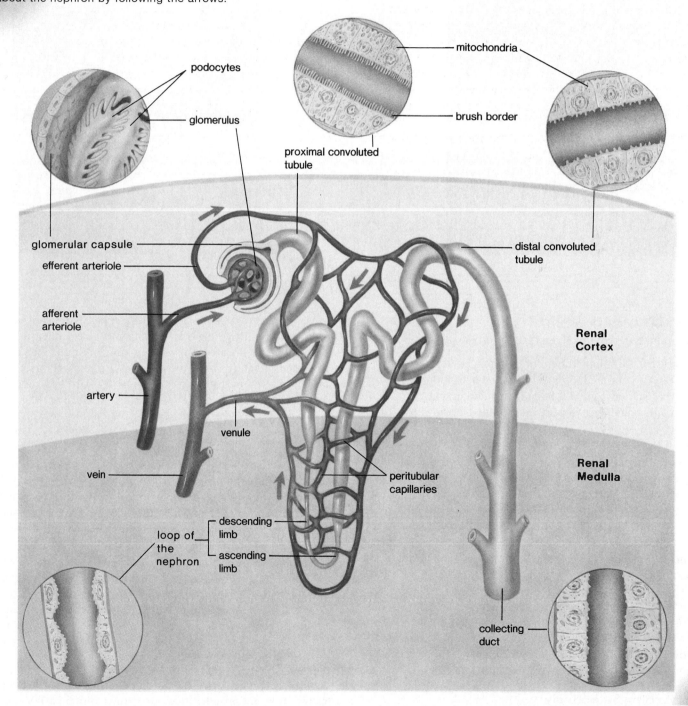

Figure 40.8

The cells that line the lumen (inside) of the proximal convoluted tubule, where selective reabsorption takes place. **a.** This photomicrograph shows that the cells have a brush border composed of microvilli, which greatly increases the surface area exposed to the lumen. The peritubular capillary surrounds the cells. **b.** Diagrammatic representation shows that each cell has many mitochondria. They supply the energy needed for active transport, the process that moves molecules (green) from the lumen to the capillary.

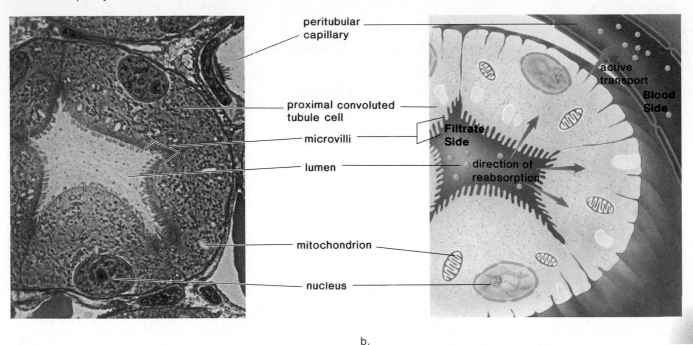

a.

b.

How Urine Is Made

Urine production requires three distinct processes:

1. Pressure filtration at the glomerular capsule;
2. Reabsorption, including selective reabsorption, at the proximal convoluted tubule, in particular; and
3. Tubular secretion at the distal convoluted tubule in particular.

Pressure Filtration

When blood enters the glomerulus, blood pressure is sufficient to cause small molecules, such as nutrients, water, salts, and wastes, to move from the glomerulus to the inside of the glomerular capsule, especially since the glomerular walls are 100 times more permeable than the walls of most capillaries elsewhere in the body. The molecules that leave the blood and enter the glomerular capsule are called the *glomerular filtrate*. Blood proteins and blood cells are too large to be part of this filtrate, so they remain in the blood as it flows into the efferent arteriole. Glomerular filtrate has the same composition as tissue fluid, and if this composition were not altered in other parts of the nephron, death from loss of water (dehydration), loss of nutrients (starvation), and lowered blood pressure would quickly follow. *Selective reabsorption,* however, prevents this from happening.

Reabsorbing Selectively

Reabsorption from the nephron to the blood takes place through the walls of the proximal convoluted tubule. Nutrients, water, and even some waste molecules diffuse passively back into the peritubular capillary network. Osmotic pressure further influences the movement of water. The nonfilterable proteins remain in the blood and exert an osmotic pressure. Also, after sodium ions (Na^+) are actively reabsorbed, chlorine ions (Cl^-) follow along, and these ions together increase the osmotic pressure of the blood so that water is further reabsorbed.

Selective reabsorption of nutrient molecules is brought about by active transport. The cells of the proximal convoluted tubule have numerous microvilli, which increase the surface area, and numerous mitochondria, which supply the energy needed for reabsorption (fig. 40.8). Reabsorption is selective since only molecules recognized by carrier molecules are actively transported through the tubule into the interstitial spaces. From there these molecules diffuse into the peritubular capillary network.

Glucose is an example of a molecule that ordinarily is reabsorbed completely because there is a plentiful supply of carrier molecules for it. However, after all its carriers are in use, any excess glucose in the filtrate will appear in the urine. In diabetes mellitus, there is an abnormally large amount of glucose in the filtrate because the liver fails to store glucose as glycogen.

Tubular Secretion

Tubular secretion refers to the transport of substances into the tubular lumen by means other than glomerular filtration. For our purposes, tubular secretion may be particularly associated with the distal convoluted tubule (fig. 40.9). Substances such as foreign

Figure 40.9

Steps in urine formation (simplified). **a.** The steps are noted within the nephron where they occur. **b.** Steps, including the molecule and the processes involved, are listed.

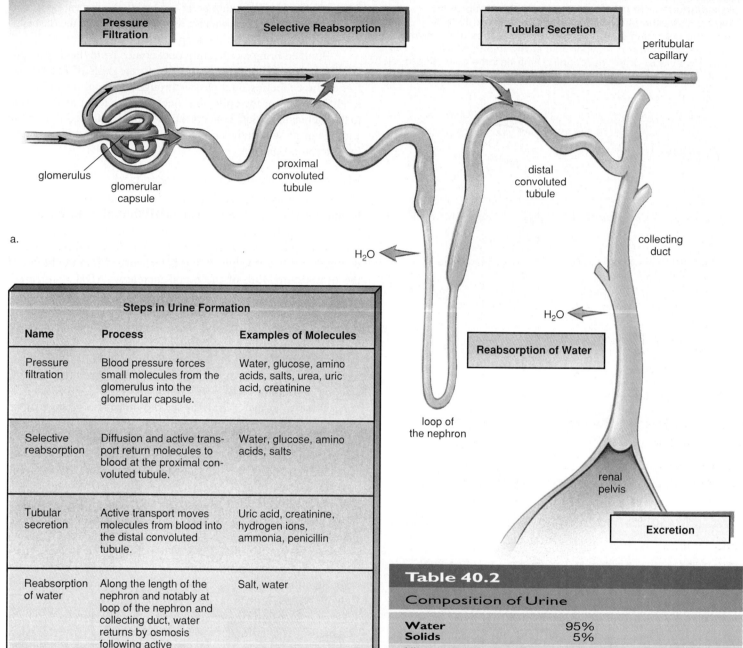

a.

Steps in Urine Formation

Name	Process	Examples of Molecules
Pressure filtration	Blood pressure forces small molecules from the glomerulus into the glomerular capsule.	Water, glucose, amino acids, salts, urea, uric acid, creatinine
Selective reabsorption	Diffusion and active transport return molecules to blood at the proximal convoluted tubule.	Water, glucose, amino acids, salts
Tubular secretion	Active transport moves molecules from blood into the distal convoluted tubule.	Uric acid, creatinine, hydrogen ions, ammonia, penicillin
Reabsorption of water	Along the length of the nephron and notably at loop of the nephron and collecting duct, water returns by osmosis following active reabsorption of salt.	Salt, water
Excretion	Urine formation rids body of metabolic wastes.	Water, salts, urea, uric acid, ammonium, creatinine

b.

Table 40.2

Composition of Urine

Water	95%
Solids	5%
Nitrogenous wastes	(per 1,500 ml of urine)
Urea	30 g
Creatinine	1–2 g
Ammonia	1–2 g
Uric acid	1 g
Ions (Salts)	25 g

Positive Ions	*Negative Ions*
Sodium	Chlorides
Potassium	Sulfates
Magnesium	Phosphates
Ammonium	
Calcium	

uric acid, hydrogen ions, ammonia, and penicillin are eliminated by tubular secretion. The process of secretion may be viewed as helping to rid the body of potentially harmful compounds that were not filtered into the glomerulus.

Following water reabsorption, which is discussed next, urine has the composition given in table 40.2.

Figure 40.10

Reabsorption of water at the loop of the nephron and the collecting duct. Salt (Na⁺Cl⁻) diffuses and is actively transported out of the ascending limb of the loop of the nephron into the renal medulla. Urea is believed to leak from the collecting duct and to enter the tissues of the renal medulla. This creates a hypertonic environment, which draws water out of the descending limb and the collecting duct. This water is returned to the circulatory system.

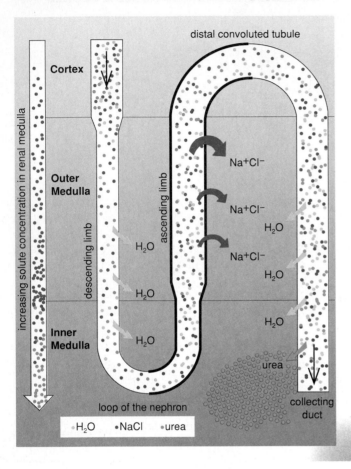

Tonicity and pH Are Regulated

Reptiles and birds rely primarily on the gut to reabsorb water, but mammals rely on the kidneys. A countercurrent mechanism enables mammals to excrete a hypertonic urine. A long loop of the nephron, which typically penetrates deep into the renal medulla, is made up of a descending (downward) limb and an ascending (upward) limb. Salt (Na⁺Cl⁻) passively diffuses out of the lower portion of the ascending limb, but the upper, thick portion of the limb actively transports salt out into the tissue of the outer renal medulla (fig. 40.10). Less and less salt is available for transport from the tubule as fluid moves up the thick portion of the ascending limb.

The arrow to the left in figure 40.10 shows that the inner medulla has the highest concentration of solutes. This is not due to salt but rather to urea, which is believed to leak from the lower portion of the collecting duct. Because of the solute concentration gradient within the renal medulla, water leaves the descending limb of the loop of the nephron along its length. This is a countercurrent mechanism because the decreasing number of water molecules in the descending limb encounter an increasing concentration of solute, and this ensures that water will continue to leave the descending limb as it approaches the loop of the nephron.

Fluid entering a collecting duct comes from the distal convoluted tubule. This fluid is isotonic to the cells of the cortex. But as the collecting duct passes through the renal medulla, water diffuses out of the collecting duct into the renal medulla due to the increasing solute concentration in the renal medulla. In the end, the urine within the collecting duct usually becomes hypertonic to blood plasma.

Hormones Keep Water Balanced

The amount of water that leaves the collecting duct is regulated by hormonal action. The hormone **ADH (antidiuretic hormone)** [Gk. *anti,* against, and *diure,* urinate], released by the posterior lobe of the pituitary, increases the permeability of the collecting duct so more water leaves it and is reabsorbed into the blood. If the osmotic pressure of the blood increases, ADH is released, more water is reabsorbed, and consequently there is less urine. On the other hand, if the osmotic pressure of the blood decreases, ADH is not released, more water is excreted, and consequently, more urine is formed. Drinking alcohol causes diuresis (increased urine flow) because it inhibits the secretion of ADH. Beer drinking, especially, causes diuresis because of increased fluid intake. Drugs called diuretics are often prescribed for high blood pressure. These drugs increase urinary excretion and thus reduce blood volume and blood pressure.

The hormone **aldosterone,** which is secreted by the adrenal cortex, helps maintain the sodium (Na⁺) and potassium (K⁺) ion balance of the blood. It causes the distal convoluted tubule to reabsorb Na⁺ and to excrete K⁺. The increase of Na⁺ in the blood causes water to be reabsorbed, leading to an increase in blood volume and blood pressure. Blood pressure is constantly monitored within the *juxtaglomerular apparatus,* a region of contact between the afferent arteriole and the distal convoluted tubule. When blood pressure is insufficient to promote pressure filtration, afferent arteriole cells secrete renin. *Renin* is an enzyme that changes angiotensinogen (a large plasma protein produced by the liver) into angiotensin I. Later, angiotensin I is converted to angiotensin II in the lungs by angiotensin-converting enzyme. Angiotensin II, a powerful vasoconstrictor, stimulates the adrenal cortex to release *aldosterone,* which allows Na⁺ to be reabsorbed and blood volume and pressure to rise. This sequence of events is called the renin-angiotensin-aldosterone system (fig. 40.11).

Notice that both ADH and aldosterone act to increase blood volume and to raise the blood pressure. When blood pressure rises, the heart produces a peptide hormone called atrial natriuretic factor (*ANF*) that inhibits the secretion of renin by the juxtaglomerular apparatus and the release of ADH by the posterior pituitary. This is an example of how hormones serve as checks and balances to one another.

Figure 40.11

The renin-angiotensin-aldosterone system. The organs named in the boxes above the blood vessel act on the substances listed in the bloodstream to bring about the release of aldosterone, which causes reabsorption of sodium ions and a subsequent rise in blood pressure.

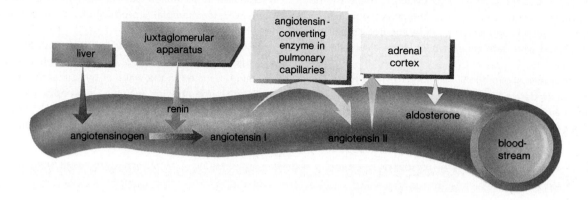

How the pH Is Adjusted

The kidneys help maintain the pH level of the blood within a narrow range, and the whole nephron takes part in this process. The excretion of hydrogen ions (H^+) and ammonia (NH_3), together with the reabsorption of sodium (Na^+) and bicarbonate ions (HCO_3^-), is adjusted to keep the pH within normal bounds. If the blood is acidic, hydrogen ions are excreted in combination with ammonia, while sodium and bicarbonate ions are reabsorbed. This will restore the pH because sodium ions promote the formation of hydroxyl ions, while bicarbonate takes up hydrogen ions when carbonic acid is formed:

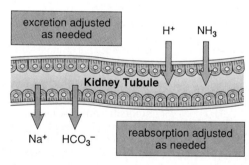

If the blood is basic, fewer hydrogen ions are excreted, and fewer sodium and bicarbonate ions are reabsorbed.

Reabsorption and/or excretion of ions (salts) by the kidneys illustrates their homeostatic ability: they maintain not only the pH of the blood but also its osmolarity.

> The kidneys excrete urea, maintain both the pH and the salt balance of blood, and regulate blood volume by regulating the reabsorption of water.

When Kidneys Fail

Because of the great importance of the kidneys to the maintenance of body fluid homeostasis, renal failure is a life-threatening event. There are a number of illnesses that cause progressive renal disease and renal failure. Recurrent infections of the urinary tract can possibly lead to kidney infections and resulting kidney failure. Patients with renal failure can sometimes undergo a kidney transplant operation. Many more lives would be saved if more people made their kidneys available for transplant upon death.

If a kidney transplant is not possible, a patient can undergo hemodialysis. In this procedure, the patient's blood is passed through a semipermeable membranous tube, which is in contact with a balanced salt (dialysis) solution. Substances more concentrated in the blood diffuse into the dialysis solution, and substances more concentrated in the dialysis solution diffuse into the blood. Accordingly, the artificial kidney can be utilized either to extract substances from the blood, including waste products or other toxic chemicals and drugs, or to add substances to blood, such as bicarbonate ions if the blood is acidic. This system is so efficient that a patient needs to undergo treatment only about twice a week.

> Kidney transplants and hemodialysis are therapies for persons who have suffered renal failure.

Biological Relationships

The liver and the kidney are two primary organs of homeostasis because they regulate the composition of blood. The liver removes poisonous substances (such as alcohol and drugs) from the blood and detoxifies them. Any products such as urea (which is made by the liver) are sent to the kidneys for excretion. Excretion is the ridding of substances that have been produced or used by the body's cells. It should not be confused with defecation, which is the elimination of nondigested remains.

There are other organs of excretion in addition to the kidneys. The liver produces products derived from the breakdown of hemoglobin, which are excreted with the bile. The lungs excrete carbon dioxide. The removal of carbon dioxide helps keep the blood pH within a normal range, and the kidneys contribute to this effort when they excrete or retain the bicarbonate ion. The kidneys also have final control over blood volume and, therefore, blood pressure. The kidneys are primarily regulated by hormones, but the brain has ultimate control. The hormone ADH, for example, is produced by a part of the brain called the hypothalamus.

Respiration is also regulated by the central nervous system. There is a respiratory center in the brain that controls the rate and depth of breathing. Located in the walls of the aorta and carotid arteries are aortic and carotid bodies, which have receptors that monitor the carbon dioxide and hydrogen ion concentrations in the blood. If these concentrations rise, the respiratory center increases the breathing rate.

Summary

1. Animals excrete nitrogenous wastes, which differ as to the amount of water and energy required to excrete them. Aquatic animals usually excrete ammonia, and land animals excrete either urea or uric acid.

2. Osmotic regulation is important to animals. Most have to balance their water and salt intake and their excretion to maintain the normal concentration in the body fluids. Marine fishes constantly drink water, excrete salts at the gills, and pass an isotonic urine. Freshwater fishes never drink water; they take in salts at the gills and pass a hypotonic urine.

3. Animals often have an excretory organ. The flame cells of planaria rid the body of excess water. Earthworm nephridia exchange molecules with the blood in a manner similar to vertebrate kidneys. Malpighian tubules in insects take up metabolic wastes and water from the hemolymph. Later, the water is absorbed by the gut.

4. Kidneys are a part of the human urinary system. Microscopically, each kidney is made up of nephrons, each of which has several parts and its own blood supply.

5. Urine formation requires three steps: pressure filtration, when nutrients, water, and wastes enter the glomerular capsule; selective reabsorption, when nutrients and some water are reabsorbed into the proximal convoluted tubule; and tubular secretion, when additional wastes are added to the tubule (e.g., the distal convoluted tubule).

6. Humans excrete a hypertonic urine. The ascending limb of the loop of the nephron actively extrudes salt so that the renal medulla is increasingly hypertonic relative to the contents of the descending limb and the collecting duct. Since urea leaks from the lower end of the collecting duct, the inner medulla has the highest concentration of solute. Therefore, a countercurrent mechanism assures that water will diffuse out of the descending limb and the collecting duct.

7. Two hormones are involved in maintaining the water content of the blood. The hormone ADH (antidiuretic hormone), which makes the collecting duct more permeable, is secreted by the posterior pituitary in response to an increase in the osmotic pressure of the blood.

8. The hormone aldosterone is secreted by the adrenal cortex after the low sodium ion (Na^+) content of the blood and the resultant low blood pressure have caused the kidneys to release renin. The presence of renin leads to the formation of angiotensin II, which causes the adrenal cortex to release aldosterone. Aldosterone causes the kidneys to retain Na^+; therefore, water is reabsorbed and blood pressure rises.

9. The kidneys adjust the pH of the blood by excreting or conserving hydrogen ions (H^+), ammonia (NH_3), and sodium (Na^+) and bicarbonate ions (HCO_3^-) as appropriate.

10. During hemodialysis, waste molecules diffuse out of the blood into the dialysis fluid. Other substances can be added to the blood.

Writing Across the Curriculum

In order to practice writing skills, students should write out the answers to any or all of the study questions and the critical thinking questions. The study questions are sequenced in the same order as the text. Answers to the objective questions, and suggested answers to the critical thinking questions, are in appendix D.

1. Relate the three primary nitrogenous wastes to the habitat of animals. 699

2. Contrast the osmotic regulation of a marine bony fish with that of a freshwater bony fish. 700

3. Give examples of how other types of animals regulate their water and salt balance. 700

4. Describe how the excretory organs of the earthworm and the insect function. 701

5. Describe the path of urine, and give a function for each structure mentioned. 702

6. Describe the macroscopic anatomy of a human kidney, and relate it to the placement of nephrons. 702–3

7. List the parts of a nephron, and give a function for each structure mentioned. 702

8. Describe how urine is made by outlining what happens at each part of the nephron. 704

9. Explain the countercurrent mechanism by which water is reabsorbed and the urine is hypertonic. 706

10. What role do ADH (antidiuretic hormone) and aldosterone play in regulating the tonicity of urine? How does this affect blood pressure? 706

11. How does the nephron regulate the pH of the blood? 707

12. How does an artificial kidney function? 707

Objective Questions

1. Which of these is mismatched?
   a. insects—excrete uric acid
   b. humans—excrete urea
   c. fishes—excrete ammonia
   d. birds—excrete ammonia

2. One advantage of urea excretion over uric acid excretion is that urea
   a. requires less energy to form.
   b. can be concentrated to a greater extent.
   c. is not a toxic substance.
   d. requires less water to excrete.

3. Freshwater bony fishes maintain water balance by
   a. excreting salt across their gills.
   b. periodically drinking small amounts of water.
   c. excreting a hypotonic urine.
   d. excreting wastes in the form of uric acid.

4. Animals with which of these are most likely to excrete a semisolid nitrogenous waste?
   a. nephridia
   b. Malpighian tubules
   c. human kidneys
   d. All of these are correct.

5. In which of these human structures are you least apt to find urine?
   a. large intestine
   b. urethra
   c. ureter
   d. bladder

6. Excretion of a hypertonic urine in humans is associated with the
   a. glomerular capsule.
   b. proximal convoluted tubule.
   c. loop of the nephron.
   d. distal convoluted tubule.

7. The presence of ADH (antidiuretic hormone) causes an individual to excrete
   a. sugars.
   b. less water.
   c. more water.
   d. Both a and c are correct.

8. In humans, water is
   a. found in the glomerular filtrate.
   b. reabsorbed from the nephron.
   c. in the urine.
   d. All of these are correct.

9. Pressure filtration is associated with the
   a. glomerular capsule.
   b. distal convoluted tubule.
   c. collecting duct.
   d. All of these are correct.

10. In humans, glucose
   a. is in the filtrate and urine.
   b. is in the filtrate and not in urine.
   c. undergoes tubular secretion and is in urine.
   d. undergoes tubular secretion and is not in urine.

11. Label this diagram of a nephron, and give the steps for urine formation in the boxes:

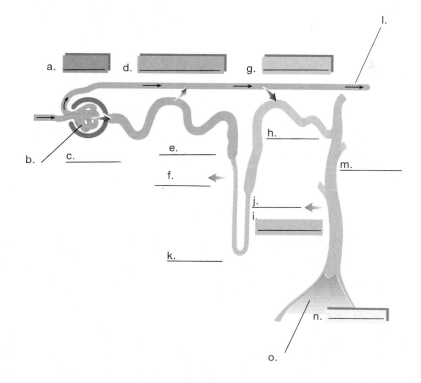

Concepts and Critical Thinking

1. The excretory system plays a primary role in homeostasis.

   Relate the need of excretion to degradative reactions in cells.

2. Animals utilize countercurrent mechanisms to increase blood concentrations of substances.

   Tell how the countercurrent mechanism in the gills of fishes and in the kidneys of mammals helps them adapt to their environments.

3. Structure suits function.

   Why would you expect the proximal convoluted tubule to be lined with cells that have many mitochondria and microvilli?

Selected Key Terms

aldosterone (al-DAHS-tuh-rohn) Hormone secreted by the adrenal cortex that regulates the sodium and potassium ion balance of the blood. 706

ADH (antidiuretic hormone) (ant-ih-DY-yuu-RET-ik) A hormone secreted by the posterior pituitary that increases the permeability of the collecting ducts in a kidney. [Gk. *anti,* against, and *diure,* urinate] 706

collecting duct A duct within the kidney that receives fluid from several nephrons; the reabsorption of water occurs here. 702

distal convoluted tubule The final portion of a nephron that joins with a collecting duct; associated with tubular secretion. [L. *dista,* distant] 702

glomerular capsule (glu-MER-uh-lur) A cuplike structure that is the initial portion of a nephron; where pressure filtration occurs. [L. *glomer,* ball, and *ula,* little] 702

glomerulus (glu-MER-uh-lus) A capillary network within a glomerular capsule of a nephron. [L. *glomer,* ball, and *ula,* little] 702

kidney One of the paired organs of the urinary system that regulates the chemical composition of the blood and produces a waste product called urine. 702

loop of the nephron The portion of a nephron between the proximal and distal convoluted tubules where water reabsorption occurs. 702

Malpighian tubule (mal-PIG-ee-un) Blind, threadlike excretory tubule near the anterior end of an insect hindgut. 701

nephridium (pl., nephridia) (ni-FRID-ee-um) Segmentally arranged, paired excretory tubules of many invertebrates, as in the earthworm, where the contents are released through a nephridiopore. [Gk. *nephri,* kidney] 701

nephron (NEF-rahn) A microscopic kidney unit that regulates blood composition by pressure filtration and selective reabsorption; there are over a million nephrons per human kidney. [Gk. *nephri,* kidney] 702

proximal convoluted tubule The portion of a nephron following the glomerular capsule where selective reabsorption of filtrate occurs. [L. *proxim,* nearest] 702

urea Main nitrogenous waste of terrestrial amphibians and mammals. [Gk. *ure,* urine] 699

ureter (YUUR-ut-ur) A tubular structure conducting urine from the kidney to the urinary bladder. 702

urethra (yuu-REE-thruh) A tubular structure that receives urine from the bladder and carries it to the outside of the body. 702

uric acid Main nitrogenous waste of insects, reptiles, birds, and some dogs. 699

urinary bladder The organ where urine is stored. 702

urine Liquid waste product made by the nephrons of the kidney through the processes of pressure filtration and selective reabsorption. [Gk. *ure,* urine] 702

NERVOUS SYSTEM

Learning Objectives

- State the overall function of the nervous system.   712

How the Nervous System Evolved

- Compare the organization and the complexity of various invertebrate nervous systems with those of the human nervous system.   712–13

Neurons Are Nerve Cells

- Describe, in general, the structure of a neuron; name three types of neurons, and state their specific functions.   714

- Describe the nerve impulse as an electrochemical change that is recorded as the action potential by the oscilloscope.   715–17

- Describe the structure and the function of a synapse, including transmission across a synapse.   718

Peripheral Nervous System Contains Nerves

- Describe the structure and the function of the peripheral nervous system.   720

- Draw a diagram depicting a spinal reflex, and explain the function of all parts included.   721

- State the parts of the autonomic system; cite similarities and differences in structure and function of its two divisions.   722–23

Central Nervous System: Brain and Spinal Cord

- Describe, in general, the structure and the function of the central nervous system.   724

- List the major parts of the brain, and give a function for each part.   724–27

- Discuss, in general, current research into learning and memory.   727

Nerve cells form a tangled web in the cerebellum, a portion of the brain.

10 µm

The ability to respond to stimuli is a characteristic of all living things. In complex animals, such as vertebrates, this ability depends on the nervous, endocrine (hormonal), sensory, and musculoskeletal systems. Working together, the nervous and endocrine systems coordinate the actions of all the other systems of the body to produce effective behavior and to keep the internal environment within safe limits for life. Because hormones are transported in the blood, it may require seconds, minutes, hours, or even longer for these chemical messengers to produce their effects. The nervous system, on the other hand, communicates rapidly, requiring only thousandths of a second. The nervous system receives and processes information before sending out signals to the muscles and glands for an appropriate response. In this way, the nervous system integrates and controls the other systems of the body.

HOW THE NERVOUS SYSTEM EVOLVED

A comparative study of animal nervous systems indicates the steps that may have led to the centralized nervous system found in vertebrates (fig. 41.1). Hydras are cnidaria composed of just two cell layers separated by a packing material called the mesoglea. Their simple nervous system that extends throughout the body within the mesoglea looks like a net of threads. The nerve net is actually composed of neurons that are in contact with one another and with muscle fibers in the outer epidermis.

Experiments with sea anemones and jellyfishes suggest that these animals, which are also cnidaria, may have two nerve nets. A fast-acting one allows major responses, particularly in times of danger, and the other coordinates slower and more delicate movements.

Planaria are bilaterally symmetrical flatworms, and they have a more complex nervous system that resembles a ladder. Cephalization is present—there is a brain, which is a concentration of neurons at the anterior end of the animal that receives sensory information from photoreceptors in the eyespots and sensory cells in the auricles. Two longitudinal nerve cords allow a rapid transfer of information from anterior to posterior. Transverse nerves between the nerve cords keep the movement of the two sides coordinated. Therefore, planaria have the rudiments of a central nervous system (brain and nerve cords) and a peripheral nervous system (transverse nerves).

The annelids (e.g., an earthworm) and arthropods have what is usually considered the typical invertebrate nervous system. The **central nervous system (CNS)** consists of a brain and a ventral solid nerve cord; the **peripheral nervous system (PNS)** [Gk. *perifer,* circumference] consists of nerves that contain both sensory and motor fibers. The ventral solid nerve cord has a ganglion in each segment, which apparently controls the muscles of that segment. Even so, the brain, which normally receives sensory information, controls the activity of the ganglia so that the entire animal is coordinated.

Vertebrates (e.g., a rabbit) also have a central nervous system and a peripheral nervous system. The central nervous system

Figure 41.1

Evolution of the nervous system. **a.** The nerve net of a hydra, a cnidarian. **b.** In the flatworm, a planarian, the paired nerve cords with transverse nerves have the appearance of a ladder. **c.** The earthworm, an annelid, has a central nervous system consisting of a brain and a ventral solid nerve cord. It also has a peripheral nervous system consisting of nerves. **d.** A rabbit, like other vertebrates, has a dorsal hollow nerve cord in its central nervous system.

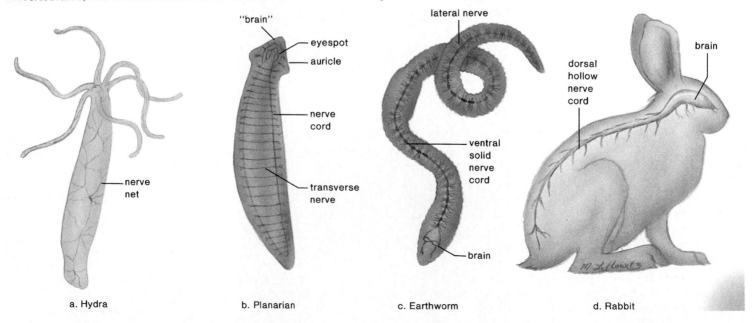

a. Hydra   b. Planarian   c. Earthworm   d. Rabbit

Figure 41.2

Overall organization of the nervous system in human beings. **a.** Pictorial representation. The central nervous system (CNS, composed of brain and spinal cord) and some of the nerves of the peripheral nervous system (PNS) are shown. **b.** The CNS communicates with the PNS, which contains nerves. In the somatic system, nerves send sensory impulses from receptors to the CNS and send motor impulses from the CNS to the skeletal muscles. In the autonomic system, consisting of the sympathetic and parasympathetic systems, motor impulses travel to smooth muscle, cardiac muscle, and the glands.

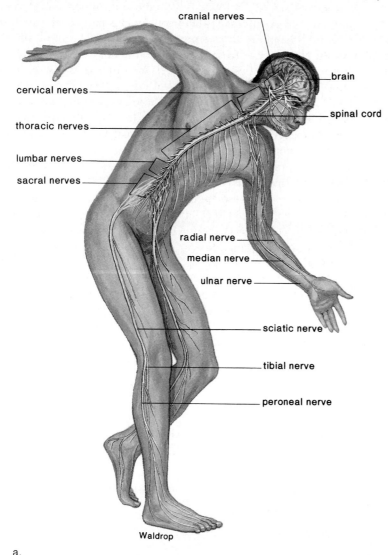

a.

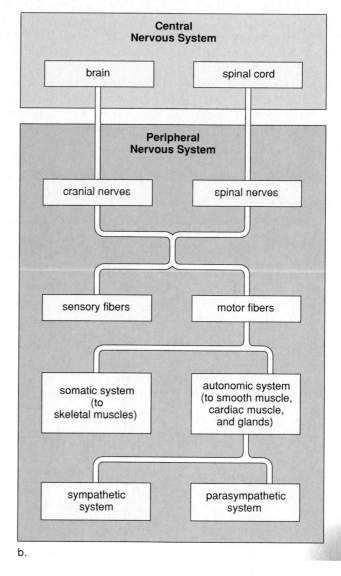

b.

contains the brain and spinal cord, consisting of a dorsal hollow nerve cord. The peripheral nervous system contains cranial and spinal nerves. In vertebrates there is a vast increase, however, in the number of neurons. For example, an insect's entire nervous system may contain a total of about one million neurons, while a vertebrate nervous system may contain many thousand to several billion times that number.

In the human nervous system, the *central nervous system* includes the brain and the spinal cord (dorsal nerve cord), which lie in the midline of the body (fig. 41.2). The skull protects the brain and the vertebrae protect the spinal cord. The *peripheral nervous system* contains the cranial nerves, which connect to the

brain, and the spinal nerves, which project from either side of the spinal cord. The peripheral nervous system is further divided into the somatic system and the autonomic (or visceral) system. The somatic system contains nerves that control skeletal muscles, skin, and joints. The autonomic system contains nerves that control the glands and smooth muscles of the internal organs.

In complex animals, the nervous system has two parts: the central nervous system and the peripheral nervous system.

NEURONS ARE NERVE CELLS

Neurons [Gk. *neuro,* nerve] are cells that vary in size and shape, but they all have three parts: the dendrite(s), the cell body, and the axon (fig. 41.3). The **dendrites** [Gk. *dendro,* tree] receive information from other neurons and generally conduct nerve impulses *toward* the cell body. The **axon** [Gk. *axo,* axis], on the other hand, conducts nerve impulses *away* from the cell body. The cell body contains the nucleus and other organelles typically found in cells. One of the main functions of the cell body is to manufacture neurotransmitters, which are chemicals stored in secretory vesicles at the ends of axons. When neurotransmitters are released, they influence the excitability of nearby neurons.

Three types of neurons are shown in figure 41.3. *Motor neurons,* each with a long axon and short dendrites, take mes-sages from the central nervous system to muscle fibers or glands. Because motor neurons cause muscle fibers or glands to react, they are said to *innervate* these structures. *Sensory neurons,* each with a long dendrite and a short axon, take messages from sense organs to the central nervous system. The third type of neuron, called an **interneuron** [L. *inter,* between, and Gk. *neuro,* nerve], is found within the central nervous system only. It conveys messages between various parts of the central nervous system, such as from one side of the brain or spinal cord to the other or from the brain to the cord, and vice versa. An interneuron has short dendrites and either a long axon or a short axon.

The dendrites and axons of these neurons are sometimes called fibers, or processes. Most long fibers, whether dendrite or axon, are covered by a white **myelin sheath** [Gk. *myelo,* spinal cord] formed from the membranes of the tightly spiraled neurolemmocytes (Schwann cells) surrounding these fibers.

Neurolemmocytes are one of the several types of neuroglial cells in the nervous system. Neuroglial cells service the neurons and have supportive and nutritive functions.

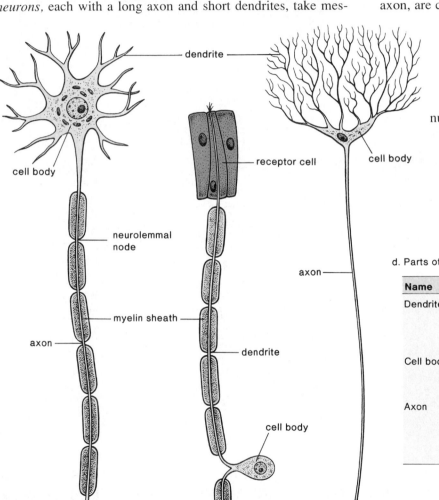

a. Motor neuron

b. Sensory neuron

c. Interneuron

d. Parts of a neuron

Name	Function	
Dendrite	A fiber that receives information and generally conducts nerve impulses to the cell body.	Both integrate (sum up excitatory and inhibitory inputs.
Cell body	Contains the nucleus and other organelles and manufactures neurotransmitters.	
Axon	A fiber that conducts nerve impulses away from the cell body and releases neurotransmitters.	

Figure 41.3

Neuron anatomy. **a.** Motor neuron. Note the branched dendrites and the single, long axon, which branches only near its tip. **b.** Sensory neuron. Note the single, long dendrite. **c.** Interneuron (from the cortex of the cerebellum) with very highly branched dendrites. **d.** Major parts of a neuron and their functions.

Figure 41.4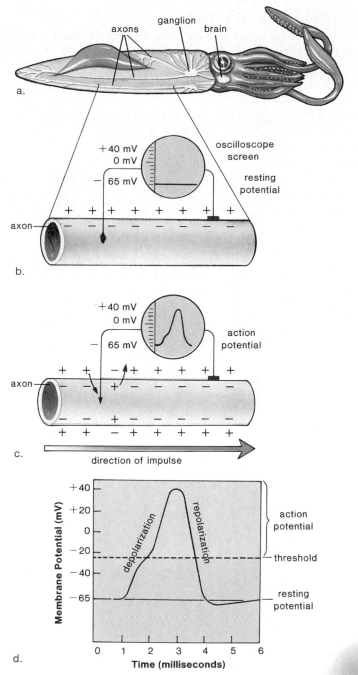

The original nerve impulse studies utilized giant squid axon and a voltage recording device known as an oscilloscope. **a.** A squid axon produces rapid muscle contraction so that the squid can move quickly. **b.** A squid axon is so large (about 1 mm in diameter) that a microelectrode can be inserted inside it. When the axon is not conducting a nerve impulse, the electrode registers and the oscilloscope records a resting potential of –65 mV. **c.** Just prior to an axon conducting a nerve impulse, the *threshold* for an action potential has been achieved, and there is a rapid change in potential from –65 mV to +40 mV (called depolarization), followed by a return to –65 mV (called repolarization). **d.** Enlargement of action potential of nerve impulse.

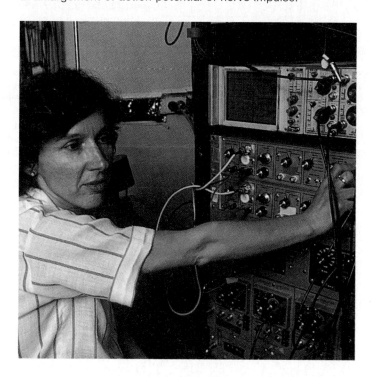

Transmitting the Nerve Impulse

Italian investigator Luigi Galvani discovered in 1786 that a nerve can be stimulated by an electric current. But it was realized later that the speed of the nerve impulse is too slow to be due simply to the movement of electrons or current within a nerve fiber. In the early 1900s, Julius Bernstein, at the University of Halle, Germany, suggested that the nerve impulse is an electrochemical phenomenon involving the movement of unequally distributed ions on either side of a neuron plasma membrane. It was not until later, however, that the investigators developed a technique that enabled them to substantiate this hypothesis. A. L. Hodgkin and A. F. Huxley, English neurophysiologists, received the Nobel prize in 1963 for their work in this field. They and a group of researchers, headed by K. S. Cole and J. J. Curtis, at Woods Hole, Massachusetts, managed to insert a very tiny electrode into the giant

axon of the squid *Loligo* (fig. 41.4). This internal electrode was then connected to a voltmeter and an *oscilloscope,* an instrument with a screen that shows a trace or pattern indicating a change in voltage with time (fig. 41.4*d*). *Voltage* is a measure of the electrical potential difference between two points, which in this case is the difference between two electrodes—one placed inside and another placed outside the axon. (An electrical potential difference across a membrane is called the membrane potential.) When a potential difference exists, we can say that a plus pole and a minus pole exist; therefore, an oscilloscope indicates the existence of polarity and records polarity changes.

Figure 41.5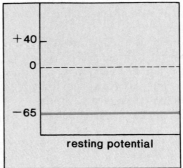

Action potential and resting potential. The action potential is the result of an exchange of sodium ions (Na⁺) and potassium ions (K⁺), and it is shown (right) as a change in polarity by an oscilloscope. So few ions are exchanged for each action potential that it is possible for a nerve fiber to repeatedly conduct nerve impulses. Whenever the fiber rests, the sodium-potassium pump restores the original distribution of ions.

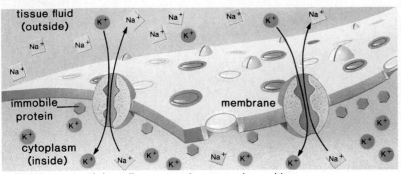

a. Resting potential: sodium-potassium pump is working.

When a neuron is not conducting a nerve impulse, the sodium (Na⁺) and potassium (K⁺) gates are closed. The sodium-potassium pump maintains the uneven distribution of these ions across the membrane. The oscilloscope registers a resting potential of −65 mV inside compared to outside.

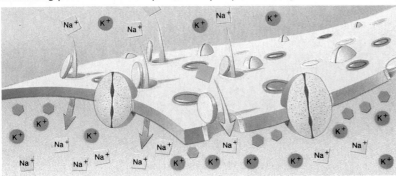

b. Action potential: sodium gates are open.

An action potential begins when the sodium gates open and sodium ions move to the inside. The oscilloscope registers a depolarization as the cytoplasm reaches +40 mV compared to tissue fluid.

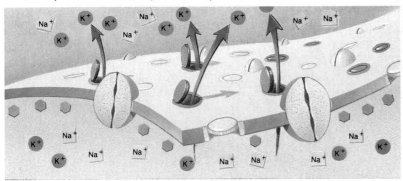

c. Action potential: potassium gates are open.

The action potential continues as the sodium gates close and the potassium gates open, allowing potassium ions to move to the outside. The oscilloscope registers repolarization as the cytoplasm again becomes −65 mV compared to tissue fluid.

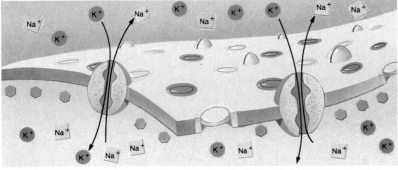

d. Refractory period: sodium-potassium pump is working.

The oscilloscope registers −65 mV again, but the sodium-potassium pump is working to restore the original sodium and potassium ion distribution. The sodium and potassium gates are now closed but will open again in response to another stimulus.

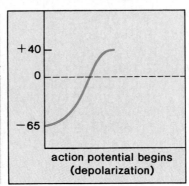

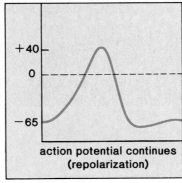

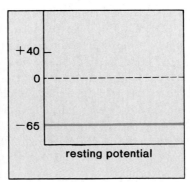

Figure 41.6

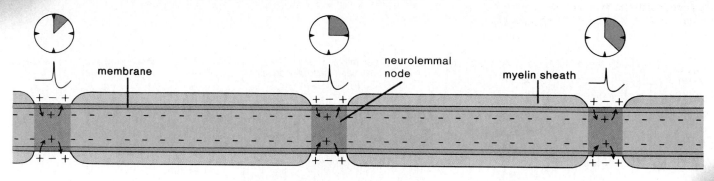

Saltatory conduction. Longitudinal section of a vertebrate axon, illustrating that the nerve impulse jumps from one neurolemmal node to the next. This greatly increases the speed of conduction.

Resting Potential Is Baseline

When the axon is not conducting an impulse, the oscilloscope records a membrane potential equal to about −65 mV (millivolts), indicating that the inside of the neuron is more negative than the outside (see fig. 41.4b). This is called the **resting potential** because the axon is not conducting an impulse.

The existence of this polarity can be correlated with a difference in ion distribution on either side of the plasma membrane of the axon. As figure 41.5a shows, there is a higher concentration of sodium ions (Na^+) outside the axon and a higher concentration of potassium ions (K^+) inside the axon. The unequal distribution of these ions is due to the action of the sodium-potassium pump. This pump is an active transport system in the plasma membrane that pumps sodium ions out of and potassium ions into the axon. The work of the pump maintains the unequal distribution of sodium and potassium ions across the membrane.

The pump is always working because the membrane is somewhat permeable to these ions and they tend to diffuse toward their lesser concentration. Since the membrane is more permeable to potassium ions than to sodium ions, there are always more positive ions outside the membrane than inside; this accounts for some of the polarity recorded by the oscilloscope. There are also large, negatively charged proteins in the cytoplasm of the axon; altogether, then, the oscilloscope records that the cytoplasm is −65 mV compared to tissue fluid. This is the resting potential.

Action Potential Brings Changes

If the axon is stimulated to conduct a nerve impulse by an electric shock, a sudden change in pH, or a pinch, there is a rapid change in the polarity recorded as a trace on the oscilloscope screen. This change in polarity is called the **action potential** (fig. 41.5b, c). First, the trace goes from −65 mV to +40 mV (called *depolarization*), indicating that the cytoplasm is now more positive than tissue fluid. Then the trace returns to −65 mV again (called *repolarization*), indicating that the inside of the axon is negative again.

The action potential is due to special protein-lined channels in the membrane, which can open to allow either sodium or potassium ions to pass through. These channels have gates, called sodium gates and potassium gates. The sodium gates open and sodium rushes into the axon during the depolarization phase of the action potential. Once this phase is complete, repolarization occurs. The potassium gates open and potassium rushes out of the axon during repolarization.

Notice that at the completion of an action potential, the original ion distribution has been altered somewhat (fig. 41.5d). There are now more sodium ions inside the axon than before, and there are more potassium ions outside the axon than before. The sodium-potassium pump is able to restore the former distribution, however.

The oscilloscope records changes at only one location in a fiber, but actually the action potential travels along the length of a fiber. It is self-propagating because the ion channels are prompted to open whenever the membrane potential decreases in an adjacent area. In invertebrates, some fibers are larger than others and a few axons are called giant axons because they are so large. The nerve impulse travels a thousand times faster in giant axons compared to thin fibers (25 m/s compared to 0.025 m/s). In vertebrates the speed of travel is improved not by increase in size but because most long fibers have a myelin sheath. There are gaps in the myelin sheath called neurolemmal nodes (nodes of Ranvier), where one neurolemmocyte ends and the next begins. The action potential simply jumps or leaps from one neurolemmal node to the next and may reach speeds of 200 m/s. This is called **saltatory conduction** [L. *saltator,* leaper] (fig. 41.6).

> **All neurons transmit the same type of nerve impulse—an electrochemical change that is self-propagating along the fiber(s).**

Figure 41.7

Synapse structure and function. **a.** A synapse occurs where an axon meets either a dendrite or a cell body. **b.** An axon bulb contains synaptic vesicles, which in turn contain neurotransmitters. **c.** Transmission across a synapse occurs when synaptic vesicles release neurotransmitters.

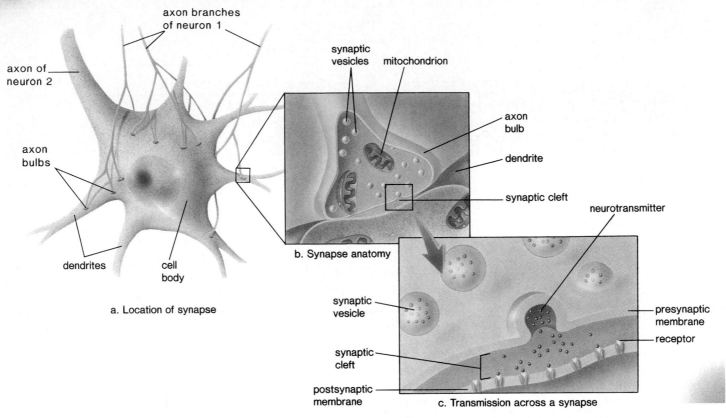

a. Location of synapse

b. Synapse anatomy

c. Transmission across a synapse

Transmitting at Synapses

In 1897, the English scientist Sir Charles Sherrington and others noted two important aspects of nerve impulse transmission between neurons. First, an impulse passing from one vertebrate nerve cell to another always moves in only one direction. Second, there is a very short delay in transmission of the nerve impulse from one neuron to another. This latter observation led to the hypothesis that there is a minute space between neurons. Sherrington called the region where the impulse moves from one neuron to another a **synapse** [Gk. *synapse,* union], meaning "to clasp." A synapse has three components: a presynaptic membrane, a gap now called the synaptic cleft, and a postsynaptic membrane (fig. 41.7).

When nerve impulses traveling along an axon reach an axon bulb, the membrane becomes permeable to calcium ions (Ca^{++}). These ions enter and then interact with actin filaments, causing the actin filaments to pull synaptic vesicles to the presynaptic membrane (fig. 41.7*b*). When the vesicles merge with this membrane, a **neurotransmitter** [Gk. *neuro,* nerve, and L. *trans,* across] is discharged into the synaptic cleft (fig. 41.7*c*). The neurotransmitter molecules diffuse across the cleft to the postsynaptic membrane, where they bind with a receptor in a lock-and-key manner. This binding process alters the membrane potential of the postsynaptic membrane in the direction of either excitation or inhibition. If excitation occurs, the membrane potential becomes less negative,

and if inhibition occurs, the membrane potential becomes more negative. This could happen if the neurotransmitter were to cause only sodium gates to open and the axon gained sodium ions (Na^{++}).

Neurotransmitters Act Quickly

Acetylcholine (ACh) and **norepinephrine (NE)** are well known neurotransmitters, active in both the peripheral nervous system and the central nervous system. These are excitatory or inhibitory, according to the type of receptor at the postsynaptic membrane.

Once a neurotransmitter has been released into a synaptic cleft, it has only a short time to act. In some synapses, the cleft contains enzymes that rapidly inactivate the neurotransmitter. For example, the enzyme **acetylcholinesterase (AChE),** or simply cholinesterase, breaks down acetylcholine. In other synapses, the synaptic ending rapidly absorbs the neurotransmitter, possibly for repackaging in synaptic vesicles or for chemical breakdown. The short existence of neurotransmitters in the synapse prevents continuous stimulation (or inhibition) of postsynaptic membranes.

Transmission of a nerve impulse across a synapse is dependent on a neurotransmitter that alters the membrane potential of the postsynaptic membrane.

Alzheimer Disease

Alzheimer disease (AD) is a disorder characterized by a gradual loss of reason. It begins with memory lapses and ends with an inability to perform any type of daily activity. Personality changes signal the onset of AD. A normal fifty- to sixty-year-old adult might forget the name of a friend not seen for years. However, people with AD forget the name of a neighbor who visits daily. With time, they have trouble traveling and cannot perform simple errands. People afflicted with AD become confused and tend to repeat questions. Signs of mental disturbances eventually appear, and patients gradually become bedridden and die of a complication such as pneumonia.

A normal neuron differs from a neuron damaged by AD. The AD neuron (fig. 41A) has bundles of fibrous protein, called neurofibrillary tangles, surrounding the nucleus in the cell, and protein-rich accumulations, called amyloid plaques, enveloping the axon branches. These abnormal neurons are especially numerous in the portions of the brain that are involved in reason and memory (frontal lobe and limbic system).

In order for scientists to examine the abnormal neurons caused by AD, brain tissue is examined microscopically after the patient dies. A chemical test is used to test brain tissue for the presence of a protein called Alzheimer disease associated protein (ADAP), which is believed to be the protein contained in the neurofibrillary tangles. Once it is proven that ADAP is the protein involved in AD, it may become routine to test patients for this protein by obtaining a sample of cerebrospinal fluid.

Over a life span of 100 years, the likelihood of developing AD is 16% for people with no family history of AD, and 24% for those having first-degree relatives with AD. This difference in susceptibility suggests that AD might have a genetic basis. Researchers have discovered that in some families whose members have a 50% chance of AD, there is a genetic defect on chromosome 21. This is of extreme interest because Down syndrome results from the inheritance of three copies of chromosome 21, and people with Down syndrome tend to develop AD. Further, the genetic defect affects the normal production of amyloid precursor protein (APP), which may be the cause of amyloid plaques.

Acetylcholine is a chemical that stimulates neurons to carry nerve impulses, and it appears that AD patients may have a reduced supply of this chemical in the brain. Drugs that enhance the production of acetylcholine are currently being tested in AD patients. Also under investigation are drugs that prevent neuron degeneration. For example, it is possible that nerve growth factor, a substance made by the body that promotes the growth of neurons, will one day be available to AD patients.

Figure 41A

Alzheimer disease (AD). An AD neuron has neurofibrillary tangles and amyloid plaques. Such neurons are particularly present in the parts of the brain noted. This accounts for the development of symptoms of AD.

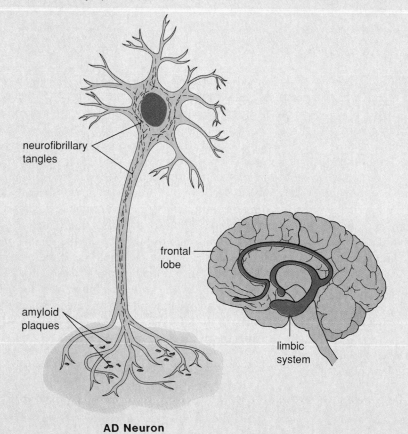

AD Neuron

Figure 41.8

Spinal cord anatomy. **a.** Cross section of the spine, showing spinal nerves. The human body has thirty-one pairs of spinal nerves. **b.** This cross section of the spinal cord shows that a spinal nerve has a dorsal root and a ventral root. Also, the cord is protected by three layers of tissue called the meninges. Spinal meningitis is an infection of these layers.

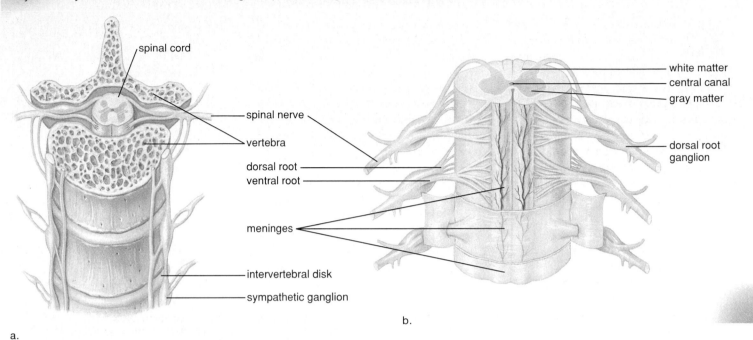

a.

b.

PERIPHERAL NERVOUS SYSTEM CONTAINS NERVES

The peripheral nervous system lies outside the central nervous system (see fig. 41.2*b*). The peripheral nervous system is made up of **nerves,** which are part of either the somatic system or the autonomic system. The somatic system contains nerves that control skeletal muscles, skin, and joints. The autonomic system contains nerves that control the smooth muscles of the internal organs and the glands. Nerves are structures that contain many long fibers—long dendrites and/or long axons. Each of these fibers is surrounded by a myelin sheath (see fig. 41.3), and therefore these nerves have a white, glistening appearance. There are no cell bodies in nerves because cell bodies are found only in the central nervous system or in the ganglia. **Ganglia** [Gk. *ganglion,* knot on a string] are collections of cell bodies found particularly within the peripheral nervous system.

Humans have twelve pairs of *cranial nerves* attached to the brain. Cranial nerves are either sensory nerves (having long dendrites of sensory neurons only), motor nerves (having long axons of motor neurons only), or mixed nerves (having both long dendrites and long axons). With the exception of the vagus nerve, all cranial nerves control the head, neck, and face. The *vagus nerve* controls the internal organs.

Humans have thirty-one pairs of *spinal nerves.* Each spinal nerve emerges from the spinal cord (fig. 41.8) by two short branches, or roots, which lie within the vertebral column. The dorsal root contains the fibers of sensory neurons, which conduct impulses to the cord. The ventral root contains the axons of motor neurons, which conduct impulses away from the cord. These two roots join just before a spinal nerve leaves the vertebral column. Therefore, all spinal nerves are mixed nerves that take impulses to and from the **spinal cord.** Their arrangement shows that humans are segmented animals: there is a pair of spinal nerves for each segment. Spinal nerves project from the spinal cord, which is a part of the central nervous system. The spinal cord is a thick, whitish nerve cord that extends longitudinally down the back, where it is protected by the vertebrae (sing., vertebra). The cord contains a tiny **central canal** filled with cerebrospinal fluid, gray matter consisting of cell bodies and short fibers, and white matter consisting of myelinated fibers.

In the peripheral nervous system, cranial nerves take impulses to and/or from the brain and spinal nerves take impulses to and from the spinal cord.

Somatic System Serves Skin and Muscles

The *somatic system* includes all nerves that serve the musculoskeletal system and the exterior sense organs, including those in the skin. Exterior sense organs are *receptors,* which receive environmental stimuli and then initiate nerve impulses. Muscle fibers are *effectors,* which bring about a reaction to the stimulus.

Reflexes Are Automatic

Reflexes [L. *reflectere,* bend back] are automatic, involuntary responses to changes occurring inside or outside the body. In the somatic system, outside stimuli often initiate a reflex action. Some reflexes, such as blinking the eye, involve the brain, but others, such as withdrawing the hand from a hot object, do not necessarily involve the brain. Figure 41.9 illustrates the path of the second type of reflex action involving the spinal cord and a spinal nerve, called a *spinal reflex,* or *reflex arc.*

If you touch a very hot object, a receptor in the skin generates nerve impulses, which move along the dendrite of a sensory neuron toward the cell body and the central nervous system. The cell body of a *sensory neuron* is located in the *dorsal-root ganglion,* just outside the cord. From the cell body, the impulses travel along the axon of the sensory nerve. The impulses then pass to many interneurons, one of which connects with a motor neuron. The short dendrites and the cell body of the *motor neuron* lead to the axon, which leaves the cord by way of the ventral root of the spinal nerve. The nerve impulses travel along the axon to *muscle fibers,* which then contract so that you withdraw your hand from the hot object. There are various other reactions—the person may look in the direction of the object, jump back, and cry out in pain. This whole series of responses occurs because the sensory neuron stimulates several interneurons. They take impulses to all parts of the central nervous system, including the cerebrum, which in turn makes the person conscious of the stimulus and his or her reaction to it.

> The reflex arc is a major functional unit of the nervous system. It allows us to react rapidly to internal and external stimuli.

Figure 41.9

A reflex arc showing the path of a reflex. When a receptor in the skin is stimulated, nerve impulses (see arrows) move along a sensory neuron to the spinal cord. (Note that the cell body of a sensory neuron is in a ganglion outside the cord.) The nerve impulses are picked up by an interneuron, which lies completely within the cord, and pass to the dendrites and the cell body of a motor neuron that lies ventrally within the cord. The nerve impulses then move along the motor neuron to an effector, such as a muscle, which contracts. The brain receives information concerning sensory stimuli by way of other interneurons, with long fibers in tracts that run up and down the cord within the white matter.

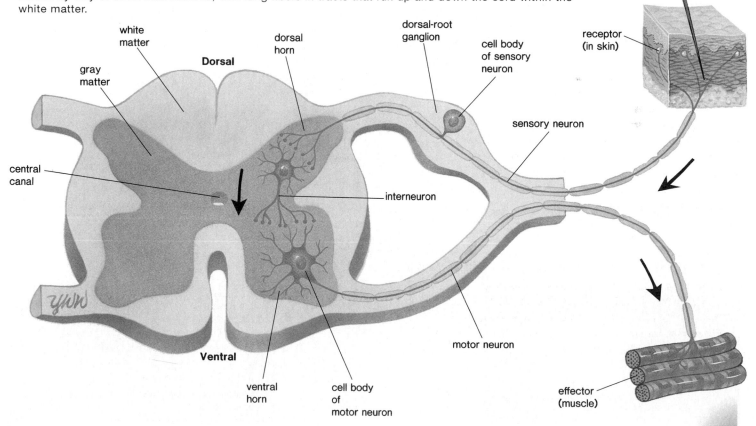

Figure 41.10 💿

Autonomic system structure and function. The sympathetic fibers arise from the thoracic and lumbar portions of the spinal cord; the parasympathetic fibers arise from the brain and the sacral portion of the spinal cord. Each system innervates the same organs but has contrary effects. For example, the sympathetic system increases the heart rate, while the parasympathetic system decreases it.

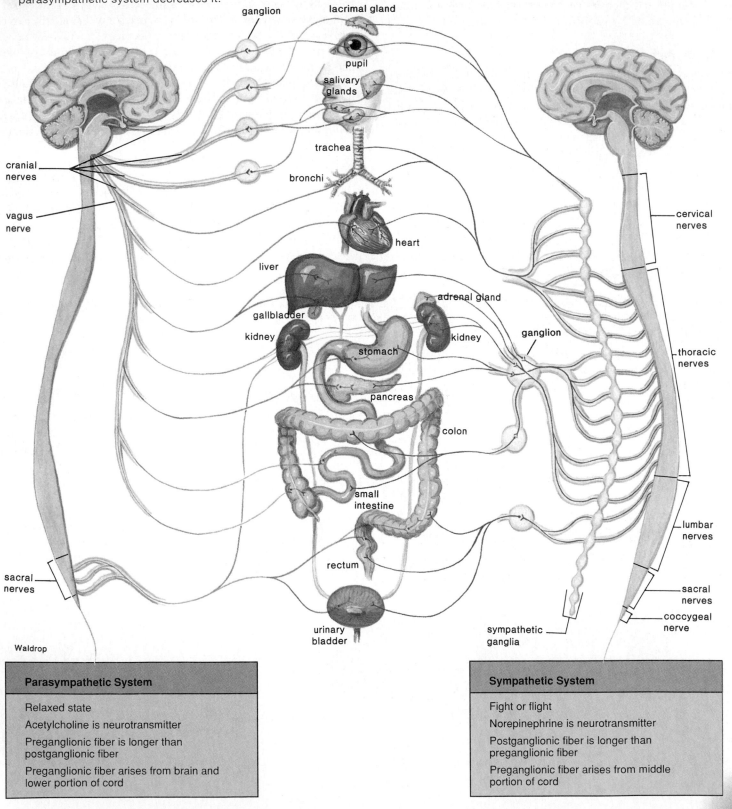

ganglion
lacrimal gland
pupil
salivary glands
trachea
bronchi
cranial nerves
vagus nerve
heart
liver
adrenal gland
gallbladder
kidney
kidney
ganglion
stomach
pancreas
colon
small intestine
rectum
sacral nerves
urinary bladder
Waldrop

cervical nerves
thoracic nerves
lumbar nerves
sacral nerves
coccygeal nerve
sympathetic ganglia

Parasympathetic System
Relaxed state
Acetylcholine is neurotransmitter
Preganglionic fiber is longer than postganglionic fiber
Preganglionic fiber arises from brain and lower portion of cord

Sympathetic System
Fight or flight
Norepinephrine is neurotransmitter
Postganglionic fiber is longer than preganglionic fiber
Preganglionic fiber arises from middle portion of cord

Autonomic System Serves Internal Organs

The **autonomic system** [Gk. *autonomia,* independence] (fig. 41.10), a part of the peripheral nervous system, is made up of motor neurons that control the internal organs automatically and usually without need for conscious intervention. The sensory neurons that come from the internal organs allow us to feel internal pain. The cell bodies for these sensory neurons are in dorsal-root ganglia, along with the cell bodies of somatic sensory neurons.

There are two divisions of the autonomic system: the sympathetic and parasympathetic systems. Both of these (1) function automatically and usually subconsciously in an involuntary manner; (2) innervate internal organs; and (3) utilize two motor neurons and one ganglion for each impulse. The first of these two neurons has a cell body within the central nervous system and a *preganglionic fiber.* The second neuron has a cell body within the ganglion and a *postganglionic fiber.*

> The autonomic system controls the function of internal organs, in the absence of conscious control.

Sympathetic System: Fight or Flight

Most preganglionic fibers of the **sympathetic system** (fig. 41.10) arise from the middle, or *thoracic-lumbar,* portion of the spinal cord and almost immediately terminate in ganglia that lie near the cord. Therefore, this system is often referred to as the thoracolumbar portion of the autonomic system. In the sympathetic system, the preganglionic fiber is short, but the postganglionic fiber that makes contact with an organ is long.

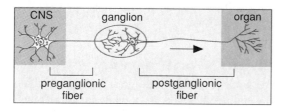

The sympathetic system is especially important during emergency situations and is associated with "fight or flight." If you need to fend off a foe or flee from danger, active muscles require a ready supply of glucose and oxygen. The sympathetic system accelerates the heartbeat, dilates the bronchi, and increases the breathing rate. On the other hand, the sympathetic system inhibits the digestive tract—digestion is not an immediate necessity if you are under attack. The neurotransmitter released by the postganglionic axon is primarily norepinephrine (NE), a chemical close in structure to epinephrine (adrenaline), a medicine used as a heart stimulant.

> The sympathetic system brings about those responses we associate with "fight or flight."

Parasympathetic System: Relaxed State

A few cranial nerves, including the vagus nerve, together with fibers that arise from the sacral (bottom) portion of the spinal cord, form the **parasympathetic system** (fig. 41.10). Therefore, this system is often referred to as the *craniosacral portion* of the autonomic system. In the parasympathetic system, the preganglionic fiber is long and the postganglionic fiber is short because the ganglia lie near or within the organ.

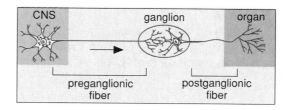

The parasympathetic system, sometimes called the "housekeeper system," promotes all the internal responses we associate with a relaxed state; for example, it causes the pupil of the eye to contract, promotes digestion of food, and retards the heartbeat. The neurotransmitter utilized by the parasympathetic system is acetylcholine (ACh).

> The parasympathetic system brings about the responses we associate with a relaxed state.

Figure 41.11

Brain functions. **a.** The medulla oblongata and hypothalamus function below the level of consciousness and maintain the vegetative functions of the body without input from the cerebrum. **b.** The cerebellum, which coordinates motor functions, is under the direct control of the cerebrum; necessary adjustments due to environmental stimuli are possible. The roller blader will stop rather than be hit by a car.

a.

b.

CENTRAL NERVOUS SYSTEM: BRAIN AND SPINAL CORD

The central nervous system (CNS) consists of the spinal cord and the brain, where nerve impulses are coordinated and interpreted. The spinal cord is surrounded by vertebrae, and, like the brain, it is wrapped in three protective membranes known as **meninges** [Gk. *menin,* membrane] (see fig. 41.8). The spaces between the meninges are filled with **cerebrospinal fluid** [L. *cereb,* brain, and *spin,* spine], which cushions and protects the central nervous system. Cerebrospinal fluid is contained in the central canal of the spinal cord and within the *ventricles* of the brain, which are interconnecting spaces that produce and serve as reservoirs for cerebrospinal fluid.

Spinal Cord Communicates

The spinal cord has two main functions: (1) it is the center for many reflex actions, which are discussed on page 721, and (2) it provides a means of communication between the brain and the spinal nerves, which leave the spinal cord.

The spinal cord has white matter and gray matter (see fig. 41.8). Unmyelinated cell bodies and short fibers give the *gray matter* its color. In cross section, the gray matter looks like a butterfly or the letter *H*. Portions of sensory neurons and motor neurons are found here, as are short interneurons that connect these two types of neurons.

Myelinated long fibers of interneurons that run together in bundles called *tracts* give *white matter* its color. These tracts connect the spinal cord to the brain. Dorsally, there are primarily ascending tracts taking information to the brain, and ventrally, there are primarily descending tracts carrying information from the brain. Because the tracts at one point cross over, the left side of the brain controls the right side of the body and the right side of the brain controls the left side of the body.

> The CNS, which lies in the midline of the body and consists of the brain and the spinal cord, initiates sensory information and motor control.

The Brain Commands

The human brain is divided into these parts: medulla oblongata, cerebellum, pons, midbrain, hypothalamus, thalamus, and cerebrum. The brain has four cavities, called **ventricles:** two lateral ventricles, the third ventricle, and the fourth ventricle.

Brain Stem

The medulla oblongata, the pons, and the midbrain lie in a portion of the brain known as the *brain stem* (figs. 41.11*a,* 41.12). The **medulla oblongata** [L. *medull,* marrow, and *oblongus,* rather long] lies between the spinal cord and the pons and is anterior to the cerebellum. It contains a number of *vital centers* for regulating heartbeat, breathing, and vasoconstriction (blood pressure). It also contains the reflex centers for vomiting, coughing, sneezing, hiccuping, and swallowing. The medulla contains tracts that ascend or descend between the spinal cord and the brain's higher centers.

The **pons** [L. *pont,* bridge] contains bundles of axons traveling between the cerebellum and the rest of the central nervous system. In addition, the pons functions with the medulla to regulate the breathing rate and has reflex centers concerned with head

Figure 41.12
The human brain. Note how large the
cerebrum is, compared to the
rest of the brain.

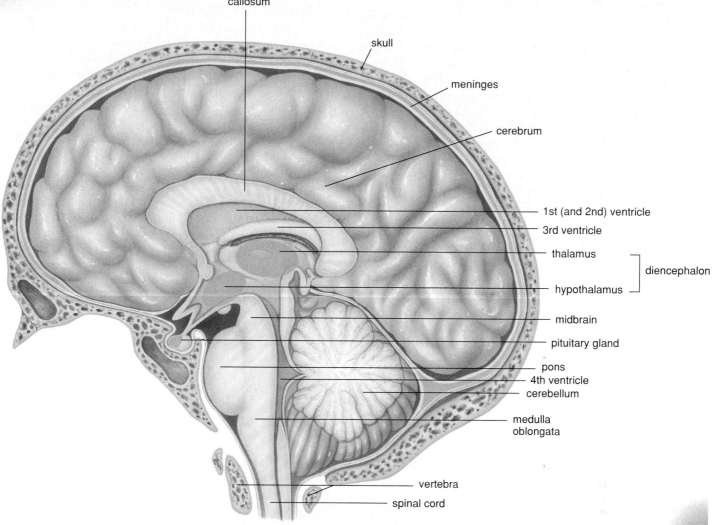

movements in response to visual and auditory stimuli. Aside from acting as a relay station for tracts passing between the cerebrum and the spinal cord or cerebellum, the **midbrain** has reflex centers for visual, auditory, and tactile responses.

Diencephalon

The hypothalamus and thalamus are in a portion of the brain known as the diencephalon, where the third ventricle is located. The hypothalamus forms the floor of the third ventricle. The **hypothalamus** [Gk. *hypo,* under] maintains homeostasis, or the constancy of the internal environment, and contains centers for regulating hunger, sleep, thirst, body temperature, water balance, and blood pressure. The hypothalamus controls the pituitary gland and thereby serves as a link between the nervous and endocrine systems.

The thalamus is in the roof of the third ventricle. The **thalamus** is the last portion of the brain for sensory input before

the cerebrum. It serves as a central relay station for sensory impulses traveling upward from other parts of the body and brain to the cerebrum. It receives all sensory impulses (except those associated with the sense of smell) and channels them to appropriate regions of the cerebrum for interpretation.

Cerebellum

The **cerebellum,** which lies below the posterior portion of the cerebrum, is separated from the brain stem by the fourth ventricle. The cerebellum functions in muscle coordination, integrating impulses received from higher centers to ensure that all of the skeletal muscles work together to produce smooth and graceful motions (fig. 41.11*b*). The cerebellum is also responsible for maintaining normal muscle tone and transmitting impulses that maintain posture. It receives information from the inner ear indicating position of the body and then sends impulses to the muscles, whose contraction maintains or restores balance.

Cerebrum

The **cerebrum,** the foremost part of the brain, is the largest part of the brain in humans (fig. 41.12). It consists of two large masses called cerebral hemispheres, which are connected by a bridge of nerve fibers called the corpus callosum. The outer portion of the cerebral hemispheres, the *cerebral cortex,* is highly convoluted and gray in color because it contains cell bodies and short fibers.

The cerebral cortex of each hemisphere contains four surface lobes: frontal, parietal, temporal, and occipital. Different functions are associated with each lobe (fig. 41.13). For example, the *frontal lobe* controls motor functions and permits us to control our muscles consciously. The *parietal lobe* receives information from receptors located in the skin, such as those for touch, pressure, and pain. The *occipital lobe* interprets visual input. The *temporal lobe* has sensory areas for hearing and smelling.

A comparative study of vertebrates indicates a progressive increase in the relative size of the cerebrum from fishes to humans, and the cerebral cortex is more convoluted in humans than other vertebrates. The function of the cerebrum has also changed. In fishes and amphibians, the cerebrum largely has an olfactory function, but in reptiles, birds, and mammals, the cerebrum receives information from other parts of the brain and coordinates sensory data and motor functions. Only the cerebrum is responsible for consciousness, and it is the portion of the brain that governs intelligence and reason. These qualities are particularly well developed in humans.

The cerebrum controls the activities of lower parts of the brain. The cerebrum can override the functioning of the brain stem and diencephalon, as when meditation or biofeedback helps control the heart rate. Acting on sensory input from the thalamus, the cerebrum initiates voluntary motor activities and controls the actions of the cerebellum. Certain areas of the cerebral cortex have been "mapped" in great detail (fig. 41.13). We know which portions of the frontal lobe control various parts of the body and which portions of the parietal lobe receive sensory information from these same parts. Each of the four lobes of the cerebral cortex contains an association area, which receives information from the other lobes and integrates it into higher, more complex levels of consciousness. These areas are concerned with intellect, artistic and creative ability, learning, and memory.

Figure 41.13

The convoluted cortex of the cerebrum is divided into four surface lobes: frontal, parietal, temporal, and occipital. It is possible to map the cerebral cortex, since each area has a particular function.

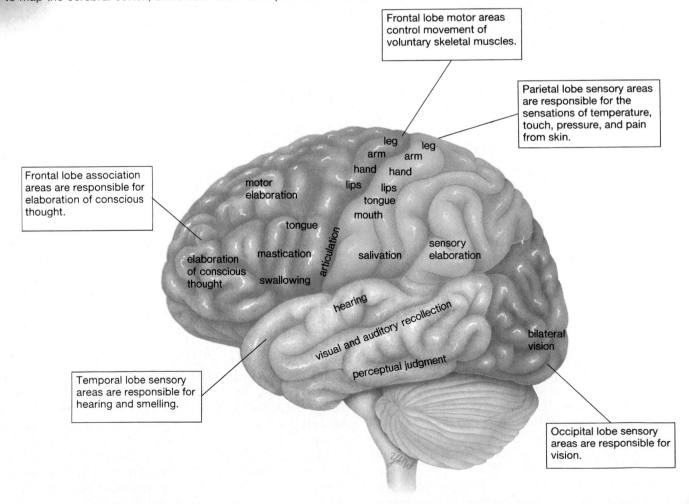

Figure 41.14

The limbic system. The limbic system, which includes portions of the cerebrum, the thalamus, and the hypothalamus, is sometimes called the emotional brain because it seems to control the emotions listed.

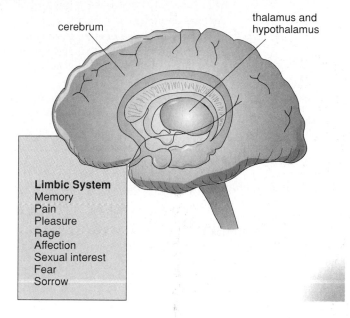

cerebrum

thalamus and hypothalamus

Limbic System
Memory
Pain
Pleasure
Rage
Affection
Sexual interest
Fear
Sorrow

Limbic System

The **limbic system** involves portions of both the unconscious and conscious brain. It lies just beneath the cortex and contains neural pathways that connect portions of the frontal lobes, the temporal lobes, the thalamus, and the hypothalamus (fig. 41.14). Several masses of gray matter that lie deep within each hemisphere of the cerebrum, termed the *basal nuclei,* are also a part of the limbic system.

Stimulation of different areas of the limbic system causes the subject to experience rage, pain, pleasure, or sorrow. By causing pleasant or unpleasant feelings about experiences, the limbic system apparently guides the individual into behavior that is likely to increase the chance of survival.

Learning and Memory

The limbic system is also involved in the processes of learning and memory. Learning requires memory, but just what permits memory development is not definitely known. Investigators have been working with invertebrates such as slugs and snails because their nervous system is very simple and yet they can be conditioned to perform a particular behavior. To study this simple type of learning, it has been possible to insert electrodes into individual cells and to alter or record the electrochemical responses of these cells (fig. 41.15). This type of research has shown that learning is accompanied by an increase in the number of synapses, while forgetting involves a decrease in the number of synapses. In other words, the nerve-circuit patterns are constantly changing as learning, remembering, and forgetting occur. Within

Figure 41.15

Individual nerve cells in a snail, *Hermissenda*, are being stimulated by microelectrodes, which produce the signals scientists previously recorded when a snail learns to avoid light. (Normally, to teach snails to avoid light, they are placed on a table that rotates every time they venture toward light.) When this snail is freed, it automatically avoids the light and does not need to be taught like other snails.

the individual neuron, learning involves a change in gene regulation and nerve protein synthesis and an increased ability to secrete transmitter substances.

At the other end of the spectrum, some investigators have been studying learning and memory in monkeys. This work has led to the conclusion that the limbic system is absolutely essential to both short-term and long-term memory. An example of short-term memory in humans is the ability to recall a telephone number long enough to dial the number; an example of long-term memory is the ability to recall the events of the day. After nerve impulses circulate within the limbic system, the basal nuclei stimulate the sensory areas where memories are stored. The involvement of the limbic system certainly explains why emotionally charged events result in our most vivid memories. The fact that the limbic system communicates with the sensory areas for touch, smell, vision, and so forth accounts for the ability of any particular sensory stimulus to awaken a complex memory.

The limbic system is particularly involved in the emotions and in memory and learning.

Five Drugs of Abuse

Alcohol

Drugs that people take to alter the mood and/or emotional state affect normal body functions, often by interfering with neurotransmitter release or uptake in the brain. It is possible to drink alcoholic beverages in moderation, but alcohol is often abused. Alcohol use becomes "abuse," or an illness, when alcohol ingestion impairs an individual's social relationships, health, job efficiency, or judgment. While it is general knowledge that alcoholics are prone to drink until they become intoxicated, there is much debate as to what causes alcoholism. Some believe that alcoholism is due to an underlying psychological disorder, while others maintain that the condition is due to an inherited physiological disorder.

Alcohol is primarily metabolized in the liver, where it disrupts the normal workings of glycolysis and the Krebs cycle. The liver contains dehydrogenase enzymes, which carry out these reactions, reducing NAD in the process.

$$NAD \longrightarrow NADH_2$$

$$alcohol \longrightarrow \longrightarrow Acetyl\text{-}CoA$$

The supply of NAD in liver cells is used up by these reactions, and there is not enough free NAD left to keep glycolysis and the Krebs cycle running. The cell begins to ferment and lactic acid builds up. The pH of the blood decreases and becomes acidic.

Since the Krebs cycle is not working, excess active acetate cannot be broken down and it is converted to fat—the liver turns fatty. Fat accumulation, the first stage in liver deterioration, begins after only a single night of heavy drinking. If heavy drinking continues, fibrous scar tissue appears during a second stage of deterioration. If heavy drinking stops, the liver can still re-cover and become normal once again. If not, the final and irrevocable stage, cirrhosis of the liver, occurs: liver cells die, harden, and turn orange ("cirrhosis" means "orange").

The surgeon general recommends that pregnant women drink no alcohol at all. Alcohol crosses the placenta freely and can cause fetal alcohol syndrome, which is characterized by mental retardation and various physical defects.

Another problem is that heavy drinking interferes with good nutrition. Alcohol is energy intensive—the $NADH_2$ molecules that result from its breakdown can be used to produce ATP (adenosine triphosphate) molecules. However, these calories are empty because they do not supply any amino acids, vitamins, and minerals as other energy sources do. Without adequate vitamins, red and white blood cells cannot be formed in the bone marrow. The immune system becomes depressed, and the chances of stomach, liver, lung, pancreas, colon, and tongue cancer increase. Protein digestion and amino acid metabolism are so upset that even adequate protein intake will not prevent amino acid deficiencies. Muscles atrophy and weakness results. Fat deposits accumulate in the heart wall and hypertension develops. There is an increased risk of cardiac arrhythmias and stroke.

Marijuana

The dried flowering tops, leaves, and stems of the Indian hemp plant *Cannabis sativa* contain and are covered by a resin that is rich in THC (tetrahydrocannabinol). The names *Cannabis* and marijuana apply to either the plant or THC.

The effects of marijuana differ depending upon the strength and the amount consumed, the expertise of the user, and the setting in which it is taken. Usually, the user reports experiencing a mild euphoria along with alterations in vision and judgment, which result in distortions of space and time. Motor incoordi-nation occurs, as well as the inability to concentrate and to speak coherently.

Intermittent use of low-potency marijuana generally is not associated with obvious symptoms of toxicity, but heavy use can produce chronic intoxication. Intoxication is recognized by the presence of hallucinations, anxiety, depression, rapid flow of ideas, body image distortions, paranoid reactions, and similar psychotic symptoms. The terms cannabis psychosis and cannabis delirium refer to such reactions.

Marijuana is classified as a hallucinogen. It is possible that, like LSD (lysergic acid diethylamide), it has an effect on the action of serotonin, an excitatory neurotransmitter in the brain.

Marijuana use does not seem to produce physical dependence, but a psychological dependence on the euphoric and sedative effects can develop. Craving can also occur as a part of regular heavy use.

Usually marijuana is smoked in a cigarette form called a joint. Since this allows toxic substances, including carcinogens, to enter the lungs, chronic respiratory disease and lung cancer are considered dangers of long-term, heavy use. Some researchers claim that marijuana use leads to long-term brain impairment as well. Others report that males and females suffer reproductive dysfunctions. Fetal cannabis syndrome, which resembles fetal alcohol syndrome, has also been reported. In addition, marijuana has been called a gateway drug because adolescents who have used marijuana also tend to try other drugs. For example, in a study of 100 cocaine abusers, 60% had smoked marijuana for more than ten years.

Some psychologists are very concerned about the use of marijuana among adolescents. Marijuana can be used to avoid dealing with the personal problems that often develop during this maturational phase.

Cocaine

Cocaine is an alkaloid derived from the shrub *Erythroxylon coca*. Cocaine is sold in powder form and as crack, a more potent extract. Users often describe the feeling of euphoria that follows intake of the drug as a rush. Snorting (inhaling) produces this effect in a few minutes, injection, within 30 seconds, and smoking, in less than 10 seconds. Persons dependent upon the drug are, therefore, most likely to smoke cocaine. The rush lasts only a few seconds and then is replaced by a state of arousal, which lasts from 5 to 30 minutes. Then the user begins to feel restless, irritable, and depressed. To overcome these symptoms, the user is apt to take more of the drug, repeating the cycle again and again. A binge of this sort can go on for days, after which the individual suffers a crash. During the binge period, the user is hyperactive and has little desire for food or sleep but has an increased sex drive. During the crash period, the user is fatigued, depressed, and irritable, has memory and concentration problems, and displays no interest in sex. Indeed, men are often impotent. Other drugs, such as marijuana, alcohol, or heroin, often are taken to ease the symptoms of the crash.

Cocaine affects the concentration of dopamine, a neurotransmitter associated with behavioral states. After release into a synapse, dopamine ordinarily is withdrawn into the presynaptic cell for recycling and reuse. Cocaine prevents the reuptake of dopamine by the presynaptic membrane; this causes an excess of dopamine in the synaptic cleft so that the user experiences the sensation of a rush. The epinephrine-like effects of dopamine account for the state of arousal that lasts for some minutes after the rush experience.

With continued cocaine use, the body begins to make less dopamine to compensate for a seemingly excess supply. The user then experiences tolerance, withdrawal symptoms, and an intense craving for the drug. Cocaine, then, is extremely addictive.

The number of deaths from cocaine and the number of emergency-room admissions for drug reactions involving cocaine have increased greatly. High doses can cause seizures and cardiac and respiratory arrest.

Individuals who snort the drug can suffer damage to the nasal tissues and even perforation of the septum between the nostrils. Whether or not long-term cocaine abuse causes brain damage is not yet known. It is known, however, that babies born to addicts suffer withdrawal symptoms and may suffer neurological and developmental problems.

Heroin

Heroin is derived from morphine, an alkaloid of opium. Heroin usually is injected. After intravenous injection, the onset of action is noticeable within one minute and reaches its peak in about five minutes. There is a feeling of euphoria along with relief of pain. Side effects can include nausea, vomiting, dysphoria, and respiratory and circulatory depression leading to death.

Heroin binds to receptors meant for the endorphins, the special neurotransmitters that kill pain and produce a feeling of tranquility. They are believed to alleviate pain by preventing the release of a neurotransmitter termed substance P from certain sensory neurons in the region of the spinal cord. When substance P is released, pain is felt, and when substance P is not released, pain is not felt. Endorphins and heroin also bind to receptors on neurons that travel from the spinal cord to the limbic system. Stimulation of these can cause a feeling of pleasure.

Individuals who inject heroin become physically dependent on the drug. With time, the body's production of endorphins decreases. Tolerance develops so that the user needs to take more of the drug just to prevent withdrawal symptoms. The euphoria originally experienced upon injection is no longer felt.

Heroin withdrawal symptoms include perspiration, dilation of pupils, tremors, restlessness, abdominal cramps, gooseflesh, defecation, vomiting, and increase in systolic pressure and respiratory rate. Those who are excessively dependent may experience convulsions, respiratory failure, and death. Infants born to women who are physically dependent also experience these withdrawal symptoms.

Methamphetamine (Ice)

Methamphetamine is related to amphetamine, a well-known stimulant. Both methamphetamine and amphetamine have been drugs of abuse for some time, but a new form of methamphetamine known as "ice" is now used as an alternative to cocaine. Ice is a pure, crystalline hydrochloride salt that has the appearance of sheetlike crystals. Unlike cocaine, ice can be illegally produced in this country in laboratories; it does not need to be imported.

Ice, like crack, will vaporize in a pipe, so it can be smoked. After rapid absorption into the bloodstream, the drug moves quickly to the brain. It has the same stimulatory effect as cocaine, and subjects report they cannot distinguish between the two drugs after intravenous administration. Methamphetamine effects, however, persist for hours instead of a few seconds. Therefore, it is the preferred drug of abuse by many.

Summary

1. In humans, the nervous system, along with the endocrine system, regulates the other systems of the body and coordinates body functions.

2. A comparative study of the invertebrates shows a gradual increase in the complexity of the nervous system. The human nervous system, like that of the earthworm, is divided into the central and peripheral nervous systems.

3. Neurons, cells that conduct nerve impulses, have three parts: dendrite(s), cell body, and axon. The dendrites and the cell body receive information from the environment, and if stimulation is sufficient, nerve impulses travel down the axon to where neurotransmitters are stored in vesicles.

4. The nerve impulse, which is recognized when the resting potential becomes an action potential, is an electrochemical phenomenon involving the movement first of sodium ions and then of potassium ions across the membrane.

    Resting potential: sodium-potassium pump at work; inside of the neuron is negative (−65 mV) compared to the outside of the neuron.

    Action potential: (1) sodium ions move to the inside, making it positive compared to outside (+40 mV); (2) potassium ions move to the outside, making the inside negative again compared to the outside (−65 mV).

5. The nerve impulse is self-propagating because the gated channels that allow sodium and potassium ions to flow down their concentration gradients are sensitive to a nearby decrease in the membrane potential.

6. Saltatory conduction occurs (in myelinated fibers) when the action potential jumps from one neurolemmal node to another. This accounts for the great speed of impulses in these fibers.

7. Transmission across a synapse usually requires neurotransmitters because there is a small space, the synaptic cleft, that separates one neuron from another. The neurotransmitters released at the ends of axons may be either excitatory or inhibitory.

8. Acetylcholine and norepinephrine are well-known neurotransmitters. After its release, acetylcholine is destroyed by acetylcholinesterase in the synaptic cleft.

9. Within the human peripheral nervous system, the somatic system includes cranial and spinal nerves. Spinal nerves extend from the spinal cord and contain both sensory and motor fibers. It is possible to use them to trace the path of a reflex arc from receptor to effector, as described here.

    Sensory neuron: receptor generates nerve impulses that travel in the dendrite to the cell body and then to the axon, which enters the cord.

    Interneuron: transmits impulses from the dorsal to the ventral root of the cord.

    Motor neuron: impulses begin in the dendrites and cell body and then pass out of the cord by way of the axon, which innervates an effector.

10. The autonomic system controls internal organs and includes the sympathetic and parasympathetic systems.

11. The human central nervous system includes the spinal cord and the brain. In the brain, the medulla oblongata and hypothalamus regulate internal organs. The thalamus receives sensory input and passes it to the cerebrum. The cerebellum functions in muscle coordination.

12. A survey of vertebrates shows a continual evolutionary increase in the relative size of the cerebrum, with its greatest development in humans. The highly convoluted cerebral cortex is divided into lobes, each of which has specific functions. In general, the cerebrum is responsible for consciousness, sensory perception, motor control, and all the higher forms of thought.

13. Research in invertebrates indicates that learning is accompanied by an increase in the number of synapses; research in monkeys indicates that the limbic system is involved. There are short-term and long-term memories; the involvement of the limbic system explains why emotionally charged events result in vivid long-term memories.

Writing Across the Curriculum

In order to practice writing skills, students should write out the answers to any or all of the study questions and the critical thinking questions. The study questions are sequenced in the same order as the text. Answers to the objective questions, and suggested answers to the critical thinking questions, are in appendix D.

Study Questions

1. What is the overall function of the nervous and endocrine systems? How do they differ in regard to this function?   712

2. Trace the evolution of the nervous system by contrasting the organization of the nervous system in hydras, planarians, earthworms, and humans.   712–13

3. Describe the structure of a neuron and give a function for each part mentioned. Name three types of neurons, and give a function for each.   714

4. What are the major events of an action potential, and what ion changes are associated with each event?   716–17

5. Describe the mode of action of a neurotransmitter at a synapse, including how it is stored and how it is destroyed.   718

6. Contrast the structure and function of the peripheral and central nervous systems.   720, 724

7. Trace the path of a spinal reflex.   721

8. Contrast the sympathetic and parasympathetic divisions of the autonomic system.   723

9. Name the major parts of the human brain and give a principal function for each part.   724–27

10. Describe the limbic system and discuss its possible involvement in learning and memory.   727

1. Which is the most complete list of animals that have both a central nervous system (CNS) and a peripheral nervous system (PNS)?
   a. hydra, planarian, earthworm, rabbit, human
   b. planarian, earthworm, rabbit, human
   c. earthworm, rabbit, human
   d. rabbit, human

2. Which of these are the first and last elements in a spinal reflex?
   a. axon and dendrite
   b. sense organ and muscle effector
   c. ventral horn and dorsal horn
   d. motor neuron and sensory neuron

3. Which term does not belong with the others?
   a. cerebrum
   b. cerebral cortex
   c. cerebral hemispheres
   d. cerebellum

4. A spinal nerve takes nerve impulses
   a. to the CNS.
   b. away from the CNS.
   c. both to and away from the CNS.
   d. only inside the CNS.

5. Which of these correctly describes the distribution of ions on either side of an axon when it is not conducting a nerve impulse?
   a. sodium ions (Na^+) outside and potassium ions (K^+) inside
   b. K^+ outside and Na^+ inside
   c. charged protein outside; Na^+ and K^+ inside
   d. Na^+ and K^+ outside and water only inside

6. When the action potential begins, sodium gates open, allowing Na^+ to cross the membrane. Now the polarity changes to
   a. negative outside and positive inside.
   b. positive outside and negative inside.
   c. There is no difference in charge between outside and inside.
   d. Any one of these could be correct.

7. Transmission of the nerve impulse across a synapse is accomplished by the
   a. movement of Na^+ and K^+.
   b. release of neurotransmitters.
   c. Both of these are correct.
   d. Neither of these is correct.

8. The autonomic system has two divisions called the
   a. CNS and PNS.
   b. somatic and skeletal systems.
   c. efferent and afferent systems.
   d. sympathetic and parasympathetic systems.

11. Label this diagram of a reflex arc.

9. Synaptic vesicles are
   a. at the ends of dendrites and axons.
   b. at the ends of axons only.
   c. along the length of all long fibers.
   d. All of these are correct.

10. Which of these is mismatched?
   a. cerebrum—consciousness
   b. thalamus—motor and sensory centers
   c. hypothalamus—internal environment regulator
   d. cerebellum—motor coordination

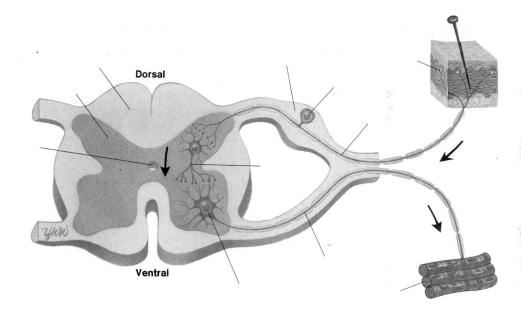

Dorsal

Ventral

▸ **Concepts and Critical Thinking**

1. *All systems of an animal's body contribute to homeostasis.*
   List several ways in which the nervous system contributes to homeostasis.

2. *Segmentation leads to specialization of parts.*
   How is segmentation, along with specialization of parts, reflected in the structure of the nervous system?

3. *Structure suits function.*
   How does the structure of a neuron suit its function?

Selected Key Terms

acetylcholine (ACh) (uh-set-ul-KOH-leen) A neurotransmitter active in both the peripheral and central nervous systems. 718

acetylcholinesterase (AChE) (uh-set-ul-koh-luh-NES-tuh-rays) An enzyme that breaks down acetylcholine bound to postsynaptic receptors within a synapse. 718

action potential Nerve impulse; the membrane potential of an active neuron. 718

autonomic system (awt-uh-NAHM-ik) A division of the peripheral nervous system that regulates internal organs. [Gk. *autonomia,* independence] 723

axon The part of a neuron that conducts impulses from the cell body to the synapse. [Gk. *axo,* axis] 714

central canal A tube within the spinal cord that is continuous with the ventricles of the brain and contains cerebrospinal fluid. 720

central nervous system (CNS) The brain and spinal cord. 712

cerebellum (ser-uh-BEL-um) Portion of the brain that coordinates skeletal muscles to produce smooth, graceful motions. 725

cerebrospinal fluid (suh-ree-broh-SPYN-ul) A fluid found in the ventricles of the brain, in the central canal of the spinal cord, and in association with the meninges. [L. *cereb,* brain, and *spin,* spine] 724

cerebrum (suh-REE-brum) The main part of the brain consisting of two large masses, or cerebral hemispheres; the largest part of the brain in mammals. 726

dendrite The part of a neuron that sends impulses toward the cell body. [Gk. *dendro,* tree] 714

ganglion (pl., ganglia) (GANG-glee-un) A knot or bundle of neuron cell bodies usually outside the central nervous system. [Gk. *ganglion,* knot on a string] 720

hypothalamus (hy-poh-THAL-uh-mus) A part of the brain that helps regulate the internal environment of the body; involved in control of heart rate, body temperature, water balance, and glandular secretions of the stomach and pituitary gland. [Gk. *hypo,* under] 725

interneuron Neuron, located within the central nervous system, conveying messages between parts of the central nervous system. [L. *inter,* between, and Gk. *neuro,* nerve] 714

limbic system Pathways linking the hypothalamus to some areas of the cerebral cortex; governs learning and memory and various emotions such as pleasure, fear, and happiness. 727

medulla oblongata (muh-DUL-uh ahb-lawng-GAHT-uh) A part of the brain stem controlling heartbeat, blood pressure, breathing, and other vital functions. It also serves to connect the spinal cord and the cerebrum. [L. *medull,* marrow, and *oblongus,* rather long] 724

meninges (sing., meninx) (muh-NIN-jeez) Protective membranous coverings about the central nervous system. [Gk. *menin,* membrane] 727

midbrain The part of the brain located below the thalamus and above the pons. 727

myelin sheath (MY-uh-lun) A white, fatty material—derived from the membrane of neurolemmocytes—that forms a covering for nerve fibers. [Gk. *myelo,* spinal cord] 714

nerve A bundle of long axons and/or dendrites outside the central nervous system. 720

neuron A nerve cell; composed of dendrite(s), a cell body, and an axon. [Gk. *neuro,* nerve] 714

neurotransmitter A chemical stored at the ends of axons that is responsible for transmission across a synapse. [Gk. *neuro,* nerve, and L. *trans,* across] 718

norepinephrine (NE) Neurotransmitter active in the peripheral and central nervous systems; a hormone secreted by adrenal medulla. 718

parasympathetic system A division of the autonomic system that is active under normal conditions; uses acetylcholine as a neurotransmitter. 723

peripheral nervous system (PNS) The nerves that branch off of the central nervous system. [Gk. *peripher,* circumference] 712

pons A part of the brain stem above the medulla oblongata and below the midbrain. It also serves to connect the cerebellar hemispheres. [L. *pont,* bridge] 724

reflex An automatic, involuntary response of an organism to a stimulus. [L. *reflectere,* bend back] 721

resting potential The membrane potential of an inactive neuron. 717

saltatory conduction The movement of nerve impulses from one neurolemmal node to another along a myelinated axon. [L. *saltator,* leaper] 717

spinal cord Part of the central nervous system; the nerve cord that is continuous with the base of the brain and housed within the vertebral column. 720

sympathetic system A division of the autonomic system that is active under "fight or flight" conditions; uses norepinephrine as a neurotransmitter. 723

synapse (SIN-aps) A junction between neurons consisting of the presynaptic (axon) membrane, the synaptic cleft, and the postsynaptic (usually dendrite) membrane. [Gk. *synapse,* union] 718

thalamus (THAL-uh-mus) A part of the brain that serves as the integrating center for sensory input, it plays a role in arousing the cerebral cortex. 725

ventricle A cavity in an organ, such as a ventricle of the brain. 724

SENSE ORGANS

Learning Objectives

- State the function of receptors within sense organs.   734

Sensing Chemicals

- Explain why the receptors for taste and smell are categorized as chemoreceptors.   734
- Describe the receptors for taste and smell in humans.   734–35

Sensing Light

- In general, contrast the eye of arthropods with that of humans.   736
- List the structures of the human eye, and give a function for each.   737

- Contrast the action of the sight receptors—the rods and the cones.   738, 740

Sensing Mechanical Stimuli

- Give examples of various types of mechanoreceptors in animals.   742
- List the structures of the human ear, and give a function for each.   742–44
- Explain how the ear serves as an organ for dynamic and static equilibrium.   744–45
- Describe the organ of Corti, and explain how it functions to permit hearing.   745

Similar sense organs lead to similar sensations for these two types of mammals.

Receptors, present in sense organs, monitor changes in the external and internal environment. Each type of receptor has a low threshold for a particular stimulus; for this reason, eyes respond to light, and ears respond to sound waves and gravity. Receptors do not interpret stimuli—they act merely as transducers that receive stimuli and generate nerve impulses. Interpretation is the function of the brain, which has a specific region for receiving nerve impulses from each of the sense organs. Impulses arriving at a particular sensory area of the brain can be interpreted in only one way; for example, those arriving at the visual area result in sight sensation, and those arriving at the olfactory area result in smell sensation. Usually the brain is able to discriminate the type of stimulus, the intensity of the stimulus, and the origin of the stimulus. On occasion, the brain can be fooled, as when a blow to the eyes causes you to "see stars."

Interoceptors located within the body monitor such conditions as blood pressure, expansion of lungs and bladder, and movement of limbs. *Exteroceptors* are located near the surface of the animal and respond to outer stimuli. Both types of receptors send information to the brain, and both are needed for homeostasis and to promote appropriate behavior. This chapter, however, concerns only exteroceptors.

Receptors only receive stimuli and generate nerve impulses, which are conducted to the spinal cord and/or brain. Sensation is dependent upon the brain.

SENSING CHEMICALS

The receptors responsible for taste and smell are termed **chemoreceptors** [Gk. *chemo,* chemistry, and L. *recept,* receive] because they are sensitive to certain chemical substances in food, liquids, and air. Chemoreception is found universally in animals and is therefore believed to be the most primitive sense. Chemoreceptors are present all over the body of planaria, but they are concentrated on the auricles at the sides of the head. In crustacea, (e.g., lobsters and crabs), chemoreceptors are widely distributed over all the appendages and antennae. They sample food and detect airborne pheromones, which are chemical messages passed between individuals. In insects, such as the housefly, chemoreceptors are found largely on the feet—flies taste with their feet instead of their mouth. In amphibians, chemoreceptors are located in the nose, in the mouth, and over the entire skin. They are

Figure 42.1

Taste buds. **a.** Elevations on the tongue are called papillae. The location of those containing taste buds responsive to sweet, sour, salt, and bitter is indicated. **b.** Enlargement of papillae. **c.** The taste buds are found along the walls of the papillae. **d.** The various cells that make up a taste bud. Taste cells in a bud end in microvilli that are sensitive to the chemicals exhibiting the tastes noted in **(a).** When the chemicals combine with membrane-bound receptors, nerve impulses are generated.

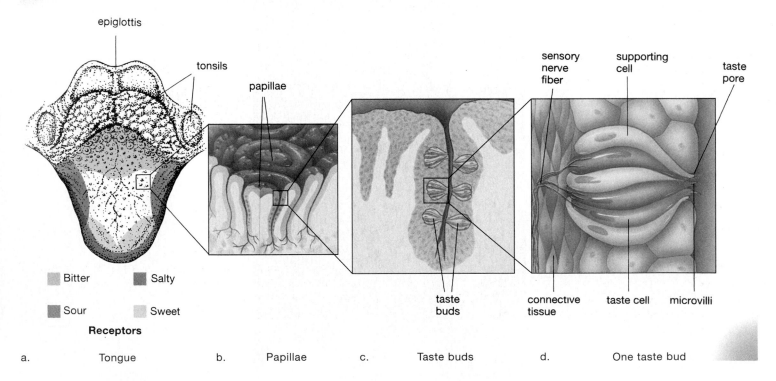

used to locate mates, detect harmful chemicals, and find food. In mammals, the receptors for taste are located in the mouth and the receptors for smell are located in the nose.

Tasting with Taste Buds

Taste buds contain the receptors for the sense of taste in humans. Many lie along the walls of the papillae, the small elevations on the tongue that are visible to the naked eye. Isolated ones are also present on the surface of the hard palate, the pharynx, and the epiglottis (fig. 42.1).

Taste buds are pockets of cells that extend through the tongue epithelium and open at a taste pore. Taste buds have supporting cells and a number of elongated taste cells that end in *microvilli,* which project through the taste pore. It is the microvilli of the cells that are stimulated by various chemicals in the environment. Humans are believed to have four types of taste buds, each type stimulated by chemicals that result in a bitter, a sour, a salty, or a sweet sensation.

Smelling with the Nose

Olfactory cells [L. *olfact,* smell], located high in the roof of the nasal cavity, are the receptors for the sense of smell in humans (fig. 42.2). The olfactory cells are actually modified neurons that synapse with the nerve fibers making up the olfactory nerve. Each olfactory cell has a tuft of about five cilia, which bear receptors for various chemicals. Research resulting in the stereochemical theory of smell has shown that different smells may be related to the various shapes of the molecules. When molecules combine with the receptor sites, nerve impulses are generated in the olfactory nerve fibers. Within the olfactory bulbs, which are paired masses of gray matter beneath the frontal lobes of the cerebrum, olfactory tracts take this sensory information to an olfactory area of the cerebrum.

In most vertebrates, the sense of smell is much more acute than the sense of taste. The human nose, for example, can detect one 25-millionth of 1 mg of mercaptan, the odoriferous chemical given off by a skunk. This averages out to approximately one molecule per sensory ending. Yet, humans have a weak sense of smell compared to other vertebrates, such as dogs.

The olfactory receptors, like touch and temperature receptors, adapt to outside stimuli. In other words, after a while, the presence of a particular chemical no longer causes the olfactory cells to generate nerve impulses, and we are no longer aware of a particular smell.

The sense of taste and the sense of smell supplement each other, creating a combined effect when interpreted by the cerebral cortex. When you have a cold, food seems to lose its taste, but actually the ability to sense its smell is temporarily absent. This may work in reverse also. When we smell something, some of the molecules move from the nose down into the mouth and stimulate certain taste buds. Thus, part of what we refer to as smell is actually taste.

Figure 42.2

Olfactory cell location and anatomy. **a.** The olfactory area in humans is located high in the nasal cavity. **b.** Enlargement of the olfactory cells shows they are modified neurons located between supporting cells. When olfactory cells are stimulated by chemicals, olfactory nerve fibers conduct nerve impulses to the olfactory bulb. An olfactory tract within the bulb takes the nerve impulses to the brain.

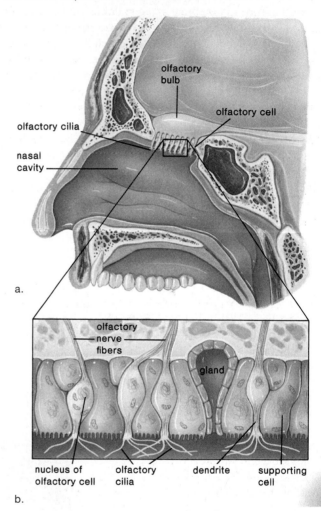

The receptors for taste (taste cells) and the receptors for smell (olfactory cells) work together to give us our sense of taste and our sense of smell.

SENSING LIGHT

Animals that lack photoreceptors largely depend on the senses of hearing and smell rather than sight. Moles, which are mammals that live underground, utilize their sense of smell and touch rather than eyesight. In its simplest form, a **photoreceptor** [Gk. *photo,* light, and L. *recept,* receive] indicates only the presence of light and its intensity. The "eyespots" of planaria also allow these animals to determine the direction of light. Image-forming eyes are found among four invertebrate groups: cnidaria, annelids, mollusks, and arthropods. Arthropods have **compound eyes** composed of many independent visual units called *ommatidia,* each possessing all the elements needed for light reception (fig. 42.3). Both the cornea and crystalline cone function as lenses to direct light rays toward the photoreceptors. The photoreceptors generate nerve impulses, which pass to the brain by way of optic nerve fibers. The outer pigment cells absorb stray light rays so that the rays do not pass from one visual unit to the other. The image, which results from all the stimulated visual units, is crude because the small size of compound eyes limits the number of visual units that still might number as many as 28,000. The advantage of a compound eye is its excellent motion detection. What we see as one continuous image becomes a series of separate images for flies and this accounts for how well they avoid capture.

Insects have color vision, but they make use of a slightly shorter range of the electromagnetic spectrum compared to humans. They can see the longest of the ultraviolet rays, and this enables them to be especially sensitive to the reproductive parts of flowers, which reflect particular ultraviolet patterns (fig. 42.4). Some fishes, reptiles, and most birds are believed to have color vision, but among mammals, only humans and other primates have color vision. It would seem, then, that this trait was adaptive for life in trees, which accounts for its retention in these few mammals.

Vertebrates and certain mollusks, like the squid and the octopus, have a *camera type of eye.* Since mollusks and vertebrates are not closely related, this similarity is an example of convergent evolution. A *single* lens focuses an image of the visual field on the photoreceptors, which are closely packed together. In vertebrates the lens changes shape to aid focusing, but in mollusks the lens moves back and forth. All of the photoreceptors taken together can be compared to a piece of film in a camera. The human eye is more complex than a camera, however, as we shall see.

Figure 42.3

Compound eye. Each visual unit of a compound eye has a cornea and a lens that focus light onto photoreceptors. The photoreceptors generate nerve impulses that are transmitted to the brain, where interpretation produces a mosaic image.

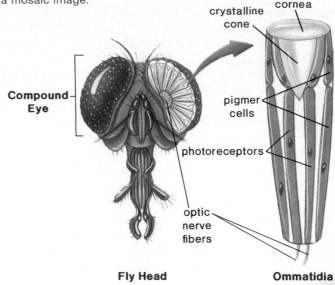

Compound Eye · Fly Head · crystalline cone · cornea · pigmer cells · photoreceptors · optic nerve fibers · Ommatidia

Figure 42.4

Evening primose, *Oenothera,* as seen by humans (*left*) and insects (*right*). Humans see no markings, but insects see distinct blotches because their eyes respond to ultraviolet rays. These types of markings often highlight the reproductive parts of flowers where insects feed on nectar and pick up pollen at the same time.

Figure 42.5

Anatomy of the human eye. Notice that the sclera becomes the cornea and that the choroid is connected to the ciliary body and the iris. The retina contains the receptors for vision; the fovea centralis is the region where vision is most acute. A blind spot occurs where the optic nerve leaves the retina. There are no receptors for light in this location.

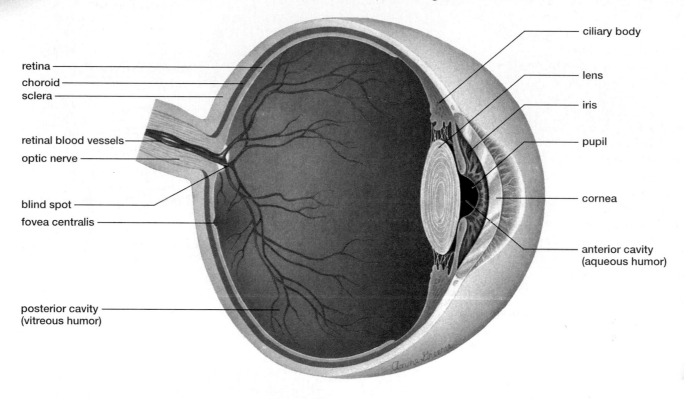

Table 42.1	
Function of Parts of the Eye	
Part	**Function**
Lens	Refracts and focuses light rays
Iris	Regulates light entrance
Pupil	Admits light
Choroid	Absorbs stray light
Sclera	Protects and supports eyeball
Cornea	Refracts light rays
Humors	Refract light rays
Ciliary body	Holds lens in place, accommodation
Retina	Contains receptors for sight
Rods	Make black-and-white vision possible
Cones	Make color vision possible
Optic nerve	Transmits impulse to brain
Fovea centralis	Makes acute vision possible

Seeing with the Eye

The most important parts of the human eye and their functions are listed in table 42.1. The human eye, which is an elongated sphere about 2.5 cm in diameter, has three layers, or coats: the sclera, the choroid, and the retina (fig. 42.5). The outer layer, the **sclera** [Gk. *scler,* hard], is an opaque, white, fibrous layer that covers most of the eye; in front of the eye the sclera becomes the transparent cornea, the window of the eye. The middle, thin, dark-brown layer, the **choroid** [Gk. *choroid,* like a membrane], contains many blood vessels and pigment that absorbs stray light rays. Toward the front of the eye, the choroid thickens and forms the ring-shaped ciliary body and finally becomes a thin, circular, muscular diaphragm, the *iris,* which regulates the size of an opening called the *pupil.* The *lens,* which is attached to the ciliary body by ligaments, divides the cavity of the eye into two portions. A basic, watery solution called *aqueous humor* fills the anterior cavity between the cornea and the lens. A viscous, gelatinous material, the *vitreous humor,* fills the large posterior cavity behind the lens.

Figure 42.6

Anatomy of the retina. The retina is the inner layer of the eye. Rods and cones are located at the back of the retina, followed by the bipolar cells and the ganglionic cells, whose fibers become the optic nerve. (Notice that rods share bipolar cells but cones do not. Cones, therefore, distinguish more detail.) The optic nerve carries impulses to the occipital lobe of the cerebrum.

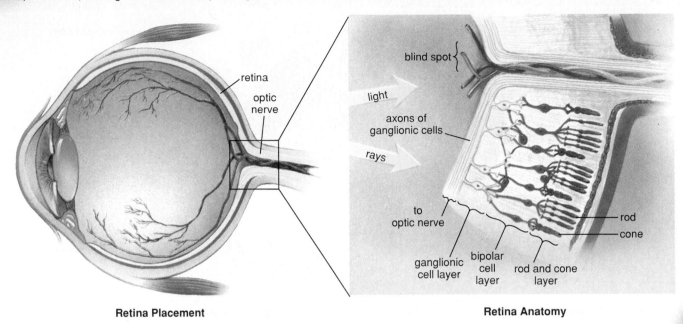

Retina Placement

Retina Anatomy

How the Retina Is Structured

The inner layer of the eye, the **retina** [L. *retin,* net], contains the receptors for sight: **rods** and **cones** (fig. 42.6). Nerve impulses initiated by the rods and the cones are passed to the bipolar cells, which in turn pass them to the ganglionic cells. The fibers of these cells pass in front of the retina, forming the **optic nerve** [Gk. *opti,* eye], which carries the nerve impulses to the brain. Notice that there are many more rods and cones than nerve fibers leaving ganglionic cells. This means that there is considerable mixing of messages and a certain amount of integration before nerve impulses are sent to the brain. There are no rods or cones at the point where the optic nerve passes through the retina; therefore, this point is called the blind spot.

The center of the retina contains a special region called the fovea centralis, an oval, yellowish area with a depression where there are only cone cells (see fig. 42.5). In the fovea centralis or fovea, color vision is most acute in daylight; at night, it is barely sensitive. At this time, the rods in the rest of the retina are active.

Blindness can have many causes, but one type of blindness that occurs generally later in life is due to glaucoma. Normally, aqueous humor produced by the ciliary body leaves the anterior cavity by way of tiny ducts. When a person has glaucoma, these drainage ducts are blocked, and aqueous humor builds up. The resulting pressure compresses the arteries that serve the nerve fibers of the retina. The nerve fibers begin to die due to lack of nutrients, and the person becomes partially blind. Over time, total blindness can result.

> **The human eye has three layers: the outer sclera, the middle choroid, and the inner retina. Only the retina contains receptors for sight.**

Focusing Uses the Lens

Light rays entering the eye are bent (refracted) as they pass through the cornea, the lens, and the humors and are brought to a focus on the retina. The lens is relatively flat when viewing distant objects but rounds up for near objects because light rays must be bent to a greater degree when viewing a near object. These changes of the lens shape are called accommodation (fig. 42.7).

Because of refraction, the image on the retina is rotated 180° from the actual, but it is believed that this image is righted in the brain. In one experiment, scientists wore glasses that inverted and reversed the field. At first, they had difficulty adjusting to the placement of objects, but they soon became accustomed to their inverted world. Experiments such as this suggest that if the retina sees the world "upside down," the brain has learned to see it right side up.

> **The lens, assisted by the cornea and the humors, focuses images on the retina.**

Figure 42.7

Focusing. **a.** Light rays from each point on an object are bent by the cornea and the lens in such a way that they are directed to a single point after emerging from the lens. By this process, an inverted image of the object forms on the retina. **b.** When focusing on a distant object, the lens is flat because the ciliary muscle is relaxed and the suspensory ligament is taut. **c.** When focusing on a near object, the lens accommodates: it becomes rounded because the ciliary muscle contracts, causing the suspensory ligament to relax.

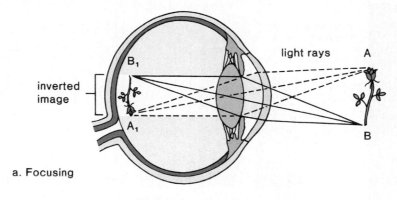

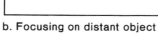

a. Focusing

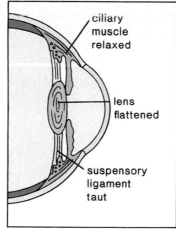

b. Focusing on distant object

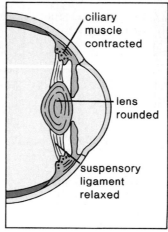

c. Focusing on near object

Helping the Eye

With normal aging, the lens loses its ability to accommodate for near objects; therefore, persons frequently need reading glasses once they reach middle age. Aging, or possibly exposure to the sun, also makes the lens subject to cataracts; the lens can become opaque and therefore incapable of transmitting light rays. Currently surgery is the only viable treatment for cataracts. First, a surgeon opens the eye near the rim of the cornea. The enzyme zonulysin may be used to digest away the ligaments holding the lens in place. Most surgeons then use a cryoprobe, which freezes the lens for easy removal. An intraocular lens attached to the iris can then be implanted so that the patient does not need to wear thick glasses or contact lenses.

Persons who can see a near object but have trouble seeing what is designated as a size 20 letter 20 feet away are said to be nearsighted. These individuals often have an elongated eyeball, and when they attempt to look at a distant object, the image is brought to focus in front of the retina. Usually these people must wear concave lenses, which diverge the light rays so that the image can be focused on the retina. There is a new treatment for nearsightedness called radial keratotomy, or radial K. From four to eight cuts are made in the cornea so that they radiate out from the center like spokes on a wheel. When the cuts heal, the cornea is flattened. Although some patients are satisfied with the result, others complain of glare and varying visual acuity.

Persons who can easily see the optometrist's chart but cannot easily see near objects are farsighted. They often have a shortened eyeball, and when they try to see near objects, the image is focused behind the retina. These persons must wear a convex lens to increase the bending of light rays so that the image can be focused on the retina. When the cornea or lens is uneven, the image is fuzzy. This condition, called **astigmatism,** can be corrected by an unevenly ground lens to compensate for the uneven cornea.

Figure 42.8

Structure and function of rods and cones. The outer segment of rods and cones contains stacks of membranous disks, which contain visual pigments. In rods, the membrane of each disk contains rhodopsin, a complex molecule containing the protein opsin and the pigment retinal. When retinal absorbs light energy, it changes shape, activating rhodopsin to begin a series of reactions that end when cGMP (cyclic guanosine monophosphate) is converted to GMP. Thereafter, ion channels close.

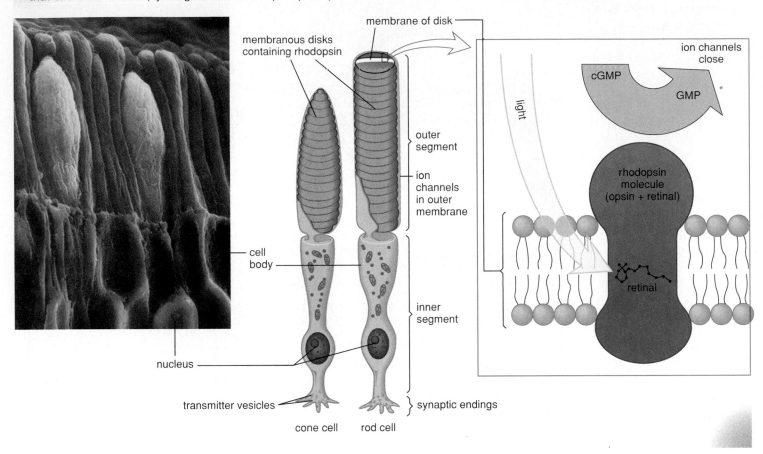

Seeing Uses Chemistry

Only dim light is required to stimulate rods; therefore, they are responsible for *night vision.* The numerous rods are also better at detecting motion than cones, but they cannot provide distinct and/or color vision. This causes objects to appear blurred and look gray in dim light. Many molecules of **rhodopsin** [Gk. *rhodo,* rose-red, and *opsis,* view] are located within the membrane of the disks (lamellae) found in the outer segment of the rods (fig. 42.8c). Rhodopsin is a complex molecule that contains protein (opsin) and a pigment molecule called *retinal,* which is a derivative of vitamin A. When light strikes retinal, it changes shape and rhodopsin is activated. As discussed in the reading on page 741, the membrane of the outer segment of a rod cell has many ion channels that are held open in the dark by cyclic guanosine monophosphate (cGMP). Activation of rhodopsin leads to a reduction in the amount of cGMP and closure of some sodium ion channels. The resulting increased negativity of the rod interior leads to change in the frequency of impulses in bipolar and ganglionic cell layers that send messages to the brain. Rod cells are sensitive

to dim light because one molecule of rhodopsin acts on many proteins that cause the cleavage of many cGMP molecules. There has been an *amplification* of the original stimulus!

The cones, located primarily in the fovea and activated by bright light, detect the fine detail and the color of an object. *Color vision* depends on three different kinds of cones, which contain pigments called the B(blue), G(green), and R(red) pigments. Each pigment is made up of retinal and opsin, but there is a slight difference in the opsin structure of each, which accounts for their individual absorption patterns. Various combinations of cones are believed to be stimulated by in-between shades of color, and the combined nerve impulses are interpreted in the brain as a particular color.

> In the human eye, the receptors for sight are the rods and the cones. The rods are responsible for vision in dim light, and the cones are responsible for vision in bright light and for color vision.

Ion Channels and Vision

My research concerns the functional properties of membrane proteins, called cGMP[1]-activated channels, which are critically involved in allowing rods to respond to light. When rhodopsin, the visual pigment located in rods, absorbs a photon of light, it begins an enzyme cascade that lowers the concentration of intracellular cGMP. In the dark, cGMP opens channels for sodium ions (Na^+) in the plasma membrane. In the light, the reduced amount of cGMP causes some ion channels to close, and the result is that the inside of the rod becomes more negatively charged. This ultimately leads to an alteration in the frequency of neurotransmitter release to other retinal cells, which relay messages to the brain.

I use amphibian rods in order to study cGMP-activated channels. In collaboration with several colleagues, my work has revealed that the channel opens rapidly after binding with several molecules of cGMP, and that the channel transports sodium ions at high rates when other ions such as calcium

[1] GMP is a nucleotide that contains the base guanine, the sugar ribose, and one phosphate group. In cyclic GMP (cGMP), the single phosphate is attached to ribose in two places.

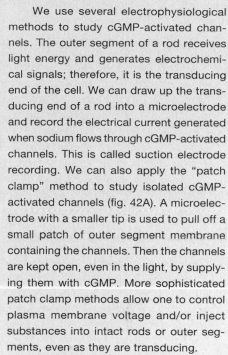

light microscope   patch clamp amplifier

Anita Zimmerman
Brown University, Providence, Rhode Island

(Ca^{++}) and magnesium (Mg^{++}) are absent. (These doubly charged ions tend to stick in the channel, falsely giving the impression that the channel might be a slow-acting carrier rather than a pore through which sodium ions freely move.) Further, we have found that the sensitivity of the channel to cGMP is modified by intracellular factors, such as enzymes and calcium-binding proteins.

We use several electrophysiological methods to study cGMP-activated channels. The outer segment of a rod receives light energy and generates electrochemical signals; therefore, it is the transducing end of the cell. We can draw up the transducing end of a rod into a microelectrode and record the electrical current generated when sodium flows through cGMP-activated channels. This is called suction electrode recording. We can also apply the "patch clamp" method to study isolated cGMP-activated channels (fig. 42A). A microelectrode with a smaller tip is used to pull off a small patch of outer segment membrane containing the channels. Then the channels are kept open, even in the light, by supplying them with cGMP. More sophisticated patch clamp methods allow one to control plasma membrane voltage and/or inject substances into intact rods or outer segments, even as they are transducing.

Probably the most powerful technique for studying cGMP-activated channels and the transduction process is the combination of electrophysiological techniques with molecular biology methodology. We modify the channels by specific mutations, and the resulting functional changes are then studied using patch clamp methods. This approach is especially applicable to our current and future work determining what role cGMP-activated channels play in light adaptation and how the channel's behavior is modified by intracellular factors. The results of these studies are expected to be applicable to the treatment of certain visual diseases.

Many other types of cells (besides rod cells) are now known to contain cGMP-activated channels. Ion channels in general play a key role in controlling hormone secretion, muscle contraction, communication among brain cells, cell homeostasis, and numerous other vital functions. Undoubtedly, the more we learn about the role of cGMP-activated channels in vision, the more we will know about ion channels in general.

Figure 42A

A salamander rod drawn into a suction electrode, with a patch clamp electrode injecting a fluorescent dye.

SENSING MECHANICAL STIMULI

Mechanoreceptors [Gk. *mechano,* instrument, and L. *recept,* receive] are sensitive to mechanical stimuli, such as pressure, sound waves, and gravity. Human skin contains various types of mechanoreceptors, such as *touch receptors* and pressure receptors. A pressure receptor, called the Pacinian corpuscle, is shaped like an onion and consists of a series of concentric layers of connective tissue wrapped around the end (dendrite) of a sensory neuron. In contrast, *pain receptors* are only the unmyelinated ("naked") ends (dendrites) of the fibers of sensory neurons. Some pain receptors are especially sensitive to mechanical stimuli; others are most sensitive to temperature or chemicals.

Hair cells, which are named for the cilia they bear, are often mechanoreceptors in various specialized vertebrate sense organs. Fishes and amphibians have a series of such receptors called the lateral line system, which detect water currents and pressure waves from nearby objects. In primitive fishes and aquatic amphibians, the receptors are located on the body surface, but in advanced fishes, they are located within a canal that has openings to the outside (fig. 42.9). A lateral line receptor is a collection of hair cells with cilia embedded in a mass of gelatinous material known as a cupula. When the cupula bends due to pressure waves, the hair cells initiate nerve impulses. The otic vesicles of fishes are derived from a portion of the lateral line system.

Figure 42.9

Lateral line system of fishes. Location of the system (*upper*); longitudinal section of the system (*lower*). A main canal has openings to the exterior. Lining the canal are hair cells (embedded in cupulae) that act as sense receptors for pressure.

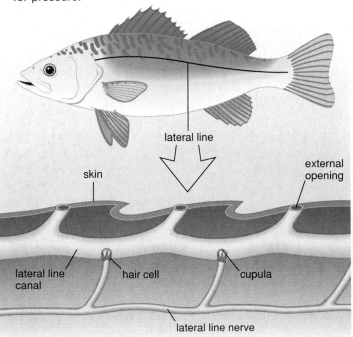

Responding to Gravity and Sound

Table 42.2 lists the most important parts of the human ear and their function. As figure 42.10 shows, the human ear has an outer, a middle, and an inner portion. The evolution of the inner ear of humans can be traced back to the lateral line system of fishes. However, the inner ear of humans contains both equilibrium and sound receptors.

The *outer ear* consists of the pinna (external flap) and *auditory canal*. The auditory canal is lined with fine hairs, which filter the air. Modified sweat glands are located in the upper wall of the canal; these secrete earwax, which helps guard the ear against entrance of foreign materials such as air pollutants.

The *middle ear* begins at the **tympanic membrane** [Gk. *tympan,* drum] and ends at a bony wall that has small openings—the *oval window* and the *round window*—covered by membranes. Three small bones are located between the tympanic membrane and the oval window. Collectively called *ossicles,* individually they are the malleus (hammer), the incus (anvil), and the stapes (stirrup), named for their structural resemblance to these objects. The auditory (eustachian) tube extends from the middle ear to the pharynx and permits the equalization of air pressure between the inside and the outside of the ear. Chewing gum, yawning, and swallowing help move air through the auditory tube during ascent and descent in airplanes or elevators. Atmospheric pressure pressing against the inner surface of the tympanic membrane then equals that pressing on its outer surface.

The middle ear is continuous with mastoid air spaces in the temporal bone of the skull. Therefore, a middle ear infection can lead to mastoiditis, a serious medical condition that should be treated promptly.

Table 42.2	
Function of the Parts of the Ear	
Part	**Function**
Outer Ear	
Pinna	Collects sound waves
Auditory canal	Filters air
Middle Ear	
Tympanic membrane and ossicles	Amplify sound waves
Auditory tube	Equalizes air pressure
Inner Ear	
Vestibule (contains utricle and saccule)	Balance (static equilibrium)
Semicircular canals	Balance (dynamic equilibrium)
Cochlea	Transmits pressure waves that cause the organ of Corti to generate nerve impulses resulting in hearing

Figure 42.10

Anatomy of the human ear. In the middle ear, the malleus (hammer), the incus (anvil), and the stapes (stirrup) amplify sound waves. Otosclerosis is a condition in which the stapes becomes attached to the inner ear and is unable to carry out its normal function. It can be replaced by a plastic piston, and thereafter the individual hears normally because sound waves are transmitted as usual to the cochlea, which contains the receptors for hearing.

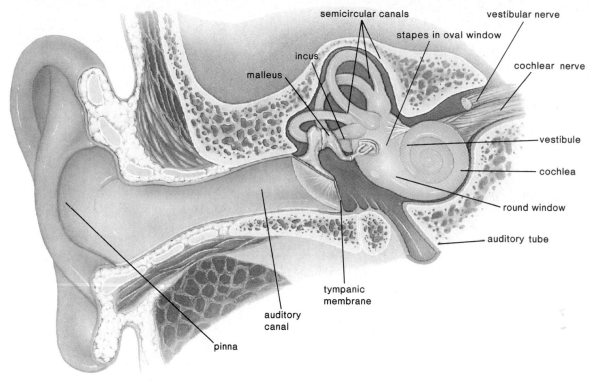

The inner ear (fig. 42.11*a*) has three spaces that form a maze called the bony labyrinth. The spaces are the semicircular canals and the vestibule, which are concerned with equilibrium, and the cochlear, which is concerned with hearing. There are membranous ducts and sacs present in the spaces that are filled with a clear fluid called the endolymph.

The **semicircular canals** are arranged so that there is one in each dimension of space. The base of each of the three canals, called the **ampulla** (fig. 42.11*b*), is slightly enlarged. Little hair cells with cilia inserted into a gelatinous material are found within the ampullae.

A vestibule, or chamber, lies between the semicircular canals and the cochlea. It contains two small membranous sacs called the **utricle** and the **saccule** (fig. 42.11*c*). Both sacs contain little hair cells with cilia that protrude into a gelatinous material. Calcium carbonate ($CaCO_3$) granules, or **otoliths,** rest on this material.

The **cochlea** [L. *cochl,* spiral] resembles the shell of a snail because it spirals. Three canals are located within the tubular cochlea: the vestibular canal, the **cochlear canal,** and the tympanic canal. Along the length of the basilar membrane, which forms the lower wall of the cochlear canal, are little hair cells with cilia that come into contact with another membrane, the **tectorial membrane** [Gk. *tect,* cover]. The hair cells of the cochlear canal are called the **organ of Corti** (fig. 42.11*d*). This organ sends nerve impulses via the cochlear (auditory) nerve to the temporal lobe of the cerebrum, where they are interpreted as sound.

The ear has three major divisions: outer ear, middle ear, and inner ear. The outer ear contains the auditory canal; the middle ear contains the ossicles; and the inner ear contains the semicircular canals, the vestibule, and the cochlea.

Figure 42.11 🔲

Anatomy of the inner ear. **a.** The inner ear contains the semicircular canals, the utricle and the saccule within a vestibule, and the cochlea. The cochlea has been cut to show the location of the organ of Corti. **b.** An ampulla at the base of each semicircular canal contains the receptors (hair cells) for dynamic equilibrium. **c.** The utricle and the saccule are small sacs that contain the receptors (hair cells) for static equilibrium. **d.** The receptors for hearing (hair cells) are in the organ of Corti.

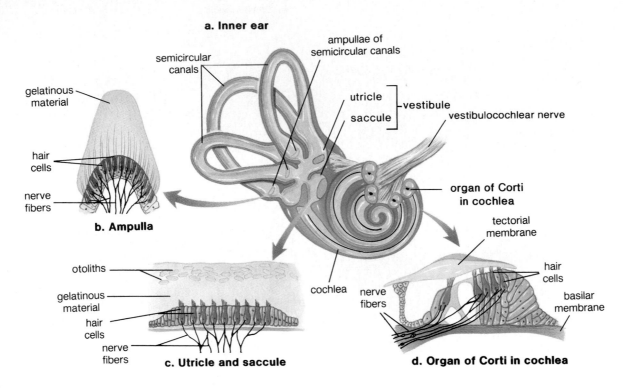

a. Inner ear

b. Ampulla

c. Utricle and saccule

d. Organ of Corti in cochlea

Hair Cells Keep Us Balanced

The semicircular canals are *dynamic equilibrium organs* because they initiate a sensation of movement (fig. 42.11*a*). At their bases are the ampullae, each one having touch-sensitive hair cells whose cilia are inserted into a gelatinous material (fig. 42.11*b*). As the body moves about, there is first a slight lag, and then the fluid within the canals moves and displaces the gelatinous material. This causes the cilia of the hair cells to bend. The three semicircular canals are each oriented in a different plane to detect movement in any direction. The brain integrates the impulses it receives from each of the three canals and therefore can determine the direction and rate of movement. Very rapid or prolonged movements of the head may cause uncomfortable side effects, such as the dizziness and nausea of seasickness.

The vestibule between the semicircular canals and the cochlea contains two small sacs, the utricle and the saccule (fig. 42.11*c*). Within each of these are groups of little hair cells; calcium carbonate granules called *otoliths* rest on the gelatinous material above the hair cells. When the head tilts, the otoliths are displaced and the gelatinous material sags, bending the cilia in a certain direction. This initiates nerve impulses that inform the brain of the position of the head. Similar types of organs, called statocysts, are also found in cnidaria, mollusks, and crustacea.

Figure 42.12 🔲

Generalized statocysts as found in mollusks and crustacea. A small particle, the statolith, moves in response to a change in the animal's position. When the statolith stops moving, it stimulates the closest cilia of hair cells. These cilia transmit impulses, indicating the position of the body.

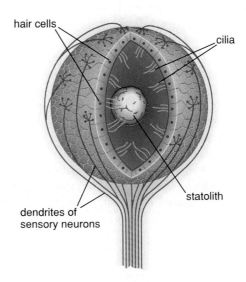

Figure 42.13

Sense of hearing. **a.** In the unwound cochlea, note that the organ of Corti consists of hair cells resting on the basilar membrane with the tectorial membrane above. The arrows represent the pressure waves that move from the oval window to the round window due to the motion of the stapes. These pressure waves cause the basilar membrane to vibrate and the cilia (or at least a portion of the over 20,000 hair cells) to bend against the tectorial membrane. The generated nerve impulses result in hearing. **b.** The micrograph shows the hair cells in the organ of Corti.

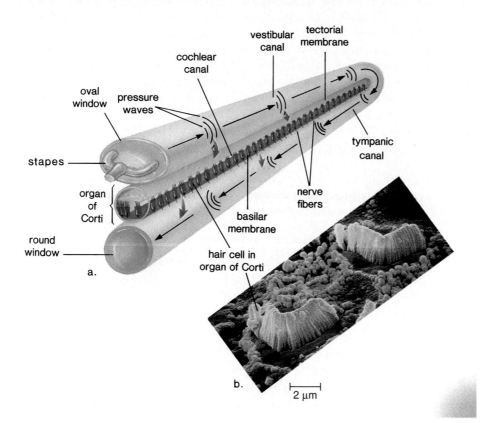

basilar membrane, which forms the floor of the cochlear canal, there are over 20,000 ciliated hair cells. Just above them is another membrane called the *tectorial membrane* (see fig. 42.11*d*). The hair cells form the organ of Corti, the sense organ for hearing.

Sound waves reach the organ of Corti by way of the outer and middle ear. Ordinarily, sound waves do not carry much energy, but when a large number of waves strike the eardrum, it moves back and forth (vibrates) very slightly. The malleus transfers the pressure from the inner surface of the eardrum to the incus, and then to the stapes (see fig. 42.10). The pressure is multiplied about twenty-fold as it moves from the eardrum to the stapes. The stapes vibrates the oval window, which transmits pressure waves to the fluid in the inner ear. These waves cause the basilar membrane to move up and down and cause the cilia of the hair cells to rub against the tectorial membrane. Bending of the cilia initiates nerve impulses, which pass by way of the auditory nerve to the brain, where the impulses are interpreted as a sound.

The organ of Corti is narrow at its base, but it widens as it approaches the tip of the cochlear canal. Various cells along it are sensitive to different wave frequencies, or pitches. Near its apex, the organ of Corti responds to low pitches, such as a bass drum, and near the base, it responds to high pitches, such as a bell or whistle. The nerve impulses from each region along the organ lead to slightly different areas in the brain. The pitch sensation we experience depends on which brain area is stimulated. Volume is a function of the *amplitude* of sound waves. Loud noises (measured in decibels, dB) cause the fluid of the cochlea to oscillate to a greater degree, and this, in turn, causes the basilar membrane to move up and down to a greater extent. The resulting increased stimulation is interpreted by the brain as loudness. Extremely loud noises can cause deafness, as discussed in the reading on page 746. It is believed that tone is interpreted by the brain according to the distribution of hair cells that are stimulated.

These organs give information only about the position of the head; they are not involved in the sensation of movement (fig. 42.12). They are therefore called *static equilibrium organs.*

> The outer ear, the middle ear, and the cochlea are necessary for hearing in humans. The vestibule—containing the utricle and the saccule—and the semicircular canals are concerned with the sense of balance.

Hair Cells Let Us Hear

The cochlea within the inner ear resembles the shell of a snail because it is spiral shaped (see fig. 42.11*a*). A cross section of the cochlea shows that it contains three canals: the vestibular, cochlear, and tympanic canals (fig. 42.13). Along the length of the

> The sense receptors for sound are ciliated hair cells on the basilar membrane (the organ of Corti).

Protect Your Hearing

Studies suggest that age-associated hearing loss can be prevented if ears are protected from loud noises, starting during infancy. Hospitals are now taking steps to make sure neonatal units and nurseries are as quiet as possible.

Today, exposure to the types of noises listed in figure 42B is a common occurrence. Noise is measured in decibels; any noise above a level of 80 decibels could result in damage to the hair cells of the organ of Corti. Eventually the cilia and then the hair cells disappear completely. If listening to city traffic for extended periods can damage hearing, it's reasonable that frequent attendance at rock concerts or frequently playing a ste-

reo loudly is also damaging to hearing. The first hint of danger could be temporary hearing loss, a "full" feeling in the ears, muffled hearing, or tinnitus (e.g., ringing in the ears). If you have any of these symptoms, modify your listening habits immediately to prevent further damage. If exposure to noise is unavoidable, specially designed noise-reduction ear muffs are available, and it is also possible to purchase earplugs made from a compressible, spongelike material. These earplugs are not the same as those worn for swimming, and they should not be used interchangeably.

Aside from loud music, noisy indoor or outdoor equipment such as a rug-cleaning machine or a chain saw are also troublesome.

Even motorcycles, snowmobiles, and motocross bikes can contribute to a gradual loss of hearing. Exposure to intense sounds of short duration, such as a burst of gunfire, can result in an immediate hearing loss. Hunters may have a significant hearing reduction in the ear opposite to the shoulder where the gun is carried.

Finally, people need to be aware that some medicines are ototoxic. Anticancer drugs, most notably cisplatin, and certain antibiotics (e.g., streptomycin) make ears especially susceptible to a hearing loss. Anyone taking such medications should protect the ears from loud noises.

Type of Noise	Sound Level (decibels)	Effect
Rock concert, shotgun, jet engine	over 125	Beyond threshold of pain; potential for hearing loss is high
Discotheque, "boom box," thunderclap	over 120	Hearing loss is likely
Chain saw, pneumatic drill, jackhammer, symphony orchestra, snowmobile, garbage truck, cement mixer	100–200	Regular exposure of more than one minute risks permanent hearing loss
Farm tractor, newspaper press, subway, motorcycle	90–100	Fifteen minutes of unprotected exposure is potentially harmful
Lawn mower, food blender	85–90	Continuous daily exposure for more than eight hours can cause hearing damage
Diesel truck, average city traffic noise	80–85	Annoying; constant exposure may cause hearing damage

Source: National Institute on Deafness and Other Communication Disorders, National Institutes of Health, January 1990.

a.

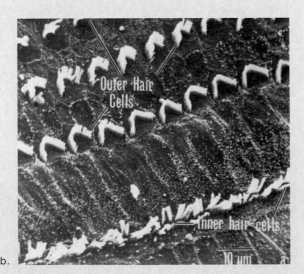
b.

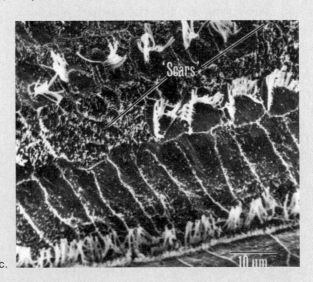
c.

Figure 42B

a. The higher the decibel reading, the more likely a noise will damage hearing. **b.** Normal hair cells in the organ of Corti of a guinea pig. **c.** Damaged cells. This damage occurred after twenty-four-hour exposure to a noise level typical of rock concerts.

Summary

1. Sense organs are transducers; they transform the energy of a stimulus to the energy of nerve impulses. It is the brain, not the sense organ, that interprets the stimulus.

2. Human olfactory cells and taste buds are chemoreceptors. They are sensitive to chemicals in water and air.

3. The human eye is a photoreceptor. The compound eye of arthropods is made up of many individual units, whereas the human eye is a camera-type eye with a single lens. Table 42.1 lists the parts of the eye and the function(s) of each part.

4. The receptors for sight in humans are the rods and the cones, which are in the retina. The rods work in minimum light and detect motion, but they do not detect color. The cones require bright light and do detect color.

5. When light strikes rhodopsin, a molecule composed of opsin and retinal, retinal changes shape and opsin is activated. Chemical reactions that produce nerve impulses follow. These impulses are eventually picked up by the optic nerve.

6. There are three kinds of cones, containing blue, green, or red pigment. Each pigment is also made up of retinal and opsin, but opsin structure varies among the three.

7. Mechanoreceptors include the touch receptors and pressure receptors in the human skin.

8. Many mechanoreceptors are hair cells with cilia, such as those found in the lateral line of fishes as well as the inner ear of humans. Table 42.2 lists the parts of the ear and the function of each part.

9. The inner ear contains the sense organs for balance. Movement of fluid past hair cells in the semicircular canals gives us a sense of dynamic equilibrium. Just like the statocysts of invertebrates, portions of the human inner ear contain calcium carbonate granules (otoliths) resting on hair cells. The movement of these granules gives us a sense of static equilibrium.

10. Hair cells on the basilar membrane (the organ of Corti) are responsible for hearing. Pressure waves, which begin at the oval window, cause the basilar membrane to vibrate so that the cilia of the hair cells touch the tectorial membrane. This causes the hair cells to initiate nerve impulses, which are carried by the auditory nerve to the brain.

Writing Across the Curriculum

In order to practice writing skills, students should write out the answers to any or all of the study questions and the critical thinking questions. The study questions are sequenced in the same order as the text. Answers to the objective questions, and suggested answers to the critical thinking questions, are in appendix D.

Study Questions

1. In what ways are all receptors similar?   734

2. Discuss the structure and the function of human chemoreceptors.   734–35

3. In general, how does the eye in arthropods differ from that in humans? What types of animals have eyes that are constructed similarly to the human eye?   736

4. Name the parts of the eye, and give a function for each part.   737

5. Contrast the location and the function of rods to those of cones.   738, 740

6. What are the types of mechanoreceptors in human skin?   742

7. Describe how the lateral line system of fishes works and why it is considered to contain mechanoreceptors.   742

8. Describe both the anatomy of the ear and how we hear.   742–43

9. Describe the role of the utricle, the saccule, and the semicircular canals in balance.   744–45

Objective Questions

1. A receptor
   a. is the first portion of a reflex arc.
   b. initiates nerve impulses.
   c. responds to only one type of stimulus.
   d. All of these are correct.

2. Which of these gives the correct path for light rays entering the human eye?
   a. sclera, retina, choroid, lens, cornea
   b. fovea centralis, pupil, aqueous humor, lens
   c. cornea, pupil, lens, vitreous humor, retina
   d. optic nerve, sclera, choroid, retina, humors

3. Which gives an incorrect function for the structure?
   a. lens—focusing
   b. iris—regulation of amount of light
   c. choroid—location of cones
   d. sclera—protection

4. Which of these contain mechanoreceptors?
   a. human skin
   b. lateral line of fishes
   c. statocysts of arthropods
   d. All of these are correct.

5. Which association is incorrect?
   a. lateral line—fishes
   b. compound eye—arthropods
   c. camera-type eye—squid
   d. statocysts—sea stars

6. Which one of these wouldn't you mention if you were tracing the path of sound vibrations?
   a. auditory canal
   b. tympanic membrane
   c. semicircular canals
   d. cochlea

7. Which one of these correctly describes the location of the organ of Corti?

   a. between the tympanic membrane and the oval window in the inner ear

   b. in the utricle and saccule within the vestibule

   c. between the tectorial membrane and the basilar membrane in the cochlear canal

   d. between the outer and inner ear within the semicircular canals

8. Which of these is mismatched?

   a. semicircular canals—inner ear

   b. utricle and saccule—outer ear

   c. auditory canal—outer ear

   d. ossicles—middle ear

9. Retinal is

   a. sensitive to light energy.

   b. a part of rhodopsin.

   c. found in both rods and cones.

   d. All of these are correct.

10. Both olfactory receptors and sound receptors have cilia, and they both

   a. are chemoreceptors.

   b. are mechanoreceptors.

   c. initiate nerve impulses.

   d. All of these are correct.

11. Label this diagram of the human eye. State a function for each structure labeled:

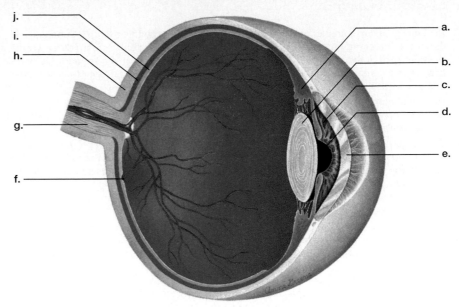

Concepts and Critical Thinking

1. *All organ systems contribute to homeostasis.*

List several ways in which the sense organs contribute to homeostasis.

2. *In the whole animal, all systems work together and influence one another.*

How do the nervous system and the sense organs work together?

3. *Animals are sensitive to only certain types of stimuli.*

Why might animals be sensitive to only certain types of stimuli?

Selected Key Terms

chemoreceptor A receptor that is sensitive to chemical stimulation—for example, receptors for taste and smell. [Gk. *chemo,* chemistry, and L. *recept,* receive]   734

choroid (KOR-oyd) The vascular, pigmented middle layer of the eyeball. [Gk. *choroid,* like a membrane]   737

cochlea (KOH-klee-uh) A spiral-shaped structure of the inner ear containing the receptors for hearing. [L. *cochl,* spiral]   743

compound eye A type of eye found in arthropods; it is composed of many independent visual units.   736

cone Photoreceptor in vertebrate eyes that responds to bright light and allows color vision.   738

mechanoreceptor A receptor that is sensitive to mechanical stimulation, such as that from pressure, sound waves, and gravity. [Gk. *mechano,* instrument, and L. *recept,* receive]   742

olfactory cell (ahl-FAK-tuh-ree) A modified neuron that is a receptor for the sense of smell. [L. *olfact,* smell]   735

optic nerve The nerve that carries impulses from the retina of the eye to the brain. [Gk. *opti,* eye]   738

organ of Corti (KORT-ee) Specialized region of the cochlea containing the hair cells for sound detection and discrimination.   743

photoreceptor A light-sensitive receptor. [Gk. *photo,* light, and L. *recept,* receive]   736

receptor In the nervous system, a specialized ending of a sensory neuron that receives stimuli from the environment and generates nerve impulses.   734

retina The innermost layer of the eyeball containing the photoreceptors—rods and cones. [L. *retin,* net]   738

rhodopsin (roh-DAHP-sun) A light-absorbing molecule in rods and cones that contains a pigment and the protein opsin. [Gk. *rhodo,* rose-red, and *opsis,* view]   740

rod A photoreceptor in vertebrate eyes that responds to dim light.   738

sclera (SKLER-uh) The outer, white, fibrous layer of the eye that surrounds the eye except for transparent cornea. [Gk. *scler,* hard]   737

semicircular canal One of three half-circle-shaped canals of the inner ear that are fluid filled and register changes in motion.   743

taste bud An oral concentration of sensory nerve endings that function as taste receptors.   735

tympanic membrane (tim-PAN-ik) Membranous region that receives air vibrations in an auditory organ. [Gk. *tympan,* drum]   742

MUSCULOSKELETAL SYSTEM

Learning Objectives

Comparing Skeletons
- Describe the functions of a skeletal system in animals. 750
- Distinguish among the three types of skeletons in the animal kingdom, and give examples of animals that have each type. 750–51

Humans Have an Endoskeleton
- Describe the anatomy of a long bone and the tissues found in a long bone. 752–53
- Explain how bone is continually being broken down and renewed. 753
- Name the two parts of the human skeleton, and list the location of the bones for both. 754–57
- Name the different types of joints, and give an example of each. 758

How Muscles Function
- Describe how whole muscles work in antagonistic pairs. 759
- Describe the anatomy of a muscle fiber and a sarcomere. 760
- Explain the sliding filament theory of muscle contraction. 761
- List the sources of ATP energy for muscle contraction, and explain the development of oxygen debt. 761
- List the series of events that occur after a muscle fiber is innervated by nervous stimulation. 762

An ant, *Atta*, carries a twig much larger than itself, proving the strength of its musculoskeletal system.

The ability to move by means of muscle fibers is one of the distinctive characteristics of animals. Being mobile helps animals obtain food, escape enemies, locate mates, and disperse the species. The title of this chapter—"Musculoskeletal System"—recognizes that the muscular system and the skeletal system work together to provide movement.

The bony skeleton of vertebrates also produces red blood cells and serves as a storage area for inorganic calcium and phosphorus salts.

To produce body movements, the force of muscle contractions is directed against a skeleton which also supports the body. In addition, a skeleton gives the body shape and often protects the internal organs, even as it facilitates movement.

We will first consider the skeleton of both invertebrates and vertebrates and later we will show how the skeletal muscles cause the bones of vertebrates to move.

COMPARING SKELETONS

Different types of skeletons are seen in the animal kingdom. A hydrostatic skeleton is seen in cnidaria, flatworms, and annelids. Some mollusks have a calcium carbonate exoskeleton while anthropods have a chitinous one. Vertebrates have a bony endoskeleton.

A Water-Filled Cavity

In animals that lack a hard skeleton, a fluid-filled gastrovascular cavity or coelom can act as a *hydrostatic skeleton*. A hydrostatic skeleton also offers support and resistance to the contraction of muscles so that mobility results. As analogies, consider that a garden hose stiffens when filled with water and that a water-filled balloon changes shape when squeezed at one end. Similarly, an animal with a hydrostatic skeleton can change shape and perform a variety of movements.

Figure 43.1

Locomotion in an earthworm. **a.** The coelom is divided by septa, and each body segment is a separate locomotor unit. There are both circular and longitudinal muscles. **b.** As circular muscles contract, the worm extends. Then longitudinal muscles contract, a portion of the body is brought forward, and so forth down the length of the worm. The worm is held in place by setae.

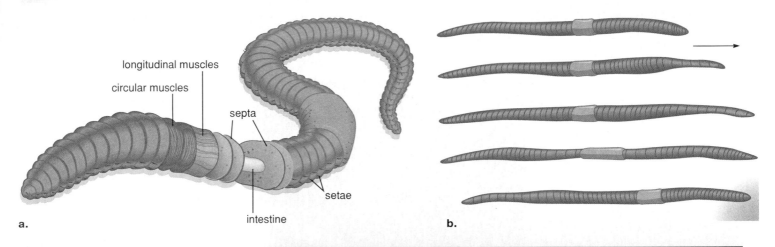

longitudinal muscles
circular muscles
septa
setae
intestine
a.
b.

Figure 43.2

Exoskeleton. Exoskeletons provide advantages by supporting muscle contraction and preventing drying out. The chitinous exoskeleton of arthropods is shed as the animal molts; until the new skeleton dries and hardens, the animal is vulnerable to predators, and muscle contractions may not translate into body movements. In this photo a dog-day cicada, *Fidicina,* has just finished molting.

Cnidaria such as hydras, and flatworms such as planaria, use their fluid-filled gastrovascular cavity as a hydroskeleton that gives support. When muscle fibers at the base of epidermal cells in a hydra contract, the body or tentacles shorten rapidly. Planaria usually glide over a substrate with the help of muscular contractions that control the body wall and cilia. Nematodes (roundworms) have a fluid-filled pseudocoelom and move in a whiplike manner when their longitudinal muscles contract. Annelids, such as earthworms, are segmented and have septa that divide their coelom into compartments (fig. 43.1). Each segment has its own set of longitudinal and circular muscles and its own nerve supply, so each segment or group of segments may function independently. When circular muscles contract, the segments become thinner and elongate. When longitudinal muscles contract, the segments become thicker and shorten. By alternating circular muscle contraction and longitudinal muscle contraction, the animal moves forward.

Exoskeletons or Endoskeletons

An exoskeleton is an exterior skeleton. Calcium carbonate forms the exoskeleton of some animals such as corals and clams, but insects and crustacea have a chitinous exoskeleton. Chitin is a strong, flexible, nitrogenous polysaccharide. Besides providing protection against wear and tear and against enemies, an exoskeleton also prevents drying out. This is an important feature for animals that live on land. Although the stiffness of an exoskeleton provides superior support for muscle contractions, an exoskeleton is not as strong as an endoskeleton (internal skeleton). Strength can be achieved by increasing the thickness of an exoskeleton, but this leaves less room for internal organs.

In mollusks, such as clams and snails, the exoskeleton grows as the animal grows. The thick and non-mobile calcium carbonate exoskeleton is largely for protection. The chitinous exoskeleton of arthropods, which is jointed and move-able, is suitable for life on land. Arthropods, however, molt to rid themselves of an exoskeleton that has become too small, and molting makes an animal vulnerable to predators (fig. 43.2).

Vertebrates have an endoskeleton, composed of bone and cartilage, which grows

with the animal. Endoskeletons do not limit the space available for internal organs, and they support greater weight. The soft tissues that surround an endoskeleton protect it, and injuries to soft tissues are apt to be easier to repair than is a broken skeleton. However, endoskeletons usually do have elements that protect vital internal organs (fig. 43.3).

Both arthropods (e.g., insects and crustacea) and vertebrates have a rigid and segmented skeleton. The exoskeleton of arthropods and the endoskeleton of vertebrates is jointed. A strong but flexible skeleton helped the arthropods and vertebrates successfully colonize the terrestrial environment.

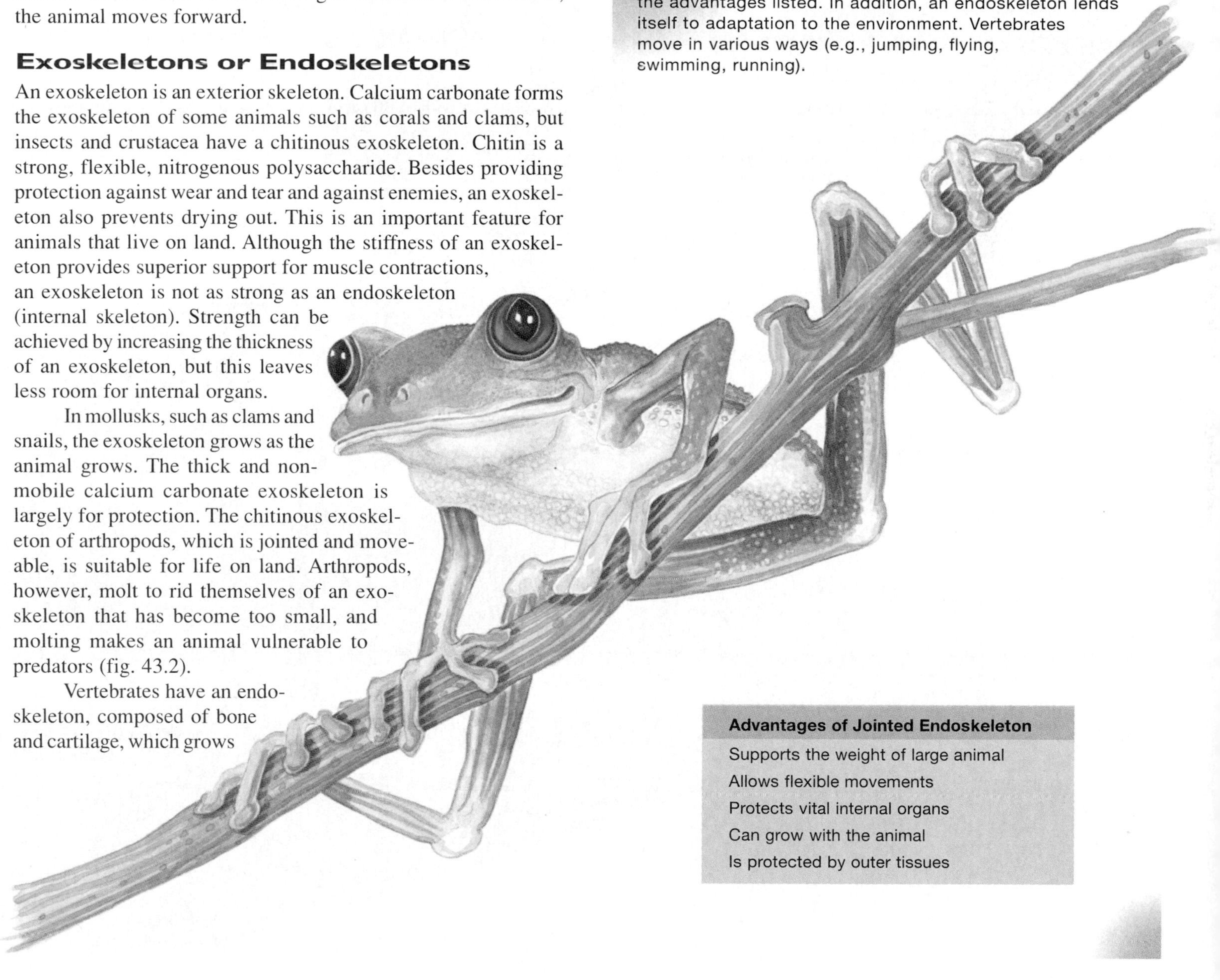

Figure 43.3
The vertebrate endoskeleton. A jointed endoskeleton has the advantages listed. In addition, an endoskeleton lends itself to adaptation to the environment. Vertebrates move in various ways (e.g., jumping, flying, swimming, running).

Advantages of Jointed Endoskeleton
Supports the weight of large animal
Allows flexible movements
Protects vital internal organs
Can grow with the animal
Is protected by outer tissues

Figure 43.4

Anatomy of a long bone. A long bone is encased by fibrous membrane except where it is covered by hyline cartilage (see micrograph). Spongy bone located beneath the cartilage may contain red bone marrow. The compact bone of the central shaft which is shown in the enlargement and micrograph contains yellow bone marrow.

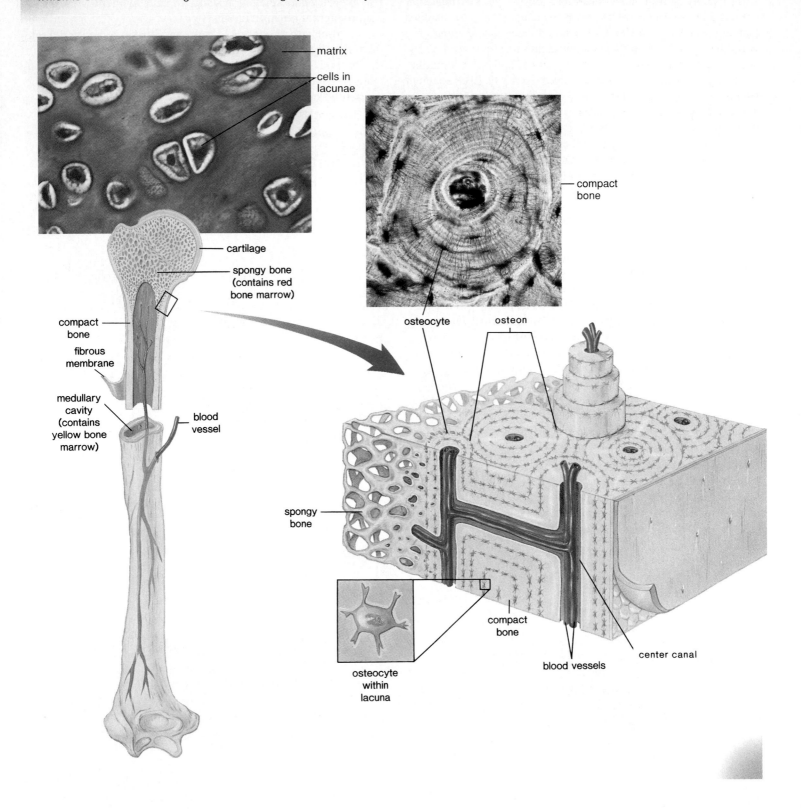

matrix

cells in lacunae

compact bone

cartilage

spongy bone (contains red bone marrow)

compact bone

fibrous membrane

medullary cavity (contains yellow bone marrow)

blood vessel

osteocyte

osteon

spongy bone

compact bone

center canal

blood vessels

osteocyte within lacuna

HUMANS HAVE AN ENDOSKELETON

The human skeleton has many functions. The large, heavy bones of the legs support the body against the pull of gravity. The skeleton protects vital internal organs. For example, the skull forms a protective encasement for the brain, as does the rib cage for the heart and the lungs. Flat bones—such as those of the skull, the ribs, and the breastbone—produce red blood cells. All bones are storage areas for inorganic calcium and phosphorous salts. Bones also provide sites for muscle attachment. The long bones, particularly those of the legs and the arms, permit flexible body movement.

> The skeleton not only permits flexible movement, it also supports and protects the body, produces red blood cells, and serves as a storehouse for certain inorganic salts.

How Bones Differ and Grow

Bone is a living tissue that continually renews itself in a manner to be described. A long bone, such as the humerus, illustrates principles of bone anatomy. When the bone is split open, as in figure 43.4, the longitudinal section shows that it is not solid but has a cavity called the medullary cavity bounded at the sides by compact bone and at the ends by spongy bone. Beyond the spongy bone there is a thin shell of compact bone and finally a layer of cartilage, another type of connective tissue in which the matrix is flexible.

Compact bone contains many osteons (formerly called Haversian systems) in which bone cells in tiny chambers called lacunae are arranged in concentric circles around center canals. The center canals contain blood vessels and nerves. The lacunae are separated by a matrix that contains protein fibers of collagen and mineral deposits, primarily of calcium and phosphorus salts.

Spongy bone contains numerous bony bars and plates separated by irregular spaces. Although lighter than compact bone, spongy bone is still designed for strength. Just as braces are used for support in buildings, the solid portions of spongy bone follow lines of stress. The spaces in spongy bone are often filled with *red bone marrow,* a specialized tissue that produces red blood cells. The cavity of a long bone usually contains *yellow bone marrow,* which is a fat-storage tissue.

> A long bone is designed for strength. It has a medullary cavity filled with yellow bone marrow and bounded by compact bone. The ends contain spongy bone and are covered by cartilage.

Bones Grow and Are Renewed

Most of the bones of the human skeleton are cartilaginous during prenatal development. Since the cartilaginous structures are shaped like the future bones, they provide "models" of these bones. The cartilaginous models are converted to bones when calcium salts are deposited in the matrix, first by certain of the cartilaginous cells and later by bone-forming cells called **osteoblasts** [Gk. *ost,* bone, and *blast,* bud]. The conversion of cartilaginous models to bones is called endochondral ossification. There are also examples of ossification that have no previous cartilaginous model. Facial bones and certain other bones of the skull are formed in this way.

During endochondral ossification in a long bone, at first, there is only a primary ossification center at the middle of a long bone, but later, secondary centers form at the ends of the bones. There remains a *cartilaginous disk* between the primary ossification center and each secondary center, which can increase in length. The rate of growth is controlled by hormones such as growth hormones and the sex hormones. Eventually the disks become ossified and the bone stops growing. The individual attains adult height when this occurs.

In the adult, bone is continually being broken down and built up again. Bone-absorbing cells, called **osteoclasts** [Gk. *ost,* bone, and *clas,* fragment], break down bone, remove worn cells, and deposit calcium in the blood. Apparently after a period of about three weeks, they disappear. The destruction caused by the work of osteoclasts is repaired by osteoblasts. As they form new bone, osteoblasts take calcium from the blood. Eventually some of these cells get caught in the matrix they secrete and are converted to **osteocytes** [Gk. *ost,* bone, and *cyt,* cell], the cells found within the lacunae of osteons.

Thus, through a process of *remodeling,* old bone tissue is replaced by new bone tissue. Because of continual remodeling, the thickness of bones can change. The physical use and hormone balance affects the thickness of bones. Strange as it may seem, adults seem to require more calcium in the diet than do children in order to promote the work of osteoblasts.

> The prenatal human skeleton is at first cartilaginous, but it is later replaced by a bony skeleton. During adult life, bone is constantly being broken down by osteoclasts and then rebuilt by osteoblasts that become osteocytes in osteons.

Bones Make Up the Skeleton

The human skeleton can be divided into two parts: the axial skeleton and the appendicular skeleton (fig. 43.5).

Axial Skeleton Is in the Midline

The **axial skeleton** [L. *axi,* axis, and Gk. *skelet,* dried body] lies in the midline of the body and consists of the skull, the vertebral column, the sternum, and the ribs.

The skull is formed by the cranium and the facial bones (fig. 43.6). The cranium protects the brain and is composed of eight bones fitted tightly together in adults. In newborns, certain bones are not completely formed and instead are joined by membranous regions called *fontanels,* all of which usually close by the age of two years. The bones of the cranium contain the **sinuses** [L. *sinu,* a hollow], air spaces lined by mucous membrane, which reduce the weight of the skull and give a resonant sound to the voice. Two sinuses called the mastoid sinuses drain into the middle ear. *Mastoiditis,* a condition that can lead to deafness, is an inflammation of these sinuses.

The major bones of the cranium have the same names as the lobes of the brain: frontal, parietal, temporal, and occipital. On the top of the cranium (fig. 43.6*a*), the *frontal bone* forms the forehead, the *parietal bones* extend to the sides, and the *occipital*

bone curves to form the base of the skull. Here there is a large opening, the **foramen magnum** [L. *foram,* opening, and *magn,* large] (fig. 43.6*b*), through which the spinal cord passes and becomes the brain stem. Below the much larger parietal bones, each *temporal bone* has an opening that leads to the middle ear. The *sphenoid bone* not only completes the sides of the skull, it also contributes to the floors and walls of the eye sockets. Likewise, the *ethmoid bone,* which lies in front of the sphenoid, is a part of the orbital wall and, in addition, is a component of the nasal septum.

> The cranium contains eight bones; the frontal, two parietal, the occipital, two temporal, the sphenoid, and the ethmoid.

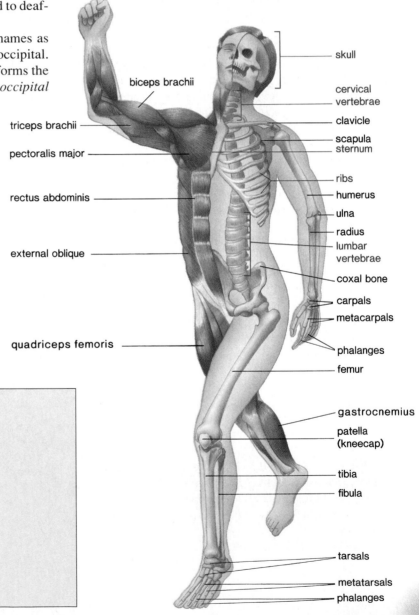

Figure 43.5
Major bones (*right*) and skeletal muscles (*left*) of the human body. The axial skeleton, composed of the skull, the vertebral column, the sternum, and the ribs (red labels), lies in the midline; the rest of the bones belong to the appendicular skeleton (black labels).

Axial skeleton
- Skull
- Vertebral column
- Sternum
- Ribs

Appendicular skeleton
- Pectoral girdle: Clavicle, scapula
- Arm: Humerus, ulna, radius
- Hand: Carpals, metacarpals, phalanges
- Pelvic girdle: Coxal bones
- Leg: Femur, tibia, fibula, patella
- Foot: Tarsals, metatarsals, phalanges

There are fourteen facial bones. The **mandible** [L. *mandibul, jaw*], or lower jaw, is the only movable portion of the skull (fig. 43.6*a*), and its action permits us to chew our food. Tooth sockets are located on this bone and on the **maxillae** [L. *maxill,* jawbone] (maxillary bones), the upper jaw that also forms the anterior portion of the hard palate. The *palatine bones* make up the posterior portion of the hard palate and the floor of the nasal cavity. The *zygomatic bones* give us our cheekbone prominences, and the nasal bones form the bridge of the nose. Each thin, scalelike *lac-* *rimal bone* lies between an ethmoid bone and a maxillary bone, and the thin, flat *vomer* joins with the perpendicular plate of the ethmoid to form the nasal septum.

The facial bones include the mandible, two maxillae, two palatine, two zygomatic, two lacrimal, two nasal, and the vomer.

Figure 43.6
Skull. **a.** Lateral view. **b.** Inferior view.

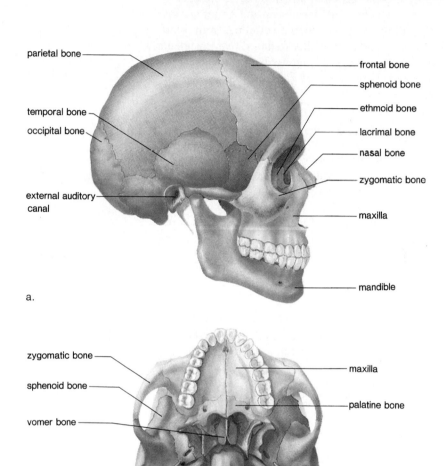

a.

parietal bone
temporal bone
occipital bone
external auditory canal

frontal bone
sphenoid bone
ethmoid bone
lacrimal bone
nasal bone
zygomatic bone
maxilla
mandible

b.

zygomatic bone
sphenoid bone
vomer bone
temporal bone

maxilla
palatine bone
foramen magnum
occipital bone

Vertebral Column Supports

The **vertebral column** [L. *vertebr,* vertebra] extends from the skull to the pelvis. Normally, the vertebral column has four curvatures that provide more resiliency and strength in an upright posture than a straight column could. The various vertebrae are named according to their location in the vertebral column (fig. 43.7). When the vertebrae join, they form a canal through which the spinal cord passes. The *spinous processes* of the vertebrae can be felt as bony projections along the midline of the back.

There are intervertebral disks between the vertebrae that act as a kind of padding. They prevent the vertebrae from grinding against one another and absorb shock caused by movements such as running, jumping, and even walking. Unfortunately, these disks become weakened with age and can slip or even rupture. Pain results when the damaged disk presses against the spinal cord and/or spinal nerves. The body may heal itself, or the disk can be removed surgically. If the latter occurs, the vertebrae can be fused together, but this limits the flexibility of the body. The presence of the disks allows motion between the vertebrae so that we can bend forward, backward, and from side to side.

The vertebral column, directly or indirectly, serves as an anchor for all the other bones of the skeleton (see fig. 43.5). All of the twelve pairs of **ribs** connect directly to the thoracic vertebrae in the back, and all but two pairs connect either directly or indirectly via shafts of cartilage to the **sternum** [Gk. *stern,* breastbone] in the front. The lower two pairs of ribs are called "floating ribs" because they do not attach to the sternum.

> The vertebral column contains the vertebrae and serves as the backbone for the body. Disks between the vertebrae provide padding and account for flexibility of the column.

Appendicular Skeleton Is Girdles and Limbs

The **appendicular skeleton** [L. *append,* hang to, and Gk. *skelet,* dried body] consists of the bones within the pectoral and pelvic girdles and the attached limbs (see fig. 43.5). The pectoral (shoulder) girdle and upper limbs (arms) are specialized for flexibility, but the pelvic girdle (hipbones) and lower limbs (legs) are specialized for strength.

Pectoral Girdle and Arm

The components of the **pectoral girdle** [Gk. *pechy,* forearm] are only loosely linked together by ligaments (fig. 43.8). Each **clavicle** (collarbone) connects with the sternum in front and the **scapula** (shoulder blade) behind, but the scapula is freely movable and held in place only by muscles. This allows it to follow freely the movements of the arm. The single long bone in the upper arm, the **humerus,** has a smoothly rounded head that fits into a socket of the scapula. The socket, however, is very shallow and much smaller than the head. Although this means that the arm can move in almost any direction, there is little stability. Therefore, this is

Figure 43.7

The vertebral column. The vertebrae are named according to their location in the column, which is flexible due to the intervertebral disks. Note the presence of the coccyx, also called the tailbone.

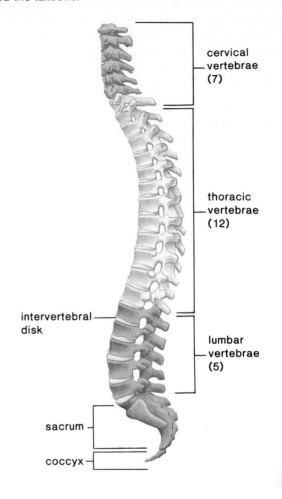

the joint that is most apt to dislocate. The opposite end of the humerus meets the two bones of the lower arm, the **ulna** and the **radius,** at the elbow. (The prominent bone in the elbow is the topmost part of the ulna.) When the arm is held so that the palm is turned frontward, the radius and ulna are about parallel to one another. When the arm is turned so that the palm is next to the body, the radius crosses in front of the ulna, a feature that contributes to the easy twisting motion of the forearm.

The many bones of the hand increase its flexibility. The wrist has eight **carpal** bones, which look like small pebbles. From these, five *metacarpal* bones fan out to form a framework for the palm. The metacarpal bone that leads to the thumb is placed in such a way that the thumb can reach out and touch the other digits. (**Digits** is a term that refers to either fingers or toes.) Beyond the metacarpals are the *phalanges,* the bones of the fingers and the thumb. The phalanges of the hand are long, slender, and lightweight.

Figure 43.8

The bones of the pectoral girdle, the arm, and the hand. The humerus is known as the "funny bone" of the elbow. The sensation upon bumping it is due to the activation of a nerve that passes across its end.

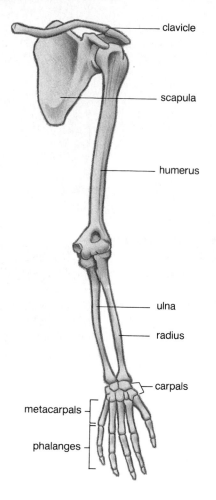

Figure 43.9

The bones of the pelvic girdle, the leg, and the foot. The femur is our strongest bone—it withstands a pressure of 540 kg per 2.5 cm³ when we walk.

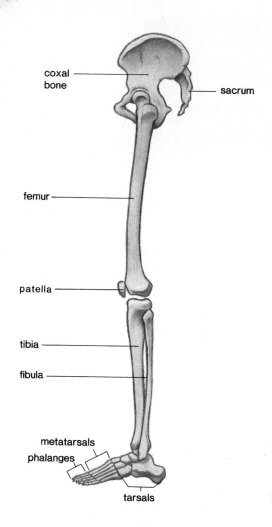

Pelvic Girdle and Leg

The **pelvic girdle** [L. *pelv,* pelvis], (fig. 43.9) consists of two heavy, large *coxal* bones (hipbones). The coxal bones are anchored to the sacrum, and together these bones form a hollow cavity that is wider in females (to accommodate childbearing) than in males. The weight of the body is transmitted through the pelvis to the legs and then onto the ground. The largest bone in the body is the femur, or thighbone. Although the femur is a strong bone, it is doubtful that the femurs of a fairytale giant could support its weight. If a giant were ten times taller than an ordinary human being, he would also be about ten times wider and thicker, making him weigh about 1,000 times as much. This amount of weight would break even giant-size femurs.

In the lower leg, the larger of the two bones, the tibia, has a ridge we call the shin. Both of the bones of the lower leg have a prominence that contributes to the ankle—the *tibia* on the inside

of the ankle and the *fibula* on the outside of the ankle. Although there are seven *tarsal bones* in the ankle, only one receives the weight and passes it on to the heel and the ball of the foot. If you wear high-heeled shoes, the weight is thrown even further anterior toward the front of your foot. The *metatarsal* bones participate in forming the arches of the foot. There is a longitudinal arch from the heel to the toes and a transverse arch across the foot. These provide a stable, springy base for the body. If the tissues that bind the metatarsals together become weakened, flat feet are apt to result. The bones of the toes are called *phalanges,* just like those of the fingers, but in the foot the phalanges are stout and extremely sturdy.

The appendicular skeleton contains the bones of the girdles and the limbs.

Figure 43.10

Knee joint, an example of a synovial joint. Notice the cavity between the bones, which is encased by ligaments and lined by synovial membrane. The patella (kneecap) serves to guide the quadriceps tendon over the joint when flexion and extension occur.

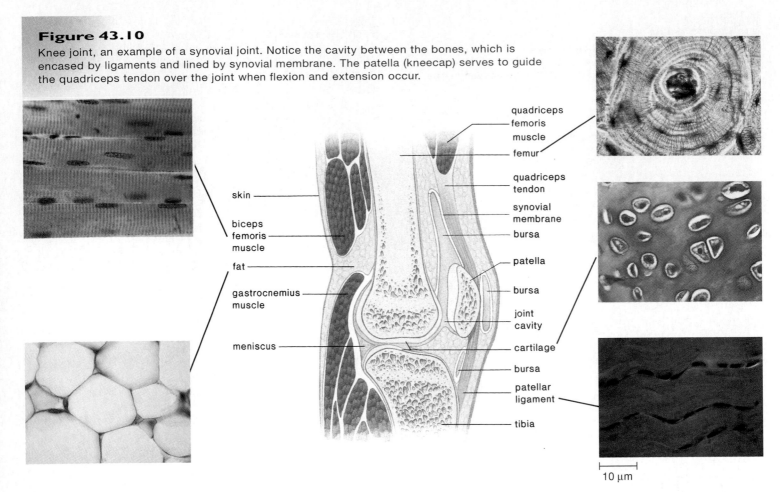

skin

biceps femoris muscle

fat

gastrocnemius muscle

meniscus

quadriceps femoris muscle

femur

quadriceps tendon

synovial membrane

bursa

patella

bursa

joint cavity

cartilage

bursa

patellar ligament

tibia

10 μm

Joints Join Bones

Bones are joined at the joints, which are classified as fibrous, cartilaginous, and synovial. Fibrous joints such as those between the cranial bones are immovable. Cartilaginous joints such as those between the vertebrae are slightly movable. The vertebrae are also separated by disks, which increase their flexibility. The two hipbones are slightly movable because they are ventrally joined by cartilage. Owing to hormonal changes, this joint becomes more flexible during late pregnancy, allowing the pelvis to expand during childbirth.

Synovial Joints Are Freely Movable

Most joints are *freely movable* **synovial joints,** in which the two bones are separated by a cavity. *Ligaments,* composed of fibrous connective tissue, bind the two bones to each other, holding them in place as they form a capsule. In a "double-jointed" individual, the ligaments are unusually loose. The joint capsule is lined by synovial membrane, which produces *synovial fluid,* a lubricant for the joint.

The knee is an example of a synovial joint (fig. 43.10). In the knee, as in other freely movable joints, the bones are capped by cartilage, although there are also crescent-shaped pieces of cartilage between the bones called **menisci** [Gk. *menisc,* crescent]. These give added stability, helping to support the weight placed on the knee joint. Unfortunately, athletes often suffer injury of the meniscus, known as torn cartilage. The knee joint also

contains thirteen fluid-filled sacs called bursae, which ease friction between tendons and ligaments and between tendons and bones. Inflammation of the bursae is called bursitis. Tennis elbow is a form of bursitis.

There are different types of movable joints. The knee and elbow joints are *hinge joints* because, like a hinged door, they largely permit movement in one direction only. More movable are the ball-and-socket joints; for example, the ball of the femur fits into a socket on the hipbone. *Ball-and-socket joints* allow movement in all planes and even a rotational movement.

Synovial joints are subject to *arthritis.* In rheumatoid arthritis, the synovial membrane becomes inflamed and thickens. Degenerative changes take place that make the joint almost immovable and painful to use. There is evidence that these effects are brought on by an autoimmune reaction. In old-age arthritis, or osteoarthritis, the cartilage at the ends of the bones disintegrates so that the two bones become rough and irregular. This type of arthritis is apt to affect the joints that have received the greatest use over the years.

> There are three kinds of joints: fibrous joints are immovable; cartilaginous joints are slightly movable; and synovial joints are freely movable.

Figure 43.11

Antagonistic muscle pairs. Muscles can exert force only by shortening. Movable joints are supplied with double sets of muscles, which work in opposite directions. As indicated by the arrows, flexor muscles decrease the angle at a joint and extensors increase the angle at a joint. **a.** Muscles in an insect's leg as an example of antagonistic muscles attached to the inside of an arthropod exoskeleton. **b.** Muscles in the human leg as an example of antagonistic muscles attached to a vertebrate endoskeleton.

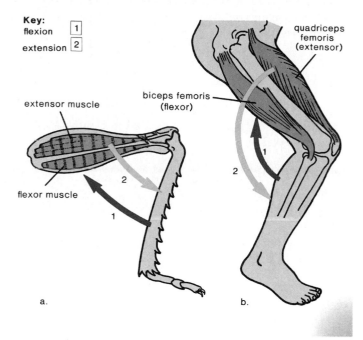

Key:
flexion ☐1
extension ☐2

extensor muscle

flexor muscle

biceps femoris (flexor)

quadriceps femoris (extensor)

a.

b.

Figure 43.12

Laboratory study of muscle fiber versus whole muscle contraction. **a.** When a muscle fiber is electrically stimulated in the laboratory, it may contract. At first the stimulus may be so weak that no contraction occurs, but as soon as the strength of the stimulus reaches the threshold, the muscle fiber contracts and then relaxes. This action, which is called a muscle fiber twitch, is divided into three stages as shown. Increasing the strength of the stimulus does not change the strength of the muscle fiber's contraction; therefore, it is said that a fiber obeys the all-or-none law. If a muscle fiber is given two stimuli in quick succession, it does not respond to the second stimulus because it is still recovering from the first stimulus. **b.** A whole muscle behaves quite differently. If the strength of the stimulus is increased, the strength of the response increases. This is because more and more fibers are being stimulated to contract. Also, quickly repeated stimuli to a whole muscle can result in a summation of twitches. This occurs because more fibers can begin to contract while others are relaxing. The muscle as a whole exhibits a greater and greater degree of contraction until tetanus, a sustained contraction, is reached. Eventually the muscle suffers fatigue and begins to relax. Fatigue in isolated muscles is associated with ATP depletion.

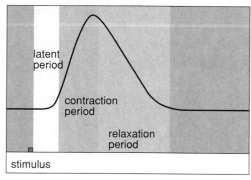

latent period

contraction period

relaxation period

stimulus

a.

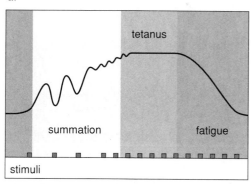

tetanus

summation

fatigue

stimuli

b.

How Muscles Function

Skeletal muscle contraction is voluntary and allows an animal to move; smooth muscle contraction pushes food along in the digestive tract, and cardiac muscle allows the heart to pump the blood. Extensive experimental work has been done to understand vertebrate skeletal muscle contraction. It is assumed that the contraction of the other types of muscles is similar to this type of muscle.

On a Macroscopic Level

Skeletal muscles, which make up over 40% of the body's weight, are attached to the skeleton by **tendons** [L. *tend,* stretch], made of fibrous connective tissue. When muscles contract, they shorten. Therefore, muscles can only pull; they cannot push. Because of this, skeletal muscles must work in *antagonistic pairs*. If one muscle of an antagonistic pair bends the joint and brings the limb toward the body, the other one straightens the joint and extends the limb. Figure 43.11 illustrates this principle and compares the actions of muscles in the limb of an arthropod, in which the muscles are attached to an exoskeleton, with those of a human, in whom the muscles are attached to an endoskeleton.

It is possible to study the contraction of individual whole muscles in the laboratory. Customarily, the gastrocnemius muscle is removed from a frog and mounted so one end is fixed and the other is movable. The mechanical force of contraction is transduced into an electrical current recorded by an apparatus called a *Physiograph.* The resulting pattern is called a *myogram* (fig. 43.12).

On a Microscopic Level

A whole skeletal muscle is composed of a number of muscle fibers in bundles (fig. 43.13). Each muscle fiber is a cell containing the usual cellular components but with special features. The plasma membrane, called the **sarcolemma** [Gk. *sarc,* flesh, and *lemma,* sheath], forms a *T* (for transverse) *system*: the *T tubules* penetrate, or dip down, into the cell so that they come into contact—but do not fuse—with expanded portions of the endoplasmic reticulum. These expanded portions, called calcium storage sacs, contain calcium ions (Ca⁺⁺), which are essential for muscle contraction. The endoplasmic reticulum encases hundreds and sometimes even thousands of **myofibrils** [Gk. *myo,* muscle, and L. *fibr,* fiber], which are the contractile portions of the fibers.

Myofibrils are cylindrical in shape and run the length of the muscle fiber. The light microscope shows that a myofibril has light and dark bands called *striations*. It is these bands that cause skeletal muscle to appear striated. The electron microscope shows that the striations of myofibrils are formed by the placement of protein filaments within contractile units called **sarcomeres** [Gk. *sarc,* flesh, and *mer,* part]. A sarcomere contains two types of protein filaments. The thick filaments are made up of a protein called **myosin,** and the thin filaments are made up of a protein called **actin.** A sarcomere extends between two dark Z lines. The I band contains only actin filaments, and the H zone contains only myosin filaments.

Figure 43.13
Skeletal muscle fiber structure and function. A muscle fiber contains many myofibrils divided into sarcomeres, which are contractile. A sarcomere contains actin (thin) filaments and myosin (thick) filaments. When a muscle fiber contracts, the thin filaments move toward the center so that the H zone gets smaller, to the point of disappearing.

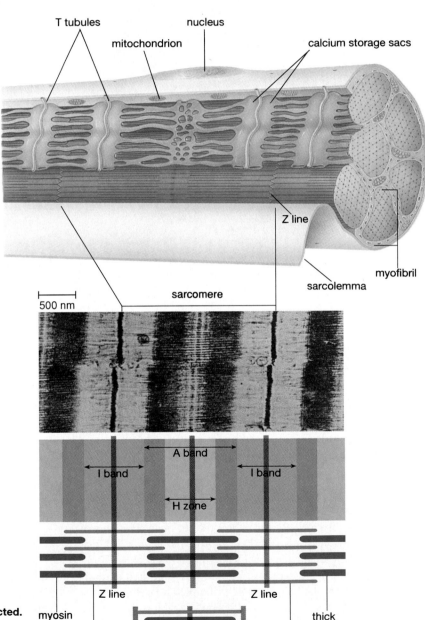

Muscle fiber has many myofibrils.

Myofibril has many sarcomeres.

Sarcomere is relaxed.

Sarcomere is contracted.

Figure 43.14

Sliding filament theory. **a.** Relaxed sarcomere. **b.** Contracted sarcomere. Note that during contraction, the I band and the H zone decrease in size. This indicates that the actin (thin) filaments slide past the myosin (thick) filaments. Even so, the myosin filaments do the work by pulling the actin filaments by means of cross-bridges.

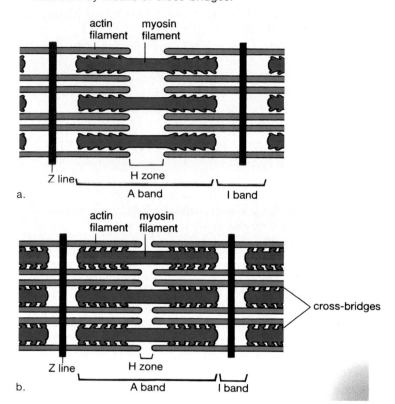

a.

actin filament   myosin filament

Z line   H zone   A band   I band

b.

actin filament   myosin filament

cross-bridges

Z line   H zone   A band   I band

Filaments Slide

As a muscle fiber contracts, the sarcomeres within the myofibrils shorten. When a sarcomere shortens (fig. 43.14b), the actin (thin) filaments slide past the myosin (thick) filaments and approach one another. This causes the I band to shorten and the H zone to nearly or completely disappear. The movement of actin filaments in relation to myosin filaments is called the **sliding filament theory** of muscle contraction. During the sliding process, the sarcomere shortens even though the filaments themselves remain the same length.

The participants in muscle contraction have the functions listed in table 43.1. Although it is the actin filaments that slide past the myosin filaments, it is the myosin filaments that do the work. In the presence of calcium ions (Ca^{++}), portions of a myosin filament called *cross-bridges* bend backward and attach to an actin filament (fig. 43.14). After attaching to the actin filament, the cross-bridges bend forward and the actin filament is pulled along. Now, ATP (adenosine triphosphate) is broken down by myosin, and detachment occurs. Note, therefore, that myosin is not only a structural protein, it is also an ATPase enzyme. The cross-bridges attach and detach some fifty to 100 times as the thin filaments are pulled to the center of a sarcomere.

Table 43.1

Muscle Contraction

Name	Function
Actin filaments	Slide past myosin, causing contraction
Ca^{++}	Needed for myosin to bind to actin
Myosin filaments	Pull actin filaments by means of cross-bridges; are enzymatic and split ATP
ATP	Supplies energy for muscle contraction

> The sliding filament theory states that actin filaments slide past myosin filaments because myosin has cross-bridges, which pull the actin filaments inward.

ATP provides the energy for muscle contraction to continue. To ensure a ready supply of ATP, muscle fibers contain creatine phosphate (phosphocreatine), a storage form of high-energy phosphate. Creatine phosphate does not directly participate in muscle contraction. Instead, it is used to regenerate ATP by the following reaction:

$$\text{creatine} \sim P + ADP \longrightarrow ATP + \text{creatine}$$

When ATP Is Needed

When all of the creatine phosphate is depleted and no oxygen (O$_2$) is available for aerobic respiration, a muscle fiber can generate ATP using fermentation, an anaerobic process. Fermentation, which is apt to occur during strenuous exercise, can supply ATP for only a short time because of lactate buildup. The buildup is noticeable when it produces muscle aches and fatigue upon exercising.

We all have had the experience of needing to continue deep breathing following strenuous exercise. This continued intake of oxygen is required to complete the metabolism of the lactate that has accumulated during exercise and that represents an **oxygen debt.** The lactate is transported to the liver, where 20% of it is completely broken down to carbon dioxide (CO$_2$) and water (H$_2$O). The ATP gained by this respiration then is used to reconvert 80% of the lactate to glucose.

> Creatine phosphate is used to generate ATP rapidly for muscle contraction. If oxygen is in limited supply, fermentation produces ATP but results in oxygen debt.

Nerves Stimulate Muscles

Muscles are innervated; that is, nerve impulses cause muscles to contract. A motor axon branches to several muscle fibers and, collectively, this is called a motor unit. Each branch ends in several axon bulbs, which contain synaptic vesicles with the neurotransmitter acetylcholine (ACh).

The region where an axon bulb lies in close proximity to the sarcolemma of a muscle fiber is called a **neuromuscular junction.** A neuromuscular junction (fig. 43.15a) has the same components as a synapse: a presynaptic membrane, a synaptic cleft, and a postsynaptic membrane. Only in this case the postsynaptic membrane is a portion of the sarcolemma of a muscle fiber. The sarcolemma, you will recall, forms T (for transverse) tubules, which dip down into the muscle fiber almost touching the calcium (Ca^{++}) storage sacs of the endoplasmic reticulum. The endoplasmic reticulum encases the myofibrils, which contain actin and myosin filaments (see fig. 43.13).

Nerve impulses travel down an axon, and it branches until nerve impulses reach the axon bulbs. Then the synaptic vesicles merge with the presynaptic membrane and ACh is released into the synaptic cleft. When ACh diffuses to and binds with receptor sites on the sarcolemma, the sarcolemma is depolarized. **Muscle action potentials** then spread over the sarcolemma and down the T system to the region of calcium storage sacs. When a muscle action potential reaches a sac, calcium ions are released. They diffuse into the cytoplasm, where they participate in muscle contraction.

It is now necessary to consider the structure of a thin filament in more detail. Figure 43.15b shows the placement of two other proteins associated with a thin filament (the double row of twisted globular actin molecules). Threads of tropomyosin wind about a thin (actin) filament, and troponin is found at intervals along the threads. After calcium ions are released, they combine with troponin. After this binding occurs, the tropomyosin threads shift their position, and myosin binding sites are exposed.

The thick (myosin) filament is a bundle of myosin molecules, each having a globular head. Each head is a cross-bridge that has an ATP-binding site. After ATP attaches to ATP-binding sites, the myosin cross-bridges reach out and attach to these binding sites, pulling the actin filaments toward the center of a sarcomere. The breakdown of ATP by myosin causes the cross-bridges to detach and then reattach to different binding sites. In this way, the actin filaments are pulled along toward the center of a sarcomere and past the myosin filaments.

The movement of the actin filaments causes muscle contraction. Contraction ceases when nerve impulses no longer stimulate the muscle fiber. With the cessation of a muscle action potential, calcium ions are pumped back into the endoplasmic reticulum by active transport. Relaxation now occurs.

> A neuromuscular junction functions like a synapse except muscle action potentials cause calcium ions (Ca^{++}) to be released from calcium storage sacs, and thereafter muscle contraction occurs.

Exercise Has Benefits

A regular exercise program, outlined in table 43.2, has many benefits. Aside from improved endurance and strength, an exercise program also helps many other organs of the body. Cardiac muscle enlarges and the heart can work harder than before. The resting heart rate decreases. Lung and diffusion capacity increase. Body fat decreases, but bone density increases so that breakage is less likely. Blood cholesterol and fat levels decrease, as does blood pressure.

Table 43.2

A Checklist for Staying Fit

Children, 7–12	Teenagers, 13–18	Adults, 19–55	Seniors, 55 and up
Pursue vigorous activity 1–2 hours daily	Pursue vigorous activity 3–5 times a week	Pursue vigorous activity for $^1/_2$ hour, 3 times a week	Pursue moderate exercise 3 times a week
Engage in free play	Build muscle with calisthenics	Exercise to prevent lower back pain: aerobics, stretching, yoga	Plan a daily walk
Build motor skills through team sports, dance, swimming	Plan aerobic exercise to control buildup of fat cells	Take active vacations: hike, bicycle, cross-country ski	Do daily stretching exercise
Encourage more exercise outside of physical education classes	Pursue tennis, swimming, horseback riding—sports that can be enjoyed for a lifetime	Find exercise partners: join a running club, a bicycle club, an outing group	Learn a new sport or activity: golf, fishing, ballroom dancing
Initiate family outings: bowling, boating, camping, hiking	Continue team sports, dancing, hiking, swimming		Try low-impact aerobics
			Consult your doctor before undertaking new exercises

Figure 43.15 〔CD〕 〔▭〕

Neuromuscular junction. The branch of an axon terminating in an axon bulb approaches, but does not touch, a muscle fiber. A synaptic cleft separates the axon bulb from the sarcolemma of the muscle fiber. When nerve impulses travel down an axon and its branches, synaptic vesicles discharge a neurotransmitter, which diffuses across the synaptic cleft. Muscle action potentials travel down the T system of a muscle fiber. Calcium ions (Ca++) are discharged from storage sacs and attach to actin filaments, exposing myosin binding sites. Myosin cross-bridges attach to and pull the actin filaments past the myosin filaments in each sarcomere within the myofibrils of a muscle fiber.

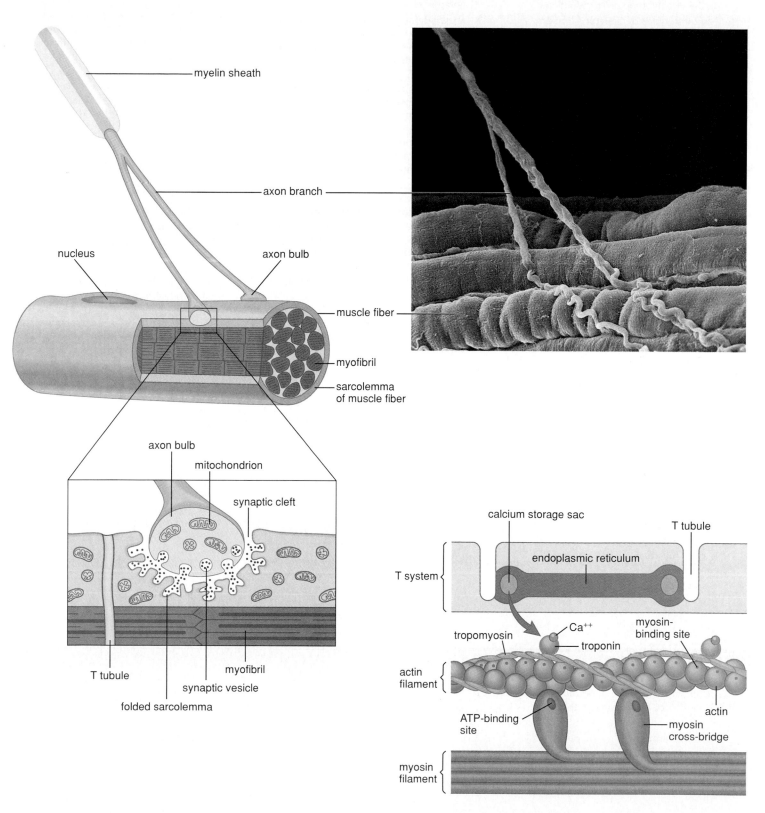

Summary

1. A rigid skeleton gives support to the body, helps protect internal organs, and assists movement. In vertebrates, the skeleton is also a storage area for calcium and phosphorous salts, as well as the site of blood cell production.

2. The three types of skeletons that are found in the animal kingdom are the hydrostatic skeleton (flatworms and segmented worms), the exoskeleton (certain mollusks and arthropods), and the endoskeleton (vertebrates).

3. Bone is constantly being renewed; osteoclasts break down bone and osteoblasts build new bone. Osteocytes are in the lacunae of osteons.

4. The human skeleton is divided into two parts: (1) the axial skeleton, which is made up of the skull, the ribs, the sternum, and the vertebrae; and (2) the appendicular skeleton, which is composed of the girdles and their appendages.

5. Joints are classified as immovable, like those of the cranium; slightly movable, like those between the vertebrae; and freely movable or synovial joints, like those in the knee and hip. In synovial joints, ligaments bind the two bones together, forming a capsule in which there is synovial fluid.

6. Whole skeletal muscles can only shorten when they contract; therefore, for a bone to be returned to its original position or the muscle to its original length, muscles must work in antagonistic pairs.

7. Muscle fibers contain a T (transverse) system, and the sarcolemma forms T tubules, which contact the endoplasmic reticulum. Here calcium ions (Ca^{++}) are stored.

8. Muscle fibers are cells that contain myofibrils in addition to the usual cellular components. Longitudinally, myofibrils are divided into sarcomeres, where it is possible to note the arrangement of actin filaments and myosin filaments.

9. When a sarcomere contracts, actin filaments slide past myosin filaments and the H zone all but disappears. Myosin has cross-bridges, which attach to and pull actin filaments along. ATP breakdown by myosin is necessary for detachment to occur.

10. The sliding filament theory of muscle contraction says that myosin filaments have cross-bridges, which attach to and detach from actin filaments, causing them to slide and the sarcomere to shorten. The H zone disappears as actin filaments approach one another.

11. Innervation of a muscle fiber begins at a neuromuscular junction. Here, synaptic vesicles release ACh into the synaptic cleft. When the sarcolemma receives ACh, a muscle action potential moves down the T system to calcium storage sacs. When calcium ions are released, contraction occurs. When calcium ions are actively transported back into the storage sacs, muscle relaxation occurs.

12. After calcium ions are released, contraction occurs because calcium combines with troponin, a protein that occurs on tropomyosin threads that wind about the actin filaments. This causes the threads to shift their position so that myosin binding sites on actin become available. When calcium ions are actively transported back into the storage sacs, muscle relaxation occurs.

Writing Across the Curriculum

In order to practice writing skills, students should write out the answers to any or all of the study questions and the critical thinking questions. The study questions are sequenced in the same order as the text. Answers to the objective questions, and suggested answers to the critical thinking questions, are in appendix D.

Study Questions

1. What are the three types of skeletons found in the animal kingdom, how do they differ, and what are some animals having each type?   750–51

2. Give several functions of the skeletal system in humans.   753

3. Describe the anatomy of a long bone; explain how bones grow and are renewed.   752–53

4. Distinguish between the axial and appendicular skeletons.   754, 756

5. List the bones that form the pectoral and pelvic girdles.   756–57

6. How are joints classified? Describe the anatomy of a freely movable joint.   758

7. Describe how muscles are attached to bones. What is accomplished by muscles acting in antagonistic pairs?   759

8. Discuss the microscopic structural features of a muscle fiber and a sarcomere. What is the sliding filament theory?   760–61

9. Discuss the availability and the specific role of ATP during muscle contraction. What is oxygen debt, and how is it repaid?   761

10. What causes a muscle action potential? How does the muscle action potential bring about sarcomere and muscle fiber contraction?   762–63

Objective Questions

For questions 1–4, match the following items with the correct locations given in the key.

Key:
- **a.** upper arm
- **b.** lower arm
- **c.** pectoral girdle
- **d.** pelvic girdle
- **e.** upper leg
- **f.** lower leg

1. ulna
2. tibia
3. clavicle
4. femur

5. Spongy bone
- **a.** contains osteons.
- **b.** contains red bone marrow where blood cells are formed.
- **c.** lends no strength to bones.
- **d.** All of these are correct.

6. Which of these is mismatched?
   a. slightly movable joint—vertebrae
   b. hinge joint—hip
   c. synovial joint—elbow
   d. immovable joint—sutures in cranium
7. In a muscle fiber
   a. the sarcolemma is connective tissue holding the myofibrils together.
   b. the T system contains calcium storage sacs.
   c. both filaments have cross-bridges.
   d. All of these are correct.
8. When muscles contract
   a. sarcomeres increase in size.
   b. myosin slides past actin.
   c. the H zone disappears.
   d. calcium is taken up by calcium storage sacs.
9. Which of these is a direct source of energy for muscle contraction?
   a. ATP
   b. creatine phosphate
   c. lactic acid
   d. Both a and b are correct.
10. Nervous stimulation of muscles
   a. occurs at a neuromuscular junction.
   b. results in an action potential that travels down the T system.
   c. causes calcium to be released from storage sacs.
   d. All of these are correct.

11. Give the function of each participant in the following reaction:

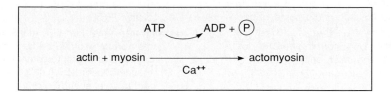

12. Label this diagram of a sarcomere:

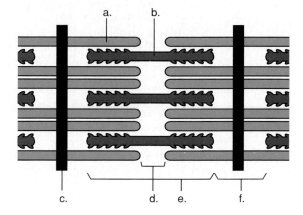

Concepts and Critical Thinking

1. *A bony skeleton determines the shape of an animal.*
   How does the skeleton aid adaptation to the environment?

2. *Movement is fundamental to the nature of animals.*
   Why is movement in animals more essential than in plants?

3. *Locomotion requires energy.*
   How do animals acquire the energy for locomotion, and specifically how is energy used to bring about locomotion?

Selected Key Terms

actin A muscle protein making up the thin filaments in a sarcomere; its movement shortens the sarcomere, yielding muscle contraction. 760

appendicular skeleton (ap-un-DIK-yuh-ler) Part of the skeleton forming the upper appendages, shoulder girdle, lower appendages, and hip girdle. [L. *append,* hang to, and Gk. *skelet,* dried body] 756

axial skeleton (AK-see-ul) Part of the skeleton forming the vertical support or axis, including the skull, the rib cage, and the vertebral column. [L. *axi,* axis, and Gk. *skelet,* dried body] 754

digit A finger or toe. 756

foramen magnum (fuh-RAY-mun MAG-num) Opening in the occipital bone of the skull through which the spinal cord passes. [L. *foram,* opening, and *magn,* large] 754

mandible The lower jaw; contains tooth sockets. [L. *mandibul,* jaw] 755

maxillae (sing., maxilla) (mak-SIL-ee) Two bones that form the upper jaw; contain tooth sockets. [L. *maxill,* jawbone] 755

menisci (sing., meniscus) (mun-NIS-ky) Fibrocartilage that separates the surfaces of bones in the knee. [Gk. *menisc,* crescent] 758

muscle action potential An electrochemical change due to increased sarcolemma permeability that is propagated down the T system and results in muscle contraction. 762

myofibril Specific muscle cell organelle containing a linear arrangement of sarcomeres, which shorten to produce muscle contraction. [Gk. *myo,* muscle, and L. *fibr,* fiber] 760

myosin (MY-uh-sun) A muscle protein making up the thick filaments in a sarcomere; it pulls actin to shorten the sarcomere, yielding muscle contraction. 760

neuromuscular junction Region where an axon bulb approaches a muscle fiber; contains a presynaptic membrane, a synaptic cleft, and a postsynaptic membrane.   762

osteoblast A bone-forming cell. [Gk. *ost,* bone, and *blast,* bud]   753

osteoclast A cell that causes erosion of bone. [Gk. *ost,* bone, and *clas,* fragment]   753

osteocyte A mature bone cell. [Gk. *ost,* bone, and *cyt,* cell]   753

oxygen debt The use of oxygen to metabolize lactate, a compound that accumulates during vigorous exercise.   761

pectoral girdle Portion of the skeleton that provides support and attachment for the arms. [Gk. *pechy,* forearm]   756

pelvic girdle Portion of the skeleton to which the legs are attached. [L. *pelv,* pelvis]   757

rib Bone hinged to the vertebral column and sternum, which, with muscle, defines the top and sides of the chest cavity.   756

sarcolemma (sahr-kuh-LEM-uh) Plasma membrane of a muscle fiber that forms the tubules of the T system involved in muscular contraction. [Gk. *sarc,* flesh, and *lemma,* sheath]   760

sarcomere (SAHR-kuh-mir) One of many units, arranged linearly within a myofibril, whose contraction produces muscle contraction. [Gk. *sarc,* flesh, and *mer,* part]   760

sinus A cavity, as with the sinuses in the human skull. [L. *sinu,* a hollow]   754

sliding filament theory The movement of actin filaments in relation to myosin filaments, which accounts for muscle contraction.   761

sternum The breastbone to which the ribs are ventrally attached. [Gk. *stern,* breastbone]   756

tendon Structure consisting of fibrous connective tissue that connects skeletal muscles to bones. [L. *tend,* stretch]   759

vertebral column The backbone of vertebrates through which the spinal cord passes. [L. *vertebr,* vertebra]   756

ENDOCRINE SYSTEM

Learning Objectives

- Discuss the relationship between the endocrine system and the nervous system; give examples to show that there are regions of overlap between their functions.   781

Hormones Affect Cellular Metabolism

- Chemically distinguish between the two major types of vertebrate hormones, and explain how each type brings about its effect on the cell.   768–69

Human Endocrine System

- Describe the location of each of the major endocrine glands of the human body.   771

- List the most important hormones produced by each endocrine gland, and describe their most important effects.   771–80

- Contrast the ways in which the hypothalamus controls the posterior and anterior pituitary.   771–73

- Explain the concept of control by negative feedback, and give several specific examples among hormones.   774

Environmental Signals in Three Categories

- Discuss environmental signals in general and three types of environmental signals in particular; discuss why the term *hormone* could be broadened to include all these categories.   781–82

The display of male birds such as this great egret, *Casmerodius,* is promoted by the male sex hormones called androgens.

The **endocrine system,** along with the nervous system, coordinates the various activities of body parts. An animal must actively find food, avoid predators, and find a mate. The internal environment must be maintained within certain limits as food is digested, nutrient molecules and oxygen are distributed to the cells, and wastes are eliminated. Both endocrine and nervous systems utilize chemical messengers to coordinate these activities. In the nervous system, neurons release neurotransmitters that influence the excitability of other neurons. In contrast, the endocrine system utilizes hormones, chemical messengers that are typically released directly into the bloodstream.

The nervous system reacts quickly to external and internal stimuli; you rapidly pull your hand away from a hot stove. The endocrine system tends to react somewhat slower because it takes time for a hormone to travel through the circulatory system to its target organ. It is important to stress that a hormone does not seek out a particular organ; to the contrary, the organ is awaiting the arrival of the hormone. Cells that can react to a hormone have specific receptors, which combine with the hormone in a lock-and-key manner. Therefore, certain cells respond to one hormone and not to another, depending on their receptors.

A **hormone** [Gk. *hormon,* excite] is defined as an organic chemical produced by one set of cells that affects a different set. Notice that this definition allows us to categorize all sorts of chemical messengers as hormones, even neurotransmitters! A certain amount of overlap between the nervous and endocrine systems is to be expected. The nervous and endocrine systems evolved simultaneously, no doubt making occasional use of the same chemical messengers and communicating not only with other systems but with each other as well. We will examine several examples of associations between the two systems on the pages that follow.

> Both the nervous and endocrine systems function to coordinate body parts and activities.

HORMONES AFFECT CELLULAR METABOLISM

Many vertebrate hormones are proteins or peptides that are coded for by genes and are synthesized within the cytoplasm at the ribosomes. Eventually, they are packaged into vesicles at the Golgi apparatus and are secreted at the plasma membrane. There are other hormones, called catecholamines, that are derived from the amino acid tyrosine. Their production requires only a series of metabolic reactions within the cytoplasm. From the viewpoint of hormonal action, we can categorize the proteins, peptides, and catecholamines as *peptide hormones.*

Other vertebrate hormones—produced by the adrenal cortex, the ovaries, and the testes—are steroids. *Steroid hormones* are derived from cholesterol by a series of metabolic reactions. These hormones are stored in fat droplets in the cell cytoplasm until their release at the plasma membrane.

Steroid Hormones Activate DNA

Steroid hormones do not bind to cell-surface receptors; they can enter the cell and the nucleus freely (fig. 44.1). Once inside the nucleus, steroid hormones such as estrogen and progesterone bind to receptors. The hormone-receptor complex is believed to bind to transcription factors that in turn bind to DNA (deoxyribonucleic acid). Particular genes are activated; transcription of DNA and translation of messenger ribonucleic acid (mRNA) follow. In this manner, steroid hormones lead to protein synthesis.

Figure 44.1

Cellular activity of steroid hormones. After passing through the plasma membrane, a steroid hormone binds to a receptor inside the cell. Recent evidence indicates that the receptors reside in the nucleus rather than the cytoplasm. The hormone-receptor complex then binds to a transcription factor, and this leads to activation of certain genes and protein synthesis.

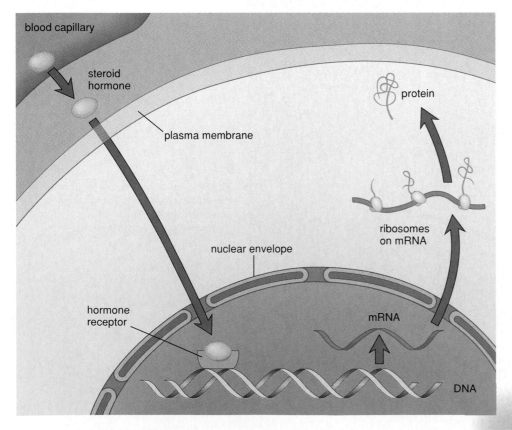

44-2

Hormones are chemical messengers that influence the metabolism of the recipient cell. Peptide hormones activate existing enzymes in the cell, and steroid hormones bring about the synthesis of new proteins. Steroids act more slowly than peptides because it takes more time to synthesize new proteins than to activate enzymes that are already present in the cell. However, steroids have a more *sustained* effect on the metabolism of the cell than do peptide hormones.

Peptide Hormones Activate Enzymes

The mode of action of peptide hormones was discovered in the 1950s by Earl W. Sutherland, Jr., who studied the effects of epinephrine on liver cells. Sutherland received a Nobel prize for his hypothesis that when this hormone binds to a cell-surface receptor, the resulting complex leads to the activation of an enzyme that produces **cyclic AMP** (adenosine monophosphate) (fig. 44.2). Cyclic AMP (cAMP) is a compound made from ATP (adenosine triphosphate), but it contains only one phosphate group, which is attached to adenosine at two locations.

Since peptide hormones never enter the cell, they are sometimes called the first messengers, while cAMP, which sets the metabolic machinery in motion, is called the second messenger. Later research has shown that there is an intermediary between the first messenger and adenylate cyclase, the enzyme that converts ATP to cAMP. G proteins, named for their ability to bind to and break down GTP (guanosine triphosphate), an energy carrier similar to ATP, are directly stimulated by the hormone-receptor interaction. G proteins are located in the membrane and regulate the action of many other membrane proteins, particularly ion channels and enzymes. In this instance, the stimulated G protein activates adenylate cyclase and cAMP results.

cAMP is a second messenger that sets an *enzyme cascade* into motion. cAMP activates only one particular enzyme in the cell, but this enzyme in turn activates another, and so forth. The activated enzymes, of course, can be used repeatedly. Therefore, at every step in the enzyme cascade, more and more reactions take place—the binding of a single hormone molecule eventually results in a 1,000-fold response. Peptide hormones tend to act relatively quickly but for a short period of time. cAMP is soon converted to an inactive product and the enzymes revert to an inactive state.

Other second messengers have been discovered in cells. Inositol triphosphate (IP_3) is a second messenger that causes the release of calcium ions (Ca^{++}) in muscle cells. Since calcium goes on to activate other proteins, it is called the third messenger. It is apparent from our discussion, then, that hormones are involved in a signal transduction pathway:

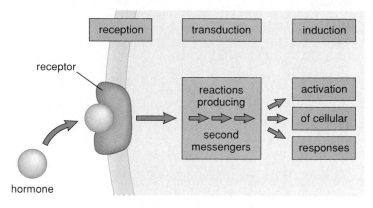

Transduction is the sequence of steps that occur between signal reception and cell response. G proteins are intimately involved in transducing the signal so that the cell responds appropriately.

Figure 44.2

Cellular activity of peptide hormones. Peptide hormones, which are called the first messengers, bind to a specific receptor protein in the plasma membrane. The hormone-receptor complex activates a G protein that binds to GTP; a portion of the complex splits off and activates adenylate cyclase. Adenylate cyclase acts on ATP to produce cAMP, the second messenger, which activates an enzyme cascade. There are also inhibitory G proteins.

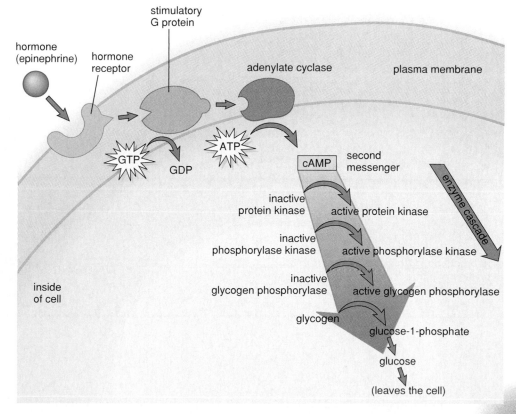

Insect Growth Hormones

All animals use chemical messengers to regulate the activities of their cells. These messengers are now being identified in a wide variety of invertebrate animals. The work on insect growth hormones began in the 1930s, so they have been studied for some time.

Insects, like other arthropods, have an exoskeleton that must be shed periodically in order to accommodate growth. Typically, the larvae of insects molt (shed their skeleton) a number of times before they pupate and metamorphose into an adult (fig. 44A). V. B. Wigglesworth showed in the 1930s that the insect brain was necessary for maturation to take place because it produced a hormone appropriately called *brain hormone*. Brain hormone stimulates the prothoracic gland, which lies in the region just behind the head, to secrete *ecdysone,* a steroid hormone. This hormone is also called the molt-and-maturation hormone because it promotes both molting and maturation. During larval stages, however, response to ecdysone is modified by the action of *juvenile hormone.* If juvenile hormone is present, the insect molts into another larval form; if it is minimally present, the insect pupates; and if it is absent, the insect undergoes metamorphosis into an adult.

Some plants produce compounds that are similar or identical to either ecdysone or juvenile hormone. These compounds apparently protect the plants by disrupting the development of the insects that feed upon them. Work is under way to extract these compounds for use as insecticides.

Figure 44A
How juvenile hormone, brain hormone, and ecdysone (the molt-and-maturation hormone) interact to bring about maturation of insects.

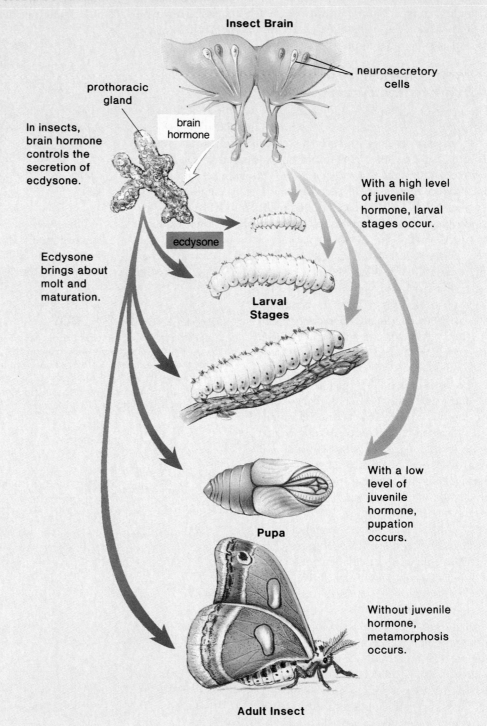

Insect Brain

neurosecretory cells

prothoracic gland

brain hormone

In insects, brain hormone controls the secretion of ecdysone.

ecdysone

Ecdysone brings about molt and maturation.

With a high level of juvenile hormone, larval stages occur.

Larval Stages

With a low level of juvenile hormone, pupation occurs.

Pupa

Without juvenile hormone, metamorphosis occurs.

Adult Insect

HUMAN ENDOCRINE SYSTEM

Endocrine glands can be contrasted with exocrine glands. The latter have ducts and secrete their products into these ducts for transport into body cavities. For example, the salivary glands send saliva into the mouth by way of the salivary ducts. Endocrine glands are ductless; they secrete their hormones directly into the bloodstream for distribution throughout the body.

The human endocrine system can be used to exemplify the vertebrate endocrine system (fig. 44.3). Even so, there are marked differences in the vertebrate hormones. Prolactin in humans stimulates female breasts to secrete milk, but in pigeons it stimulates the secretion of crop milk, a product of the gut. Some hormones have entirely different functions in different vertebrates. Thyroxin in humans stimulates metabolism, but in frogs it induces metamorphosis (the transformation of tadpole to adult). Other hormones are species-specific; that is, they function only in one species.

Hypothalamus Controls the Pituitary Gland

The hypothalamus is the portion of the brain that regulates the internal environment; it helps to control heart rate, body temperature, and water balance, as well as the glandular secretions of the **pituitary gland.** The pituitary, a small gland about 1 cm in diameter, lies just below the hypothalamus and is divided into two portions called the posterior pituitary and the anterior pituitary.

Posterior Pituitary Stores Two Hormones

The structural and functional relation between the hypothalamus and the posterior pituitary illustrates the overlap between the nervous and endocrine systems. The posterior pituitary is connected to the hypothalamus by means of a stalklike structure. There are neurons in the hypothalamus that are called neurosecretory cells because they both respond to neurotransmitters and produce the hormones that are stored in and released from the posterior pituitary. The hormones pass from the hypothalamus through axons that terminate in the posterior pituitary.

The axon endings in the posterior pituitary store **antidiuretic hormone (ADH)** [Gk. *anti,* against, and *diure,* urinate]—sometimes called vasopressin—and oxytocin (table 44.1). ADH promotes the reabsorption of water from the collecting ducts, which receive urine produced by nephrons within the kidneys. The hypothalamus contains other nerve cells that act as a sensor because they are sensitive to the tonicity of the blood. When these cells determine that the blood is too concentrated, ADH is released into the bloodstream from the axon endings in the posterior pituitary. As the blood becomes dilute, the hormone no longer is released. This is an example of control by negative feedback because the effect of the hormone (to dilute blood) acts to shut down the release of the hormone.

Oxytocin [Gk. *oxy,* sharp, and *toc,* birth] is the other hormone that is made in the hypothalamus and stored in the posterior pituitary. Oxytocin causes the uterus to contract and is used to artificially induce labor. It also stimulates the release of milk from the mammary glands for nursing.

> The posterior pituitary stores two hormones, ADH and oxytocin, both of which are produced by and released from neurosecretory cells in the hypothalamus.

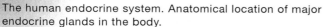

Figure 44.3 🔘

The human endocrine system. Anatomical location of major endocrine glands in the body.

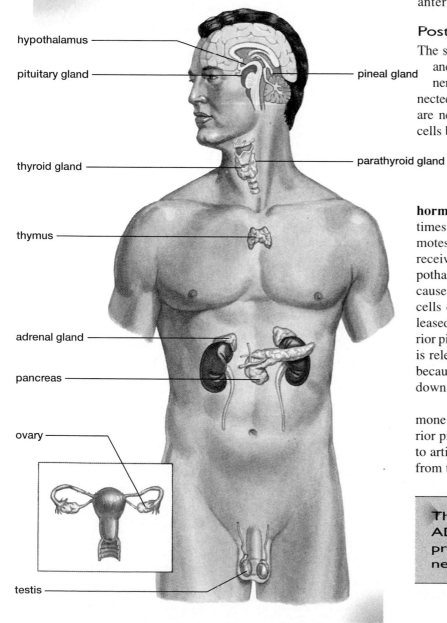

hypothalamus

pituitary gland

pineal gland

thyroid gland

parathyroid gland

thymus

adrenal gland

pancreas

ovary

testis

Table 44.1

Human Endocrine Glands and Their Hormones

Endocrine Gland	Hormone Released	Chemical Structure of Hormone	Target Tissues/ Organ	Chief Function(s) of Hormone
Hypothalamus	Hypothalamic-releasing hormones Hypothalamic-release-inhibiting hormones	Peptide	Anterior pituitary	Regulate anterior pituitary hormones
Anterior pituitary	Thyroid-stimulating (TSH, thyrotropic)	Glycoprotein	Thyroid	Stimulates thyroid
	Adrenocorticotropic (ACTH)	Polypeptide	Adrenal cortex	Stimulates adrenal cortex
	Gonadotropic (follicle-stimulating [FSH], luteinizing [LH])	Glycoprotein	Gonads	Controls egg and sperm production Controls sex hormone production
	Prolactin (PRL)	Protein	Mammary glands	Stimulates milk production
	Growth (GH, somatotropic)	Protein	Soft tissues, bones	Stimulates cell division, protein synthesis, and bone growth
	Melanocyte-stimulating (MSH)	Polypeptide	Melanocytes in skin	Unknown function in humans; regulates skin color in lower vertebrates
Posterior pituitary	Antidiuretic (ADH, vasopressin)	Peptide	Kidneys	Stimulates water reabsorption by kidneys
	Oxytocin	Peptide	Uterus, mammary glands	Stimulates uterine muscle contraction and release of milk by mammary glands
Thyroid	Thyroxin (T4) and triiodothyronine (T3)	Iodinated amino acid	All tissues	Increase metabolic rate; help regulate growth and development
	Calcitonin	Peptide	Bones, kidneys, intestine	Lowers blood calcium level
Parathyroids	Parathyroid (PTH)	Polypeptide	Bones, kidneys, intestine	Raises blood calcium level
Adrenal cortex	Glucocorticoids (cortisol)	Steroid	All tissues	Raise blood glucose level; stimulate breakdown of protein
	Mineralocorticoids (aldosterone)	Steroid	Kidneys	Stimulate kidneys to reabsorb sodium and to excrete potassium
	Sex hormones	Steroid	Gonads, skin, muscles, bones	Stimulate development of secondary sex characteristics (particularly in male)
Adrenal medulla	Epinephrine and norepinephrine	Catecholamine	Cardiac and other muscles	Stimulate fight-or-flight reactions; raise blood glucose level
Pancreas	Insulin	Polypeptide	Liver, muscles, adipose tissue	Lowers blood glucose level; promotes formation of glycogen, proteins, and fats
	Glucagon	Polypeptide	Liver, muscles, adipose tissue	Raises blood glucose level; promotes breakdown of glycogen, proteins, and fats
Gonads				
Testes	Androgens (testosterone)	Steroid	Gonads, skin, muscles, bones	Stimulate spematogenesis; develop and maintain secondary male sex characteristics
Ovaries	Estrogens and progesterone	Steroid	Gonads, skin, muscles, bones	Stimulate growth of uterine lining; develop and maintain secondary female sex characteristics
Thymus	Thymosins	Peptide	T lymphocytes	Stimulate production and maturation of T lymphocytes
Pineal gland	Melatonin	Catecholamine	Circadian rhythms	Involved in circadian and circannual rhythms; possibly involved in maturation of sex organs
Digestive tract	Gastrin	Peptide	Stomach lining	Stimulates secretion of gastric juices
	Secretin	Peptide	Pancreas	Stimulates secretion of pancreatic juices
	Cholecystokinin (CCK)	Peptide	Pancreas, gall-bladder	Stimulates secretion of pancreatic juices and flow of bile from gallbladder

Anterior Pituitary Is the Master Gland

By the 1930s, biologists knew that the hypothalamus also controls the release of the anterior pituitary hormones. Electrical stimulation of the hypothalamus causes the release of anterior pituitary hormones, but *direct* stimulation of the anterior pituitary itself has no effect. Detailed anatomical studies show that there is a *portal* system consisting of blood vessels connecting a capillary bed in the hypothalamus with one in the anterior pituitary (fig. 44.4). Some scientists believed that a different set of neurosecretory cells in the hypothalamus synthesizes a number of different releasing hormones that are sent to the anterior pituitary by way of the vascular portal system. There began a long and competitive struggle between two groups of investigators to identify one of these *hypothalamic-releasing hormones,* which cause the anterior pituitary to release hormones. The group headed by R. Guillemin processed nearly 2 million sheep hypothalami, and the group headed by A. V. Schally processed more than a million pig hypothalami until each group announced, in November of 1969, that it had isolated and determined the structure of one of these hormones, a peptide containing only three amino acids.

Later, it was found that some of the hypothalamic hormones inhibit the release of anterior pituitary hormones. Therefore, today, it is customary to speak of *hypothalamic-releasing hormones* and *hypothalamic-release-inhibiting hormones.* There is a *gonadotropic-releasing hormone (GnRH)* and a gonadotropic-release-inhibiting hormone (GnRIH). The first hormone stimulates the anterior pituitary to release gonadotropic hormones, and the second inhibits the anterior pituitary from releasing the same hormones.

Figure 44.4

Hypothalamus and anterior pituitary. The hypothalamus controls the secretions of the anterior pituitary, and the anterior pituitary controls the secretions of these other endocrine glands.

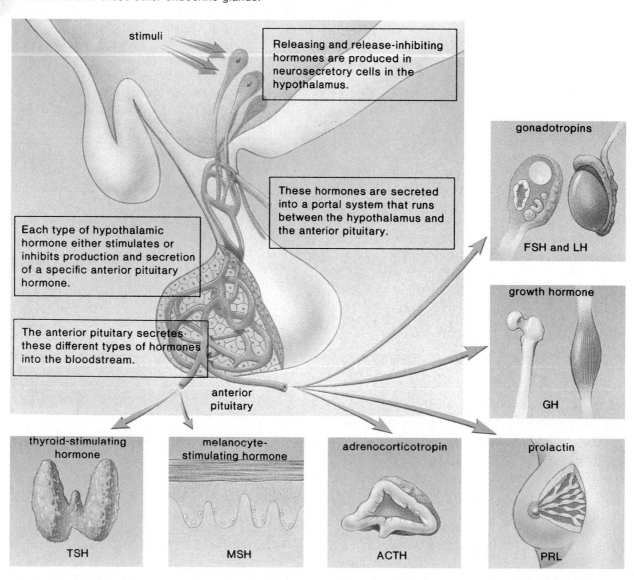

stimuli

Releasing and release-inhibiting hormones are produced in neurosecretory cells in the hypothalamus.

gonadotropins

These hormones are secreted into a portal system that runs between the hypothalamus and the anterior pituitary.

Each type of hypothalamic hormone either stimulates or inhibits production and secretion of a specific anterior pituitary hormone.

FSH and LH

growth hormone

The anterior pituitary secretes these different types of hormones into the bloodstream.

anterior pituitary

GH

thyroid-stimulating hormone

melanocyte-stimulating hormone

adrenocorticotropin

prolactin

TSH

MSH

ACTH

PRL

The anterior pituitary produces at least six different types of hormones, each by a distinct cell type (see fig. 44.4). Three of these hormones have a direct effect on the body. **Growth hormone (GH),** or somatotropic hormone, dramatically affects physical appearance since it determines the height of the individual. If too little GH is produced during childhood, the individual becomes a pituitary dwarf, and if too much is produced, the individual is a pituitary giant. In both instances, the individual has normal body proportions. On occasion, however, there is overproduction of growth hormone in the adult, and a condition called *acromegaly* results. Since only the feet, hands, and face (particularly chin, nose, and eyebrow ridges) can respond, these portions of the body become overly large.

GH promotes cell division, protein synthesis, and bone growth. It stimulates the transport of amino acids into cells and increases the activity of ribosomes, both of which are essential to protein synthesis. In bones, it promotes growth of the cartilaginous plates and causes osteoblasts to form bone. Evidence suggests that the effects on cartilage and bone may actually be due to hormones called *somatomedins,* which are released by the liver in response to GH.

Prolactin (PRL) [Gk. *pro,* before, and L. *lact,* milk] is produced in quantity only after childbirth. It causes the mammary glands in the breasts to develop and produce milk. It also plays a role in carbohydrate and fat metabolism.

Melanocyte-stimulating hormone (MSH) [Gk. *melano,* black, and *cyt,* cell] causes skin color changes in many fishes, amphibians, and reptiles who have melanophores, special skin cells that produce color variations. In humans, MSH stimulates melanocytes to increase their synthesis of melanin. It is derived from a molecule that is also the precursor for both ACTH and the anterior pituitary endorphins. These endorphins are structurally and functionally similar to the endorphins produced in brain nerve cells.

The anterior pituitary is sometimes called the *master gland* because it controls the secretion of some other endocrine glands (see fig. 44.4). As indicated in table 44.1, the anterior pituitary secretes the following hormones, which have an effect on other glands:

1. **Thyroid-stimulating hormone (TSH)**

2. **Adrenocorticotropic hormone (ACTH),** which stimulates the adrenal cortex

3. **Gonadotropic hormones (FSH and LH),** which stimulate the gonads—the testes in males and the ovaries in females

TSH causes the thyroid to produce thyroxin; ACTH causes the adrenal cortex to produce cortisol; and gonadotropic hormones cause the gonads to secrete sex hormones. A three-tiered relationship exists among the hypothalamus, the anterior pituitary, and the other endocrine glands; the hypothalamus produces releasing hormones, which control the anterior pituitary, and the anterior pituitary produces hormones that control the thyroid, the adrenal cortex, and the gonads. In turn these glands produce hormones that, through a negative feedback mechanism, regulate the secretion of the appropriate hypothalamic-releasing hormone.

> The hypothalamus, the anterior pituitary, and the other endocrine glands controlled by the anterior pituitary are all involved in a self-regulating negative feedback mechanism.

Thyroid Gland Speeds Metabolism

The **thyroid gland** [Gk. *thyro,* door] is a large gland located in the neck, where it is attached to the trachea just below the larynx (fig. 44.5a). The two hormones produced by the thyroid both contain iodine. **Thyroxin,** or T_4, contains four atoms of iodine; it is secreted in greater amounts but is less potent than triiodothyronine, or T_3, which has only three atoms of iodine. Iodine is actively transported into the thyroid gland, and it may reach a concentration as much as twenty-five times greater than that of the blood.

Even before the structure of thyroxin was known, it was surmised that the hormone contained iodine because when iodine is lacking in the diet, the thyroid gland enlarges, producing a **goiter.** The cause of the enlargement becomes clear if we consider the relationship between the thyroid and the anterior pituitary.

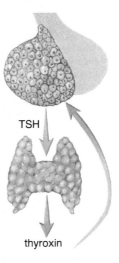

TSH

thyroxin

Figure 44.5

Thyroid and parathyroid glands. **a.** The thyroid gland is located in the neck in front of the trachea. **b.** The four parathyroid glands are embedded in the posterior surface of the thyroid gland. Yet the parathyroid and thyroid glands have no anatomical or physiological connection with one another. **c.** Regulation of parathyroid hormone (PTH) secretion. A low blood calcium level causes the parathyroids to secrete PTH, which causes the kidneys and the intestine to retain calcium and osteoclasts to break down bone. The result is a higher blood calcium level. A high blood calcium level then inhibits the secretion of PTH.

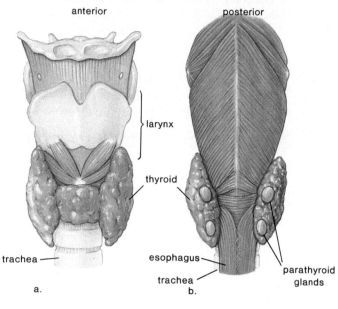

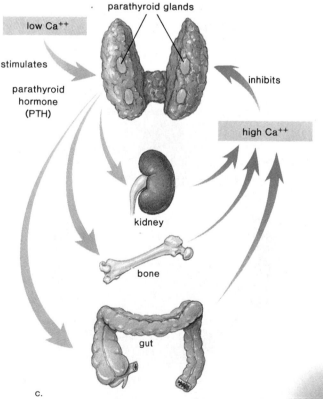

The anterior pituitary produces TSH, which stimulates the thyroid to secrete thyroxin. The increased level of thyroxin exerts feedback control over the anterior pituitary, which ceases to produce TSH. When there is a low level of thyroxin in the blood, the anterior pituitary continues to produce TSH. The thyroid responds by increasing in size and producing a goiter, but this increase in size is ineffective because active thyroxin cannot be produced without iodine. Eventually scientists discovered that a goiter can be prevented by consumption of iodized salt.

In general thyroxin increases the metabolic rate in all cells; the number of respiratory enzymes increases, as does oxygen uptake. Thyroxin is necessary in vertebrates for proper growth and development. For example, without thyroxin, frogs do not metamorphose properly, and humans do not mature properly. *Cretinism* occurs in individuals who have suffered from hypothyroidism (low thyroid function) since birth. They show reduced skeletal growth, sexual immaturity, and abnormal protein metabolism. The latter leads to mental retardation.

In addition to thyroxin, the thyroid gland also produces the hormone *calcitonin*. This hormone lowers the level of calcium in the blood and opposes the action of the parathyroid hormone, which we will discuss in the next section.

> **Thyroxin speeds up metabolism and helps regulate growth and development in immature animals.**

Parathyroid Glands Regulate Calcium

The four **parathyroid glands** are embedded in the posterior surface of the thyroid gland (fig. 44.5*b*). They produce a hormone called **parathyroid hormone (PTH).** Under the influence of PTH, the calcium (Ca^{++}) level in the blood increases and the phosphate (PO_4) level decreases. PTH stimulates the *absorption* of calcium from the gut by activating vitamin D, the *retention* of calcium (the excretion of phosphate) by the kidneys, and the *demineralization* of the bone by promoting the activity of the osteoclasts, the bone-reabsorbing cells. When the blood calcium level reaches the appropriate level, the parathyroid glands no longer produce PTH (fig. 44.5*c*).

If PTH is not produced in response to low blood calcium, *tetany* results because calcium plays an important role in both nervous conduction and muscle contraction. In tetany, the body shakes from continuous muscle contraction. The effect is brought about by increased excitability of the nerves, which fire spontaneously and without rest.

> **Parathyroid hormone (PTH) maintains a high blood calcium level. Its actions are opposed by calcitonin, which is produced by the thyroid.**

Adrenal Glands Contain Two Parts

Each of the two **adrenal glands** [L. *ad,* toward, and *rena,* kidney], lies atop a kidney (see fig. 44.3). Each consists of an inner portion called the medulla and an outer portion called the cortex. These portions, like the anterior pituitary and the posterior pituitary, have no physiological connection with one another.

Adrenal Medulla Is for Fight or Flight

The adrenal medulla secretes *epinephrine* and *norepinephrine* under conditions of stress. They bring about all those responses we associate with the "fight-or-flight" reaction: the blood glucose level and the metabolic rate increase, as do breathing and the heart rate. The blood vessels in the intestine constrict, and those in the muscles dilate. This increased circulation to the muscles causes them to have more stamina than usual. In times of emergency, the sympathetic nervous system *initiates* these responses, but they are *maintained* by secretions from the adrenal medulla.

The adrenal medulla is innervated by one set of sympathetic nerve fibers. Recall that usually there are preganglionic and postganglionic nerve fibers for each organ stimulated. In this instance, what happened to the postganglionic neurons? It appears that the adrenal medulla may have evolved from a modification of the postganglionic neurons. Like the neurosecretory neurons in the hypothalamus, these neurons also secrete hormones into the bloodstream. This is another example of a connection between the nervous and endocrine systems.

Adrenal Cortex Keeps Things Steady

Although the adrenal medulla may be removed with no ill effects, the adrenal cortex is essential to life. The two major classes of hormones made by the adrenal cortex are the *glucocorticoids* and the *mineralocorticoids.* The cortex also secretes a small amount of male and an even smaller amount of female sex hormones. All of these hormones are steroids.

Of the various glucocorticoids, the hormone responsible for the greatest amount of activity is *cortisol.* Cortisol promotes the hydrolysis of muscle protein to amino acids that enter the blood. This leads to an increased level of glucose when the liver converts these amino acids to glucose. Cortisol also favors metabolism of fatty acids rather than carbohydrates. In opposition to insulin, therefore, cortisol raises the blood glucose level. Cortisol also counteracts the inflammatory response, which leads to the pain and swelling of joints in arthritis and bursitis. The administration of cortisol eases the symptoms of these conditions because it reduces inflammation.

The secretion of cortisol by the adrenal cortex is under the control of the anterior pituitary hormone ACTH. The hypothalamus produces corticotropin-releasing hormone (CRH) that stimulates the anterior pituitary to release ACTH. ACTH in turn stimulates the adrenal cortex to secrete cortisol, which regulates its own synthesis by negative feedback of both CRH and ACTH synthesis.

The secretion of mineralocorticoids, the most significant of which is **aldosterone** [Gk. *aldainein,* nourish, and *stereos,* solid], is not under the control of the anterior pituitary. Aldosterone regulates the level of sodium ions (Na$^+$) and potassium ions (K$^+$) in the blood. Its primary target organ is the kidney, where it promotes renal absorption of sodium and renal excretion of potassium. The blood sodium level is particularly important to the maintenance of blood pressure, and the concentration of this ion indirectly regulates the secretion of aldosterone. When the blood sodium level is low, the kidneys secrete renin (fig. 44.6). Renin is an enzyme that converts the plasma protein angiotensinogen to angiotensin I, which becomes angiotensin II in the lungs. Angiotensin II stimulates the adrenal cortex to release aldosterone. This is called the renin-angiotensin-aldosterone homeostatic system. The effect of this system raises the blood pressure in two ways. First, angiotensin constricts the arteries directly, and second, aldosterone causes the kidneys to reabsorb sodium. When blood sodium level is high, water is reabsorbed, and blood volume and pressure are maintained.

Cortisol, which raises the blood glucose level, and aldosterone, which raises the blood sodium level, are two hormones secreted by the adrenal cortex.

Figure 44.6

Renin-angiotensin-aldosterone homeostatic system. If the blood level of sodium is low, the kidneys secrete renin. The increased renin acts via the increased production of angiotensin I and II to stimulate aldosterone secretion. Aldosterone promotes reabsorption of sodium by the kidneys; when the blood sodium level rises, the kidneys stop secreting renin.

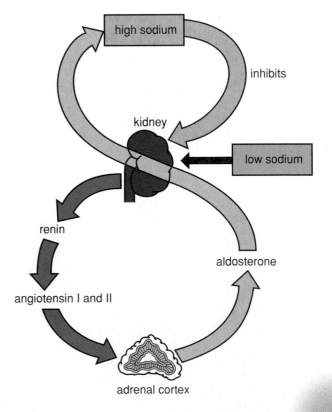

Figure 44.7

The pancreas is both an exocrine gland and an endocrine gland. It sends digestive juices to the duodenum by way of the pancreatic duct, and it sends the hormones insulin and glucagon into the bloodstream. In 1920, physician Frederick Banting decided to try to isolate insulin. Previous investigators had been unable to do this because the enzymes in the digestive juices destroyed insulin (a protein) during the isolation procedure. He hit upon the idea of tying off the pancreatic duct, which he knew from previous research would lead to the degeneration only of the cells that produce digestive juices and not of the pancreatic islets (of Langerhans), where insulin is made. J. J. Macleod made a laboratory available to him at the University of Toronto and also assigned a graduate student, Charles Best, to assisting him. Banting and Best had limited funds and spent that summer working, sleeping, and eating in the lab. By the end of the summer, they had obtained pancreatic extracts that did lower the blood glucose level in diabetic dogs. Macleod then brought in biochemists, who purified the extract. Insulin therapy for the first human patient began in 1922, and large-scale production of purified insulin from pigs and cattle followed. Banting and Macleod received a Nobel Prize for their work in 1923. The amino acid sequence of insulin was determined in 1953. Insulin is presently synthesized using recombinant DNA technology. Banting and Best followed the required steps given in the chart to identify a chemical messenger.

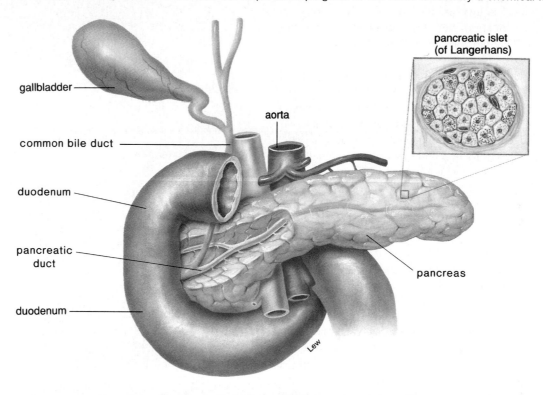

Steps	Example
Identify the source of the chemical	Pancreas is source
Identify the effect to be studied	Presence of pancreas in body lowers blood sugar
Isolate the chemical	Insulin isolated from pancreatic secretions
Show that the chemical alone has the effect	Insulin alone lowers blood sugar

Pancreas Is Both Endocrine and Exocrine Gland

The **pancreas** is a long organ that lies transversely in the abdomen between the kidneys and near the duodenum of the small intestine (fig. 44.7). It is composed of two types of tissue. Exocrine tissue produces and secretes *digestive juices* that go by way of ducts to the small intestine. Endocrine tissue, called the **pancreatic islets** (of Langerhans), produces and secretes the hormones **insulin** and **glucagon** [Gk. *gluc*, sweet, and *ago*, lead toward] directly into the blood.

All the cells of the body use glucose as an energy source; to preserve the health of the body, it is important that the glucose concentration remain within normal limits. Insulin is secreted when there is a high blood glucose level, which usually occurs just after eating. Insulin has three different actions: (1) it stimulates liver, fat, and muscle cells to take up and metabolize glucose; (2) it stimulates the liver and the muscles to store glucose as glycogen; and (3) it promotes the buildup of fats and proteins and inhibits their use as an energy source. Therefore, insulin is a hormone that promotes storage of nutrients so that they are on hand during leaner times. It therefore helps to lower the blood glucose level.

Glucagon is secreted from the pancreas in between eating, and its effects are opposite to those of insulin. Glucagon stimulates the breakdown of stored nutrients and causes the blood glucose level to rise (fig. 44.8).

Diabetes Mellitus Is Deficient Insulin

Diabetes mellitus is a fairly common disease caused by a defect in insulin production or utilization. The most common laboratory test for diabetes mellitus (usually called diabetes) is to look for sugar, or glucose, in the urine. Glucose in the urine means that the blood glucose level is high enough to cause the kidneys to excrete glucose. This indicates that the liver is not storing glucose as glycogen and that the cells are not utilizing glucose as an energy source.

Since carbohydrate is not being metabolized, the body turns to the breakdown of protein and fat for energy. Unfortunately, the breakdown of these molecules leads to the buildup of ketones in the blood. The resulting reduction in blood volume and acidosis (acid blood) can eventually lead to coma and death of the diabetic.

There are two types of diabetes. In *type I* (*insulin-dependent*) *diabetes*, the pancreas is not producing insulin. The condition is believed to be brought on by exposure to an environmental agent, most likely a virus, whose presence causes cytotoxic T cells to destroy the pancreatic islets (of Langerhans). As a result, the individual must have daily insulin injections. Although these injections control the diabetic symptoms, either an overdose of insulin or the absence of regular eating can bring on the symptoms of hypoglycemia (low blood sugar). These symptoms appear when the blood glucose level falls below normal levels. Since the brain requires a constant supply of sugar, unconsciousness can result. The cure is quite simple: an immediate source of sugar, such as a sugar cube or fruit juice, can very quickly counteract hypoglycemia.

Obviously, receiving insulin injections is not the same as having a fully functioning pancreas that supplies insulin on demand. For this reason, some doctors advocate an islet transplant for type I diabetes.

Of the 12 million people who now have diabetes in the United States, at least 10 million have *type II* (*insulin-independent*) *diabetes*. This type of diabetes usually occurs in people of any age who are obese and inactive. The pancreas produces insulin, but the cells do not respond to it. At first, cells lack the receptors necessary to detect the presence of insulin, and later, the organs and tissues listed in figure 44.8 are even incapable of taking up glucose. If type II diabetes is untreated, the results can be as serious as those of type I diabetes. (Diabetics are prone to blindness, kidney disease, and circulatory disorders, including strokes. Pregnancy carries an increased risk of diabetic coma, and the child of a diabetic is somewhat more likely to be stillborn or to die shortly after birth.) It is important, therefore, to prevent or to at least control type II diabetes. The best defense is a low-fat diet and regular exercise. If this fails, there are oral drugs that make the cells more sensitive to the effects of insulin or that stimulate the pancreas to make more insulin.

Figure 44.8

Insulin and glucagon homeostatic system. When blood glucose level is high, the pancreas secretes insulin. Insulin promotes the storage of glucose as glycogen and the synthesis of proteins and fats (as opposed to their use as energy sources). Therefore, insulin lowers the blood glucose level. When the blood glucose level is low, the pancreas secretes glucagon. Glucagon acts in opposition to insulin in all respects; therefore, glucagon raises the blood glucose level.

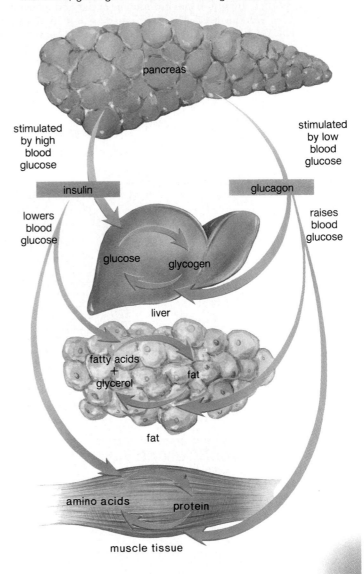

Diabetes mellitus is due to a lack of insulin or a lack of sensitivity to insulin. Insulin lowers the blood glucose level by promoting glucose up-take by cells and conversion of glucose to glycogen by the liver.

Dangers of Anabolic Steroids

 nabolic steroids are synthetic forms of the male sex hormone testosterone. Trainers may have been the first to acquire anabolic steroids for weight lifters, body builders, and other athletes such as professional football players. When taken in large doses (ten to 100 times the amount prescribed by doctors for illnesses), anabolic steroids promote larger muscles when accompanied by exercise. Occasionally steroid abuse makes the news

because an Olympic winner tests positive for the drug and must relinquish a medal. Steroid use has been outlawed by the International Olympic Committee.

The U.S. Food and Drug Administration bans the importation of most steroids, but they are brought into the country illegally and sold through the mail or in gyms and health clubs. According to federal officials, 1 million to 3 million Americans now take anabolic steroids. Their increased use by teenagers, wishing to build bulk quickly, is of special concern. Some attribute this to society's emphasis on physical

appearance and the need of insecure youngsters to feel better about how they look.

Physicians, teachers, and parents are quite alarmed about anabolic steroid abuse. It's even predicted that two or three months of high-dosage use in a youngster can cause death two or three decades later. The many harmful effects of anabolic steroids on the body are listed in figure 44B. In addition, these drugs increase aggression and make a person feel invincible. One abuser even had his friend videotape him as he drove his car at 40 miles per hour into a tree!

Figure 44B

The effects of anabolic steroid use.

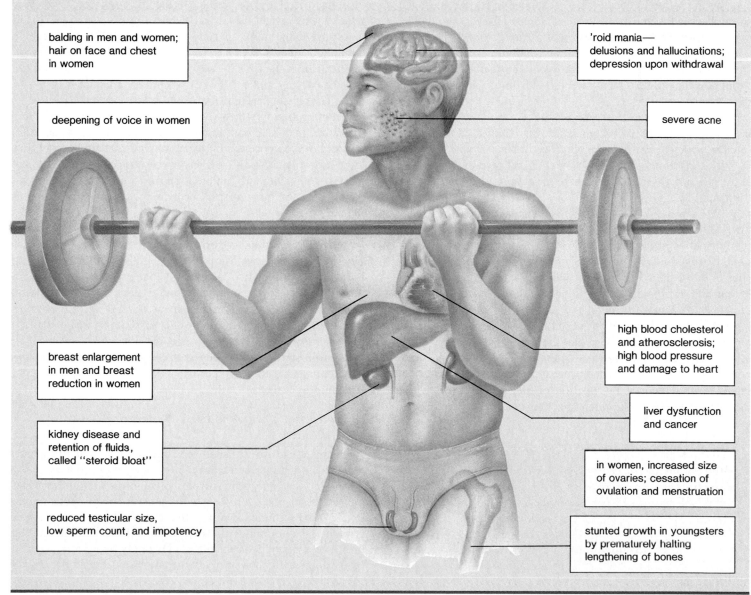

balding in men and women; hair on face and chest in women

deepening of voice in women

breast enlargement in men and breast reduction in women

kidney disease and retention of fluids, called "steroid bloat"

reduced testicular size, low sperm count, and impotency

'roid mania— delusions and hallucinations; depression upon withdrawal

severe acne

high blood cholesterol and atherosclerosis; high blood pressure and damage to heart

liver dysfunction and cancer

in women, increased size of ovaries; cessation of ovulation and menstruation

stunted growth in youngsters by prematurely halting lengthening of bones

Testes Are in Males and Ovaries Are in Females

The sex organs are the testes in the male and the ovaries in the female. The *testes* are located in the scrotum, and the ovaries are located in the abdominal cavity. The testes produce the *androgens* (e.g., *testosterone*), which are the male sex hormones, and the *ovaries* produce estrogen and progesterone, the female sex hormones. The hypothalamus and the pituitary gland control the hormonal secretions of these organs in the same manner that was described for the thyroid gland previously.

The male sex hormone, testosterone, has many functions. It is essential for the normal development and functioning of the sex organs in males. It is also necessary for the maturation of sperm.

Greatly increased testosterone secretion at the time of puberty stimulates the growth of the penis and the testes. Testosterone also brings about and maintains the secondary sex characteristics in males that develop at the time of puberty. Testosterone causes growth of a beard, axillary (underarm) hair, and pubic hair. It prompts the larynx and the vocal cords to enlarge, causing the voice to change. It is responsible for the muscular strength of males, and this is the reason some athletes take supplemental amounts of **anabolic steroids,** which are either testosterone or related chemicals. The contraindications of taking anabolic steroids are discussed in the reading on the previous page. Testosterone also causes oil and sweat glands in the skin to secrete; therefore, it is largely responsible for acne and body odor. Another side effect of testosterone is baldness. Genes for baldness probably are inherited by both sexes, but baldness is seen more often in males because of the presence of testosterone.

Testosterone is believed to be largely responsible for the sex drive. It may even contribute to the supposed aggressiveness of males.

The female sex hormones, *estrogens* and *progesterone,* have many effects on the body. In particular, estrogens secreted at the time of puberty stimulates the growth of the uterus and the vagina. Estrogen is necessary for egg maturation and is largely responsible for the secondary sex characteristics in females. It is responsible for female body hair and fat distribution. In general, females have a more rounded appearance than males because of a greater accumulation of fat beneath the skin. Also, the pelvic girdle enlarges in females so that the pelvic cavity has a larger relative size compared to males; this means that females have wider hips. Both estrogen and progesterone also are required for breast development and regulation of the uterine cycle, which includes monthly menstruation (discharge of blood and muscosal tissues from the uterus).

> The androgens, primarily testosterone, are the male sex hormones produced by the testes; estrogen and progesterone are the female sex hormones produced by the ovaries. The sex hormones maintain the sex organs and the secondary sex characteristics.

Still Other Endocrine Glands

There are some other glands in the body that produce hormones, and we will discuss some of these here.

Thymus Is Most Active in Children

The *thymus* is a lobular gland that lies in the upper thoracic cavity (see fig. 44.3). This organ reaches its largest size and is most active during childhood. With aging, the organ gets smaller and becomes fatty. Certain lymphocytes that originate in the bone marrow and then pass through the thymus are transformed into T cells. The thymus produces various hormones called *thymosins,* which aid the differentiation of T cells and may stimulate immune cells in general. There is hope that these hormones can be used in conjunction with lymphokine therapy to restore or to stimulate T cell function in patients suffering from AIDS or cancer.

Pineal Gland and Daily/Yearly Rhythms

The **pineal gland** produces the hormone called *melatonin*; this occurs primarily at night. In fishes and amphibians, the pineal gland is located near the surface of the body and is a "third eye," which receives light rays directly. In mammals, the pineal gland is located in the third ventricle of the brain and cannot receive direct light signals (see fig. 44.3). However, it does receive nerve impulses from the eyes by way of the optic tract. Again, we see that the nervous and endocrine systems are connected.

The pineal gland and melatonin are involved in daily cycles called **circadian rhythms** [L. *circa,* about, and *dies,* day]. Normally we grow sleepy at night when melatonin levels are high and we awaken once daylight returns and melatonin levels are low. Shift work is usually troublesome because it upsets this normal daily rhythm. Similarly, international travel often results in jet lag because the body is still producing melatonin according to the old schedule.

Many animals go through a yearly cycle that includes enlargement of reproductive organs during the summer when melatonin levels are low. Mating occurs in the fall and young are born in the spring. It is of interest that children with a brain tumor that destroys the pineal gland experience early puberty. Therefore, it's possible that the pineal gland is also involved in human sexual development. Another disorder is seasonal affective disorder (SAD); sufferers become depressed and have an uncontrollable desire to sleep with the onset of winter. Giving melatonin makes their symptoms worse, but exposure to a bright light improves them.

Hormones That Are Not Associated with Glands

Even organs that are not usually considered to be endocrine glands have been found to secrete hormones. The heart produces *atrial natriuretic hormone,* which helps to regulate the sodium and water balance of the body. It lowers blood pressure by promoting renal excretion of sodium and water, and it also inhibits the release of renin and the hormones aldosterone and ADH. Atrial natriuretic hormone is a peptide that is released not only by the atria but also by the aortic arch, the ventricles, the lungs, and the pituitary gland in response to increases in blood pressure. The stomach and the small intestine produce the peptide hormones.

A number of different types of organs and cells produce peptide *growth factors*, which stimulate cell division and mitosis. They are like hormones in that they act on cells that have specific receptors to receive them. Some, including lymphokines and blood cell growth factors, are released into blood; others diffuse to nearby cells. Other growth factors are described in the following listing:

Platelet-derived growth factor is released from platelets and many other cell types. It helps in wound healing and causes an increase in the number of fibroblasts, smooth muscle cells, and certain cells of the nervous system.
Epidermal growth factor and *nerve growth factor* stimulate the cells indicated by their names as well as many others. These growth factors are also important in wound healing.
Tumor angiogenesis factor stimulates the formation of capillary networks and is released by tumor cells. One treatment for cancer is to prevent the activity of this growth factor.

Prostaglandins (PG) are another class of chemical messengers that also are produced and act locally. (The first prostaglandin was found in secretions of the prostate gland, accounting for the name.) They are derived from fatty acids stored in plasma membranes as phospholipids. When a cell is stimulated by reception of a hormone or even by trauma, a series of synthetic reactions takes place in the plasma membrane, and PG is first released into the cytoplasm and then secreted from the cell. There are many different types of prostaglandins produced by many different tissues. In the uterus, certain prostaglandins cause muscles to contract; therefore, they are implicated in the pain and discomfort of menstruation in some women. (Antiprostaglandin therapy is useful in these cases.) On the other hand, certain prostaglandins are used to (1) treat ulcers, because they reduce gastric secretion, (2) treat hypertension, because they lower blood pressure, and (3) prevent thrombosis, because they inhibit platelet aggregation. Because different prostaglandins can have contrary effects, it has been very difficult to standardize their use, and in most instances, prostaglandin therapy is still considered experimental.

ENVIRONMENTAL SIGNALS IN THREE CATEGORIES

In this chapter, we concentrated on describing the functions of the human endocrine glands and their hormonal secretions. We already know that hormones are only one type of chemical messenger or environmental signal between cells. In fact, the concept of the environmental signal now has been broadened to include at least the following three different categories of messengers (fig. 44.9):

1. *Environmental signals that act at a distance between individuals.* Many organisms release chemical messengers, called *pheromones,* into the air or in externally deposited body fluids. These are intended to be messages for other members of the species. Ants lay down a pheromone trail to direct other ants to food, and the female silkworm moth releases bombykol, a sex attractant that is received by male moth antennae even several miles away. This chemical is so potent that it has been estimated that only forty out of 40,000 receptors on the male antennae need to be activated in order for the male to respond. Mammals, too, release pheromones—the urine of dogs serves as a territorial marker. Studies are being conducted to determine if humans also have pheromones.

2. *Environmental signals that act at a distance between body parts.* This category includes the endocrine secretions, which traditionally have been called hormones. It also includes the secretions of the neurosecretory cells in the hypothalamus; the production and action of ADH and oxytocin illustrate the close relationship between the nervous system and the endocrine system. Neurosecretory cells produce these hormones, which are released when these cells receive nerve impulses. As another example of the overlap between the nervous and endocrine systems, consider that endorphins on occasion travel in the bloodstream, but they act on nerve cells to alter their membrane potential. Also, norepinephrine is both a neurotransmitter and hormone secreted by the adrenal medulla.

3. *Environmental signals that act locally between adjacent cells.* Neurotransmitters released by neurons belong in this category, as do substances like prostaglandins and growth factors, which are sometimes called local hormones. Also, when the skin is cut, histamine is released by mast cells and promotes the inflammatory response.

Redefinition of a Hormone

Traditionally, a hormone was considered to be a secretion of an endocrine gland that was carried in the bloodstream to a target organ. In recent years, some scientists have broadened the definition of a hormone to include *all* types of chemical messengers. This change seemed necessary because those chemicals traditionally considered to be hormones now have been found in all sorts of tissues in the human body. It is impossible for insulin produced by the pancreas to enter the brain because of the blood-brain barrier—a tight fusion of endothelial cells of the capillary walls that prevents passage of larger molecules like peptides. Yet, insulin has been found in the brain. It now appears that the brain cells themselves can produce insulin, which is used locally to influence the metabolism of adjacent cells. Also, some chemicals identical to the hormones of the endocrine system have been found in lower organisms, even in bacteria! A moment's thought about the evolutionary process helps to explain this; these regulatory chemicals may have been present in the earliest cells and only became specialized as hormones as evolution proceeded.

Figure 44.9

The three categories of environmental signals. Pheromones are chemical messengers that act at a distance between individuals. Endocrine hormones and neurosecretions typically are carried in the bloodstream and act at a distance within the body of a single organism. Some chemical messengers have local effects only; they pass between cells that are adjacent to one another. This, of course, includes neurotransmitters.

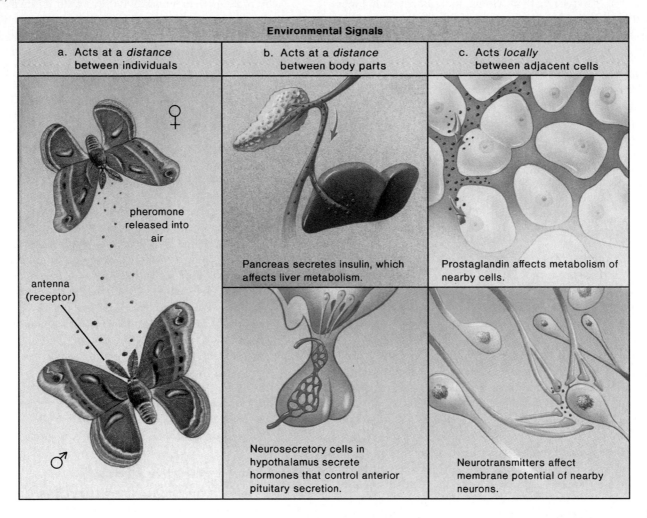

Environmental Signals

a. Acts at a *distance* between individuals

pheromone released into air

antenna (receptor)

♀

♂

b. Acts at a *distance* between body parts

Pancreas secretes insulin, which affects liver metabolism.

Neurosecretory cells in hypothalamus secrete hormones that control anterior pituitary secretion.

c. Acts *locally* between adjacent cells

Prostaglandin affects metabolism of nearby cells.

Neurotransmitters affect membrane potential of nearby neurons.

▶ Summary

1. There are two major types of compounds used as hormones; a few hormones are steroids; most hormones are classified as peptides.

2. The steroid hormones are lipid soluble and can pass through plasma membranes. Once inside the nucleus, they combine with a receptor molecule, and the complex attaches to transcription factors which activate DNA. Transcription and translation lead to protein synthesis; in this way, steroid hormones alter the metabolism of the cell.

3. The peptide hormones are usually received by a receptor located in the plasma membrane. Most often their reception leads to activation of an enzyme that changes ATP to cyclic AMP (cAMP). cAMP then activates another enzyme, which activates another, and so forth.

4. The endocrine glands in humans, which are shown in figure 44.3, produce hormones that are secreted into the bloodstream and circulate about the body until they are received by their target organs.

5. Neurosecretory cells in the hypothalamus produce antidiuretic hormone (ADH) and oxytocin, which are stored in axon endings in the posterior pituitary until they are released.

6. The hypothalamus produces hypothalamic-releasing and hypothalamic-release-inhibiting hormones, which pass to the anterior pituitary by way of a portal system. These hormones either stimulate or inhibit the release of a particular anterior pituitary hormone.

7. The anterior pituitary produces at least six types of hormones (see table 44.1). Because the anterior pituitary also stimulates certain other hormonal glands, it is sometimes called the master gland.

8. The thyroid gland produces thyroxin and triiodothyronine, hormones that play a role in growth and development of immature forms; in mature individuals they increase the metabolic rate. The thyroid gland also produces calcitonin, which helps lower the blood calcium level.

9. The parathyroid glands raise the blood calcium and decrease the blood phosphate level.

10. The adrenal medulla secretes epinephrine and norepinephrine, which bring about responses we associate with the fight-or-flight reaction.

11. The adrenal cortex primarily produces the glucocorticoids (cortisol) and the mineralocorticoids (aldosterone). Cortisol stimulates hydrolysis of proteins to amino acids that are converted to glucose; in this way, it raises the blood glucose level. It also counteracts the inflammatory reaction. Aldosterone causes the kidneys to reabsorb sodium ions (Na^+) and excrete potassium ions (K^+).

12. The islets of the pancreas secrete insulin, which lowers the blood glucose level, and glucagon, which has the opposite effect.

13. The gonads produce the sex hormones; the thymus secretes thymosins, which stimulate T lymphocyte production and maturation; the pineal gland produces melatonin, whose function in mammals is uncertain—it may affect development of the reproductive organs.

14. There are three categories of chemical messengers: those that act at a distance between individuals (pheromones); those that act at a distance within the individual (traditional endocrine hormones and secretions of neurosecretory cells); and local messengers (such as prostaglandins, growth factors, and neurotransmitters). Since there is great overlap between these categories, perhaps the definition of a hormone should be expanded to include all of them.

Writing Across the Curriculum

In order to practice writing skills, students should write out the answers to any or all of the study questions and the critical thinking questions. The study questions are sequenced in the same order as the text. Answers to the objective questions, and suggested answers to the critical thinking questions, are in appendix D.

Study Questions

1. Give a definition of endocrine hormones that includes how they are transported in the body, and how they are received. What does "target" organ mean?   768

2. Categorize endocrine hormones according to their chemical makeup.   768

3. Explain how the two major types of hormones influence the metabolism of the cell.   768–69

4. Give the location in the human body of all the major endocrine glands. Name the hormones secreted by each gland, and describe their chief functions.   772

5. Explain the relationship of the hypothalamus to the posterior pituitary gland and to the anterior pituitary gland.   771, 773–74

6. Explain the concept of negative feedback and give an example involving antidiuretic hormone (ADH).   771

7. Give an example of the three-tiered relationship among the hypothalamus, the anterior pituitary, and other endocrine glands. Explain why the anterior pituitary can be called the master gland.   773

8. Draw a diagram to explain the contrary actions of insulin and glucagon. Use your diagram to explain the symptoms of type I diabetes mellitus.   777–78

9. Categorize chemical messengers into three groups, and give examples of each group.   781

10. Give examples to show that there is an overlap between the mode of operation of the nervous system and that of the endocrine system. Explain why the traditional definition of a hormone may need to be expanded.   781

Objective Questions

Match the hormone in questions 1–5 to the correct gland in the key.

Key:
   a. pancreas
   b. anterior pituitary
   c. posterior pituitary
   d. thyroid
   e. adrenal medulla
   f. adrenal cortex

1. cortisol
2. growth hormone (GH)
3. oxytocin storage
4. insulin
5. epinephrine

6. The anterior pituitary controls the secretion(s) of
   a. both the adrenal medulla and the adrenal cortex.
   b. both cortisol and aldosterone.
   c. thyroxin.
   d. All of these are correct.

7. Peptide hormones
   a. are received by a receptor located in the plasma membrane.
   b. are received by a receptor located in the cytoplasm.
   c. bring about the transcription of DNA.
   d. Both b and c are correct.

8. Aldosterone causes the
   a. kidneys to release renin.
   b. kidneys to reabsorb sodium.
   c. blood volume to increase.
   d. All of these are correct.

9. Diabetes mellitus is associated with
   a. too much insulin in the blood.
   b. too high a blood glucose level.
   c. blood that is too dilute.
   d. All of these are correct.

10. The blood cortisol level controls the secretion of
    a. a releasing hormone from the hypothalamus.
    b. adrenocorticotropic hormone (ACTH) from the anterior pituitary.
    c. cortisol from the adrenal cortex.
    d. All of these are correct.

11. One of the chief differences between pheromones and local hormones is
    a. the distance over which they act.
    b. that one is a chemical messenger and the other is not.
    c. that one is made by invertebrates and the other is made by vertebrates.
    d. All of these are correct.

12. Label this diagram and explain how a negative feedback system keeps the hormone level constant in the body:

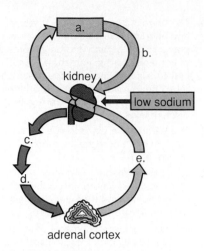

adrenal cortex

Concepts and Critical Thinking

1. *Hormone levels are maintained by feedback control.*

   Contrast control of neurotransmitter levels in the nervous system with control of hormone levels in the endocrine system.

2. *The nervous system is fast acting, and the endocrine system is fairly slow moving.*

   Contrast message delivery in the nervous system with that in the endocrine system.

3. *Hormone levels greatly affect the phenotype.*

   Use the effect of sex hormones to substantiate this concept.

Selected Key Terms

adrenal gland (uh-DREEN-ul) A gland that lies atop a kidney; the adrenal medulla produces the hormones epinephrine and norepinephrine and the adrenal cortex produces the corticoid hormones. [L. *ad,* toward, and *rena,* kidney]   776

adrenocorticotropic hormone (ACTH) (uh-DREE-noh-kawrt-ih-koh-TROH-pik) A hormone secreted by the anterior lobe of the pituitary gland that stimulates activity in the adrenal cortex.   774

aldosterone (al-DAHS-tuh-rohn) A hormone secreted by the adrenal cortex that regulates the sodium and potassium balance of the blood.   776

antidiuretic hormone (ADH) (ANT-ih-dy-yuu-RET-ik) A hormone secreted by the posterior pituitary that promotes the reabsorption of water from the collecting ducts, which receive urine produced by nephrons within the kidneys. [Gk. *anti,* against, and *diure,* urinate]   771

cyclic AMP An ATP-related compound that promotes chemical reactions in cells; as the second messenger in peptide hormone transduction, it initiates activity of the metabolic machinery.   769

endocrine system One of the major systems involved in the coordination of body activities; uses messengers called hormones, which are secreted into the bloodstream. [Gk. *end,* within, and *krinein,* separate]   768

glucagon A hormone secreted by the pancreas which causes the liver to break down glycogen and raises the blood glucose level.   777

gonadotropic hormone (goh-nad-uh-TRAHP-ik) A type of hormone that regulates the activity of the ovaries and testes; principally follicle-stimulating hormone (FSH) and luteinizing hormone (LH).   774

growth hormone (GH) A substance secreted by the anterior pituitary; it promotes cell division, protein synthesis, and bone growth.   774

hormone A chemical produced in one part of the body that controls the activity of other parts. [Gk. *hormon,* excite]   768

insulin A hormone secreted by the pancreas that lowers the blood glucose level by promoting the uptake of glucose by cells and the conversion of glucose to glycogen by the liver. [L. *insul,* island]   777

pancreas An abdominal organ that produces digestive enzymes and the hormones insulin and glucagon.   777

parathyroid gland (par-uh-THY-royd) A gland embedded in the posterior surface of the thyroid gland; it produces parathyroid hormone. [Gk. *para,* beside, and *thyro,* door]   775

parathyroid hormone (PTH) (par-uh-THY-royd) A hormone secreted by the four parathyoid glands that increases the blood calcium level and decreases the blood phosphate level. [Gk. *para,* beside, and *thyro,* door]   775

pineal gland (PY-nee-ul) A gland—either at the skin surface (fish, amphibians) or in the third ventricle of the brain, (mammals)—that produces melatonin.   780

pituitary gland A small gland that lies just inferior to the hypothalamus; the anterior pituitary produces several hormones, some of which control other endocrine glands; the posterior pituitary produces oxytocin and antidiuretic hormone.   771

thyroid gland A large gland in the neck that produces several important hormones, including thyroxin and calcitonin. [Gk. *thyro,* door]   774

thyroxin (thy-RAHK-seen) A substance (also called T4) secreted from the thyroid gland that promotes growth and development in vertebrates; in general, it increases the metabolic rate in cells. [Gk. *thyro,* door]   774

45

REPRODUCTION IN ANIMALS

Learning Objectives

How Animals Reproduce

- Contrast asexual reproduction with sexual reproduction, and relate their advantages to environmental conditions. 786
- Contrast primary and accessory organs of reproduction; discuss various means by which animals protect the zygote and the developing embryo. 787–89

Males Have Testes

- Name and give a function for the organs of the human male reproductive system; trace the path of sperm from the testes to the penis. 790–91
- Describe the microscopic anatomy of the testes, including the stages of spermatogenesis; relate the action of the hormones FSH and LH (ICSH) to the functions of the testes. 792–93
- Describe hormonal control in the male, mentioning the hypothalamus, the anterior pituitary, and testosterone; list several actions of testosterone. 793

Females Have Ovaries

- Name and give a function for the organs of the human female reproductive system. 794
- Describe the microscopic anatomy of the ovary, including a description of the ovarian cycle. 795
- Describe the uterine cycle; explain the relationship among the hormones GnRH, FSH, LH, and the female sex hormones; give several functions of estrogen and progesterone. 796
- Explain the cessation of the ovarian and uterine cycles in the pregnant female. 797

Humans Vary in Fertility

- List several means of birth control, and compare their effectiveness. 798–99

Sexually Transmitted Diseases

- Describe the cause and symptoms of the following sexually transmitted diseases: AIDS, genital herpes, genital warts, gonorrhea, chlamydia, and syphilis. 799–800

Baby and mother masai giraffe, *Giraffa*. Organisms use reproduction to make copies of themselves.

nimals expend a considerable amount of energy and time on reproduction. After all, reproduction ensures that the animal's genes are passed on to the next generation. The life cycle of any particular animal comes to an end, but its genes can be perpetuated as long as reproduction has taken place.

How Animals Reproduce

Most animals reproduce sexually. They have both primary sex organs for the production of gametes and accessory organs for the storage and transport of gametes. Both aquatic and terrestrial animals have means by which they protect both the zygote and the embryo until development is complete. Since sexual reproduction usually occurs between separate sexes, various methods have evolved to assure that male and female or their gametes find each other.

Asexual Versus Sexual Reproduction

There are two fundamental patterns of reproduction—asexual and sexual:

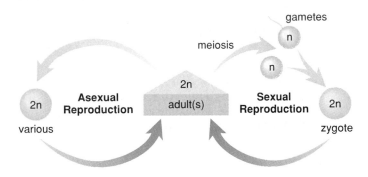

In **asexual reproduction,** there is only one parent, and the offspring have the same phenotype and genotype as that parent. This lack of variation is not a disadvantage as long as the environment stays the same. Organisms that reproduce asexually often have the tremendous advantage of being able to produce a large number of offspring within a limited amount of time.

Only certain methods of asexual reproduction are found among animals. Many flatworms can constrict into two halves, each of which can become a new individual. This form of *regeneration* is also seen among sponges and echinoderms. Chopping up a sea star does not kill it; instead, each fragment grows into another animal. Some cnidaria, such as hydras, reproduce by *budding* (fig. 45.1), during which the new individual arises as an outgrowth (bud) of the parent. Some insects and several other types of arthropods have the ability to reproduce parthenogenetically. **Parthenogenesis** [Gk. *partheno,* without fertilization, and *gene,* origin] is a modification of sexual reproduction in which an unfertilized egg develops into a complete individual. Some organisms such as aphids, also called plant lice, can be alter-

Figure 45.1
Reproduction in *Hydra.* Hydras reproduce asexually and sexually. During asexual reproduction, a new polyp buds from the parental polyp. During sexual reproduction, temporary gonads develop in the body wall.

nately parthenogenetic and then fully sexual. In the summer, many generations of aphid females produce up to 100 young without prior fertilization. In the autumn, however, aphids reproduce sexually and the zygotes over winter.

Usually animals practice **sexual reproduction,** which involves sex cells (gametes). The gametes may be specialized into eggs or sperm, and even if egg and sperm are produced by the same individual, animals usually practice cross-fertilization. This is the case with earthworms, which are hermaphroditic—each worm has both male and female sex organs. When animals reproduce sexually, an offspring inherits half its genes from one parent and the other half from the other parent. Therefore, an offspring has a different combination of genes than either parent. In this way, variation is introduced and maintained. Such variation is an advantage to the species if the environment is changing, because an offspring might be better adapted to the new environment than is either parent.

In some cnidaria there is an alternation of generations. The polypoid stage of *Obelia,* which is a colony made up of many hydralike polyps, is sessile and produces medusae by budding. The medusan stage, which looks like a jellyfish, is motile and produces egg and sperm. The motile stage disperses the species.

Reproductive Organs Are Primary or Accessory

Animals usually produce gametes in specialized organs called **gonads** [Gk. *gon,* seed]. Sponges are an exception to this rule because in sponges the collar cells lining the central cavity give rise to sperm and eggs. Cnidaria, such as hydras, produce only temporary gonads in the fall when sexual reproduction occurs (fig. 45.1). The animals in the other phyla have permanent reproductive organs. The gonads are **testes** for the production of sperm and **ovaries** [L. *ovi,* egg] for the production of eggs. These gametes are produced by germ cells, cells set aside early in development for this specific purpose. The other cells in a gonad support and nourish the developing gametes or produce hormones necessary to the reproductive process.

There are also accessory organs—ducts and storage areas which aid in bringing the gametes together. Notice that the earthworm (fig. 45.2) contains the following accessory organs:

Sperm ducts and oviducts:	passageways for the gametes from the gonad to the exterior.
Seminal vesicle:	a storage area that receives sperm from the testes and holds them until they are released.
Seminal receptacle:	a storage area that receives sperm from a partner and holds them until they are used to fertilize the eggs.

Earthworms are hermaphroditic, and partners exchange sperm as the worms lie parallel to each other facing opposite directions. After the worms separate, the clitellum of each produces a slime tube that is moved along over the head by muscle contractions. As it passes, eggs and the sperm received from the partner are deposited in the tube where development occurs.

Copulation [L. *copul,* link] is sexual union to facilitate the reception of sperm by a partner, usually a female. Earthworms do not have a copulatory organ, but other animals do have a copulatory organ among their accessory organs of reproduction. In terrestrial animals, males typically have a **penis** for depositing sperm into the vagina of females. Aquatic animals also have other types of copulatory organs. Lobsters and crayfish have a modified leg;

Figure   45.2

Reproduction in earthworms, *Lumbricus.* **a.** Earthworms are hermaphroditic; they contain the primary and accessory organs of both sexes. **b.** When earthworms exchange sperm, they pass it from the seminal vesicles of one to the seminal receptacles of the other.

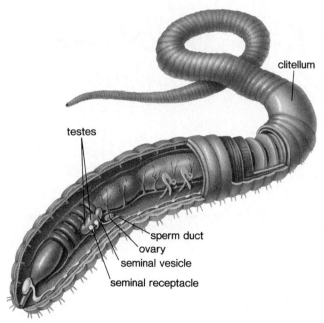

a.

b.

cuttlefish and octopuses use a tentacle; and sharks have a modified pelvic fin that passes packets of sperm to the female. Among terrestrial animals, most birds lack a penis and vagina. They have a cloaca, a chamber that receives products from the digestive, urinary, and reproductive tracts. A male transfers sperm to a female after placing his cloacal opening adjacent to hers.

Figure 45.3

Life cycle of a moth. Moths are oviparous and deposit fertilized eggs in a suitable location for their development. The eggs develop into larvae. There are several larval stages before pupation occurs and metamorphosis results in the adult.

egg mass

adult stage

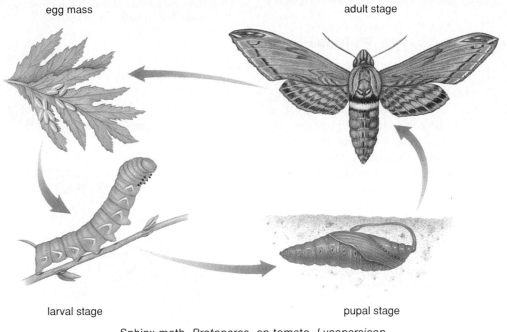

larval stage

pupal stage

Sphinx moth, *Protoparce,* on tomato, *Lycopersicon*

Protecting Zygote and Embryo

Many aquatic animals practice external fertilization; that is, eggs and sperm join outside the body in the water. Terrestrial animals tend to practice internal fertilization, meaning that egg and sperm join inside the female's body. Both types of animals are usually *oviparous,* meaning that they deposit eggs in the external environment. Consider the life cycle of insects (fig. 45.3). Their eggs are produced in the ovaries, and as they mature they increase in size because yolk has been added to them. **Yolk** is stored food to be used by the developing embryo. Then, to prevent the eggs from drying out, they are covered by a shell consisting of several layers of protein- and wax-containing material. Small holes are left at one end of the egg for the entry of sperm. Some insects have a special internal organ for storing sperm for some time after copulation so that the eggs can be fertilized internally before they are deposited in the environment.

A **larva** is an independent form that is often quite different in appearance and way of life from the adult. A larva is able to seek its own food to sustain itself until it becomes an adult. In some terrestrial insects, there are several larval stages and then the animal pupates. A *pupa* is enclosed by a hardened cuticle, often within a cocoon. Here **metamorphosis** [Gk. *met,* change, and *morph,* form], which is a dramatic change in shape, takes place. Then the adult insect emerges and flies off to find a mate and reproduce. Other insects (e.g., grasshoppers) undergo incomplete metamorphosis; pupation does not occur and there are a number of nymph stages, each one looking more like the adult.

Many aquatic forms also have a larval stage. Since the larva has a different life-style, it is able to make use of a different food source than the adult. In sea stars, the bilaterally symmetrical larva simply attaches itself to a substratum and undergoes metamorphosis to become a radially symmetrical juvenile. Among barnacles, the free-swimming larva metamorphoses into the sessile adult with calcareous plates. Crayfish, on the other hand, do not have a larval stage; the egg hatches into a tiny juvenile with the same form as the adult.

Reptiles and particularly birds provide their eggs with plentiful yolk; there is no larval stage. Complete development takes place within a shelled egg containing **extraembryonic membranes** [L. *extra,* outside] to serve the needs of the embryo. The outermost membrane, the *chorion,* lies next to the shell and functions in gas exchange. The *amnion* forms a water-filled sac around the embryo, ensuring that it will not dry out. The *yolk sac* holds the yolk, which nourishes the embryo, and the *allantois* holds nitrogen waste products. The shelled egg frees these animals from the need to reproduce in the water and increases their adaptation to the terrestrial environment.

Birds in particular tend their eggs, and newly hatched birds usually have to be fed before they are able to fly away and seek food for themselves. Complex hormones and neural regulation are involved in reproductive behavior of parental birds (fig. 45.4). Some animals take a different tactic. They do not deposit and tend their eggs; instead they are *ovoviviparous,* meaning that their eggs are retained in the body until they hatch. Then fully devel-

Figure 45.4

Parenting in birds. Birds are oviparous and lay hard-shelled eggs. They are well-known for incubating their eggs and caring for their offspring after they hatch. This road runner, *Geococcyx,* feeds its young.

oped offspring, which have a way of life like the parent, are released. Oysters retain their eggs in the mantle cavity, and male sea horses have a special brood pouch in which the eggs complete development.

Finally some animals, particularly mammals, practice internal fertilization and are *viviparous.* After offspring are born, the nutrients needed for development are supplied by the mother. Viviparity represents the ultimate in caring for the zygote and embryo. How did viviparity among certain mammals come about?

Some mammals, such as the duckbill platypus and the spiny ant-eater, are egg-laying mammals. Marsupial offspring are born in a very immature state; they finish their development within a pouch, where they are nourished on milk. In marsupials, the embryos develop within a duplex uterus, having two chambers. The uterus of most placental mammals has two so-called horns where several embryos can attach and develop in sequence. Only among primates, including humans, is there a simplex uterus where usually a single embryo develops. The **placenta** is a complex structure derived in part from the chorion of a shelled egg. Its evolution allowed the developing offspring to exchange materials with the mother and made the shelled egg unnecessary.

Finding a Mate

Sexually reproducing animals have all sorts of ways of making sure that the gametes find each other. Aquatic animals that practice external fertilization are programmed to release their eggs in the water only at certain times. One environmental signal that seems to work is the lunar cycle. Each month the moon moves closer to the earth and the tides become somewhat higher. Aquatic animals able to sense this change can release their gametes at the same time. Hundreds of thousands of palolo worms rise to the surface of the sea and release their eggs during a two- to four-hour period on two or three specific successive days of the year. Most likely they are under the control of a biological clock that can sense the passage of time so that their reproductive behavior is synchronized.

Among terrestrial animals, reproductive cycles are often tied to day-length changes. The photoperiod reliably indicates the proper time for reproductive behavior, including migration to distant places. Researchers have found that melatonin is produced by the pineal gland during the night, and that this hormone seems to be involved in reproductive cycles. It has been observed that fall-breeding animals can be induced to breed in the spring if they are subjected to artificially shortened day lengths.

Animals that copulate have courtship rituals—specific mating activities that bring the sexes together. These rituals ensure that male and female are of the same species and reduce any aggressive tendencies between the mating pair. They also promote hormonal responses that prepare the body for reproductive success. Reproductive success is evaluated in terms of how many fertile offspring an individual contributes to the next generation. The individual is motivated to reproduce; but in terms of the species, adaptation to the environment is dependent upon the reproductive success of the more fit individuals of a population.

Sexually reproducing animals usually have primary and accessory sex organs, and they have various ways to protect developing offspring after finding a mate.

MALES HAVE TESTES

The male reproductive system includes the organs pictured in figure 45.5 and listed in table 45.1. The male gonads are paired testes, which are suspended within the *scrotal sacs* of the scrotum. The testes begin their development inside the abdominal cavity, but they descend into the scrotal sacs as development proceeds. If the testes do not descend—and the male does not receive hormone therapy or undergo surgery to place the testes in the scrotum—sterility (the inability to produce offspring) results. Sterility occurs because normal sperm production is inhibited at body temperature; a cooler temperature is required.

Sperm produced by the testes mature within the *epididymides* (sing., epididymis), which are tightly coiled tubules lying just outside the testes. Maturation seems to be required for the sperm to swim to the egg. Once the sperm have matured, they are propelled into the **vasa deferentia** (sing., vas deferens) by muscular contractions. Sperm are stored in both the epididymides and the vasa deferentia. When a male becomes sexually aroused, sperm enter the urethra, part of which is located within the penis.

The penis is a cylindrical organ that usually hangs in front of the scrotum. Spongy, erectile tissue containing distensible blood spaces extends through the shaft of the penis (fig. 45.6). During sexual arousal, nervous reflexes cause an increase in arterial blood flow to the penis. This increased blood flow fills the blood space in

Table 45.1

Male Reproductive System

Organ	Function
Testes	Produce sperm and sex hormones
Epididymides	Maturation and some storage of sperm
Vasa deferentia	Conduct and store sperm
Seminal vesicles	Contribute fluid to semen
Prostate gland	Contributes fluid to semen
Urethra	Conducts sperm
Bulbourethral glands	Contribute fluid to semen
Penis	Organ of copulation

Figure 45.5

Side view of the male reproductive system. Notice that the urethra in males carries either urine from the bladder or semen from the testes.

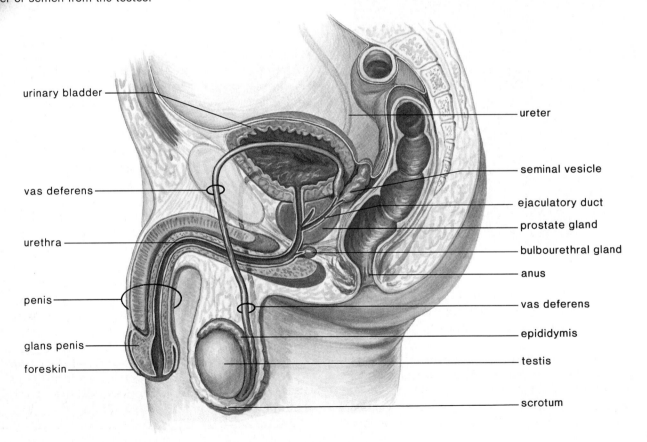

the erectile tissue, and the penis, which is normally limp (flaccid), stiffens and increases in size. These changes are called *erection*. If the penis fails to become erect, the condition is called *impotency*.

Semen [L. *semen,* sperm] (seminal fluid) is a thick, whitish fluid that contains sperm and fluids. As table 45.1 indicates, three types of glands contribute fluids to semen. The *seminal vesicles* lie at the base of the bladder. Each joins a vas deferens to form an ejaculatory duct that enters the urethra. As sperm pass from the vasa deferentia into the urethra, these vesicles secrete a thick, viscous fluid containing nutrients for possible use by the sperm. Just below the bladder is the *prostate gland,* which secretes a milky alkaline fluid believed to activate or increase the motility of the sperm. In older men, the prostate gland may become enlarged, thereby constricting the urethra and making urination difficult. Slightly below the prostate gland, on either side of the urethra, is a pair of small glands called *bulbourethral glands,* which have mucous secretions with a lubricating effect. Notice from figure 45.5 that the urethra also carries urine from the bladder during urination.

> Sperm produced by the testes mature in the epididymides and pass from the vasa deferentia to the urethra, where certain glands add fluid to semen.

Ejaculation

If sexual arousal reaches its peak, **ejaculation** follows an erection. The first phase of ejaculation is called *emission.* During emission, the spinal cord sends nerve impulses via appropriate nerve fibers to the epididymides and vasa deferentia. Their subsequent motility causes sperm to enter the ejaculatory duct, whereupon the seminal vesicles, prostate gland, and bulbourethral glands release their secretions. At this time, a small amount of secretion from the bulbourethral glands may leak from the end of the penis. Since this is a mucoid secretion, it is believed that this leakage may aid the process of intercourse by providing a certain amount of lubrication. During the second phase of ejaculation, call *expulsion,* rhythmical contractions of muscles at the base of the penis and within the urethral wall expel semen in spurts from the opening of urethra. These rhythmical contractions are an example of release from *myotonia,* or muscle tenseness. Myotonia is another important sexual response.

An erection lasts for only a limited amount of time. The penis now returns to its normal flaccid state. Following ejaculation, a male may typically experience a period of time, called **refractory period,** during which stimulation does not bring about an erection. The contractions that expel semen from the penis are a part of male **orgasm,** the physiological and psychological sensations that occur at the climax of sexual stimulation.

Figure 45.6

Penis anatomy. **a.** Beneath the skin and the connective tissue lies the urethra, surrounded by erectile tissue. This tissue expands to form the glans penis, which in uncircumcised males is partially covered by the prepuce (foreskin). **b.** Two other columns of erectile tissue in the penis are dorsally located.

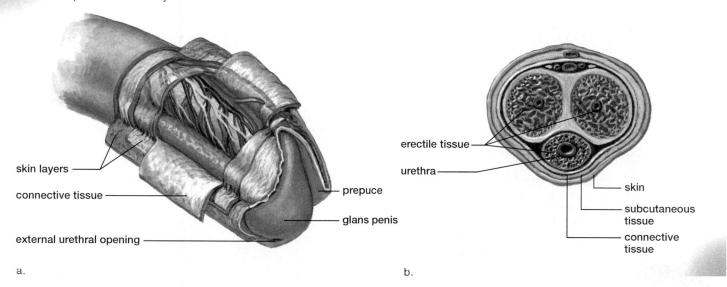

skin layers

connective tissue

external urethral opening

prepuce

glans penis

a.

erectile tissue

urethra

skin

subcutaneous tissue

connective tissue

b.

Figure 45.7

Testis and sperm. **a.** Longitudinal section showing lobules containing seminiferous tubules. **b.** Light micrograph of cross section of seminiferous tubules. **c.** Diagrammatic representation of spermatogenesis, which occurs in the wall of the tubules. **d.** Mature sperm consist of a head, a middle piece, and a tail. The nucleus is in the head, capped by an enzyme-containing acrosome.

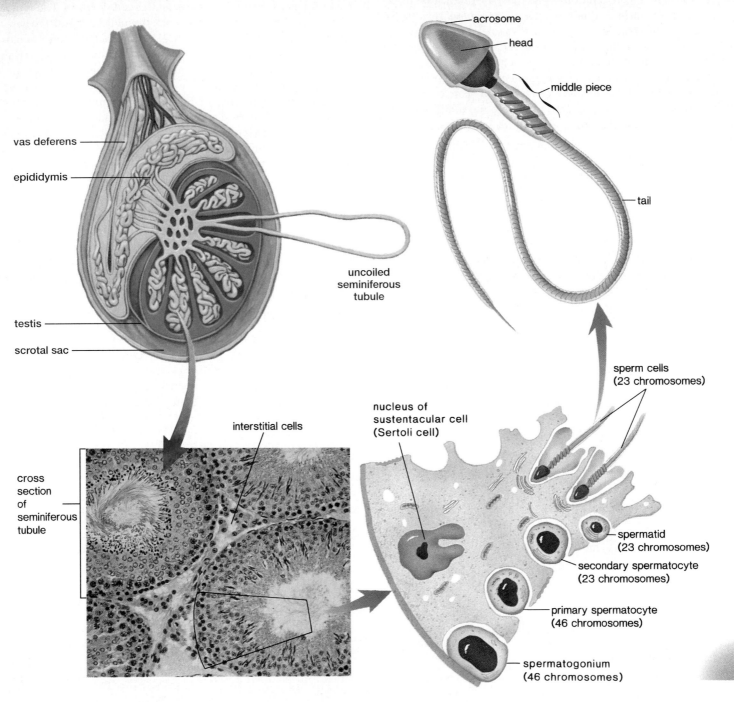

vas deferens

epididymis

testis

scrotal sac

uncoiled seminiferous tubule

acrosome

head

middle piece

tail

cross section of seminiferous tubule

interstitial cells

nucleus of sustentacular cell (Sertoli cell)

sperm cells (23 chromosomes)

spermatid (23 chromosomes)

secondary spermatocyte (23 chromosomes)

primary spermatocyte (46 chromosomes)

spermatogonium (46 chromosomes)

Testes Produce Sperm and Hormones

A longitudinal section of a testis shows that it is composed of compartments called lobules, each of which contains one to three tightly coiled *seminiferous tubules* (fig. 45.7*a*). Altogether, these tubules have a combined length of approximately 250 meters. A microscopic cross section of a seminiferous tubule shows that it is packed with cells undergoing *spermatogenesis* (fig. 45.7*b*), which involves meiosis. Also present are sustentacular (Sertoli) cells, which support, nourish, and regulate the spermatogenic cells (fig. 45.7*c*).

Mature **sperm,** or spermatozoa, have three distinct parts: a head, a middle piece, and a tail (fig. 43.5*d*). The middle piece and the tail contain microtubules, in the characteristic 9 + 2 pattern of cilia and flagella. In the middle piece, mitochondria are wrapped around the microtubules and provide the energy for movement. The head contains a nucleus covered by a cap called the *acrosome,* which stores enzymes needed to penetrate the egg. The human egg is surrounded by several layers of cells and a thick membrane—these acrosomal enzymes play a role in allowing a sperm to reach the surface of the egg. The normal human male usually produces several hundred million sperm per ejaculation, assuring an adequate number for fertilization to take place. Fewer than 100 ever reach the vicinity of the egg, however, and only one sperm normally enters an egg.

Hormonal Regulation in Males

The hypothalamus has ultimate control of the testes' sexual function because it secretes a hormone called gonadotropic-releasing hormone, or GnRH, that stimulates the anterior pituitary to produce the gonadotropic hormones. There are two gonadotropic hormones—follicle-stimulating hormone (FSH) and luteinizing hormone (LH)—in both males and females. In males, FSH promotes spermatogenesis in the seminiferous tubules, which also release the hormone inhibin.

LH in males is sometimes given the name *interstitial cell-stimulating hormone* (*ICSH*) because it controls the production of testosterone by the interstitial cells, scattered in the spaces between the seminiferous tubules (fig. 45.7*b*). All these hormones are involved in a negative feedback relationship that maintains the fairly constant production of sperm and testosterone (fig. 45.8).

Testosterone Is the Male Sex Hormone

Testosterone is the main sex hormone in males. It is essential for the normal development and functioning of the organs listed in table 45.1. Testosterone is also necessary for the maturation of sperm.

Testosterone brings about and maintains the male secondary sex characteristics that develop at the time of puberty. Testosterone causes growth of a beard, axillary (underarm) hair, and pubic hair. It prompts the larynx and vocal cords to enlarge, causing the voice to change. It is responsible for the greater muscle

Figure 45.8

The hypothalamus-pituitary-testis control relationship. Testosterone acts on various body tissues and also regulates the amount of hypothalamic gonadotropic-releasing hormone (GnRH) being sent to the pituitary. GnRH affects gonadotropic hormone production by the pituitary. Luteinizing hormone (LH) regulates the amount of testosterone produced, and follicle-stimulating hormone (FSH) controls spermatogenesis. The seminiferous tubules release a substance called inhibin, which is also involved in feedback inhibition.

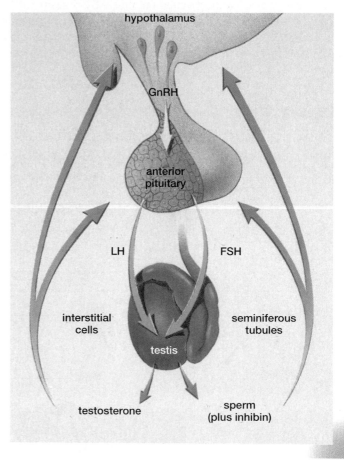

strength of males, and this is the reason some athletes take supplemental amounts of anabolic steroids, which are either testosterone or related chemicals. The practice can lead to health problems involving the kidneys, the circulatory system, and hormonal imbalances, resulting in feminization of males and masculinization of females. Testosterone is believed to be largely responsible for the sex drive and may even contribute to the supposed aggressiveness of males.

Testosterone also causes oil and sweat glands in the skin to secrete; therefore, it is largely responsible for acne and body odor. Another side effect of testosterone is baldness.

FEMALES HAVE OVARIES

The female reproductive system includes the ovaries, the oviducts, the uterus, and the vagina (fig. 45.9 and table 45.2). The ovaries, which produce an egg each month, lie in shallow depressions, one on each side of the upper pelvic cavity. The **oviducts** [L. *ovi*, egg, and *duc*, lead], also called uterine or fallopian tubes, extend from the ovaries to the uterus; however, the oviducts are not attached to the ovaries. Instead, they have fingerlike projections called *fimbriae* that sweep over the ovaries. When an egg bursts from an ovary during ovulation, it usually is swept into an oviduct by the combined action of the fimbriae and the beating of cilia that line the oviducts. Fertilization, if it occurs, normally takes place in an oviduct, and the developing embryo is propelled slowly by ciliary movement and tubular muscle contrac-

tion to the uterus. The **uterus** [L. *uter*, womb] is a thick-walled muscular organ about the size and shape of an inverted pear. The embryo completes its development after embedding itself in the uterine lining, called the **endometrium** [Gk. *endo*, within, and *metri*, uterus]. A small opening at the cervix leads to the vaginal canal. The **vagina** [L. *vagin*, sheath] is a tube at a 45° angle with the small of the back. The mucosal lining of the vagina lies in folds and can extend. This is especially important when the vagina serves as the birth canal, and it also can facilitate intercourse, when the vagina receives the penis during copulation.

The external genital organs of the female are known collectively as the *vulva* (fig. 45.9*b*). The *mons pubis* and two folds of skin called *labia minora* and *labia majora* are on either side of the urethral and vaginal openings. At the juncture of the labia minora is the *clitoris*, which is homologous to the penis in males. The clitoris has

Figure 45.9

Female reproductive system. **a.** Side view of organs. The ovaries produce one egg per month. Fertilization occurs in the oviduct, and development occurs in the uterus. The vagina is the birth canal and organ of copulation. **b.** Vulva. At birth, the opening of the vagina is partially occluded by a membrane called the hymen. Physical activities and sexual intercourse disrupt the hymen.

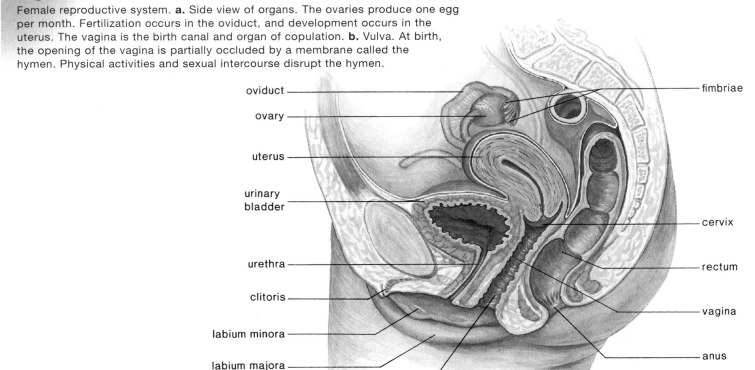

a.

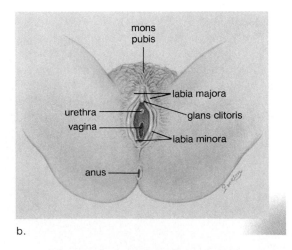

b.

Table 45.2	
Female Reproductive Organs	
Organ	**Function**
Ovaries	Produce egg and sex hormones
Oviducts (fallopian tubes)	Conduct egg; location of fertilization
Uterus (womb)	Houses developing fetus
Cervix	Contains opening to uterus
Vagina	Receives penis during copulation and serves as birth canal

a shaft of erectile tissue and is capped by a pea-shaped glans. The many sense receptors of the clitoris allow it to function as a sexually sensitive organ. Orgasm in the female is a release of neuromuscular tension in the muscles of the genital area, vagina, and uterus.

Ovaries Produce Eggs and Hormones

The ovaries, which alternate in producing one egg each month, also produce the female sex hormones, **estrogen** and **progesterone,** during the ovarian cycle.

Ovarian Cycle

A longitudinal section through an ovary shows many **follicles** [L. *follicul,* little bag], each containing an oocyte (fig. 45.10). A female is born with as many as 2 million follicles, but the number is reduced to 300,000–400,000 by the time of puberty. Only a small number of follicles (about 400) ever mature, because a female usually produces only one egg per month during her reproductive years.

As the follicle undergoes maturation, it develops from a primary follicle to a secondary follicle to a Graafian follicle. *Oogenesis* is occurring (during which time the chromosomal num-

ber is reduced), and a secondary follicle contains a secondary oocyte pushed to one side of a fluid-filled cavity. In a *Graafian follicle,* the fluid-filled cavity increases to the point that the follicle wall balloons out on the surface of the ovary and bursts, releasing the secondary oocyte surrounded by a clear membrane and follicular cells. This is referred to as **ovulation,** and for the sake of convenience, the released oocyte is often called an ovum, or egg. Actually, the second meiotic division is not completed unless fertilization occurs. In the meantime, the follicle is developing into the **corpus luteum** [L. *corpusc,* little body, and *lut,* yellowish]. If pregnancy does not occur, the corpus luteum begins to degenerate after about ten days.

The ovarian cycle is under the control of the gonadotropic hormones, **follicle-stimulating hormone (FSH)** and **luteinizing hormone (LH)** (fig. 45.11 and table 45.3). The gonadotropic hormones are not present in constant amounts and instead are secreted at different rates during the cycle. For simplicity's sake, it is convenient to emphasize that during the first half, or *follicular phase,* of the cycle, FSH promotes the development of a follicle, which secretes estrogen. As the estrogen level in the blood rises, it exerts feedback control over the anterior pituitary secretion of FSH so that the follicular phase comes to an end.

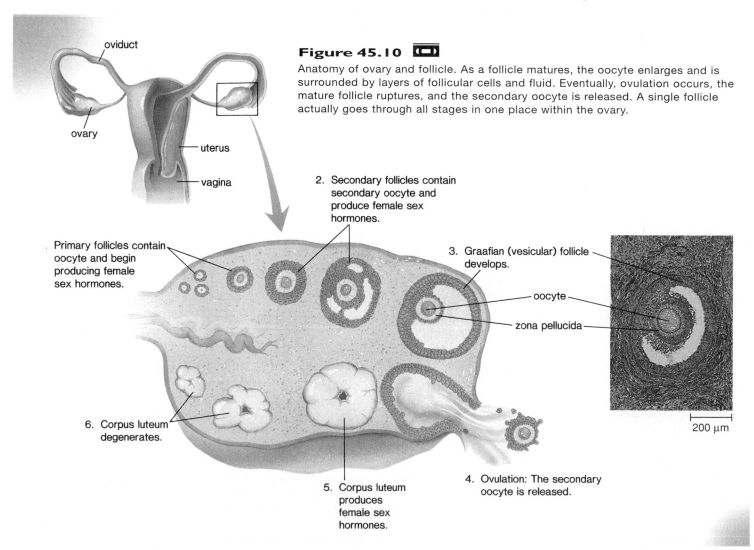

Figure 45.10

Anatomy of ovary and follicle. As a follicle matures, the oocyte enlarges and is surrounded by layers of follicular cells and fluid. Eventually, ovulation occurs, the mature follicle ruptures, and the secondary oocyte is released. A single follicle actually goes through all stages in one place within the ovary.

2. Secondary follicles contain secondary oocyte and produce female sex hormones.

Primary follicles contain oocyte and begin producing female sex hormones.

3. Graafian (vesicular) follicle develops.

oocyte

zona pellucida

200 µm

6. Corpus luteum degenerates.

5. Corpus luteum produces female sex hormones.

4. Ovulation: The secondary oocyte is released.

Table 45.3

Ovarian and Uterine Cycles (Simplified)

Ovarian Cycle	Events	Uterine Cycle	Events
Follicular phase—Days 1–13	FSH Follicle maturation Estrogen	Menstruation—Days 1–5 Proliferative phase—Days 6–13	Endometrium breaks down Endometrium rebuilds
Ovulation—Day 14*	LH spike		
Luteal phase—Days 15–28	LH Corpus luteum Progesterone	Secretory phase—Days 15–28	Endometrium thickens and glands are secretory

Figure 45.11

Hypothalamic-pituitary-ovary control relationship. GnRH is a hypothalamic-releasing hormone that stimulates the anterior pituitary to secrete FSH and LH. These gonadotropic hormones act on the ovaries. FSH promotes the development of the follicle that later, under the influence of LH, becomes the corpus luteum. Negative feedback controls the level of all hormones involved.

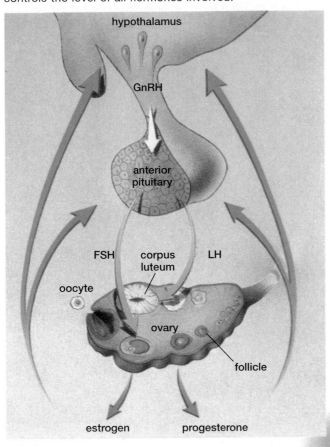

Presumably, the high level of estrogen in the blood also causes the hypothalamus suddenly to secrete a large amount of GnRH. This leads to a surge of LH production by the anterior pituitary and to ovulation at about the fourteenth day of a twenty-eight-day cycle (fig. 45.12).

During the second half, or *luteal phase,* of the ovarian cycle, it is convenient to emphasize that LH promotes the development of the corpus luteum, which secretes progesterone. Progesterone causes the uterine lining to build up. As the blood level of progesterone rises, it exerts feedback control over anterior pituitary secretion of LH so that the corpus luteum begins to degenerate. As the luteal phase comes to an end, menstruation occurs.

One ovarian follicle per month produces a secondary oocyte. Following ovulation, the follicle develops into the corpus luteum.

Uterine Cycle

The female sex hormones, estrogen and progesterone, have numerous functions. The effects of these hormones on the endometrium of the uterus causes the uterus to undergo a cyclical series of events known as the **uterine cycle** (table 45.3 and fig. 45.12). Twenty-eight-day cycles are divided as follows.

During *days 1–5,* there is a low level of female sex hormones in the body, causing the uterine lining to disintegrate and its blood vessels to rupture. A flow of blood, known as the *menses,* passes out of the vagina during **menstruation** [L. *menstru,* monthly], also known as the menstrual period.

During *days 6–13,* increased production of estrogen by an ovarian follicle causes the endometrium to thicken and to become vascular and glandular. This is called the proliferative phase of the uterine cycle.

Ovulation usually occurs on the fourteenth day of the twenty-eight-day cycle.

During *days 15–28,* increased production of progesterone by the corpus luteum causes the endometrium to double in thickness and the uterine glands to mature, producing a thick mucoid secretion. This is called the secretory phase of the uterine cycle. The endometrium now is prepared to receive the developing embryo. If pregnancy does not occur, the corpus luteum degenerates and the low level of sex hormones in the female body causes the uterine lining to break down. The menstrual discharge begins at this time. Even while menstruation is occurring, the anterior pituitary begins to increase its production of FSH and a new follicle begins to mature. Table 45.3 indicates how the ovarian cycle controls the uterine cycle.

Figure 45.12

Blood hormone levels associated with the ovarian and uterine cycles. Before ovulation, FSH stimulates a follicle to produce increasing amounts of estrogen, and the endometrium thickens. After ovulation, LH stimulates the corpus luteum to produce increasing amounts of progesterone, and the endometrium becomes secretory. Menstruation begins when progesterone production declines to a low level.

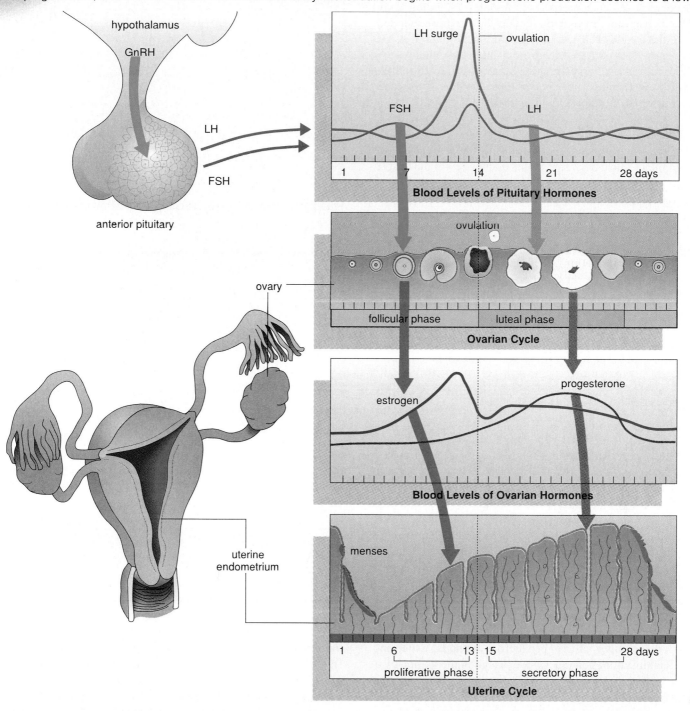

Events Following Fertilization

If fertilization does occur, an embryo begins development even as it travels down the oviduct to the uterus. The endometrium is now prepared to receive the developing embryo, which becomes embedded in the lining several days following fertilization. The *placenta* originates from both maternal and fetal tissues. It is the region of exchange of molecules between fetal and maternal blood, although there is rarely any mixing of the two. At first the placenta produces human chorionic gonadotropin (HCG), which maintains the corpus luteum until the placenta begins its own production of progesterone and estrogen. Progesterone and estrogen have two effects. They shut down the anterior pituitary so that no new follicles mature, and they maintain the lining of the uterus so that the corpus luteum is not needed. There is no menstruation during pregnancy.

Estrogen and Progesterone Are Female Sex Hormones

Estrogen and progesterone not only affect the uterus; they affect other parts of the body as well. Estrogen is largely responsible for the secondary sex characteristics in females, including body hair and fat distribution. In general, females have a more rounded appearance than males because of a greater accumulation of fat beneath the skin. Also, the pelvic girdle enlarges in females, and the pelvic cavity has a larger relative size compared to males. This means that females have wider hips. Both estrogen and progesterone are also required for breast development.

Breasts Produce Milk

A female breast contains one or two dozen lobules, each with its own mammary duct (fig. 45.13). This duct begins at the nipple and divides into numerous other ducts, which end in blind sacs called *alveoli*. In a nonlactating breast, the ducts far outnumber the alveoli because alveoli are made up of cells that can produce milk.

Milk is not produced during pregnancy. Prolactin is needed for lactation (milk production) to begin, and production of this hormone is suppressed by the feedback inhibition estrogen and progesterone have on the anterior pituitary during pregnancy. It takes a couple of days after delivery of a baby for milk production to begin. In the meantime, the breasts produce a watery, yellowish white fluid called *colostrum*, which has a similar composition to milk but contains more protein and less fat.

HUMANS VARY IN FERTILITY

The two major causes of infertility in females are blocked oviducts, possibly due to a sexually transmitted disease, and failure to ovulate due to low body weight. *Endometriosis*, the spread of uterine tissue beyond the uterus, is also a cause. If no obstruction is apparent and body weight is normal, it is possible to give females HCG extracted from the urine of pregnant women, along with HMG (human menopausal gonadotropin) extracted from the urine of postmenopausal women. This treatment causes multiple ovulations and sometimes multiple pregnancies. The most frequent causes of sterility and infertility in males are low sperm count and/or a large proportion of abnormal sperm. Disease, radiation, chemical mutagens, too much heat near the testes, and the use of psychoactive drugs can contribute to this condition.

When reproduction does not occur in the usual manner, couples often seek alternative reproductive methods, which include artificial insemination (sperm are placed in the vagina by a physician), in vitro fertilization (fertilization takes place in laboratory glassware and the zygote is inserted into the uterus), and surrogate motherhood (a woman has another couple's child).

Sometimes couples wish to prevent a possible pregnancy. Several means of *birth control* are readily available in the United States, and the most common are listed in table 45.4. The effec-

Figure 45.13

Anatomy of breast. The female breast contains lobules consisting of ducts and alveoli. The alveoli are lined by milk-producing cells in the lactating (milk-producing) breast.

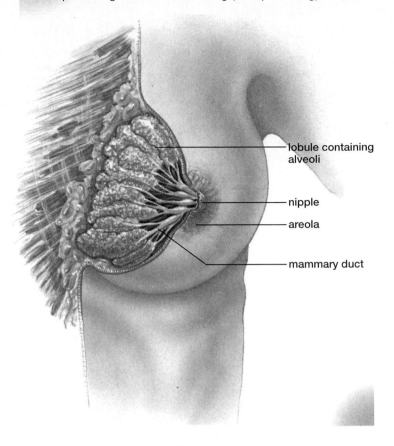

lobule containing alveoli

nipple

areola

mammary duct

tiveness of the method for all but abstinence refers to the number of women per year who will not get pregnant even though they are regularly engaging in sexual intercourse.

SEXUALLY TRANSMITTED DISEASES

Sexually transmitted diseases (*STDs*) are caused by organisms ranging from viruses to arthropods; however, we will discuss only certain STDs caused by viruses and bacteria. Unfortunately, for unknown reasons, humans cannot develop good immunity to any STDs. Therefore, prompt medical treatment should be received when exposed to an STD. To prevent the spread of STDs, a condom can be used; the concomitant use of a spermicide containing nonoxynol 9 gives added protection.

It is difficult to cure the STDs caused by viruses (e.g., AIDS, genital herpes, and genital warts) but treatment is available for AIDS and genital herpes. Those STDs caused by bacteria (e.g., gonorrhea, chlamydia, and syphilis) are treatable with antibiotics.

Table 45.4

Common Birth-Control Methods

Name	Procedure	Methodology	Effectiveness	Risk
Abstinence	Refrain from sexual intercourse	No sperm in vagina	100%	None
Vasectomy	Vasa deferentia are cut and tied	No sperm in seminal fluid	Almost 100%	Irreversible sterility
Tubal ligation	Oviducts are cut and tied	No eggs in oviduct	Almost 100%	Irreversible sterility
Oral contraception (birth-control pill)	Hormone medication is taken daily	Anterior pituitary does not release FSH and LH	Almost 100%	Thromboembolism, especially in smokers
Depo-Provera	Four injections of progesterone-like steroid are given per year	Anterior pituitary does not release FSH and LH	About 99%	Breast cancer? Osteoporosis?
Norplant	Tubes of progestin (form of progesterone) are implanted under skin	Anterior pituitary does not release FSH and LH	More than 90%	Presently none known
IUD	Plastic coil is inserted into uterus by physician	Prevents implantation	More than 90%	Infection (pelvic inflammatory disease, PID)
Diaphragm	Plastic cup is inserted into vagina to cover cervix before intercourse	Blocks entrance of sperm to uterus	With jelly, about 90%	Presently none known
Cervical cap	Rubber cup is held by suction over cervix	Delivers spermicide near cervix	Almost 85%	Cancer of cervix?
Male condom	Latex sheath is fitted over erect penis	Traps sperm and prevents STDs	About 85%	Presently none known
Female condom	Plastic tubing is fitted inside vagina	Blocks entrance of sperm to uterus and prevents STDs	About 85%	Presently none known
Coitus interruptus (withdrawal)	Male withdraws penis before ejaculation	Prevents sperm from entering vagina	75%`	Presently none known
Jellies, creams, foams	These spermicidal products are inserted before intercourse	Kill a large number of sperm	About 75%	Presently none known
Natural family planning	Day of ovulation is determined by record keeping; various methods of testing	Intercourse avoided on certain days of the month	About 70%	Presently none known
Douche	Vagina and uterus are cleansed after intercourse	Washes out sperm	Less than 70%	Presently none known

AIDS Is Preventable

The organism that causes **acquired immunodeficiency syndrome (AIDS)** is a virus called **human immunodeficiency virus (HIV).** HIV attacks the type of lymphocyte known as helper T cells. Helper T cells, you will recall, stimulate the activities of B lymphocytes, which produce antibodies. After an HIV infection sets in, helper T cells begin to decline in number and the person becomes more susceptible to other types of infections.

Symptoms

AIDS has three stages of infection. During the first stage, which may last about a year, the individual is an asymptomatic carrier. The AIDS blood test (an antibody test) is positive, and the individual can pass on the infection, yet there are no symptoms. During the second stage, called AIDS-related complex (ARC), which may last six to eight years, the lymph nodes swell and there may also be weight loss, night sweats, fatigue, fever, and diarrhea. Infections like thrush (white sores on the tongue and in the mouth) and herpes reoccur. Finally, the person may develop full-blown

AIDS, which is characterized by nervous disorders and by the development of an opportunistic disease such as an unusual type of pneumonia or skin cancer. Opportunistic diseases are ones that occur only in individuals who have little or no capability of fighting an infection. The AIDS patient usually dies about seven to nine years after infection.

Transmission

AIDS is transmitted by infected blood, semen, and vaginal secretions. In the United States, the two main affected groups are intravenous (IV) drug users and homosexual men. However, the number of HIV infections in male homosexuals appears to have peaked; in 1988, male homosexuals accounted for 61% of U.S. AIDS cases; now they account for 58%. In contrast, the percentage of infected heterosexuals is rising—20% of new infections are women. The potential for heterosexual infections is of extreme concern to everyone. The AIDS virus can cross the placenta, and infected infants presently account for about 1% of all AIDS cases.

Genital Herpes Can Reoccur

Genital herpes is caused by herpes simplex virus—type 1 usually causes cold sores and fever blisters, while type 2 more often causes genital herpes. Many times a person infected with type 2 has no symptoms, but if symptoms are present, there are painful ulcers on the genitals that heal and then reappear. The ulcers may be accompanied by fever, pain upon urination, and swollen lymph nodes. At this time, the individual has an increased risk of acquiring an AIDS infection. Exposure in the birth canal can cause an infection in the newborn, which leads to neurological disorders and even death. Birth by cesarean section prevents this possibility.

Genital Warts Can Cause Cancer

Genital warts are caused by the human papillomaviruses (HPVs). Many times, carriers do not have any sign of warts, or merely flat lesions may be present. If visible warts are removed, they may recur. HPVs are now associated with cancer of the cervix, as well as tumors of the vulva, the vagina, the anus, and the penis. Some researchers believe that the viruses are involved in 90–95% of all cases of cancer of the cervix.

Gonorrhea Can Cause PID

Gonorrhea is caused by the bacterium *Neisseria gonorrhoeae*. Diagnosis in the male is not difficult, since typical symptoms are pain upon urination and a thick, greenish yellow urethral discharge. In males and females, a latent infection leads to pelvic inflammatory disease (PID), in which the vasa deferentia or oviducts are affected. As the inflamed tubes heal, they may become partially or completely blocked by scar tissue, resulting in sterility or infertility. If a baby is exposed during birth, an eye infection leading to blindness can result. All newborns are given eye drops to prevent this possibility.

Chlamydia Can Be Confused with Gonorrhea

Chlamydia is named for the tiny bacterium that causes it (*Chlamydia trachomatis*). Chlamydia is the most common cause of nongonococcal urethritis (NGU), which is often difficult to distinguish from gonococcal urethritis. Since an infection can also cause PID, physicians routinely prescribe medicines for both gonorrhea and chlamydia at the same time. Chlamydia also causes cervical ulcerations, which increase the risk of acquiring AIDS. If a baby comes in contact with chlamydia during birth, inflammation of the eyes or pneumonia can result.

Syphilis Has Three Stages

Syphilis, which is caused by the bacterium *Treponema pallidum,* has three stages, which are typically separated by latent periods. In the primary stage, a hard chancre (ulcerated sore with hard edges) appears. In the secondary stage, a rash appears all over the body—even on the palms of the hands and the soles of the feet. During the tertiary stage, syphilis may affect the cardiovascular and/or nervous system. An infected person may become mentally retarded, become blind, walk with a shuffle, or show signs of insanity. *Gummas,* which are large destructive ulcers, may develop on the skin or within the internal organs. Syphilitic bacteria can cross the placenta, causing birth defects or a stillbirth. Unlike the other STDs discussed, there is a blood test to diagnose syphilis.

Summary

1. Asexual reproduction may quickly produce a large number of offspring genetically identical to the parent. This is advantageous when environmental conditions are static.

2. Sexual reproduction involves gametes and produces offspring that are genetically slightly different from the parents. This may be advantageous if the environment is changing.

3. The gonads are the primary sex organs but there are also accessory organs. The accessory organs consist of storage areas for sperm and ducts that conduct the gametes.

4. Animals typically protect their eggs and embryos. Those that are oviparous provide them with yolk, and if the animal is terrestrial there is typically a shell to prevent drying out. The amount of yolk is dependent on whether there is a larval stage.

5. Reptiles and birds have extraembryonic membranes that allow vertebrates to develop on land; these same membranes are modified for internal development in mammals.

6. Ovoviviparous animals retain their eggs until the offspring have hatched, and viviparous animals retain the embryo. Placental mammals exemplify viviparous animals.

7. In human males, sperm are produced in the testes, mature in the epididymides, and may be stored in the vasa deferentia before entering the urethra, along with seminal fluid (produced by seminal vesicles, prostate gland, and bulbourethral glands). Sperm are ejaculated during male orgasm, when the penis is erect.

8. Spermatogenesis occurs in the seminiferous tubules of the testes, which also produce testosterone in interstitial cells. Testosterone maintains the secondary sex characteristics of males, such as low voice, facial hair, and increased muscle strength.

9. Follicle-stimulating hormone (FSH) from the anterior pituitary stimulates spermatogenesis, and luteinizing hormone (LH, also called ICSH) stimulates testosterone production. A hypothalamic-releasing hormone, gonadotropic-releasing hormone (GnRH), controls anterior pituitary production and FSH and LH release. The level of testosterone in the blood controls the secretion of GnRH and the anterior pituitary hormones by a negative feedback system.

10. In females, an egg produced by an ovary enters an oviduct, which leads to the uterus. The uterus opens into the vagina. The external genital area of women includes the vaginal opening, the clitoris, the labia minora, and the labia majora.

11. In either ovary, one follicle a month matures, produces a secondary oocyte, and becomes a corpus luteum. This is called the ovarian cycle. The follicle and the corpus luteum produce estrogen and progesterone, the female sex hormones.

12. The uterine cycle occurs concurrently with the ovarian cycle. In the first half of these cycles (days 1–13, before ovulation), the anterior pituitary produces FSH and the follicle produces estrogen. Estrogen causes the uterine lining to increase in thickness. In the second half of these cycles (days 15–28, after ovulation), the anterior pituitary produces LH and the follicle produces progesterone. Progesterone causes the uterine lining to become secretory. Feedback control of the hypothalamus and anterior pituitary causes the levels of estrogen and progesterone to fluctuate. When they are at a low level, menstruation begins.

13. If fertilization occurs, the corpus luteum is maintained because of HCG production. Progesterone production does not cease, and the zygote implants itself in the thick uterine lining.

14. Estrogen and progesterone maintain the secondary sex characteristics of females, including less body hair than males, a wider pelvic girdle, a more rounded appearance, and development of breasts.

15. Infertile couples are increasingly resorting to alternative methods of reproduction. Numerous birth-control methods and devices are available for those who wish to prevent pregnancy.

16. Acquired immunodeficiency syndrome (AIDS) is caused by human immuno-deficiency virus (HIV), which infects helper cells. First, the symptoms of AIDS-related complex, and then those of full-blown AIDS, appear. All persons should take the proper steps to prevent the spread of AIDS.

17. Sexually transmitted diseases include AIDS; herpes, which can recur; genital warts, which lead to cancer of the cervix; gonorrhea and chlamydia, which cause pelvic inflammatory disease (PID); and syphilis, which has cardiovascular and neurological complications if untreated.

Writing Across the Curriculum

In order to practice writing skills, students should write out the answers to any or all of the study questions and the critical thinking questions. The study questions are sequenced in the same order as the text. Answers to the objective questions, and suggested answers to the critical thinking questions, are in appendix D.

Study Questions

1. Give examples of asexual and sexual reproduction among animals. Relate these practices to environmental conditions.   786–87

2. What are the primary sex organs and the usual accessory sex organs? Give examples in reference to the earthworm. How does the reproductive system of earthworms differ from that of most animals?   787

3. Describe the life cycle of an insect utilizing these terms: internal fertilization, oviparous, larva, and metamorphosis. Would you expect an insect egg to contain much yolk? Why?   788

4. Outline the path of sperm. What glands contribute fluids to semen?   790–91

5. Discuss the anatomy and physiology of the testes. Describe the structure of sperm.   792–93

6. Name the endocrine glands involved in maintaining the sex characteristics of males and the hormones produced by each.   793

7. Discuss the anatomy and physiology of the ovaries. Describe ovulation.   794–95

8. Outline the path of the egg. Where do fertilization and implantation occur? Name two functions of the vagina.   794–95

9. Discuss hormonal regulation in the female by listing the events of the uterine cycle and relating these to the ovarian cycle. In what way is menstruation prevented if pregnancy occurs?   796

10. What means of birth control help prevent the spread of AIDS? What other measures can be taken to protect oneself from AIDS?   799

11. Describe at least three other common sexually transmitted diseases.   800

Objective Questions

1. Which of these is a requirement for sexual reproduction?
   a. male and female parents
   b. production of gametes
   c. optimal environmental conditions
   d. aquatic habitat

2. Internal fertilization
   a. prevents the drying out of gametes and zygotes.
   b. must take place on land.
   c. is practiced by humans.
   d. Both a and c are correct.

3. Which of these is mismatched?
   a. interstitial cells—testosterone
   b. seminiferous tubules—sperm production
   c. vasa deferentia—seminal fluid production
   d. urethra—conducts sperm

4. Follicle-stimulating hormone (FSH)
   a. is secreted by females but not males.
   b. stimulates the seminiferous tubules to produce sperm.
   c. secretion is controlled by gonadotropic-releasing hormone (GnRH).
   d. Both b and c are correct.

5. Which of these combinations is most likely to be present before ovulation occurs?
   a. FSH, corpus luteum, estrogen, secretory uterine lining
   b. Luteinizing hormone (LH), follicle, progesterone, thick uterine lining
   c. FSH, follicle, estrogen, uterine lining becoming thick
   d. LH, corpus luteum, progesterone, secretory uterine lining

6. In tracing the path of sperm, you would mention vasa deferentia before
   a. testes.   c. urethra.
   b. epididymides.   d. uterus.

7. An oocyte is fertilized in the
   a. vagina.   c. oviduct.
   b. uterus.   d. ovary.

8. During pregnancy,
   a. the ovarian and uterine cycles occur more quickly than before.
   b. GnRH is produced at a higher level than before.
   c. the ovarian and uterine cycles do not occur.
   d. the female secondary sex characteristics are not maintained.

9. Which of the following means of birth control is most effective in preventing AIDS?

   a. condom

   b. pill

   c. diaphragm

   d. spermicidal jelly

10. Which of these sexually transmitted diseases is mismatched with its cause?

   a. AIDS—bacterial infection of red blood cells

   b. gonorrhea—bacterial infection of genital tract

   c. chlamydia—bacterial infection of genital tract

   d. syphilis—bacterial infection of body

11. Label this diagram of the male reproductive system and trace the path of sperm:

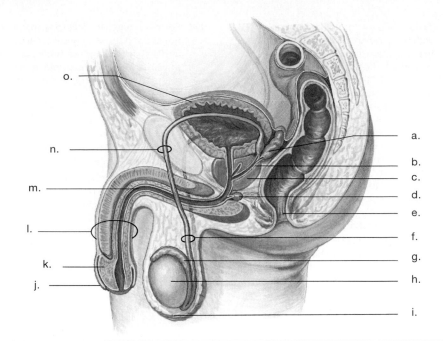

Concepts and Critical Thinking

1. *Successful reproduction on land requires certain adaptations.*

Contrast the manner in which reptiles are adapted to reproduce on land with the manner in which humans are adapted to reproduce on land.

2. *Reproduction is under hormonal rather than nervous control.*

Why would you have predicted hormonal rather than nervous control of reproduction?

Selected Key Terms

copulation A sexual union between a male and a female. [L. *copul,* link]   787

corpus luteum (KOR-pus LOOT-ee-um) A follicle that has released an egg and increases its secretion of progesterone. [L. *corpusc,* little body, and *lut,* yellowish]   795

endometrium (en-doh-MEE-tree-um) A mucous membrane lining the interior surface of the uterus. [Gk. *endo,* within, and *metri,* uterus]   794

estrogen One of several female ovarian sex hormones that causes the endometrium of the uterus to proliferate during the uterine cycle; along with progesterone, estrogen maintain secondary sex characteristics in females.   795

follicle Structure in the ovary of animals that contains oocytes; site of egg production. [L. *follicul,* little bag]   795

follicle-stimulating hormone (FSH) Gonadotropic hormone secreted by the anterior pituitary; it promotes production of eggs in females and sperm in males.   795

gonad An organ that produces sex cells; the ovary, which produces eggs, and the testis, which produces sperm. [Gk. *gon,* seed]   787

larva (pl., larvae) An immature form in the life cycle of some animals; the stage of development between the embryo and the adult form. It undergoes metamorphosis to become the adult form.   788

luteinizing hormone (LH) (LOOT-ee-ny-zing) Gonadotropic hormone secreted by the anterior pituitary that stimulates the production of sex hormones in males and females.   795

menstruation The periodic shedding of tissue and blood from the inner lining of the uterus. [L. *menstru,* monthly]   796

metamorphosis A change in shape and form that some animals, such as insects, undergo during development. [Gk. *met,* change, and *morph,* form]   788

ovulation Bursting of a follicle when an egg is released from the ovary.   795

parthenogenesis (par-thuh-noh-JEN-uh-sus) The development of an egg cell into a whole organism without fertilization. [Gk. *partheno,* without fertilization, and *gene,* origin]   786

penis Male copulatory organ.   787

progesterone (proh-JES-tuh-rohn) Female ovarian sex hormone that causes the endometrium of the uterus to become secretory during the uterine cycle; along with estrogen, it maintains secondary sex characteristics in females.   795

semen Thick, whitish fluid consisting of sperm and secretions from several glands of the male reproductive tract. [L. *semen,* sperm]   791

testosterone (teh-STAHS-tuh-rohn) Male sex hormone produced by interstitial cells in the testis; it maintains secondary sex characteristics in males.   793

uterine cycle A cycle that runs concurrently with the ovarian cycle; it prepares the uterus to receive a developing zygote.   796

uterus The pear-shaped portion of the female reproductive tract that lies between the oviducts and the vagina; the site of embryo and fetal development. [L. *uter,* womb]   794

vagina A muscular tube leading from the uterus; the female copulatory organ and the birth canal. [L. *vagin,* sheath]   794

46

DEVELOPMENT IN ANIMALS

Learning Objectives

- Name and define three processes that occur whenever there is a developmental change.   804

Development Has Stages

- Explain the germ layer theory of development, and give examples.   805
- Compare the early developmental stages of the lancelet, frog, and the chick.   806
- Draw and label a cross section of a typical vertebrate embryo at the neurula stage of development.   807

Cells Become Specialized and Embryos Take Shape

- Give evidence that differentiation probably begins soon after formation of the zygote.   808

- Explain how morphogenesis can be accounted for by interactions between tissues.   809–810

Humans Are Embryos and Then Fetuses

- List the extraembryonic membranes, and give their function in chicks and in humans.   811
- State the stages of embryonic development in humans, and compare them to those in the chick; outline fetal development in humans.   813–16

Development Continues

- Briefly outline the developmental changes in humans from infancy through old age.   817

All animal embryos develop in a fluid medium. Calf embryo, *Bos,* of approximately 3¹/₂ months is surrounded by amniotic fluid within the uterus of its mother.

evelopment includes the events and processes that occur as a single cell becomes a complex organism. These same processes are also seen as the newly born or hatched organism matures, as lost parts regenerate, as a wound heals, and even as organisms age. Therefore, it is important that the study of development encompasses not only embryology (development of the embryo) but these other events as well.

Development requires growth, differentiation, and morphogenesis. When an organism increases in size, we say that it has grown. During **growth,** cells divide, get larger, and divide once again. **Differentiation** occurs when cells become specialized in structure and function; a muscle cell looks different and acts differently than a nerve cell. **Morphogenesis** [Gk. *morph,* form, and *gene,* origin] goes one step beyond growth and differentiation. It occurs when body parts take on a certain form. There is a great deal of difference between your arm and leg, even though they contain the same types of tissues.

We will discuss these processes as they apply to development of the embryo, but keep in mind that they also occur whenever an organism goes through any developmental change.

> Growth, differentiation, and morphogenesis are three processes that are seen whenever a developmental change occurs.

DEVELOPMENT HAS STAGES

All chordate embryos go through the same early developmental stages of zygote, morula, blastula, early gastrula, and late gastrula. The presence of yolk, which is dense nutrient material, however, affects the manner in which embryonic cells complete the first three stages, and hence the appearance of the embryo at the end of each stage. Considering this, we will take as our example the lancelet, an animal whose egg has little yolk.

Fertilization [L. *fertil,* fruitful], which results in a zygote, requires that the sperm and egg interact. A sperm has three distinct parts: a head, a middle piece, and a tail. The tail is a flagellum, which allows the sperm to swim toward the egg, and the middle piece contains energy-producing mitochondria. The head contains a haploid nucleus capped by a membrane-bounded acrosome containing enzymes that allow the sperm to penetrate the egg.

Several mechanisms have evolved to assure that fertilization takes place and in a species-specific manner (fig. 46.1). Males release so many sperm that the egg is literally covered by them. The egg has a plasma membrane, a vitelline membrane, and a jelly coat. The acrosome enzymes digest away the jelly coat as the acrosome extrudes a filament that attaches to receptors located in the vitelline membrane. This is a lock-and-key reaction that is species-specific. Then, the egg plasma membrane and sperm nuclear membrane fuse allowing the sperm nucleus to enter. Fusion takes place and the zygote begins development.

As soon as the plasma membrane of sperm and egg fuse, the plasma membrane and the vitelline membrane undergo changes that prevent the entrance of any other sperm. The vitelline membrane is now called the fertilization membrane.

Following fertilization, the zygote undergoes **cleavage,** which is cell division without growth (fig. 46.2). DNA (deoxyribonucleic acid) replication and mitosis occur repeatedly, and the cells get smaller with each division. Lancelet, being deutero-

Figure 46.1

Fertilization. A head of a sperm contains a haploid nucleus capped by a membrane-bounded acrosome. The acrosome releases enzymes that digest away the jelly coat around the egg, and it extrudes a filament that attaches to a receptor on the vitelline membrane. Following fusion of the sperm and cell plasma membranes, the sperm nucleus enters the egg. The nuclei fuse, and the resulting zygote begins to divide. The vitelline membrane becomes the fertilization membrane, which prohibits any more sperm from entering the egg.

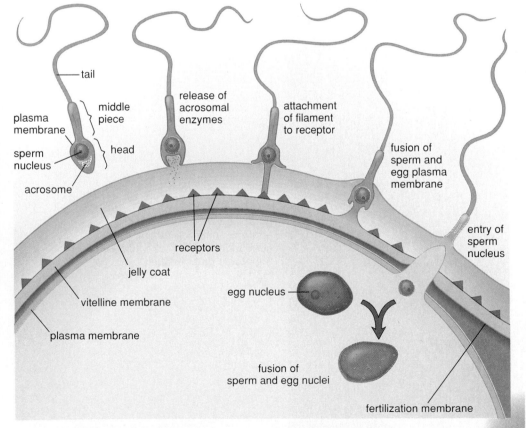

stomes, have a pattern of cleavage that is radial and indeterminate. The term *radial* means that any plane passing through the major axis will divide the embryo into two symmetrical halves. The term *indeterminate* means that the cleavage cells have not differentiated, and therefore their developmental fate is not yet set.

Because the lancelet has little yolk, the cell divisions are equal, and the cells are of uniform size in the resulting **morula** [L. *morul,* a little mulberry]. Then a cavity called the **blastocoel** [Gk. *blast,* bud, and *coel,* hollow] develops and a hollow ball known as the **blastula** [Gk. *blast,* bud, and L. *ula,* little] forms.

The **gastrula** [Gk. *gastr,* stomach, and L. *ula,* little] stage is evident in a lancelet when certain cells begin to push, or invaginate, into the blastocoel, creating a double layer of cells. The outer layer is called the **ectoderm,** and the inner layer is called the **endoderm.** The space created by invagination becomes the gut, but at this point it is termed either the primitive gut or the *archenteron.* The pore, or hole, created by invagination is the *blastopore,* and in a lancelet the blastopore eventually becomes the anus.

Gastrulation is not complete until three layers of cells are present. The third, or middle, layer of cells is called the **mesoderm.** In a lancelet, this layer begins as outpocketings from the primitive gut. These outpocketings grow in size until they meet and fuse. In effect then, two layers of mesoderm are formed, and the space between them is the coelom.

Ectoderm, mesoderm, and endoderm are called the embryonic **germ layers** of the embryo. No matter how gastrulation takes place, the end result is the same: three germ layers are formed. It is possible to relate the development of future organs to these germ layers:

Embryonic Germ Layer	Vertebrate Adult Structures
Ectoderm (outer layer)	Epidermis of skin; epithelial lining of mouth and rectum; nervous system
Mesoderm (middle layer)	Skeleton; muscular system; dermis of skin; circulatory system; excretory system; reproductive system—including most epithelial linings; outer layers of respiratory and digestive systems
Endoderm (inner layer)	Epithelial lining of digestive tract and respiratory tract; associated glands of these systems; epithelial lining of urinary bladder

Karl E. Von Baer, the nineteenth-century embryologist, first related development to the formation of germ layers. This is called the *germ layer theory.*

The three embryonic germ layers arise during gastrulation, when cells invaginate into the blastocoel. The development of organs can be related to the three germ layers: ectoderm, mesoderm, and endoderm.

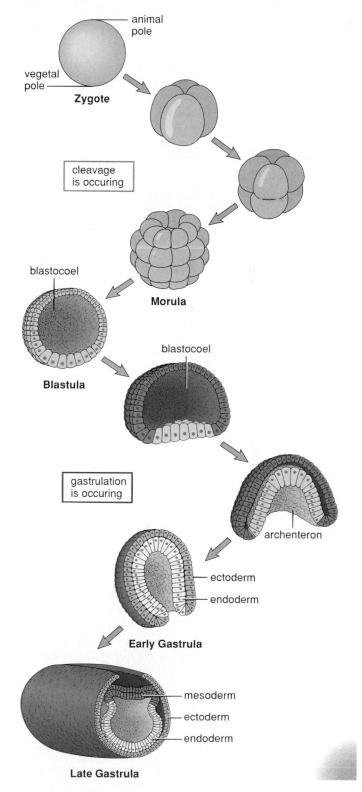

Figure 46.2

Early development in a lancelet. A lancelet has little yolk as an embryo, and it can be used to exemplify the early stages of development in such animals. Cleavage produces a number of cells that form a cavity. Invagination during gastrulation produces the germ layers ectoderm and endoderm. Mesoderm arises from pouches that pinch off from the endoderm.

animal pole

vegetal pole

Zygote

cleavage is occuring

blastocoel

Morula

blastocoel

Blastula

gastrulation is occuring

archenteron

ectoderm

endoderm

Early Gastrula

mesoderm

ectoderm

endoderm

Late Gastrula

How Yolk Affects the Stages

Table 46.1 indicates the amount of yolk in four types of embryos and relates the amount of yolk to the environment in which the animal develops. The lancelet and frog develop in water, and they have less yolk than the chick because their development proceeds quickly to a swimming larval stage that can feed itself. The chick is representative of vertebrate animals that have solved, in part, the problem of reproduction on land by providing a great deal of yolk within a hard shell. Development continues in the shell until there is an offspring capable of land existence.

Early stages of human development resemble those of the chick embryo, yet this resemblance cannot be related to the amount of yolk because the human egg contains little yolk. But the evolutionary history of these two animals can provide an answer for this similarity. Both birds and mammals are related to reptiles; this explains why all three groups develop similarly, despite a difference in the amount of yolk in the eggs.

> **The amount of yolk affects the manner in which animals complete the first three stages of development.**

Figure 46.3 compares the appearance of early developmental stages in the lancelet, the frog, and the chick. In the frog embryo, cells at the animal pole have little yolk while those at the vegetal pole contain more yolk. The presence of yolk causes cells to cleave more slowly, and you can see that the cells of the animal pole are smaller than those of the vegetal pole. In the chick, cleavage is incomplete—only those cells lying on top of the yolk cleave. This means that although cleavage in the lancelet and the frog results in a morula, no such ball of cells is seen in the chick (fig. 46.3*a*). Instead, during the morula stage the cells spread out on a portion of the yolk.

In the frog, the blastocoel is formed at the animal pole only. The heavily laden yolk cells of the vegetal pole do not participate in this step. In a chick, the blastocoel is created when the cells lift up from the yolk and leave a space between the cells and the yolk (fig. 46.3*b*).

Figure 46.3

Comparative stages of development. **a.** Morula stages for a lancelet, a frog, and a chick. **b.** Blastula stages. **c.** Early gastrula stages. **d.** Late gastrula stages.

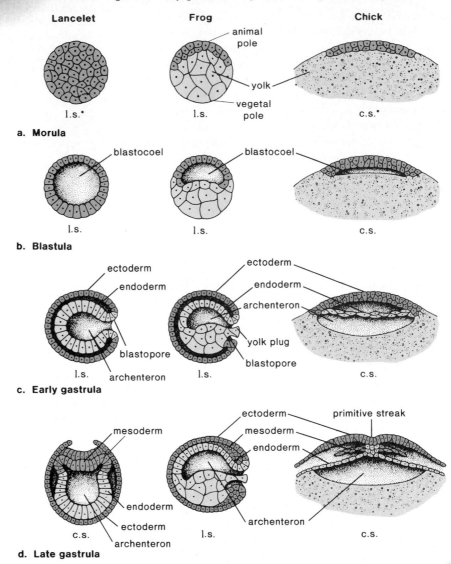

*l.s. = longitudinal section; c.s. = cross section

Table 46.1

Amount of Yolk in Eggs Versus Location of Development

Animal	Yolk	Location of Development
Lancelet	Little	External in water
Frog	Some	External in water
Chick	Much	Within hard shell
Human	Little	Inside mother

Figure 46.4

Development of neural tube and coelom in a frog embryo. **a.** Ectoderm cells that lie above the future notochord (called presumptive notochord) thicken to form a neural plate. **b.** The neural groove and folds are noticeable as the neural tube begins to form. **c.** A splitting of the mesoderm produces a coelom, which is completely lined by mesoderm. **d.** A neural tube and a coelom have now developed.

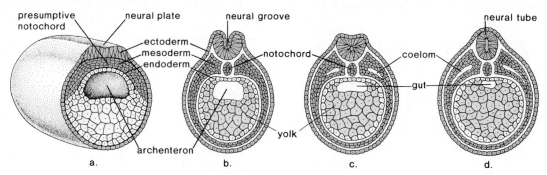

In the frog, the cells containing yolk do not participate in gastrulation and therefore they do not invaginate. Instead, a slitlike blastopore is formed when the animal pole cells begin to invaginate from above. Following this, other animal pole cells move down over the yolk, and the blastopore becomes rounded when these cells also invaginate from below. At this stage, there are some yolk cells temporarily left in the region of the pore; these are called the yolk plug. In the chick, there is so much yolk that endoderm formation does not occur by invagination. Instead, an upper layer of cells differentiates into ectoderm, and a lower layer differentiates into endoderm (fig. 46.3*c*).

In the frog, cells from the dorsal lip of the blastopore migrate between the ectoderm and endoderm, forming the mesoderm. Later, a splitting of the mesoderm creates the coelom. In the chick, the mesoderm layer arises by an invagination of cells along the edges of a longitudinal furrow in the midline of the embryo. Because of its appearance, this furrow is called the *primitive streak* (fig. 46.3*d*). Later, the newly formed mesoderm will split to produce a coelomic cavity.

Neurulation Produces the Nervous System

In chordate animals, newly formed mesoderm cells that lie along the main longitudinal axis of the animal coalesce to form a dorsal supporting rod called the **notochord** [Gk. *noto,* back, and *chord,* string]. The notochord persists in lancelets but in frogs, chicks, and humans, it is later replaced by the vertebral column.

The nervous system develops from midline ectoderm located just above the notochord. At first, a thickening of cells called the *neural plate* is seen along the dorsal surface of the embryo. Then, *neural folds* develop on either side of a neural groove, which becomes the *neural tube* when these folds fuse. Figure 46.4 shows cross sections of frog development to illustrate the formation of the neural tube. At this point, the embryo is called a *neurula*. Later, the anterior end of the neural tube develops into the brain.

Midline mesoderm cells that did not contribute to the formation of the notochord now become two longitudinal masses of

Figure 46.5

Typical cross section of a chordate embryo at the neurula stage. Each of the germ layers, indicated by color (see key), can be associated with the later development of particular parts. The somites give rise to the muscles of each segment and to the vertebrae, which replace the notochord.

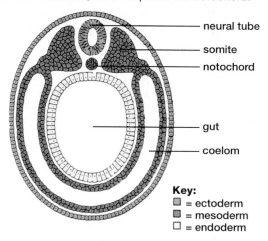

tissue. These two masses become blocked off into the somites, which give rise to segmental muscles in all chordates. In vertebrates, the somites also produce the vertebral bones.

The chordate embryo in figure 46.5 shows the location of various parts. This figure and the chart on page 805 will help you relate the formation of chordate structures and organs to the three embryonic layers of cells: the ectoderm, the mesoderm, and the endoderm.

> During neurulation, the neural tube develops just above the notochord. At the neurula stage of development, a cross section of all chordate embryos is similar in appearance.

CELLS BECOME SPECIALIZED AND EMBRYOS TAKE SHAPE

Differentiation and morphogenesis are two developmental processes. They account for the specialization of tissues and the formation of organs, and they determine the overall shape and form of an animal.

How Cells Become Specialized

Differentiation has occurred when cells become specialized in structure and function. The process of differentiation most likely starts long before we can recognize different types of cells. Ectodermal, endodermal, and mesodermal cells in the gastrula look quite similar, but yet they must be different because they develop into different organs. What causes differentiation to occur, and when does it begin?

We know that differentiation cannot be due to a parceling out of genes into embryonic cells, because each cell in the body contains a full complement of chromosomes and, therefore, genes. However, we can note that the cytoplasm of a frog's egg is not uniform. It is polar and has both an anterior/posterior axis and a dorsal/ventral axis, which can be correlated with the gray crescent, a gray area that appears after the sperm fertilizes the egg (fig. 46.6*a*). Hans Spemann, who received a Nobel prize in 1935 for his extensive work in embryology, showed that if the gray crescent is divided equally by the first cleavage, each experimentally separated daughter cell develops into a complete embryo

(fig. 46.6*b*). If the egg divides so that only one daughter cell receives the gray crescent, however, only that cell becomes a complete embryo (fig. 46.6*c*). We can therefore speculate that particular chemical signals within the gray crescent turn on the genes that control development in the frog.

It is hypothesized that genes are turned on/off due to *ooplasmic segregation,* which is the distribution of maternal cytoplasmic contents to the various cells of the morula:

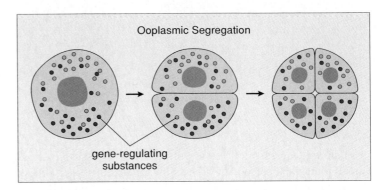

Ooplasmic Segregation

gene-regulating substances

Cytoplasmic substances, parceled out during cleavage, initially influence which genes are activated and how cells differentiate.

Figure 46.6

Cytoplasmic influence on development. **a.** A frog's egg has anterior/posterior and dorsal/ventral axes that correlate with the position of the gray crescent. **b.** The first cleavage normally divides the gray crescent in half, and each daughter cell is capable of developing into a complete tadpole. **c.** But if only one daughter cell receives the gray crescent, then only that cell can become a complete embryo. This shows that chemical messengers are not uniformly distributed in the egg's cytoplasm of frogs.

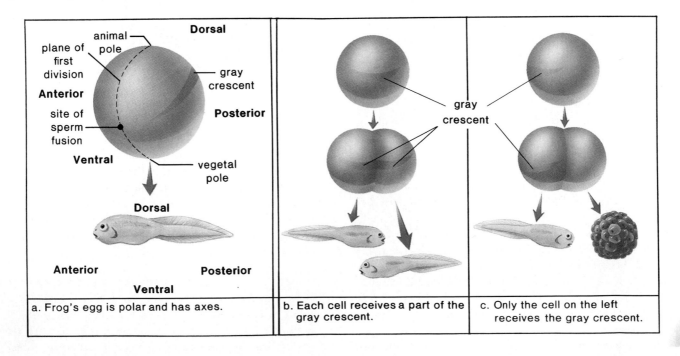

a. Frog's egg is polar and has axes.

b. Each cell receives a part of the gray crescent.

c. Only the cell on the left receives the gray crescent.

How Morphogenesis Occurs

As development proceeds, a cell's differentiation is influenced not only by its cytoplasmic content, but also by signals given off by neighboring cells. Migration of cells occurs during gastrulation, and there is evidence that one set of cells can influence the migratory path taken by another set of cells. Some cells produce an extracellular matrix that contains fibrils, and in the laboratory, it can be shown that the orientation of these fibrils influences migratory cells. The cytoskeletons of the migrating cells are oriented in the same direction as the fibrils. Although this may not be an exact mechanism at work during gastrulation, it suggests that formation of the germ layers is probably influenced by environmental factors.

Spemann showed that a frog embryo's gray crescent becomes the dorsal lip of the blastopore, where gastrulation begins. Since this region is necessary for complete development, he called the dorsal lip of the blastopore the primary organizer. The cells closest to Spemann's primary organizer become endoderm, those farther away become mesoderm, and those farthest away become ectoderm. This suggests that there may be a molecular concentration gradient that acts as a signal to induce germ layer differentiation. **Induction** [L. *in,* into, and *duct,* lead] is the ability of a chemical or a tissue to influence the development of another tissue. The inducing chemical is called a *signal.*

Experiments performed by Jim Smith of the National Institute of Medical Research in London indicate that the peptide growth factor called activin may play a role in the signaling process. At low concentrations of activin, animal pole cells become epidermis, an ectoderm-derived tissue, and at higher concentrations they become muscle and notochord, a mesoderm-derived tissue.

The gray crescent of a frog egg marks the dorsal side of the embryo where the notochord and nervous system develop. Spemann and his colleague Hilde Mangold showed that presumptive (potential) notochord tissue induces the formation of the nervous system (fig. 46.7). If presumptive nervous system tissue, located just above the presumptive notochord, is cut out and transplanted to the belly region of the embryo, it does not form a neural tube. On the other hand, if presumptive notochord tissue is cut out and transplanted beneath what would be belly ectoderm, this ectoderm differentiates into neural tissue. Still other

Figure 46.7

Experiments showing importance of presumptive notochord. **a.** In this experiment, the presumptive nervous system (blue) does not develop into the neural plate if moved from its normal location. **b.** In this experiment, the presumptive notochord (red) can cause the belly ectoderm to develop into the neural plate (blue). This shows that the notochord induces ectoderm to become a neural plate, most likely by sending out chemical signals.

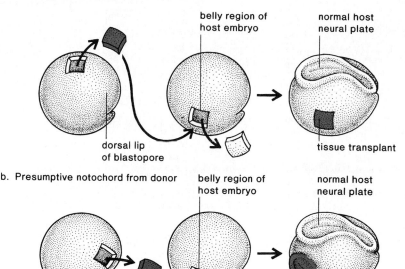

a. Presumptive nervous system from donor

belly region of host embryo

normal host neural plate

dorsal lip of blastopore

tissue transplant

b. Presumptive notochord from donor

belly region of host embryo

normal host neural plate

induced neural plate

examples of induction are now known. In 1905, Warren Lewis studied the formation of the eye in frog embryos. He found that an optic vesicle, which is a lateral outgrowth of developing brain tissue, induces overlying ectoderm to thicken and become a lens. The developing lens in turn induces an optic vesicle to form an optic cup, where the retina develops.

Today investigators believe the process of induction goes on continuously—neighboring cells are always influencing one another. Either direct contact or the production of a chemical acts as a signal that activates certain genes and brings about protein synthesis. This diagram shows how morphogenesis can be a sequential process:

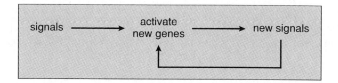

signals ⟶ activate new genes ⟶ new signals

Genes That Control Pattern Formation

Investigators studying morphogenesis in *Drosophila* (fruit fly) have discovered that there are some genes that determine the animal's anterior/posterior and dorsal/ventral axes, others that determine the number and polarity of its segments, and still others, called *homeotic genes,* that determine how these segments develop. Homeotic genes have now been found in many other organisms and, surprisingly, they all contain the same particular sequence of nucleic acids, called a *homeobox.*

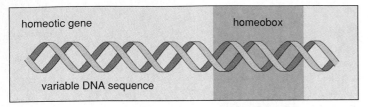

homeotic gene — homeobox

variable DNA sequence

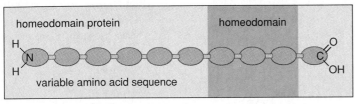

homeodomain protein — homeodomain

variable amino acid sequence

Since homeoboxes have been found in almost all eukaryotic organisms, it is believed that homeoboxes are derived from an original nucleic acid sequence that has been largely conserved (maintained from generation to generation) because of its importance in the regulation of animal development.

In *Drosophila,* a homeotic mutation causes body parts to be misplaced—a homeotic mutant fly can have two pairs of wings or extra legs where antennae should be (fig. 46.8). Similarly, in the frog *Xenopus,* if the expression levels of the homeotic genes are altered, headless and tailless embryos are produced.

Homeotic genes are clearly involved in *pattern formation*—that is, the shaping of an embryo so that the adult has a normal appearance. Homeotic genes are arranged in a definite order on a chromosome; those first in line determine the anterior portion of the embryo, while those later in the sequence determine the posterior portion of the embryo. A homeotic gene codes for a homeodomain protein. Each of these proteins has a homeodomain, a sequence of sixty amino acids that is found in all other homeodomain proteins. Homeodomain proteins stay in the nucleus and regulate transcription of other genes during development. Researchers envision that a homeodomain protein produced by one homeotic gene binds to and turns on the next homeotic gene, and this orderly process determines the overall pattern of the embryo. It appears that homeotic genes also establish homeodomain protein gradients that affect the pattern development of specific parts,

Figure 46.8

Homeotic mutations in *Drosophila*. Homeotic genes control pattern formation, an aspect of morphogenesis. In these instances, homeotic genes were activated at inappropriate times. **a.** A fly with four wings resulted. **b.** A fly with legs on its head resulted.

a.

b.

such as the limbs. One well-known gradient that determines wing formation in the chick involves retinoic acid, a chemical related to retinal, which is present in rods and cones of the eye.

Many laboratories are engaged in discovering much more about homeotic genes and homeodomain proteins. We need to know, for example, how homeotic genes are turned on and how protein gradients are maintained in tissues. The roles of the cytoskeleton and extracellular matrix are being explored.

Morphogenesis is dependent upon signals (either contact or chemical) from neighboring cells. These signals are believed to activate particular genes, including homeotic genes.

HUMANS ARE EMBRYOS AND THEN FETUSES

Development encompasses the time from conception (fertilization followed by implantation) to birth (parturition). In humans, the gestation period, or length of pregnancy, is approximately nine months. It is customary to calculate the time of birth by adding 280 days to the start of the last menstruation, because this date is usually known, whereas the day of fertilization is usually unknown. Because the time of birth is influenced by so many variables, only about 5% of babies actually arrive on the forecasted date.

Human development is often divided into embryonic development (months 1 and 2) and fetal development (months 3–9). The embryonic period consists of early formation of the major organs, and fetal development is the refinement of these structures.

Before we consider human development chronologically, we must understand the placement of **extraembryonic membranes** [L. *extra,* outside]. Extraembryonic membranes are best understood by considering their function in reptiles and birds. In reptiles, these membranes made development on land first possible. If an embryo develops in the water, the water supplies oxygen for the embryo and takes away waste products. The surrounding water prevents desiccation, or drying out, and provides a protective cushion. For an embryo that develops on land, all these functions are performed by the extraembryonic membranes.

In the chick, the extraembryonic membranes develop from extensions of the germ layers, which spread out over the yolk. Figure 46.9 shows the chick surrounded by the membranes. The **chorion** [Gk. *chori,* membrane] lies next to the shell and carries on gas exchange. The **amnion** [Gk. *amnio,* fetal membrane] contains the protective amniotic fluid, which bathes the developing embryo. The **allantois** [Gk. *allant,* sausage, and *eidos,* form] collects nitrogenous wastes, and the **yolk sac** surrounds the remaining yolk, which provides nourishment.

As figure 46.9 indicates, humans (and other mammals) also have these extraembryonic membranes. The chorion develops into the fetal half of the placenta; the yolk sac, which lacks yolk, is the first site of blood cell formation; the allantoic blood vessels become the umbilical blood vessels; and the amnion contains fluid to cushion and protect the fetus. Therefore, the function of the membranes in humans has been modified to suit internal development, but their very presence indicates our relationship to birds and to reptiles. It is interesting to note that all chordate animals develop in water, either in bodies of water or within amniotic fluid.

> The presence of extraembryonic membranes in reptiles made development on land possible. Humans also have these membranes, but their function has been modified for internal development.

Figure 46.9

Extraembryonic membranes. The membranes, which are not part of the embryo, are found during the development of chicks and humans, where each has a specific function.

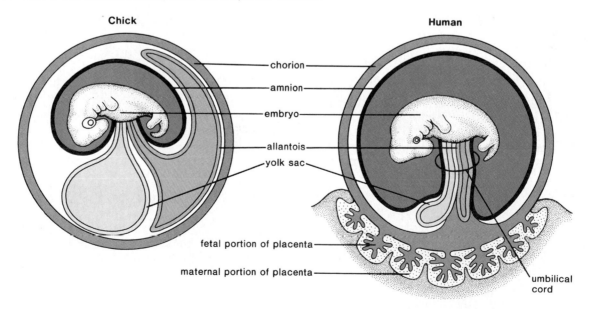

Embryos Don't Look Human

Embryonic development includes the first two months of development.

First Week

Fertilization occurs in the upper third of an oviduct (fig. 46.10), and cleavage begins even as the embryo passes down this tube to the uterus. By the time the embryo reaches the uterus on the third day, it is a *morula*. The morula is not much larger than the zygote because, even though multiple cell divisions have occurred, there has been no growth of these newly formed cells. By about the fifth day, the morula is transformed into the blastocyst. The blas-

tocyst has a fluid-filled cavity, a single layer of outer cells called the **trophoblast** [Gk. *troph*, nourish, and *blast*, bud], and an inner cell mass. Later, the trophoblast, reinforced by a layer of mesoderm, gives rise to the *chorion*, one of the extraembryonic membranes (see fig. 46.9). The *inner cell* mass eventually becomes the fetus.

Second Week

At the end of the first week, the embryo begins the process of *implanting* in the wall of the uterus. The trophoblast secretes enzymes to digest away some of the tissue and blood vessels of the uterine wall (fig. 46.10). The embryo is now about the size of

Figure 46.10

Human development before implantation. Structures and events proceed counterclockwise. At ovulation, the secondary oocyte leaves the ovary. A single sperm penetrates the zona pellucida, and fertilization occurs in the oviduct. As the zygote moves along the oviduct, it undergoes cleavage to produce a morula. The blastocyst forms and implants itself in the uterine lining.

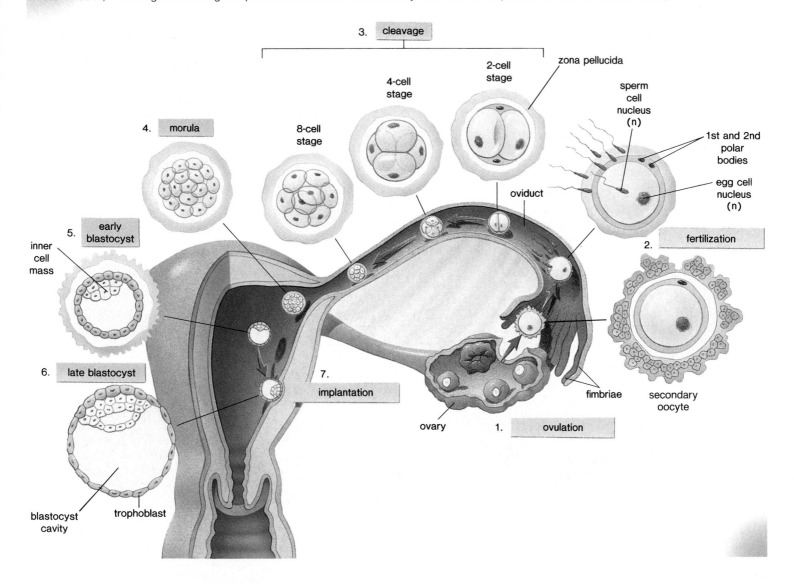

the period at the end of this sentence. The trophoblast begins to secrete **human chorionic gonadotropic hormone (HCG),** the hormone that is the basis for the pregnancy test and that serves to maintain the corpus luteum past the time it normally disintegrates. Because of this, the endometrium is maintained and menstruation does not occur.

As the week progresses, the inner cell mass detaches itself from the trophoblast, and two more extraembryonic membranes form (fig. 46.11*a*). The *yolk sac,* which forms below the embryonic disk, has no nutritive function as in chicks, but it is the first site of blood cell formation. However, the *amnion* and its cavity are where the embryo (and then the fetus)

develops. In humans, amniotic fluid acts as an insulator against cold and heat and also absorbs shock, such as that caused by the mother exercising.

Gastrulation occurs during the second week. The inner cell mass now has flattened into the *embryonic disk,* composed of two layers of cells: *ectoderm* above and *endoderm* below. Once the embryonic disk elongates to form the *primitive streak,* similar to that found in birds, the third germ layer, mesoderm, forms by invagination of cells along the streak. The trophoblast is reinforced by mesoderm and becomes the chorion.

It is possible to relate the development of future organs to these germ layers (see p. 805).

Figure 46.11

Stages showing the early appearance of the extraembryonic membranes and the formation of the umbilical cord in the human embryo. **a.** At 14 days, the amniotic cavity appears. **b.** At 21 days, the chorion and the yolk sac are apparent. **c.** At 28 days, the body stalk and the allantois form. **d.** At 35 days, the embryo begins to take shape as the umbilical cord starts forming. **e.** Eventually, at 42+ days, the umbilical cord is fully formed.

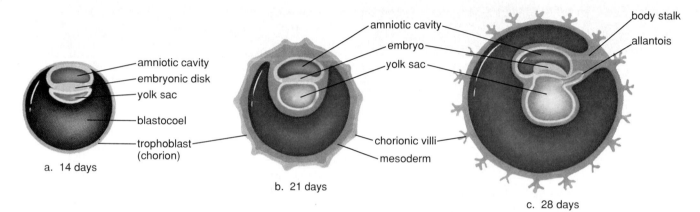

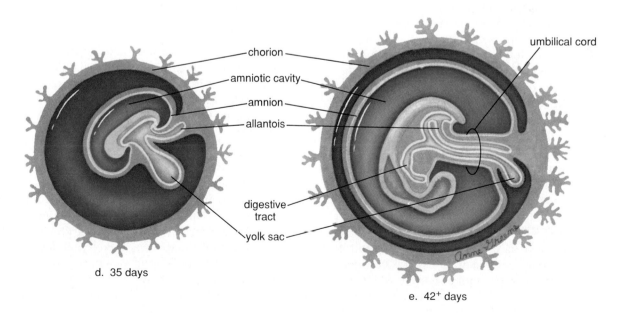

Figure 46.12 📼

Human embryo at beginning of fifth week. **a.** Scanning electron micrograph. **b.** The embryo is curled so that the head touches the heart, the two organs whose development is further along than the rest of the body. The organs of the gastrointestinal tract are forming, and the arms and the legs develop from the bulges that are called limb buds. The tail is an evolutionary remnant; its bones regress and become those of the coccyx (tailbone). The pharyngeal arches become functioning gills only in fishes and amphibian larvae; in humans, the first pair of pharyngeal pouches becomes the eustachian tubes. The second pair becomes the tonsils, while the third and fourth become the thymus gland and the parathyroids.

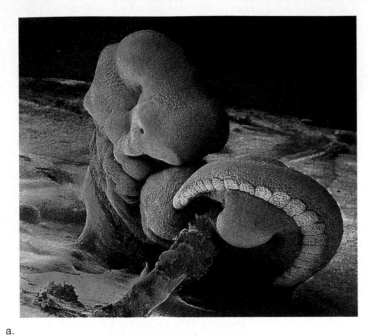

a.

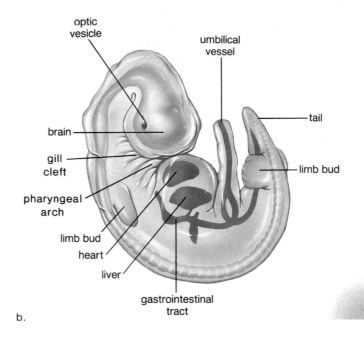

b.

Third Week

Two important organ systems make their appearance during the third week. The nervous system is the first organ system to be visually evident. At first, a thickening appears along the entire dorsal length of the embryo, and then invagination occurs as neural folds appear. When the neural folds meet at the midline, the neural tube, which later develops into the brain and the nerve cord, is formed (see fig. 46.4). After the notochord is replaced by the vertebral column, the nerve cord is called the spinal cord.

Development of the heart begins in the third week and continues into the fourth week. At first, there are right and left heart tubes; when these fuse, the heart begins pumping blood, even though the chambers of the heart are not fully formed. The veins enter posteriorly and the arteries exit anteriorly from this largely tubular heart, but later the heart twists so that all major blood vessels are located anteriorly.

Fourth and Fifth Weeks

At four weeks, the embryo is barely larger than the height of this print. A bridge of mesoderm called the body stalk connects the caudal (tail) end of the embryo with the chorion, which has projections called chorionic villi (see fig. 46.11c). The fourth extraembryonic membrane, the *allantois,* is contained within this stalk, and its blood vessels become the umbilical blood vessels. The head and the tail then lift up, and the body stalk moves anteriorly by constriction (see fig. 46.11d). Once this process is complete, the **umbilical cord** [L. *umbilic,* navel], which connects the developing embryo to the placenta, is fully formed (see fig. 46.11e).

Little flippers called limb buds appear (fig. 46.12); later, the arms and the legs develop from the limb buds, and even the hands and the feet become apparent. At the same time—during the fifth week—the head enlarges and the sense organs become more prominent. It is possible to make out the developing eyes, ears, and even nose.

Sixth through Eighth Weeks

There is a remarkable change in external appearance during the sixth through eighth weeks of development—a form that is difficult to recognize as human becomes easily recognized as human. Concurrent with brain development, the head achieves its normal relationship with the body as a neck region develops. The nervous system is developed well enough to permit reflex actions, such as a startle response to touch. At the end of this period, the embryo is about 38 mm (1.5 in) long and weighs no more than an aspirin tablet, even though all organ systems are established.

Figure 46.13

Anatomy of the placenta in a fetus at six to seven months. The placenta is composed of both fetal and maternal tissues. Chorionic villi penetrate the uterine lining and are surrounded by maternal blood. Exchange of molecules between fetal and maternal blood takes place across the walls of the chorionic villi.

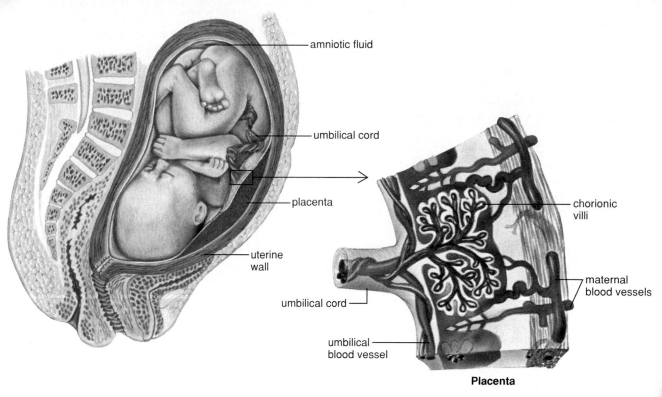

Placenta

The Placenta Fulfills Needs

The **placenta** begins formation once the embryo is fully implanted. Treelike extensions of the chorion called **chorionic villi** [Gk. *chori,* membrane, and L. *vill,* shaggy hair] project into the maternal tissues. Later, these disappear in all areas except where the placenta develops. By the tenth week, the placenta (fig. 46.13) is fully formed and has already begun to produce progesterone and estrogen. These hormones have two effects: due to their negative feedback control of the hypothalamus and the anterior pituitary, they prevent any new follicles from maturing, and they maintain the lining of the uterus—now the corpus luteum is not needed. There is no menstruation during pregnancy.

The placenta has a fetal side contributed by the chorion and a maternal side consisting of uterine tissues. Notice in figure 46.13 how the chorionic villi are surrounded by maternal blood sinuses; yet maternal and fetal blood never mix, since exchange always takes place across plasma membranes. Carbon dioxide and other wastes move from the fetal side to the maternal side, and nutri-

ents and oxygen move from the maternal side to the fetal side of the placenta. The umbilical cord stretches between the placenta and the fetus. Although it may seem that the umbilical cord travels from the placenta to the intestine, actually the umbilical cord is simply taking fetal blood to and from the placenta. The umbilical cord is the lifeline of the fetus because it contains the umbilical arteries and vein, which transport waste molecules (carbon dioxide and urea) to the placenta for disposal and take oxygen and nutrient molecules from the placenta to the rest of the fetal circulatory system.

Harmful chemicals can also cross the placenta. This is of particular concern during the embryonic period, when various structures are first forming. Each organ or part seems to have a sensitive period during which a substance can alter its normal development. For example, if a woman takes the drug thalidomide, a tranquilizer, between days 27 and 40 of her pregnancy, the infant is likely to be born with deformed limbs. After day 40, however, the infant is born with normal limbs.

Fetuses Look Human

Fetal development (months 3–9) is marked by an extreme increase in size. Weight multiplies 600 times, going from less than 28 g to 3 kg. In this time, too, the fetus grows to about 50 cm in length. The genitalia appear in the third month, so it is possible to tell if the fetus is male or female.

Soon, hair, eyebrows, and eyelashes add finishing touches to the face and head. In the same way, fingernails and toenails complete the hands and feet. A fine, downy hair (**lanugo**) covers the limbs and trunk, only to later disappear. The fetus looks very old because the skin is growing so fast that it wrinkles. A waxy, almost cheeselike substance (**vernix caseosa**) protects the wrinkly skin from the watery amniotic fluid.

The fetus at first only flexes its limbs and nods its head, but later it can move its limbs vigorously to avoid discomfort. The mother feels these movements from about the fourth month on. The other systems of the body also begin to function. The fetus begins to suck its thumb, swallow amniotic fluid, and urinate.

After sixteen weeks, the fetal heartbeat is heard through a stethoscope. A fetus born at twenty-four weeks has a chance of surviving, although the lungs are still immature and often cannot capture oxygen adequately. Weight gain during the last couple of months increases the likelihood of survival.

Birth Has Three Stages

As pregnancy progresses, the level of estrogen in the bloodstream exceeds the level of progesterone. This may help bring on birth of the fetus, because estrogen promotes uterine sensitivity to nervous stimulation. It is also possible that the fetus itself initiates the birth process by releasing a chemical messenger. Researchers have found in studies with sheep that if the fetal hypothalamus or pituitary is destroyed, birth can be postponed indefinitely.

The process of birth (parturition) includes three stages: dilation of the cervix, expulsion of the fetus, and delivery of the afterbirth (the placenta and the extraembryonic membranes) (fig. 46.14).

Figure 46.14

Three stages of parturition. **a.** Position of fetus just before birth begins. **b.** Dilation of cervix. **c.** Birth of baby. **d.** Expulsion of afterbirth.

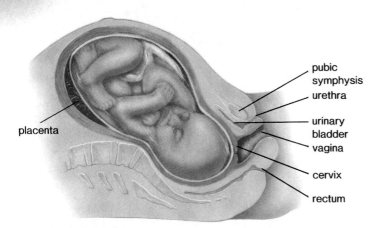

placenta — pubic symphysis — urethra — urinary bladder — vagina — cervix — rectum

a. 9-month-old fetus

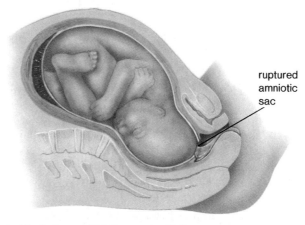

ruptured amniotic sac

b. First stage of birth: cervix dilates

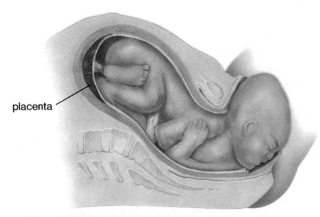

placenta

c. Second stage of birth: baby emerges

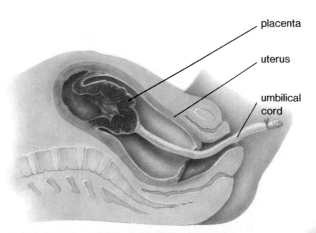

placenta — uterus — umbilical cord

d. Third stage of birth: expelling afterbirth

DEVELOPMENT CONTINUES

Development does not cease once birth has occurred; it continues throughout the stages of life: infancy, childhood, adolescence, and adulthood.

Infancy lasts until about two years of age. It is characterized by tremendous growth and sensorimotor development. During *childhood,* the individual grows and the body proportions change. *Adolescence* begins with **puberty** [L. *puber,* adult], when the secondary sex characteristics appear and the sexual organs become functional. At this time, there is an acceleration of growth leading to changes in height, weight, fat distribution, and body proportions. Males commonly experience a growth spurt later than females; therefore, they grow for a longer period of time. Males are generally taller than females and have broader shoulders and longer legs relative to their trunk length.

Young adults are at their physical peak in muscle strength, reaction time, and sensory perception. The organ systems at this time are best able to respond to altered circumstances in a homeostatic manner. From now on, however, there is an almost imperceptible, gradual loss of some of the body's abilities.

> Developmental changes occur throughout infancy, childhood, adolescence, and adulthood.

Aging Has Causes

Aging encompasses the progressive changes that contribute to an increased risk of infirmity, disease, and death. There are many theories about what causes aging. Perhaps aging is due to a change in the genes affecting the structure and the function of cells; perhaps it is due to a systematic change especially in regard to hormones and the immune system; or perhaps it is due to extrinsic factors outside the body. The study of **gerontology** [Gk. *geron,* an old man, and *logy,* study of] is devoted to increasing the number of years an individual enjoys the full functions of all body parts and processes. Just as it is wise to make the proper preparations to remain financially independent when older, it is also wise to realize that biological success in old age begins with the health habits developed when we are younger.

Biological Relationships

Biology is almost synonymous with reproduction in some persons' minds, and for good reason. Reproduction is the means by which an organism passes on its genetic material and the species is assured of continuance. Reproduction is central to the fields of genetics and evolution. In evolutionary terms, when fit individuals enjoy reproductive success, adaptive traits become more prevalent in a population. Reproduction is itself adapted to the environment—some organisms are adapted to reproducing in water and some to reproducing on land. The reproductive strategies of organisms also include other considerations, such as the number of offspring and the care given to them.

Development shows how animals are related. Closely related organisms go through the same developmental stages because they share a common ancestor. We have extraembryonic membranes as does a chick, but our early developmental stages even resemble that of a lancelet, an invertebrate chordate. Just as mammalian hormones are identical to chemicals found even in bacteria, the chemical signals that control development are most likely fundamental to life itself. Research into the regulation of development is beginning to bear fruit, and no doubt there will be many revelations in the near future.

Summary

1. Any developmental change requires three processes: growth, differentiation, and morphogenesis.

2. Development occurs after fertilization. The acrosome of a sperm releases enzymes that digest away the jelly coat around the egg; the acrosome extrudes a filament that attaches to a receptor on the vitelline membrane. The sperm nucleus enters the egg and fuses with the egg nucleus. The resulting zygote begins to divide.

3. The early developmental stages in animals includes these events. During cleavage, division occurs, but there is no overall growth. The result is a morula, which becomes the blastula when an internal cavity (the blastocoel) appears. During the gastrula stage, invagination of cells into the blastocoel results in formation of the germ layers: ectoderm, mesoderm, and endoderm. Later development of organs can be related to these layers.

4. The development of three types of animals (lancelet, frog, and chick) is compared. The first three stages (cleavage, blastulation, and gastrulation) differ according to the amount of yolk in the egg.

5. During neurulation, the nervous system develops from midline ectoderm, just above the notochord. At this point, it is possible to draw a typical cross section of a vertebrate embryo (see fig. 46.4).

6. In many species, differentiation begins with cleavage, when the egg's cytoplasm is partitioned among the numerous cells. The cytoplasm is not uniform in content, and presumably each of the first few cells differ as to their cytoplasmic contents. Some probably contain substances that can influence gene activity—turning some genes on and others off.

7. After the first cleavage of a frog embryo, only a daughter cell that receives a portion of the gray crescent is able to develop into a complete embryo. This illustrates the importance of cytoplasmic inheritance to early development especially in amphibians.

8. Morphogenesis involves the process of induction. The notochord induces the formation of the neural tube in frog embryos. The reciprocal induction that occurs between the lens and the optic vesicle is another good example of this phenomenon.

9. Today we envision induction as always present because cells are believed to constantly give off signals that influence the genetic activity of neighboring cells.

10. Studies of homeotic genes and pattern formation further indicate that morphogenesis involves genetic and environmental influences.

11. Human development can be divided into embryonic development (months 1 and 2) and fetal development (months 3–9). The early stages in human development resemble those of the chick. The similarities are probably due to their evolutionary relationship, not the amount of yolk the eggs contain, because the human egg has little yolk.

12. The extraembryonic membranes appear early in human development. The trophoblast of the blastocyst is the first sign of the chorion, which goes on to become the fetal part of the placenta. The placenta is where exchange occurs between fetal and maternal blood. The amnion contains the amniotic fluid, which cushions and protects the embryo. The yolk sac and allantois are also present.

13. Fertilization occurs in the oviduct, and cleavage occurs as the embryo moves toward the uterus. The morula becomes the blastocyst before implanting in the uterine lining.

14. Organ development begins with neural tube and heart formation. There follows a steady progression of organ formation during embryonic development. During fetal development, refinement of features occurs, and the fetus adds weight. Birth occurs about 280 days after the start of the mother's last menstruation.

15. Development after birth consists of infancy, childhood, adolescence, and adulthood. Young adults are at their prime, and then the aging process begins. Aging may be genetic in origin, due to cellular repair changes, body processes, or extrinsic factors.

Writing Across the Curriculum

In order to practice writing skills, students should write out the answers to any or all of the study questions and the critical thinking questions. The study questions are sequenced in the same order as the text. Answers to the objective questions, and suggested answers to the critical thinking questions, are in appendix D.

Study Questions

1. Define and give examples of the three processes that occur whenever a developmental change occurs.   804

2. State the germ layer theory, and tell which organs are derived from each of the germ layers.   805

3. Compare the process of cleavage and the formation of the blastula and gastrula in lancelets, frogs, and chicks.   806

4. Draw a cross section of a typical chordate embryo at the neurula stage, and label your drawing.   807

5. Explain how differentiation and morphogenesis are dependent upon signals given off by neighboring cells. What do the signals bring about in the receiving cells?   808–10

6. Describe an experiment performed by Spemann suggesting that the notochord induces formation of the neural tube. Give another well-known example of induction between tissues.   809

7. List the human extraembryonic membranes, give a function for each, and compare their functions to those in the chick.   811

8. Tell where fertilization, cleavage, the morula stage, and the blastocyst stage occur in humans. What happens to the embryo in the uterus?   812

9. Describe the structure and the function of the placenta in humans.   815

10. Outline the developmental changes that occur in humans from fetal development to adulthood.   816–17

Objective Questions

1. Which of these stages is the first one out of sequence?
   a. cleavage
   b. blastula
   c. morula
   d. gastrula

2. Which of these stages is mismatched?
   a. cleavage—cell division
   b. blastula—gut formation
   c. gastrula—three germ layers
   d. neurula—nervous system

3. Which of the germ layers is best associated with development of the heart?
   a. ectoderm
   b. mesoderm
   c. endoderm
   d. All of these are correct.

4. In many embryos, differentiation begins at what stage?
   a .cleavage
   b .blastula
   c .gastrula
   d .neurula

5. Morphogenesis is best associated with
   a. overall growth.
   b. induction of one tissue by another.
   c. genetic mutations.
   d. All of these are correct.

6. In humans, the placenta develops from the chorion. This indicates that human development
   a. resembles that of the chick.
   b. is dependent upon extraembryonic membranes.
   c. cannot be compared to lower animals.
   d. begins only upon implantation.

7. In humans, the fetus
   a. is surrounded by four extraembryonic membranes.
   b. has developed organs and is recognizably human.
   c. is dependent upon the placenta for excretion of wastes and acquisition of nutrients.
   d. Both b and c are correct.

8. Developmental changes
   a. require growth, differentiation, and morphogenesis.
   b. stop occurring when one is grown.
   c. are dependent upon a parceling out of genes into daughter cells.
   d. Both a and c are correct.

9. Mesoderm forms by invagination of cells in the
   a. lancelet.
   b. frog.
   c. chick.
   d. All of these are correct.

10. Which of these is mismatched?
   a. brain—ectoderm
   b. gut—endoderm
   c. bone—mesoderm
   d. lens—endoderm

11. Label this diagram illustrating the placement of the extraembryonic membranes, and give a function for each membrane in humans:

Human

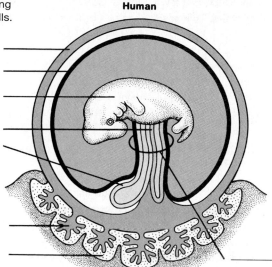

Concepts and Critical Thinking

1. *Development occurs throughout the life of an animal.*
Why is aging considered a part of development?

2. *Chemical signals are involved in development.*
Should these chemical signals be considered hormones? Why or why not?

3. *Genes control development.*
Reconcile this statement with the observation that development is sequential in nature.

Selected Key Terms

allantois (uh-LANT-uh-wus) An extraembryonic membrane that accumulates nitrogenous wastes in birds and reptiles and contributes to the formation of umbilical blood vessels in mammals. [Gk. *allant,* sausage, and *eidos,* form]   811

amnion (AM-nee-ahn) An extraembryonic membrane of birds, reptiles, and mammals that forms an enclosing, fluid-filled sac. [Gk. *amnio,* fetal membrane]   811

blastula (BLAST-chuh-luh) A hollow, fluid-filled ball of cells occurring during animal development prior to gastrula formation. [Gk. *blast,* bud, and L. *ula,* little]   805

chorion (KOR-ee-ahn) An extraembryonic membrane functioning for respiratory exchange in birds and reptiles; contributes to placenta formation in mammals. [Gk. *chori,* membrane]   811

cleavage Cell division without cytoplasmic addition or enlargement; occurs during first stage of animal development.   804

differentiation The specialization of early embryonic cells with regard to structure and function.   804

extraembryonic membrane A membrane that is not a part of the embryo but is necessary to the continued existence and health of the embryo. [L. *extra,* outside]   811

gastrula (GAS-truh-luh) The stage of animal development during which the germ layers form, at least in part, by invagination. [Gk. *gastr,* stomach, and L. *ula,* little]   805

germ layer A developmental layer of the body—that is, ectoderm, mesoderm, or endoderm.   805

induction The ability of a chemical or a tissue to influence the development of another tissue. [L. *in,* into, and *duct,* lead]   809

morphogenesis (mor-fuh-JEN-uh sus) The movement of early embryonic cells to establish body outline and form. [Gk. *morph,* form, and *gene,* origin]   804

morula (MOR-yuh-luh) A spherical mass of cells resulting from cleavage during animal development prior to the blastula stage. [L. *morul,* a little mulberry]   805

placenta The structure during the development of placental mammals that forms from the chorion and the uterine wall and allows the embryo, and then the fetus, to acquire nutrients and rid itself of wastes.   815

trophoblast (TROH-fuh-blast) The outer membrane surrounding the embryo in mammals, when thickened by a layer of mesoderm, it becomes the chorion, an extraembryonic membrane. [Gk. *troph,* nourish, and *blast,* bud]   812

umbilical cord The cord connecting the fetus to the placenta through which blood vessels pass. [L. *umbilic,* navel]   814

Alcamo, I. E. 1993. *AIDS: The biological basis*. Dubuque, Iowa: Wm. C. Brown Publishers. This easily understood book focuses on the biological basis of AIDS.

Aral, S. O., and Holmes, K. K. 1991. Sexually transmitted diseases in the AIDS era. *Scientific American* 264(2):62. Gonorrhea and syphilis have nearly disappeared, except in the United States.

Benjamini, E., and Leskowitz, S. 1993. *Immunology: A short course*. 2d ed. New York: John Wiley & Sons. Presents the essential principles of immunology.

Bolognesi, D. P. 1994. Prospects for an HIV vaccine. *Science & Medicine* 1(1):44. Development of an HIV vaccine requires a greater understanding of the infection and the virus.

Cooper, G. 1993. *The cancer book*. Boston: Jones and Bartlett Publishers. This non-technical book explains the basic nature and causes of cancer, and it gives current cancer prevention and treatment strategies.

Crowley, L. 1992. *Introduction to human disease*. 3d ed. Boston: Jones and Bartlett Publishers. Presents the general concepts of disease and organ system diseases.

Edge, V., and Miller, M. 1994. *Women's health care*. St. Louis: Mosby-Year Book, Inc. Provides an overview of disorders that occur mainly in women.

Ewald, P. W. 1993. The evolution of virulence. *Scientific American* 286(4):86. Directing the evolution of pathogens may result in a new approach to medicine.

Garnick, M. 1994. The dilemmas of prostate cancer. *Scientific American* 270(4):72. Prostate cancer has been detected with increasing frequency in recent years.

Hampton, J. 1991. *The biology of human aging*. Dubuque, Iowa: Wm. C. Brown Publishers. This is an introductory text written for those interested in gerentology.

Lawn, R. M. 1992. Lipoprotein (a) in heart disease. *Scientific American* 266(6):54. The agent of heart disease in individuals with low-risk profiles may be a blood particle known as lipoprotein a, which also functions in repairing damaged blood vessels.

Liotta, L. A. 1992. Cancer cell invasion and metastasis. *Scientific American* 266(2):54. Regulatory genes and proteins that control metastasis have produced a promising class of synthetic drugs.

Matthews, G. 1991. *Cellular physiology of nerve and muscle*. 2d ed. Boston: Blackwell Scientific Publications. Provides a detailed look at the principles of the cellular physiology of nerve and muscle.

McGinnis, W., and Kuziora, M. 1994. The molecular architects of body design. *Scientific American* 270(2):58. The ability to transfer genes between species provides a way to study how genes control development.

Mellion, M. 1994. *Sports medicine secrets*. St. Louis: Mosby-Year Book, Inc. This book covers frequently asked questions in sports medicine.

Nilsson, L. 1990. *A child is born*. 2d ed. New York: Delacorte Press. This well-illustrated book depicts the steps from fertilization to birth.

Nolte, J. 1993. *The human brain*. 3d ed. St. Louis: Mosby-Year Book, Inc. Beginners are guided through the basic aspects of brain structure and function.

Ray, O., and Ksir, C. 1993. *Drugs, society, & human behavior*. 6th ed. St. Louis: Mosby-Year Book, Inc. This textbook addresses drugs from psychological, pharmacological, historical, and legal perspectives.

Sataloff, R. T. 1992. The human voice. *Scientific American* 267(6):108. Discusses how vocal sounds originate and change, as well as treatments for vocal problems.

Science & Medicine. 1994. 1(3). This issue includes information on the actions of estrogens and on the possible link between fetal nutrition and diabetes.

Scientific American. 1993. 269(3). This special issue is devoted entirely to the immune system and its function; it includes discussions of AIDS, allergies, and therapeutic agents.

Valtin, H. 1994. *Renal function*. 3d ed. Boston: Little, Brown and Company. Written for advanced students, this text discusses mechanisms for preserving fluid and solute balance in renal function.

Wardlaw, G., et al. 1994. *Contemporary nutrition*. 2d ed. St. Louis: Mosby-Year Book, Inc. This text gives a clear understanding of nutritional information found on product labels.

Most animals have specialized respiratory organs (e.g., gills or lungs) for gas exchange. Many animals, especially amphibians, are also capable of skin breathing, or exchanging gases across the skin. Physiologists decided to test the hypothesis that *amphibians have physiological adaptations that favor skin breathing under appropriate conditions.*

Skin capillaries can be open (carrying blood) or closed (not carrying blood). The amount of open capillaries was determined in normal frogs and in frogs prevented from using their lungs. What do you predict about the amount of open capillaries in the skin of frogs prevented from using their lungs compared to those that use their lungs?

Prediction 1   There will be more open capillaries in the skin of frogs prevented from using their lungs.

Result 1   The predicted results were observed. Apparently amphibians are capable of regulating the amount of open capillaries in the skin to make more blood available for skin breathing.

> **Question 1.**   In another experiment, frogs that had been submerged and were skin breathing in the water were transferred to air. For what two reasons would you expect a decreased amount of open capillaries in the skin?

Decreased distance between skin capillaries and the external medium speeds the process of diffusion, and this facilitates skin breathing. One group of tadpoles was raised in oxygen-rich water, and another group was raised in oxygen-poor water. What do you predict about the distance of skin capillaries from the external environment in these two groups of tadpoles?

Prediction 2   Tadpoles raised in oxygen-poor water will have skin capillaries closer to the external environment than tadpoles raised in oxygen-rich water.

Result 2   Examination revealed that tadpoles raised in the oxygen-poor environment had skin capillaries 20 μm closer to the environment than tadpoles raised in an oxygen-rich environment. Moreover, these skin capillaries were finer and grew in a more dense network.

> **Question 2.**   What are the relative chances of effective skin breathing if tadpoles raised in an oxygen-poor environment are placed in an oxygen-rich environment? if tadpoles raised in an oxygen-rich environment are placed in an oxygen-poor environment?

Flowing water, as opposed to stagnant water, makes more oxygen available to the skin and therefore favors skin breathing. Amphibians are sometimes observed to have rhythmic body movements when submerged in water. Such movement may facilitate skin breathing. A frog immobilized in a wire cage was immersed in a water bath so that only its mouth and nostrils were exposed to air. Oxygen uptake from the water was determined when the water was stirred and when the water was not stirred. (Oxygen uptake was determined by periodically measuring the oxygen concentration in the water bath. A layer of mineral oil was placed on the surface of the water to prevent atmospheric oxygen from replacing the oxygen consumed.) What do you predict regarding oxygen consumption when the water was stirred and when it was not stirred?

Prediction 3   There will be more oxygen consumption when the water is stirred as opposed to when it is not stirred.

Result 3   The results of this experiment are shown in figure A. These data indicate that oxygen consumption is greater when the water bath is stirred than when it is not stirred. These results suggest that the body movements of amphibians are a behavioral adaptation to promote skin breathing.

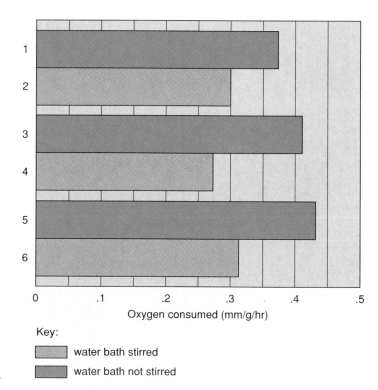

Figure A

Oxygen consumed by frog via skin breathing.

Adapted from "Skin Breathing in Vertebrates" by Martin E. Feder and Warren W. Burggran. Copyright © 1985 Scientific American, Inc. All rights reserved.

Key:
water bath stirred
water bath not stirred

Question 3. **(a)** What would be the results in figure A if mineral oil hadn't been placed on the water?

(b) What would be the results in figure A if the experiment was repeated with no frog? Could this experiment serve as a control? Why?

(c) Would a frog have more skin capillaries open when the water was stirred or not stirred? Why?

Figure B diagrams the circulatory system of an amphibian. Note the muscular sphincters, which apparently can control blood flow to the lungs or the skin. It is possible to measure blood flow in the pulmonary artery, which carries blood to the lungs, and in the cutaneous artery, which takes blood to the skin. Which blood vessel do you predict will carry more blood when a toad is prevented from using its lungs? when a toad is using its lungs?

Prediction 4 If a toad is prevented from using its lungs, the cutaneous artery will carry more blood. If a toad is using its lungs, the pulmonary artery will carry more blood.

Result 4 Subsequent observations were consistent with the prediction.

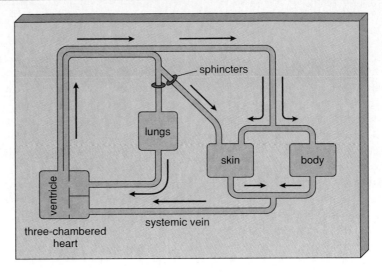

Figure B

Circulatory system in amphibian showing the three-chambered heart and circulation to lungs, skin, and body. The muscle sphincters can shunt deoxygenated blood to skin or lungs depending on the environmental conditions.

Question 4. **(a)** Suppose the data show that there is always more blood in the cutaneous artery even when a frog is using its lungs. What would be the implication regarding skin breathing in amphibians?

(b) Would this refute the hypothesis? Why?

Many experiments find support for the hypothesis that amphibians have physiological adaptations that favor skin breathing under appropriate conditions.

References

Feder, M. E., and Burggren, W. W. 1985. Cutaneous gas exchange in vertebrates: Design, patterns, control, and implications. *Biological Reviews* 60:1–45.

———. 1985. Skin breathing in vertebrates. *Scientific American* 253(5):126.

Part VII

BEHAVIOR AND ECOLOGY

The behavior of organisms allows them to interact with their own kind and with other species. These interactions are the framework for ecosystems, units of the biosphere in which energy flows and chemicals cycle. In mature natural ecosystems, populations usually remain constant in size and require the same amount of energy and chemicals each year. In contrast, the human population constantly increases in size and uses ever-greater amounts of energy and raw materials each year. This puts a strain on natural ecosystems, which act as a support system for the human population. Therefore, it is necessary to find ways to use energy more efficiently and recycle raw materials in order to prevent the buildup of pollutants which can destroy natural ecosystems. The preservation of natural communities, called biomes, is a top priority not only for the species that live there but also for the human population.

Organisms such as these elephants, *Loxodonta*, live in an ecosystem where they interact with other populations and the physical environment.

Many of the figures and concepts discussed in *Biology,* fifth edition, are further explored in technology products. The following is a list of figures in part VII that correlates to technology products.

[icon] A set of five videotapes contains 53 animations of physiological processes integral to the study of biology. These videotapes, entitled *Life Science Animations*, cover such topics as chemistry, genetics, and reproduction. A videotape icon appears in appropriate figure legends to alert the reader to these animations.

[icon] *Explorations in Human Biology* and *Explorations in Cell Biology, Metabolism, and Genetics* by George B. Johnson are interactive CD-ROMs with activities that can be used by an instructor in lecture and/or placed in a lab or resource center for student use. This interactive software consists of modules that cover key topics discussed in a biology course. The CD-ROMs are available for use with Macintosh and IBM Windows computers. A CD-ROM icon appears in appropriate figure legends to alert the reader to these activities.

Corresponding Figures		[icon] Videotape Concepts	[icon] CD-Rom Modules
48A	Age structure diagrams	—	Life Span and Lifestyle
50.1	Ecosystem composition	52. Energy Flow through an Ecosystem	—
50.7	Pyramid of energy	52. Energy Flow through an Ecosystem	—
50.8	Components of a biochemical cycle	52. Energy Flow through an Ecosystem	—
50.9	Carbon cycle	51. Carbon and Nitrogen Cycles;	—
		52. Energy Flow through an Ecosystem	—
50.10	Nitrogen cycle	51. Carbon and Nitrogen Cycles	—
51.1	Lake life zones	—	Pollution in a Freshwater Lake
52.7	Sources of surface water pollution	—	Pollution in a Freshwater Lake
52.8	Biological magnification	—	Pollution in a Freshwater Lake

ANIMAL BEHAVIOR

Learning Objectives

- Describe the two types of questions considered by biologists who study animal behavior. 826

Behavior Has a Genetic Basis

- Support, with examples, the premise that behavior has a genetic basis. 828
- State, with examples, the two body systems that control behavior. 827

Behavior Undergoes Development

- Give examples to show that behaviors sometimes undergo development after birth. 828–29
- Discuss different types of learning and how learning affects behavior. 828–29

Behavior Is Adaptive

- Explain why you would expect behavior to be adaptive. 830

- Discuss sexual selection in relation to female selectivity and male competition for mates. 830–32
- Show how an animal's way of capturing resources may be related to its reproductive behavior. 830

Animals Are Social

- List and give examples of the different types of communication between animals. 833–34
- Use a cost-benefit analysis to show that social living is sometimes adaptive. 835

Sociobiology and Animal Behavior

- Explain how altruism might evolve under certain circumstances. 835–36

A leatherback sea turtle, *Dermochelys,* instinctively makes its way to the sea upon hatching.

t the start of the breeding season, male bower-birds use small sticks and twigs to build elaborate display areas called bowers. They clear the space around the bowers, removing leaves and debris, and decorate the area with fresh flowers, fruits, moss, mushrooms, pebbles, or shells. Each species has its own preference in decorations. The satin bowerbird of eastern Australia prefers blue objects, a color that harmonizes with the male's glossy blue-black plumage (fig. 47.1).

After the bower is complete, a male spends most of his time near his bower, calling to females, renewing his decorations and guarding his work against possible raids by other males. After inspecting many bowers and their owners, a female approaches one and the male begins a display. He faces her, fluffs up his feathers, and flaps his wings to the beat of a call. The female enters the bower, and if she crouches, the two mate.

An ethologist (a scientist who studies behavior) might seek answers to two main types of questions about the behavior of the male bowerbird. *Causal questions* are answered by describing how an animal is biologically organized and equipped to carry out the behavior. *Survival value questions* are answered by describing how the behavior helps an animal exploit resources, avoid predators, or secure a mate. Both types of questions are grounded in the recognition that **behavior,** observable and coordinated responses to environmental stimuli, has a genetic basis.

> Ethologists ask causal questions and survival value questions about behavior. The answers to the first type of question describe how the behavior is controlled, and the answers to the second type of question describe how the behavior helps the animal survive and reproduce.

BEHAVIOR HAS A GENETIC BASIS

Various types of experiments have been performed to determine if behavior has a genetic basis. William Dilger studied the nest-building behavior of small parrots known as lovebirds. A peach-faced lovebird, *Agapornis roseicollis,* cuts long, regular strips of material with its strong beak and then tucks them in its rump feathers for transport to the nest. A Fisher's lovebird, *Agapornis fischeri,* carries stronger materials, such as sticks, directly in its beak.

Dilger reasoned that if the behavior for obtaining and carrying nesting material is inherited, then hybrids might show intermediate behavior. He mated two species of birds and observed that the

Figure 47.1

Female satin bowerbird, *Ptilonorhynchus violaceus,* has chosen to mate with this male. Most likely she was attracted by his physique and the blue decorations of his bower.

hybrid birds have difficulty carrying nesting materials. They cut strips and try to tuck them in their rump feathers, but they are unsuccessful. After a long period of time (about three years) a hybrid learns to carry the cut strips in its beak but still briefly turns its head toward its rump before flying off. Therefore, Dilger's studies support the hypothesis that behavior has a genetic basis.

Steven Arnold performed several experiments with the garter snake *Thamnophis elegans* after he observed a distinct difference between two different types of snake populations in California. Inland populations are aquatic and commonly feed underwater on frogs and fish. Coastal populations are terrestrial and feed mainly on slugs. In the laboratory, inland adult snakes refused to eat slugs while coastal snakes readily did so. To test for possible genetic differences between the two populations, Arnold arranged matings between inland and coastal individuals and found that isolated newborns show an overall intermediate incidence of slug acceptance.

The difference between slug acceptors and slug rejecters appears to be inherited, but what physiological difference have the genes brought about? Arnold devised a clever experiment to answer this causal question. When snakes eat, their tongues carry chemicals to an odor receptor in the roof the mouth. They use tongue flicks to recognize their prey! Even newborns will flick their tongues at cotton swabs dipped in fluids of their prey. Arnold dipped swabs in slug extract and counted the number of tongue flicks for newborn inland and coastal snakes. Coastal snakes had a higher number than in-

Figure 47.2

The number of tongue flicks by inland and coastal garter snakes, *Thamnophis elegans,* as a response to slug extract on cotton swabs. Coastal snakes tongue-flicked more than inland snakes.

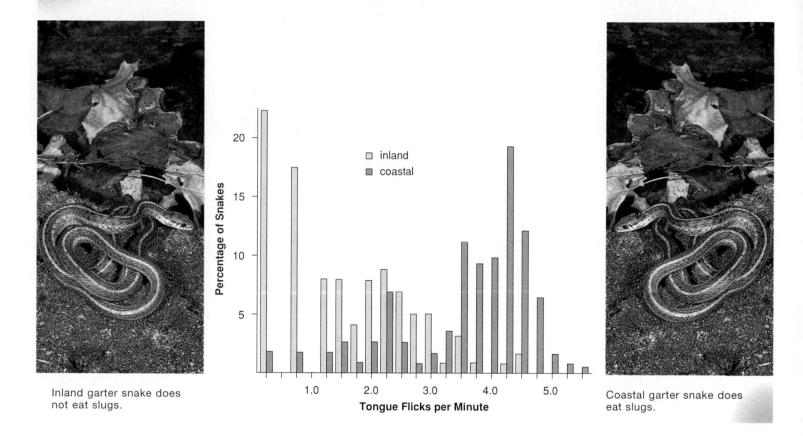

Inland garter snake does not eat slugs.

Coastal garter snake does eat slugs.

land snakes (fig. 47.2). Although hybrids showed a great deal of variation in the number of tongue flicks, they were generally intermediate as predicted by the genetic hypothesis. These findings suggest that inland snakes do not eat slugs because they are not sensitive to their smell. It would seem that the genetic differences between the two populations of snakes has resulted in a physiological difference in their nervous systems.

Both nervous and endocrine systems are responsible for the integration of body systems. Is the endocrine system also involved in behavior? Various studies have been done to show that it is. For example, the egg-laying behavior in the snail *Aplysia* involves a set sequence of movements. Following copulation, the animal extrudes long strings of more than a million egg cases. It takes the egg case string in its mouth, covers it with mucus, and waves its head back and forth to wind the string into an irregular mass, which attaches it to a solid object, like a rock. Several years ago, scientists isolated and analyzed an egg-laying hormone (ELH) that causes the snail to lay eggs even if it had not

mated. ELH was found to be a small protein of thirty-six amino acids that diffuses into the circulatory system and excites the smooth muscle cells of the reproductive duct, causing them to contract and expel the egg string. Using recombinant DNA (deoxyribonucleic acid) techniques, the investigators isolated the ELH gene. The gene's product turned out to be a protein with 271 amino acids. The protein can be cleaved into as many as eleven possible products, and ELH is one of these. ELH alone, or in conjunction with these other products, is thought to control all the components of egg-laying behavior in *Aplysia.*

The results of many types of studies support the hypothesis that behavior has a genetic basis and that genes influence the development of neural and hormonal mechanisms that control behavior.

BEHAVIOR UNDERGOES DEVELOPMENT

Given that all behaviors have a genetic basis, we can go on to ask if environmental experiences after hatching or birth also shape the behavior. Some behaviors seem to be stereotyped—they are always performed the same way each time. These were called fixed action patterns (FAP), and it is said that FAPs were elicited by a sign stimulus, a cue that sets the behavior in motion. For example, human babies will smile when a flat but face-sized mask with two dark spots for eyes is brought near them. It's possible that some behaviors are FAPs, but increasingly investigators are finding that many behaviors, formerly thought to be FAPs, develop after practice.

One investigator, Jack Hailman, has exhaustively studied laughing gull chicks' begging behavior, which is always performed the same way in response to the parent's red beak. A chick directs a pecking motion toward the parent's beak, grasps it, and strokes it downward (fig. 47.3). He noticed that sometimes a parent stimulates the begging behavior by swinging its beak gently from side to side. After the chick responds, the parent regurgitates food onto the floor of the nest. If need be, the parent then encourages the chick to eat. This interaction between the chicks and their parents made Hailman think the begging behavior might involve learning. (**Learning** is defined as a durable change in behavior brought about by experience.) To test this hypothesis, Hailman painted diagrammatic pictures of gull heads on small cards and then collected eggs in the field. The eggs were hatched in a dark incubator to eliminate visual stimuli before the test. On the day of hatching, each chick was allowed to make about a dozen pecks at the model. The chicks were returned to the nest and were each retested. The tests showed that on the average, only one-third of the pecks by a newly hatched chick strike the model. But one day after hatching more than half of the pecks are accurate, and two days after hatching the accuracy reaches a level of more than 75%. His treatment and testing of other groups allowed him to conclude that improvement in motor skills, as well as visual experience, strongly effect development of chick begging behavior.

> **Behavior has a genetic basis, but the development of mechanisms that control behavior is subject to environmental influences, such as practice after birth.**

Hailman went on to test how chicks recognize a parent. He found that newly hatched chicks peck equally at any model as long as it has a red beak. Chicks a week old, however, will peck only at models that closely resemble the parent. Hailman speculated that operant conditioning with a reward of food could account for this change in behavior.

Operant conditioning, which is one of many forms of learning, is often defined as the gradual strengthening of stimulus-response connections. In everyday life, most people know that animals can be taught tricks by giving rewards such as food or affection. The trainer presents the stimulus, say a hoop, and then gives a reward (food) for the proper response (jumping through the hoop). B. F. Skinner is well known for studying this type of learning in the laboratory. In the simplest type of experiment

Figure 47.3

Pecking behavior of laughing gull, *Larus atricilla,* chicks. At about three days, laughing gull chicks grasp the beak of a parent, stroking it downward and the parent then regurgitates food.

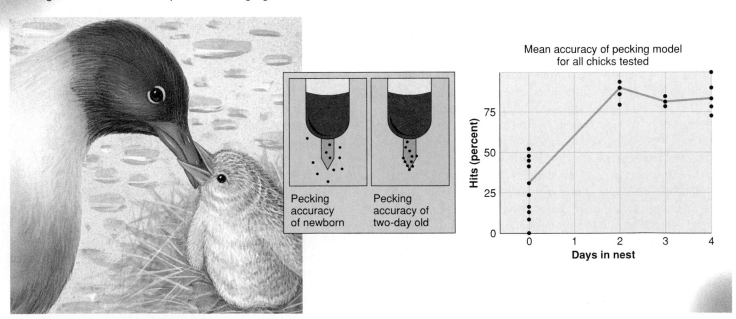

performed by Skinner, a caged rat happens to press a lever and is rewarded with sugar pellets, which it avidly consumes. Thereafter, the rat regularly presses the lever whenever it is hungry. In more sophisticated experiments, Skinner even taught pigeons to play ping-pong by reinforcing desired responses to stimuli.

Imprinting is another form of learning; chicks, ducklings and goslings will follow the first moving object they see after hatching. This object is ordinarily their mother, but they seemingly can be imprinted on any object—a human or a red ball—if it is the first moving object they see during a sensitive period of two to three days after hatching. The term *sensitive period* means that the behavior only develops during this time. Although the Englishman Douglas Spalding first observed imprinting, the Austrian Konrad Lorenz is well known for investigating it. He found that imprinting not only served the useful purpose of keeping chicks near their mother, it also caused male birds to court a member of the correct species—someone who looks like mother! The goslings who had been imprinted on Lorenz courted human beings later in life. In-depth studies on imprinting have shown that the process is more complicated than originally thought. Eckhard Hess found that mallard ducklings imprinted on humans in the laboratory would switch to a female mallard that had hatched a clutch of ducklings several hours before. He found that vocalization before and after hatching was an important element in the imprinting process. Female mallards cluck during the entire time that imprinting is occurring. Does experience such as social interactions influence learning in situations other than imprinting? Song learning in birds seems to say it does.

Birds Which Learn to Sing

During the past several decades, an increasing number of investigators have studied song learning in birds. White-crowned sparrows sing a species-specific song, but males of a particular region have their own dialect. This caused Peter Marler to hypothesize that young birds learn how to sing from older birds. To test his hypothesis, Marler housed the birds in cages where he could completely control the songs they heard (fig. 47.4). A group of birds that *heard no songs at all* sang a song, but it was not fully developed. Birds that *heard tapes of white-crowns singing* sang in that dialect, as long as the tapes were played during a sensitive period from about age ten to fifty days. White-crowned sparrows' dialects (or other species' songs) played before or after this sensitive period had no effect on their song. Apparently, their brain is especially primed to respond to acoustical stimuli during the sensitive period. Neurons that are critical for song production have been located, and they fire when the bird's own song is played or when a song of the same dialect is played. Other investigators have shown that birds *given an adult tutor* will sing the song of even a different species—no matter when the tutoring begins! It would appear that social experience has a very strong influence over the development of singing.

> Animals have an ability to benefit from experience; learning occurs when a behavior changes with practice.

Figure 47.4

Song learning by white-crowned sparrow, *Zonotrichia leucophrys*. Three different experimental procedures are depicted and the results noted. These results suggest that there is both a genetic basis and an environmental basis for song learning in birds.

Isolated bird sings but song is not developed.

Bird sings developed song played during a sensitive period.

Bird sings song of social tutor without regard to sensitive period.

BEHAVIOR IS ADAPTIVE

Since genes influence the development of behavior, it is reasonable to assume that behavioral traits (like other traits) could evolve. Our discussion will focus on reproductive behavior—specifically the manner in which animals secure a mate. But we will also touch on the other two survival issues—capturing resources and avoiding predators—because these help an animal survive, and without survival reproduction is impossible. Investigators studying survival value seek to test hypotheses that specify how a given trait might improve reproductive success.

Among birds and mammals, males can father many offspring because they continually produce sperm in great quantity. We would then expect competition among males to inseminate as many different females as possible. In contrast, females produce few eggs, so the choice of a mate becomes a prevailing consideration. Sexual selection can bring about evolutionary changes in the species. Natural selection due to competition among males and mate choice by females is called **sexual selection.**

Females Choose

Courtship displays are rituals that serve to prepare the sexes for mating. They help male and female recognize each other so that mating will be successful. They also play a role in a female's choice of a mate.

Gerald Borgia conducted a study of satin bowerbirds (see fig. 47.1) to test these two opposing hypotheses regarding female choice:

Good genes hypothesis: females choose mates on the basis of traits that improve their chances of survival.

Run-away hypothesis: females choose mates on the basis of traits that make them attractive to females.

Borgia and his assistants watched bowerbirds at feeding stations and also monitored the bowers. They discovered that although males tend to steal blue feathers and/or actively destroy a neighbor's bower, more aggressive and vigorous males were able to keep their bowers in good condition. These were the males usually chosen as mates by females.

Borgia felt that the investigation did not clearly support either hypothesis. It could be that aggressiveness, if inherited, does improve the chances of survival, or it could be that females simply preferred bowers with the most blue feathers.

Bruce Beehler studied the behavior of the birds of paradise in New Guinea (fig. 47.5). The raggiana bird of paradise is remarkably dimorphic—the males are larger than females and have beautiful orange flank plumes. In contrast, the females are drab. Courting males, called a lek, gathers and begin to call. If a female joins them, the males raise their orange display plumes, shake their wings and hop from side to side, while continuing to call. They then stop calling and lean upside down with the wings projected forward to show off their beautiful feathers.

Female choice can explain why male birds are so much more showy than females, even if it is not known which of Borgia's two hypotheses applies. It's possible that the remarkable plumes of the male do signify health and vigor, just as a well-constructed bower might, or it's possible that females choose the flamboyant males on the basis that their sons will also be attractive to females. Beehler then questioned whether reproductive behavior could be related to food source. Raggiana birds forage far and wide for their food (nutritious, complex fruits), and lekking is one way for males to attract the wide-ranging females. The male raggiana is polygynous (has more than one mate) and does not help raise the offspring. On the other hand a related species, the trumpet manucode, *Manucodia keraudrenit,* feeds on figs, which are more prevalent but not as nutritious as complex fruits. These birds are monogamous—the pair bonds perhaps for life—and both sexes are needed to successfully raise the young (fig. 47.5).

Since raggiana offspring are fed a more nutritious source of food, perhaps it leaves the males free to follow their best reproductive strategy (inseminating many females). And perhaps because trumpet manucode offspring are fed a less nutritious food source, the best reproductive strategy for males includes monogamy and helping to raise the young.

Figure 47.5

Mating behavior in birds of paradise, *Paradisaea raggiana,* is influenced by species foraging habits. The raggiana male has resplendent plumage brought about by sexual selection. The females are widely scattered, foraging for complex fruits; the males form leks that females visit to choose a mate.

male

female

mahogany tree

fruit

Figure 47.6

A male olive baboon, *Papio anubis,* displaying full threat. Males are larger than females and have enlarged canines. Competition between males establishes a dominance hierarchy for the distribution of resources.

Figure 47.7

Female choice and male dominance among baboons. Although it may appear that females mate indiscriminately, actually they mate more often with a dominant male when they are most fertile.

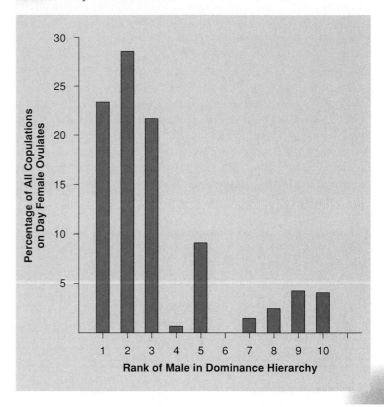

Males Compete

Studies have been done to determine if the benefit gained is worth the cost of competition among males. When costs are high, it is unlikely that a trait will evolve, but when benefits are high the trait is expected to evolve. A trait that helps a male compete can lead to a positive effect (e.g., more mates), but what are the possible negative effects (e.g., early death)? Only if the positive effects outweigh the negative effects will the animal enjoy reproductive success.

Baboons Have a Dominance Hierarchy

Baboons, a type of Old-World monkey, live together in a troop. Males and females have separate **dominance hierarchies** in which a higher ranking animal has greater access to resources than a lower ranking animal. Dominance is decided by confrontations, resulting in one animal giving way to the other.

Baboons are dimorphic; the males are larger than the females and they can threaten others with their long, sharp canines (fig. 47.6). The baboons travel within a home range, hunting food each day and sleep in trees at night. The dominant males decide where and when the troop will move and, if the troop is threatened, they cover the troop as it retreats and attack when necessary.

Females undergo a period known as estrus, during which they ovulate and are willing to mate. When first receptive, a female mates with subordinate males and older juveniles. Later a female approaches a dominant male, which becomes very interested once ovulation is near. They form a consort pair which lasts only for an hour or several days. Dominant males are interested in and protective of young baboons, regardless of the true father.

However, the male baboon pays a cost for his dominant position. Being larger means that he needs more food, and being willing and able to fight predators means that he may get hurt, and so forth. Is there a reproductive benefit to his behavior? Glen Hausfater counted copulations of dominant males and found that they do indeed monopolize estrous females when he judged them to be most fertile (fig. 47.7). Nevertheless, there are other avenues to fathering offspring. Some males act as helpers to particular females and her offspring; the next time she is in estrus she may mate preferentially with him instead of a dominant male. Or subordinate males may form a friendship group that can oppose a dominant male, making him give up a receptive female.

Red Deer Stake Out a Territory

A territory is an area that is defended against competitors. **Territoriality** includes the type of defensive behavior needed to defend a territory. Vocalization and displays, rather than outright fighting, may be sufficient to defend a territory (fig. 47.8). Male song birds use singing to announce their willingness to defend a territory—so other males of the species become reluctant to make use of the same area.

T. H. Clutton-Brock has studied reproductive success among red deer on the Scottish island of Rhum. Stags (males) compete for a harem, a group of hinds (females) that mate only with one stag, called the harem master. This reproductive group occupies a particular home range where the harem master fights any challenger. If the harem master cannot frighten a challenger away, they lock antlers and push against one another. If the challenger now withdraws, the master pursues him for a short distance, roaring the whole time. If the challenger wins, he becomes the harem master.

After studying the red deer for more than twelve years, Clutton-Brock concluded that a harem master can father two dozen offspring at most, because he is at the peak of his fighting ability for only a short time. And what does it cost him to be able to father offspring? Stags must be large and powerful in order to fight; therefore, they grow faster and have less body fat. During bad times they are more likely to die of starvation and in general have shorter lives. Therefore the benefit of reproduction is not without its cost. If these costs of reproducing exceed the benefits (number of offspring), then these traits will no longer be passed on.

> It is hypothesized that evolution by sexual selection stems from the opportunity of females to choose among potential partners, and from male competition to inseminate as many partners as possible.

Figure 47.8

Male red deer, *Cervus elaphus,* compete for a harem within a particular territory. **a.** Roaring alone may frighten off a challenger. **b.** But outright fighting may be necessary, and the victor is most likely the stronger of the two animals.

a.

b.

ANIMALS ARE SOCIAL

There is a wide diversity of social behavior among animals. Some animals are largely solitary and join with a member of the opposite sex only for the purpose of reproduction. Others pair, bond, and cooperate in raising offspring. Still others form a **society** in which members of species are organized in a cooperative manner, extending beyond sexual and parental behavior. We have already had occasion to mention the social groups of baboons and red deer. Social behavior in these and other animals requires that they communicate with one another.

Communication Is Varied

Communication is an action by a sender that influences the behavior of a receiver. When the sender and receiver are members of the same species, it is expected that signals will benefit both sender and receiver.

What about signals between different species? Bats send out a series of sound pulses and listen for the corresponding echoes in order to find their way through dark caves and locate food at night. Some moths have an ability to hear these sound pulses, and they begin evasive tactics when they sense that a bat is near. Are the bats purposefully communicating with the moths? No, bat sounds are simply a *cue* to the moths that danger is near.

> Communication is an action by a sender that affects the behavior of a receiver.

Chemical Communication

Chemical signals have the advantage of working both night and day. The term **pheromone** [Gk. *pher,* carry, and *mon,* one] is used to designate chemical signals that are passed between members of the same species. Female moths secrete chemicals from special abdominal glands which are detected downwind by receptors on male antennae. The antennae are especially sensitive, and this assures that only male moths of the correct species (and not predators) will be able to detect them.

Cheetahs and other cats mark their territories by depositing urine, feces, and anal gland secretions at the boundaries (fig. 47.9). Klipspringers (small antelope) use secretions from a gland below the eye to mark twigs and grasses of their territory.

Auditory Communication

Auditory (sound) *communication* has some advantages over other kinds of communication (fig. 47.10). It is faster than chemical communication, and it also is effective both night and day. Further, auditory communication can be modified not only by loudness but also by pattern, duration, and repetition. In an experiment with rats, a researcher discovered that an intruder can avoid attack by increasing the frequency with which it makes an appeasement sound.

Male crickets have calls, and male birds have songs for a number of different occasions. For example, birds may have one song for distress, another for courting, and still another for marking territories. Sailors have long heard the songs of humpback whales because they are transmitted through the hull of a ship. But only recently has it been shown that the song has six basic themes, each with its own phrases, that can vary in length and be

Figure 47.9
This male cheetah, *Acinonyx,* is spraying a pheromone onto a tree in order to mark its territory.

Figure 47.10
A chimpanzee, *Pan,* with a researcher. Chimpanzees are unable to speak but can learn to use a visual language consisting of symbols. Some believe chimps only mimic their teachers and never understand the cognitive use of a language. Here the experimenter shows Nim the sign for "drink." Nim copies.

interspersed with sundry cries and chirps. The purpose of the song is probably sexual and serves to advertise the availability of the singer. Language is the ultimate auditory communication, but only humans have the biological ability to produce a large number of different sounds and to put them together in many different ways. Nonhuman primates have at most only forty different vocalizations, each having a definite meaning, such as the one meaning "baby on the ground," which is uttered by a baboon when a baby baboon falls out of a tree. Although chimpanzees can be taught to use an artificial language, they never progress beyond the capability level of a two-year-old child. It has also been difficult to prove that chimps understand the concept of grammar or can use their language to reason. It still seems as if humans possess a communication ability unparalleled by other animals.

Visual Communication

Visual signals are most often used by species that are active during the day. Contests between males make use of threat postures and possibly prevent outright fighting that might result in reduced fitness. A male baboon displaying full threat is an awesome sight that establishes his dominance and keeps peace within the baboon troop (see fig. 47.6). Hippopotamuses have territorial displays that include mouth opening.

The plumage of a male raggiana bird of paradise allows him to put on a spectacular courtship dance to attract females and to give her a basis on which to select a suitable mate (see fig. 47.5). Defense and courtship displays are exaggerated and are always performed in the same way so that their meaning is clear.

Tactile Communication

Tactile communication occurs when one animal touches another. For example, gull chicks peck at the parent's beak in order to induce the parent to feed them (see fig. 47.3). A male leopard nuzzles the female's neck to calm her and to stimulate her willingness to mate. In primates, grooming—one animal cleaning the coat and skin of another—helps cement social bonds within a group.

Honeybees use a combination of tactile and auditory communication to impart information about the environment. Karl von Frisch, another famous ethologist, did many detailed bee experiments in the 1940s. He discovered that when a foraging bee returns to the hive, it performs a waggle dance that indicates the distance and the direction of a food source (fig. 47.11). As the bee moves between the two loops of a figure 8, it buzzes noisily and shakes its entire body in so-called waggles. Outside the hive, the dance is done on a horizontal surface and the straight run indicates the direction of the food. Inside the hive, the angle of the straight run to that of the direction of gravity is the same as the angle of the food source to the sun. In other words, a 40° angle to the left of vertical means that food is 40° to the left of the sun. Distance to the food source is believed to be indicated by the number of waggles and/or the amount of time taken to complete the straight run.

> Animals use a number of different ways to communicate, and communication facilitates cooperation.

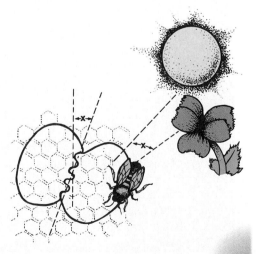

Figure 47.11
Communication among bees. **a**. Honeybees, *Apis mellifera,* do a waggle dance to indicate the direction of food. **b**. If the dance is done outside the hive on a horizontal surface, the straight run of the dance will point to the food source. If the dance is done inside the hive on a vertical surface, the angle of the straightaway to that of the direction of gravity is the same as the angle of the food source to the sun.

a.   Waggle dance

b.   Components of dance

SOCIOBIOLOGY AND ANIMAL BEHAVIOR

Sociobiology applies the principles of evolutionary biology to the study of social behavior in animals. Sociobiologists develop hypotheses about social living based on the assumption that a social individual derives more reproductive benefits than costs from living in a society. Then they perform a cost-benefit analysis to see if their hypotheses are correct.

Group living does have benefits under certain circumstances. It can help an animal avoid predators, rear offspring, and find food. A group of impalas is more likely to hear an approaching predator than a solitary one. Many fish moving rapidly in many directions might distract a would-be predator.

The pair bonding of trumpet manucode helps the birds raise their young. Due to their particular food source, the female cannot rear as many offspring alone as she can with the male's help. Weaver birds form giant colonies that help protect them from predators, but the birds may also share information about food sources. Primate members of the same troop signal to one another when they have found an especially bountiful fruit tree. Lions working together are able to capture large prey, such as zebra and buffalo.

Group living also has its disadvantages. When animals are crowded together into a small area, disputes can arise over access to the best feeding places and sleeping sites. Dominance hierarchies are one way to apportion resources, but this puts subordinates at a disadvantage. Among red deer, the ability of a hind to rear sons is dependent on her dominance. Clutton-Brock found that only large, dominant females can successfully rear sons; small subordinate females tend to rear daughters. Sons result in more grandchildren, but subordinate females do not have access to enough resources to rear sons whose larger size and rapid growth require an extended period of nursing. Like the subordinate males in a baboon troop, females may be better off in fitness terms if they stay with a group, despite the cost involved.

Living in close quarters means that illness and parasites can pass from one to the other more rapidly. Baboons and other types of social primates invest much time in grooming one another.

> Social living has both advantages and disadvantages. Only if the benefits, in terms of individual reproductive success, outweigh the disadvantages will societies evolve.

Altruism Versus Self-Interest

Altruism [L. *altru,* other] is behavior that has the potential to decrease the lifetime reproductive success of the altruist while benefiting the reproductive success of another member of the group. In insect societies, especially, reproduction is limited to only one pair, the queen and her mate. For example, among army ants the queen is inseminated only during her nuptial flight, and thereafter she spends her time reproducing. The society has three different sizes of sterile female workers. The smallest workers (3 mm), called the nurses, take care of the queen and larvae, feeding them and keeping them clean. The intermediately sized workers, constituting most of the population, go out on raids to collect food. The soldiers (14 mm), with huge heads and powerful jaws, run along the sides and rear of raiding parties where they can best attack any intruders.

Can the altruistic behavior of sterile workers be explained in terms of reproductive success? In 1964, the English biologist William Hamilton pointed out that a given gene can be passed from one generation to the next in two quite different ways. The first way is direct: a parent can pass the gene directly to an offspring. The second way is indirect: an animal can help a relative reproduce and thereby pass the gene to the next generation via this relative. Direct selection is natural selection that can result in adaptation to the environment when the reproductive success of individuals differ. Indirect selection is natural selection that can result in adaptation to the environment when individuals differ in their effects on the reproductive success of relatives. The **inclusive fitness** of an individual includes personal reproduction and reproduction of relatives.

Among social insects, the queen is diploid but her mate is haploid. If the queen has had only one mate, sisters inherit the same set of genes from their father and a half a set from their mother, meaning that it's possible for sisters to share 75% of their genes in common:

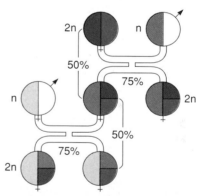

Under these circumstances, altruistic behavior is more likely to evolve.

Indirect selection can also occur among animals whose offspring receive only a half set of genes from both parents. Consider that your brother or sister shares 50% of your genes, your niece or nephew shares 25%, and so forth. This means that the survival of two nieces (or nephews) is worth the survival of one sibling, assuming they both go on to reproduce.

Michael Ghiglieri, when studying chimpanzees in Africa, observed that a female in estrus frequently copulates with several members of the same group and that the males make no attempt to interfere with each other's matings. How can they be acting in their own self-interest? Genetic relatedness of the males appears to underlie their apparent altruism; they all share genes in common because males never leave the territory in which they are born.

Figure 47.12

Inclusive fitness. A meerkat, *Suricata,* is acting as a baby-sitter for its young sisters and brothers while their mother is away. Could this helpful behavior contribute to the baby-sitter's inclusive fitness?

Helpers at the Nest

It has been observed among birds that offspring from the same clutch of eggs often stay on with their parents to help rear and feed the next batch of offspring. In a study of Florida scrub jays, the number of fledglings produced by an adult pair doubled when they had helpers. Mammalian offspring are also observed to help their parents (fig. 47.12). Among jackals in Africa, pairs alone managed to rear an average of 1.4 pups, whereas pairs with helpers reared 3.6 pups.

Is the reproductive success of the helpers increased by their altruistic behavior? It could be if the chance of their reproducing on their own is limited. David and Sandra Ligon studied the breeding behavior of green wood-hoopoes (*Phoeniculus purpurens*), an insect-eating bird of Africa. A flock may have as many as sixteen members but only one breeding pair; the other sexually mature members help feed and protect the fledglings and protect the home territory from invasion by other green wood-hoopoes. Resources are limited, particularly since there are few acacia trees to provide roost holes at night when predation is intense. Therefore, there is rarely the opportunity to immediately have a territory of one's own.

When an opportunity arises for a green wood-hoopoe to start its own territory, it takes a younger flock member with it. The younger bird, which serves as a helper, was raised by the older bird! The younger bird is not acting contrary to its own long-term genetic interests because if the older bird dies (the death rate among breeders is high), the younger bird takes over the sibling's reproductive duties.

The Ligons identified three theories that are relevant to their study: (1) direct selection is operative when a breeding pair has their own offspring, (2) indirect selection is operative when helpers assist their parents or siblings raise offspring, and (3) reciprocity can be at work when, as has been observed, nonrelatives help a breeding pair. Reciprocity occurs when an individual provides aid to another with some chance that it will be repaid in the future, such as when a nest helper inherits the territory of a breeding bird.

> Altruism can be adaptive when individuals help their parents raise siblings. Inclusive fitness is measured by the genes an individual contributes to the next generation, either directly or indirectly by way of relatives.

Summary

1. Behavior refers to observable and coordinated responses an animal makes to environmental stimuli.

2. Ethologists can ask causal questions and survival questions about a behavior. Causal questions pertain to mechanisms of behavior and survival value questions pertain to the adaptive nature of behavior.

3. Hybrid studies with lovebirds produce results consistent with the hypothesis that behavior has a genetic basis.

4. Garter snake experiments indicate that the nervous system controls behavior. *Aplysia* DNA studies indicate that the endocrine system also controls behavior.

5. The environment is influential in the development of behavioral responses, as exemplified by an improvement in laughing gull chick begging behavior and an increased ability of chicks to recognize parents.

6. Modern studies suggest that most behaviors improve with experience. Even behaviors that were formerly thought to be fixed action patterns (FAPs) or otherwise thought to be inflexible sometimes can be modified.

7. Song learning in birds involves various elements—including the existence of a sensitive period when an animal is primed to learn—and the effect of social interactions.

8. We can assume that since behavior has a genetic basis, those traits will evolve that are adaptive to the individual. Traits that promote reproductive success should have advantages that exceed their disadvantages.

9. The reproductive behavior of males and females is related to their anatomy and physiology. Males who produce many sperm for a long time are expected to compete to inseminate females. Females who produce few eggs are expected to be selective about their mates.

10. Experiments with satin bowerbirds and birds of paradise support these bases for sexual selection.

11. The raggiana bird of paradise males gather in a lek—most likely because females are widely scattered, as is their customary food source. The food source for a related species, the trumpet manucode, is readily available but less nutritious. These birds are monogamous—it takes two parents to rear the young.

12. A cost-benefit analysis applies to competition between males for mates in reference to a dominance hierarchy (e.g., baboons) and territoriality (e.g., red deer).

13. Animals that form social groups communicate with one another. Communications such as chemical, auditory, visual, and tactile signals foster cooperation that benefits both the sender and the receiver.

14. There are benefits and costs to living in a social group. If animals live in a social group it is expected that the advantages (e.g., help to avoid predators, raise young, and find food) will outweigh the disadvantages (e.g., tension between members, spread of illness and parasites, and reduced reproductive potential). This expectation can sometimes be tested.

15. In most instances, the individuals of a society act to increase their own reproductive success. Sometimes animals perform altruistic acts, as when individuals help their parents rear siblings. There is a benefit to this behavior when one considers inclusive fitness, which involves both direct selection and indirect selection.

16. In social insects, altruism but can be explained on th they are helping a reproduci survive. A study of wood-hoop African bird, shows that younger siblings may help older siblings who reared them until the younger get a chance to reproduce themselves.

Writing Across the Curriculum

In order to practice writing skills, students should write out the answers to any or all of the study questions and the critical thinking questions. The study questions are sequenced in the same order as the text. Answers to the objective questions, and suggested answers to the critical thinking questions, are in appendix D.

Study Questions

1. State the two types of questions asked by ethologists and explain how they differ. 826

2. Describe Dilger's experiment with lovebirds, and explain how it shows that behavior has a genetic basis. 826

3. Arnold's experiment with garter snakes showed that what system is involved in behavior? Explain the experiment and the results. 826–27

4. Studies of *Aplysia* DNA show that the endocrine system is also involved in behavior. Explain. 827

5. Some behaviors require practice before developing completely. How does Hailman's experiment with laughing gull chicks support this statement? 828

6. An argument can be made that social contact is an important element in learning. Explain with reference to imprinting in mallard ducks and song learning in white-crowned sparrows. 829

7. Why would you expect behavior to be subject to natural selection and be adaptive? 830

8. How do Borgia's studies of satin bowerbird behavior and Clutton-Brock's studies with red deer support the belief that reproductive behavior is related to male and female anatomy and physiology? 830, 832

9. Reproductive behavior sometimes seems tied to how an animal acquires food. Explain with reference to the two bird of paradise species discussed in this chapter. 830

10. Give examples of the different types of communication among members of a social group. 833–34

11. What is a cost-benefit analysis and how does it apply to living in a social group? Give examples. 835

12. How can altruism, as defined on page 835, be explained on the basis of self-interest? 835–36

Objective Questions

1. Which of these questions is least likely to interest a behaviorist?
   a. How do genes control the development of the nervous system?
   b. Why do animals living in the tundra have white coats?
   c. Does aggression have a genetic basis?
   d. Why do some animals feed in groups and others feed singly?

2. Female sage grouse are widely scattered throughout the prairie. Which of these would you expect?
   a. A male will maintain a territory large enough to contain at least one female.
   b. Male and female birds will be monogamous and both will help feed the young.
   c. Males will form a lek where females will choose a mate.
   d. Males will form a dominance hierarchy for the purpose of distributing resources.

3. White-crowned sparrows from two different areas sing with a different dialect. If the behavior is primarily genetic, newly hatched birds from each area will
   a. sing with their own dialect.
   b. need tutors in order to sing in their dialect.
   c. sing only when a female is nearby.
   d. Both a and c are correct.

4. Orangutans are solitary but territorial. This would mean orangutans defend their territory's boundaries against
   a. other male orangutans.
   b. female organutans.
   c. all types of animals.
   d. Both a and b are correct.

es of a raggiana
...ue to the fact that
...play
...other birds.
...rritories.
...y females as mates.
...e are correct.

...e females in a baboon troop
...not produce offspring as often as
dominant females. It is clear that

a. the cost of being in the troop is too
high.

b. the dominant males do not mate
with subordinate females.

c. subordinate females must benefit
from being in the troop.

d. Both a and b are correct.

7. Peach-faced lovebirds carry nesting
material in the rump feathers; Fisher's
lovebirds carry nesting material in their
beaks. The fact that hybrids of these
two are intermediate shows that

a. the trait is controlled by the nervous
system.

b. nesting is controlled by hormones.

c. the behavior is genetic.

d. Both a and c are correct.

8. At first laughing gull chicks peck at any
model that looks like a red beak; later
they will not peck at any model that
does not look like a parent. This shows
that the behavior

a. is a fixed action pattern.

b. undergoes development after birth.

c. is controlled by the nervous system.

d. All of these are correct.

9. Which of these could be an answer to a
causal question? Males compete
because

a. they have the size and weapons
with which to compete.

b. they produce many sperm for a long
time.

c. the testes produce the hormone
testosterone.

d. Both a and c are correct.

10. Which of these could be an answer to a
survival value question? Females are
choosy because

a. they do not have the size and
weapons with which to compete.

b. they invest heavily in the offspring
they produce.

c. the ovaries produce the hormones
estrogen and progesterone.

d. All of these are correct.

Concepts and Critical Thinking

1. *All behavior both has a genetic basis
and is influenced by lifetime
experiences, including learning.*
Explain why you would expect this
statement to apply even to human
reasoning.

2. *Behavior increases the individual fitness
of the individual.*
Why would you expect feeding
behavior patterns, territoriality, and
reproductive behavior patterns to
increase individual fitness?

3. *Individuals live in a society when the
benefits to the individual outweigh
the costs.*
Show that altruistic acts are actually
selfish acts.

Selected Key Terms

altruism A social interaction that has the
potential to decrease the lifetime
reproductive success of the member
exhibiting the behavior. [L. *altru,*
other]   835

behavior Observable, coordinated responses
to environmental stimuli.   826

communication A signal by a sender that
influences the behavior of a
receiver.   833

dominance hierarchy Social ranking within a
group in which a higher ranking
individual acquires more resources than
a lower ranking individual.   831

imprinting A form of learning that occurs
early in the lives of animals; a close
association is made that later
influences sexual behavior.   829

inclusive fitness Fitness that results from
direct selection and indirect
selection.   835

learning A relatively permanent change in an
animal's behavior that results from
practice and experience.   828

operant conditioning A form of learning that
results from rewarding or reinforcing a
particular behavior.   828

pheromone A chemical released by the body
that causes a predictable reaction of
another member of the same species.
[Gk. *pher,* carry, and *mon,* one]   833

sexual selection Changes in males and
females due to male competition and
female selectivity.   830

society A group in which members of
species are organized in a cooperative
manner, extending beyond sexual and
parental behavior.   833

sociobiology The application of evolutionary
biology principles to the study of social
behavior in animals.   835

territoriality Behavior related to the act of
marking or defending a particular area
against invasion by another species
member; area often used for the
purpose of feeding, mating, and caring
for young.   832

48

ECOLOGY OF POPULATIONS

Learning Objectives

Populations Tend to Grow

- Calculate the rate of natural increase for a population when provided with the number of individuals in the population, the birthrate, and the death rate.   840

- Contrast a **J**-shaped growth curve with an **S**-shaped growth curve.   840–41

- Indicate which parts of an **S**-shaped growth curve represent biotic potential, environmental resistance, and carrying capacity.   841

- Give examples of density-independent and density-dependent effects of environmental resistance.   842

- Contrast three likely types of survivorship curves for a population.   843

- Contrast three common age structure diagrams for a population.   843

Strategies for Existing

- Contrast an *r*-strategist population with a *K*-strategist population in regard to growth curves, survivorship curves, and age structure diagrams.   844

The Human Population Is Growing

- Describe the growth curve for the world's human population.   845

- Contrast the demography of more developed and less developed countries; tell why both types of countries contribute heavily to resource consumption.   845

The human, *Homo sapiens*, population ever increases in size.

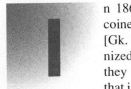

n 1869, the German zoologist Ernst Haeckel coined the word *ecology* from two Greek roots: [Gk. *eco,* house, and *logy,* study of]. He recognized that organisms do not exist alone; rather, they are part of a household, a functional unit that includes other types of organisms and their physical surroundings. Today, we define **ecology** as the study of the interactions of organisms with both their *biotic* (living) environment and their *abiotic* (physical) environment.

Various environmental factors can affect the size of a **population,** all the organisms of the same species at the locale (fig. 48.1*a*). We will begin by taking a look at some of these factors in this and the next chapter. Ecology seeks to understand how environmental factors and interactions determine the sizes of populations found in a certain locale at any particular time.

> Ecology is the study of interactions of populations with one another and with the physical environment.

POPULATIONS TEND TO GROW

Populations increase in size whenever the number of births exceeds the number of deaths. Suppose, for example, that a population has a size of 1,000 individuals, the birthrate is 30 per year, and the death rate is 10 per year. What is the rate of natural increase?

$$\text{rate of natural increase} \atop (r) = \frac{\text{birth} - \text{death} \atop (b) \qquad (d)}{\text{population size} \atop (N)}$$

$$r = \frac{b - d}{N} = \frac{30 - 10}{1{,}000} = 0.02 = 2\% \text{ per year}$$

The rate of natural increase is the percent increase in population size each year due to reproduction of members. It does not include any change in population size from either immigration or emigration, which for the purpose of our discussion can be assumed to be equivalent.

Populations with a positive rate of natural increase grow larger each year.

$$\text{increase} \atop (I) = \text{rate of natural increase} \atop (r) \times \text{population size} \atop (N)$$

$$I = rN = 0.02 \times 10{,}000 = 200$$

If the population size is now 10,200 individuals and the rate of natural increase remains at 2%, the next year's increase will be 204 individuals instead of 200, and so forth. Therefore, the population is undergoing **exponential growth:** at the end of each year, N is larger and therefore I is also larger. This is apparent when population size is plotted against time. When an arithmetic scale

Figure 48.1
Population growth. **a.** Each species in this deciduous forest is a member of a population. **b.** A J-shaped growth curve results when a population is expressing its biotic potential. The rate of natural increase is as great as it can be.

a.

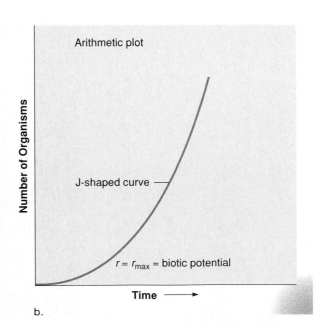

Arithmetic plot

Number of Organisms

J-shaped curve

$r = r_{max}$ = biotic potential

Time ⟶

b.

is used for population size, the resulting growth curve resembles that in figure 48.1*b*. It starts off slowly and then increases dramatically, producing a **J**-*shaped curve*.

Uninhibited Growth Is Rare

The **biotic potential** [Gk. *bio,* life] of a population is the maximum rate of natural increase (r_{max}) that can possibly occur under ideal circumstances. These circumstances include plenty of room for each member of the population, unlimited resources, and no hindrances, such as predators or parasites. Resources include food, water, and a suitable place to exist. Because these conditions rarely occur, it is very difficult to determine the r_{max} for most species; 2–5% is believed to be typical of large mammals, while insects can have a biotic potential as high as 50%.

Whether the biotic potential is high or low depends on such factors as the following:

1. usual number of offspring per reproduction;
2. chances of survival until age of reproduction;
3. how often each individual reproduces;
4. age at which reproduction begins.

Maximum growth rate is not experienced by any population for any length of time. This is readily apparent when considering that if a single female pig had her first litter at nine months, and produced two litters a year, each of which contained an average of four females (which, in turn, reproduced at the same rate), there would be 2,220 pigs by the end of three years. Because of exponential growth, even species with a low biotic potential would soon cover the face of the earth with their own kind. For example, as Charles Darwin calculated, a single pair of elephants would have over 19 million live descendants after 750 years.

Inhibited Growth Is Common

Populations do not undergo exponential growth for very long. Even in the laboratory setting, where crowding may be the only limiting factor, growth of populations eventually levels off. Figure 48.2 gives the actual growth curve for a fruit fly population reared in a culture bottle. This type of curve is often called a sigmoid or **S**-*shaped growth curve*. During an acceleration phase, when births exceed deaths, *r* is positive; during a deceleration phase, when births and deaths are more nearly equal, *r* is declining. Finally, when births exactly equal deaths, *r* is zero, and the population maintains a steady state.

Population size is believed to level off at the **carrying capacity** (*K*) of the environment. In other words, the environment is capable of sustaining a population of a limited size. As the population increases in size, there will be more and more competition for available space and food. Eventually, this will affect population size. It is said that the environment increasingly resists the biotic potential of the population. **Environmental resistance** contains the effects in table 48.1. The expression

$$\frac{K - N}{K}$$

pertains to density-dependent resistance. It also tells us what proportion of the carrying capacity still remains. If *N* is small, the expression approximates one, and most of the carrying capacity still remains. If *N* is large, the expression approaches zero, which indicates that the carrying capacity has almost been reached. Insert real numbers in the equation to show that this is the case.

Figure 48.2

S-shaped growth curve. **a.** This growth curve is based on the number of flies in a fruit fly culture bottle. At first the population grew exponentially but then slowed when resources dwindled and environmental resistance set in. **b.** In nature, S-shaped growth curves level off at the carrying capacity of the environment, after having gone through the phases noted.

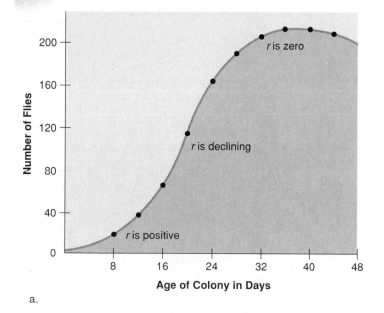

a.

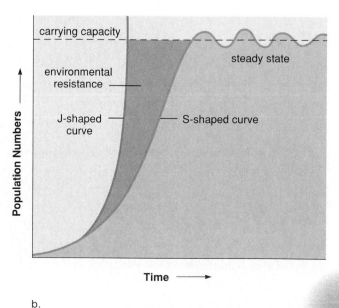

b.

If our argument to this point is sound, then insertion of the expression

$$\frac{K - N}{K}$$

into the equation for exponential growth should result in an S-shaped curve.

$$I = r\left(\frac{K - N}{K}\right)N$$

At low population densities, when the expression approximates one, growth I would be nearly equal to rN; therefore, growth is exponential. But as the density increases, the expression approaches zero, and growth levels off. Therefore, it seems that the concept of carrying capacity explains the logistic growth curve. Further, we can predict that if a population happens to overshoot the carrying capacity, it will have to decline once again because the expression

$$\frac{K - N}{K}$$

then will have a negative value.

Fluctuations are often seen in population sizes, as when there is an abrupt change in carrying capacity from season to season. During the summer, when resources are plentiful, a population increases in size. In winter, when the environment is less favorable, a population declines. As a result, population size can fluctuate from year to year. The mean of the increases and decreases over time represents the average carrying capacity of the environment.

Among some species, notably insects and certain plants, populations grow rapidly for a limited period of time and then quickly die out. The growth curve for these populations is at first J-shaped, but the exponential growth is followed by a sharp decline. For example, a reindeer herd introduced on St. Matthew Island, Alaska, underwent a rapid expansion and then declined just as quickly when food resources were depleted by the overgrazing of the herd, which had grown too large (fig. 48.3).

Table 48.1

Environmental Resistance to Biotic Potential (r_{max})

Density-Independent Effects	
Climate and weather	Effects that are independent of population density
Natural disasters	
Requirements for growth	
Density-Dependent Effects	
Competition	Effects that intensify with increased population density
Emigration	
Predation	
Parasitism	

Biotic potential is normally held in check by environmental resistance so that the growth curve is S shaped and levels off at the carrying capacity of the environment.

Figure 48.3

Exceeding the carrying capacity. **a.** Reindeer, *Rangifer,* on St. Matthew Island, Alaska. **b.** The herd grew exponentially for several decades and then underwent a sharp decline as a result of overgrazing the available range.

a.

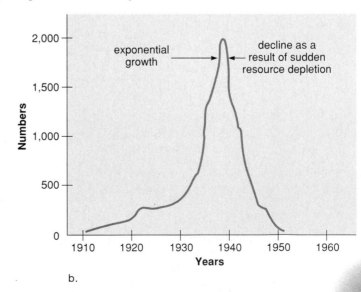

b.

Figure 48.4

The three basic types of survivorship curves. The type I curve occurs when the members of a species usually live the full physiological life span. The type II curve occurs when the rate of mortality is fairly constant at all age levels. The type III curve occurs when there is a high mortality early in life.

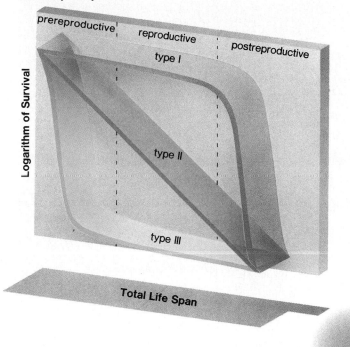

Figure 48.5

Growth of a honeybee population during a single season. Age structure patterns are shown for the following. **a.** An expanding population. **b.** A stable population. **c.** A diminishing population. In each diagram, the red color represents the prereproductive individuals, blue the reproductive individuals, and green the postreproductive individuals.

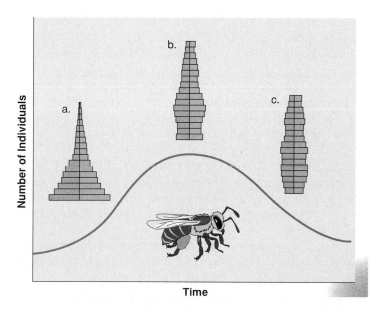

Who Survives Best?

Members of a population have a limited life span, and death is the means by which most individuals are lost from a population. (The other means is emigration—departure.) The number of members of a population that are dying per unit of population per unit time is the death rate. The death rate is usually determined by dividing the number of individuals that have died during a given time period by the number alive at the beginning of that period of time.

Rates of natural increase in population size are a function of additions by birth and losses by death. The rate of increase sometimes becomes greater, not because of a growing birthrate but because of a decline in the death rate. This decline in deaths is one reason for the explosive growth of the human population in certain countries of the world.

Another way of looking at mortality is to calculate **survivorship,** which is the number of individuals in a given population alive at the beginning of each age interval. A survivorship curve can be drawn by plotting the number of survivors against time.

Three types of survivorship curves are shown in figure 48.4. The type I curve shows that most individuals within a designated group live out their allotted life span and then die of old age. Under very favorable environmental conditions, certain mammals, such as humans, and annual plants, which live one season, tend to approach this curve. The type II curve results when organisms die at a constant rate through time. Such curves are typical of birds, rodents, and some perennial plants that live more than one season. The type III curve indicates that many organisms die early in life. This curve is typical of fishes, many invertebrates, and many plants that produce a vast number of eggs or seeds that die early.

Age Structure Predicts Population Growth

Populations have three age groups: *prereproductive, reproductive,* and *postreproductive.* One way of characterizing populations is by these age groups. This is best visualized when the proportion of individuals in each group is plotted on a bar graph, thereby producing an **age structure diagram.** If the birthrate is high and the population is undergoing exponential growth, a *pyramid-shaped* figure results, because each successive generation is larger than the previous one. When the birthrate equals the death rate, a *bell-shaped* age diagram is expected, because the dependency and reproductive age groups become more nearly equal. The postreproductive group is still the smallest, however, because of mortality. If the birthrate falls below the death rate, the dependency group will become smaller than the reproductive group. The age structure diagram will then be *urn shaped* because the postreproductive group is now the largest.

In a study of a honeybee hive, these changes in the age structure diagram were observed in a single season (fig. 48.5).

Figure 48.6
Existence strategies. **a.** *r*-strategists, like the dandelion, *Taraxacum,* have the characteristics listed. **b.** *K*-strategists, like the grizzly bear, *Ursus,* have the characteristics noted.

r-strategists

Small individuals
Short life span
Fast to mature
Many offspring
Little or no care of offspring

K-strategists

Large individuals
Long life span
Slow to mature
Few offspring
Much care of offspring

STRATEGIES FOR EXISTING

Populations do not increase in size year after year because environmental resistance, including both *density-independent* and *density-dependent* effects (see table 48.1), regulates number. Some populations are regulated primarily by density-independent effects. These tend to have **J**-shaped growth curves until some environmental change causes them to decline, usually within a short time. Most likely these populations are *opportunistic species,* which move in and occupy new environments. Dandelions in lawns and along roadsides and tent caterpillars in cherry and apple trees are opportunistic species. During a short period of time, they produce many offspring, which require little care. Therefore, these populations usually have a survivorship curve similar to type III in figure 48.4. But chances are that some of these offspring will quickly disperse to colonize new habitats, because opportunistic species usually have efficient dispersal mechanisms. From an evolutionary point of view, such species have undergone selection to maximize their rate of natural increase, and for this reason they are said to be *r*-selected or to be ***r*-strategists** (fig. 48.6*a*).

Other populations are regulated primarily by density-dependent effects. These tend to produce **S**-shaped growth curves. Such populations are termed *equilibrium species.* For example, whales are relatively large, long-lived, and slow to mature. They produce a small number of offspring and expend considerable energy in producing each individual, because resources are limited and competitive superiority is a necessity for survival. These organisms tend to have a survivorship curve like type I in figure 48.4. Equilibrium species are strong competitors and, once established, can dominate or exclude opportunistic species. They are specialists rather than colonizers, and they tend to become extinct when their normal way of life is destroyed. When undisturbed, the population size remains stable at or near the carrying capacity of the environment. Equilibrium species are said to be *K*-selected or to be ***K*-strategists** (fig. 48.6*b*).

Most populations cannot be characterized as either *r*- or *K*-strategists because they have intermediate characteristics. Such populations tend to have the type II survivorship curve.

THE HUMAN POPULATION IS GROWING

The rate of natural increase, or growth rate, of the human population of the world is now 1.8%. The growth curve is J-shaped and exponential but may eventually level off (fig. 48.7). There were two phases of exponential growth before the present one. The first phase occurred after tool making and the second occurred after the adoption of plant cultivation and animal husbandry, but neither added significantly to our numbers today. The latest phase of exponential growth, which is due to the Industrial Revolution, began about 1850 and has resulted in the enormous increase we see in figure 48.7.

Countries Differ in Their Growth

The countries of Europe and North America, along with Russia and Japan, were the first nations to become industrialized. These nations, often referred to collectively as the *more developed countries* (*MDCs*), doubled their populations between 1850 and 1950. This was largely due to a decline in the death rate caused by the rise of modern medicine and improved socioeconomic conditions. The death rate decline was followed shortly thereafter by a decline in the birthrate, so the populations in the MDCs showed only modest growth between 1950 and 1975. This sequence of events is termed a **demographic transition.**

The growth rate for the MDCs as a whole has now stabilized at about 0.6%. A few of the MDCs—Italy, Denmark, Germany, Hungary, and Sweden—are not growing or are actually losing population. The United States has a higher growth rate (0.7%) than average, because, as discussed in the reading on page 846, many people continue to immigrate to the United States. In addition, a baby boom between 1947 and 1964 resulted in an unusually large number of women who are still of reproductive age.

Most countries in Africa, Asia, and Latin America are collectively known as the *less developed countries* (*LDCs*) because they are not yet fully industrialized. Although mortality began to decline steeply in these countries following World War II with the importation of modern medicine from the MDCs, the birthrate did not decline to the same extent. Therefore, the populations of the LDCs began to increase dramatically. The LDCs were unable to cope adequately with such rapid population expansion, and many people in these countries are underfed, ill-housed, unschooled, and living in abject poverty.

The growth rate of the LDCs peaked at 2.4% between 1960 and 1965. Since that time, the mortality decline has slowed and the birthrate has fallen. The growth rate is expected to be 1.8% by the end of the century. At that time, however, more than two-thirds of the world population will be in the LDCs.

Increasing world population is putting extreme pressure on the earth's resources, environment, and social organization. Al-

Figure 48.7

Growth curve for world human population. The human population is now undergoing rapid exponential growth. The population size may level off at 8, 10.5, or 14.2 billion, depending upon the speed with which the growth rate may decline.

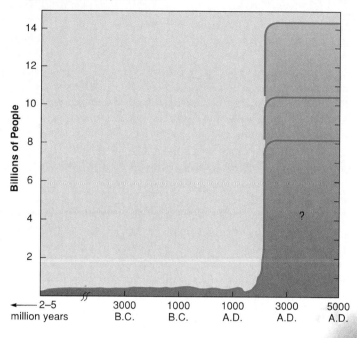

though population increases in LDCs might seem to be of the gravest concern, this is not necessarily the case. Each person in a MDC consumes more resources, and is therefore responsible for a greater amount of pollution than a person in a LDC. Environmental impact (EI) is measured not only in terms of population size but also in terms of the resources used and the pollution caused by each person in the population. Therefore, there are two possible types of overpopulation. The first type is due to increased population, and the second is due to increased resource consumption. The first type of overpopulation is more obvious in LDCs, and the second type is more obvious in MDCs.

The more developed countries have a low growth rate but greater resource consumption per individual. The less developed countries have a higher growth rate but lower resource consumption per individual.

U.S. Population Will Grow

Based on the 1990 census, the Census Bureau has projected that the U.S. population will reach 274.8 million by the year 2000, and ultimately 382.7 million by 2050. The projected population for 2050 is more than 80 million higher than previous expectations. In the new projections, there is no leveling off and no end in sight to population growth. Figure 48A shows that the U.S. population has gone through the stages described in figure 48.5. Even so, growth will continue as long as the prereproductive group is larger than the postreproductive group.

The U.S. racial/ethnic mix will grow increasingly diverse, due to a combination of factors: slow growth among non-Hispanic whites, steady growth among African Americans and Native Americans, and rapid growth among Hispanics and Asian Americans. Over the next 60 years, the share of the population that is non-Hispanic white should decline steadily—from 76% in 1990 to 68% in 2010 and 60% in 2030. By 2050, a bare majority of Americans (53%) will be non-Hispanic whites.

The nonwhite population itself is expected to become more diverse as well. While the numbers of African Americans are expected to grow steadily, reaching 38.2 million in 2010 and 57.3 million in 2050, their share of the population is expected to grow more slowly, reaching 13% in 2010 and 15% in 2050.

By contrast, Hispanics and Asian Americans are expected to grow fairly rapidly, the result of immigration and natural increase. Between 1990 and 2010, Hispanics are expected to grow from 22.4 million to 39.3 million. About that time, Hispanics should replace African Americans as the nation's largest minority group. By 2050, 20% of Americans—a total of over 80 million persons—will be Hispanic. Asian Americans are expected to grow even more rapidly—from 7 million in 1990 to 16.5 million in 2010 and 38.8 million in 2050. By 2050, 10% of Americans will be of Asian descent. As for Native Americans, they should continue to grow steadily, reaching over 4 million by 2050. However, they will compose barely 1% of all Americans.

The report also projects the pace of the graying of America, as the baby-boom generation (those born between 1947 and 1964) continues to age. For example, the population aged 65 and older will continue growing—steadily at first, from 31 million persons (12.5% of the total) in 1990 to 39.7 million (13%) in 2010. After 2010, however, the elderly population is projected to grow rapidly as the baby boomers enter its ranks. By 2030, when the younger boomers reach age 65, more than 20% of Americans—nearly 70 million—will be age 65 and over.

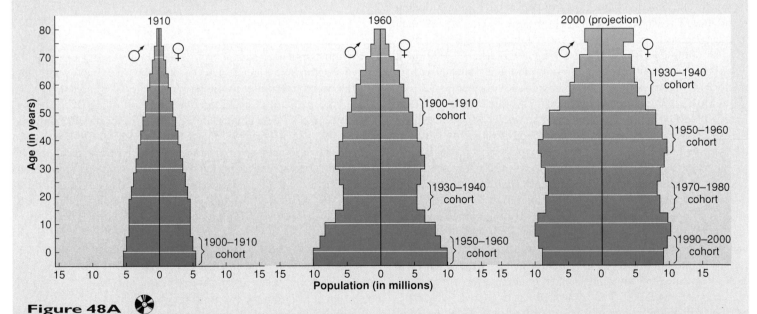

Figure 48A

Age structure diagrams of the U.S. population. In 1910, the diagram was shaped like a pyramid. This diagram resembles that of the less developed countries today, although they have an even larger base. In 1960, the diagram was shifting toward a more rectangular one. This diagram projects that by the year 2000 the age forty group will be the same size as that of the teenage group. Others suggest that the prereproductive group will still be larger than the postreproductive group. Note that these diagrams track various cohorts (people born in the same time period): the 1900–1910 cohort is seen in the first two diagrams but is gone by the last diagram.

1. Ecology is the study of the interactions of organisms with the physical environment and with one another. Organisms of the same species living in one locale form a population.

2. Populations with a positive rate of natural increase (r) have an increase in size expressed as $I = rN$, where N is the number of individuals in the population. Because N is larger each year, so is I. This means the population is increasing in size exponentially, and the growth curve is J shaped, or exponential.

3. The maximum rate of natural increase (biotic potential) for a population (r_{max}) occurs only when there is no environmental resistance, which includes density-independent and density-dependent effects.

4. An r_{max} may be observed for a short time during exponential growth, but eventually environmental resistance causes the growth curve to become S shaped as the population size levels off at the carrying capacity of the environment.

5. Sometimes populations exhibit a J-shaped curve followed by a sharp decline. Opportunistic species often colonize an area and then are cut back by the first frost, for example. Or unrestricted growth is often followed by a crash, as the population greatly exceeds the environment's carrying capacity.

6. Populations tend to have one of three types of survivorship curves, depending on whether most individuals live out the normal life span, die at a constant rate regardless of age, or die early.

7. Each population also has a particular type of age structure diagram, which indicates the number of individuals in the prereproductive, reproductive, and postreproductive age groups. The shape of the diagram tells whether the population is a young, expanding one, a stable one, or a dying one.

8. Populations seem to have a particular overall strategy for continued existence. Those that are opportunists produce many young within a short period of time and rely on rapid dispersal to new, unoccupied environments. These populations tend to have a J-shaped growth curve and to be regulated by density-independent effects. Such populations belong to species that are r-selected.

9. Other populations produce a limited number of young, which they nurture for a long time. These populations tend to be regulated by density-dependent effects and belong to species that are K-selected.

10. The human population is now in an exponential part of its growth curve. More developed countries underwent a demographic transition between 1950 and 1975, with the result that their growth rate is now only about 0.6%. Less developed countries are just now undergoing demographic transition. Because this transition was delayed, their growth rate at one time was as high as 2.4%, but it is declining slowly now.

11. Resource consumption depends on population size and on consumption per individual. Less developed countries are responsible for the first type of environmental impact, and more developed countries are responsible for the second type.

Writing Across the Curriculum

In order to practice writing skills, students should write out the answers to any or all of the study questions and the critical thinking questions. The study questions are sequenced in the same order as the text. Answers to the objective questions, and suggested answers to the critical thinking questions, are in appendix D.

> **Study Questions**

1. Draw a J-shaped growth curve and discuss why populations characterized by such curves may suddenly decline in size.   840

2. Show that a population of 10,000 persons will add more individuals with each generation, even if the growth rate remains constant. Is it possible that even with a declining growth rate the same number of individuals could be added each generation?   840

3. Draw an S-shaped growth curve and relate the concepts of biotic potential, environmental resistance, and carrying capacity to the curve.   841

4. Name four types of density-dependent effects, and explain what is meant by this term.   842

5. Draw three different survivorship curves, and explain what each curve indicates about the expected time of death.   843

6. Draw three different age structure diagrams, and explain what each one indicates about a population.   843

7. What is an r-strategist? a K-strategist?   844

8. Define demographic transition. When did the more developed countries (MDCs) undergo demographic transition? When did the less developed countries (LDCs) undergo demographic transition?   845

9. Give at least three differences between the MDCs and the LDCs.   845

Objective Questions

1. A population contains all the
   a. organisms that live at one locale.
   b. organisms that are members of the same species at one locale.
   c. similar types of organisms at one locale.
   d. organisms that are interacting with one another at one locale.

2. In a population $N = 1,500$, if the birthrate is 42 per year and the death rate is 27 per year, the rate of natural increase will be
   a. 42%.
   b. 27%.
   c. 1%.
   d. 0.1%.

3. Whether the biotic potential for a species is high or low depends on such factors as the
   a. usual number of offspring per reproduction.
   b. chances of survival until age of reproduction.
   c. age at which reproduction begins.
   d. All of these are correct.

4. When a population is undergoing exponential growth, it
   a. decreases by the same amount each year.
   b. remains the same size each year.
   c. increases by the same amount each year.
   d. increases by a larger amount each year.

5. Environmental resistance
   a. prevents exponential growth from occurring.
   b. includes density-independent effects.
   c. helps determine the carrying capacity.
   d. Both b and c are correct.

6. Populations termed *r*-strategists
   a. have J-shaped growth curves.
   b. have type III survivorship curves.
   c. are usually pioneer species.
   d. All of these are correct.

7. Once the demographic transition has occurred
   a. both the death rate and birthrate are high.
   b. both the death rate and birthrate are low.
   c. the death rate is high but the birthrate is low.
   d. the death rate is low but the birthrate is high.

8. Which shape best describes the age structure for a country whose population has stabilized?
   a. pyramid shaped
   b. urn shaped
   c. bell shaped
   d. exponential

9. Label this diagram of a growth curve. What does *r* stand for?

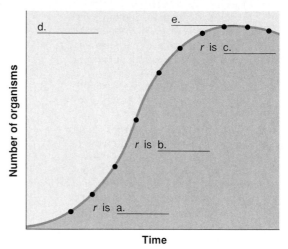

Concepts and Critical Thinking

1. *Population growth is always finite.*
   Under what circumstances is population growth maximal?

2. *Each population has a life strategy.*
   How is the human life strategy like that of an *r*-strategist? like that of a *K*-strategist?

Selected Key Terms

age structure diagram A representation of the number of individuals in each age group in a population.   843

biotic potential The maximum rate of natural increase of a population that can occur under ideal circumstances. [Gk. *bio*, life]   841

carrying capacity The maximum size of a population that can be supported by the environment in a particular locale.   841

demographic transition A decline in death rate, followed shortly by a decline in birthrate, resulting in slower population growth.   845

ecology The study of the interactions of organisms with their living and physical environment. [Gk. *eco*, house, and *logy*, study of]   840

environmental resistance The opposing force of the environment on the biotic potential of a population.   841

exponential growth A geometrically multiplying, rapid population growth rate.   840

K-strategist A species that has evolved characteristics that keep its population size near carrying capacity—for example, few offspring, longer generation time.   844

population A group of organisms of the same species occupying a certain area and sharing a common gene pool.   840

r-strategist A species that has evolved characteristics that maximize its rate of natural increase—for example, high birthrate.   844

survivorship Percentage of remaining survivors of a population over time; usually shown graphically, it can be used to depict death rates.   843

INTERACTIONS WITHIN COMMUNITIES

Learning Objectives

When Organisms Compete

- Discuss the effect that interspecific competition can have on population size.   850–51
- State the competitive exclusion principle, and relate this principle to the diversity of organisms.   851
- Distinguish between the niche and the habitat of an organism.   851

When Organisms Are Predators

- Discuss the effect that predation can have on the size of the prey population and on the diversity of the community.   852

- Give examples to show that human interference can upset the natural balance of a community.   852
- Give examples of plant and animal antipredator defenses.   853
- Explain the principle of mimicry, and give examples of the two kinds of mimicry.   853

When Organisms Depend on Another

- Give examples of the three types of symbiotic relationships, and explain what effect they can have on population size.   854–56

Oxpeckers, *Buphagus,* on the neck of an impala, *Aepyceros,* are gathering a meal of ticks and maggots. Their hissing when danger is near may help to alert their host.

W henever we walk into a forest or stop by the side of a pond, we are in a **community** of populations interacting with one another. The types of interactions vary, but we will primarily consider interactions involving competition, predation, and symbiosis. These interactions are important in controlling the diversity and size of populations. Only when populations remain at an appropriate size—one to the other— can a community of populations continue to sustain itself.

Figure 49.1

Competition between two species of paramecia. When grown alone in pure culture, *Paramecium caudatum* and *Paramecium aurelia* exhibit sigmoidal growth. When the two species are grown together in mixed culture, *P. aurelia* is the better competitor, and its population increases. *P. caudatum* cannot grow in the presence of a growing population of P. aurelia, so it dies out.

Source: Data from G. F. Gause, The Struggle for Existence, *1934, Williams & Wilkins Company, Baltimore, MD.*

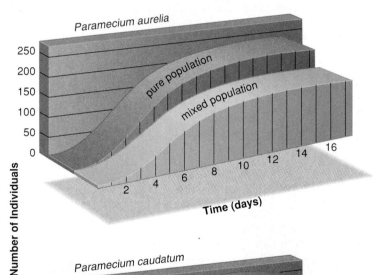

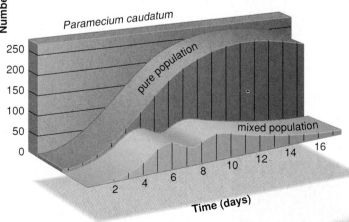

WHEN ORGANISMS COMPETE

Intraspecific competition, which occurs among members of a population, helps to limit the size of a population. Some animals live in groups with *dominance hierarchies* that determine the social position and importance of each animal. Dominance is determined by a contest—either actual fighting or simply a ritual contest of who can frighten whom. The dominant animals eat first and may have a chance to mate before lower ranking animals. The other animals either assist the dominant individuals or leave the group. In either case, they may not produce offspring.

Another social interaction that may affect population size is *territoriality,* in which successful competitors establish territories that they defend against other animals. Many animals mate and produce offspring within the territory. The best territory defenders often have the best territories—those with the best food resources and, among birds, the best nesting sites. The less successful defenders must make do with less desirable territories, and some have no territories at all. Therefore, these animals produce fewer offspring than those in better territories, or they produce no offspring at all.

Interspecific competition, which occurs when members of different species compete with one another, can lead to the predominance of one species and the virtual elimination of the other. This was demonstrated in the laboratory by G. F. Gause, who grew two species of paramecia in one test tube containing a fixed amount of bacterial food. Although each population survived

Figure 49.2

Effects of competition. Competition prevents two species of barnacles from occupying as much of the intertidal zone as possible. Both exist in the area of competition between *Chthamalus* and *Balanus.* Above this area only *Chthamalus* survives and below it only *Balanus* survives.

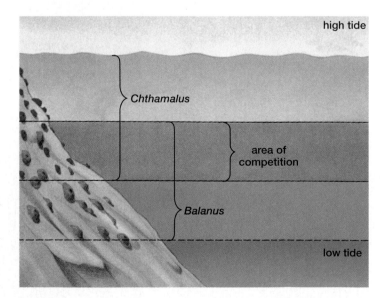

Figure 49.3

Resource partitioning among five species of coexisting warblers. The diagrams represent spruce trees. The time each species spent in various portions of the trees was determined, and it was discovered that each species spends more than half its time in the blue regions.

| Cape May warbler | Black-throated green warbler | Yellow-rumped warbler | Bay-breasted warbler | Blackburnian warbler |

when grown separately, only one survived when they were grown together (fig. 49.1). The successful paramecium population had a higher rate of natural increase than the unsuccessful population. This is an example of local extinction resulting from interspecific competition.

Instead of extinction in natural ecosystems, there may be restriction in the range of one of the species, as observed by Joseph Connell when he studied the distribution of barnacles on the Scottish coast. *Chthamalus stellatus* lives on the high part of the intertidal zone, and *Balanus balanoides* lives on the lower part (fig. 49.2). Free-swimming larvae of both species attach themselves to rocks at any point in the intertidal zone, where they develop into the sessile adult form. In the lower zone, the faster-growing *Balanus* individuals either force *Chthamalus* individuals off the rocks or grow over them. *Balanus,* however, is not as resistant to drying out as is *Chthamalus* and does not survive well in the upper intertidal zone, thus allowing *Chthamalus* to grow there.

Humans Intervene

The fact that successful competition can cause one species to increase in size at the expense of another has been demonstrated inadvertently by human intervention. The carp, a fish imported to the United States from the Orient, is able to tolerate polluted water. Therefore, this fish now is often more prevalent than our own native fishes. Melaleuca, an ornamental tree that was introduced into Florida, thrives in wet habitats and became a pest in the Everglades National Park. The burro, which originated in Ethiopia and Somalia and is adapted to a dry environment, now is threatening the existence of deer, pronghorn antelope, and desert bighorn sheep in the Grand Canyon.

Competition Affects Niches

Competition between species does not always lead to expansion of one population and restriction of another. Gause showed in another laboratory experiment that when two different species of paramecia occupied the same tube, both survived because one species fed on bacteria on the bottom and the other fed on bacteria suspended in solution. Such experiments have led some biologists to formulate and support a **competitive exclusion principle,** which states that no two species can occupy the same niche at the same time.

Niche comprises the *resources* that the organism exploits to meet its energy, nutrient, and survival demands. Competition results when resources are exploited (used by some organisms in a way that make them temporarily or permanently unavailable to others). **Habitat** comprises the *conditions* that influence an organism's life activities and describe the location where the organism is able to survive and reproduce.

Robert MacArthur recorded the length of time each of five species of warblers spent in different spruce tree zones to determine where each species did most of its feeding (fig. 49.3). He discovered that the various species primarily use different parts of the tree canopy and therefore use different food resources.

> The competitive exclusion principle states that no two species can occupy the same niche. Therefore, several species living in the same ecosystems are partitioning available resources.

WHEN ORGANISMS ARE PREDATORS

Predation, simply defined, is one organism feeding on another, called the *prey*. Through the evolutionary process, predators become adapted to capturing their prey. The anatomy of browsers enables them to reach high into trees—giraffes have long necks and elephants have long trunks. Birds of prey have talons and sharp beaks, which enable them to capture, hold, and kill their prey. Carnivores also need keen eyesight. Hawk eyes have a resolving power eight times that of the human eye due to the concentration of cones in two foveas instead of one.

Prey Population Size Is Affected

In one laboratory experiment, Gause placed didinia and paramecia in a test tube. In this environment, the didinia actually captured all the paramecia and then died out from starvation. If Gause provided refuge for the prey, however—in this case sediment on the bottom of the laboratory glassware—part of the prey population survived. This suggests that predator-prey relationships can stabilize when predator pressure eases as the prey population decreases in size. In nature, this can be the result of prey being able to hide and/or of predators switching to a more abundant, and hence more economical, prey species.

Data based on the number of pelts sold by fur trappers suggests that the size of lynx populations fluctuates with the size of the snowshoe hare populations. Figure 49.4 shows that as the prey (hare) population increases, so does the predator (lynx) population. Then with increased predation, first the prey population and then the predator population declines. It's possible that over-winter food shortages trigger the decline and make the hares more vulnerable to predators.

Robert Paine demonstrated in the 1960s that if the large sea star *Pisaster* is removed from an intertidal community of the Washington Coast, the mussel *Mytilus* outcompetes all the other species on the rocks. He said that *Pisaster* was a *keystone predator* because its predation effects determine the biotic structure of the entire community. Sea otters that feed on invertebrates are a classic example of a keystone predator. When they arrive in a coastal marine environment, invertebrate populations decline and the kelp (a type of brown algae) population increases dramatically.

Humans Interfere

Sometimes humans have neglected to take into consideration that predators help to keep prey populations in check. For example, in the past, coyotes have been killed indiscriminately in the West without regard for the fact that they help to keep the prairie dog population under control. Similarly, when the dingo, a wild dog in Australia, was killed off because it attacked sheep, the rabbit and wallaby populations greatly increased. In contrast, humans formerly kept the burro population in the Grand Canyon within reasonable limits by killing them for meat. Since the killing of burros was outlawed in 1971, their numbers have increased until they now are destructive pests and threaten the existence of native animals.

> Predators help to control the size of prey populations. The oscillations in predator and prey populations are still being investigated.

Figure 49.4

a. Montana lynx, *Felis,* a solitary predator. A long, strong forelimb with sharp claws grabs its main prey, the snowshoe hare. A lynx lives in northern forests. Its brownish gray coat blends in well against tree trunks, and its long legs enable it to walk through deep snow. **b.** Example of predator-prey cycling. As the hare population increases in size, so does the lynx population; but then the hare population, followed by the lynx population, suffers a dramatic decrease in size. While it may seem as if this cycling is due to "overkill" by the lynx population, other factors could be involved.

(These data are based on the number of lynx and snowshoe hare pelts received by the Hudson Bay Company in the years indicated.)

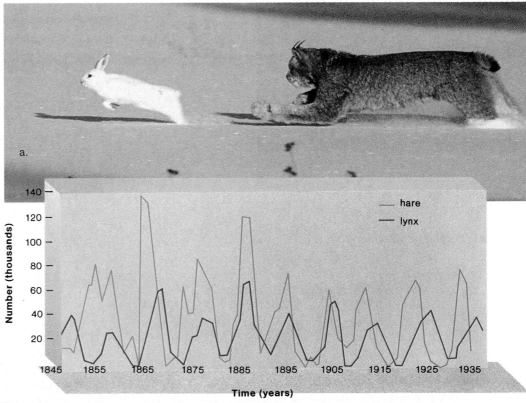

Figure 49.5

Antipredator defenses. **a.** Concealment. Flounder can take on the same coloration as their background. **b.** Fright. The South American lantern fly has a large false head that resembles that of an alligator. This may frighten a predator into thinking it is facing a dangerous animal. **c.** Warning coloration. The skin secretions of dart-poison frogs are so poisonous that they were used by natives to make their arrows instant lethal weapons. The coloration of these frogs warns others to beware.

a.   Flounder, *Platichthys*

b. South American lantern fly, *Lanternaria*

c. Dart-poison frog, *Dendrobates*

Prey Defend Themselves

While predators have evolved strategies to secure the maximum amount of food with minimal expenditure of energy, prey organisms have evolved strategies to escape predation.

In plants, the sharp spines of the cactus, the pointed leaves of the holly, and the tough, leathery leaves of the oak tree all discourage predation by insects. Plants even produce poisonous chemicals—some interfere with the normal metabolism of the adult insect and others act as hormone analogues, interfering with the development of insect larvae.

Animals have varied *antipredator defenses*. Some of the more effective defenses are concealment, fright, warning coloration, and vigilance (fig. 49.5).

Mimicry Can Help

Mimicry [Gk. *mim,* imitation] occurs when one species resembles another for its own benefit. Mimicry can help a predator capture food or it can help a prey avoid capture. For example, snapping turtles have tongues and angler fishes have lures that resemble worms for the purpose of bringing small fish within reach. To avoid capture, there are inch worms that resemble twigs and caterpillars that can transform themselves into shapes that resemble snakes.

Batesian mimicry (named for Henry Bates, who discovered it) occurs when a prey mimics another species that has a successful antipredator defense. Many examples of Batesian mimicry involve warning coloration. Among flies of the family Syrphidae, which feed on the nectar and pollen of flowers, one species resembles the wasp *Vespula arenaria* so closely it is difficult to tell them apart (fig. 49.6). Once a predator experiences the defense of a wasp it remembers the coloration and avoids all animals that look similar.[1]

---

[1] It has long been said that the viceroy butterfly is a mimic of the monarch butterfly, which is poisonous to birds. This is being questioned because (1) birds don't often eat monarch butterflies in the wild; (2) when flycatchers are fed monarch butterflies in the laboratory, they don't get sick; and (3) the viceroy butterfly is toxic when its larvae have fed on willow plants.

Figure 49.6

Flies of the family Syrphidae are called flower flies because they are likely to be found on flowers where they drink nectar and eat pollen. Some species, like *Syrphus*, mimic a wasp, which is protected from predation by its sting.

There are also examples of species that have the same defense and resemble each other. For example, many coral snake species have brilliant red, black, and yellow body rings. And the stinging insects—bees, wasps, and hornets—all have the familiar black and yellow color bands. Mimics that share the same protective defense are called *Müllerian mimics* after Fritz Müller, who discovered this form of mimicry.

Antipredator defenses are varied. Sometimes one species mimics another that has a successful defense (Batesian mimic), and sometimes several different species with the same defense mimic one another (Müllerian mimic).

Lyme Disease, a Parasitic Infection

ith the exception of AIDS, Lyme disease is the most serious newly recognized infectious disease in the United States in terms of number of cases and potential for severe illness. Lyme disease has been reported in many states, but most cases occur in the Northeast (New York, New Jersey, Connecticut, and Massachusetts), the upper Midwest (Minnesota and Wisconsin), and the Pacific Northwest (California and Oregon). Lyme disease takes its name from Lyme, Connecticut, where the disease first was recognized in 1975.

The cause of Lyme disease is a spirochete, *Borrelia burgdorferi,* a coiled bacterium that is spread by the bite of a deer tick, *Ixodes dammini* in the East and *I. ricinus* in the West. Adult deer ticks are only about two-thirds the size of dog ticks. They are so named because adult ticks feed and mate on white-tailed deer. Ticks feed on the blood of their host and triple in size following a meal (fig. 49A). Ticks are arthropods that go through a number of states (egg, larva, nymph, adult) as they develop; molting occurs between the stages.

After a female tick has fed and mated in the fall, she falls to the ground and lays her eggs. When these eggs hatch in the spring, they become larvae that feed primarily on white-footed mice. These mice are an important reservoir for the Lyme disease bacterium; when mice are infected, the tick becomes infected. The fed larvae overwinter and molt the next spring to become nymphs that are not much larger than the head of a pin. It is during the nymph stage, between May and September, that ticks are most apt to feed on humans and to pass on to them the bacterium that causes Lyme disease. The nymph is dark brown and hard bodied and is mistaken easily for a scab or a piece of dirt on the skin. Other likely hosts for nymphs are white-footed mice, raccoons, and skunks. After feeding, the nymph develops into an adult, and the life cycle repeats itself.

Altogether, ticks remain on their hosts only about eighteen days. The unfed adults, larvae, and nymphs spend most of their time attached to grasses or shrubs waiting for an appropriate host. Infestation is greatest in wooded areas, but people also have been bitten in their own backyards, especially if the yards are adjacent to wooded areas.

The effects of Lyme disease vary from mild to severe. First, some victims, but not all, get a rash that is called a bull's-eye rash because it has a red center encircled by a light area and then a red area again. The rash can get as large as a dinner plate. At this time, infected persons possibly feel like they have a mild case of flu. In about a month or so, nausea and neck and joint pain similar to that caused by arthritis may develop. Finally, a few may experience heart blockage—sometimes even requiring implantation of a pacemaker—and neurological disorders that mimic the symptoms of meningitis and encephalitis. Fierce headaches, facial paralysis, depression, and a temporary loss of memory also can occur. Loss of muscular coordination sometimes makes the disease seem like multiple sclerosis. Lyme disease is called "the great imitator" because it easily is misdiagnosed as a number of other illnesses.

It is never too late to be treated for Lyme disease. A blood test can detect antibodies to the bacterium in the system. If the blood test is positive, the administration of an antibiotic (penicillin, tetracycline, or erythromycin) cures the condition. Antitick sprays, which discourage ticks from choosing a human host in the first place, are available. Some home owners are trying to control the tick population in their vicinity by killing off the mice and ticks with chemicals. A more natural solution can be attempted by local governments. It is possible to release into the environment tiny parasitic wasps that lay their eggs only in ticks. The developing wasp larvae kill the ticks.

WHEN ORGANISMS DEPEND ON ANOTHER

Symbiosis [Gk. *symbio,* living together] is a close relationship between two species in which at least one of the species is dependent upon the other (table 49.1). As with predation, coevolution occurs, and the species become closely adapted to one another. In parasitism, the parasite benefits, but the host is harmed; in commensalism, one species benefits, but the other is unaffected; and in mutualism, both species benefit.

Parasitism Is Destructive

Parasitism [Gk. *parasit,* eat at another's table] is similar to predation in that the *parasite* derives nourishment from the host (just as the predator derives nourishment from its prey). Usually, however, the host is larger than the parasite, and an efficient parasite does not kill the host—at least not until its own life cycle is complete. Viruses are always parasites, as are a number of bacteria, protochtists, plants, and animals. The smaller parasites tend to be endoparasites that live in the bodies of the hosts. Larger parasites tend to be ectoparasites that remain attached to the exterior of the host by means of specialized organs and appendages.

Table 49.1

Symbiosis

	Species 1	Species 2
Parasitism	Benefited	Harmed
Commensalism	Benefited	No effect
Mutualism	Benefited	Benefited

Figure 49A

The life cycle of a deer tick. **a.** Adult ticks feed and mate on white-tailed deer, which accounts for the common name of the ticks. Female adults lay their eggs in soil and then die. **b.** In the spring and summer, larvae feed mainly on white-footed mice. They then overwinter. **c.** During the next summer, nymphs feed on white-footed mice or other animals, including humans. If a nymph is infected with the bacterium, humans get Lyme disease. **d.** Deer tick before feeding and after feeding. Actual size is shown along with enlarged size.

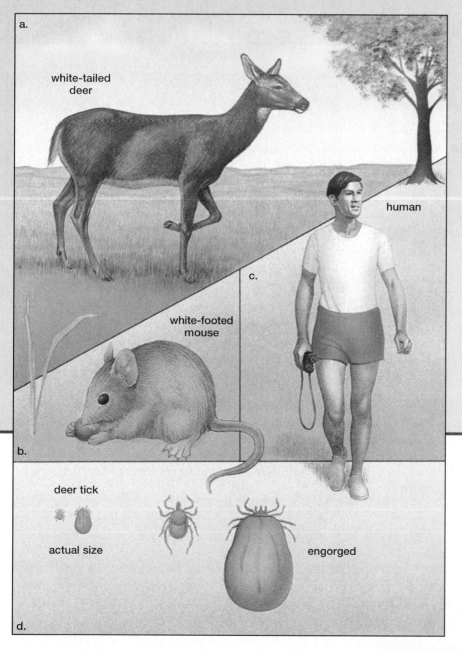

a.

white-tailed
deer

human

c.

white-footed
mouse

b.

deer tick

actual size

engorged

d.

Just as predators can dramatically reduce the size of a prey population that lacks a suitable defense, so parasites can reduce the size of a host population that has no defense. Thousands of elm trees have died in the United States from the inadvertent introduction of Dutch elm disease, which is caused by a parasitic fungus. A new method of treating Dutch elm disease utilizes bacteria that produce a fungicide when injected into the tree. Another means of curbing this fungal infection of trees is to control the bark beetle that spreads the disease.

Many other parasites use a secondary host for dispersal or completion of the stages of development. An example is the deer tick, which is discussed in the reading on the facing page.

> In parasitism, the host species is harmed. Parasites, which sometimes help to control the size of their host population, may require a secondary host for dispersal.

Commensalism Is Not Harmful

Commensalism [L. *com,* together, and *mensa,* table] is a relationship between two species in which one species is benefited and the other is neither benefited nor harmed. Often, the host species provides a home and/or transportation for the other species. Barnacles that attach themselves to the backs of whales and the shells of horseshoe crabs are provided with both a home and transportation. Remoras are fishes that attach themselves to the bellies of sharks by means of a modified dorsal fin acting as a suction cup. The remoras obtain a free ride and also feed on the remains of the shark's meals. Epiphytes grow in the branches of trees, where they receive light, but they take no nourishment from the trees. Instead, their roots obtain nutrients and water from the air. Clownfishes live within the waving mass of tentacles of sea anemones. Because most fishes avoid the poisonous tentacles of the anemones, the clownfishes are protected from predators. Perhaps this relationship borders on mutualism because the clownfishes actually may attract other fishes on which the anemone can feed.

> In commensalism, one species is benefited and the other is unaffected. Often the host simply provides a home and/or transportation.

Figure 49.7

The bullhorn acacia tree, *Acacia*, is adapted to provide a home for ants of the species *Pseudomyrmex ferruginea*. **a.** The thorns are hollow and the ants live inside. **b.** The base of leaves have nectaries (openings) where ants can feed. **c.** Leaves of the bullhorn acacia have bodies at the tips that ants harvest for larval food.

b.

c.

a.

Mutualism Is Beneficial to Both

Mutualism [L. *mutu,* reciprocal] is a symbiotic relationship in which both members of the association benefit. Mutualistic relationships often allow organisms to obtain food or to avoid predation.

Bacteria that reside in the human intestinal tract are provided with food, but they also provide humans with vitamins, which are molecules we are unable to synthesize for ourselves. Termites would not even be able to digest wood if not for the protozoans that inhabit their intestinal tract; it is the bacteria in the protozoans that digest cellulose. Mycorrhizae, also called fungal roots, are symbiotic associations between the roots of plants and fungal hyphae. Mycorrhizal hyphae improve the uptake of nutrients for the plant, protect the plant's roots against pathogens, and produce plant growth hormones. In return, the fungus obtains carbohydrates from the plant. As another example, flowers and their pollinators have coevolved and are dependent upon one another. The flower is benefited when the pollinator carries pollen to another flower, ensuring cross-fertilization, and the flower provides food for the pollinator.

In tropical America, the bullhorn acacia tree is adapted to provide a home for ants of the species *Pseudomyrmex ferruginea* (fig. 49.7). Unlike other acacias, this species has swollen thorns with a hollow interior, where ant larvae can grow and develop. In addition to housing the ants, the acacias provide them with food. The ants feed from nectaries at the base of the leaves and eat fat- and protein-containing nodules called Beltian bodies, which are found at the tips of some of the leaves. Bullhorn acacias have leaves throughout the year, while related acacia species lose their leaves during the dry season. The ants constantly protect the plant from herbivores and other plants that might shade it because, unlike other ants, they are active twenty-four hours a day.

> In mutualism, both species benefit.
> The two species often are closely adapted to one another.

1. A community is a group of populations that are interacting with one another.

2. Competition may be intraspecific or interspecific. Interspecific competition occurs only for a short period of time, because either one population replaces the other or the two species evolve to occupy different niches. Although it may seem that similar species are occupying the same niche, actually there are slight differences.

3. Two very important concepts in ecology are habitat and niche. Habitat indicates the conditions and describes the location where a population lives. Niche comprises the resources an organism uses. Several similar species that live in the same ecosystem occupy different niches.

4. Evidence suggests that predation tends to control the size of prey population, but the relationship may involve other factors as well. For example, the availability of food affects population sizes.

5. Just as predators are adapted to capture prey, prey are adapted to escape predators. Plants have both physical and chemical defenses. Animals have defenses that include concealment, fright of the predator, warning coloration, and vigilance.

6. Some animals mimic other animals that have a defense, especially those that are poisonous.

7. Symbiotic relationships include parasitism, commensalism, and mutualism. Parasitism may control the size of the host populations.

8. In commensalism, one species is benefited and the other is unaffected. Often the host simply provides a home and/or transportation.

9. In mutualism, both species benefit. The two species are often closely adapted to each other, as are flowers and their pollinators. There are also examples of mutualistic species that live together in the same locale, such as ants and bullhorn acacia trees.

Writing Across the Curriculum

In order to practice writing skills, students should write out the answers to any or all of the study questions and the critical thinking questions. The study questions are sequenced in the same order as the text. Answers to the objective questions, and suggested answers to the critical thinking questions, are in appendix D.

Study Questions

1. Why doesn't interspecific competition between similar populations always lead to the extinction of one of them? 850–51

2. What is the competitive exclusion principle, and how is it related to diversity of organisms? 851

3. Explain what is meant by the niche of an organism and why it is possible for similar types of organisms to be found in the same general area. 851

4. What evidence is there that predators might overkill their prey? that they do not do so? 852

5. Why would you recommend that humans not kill animals, such as coyotes, which sometimes prey on farm animals? 852

6. Describe some antipredator defenses of plants and animals. 853

7. What is mimicry? What is the difference between Batesian and Müllerian mimicry? 853

8. Give examples of parasitism, and explain the effects on the host organism. 854–55

9. Give examples of commensalism, and explain the effects on the host organism. 855

10. Give examples of mutualism, and explain the benefits to each organism. 856

Objective Questions

1. Six species of monkeys are found in a tropical forest. Most likely, they
   a. occupy the same niche.
   b. eat different foods and occupy different ranges.
   c. spend much time fighting each other.
   d. All of these are correct.

2. Leaf cutter ants keep fungal gardens. The ants provide food for the fungus but also feed on the fungus. This is an example of
   a. competition.
   b. predation.
   c. commensalism.
   d. mutualism.

3. Clownfishes live among sea anemone tentacles, where they are protected. If the clownfish provides no service to the anemone, this is an example of
   a. competition.   c. commensalism.
   b. predation.   d. mutualism.

4. Two species of barnacles vie for space in the intertidal zone. The one that remains is
   a. the better competitor.
   b. better adapted to the area.
   c. the better predator on the other.
   d. Both a and b are correct.

5. Territoriality occurs as a result of
   a. predation.
   b. parasitism.
   c. competition.
   d. cooperation.

6. A bullhorn acacia provides a home and nutrients for ants. Which statement is correct?
   a. The plant is under the control of pheromones produced by the ants.
   b. The ants protect the plant.
   c. They have coevolved to occupy different niches.
   d. All of these are correct.

7. The niche of an organism
   a. is the same as its habitat.
   b. includes how it competes and acquires food.
   c. is specific to the organism.
   d. Both b and c are correct.

8. The frilled lizard of Australia suddenly opened its mouth wide and unfurled folds of skin around its neck. Most likely this was a way to
   a. conceal itself.
   b. warn that it was noxious to eat.
   c. scare a predator.
   d. All of these are correct.

9. When one species mimics another species, the mimic sometimes
   a. lacks the defense of the model.
   b. possesses the defense of the model.
   c. is brightly colored.
   d. All of these are correct.

10. An experimenter introduced didinia into a culture of paramecia. Knowing that didinia prey on paramecia, explain this graph.

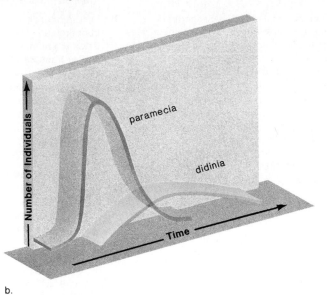

b.

11. On the line provided, identify each example, as parasitism, commensalism, or mutualism.

a. A heterotroph provides a home for an autotroph, who supplies it with organic molecules.

_____

b. A fish attaches to and receives nutrients directly from another fish.

_____

c. An organism lives in the tube along with a tube worm.

_____

Concepts and Critical Thinking

1. *Communities vary in their diversity.*
Why do more diverse communities have more niches?

2. *Population sizes in a community are in part controlled by predation.*
If predation acts as a check on prey population size, what are the counterchecks?

3. *Symbiotic relationships are important to the fabric of a community.*
Why could parasitism affect both population sizes and diversity within a community?

Selected Key Terms

commensalism A symbiotic relationship in which one species is benefited and the other is neither harmed nor benefited. [L. *com,* together, and *mensa,* table] 855

community A group of many different populations that interact with one another. 850

competitive exclusion principle The theory that no two species can occupy the same niche. 851

habitat The conditions of the environment that influence an organism's life activities and describe the location where the organism is able to survive and reproduce. 851

mimicry The superficial resemblance of one organism to another organism of a different species; often used to avoid predation. [Gk. *mim,* imitation] 853

mutualism A symbiotic relationship in which both species benefit. [L. *mutu,* reciprocal] 856

niche The resources that an organism exploits to meet its energy, nutrient, and survival demands. 851

parasitism A symbiotic relationship in which one species (parasite) benefits in terms of growth and reproduction to the harm of the other species (host). [Gk. *parasit,* eat at another's table] 854

symbiosis A relationship that occurs when two different species live together in a unique way; it may be beneficial, neutral, or detrimental to one and/or the other species. [Gk. *symbio,* living together] 854

50

ECOSYSTEMS: THE FLOW OF ENERGY AND THE CYCLING OF MATERIALS

Learning Objectives

Ecosystems Are Organized

- Give examples of biotic components within an ecosystem.   860
- Describe the process of primary and secondary succession on land; contrast the properties of the early stages of succession with the climax stage of succession.   860–61

Energy Flows in an Ecosystem

- Name two types of food chains, and give an example of each type.   863
- Give an example of a food web, and define trophic level.   863
- Give examples to show how environmental disturbances can affect a food web.   863

- Construct a generalized pyramid of energy and use it as a basis to explain why energy flows through an ecosystem.   865

Chemicals Cycle in an Ecosystem

- Name and give a function for each part of a generalized biochemical cycle.   866
- Describe the carbon, nitrogen, phosphorus and water cycles.   866–70
- Describe the human influence on each of these cycles.   866, 868, 869, 870

Human Food Chain Versus Natural Food Web

- Contrast the human food chain with a natural food web.   871

Praying mantis, *Mantis,* feeds on a bumble bee, *Bombus*, which has taken nectar from a flower. There is a flow of energy from the sun through all living things.

n this chapter we consider the characteristics and composition of ecosystems. An **ecosystem** [Gk. *eco,* house, and *sys,* together] comprises all of the populations in a given area, together with the physical environment. Therefore, an ecosystem possesses both biotic (living) and abiotic (nonliving) components. The nonliving components include soil, water, light, inorganic nutrients, and weather variables.

ECOSYSTEMS ARE ORGANIZED

The living components of the ecosystem can be categorized as either producers or consumers. **Producers** are autotrophic organisms with the capability of carrying on photosynthesis and making food for themselves (and indirectly for the other populations as well). In terrestrial ecosystems, the producers are predominantly green plants, while in freshwater and marine ecosystems, the dominant producers are various species of algae.

Consumers are heterotrophic organisms that use preformed food. It is possible to distinguish four types of consumers, depending on their food source. **Herbivores** [L. *herb,* grass, and *vor,* eat] feed directly on green plants; they are termed primary consumers. **Carnivores** [L. *carn,* flesh, and *vor,* eat] feed only on other animals and are thus secondary, or tertiary, consumers. **Omnivores** [L. *omni,* all, and *vor,* eat] feed on both plants and animals. Therefore, a caterpillar feeding on a leaf is a herbivore; a green heron feeding on a fish is a carnivore; a human being eating both leafy green vegetables and beef is an omnivore.

Decomposers are a fourth type of consumer, which feed on detritus. **Detritus** [L. *detrit,* wear off] is the remains of plants and animals following their death and fragmentation by soil organisms. The bacteria and fungi of decay are important detritus feeders, but so are other soil organisms, such as earthworms and various small arthropods. The importance of the latter can be demonstrated by placing leaf litter in bags with mesh too fine to allow soil animals to enter; the leaf litter does not decompose well, even though bacteria and fungi are present. Small soil organisms precondition the detritus so that bacteria and fungi can break it down to inorganic matter that producers can use again.

When we diagram all the biotic components of an ecosystem, as in figure 50.1, it is possible to illustrate that every ecosystem is characterized by two fundamental phenomena: energy flow and chemical cycling. Energy flow begins when producers absorb solar energy, and chemical cycling begins when producers take in inorganic nutrients from the physical environment. Energy flow occurs because all the energy content of organic food is eventually lost to the environment as heat. The original inorganic nutrients, however—the individual chemical elements that make up organisms—are cycled through the abiotic environment and eventually cycled back to the producers.

> **Within an ecosystem, energy flows and chemicals cycle.**

Communities Undergo Succession

When life first arose, it was confined to the oceans, but about 450 million years ago, organisms began to colonize the bare land. Eventually, the land supported many complex communities of living things. Similarly, today we can observe a sequence of stages by which bare rock becomes capable of sustaining many organisms. We call this primary succession (fig. 50.2). During **succession,** a community undergoes successive changes until finally there is a climax community, a mix of plants and animals that is at its most diverse state. Secondary succession is also observed when a climax community that has been disturbed returns to a state of diversity again. Abandoned farmland goes

Figure 50.1

Ecosystem composition. **a.** Chemicals cycle but energy flows through an ecosystem because all the energy derived from the sun eventually dissipates as heat. **b.** Terms that pertain to the study of ecology.

a.

Term	Definition
Ecology	Study of the interactions of organisms with the physical environment and with each other.
Biosphere	That portion of the surface of the earth (air, water, and land) where living things exist.
Ecosystem	A community, along with its physical environment; has a living (biotic) component and a nonliving (abiotic) component.
Community	All the populations that are found in a particular area.
Population	All the members of the same species that inhabit a particular area.

b.

Figure 50.2

Possible sequence of stages during primary succession. **a.** Lichens grow on bare rock. **b.** Individual plants take hold. **c.** Perennial herbs spread throughout the area. **d.** Trees can become established in the final stage of succession.

a.

b.

c.

d.

Figure 50.3

Secondary succession. This includes the stages by which defoliated land areas, such as abandoned farmland or strip-mined land, become a climax community again. During secondary succession, grass and weeds are followed by shrubs and trees and finally by a mature climax forest.

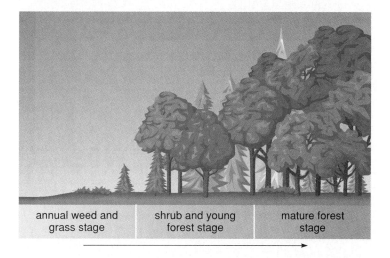

| annual weed and grass stage | shrub and young forest stage | mature forest stage |

Table 50.1

Properties of Communities

Pioneer Community	Climax Community
Harsh environment	Most favorable environment
Biomass increasing	Biomass stable
Energy consumption inefficient	Energy consumption efficient
Some nutrient loss	Nutrient cycling
Low species diversity	High species diversity
Fluctuations common	Fluctuations do not usually occur
Little stability	Great stability

the most productive. But the pioneer community lacks the diversity to make full use of inputs such as energy and nutrients and therefore the outputs (heat and loss of nutrients) are high. As succession proceeds, diversity increases, nutrients recycle more, and there is more efficient energy use. Climax communities are able to make full use of inputs and this helps them to maintain their stability.

Humans often replace climax communities, which tend to have the characteristics listed in table 50.1, with simpler communities, which tend to have the same characteristics as those of the pioneer communities listed in table 50.1. Agricultural fields and managed forests show an increase in biomass and have high yields because they are given large inputs, such as fertilizer applications. The price paid for this growth potential, however, is a certain amount of waste and loss of stability. We should keep in mind that stable climax communities aid in many ecological services, such as purification of the air and water, that are necessary to our well-being. For this reason, it would be wise to make sure that a large portion of every biome is kept in its natural state.

through a series of stages and may eventually become a forest community as depicted in figure 50.3.

When we study a community, we are considering only the populations of organisms that make up that community, but when we study an ecosystem, we are concerned with the community plus its physical environment. **Ecology** is the study of the interactions of organisms with each other and with the physical environment.

Climax Communities Are More Stable

Researchers find that the early stages of succession, also called pioneer communities, show the most growth and are therefore

Figure 50.4

Examples of food chains.
a. Terrestrial. **b.** Aquatic.

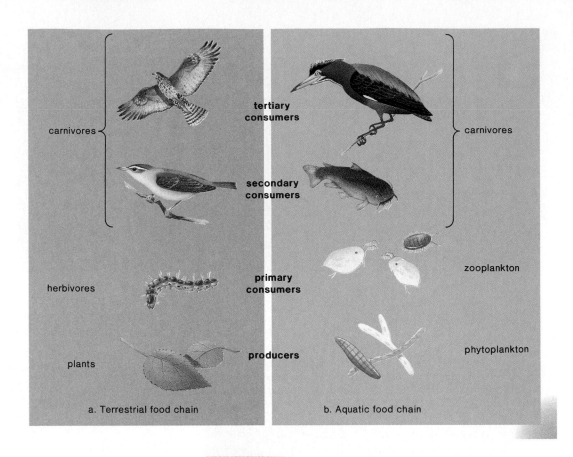

carnivores {

tertiary consumers

carnivores

secondary consumers

zooplankton

herbivores

primary consumers

plants

producers

phytoplankton

a. Terrestrial food chain

b. Aquatic food chain

Figure 50.5

Deciduous forest ecosystem. The arrows indicate the flow of energy in a food web.

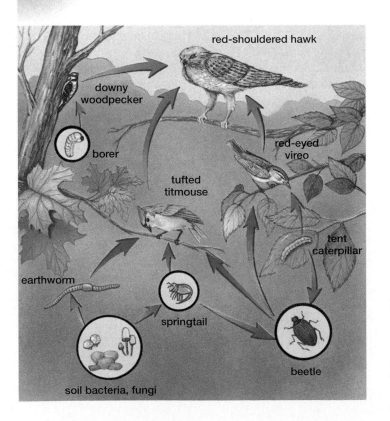

red-shouldered hawk

downy woodpecker

borer

red-eyed vireo

tufted titmouse

tent caterpillar

earthworm

springtail

beetle

soil bacteria, fungi

Figure 50.6

Freshwater pond ecosystem. The arrows indicate the flow of energy in a food web.

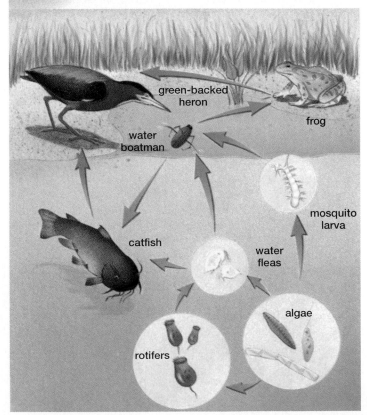

green-backed heron

frog

water boatman

mosquito larva

catfish

water fleas

algae

rotifers

ENERGY FLOWS IN AN ECOSYSTEM

Energy flow in an ecosystem is a consequence of two fundamental laws of thermodynamics. The first law states that energy cannot be created or destroyed, and the second law states that when energy is transformed from one form to another, there is always a loss of some usable energy as heat. Since energy cannot be created or completely transformed from one form to another, ecosystems are unable to function unless there is a constant energy input. This input comes from the sun, the ultimate source of energy for our planet.

Food Chains Become Food Webs

Energy flows through an ecosystem as the individuals of one population feed on those of another. A **food chain** indicates who eats whom in an ecosystem. Figure 50.4*a* depicts a possible terrestrial food chain, and figure 50.4*b* depicts a possible aquatic food chain. It is important to realize that each represents just one path of energy flow through an ecosystem. Natural ecosystems have numerous food chains, each linked to others to form a complex food web. For example, figure 50.5 shows a deciduous forest **food web** in which plants are eaten by a variety of insects, and these, in turn, are eaten by several different birds, which may then be eaten by a larger bird, such as a hawk. Therefore, energy flow is better described in terms of **trophic levels** [Gk. *troph,* feeder] (feeding levels), each one further removed from the producer population, the first (photosynthetic) level. All animals acting as primary consumers are part of a second trophic level; all animals acting as secondary consumers are part of the third trophic level; and so on. The populations in an ecosystem form food chains in which the producers produce food for the other populations, which are consumers. While it is convenient to study food chains, the populations in an ecosystem actually form a food web in which food chains join and overlap with one another.

The food chain depicted in figure 50.4*a* is part of the forest food web shown in figure 50.5, and the food chain depicted in figure 50.4*b* is part of the aquatic food web shown in figure 50.6. Both these food chains are called *grazing food chains* because the primary consumer feeds on a photosynthesizer. In some ecosystems (forests, rivers, and marshes) there are food chains in which the primary consumer feeds mostly on detritus. *Detritus food chains* can account for more energy flow than grazing food chains because most organisms die without having been eaten. In the forest, an example of a detritus food chain is

detritus ⟶ soil bacteria ⟶ earthworms

A detritus food chain is often connected to a grazing food chain, as when earthworms are eaten by a tufted titmouse. When dead organisms have decomposed, all the solar energy that was

Table 50.2	
Population Size	
Density-Independent Effects Climate and weather Natural disasters Requirements for growth	Effects that are independent of population density
Density-Dependent Effects Competition Emigration Predation Parasitism	Effects that intensify with increased population density

taken up by the producer populations dissipates as heat. Therefore, energy does not cycle.

> In an ecosystem, food chains containing a producer and consumers join and overlap in a food web. Decomposers feed on the remains of these organisms when they die.

Populations Maintain Their Size

In an ecosystem, population sizes are held in check by the density-independent and density-dependent effects listed in table 50.2. Just now we are interested in the effects of competition and predation. Interspecific competition occurs when populations make use of the same food sources. Predation occurs when one population feeds on a prey population.

In figure 50.5, tufted titmice and red-eyed vireos both prey on beetles. What would happen if a selective pesticide was used to reduce the size of the beetle population? More intense competition between tufted titmouse and red-eyed vireo populations would cause their sizes to decline. How might the earthworm population size be affected? Tufted titmice would most likely increase their predation on earthworms, whose population would now decline. How might the red-shouldered hawk population be affected? A reduction in the size of prey populations would eventually cause a reduction in the size of the hawk population also. Would the size of the decomposer population change if many more beetles die than usual?

Our discussion supports the ecological truism "everything is connected to everything else." A disturbance in the food chains within a food web can have diverse consequences and can even lead to a total collapse of an ecosystem.

> Because food chains join and overlap, a disturbance in one chain can affect the other chains.

Marine Enclosures for Whole-Ecosystem Studies

The MERL (Marine Ecosystems Research Laboratory) enclosures shown in figure 50A provide marine researchers with a unique ability to experiment with whole marine ecosystems. When set up in a configuration to simulate lower Narragansett Bay, unmanipulated enclosures maintain healthy ecosystems for many months with properties that are similar to those actually found in the bay. This allows scientists to conduct experiments to determine the effect of a contaminant on an entire coastal ecosystem. The enclosures also make possible well-constrained experiments to study the fate of chemicals in a near-natural ecosystem.

The enclosures are large enough to allow repetitive sampling of all the biological populations. The ability of the enclosures to be self-maintaining allows experiments to be conducted over months or years. The proximity of the enclosures to laboratory facilities enables sampling at shorter time intervals than are usually practical in the field. There are fourteen individual enclosures to allow for replication of treatments and untreated controls.

Each enclosed ecosystem is contained in a tank 1.8 meters in diameter and 5 meters deep. They are outdoors and exposed to natural sunlight. To initiate a typical experiment, a benthic (bottom of the ocean) community is collected, usually from a silt-clay area in Narragansett Bay, with a box corer that maintains the sediments in a nearly undisturbed condition. The 37-cm-thick beds of sediment placed into each tank weigh roughly a ton each. Thirteen cubic meters of unfiltered seawater, with its water column community intact, is transferred from the adjacent bay with nondisruptive displacement pumps. Mechanical mixing provides water movement in the enclosures to simulate wind and wave movement in the field. In the summer, cooling is provided, and in the winter, heat is provided to keep the enclosure temperatures similar to those in the bay.

Figure 50A

MERL (Marine Ecosystem Research Laboratory) enclosures at the University of Rhode Island's Graduate School of Oceanography.

One set of MERL experiments addressed the problem of chronic additions of oil hydrocarbons to coastal waters. Water runoff from land, especially in urban areas, carries a continuous trickle of oil to coastal environments. The total amounts of petroleum hydrocarbons introduced into coastal waters through urban runoff and river runoff are believed to be greater than introductions through oil spills. Daily additions of fuel oil, of the type regularly used in home furnaces, were made into three replicate enclosures. Two experiments were conducted. The first 5.5-month experiment added oil to achieve about 0.2 ppm total hydrocarbons in the water column, while the second 4-month experiment achieved about 0.1 ppm total hydrocarbons. These levels of fuel hydrocarbons are below the acute toxicity of hydrocarbons to most tested marine species. Populations were also studied over a one-year recovery period. An objective of the experiment was to see if some aggregate index or measure could be used to determine the health of the ecosystem. It was hypothesized that community diversity and primary production would be lower in the treated enclosures than in the controls.

The oil additions had a clear effect on the populations in the enclosures. Zooplank-ton and benthic macroorganisms were greatly reduced in abundance. Benthic populations remained depressed for at least a year after the treatments were stopped. Even though the additions of oil clearly had a major impact on the communities in the enclosures, neither of the original hypotheses turned out to be correct. Although the population levels were quite different in treated and control tanks, measures of the diversity of benthic organisms in treated and control enclosures were indistinguishable. With oil treatments, there were increases in phytoplankton abundance and primary production instead of the expected decrease. In hindsight, the reason for the increase in phytoplankton abundance was clear. The oil was more toxic to the organisms that may graze the phytoplankton than to the phytoplankton itself. With the population of grazers reduced, the abundance and production of phytoplankton increased.

This is a good example of the connections within an ecosystem, and the inherent difficulty of predicting how any component of an ecosystem will respond to stress.

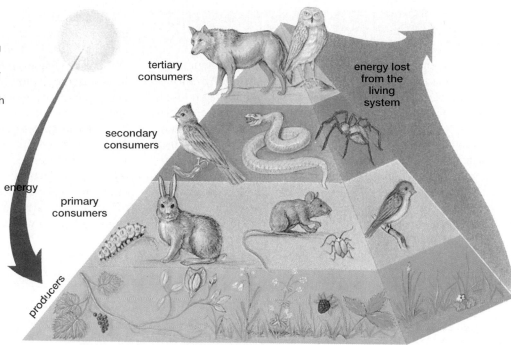

Figure 50.7

Pyramid of energy. At each succeeding trophic level in the pyramid, an appreciable portion of energy originally trapped by the producer is dissipated as heat. Accordingly, organisms in each trophic level pass on less energy than they received.

tertiary consumers

secondary consumers

energy

primary consumers

producers

energy lost from the living system

energy retained in the living system

Populations Form a Pyramid

The trophic structure of an ecosystem can be summarized in the form of an **ecological pyramid.** The base of the pyramid represents the producer trophic level, and the apex is the highest level of consumer called the top predator. The other consumer trophic levels are in between the producer and the top-predator level.

There are three possible kinds of pyramids. One is the *pyramid of numbers,* based on the number of organisms at each trophic level. A second is the *pyramid of biomass.* Biomass is the weight of living material at some particular time. To calculate the biomass for each trophic level, first an average weight for the organisms at each level is determined, and then the number of organisms at each level is estimated. Multiplying the average weight by the estimated number gives the approximate biomass for each trophic level. A third pyramid, the *pyramid of energy,* shows that there is a decreasing amount of energy available at each successive tropic level (fig. 50.7). Less energy is found in each succeeding trophic level for the following reasons:

1. Only a certain amount is captured and eaten by the next trophic level.
2. Some of the food that is eaten cannot be digested and exits the digestive tract as waste.
3. Only a portion of the food that is digested becomes part of the organisms's body. The rest is used as a source of energy.

In regard to the last point, we have to realize that a significant portion of food molecules is used as an energy source for ATP (adenosine triphosphate) buildup in mitochondria. This ATP is needed to build the proteins, carbohydrates, and lipids that compose the body. ATP is also needed for such activities as muscle contraction, nerve conduction, and active transport.

The unavoidable loss of usable energy between feeding levels explains why food chains are relatively short—at most, four or five links—and why mice (herbivores) are more common than weasels, foxes, or hawks (carnivores). The population sizes are appropriate to the amount of energy available at each trophic level, until finally there is an insufficient amount of energy to support another level. The largest populations in an ecological pyramid are the producer populations at the base of the pyramid, and the smallest populations are the top predators. As with all organisms, the population size of top predators is controlled by the amount of food energy available to them.

The energy considerations associated with ecological pyramids have implications for the human population. In general, only about 10% of the energy available at a particular trophic level is incorporated into the tissues of the next level. This being the case, it can be estimated that 100 kg of grain would, if consumed directly, result in 10 human kg, but if fed to cattle, it would result in only 1 human kg. Therefore, a larger human population can be sustained by eating grain than by eating grain-consuming animals.

> In a food web, each successive trophic level has less total energy content because when energy is transferred from one level to the next, some energy is lost to the environment as heat.

CHEMICALS CYCLE IN AN ECOSYSTEM

In contrast to energy, inorganic nutrients do cycle through large natural ecosystems. Because there is minimal input from the outside, the various chemical elements essential to life are used over and over. Since the pathways by which chemicals circulate through ecosystems involve both living (biosphere) and nonliving (geological) areas, they are known as **biogeochemical cycles.** For each element, the cycling process involves (1) a reservoir— that portion of the earth that acts as a storehouse for the element; (2) an exchange pool—that portion of the environment from which the producers take their nutrients; and (3) the biotic community— through which chemicals move along food chains to and from the exchange pool (fig. 50.8).

Carbon Cycles

The relationship between photosynthesis and aerobic cellular respiration should be kept in mind when discussing the carbon cycle. Recall that for simplicity's sake, this equation in the forward direction represents aerobic cellular respiration, and in the reverse direction it is used to represent photosynthesis.

$$\underset{\text{photosynthesis}}{\overset{\text{aerobic cellular respiration}}{C_6H_{12}O_6 + 6O_2 \rightleftharpoons 6CO_2 + 6H_2O}}$$

The equation tells us that aerobic cellular respiration releases carbon dioxide, the molecule needed for photosynthesis. However, photosynthesis releases oxygen, the molecule needed for aerobic respiration. Animals are dependent on green organisms, not only to produce organic food and energy but also to supply the biosphere with oxygen. However, since producers both photosynthesize and respire, they can function independently of the animal world.

In the carbon cycle, organisms in both terrestrial and aquatic ecosystems exchange carbon dioxide with the atmosphere (fig. 50.9). On land, plants take up carbon dioxide from the air, and through photosynthesis they incorporate carbon into food that is used by autotrophs and heterotrophs alike. When organisms respire, a portion of this carbon is returned to the atmosphere as carbon dioxide.

In aquatic ecosystems, the exchange of carbon dioxide with the atmosphere is indirect. Carbon dioxide from the air combines with water to produce bicarbonate (HCO_3^-), a source of carbon for algae that produce food for themselves and for heterotrophs. Similarly, when aquatic organisms respire, the carbon dioxide they give off becomes bicarbonate. The amount of bicarbonate in the water is in equilibrium with the amount of carbon dioxide in the air.

Reservoirs Hold Carbon

Living and dead organisms contain organic carbon and serve as one of the reservoirs for the carbon cycle. The world's biota, particularly trees, contain 800 billion tons of organic carbon, and an additional 1,000–3,000 billion metric tons are estimated to be held in the remains of plants and animals in the soil. Before decomposition can occur, some of these remains are subjected to physical processes that transform them into coal, oil, and natural gas. We call these materials the fossil fuels. Most of the fossil fuels were formed during the Carboniferous period, 286–360 million years ago, when an exceptionally large amount of organic matter was buried before decomposing. Another reservoir is the inorganic carbonate that accumulates in limestone and in calcium carbonate shells. The oceans abound in organisms, some microscopic, that are composed of calcium carbonate shells and that accumulate in ocean bottom sediments. Limestone is formed from these sediments by geological transformation.

Humans Alter the Balances

The activities of human beings have increased the amount of carbon dioxide and other gases in the atmosphere. Data from monitoring stations record an increase of 20 ppm (parts per

Figure 50.8

Components of a biochemical cycle. The reservoir stores the chemical, and the exchange pool makes it available to producers. The chemical then cycles through food chains. Decomposition returns the chemical to the exchange pool once again (if it has not already returned by another process).

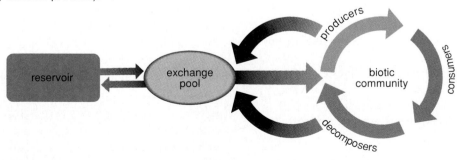

million) in carbon dioxide in only 22 years. (This is equivalent to 42 billion metric tons of carbon.) This buildup is primarily attributed to the burning of fossil fuels and wood. The oil well fires that were set during the Gulf War added carbon dioxide to the atmosphere, but the ongoing burning of tropical rain forests is of even more concern. When we do away with forests, we reduce a reservoir that takes up excess carbon dioxide. At this time, the oceans are believed to be taking up most of the excess carbon dioxide; the burning of fossil fuels in the last 22 years has probably released 78 billion metric tons of carbon, yet the atmosphere registers an increase of "only" 42 billion metric tons.

There is much concern that an increased amount of carbon dioxide (and other gases) in the atmosphere is causing a global warming. These gases allow the sun's rays to pass through, but they absorb and reradiate heat back to the earth, a phenomenon called the *greenhouse effect*.

In the carbon cycle, photosynthesis removes but respiration returns carbon dioxide to the atmosphere. Forests and dead organisms are carbon reservoirs, as is the ocean.

Figure 50.9

Carbon cycle. Photosynthesizers take up carbon dioxide (CO_2) from the air or bicarbonate ion (HCO_3^-) from the water. They and all other organisms return carbon dioxide to the environment. The carbon dioxide level is also increased when volcanoes erupt and fossil fuels are burned. Presently, the oceans are a primary reservoir for carbon in the form of limestone and calcium carbonate shells.

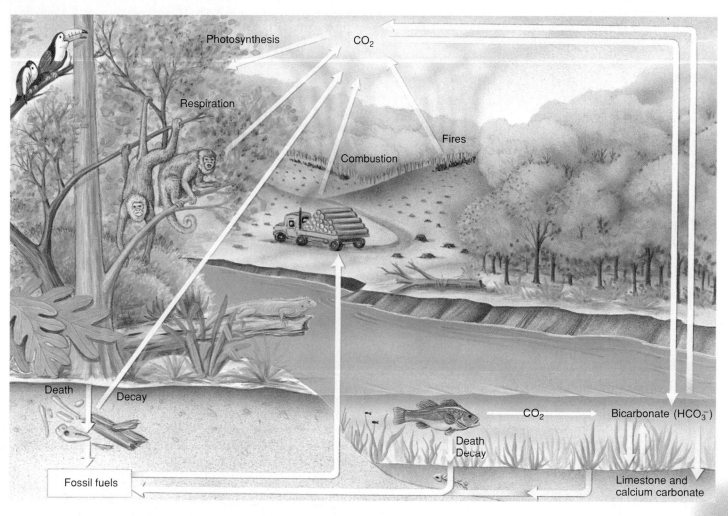

Figure 50.10

Nitrogen cycle. Several types of bacteria are at work: nitrogen-fixing bacteria reduce nitrogen gas (N_2); nitrifying bacteria, which include both nitrite-producing and nitrate-producing bacteria, convert ammonium (NH_4^+) to nitrate; and denitrifying bacteria convert nitrate back to nitrogen gas. Humans contribute to the cycle by using nitrogen gas to produce nitrate for fertilizers.

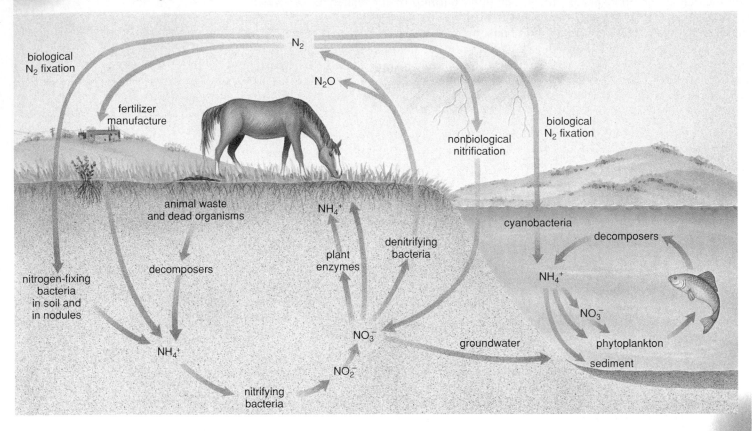

Nitrogen Cycles

Nitrogen is an abundant element in the atmosphere. Nitrogen (N_2) makes up about 78% of the atmosphere by volume, yet nitrogen deficiency commonly limits plant growth. Plants cannot incorporate nitrogen into organic compounds and therefore depend on various types of bacteria to make nitrogen available to them (fig. 50.10).

Nitrogen Gas Becomes Fixed

Nitrogen fixation occurs when nitrogen (N_2) is reduced and added to organic compounds. Some cyanobacteria in aquatic ecosystems and some free-living bacteria in soil are able to reduce nitrogen gas to ammonium (NH_4^+). Other nitrogen-fixing bacteria live in nodules on the roots of legumes (fig. 50.10). They make reduced nitrogen and organic compounds available to the host plant.

Plants take up both NH_4^+ and nitrate (NO_3^-) from the soil. After plants take up NO_3^- from the soil, it is enzymatically reduced to NH_4^+ and is used to produce amino acids and nucleic acids.

Nitrogen Gas Becomes Nitrates

Nitrification is the production of nitrates. Nitrogen gas (N_2) is converted to nitrate (NO_3^-) in the atmosphere when cosmic radiation, meteor trails, and lightning provide the high energy needed

for nitrogen to react with oxygen. Also, humans make a most significant contribution to the nitrogen cycle when they convert nitrogen gas to ammonium and urea for use in fertilizers.

Ammonium (NH_4^+) in the soil is converted to nitrate by certain soil bacteria in a two-step process. First, nitrite-producing bacteria convert ammonium to nitrite (NO_2^-), and then nitrate-producing bacteria convert nitrite to nitrate. These two groups of bacteria are called the nitrifying bacteria. Notice the subcycle in the nitrogen cycle that involves only ammonium, nitrites, and nitrates. This subcycle does not depend on the presence of nitrogen gas at all (fig. 50.10).

Denitrification is the conversion of nitrate to nitrous oxide and nitrogen gas. There are denitrifying bacteria in both aquatic and terrestrial ecosystems. Denitrification counterbalances nitrogen fixation, but not completely. More nitrogen fixation occurs, especially due to fertilizer production.

In the nitrogen cycle: nitrogen-fixing bacteria (in nodules and in the soil) reduce nitrogen gas; nitrifying bacteria convert ammonium to nitrate; denitrifying bacteria convert nitrate back to nitrogen gas.

Figure 50.11

The phosphorus cycle. Weathering of rocks releases phosphate which enters producers and then cycles through organisms. Run-off from the land takes phosphate into the oceans where it is incorporated into sediments that are sometimes uplifted by geological upheavals. When humans mine phosphate for inclusion in fertilizers, they increase the amount of available phosphate ions in ecosystems.

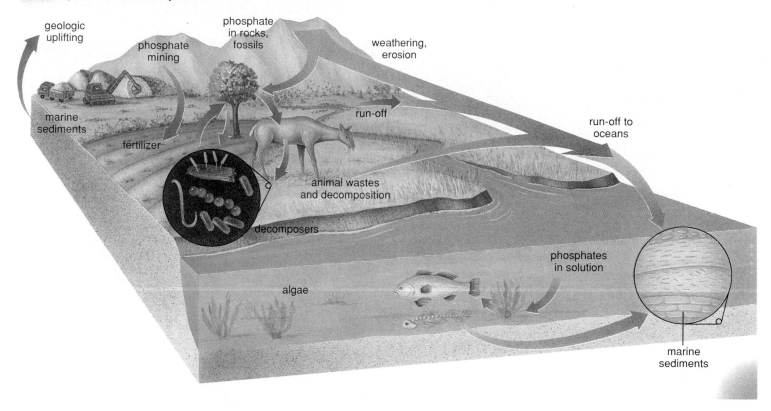

PHOSPHORUS CYCLES

On land, the weathering of rocks makes phosphate ions ($PO_4^=$ and $HPO_4^=$) available to plants which take it up from the soil (fig. 50.11). Some of this phosphate runs off into aquatic ecosystems where algae take phosphate up from the water before it becomes trapped in sediments. Phosphate in sediments only becomes available when a geological upheaval exposes sedimentary rocks to weathering once more. Phosphorus does not enter the atmosphere and, therefore, the phosphorus cycle is called a sedimentary cycle.

The phosphate taken up by producers is incorporated into a variety of molecules, including phospholipids and ATP or the nucleotides that become a part of DNA and RNA. Animals eat producers and incorporate some of the phosphate into teeth, bones, and shells that do not decompose for very long periods. Death and decay of all organisms and also decomposition of animals wastes does, however, makes phosphate ions available to producers once again. Because available phosphate is generally taken up very quickly, it is usually a limiting nutrient in most ecosystems.

Humans Influence the Phosphorus Cycle

Human beings boost the supply of phosphate by mining phosphate ores for fertilizer production, animal feed supplements, and detergents. One well known region where phosphorus is strip-mined (so-called because earth is removed in strips) lies east of Tampa, Florida. Here fossilized remains of marine animals were laid down some 10 to 15 million years ago. Phosphate ore is slightly radioactive and, therefore, mining phosphate poses a health threat to all organisms even those that do the mining! Also, only a portion of this land has been properly reclaimed and the rest is subject to severe soil erosion.

Run-off of animals wastes from livestock feedlots and commercial fertilizers from cropland as well as discharge of untreated and treated municipal sewage can all add excess phosphate to near-by waters. Then, an excess growth of algae, called an algal bloom, may occur.

In the phosphorus cycle, weathering makes phosphate available to producers followed by consumers. Death and decay of all organisms makes phosphate available to consumers once again. Phosphate trapped in sedimentary rock only becomes available following a geological upheaval.

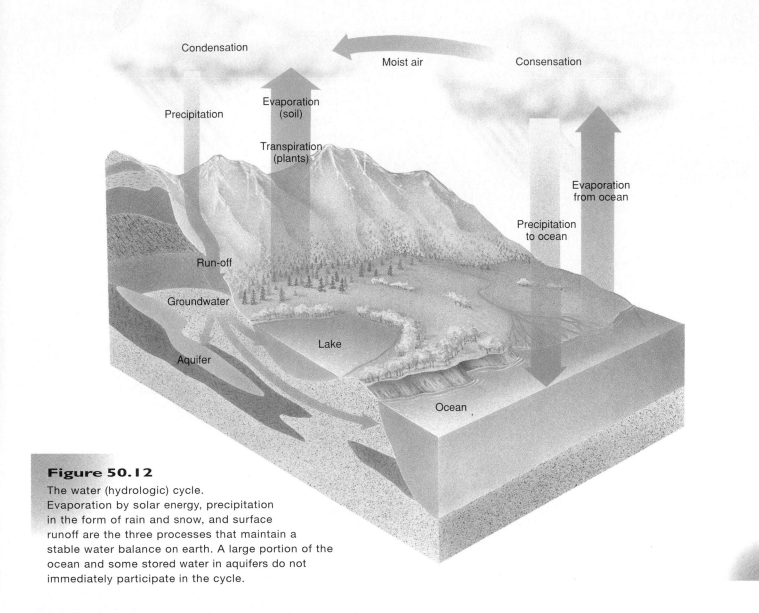

Figure 50.12
The water (hydrologic) cycle.
Evaporation by solar energy, precipitation
in the form of rain and snow, and surface
runoff are the three processes that maintain a
stable water balance on earth. A large portion of the
ocean and some stored water in aquifers do not
immediately participate in the cycle.

WATER CYCLES

Water cycles through the biosphere in the manner described in figure 50.12. Freshwater is distilled from salt water. The sun's rays cause fresh water to evaporate from seawater and the salts are left behind. Vaporized fresh water rises into the atmosphere, cools, and falls as rain over the oceans and the land. A lesser amount of water also evaporates from bodies of fresh water. Since land lies above sea level, gravity eventually returns all fresh water to the sea, but in the meantime, it is contained within standing waters (lakes and ponds), flowing water (streams and rivers), and groundwater.

When rain falls, some of the water sinks or percolates into the ground and saturates the earth to a certain level. The top of the saturation zone is called the groundwater table, or simply, the water table. Sometimes ground water is also located in a porous layer, called an aquifer, that lies between two sloping layers of impervious rock. Wells can be used to remove some of this water.

Freshwater, which makes up only about 3% of the world's supply of water, is called a renewable resource because a new supply is always being produced. Even so we can run out of fresh water when the available supply is not adequate and/or is polluted so that it is not usable. Also, groundwater mining occurs when water is removed from aquifers for the purpose of irrigation or for household use.

In the water (hydrologic) cycle, fresh water evaporates from the bodies of water and falls to the earth. Water that falls on land enters the ground or surface waters or aquifers. Water remains in aquifers for some time; otherwise it soon returns to the ocean.

HUMAN FOOD CHAIN VERSUS NATURAL FOOD WEB

Mature natural webs tend to be stable. The sizes of the many and varied populations are held in check by the interactions between species, such as competition and predation. The amount of energy that enters and the amount of matter that cycles is appropriate to support these populations. Pollution, defined as any undesirable change in the environment that can be harmful to humans and other life, does not normally occur (fig. 50.13).

Today, humans largely depend on a food chain of their own making. Domesticated plants or animals are kept in highly unnatural conditions, with a minimum of species diversity and a high degree of energy input in the form of human care and fossil fuel. Adding to the lack of diversity is the tendency of farmers to plant the same hybrid variety of wheat or corn year after year because it produces the highest yield. This so-called monoculture farming contributes to instability, since any one environmental factor, either biological or physical, can cause a crop failure in all regions.

The size of the populations in the human food chain is not constant. The human population has tripled since 1900, and the overall size of the population continues to increase dramatically. Fertilizers, pesticides, water, and fossil fuels are used as a way to ever increase the food supply.

Figure 50.13
Natural food web versus human food chain.

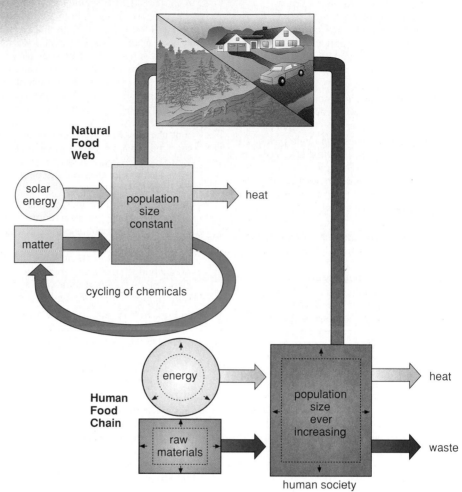

The human food chain is largely noncyclic (fig. 50.13). There is a large input of fossil fuel energy (in addition to solar energy) and other substances that do not cycle back to the producers. Unfortunately, this means there is also a large output of wastes. Excess fertilizers and pesticides from farmlands and lawns are often transported by water and wind to aquatic ecosystems. Animal and human sewage are also added to natural waters, where the bacteria of decay are often unable immediately to break down the quantity that is disposed. Therefore, it is customary for each community to pretreat sewage in sewage treatment plants before the effluent is added to nearby bodies of water.

The human food chain is in reality dependent on natural ecosystems since they lend stability to the biosphere and absorb wastes such as excess fertilizers, pesticides, and fuel breakdown products. But due to the increase in size of human populations, the natural communities are often overwhelmed. It is then that humans recognize that something is amiss and realize that pollutants have harmed the environment.

It is best to begin finding ways in which humans can "work with nature rather than against nature." If we continue practices that create environmental problems, we must ask ourselves if we are willing to bear the cost. As ecologists are fond of saying, "There is no free lunch." By this they mean that for every artificial benefit, there is a price. For example, if we kill off coyotes because they prey on chickens, we then have to realize that the mouse population (mice are a common food for coyotes) will probably increase. In an ecosystem, as we have seen, "everything is connected to everything else."

Summary

1. Ecosystems contain both abiotic (physical) and biotic (living) components. Biotic components are either producers or consumers. Consumers may be herbivores, carnivores, omnivores, or decomposers.

2. Energy flow and chemical cycling are two phenomena observed in ecosystems.

3. Climax communities arise by a process called succession. The first stage of succession, called the pioneer community, produces new growth but tends to be unstable. The final stage, called the climax community, produces little new growth but tends to be stable.

4. Food chains are paths of energy flow through an ecosystem. Grazing food chains always begin with a producer population, which is capable of producing organic food, followed by a series of consumer populations. Detritus food chains begin with dead organic matter, which is consumed by decomposers, including bacteria and fungi as well as various soil animals. Eventually, all members of food chains die and decompose. The very same chemicals are then made available to the producer population again, but the energy has been dissipated as heat. Therefore, energy does not cycle through an ecosystem.

5. If we consider the various food chains together, we realize that they form an intricate food web in which there are various trophic (feeding) levels. All producers are on the first level, all primary consumers are on the second level, and so forth. To illustrate that energy does not cycle, it is customary to arrange the various trophic levels to form an energy pyramid. Then we see that each level contains less energy than the previous level. It is estimated that only 10% of the available energy is actually incorporated into the body tissues of the next level.

6. Chemical cycling through an ecosystem involves not only the biotic components of an ecosystem but also the physical environment. Each cycle involves a reservoir where the element is stored, an exchange pool from which the populations take and return nutrients, and the populations themselves.

7. In the carbon cycle, the reservoir is organic matter, calcium carbonate shells, and limestone. The exchange pool is the atmosphere: photosynthesis removes carbon dioxide, and respiration and combustion add carbon dioxide.

8. In the nitrogen cycle, the reservoir is the atmosphere, but nitrogen (N_2) gas must be converted to nitrate (NO_3^-) for use by producers. Nitrogen-fixing bacteria, particularly in root nodules, make organic nitrogen available to plants.

Other bacteria active in the nitrogen cycle are the nitrifying bacteria, which convert ammonium to nitrate, and the denitrifying bacteria, which reconvert nitrate to N_2.

9. In mature natural food webs, usually a constant amount of energy is required and additional material inputs are minimal because matter cycles. In contrast, the human food chain tends to be unstable. The human food chain is quite short, usually containing at most only three links. Adding to this lack of diversity is the tendency of farmers to use only certain high-yield varieties of agricultural plants, which require such supplements as fertilizers, pesticides, and water. The human food chain is noncyclic, and worse yet, more fossil fuel energy and material supplements are needed each year to produce more food for the human population, which continues to increase in size. Pollution is a side effect; it would be beneficial for us to find ways to fulfill our needs in a more natural way.

Writing Across the Curriculum

In order to practice writing skills, students should write out the answers to any or all of the study questions and the critical thinking questions. The study questions are sequenced in the same order as the text. Answers to the objective questions, and suggested answers to the critical thinking questions, are in appendix D.

Study Questions

1. Name four different types of consumers found in natural ecosystems.   860

2. Describe the stages of succession by which bare land and an abandoned field can become a forest.   860–61

3. What properties distinguish a pioneer community from a climax community and account for the lower productivity of the pioneer community?   861

4. Give an example of a grazing and a detritus food chain for a terrestrial and for an aquatic ecosystem.   863

5. Why is the term *trophic level* more appropriately applied to a food web rather than a food chain?   863

6. How would other population sizes be affected if the tufted titmouse population were to be decimated in figure 50.5? if a pesticide were used to kill the mosquito larvae in figure 50.6?   862

7. What are the three possible kinds of pyramids? Draw a pyramid of energy and explain why such a pyramid can be used to verify that energy does not cycle.   865

8. Explain what is meant by a *reservoir* and *exchange pool* for a biochemical cycle.   866

9. Draw a diagram to illustrate the carbon, nitrogen, phosphorus and water biochemical cycles and include in your diagram the manner in which humans disturb the equilibrium of these cycles.   866–70

10. Compare and contrast the basic characteristics of a natural food web to the characteristics of the human food chain.   871

Objective Questions

1. Compare this food chain: algae → water fleas → catfish → green herons to this food chain: trees → tent caterpillars → red-eyed vireos → hawks. Both water fleas and tent caterpillars are
   a. carnivores.
   b. primary consumers.
   c. detritus feeders.
   d. Both a and b are correct.

2. Consider the components of a food chain: producers → herbivores → carnivores → top carnivores. Which level contains the most energy?
   a. producers
   b. herbivores
   c. carnivores
   d. top carnivores

3. Consider the components of a food chain: producers → herbivores → carnivores → top carnivores. Eventually what happens to all the energy passed from one element to the next?
   a. It recycles back to the producers.
   b. It results in a much larger decomposer population.
   c. It is dissipated into the environment.
   d. It is recaptured by another food chain.

4. Which of the following contribute to the carbon cycle?
   a. respiration
   b. photosynthesis
   c. fossil fuel combustion
   d. All of these are correct.

5. A natural food web
   a. contains only grazing food chains.
   b. contains several trophic levels.
   c. is usually unstable.
   d. All of these are correct.

6. How do plants contribute to the carbon cycle?
   a. When they respire, they release carbon dioxide (CO_2) into the atmosphere.
   b. When they photosynthesize, they consume CO_2 from the atmosphere.
   c. They do not contribute to the carbon cycle.
   d. Both a and b are correct.

7. How do nitrogen-fixing bacteria contribute to the nitrogen cycle?
   a. They return nitrogen (N_2) to the atmosphere.
   b. They change ammonium to nitrate.
   c. They change N_2 to ammonium.
   d. They withdraw nitrate from the soil.

8. In what way are decomposers like producers?
   a. Either one may be the first member of a grazing food chain.
   b. Both produce oxygen for other forms of life.
   c. Both require a source of nutrient molecules and energy.
   d. Both supply organic food for the biosphere.

9. How is a primary consumer like a secondary consumer?
   a. Both pass on less energy to the next trophic level than they received.
   b. Both pass on the same amount of energy to the next trophic level.
   c. Both tend to be herbivores that produce nutrients for plants.
   d. Both are able to convert organic compounds to ATP without the loss of energy.

10. Which statement is true concerning this food chain: grass → rabbits → snakes → hawks?
    a. Each predator population has a greater biomass than its prey population.
    b. Each prey population has a greater biomass than its predator population.
    c. Each population is omnivorous.
    d. Both a and c are correct.

11. Add these trophic levels to this diagram representing a pyramid of energy: algae, large fishes, humans, small fishes, zooplankton:

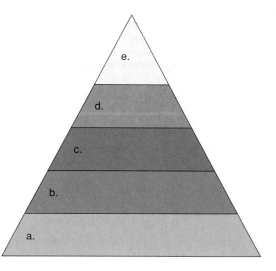

Concepts and Critical Thinking

1. *Chemicals cycle through an ecosystem.*
   How does chemical cycling involve both abiotic and biotic components of an ecosystem?

2. *Energy flows through an ecosystem.*
   Relate energy flow through an ecosystem to the laws of thermodynamics.

3. *Human activities can lead to more pollution.*
   What do ecologists mean by the expression, "There is no free lunch"?

biogeochemical cycle (by-oh-jee-oh-KEM-i-kal) The circulating pathway of an element through the biotic and abiotic components of an ecosystem.   866

carnivore A secondary consumer in a food chain that eats other animals. [L. *carn,* flesh, and *vor,* eat]   860

consumer An organism that feeds on another organism in a food chain; primary consumers eat plants, and secondary consumers eat animals.   860

decomposer An organism, usually a bacterial or fungal species, that breaks down large organic molecules into elements that can be recycled in the environment.   860

detritus (dih-TRYT-us) Partially decomposed remains of plants and animals found in soil and on the beds of bodies of water. [L. *detrit,* wear off]   860

ecological pyramid Pictorial graph representing biomass, organism number, or energy content of each trophic level in a food web—from the producer to the final consumer populations.   865

ecology The study of the interaction of organisms with their living and physical environment. [Gk. *eco,* house, and *logy,* study of]   861

ecosystem A biological community together with the associated abiotic environment. [Gk. *eco,* house, and *sys,* together]   860

food chain A succession of organisms in an ecosystem that are linked by an energy flow and by the order of who eats whom.   863

food web A complex pattern of interlocking and crisscrossing food chains.   863

herbivore A primary consumer in a food chain; a plant eater. [L. *herb,* grass, and *vor,* eat]   860

nitrogen fixation The process whereby free atmospheric nitrogen is converted into compounds, such as ammonium and nitrates, usually by soil bacteria.   868

omnivore An organism in a food chain that feeds on both plants and animals. [L. *omni,* all, and *vor,* eat]   860

producer An organism at the start of a food chain that makes its own food (e.g., green plants on land and algae in water).   860

succession An orderly sequence of community replacement—one following the other—that leads eventually to a climax community.   860

trophic level Feeding level of one or more populations in a food web. [Gk. *troph,* feeder]   863

THE BIOSPHERE

Learning Objectives

Aquatic Communities

- Distinguish between freshwater communities and marine communities.   876
- List and describe the life zones of a lake and the types of organisms that reside in these zones.   876
- Distinguish between coastal communities and the oceans.   876–79
- Explain why coastal communities are more productive than communities in the open ocean.   876–79
- Describe the life zones of the ocean and the types of organisms that reside in these zones.   878–79

Terrestrial Biomes

- Describe the characteristics of the treeless biomes: deserts, tundra, grasslands, and scrubland.   882–85
- Describe the characteristics of forests: taiga, temperate forests, and tropical forests.   885–87
- Relate the location of the various terrestrial biomes to latitude and altitude.   887
- Contrast and explain the productivity of the various aquatic communities and terrestrial biomes.   888

The biosphere contains terrestrial, aquatic, and aerial habitats at varying altitudes.

he earth is enveloped by the **biosphere** [Gk. *bio,* life, and *spher,* ball]—a thin realm composed of water, land, and air—where organisms are found. The biosphere contains communities of populations that interact with each other and the physical environment. The largest communities on land are called **biomes.** There is no equivalent term for large aquatic communities, which is unfortunate because both the aquatic environment and the land environment contain large communities that have unique, defined characteristics.

AQUATIC COMMUNITIES

Aquatic communities can be divided into two types: freshwater (inland) communities and marine (saltwater or oceanic) communities.

Freshwater Communities

Freshwater communities are found in lakes, ponds, rivers, and streams. Here, we consider only the composition of a *lake* whose mixture of organisms is similar to that of the other freshwater communities.

Lakes

The body of a lake has three life zones: the littoral zone, which is closest to the shore, the limnetic zone, which is the sunlit main body of the lake; and the profundal zone, which is the deep part where light does not penetrate (fig. 51.1).

Aquatic plants are rooted in the shallow littoral zone of a lake, and various microscopic organisms cling to these plants and to rocks. Microscopic, suspended organisms known as **plankton** [Gk. *plankt,* wandering] are present in both the littoral and limnetic zones. *Phytoplankton* [Gk. *phyt,* plant, and *plankt,* wandering] are photosynthesizing algae, and *zooplankton* [Gk. *zoo,* animal] are protozoa and tiny crustacea. Small fishes feed on plankton and also serve as food for large fishes. In the profundal zone, there are mollusks, crustacea, and worms that feed on debris that falls from above.

A few insect larvae are in the limnetic zone but they are far more prominent in both the littoral and profundal zones. Midge larvae and ghost worms are common members of the *benthos,* bottom-dwelling organisms living in the benthic zone at the soil-water interface.

Marine Communities

Marine (saltwater) communities begin along the shoreline—coastal communities. Later we will discuss the oceans.

Coastal Communities

An **estuary** forms where a large river flows into the ocean (fig. 51.2). The river brings fresh water into the estuary. Because of

Figure 51.1

Life zones of a lake. Rooted plants and clinging organisms live in the littoral zone. Phytoplankton, zooplankton, and fishes are in the sunlit limnetic zone. Bottom-dwelling organisms, like crayfishes and mollusks, are in the profundal zone.

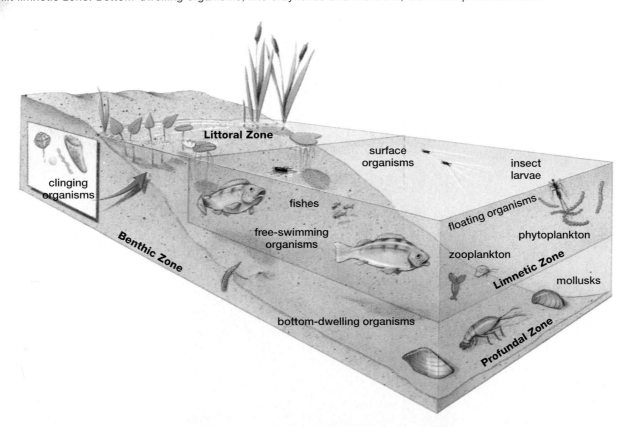

Figure 51.2

Estuary structure and function. Since an estuary is located where a river flows into the ocean, it receives nutrients from land and also from the sea by way of the tides. Decaying grasses also provide nutrients. Estuaries serve as a nursery for the spawning and rearing of the young for many species of fishes, mollusks, shrimp, and other crustacea.

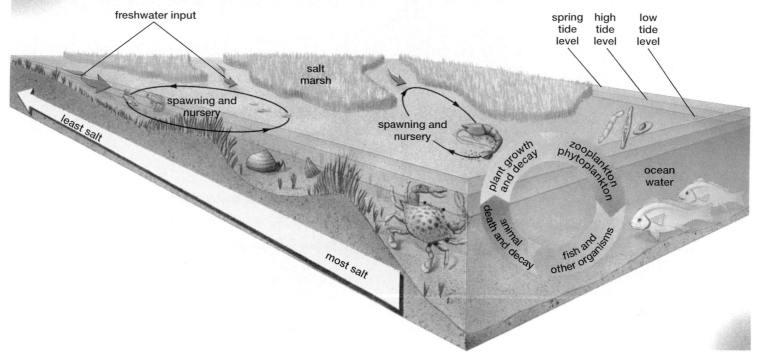

the tides, the sea brings salt water into this same area. Therefore, an estuary is characterized by a mixture of fresh water and salt water; this is called brackish water. Most estuaries are rather shallow with good sunlight penetration. The temperature of estuarine waters is generally higher than that of the surrounding marine or freshwater environments. Further, an estuary acts as a nutrient trap; the tides bring nutrients from the sea, and at the same time, they prevent the seaward escape of nutrients brought by the river.

Only a few types of small fishes live permanently in an estuary, but many types develop there; therefore, both larval and immature fishes are present in large numbers. It has been estimated that well over half of all marine fishes develop in the protective environment of an estuary; this is why estuaries are called the nurseries of the sea. Shrimps and mollusks, too, use the estuary as a nursery.

Coral reefs are found in warm tropical seas, where the water is still shallow (fig. 51.3). Their chief constituents are stony corals (phylum Cnidaria), which have a calcium carbonate exoskeleton, and carbonaceous red and green algae. Most of the solid part of a coral reef is composed of the skeletons of dead coral; the outer layer contains living organisms.

A reef is densely populated with diverse animal life. There are many types of small fishes, all of which are beautifully colored. In addition, the numerous crevices and caves provide shelter for filter feeders (sponges, sea squirts, fan worms) and for scavengers (crabs and sea urchins). The barracuda and the moray eel prey on these animals.

Figure 51.3

Coral reef. A coral reef is a unique community of marine organisms. The abundance of life is the result of the optimal environmental conditions of tropical seas.

Figure 51.4

Marine environment. Organisms reside in the pelagic division (blue), where waters are divided as indicated. Organisms also reside in the benthic division (brown), with surfaces divided and in the zones indicated.

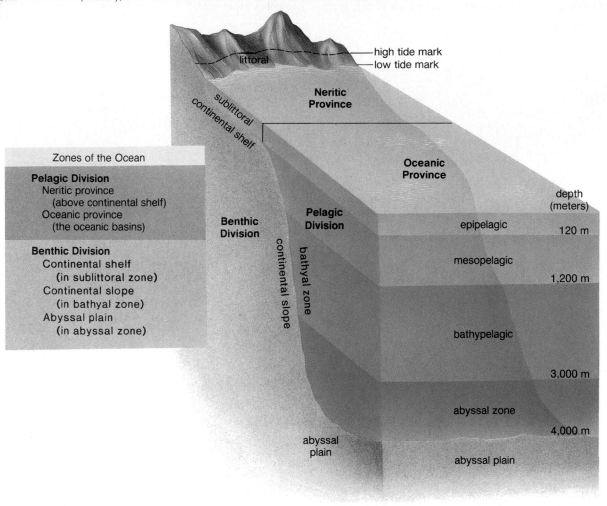

Oceans

The oceans cover approximately three-quarters of our planet. The geographic areas and zones of an ocean are shown in figure 51.4. It is customary to place the organisms of the oceans into either the **pelagic division** [Gk. *pelagi,* the sea] (open waters) or the **benthic division** [Gk. *bentho,* depths of the sea] (ocean floor).

Pelagic Division

The pelagic division includes the neritic province and the oceanic province. There is a greater concentration of organisms in the neritic province than in the oceanic province because sunlight penetrates the waters of the former, and this is where you find the most nutrients. Phytoplankton is food not only for zooplankton but also for small fishes. These small fishes in turn are food for commercially valuable fishes—herring, cod, and flounder.

In the oceanic province, the epipelagic zone does not have a high concentration of phytoplankton because it lacks nutrients (fig. 51.4). These photosynthesizers, however, still support a large assembly of zooplankton because the oceans are so large. The zooplankton are food for herrings and bluefishes, which in turn are eaten by larger mackerels, tunas, and sharks. Flying fishes, which glide above the surface, are preyed upon by dolphins (not to be confused with mammalian porpoises, which also are present). Whales are other mammals found in the epipelagic zone. Baleen whales strain krill (small crustacea) from the water, and the toothed sperm whales feed primarily on the common squid.

Animals in the mesopelagic zone are carnivores, are adapted to the absence of light, and tend to be translucent, red colored, or even luminescent. There are luminescent shrimps, squids, and fishes, such as lantern and hatchet fishes.

The bathypelagic zone is in complete darkness except for an occasional flash of bioluminescent light. Carnivores and scavengers are found in this zone. Strange-looking fishes with distensible mouths and abdomens and small, tubular eyes feed on infrequent prey.

Figure 51.5

Pelagic division. Organisms of the epipelagic, mesopelagic, and bathypelagic zones are shown. The abyssal zone is a part of the benthic division.

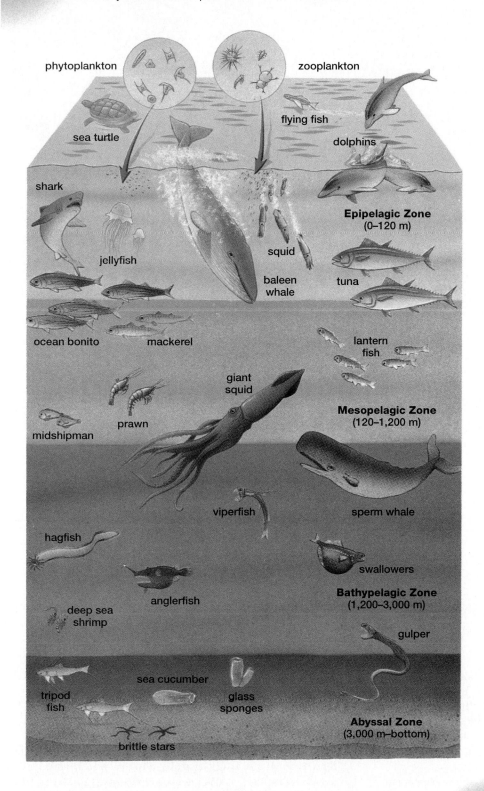

phytoplankton

zooplankton

sea turtle

flying fish

dolphins

shark

Epipelagic Zone
(0–120 m)

jellyfish

squid

baleen
whale

tuna

ocean bonito

mackerel

lantern
fish

giant
squid

prawn

Mesopelagic Zone
(120–1,200 m)

midshipman

viperfish

sperm whale

hagfish

swallowers

anglerfish

Bathypelagic Zone
(1,200–3,000 m)

deep sea
shrimp

gulper

sea cucumber

tripod
fish

glass
sponges

Abyssal Zone
(3,000 m–bottom)

brittle stars

Benthic Division

The benthic division includes organisms that live on the continental shelf, the continental slope, and the abyssal plain (figs. 51.4, 51.5). These are the organisms of the sublittoral, bathyal, and abyssal zones.

Seaweed grows in the sublittoral zone, and it can be found in batches on outcroppings as the water gets deeper. Nearly all benthic organisms, however, are dependent on the slow rain of plankton and detritus from the sunlit waters above. There is more diversity of life in the sublittoral and bathyal zones than in the abyssal zone. In these first two zones, clams, worms, and sea urchins are preyed upon by starfishes, lobsters, crabs, and brittle stars.

The abyssal zone is inhabited by animals that live just above and in the dark abyssal plain. It once was thought that few animals exist in this zone because of the intense pressure and the extreme cold. Yet many invertebrates live here by feeding on debris floating down from the mesopelagic zone. Sea lilies rise above the seafloor; sea cucumbers and sea urchins crawl around on the sea bottom; and tubeworms burrow in the mud.

The flat abyssal plain is interrupted by enormous underwater mountain chains called oceanic ridges. Along the axes of the ridges, crustal plates spread apart and molten magma rises to fill the gap. At specific sites of these tectonic spreading zones, seawater percolates through cracks and is heated to about 350° C, causing sulfate to react with water and form hydrogen sulfide (H_2S). The water temperature–hydrogen sulfide combination has been found to support communities that contain huge tubeworms and clams. Chemosynthetic bacteria that obtain energy from oxidizing hydrogen sulfide live within these organisms.

The neritic province and the epipelagic zone of the oceanic province receive sunlight and contain the organisms with which we are most familiar. The organisms of the benthic division are dependent upon debris that floats down from above.

Figure 51.6

Biomes. **a.** Temperature and rainfall determine the nature of the biome to a large extent. For example, rain forests are found in tropical regions where temperatures are warm and rainfall is plentiful year-round. Deserts, on the other hand, are found in tropical and temperate regions where rainfall is minimal. **b.** A map showing the major biomes of the world as they would be distributed if undisturbed by humans.

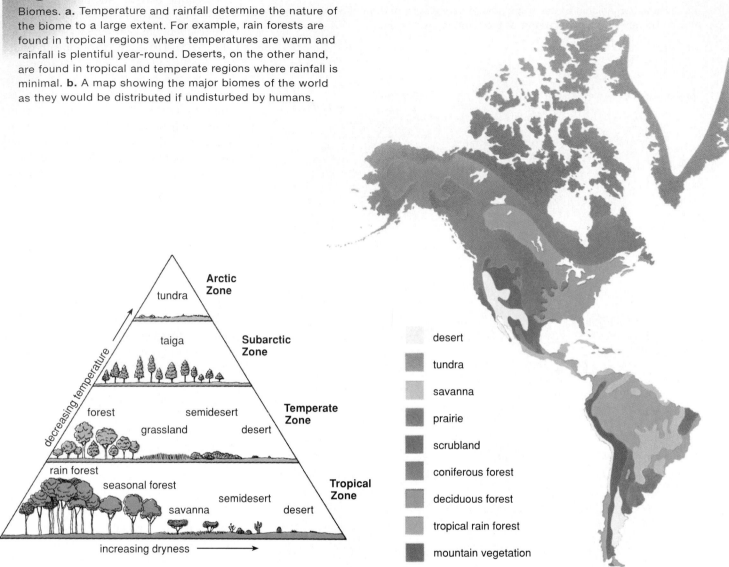

TERRESTRIAL BIOMES

The earth's surface can be divided into various zones, each of which contains one or more biomes (fig. 51.6a). For example, whereas the subarctic zone includes only the taiga, a coniferous forest, the tropical zone includes forests, grasslands, and deserts.

Climate, which can be described largely in terms of temperature and rainfall, determines the geographic location of a biome. The tundra is found where temperatures are the coldest, and tropical rain forests are found near the equator where there is plenty of sunshine and rainfall throughout the year.

The distribution of heat and rainfall are not solely dependent on latitude. The sun's rays fall perpendicular to the equator, but solar energy also creates air and ocean currents, which distribute this heat. Gigantic ocean currents bring the equator's warmth to certain continents while cooling others. In addition, solar energy drives the water cycle. Fresh water evaporates from seawater and then rises into the atmosphere. After cooling, it falls as rain over the oceans and the land. Rain is not distributed evenly; it is heaviest along the equator and tapers off toward the poles. Other features—like mountain ranges and ocean and wind currents—determine how much rain falls on the various parts of a continent.

> Temperature and rainfall influences climate and, therefore, where the different biomes are found on the surface of the earth.

Figure 51.6*b* shows the location of the various biomes more specifically. Deserts, tundra, grasslands (both the prairies of the temperate zone and the savanna of the tropical zone), and scrubland all lack trees. They are treeless because they do not receive enough rainfall to support the growth of forests.

Other biomes receive water in good supply and do have trees. The forests we will be discussing are of three types: the taiga, which is found in the subarctic zone, and the temperate and tropical forests, which are found in the zones of those names. The taiga receives the least amount of rainfall and is composed primarily of evergreen trees whose needle-like leaves conserve water. Within a temperate forest the broad-leafed trees lose their leaves when the weather turns cold but in a tropical rain forest the temperature and rainfall are suitable for broad-leafed trees to retain their leaves throughout the year.

For the purpose of discussion, biomes are divided into those that have trees and those that do not.

Figure 51.7

Desert vegetation. These plants are adapted to retain water so that they can live in areas with little rain.

Figure 51.8

Tundra biome in the autumn. Caribou bull, *Rangifer,* grazes on the low-lying vegetation.

Treeless Biomes

The treeless biomes include deserts, tundra, grasslands, and scrubland. These biomes contain few, if any, trees.

Deserts

Deserts are found in regions where annual rainfall is less than 25 cm (fig. 51.7). The days are hot because the lack of cloud cover allows the sun's rays to penetrate easily, but the nights are cold because the heat escapes easily into the atmosphere.

The Sahara in Africa and a few other deserts have little or no vegetation, but most have a variety of plants. The best-known desert perennials in North America are the succulent, leafless cacti, which have stems that store water and carry on photosynthesis. Also common are nonsucculent shrubs, such as the many-branched sagebrush with silvery gray leaves and the spiny-branched ocotillo that produces leaves during wet periods and sheds them during dry periods.

Some animals are adapted to the desert environment. A desert has numerous insects, which pass through the stages of development from pupa to pupa when there is rain. Reptiles, especially lizards and snakes, are perhaps the most characteristic group of vertebrates found in deserts, but running birds (e.g., the roadrunner) and rodents (e.g., the kangaroo rat) are also well known. Larger mammals, like the coyote, prey on the rodents, as do the hawks.

Tundra

The arctic **tundra** biome encircles the earth just south of ice-covered polar seas in the Northern Hemisphere (fig. 51.8). (A similar community, called the alpine tundra, occurs above the timberline on mountain ranges.) The arctic tundra is cold and dark much of the year. Because rainfall amounts to only about 20 cm a year, the tundra could possibly be considered a desert, but melting snow makes water plentiful in the summer, especially because so little evaporates. Only the topmost layer of earth thaws; the *permafrost* beneath this layer is always frozen.

Trees are not found in the tundra because the growing season is too short, their roots cannot penetrate the permafrost, and they cannot become anchored in the boggy soil of summer. In the summer, the ground is just about covered with sedges and short-grasses, but there also are numerous patches of lichens and mosses. Dwarf woody shrubs flower and seed quickly while there is plentiful sun for photosynthesis.

A few animals live in the tundra year-round. For example, the ratlike lemming stays beneath the snow; the ptarmigan, a grouse, burrows in the snow during storms; and the musk-ox conserves heat because of its thick coat and short, squat body. In the summer, the tundra is alive with numerous insects and birds, particularly shorebirds and waterfowl that migrate inland. Caribou and reindeer also come, along with the wolves that prey upon them. Polar bears are common near the coast.

Eloy Rodriguez and the Search for Medicinal Plants

Eloy Rodriguez (fig. 51A), a plant biologist at the University of California-Irvine, has spent twenty years traveling throughout the deserts and jungles of Africa, China, India, and the Americas to learn about medicinal plants used by native healers. A leader of twentieth-century American ethobotany (the study of plants used traditionally by indigenous people for food, medicine, shelter, and other purposes), Rodriguez is one of the first modern scientists to extract medicinal compounds from jojoba and candelilla in the laboratory. Yet he reminds his students that these two plants were probably used by ancient desert dwellers as well.

Plants that grow only in tropical rain forests are currently the direct or indirect source of more than 25% of modern prescription drugs, yet only 1% of our tropical forests has been investigated for medicinal purposes, according to Rodriguez. He is also concerned that while only 5% of the plants in the Sonoran desert have been studied by western pharmacologists, half of its 3,000 plant species may have medicinal properties recognized for centuries by indigenous people.

Rodriguez is working vigorously to save endangered plants while filling the gap of knowledge between age-old native use of plants and their scientific investigation in modern labs. As he told a *Wildlife Conservation* journalist in 1991, "We've only just scratched the surface and we've discovered the first drug against malaria (quinine), and the first drug against the cough (codeine), and the first drug against cancer (vincristine)."

By combining modern science with the age-old observations of indigenous people

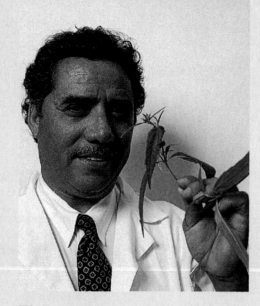

Figure 51A

Eloy Rodriguez believes that animals use plants to cure their illnesses and that we can learn to do the same.

around the world, Rodriguez has learned that creosote (*Larrea tridentata*), a plant of the Sonoran desert which natives call "hedionda" or "bad little smeller," contains over 1,000 potential drugs. Native Americans have used creosote for generations to treat colds, chest infections, intestinal problems, menstrual pains, dandruff, toothaches, and other ills. Referring to its chemical properties, Rodriguez calls creosote a "botanical superstar."

Another potential superstar comes from Africa. Rodriguez discovered strong antibiotic properties in a red oil (thiarubrine-A) extracted from the leaves of an *Aspilia* (in the *Compositae* family) brought to him by Harvard University anthropologist Richard Wrangham, who discov-

ered that sick chimps in Tanzania would swallow these leaves. Thiarubrine-A destroys *Candida albicans* and other fungi, is anthelmintic (toxic to parasitic nematodes [worms] found in plants and animals), and is effective against some viruses and human tumor cells in the colon and lung. Although the full extent of thiarubrine-A's antibiotic properties are not yet known, Rodriguez is delighted that "One of the first drugs that we discovered in studying the apes turned out to be a very good antitumor and antiviral drug." He believes that thiarubrine-A could even be an effective pesticide in third-world countries.

Rodriguez and Wrangham, who plan to donate part of their profits from the patent on thiarubrine-A to the conservation of African chimps and plants, invented the word "zoopharmacognosy" in 1987 to refer to animals' deliberate use of medicinal plants to treat their illnesses. As Rodriguez explained in *National Wildlife,*

> "We think there is some learning and that knowledge is passed on—and that this has been going on for a long time . . . Wild apes five or six million years ago were already using plants . . . And as the human line evolved, we obviously learned from animals. We observed them. It gives us a peek into how we came about selecting medicinal plants." (1994. *National Wildlife* 32 [1]:46.)

Rodriguez obtained his Ph.D. at the University of Texas in 1970. He was named U.C. Irvine's first professor of phytochemistry in 1976. In recognition of his work, he was named Hispanic Educator of the Year in 1969.

Figure 51.9

Soil profiles. **a.** Soil has horizontal layers called horizons. The top layer, the A horizon, contains most of the organic matter consisting of litter and humus. It also has a zone of leaching through which dissolved materials move downward. The middle layer, the B horizon, accumulates minerals and particles as water moves from the A to B horizons. The last layer, the C horizon, consists of weathered rock. This layer determines the pH of the soil and its ability to absorb and retain moisture. **b.** Soils formed in grasslands have a deep A horizon built up from decaying grasses over many years. The shallow B horizon does not have sufficient nutrients to support growth because the low amount of rainfall in the grassland areas limits the amount of leaching from the topsoil. **c.** In forest soils, both the A and B horizons have enough nutrients to allow for root growth. In tropical rain forests, the A horizon is more shallow than this generalized profile and the B horizon is deeper, signifying that leaching is more extensive. Since the topsoil of rain forests lacks nutrients, it has only a limited ability to support crops.

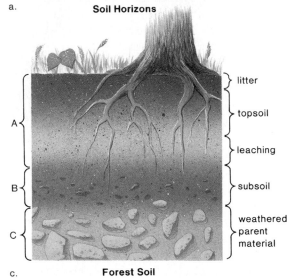

litter: leaves and other debris

topsoil: humus plus living organisms

leaching: removal of nutrients

subsoil: accumulation of minerals and organic materials

parent material: weathered rock

a. **Soil Horizons**

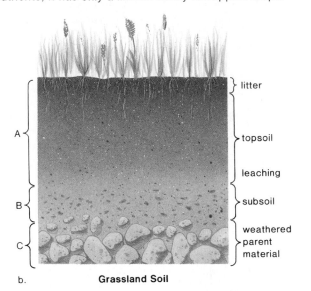

litter

topsoil

leaching

subsoil

weathered parent material

b. **Grassland Soil**

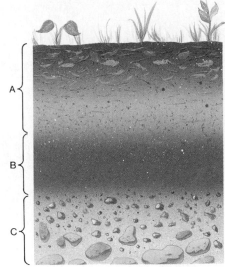

litter

topsoil

leaching

subsoil

weathered parent material

c. **Forest Soil**

Figure 51.10

Vegetation and animal life of the African savanna. There are more types of grazers in the savanna than in any other biome.

Grasslands

Grasslands occur where rainfall is greater than 25 cm but is generally insufficient to support trees. The extensive root system of grasses allows them to recover quickly from drought and fire, which occur frequently in this biome. The matted roots also efficiently absorb surface water and prevent invasion by most trees. Over the years, organic matter builds up in the rich soil, which often is exploited for agriculture (fig. 51.9).

In the tropics, particularly in much of Africa, there is a tropical grassland called the **savanna** (fig. 51.10). One tree that can survive the severe dry season is the flat-topped acacia, which sheds its leaves during a drought. The African savanna supports the greatest variety and number of large herbivores of all the biomes. Elephants and giraffes are browsers that feed on tree vegetation. Antelopes, zebras, wildebeests, water buffalo, and rhinoceroses are grazers that feed on grasses. Any plant litter that is not consumed by grazers is attacked by a variety of small organisms, among them termites. Termites build towering nests in which they tend fungal gardens, their source of food. The herbivores support a large population of carnivores. Lions and hyenas hunt in packs, cheetahs hunt singly by day, and leopards hunt singly by night.

A **prairie** is a temperate grassland. When traveling east to west across the U.S. Midwest, the tall-grass prairie gradually gives way to the short-grass prairie. Although grasses dominate both types of prairie, they are interspersed by forbs, herbs other than grasses. These often catch the eye because they have colorful flowers, whereas grasses do not.

Large herds of buffalo—estimated at hundreds of thousands—once roamed the prairies and plains, as did herds of pronghorn antelope. Small mammals, such as mice, prairie dogs, and rabbits, typically burrow in the ground, although they usually feed above ground. Hawks, snakes, badgers, coyotes, and foxes feed on these mammals.

Scrubland

In parts of South Africa, western Australia, and central Chile, around the Mediterranean Sea, and in California, most of the rain falls in winter and the summers are very dry. There is a dense scrubland known as *chaparral* in this country. The shrubs have small but thick evergreen leaves that often are coated with a waxy material that prevents loss of moisture from the leaves. Their thick underground stems survive the dry summers and frequent fires and can sprout new growth. Rodents and reptiles abound in this biome.

Forests

The forests include the taiga, temperate forests, and the tropical forests.

Taiga

The **taiga** is a coniferous forest extending in a broad belt across northern Eurasia and North America. The climate is characterized by cold winters and cool summers, with a growing season of about 130 days. Rainfall ranges between 40 cm and 100 cm per year, with much of it in the form of heavy snows. The great stands of evergreen, narrow-leaved trees—such as spruce, fir, and pine—are interrupted by many lakes and swamps (fig. 51.11). (*Taiga* is Russian for swampland.) Beneath the dense tree canopy (upper layer of leaves, which is the first to receive sunlight) there is little light, but a ground cover of lichens, mosses, and ferns usually is found.

Compared to other forests, the taiga has relatively few consumer species. In the summer, insects attack the trees and are eaten by warblers and flycatchers. Other birds, such as crossbills and grosbeaks, extract seeds from the cones of the trees. Birds of prey and other carnivores—weasel, lynx, and wolf—feed on small animals, such as the plentiful rodents. The large herbivores—moose and bear—are apt to be found in clearings or near the water's edge, where small trees and shrubs are found.

Figure 51.11

The taiga biome stretches around the globe in the northern temperate zone and contains narrow-leated evergreen trees that are adapted to harsh conditions.

Temperate Forests

Temperate forests are found south of the taiga in eastern North America, eastern Asia, and much of Europe. The climate in these areas is moderate, with relatively high rainfall (75–150 cm per year). The seasons are well defined, and the growing season ranges between 140 and 300 days. The trees, such as oak, beech, and maple, have broad leaves and are termed deciduous trees; they lose their leaves in the fall and grow them in the spring. A forest dominated by these trees is called a temperate deciduous forest (fig. 51.12).

In a temperate deciduous forest, enough sunlight penetrates the canopy for the growth of a well-developed understory—a layer of shrubs, a layer of herbaceous plants, and then often a ground cover of mosses and ferns. Animal life is plentiful. Birds and rodents provide food for bobcats, wolves, and foxes. The white-tailed deer has recently increased in number, while the black bear, an omnivore, has decreased in number, although it is still commonly found in some areas.

Tropical Forests

In tropical regions, some forests are deciduous—the broad-leaved trees lose their leaves because of a dry season. We are more interested in the *tropical rain forests* of South America, Africa, and the Indo-Malayan region near the equator. Here, the weather is always warm (between 20° C and 25° C) and rainfall is plentiful (with a minimum of 190 cm per year). This is the richest biome, both in the different kinds of species found and the total biomass (that is, the amount of living matter). The beneficial uses of plants found in tropical rain forests is discussed in the reading on page 883.

The tropical rain forest has a complex structure, with many levels of life (fig. 51.13). Some of the broad-leaved evergreen trees grow from 15 to 50 meters or more. These tall trees often have trunks buttressed at ground level to prevent their toppling over. Lianas, or woody vines, that encircle the tree as it grows, also help to strengthen the trunk. The rain forest understory becomes dense in open areas or clearings, where light contributes to the development of a thick jungle.

Although there is animal life on the ground (pacas, agoutis, peccaries, armadillos, and coatis), most animals live in the trees. Insect life is so abundant that the majority of species have not been identified yet. The various birds, such as hummingbirds, parakeets, parrots, and toucans, are often beautifully colored. Amphibians and reptiles are well represented by many types of frogs, snakes, and lizards. Monkeys are well-known primates that feed on the fruits of the trees. The largest carnivores are the big cats—the jaguars in South America and the leopards in Africa and Asia.

Many animals spend their entire life in the canopy, as do some plants. Epiphytes are plants that grow on other plants but do not parasitize them. Instead, some have roots that absorb moisture and minerals leached from the canopy; others catch rain and debris in hollows produced by overlapping leaf bases. The most common epiphytes are related to pineapples, orchids, or ferns.

Productivity of a tropical rain forest is high (fig. 51.14) because of high temperatures, a year-long growing season, and the rapid recycling of nutrients from the litter. The soil of a mature tropical rain forest, however, is not always suitable for agriculture. Numerous organisms quickly break down any litter, and nutrients are recycled immediately to the plants. Of the minerals, aluminum and iron sometimes remain near the surface, producing a red-colored soil known as laterite. When

Figure 51.12

Deciduous forest. The forest as it would appear in the summer. Notice that sunlight can penetrate through the leaf canopy and that plants are growing on the forest floor.

the trees are cleared, laterite bakes in the hot sun to a bricklike consistency that will not support crops. Slash-and-burn agriculture is a type of agriculture that has been successful in the tropics. Trees are felled and burned, and the ashes produced provide enough nutrients for several harvests. Thereafter, the forest is allowed to regrow, and a new section is utilized for agriculture.

> The taiga has the least amount of rainfall for a forest. The temperate deciduous forest has trees that grow and shed their leaves with the seasons. The tropical rain forest is the least studied and the most complex of all the biomes.

Latitude and Altitude

If you travel from the equator to the North Pole, it is possible to observe first a tropical rain forest, followed by a temperate deciduous forest, taiga, and a tundra, in that order. This shows that the location of the biomes is influenced by latitude because latitude determines temperature.

It is also possible to observe a similar sequence of biomes by traveling from the bottom to the top of a mountain. These transitions are largely due to decreasing temperature as the altitude increases, but soil conditions and rainfall are also important.

> In general, the same sequence of biomes is observed when latitude increases or when altitude increases.

Figure 51.13

Levels of life in a tropical rain forest. Even the canopy (solid layer of leaves) has levels, and some organisms spend their entire life in one particular level. Long lianas (hanging vines) climb into the canopy, where they produce leaves. Epiphytes are air plants that grow on the trees but do not parasitize them.

canopy

understory

forest floor

lianas

epiphyte

Figure 51.14

Average net primary productivity for several communities. It is influenced by such factors as temperature and rainfall. Also important is the availability of sunlight and nutrients and the length of the growing season. The more productive a community, the more life it can support per unit area.

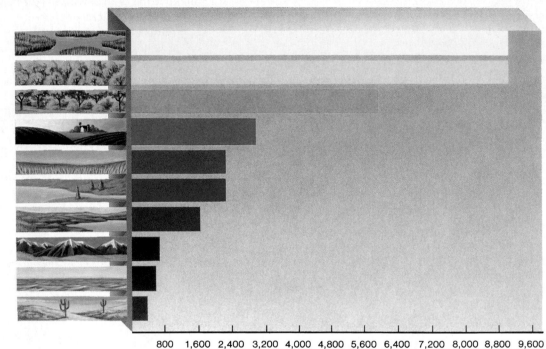

Average Net Primary Productivity (kcal/m²/yr)

Gross primary productivity (GPP): Total rate of photosynthesis in a specified area, usually expressed as kilocalories of energy produced per square meter per year (kcal/m²/yr).

Autotrophs (mostly photosynthetic plants and algae) absorb the energy of the sun and produce food for all organisms in a community.

Net primary productivity (NPP): The rate at which plants produce usable food, which contains chemical energy (also expressed as kilocalories per square meter per year).

$$NPP = GPP - RS$$

where RS is the energy used by the autotrophs for respiration.

Since plants respire, they use some of the food they produce (GPP) for respiration, and what is left (NPP) is available for growth and storage and can be used as food for heterotrophs. Usually, between 50% and 90% of GPP remains as NPP.

Summary

1. Aquatic communities are divided into freshwater communities and marine communities.

2. Lakes are freshwater communities with three life zones and a different mix of organisms in each zone.

3. Marine communities are divided into coastal communities and the oceans. The coastal communities, especially estuaries, are more productive than the oceans.

4. Coral reefs are extremely productive communities found in shallow tropical waters.

5. An ocean is divided into the pelagic division and the benthic division.

6. The pelagic division (open waters) has three zones. The epipelagic zone receives adequate sunlight and supports the most life. The mesopelagic zone contains organisms adapted to minimum and no light, respectively.

7. The benthic division (ocean floor) includes the organisms that live on: the continental shelf in the sublittoral zone; the continental slope in the bathyal zone; and the abyssal plain in the abyssal zone.

8. The treeless biomes include deserts, tundra, grasslands, and scrubland.

9. The organisms of a desert are adapted to heat and minimum rainfall. Those in the tundra are adapted to cold; there is water only because melting snow does not rapidly evaporate in the summer.

10. Among grasslands, the savanna, a tropical grassland, supports the greatest number of different types of large herbivores. The prairie, found in the United States, has a limited variety of vegetation and animal life.

11. Forests require adequate rainfall. The taiga, a coniferous forest, has the least amount of rainfall. The temperate deciduous forest has trees that gain and lose their leaves because of the alternating seasons of summer and winter. Tropical rain forests are the most complex and productive of all biomes.

Writing Across the Curriculum

In order to practice writing skills, students should write out the answers to any or all of the study questions and the critical thinking questions. The study questions are sequenced in the same order as the text. Answers to the objective questions, and suggested answers to the critical thinking questions, are in appendix D.

Study Questions

1. Describe the life zones of a lake and the organisms you would expect to find in each zone.   876
2. Describe the coastal communities, including coral reefs, and discuss the importance of estuaries to the productivity of the ocean.   876–79
3. Describe the zones of the open ocean and the organisms you would expect to find in each zone.   878–79
4. Describe the climate and the populations of a desert in North America.   882
5. Describe the location, the climate, and the populations of the arctic tundra.   882
6. Describe the climate and the populations of the African savanna.   885
7. Describe the location, the climate, and the populations of the North American prairie.   885
8. Describe the location, the climate, and the populations of the taiga.   885
9. Describe the location, the climate, and the populations of temperate deciduous forests in North America.   886
10. Describe the location, the climate, and the populations of tropical rain forests.   886–87
11. Name the terrestrial biomes you would expect to find when going from the base to the top of a mountain.   887

Objective Questions

1. Phytoplankton are more likely to be found in which zone of the ocean?
   a. epipelagic zone
   b. mesopelagic zone
   c. bathypelagic zone
   d. continental slope
2. An estuary acts as a nutrient trap because of the
   a. action of rivers and tides.
   b. depth at which photosynthesis can occur.
   c. amount of rainfall received.
   d. height of the water table.
3. Which area of an ocean has the greatest concentration of nutrients?
   a. epipelagic zone and benthic zone
   b. epipelagic zone only
   c. benthic zone only
   d. neritic province
4. The forest with a multilevel understory is the
   a. tropical rain forest.
   b. coniferous forest.
   c. tundra.
   d. temperate deciduous forest.

5. All of these phrases describe a tropical rain forest except
   a. nutrient-rich soil.
   b. many arboreal plants and animals.
   c. canopy composed of many layers.
   d. broad-leaved evergreen trees.
6. Which type of animal would you be least likely to find in a grassland biome?
   a. hoofed herbivore
   b. active carnivore
   c. arboreal primate
   d. flying insect
7. All of these phrases describe the tundra except
   a. low-lying vegetation.
   b. northernmost biome.
   c. short growing season.
   d. many different types of species.
8. Which of these is mismatched?
   a. tundra—permafrost
   b. savanna—acacia trees
   c. prairie—epiphytes
   d. coniferous forest—evergreen trees

9. Which of these lists the least productive to the most productive communities?
   a. ocean, rocky beach, temperate forest, estuary
   b. agricultural land, tundra, tropical rain forest, desert
   c. lakes and streams, tropical rain forest, open ocean
   d. estuary, agricultural land, lakes and streams, tundra
10. Use plus signs (4 + is maximum) to indicate the degree of temperature and the amount of rainfall for these biomes.

	Temperature	Rainfall
a. tropical rain forest		
b. savanna		
c. taiga		
d. tundra		

Concepts and Critical Thinking

1. *The productivity of communities varies.* Use figure 51.4 to explain why a neritic province is more productive but more polluted than the oceanic province.

2. *The productivity of communities varies.* Why is the productivity of the ocean equivalent to that of a desert?

3. *The gross and net primary productivity of communities varies.* Explain why you might see this sequence of communities from the base to the top of a mountain: temperate forest, coniferous forest, tundra.

Selected Key Terms

benthic division (BEN-thik) The ocean floor, which supports a unique set of organisms in contrast to the pelagic division. [Gk. *bentho,* depths of the sea] 878

biome (BY-ohm) A major terrestrial community characterized by certain climatic conditions and dominated by particular types of plants. 876

biosphere The thin shell of air, land, and water around the earth that supports life. [Gk. *bio,* life, and *spher,* ball] 876

desert Treeless biome where the annual rainfall is less than 25 cm; the rain that does fall is subject to rapid runoff and evaporation. 882

estuary The end of a river where fresh water and salt water mix as they meet. 876

pelagic division (puh-LAJ-ik) The open portion of the sea. [Gk. *pelagi,* the sea] 878

plankton Freshwater and marine organisms that float on or near the surface of the water. [Gk. *plankt,* wandering] 876

prairie Terrestrial biome that is a temperate grassland, changing from tall-grass prairies to short-grass prairies when traveling east to west across the Midwest of the United States. 885

savanna Terrestrial biome that is a tropical grassland in Africa, characterized by few trees and a severe dry season. 885

taiga (TY-guh) Terrestrial biome that is a coniferous forest extending in a broad belt across northern Eurasia and North America. 885

tundra Treeless terrestrial biome of cold climates; is found on high mountains and in polar regions. 882

52

ENVIRONMENTAL CONCERNS

Learning Objectives

Air Pollutants Interact

- List the substances that contribute to air pollution; note their sources and associate each one with the global warming, the destruction of the ozone shield, acid deposition, or development of photochemical smog.   892–95

- List the environmental effects of global warming, destruction of the ozone shield, acid deposition, and smog.   892–95

- Explain how greenhouse gases bring about global warming, how chlorofluorocarbons break down the ozone shield, and how smog develops.   893–95

Water Pollutants Spoil Drinking Water

- Explain why we may be running out of fresh water.   896

- Give reasons why underground water supplies are being polluted, and tell how the ocean becomes polluted.   896–97

How People Degrade Land

- List ways in which quality of the land is being degraded today.   899–901

- Using DDT as an example, explain how biological magnification occurs.   899

- Discuss the adverse effects of forest destruction and a loss of biodiversity.   900–901

A Sustainable World Is Possible

- Compare the environmental impact of more developed and less developed countries.   902

- Discuss the concept of a sustainable world.   902

All types of forests around the world are being destroyed by humans.

s the human population increases in size, the space allotted to natural ecosystems is reduced in size. Natural ecosystems are then no longer able to process and rid the biosphere of wastes, which accumulate and are called pollutants. **Pollutants** [L. *pollut,* defiled] are substances added to the environment, particularly by human activities, that lead to undesirable effects for all living things. Human beings add pollutants to all parts of the biosphere—air, water, and land.

AIR POLLUTANTS INTERACT

Four major concerns (global warming, destruction of the ozone shield, acid deposition, and photochemical smog) are associated with the air pollutants listed in figure 52.1. You can see that fossil

fuel burning and vehicle exhaust are primary causes of air pollution gases. These two are related because gasoline is derived from petroleum (oil), a fossil fuel. The fossil fuels (oil, coal, and natural gas) are burned in the home to provide heat and in power plants to generate electricity.

U.S. citizens have begun to practice energy conservation, and it is estimated that in so doing they have saved $150 billion a year. But it is projected even more energy conservation is possible by making use of renewable energy sources such as solar and wind energy, falling water, and geothermal energy.

Global Warming Melts Ice Cap

Certain air pollutants allow the sun's rays to pass through but then absorb and reradiate the heat back toward the earth (fig. 52.2*a*). This is called the **greenhouse effect** because it is like the

Figure 52.1

Air pollutants. These are the gases, along with their sources, that contribute to four environmental effects of major concern: global warming, ozone shield destruction, acid deposition, and photochemical smog. An examination of the sources of these gases shows that vehicle exhaust and fossil fuel burning are the chief contributors.

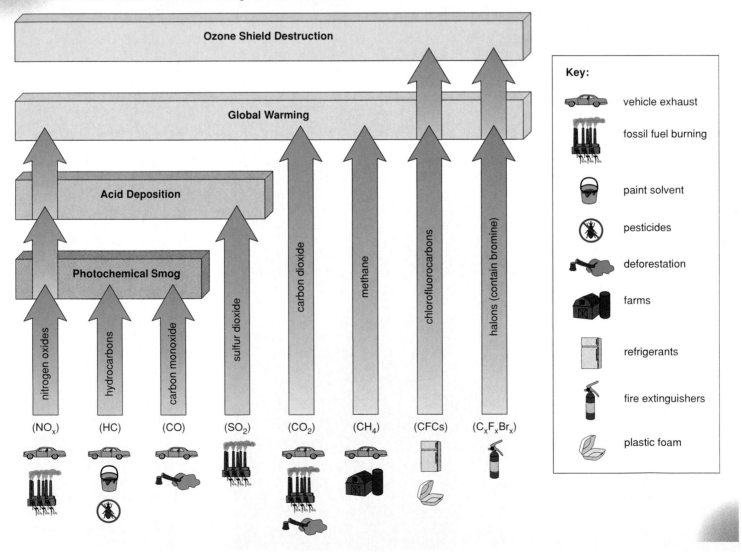

Figure 52.2

Global warming. **a.** The greenhouse effect is caused by the atmospheric accumulation of certain gases that allow the rays of the sun to pass through but absorb and reradiate heat to the earth. **b.** The greenhouse gases. The increase in warming caused by these gases is listed for 1950 to 2020.

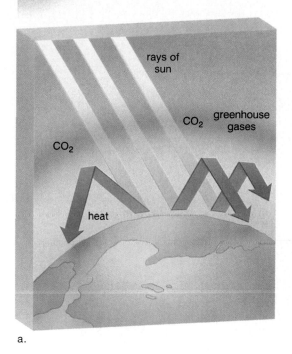

a.

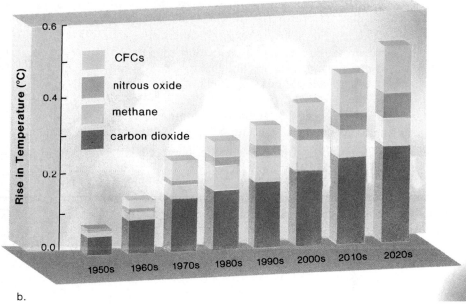

b.

glass of a greenhouse that allows sunlight to pass through and then traps the resulting heat inside the structure. The air pollutants responsible for the greenhouse effect are known as the greenhouse gases. They are as follows:

Gas	From
Carbon dioxide (CO_2)	Fossil fuel and wood burning
Nitrous oxide (NO_2)	Fertilizer use and animal wastes
Methane (CH_4)	Biogas (bacterial decomposition, particularly in the guts of animals, in sediments, and in flooded rice paddies)
Chlorofluorocarbons (CFCs)	Freon, a refrigerant
Halons (halocarbons, $C_xF_xBr_x$)	Fire extinguishers

If nothing is done to control the level of greenhouse gases in the atmosphere, a rise in global temperature is expected. Figure 52.2*b* predicts a rise of over 0.5° C by 2020, but some authorities predict the rise in temperature could be as high as 5° C by 2050.

The ecological effects of a 5° C rise in global temperature would be severe. The sea level would rise—melting of the polar ice caps would add more water to the sea, and in any case water expands when it heats up. There would be coastal flooding and the possible loss of many cities, like New York, Boston, Miami, and Galveston in the United States. Coastal ecosystems, such as marshes, swamps, and bayous, would normally move inland to higher ground as the sea level rises, but many of these ecosys-

tems are blocked by artificial structures and may be unable to move inland. If so, the loss of fertility would be immense.

There may also be food loss because of regional changes in climate. Because of greater heat and also drought in the midwestern United States, the suitable climate for growing wheat and corn may shift as far north as Canada, where the soil is not as suitable.

It is clear from figure 52.2*b* that carbon dioxide accounts for at least 50% of the predicted rise in global temperature. Therefore, a sharp decrease in the consumption of fossil fuels is recommended, and we must find more efficient ways to acquire energy from cleaner fuels, such as natural gas. We must also use alternative energy sources, such as solar and geothermal energy and even perhaps nuclear power. In addition to fossil fuel consumption, deforestation is a major contributor to the rise in carbon dioxide. Burning one acre of primary forest releases 200,000 kg of carbon dioxide into the air; moreover, the trees are no longer available to act as a sink to take up carbon dioxide during photosynthesis. Therefore, tropical rain forest deforestation should be halted and extensive reforestation should take place all over the globe.

The other greenhouse gases combined account for the other 50% predicted rise in global temperature. A complete phaseout of chlorofluorocarbon use would be most beneficial. Fortunately, in an effort to arrest ozone shield destruction, the United States and the European countries have agreed to reduce CFC production by 85% as soon as possible and to stop their production altogether by the end of the century.

Ozone Shield Holes Cause Skin Cancer

The earth's atmosphere is divided into layers. The troposphere envelopes us as we go about our day-to-day lives. In the stratosphere, some 50 km above the earth, there is a layer of ozone (O_3) called an **ozone shield** that absorbs the ultraviolet (UV) rays of the sun so that they do not strike the earth. UV radiation causes mutations that can lead to skin cancer and can make the lens of the eyes develop cataracts. It also is believed to adversely affect the immune system and our ability to resist infectious diseases. Crop and tree growth is impaired, and UV radiation also kills off plankton (microscopic plant and animal life) that sustain oceanic life. Without an adequate ozone shield, our health and food sources are threatened.

Depletion of the ozone layer within the stratosphere in recent years is, therefore, of serious concern. It became apparent in the 1980s that some worldwide depletion of ozone had occurred and that there was a severe depletion of some 40–50% above the Antarctic every spring. Severe depletions of the ozone layer are commonly called "ozone holes." Detection devices now tell us that there is an ozone hole above the Arctic as well, and ozone holes could also develop within northern and southern latitudes, where many people live. Whether or not these holes develop depends on prevailing winds, weather conditions, and the type of particles in the atmosphere. A United Nations Environment Program report predicts a 26% rise in cataracts and nonmelanoma skin cancers for every 10% drop in the ozone level. A 26% increase translates into 1.75 million additional cases of cataracts and 300,000 more cases of skin cancer every year, worldwide.

The cause of ozone depletion can be traced to the release of chlorine atoms (Cl) into the stratosphere (fig. 52.3). Chlorine atoms combine with ozone and strip away the oxygen atoms one by one. One atom of chlorine can destroy up to 100,000 molecules of ozone before settling to the earth's surface as chloride years later. These chlorine atoms come from the breakdown of chlorofluorocarbons (CFCs), chemicals much in use by humans. The best known CFC is Freon, a heat transfer agent found in refrigerators and air conditioners. CFCs are also used as cleaning agents and foaming agents during the production of styrofoam found in coffee cups, egg cartons, insulation, and paddings. Formerly, CFCs were used as propellants in spray cans, but this application is now banned in the United States and several European countries. Most countries of the world have agreed to stop using CFCs by the year 2000, but the United States is halting production by 1995. Scientists are now searching for CFC substitutes that will not release chlorine atoms (nor bromine atoms) to harm the ozone shield.

Acid Deposition Kills Trees

The coal and oil routinely burned by power plants release sulfur dioxide into the air. Kuwait oil has a high sulfur content, and therefore the oil well fires started during the Gulf War released much sulfur dioxide into the atmosphere. Automobile exhaust routinely puts nitrogen oxides in the air. Both sulfur dioxide and nitrogen

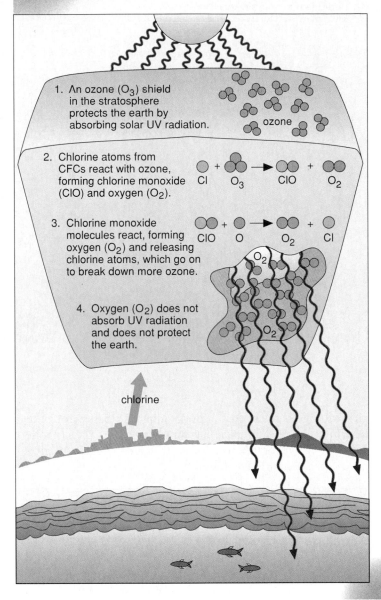

Figure 52.3

The development of an ozone hole due to the release of chlorine atoms from chlorofluorocarbons (CFCs).

1. An ozone (O_3) shield in the stratosphere protects the earth by absorbing solar UV radiation.

2. Chlorine atoms from CFCs react with ozone, forming chlorine monoxide (ClO) and oxygen (O_2). $Cl + O_3 \rightarrow ClO + O_2$

3. Chlorine monoxide molecules react, forming oxygen (O_2) and releasing chlorine atoms, which go on to break down more ozone. $ClO + O \rightarrow O_2 + Cl$

4. Oxygen (O_2) does not absorb UV radiation and does not protect the earth.

chlorine

oxides are converted to acids when they combine with water vapor in the atmosphere, a reaction that is promoted by ozone in smog. These acids return to earth as either wet deposition (acid rain or snow) or dry deposition (sulfate and nitrate salts).

Acid deposition is now associated with dead or dying lakes and forests, particularly in North America and Europe (fig. 52.4). Acid deposition also corrodes marble, metal, and stonework, an effect that is noticeable in cities. It can also degrade our water supply by leaching heavy metals from the soil into drinking-water supplies. Similarly, acid water dissolves copper from pipes and from lead solder, which is used to join pipes.

Figure 52.4

Acid deposition in the United States. The numbers in this map are average pH recordings of deposition. The northeast is the hardest hit area because winds carry the acid pollutants from other parts of the country in this direction.

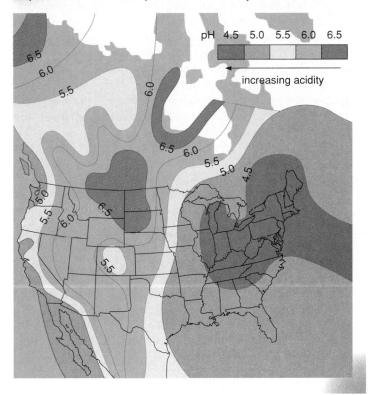

pH 4.5 5.0 5.5 6.0 6.5

← increasing acidity

Figure 52.5

Ozone effects. **a.** This milkweed, *Asclepias,* was exposed to ozone and appears unhealthy—leaf mottling is apparent. **b.** This milkweed was grown in an enclosure with filtered air and appears healthy.

a.   b.

Photochemical Smog Affects Breathing

Photochemical smog [Gk. *photo,* light, and *chem,* chemical] contains two air pollutants—nitrogen oxides (NO_x) and hydrocarbons (HC)—that react with one another in the presence of sunlight to produce ozone (O_3) and PAN (peroxylacetyl nitrate). Both nitrogen oxides and hydrocarbons come from fossil fuel combustion, but additional hydrocarbons come from various other sources as well, including paint solvents and pesticides.

Ozone and PAN are commonly referred to as oxidants. Breathing ozone affects the respiratory and nervous systems, resulting in respiratory distress, headache, and exhaustion. These symptoms are particularly apt to appear in young people; therefore, in Los Angeles, where ozone levels are often high, schoolchildren must remain inside the school building whenever the ozone level reaches 0.35 ppm (parts per million by weight). Ozone is especially damaging to plants, resulting in leaf mottling and reduced growth (fig. 52.5).

Carbon monoxide (CO) is another gas that comes from the burning of fossil fuels in the industrial Northern Hemisphere. High levels of carbon monoxide increase the formation of ozone. Carbon monoxide also combines preferentially with hemoglobin and thereby prevents hemoglobin from carrying oxygen. Breathing large quantities of automobile exhaust can even result in death because of this effect. Of late, it has been discovered that the amount of carbon monoxide over the Southern Hemisphere—from the burning of tropical forests—is equal to that over the Northern Hemisphere.

Normally, warm air near the ground is able to escape into the atmosphere. Sometimes, however, air pollutants, including smog and soot, are trapped near the earth due to a long-lasting thermal inversion. During a **thermal inversion** [Gk. *therm,* heat, and L. *vers,* turn], there is the cold air at ground level beneath a layer of warm stagnant air above. This often occurs at sunset, but turbulence usually mixes these layers during the day. Some areas surrounded by hills are particularly susceptible to the effects of a temperature inversion because the air tends to stagnate and there is little turbulent mixing.

> Air pollutants are involved in causing four major environmental effects: global warming, ozone shield destruction, acid deposition, and photochemical smog. Each pollutant may be involved in more than one of these.

While each of these environmental effects is bad enough when considered separately, they actually feed on one another, making the total effect much worse than is predicted for each separately.

Fresh water is required not only for domestic purposes, including drinking water, but also for crop irrigation, industrial use, and energy production. Surface water from rivers, lakes, and underground rivers called aquifers are used to meet these needs (fig. 52.6). The water in **aquifers** [L. *aqua,* water, and *fer,* bear] is a vast natural resource, but to ensure a continual supply withdrawals cannot exeed deposits. In this country, the farmers of the Midwest withdraw water from aquifers up to fifty times faster than nature replaces it. China, with a population of one billion, is also mining its water to meet the needs of its people, despite the estimate that its aquifers can sustain only 650 million people. In the United States, the government still heavily subsidizes water so that the incentive to use water carefully and efficiently is lacking.

Pollution of surface water, groundwater, and the oceans is another reason why we are running out of fresh water.

Surface Water Is Ponds and Lakes

All sorts of pollutants from various sources enter surface waters, as depicted in figure 52.7. Sewage treatment plants can help degrade organic wastes, which otherwise can cause oxygen depletion in lakes and rivers. As the oxygen level decreases, the diversity of life is greatly reduced. Also, human feces can contain patho-

Figure 52.6

Crop irrigation. Forty percent of the water used for irrigation comes from under the ground. In the Texas high plains, central Arizona, and southern Florida, withdrawals from aquifers exceed any possibility of recharge. This is called "groundwater mining," which causes sinkholes due to the collapse of underground caverns and also causes saltwater intrusion into freshwater supplies.

genic microorganisms that cause cholera, typhoid fever, and dysentery. In less developed countries, where the population is growing and where waste treatment is practically nonexistent, many children die each year from these diseases.

Typically, sewage treatment plants use bacteria to break down organic matter to inorganic nutrients, like nitrates and phosphates, which then enter surface waters. These types of nutrients, which also can enter waters by fertilizer runoff and soil erosion, lead to *cultural eutrophication,* an acceleration of the natural process by which bodies of water fill in and disappear. First, the nutrients cause overgrowth of algae. Then, when the algae die, oxygen is used up by the decomposers, and the water's capacity to support life is reduced. Massive fish kills are sometimes the result of cultural eutrophication.

Industrial wastes can include heavy metals and organochlorides, such as pesticides. These materials are not degraded readily under natural conditions nor in conventional sewage treatment plants. Sometimes, they accumulate in the mud of deltas and estuaries of highly polluted rivers and cause environmental problems if they are disturbed. Industrial pollution is being addressed in many industrialized countries but usually has low priority in less developed countries.

Some pollutants enter bodies of water from the atmosphere. Acid deposition has caused many lakes to become sterile in the industrialized world because acid leaches aluminum and iron out of the soil. A high concentration of these ions kills fishes and other forms of aquatic life. Lime is sometimes helpful against acidification of a lake.

Groundwater Is Aquifers

In areas of intensive animal farming or where there are many septic tanks, ammonium (NH_4^+) released from animal and human waste is converted by soil bacteria to soluble nitrate, which moves down through the soil (percolates) into underground water supplies. Between 5 and 10% of all wells examined in the United States have nitrate levels higher than the recommended maximum.

Industry also pollutes aquifers. Previously, industry ran wastewater into a pit, from which pollutants could seep into the ground. Wastewater and chemical wastes were also injected into deep wells, from which pollutants constantly discharge. Both of these customs have been or are in the process of being phased out. It is very difficult for industry to find other ways to dispose of wastes, especially since citizens do not wish to live near waste treatment plants. As mentioned previously, the emphasis today is on prevention of wastes in the first place. Industry is trying to use processes that do not create wastes and/or to recycle the wastes they do generate.

Ocean Water Needs Protection, Too

Coastal regions are not only the immediate receptors for local pollutants, they are also the final receptors for pollutants carried by rivers that empty at a coast. Waste dumping also occurs at sea, and ocean currents sometimes transport both trash and pollutants back to shore. Examples are the nonbiodegradable plastic bottles, pellets, and containers that now commonly litter beaches and the oceans' surfaces. Some of these, such as the plastic that holds a six-pack of cans, cause the death of birds, fishes, and marine mammals that mistake them for food and get entangled in them.

Offshore mining and shipping add pollutants to the oceans. Some 5 million metric tons of oil a year—or more than one gram per 100 square meters of the oceans' surfaces—end up in the oceans. Large oil spills kill plankton, fish larvae, and shellfishes, as well as birds and marine mammals. The largest tanker spill in U.S. territorial waters occurred on March 24, 1989, when the tanker *Exxon Valdez* struck a reef in Alaska's Prince William Sound and leaked 44 million liters of crude oil. During the war with Iraq, 120 million liters were released from damaged on-shore storage tanks into the Persian Gulf—an event that was called

environmental terrorism. Although petroleum is biodegradable, the process takes a long time because the low-nutrient content of seawater does not support a large bacterial population. Once the oil washes up onto beaches, it takes many hours of work and millions of dollars to clean it up.

> Adequate sewage treatment and waste disposal are necessary to prevent the pollution of rivers and oceans. New methods also are needed to prevent pollution of underground water supplies.

Figure 52.7

Sources of surface water pollution. **a.** So many different pollutants enter rivers (and also lakes) that they are in danger of dying. **b.** Listing of pollutants.

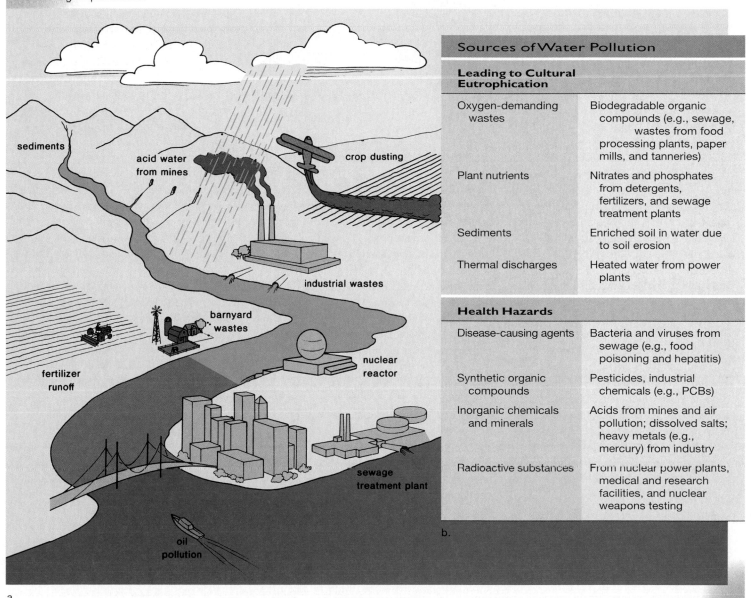

Sources of Water Pollution

Leading to Cultural Eutrophication

Oxygen-demanding wastes	Biodegradable organic compounds (e.g., sewage, wastes from food processing plants, paper mills, and tanneries)
Plant nutrients	Nitrates and phosphates from detergents, fertilizers, and sewage treatment plants
Sediments	Enriched soil in water due to soil erosion
Thermal discharges	Heated water from power plants

Health Hazards

Disease-causing agents	Bacteria and viruses from sewage (e.g., food poisoning and hepatitis)
Synthetic organic compounds	Pesticides, industrial chemicals (e.g., PCBs)
Inorganic chemicals and minerals	Acids from mines and air pollution; dissolved salts; heavy metals (e.g., mercury) from industry
Radioactive substances	From nuclear power plants, medical and research facilities, and nuclear weapons testing

The PCB Menace

A s a Ph.D. recently out of graduate school in 1975, I was eager to start a research program that would be meaningful and not just an academic exercise. Occasionally, scientific inspiration comes from the least likely sources. I became intrigued by a newspaper article reporting that Congress had passed the Toxic Substance Control Act that gave the Environmental Protection Agency (EPA) the authority to regulate selected chemical substances and mixtures. In addition, this act prohibited the production of polychlorinated biphenyls (PCBs) after 1979. I wondered what it was about these chemicals that prompted Congress to single them out for such a fate? A cursory review of the scientific literature quickly revealed the answer.

By 1966, pesticide toxicologists and environmental scientists had become increasingly alarmed by the presence of PCB residues in fishes, feathers, and even human hair. By the mid 1970s, research studies revealed that PCBs exert toxicological, teratogenic (developmental anomalies), and physiological effects. In 1975, the EPA estimated that 50% of the human population of the United States contained one to three parts per million of PCBs in fat tissue.

PCBs, first manufactured in the United States in 1929, are chemically related to other chlorinated hydrocarbons such as DDT. They are thermally stable, soluble in organic solvents and lipids, but resistant to oxidation, hydrolysis, and degradation. These properties give PCBs important industrial applications in the manufacture of plastics, paints, lubricants, hydraulic fluids, adhesives, printing products, and electrical insulators. However, the chemical properties that made PCBs important industrial chemicals also account for their impact on the environment, and for their effects on biological systems.

The scientific literature before 1977 had already recorded various pathological effects associated with PCB exposure, including reproductive dysfunction, chromosomal defects, premature births, congenital abnor-

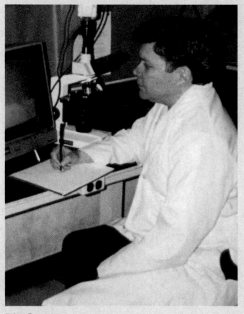

Ric Garcia
Clemson University

malities, induced tumors, and metabolic disorders, including altered enzyme activity. The list of research organisms read like a roll call of the living world, with most of PCB experimentation conducted on birds, rats, and mice. I did not consider rodents appropriate research animals for this area of investigation. Rodents are not likely to be early victims of environmental PCB pollution, nor are they directly situated in the food web of those organisms that are. It was obvious to me that fish are more appropriate research animals for this type of investigation. The research organism is the single most important factor in the success of scientific investigations as is shown by Mendel's work with pea plants, T. H. Morgan's work with fruit flies, Beadle and Tatum's work with *Neurospora*, and any number of other classic studies.

Could there be one fish that is the ideal research organism for all these studies? After an exhaustive search, the answer was yes, the common zebra fish, *Brachydanio rerio*. This fish is a member of the subclass Actinopterigii, which includes such important game fish as trout and salmon. Zebra fish have many characteristics that ideally suited them for the various aspects of the proposed investigations.

They are small (20–30 mm in length), and easy to maintain and handle so that many individuals can be kept in laboratory aquaria. A single female will lay many eggs without regard to season. The embryos develop at a uniform rate with successive stages reached simultaneously. The eggs are transparent, making photographic recording of development possible. Zebra fish do have one annoying habit, however. They will eat all the newly laid eggs that they can find. In nature, some eggs escape predation by falling into crevasses, by sliding behind shells, or by being camouflaged by vegetation. This seemingly insignificant problem stymied initial work on the research for several weeks until the answer came, as it often does in scientific research, from an unexpected source. One of my research assistants mentioned the problem to a graduate student not associated with the project. She quickly suggested using bobbinet, a machine-woven net fabric. We found that the mesh was large enough to allow the eggs to pass, but much too small to let the adult fish reach the eggs. It was a simple matter to stretch the mesh across the aquarium about one inch above the bottom. Unexpected details like this one often arise in research and must be solved before the planned significant aspects of the research can be accomplished.

My research team and I went on to discover that PCBs are toxic to zebra fish at levels lower than are found in some municipal sludge, but not as low as those presently found in natural aquatic environments. The team also found that low levels of PCBs have profound effects on the embryological and neurological development of the fish.

The single most important result of this research is probably the realization that, despite the onerous expense of cleaning up the environment, no expense is too great to protect biological systems from the detrimental effects of chemical pollutants. These compounds are steadily making their way into the environment and contaminating food webs at every level.

HOW PEOPLE DEGRADE LAND

Whereas 20% of the world's population lived in cities in 1950, it is predicted that 60% will live in cities by the year 2000. Near cities the development of new housing areas has led to urban sprawl. Such areas tend to take over agricultural land or simply further degrade the land in the area.

The land has been degraded in many ways. Here, we will discuss some of the greatest concerns.

Waste Disposal and Dangerous Trash

Every year, the U.S. population discards billions of tons of solid wastes, much of it on land. Solid wastes include not only household trash but also sewage sludge, agricultural residues, mining refuse, and industrial wastes. Opening dumping, sanitary landfills, or incineration have been the most common practices of disposing trash. These disposal methods are increasingly expensive and also cause pollution problems. It would be far more satisfactory to recycle materials as much as possible and/or to use organic substances as a fuel to generate electricity. One study showed that it was possible to achieve 70–90% public participation in recycling by spending only thirty cents per household. A city the size of Washington, D.C., where 500,000 tons of waste are generated per year, could have an increase of 1,300 jobs if the community utilized solid wastes as a resource instead of throwing them away.

Hazardous Wastes

Some solid wastes, called hazardous wastes, endanger our health as discussed in the reading on page 898. Hazardous wastes include:

> **Heavy metals,** such as lead, mercury, cadmium, nickel, and beryllium, contaminate many wastes. These metals can accumulate in various organs, interfering with normal enzymatic actions and causing illness.
> **Chlorinated hydrocarbons,** also called *organochlorides,* include various pesticides and PCBs (polychlorinated biphenyls), which are often cancer-producing in laboratory animals.
> **Nuclear wastes** include radioactive elements that will be dangerous for thousands of years. ^{239}Plutonium takes 200,000 years to lose its radioactivity.

These wastes enter bodies of water and are subject to **biological magnification** (fig. 52.8). Decomposers are unable to break down these wastes. They enter and remain in the body

Figure 52.8

Biological magnification. A poison (dots) such as DDT, which is minimally excreted (arrows), becomes maximally concentrated as it passes along a food chain due to the reduced size of the trophic levels.

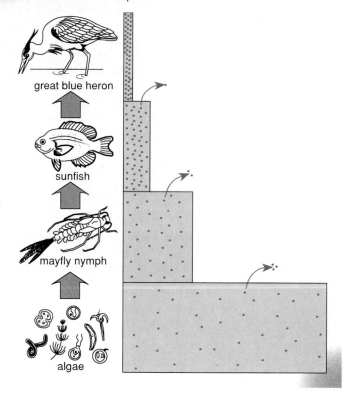

because they are not excreted. Therefore, they become more concentrated as they pass along a food chain. Notice in figure 52.8 that the dots representing DDT become more concentrated as they pass from producer to tertiary consumer. Biological magnification is most apt to occur in aquatic food chains, since there are more links in aquatic food chains than there are in terrestrial food chains. Humans are the final consumers in both types of food chains, and in some areas, human milk contains detectable amounts of DDT and PCBs, which are organochlorides.

The U.S. spends $9 billion a year on cleanup but only $200 million yearly to prevent contamination. It would be best to place the emphasis on preventing contaminants from entering the environment rather than cleaning up pollution. Likewise, recycling can save industry money as witnessed by the 3M Corporation, which reported savings of $1.2 billion by recycling waste and preventing pollution.

Soil Erodes and Deserts Grow

In agricultural areas, wind and rain carry away about 25 billion tons of topsoil yearly, worldwide. If this rate of loss continues, we will lose practically all our topsoil by the middle of the next century. Soil erosion causes a loss of productivity that is compensated by increased use of fertilizers, pesticides, and fossil fuel energy. One answer to the problem of erosion is to adopt soil conservation measures. For example, farmers could use strip-cropping and contour farming (fig. 52.9). Thanks to a U.S. program offering incentives to farmers to use these techniques, erosion dropped by one-third between 1985 and 1990, and similar results are expected again by the mid-1990s.

Desertification is the transformation of marginal lands to desert conditions because of overgrazing and overfarming. Desertification has been particularly evident along the southern edge of the Sahara Desert in Africa, where it is estimated that 350,000 square miles of once-productive grazing land has become desert in the last fifty years. However, desertification also occurs in this country. The U.S. Bureau of Land Management, which opens up federal lands for grazing, reports that much of the rangeland it manages is in poor or bad condition, with much of its topsoil gone and with greatly reduced ability to support forage plants.

> Humans often used land for their cities and for agriculture. Agricultural land quality is threatened by soil erosion, which can lead to desertification.

Wars Cause Land Spoilage

Many plants and animals are killed because of wars. For example, during a civil war in Angola, rhinos and elephants were shot, and their tusks and horns were sold to buy uniforms and weapons. During a war between Uganda and Tanzania, hippos were used as target practice, and other animals were killed for food and for their ivory tusks.

However, habitat destruction caused by wars probably leads to more loss of life than direct killing. Scientists estimate that during the Vietnam War 5.45 million acres of tropical forests were destroyed due to bombing, bulldozing, and the spraying of defoliants such as Agent Orange. Also, about half of South Vietnam's wetlands are now devoid of their mangrove trees due to the effects of war. The Gulf War was similarly destructive. Although the sands of Kuwait may seem lifeless, they are actually home to a variety of spiders, snakes, and scorpions, as well as sheep, gazelles, and camels.

Forests Need Protection

In Canada, vast stands of trees are scheduled to be felled and turned into paper and wood products like posts and particleboard. Thousands of miles of new logging roads are to be built during the next five to ten years, and this no doubt will bring many visitors to hunt and fish where only indigenous people did so previously. The animals that live there—moose, porcupine, lynx, and snowshoe hare—will also be displaced. Songbirds who migrate there during the summer will no longer find shelter. Although the logging companies are to replant, conservationists wonder if companies have the necessary expertise or if wildlife can sustain themselves in the meantime.

Tropical rain forests are much more biologically diverse than temperate forests. For example, temperate forests across the entire United States contain about 400 tree species. In the rain forest, a typical ten-hectare area holds as many as 750 types of trees. The fresh waters of South America are inhabited by an estimated 5,000 fish species; on the eastern slopes of the Andes, there are 80 or more species of frogs and toads, and in Ecuador, there are more than 1,200 species of birds—roughly twice as many as those inhabiting all of the United States and Canada. Therefore, a very serious side effect of deforestation in tropical countries is the loss of biological diversity.

Figure 52.9

Contour farming. Crops are planted according to the lay of the land to reduce soil erosion. This farmer has planted alfalfa, *Medicago,* whose roots hold the soil, in between the strips of corn, *Zea,* to replenish the nitrogen content of the soil. Alfalfa, a legume, also has root nodules that contain nitrogen-fixing bacteria.

A National Academy of Sciences study estimated that a million species of plants and animals are in danger of disappearing within twenty years as a result of deforestation in tropical countries. Many of these life forms have never been studied, and yet they may be useful sources of food or medicines.

Logging of tropical forests occurs because industrialized nations prefer furniture made from costly tropical woods and because people want to farm the land (fig. 52.10). In Brazil, the government allows citizens to own any land they clear in the Amazon forest (along the Amazon River). When they arrive, the people practice slash-and-burn agriculture, in which trees are cut down and burned to provide nutrients and space to raise crops. Unfortunately, the fertility of the land is sufficient to sustain agriculture for only a few years. Once the cleared land is incapable of sustaining crops, the farmer moves on to another part of the rain forest to slash and burn again. In the meantime, cattle ranchers move in. Cattle ranchers are the greatest beneficiaries of deforestation, and increased ranching is therefore another reason for tropical rain forest destruction. A newly begun pig-iron industry in Brazil also indirectly results in further exploitation of the rain forest. The pig iron must be processed before it is exported, and smelting the pig iron requires the use of charcoal (burnt wood).

> There is much concern worldwide about the loss of biological diversity due to the destruction of tropical rain forests. The myriad plants and animals that live there could possibly benefit human beings.

While it may seem like an either-or situation— either preservation of the forests or human survival—there is a growing recognition that this is not the case. Natives who harvest rubber from the trees can have a sustainable income from the same trees year after year. A recent study calculated the market value of rubber and exotic produce, like the aguaje palm fruit, that can be harvested continually from the Amazon forest. It concluded that selling these products would yield more than twice the income from either lumbering or cattle ranching, and it would help achieve a sustainable world (fig. 52.11).

Figure 52.10
Forest destruction leads to the detrimental effects mentioned.

Forest Destruction:

Loss of a CO_2 sink:	forests take up carbon dioxide from the atmosphere
Loss of biodiversity:	forests are home for plants and animals
Loss of possible medicinal plants	tropical rain forests contain unique plants
Soil erosion:	trees hold the soil
Water pollution:	saw mills and paper mills pollute
Ecosystems destruction:	first step toward converting land to industrialized or urbanized areas

Figure 52.11

Figure 52.11

Sustainable life in the tropics. In its natural state, a tropical rain forest is immensely rich in wildlife. If the rubber trees, *Hevea,* are not cut down, rubber tappers can earn a sustainable living by tapping the same trees year after year.

A Sustainable World Is Possible

The world's population is expanding rapidly, and the doubling time is now less than 50 years. Population size is just about stable in the more developed countries; most of this expansion will occur in the less developed countries of the world. The rapid increase in population is putting a strain on the environment and there is doubt that it will be possible to produce enough food to feed such a large increase in numbers. However, many couples in the developing countries want to practice family planning; they just need the education and means to do so. Thailand's average family size was 6.5 children in 1969; today it is two children. Similar results are possible in other countries as well.

It is important to realize that environmental impact is measured not only in terms of the population size but also in terms of the resource used and the pollution caused by each person in the population. Therefore, there are two types of overpopulation. The first type is due to increased population as seen in the less developed countries, and the second type is due to increased resource consumption as seen in the more developed countries. An average American family, in terms of per capita resource consumption and waste production, is the equivalent of thirty people in a less developed country.

Overpopulation and overconsumption account for increased pollution and also for the mass extinction of wildlife that is going on. We are expected to lose one-third to two-thirds of the earth's species, any one of which could possibly have made a significant contribution to agriculture or medicine. Before the establishment of industrialized societies, people felt connected to the plants and animals on which they depended, and they were then better able to live in a sustainable way. This was replaced with the idea that we are separate from nature and have the right to exploit nature as much as possible. Our industrial society lives on *borrowed carrying capacity*—our cities not only borrow resources from local communities, our entire population borrows from the past and future. The forests of the Carboniferous have become the fossil fuels that sustain our way of life, and the environmental degradation we cause is going to be paid for by our children.

It is clearly time for a new philosophy. In a **sustainable world,** development will meet economic needs of all peoples while protecting the environment for future generations. Various organizations have singled out communities to serve as models of how to balance ecological and economic goals. For example, in Clinch Valley of southwest Virginia, the Nature Conservancy is helping to revive the traditional method of logging with draft horses. This technique, which allows the selective cutting of trees, preserves the forest and prevents soil erosion so damaging to the environment. The United Nations has an established bioreserve system, a global network of sites that combine preservation with research on sustainable management for human welfare. More than 100 countries are now participants in the program.

All peoples can benefit from a sustainable world where economic development and environmental preservation are considered complementary rather than opposing processes.

Biological Relationships

Ecologists have two favorite sayings: (1) Everything is connected to everything else, and (2) there is no free lunch. We have seen how everything is connected. If you affect one part of the carbon cycle, you affect the entire balance of carbon in the entire world. Ecological effects know no boundaries. Coal that is burned in the Midwest releases acids into the atmosphere that affect lakes in the Northeast. And plants and animals aren't the only organisms affected. Humans are dependent on natural cycles just as much as any organism in the biosphere. What we do to natural ecosystems will eventually be felt by us also.

The second saying means that we have to pay for what we do. If we build a home on a flood plain, we can expect that it will be flooded once in a while. When we burn fossil fuels, we can expect acid rain and global warming as a consequence. Many times it is difficult to predict the particular consequences, but we can be assured that eventually they will become apparent. As we do away with plant and animal diversity, it should never be said, "What use is this organism?" One never knows how a particular organism might someday be useful to humans. Adult sea urchin skeletons are now used as molds for the production of small artificial blood vessels, and armadillos are used in leprosy research.

Summary

1. An increasing human population is causing land, water, and air pollution.

2. Various substances are associated with air pollution, such as sulfur dioxide, hydrocarbons, nitrogen oxides, methane, chlorofluorocarbons (CFCs), carbon dioxide, and carbon monoxide. These have various sources but most come from vehicle exhaust and fossil fuel burning.

3. Carbon dioxide, nitrous oxide, methane, and CFCs trap solar heat just like the panes of a greenhouse, leading to the so-called greenhouse effect. It is predicted that a buildup in these "greenhouse gases" will lead to a global warming. The effects of global warming could be a rise in sea level and a change in climate patterns. Food shortages could follow.

4. To control global warming, it is recommended that we reduce our consumption of fossil fuel energy and halt tropical rain forest destruction. Also, we should increase the amount of land devoted to forests. A ban on the manufacture of CFCs has already begun.

5. Ozone shield destruction is particularly associated with CFCs. CFCs rise into the stratosphere and release chlorine.

Chlorine causes ozone to break down. Since ozone prevents harmful ultraviolet radiation from reaching the surface of the earth, reduction in the amount of ozone will lead to skin cancer in humans and decreased productivity of the oceans.

6. Sulfur dioxide and nitrogen oxide react with water vapor to form acids that contribute to acid deposition. Acid deposition is killing lakes and forests and also corrodes marble, metal, and stonework.

7. Hydrocarbons and nitrogen oxides react to form smog, which contains ozone and PAN (peroxyacetyl nitrate). These oxidants are harmful to animal and plant life.

8. Solid wastes, including hazardous wastes, are deposited on land. The latter, including metals, organochlorides, and nuclear wastes, may contaminate water supplies. The oceans are the final recipients of wastes deposited in rivers and along the coasts.

9. Water in aquifers is being withdrawn up to fifty times faster than it can be replaced. Pollution of underground water supplies—as well as of lakes and oceans—is also a serious problem.

10. Soil erosion reduces the quality of land and leads to desertification.

11. The Canadian forests and the tropical rain forests in Southeast Asia and Oceania, Central and South America, and Africa are being cut to provide wood for export. Slash-and-burn agriculture also reduces tropical rain forests.

12. The loss of biological diversity due to the destruction of tropical rain forests will be immense. Many of these threatened organisms could possibly be of benefit to humans if we had time to study and domesticate them.

13. In a sustainable world, economic development will be tied to environmental preservation and we will no longer borrow carrying capacity from past ages and future generations.

Writing Across the Curriculum

In order to practice writing skills, students should write out the answers to any or all of the study questions and the critical thinking questions. The study questions are sequenced in the same order as the text. Answers to the objective questions, and suggested answers to the critical thinking questions, are in appendix D.

Study Questions

1. What are the environmental effects of global warming, and what can be done to prevent global warming?   892–93

2. What substances contribute to air pollution? What are their sources? Which ones are associated with photochemical smog, acid deposition, global warming, and destruction of the ozone shield?   892–95

3. How does smog develop? How do acids develop in the atmosphere? How do chlorofluorocarbons (CFCs) break down the ozone shield? How do the greenhouse gases bring about global warming?   893–95

4. What are several ways in which underground water supplies can be polluted?   896–97

5. What are the three types of hazardous wastes that contribute to pollution on land?   899

6. Give three reasons why the quality of the land is being degraded today. What is desertification?   899–900

7. Give three reasons why tropical rain forests are being destroyed. What is another possible reason in the future?   900–901

8. What are the primary ecological concerns associated with the destruction of rain forests?   901

9. How do less developed countries contribute to environmental degradation? more developed countries?   902

Objective Questions

For questions 1–4, match the terms with those in the key:

Key:
  a. sulfur dioxide
  b. ozone
  c. carbon dioxide
  d. chlorofluorocarbons (CFCs)

1. acid deposition
2. ozone shield destruction
3. greenhouse effect
4. photochemical smog
5. Which of these is a true statement?
   a. More developed countries do not contribute to the destruction of tropical rain forests.

   b. Carbon dioxide from fossil fuel combustion is the primary greenhouse gas.

   c. Water from underground sources is never subject to contamination.

   d. Sulfur dioxide is given off to the same degree by the burning of all fossil fuels.

6. Which of these is a true statement?

   a. Global warming is of no immediate concern.

   b. Global warming is so imminent that nothing can be done.

   c. Reduction in fossil fuel burning will lessen the greenhouse effect.

   d. Since gases not derived from fossil fuel combustion are involved, reduction in fossil fuel burning will not help the greenhouse effect.

7. Tropical rain forest destruction is extremely serious because

   a. it will lead to a severe reduction in biological diversity.

   b. tropical soils cannot support agriculture for long.

   c. large tracts of forest absorb carbon dioxide, reducing the threat of global warming.

   d. All of these are correct.

8. Which of these is mismatched?

   a. fossil fuel burning—carbon dioxide given off

   b. nuclear power—radioactive wastes

   c. solar energy—greenhouse effect

   d. biomass burning—carbon dioxide given off

9. Acid deposition causes

   a. lakes and forests to die.

   b. acid indigestion in humans.

   c. the greenhouse effect to lessen.

   d. All of these are correct.

10. Water is a renewable resource, and

   a. there will always be a plentiful supply.

   b. the oceans can never become polluted.

   c. it is still subject to pollution.

   d. primary sewage treatment plants assure clean drinking water.

Concepts and Critical Thinking

1. *Air pollutants have far-reaching effects.*
Use figure 52.1 to substantiate that air pollutants have combined effects.

2. *Tropical rain forests play a major role in the biosphere.*
Explain why the tropical rain forests should be saved.

Selected Key Terms

acid deposition The return to earth as rain or snow of the sulfate or nitrate salts of acids produced by commercial and industrial activities. 894

aquifer (AHK-wuh-fur) An underground river that lies between two nonporous layers of rock. [L. *aqua,* water, and *fer,* bear] 896

biological magnification The process by which substances become more concentrated in organisms in the higher trophic levels of the food chain. 899

desertification (di-zurt-uh-fuh-KAY-shun) The transformation of marginal lands to desert conditions. 900

greenhouse effect The reradiation of solar heat toward the earth, caused by gases in the atmosphere. 892

ozone shield Formed from oxygen in the upper atmosphere, it protects the earth from ultraviolet radiation. 894

photochemical smog Air pollution that contains nitrogen oxides and hydrocarbons which react to produce ozone and PAN (peroxylacetyl nitrate). [Gk. *photo,* light, and *chem,* chemical] 895

pollutant A substance that is added to the environment and leads to undesirable effects for living organisms. [L. *pollut,* defiled] 892

sustainable world A global way of life that can continue indefinitely because the economic needs of all peoples are met while still protecting the environment. 902

thermal inversion Temperature inversion that traps cold air and its pollutants near the earth with the warm air above it. [Gk. *therm,* heat, and L. *vers,* turn] 895

Suggested Readings for Part VII

Anderson, D. M. 1994. Red tides. *Scientific American* 271(2):62. The frequency of toxic red tides has been increasing because pollution provides rich nutrients, which encourages algal bloom.

Brown, B. E., and Ogden, J. C. 1993. Coral bleaching. *Scientific American* 268(1):64. Coral bleaching usually occurs due to abnormally high seawater temperatures, and this could indicate global warming.

Charlson, R., and Wigley, T. L. 1994. Sulfate aerosol and climatic change. *Scientific American* 270(2):48. Sulfur aerosols scatter sunlight back into space before it can contribute to global warming.

Cox, G. 1993. *Conservation ecology.* Dubuque, Iowa: Wm. C. Brown Publishers. Discusses the nature of the biosphere, the threats to its integrity, and ecologically sound responses.

Cox, P. A., and Balick, M. J. 1994. The ethnobotanical approach to drug discovery. *Scientific American* 270(6):82. Many rain forest plants are used by indigenous cultures for medicinal purposes; these flora should be screened for pharmaceutical compounds.

Duellman, W. E. 1992. Reproductive strategies of frogs. *Scientific American* 267(1):80. Frogs have mananged to colonize niches throughout the terrrestrial environment.

Eisner, T., and Wilson, E. O., editors. 1975. *Readings from* Scientific American*: Animal behavior.* San Francisco: W. H. Freeman and Co. A collection of articles on animal behavior.

Glass, L., and Mackey, M. C. 1988. *From clocks to chaos: The rhythms of life.* Princeton University Press. Princeton, N.J.: An advanced presentation of the application of mathematics to the study of biological rhythms.

Goulding, M. 1993. Flooded forests of the Amazon. *Scientific American* 266(3):114. Unique adaptations allow creatures to thrive in the aquatic ecosystems of the rain forest.

Grier, J., and Burk, T. 1992. *Biology of animal behavior.* 2d ed. St. Louis: Mosby-Year Book, Inc. Essays integrate the structure and function of behavior with topics of ethology, comparative psychology, and neurobiology.

Holloway, M. 1993. Sustaining the Amazon. *Scientific American* 269(1):90. Harvesting Brazil nuts and other products may allow economic growth without destroying the Amazon.

Holloway, M. 1994. Diversity blues. *Scientific American* 271(2):16. Toxic tides, coastal development, and pollution are increasing; oceanic biodiversity is suffering.

Holloway, M. 1994. Nurturing nature. *Scientific American* 270(4):98. Florida's Everglades are serving as a testing ground—and battlefield—for an epic attempt to restore an environment damaged by human activity.

Holloway, M., and Horgan, J. 1991. Soiled shores. *Scientific American* 265(4):102. An evaluation of the effectiveness of cleanup techniques after the Exxon Valdez spill, and the implications for Persian Gulf cleanup.

Kirchner, W., and Towne, W. 1994. The sensory basis of the honeybee's dance language. *Scientific American* 270(6):74. The honeybees' elaborately choreographed dance and its sounds communicate to nestmates where food outside the hive is located.

Lents, J. M., and Kelly, W. J. 1993. Clearing the air in Los Angeles. *Scientific American* 269(4):32. During the past two decades, pollution has been cut dramatically, even as population and the number of automobiles soared.

Lohmann, K. 1992. How sea turtles navigate. *Scientific American* 266(1):100. A combination of cues from the earth's magnetic field and the steady seasonal pattern of waves may be the sources of sea turtles' biological maps and compass.

May, R. M. 1992. How many species inhabit the earth? *Scientific American* 267(4):42. Author argues that an accurate census of species is crucial to preserve biological diversity and to manage the earth's resources.

Morgan, M. et al. 1993. *Environmental science: Managing biological and physical resources.* Dubuque, Iowa: Wm. C. Brown Publishers. Written for the undergraduate, this book explains how various environmental issues are linked.

Newman, E. 1993. *Applied ecology.* Oxford: Blackwell Scientific Publications. Presents the role of biological science in environmental preservation (a basic knowledge of related fields of science and math is assumed).

Odum, E. 1993. *Ecology: And our endangered life-support systems.* 2d ed. Sunderland, Mass.: Sinauer Associates. Introduces the principles of modern ecology as they relate to threats to the biosphere.

Pollack, H., and Chapman, D. 1993. Underground records of changing climate. *Scientific American* 268(6):44. More is being learned about global climate through geological studies.

Reganold, J. P., et al. 1990. Sustainable agriculture. *Scientific American* 262(6):112. Conservation-minded farming methods combined with modern technology can reduce farmers' dependence on dangerous chemicals.

Rennie, J. 1992. Living together. *Scientific American* 266(1):122. Ecologists are studying intimate associations that develop between host and parasite; these associations may have fundamentally shaped the evolution of all living things.

Strobel, G. A. 1991. Biological control of weeds. *Scientific American* 265(1):72. Presents environmentally compatible alternatives to chemical herbicides.

Toon, O. B., and Turco, R. P. 1991. Polar stratospheric clouds and ozone depletion. *Scientific American* 264(6):68. Clouds and CFCs create the ozone hole in Antarctica.

Tumlinson, J. H., et al. 1993. How parasitic wasps find their hosts. *Scientific American* 266(3):100. Besides recognizing odors from their caterpillar hosts, wasps also learn to identify compounds released by the plant on which the caterpillars feed.

When observed over several years, the population size of many organisms can fluctuate or oscillate in a regular way. Several species of insects exhibit spectacular population size fluctuations. One species that has been studied in detail is the forest tent caterpillar that feeds on deciduous trees throughout North America (fig. A).[1]

Populations of the tent caterpillar can increase to such a large size that the leaves in wide areas of the forest are completely consumed. The populations will, however, later decrease for several years before another increase occurs (fig. B). These periodic, regular cycles of population growth and decline have proven extremely puzzling to biologists. In the natural environment where conditions are often irregular and chaotic, there appears to be no simple reason for such regular population cycles.

What causes and controls these fluctuations in population size? Several hypotheses have been proposed. Perhaps the most obvious is that the food supply controls caterpillar populations.

Hypothesis I   *Caterpillar population size will be related to the amount of food available as forest vegetation.*

Prediction I   Based on this hypothesis, it is possible to predict that if food is plentiful, caterpillar populations increase. When caterpillars exhaust their food supply (tree leaves), the populations decrease.

Result I   Careful observations revealed that the populations often start to decline well before vegetation was completely consumed. In one specific experiment, tent caterpillar colonies were taken from an area where population density was high and placed in an uninfested area where there was ample vegetation. These new colonies, however, decreased in population size at the same time as

did colonies in heavily infested areas even though the food supply was plentiful for the new colonies!

> **Question I.**   **(a)** Outline the experimental design in the experiment described above. What variable was measured? What variable was held constant? What was the control?

A slightly different experiment was also performed to test Hypothesis 1. In this study, caterpillar colonies were removed from an area where the population was growing. This procedure artificially maintained a low population density and prevented the caterpillars from significantly reducing the food supply. Under these conditions, the caterpillar population again declined when the populations in other areas decreased, even though food was plentiful.

Figure A
Tent caterpillars, *Malacosoma,* form colonies in the branches of infested wild plum trees, *Prunus.* Severe outbreaks of caterpillar populations can completely defoliate trees.

These results—which clearly indicate that there is little, if any, relation between food supply and population size—contradict Hypothesis 1.

Since widely separated populations increase and decline at the same time, some factor that would affect them all in the same way could account for the changes in population size. Weather is an obvious factor that affects widespread populations in the same way.

Hypothesis 2 Fluctuations in tent caterpillar populations are related to favorable and unfavorable weather conditions.

Prediction 2 During favorable climatic conditions, caterpillar populations increase; during harsh weather conditions, populations decrease or remain low.

Result 2 Careful examination of extensive weather records and caterpillar outbreaks have revealed no link between weather conditions and tent caterpillar outbreaks. Even though a wide variety of seasonal variations in temperature, rainfall, and incident sunlight were exam-ined, no relation could be detected between any weather condition and population cycles. In another study, populations were examined in mountainous areas where there are large variations in temperature and rainfall with altitude. Even in this case, caterpillar populations at low and high elevations exhibited the same population cycles at the same times.

Clearly Hypothesis 2 must also be rejected. Another series of experiments suggested that a completely different factor may account for population oscillations. In these studies, tent caterpillar eggs were collected from natural populations and the resulting caterpillars were reared in the laboratory under constant, controlled conditions. Even in the laboratory, these populations decreased at the same time as those in the field! These experiments suggested that something carried by the caterpillars and/or the eggs was controlling fluctuations.

It has long been known that insect viruses can infect a wide variety of forest caterpillars. Could periodic outbreaks of infection reduce caterpillar populations?

Hypothesis 3 Infection of caterpillar populations with a lethal virus causes growing populations to decrease and maintains small populations at a low level.

Prediction 3 When increasing caterpillar populations are artificially infected with a lethal virus, the population decreases.

Result 3 In an aerial and ground spraying program using a lethal virus in Canadian forests, caterpillar populations were reduced to zero. At other untreated sites, populations continued to grow, reaching a peak the next year. Spraying with the virus stopped the caterpillar outbreak well before growth reached a maximum. Indeed, spraying with the virus has proven to be the only effective means of controlling population cycles.

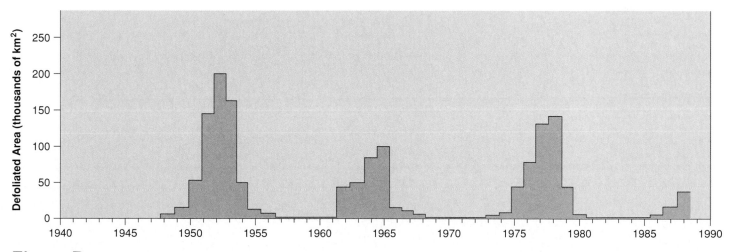

Figure B
Population cycles of tent caterpillars in Ontario, Canada. Severe outbreaks were observed in 1952, 1965, and 1977.

These results seem to provide strong support for Hypothesis 3. Additional experiments are needed to test the hypothesis, but this is a difficult endeavor. The mechanism of transmission of the virus is not known, and detecting the virus at low concentrations can be difficult. As experimental techniques improve, it will be possible to investigate this hypothesis in more detail.

Question 3. **(d)** Of approximately 80 species of forest insects that can exhibit explosive population growth, 18 species show population cycles. How could the viral infection hypothesis explain why some species are cyclic and others are not?

This case study is an excellent example of an investigation where several hypotheses initially seem reasonable. Subsequent testing of *each* hypothesis is necessary to establish which should be eliminated and which has the most support.

References

1 Myers, J. H. 1993. Population outbreaks in forest Lepidoptera. *American Scientist* 81(3):240.

Kingdom Prokaryotae

Prokaryotic, unicellular organisms; heterotrophic by absorption, autotrophic by chemosynthesis or by photosynthesis; primarily asexual reproduction by binary fission but genetic exchange occurs by conjugation, transformation, transduction; motile forms move by flagella.

Subkingdom Archaebacteria   Bacteria that lack peptidoglycan walls. Methanogens, halophiles, thermoacidophiles.

Subkingdom Eubacteria   Bacteria having peptidoglycan walls:

Gram-negative bacteria   (thin layer of peptidoglycan)

Phylum Chemoautotrophs   Rod-shaped; derive energy from oxidizing inorganic compounds. Nitrobacteria.

Phylum Photoautotrophs   Rod-shaped; derive energy from sunlight. Includes the anoxygenic photosynthesizers such as the purple nonsulfur bacterium *Rhodospirillum* and the oxygenic photosynthesizers such as the cyanobacteria, *Anabena* and *Oscillatoria*.

Phylum Enterobacteria   Rod-shaped, heterotrophic bacteria. *Salmonella, Escherichia coli, Vibrio cholerae*.

Phylum Myxobacteria   Rod-shaped, form masses; some are spore-bearing. Myxobacteria.

Phylum Pseudomonads   Rod-shaped, flagellated soil bacteria. *Pseudomonas*.

Phylum Rickettsias   Obligate parasites of vertebrates and arthropods. *Rickettsia*.

Phylum Spirochaetes   Spiral-shaped, flagellated bacteria. *Borrelia, Treponema*.

Phylum Cyanobacteria   Photosynthetic bacteria; chlorophyll *a* and phycobilin. *Anabena, Oscillatoria, Spirulina*.

Gram-positive bacteria   (thick layer of peptidoglycan)

Phylum Actinobacteria   Spore-producing, filamentous bacteria. *Actinomyces, Streptomyces, Mycobacterium*.

Kingdom Protoctista

Eukaryotic, unicellular microorganisms and their immediate multicellular descendants; asexual and sexual reproduction; flagella and cilia with 9 + 2 microtubules. Nucleated algae, protozoa, slime molds, and water molds.

The Algae*

Phylum Chlorophyta   Mostly freshwater unicellular, colonial, or multicellular; chlorophylls *a* and *b*; starch accumulates within chloroplast. Cell wall; some with flagella. Green algae: *Chlamydomonas, Spirogyra, Oedogonim, Ulva*. 7,000 species.

Phylum Phaeophyta   Almost all marine, often multicellular; common along rocky coasts; chlorophylls *a* and *c*. Brown algae: *Fucus, Laminaria, Nereocystis, Sargassum*. 1,500 species.

Phylum Chrysophyta   Marine and freshwater, mostly unicellular; chlorophylls *a* and *c*. Cell wall in some contains silica. Diatoms and allies. 11,000 species.

Phylum Dinoflagella   Mostly marine, unicellular; chlorophylls *a* and *c*. Cellulose plates for cell wall, two unequal flagella beat in grooves at right angles. Many are symbiotic and then known as zooxanthellae. Dinoflagellates. 1,000 species.

Phylum Euglenophyta   Mostly freshwater, unicellular; often chlorophylls *a* and *b*. No cell wall; two flagella. Euglenoids: *Euglena*. 1,000 species.

Phylum Rhodophyta   Mostly marine, multicellular; chlorophyll *a* and phycobilin like the cyanobacteria. Red algae. 4,000 species.

The Protozoa*

Phylum Sarcodina   Freshwater and marine unicellular heterotrophs by ingestion; movement by pseudopods; no cell wall but marine forms may have shells; asexual reproduction. Amoebas and allies: *Amoeba proteus, Entamoeba histolytica*. 40,000 species.

Phylum Ciliophora   Freshwater unicellular heterotrophs by ingestion; movement by cilia; no cell wall but some have a flexible pellicle; asexual reproduction with complex sexual exchange through conjugation. Ciliates: *Paramecium, Stentor, Vorticella*. 8,000 species.

Phylum Zoomastigophora   Freshwater or parasitic unicellular heterotrophs by ingestion or absorption; movement by flagella. Asexual reproduction. Zooflagellates: *Giardia, Trichomonas, Trypanosoma* (African sleeping sickness).

Phylum Sporozoa   Unicellular heterotrophs by absorption; nonmotile, spore-forming parasites of animals; complex life cycles. Sporozoa: *Plasmodium* (malaria), *Pneumocystis* (pneumonia), *Toxoplasma* (toxoplasmosis). 3,600 species.

The Slime Molds and Water Molds*

Phylum Gymnomycota   Individual amoeboid cells or multinucleated mass; heterotrophic by ingestion; nonmotile spores with rigid cell walls and motile cells with flexible walls are produced. Slime molds. 560 species.

Phylum Oomycota   Filamentous mildews or molds with cellulose cell walls; heterotrophic by saprotrophism or parasitism; asexual reproduction by formation of zoospores; oogamy during sexual reproduction. Water molds. 580 species.

Kingdom Fungi

Multicellular eukaryotes; heterotrophic by absorption; lack flagella; nonmotile spores form during both asexual and sexual reproduction.

Division Zygomycota   Hyphae nonseptate; asexual reproduction common by sporangiospores; sexual reproduction involves thick-walled zygospore. Zygospore fungi: soil and dung molds, black bread molds (*Rhizopus*). 600 species.

Division Ascomycota   Hyphae septate; asexual reproduction common by conidiospores; sexual reproduction involves dikaryotic hyphae with formation of ascospores in asci. Sac fungi: many small wood-decaying fungi, yeasts (*Saccharomyces*), molds (*Neurospora*), morels, cup fungi, truffles; plant parasites: powdery mildews, ergots. 30,000 species.

Division Basidiomycota   Hyphae septate; asexual reproduction by conidiospores; sexual reproduction common by long-lasting dikaryotic mycelium with formation of basidiospores on basidia. Club fungi: mushrooms, stinkhorns, puffballs, bracket and shelf fungi, coral fungi; plant parasites: rusts, smuts. 16,000 species.

Division Deuteromycota   Hyphae septate; asexual reproduction common by conidiospores; sexual reproductive structures are not known. Imperfect fungi: athlete's foot, ringworm, candidiasis. 25,000 species.

Kingdom Plantae

Multicellular, primarily terrestrial eukaryotes with well-developed tissues; autotrophic by photosynthesis; alternation of generations life cycle. Like green algae, plants contain chlorophylls *a* and *b*, carotenoids; store starch in chloroplasts; cell wall contains cellulose.

Division Hepatophyta   Strap-shaped (some leafy, some thallose), that creep along the substrate; dominant gametophyte and dependent sporophyte; mostly moist and shaded habitats. Liverworts. 10,000 species.

Division Bryophyta   Stemlike, leaflike, and rootlike structures; dominant gametophyte and dependent sporophyte; mostly moist and shaded habitats. Mosses. 12,000 species.

Division Anthocerotophyta   Thallose plants with green gametophytes; photosynthetic sporophytes at the upper surface of gametophyte; dominant gametophyte and dependent sporophyte; mostly moist and shaded habitats. Hornworts. 100 species.

The Vascular Plants*

Division Psilotophyta   Rhizome with erect branched stems; no roots or leaves; terminal sporangia borne on stems; tropical and subtropical habitats. Whisk ferns. Several species.

Division Lycopodophyta   In *Lycopodium*, rhizome with upright branches and roots; scalelike leaves (microphylls) cover stems and branches; sporangia mostly borne in terminal cones; mostly tropical and subtropical but also temperate to Arctic and dry habitats. Club mosses, spike mosses, quillworts. 1,000 species.

Division Equisetophyta   In *Equisetum*, horizontal underground rhizome jointed stems; whorled branches and scalelike leaves; sporangia borne in terminal cones; moist habitats. Horsetails. 15 species.

Division Pteridophyta   Well-developed leaves (megaphylls) called fronds; sporangia on sporophylls; moist, shaded habitats common; sometimes dry areas. Ferns. 12,000 species.

The Seed Plants*
Gymnosperms*

Division Pinophyta   Woody tree with thick trunk; needle-like or scalelike evergreen leaves (some shrubby); reproductive organs in pollen and seed cones; widespread distribution. Conifers: pines, firs, yews, redwoods, spruces. 550 species.

Division Cycadophyta   Thick woody stem; large leaves resembling palm fronds; massive male and female cones; mostly tropical and subtropical. Cycads. 100 species.

Division Ginkgophyta   Woody tree with long side branches; fan-shaped deciduous leaves; microsporangia in cones, naked ovules on stalks; gardens and parks. Maidenhair tree. One living species.

Division Gnetophyta   In *Gnetum*, trees and climbing vines with large leathery leaves; moist tropical habitat. In *Ephedra*, a profusely branched shrub with small, scalelike leaves; desert habitat. In *Welwitschia*, massive woody, disk-shaped stem with straplike leaves; desert habitat. Gnetophytes. 70 species.

The Angiosperms*

Division Magnoliophyta   Trees, shrubs, herbs; most with broad leaves; herbs are perennials or annuals; reproductive organs in flower; pollen often carried by insects; double fertilization; seeds enclosed by fruits; widespread distribution; some aquatic. Flowering plants.

Class Liliopsida (monocot) Flower parts in threes or multiples of threes; parallel-veined leaves; one cotyledon. Grasses, lilies, pineapple. 65,000 species.

Class Magnoliopsida (dicot) Flower parts in fours, fives, or multiples of these; net-veined leaves; two cotyledons. Most flowering herbs, shrubs, trees. 170,000 species.

Kingdom Animalia

Multicellular organisms with well-developed tissues; usually motile; heterotrophic by ingestion, generally in a digestive cavity; diplontic life cycle.

Phylum Porifera Multicellular bodies perforated by many pores that admit water which exits through the only opening; internal skeleton of spicules; digestion within collar cells (choanocytes); regeneration possible. Mostly marine sponges. 5,000 species.

Phylum Cnidaria Two-layered radially symmetrical body; gastrovascular cavity has only one opening; characterized by presence of stinging cells (cnidocytes); regeneration possible; all aquatic and most marine. Hydras, jellyfishes. 9,000 species.

Class Cubozoa Medusa form square with toxic sting. Sea wasps, box jellyfish.

Class Anthozoa Polyp forms with no medusae. Sea anemones, corals.

Class Hydrozoa Polyp form dominant, often colonial, frequently with an alternation of generations. *Hydra, Obelia.*

Class Monogenea Parasitic, with hooks. Anchor worms.

Class Scyphozoa Medusa form dominant. *Aurelia.*

Phylum Ctenophora Free-swimming, often almost spherical animals; translucent, sometimes bioluminescent; plates of cilia and a thick layer of mesoglea; radially symmetrical with two very long, specialized tentacles. Comb jellies, sea walnuts. 90 species.

Phylum Platyhelminthes Three-layered bilaterally symmetrical body; gastrovascular cavity has only one opening; excretion by means of flame cells; complex hermaphroditic reproductive systems; regeneration possible. Flatworms. 13,000 species.

Class Turbellaria Ciliated, carnivorous with eyespots. Planaria.

Class Trematoda Parasitic with oral and ventral suckers; digestive cavity. Flukes.

Class Cestoda Parasitic with scolex having hooks and suckers and proglottids; no digestive cavity. Tapeworms.

Phylum Nemertea Usually marine worms with proboscis apparatus; acoelomate; a complete digestive system. Ribbon worms. 650 species.

Phylum Nematoda Nonsegmented worms; pseudocoelom and a tube-within-a-tube body plan; free living and parasitic. Roundworms: *Ascaris.* 12,000 species.

Phylum Rotifera Microscopic, pseudocoelomate wormlike or spherical animals with a corona (circle of cilia) on the head, the beating of which resembles a revolving wheel. Rotifers. 2,000 species.

The Protostomes* Schizocoelomates; the first embryonic opening is associated with the mouth; cleavage is spiral and determinate.

Phylum Mollusca Body divided into foot, visceral mass, and mantle; usually also radula and shell; reduced coelom. Mollusks. 110,000 species.

Class Polyplacophora Body flattened dorsoventrally; shell consisting of eight dorsal plates; grazing marine herbivores. Chitons.

Class Bivalvia Body enclosed by a shell consisting of two valves; no head or radula; wedge-shaped foot; marine and freshwater sessile filter feeders. Clams, scallops, oysters, mussels.

Class Cephalopoda Tentacles about head; shell may be reduced or absent; head in line with elongated visceral mass, closed circulatory system; well-developed nervous system with cephalization; marine active predators. Squids, chambered nautilus, octopus.

Class Gastropoda Shell is coiled if present; body symmetry distorted by torsion; head with tentacles; marine, freshwater, and terrestrial grazing herbivores. Snails, slugs, nudibranchs.

Phylum Annelida Segmented worms with a long, cylindrical, soft body; protostome coelomates with internal septa; specialized digestive tract; definite central nervous system with brain and ventral solid nerve cord; closed circulatory system. Annelids. 12,000 species.

Class Polychaeta Marine with good cephalization; bundles of setae on parapodia. Clam worms (*Nereis*), tube worms.

Class Oligochaeta Fewer setae with no parapodia; no distinct head in terrestrial forms. Earthworms.

Class Hirudinea External parasites or scavengers, or with anterior and posterior suckers; parapodia and setae absent. Leeches.

Phylum Arthropoda Chitinous exoskeleton with jointed appendages specialized in structure and function; well-developed central nervous system with brain and ventral paired nerve cord; reduced coelom; hemocoel. Arthropods. Over 6 million species.

Subphylum Trilobitomorpha Three-lobed body with distinct head, thorax, and abdomen; serially repeated biramous appendages; extinct.

Subphylum Chelicerata Chelicerae, pedipalps, and four pairs of walking legs attached to a cephalothorax; no antennae, mandibles, or maxillae. Spiders, scorpions, horseshoe crabs.

Subphylum Crustacea   Compound eyes and five pairs of walking appendages; antennae and antennules, mandibles and maxillae on head; biramous appendages on thorax and abdomen. Lobsters, crayfish, shrimps, crabs, many others.

Subphylum Uniramia   Uniramous appendages; one pair of antennae, one pair of mandibles, and one or two pairs of maxillae; terrestrial with tracheae. Millipedes, centipedes, insects.

The Deuterostomes*   Enterocoelomates; the second embryonic opening is associated with mouth; cleavage is radial and indeterminate.

Phylum Echinodermata   Radial symmetry; endoskeleton of spine-bearing plates; water vascular system with tube feet. Echinoderms. 6,000 species.

Class Crinoidea   Filter feeders with feathery arms. Sea lilies, feather stars. 600 species.

Class Asteroidea   Five arms project from central disk; movement by tube feet. Sea stars. 1,500 species.

Class Ophiuroidea   Slender, long, often spiny, highly flexible arms from central disk. Brittle stars. 2,000 species.

Class Echinoidea   No distinct arms; spines used for locomotion, defense, burrowing. Sea urchins, sand dollars. 950 species.

Class Holothuroidea   Long, leathery body with tentacles about mouth. Sea cucumbers. 1,500 species.

Phylum Hemichordata   Marine; wormlike body divided into proboscis, collar, trunk; pharyngeal gill slits and dorsal hollow nerve cord in proboscis. Hemichordates: acorn worms. 90 species.

Phylum Chordata   Pharyngeal pouches; dorsal hollow nerve cord; notochord; post-anal tail. Chordates. 45,000 species.

Subphylum Urochordata   Larva free swimming with three chordate characteristics; adults sessile filter feeders with plentiful gill slits. Tunicates. 1,250 species.

Subphylum Cephalochordata   Marine fishlike animals with three chordate characteristics as adults. Lancelets. 23 species.

The Vertebrates*

Subphylum Vertebrata   Notochord replaced by vertebrae that protect the nerve cord; skull that protects the brain; segmented with jointed appendages. Vertebrates. 43,700 species.

Superclass Agnatha   Marine and freshwater fishes; lack jaws and paired appendages; cartilaginous plates added to notochordal skeleton; notochord. Lampreys, hagfishes. 63 species.

Superclass Gnathostomata   Hinged jaws; paired appendages. Jawed fishes, tetrapods.

Class Chondrichthyes   Marine cartilaginous fishes; lack operculum and swim bladder; tail fin usually asymmetrical. Sharks, skates, rays. 850 species.

Class Osteichthyes   Marine and freshwater bony fishes; operculum; swim bladder or lungs; tail fin usually symmetrical. Lungfishes, lobe-finned fishes, ray-finned fishes (herring, salmon, sturgeon, eels, sea horse). 20,000 species.

Class Amphibia   Tetrapod with nonamniote egg; nonscaly skin; metamorphosis; three-chambered heart; ectothermic. Urodeles (salamanders, newts), anurans (frogs, toads). 3,900 species.

Class Reptilia   Tetrapod with amniotic egg; scaly skin; ectothermic. Squamata (snakes, lizards), chelonians (turtles, tortoises); crocodilians (crocodiles and alligators). 6,000 species.

Class Aves   Tetrapod with feathers; bipedal with wings; double circulation; endothermic. Sparrows, penguins, ostriches. 9,000 species.

Class Mammalia   Tetrapods with hair, mammary glands; double circulation; endothermic; teeth differentiated. Monotremes (spiny anteater, duckbill platypus), marsupials (opossum, kangaroo), placental mammals (whales, rodents, dogs, cats, elephants, horses, bats, humans). 4,500 species.

---

* Not in the classification of organisms, but added here for clarity

APPENDIX B
TABLE OF CHEMICAL ELEMENTS

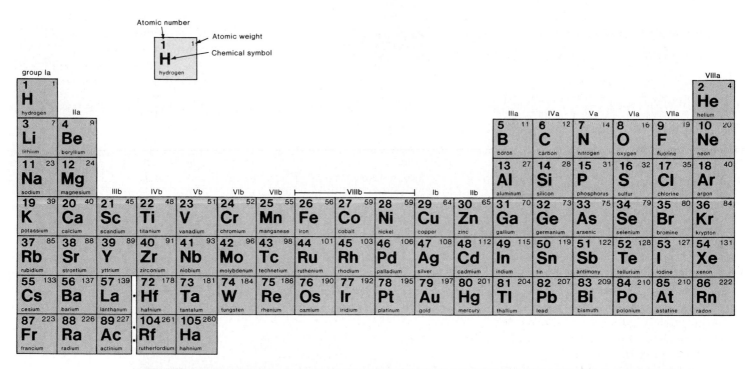

APPENDIX C
METRIC SYSTEM

Unit and Abbreviation	Metric Equivalent	Approximate English-to-Metric Conversion Factor	Units of Temperature
Length			
nanometer (nm)	$= 10^{-9}$ m $(10^{-3}$ μm)		
micrometer (μm)	$= 10^{-6}$ m $(10^{-3}$ mm)		
millimeter (mm)	$= 0.001\ (10^{-3})$ m		
centimeter (cm)	$= 0.01\ (10^{-2})$ m	1 inch = 2.54 cm	
		1 foot = 30.5 cm	
meter (m)	$= 100\ (10^{2})$ cm	1 foot = 0.30 m	
	$= 1{,}000$ mm	1 yard = 0.91 m	
kilometer (km)	$= 1{,}000\ (10^{3})$ m	1 mi = 1.6 km	
Weight (mass)			
nanogram (ng)	$= 10^{-9}$ g		
microgram (μg)	$= 10^{-6}$ g		
milligram (mg)	$= 10^{-3}$ g		
gram (g)	$= 1{,}000$ mg	1 ounce = 28.3 g	
		1 pound = 454 g	
kilogram (kg)	$= 1{,}000\ (10^{3})$ g	= 0.45 kg	
metric ton (t)	$= 1{,}000$ kg	1 ton = 0.91 t	
Volume			
microliter (μ*l*)	$= 10^{-6}$ *l* $(10^{-3}$ m*l*)		
milliliter (m*l*)	$= 10^{-3}$ *l*	1 tsp = 5 m*l*	
	$= 1$ cm^3 (cc)	1 fl oz = 30 m*l*	
	$= 1{,}000$ mm^3		
liter (*l*)	$= 1{,}000$ m*l*	1 pint = 0.47 *l*	
		1 quart = 0.95 *l*	
		1 gallon = 3.79 *l*	
kiloliter (k*l*)	$= 1{,}000$ *l*		

To convert temperature scales:
Fahrenheit to Centigrade °C $= \frac{5}{9}$ (°F − 32)

°C	°F	
100	212	Water boils at standard temperature and pressure
71	160	Flash pasteurization of milk
57	134	Highest recorded temperature in the United States, Death Valley, July 10, 1913
41	105.8	Average body temperature of a marathon runner in hot weather
37	98.6	Human body temperature
20.3	68.6	Lowest recorded body temperature to be survived by a human
0	32.0	Water freezes at standard temperature and pressure

APPENDIX D
ANSWERS

Chapter 1

Objective Questions

1. d
2. c
3. a
4. b
5. e
6. c
7. b
8. c

9. **a.** plants; **b.** animals; **c.** nutrients for plants; **d.** death and decay

Concepts and Critical Thinking

1. A common ancestor has passed on to all living things common characteristics, such as using DNA genes.
2. Ways of life are diverse; therefore, organisms are diverse.
3. Nonliving things may have levels of organization, but they do not demonstrate emergent properties, where the whole is greater than the sum of the parts. For example, a cell is alive, but the structures that make up a cell are not alive.

Chapter 2

Objective Questions

1. c, d, a, b
2. d
3. a
4. b
5. c
6. a
7. d

Concepts and Critical Thinking

1. Even though the results of experimentation or observation support a hypothesis, it could be that the further studies will prove it false.
2. In the everyday sense, a theory means a supposition; in the scientific sense, a theory means a hypothesis that has been supported by many experiments and observations.

3. A scientist does studies to understand the natural world; citizens make decisions as to how these results should be used.

Chapter 3

Objective Questions

1. c
2. b
3. c
4. d
5. d
6. d
7. b
8. c
9. a

10. 7p and 7n in nucleus; two electrons in inner shell, and five electrons in outer shell. This means that nitrogen needs three more electrons to complete its outer shell; therefore the formula for ammonia is NH_3, since hydogen contributes one electron each.

Concepts and Critical Thinking

1. For example, people take supplemental calcium to keep their bones strong.
2. Molecules form by bonding between atoms, which requires that electrons be lost, gained, or shared. The bonds that result are energy relationships, and without molecules, living things could not exist. Also, living things are dependent upon chemical reactions such as those that occur during photosynthesis. These reactions involve the excitation of electrons and the release of their gained energy.
3. For example, if water was not slow to heat up and slow to cool down, living things might be subject to the killing effects of rapid heating

and cooling. The density of water is less at $O°$ C, and therefore the cold layer rises, allowing plants and especially animals to live below the surface during cold weather.

Chapter 4

Objective Questions

1. c
2. a
3. d
4. b
5. c
6. b
7. c
8. c
9. d
10. c
11. a

12. **a.** monomer; **b.** condensation; **c.** polymer; **d.** hydrolysis. The diagram shows the manner in which macromolecules are synthesized and degraded in cells.
13. **a.** primary level; **b.** secondary level; **c.** tertiary level; **d.** quaternary level
14. c

Concepts and Critical Thinking

1. They are unified in the use of carbohydrate as a structural molecule, but they are diversified as to the particular carbohydrate.
2. Butter is solid, and an oil is a liquid at room temperature because a fat containing saturated hydrocarbon chains melts at a higher temperature than one containing unsaturated chains.
3. Phospholipids have a polar head and nonpolar tails; they make up the plasma membrane, which is selectively permeable. Keratin, a fibrous protein that contains only helix polypeptides, is found in tough structures such as hair and nails.

Chapter 5

Objective Questions

1.	c	6.	c
2.	c	7.	a
3.	d	8.	d
4.	a	9.	b
5.	c	10.	d

11. **a.** example; **b.** Mitochondria and chloroplasts are a pair because they are both membranous structures involved in energy metabolism. **c.** Centrioles and flagella are a pair because they both contain microtubules; centrioles give rise to the basal bodies of flagella. **d.** ER and ribosomes are a pair because together they are rough ER, which produces proteins.

12. **a.** Golgi apparatus further modified; **b.** smooth ER modifies; **c.** rough ER produces; **d.** chromatin-DNA directs; **e.** nucleolus-RNA helps.

Concepts and Critical Thinking

1. Show them microscopic slides of all sorts of tissues from different organisms. You would have to find an organism whose tissues did not contain cells.
2. The various organelles listed in table 5.1 show that the cell is compartmentalized; each organelle has a separate function.
3. All the structures labeled in question 12 above, plus mitochondria, supply ATP energy. All the other parts of a cell assist to some degree also.

Chapter 6

Objective Questions

1.	b	6.	d
2.	b	7.	d
3.	a	8.	b
4.	c	9.	b
5.	c		

10. **a.** hypertonic—Cell shrinks due to loss of water; **b.** hypotonic—Cell has swelled due to gain of water.

Concepts and Critical Thinking

1. Structurally, the plasma membrane is the outer boundary of the cell. Functionally, the plasma membrane regulates what enters and leaves a cell.
2. A cell can die in either a severely hypertonic or a severely hypotonic solution because of the passage of water.
3. The plasma membrane secretes chemical messengers that communicate with distant cells; the plasma membrane participates in the structure of junctions between adjacent cells.

Chapter 7

Objective Questions

1.	a	5.	d
2.	d	6.	c
3.	c	7.	d
4.	a	8.	c

9. **a.** macromolecules; **b.** degradative reactions; **c.** ADP + ⓟ→ ATP; **d.** NADP → NADPH; **e.** small molecules; **f.** synthetic reactions; **g.** macromolecules

10 **a.** high H^+ concentration; **b.** low H^+ concentration; **c.** H^+ pump in electron transport system; **d.** H^+; **e.** ATP synthase complex; **f.** ADP; **g.** P; **h.** ATP. See also figure 7.10, page 115.

Concepts and Critical Thinking

1. Both the rough ER and the Golgi apparatus produce molecules that are used for structural purposes. It takes energy to produce molecules.
2. When glucose energy is converted to ATP, there is a loss, and the energy released when ATP is broken down eventually becomes heat.
3. The temperature of the body is not high, and enzymes are needed to bring reactants together.

Chapter 8

Objective Questions

1.	d	5.	c
2.	d	6.	d
3.	a	7.	c
4.	d	8.	d

9. **a.** outer membrane; **b.** inner membrane; **c.** stroma; **d.** thylakoid; **e.** grana; **f.** thylakoid; **g.** stroma

10. **a.** water; **b.** oxygen; **c.** carbon dioxide; **d.** carbohydrate; **e.** ADP + ⓟ → ATP; **f.** $NADP^+$ → NADPH

Concepts and Critical Thinking

1. Show that solar energy is needed for photosynthesis, and photosynthetic organisms are the food for the biosphere, including humans. The bodies of plants became the fossil fuels, which we use to produce electricity, heat houses, and convert to gasoline for cars.
2. Chlorophyll captures solar energy, which is converted to ATP energy and used to produce NADPH. ATP and NADPH are used to reduce CO_2 to a carbohydrate.
3. The thylakoid space is separated from the stroma by the thylakoid membrane; the buildup of hydrogen ions in the thylakoid space leads to ATP production by chemiosmotic means.

Chapter 9

Objective Questions

1.	b	11.	c
2.	c	12.	a
3.	a	13.	b
4.	c	14.	d
5.	c	15.	b
6.	c	16.	a
7.	a	17.	d
8.	b	18.	a
9.	c	19.	c
10.	d	20.	b

21. **a.** outer membrane; **b.** inner membrane; **c.** cristae; **d.** matrix

22. **a.** glucose; **b.** 2 ATP; **c.** pyruvate; **d.** CO_2; **e.** acetyl-CoA; **f.** Krebs cycle; **g.** 2 ATP; **h.** CO_2; **i.** NADH; **j.** NADH; **k.** NADH; **l.** electron transport system; **m.** 32 ATP; **n.** H_2O

Concepts and Critical Thinking

1. Flow of energy: photosynthesis converts the energy of the sun into carbohydrates that are converted to ATP energy by cellular respiration. Recycling of matter: Carbohydrates and oxygen from photosynthesis participate in cellular respiration, whose end product, carbon dioxide, reenters plants.
2. Nutrient molecules are broken down to molecules that participate in cellular respiration, with the concomitant buildup of ATP. It is the ATP that is used by cells.
3. Glycolysis is a metabolic pathway that is almost universally found in organisms; it must have evolved in an ancestor common to all organisms.

Chapter 10

Objective Questions

1. c
2. b
3. d
4. d
5. a
6. c
7. b
8. c
9. b
10. b
11. a. centrosome; b. nuclear envelope fragment; c. kinetochore; d. aster; e. nucleolus; f. spindle fibers. See also figure 10.5, page 162.

Concepts and Critical Thinking

1. As cells grow, they become ready for reproduction by producing more plasma membrane, cytoplasm, and organelles.
2. The daughter cells inherit DNA, along with its inherent regulation, from the parent cell.
3. Mitosis involves the use of a spindle, a structure that ensures that each daughter cell receives a copy of each chromosome. It also occurs in an orderly manner.

Chapter 11

Objective Questions

1. b
2. c
3. c
4. b
5. a
6. c
7. d
8. d
9. c
10. a—It shows bivalents at the metaphase plates.

Concepts and Critical Thinking

1. Asexual reproduction and sexual reproduction begin with cells, usually single cells. This shows how fundamental the cell is to the life of an organism.
2. Variation during asexual reproduction is limited to the occurrence of mutations.
3. Advantage: favorable mutations may be of immediate advantage. Disadvantage: unfavorable mutations may be of immediate disadvantage.

Chapter 12

Practice Problems 1

1. a. 100% W; b. 50% W, 50% w; c. 50% T, 50% t; d. 100% T
2. a. gamete; b. genotype; c. gamete

Practice Problems 2

1. bb
2. 75% yellow; 25% green
3. $^3/_4$ or 75%
4. $Tt \times tt$, tt

Practice Problems 3

1. Testcross
2. Ll, ll, 50% Ll, 50% ll
3. 200 have wrinkled seeds

Practice Problems 4

1. a. 50% TG, 50% tG; b. 25% TG, 25% Tg, 25% tG, 25% tg; c. 50% TG, 50% Tg
2. a. gamete; b. genotype; c. gamete

Practice Problems 5

1. $BbTt$ only
2. a. $LlGg$, $llgg$; b. $LlGg$, $LlGg$
3. $^9/_{16}$

Objective Questions

1. b
2. a
3. c
4. d
5. c
6. d
7. a
8. b
9. b
10. b
11. c
12. d

Additional Genetics Problems

1. 100% chance for widow's peak and 0% chance for continuous hairline
2. ee (recessive)
3. 50%

4. 210 gray bodies and 70 black bodies; 140 = heterozygous; cross fly with recessive (black body)
5. F_1 = all black with short hair; F_2 = 9 black, short: 3 black, long: 3 brown, short: 1 brown, long; offspring would be 1 brown long : 1 brown short : 1 black long : 1 black short
6. $Bbtt \times bbTt$ and $bbtt$
7. $GGLl$
8. 25%

Concepts and Critical Thinking

1. You inherit chromosomes containing the same types of genes from your parents, but each parent contributes one-half of the genes inherited.
2. Plants and animals both have chromosomes containing the genetic material, DNA.
3. The individual's genes were not modified by the accident.

Chapter 13

Practice Problems 1

1. Cc^h (wild), $c^{ch}c^h$ (light gray), Cc^{ch} (wild), c^hc^h (Himalayan)
2. 1 pink, 1 white; or 50% pink, 50% white
3. 7
4. pleiotropy, epistasis

Practice Problems 2

1. females: X^RX^R, X^RX^r, X^rX^r males: XRY (gametes X^R, Y), X^rY (gametes X^RYX^r, Y)
2. b in 1:1
3. 100%; none; 100%

Practice Problems 3

1. 9:3:3:1; linkage
2. 12
3. bar eye, scalloped wings, garnet eye

Objective Questions

1. b
2. c
3. e
4. a
5. b
6. b
7. d
8. b
9. c
10. d

Additional Genetics Problems

1. pleiotropy
2. codominance; $F^B F^B, F^W F^W, F^B F^W$
3. 50%
4. 6; yes
5. linkage; 10
6. Both males and females are 1:1.
7. $X^B X^B \times X^b Y$ = both males all and females bar-eyed, $X^b X^b \times X^B Y$ = females bar-eyed, males all normal
8. $X^b X^b Ww$
9. females—1 short-haired tortoise shell : 1 short-haired yellow. males—1 short-haired black : 1 short-haired yellow

Concepts and Critical Thinking

1. Most human traits, such as height and color of skin, are examples of polygenic inheritance.
2. The genes behave similarly to the chromosomes (i.e., they come in pairs, they segregate during meiosis, and there is only one in the gametes).
3. Almost all males have a Y chromosome; XO individuals are females. This shows that most likely sex-determining alleles on the Y chromosome have some degree of dominance to sex-determining alleles on the X chromosome.

Chapter 14

Practice Problems 1

1. 50%
2. heterozygous—unless it is a new mutation, which is a fairly common cause of neurofibromatosis.

Practice Problems 2

1. heterozygous
2. $Hb^A Hb^S$; either $Hb^S Hb^S$ or $Hb^A Hb^S$
3. A, B, AB, O

Practice Problems 3

1. mother $X^H X^h$, father $X^H Y$, son $X^h Y$; 50%
2. color-blind father

Objective Questions

1. c
2. a
3. b
4. c
5. d
6. c
7. b
8. d
9. c
10. a

11. autosomal dominant condition

Additional Genetics Problems

1. 0%; 0%; 100%
2. 25%
3. *AB;* yes; A, B, AB, or O
4. $X^C X^c Ww, X^C Y Ww;$ normal vision with widow's peak
5. sex-linked recessive, $X^A X^a$

Concepts and Critical Thinking

1. Similarities include all the basic principles of genetics pertaining to Mendel's laws. Plants do not have sex chromosomes; therefore sex-linkage, bar bodies, etc., do not pertain to them. Also, polyploidy becomes a common chromosomal mutation. Yes, the concept still holds, because any differences don't negate the basic similarities.
2. Divide the cells of an early embryo to produce as large a number of identical children as possible. (This solves the nature question.) Raise each child under entirely different circumstances and then see how similar the children are.
3. This is a question that individuals must decide on their own. Genetic counseling and genetic testing can sometimes tell parents their chances of having a child with a genetic disease.

Chapter 15

Objective Questions

1. b
2. d
3. a
4. c
5. d
6. c
7. a
8. d
9. d

10. The parental helix is heavy-heavy, and each daughter helix is heavy-light. This shows that each daughter helix is composed of one template strand and one new strand, which is consistent with semiconservative replication.

Concepts and Critical Thinking

1. Hershey and Chase reasoned that which ever phage molecule—DNA or protein—entered bacteria, this molecule was the genetic material because it directed the production of a virus with specific characteristics.
2. Replication is a part of duplication of the chromosomes. Replication before mitosis ensures that each daughter cell will have the diploid number of chromosomes, and replication before meiosis ensures that the sperm and egg will have the haploid number of chromosomes.
3. Mutation is the ultimate source of genetic variation. Without variation, new organisms would never evolve.

Chapter 16

Objective Questions

1. b
2. a
3. c
4. a
5. a
6. c
7. b
8. c
9. d

10. **a.** ACU CCU GAA UGC AAA; **b.** UGA GGA CUU ACG UUU; **c.** threonine-proline-glutamate-cysteine-lysine

Concepts and Critical Thinking

1. The genetic information stored by DNA is the sequence of amino acids in a protein; this is stored in the sequence of DNA bases.
2. A universal code means that the ancestry of all types of organisms can be traced to a common origin.
3. The sequence of bases of DNA ultimately determines the sequence of amino acids in a protein.

Chapter 17

Objective Questions

1. c
2. d
3. a
4. a
5. b
6. b
7. b
8. d
9. d
10. d

11. **a.** DNA; **b.** regulator gene; **c.** promoter; **d.** operator; **e.** structural genes; **f.** mRNA; **g.** active repressor protein; **h.** RNA polymerase (see also figure 17.1*a*, *page 261*)
12. For the *trp* operon to be in the off position, a corepressor has to be attached to the repressor.

Concepts and Critical Thinking

1. Only certain mRNA molecules are present in cells at any particular time.
2. Gene expression necessitates a functioning protein product. Posttranslational control involves regulation of the activity of the protein product.
3. Checks and balances are often seen in biological systems. This is a safety feature that allows greater control.

Chapter 18

Objective Questions

1.	a	**6.**	c
2.	d	**7.**	c
3.	d	**8.**	d
4.	d	**9.**	a
5.	d		

10. **a.** AATT; **b.** TTAA
11. **a.** retrovirus; **b.** recombinant RNA; **c.** human genome; **d.** recombinant DNA; **e.** reverse transcription; **f.** recombinant DNA; **g.** defective gene. See also figure 18.8, page 285.

Concepts and Critical Thinking

1. It is possible to make recombinant DNA, to modify natural DNA in the laboratory, to perform PCR analysis, to do DNA fingerprinting, and to determine the sequence of the bases of DNA. This is disturbing to people who resist thinking of humans as physical and chemical machines.
2. Human genes can be placed in a bacterium, where they function normally.

Chapter 19

Objective Questions

1.	d	**5.**	d
2.	b	**6.**	d
3.	b	**7.**	d
4.	d	**8.**	b

9. All the continents of today were one continent during the Triassic period, and the reptiles spread throughout the land.
10. All vertebrates share a common ancestor, who had pharyngeal pouches during development.
11. Two different continents can have similar environments and, therefore, unrelated organisms that are similarly adapted.
12. Life has history, and it's possible to trace the history of individual organisms.

Concepts and Critical Thinking

1. Both bacteria and humans use DNA as the hereditary material and have similar metabolic pathways.
2. If adaptation were purposeful, organisms would not have structures that serve no current function.
3. It is possible to formulate a hypothesis about evolution and then make observations to see if the hypothesis is correct.

Chapter 20

Practice Problems 1

1. $q = 0.3$, $p = 0.7$; 9% are homozygous recessive (*t*), 49% are homozygous dominant (*T*), 42% are heterozygous
2. $Ll = 60\%$, $ll = 40\%$

Objective Questions

1.	c	**7.**	d
2.	c	**8.**	d
3.	c	**9.**	c
4.	c	**10.**	b
5.	d	**11.**	b
6.	b		

12. **a.** See figure 20.5, page 319. **b.** See figure 20.6, page 320. **c.** See figure 20.7, page 320.

13. **a.** Label each circle "population" and each arrow "gene flow." **b.** Do away with five middle arrows so that two sets of circles remain. The circles of each set are connected by arrows.

Additional Genetics Problems

1. 16%
2. 99%
3. recessive allele = 0.2, dominant allele = 0.8; homozygous recessive = 0.04, homozygous dominant = 0.64, heterozygous = 0.32

Concepts and Critical Thinking

1. The recessive and dominant characteristics are maintained in a population and neither tends to disappear.
2. The more fit organisms have more offspring, and this is the way by which adaptive traits accumulate in a population.
3. The higher taxa show how species are related. Species in different kingdoms are distantly related, and those in the same genus are closely related.

Chapter 21

Objective Questions

1.	d	**7.**	b
2.	c	**8.**	a
3.	b	**9.**	a
4.	c	**10.**	d
5.	b	**11.**	c
6.	b		

12. **a.** Cambrian era begins; **b.** multicellularity; **c.** origin of eukaryotic cells; **d.** oxidizing atmosphere; **e.** oldest known fossils; **f.** formation of earth

Concepts and Critical Thinking

1. All three hypotheses suggest that a chemical evolution produced the first cell(s).
2. Under the conditions of the primitive earth, a chemical evolution produced the first cell(s). Under the conditions of today's earth, life comes only from life.

3. Both the phyletic gradualism and the punctuated equilibrium models of evolutionary change would support the statement that speciation accounts for the diversity of life. These two models disagree as to how rapidly speciation might occur; with phyletic gradualism, the process is more gradual than with punctuated equilibrium which, relatively speaking, proposes more rapid change within a given period of time.

Chapter 22

Objective Questions

1. a
2. b
3. d
4. d
5. d
6. c
7. c
8. b
9. c
10. a. Chordata; b. Vertebrata; c. Class; d. Order; e. Anthropoidea; f. Hominoidea; g. Hominidae; h. Genus; i. *sapiens*

Concepts and Critical Thinking

1. We are closely related to the African apes on the basis of structure, function, behavior, and genetics. Our bodies are structured similarly and our internal organs function similarly. The young of both apes and humans have an extended period of dependency during which they learn from the adults. Molecular data suggests that African apes and humans diverged about 6 MYA.
2. Hominids evolved in eastern Africa after formation of the rift valley, which separated eastern Africa from the rest of the continent. The evolution of humans may be associated with adaptations to the increasingly dry environmental conditions.
3. DNA similarities show relatedness because it shows that the genes of the two species being compared are similar. Genes govern the structure and function of organisms. Two examples: (1) comparison of modern human DNA with that of African apes suggests that they diverged much later than previously thought and (2) comparison of mitochondrial DNA among modern human races supports the out-of-Africa hypothesis.

Chapter 23

Objective Questions

1. a
2. c
3. d
4. a
5. c
6. a
7. d
8. b
9. b
10. d
11. a. 3; by color—eel, newt, snake, and lizard; b. vertebra; amniote egg, internal fertilization; c. the clades; they share derived characters. See also figure 23B, page 392.

Concepts and Critical Thinking

1. The classification of humans tells you that humans trace their ancestry back to the evolution of animals, chordates, mammals, and primates, in that sequence. Humans share these classification categories with the apes from which they diverged when the hominids evolved. They are closely related to the other extinct hominids but became *Homo* when their brains underwent greater development and they began to use tools. *Homo sapiens* is the only species to have a conceptual language and the ability to manipulate the environment at will.
2. If you want to define a species in terms of structure, then you have to contend with the recognition that each species contains individuals with variant features. If you want to define a species in terms of reproductive isolation you have to concede that some species do hybridize with other species. To define a species simply as the lowest ranking taxon does not tell you how species function in nature.
3. Cladists believe traditionalists are being subjective when they give more weight to adaptations to new environments than they do to the characters themselves. They are judging the "quality" of characters when they say that the adaptations of birds warrent placing birds in their own class rather than with the reptiles.

Chapter 24

Objective Questions

1. c
2. c
3. b
4. c
5. c
6. c
7. c
8. c
9. b
10. d
11. a. attachment; b. bacterial chromosome; c. penetration; d. integration; e. prophage; f. maturation; g. release. See also figure 24.3, page 399.

Concepts and Critical Thinking

1. Viruses are unable to carry on reproduction outside a living cell. They reproduce by taking over the machinery of the cell; therefore, they are obligate parasites.
2. Prokaryotes are metabolically diverse, as witnessed by the fact that there is probably no single type of organic compound that some prokaryotes cannot digest.
3. Prokaryotes are structurally simple but biochemically diverse. The statement that life from simple to complex refers to structure, not biochemistry.

Chapter 25

Objective Questions

1. c
2. b
3. b
4. d
5. b
6. b
7. d
8. c
9. d
10. b
11. a. sexual reproduction; b. isogametes pairing; c. zygote (2n); d. zygospore (2n); e. asexual reproduction; f. zoospores (n); g. nucleus; h. chloroplast; i. pyrenoid; j. starch granule; k. flagellum; l. eyespot; m. gamete formation.
12. Asexual: one parent, no gametes produced, no genetic recombination. Sexual: two parents, gametes produced, genetic recombination. See also figure 25.2, page 414.

Concepts and Critical Thinking

1. If chloroplasts evolved from endocytosis, we cannot rely on the presence of similar pigments in two groups to indicate an evolutionary relationship.
2. Protoctists are classified because they do not conform to the categories of the other kingdoms, not because of specific characteristics of the organisms.
3. Sporozoa are nonmotile and parasitic.

Chapter 26

Objective Questions

1.	b	6.	a
2.	c	7.	d
3.	b	8.	c
4.	a	9.	d
5.	c	10.	d

11. **a.** meiosis; **b.** basidiospores; **c.** dikaryotic mycelium; **d.** fruiting body (basidiocarp); **e.** stalk; **f.** gill; **g.** cap; **h.** dikaryotic (n + n); **i.** diploid (2n); **j.** zygote. See also figure 26.7, page 436.

Concepts and Critical Thinking

1. All fungi carry out extracellular digestion and reproduce by means of spores. Fungi are composed of filaments of cells (hyphae) which are submerged in a substrate into which they send digestive juices and from which they acquire nutrient molecules. Fungi live on the land and produce spores that are frequently windblown.
2. Each group of fungi reproduce slightly differently and this provides the means by which they are classified.
3. We do not know what data should be used to indicate evolutionary relationships among fungi and, as yet, DNA analysis has not been carried out.

Chapter 27

Objective Questions

1.	d	6.	b
2.	c	7.	b
3.	c	8.	b
4.	c	9.	d
5.	d		

10. **a.** sporophyte (2n); **b.** meiosis; **c.** gametophyte (n); **d.** fertilization. See also figure 27B, page 459.

Concepts and Critical Thinking

1. The five-kingdom system of classification is based in part on mode of nutrition. From this standpoint, it would seem that all photosynthesizers should be in the same kingdom. On the other hand, in this text all organisms in the plant kingdom are multicellular with some degree of complexity. Also, all organisms in the plant kingdom protect the zygote.
2. Roots enable a plant to take water out of the soil, stems hold the leaves aloft to catch solar energy, and the leaves also take in carbon dioxide at stomates.
3. Advantages to having a dominant sporophyte: (a) the sporophyte is the diploid generation, and a harmful gene can be masked by a normal gene; (b) the sporophyte is the generation that has vascular tissue, which is a beneficial adaptation to life on land; (c) the sporophyte is the generation that can grow larger and best protects the gametophyte as it does in seed plants.

Chapter 28

Objective Questions

1.	d	5.	b
2.	c	6.	d
3.	d	7.	a
4.	d		

8. **a.** polyp; **b.** budding; **c.** medusa; **d.** zygote; **e.** planula; **f.** mesoglea; **g.** mouth; **h.** tentacle. See also figure 28.5, page 471.

9. Sponges (no items)
Cnidaria
    radial symmetry
    tissue level of organization
Flatworms
    three tissue layers
Roundworms
    pseudocoelom
    three tissue layers
    tube-within-a tube body plan

Concepts and Critical Thinking

1. You would expect them to lack photosynthetic pigments, have some means of digesting food, distribute the products of digestion to cells, and rid the body of wastes. Each group of animals is adapted to its own means of acquiring food.
2. A common ancestor would have to have those features shared by both types of organisms: bilateral symmetry, three tissue layers, and organs.
3. Internal parasites need to have a means of protecting themselves from host attack, absorbing nutrients from the host, and reproducing that allows dispersal to new hosts.

Chapter 29

Objective Questions

1.	b	6.	a
2.	d	7.	d
3.	b	8.	c
4.	c	9.	a
5.	c		

10. **a.** all three; **b.** annelids, arthropods; **c.** all three; **d.** all three; **e.** all three; **f.** all three; **g.** arthropods; **h.** mollusks
11. **a.** earthworms; **b.** clams; **c.** clams; **d.** clams; **e.** earthworms; **f.** earthworms; **g.** clams; **h.** clams; **i.** earthworms; **j.** earthworms
12. **a.** head; **b.** antenna; **c.** simple eye; **d.** compound eye; **e.** thorax; **f.** tympanum; **g.** abdomen; **h.** forewing; **i.** hindwing; **j.** ovipositor; **k.** spiracles; **l.** air sac; **m.** spiracle; **n.** tracheae. See also figure 29.14a, page 498.

Concepts and Critical Thinking

1. Segmentation is obvious in an earthworm due to the uniform external rings and presence of setae on every ring. In an arthropod such as the grasshopper, segmentation has led to specialization of parts. There is a head region, a thorax, and an abdominal region. The segments devoted to the head bear mouthparts; those of the thorax bear legs and wings, and the abdomen has no appendages.
2. For example, a clam (phylum Mollusca) is a filter feeder. There is no head and the clam burrows in the soil with its hatchet foot. Small particles that enter the mantle cavity are trapped by mucus on the gills and directed by cilia toward the mouth. Clam worms (phylum Annelida) are predators with a head that bears sense organs and strong chitinous jaws for eating prey. Spiders (phylum Arthropoda) have chelicerae modified as fangs, with ducts from poison glands, and pedipalps to hold and chew prey.
3. Wings (for flying in air); spiracles and tracheae (for breathing air); tympanum (for picking up sound waves); ovipositor (for laying eggs in earth); digestive system (for eating grass); Malpighian tubules (for excretion without loss of water); vagina and seminal receptacles (for reception and storage of sperm without desiccation).

Chapter 30

Objective Questions

1.	b	6.	d
2.	b	7.	a
3.	d	8.	c
4.	a	9.	d
5.	b	10.	b

11. a. pharyngeal pouches; b. dorsal hollow nerve cord; c. notochord; d. post-anal tail. See illustration, page 506.

Concepts and Critical Thinking

1. Both arthropods and chordates have the same body plan (tube-within-a-tube with specialization of parts), are bilateral with cephalization, have three tissue layers, have organ systems, have a true coelum, and are segmented with specialization of parts.
2. The skeleton of arthropods and vertebrates is rigid and segmented. A rigid skeleton provides the support needed when water no longer provides buoyancy, and a segmented skeleton permits the complex body movements required for locomotion on land.
3. How gametes are protected from drying out: reptiles pass sperm directly from male to female; angiosperms rely on the pollen grain. How embryo is protected from drying out: reptiles develop in a shelled egg; angiosperms produce seeds that protect the embryo until germination under favorable conditions occurs.

Chapter 31

Objective Questions

1.	c	6.	b
2.	b	7.	b
3.	c	8.	c
4.	c	9.	c
5.	b	10.	b

11. a. epidermis; b. cortex; c. endodermis; d. phloem; e. xylem. See also figure 31.8, page 536.
12. a. cork; b. phloem; c. vascular cambium; d. bark; e. xylem (wood); f. pith; g. annual ring. See also figure 31.15, page 542.
13. a. upper epidermis; b. palisade mesophyll; c. leaf vein; d. spongy mesophyll; e. lower epidermis. See also figure 31.18, page 546.

Concepts and Critical Thinking

1. A leaf that is broad and flat is well shaped to catch the sun's rays; the cells contain chloroplasts; the leaf veins bring water from the roots; and the stomates admit carbon dioxide into the air spaces of the spongy layer.
2. Write out your answer and check it against figure 31.1 (page 530) and table 31.1 (page 548).

3. Wood helps a plant resist the pull of gravity. It serves as an internal skeleton and allows the plant to lift its leaves, exposing them to the solar rays.

Chapter 32

Objective Questions

1.	d	5.	c
2.	a	6.	c
3.	c	7.	c
4.	b	8.	d

9. The diagram shows that air pressure pushing down on mercury in the pan can raise a column of mercury only to 76 cm. When water above the column is transpired, it pulls on the mercury and raises it higher. This suggests that transpiration would be able to raise water to the top of trees.
10. See figure 32.6, page 556. After K^+ enters guard cells, water follows by osmosis and the stomate opens.
11. There is more solute in the left bulb than in the right; therefore water enters the left bulb. This creates a pressure that causes water, along with solute, to flow toward the right bulb.

Concepts and Critical Thinking

1. A physical process accounts for the transport of water in xylem, causes a stomate to open, and accounts for the transport of organic substances in phloem.
2. Because vessel cells are hollow and nonliving, they form a continuous pipeline from the roots to the leaves. This allows plants to transport water and minerals from the roots to the leaves.

Chapter 33

Objective Questions

1.	d	7.	d
2.	b	8.	b
3.	e	9.	d
4.	a	10.	d
5.	c	11.	a
6.	b		

12. **a.** abscissic acid (ABA) in; **b.** K⁺ ions out; **c.** guard cell. K⁺ ions leave guard cells under the influence of ABA when a plant is water stressed. Water osmotically follows the movement of K⁺, and the stomate closes.

Concepts and Critical Thinking

1. The best example is that the ratio of auxin to cytokinin determines whether a plant tissue will form an undifferentiated mass or form roots, vegetative shoots and leaves, or flowers.
2. **a.** It is adaptive, for example, for leaves to unfold and stomates to open during the day, when photosynthesis can occur. **b.** A biological clock system needs a receptor that is sensitive to light and dark, a timekeeper (a biological clock), and a means of communication within the body of the organism. In regard to flowering, phytochrome is the receptor and hormones are probably the means of communication. The possible timekeeper is not known.
3. Reception occurs when auxin binds to receptors on cells. After reception the cell produces cellulase enzyme. This is transduction. Then cellulase brings about a breakdown of the cell wall to produce elongation of cells and bending of the stem toward the light. The response to auxin has now occurred.

Chapter 34

Objective Questions

1.	c	**6.**	b
2.	a	**7.**	a
3.	b	**8.**	d
4.	a	**9.**	c
5.	a	**10.**	d

11. **a.** sporophyte; **b.** meiosis; **c.** microspore; **d.** megaspore; **e.** microgametophyte (pollen grain); **f.** megagametophyte (embryo sac); **g.** egg and sperm; **h.** fertilization; **i.** zygote; **j.** seed. See also figure 34.1, page 586.

Concepts and Critical Thinking

1. Flowering plants follow the alternation of generations life cycle, but the gametophyte is reduced to a microscopic size and is protected by the sporophyte. The gametes are also protected; the egg stays within the ovule in the ovary and awaits the sperm. A pollen grain is transported to the pistil by wind or animals and then germinates, allowing the sperm to move down the style to the egg. The zygote (new sporophyte) develops into an embryo within the ovule, which becomes the seed enclosed by fruit. Fruit is dispersed in various ways.
2. As stated, the gametophyte is protected by the sporophyte and the embryonic sporophyte is protected by the seed.
3. Coevolution results in one type of pollinator gathering food from a particular plant. This reduces competition and assures the pollinator of food from this particular source.

Chapter 35

Objective Questions

1.	b	**6.**	d
2.	b	**7.**	b
3.	a	**8.**	d
4.	d	**9.**	d
5.	d	**10.**	c

11. **a.** smooth muscular tissue; **b.** blood cells—connective tissue; **c.** nervous tissue; **d.** ciliated columnar epithelium

Concepts and Critical Thinking

1. The cell is alive, but the organelles making up a cell are not alive; a tissue performs functions that the individual cell in the tissue cannot perform, and so forth from level to level.
2. Acquiring food is located to the right and left of the diagram. Cellular respiration is a degradative pathway requiring an exchange of gases. Excretion of waste accompanies degradation.
3. Acquiring food provides materials and energy; the musculoskeletal system helps us get food; exchange of gases gets rid of carbon dioxide

and brings in oxygen; transporting materials brings nutrients to and takes wastes away from cells.

Chapter 36

Objective Questions

1.	b	**7.**	b
2.	b	**8.**	b
3.	a	**9.**	d
4.	d	**10.**	b
5.	d	**11.**	d
6.	c		

12. **a.** aorta; **b.** left pulmonary artery; **c.** pulmonary trunk; **d.** left pulmonary veins; **e.** left atrium; **f.** semilunar valves; **g.** atrioventricular (mitral) valve; **h.** left ventricle; **i.** septum; **j.** inferior vena cava; **k.** right ventricle; **l.** chordae tendineae; **m.** atrioventricular (tricuspid) valve; **n.** right atrium; **o.** right pulmonary veins; **p.** branches of right pulmonary artery; **q.** superior vena cava. See also figure 36.6, page 633.

Concepts and Critical Thinking

1. Tissue fluid remains relatively constant because materials are continuously being added and removed at the capillaries.
2. The cells are far removed from the organism's exterior surface, and therefore they have to have nutrients brought to them and wastes removed from them.
3. ATP energy keeps the heart pumping (arterial flow) and the skeletal muscles contracting (venous flow). ATP energy is produced by mitochondria, where chemical energy is transformed into usable energy.

Chapter 37

Objective Questions

1.	d	**6.**	b
2.	d	**7.**	a
3.	a	**8.**	a
4.	b	**9.**	b
5.	c	**10.**	d

11. **a.** Helper T cells secrete lymphokines and stimulate other immune cells; **b.** suppressor T cells suppress further development of helper T cells, and prevent B and T cell immune responses from getting

out of hand; **c.** memory T cells respond to particular antigens, resulting in active immunity; **d.** cytotoxic T cells search out and destroy antigen-bearing cells.

Concepts and Critical Thinking

1. Death occurs when immunity fails to prevent microorganisms from taking over the body.
2. Immunity consists of immediate defense mechanisms and specific defense mechanisms, which work more slowly.
3. Bones are of course part of the skeletal system. Red bone marrow is the site of red and white blood cell formation; therefore, it is part of the circulatory and lymphatic systems.

Chapter 38

Objective Questions

1.	d	**7.**	c
2.	b	**8.**	c
3.	d	**9.**	d
4.	b	**10.**	c
5.	c	**11.**	d
6.	c	**12.**	c

13. Test tube 1: no digestion; no enzyme and no HCl
    Test tube 2: some digestion; no HCl
    Test tube 3: no digestion; no enzyme
    Test tube 4: digestion; both enzyme and HCl are present

Concepts and Critical Thinking

1. In humans, the digestive system takes in nutrients, excretes certain metabolites like heavy metals, and prevents bacterial invasion by the low pH of the stomach.
2. A clam is aquatic and filters debris from the water which enters and exits the mantle cavity. An earthworm lives in the soil and obtains organic matter by sucking up soil. An earthworm has many specific organs: crop for storage, gizzard for grinding and intestine for absorption. A squid is an active predator which has tentacles to seize prey and jaws to bite off suitably sized pieces. A grasshopper, which is terrestrial and feeds on most any plant, has many

specific organs: a crop (storage), stomach (digestion) and gastric ceca (absorption).

3. Human beings are omnivores—we eat both plant and animal material. The meat we eat is from animals that have fed on plants; therefore, all sources of food can ultimately be traced to plants. Food is used as a source of building blocks and energy. Also important is the fact that plants supply us with oxygen needed for the breakdown of glucose products in mitochondria, where ATP is produced.

Chapter 39

Objective Questions

1.	a	**6.**	b
2.	b	**7.**	c
3.	b	**8.**	b
4.	d	**9.**	d
5.	c	**10.**	b

11. **a.** nasal cavity; **b.** nostril; **c.** pharynx; **d.** epiglottis; **e.** glottis; **f.** larynx; **g.** trachea; **h.** bronchus; **i.** bronchiole; **j.** lung; **k.** diaphragm; **l.** pulmonary venule; **m.** pulmonary arteriole; **n.** alveolus; **o.** capillary network. See also figure 39.6, page 705.

Concepts and Critical Thinking

1. The respiratory system carries out exchange of gases and helps maintain the pH of the blood.
2. Gills are external extensions and lungs are internal cavities. Both are minutely divided and highly vascularized for the exchange of gases.
3. In humans, the lungs expand when the chest moves up and out and deflate when the chest moves down and in. The lungs contain many alveoli (air sacs) and are highly vascularized. Oxygen enters the blood following inhalation, and carbon dioxide leaves the body upon exhalation.

Chapter 40

Objective Questions

1.	d	**6.**	c
2.	a	**7.**	b
3.	c	**8.**	d
4.	b	**9.**	a
5.	a	**10.**	b

11. **a.** pressure filtration; **b.** glomerulus; **c.** glomerular capsule; **d.** selective reabsorption; **e.** proximal convoluted tubule; **f.** water; **g.** tubular secretion; **h.** distal convoluted tubule; **i.** reabsorption of water; **j.** reabsorption of H_2O; **k.** loop of the nephron; **l.** peritubular cavity; **m.** collecting duct; **n.** excretion; **o.** renal pelvis. See also figure 40.9, page 705.

Concepts and Critical Thinking

1. When molecules undergo degradation, wastes result. For example, following glucose metabolism, carbon dioxide must be excreted. Following amino acid breakdown, urea must be excreted.
2. Water contains a lower amount of oxygen than air. The countercurrent mechanism in the gills of fishes helps them extract oxygen out of water. Mammals evolved on land; a countercurrent mechanism in the kidneys helps them conserve water.
3. Reabsorption, in part by active transport, takes place in the proximal convoluted tubule. An increased surface area (microvilli) helps reabsorption, and mitochondria supply the ATP energy for active transport.

Chapter 41

Objective Questions

1.	c	**6.**	a
2.	b	**7.**	b
3.	d	**8.**	d
4.	c	**9.**	b
5.	a	**10.**	b

11. **a.** receptor; **b.** sensory neuron; **c.** cell body of sensory neuron; **d.** dorsal root ganglion; **e.** white matter; **f.** gray matter; **g.** central canal; **h.** cell body of motor neuron; **i.** interneuron; **j.** motor neuron; **k.** effector (brings about adaptive response).

Concepts and Critical Thinking

1. The nervous system controls internal organs like the beating of the heart and skeletal muscles, which allow an animal to seek environments compatible with a constant internal environment.
2. There is a spinal nerve in each segment, but the brain is an obvious specialization of part of the spinal cord.
3. A neuron has long processes that conduct nerve impulses. The postsynaptic membrane is part of a dendrite, and the presynaptic membrane is part of an axon. Impulses always flow in this direction because only an axon contains synaptic vesicles.

Chapter 42

Objective Questions

1.	d	**6.**	c
2.	c	**7.**	c
3.	c	**8.**	b
4.	d	**9.**	d
5.	d	**10.**	c

11. **a.** ciliary body (holds lens in place, accommodation); **b.** lens (refracts and focuses light rays); **c.** iris (regulates light entrance); **d.** pupil (admits light); **e.** cornea (refracts light rays); **f.** fovea centralis (makes acute vision possible); **g.** optic nerve (transmits impulse to brain); **h.** sclera (protects and supports eyeball); **i.** choroid (absorbs stray light); **j.** retina (contains receptors for sight). See also figure 42.5, page 737.

Concepts and Critical Thinking

1. The sense organs help animals find favorable environments and avoid unfavorable ones; they help animals find food and avoid

predators; they help animals communicate with others for the purpose of cooperation.
2. The sense organs are receptors for external and internal stimuli; they generate nerve impulses, which supply information to the central nervous system.
3. Relative fitness determines what structures characterize a species. Therefore, animals have those sense organs that are most adaptive.

Chapter 43

Objective Questions

1.	b	**6.**	b
2.	f	**7.**	b
3.	c	**8.**	c
4.	e	**9.**	d
5.	b	**10.**	d

11. See table 43.2, page 761.
12. **a.** actin filament; **b.** myosin filament; **c.** Z line; **d.** H zone; **e.** A band; **f.** I band. See also figure 43.14, page 761.

Concepts and Critical Thinking

1. Compare, for example, the skeleton of a fish to that of a primate, such as monkey. The skeleton of a fish is adapted to moving through water and that of a monkey to climbing in trees.
2. Animals have to seek food; therefore, locomotion is essential to them.
3. Nutrient molecules from the digestive system travel in the blood to muscle cells. Here, glucose energy is converted to ATP energy, largely within mitochondria. ATP energy is used by myosin filaments to pull actin filaments, and muscle contraction occurs.

Chapter 44

Objective Questions

1.	f	**7.**	a
2.	b	**8.**	d
3.	c	**9.**	b
4.	a	**10.**	d
5.	e	**11.**	a
6.	c		

12. **a.** high sodium; **b.** inhibits; **c.** renin; **d.** angiotensin I and II; **e.** aldosterone. When the blood sodium level is low, the kidneys secrete renin. Renin stimulates the production of angiotensin I and II, which stimulate the adrenal cortex to release aldosterone. The kidneys absorb sodium. See also figure 44.6, page 776.

Concepts and Critical Thinking

1. Neurotransmitters are released when needed and then reabsorbed by the presynaptic membrane or broken down within the synaptic cleft by an enzyme. The level of a hormone is controlled typically by using negative feedback to regulate its production.
2. Specialized structures (i.e., neurons) deliver messages in the nervous system, whereas the endocrine system uses the circulatory system.
3. The human body undergoes a dramatic change following puberty.

Chapter 45

Objective Questions

1.	b	**6.**	c
2.	d	**7.**	c
3.	c	**8.**	c
4.	d	**9.**	a
5.	c	**10.**	a

11. **a.** seminal vesicle; **b.** ejaculatory duct; **c.** prostate gland; **d.** bulbourethral gland; **e.** anus; **f.** vas deferens; **g.** epididymis; **h.** testis; **i.** scrotum; **j.** foreskin; **k.** glans penis; **l.** penis; **m.** urethra; **n.** vas deferens; **o.** urinary bladder. Path of sperm: testis, epididymis, vas deferens, urethra (in penis). See also figure 45.5, page 790.

Concepts and Critical Thinking

1. Reptiles and humans are similarly adapted, except the embryos of reptiles develop in shelled eggs while the embryos of placental mammals develop within the uterus of the female. Even so, the same extraembryonic membranes surround the embryo.

2. Reproduction is a process that takes some time; it is not like movement, which takes place rapidly.

Chapter 46

Objective Questions

1.	b	6.	b
2.	b	7.	d
3.	b	8.	a
4.	a	9.	d
5.	b	10.	d

11. **a.** chorion (exchanges wastes for nutrients with the mother); **b.** amnion (protects and prevents desiccation); **c.** embryo; **d.** allantois (blood vessels become umbilical blood vessels); **e.** yolk sac (first site of blood cell formation); **f.** fetal portion of placenta; **g.** maternal portion of placenta; **h.** umbilical cord (connects developing embryo to the placenta). See also figure 46.9, page 811.

Concepts and Critical Thinking

1. Senescence is a change that is part of the normal life cycle from fertilization to death.
2. They should be considered local hormones because they are messengers that are produced by one cell and act on another cell.
3. Perhaps a gene produces a molecule that acts as signal to control a certain developmental event, and this turns on the next gene in the sequence.

Chapter 47

Objective Questions

1.	b	6.	c
2.	c	7.	c
3.	a	8.	b
4.	d	9.	d
5.	c	10.	b

Concepts and Critical Thinking

1. The genes control the development of the brain and therefore even insight learning has a genetic basis.
2. Feeding behavior patterns affect fitness because an animal needs a body in good working order for reproduction to be successful. Territoriality affects fitness because an animal needs enough food to nourish its offspring. Reproductive patterns affect fitness because an animal needs to have a mate to reproduce.
3. Altruistic acts can be shown to increase inclusive fitness.

Chapter 48

Objective Questions

1.	b	5.	d
2.	c	6.	d
3.	d	7.	b
4.	d	8.	c

9. **a.** positive; **b.** declining; **c.** zero; **d.** carrying capacity; **e.** steady state

Concepts and Critical Thinking

1. Population growth could be infinite when there are unlimited resources, such as space, food, and shelter, and where there are no deaths due to natural disasters.
2. Human life strategy is only like that of a *K*-strategist. See also figure 48.6, page 844.

Chapter 49

Objective Questions

1.	b	6.	b
2.	d	7.	d
3.	c	8.	c
4.	d	9.	d
5.	c		

10. Predation has caused the number of paramecia to decline and when they die out, so do the didinia. The graph suggests that predators can over-exploit a food resource.
11. **a.** mutualism; **b.** parasitism; **c.** commensalism

Concepts and Critical Thinking

1. The organisms themselves provide niches for other organisms. For example, several types of warblers find niches in spruce trees.
2. As prey populations decrease in size, it is less likely that a predator will find that type of prey, and prey populations have defenses against predation.
3. Parasites keep down population sizes when they weaken or directly kill off their hosts. Parasites increase diversity because, for example, even parasites have parasites. As mentioned in number 1, organisms themselves provide niches for other organisms.

Chapter 50

Objective Questions

1.	b	6.	d
2.	a	7.	c
3.	c	8.	c
4.	d	9.	a
5.	b	10.	b

11. **a.** algae; **b.** zooplankton; **c.** small fishes; **d.** large fishes; **e.** humans

Concepts and Critical Thinking

1. For example, the atmosphere is the abiotic component of the nitrogen cycle, and the passage of nitrogen compounds from producer to consumers is the biotic component of the nitrogen cycle.
2. It is impossible to create energy to keep an ecosystem going (first law), and as energy is passed from one trophic level to the next, there is always some loss of energy (second law). Therefore, there is a flow of energy from the sun through an ecosystem.
3. The statement "There is no free lunch" means that for every artificial benefit, there is a price. For example, if we kill off coyotes because they prey on chickens, we then have to realize that the mouse population (mice are a common food for coyotes) will probably increase. In an ecosystem, as we have seen, "everything is connected to everything else".

Chapter 51

Objective Questions

1. a
2. a
3. d
4. a
5. a
6. c
7. d
8. c
9. a

10. **a.** 4+ for both; **b.** 3+ for both; **c.** 2+ for both; **d.** 1+ for both

Concepts and Critical Thinking

1. The neritic province is more productive because it receives both nutrients and sunlight. In contrast, only the epipelagic zone of the oceanic province receives adequate sunlight but it is not as nutrient rich. Unfortunately the neritic province is the first to receive water-borne pollutants from land and this coupled with seaside development and the filling in of wetlands makes this province more polluted than the oceanic province.

2. A desert has low productivity due to the lack of water which even when present drains quickly away. An ocean has low productivity because of the lack of nutrients—recyling is difficult because debris tends to settle on the ocean floor.

3. It gets colder as you go from the base of a mountain to the top; therefore, the communities will change as noted. Temperature has an effect on productivity.

Chapter 52

Objective Questions

1. a
2. d
3. c
4. b
5. b
6. c
7. d
8. c
9. a
10. c

Concepts and Critical Thinking

1. The figure shows, for example, that nitrous dioxide (NO_2), nitrous oxide, carbon dioxide, methane, CFCs, and halons all contribute to the greenhouse effect, and of these CFCs and halons also caused ozone shield destruction.

2. The tropical rain forests should be saved to (a) preserve biodiversity, (b) save soil, (c) provide homes for indigenous people, (d) prevent climate changes and pollution, and (e) preserve plants useful to us.

GLOSSARY

A

abscisic acid (ABA) (ab-SIZ-ik) A plant hormone that causes stomates to close and that initiates and maintains dormancy. 579

abscission (ab-SIZH-un) The dropping of leaves, fruits, or flowers from a plant. [L. *ab*, away, and *sciss*, cut] 579

acetylcholine (ACh) (uh-set-ul-KOH-leen) A neurotransmitter active in both the peripheral and central nervous systems. 718

acetylcholinesterase (AChE) (uh-set-ul-koh-luh-NES-tuh-rays) An enzyme that breaks down acetylcholine bound to postsynaptic receptors within a synapse. 718

acetyl-CoA A molecule made up of a two-carbon acetyl group attached to coenzyme A. The acetyl group enters the Krebs cycle for further oxidation. 145

acid A compound tending to raise the hydrogen ion concentration in a solution and to lower its pH numerically. [L. *acidus*, sour] 36

acid deposition The return to earth as rain or snow of the sulfate or nitrate salts of acids produced by commercial and industrial activities. 894

acquired immunodeficiency syndrome (AIDS) A disease caused by HIV and transmitted via body fluids; characterized by failure of the immune system. 799

actin A muscle protein making up the thin filaments in a sarcomere; its movement shortens the sarcomere, yielding muscle contraction. 760

action potential Nerve impulse, the membrane potential of an active neuron. 718

active site That part of an enzyme molecule where the substrate fits and the chemical reaction occurs. 109

active transport Use of a plasma membrane carrier protein to move particles from a region of lower to higher concentration; it opposes equilibrium and requires energy. 94

adaptation An organism's modification in structure, function, or behavior which increases the likelihood of continued existence. [L. *ad*, toward, and *apt*, adjust] 5, 303

adaptive radiation The formation of a large number of species from a common ancestor. 235

adenine (A) (AD-un-een) One of four nitrogen-containing bases in nucleotides composing the structure of DNA and RNA. 235

ADH (antidiuretic hormone) (ant-ih-DY-yuu-RET-ik) A hormone secreted by the posterior pituitary that increases the permeability of the collecting ducts in a kidney. [Gk. *anti*, against, and *diure*, urinate] 706

adipose tissue A connective tissue in which fat is stored. [L. *adeps*, fat] 614

ADP (adenosine diphosphate) (ah-den-ah-SEEN dy-FAHS-fayt) One of the products of the hydrolysis of ATP, a process that liberates energy. 57, 114

adrenal gland (uh-DREEN-ul) A gland that lies atop a kidney; the adrenal medulla produces the hormones epinephrine and norepinephrine and the adrenal cortex produces the corticoid hormones. [L. *ad*, toward, and *rena*, kidney] 776

adrenocorticotropic hormone (ACTH) (uh-DREE-noh-kawrt-ih-koh-TROH-pik) A hormone secreted by the anterior lobe of the pituitary gland that stimulates activity in the adrenal cortex. 774

aerobic respiration The aerobic breakdown of pyruvate within mitochondria; results in 34 ATP, carbon dioxide, and water. [Gk. *aer*, air] 112, 144

age structure diagram A representation of the number of individuals in each age group in a population. 843

agglutination (uh-gloot-un-AY-shun) Clumping of red blood cells due to a reaction between antigens on red blood cell membranes and antibodies in the plasma. [L. *agglutin*, glued together] 644

aldosterone (al-DAHS-tuh-rohn) Hormone secreted by the adrenal cortex that regulates the sodium and potassium ion balance of the blood. 644, 706

alga (pl., algae) Aquatic, plantlike organism carrying out photosynthesis and belonging to the kingdom Protoctista. [L. *alg*, seaweed] 413

allantois (uh-LANT-uh-wus) An extraembryonic membrane that accumulates nitrogenous wastes in birds and reptiles and contributes to the formation of umbilical blood vessels in mammals. [Gk. *allant*, sausage, and *eidos*, form] 811

allele (uh-LEEL) Alternative forms of a gene which occur at the same locus on homologous chromosomes. [Gk. *allelo*, one another, parallel] 187

allopatric speciation (al-uh-PA-trik) The origin of new species in populations that are separated geographically. [Gk. *allo*, different, and *patri*, fatherland] 324

altruism A social interaction that has the potential to decrease the lifetime reproductive success of the member exhibiting the behavior. [L. *altru*, other] 835

alveolus (pl., alveoli) (al-VEE-uh-lus) Terminal, microscopic, grapelike air sac found in vertebrate lungs. [L. *alve*, cavity] 689

amino acid An organic molecule having an amino group and an acid group, that covalently bonds to produce protein molecules. 52

amnion (AM-nee-ahn) An extraembryonic membrane of birds, reptiles, and mammals that forms an enclosing, fluid-filled sac. [Gk. *amnio*, fetal membrane] 811

amniote egg An egg that has an amnion, as seen during the development of reptiles, birds, and mammals. 514

amoeboid Protoctist that moves and engulfs prey with pseudopods; amoebalike in movement. 420

amphibian A member of a class of terrestrial vertebrates that includes frogs, toads, and salamanders; they are still tied to a watery environment for reproduction. [Gk. *amph*, on both sides] 512

amylase A starch digesting enzyme secreted by salivary glands and pancreas. 671

angiosperm A flowering plant; the seeds are borne within a fruit. [Gk. *ang*, vessel, and *sperm*, seed] 457

annelid A member of the phylum Annelida, which includes clam worms, tubeworms, earthworms and leeches; characterized by a segmented body. [L. *annelus*, little ring] 490

anther Part of stamen where pollen grains develop. 458, 587

antheridium (pl., antheridia) (an-thuh-RID-ee-um) A reproductive organ found in bryophytes and some vascular plants which produces flagellated sperm. [Gk. *anth*, flower, and *idia*, small] 446

anthropoid (AN-thruh-poyd) A group of primates that includes monkeys, apes, and humans. [Gk. *anthrop*, man, and *oid*, like] 359

antibiotic A medicine that specifically interferes with bacterial metabolism and in that way cures humans of a bacterial disease. [Gk. *anti*, against, and *bio*, life] 407

antibody A protein produced in response to the presence of an antigen; each antibody combines with a specific antigen. [Gk. *anti*, against] 641, 654

antibody-mediated immunity Body line of resistance due to antibody-producing B cells. 655

anticodon Three nucleotides on a tRNA molecule attracted to a complementary codon on mRNA. [Gk. *anti*, against, and L. *cod*, tail] 252

antidiuretic hormone (ADH) (ANT-ih-dy-yuu-RET-ik) A hormone secreted by the posterior pituitary that promotes the reabsorption of water from the collecting ducts, which receive urine produced by nephrons within the kidneys. [Gk. *anti*, against, and *diure*, urinate] 771

antigen A foreign substance, usually a protein or a polysaccharide, that stimulates the immune system to react, such as to produce antibodies. [Gk. *anti*, against, and *gene*, origin] 654

antigen A foreign substance, usually a protein, that stimulates the immune system to react, such as to produce antibodies. [Gk. *anti*, against, and *gene*, origin] 641

aorta Major systemic artery that takes blood from the heart to the tissues. [L. *aorta*, great artery] 636

appendicular skeleton (ap-un-DIK-yuh-ler) Part of the skeleton forming the upper appendages, shoulder girdle, lower appendages, and hip girdle. [L. *append*, hang to, and Gk. *skelet*, dried body] 756

aquifer (AHK-wuh-fur) An underground river that lies between two nonporous layers of rock. [L. *aqua*, water, and *fer*, bear] 896

archaebacterium (ar-kee-bak-TEE-ree-um) Probably the earliest prokaryote; the cell wall and ribosomal RNA differ from those in other bacteria, and many live in extreme environments. [Gk. *archae*, ancient, and *bact*, rod] 405

archegonium (pl., archigonia) (ar-ki-GOH-nee-um) A reproductive organ found in bryophytes and some vascular plants which produces an egg. [Gk. *archeg*, first] 446

arteriole Vessel that takes blood from an artery to capillaries. 630

artery A blood vessel that transports blood away from the heart. 630

arthropod (AR-throh-pad) A member of the phylum Arthropoda, which includes lobsters, insects and spiders; characterized by jointed appendages. [Gk. *arthron*, joint, and *pod*, foot] 493

ascus (pl., asci) A fingerlike sac in which nuclear fusion, meiosis, and ascospore formation occur during the sexual reproduction of the sac fungi. [Gk. *asc*, bag] 435

asexual reproduction Reproduction that requires only one parent and does not involve gametes. 786

aster Short, radiating fibers produced by the centrioles in animal cells. [Gk. *aster*, star] 162

asymmetry Body plan having no particular symmetry. 466

atom The smallest particle of an element that displays its properties. [Gk. *atomos*, individual] 25

ATP (adenosine triphosphate) (ah-den-ah-SEEN try-FAHS-fayt) A compound containing adenine, ribose, and three phosphates. The breakdown of ATP to ADP makes energy available for energy-requiring processes in cells. 57, 114

atrioventricular valve A heart valve located between an atrium and a ventricle. 632

atrium (pl., atria) Chamber; particularly an upper chamber of the heart lying above the ventricle(s). 632

australopithecine (aw-stray-loh-PITH-uh-syn) One of several species of *Australopithecus*, a genus that contains the first generally recognized hominids. [L. *austr*, southern, and Gk. *pithec*, ape] 362

autonomic system (awt-uh-NAHM-ik) A division of the peripheral nervous system that regulates internal organs. [Gk. *autonomia*, independence] 723

autosome Any chromosome other than a sex chromosome. [Gk. *aut*, self, and *soma*, body] 202, 212

autotroph An organism that can make organic molecules from inorganic nutrients. [Gk. *aut*, self, and *troph*, feeder] 335

auxin (AHK-sun) A plant hormone regulating growth, particularly cell elongation; most often indoleacetic acid (IAA). [Gk. *aux*, grow] 572

axial skeleton (AK-see-ul) Part of the skeleton forming the vertical support or axis, including the skull, the rib cage, and the vertebral column. [L. *axi*, axis, and Gk. *skelet*, dried body] 754

axon The part of a neuron that conducts impulses from the cell body to the synapse. [Gk. *axo*, axis] 714

bacteriophage (bak-TEER-ee-uh-fayj) A virus that parasitizes a bacterial cell as its host, often destroying it by lytic action. [Gk. *bact*, rod, and *phag*, eat] 233, 398

bacterium (pl., bacteria) A unicellular organism that lacks a nucleus and cytoplasmic organelles other than ribosomes; reproduces by binary fission and occurs in one of three shapes (rod, sphere, spiral). [Gk. *bact*, rod] 66, 401

Barr body A dark-staining body (discovered by M. Barr) in the nuclei of female mammals which contains a condensed, inactive X chromosome. 263

base A compound tending to lower the hydrogen ion concentration in a solution and raise its pH numerically. 36

basidium (pl., basidia) (buh-SID-ee-um) A club-shaped structure in which nuclear fusion, meiosis, and basidiospore production occur during the sexual reproduction of club fungi. [L. *basidi*, small pedestal] 437

behavior Observable, coordinated responses to environmental stimuli. 826

benthic division (BEN-thik) The ocean floor, which supports a unique set of organisms in contrast to the pelagic division. [Gk. *bentho*, depths of the sea] 878

bicarbonate ion The form in which most of the carbon dioxide is transported in the bloodstream; HCO_3^-.   691

bilateral symmetry Body plan having two corresponding or complementary halves.   466

bile A secretion of the liver that is temporarily stored in the gallbladder before being released into the small intestine, where it emulsifies fat.   674

binary fission Splitting of a parent cell into two daughter cells; serves as an asexual form of reproduction in bacteria. [L. *bi*, two, and *fiss*, cleft]   403

biogeochemical cycle (by-oh-je-oh-KEM-i-kal) The circulating pathway of an element through the biotic and abiotic components of an ecosystem.   866

biogeography The study of the geographical distribution of organisms. [Gk. *bio*, life, *geo*, earth, and *graph*, writing]   298

biological clock Internal mechanism that maintains a biological rhythm in the absence of environmental stimuli.   571

biological magnification The process by which substances become more concentrated in organisms in the higher trophic levels of the food chain.   899

biome (BY-ohm) A major terrestrial community characterized by certain climatic conditions and dominated by particular types of plants.   876

biosphere The thin shell of air, land, and water around the earth that supports life. [Gk. *bio*, life, and *spher*, ball]   6, 876

biotic potential The maximum rate of natural increase of a population that can occur under ideal circumstances. [Gk. *bio*, life]   841

bivalent (by-VAY-lent) Homologous chromosomes, each having sister chromatids, that are joined by a nucleoprotein lattice during meiosis; also called a tetrad. [L. *bi*, two, and *valent*, strength]   172

blastocoel The fluid-filled cavity of a blastula. [Gk. *blast*, bud, and *coel*, hollow]   805

blastula (BLAST-chuh-luh) A hollow, fluid-filled ball of cells occuring during animal development prior to gastrula formation. [Gk. *blast*, bud, and L. *ula*, little]   805

blood A type of connective tissue in which cells are separated by a liquid called plasma.   615

blood pressure Force of blood pushing against the inside wall of an artery.   637

B lymphocyte (LIM-fuh-syt) A lymphocyte that matures in the bone marrow and, when stimulated by the presence of a specific antigen, gives rise to antibody-producing plasma cells. [L. *lymph*, water, and *cyt*, cell]   654

bone Connective tissue in which the cells lie within lacunae embedded in a hard matrix of calcium salts deposited around protein fibers.   615

bronchiole (BRAHNG-kee-ohl) A small tube that conducts air from a bronchus to the alveoli. [Gk. *bronch*, windpipe, and *iol*, little]   689

bronchus (pl., bronchi) (BRAHNG-kus) One of two main branches of the trachea in vertebrates that have lungs. [Gk. *bronch*, windpipe]   689

bryophyte A nonvascular plant in the group that includes mosses (division Bryophyta) and liverworts (division Hepatophyta) and hornworts (division Anthocerotophyta). [Gk. *bryo*, moss, and *phyt*, plant]   445

buffer A substance or group of substances that tend to resist pH changes in a solution, thus stabilizing its relative acidity.   37

C_3 plant A plant that directly uses the Calvin cycle; the first detected molecule during photosynthesis is PGA, a three-carbon molecule.   130

C_4 plant A plant that fixes carbon dioxide to produce a C_4 molecule that releases carbon dioxide to the Calvin cycle.   130

Calvin cycle A series of photosynthetic reactions in which carbon dioxide is fixed and reduced in the chloroplast.   127

CAM plant A plant that fixes carbon dioxide at night to produce a C_4 molecule that releases carbon dioxide to the Calvin cycle during the day; CAM stands for crassulacean-acid metabolism.   130

cancer A malignant tumor whose nondifferentiated cells exhibit loss of contact inhibition, uncontrolled growth, and the ability to invade tissues and metastasize.   268

capillary A microscopic blood vessel; gas and nutrient exchange occurs across the walls of a capillary. [L. *capilla*, hair]   630

carbohydrate A class of organic compounds consisting of carbon, hydrogen, and oxygen atoms; includes monosaccharides, disaccharides, and polysaccharides. [L. *carbo*, charcoal, and Gk. *hydr*, water]   45

carbon dioxide (CO_2) fixation Photosynthetic reaction in which carbon dioxide is attached to an organic compound.   128

carbonic anhydrase An enzyme in red blood cells that speeds the formation of carbonic acid from water and carbon dioxide. [Gk. *an*, without, and *hydr*, water]   691

carcinogen (kar-SIN-uh-jen) An environmental agent that causes mutations leading to the development of cancer. [Gk. *carcino*, ulcer, and *gene*, origin]   269

cardiac muscle Striated, involuntary muscle tissue found only in the heart. [Gk. *card*, heart]   616

cardiovascular system Organ system consisting of the blood, heart, and a series of blood vessels that distribute blood under the pumping action of the heart. [Gk. *card*, heart, and L. *vascul*, little vessel]   630

carnivore A secondary or higher consumer in a food chain; eats other animals. [L. *carn*, flesh, and *vor*, eat]   860

carpel (KAHR-pul) In flowering plants, a reproductive unit of a pistil; consisting of three parts—the stigma, the style, and the ovary. [Gk. *carpus*, fruit]   587

carrier An individual that appears nomal but who is capable of transmitting an infectious or genetic disorder.   219

carrier protein A protein that combines with and transports a molecule across the plasma membrane.   94

carrying capacity The maximum size of a population that can be supported by the environment in a particular locale.   841

cartilage A connective tissue in which the cells lie within lacunae embedded in a flexible proteinaceous matrix. [L. *cartilago*, gristle]   614

Casparian strip (kas-PAIR-ee-un) A layer of impermeable lignin and suberin bordering four sides of root endodermal cells; prevents water and solute transport between adjacent cells.   537

catastrophism (ka-TAS-truh-fism) The belief espoused by Cuvier that periods of catastrophic extinctions occurred, after which repopulation of surviving species took place giving the appearance of change through time. [Gk. *cata*, downward, and *trop*, change]   296

cell The smallest unit that displays properties of life; composed of cytoplasmic regions, possibly organelles, and surrounded by a plasma membrane.   62

cell plate The structure across a dividing plant cell that signals the location of new plasma membranes and cell walls.   165

cell theory The tenet that says a cell is the structural and functional unit of organisms; cells are capable of self-reproduction and come only from preexisting cells.   63

cellular respiration Metabolic reactions that use the energy from carbohydrate or fatty acid or amino acid oxidation to produce ATP molecules; includes fermentation and aerobic respiration.   139

cellulose A polysaccharide composed of glucose molecules; the chief constituent of a plant's cell wall.   46

cell wall A tough layer of material outside the plasma membrane of a bacterium, a fungal cell, an algal cell, or a plant cell, which provides mechanical protection.   67

central canal A tube within the spinal cord that is continuous with the ventricles of the brain and contains cerebrospinal fluid.   720

central nervous system (CNS) The brain and spinal cord.   712

centriole Cell organelle, existing in pairs, that occurs in the centrosome and may help organize a mitotic spindle for chromosome movement during cell division. [Gk. *centr*, center]   78, 162

centromere (SEN-truh-mir) A constriction where sister chromatids of a chromosome are held together. [Gk. *centr*, center, and *mer*, part]   159

centrosome (SEN-truh-sohm) The central microtubule organizing center of cells consisting of granular material. In animal cells, it contains two centrioles. [Gk. *centr*, center, and *soma*, body]   78, 162

cephalization (sef-uh-luh-ZAY-shun) Development of a well-recognized anterior head with concentrated nerve masses and receptors. [Gk. *cephal*, head]   474

cerebellum (ser-uh-BEL-um) Portion of the brain that coordinates skeletal muscles to produce smooth, graceful motions.   725

cerebrospinal fluid (suh-ree-broh-SPYN-ul) A fluid found in the ventricles of the brain, in the central canal of the spinal cord, and in association with the meninges. [L. *cereb*, brain, and *spin*, spine]   724

cerebrum (suh-REE-brum) The main part of the brain consisting of two large masses, or cerebral hemispheres; the largest part of the brain in mammals.   726

chemical evolution An increase in the complexity of chemicals that could have led to the first cells.   333

chemiosmotic phosphorylation (kem-ee-ahz-MAHT-ik fahs-for-ah-LAY-shun) The production of ATP by utilizing the energy released when H^+ flows through an ATP synthase complex in mitochondria and chloroplasts. [Gk. *chem*, juice, *osmo*, pushing, *phos*, light, and *phor*, movement]   114

chemoreceptor A receptor that is sensitive to chemical stimulation—for example, receptors for taste and smell. [Gk. *chemo*, chemistry, and L. *recept*, receive]   734

chemosynthesis The process of making food by using energy derived from the oxidation of inorganic compounds in the environment. [Gk. *chemo*, chemistry, *syn*, together, and *thesis*, an arranging]   404

chitin (KYT-un) A strong but flexible, nitrogenous polysaccharide found in the exoskeleton of arthropods. [Gk. *chit*, a tunic]   46, 493

chlorophyll A green pigment that absorbs solar energy and is important in photosynthesis. [Gk. *chlor*, green, and *phyll*, leaf]   123

chloroplast A membrane-bounded organelle with chlorophyll-containing membranous grana; where photosynthesis takes place. [Gk. *chlor*, green, and *plast*, formed, molded]   75, 122

cholesterol A steroid that occurs in animal plasma membranes and in humans; is known to contribute to the development of plaque on blood vessel walls.   86

chorion (KOR-ee-ahn) An extraembryonic membrane functioning for respiratory exchange in birds and reptiles; contributes to placenta formation in mammals. [Gk. *chori*, membrane]   811

choroid (KOR-oyd) The vascular, pigmented middle layer of the eyeball. [Gk. *choroid*, like a membrane]   737

chromatin (KROH-mut-un) The mass of DNA and associated proteins observed within a nucleus that is not dividing. [Gk. *chrom*, color, and *tin*, stretch]   70, 159

chromosomal theory of inheritance Theory that the genes are on the chromosomes, accounting for their similar behavior.   202

chromosome Association of DNA and proteins in which genes are arranged linearly; visible only during cell division. [Gk. *chrom*, color, and *soma*, both]   70, 158

cilium (pl., cilia) Short, hairlike projection from the plasma membrane, occurring usually in large number.   78

circadian rhythm A biological rhythm with a twenty-four-hour cycle. [L. *circa*, about, and *dies*, day]   570, 780

clade In cladistics, a common ancestor and all the species descended from this common ancestor. [Gk. *klados*, having branches]   392

cladistics (kluh-DIS-tiks) A school of systematics that determines the degree of relatedness by analyzing primitive and derived characters then constructs cladograms.   391

cladogram (KLAD-uh-gram) In cladistics, a branching diagram that shows the relationship among species in regard to their shared, derived characters. [Gk. *klados*, having branches]   391

classification A set of categories to which species are assigned on the basis of their relationship to other species.   382

cleavage Cell division without cytoplasmic addition or enlargement; occurs during the first stage of animal development.   484, 804

cloaca A posterior portion of the digestive tract in certain vertebrates that receives feces and urogenital products.   513

cloned The production of identical copies; in genetic engineering, the production of many identical copies of a gene. [Gk. *clon*, young shoot]   278

cochlea (KOH-klee-uh) A spiral-shaped structure of the inner ear containing the receptors for hearing. [L. *cochl*, spiral]   743

codominance A pattern of inheritance in which both alleles of a gene are expressed.   198

codon Three nucleotides of DNA or mRNA; it codes for a particular amino acid or termination of translation. [L. *cod*, tail]   249

coelom (SEE-lum) A body cavity lying between the digestive tract and body wall that is completely lined by mesoderm. [Gk. *coel*, hollow]   466, 484

coenzyme A nonprotein organic part of an enzyme structure, often with a vitamin as a subpart.   111

cohesion-tension model An explanation for the transport of water to great heights in a plant due to a negative water potential (compared to the roots). This movement is brought about by transpiration and is dependent upon the ability of water molecules to cohere and to adhere to cell walls.   555

collecting duct A duct within the kidney that receives fluid from several nephrons; the reabsorption of water occurs here. 702

colon The large intestine. 677

commensalism A symbiotic relationship in which one species is benefited and the other is neither harmed nor benefited. [L. *com*, together, and *mensa*, table] 855

common ancestor An ancestor held in common by at least two lines of descent. 382

communication A signal by a sender that influences the behavior of a receiver. 833

community A group of many different populations that interact with one another. 850

competitive exclusion principle The theory that no two species can occupy the same niche. 851

complementary base pairing Bonding between a particular purine and a particular pyrimidine in DNA. 57, 236

complement system A series of proteins in plasma that form a nonspecific defense mechanism against a microbe invasion; it complements the antigen-antibody reaction. 654

compound A chemical substance having two or more different elements in fixed ratio. 30

compound eye A type of eye found in arthropods; it is composed of many independent visual units. 736

condensation A chemical change resulting in the covalent bonding of two monomers with the accompanying loss of a water molecule. 44

cone Photoreceptor in vertebrate eyes that responds to bright light and allows color vision. 738

conidiospore (kuh-NID-ee-uh-spohr) Spore produced by sac and club fungi during asexual reproduction. 435

conifer One of the four groups of gymnosperm plants; cone-bearing trees that include pine, cedar, and spruce. [Gk. *con*, pine cone, and L. *fer*, bear, carry] 454

conjugation A union that results in the transfer of genetic material from one cell to another. [L. *conjug*, joined together] 416

connective tissue A type of animal tissue that binds structures together, provides support and protection, fills spaces, stores fat, and forms blood cells; adipose tissue, cartilage, bone, and blood are types of connective tissue. 614

consumer An organism that feeds on another organism in a food chain; primary consumers eat plants, and secondary consumers eat animals. 860

continental drift The movement of continents with respect to one another over the earth's surface. 338

control group A sample that goes through all the steps of an experiment except the one being tested; a standard against which results of an experiment are checked. 16

convergent evolution Similarity in structure in distantly related groups due to adaptation to the environment. 388

copulation A sexual union to facilitate the reception of sperm by a partner, usually a female. [L. *copul*, link] 787

corepressor A molecule that binds to a repressor, allowing the repressor to bind to an operator in a repressible operon. 260

cork Outer covering of bark of trees; made of dead cells that may be sloughed off. 533

cork cambium A lateral meristem that produces cork. [L. *cambi*, exchange] 543

corpus luteum (KOR-pus LOOT-ee-um) A follicle that has released an egg and increases its secretion of progesterone. [L. *corpusc*, little body, and *lut*, yellowish] 795

cotyledon (kaht-ul-EED-un) Seed leaf for the embryo of a flowering plant; provides nutrient molecules for the developing plant before it begins to photosynthesize. [Gk. *cotyl*, cup-shaped cavity] 532, 593

covalent bond (koh-VAY-lent) A chemical bond in which the atoms share one pair of electrons. [L. *co*, with, and *valent*, strength] 31

cristae Shelflike projections that extend into the matrix of a mitochondrion. 76

Cro-Magnon Hominid who lived 40,000 years ago; these people were accomplished hunters, made compound stone tools, and possibly had a language. 368

crossing-over An exchange of segments between nonsister chromatids of a bivalent during meiosis. 173

cuticle A waxy layer covering the epidermis of plants that protects the plant against water loss and disease-causing organisms. [L. *cut*, skin] 546

cyanobacterium (sy-ah-noh-bak-TEE-ree-um) A photosynthetic eubacterium that contains chlorophyll and releases oxygen; formerly called a blue-green alga. [Gk. *cyano*, blue, and *bact*, rod] 406

cyclic AMP An ATP-related compound that promotes chemical reactions in cells; as the second messenger in peptide hormone transduction, it initiates activity of the metabolic machinery. 769

cyclin A protein that cycles in quantity as the cell cycle progresses; combines with and activates the kinases that function to promote the events of the cycle. 160

cyst A resting stage enveloped by a protective capsule in the life cycle of certain organisms; a saclike abnormal growth. 477

cytokinesis (syt-oh-kuh-NEE-sus) The division of the cytoplasm following mitosis and meiosis. [Gk. *cyt*, cell, and *kine*, movement] 159

cytokinin (syt-uh-KY-nun) A plant hormone that promotes cell division; often works in combination with auxin during organ development in plant embryos. 577

cytoplasm Contents of a cell between the nucleus (nucleoid) and the plasma membrane. [Gk. *cyt*, cell, and *plasm*, something modeled] 66

cytosine (C) (SYT-uh-seen) One of four nitrogen-containing bases in nucleotides composing the structure of DNA and RNA. 235

cytoskeleton Internal framework of the cell, consisting of microtubules, actin filaments, and intermediate filaments. [Gk. *cyt*, cell, and *skelet*, dried body] 67, 76

cytosol The solution phase of the cytoplasm. [Gk. *cyt*, cell, and *sol*, sun] 66

datum (pl., data) A fact or a piece of information collected through observation and/or experimentation. [L. *datum*, gift] 14

decomposer An organism, usually a bacterial or fungal species, that breaks down large organic molecules into elements that can be recycled in the environment. 404, 860

deductive reasoning A process of logic and reasoning, using "if . . . then" statements. 15

demographic transition A decline in death rate, followed shortly by a decline in birthrate, resulting in slower population growth. 841

denatured The condition of an enzyme when its shape is changed so that its active site cannot bind substrate molecules. 110

dendrite The part of a neuron that sends impulses toward the cell body. [Gk. *dendro*, tree]   714

dependent variable A result or change that occurs when an experimental variable is utilized in an experiment.   16

derived character A structural, physiological, or behavioral trait that is present in a specific lineage and is not present in the common ancestor for several lineages.   387

dermis The deeper, thicker layer of the skin that consists of fibrous connective tissue and contains various structures such as sense organs. [Gk. *derm*, skin]   619

desert Treeless biome where the annual rainfall is less than 25 cm; the rain that does fall is subject to rapid runoff and evaporation.   882

desertification (di-zurt-uh-fuh-KAY-SHUN) The transformation of marginal lands to desert conditions.   900

detritus (dih-TRYT-us) Partially decomposed remains of plants and animals found in soil and on the beds of bodies of water. [L. *detrit*, wear off]   860

deuterostome (DOOT-uh-ruh-stohm) A group of coelomate animals in which the second embryonic opening is associated with the mouth; the first embryonic opening, the blastopore, is associated with the anus. [Gk. *deutero*, second, and *stoma*, mouth]   484, 504

diaphragm A dome-shaped muscularized sheet separating the thoracic cavity from the abdominal cavity in mammals. [Gk. *dia*, separate, and *phragm*, partition]   687

diastole (dy-AS-tuh-lee) The relaxation period of a heart during the cardiac cycle. [Gk. *diastol*, standing apart]   634

diatom A freshwater or marine unicellular golden-brown alga, with a cell wall consisting of two silica-impregnated valves, which is extremely numerous in phytoplankton. [Gk. *dia*, through, and *tom*, cut]   418

dicotyledon (dy-KAHT-ul-eed-un) A flowering plant group; members show two embryonic leaves, net-veined leaves, cylindrical arrangement of vascular bundles, and other characteristics. [Gk. *di*, two, and *kotyl*, cavity]   458

differentially permeable Ability of plasma membranes to regulate the passage of substances into and out of the cell, allowing some to pass through and preventing the passage of others.   90

differentiation The specialization of early embryonic cells with regard to structure and function.   804

diffusion The movement of molecules from a region of higher to lower concentration; it requires no energy and tends to lead to an equal distribution.   91

digit A finger or toe.   756

dinoflagellate (dy-noh-FLAJ-uh-lut) A unicellular alga, with two flagella, one whiplash and the other located within a groove between protective cellulose plates, whose numbers periodically explode to cause a toxic "red tide" in ocean waters.[Gk. *din*, whirling, and L. *flagell*, whip]   418

diploid (2n) number A cell condition in which two of each type of chromosome is present. [Gk. *dipl*, double, and *oid*, form]   159, 170

directional selection An outcome of natural selection in which an extreme phenotype is favored, usually in a changing environment.   318

disruptive selection An outcome of natural selection in which extreme phenotypes are favored over the average phenotype and can lead to more than one distinct form.   320

distal convoluted tubule The final portion of a nephron that joins with a collecting duct; associated with tubular secretion. [L. *dista*, distant]   702

DNA (deoxyribonucleic acid) A nucleic acid polymer produced from covalent bonding of nucleotide monomers that contain the sugar deoxyribose; the genetic material of nearly all organisms.   56, 232

DNA fingerprinting Using DNA fragment lengths, resulting from restriction enzyme cleavage, to identify particular individuals.   282

DNA ligase (LY-gays) An enzyme that links DNA fragments; used during production of recombinant DNA to join foreign DNA to the vector DNA. [L. *liga*, tied]   279

DNA polymerase (PAHL-uh-muh-rays) During replication, an enzyme that joins the nucleotides complementary to a DNA template.   238

DNA probe Known sequences of DNA that are used to find complementary DNA strands; can be used diagnostically to determine the presence of particular genes.   281

dominance hierarchy Social ranking within a group in which a higher ranking individual acquires more resources than a lower ranking individual.   831

dominant allele (uh-LEEL) An allele that exerts its phenotypic effect in the heterozygote; it hides the expression of the recessive allele.   187

duodenum (doo-uh-DEE-num) The first part of the small intestine where chyme enters from the stomach.   672

echinoderm (i-KY-nuh-durm) A number of a phylum of marine animals that includes sea stars, sea urchins, and sand dollars; characterized by radial symmetry and a water vascular system. [L. *echinatus*, set with prickles, and *derm*, skin]   504

ecological pyramid Pictorial graph representing biomass, organism number, or energy content of each trophic level in a food web—from the producer to the final consumer populations.   865

ecology The study of the interaction of organisms with their living and physical environment. [Gk. *eco*, house, and *logy*, study of]   840, 861

ecosystem A biological community together with the associated abiotic environment. [Gk. *eco*, house, and *sys*, together]   3, 860

ectoderm The outer germ layer of the embryonic gastrula; it gives rise to the nervous system and skin. [Gk. *ecto*, outer, and *derm*, skin]   805

ectothermic Having a body temperature that varies according to the environmental temperature. [Gk. *ecto*, outer, and *therm*, heat]   512

electromagnetic spectrum Solar radiation divided on the basis of wavelength, with gamma rays having the shortest wavelength and radio waves having the longest wavelength.   120

electron A negative subatomic particle, moving about in energy levels around the nucleus of the atom. [Gk. *electr*, amber, electricity]   25

electron transport system A mechanism whereby electrons are passed along a series of carrier molecules, releasing energy for the synthesis of ATP.   112, 124, 146

element A substance, consisting of only one type of atom; e.g., carbon, hydrogen, oxygen.   24

embryo The early developmental stage of a plant or animal, produced from a zygote.   592

embryo sac The megagametophyte of flowering plants that contains an egg cell.   589

endocrine system One of the major systems involved in the coordination of body activities; uses messengers called hormones, which are secreted into the bloodstream. [Gk. *end*, within, and *krinein*, separate]   768

endocytosis (en-doh-sy-TOH-sis) A process by which particles or debris are moved into the cell from the environment by phagocytosis (cellular eating) or pinocytosis (cellular drinking); includes receptor-mediated endocytosis. [Gk. *endo*, inside, and *cyt*, cell] 96

endoderm An inner layer of cells that lines the primitive gut of the gastrula; it becomes the lining of the digestive tract and associated organs. [Gk. *endo*, inner, and *derm*, skin] 805

endodermis Internal plant root tissue forming a boundary between the cortex and the vascular cylinder. [Gk. *endo*, within, and *derm*, skin] 537

endometrium (en-doh-MEE-tree-um) A mucous membrane lining the interior surface of the uterus. [Gk. *endo*, within, and *metri*, uterus] 794

endoplasmic reticulum (en-doh-PLAZ-mik reh-TIK-yoo-lum) A system of membranous saccules and channels in the cytoplasm. [Gk. *endo*, within, and *plasm*, something molded, and L. *reticul*, network] 71

endosperm The nutritive tissue in a seed; often triploid from a fusion of sperm cell with two polar nuclei. 592

endospore A bacterium that has shrunk its cell, rounded up within the former plasma membrane, and secreted a new and thicker cell wall in the face of unfavorable environmental conditions. [Gk. *endo*, within, and *spor*, seed] 403

endothermic Having a body temperature that is derived from the oxidative metabolism of the organism. [Gk. *endo*, within, and *therm*, heat] 519

energy The capacity to do work and bring about change; occurs in a variety of forms. 4, 27, 104

environmental resistance The opposing force of the environment on the biotic potential of a population. 841

enzyme An organic catalyst, usually a protein molecule, that speeds chemical reactions in living systems. 52, 107

epidermis In plants, the covering tissue of plant roots and leaves, and also stems of nonwoody organisms. In animals, the outer, protective layer of the skin. [Gk. *epi*, upon, and *derm*, skin] 533, 619

epiglottis (ep-uh-GLAHT-us) A structure that covers the glottis, the air-tract opening, during the process of swallowing. [Gk. *epi*, upon, and *glotti*, tongue] 672, 688

epiphyte (EP-uh-fyt) A plant that takes its nourishment from the air because its attachment to other plants gives it an aerial position. [Gk. *epi*, upon, and *phyt*, plant] 561

epithelial tissue A type of animal tissue forming a continuous layer over most body surfaces (i.e., skin) and inner cavities; squamous, cuboidal, and columnar are the three types of epithelial tissue. [Gk. *epi*, upon, and *thec*, a case] 612

erythrocyte A red blood cell that contains hemoglobin and carries oxygen from the lungs or gills to the tissues in vertebrates. [Gk. *erythr*, red, and *cyt*, cell] 641

esophagus (i-SAHF-uh-gus) A muscular tube for moving swallowed food from the pharynx to the stomach. [Gk. *eso*, within, and *phag*, eat] 672

estrogen One of several female ovarian sex hormones that causes the endometrium of the uterus to proliferate during the uterine cycle; along with progesterone, estrogens maintain secondary sex characteristics in females. 795

estuary The end of a river where fresh water and salt water mix as they meet. [L. *estuar*, sea] 876

ethylene (ETH-uh-leen) A plant hormone that causes ripening of fruit and is also involved in abscission. 579

eubacterium (yoo-bak-TEE-ree-um) Most common type of bacteria, including the cyanobacteria. 405

euchromatin (yoo-KROH-mut-un) Diffuse chromatin, which is being transcribed. [Gk. *eu*, good, *chrom*, color, and *tin*, stretch] 263

euglenoid (yuu-GLEE-noyd) A flagellated and flexible freshwater unicellular organism which usually contains chloroplasts and is often characterized as having both animal-like and plantlike characteristics. 418

eukaryotic cell (yoo-kair-ee-AHT-ik) Typical of most types of organisms (except bacteria) having a well-defined nucleus and organelles. [Gk. *eu*, good, and *karyo*, nucleus] 67

evolution The descent of organisms from common ancestors with the development of genetic and phenotypic changes over time that make them more suited to the local environment. [L. *evolut*, an unrolling] 6, 295

exhalation Stage during respiration when air is pushed out of the lungs; expiration. 687

exocytosis (ek-soh-sy-TOH-sis) A process by which particles or debris are moved out of the cell by vesicles that fuse with the plasma membrane. [Gk. *exo*, outside, and *cyt*, cell] 96

exon In a gene, the portion of the DNA code that is expressed as the result of polypeptide formation. [Gk. *exo*, outside] 251

exoskeleton (ek-soh-SKEL-ut-un) A protective external skeleton, as in arthropods. [Gk. *exo*, outside, and *skelet*, dried body] 493

experimental variable The condition that is tested in an experiment by manipulating it and observing the results. 16

exponential growth A geometrically multiplying, rapid population growth rate. 840

extinction The total disappearance of a species or higher group. 343

extraembryonic membrane A membrane that is not a part of the embryo but is necessary to the continued existence and health of the embryo. [L. *extra*, outside] 811

facilitated transport Process whereby molecules pass through a plasma membrane, utilizing a carrier protein without the expenditure of energy. 94

FAD (flavin-adenine dinucleotide) (FLAY-vun AD-un-een dy-NOO-klee-uh-tyd) A coenzyme that functions as an electron acceptor in cellular oxidation-reduction reactions. 112

fat A solid lipid formed when three fatty acids with limited double bonds combine with glycerol; found in human adipose tissue and also called a triglyceride. 48

feedback inhibition A process by which a substance, often an end product of a reaction or a metabolic pathway, controls its own continued production by binding with the enzyme that produced it. 110

fermentation The anaerobic breakdown of glucose that results in two ATP and products such as alcohol and lactate. [L. *ferment*, yeast] 142

fertilization The union of a sperm nucleus and an egg nucleus, which creates the zygote with the diploid number of chromosomes. [L. *fertil*, fruitful] 592, 804

fibroblast Cell type of loose and fibrous connective tissue with cells at some distance from one another and separated by a jellylike matrix containing collagen and elastin fibers. [L. *fibr*, fiber, and Gk. *blast*, bud] 614

filament The elongated stalk of a stamen bearing the anther at the tip. 587

fitness The ability of an organism to survive and reproduce in its environment. 300, 318

flagellum (pl., flagella) Slender, long extension used for locomotion by some bacteria, protozoa, and sperm. [L. *flagell*, whip]   78

flower The reproductive organ of a flowering plant, consisting of several kinds of modified leaves arranged in concentric rings and attached to a modified stem called the receptacle.   587

fluid-mosaic model Model for the plasma membrane based on the changing location and pattern of protein molecules in a fluid phospholipid bilayer.   85

follicle Structure in the ovary of animals that contains oocytes; site of egg production. [L. *follicul*, little bag]   795

follicle-stimulating hormone (FSH) Gonadotropic hormone secreted by the anterior pituitary; it promotes production of eggs in females and sperm in males.   795

food chain A succession of organisms in an ecosystem that are linked by an energy flow and by the order of who eats whom.   863

food web A complex pattern of interlocking and crisscrossing food chains.   863

foramen magnum (fuh-RAY-mun MAG-num) Opening in the occipital bone of the skull through which the spinal cord passes. [L. *foram*, opening, and *magn*, large]   754

fossil The remains or tangible traces of an ancient organism preserved in sediment or rock. [L. *fossil*, dug up]   336

fruit A flowering plant structure consisting of one or more ripened ovaries that usually contain seeds.   458, 594

fruiting body A spore-producing and spore-disseminating structure found in sac and club fungi.   435

fungus (pl., fungi) A saprotrophic decomposer; the body is made up of filaments called hyphae that form a mass called a mycelium.   430

gallbladder An organ attached to the liver that serves as a storage organ for bile.   674

gamete (GAM-eet) Haploid sex cell. [Gk. *gamet*, wife or husband]   170

gametophyte (guh-MEET-uh-fyt) The haploid generation of the alternation of generations life cycle of a plant; it produces gametes that unite to form a diploid zygote. [Gk. *gamet*, wife or husband, and *phyt*, plant]   445

ganglion (pl., ganglia) (GANG-glee-un) A knot or bundle of neuron cell bodies usually outside the central nervous system. [Gk. *ganglion*, knot on a string]   720

gastrovascular cavity A blind digestive cavity that also serves a circulatory (transport) function in animals that lack a circulatory system. [Gk. *gastro*, stomach, and L. *vascul*, little vessel]   470

gastrula (GAS-truh-luh) The stage of animal development during which the germ layers form at least in part by invagination. [Gk. *gastro*, stomach, and L. *ula*, little]   805

gene The unit of heredity passed on to offspring. [Gk. *gene*, origin]   5

gene flow The sharing of genes between two populations through interbreeding.   315

gene locus The specific location of a particular gene on homologous chromosomes.   187

gene pool The total of all the genes of all the individuals in a population.   313

gene therapy The use of bioengineered cells or other biotechnology techniques to treat human genetic disorders.   285

genetic drift A change in the genetic makeup of a population due to chance (random) events; important in small populations or when only a few individuals mate.   316

genetic engineering The use of technology to alter the genome of a living cell for medical or industrial use.   278

genotype The alleles of an organism for a particular trait or traits; for example, *BB* or *Aa*. [Gk. *geno*, race, and *typos*, image]   187

genus (pl., genera) A group of related species with taxonomic rank below family. The scientific name includes the genus and the specific epithet.   383

germinate The resumption of growth by a seed or any other reproductive structure of a plant or protoctist   596

germ layer A developmental layer of the body—that is, ectoderm, mesoderm, or endoderm.   805

gibberellin (jib-uh-REL-un) A plant hormone producing increased stem growth; also involved in flowering and seed germination. [L. *gibb*, humped]   574

gills Respiratory organ in most aquatic animals; in fish an outward extension of the pharynx.   685

girdling Removing a strip of bark from around a tree.   562

glomerular capsule (glu-MER-uh-lur) A cuplike structure that is the initial portion of a nephron; where pressure filtration occurs. [L. *glomer*, ball, and *ula*, little]   702

glomerulus (glu-MER-uh-lus) A capillary network within a glomerular capsule of a nephron. [L. *glomer*, ball, and *ula*, little]   702

glottis (GLAHT-us) An opening for airflow in the larynx. [Gk. *glotti*, tongue]   688

glucagon A hormone secreted by the pancreas which causes the liver to break down glycogen and raises the blood glucose level.   777

glucose The six-carbon sugar that most organisms degrade as a source of energy during cellular respiration. [Gk. *gluco*, sweet, and *ose*, full of]   45

glycogen The storage polysaccharide found in animals that is composed of glucose molecules joined in a linear fashion but having numerous branches. [Gk. *glyc*, sweet, and *gen*, produce]   46

glycolysis (gly-KAHL-uh-sis) A pathway of metabolism converting glucose to pyruvate; resulting in a net gain of two ATP and two NADH molecules. [Gk. *glyc*, sweet, and *lys*, loosening]   140

Golgi apparatus An organelle consisting of a central region of saccules and vesicles that modifies proteins and produces lysosomes.   73

gonad An organ that produces sex cells; the ovary, which produces eggs, and the testis, which produces sperm. [Gk. *gon*, seed]   787

gonadotropic hormone (goh-nad-uh-TRAHP-ik) A type of hormone that regulates the activity of the ovaries and testes; principally follicle-stimulating hormone (FSH) and luteinizing hormone (LH).   774

granum (pl., grana) (GRAY-num) A stack of chlorophyll-containing thylakoids in a chloroplast.   75, 123

gravitropism (grav-ih-TRUH-piz-um) Directional growth of plants in response to the earth's gravity; roots demonstrate positive gravitropism, and stems demonstrate negative gravitropism. [Gk. *grav*, heavy, and *trop*, turn]   569

green alga A type of protoctista in the phylum Chlorophyta that contains chlorophylls *a* and *b* and has other biochemical characteristics like those of plants.   413

greenhouse effect The reradiation of solar heat toward the earth, caused by gases in the atmosphere.   892

growth An increase in the number of cells and/or the size of these cells.   804

growth hormone (GH) A substance secreted by the anterior pituitary; it promotes cell division, protein synthesis, and bone growth. 774

guanine (G) (GWAHN-een) One of four nitrogen-containing bases in nucleotides composing the structure of DNA and RNA. 235

guard cell A type of plant cell that is found in pairs, with one on each side of a leaf stomate; changes in the turgor pressure of these cells regulate the size and passage of gases through the stomate. 556

guttation (guh-TAY-shun) The liberation of water droplets from the edges and tips of leaves. [L. *gutt*, a drop] 554

gymnosperm (JIM-nuh-sperm) A vascular plant producing naked seeds, as in conifers. [Gk. *gymn*, naked, and *sperm*, seed] 454

habitat The conditions of the environment that influence an organism's life activities and describe the location where the organism is able to survive and reproduce. 851

haploid (n) number A cell condition in which only one of each type of chromosome is present. [Gk. *hapl*, single, and *oid*, form] 159, 170

Hardy-Weinberg law A law stating that the frequency of an allele in a population remains stable under certain assumptions, such as random mating; therefore, no change or evolution occurs. 314

heart A muscular organ that pumps the blood, propelling it through blood vessels. 632

hemocoel Residual coelom found in arthropods that is filled with hemolymph.[Gk. *hem*, blood, and *coel*, hollow] 496

hemoglobin Red respiratory pigment of erythrocytes used for transport of oxygen. [Gk. *hem*, blood, and L. *glob*, ball] 641, 691

herbaceous plant A plant that lacks persistent woody tissue. [L. *herb*, grass] 457

herbaceous stem A nonwoody stem. [L. *herb*, grass] 540

herbivore A primary consumer in a food chain; a plant eater. [L. *herb*, grass, and *vor*, eat] 860

hermaphroditic (hur-maf-ruh-DIT-ik) Characterizes an animal having both male and female sex organs. 475

heterochromatin (het-uh-roh-KROH-mut-un) Highly compacted chromatin that is not being transcribed. 263

heterotroph An organism that cannot synthesize organic compounds from inorganic substances and therefore must take in preformed food. [Gk. *hetero*, different, and *troph*, feeder] 335

heterozygous Possessing unlike alleles for a particular trait. [Gk. *heter*, different, and *zyg*, yoke] 187

homeostasis The maintenance of internal conditions in a cell or an organism by means of a self-regulation mechanism. [Gk. *homeo*, like, and *stasis*, standing] 4, 622

homeotherm An animal (bird or mammal) that maintains a uniform body temperature independent of the environmental temperature. [Gk. *homeo*, like, same, and *therm*, heat] 519

hominid A member of the family Hominid containing humans and their direct ancestors known only by the fossil record. [L. *hom*, man, and *id*, a condition of] 361

hominoid A member of a superfamily containing humans and the great apes. [L. *hom*, man, and Gk. *oid*, like] 359

Homo erectus Hominid who lived during the Pleistocene epoch; had a posture and locomotion similar to modern humans. [L. *hom*, man, and *erect*, upright] 366

Homo habilis Hominid of 2 million years ago; possibly a direct ancestor of modern humans. [L. *hom*, man, and *habilis*, handy] 365

homologous chromosome (hoh-MAHL-uh-gus) A member of a pair of chromosomes that carry genes for the same traits and synapse during prophase of the first meiotic division. [Gk. *homo*, alike] 170

homologous structure (hoh-MAHL-uh-gus) In evolution, a structure that is similar in different organisms because these organisms are derived from a common ancestor. [Gk. *homo*, alike] 306

homologue (HOH-muh-log) A member of a homologous pair of chromosomes. [Gk. *homo*, alike] 170

homology Similarity in structure due to having a common ancestor. [Gk. *homologia*, conformity, and *logy*, study of] 388

homozygous Possessing two identical alleles for a particular trait. [Gk. *homo*, alike, and *zyg*, yoke] 187

hormone A chemical messenger produced in one part of the body that controls the activity of other parts. [Gk. *hormon*, excite] 572, 768

human immunodeficiency virus (HIV) Virus responsible for AIDS. 799

hybridization The crossing of different varieties or species. [L. *hybrid*, mongrel] 600

hydrogen bond A weak bond that arises between a partially positive hydrogen and a partially negative oxygen, often on different molecules or separated by some distance. 33

hydrolysis (hy-DRAH-lih-sis) Splitting of a compound by the addition of water, with the H^+ being incorporated in one fragment and the OH^- in the other. [Gk. *hydr*, water, and *lysis*, loosening, dissolving] 44

hydrophilic (hy-druh-FIL-ik) A type of molecule that interacts with water by dissolving in water or forming hydrogen bonds with water molecules. [L. *hydr*, water, and Gk. *phil*, loving] 34, 43

hydrophobic (hy-druh-FOH-bik) A type of molecule that does not interact with water because it is nonpolar. [L. *hydr*, water, and Gk. *phobos*, dreading] 35, 43

hydroponics (hy-druh-PAHN-iks) A water culture method of growing plants that allows an experimenter to vary the nutrients and minerals provided so as to determine the essential nutrients. [Gk. *hydr*, water, and *pono*, toil] 558

hypertonic solution Higher solute concentration (less water) than the cytoplasm of a cell; causes cell to lose water by osmosis. [Gk. *hyper*, over, and *ton*, tension] 93

hypha (pl., hyphae) A filament of the vegetative body of a fungus. [Gk. *hyph*, web] 431

hypothalamus (hy-poh-THAL-uh-mus) A part of the brain that helps regulate the internal environment of the body; involved in control of heart rate, body temperature, water balance, and glandular secretions of the stomach and pituitary gland. [Gk. *hypo*, under] 725

hypothesis A supposition that is established by reasoning after consideration of available evidence; it can be tested by obtaining more data, often by experimentation. [Gk. *hypothesis*, foundation] 14

hypotonic solution Lower solute concentration (more water) than the cytoplasm of a cell; causes cell to gain water by osmosis. [Gk. *hypo*, under, and *ton*, tension] 93

immunity The ability of the body to protect itself from foreign substances and cells, including infectious microbes. [L. *immun*, safe, free] 652

imprinting A form of learning that occurs early in the lives of animals; a close association is made that later influences sexual behavior. 829

inclusive fitness Fitness that results from direct selection and indirect selection. 835

incomplete dominance A pattern of inheritance in which the offspring shows characteristics intermediate between two extreme parental characteristics—for example, a red and a white flower producing pink offspring. 198

inducer A molecule that brings about activity of an operon by joining with a repressor and preventing it from binding to the operator. 260

inducible operon An operon that is normally inactive but is turned on when an inducer is present. 260

induction The ability of a chemical or a tissue to influence the development of another tissue. [L. *in*, into, and *duct*, lead] 809

inductive reasoning A process of logic and reasoning, such as using specific observations to arrive at a hypothesis. 15

inflammatory reaction A tissue response to injury that is characterized by redness, swelling, pain, and heat. [L. *in*, into, and *flamm*, burn] 652

inhalation Stage during respiration when air is drawn into the lungs; inspiration. 687

inheritance of acquired characteristics Lamarckian belief that organisms become adapted to their environment during their lifetime and pass on these adaptations to their offspring. 296

inorganic molecule A type of molecule that is not a compound of carbon and hydrogen. 42

insulin A hormone secreted by the pancreas that lowers the blood glucose level by promoting the uptake of glucose by cells and the conversion of glucose to glycogen by the liver. [L. *insul*, island] 777

interferon A protein formed by a cell infected with a virus that can increase the resistance of other cells to the virus. [L. *inter*, between, and *fero*, fierce] 654

interneuron A neuron, located within the central nervous system, conveying messages between parts of the central nervous system. [L. *inter*, between, and Gk. *neuro*, nerve] 714

interphase The stage of the cell cycle during which DNA synthesis occurs and the nucleus is not actively dividing. [L. *inter*, between, and Gk. *phase*, appearance] 160

intron Noncoding segments of DNA that are transcribed but removed before mRNA leaves the nucleus. [L. *intra*, within] 251

invertebrate Referring to an animal without a serial arrangement of vertebrae, or a backbone. [L. *in*, without, and *vertebr*, vertebra] 466

ion Charged derivative of an atom—positive if the atom loses electrons and negative if the atom gains electrons. 31

ionic bond A chemical bond in which ions are attracted to one another by opposite charges. 31

isomers (EYE-suh-mur) Molecules with the same molecular formula but different structure and, therefore, shape. [Gk. *iso*, equal, and *meris*, part] 43

isotonic solution A solution that is equal in solute and water concentration to that of the cytoplasm of a cell; causes cell to neither lose nor gain water by osmosis. [Gk. *iso*, equal, and *ton*, tension] 92

isotopes Atoms having the same atomic number but a different atomic weight due to the number of neutrons. [Gk. *iso*, equal, and *topos*, place] 26

jointed appendage A freely moveable appendage of arthropods. 493

karyotype (KAR-ee-uh-typ) Chromosomes arranged by pairs according to their size, shape, and general appearance in mitotic metaphase. 212

kidney One of the paired organs of the urinary system that regulates the chemical composition of the blood and produces a waste product called urine. 702

kinase (KY-nays) Any one of several enzymes that phosphorylate their substrates. 160

kingdom A taxonomic category grouping related phyla (animals) or divisions (plants). 383

kingdom Animalia The kingdom to which all animals are assigned. 384

kingdom Fungi The kingdom to which fungi (e.g., mushrooms and molds) are assigned. 384, 432

kingdom Plantae The kingdom to which plants are assigned. 384, 444

kingdom Prokaryotae (proh-kar-ee-OH-tee) The kingdom to which prokaryotes (bacteria and cyanobacteria) are assigned. [Gk. *pro*, before, and *karyo*, nucleus] 384, 401

kingdom Protoctista The kingdom to which protoctists (algae, including multicellular forms; protozoa, including multicellular forms; water molds; and slime molds) are assigned. [Gk. *proto*, first, and *ktistos*, to establish] 384, 413

Krebs cycle A cycle of reactions in mitochondria that begins and ends with citric acid; it produces CO_2, ATP, NADH, and $FADH_2$; also called the citric acid cycle. 145

K-strategist A species that has evolved characteristics that keep its population size near carrying capacity—for example, few offspring, longer generation time. 844

lacteal (LAK-tee-ul) A lymphatic vessel in an intestinal villus, it aids in the absorption of fats. [L. *lac*, milk] 675

larva (pl., larvae) An immature form in the life cycle of some animals; the stage of development between the embryo and the adult form. It undergoes metamorphosis to become the adult form. 788

larynx (LAR-ingks) Cartilaginous organ located between the pharynx and the trachea in tetrapods which contains the vocal cords; voice box. [Gk. *laryn*, gullet] 688

leaf Usually broad, flat structure of a plant shoot system, containing cells that carry out photosynthesis. 531

learning A relatively permanent change in an animal's behavior that results from practice and experience. 828

leukocyte White blood cell of which there are several types, each having a specific function in protecting the body from invasion by foreign substances and organisms. [Gk. *leuko*, white, and *cyt*, cell] 641

lichen (LY-kun) A symbiotic relationship between certain fungi and algae, which has long been thought to be mutualistic, in which the fungi provide inorganic food and the algae provide organic food. 439

light-dependent reactions A set of photosynthetic reactions that require solar energy to proceed; it produces ATP and NADPH. 123

light-independent reactions A set of photosynthetic reactions that does not directly require solar energy; it uses the products of the light-dependent reactions to reduce carbon dioxide to a carbohydrate. 123

limbic system Pathways linking the hypothalamus to some areas of the cerebral cortex; governs learning and memory and various emotions such as pleasure, fear, and happiness. 727

lineage A line of evolutionary descent from a common ancestor. 350

linkage group Alleles of different genes that are located on the same chromosome and tend to be inherited together. 204

lipase A fat-digesting enzyme secreted by the pancreas. 674

lipid (LIP-id) A class of organic compounds that tend to be soluble in nonpolar solvents such as alcohol; includes fats and oils. [Gk. *lipos*, fat] 48

liposome Droplet of phospholipid molecules formed in a liquid environment. [Gk. *lipo*, fat, and *soma*, body] 334

loop of the nephron The portion of a nephron between the proximal and distal convoluted tubules where water reabsorption occurs. 702

lung An internal respiratory organ containing moist surfaces for gas exchange. 686

luteinizing hormone (LH) (LOOT-ee-ny-zing) Gonadotropic hormone secreted by the anterior pituitary that stimulates the production of sex hormones in males and females. 795

lymph Fluid, derived from tissue fluid, that is carried in lymphatic vessels. [L. *lymph*, water] 650

lymphatic system Mammalian organ system consisting of lymphatic vessels and lymphoid organs. [L. *lymph*, water] 650

lymph nodes A mass of lymphoid tissue located along the course of a lymphatic vessel. [L. *lymph*, water] 651

lymphocyte Specialized white blood cell; occurs in two forms—T lymphocyte and B lymphocyte. [L. *lymph*, water, and *cyt*, cell] 641

lymphokine (LIM-fuh-kyn) A molecule secreted by T lymphocytes that has the ability to affect the activity of all types of immune cells. [L. *lymph*, water, and *kine*, movement] 658

lysogenic cycle A bacteriophage life cycle in which the virus incorporates its DNA into that of the bacterium; only later does it begin a lytic cycle, which ends with the destruction of the bacterium. [Gk. *lyso*, loose, and *genos*, descent] 399

lysosome Membrane-bounded vesicle that contains hydrolytic enzymes for digesting macromolecules. [Gk. *ly*, loose, and *soma*, body] 73

lytic cycle One of the bacteriophage life cycles in which the virus takes over the operation of the bacterium immediately upon entering it and subsequently destroys the bacterium. [Gk. *ly*, loose] 398

M

macrophage A large phagocytic cell derived from a monocyte that ingests microbes and debris. [Gk. *macr*, large, and *phag*, eat] 641, 653

Malpighian tubule (mal-PIG-ee-un) Blind, threadlike excretory tubule near anterior end of an insect hindgut. 498, 701

mammal A member of a class of vertebrates characterized especially by the presence of hair and mammary glands. [Gk. *mammil*, teat] 356, 519

mandible The lower jaw; contains tooth sockets. [L. *mandibul*, jaw] 755

marsupial (mar-SOO-pee-ul) A mammal bearing immature young nursed in a marsupium, or pouch—for example, kangaroo and opossum. [Gk. *marsupi*, bag] 520

mass extinction An episode of large-scale extinction in which large numbers of species disappear in a few million years or less. 343

matrix Unstructured semifluid substance that fills the space in tissues, inside a cell or organelle. 76

matter Anything that takes up space and has mass; can exist as a solid, liquid, or gas. 24

maxillae (sing., maxilla) (mak-SIL-ee) Two bones that form the upper jaw; contain tooth sockets. [L. *maxill*, jawbone] 755

mechanoreceptor A receptor that is sensitive to mechanical stimulation, such as that from pressure, sound waves, and gravity. [Gk. *mechano*, instrument, and L. *recept*, receive] 742

medulla oblongata (muh-DUL-uh ahb-lawng-GAHT-uh) A part of the brain stem controlling heartbeat, blood pressure, breathing, and other vital functions. It also serves to connect the spinal cord and cerebrum. [L. *medull*, marrow, and *oblongus*, rather long] 724

megagametophyte In seed plants, the gametophyte that produces an egg; in flowering plants, an embryo sac. [Gk. *mega*, large, *gamet*, wife, and *phyt*, plant] 589

megaspore The spore produced by the megasporocyte of a seed plant; of the four produced, one develops into a megagametophyte (embryo sac). 586

meiosis (my-OH-sus) The type of nuclear division that occurs as part of sexual reproduction in which the daughter cells receive the haploid number of chromosomes. [Gk. *mei*, less, and *sis*, the act of] 170

meninges (sing., meninx) (muh-NIN-jeez) Protective membranous coverings about the central nervous system. [Gk. *menin*, membrane] 724

menisci (sing., meniscus) (mun-NIS-ky) Fibrocartilage that separates the surfaces of bones in the knee. [Gk. *menisc*, crescent] 758

menstruation The periodic shedding of tissue and blood from the inner lining of the uterus. [L. *menstru*, monthly] 796

meristem Undifferentiated embryonic tissue in the active growth regions of plants. [Gk. *meristo*, divided] 533

mesoderm The middle germ layer of embryonic gastrula; gives rise to the muscles, the connective tissue, and the circulatory system. [Gk. *meso*, middle, and *derm*, skin] 805

mesoglea (mez-uh-GLEE-uh) A jellylike layer between the epidermis and the gastrodermis of cnidaria. [Gk. *meso*, middle, and *gle*, glue] 470

mesophyll Inner, thickest layer of a leaf consisting of palisade and spongy mesophyll; the site of most of photosynthesis. [Gk. *meso*, middle, and *phyll*, leaf] 546

messenger RNA (mRNA) A type of RNA formed from a DNA template and bearing coded imformation that directs the amino acid sequence of a polypeptide. 248

metabolic pool Metabolites that are the products of and/or the substrates for key reactions in cells allowing one type of molecule to be changed into another type, such as the conversion of carbohydrates to fats. [Gk. *metab*, change] 149

metabolism All of the chemical reactions that occur in a cell during growth and repair. [Gk. *metab*, change] 4, 107

metamorphosis A change in shape and form that some animals, such as insects, undergo during development. [Gk. *met*, change, and *morph*, form] 493, 788

metastasis (meh-TAS-tuh-sus) The spread of cancer from the place of origin throughout the body; caused by the ability of cancer cells to migrate and invade tissues. [Gk. *meta*, between, and L. *stasis*, standing] 268

MHC (major histocompatibility complex) protein A membrane protein that serves to identify the cells of a particular individual.   659

microbe A microscopic infectious agent, such as a bacterium or a virus. [Gk. *micr*, small]   652

microbody Membrane-bounded vesicle containing specific enzymes involved in lipid and alcohol metabolism, photosynthesis, and germination. [Gk. *micr*, small]   74

microgametophyte In seed plants, the gametophyte that produces sperm; a pollen grain. [Gk. *micr*, small, *gamet*, husband, and *phyt*, plant]   589

microsphere Formed from proteinoids exposed to water; has properties similar to today's cells. [Gk. *micr*, small, and *spher*, ball]   334

microspore The spore produced by a microsporocyte of a seed plant; it develops into a microgametophyte (pollen grain).   586

microtubule Small cylindrical organelle that is believed to be involved in maintaining the shape of the cell and is present in cilia and flagella. [Gk. *micr*, small, and L. *tubul*, little pipe]   77

midbrain The part of the brain located below the thalamus and above the pons.   724

mimicry The superficial resemblance of one organism to another organism of a different species; often used to avoid predation. [Gk. *mim*, imitation]   853

mitochondrion A membranous organelle in which aerobic respiration produces ATP molecules. [Gk. *mito*, thread, and *chondro*, grain]   75

mitosis (my-TOH-sus) A process in which a parent nucleus reproduces two daughter nuclei, each identical to the parent nucleus. This division is necessary for growth and development. [Gk. *mito*, thread, and *sis*, the act of]   159

molecular clock The idea that the rate at which mutation changes accumulate in certain types of genes is constant over time and is not involved in adaptation to the environment.   361

molecule The smallest part of a compound that retains the properties of the compound; formed by the union of two or more atoms by covalent or ionic bonding. [L. *moles*, mass]   30

mollusk Member of the phylum Mollusca that includes squids, clams, snails and chitons; characterized by a visceral mass, a mantle, and a foot.   486

molt Periodic shedding of the exoskeleton in arthropods.   493

monocotyledon (mahn-uh-KAHT-ul-eed-un) A flowering plant group; members show one embryonic leaf, parallel-veined leaves, scattered vascular bundles, and other characteristics. [Gk. *mono*, one, and *kotyl*, cavity]   458

monotreme (MAHN-uh-treem) An egg-laying mammal—for example, duckbill platypus and spiny anteater. [Gk. *mono*, one, and *trema*, hole]   519

morphogenesis (mor-fuh-JEN-uh sus) The movement of early embryonic cells to establish body outline and form. [Gk. *morph*, form, and *gene*, origin]   804

morula (MOR-yuh-luh) A spherical mass of cells resulting from cleavage during animal development prior to the blastula stage. [L. *morul*, a little mulberry]   805

multiple allele A pattern of inheritance in which there are more than two alleles for a particular trait, although each individual has only two of these alleles.   199 224

muscle action potential An electrochemical change due to increased sarcolemma permeability that is propagated down the T system and results in muscle contraction.   762

muscular(contractile) tissue A type of animal tissue composed of fibers that shorten and lengthen to produce movements; skeletal, cardiac, and smooth (visceral) are the three types of vertebrate muscles.   616

mutagen (MYOOT-uh-jun) An agent, such as radiation or a chemical, that brings about a mutation in DNA. [L. *muta*, change]   256

mutation An alteration in chromosome structure or number and also an alteration in a gene due to a change in DNA composition. [L. *muta*, change]   206, 232

mutualism A symbiotic relationship in which both species benefit. [L. *mutu*, reciprocal]   856

mycelium (my-SEE-lee-um) A tangled mass of hyphal filaments composing the vegetative body of a fungus. [Gk. *myc*, fungus, and *ium*, small]   431

mycorrhiza (my-kuh-RY-zuh) A symbiotic relationship between fungal hyphae and roots of vascular plants; it assists in the uptake of minerals by the plant and receives organic nutrients from the plant. [Gk. *myc*, fungus, and *rhiz*, root]   440, 561

myelin sheath (MY-uh-lun) A white, fatty material—derived from the membrane of neurolemmocytes—that forms a covering for nerve fibers. [Gk. *myelo*, spinal cord]   714

myocardium Muscle of the heart [Gk. *myo*, muscle, and *card*, heart]   632

myofibril Specific muscle cell organelle containing a linear arrangement of sarcomeres, which shorten to produce muscle contraction. [Gk. *myo*, muscle, and L. *fibr*, fiber]   760

myosin (MY-uh-sun) A muscle protein making up the thick filaments in a sarcomere; it pulls actin to shorten the sarcomere, yielding muscle contraction.   760

NAD⁺ (nicotinamide adenine dinucleotide) (nik-uh-TEE-nuh-myd AD-un-een dy-NOO-klee-uh-tyd) A coenzyme that functions as an electron carrier and a hydrogen ion carrier in cellular oxidation-reduction reactions of glycolysis and cellular respiration.   112

NADP⁺ (nicotinamide adenine dinucleotide phosphate) (nik-uh-TEE-nuh-myd AD-un-een dy-NOO-klee-uh-tyd FAHS-fayt) A coenzyme that functions as an electron carrier and a hydrogen ion carrier in cellular oxidation-reduction reactions of photosynthesis.   112

natural selection The guiding force of evolution caused by environmental selection of organisms most fit to reproduce, resulting in adaptation.   300

Neanderthal Hominid who lived during the last Ice Age in Europe and the Middle East; these people made stone tools, hunted large game, and lived together in a kind of society.   368

negative feedback A mechanism of homeostatic response in which the output is counter to and cancels the input.   622

nematocyst (NEM-ut-uh-sist) In cnidaria, a capsule that contains a threadlike fiber whose release aids in the capture of prey. [Gk. *nem*, thread, and *cyst*, bag]   470

nephridium (pl., nephridia) (nih-FRID-ee-um) Segmentally arranged, paired excretory tubules of many invertebrates, as in the earthworm, where the contents are released through a nephridiopore. [Gk. *nephri*, kidney]   490, 701

nephron (NEF-rahn) A microscopic kidney unit that regulates blood composition by pressure filtration and selective reabsorption; there are over a million nephrons per human kidney. [Gk. *nephri*, kidney]   702

nerve A bundle of long axons and/or dendrites outside the central nervous system.   720

nervous tissue A type of animal tissue; contains nerve cells (neurons), which conduct impulses, and neuroglial cells, which support, protect, and provide nutrients to neurons.   617

neuromuscular junction Region where an axon bulb approaches the sarcolemma of a muscle fiber; contains a presynaptic membrane, a synaptic cleft, and a postsynaptic membrane.   762

neuron Nerve cell that characteristically has three parts: dendrites, cell body, and axon. [Gk. *neuro*, nerve]   617, 714

neurotransmitter A chemical made at the ends of axons that is responsible for transmission across a synapse or a neuromuscular junction. [Gk. *neuro*, nerve, and L. *trans*, across]   718

neutron A subatomic particle that has a weight of one atomic mass unit, carries no charge, and is found in the nucleus of an atom.   25

neutrophil Granular leukocyte that is the most abundant of the white blood cells; first to respond to infection. [L. *neutro*, neither, and *phil*, loving]   641

niche The resources that an organism exploits to meet its energy, nutrient, and survival demands.   851

nitrogen fixation The process whereby free atmospheric nitrogen is converted into compounds, such as ammonium and nitrates, usually by soil bacteria.   405, 868

nodule A structure on plant roots that contains nitrogen-fixing bacteria. [L. *nodul*, little knot]   560

nondisjunction The failure of homologous chromosomes or daughter chromosomes to separate during meiosis I and meiosis II, respectively.   213

norepinephrine (NE) Neurotransmitter active in the peripheral and central nervous systems; a hormone secreted by the adrenal medulla.   718

notochord Dorsal supporting rod that exists in all chordates sometime in their life history; replaced by the vertebral column in vertebrates. [Gk. *noto*, back, and *chord*, string]   506, 807

nuclear envelope The double membrane that surrounds the nucleus and is continuous with the endoplasmic reticulum.   70

nucleic acid A polymer of nucleotides; both DNA and RNA are nucleic acids.   56, 232

nucleoid Area in prokaryotic cell where DNA is found. [L. *nucle*, nucleus]   66, 166

nucleolus (pl., nucleoli) Dark-staining, spherical body in the cell nucleus that contains ribosomal RNA. [L. *nucleol*, little nucleus]   70

nucleotide Monomer of DNA and RNA consisting of a five-carbon sugar bonded to a nitrogenous base and a phosphate group.   56

nucleus (NOO-klee-us) Region of a eukaryotic cell, containing chromosomes, that controls the structure and function of the cell.   70

ocean ridge The ridge on the ocean floor where oceanic crust forms and from which it moves laterally in each direction.   339

oil A liquid lipid formed when three fatty acids with many double bonds combine with glycerol; common to plants and also called a triglyceride.   48

olfactory cell (ahl-FAK-tuh-ree) A modified neuron that is a receptor for the sense of smell. [L. *olfact*, smell]   735

omnivore An organism in a food chain that feeds on both plants and animals. [L. *omni*, all, and *vor*, eat]   860

oncogene (ONG-koh-jeen) A cancer-causing gene. [Gk. *onco*, tumor]   269

oogamy Sexual reproduction in which the gametes are dissimilar; the egg is large and nonmotile and the sperm is smaller and motile. [Gk. *oo*, egg, and *gamy*, reproduction]   414

oogenesis (oh-uh-JEN-uh-sus) The production of eggs in females by the process of meiosis and maturation. [Gk. *oo*, egg, and *gene*, origin]   176

operant conditioning A form of learning that results from rewarding or reinforcing a particular behavior.   828

operator In an operon, the sequence of DNA to which the repressor protein binds.   260

operon (OP-er-on) A group of structural and regulating genes that functions as a single unit. [L. *opera*, work]   260

optic nerve The nerve that carries impulses from the retina of the eye to the brain. [Gk. *opti*, eye]   738

orbital A volume of space around a nucleus where electrons can be found most of the time.   27

organ A combination of two or more different tissues performing a common function.   618

organelle Small, membranous structure in the cytoplasm having a specific function.   67

organic molecule A type of molecule that contains carbon and hydrogen; it usually also has oxygen attached to the carbon(s).   42

organ of Corti (KORT-ee) Specialized region of the cochlea containing the hair cells for sound detection and discrimination.   743

organ system A group of related organs working together.   618

osmosis The diffusion of water through a differentially permeable membrane. [Gk. *osmo*, pushing]   92

osmotic pressure Measure of the tendency of water to move across a differentially permeable membrane; visible as an increase in liquid on the side of the membrane with higher solute concentration.   92

osteoblast A bone-forming cell. [Gk. *ost*, bone, and *blast*, bud]   753

osteoclast A cell that causes erosion of bone. [Gk. *ost*, bone, and *clas*, fragment]   753

osteocyte A mature bone cell. [Gk. *ost*, bone, and *cyt*, cell]   753

ovary In flowering plants, enlarged, base portion of the pistil that eventually develops into the fruit; in animals, the organ that produces eggs, estrogen, and progesterone. [L. *ovi*, egg]   458, 587, 787

oviduct A tube that transports eggs to outside or to the uterus; also called uterine tube. [L. *ovi*, egg, and *duc*, lead]   794

ovulation Bursting of a follicle when an egg is released from the ovary.   795

ovule In seed plants, a structure that contains the megasporangium, where meiosis occurs and the megagametophyte is produced; develops into the seed.   454, 587

oxidation (ahk-sih-DAY-shun) A loss of one or more electrons from an atom or molecule with a concurrent release of energy; in biological systems, generally the loss of hydrogen atoms.   33

oxidative phosphorylation (fahs-for-ah-LAY-shun) The process by which ATP production is tied to an electron transport system that uses oxygen as the final receptor; occurs in mitochondria. [Gk. *phos*, light, and *phor*, movement]   146

oxygen debt The use of oxygen to metabolize lactate, which builds up due to anaerobic conditions.   142, 761

ozone shield Formed from oxygen in the upper atmosphere, it protects the earth from ultraviolet radiation.   339, 894

P

paleontology (pay-lee-ahn-TAHL-uh-jee) Study of fossils that results in knowledge about the history of life. [Gk. *paleo*, ancient, and *logy*, study of] 296, 337

palisade mesophyll In a plant leaf, the layer of mesophyll containing elongated cells with many chloroplasts. [L. *pali*, stake, Gk. *meso*, middle, and *phyll*, leaf] 546

pancreas An abdominal organ that produces digestive enzymes and the hormones insulin and glucagon. 777

pancreatic islets (of Langerhans) Distinctive group of cells within the pancreas that secretes insulin and glucagon. 777

parallel evolution Similarity in structure in related groups that cannot be traced to a common ancestor. 388

parasitism A symbiotic relationship in which one species (parasite) benefits in terms of growth and reproduction to the harm of the other species (host). [Gk. *parasit*, eat at another's table] 854

parasympathetic system A division of the autonomic system that is active under normal conditions; uses acetylcholine as a neurotransmitter. 723

parathyroid gland (par-uh-THY-royd) A gland embedded in the posterior surface of the thyroid gland; it produces parathyroid hormone. [Gk. *para*, beside, and *thyro*, door] 775

parathyroid hormone (PTH) (par-uh-THY-royd) A hormone secreted by the four parathyoid glands that increases the blood calcium level and decreases the blood phosphate level. [Gk. *para*, beside, and *thyro*, door] 775

parenchyma (puh-REN-kuh-muh) The least specialized of all plant cell or tissue types; contains plastids and is found in all organs of a plant. [Gk. *para*, beside, and *enchyma*, infusion] 534

parthenogenesis (par-thuh-noh-JEN-uh-sus) The development of an egg cell into a whole organism without fertilization. [Gk. *partheno*, without fertilization, and *gene*, origin] 786

pectoral girdle Portion of the skeleton that provides support and attachment for the arms. [Gk. *pechy*, forearm] 756

pelagic division The open portion of the sea. [Gk. *pelagi*, the sea] 878

pelvic girdle Portion of the skeleton to which the legs are attached. [L. *pelv*, pelvis] 757

penis Male copulatory organ. 787

pepsin A protein-digesting enzyme secreted by gastric glands. 672

peptide Two or more amino acids joined together by covalent bonding. 52

peptide bond The covalent bond that joins two amino acids. 52

pericycle The external layer of cells in the vascular cylinder of a plant root, producing branch and secondary roots. 537

peripheral nervous system (PNS) The nerves that branch off of the central nervous system. [Gk. *peripher*, circumference] 712

peristalsis (per-uh-STAWL-sus) The rhythmic, wavelike contraction that moves food through the digestive tract. [Gk. *peristole*, contraction] 672

petal The plant structure belonging to an inner whorl of the flower; colored and internal to the outer whorl of sepals. 587

phagocytize The taking in of a cell and/or debris by endocytosis: cell eating. [Gk. *phag*, eat, and *cyt*, cell] 420

phagocytosis (fag-oh-suh-TOH-sis) A process by which amoeboid-type cells engulf large material, forming an intracellular vacuole. [Gk. *phag*, eat, and *cyt*, cell] 96

pharynx (FAR-ingks) A common passageway for both food intake and air movement, located between the mouth and the esophagus. [Gk. *pharyn*, throat] 688

phenotype The visible expression of a genotype—for example, brown eyes or attached earlobes. [Gk. *pheno*, appear, and *typos*, image] 187

pheromone A chemical released by the body that causes a predictable reaction of another member of the same species. [Gk. *pher*, carry, and *mon*, one] 833

phloem (FLOH-um) The vascular tissue that conducts organic solutes in plants; it contains sieve-tube cells and companion cells. [Gk. *phloe*, tree bark, and L. *em*, in] 448, 534

phospholipid (fahs-foh-LIP-id) A molecule having the same structure as a neutral fat except one bonded fatty acid is replaced by a group that contains phosphate; an important component of plasma membranes. [Gk. *phos*, light, and *lipar*, oil] 51, 86

photochemical smog Air pollution that contains nitrogen oxides and hydrocarbons which react to produce ozone and PAN (peroxylacetyl nitrate). [Gk. *photo*, light, and *chem*, chemical] 895

photon A discrete packet of solar energy; the amount of energy in a photon is inversely related to the wavelength of the photon. [Gk. *photo*, light] 120

photoperiodism (foht-oh-PIR-ee-ud-iz-um) The relative lengths of daylight and darkness that affect the physiology and behavior of an organism. [Gk. *photo*, light, and *perio*, on the other side] 580

photoreceptor A light sensitive receptor. [Gk. *photo*, light, and L. *recept*, receive] 736

photosynthesis A process usually occurring within chloroplasts whereby chlorophyll traps solar energy and carbon dioxide is reduced to a carbohydrate. [Gk. *photo*, light, and *synthesis*, putting together] 4, 112, 120

photosystem A photosynthetic unit where solar energy is absorbed; contains an antenna (photosynthetic pigments) and an electron acceptor; photosystem I (PS I) and a PS II. 124

phototropism (foh-TAH-truh-piz-um) Directional growth of plants in response to light; stems demonstrate positive phototropism. [Gk. *photo*, light, and *trop*, turn] 569

pH scale A measurement scale for the relative hydrogen ion concentration [H^+] and hydroxyl ion concentration [OH^-]. 36

phyletic gradualism (fy-LET-ik) An evolutionary model that proposes evolutionary change resulting in a new species can occur gradually in an unbranched lineage. [Gk. *phyl*, tribe] 351

phylogenetic tree (fy-loh-JEN-et-ik) A diagram that indicates common ancestors and lines of descent. 387

phylogeny (fy-LAHJ-uh-nee) The evolutionary history of a group of organisms. [Gk. *phyl*, tribe] 387

phytochrome (FYT-uh-krohm) A photoreversible plant pigment whose active form seems to be involved in regulating transcription of certain genes. [Gk. *phyt*, plant, and *chrom*, color] 580

phytoplankton (fyt-oh-PLANGK-tuh) The part of plankton containing organisms that (1) photosynthesize and produce much of the oxygen in the atmosphere and (2) serve as food producers in aquatic ecosystems. [Gk. *phyt*, plant, and *plankt*, wandering] 413

pineal gland (PY-nee-ul) A gland—either at the skin surface (fish, amphibians) or in the third ventricle of the brain, (mammals)—that produces melatonin. 780

pinocytosis (pin-oh-suh-TOH-sis) A process by which vesicles form around and bring macromolecules into the cell. [Gk. *pin*, drink, and *cyt*, cell] 96

pistil A female flower structure consisting of an ovary, a style, and a stigma. [L. *pistill*, pestle]   458, 587

pituitary gland A small gland that lies just inferior to the hypothalamus; the anterior pituitary produces several hormones, some of which control other endocrine glands; the posterior pituitary produces oxytocin and antidiuretic hormone.   771

placenta The structure during the development of placental mammals that forms from the chorion and the uterine wall and allows the embryo and then the fetus to acquire nutrients and rid itself of wastes.   789, 815

placental mammal A member of a mammalian subclass characterized by a placenta, an organ of exchange between maternal and fetal blood that supplies nutrients to the growing offspring.   520

plankton Fresh and marine organisms that float on or near the surface of the water. [Gk. *plankt*, wandering]   413, 876

plasma The liquid portion of blood; contains nutrients, wastes, salts, and proteins. [Gk. *plasma*, something molded]   641

plasma cell A cell derived from a B-cell lymphocyte that is specialized to mass-produce antibodies. [Gk. *plasm*, something molded]   655

plasma membrane Flexible bilayer of phospholipids and proteins that defines the boundary of the cell and regulates the flow of materials into and out of the cell; also called the cell membrane.   66

plasmid A self-duplicating ring of accessory DNA in the cytoplasm of bacteria.   278

plasmodesmata (sing., plasmodesma) The minute cytoplasmic threads that extend through openings in cell walls and connect the cytoplasm of adjacent plant cells. [Gk. *plasma*, form, and *desma*, bond]   99

plasmolysis Contraction of the cell contents due to the loss of water. [Gk. *plasm*, something molded, and *lys*, loosening]   93

platelet A component of blood that is necessary to blood clotting. [Gk. *plate*, flat]   642

plate tectonics (tek-TAHN-iks) The study of the behavior of the earth's crust in terms of moving plates that are formed at ocean ridges and destroyed at subduction zones. [Gk. *tect*, a covering]   339

plumule (PLOO-myool) In flowering plants, the embryonic plant shoot that bears young leaves. [L. *plum*, feather]   597

polar body In oogenesis, a nonfunctional product; three of the four meiotic products are of this type.   178

polar covalent bond A bond in which the sharing of electrons between atoms is unequal.   33

pollen grain A microgametophyte in seed plants. [L. *pollen*, fine dust]   454, 589

pollination In seed plants, the transfer of pollen from microsporangium to the ovule, which by this time contains a megagametophyte. [L. *pollen*, fine dust]   454, 592

pollutant A substance that is added to the environment and leads to undesirable effects for living organisms. [L. *pollut*, defiled]   892

polygenic inheritance A pattern of inheritance in which a trait is controlled by several allelic pairs; each dominant allele contributes in an additive and like manner. [Gk. *poly*, many, and *genic*, producing]   200

polymer Macromolecule consisting of covalently bonded monomers; for example, a protein is a polymer of monomers called amino acids. [Gk. *poly*, many, and *meris*, part]   44

polyploid (polyploidy) A condition in which an organism has more than two complete sets of chromosomes. [Gk. *poly*, many, and *ploid*, sets]   206

polysome A string of ribosomes, simultaneously translating the same mRNA strand during protein synthesis. [Gk. *poly*, many, and *soma*, body]   252

pons A part of the brain stem above the medulla oblongata and below the midbrain. It also serves to connect the cerebral hemispheres. [L. *pont*, bridge]   724

population A group of organisms of the same species occupying a certain area and sharing a common gene pool.   312, 840

portal system A pathway of blood flow that begins and ends in capillaries, such as the one found between the small intestine and liver. [L. *porta*, door]   636

positive feedback A mechanism of homeostatic response in which the output intensifies and increases the likelihood of response, instead of countering it and canceling it.   622

postmating isolating mechanism An anatomical or physiological difference between two species that prevents successful reproduction after mating has taken place.   323

prairie Terrestrial biome that is a temperate grassland. When travelling east to west in the midwest of the United States, a tall-grass prairie changes to a short grass prairie.   855

premating isolating mechanism An anatomical or behavioral difference between two species that prevents the possibility of mating.   322

pressure-flow model Model explaining transport through sieve tubes of phloem by a positive pressure potential (compared to a sink) due to the active transport of sucrose and the passive transport of water.   562

primate Animal that belongs to the order Primates, the order of mammals that includes prosimians, monkeys, apes, and humans.   357

primitive character A structural, physiological, or behavioral trait that is present in a common ancestor and all members of a group.   387

Proconsul A possible hominoid ancestor; a forest-dwelling primate with some characteristics of living apes.   359

producer An organism at the start of a food chain that makes its own food (e.g., green plants on land and algae in water).   860

progesterone (proh-JES-tuh-rohn) Female ovarian sex hormone that causes the endometrium of the uterus to become secretory during the uterine cycle; along with estrogen, it maintains secondary sex characteristics in females.   795

prokaryotic cell (proh-kair-ee-AHT-ik) Typical of bacteria, lacking a membrane-bounded nucleus and most organelles.   66

promoter In an operon, a sequence of DNA where RNA polymerase begins transcription.   250, 260

prosimian (proh-SIM-ee-un) A group of primates that includes lemurs and tarsiers and may resemble the first primates to have evolved. [Gk. *pro*, before, and *simos*, monkey, ape]   357

protein A polymer having, as its primary structure, a sequence of amino acids united through covalent bonding.   52

proteinoid (PROHT-en-oyd) Abiotically polymerized amino acids that are joined in a preferred manner; possible early step in cell evolution.   334

protocell A cell forerunner developed from cell-like microspheres. [Gk. *proto*, first]   334

protoctist Organism belonging to the kingdom Protoctista; for example, protozoa, algae, slime or water molds. [Gk. *proto*, first, and *ktistos*, to establish]   413

proton A subatomic particle found in the nucleus of an atom that has a weight of one atomic mass unit and carries a positive charge; a hydrogen ion.   25

proto-oncogene (PROH-toh-ONG-koh-jeen) A normal gene that can become an oncogene through mutation. [Gk. *proto*, first, *onco*, tumor]   271

protoplast A plant cell from which the cell wall has been removed. [Gk. *proto*, first, and *plast*, formed, molded]   602

protostome (PROH-toh-stohm) A group of coelomate animals in which the first embryonic opening (the blastopore) is associated with the mouth. [Gk. *proto*, first, and *stom*, mouth]   484

protozoan (pl., protozoa) Animal-like, heterotrophic, unicellular organism. [Gk. *proto*, first, and *zoa*, animal]   420

proximal convoluted tubule The portion of a nephron following the glomerular capsule where selective reabsorption of filtrate occurs. [L. *proxim*, nearest]   702

pseudocoelom (soo-doh-SEE-lum) A body cavity lying between the digestive tract and body wall that is incompletely lined by mesoderm. [Gk. *pseudo*, false, and *coel*, hollow]   478

pseudopod Cytoplasmic extension of amoeboid protoctists; used for locomotion and engulfing food. [Gk. *pseudo*, false, and *pod*, foot]   420

pulmonary circuit A circulatory pathway between the lungs and the heart. [L. *pulmo*, lung]   636

punctuated equilibrium An evolutionary model that proposes there are periods of rapid change dependent on speciation followed by long periods of stasis.   351

Punnett square A grid that enables one to calculate the results of simple genetic crosses by lining up alleles within the gametes of two parents on the outside margin and their recombination in boxes inside the grid.   189

purine (PYUR-een) A type of nitrogen-containing base, such as adenine and guanine, having a double-ring structure.   235

pyrimidine (py-RIM-uh-deen) A type of nitrogen-containing base, such as cytosine, thymine, and uracil, having a single-ring structure.   235

pyruvate (py-ROO-vayt) The end product of glycolysis; its further fate, involving fermentation or entry into a mitochondrion, depends on oxygen availability.   140

radial symmetry Body plan in which similar parts are arranged around a central axis, like spokes of a wheel.   466

receptor Portion of a sensory neuron that responds to an external stimulus; also, any molecule on the surface of a cell that binds specifically to other molecules (such as hormones, neurotransmitters). [L. *recept*, receive]   721, 734

receptor-mediated endocytosis Pinocytic uptake of macromolecules that bind to specific receptors on the cell surface.   97

recessive allele (uh-LEEL) An allele that exerts its phenotypic effect only in the homozygote; its expression is masked by a dominant allele.   187

recombinant DNA (rDNA) DNA that contains genes from more than one source.   278

reduction A gain of electrons by an atom or molecule with a concurrent storage of energy; in biological systems, generally the gain of hydrogen atoms.   33

reflex An automatic, involuntary response of an organism to a stimulus. [L. *reflectere*, bend back]   721

regulator gene In an operon, a gene that codes for a repressor.   260

repressible operon (OP-er-on) An operon that is normally active because the repressor must combine with a corepressor before the complex can bind to the operator.   260

repressor In an operon, protein molecule that binds to an operator, preventing RNA polymerase from binding to the promoter site.   260

reproduce To produce a new individual of the same kind.   5

reptile A member of a class of terrestrial vertebrates with internal fertilization, scaly skin, and an egg with a leathery shell; includes snakes, lizards, turtles, and crocodiles. [L. *reptil*, creep, crawl]   514

resting potential The membrane potential of an inactive neuron.   717

restriction enzyme Bacterial enzyme that stops viral reproduction by cleaving viral DNA; used to cut DNA at specific points during production of recombinant DNA.   279

retina The innermost layer of the eyeball containing the photoreceptors—rods and cones. [L. *retin*, net]   738

retrovirus RNA virus containing the enzyme reverse transcriptase that carries out RNA/DNA transcription; retroviruses include oncogenes and the AIDS viruses. [L. *retro*, backward, and *viro*, poison]   400

rhizoid A rootlike hair that anchors a plant and absorbs minerals and water from the soil. [Gk. *rhiz*, root, and *oid*, like]   446

rhizome A rootlike, underground stem. [Gk. *rhizo*, root]   544

rhodopsin (roh-DAHP-sun) A light-absorbing molecule in rods that contains a pigment and the protein opsin. [Gk. *rhodo*, rose-red, and *opsis*, view]   740

rib Bone hinged to the vertebral column and sternum, which, with muscle, defines the top and sides of the chest cavity.   756

rib cage The top and side of the thoracic cavity in vertebrates; contains ribs and intercostal muscles.   687

ribosomal RNA (rRNA) A type of RNA found in ribosomes that coordinates the coupling of anticodons with codons during polypeptide synthesis.   248

ribosome RNA and protein in two subunits; site of protein synthesis.   71

ribozyme Enzyme that carries out mRNA processing.   251

RNA (ribonucleic acid) A nucleic acid polymer produced from covalent bonding of nucleotide monomers that contain the sugar ribose; RNA helps DNA carry out protein synthesis.   56

RNA (ribonucleic acid) A nucleic acid polymer produced from covalent bonding of nucleotide monomers that contain the sugar ribose; RNA helps DNA carry out protein synthesis.   232

RNA polymerase (PAHL-uh-muh-rays) An enzyme that speeds the formation of RNA from a DNA template. [Gk. *poly*, many, and *meris*, part]   250

rod A photoreceptor in vertebrate eyes that responds to dim light.   738

root hair An extension of a root epidermal cell that collectively increases the surface area for the absorption of water and minerals.   533

root pressure A force generated by an osmotic gradient that serves to elevate sap through xylem for a short distance.   554

r-strategist A species that has evolved characteristics that maximize its rate of natural increase—for example, high birthrate.   844

RuBP (ribulose bisphosphate) A five-carbon compound that combines with and fixes carbon dioxide during the Calvin cycle and is later regenerated by the same cycle.   127

sac body plan A body with a digestive cavity that has only one opening, as in cnidaria and flatworms.   474

salivary gland A gland associated with the mouth that secretes saliva.   671

saltatory conduction The movement of nerve impulses from one neurolemmal node to another along a myelinated axon. [L. *saltator*, leaper] 717

saprotroph (SAP-roh-trohf) An organism, usually a bacterium or fungus, that digests dead organic matter; secretes digestive enzymes and absorbs the resulting nutrients back across the plasma membrane. [Gk. *sapro*, putrid, and *troph*, feeder] 404

sarcolemma (sahr-kuh-LEM-uh) Plasma membrane of a muscle fiber that forms the tubules of the T system involved in muscular contraction. [Gk. *sarc*, flesh, and *lemma*, sheath] 760

sarcomere (SAHR-kuh-mir) One of many units, arranged linearly within a myofibril, whose contraction produces muscle contraction. [Gk. *sarc*, flesh, and *mer*, part] 760

savanna Terrestrial biome that is a tropical grassland in Africa, characterized by a few trees and a severe dry season. 885

scientific method A step-by-step process for discovery and generation of knowledge—ranging from observation and hypothesis to theory and principle. 14

sclera (SKLER-uh) The outer, white, fibrous layer of the eye that surrounds the eye except for the transparent cornea. [Gk. *scler*, hard] 737

secondary oocyte (OH-uh-syt) In oogenesis, the functional product of meiosis I; becomes the egg. [Gk. *oo*, egg, and *cyt*, cell] 178

sedimentation The process by which particulate material accumulates and forms a stratum. [L. *sedimentum*, a settling] 336

seed A mature ovule that contains an embryo, with stored food enclosed in a protective coat. 454, 594

segmentation Repetition of body units as is seen in the earthworm. 490

semen Thick, whitish fluid consisting of sperm and secretions from several glands of the male reproductive tract. [L. *semen*, sperm] 791

semicircular canal One of three half-circle-shaped canals of the inner ear that are fluid filled and register changes in motion. 743

semiconservative replication Duplication of DNA resulting in a double helix having one parental and one new strand. 238

sepal The protective leaflike structure enclosing the flower when in bud. 587

sessile Organisms that lack locomotion and remain stationary in one place, such as plants or sponges. 466

sessile filter feeder An organism that stays in one place and filters its food from the water. 469

sex chromosome A chromosome that determines the sex of an individual; in many animals, females have two X chromosomes and males have an X and Y chromosome. 202, 212

sex-influenced trait An autosomal phenotype controlled by an allele that is expressed differently in the two sexes; for example, the possibility of pattern baldness is increased by the presence of testosterone in males. 227

sexual reproduction Reproduction involving meiosis, gamete formation, and fertilization; produces offspring with chromosomes inherited from each parent. 170, 786

sexual selection Changes in males and females due to male competition and female selectivity. 830

sinus A cavity, as with the sinuses in the human skull. [L. *sinu*, a hollow] 54

sister chromatid (KROH-muh-tud) One of two genetically identical chromosomal units that are the result of DNA replication and are attached to each other at the centromere. 159

skeletal muscle Striated, voluntary muscle tissue that comprises skeletal muscles; also called striated muscle. 616

sliding filament theory The movement of actin filaments in relation to myosin filaments, which accounts for muscle contraction. 761

smooth (visceral) muscle Nonstriated, involuntary muscles found in the walls of internal organs. 616

society A group in which members of species are organized in a cooperative manner, extending beyond sexual and parental behavior. 833

sociobiology The application of evolutionary biology principles to the study of social behavior in animals. 835

sodium-potassium pump A transport protein in the plasma membrane that moves sodium ions out of and potassium into animal cells; important in nerve and muscle cells. 94

solute A substance dissolved in a solvent to form a solution. 91

solvent A fluid, such as water, that dissolves solutes. 91

speciation The process whereby a new species originates or is produced. 322

species A taxonomic category that is the subdivision of a genus; its members can breed successfully with each other but not with members of another species. [L. *speci*, a kind] 5, 322, 383

sperm Male sex cell or gamete, usually motile and smaller than female gamete. 793

spermatogenesis (spur-mat-uh-JEN-uh-sus) The production of sperm in males by the process of meiosis and maturation. [Gk. *sperm*, seed, and *gene*, origin] 176

spicule (SPIK-yool) A skeletal structure of sponges composed of calcium carbonate or silicate. [L. *spic*, spike, and *ule*, little] 469

spinal cord Part of the central nervous system; the nerve cord that is continuous with the base of the brain and housed within the vertebral column. 720

spindle A microtubule structure that brings about chromosomal movement during cell division. 162

spongy mesophyll In a plant leaf, the layer of mesophyll containing loosely packed, irregularly spaced cells that increase the amount of surface area for gas exchange; along with palisade mesophyll, it is the site of most of photosynthesis. [Gk. *spong*, sponge, *meso*, middle, and *phyll*, leaf] 546

sporangium (pl., sporangia) (spuh-RAN-jee-um) A capsule that produces sporangiospores. [Gk. *spor*, seed, *ang*, vessel, and *ium*, small] 432

spore An asexual reproductive structure that is resistant to unfavorable environmental conditions and develops into a haploid generation. [Gk. *spor*, seed] 414, 431

sporophyte (SPOR-uh-fyt) The diploid generation of the alternation of generations life cycle of a plant; meiosis produces haploid spores that develop into the haploid generation. [Gk. *spor*, seed, and *phyt*, plant] 445

stabilizing selection An outcome of natural selection in which extreme phenotypes are eliminated and the average phenotype is conserved. 320

stamen A pollen-producing flower structure consisting of an anther on a filament tip. 458, 587

starch The storage polysaccharide found in plants that is composed of glucose molecules joined in a linear fashion. 46

stem Usually the upright, vertical portion of a plant, which transports substances to and from the leaves. 530

sternum The breastbone to which the ribs are ventrally attached. [Gk. *stern*, breastbone] 756

steroid A type of lipid molecule having four interlocking rings; examples are cholesterol, progesterone, and testosterone. 51

stigma Enlarged, sticky knob at one end of the pistil where pollen grains are received during pollination. 458, 587

stolon A stem that grows horizontally along the ground and establishes plantlets periodically when it contacts the soil (e.g., the runners of a strawberry plant). [L. *stolo*, shoot] 544

stomate Small opening with two guard cells in leaf epidermis and stems; their opening controls the rate of gas exchange. 448

striated Having bands; cardiac and skeletal muscle are striated with bands of light and dark. [L. *stria*, streaked] 616

stroma (STROH-muh) A large, central space in a chloroplast that is fluid filled and contains enzymes used in photosynthesis. [Gk. *stroma*, spread out] 75, 123

structural gene Gene that codes for an enzyme in a metabolic pathway. 260

style The tubular part of the pistil of a flower where a pollen tube develops from a transferred pollen grain. 458, 587

substrate The reactant in an enzymatic reaction; each enzyme has a specific substrate. [L. *sub*, below, and *strat*, layer] 107

substrate-level phosphorylation (fahs-for-ah-LAY-shun) An enzymatic process in which ATP is formed by transferring a phosphate from a metabolic substrate to ADP. [Gk. *phos*, light, and *phor*, movement] 114, 140

succession An orderly sequence of community replacement—one following the other-that leads eventually to a climax community. 860

survivorship Percentage of remaining survivors of a population over time; usually shown graphically, it can be used to depict death rates. 843

sustainable world A global way of life that can continue indefinitely because the economic needs of all peoples are met while still protecting the environment. 902

symbiosis A relationship that occurs when two different species live together in a unique way; it may be beneficial, neutral, or detrimental to one and/or the other species. [Gk. *symbio*, living together] 854

symbiotic A close relationship between two species; includes parasitism, mutualism, and commensalism. [Gk. *symbio*, living together] 404

sympathetic system A division of the autonomic system that is active under "flight or fight" conditions; uses norepinephrine as a neurotransmitter. 723

sympatric speciation (sim-PA-trik) The origin of new species in populations that overlap geographically. [Gk. *sym*, together, and *patri*, fatherland] 324

synapse (SIN-aps) A junction between neurons consisting of the presynaptic (axon) membrane, the synaptic cleft, and the postsynaptic (usually dendrite) membrane. [Gk. *synapse*, union] 718

synapsis The pairing of homologous chromosomes during meiosis I. [Gk. *synap*, union] 172

systematics The study of the diversity of organisms at all levels of organization, from the cellular level to the population level. [Gk. *sys*, together] 387

systemic circuit A circulatory pathway of blood flow between the tissues and the heart. 636

systole (SIS-tuh-lee) The contraction period of a heart during the cardiac cycle. [Gk. *systol*, contraction] 634

taiga (TY-guh) Terrestrial biome that is a coniferous forest extending in a broad belt across northern Eurasia and North America. 885

taste bud A concentration of sensory nerve endings in the oral cavity that functions as taste receptors. 735

taxon (pl., taxa) Group of organisms that fills a particular classification category. [Gk. *taxis*, arrangement] 382

taxonomy The branch of biology concerned with identifying and naming organisms. [Gk. *taxis*, arrangement, and *nomy*, science of] 10, 380

tendon Strap of fibrous connective tissue that joins skeletal muscle to bone.[L. *tend*, stretch] 614, 759

territoriality Behavior related to the act of marking or defending a particular area against invasion by another species member; area often used for the purpose of feeding, mating, and caring for young. 832

testcross A cross between an individual with the dominant phenotype and an individual with the recessive phenotype to see if the individual with the dominant phenotype is homozygous or heterozygous. 190

testosterone (teh-STAHS-tuh-rohn) Male sex hormone produced by interstitial cells in the testis; it maintains secondary sex characteristics in males. 793

tetrad Following synapsis, the set of four chromatids of a homologous chromosome pair, visible during prophase of meiosis I; also called bivalent. [Gk. *tetr*, four] 172

thalamus (THAL-uh-mus) A part of the brain that serves as the integrating center for sensory input, it plays a role in arousing the cerebral cortex. 725

theory A conceptual scheme arrived at by the scientific method and supported by innumerable observations and experimentations. 14

thermal inversion Temperature inversion that traps cold air and its pollutants near the earth with the warm air above it. [Gk. *therm*, heat, and L. *vers*, turn] 895

thigmotropism (thig-MAH-truh-piz-um) In plants, unequal growth due to contact with solid objects, as the coiling of tendrils around a pole. [Gk. *thigm*, touch, and *trop*, turn] 570

thoracic cavity The internal body space of some animals that contains the lungs and the heart protecting them from desiccation; the chest. 687

thrombocyte Platelet; cell fragment in the blood that initiates the process of blood clotting [Gk. *thrombo*, blood clot, and *cyt*, cell] 641

thylakoid (THY-luh-koyd) A flattened sac within a granum whose membrane contains the photosynthetic pigments (e.g., chlorophyll); where the light-dependent reactions occur. [Gk. *thylac*, sack, and *oid*, like] 75, 123

thymine (T) (THY-meen) One of four nitrogen-containing bases in nucleotides composing the structure of DNA. 235

thyroid gland A large gland in the neck that produces several important hormones, including thyroxin and calcitonin. [Gk. *thyro*, door] 774

thyroxin (thy-RAHK-seen) A substance (also called T4) secreted from the thyroid gland that promotes growth and development in vertebrates; in general, it increases the metabolic rate in cells. [Gk. *thyro*, door] 774

tissue A group of similar cells combined to perform a common function. 612

tissue culture The process of growing tissue artificially in a usually liquid medium in laboratory glassware. 600

tissue fluid A filtrate containing all the small molecules of blood plasma that bathes all the cells of the body. 642

T lymphocyte (LIM-fuh-syt) A lymphocyte that matures in the thymus and exists in four varieties, one of which kills antigen-bearing cells outright. [L. *lymph*, water, and *cyt*, cell] 654

tonicity The degree to which the concentration of solute versus solvent causes fluids to move into or out of cells. 92

trachea (TRAY-kee-uh) An air tube (windpipe) in tetrapod vertebrates that runs between the larynx and the bronchi; also an air tube in insects that is located between the spiracles and the tracheoles. [L. *trache*, windpipe] 493, 688

transcription The process whereby a DNA strand serves as a template for the formation of mRNA. [L. *trans*, across, and *scribere*, to write] 248

transcription factor In eukaryotes, protein required for the initiation of transcription by RNA polymerase. 266

transfer RNA (tRNA) A type of RNA that transfers a particular amino acid to a ribosome during protein synthesis; at one end it binds to the amino acid and at the other end it has an anticodon that binds to an mRNA codon. 248

transgenic organism Free-living organisms in the environment that have had a foreign gene inserted into them. [L. *trans*, across, and Gk. *gene*, origin] 283

transition reaction A reaction that oxidizes pyruvate with the release of carbon dioxide; results in acetyl-CoA and connects glycolysis to the Krebs cycle. 144

translation The process whereby the sequence of codons in mRNA determines (is translated into) the sequence of amino acids in a polypeptide. [L. *trans*, across, and *latus*, carried] 248

transpiration A plant's loss of water to the atmosphere, mainly through evaporation at leaf stomates. [L. *trans*, across, and *spir*, breathe] 555

trophic level Feeding level of one or more populations in a food web. [Gk. *troph*, feeder] 863

trophoblast (TROH-fuh-blast) The outer membrane surrounding the embryo in mammals; when thickened by a layer of mesoderm, it becomes the chorion, an extraembryonic membrane. [Gk. *troph*, nourish, and *blast*, bud] 812

tropism In plants, a growth response toward or away from a directional stimulus. [Gk. *trop*, turn] 568

trypanosome (trip-AN-uh-sohm) A member of a genus of parasitic zooflagellates that cause severe disease in human beings and domestic animals, including a condition called sleeping sickness. [Gk. *tryp*, hole, and *soma*, body] 422

trypsin A protein-digesting enzyme secreted by the pancreas. 674

tube-within-a-tube body plan A body with a digestive tract that has both a mouth and an anus. 474

tumor Cells derived from a single mutated cell that has repeatedly undergone cell division; benign tumors remain at the site of origin and malignant tumors metastasize. [L. *tumor*, swelling] 268

tumor-suppressor gene Gene that codes for a protein that ordinarily suppresses cell division. 269

tundra Treeless terrestrial biome of cold climates; is found on high mountains and in polar regions. 882

turgor pressure The pressure of the cell contents against the cell wall, in plant cells, determined by the water content of the vacuole; gives internal support to the plant cell. [L. *turg*, swell] 93

tympanic membrane (tim-PAN-ik) Membranous region that receives air vibrations in an auditory organ. [Gk. *tympan*, drum] 742

U

umbilical cord The cord connecting the fetus to the placenta through which blood vessels pass. [L. *umbilic*, navel] 814

urea Main nitrogenous waste of terrestrial amphibians and mammals. [Gk. *ure*, urine] 699

ureter (YUUR-ut-ur) A tubular structure conducting urine from the kidney to the urinary bladder. 702

urethra (yuu-REE-thruh) A tubular structure that receives urine from the bladder and carries it to the outside of the body. 702

uric acid Main nitrogenous waste of insects, reptiles, birds, and some dogs. 699

urinary bladder The organ where urine is stored. 702

urine Liquid waste product made by the nephrons of the kidney through the processes of pressure filtration and selective reabsorption. [Gk. *ure*, urine] 702

uterine cycle A cycle that runs concurrently with the ovarian cycle; it prepares the uterus to receive a developing zygote. 796

uterus The pear-shaped portion of the female reproductive tract that lies between the oviducts and the vagina; the site of embryo and fetal development. [L. *uter*, womb] 794

V

vaccine Antigens prepared in such a way that they can promote active immunity without causing disease. [L. *vaccin*, of a cow] 440, 661

vacuole A membranous cavity, usually filled with fluid. 74

vagina A muscular tube leading from the uterus; the female copulatory organ and the birth canal. [L. *vagin*, sheath] 794

valve Membranous extension of a vessel or the heart wall that opens and closes, ensuring one-way flow; common to the systemic veins, the lymphatic veins, and the heart. 632

vascular cambium A lateral meristem that produces secondary phloem and secondary xylem. [L. *vascula*, little vessel, and *cambi*, exchange] 540

vascular plant A plant that contains the vascular tissues xylem and phloem as part of its structure. 448

vas deferens (pl., vasa deferentia) Tube that leads from the testes to the urethra in mammals. 790

vector In genetic engineering, a means used to transfer foreign genetic material into a cell—for example, a plasmid. [L. *vect*, carried] 278

vein A blood vessel that arises from venules and transports blood toward the heart. [L. *ven*, vein] 630

vena cava A large systemic vein that returns blood to the right atrium of the heart in tetrapods; either the superior or inferior vena cava. [L. *ven*, vein, and *cav*, hollow] 636

ventricle A cavity in an organ, such as a lower chamber of the heart; or the ventricles of the brain. 632, 724

venule Vessel that takes blood from capillaries to a vein. 631

vertebral column The backbone of vertebrates through which the spinal cord passes. [L. *vertebr*, vertebra] 756

vertebrate Animal possessing a backbone composed of vertebrae. 509

vestigial structure (ve-STIJ-(ee-)-ul) The remains of a structure that was functional in some ancestor but is no longer functional in the organism in question. [L. *vestig*, trace] 306

villus (pl., villi) (VIL-us) A small, fingerlike projection of the inner small intestinal wall. [L. *vill*, shaggy hair] 674

virus A nonliving, obligate, intracellular parasite consisting of an outer capsid and an inner core of nucleic acid. [L. *viro*, poison] 396

vitamin An organic molecule that is required in small quantities for various biological processes and must be in an organism's diet because it cannot be synthesized by the organism; becomes part of coenzyme structure. [L. *vit*, life] 111, 678

vocal cord Fold of tissue within the larynx; creates vocal sounds when it vibrates. 688

W

water potential The potential energy of water; it is a measure of the capability to release or take up water. 000

woody plant A plant that contains wood; usually trees such as evergreen trees (gymnosperms) and flowering trees (angiosperms). Alternative is a herbaceous plant. 457

X

X-linked gene Gene located on the X chromosome that does not control a sexual feature of the organism. 202

xylem (ZY-lum) The vascular tissue that transports water and mineral solutes upward through the plant body; it contains vessel elements and tracheids. [Gk. *xyl*, wood, and L. *em*, in] 448, 534

Y

yolk A rich nutrient material in the egg that nourishes embryos. 788

yolk sac The extraembryonic membrane that encloses yolk, except in most mammals. 811

Z

zooflagellate (zoh-uh-FLAJ-uh-layt) Protozoan that moves by means of flagella. [Gk. *zoo*, animal, and L. *flagell*, whip] 422

zooplankton (zoh-uh-PLANGK-tun) The part of plankton containing protozoa and microscopic animals. [Gk. *zoo*, animal, and *plankt*, wandering] 420

zygospore (ZY-guh-spohr) A thick-walled, resting cell formed during sexual reproduction of zygospore fungi. 432

CREDITS

Photographs

Part Openers

1: © D.W. Fawcett/Photo Researchers, Inc.; **2:** © Kathy Bushve/Tony Stone Images; **3:** © Michael Fogden/Animals Animals/Earth Scenes; **4:** © Brian Parker/Tom Stack & Associates; **5:** © Heather Angel/Biofotos; **6:** © Robert P. Falls, Sr./Bruce Coleman, Inc.; **7:** © James Martin/Tony Stone Images

Chapter 1

Opener: © Rod Kieft/Visuals Unlimited; **1.2a:** © Gunter Ziesler/Peter Arnold, Inc.; **1.2b:** © Fritz Polking/Peter Arnold, Inc.; **p.2:** © John D. Cunningham/Visuals Unlimited; **1.3a:** © Rod Allin/Tom Stack & Associates; **1.3b:** © Kjell B. Sandved; **1.5 (coral reef):** © Ed Robinson/Tom Stack & Associates; **(tubastraea coral):** © F. Stuart Westmorland/Tom Stack & Associates; **(moray eel):** © Davie Fleetham/Tom Stack & Associates; **(red grouper):** © C. Ressler/Animals Animals/Earth Scenes; **(lionfish):** © Tom Stack/Tom Stack & Associates; **1.6 (rainforest):** © Barbara von Hoffmann/Tom Stack & Associates; **1.6 (toucan):** © Ed Reschke/Peter Arnold, Inc.; **(dart frog):** © Kevin Schafer & Martha Hill/Tom Stack & Associates; **(butterfly):** © Kjell Sandved; **(jaguar):** © BIOS (Seitre)/Peter Arnold, Inc.; **(epiphytic):** © Max & Bea Hunn/Visuals Unlimited; **1.7 (top):** © Eric Grave/Photo Researchers, Inc.; **1.7b1:** © John Cunningham/Visuals Unlimited; **(bottom, left to right):** © Rod Planck/Tom Stack & Associates; © Farell Grehan/Photo Researchers, Inc.; © Leonard Lee Rue Enterprises

Chapter 2

Opener: © David Joel/Tony Stone Images; **2.2 (left):** © J. A. Bishop & L. M. Cook; **(right):** © Michael Tweedy/Photo Researchers, Inc.

Chapter 3

Opener: © Bill Ivy/Tony Stone Images; **3.1 (earth's crust):** © Jeffery Howe/Visuals Unlimited; **(fish):** © Dave Fleetham/Tom Stack & Associates; **3A:** © Clinique STE Catherine/CNRI/SPL/Photo Researchers, Inc.; **3B:** © Scott Camazine/Photo Researchers, Inc.; **3.7c:** © Charles M. Falco/Photo Researchers, Inc.; **3.8:** © Douglas Faulkner/ Sally Faulkner Collection; **3.11a:** © Clyde H. Smith/Peter Arnold, Inc.; **3.11b:** © Di Maggio/Peter Arnold, Inc.; **3.11c:** © Holt Confer/Grant Heilman Photography

Chapter 4

Opener: © Ken Eward/Science Source/Photo Researchers, Inc.; **4.1a:** © John Gerlach/Tom Stack & Associates; **4.1b:** © Leonard Lee Rue III/Photo Researchers, Inc.; **4.1c:** © H. Pol/CNRI/SPL/Photo Researchers, Inc.; **4.6a:** © Joyce Photographics/Photo Researchers, Inc.; **4.7a:** © Jeremy Burgess/SPL./Photo Researchers, Inc.; **4.7b:** © Don Fawcett/Photo Researchers, Inc.; **4.8:** © Biophoto Associates/Photo Researchers, Inc.; **4.11a:** © Anthony Mercieca/Photo Researchers, Inc.; **4.11b:** © Treat Davidson Warren/Photo Researchers, Inc.; **4.17:** © T. Edwards/Visuals Unlimited

Chapter 5

Opener: © Don W. Fawcett/Visuals Unlimited; **5.1a:** © Tony Stone Images; **5.1b:** © Carolina Biological Supply/Phototake; **5.1c:** © B. Miller/Biological Photo Service; **5.1d:** © Ed Reschke; **5A (left):** © M. Abbey/Visuals Unlimited; **5A (middle):** © M. Schliwa/Visuals Unlimited; **5A (right):** © Drs. Kessel/Shih/Peter Arnold, Inc.; **5B (Brightfield):** © Biophoto Assoc./Photo Researchers, Inc.; **(Brightfield Stained):** © Ed Reschke; **(Diggerential, Phase, Darkfield):** © David M. Phillips/Visuals Unlimited; **5.3a:** © David M. Phillips/Visuals Unlimited; **5.3b:** © Biophoto Associates/Photo Researchers, Inc.; **5.4b:** © Richard Rodewald/Biological Photo Service; **5.5b:** © E.H. Newcomb & W.P. Wergin/Biological Photo Service; **5.6:** © Don Fawcett/Photo Researchers Inc.; **5.7a:** © W. Rosenberg/Iona College/Biological Photo Service; **5C (middle):** © Richard Rodewald/University of Virginia/Biological Photo Service; **5C (right):** © W. Rosenberg/Iona College/Biological Photo Service; **5.8a:** © David M. Phillips/Visuals Unlimited; **5.9:** © G.E. Frederick, courtesy of E.H. Newcomb, University of Wisconsin/Biological Photo Service; **5.11a:** Courtesy of Herbert W. Israel, Cornell University; **5.12a:** Courtesy of Dr. Keith Porter; **5.13 (actin):** © M. Schliwa/Visuals Unlimited; **(intermediate & microtubules)):** © K.G. Mutri/Visuals Unlimited; **5.14b:** Courtesy of Kent McDonald, University of Colorado at Boulder; **5.15 (all):** © W.L. Dentler/Biological Photo Service

Chapter 6

Opener: © Dr. C.K.S. Kim/Peter Arnold, Inc.; **6.1a:** © W. Rosenberg/Biological Photo Service; **6.1d:** © Don Fawcett/Photo Researchers, Inc.;

P. 89: Courtesy of Robin Wright; **6.13b:** Courtesy of Mark Bretscher; **6.15 (top, left):** © David Phillips/Visuals Unlimited; **(top, right):** © Don Fawcett/Visuals Unlimited; **(bottom, right):** © D. Allbertini/D. Fawcett/Visuals Unlimited

Chapter 7

Opener: © Keith Porter/Photo Researchers, Inc.; **7.1:** © Joe Distefano/Photo Researchers, Inc.

Chapter 8

Opener: © Milton Rand/Tom Stack & Associates; **8.1:** © Jeff Lepore/Photo Researchers, Inc.; **8.3:** Courtesy of Herbert W. Israel, Cornell University; **8.8a:** Courtesy of Dr. Melvin Calvin; **p. 132:** Courtesy of Dennis Clark

Chapter 9

Opener: © Christoph Burki/Tony Stone Images; **9.1a:** © Dieter Blum/Peter Arnold, Inc.; **p.143:** © Tim Davis/Photo Researchers, Inc.; **9.6:** Courtesy of Dr. Keith Porter

Chapter 10

Opener: © Carolina Biological Supply/Phototake; **10.1:** © Prof. Motta/Photo Researchers, Inc.; **10.2a:** © Biophoto Associates/Science Source/Photo Researchers, Inc.; **10.5, 10.6, 10.7, 10.8:** © Ed Reschke; **10.9a:** © C.Y. Shih & Richard Kessel; **10.10 (all):** Courtesy of Dr. Andrew Bajer; **10.11:** © S.C. Holt, Univ. of Texas Health Science Center/ Biological Photo Service

Chapter 11

Opener: © David M. Phillips/Visuals Unlimited; **11.3a:** Courtesy of Dr. D. Von Wettstein; **11.4:** Courtesy of B. John

Chapter 12

Opener: © D. Cavagnaro/Visuals Unlimited; **12.1:** © William Ferguson

Chapter 13

Opener: © Alfred Pasieka/SPL/Photo Researchers, Inc.; **13.3 (wild rabbit):** © Richard Kolar/Animals Animals/Earth Scenes; **(chinchilla):** © Richard Kolar/Animals Animals/Earth Scenes; **(himalayan):** © Barry L. Runk/Grant Heilman Photography; **(albino rabbit):** © John Cunningham/Visuals Unlimited; **13.9a-c:** © Bob Coyle

Chapter 14

Opener: © Omikron/Photo Researchers, Inc.; **14.1a:** © CNRI/SPL/Photo Researchers, Inc.; **14.3a:** © Jill Cannafax/EKM-Nepenthe; **14.4:** Courtesy of F.A. Davis Company and Dr. R.H. Kampmeier; **14.5:** © Dr. Dorothy Warburton/Peter Arnold, Inc.; **14.8:** © Steve Uzzell; **14.9b:** © Bill Longcore/Photo Researchers, Inc.; **14.10c:** © IMS Creative/Custom Medical Stock Photos; **14.11:** Courtesy The Cystic Fibrosis Foundation

Chapter 15

Opener: © Ken Edward/Science Source/Photo Researchers, Inc.; **15.2 (both):** © Lee Simon/Photo Researchers, Inc.; **15.5b:** Courtesy of the Biophysics Department, Kings College, London; **15.6a:** © Dr. Nelson Max/Peter Arnold, Inc.; **15B:** Cold Spring Harbor Laboratory; **15C:** © Biological Photo Service

Chapter 16

Opener: © Ken Edward/Science Source/Photo Researchers, Inc.; **16.2a:** © Bill Longcore/Photo Researchers, Inc.; **16.6a:** © Oscar L. Miller SPL/Photo Researchers, Inc.; **16.8b:** Courtesy of Alexander Rich; **16.9b:** Courtesy of Dr. Nelson Max

Chapter 17

Opener: © Omikron/Science Source/Photo Researchers, Inc.; **17.4a:** © George Wilder/Visuals Unlimited; **17B:** Courtesy of Dr. Stephen Wolfe; **17.5:** From M.B. Roth and J.G. Gall, *Cell Biology*, 105:1047-1054, 1987. © Rockefeller University Press; **p. 269:** Courtesy of Thomas Gilmore; **17.12:** © Wm. C. Brown Communications/Bob Coyle, photographer

Chapter 18

Opener: © Cetus Corp./Peter Arnold, Inc.; **18.5 (both):** Courtesy of General Electric Research and Development Center; **18.6:** Courtesy of Monsanto Company; **18.7:** Courtesy of Gene Pharming Europe

Chapter 19

Opener: © Jacana/Photo Researchers, Inc.; **19.1b:** © Tom Stack/Tom Stack & Associates; **19.1c:** © C. Luiz Claudio Marigo/Peter Arnold, Inc.; **19.1d:** © John James/Biological Photo Service; **19.1e:** © C. Luiz Claudio Marigo/Peter Arnold, Inc.; **19.1f:** © Ken Lucas/Biological Photo Service; **19.1g:** © Miguel Castro/Photo Researchers, Inc.; **19.2:** The Bettmann Archives; **19.3:** © John Cunningham/Visuals Unlimited; **19.4:** © Malcolm Boulton/Photo Researchers, Inc.; **19.5b:** © J. and L. Weber/Peter Arnold, Inc.; **19.7:** © Don Fawcett/Visuals Unlimited; **19.8a:** © Walt Anderson/Visuals Unlimited; **19.8b:** © Michael Dick/Animals Animals/Earth Scenes; **19.9a:** © F.B. Gill/VIERO; **19.9b:** © Miguel Castro/Photo Researchers, Inc.; **19.9c:** © Alan Root/Bruce Coleman, Inc.; **19.10:** © Wendell Metzen/Bruce Coleman, Inc.; **19A:** © Stock Montage/Historical Picture Service; **19.11 (wolf):** © Gary Milburn/Tom Stack & Associates; **(terrier):** © Mary Bloom/Peter Arnold, Inc.; **(beagle):** © Mary Bloom/Peter Arnold, Inc.; **(dalmation):** © Alexander Kowry/Photo Researchers, Inc.; **(bulldog):** © Salana/Jacana/Photo Researchers, Inc.; **(chihuahua):** © Mary Eleanor Brawning/Photo Researchers, Inc.; **(sheepdog):** © Carolyn McKeone/Photo Researchers, Inc.; **(bloodhound):** © Mary Bloom/Peter Arnold, Inc.; **(chow):** © Jeanne White/Photo Researchers, Inc.; **19.12a-c:** Courtesy of W. Atlee Burpee Company; **19.13a:** © John Cunningham/Visuals Unlimited; **19.13b:** Transparency #213, Courtesy Department of Library Services, American Museum of Natural History; **19.14 (wombat:)** © Adrienne Gibson/Animals Animals/Earth Scenes; **(kangaroo):** © George Holton/Photo Researchers, Inc.; **(glider):** © John Sundance/Jacana/Photo Researchers, Inc.; **(cat):** © Tom McHugh/Photo Researchers, Inc.; **(wolf):** © Tom McHugh/Photo Researchers, Inc.; **19.16a, b:** © Carolina Biological Supply/Phototake

Chapter 20

Opener: © Fritz Polking/Peter Arnold, Inc.; **20.2 (left):** © J.A. Bishop & L.M. Cook; **(right):** © Michael Tweedy/Photo Researchers, Inc.; **20.4:** Courtesy of Dr. Mckusick; **20.7:** © Bob Evans/Peter Arnold, Inc.; **20.9 (top):** © Stanley Maslowski/Visuals Unlimited; **(middle):** © Karl Maslowski/Visuals Unlimited; **(bottom):** © Ralph Reinhold/Animals Animals/Earth Scenes; **p.326, 20A-C:** Courtesy of Gerald Carr

Chapter 21

Opener: © U. Englebert/Photo Researchers, Inc.; **21.3a:** © Science VV/Visuals Unlimited; **21.3b:** Courtesy of Dr. David Deamer; **21.6:** © Sylvain Grandadam/Photo Researchers, Inc.; **21.8b:** © David Parker/SPL/Photo Researchers, Inc.; **21.8c:** © Matthew Shipp/SPL/Photo Researchers, Inc.; **21.9a:** Courtesy of J. William Schopf; **21.9b:** © Francois Gohier/Photo Researchers, Inc.; **21.10a:** © Field Museum of Natural History, Neg. # GEO80872C, Chicago; **21.10b:** Courtesy of B. Runnegar; **21.12:** © Field Museum of Natural History, Neg. # 75400C, Chicago; **21.13a:** © Field Museum of Natural History, Neg. # CK5T, Chicago; **21.13b:** © Field Museum of Natural History, Neg. # CK9T, Chicago; **21A (both):** Museum of the Rockies; **21.14:** © Field Museum of Natural History, Neg. # CK121T, Chicago; **21.15:** © The Field Museum, # CK30T, Chicago; **21.17a:** Courtesy of the Senckenberg Museum; **21.17b:** © Ronald Seitre/Peter Arnold, Inc.

Chapter 22

Opener: © Peggy/Yoram Kahana; **22.2b:** © Ron Austing/Photo Researchers, Inc.; **22.2c:** © Howard Uible/Photo Researchers, Inc.; **22.4c:** © A. Walker/National Museums of Kenya; **22.5a:** © Martha Reeves/Photo Researchers, Inc.; **22.5b:** © BIOS/Peter Arnold, Inc.; **22.5c:** © George Holton/Photo Researchers, Inc.; **22.5d:** © Tom McHugh/Photo Researchers, Inc.; **22.7a:** © Dan Dreyfus & Associates Photography; **22.7b:** © John Reader/SPL/Photo Researchers, Inc.; **22.8a:** © Institute of Human Origins; **p. 364:** © Jon Goell; **22A:** © Margaret Miller/Photo Researchers, Inc. **22.10:** © A. Walker/National Museums of Kenya; **22.12:** © Field Museum of Natural History, Neg. # 102513C, Chicago; **22.13:** Transparency # 608, Courtesy Department of Library Services, American Museum of Natural History; **22.15a:** © M. & D. Long/Visuals Unlimited; **22.15b:** © David Madison/Bruce Coleman, Inc.; **22.15c:** © Jocelyn Burt/Bruce Coleman, Inc.; **22.15d:** © Van Butcher/Photo Researchers, Inc.; **22.15e:** © Stephen Trimble

Chapter 23

Opener: © WHOI/D. Foster/Visuals Unlimited; **23.2a:** © Universitetsbiblioteket, Uppsala; **23.2b:** © John Sohlden/Visuals Unlimited; **23.2c:** © P. Cavagnaro/Visuals Unlimited; **23.3:** © Tim Davis/Photo Researchers, Inc.; **23.4:** © Jen and Des Bartlett/Bruce Coleman, Inc.; **23.7 (bacteria):** © David M. Phillips/Visuals Unlimited; **23.7 (black-eyed Susan):** © Ed Reschke/Peter Arnold, Inc.; **23.7 (mushroom):** © Rod Planck/Tom Stack & Associates; **23.7 (Paramecium):** © M. Abbey/Visuals Unlimited; **23.7 (wolf):** © Art Wolfe/Tony Stone Images; **p.386 (web):** © Charles Krebs/Tony Stone Images; **p.386:** Courtesy of William Shear; **23.9 (left):** © John Cunningham/Visuals Unlimited; **(right):** © John Shaw/Tom Stack & Associates

Chapter 24

Opener: © A.B. Dowsett/SPL/Photo Researchers, Inc.; **24.1a:** © Robert Caughey/Visuals Unlimited; **24.1b:** © Michael Wurtz/Biozentrum, University of Basel/SPL/ Photo Researchers, Inc.; **24.1c:** © Science Source/Photo Researchers, Inc.; **24.1d:** © K.G. Murti/Visuals Unlimited; **24.2:** © Ed Degginger/Color Pic, Inc.; **24.4:** Courtesy of Organon Teknika Corp.; **24.7:** Courtesy of Dr. Jerald S. Feitelson; **24.8:** Courtesy of The Nitragin Company, Inc.; **24.9a, b:** © David M. Phillips/Visuals Unlimited; **24.9c:** © R.G. Kessel-C.Y. Shih/Visuals Unlimited; **24.10a:** © R. Knauft/Biology Media/Photo Researchers, Inc.; **24.10b:** © Eric Grave/Photo Researchers, Inc.

Chapter 25

Opener: © Nuridsany et Perennou/Photo Researchers, Inc.; **25.3:** © R. Knauft/Photo Researchers, Inc.; **p. 415 (both):** Courtesy of Susan Dutcher; **25.4 (right):** © M.I. Walker/Science Source/Photo Researchers, Inc.; **25.5 (top):** © E.R. Degginger/Photo Researchers, Inc.; **25.6:** © D.P. Wilson/Eric & David Hosking/Photo Researchers, Inc.; **25.7a:** © Dr. Ann Smith/Photo Researchers, Inc.; **25.7b:** © Biophoto Associates/Photo Researchers, Inc.; **25.9:** © Randy Morse/Tom Stack & Associates; **25.10b:** © Manfred Kage/Peter Arnold, Inc.; **25.10c:** © Cabisco/Visuals Unlimited; **25.11a, b:** © Eric Grave/Photo Researchers, Inc.; **25.11c:** © Carolina Biological Supply/Phototake; **25.12a:** © M. Abbey/Visuals Unlimited; **25.12b:** © Ed Reschke/Peter Arnold, Inc.; **25.14 (bottom):** © Cabisco/Visuals Unlimited; **25.14 (top):** © V. Duran/Visuals Unlimited

Chapter 26

Opener: © Jeff Lepore/Photo Researchers, Inc.; **26.1a:** © Gary R. Robinson/Visuals Unlimited; **26.1c:** © Garry T. Cole/Biological Photo Service; **26.2a:** © C.Y. Shih & Richard Kessel; **26.2b:** © Jeffrey Lepore/Photo Researchers,

Inc.; **26.3:** © David M. Phillips/Visuals Unlimited; **26.4:** © John E. Hodgin; **26.5a:** © Walter H. Hodge/Peter Arnold, Inc.; **26.5b (bottom):** © Michael Viard/Peter Arnold, Inc.; **(top):** © James Richardson/Visuals Unlimited; **26.5c:** Courtesy of Kingsley R. Stern; **26.6:** © J. Forsdyke/Gene Cox/SPL/Photo Researchers, Inc.; **26.7a (right):** © Biophoto Associates; **26.7b:** © Glenn Oliver/Visuals Unlimited; **26.7c:** M. Eichelberger/Visuals Unlimited; **26.7d (left):** © Dick Poe/Visuals Unlimited; **(right):** © L. West/Photo Researchers, Inc.; **26.8a:** © L. Lee Rue III/Photo Researchers, Inc.; **26.8b:** © Arthur M. Siegelman/Visuals Unlimited; **26A:** © G. Tomsich/Photo Researchers, Inc.; **26B:** © R. Calentine/Visuals Unlimited; **26.9:** © G.L. Barron/Univ. of Guelph; **26.10b:** © Stephen Kraseman/Peter Arnold, Inc.; **26.10c:** © John Shaw/Tom Stack & Associates; **26.10d:** © Kerry T. Givens/Tom Stack & Associates; **26.11:** © R. Roncadori/Visuals Unlimited

Chapter 27

Opener: © Wolfgang Kaehler; **p. 445:** © Jack W. Dykinga/Bruce Coleman, Inc.; **27.2a:** © Ed Reschke/Peter Arnold, Inc.; **27.2b(left):** © John D. Cunningham/Visuals Unlimited; **(right):** © R. Calentine/Visuals Unlimited; **27.3:** © John Gerlach/Visuals Unlimited; **27.4:** © Doug Sokell/Tom Stack & Associates; **27.5:** © Carolina Biological Supply/Phototake; **27.6:** © Steve Solum/Bruce Coleman, Inc.; **27.7:** © Robert P. Carr/Bruce Coleman, Inc.; **27.8a:** © John Gerlach/Visuals Unlimited; **27.8b:** © W.H. Hodge/Peter Arnold, Inc.; **27.8c:** Forest W. Buchanan/Visuals Unlimited; **27.9:** © Matt Meadows/Peter Arnold, Inc.; **27.10:** © Carolina Biological Supply/Phototake; **27.11a:** © D. Cavagnaro/Visuals Unlimited; **27.11b:** Courtesy of Kingsley R. Stern; **27.11c:** © E.S. Ross

Chapter 28

Opener: © Brian Parker/Tom Stack & Associates; **28.1 (bottom):** © Joe McDonald/Visuals Unlimited; **(top):** © Bio Media Associates; **28.4a:** © J. Mcullagh/Visuals Unlimited; **28.4b:** © Jeff Rotman; **28.5b:** © Carolina Biological Supply/Phototake; **28.5c:** © Ron Taylor/Bruce Coleman, Inc.; **28.5d:** © Runk/Schoenberger/Grant Heilman Photography; **28.5e:** © Bill Curtsinger/Photo Researchers, Inc.; **28.6:** © Cabisco/Visuals Unlimited; **28.7:** © Runk/Schoenberger/Grant Heilman Photography; **28.8:** © Stan Elems/Visuals Unlimited; **28.9a:** © Carolina Biological Supply/Phototake; **28.11:** Courtesy of Dr. Fred Whittaker; **28.12 (top):** © Arthur Siegelman/Visuals Unlimited; **28.12 (bottom):** © James Solliday/Biological Photo Service; **28.13:** From E.K. Markell and M. Voge, *Medical Parasitology,* 7 ed., 1992 W.B. Saunders, Co.

Chapter 29

Opener: © C. Allan Morgan/Peter Arnold, Inc.; **29.2a:** © Biophoto Associates; **29.2b:** © Fred Bavendam/Peter Arnold, Inc.; **29.2c:** © Douglas Faulkner/Photo Researchers, Inc.; **29.2d:** © Marty Snyderman/Visuals Unlimited; **29.4:** © Michael DiSpezio; **29.5:** © William Ferguson; **29.6a:** © Michael DiSpezio; **29.6b:**

© W.H. Hughes/Visuals Unlimited; **29.7b:** © Roger K. Burnard/Biological Photo Service; **29A:** © St. Bartholomew's Hospital/SPU/Photo Researchers, Inc.; **29.9a:** © Tom McHugh/Photo Researchers, Inc.; **29.9b:** © Zig Leszczynski/Animals Animals/Earth Scenes; **29.9c:** © J. Robinson/Photo Researchers, Inc.; **29.11a:** © Dwight Kuhn; **29.11b:** © John MacGregor/Peter Arnold, Inc.; **29.12 (dragonfly):** © John Gerlach/Tony Stone Images; **(beetle):** © Kjell Sandved/Bruce Coleman, Inc.; **(grasshopper):** © A. Kerstitch/Visuals Unlimited; **(walking stick):** © Art Wolfe/Tony Stone Images; **(tortoise shell):** © Science VU/Visuals Unlimited; **29.12 (lacewing):** © Glenn Oliver/Visuals Unlimited **29.13 (bottom,right):** © L. West/Bruce Coleman, Inc.; **(top,right):** © Bill Beatty/Visuals Unlimited; **29B:** © Edward S. Ross

Chapter 30

Opener: © Joe McDonald/Tom Stack & Associates; **30.1a:** © Randy Morse/Tom Stack & Associates, **30.1b:** © A. Kerstitch/Visuals Unlimited; **30.1c:** © John Cunningham/Visuals Unlimited; **30.2:** © D.P. Wilson/FLPA; **30.3:** © Rick Harbo; **30.4:** © Heather Angel/Biofotos; **30.6:** © Heather Angel/Biofotos; **30.7a:** © Ron & Valarie Taylor/Bruce Coleman, Inc.; **30.8:** © Estate of Dr. Jerome Metzner/Peter Arnold, Inc.; **30.11a-d:** © Jane Burton/Bruce Coleman, **30.12:** © Bruce Davidson/Animals Animals/Earth Scenes; **30A:** © W. Weber/Visuals Unlimited; **30.14:** © R.F. Ashley/Visuals Unlimited; **30.15b(both):** © Daniel J. Cox/Tony Stone Images; **30.16a:** © Tom McHugh/Photo Researchers, Inc.; **30.16b:** © Tony Stone Images; **30.16c:** © Leonard Lee Rue

Chapter 31

Opener: © Bob Gossington/Bruce Coleman, Inc.; **31.2a:** © Michael Gadomski/Photo Researchers, Inc.; **31.2b:** © Norman Tomalin/Bruce Coleman, Inc.; **31.2c:** © Brian Stablyk/Tony Stone Images; **31.4a:** © John Cunningham/Visuals Unlimited; **31.4b:** © Ed Reschke/Peter Arnold, Inc.; **31.4c:** © Biophoto Associates/Photo Researchers, Inc.; **31.5a:** © Biological Photo Service; **31.5b,c:** © Biophoto Associates/Photo Researchers, Inc.; **31.6b:** © Biological Photo Service; **31.7b:** © George Wilder/Visuals Unlimited; **31.8b:** © Carolina Biological Supply/Phototake; **31.9:** © Dwight Kuhn; **31.10a:** © John Cunningham/Visuals Unlimited; **31.10b:** Photomicrograph by G.S. Ellmore; **31.11a:** © G.R. Roberts; **31.11b:** © Ed Degginger/Color Pic., Inc.; **31.11c:** © David Newman/Visuals Unlimited; **31.12a:** © J.R. Waaland, University of Washington/Biological Photo Service; **31.13a, 31.14a:** © Carolina Biological Supply/Phototake; **31.14b,c:** © Runk/Schoenberger/Grant Heilman Photography; **31.15b:** © Ardea London Ltd.; **31b:** © James Schnepf Photography, Inc.; **31.18b:** © Dr. Jeremy Burgess/SPL/Photo Researchers, Inc.; **31.20a:** © Patti Murray/Animals Animals/Earth Scenes; **31.20b:** © Michael Gadomski/Photo Researchers, Inc.; **31.20c:** © Carolina Biological Supply/Phototake

Chapter 32

Opener: © Runk/Schoenberger/Grant Heilman Photography; **32.2(both):** © Dwight Kuhn; **32.4:** © Ed Reschke/Peter Arnold, Inc.; **32.6a:** © Dr. Jeremy Burgess/SPL/Photo Researchers, Inc.; **32.6b:** © Dr. Jeremy Burgess/SPL/Photo Researchers, Inc.; **p. 557:** Courtesy of G. David Tilman; **32.7a-c:** Courtesy of Dr. Mary E. Doohan; **32.9:** © Dwight Kuhn; **32.10:** © Stanley Flegler/Visuals Unlimited

Chapter 33

Opener: © Dwight Kuhn; **33.1:** © Kim Taylor/Bruce Coleman, Inc.; **33.2:** © Kingsley Stern; **33.2b:** © Professor Malcom B. Wilkins, Botany Department, Glasgow University; **33.2c:** © BioPhot; **33.3:** © John Cunningham/Visuals Unlimited; **33.4a,b:** © John Kaprielian/Photo Researchers, Inc.; **33.5a,b:** © Tom McHugh/Photo Researchers, Inc.; **33.6:** Courtesy of Kingsley R. Stern; **33.9:** © Robert E. Lyons/Visuals Unlimited; **p. 575:** Courtesy of Donald Briskin & Margaret Gawienowski; **33A:** Courtesy R.J. Weaver; **33.11a-d:** © Kiem Tran Thanh Van and her Colleagues; **33B-D:** © Elliot Meyerowitz; **33.13:** © Runk/Schoenberger/Grant Heilman Photography; **33.16:** © Frank Salisbury

Chapter 34

Opener: © Telegraph Colour Library/FPG International; **34.2 (right):** © Michel Viard/Peter Arnold, Inc.; **34Aa:** © Comstock; **34Ab:** © H. Eisenbeiss/Photo Researchers, Inc.; **34Ac:** © Anthony Mercieca/Photo Researchers, Inc.; **34Ad:** © Donna Howell; **34.4a:** © Biophoto Associates/Photo Researchers, Inc.; **34.4b:** © Dr. Jeremy Burgess/SPL/Photo Researchers, Inc.; **34.7a(left):** © Joe Munroe/Photo Researchers, Inc.; **(right):** Courtesy of Kingsley R. Stern; **34.7b(left):** © Ralph A. Reinhold/Animals Animals/Earth Scenes; **(right):** © W. Ormerod/Visuals Unlimited; **34.7c(both):** © Dwight Kuhn; **34.7d(left):** © C.S. Lobban/Biological Photo Service; **(right):** © Biological Photo Service; **34B (corn plant):** © Adam Hart-Davis/SPL/Photo Researchers, Inc.; **(corn kernels):** © Mark S. Skalny/Visuals Unlimited; **(wheat plant):** © C.P. Hickman/Visuals Unlimited; **(wheat grain):** © Phillip Hayson/Photo Researchers, Inc.; **(rice plant):** © Scott Camazine; **(rice grains):** © John Tiszler/Peter Arnold, Inc.; **34C (both):** © Heather Angel/BioFotos; **34Cb:** © Dale Jackson/Visuals Unlimited. **Inset:** © B. Daemmrich/The Image Works; **34Cc:** © Steven King/Peter Arnold, Inc. **Inset:** © W. and D. MeIntyre/Photo Researchers, Inc.; **34.10:** © G.I. Bernard/Animals Animals/Earth Scenes; **34.11a-d:** © Runk Schoenberger/Grant Heilman Photography; **34.12b:** © Biophoto Associates/Photo Researchers, Inc.; **34.12c (bottom):** © Laboratories Carlsberg; **34.13:** Courtesy of Keith V. Wood; **34.14a-c:** Courtesy of Monsanto Co.

Chapter 35

Opener: © Professors P.M. Motta & T. Fujita/University "La Sapienza", Rome,/SPL/Photo Researchers, Inc.; **35.2 (simple columnar):** © Edwin Reschke/Peter Arnold, Inc.; **(rest):**

© Edwin Reschke; **35.3a-d:** © Edwin Reschke; **35.4b:** © Francis Leroy/Photo Researchers, Inc.; **35.6a-c, 35.7b:** © Edwin A. Reschke; **35A:** © Steve Bourgeois/Unicorn Stock Photos

Chapter 36
Opener: © Manfred Kage/Peter Arnold, Inc.; **36.1a:** © Eric Grave/Photo Researchers, Inc.; **36.1b:** © Carolina Biological Supply Company/Phototake; **36.1c:** © Michael Dispezio; **36A:** The Bettmann Archives; **36Ba:** © Lewis Lainey; **36.12b:** © SPL/Photo Researchers, Inc.; **36.15a:** Courtesy of Stuart I. Fox

Chapter 37
Opener: © CDC/RG/Peter Arnold, Inc.; **37.3all:** © Ed Reschke/Peter Arnold, Inc.; **37.7b:** © R. Feldmann/D. McCoy/Rainbow; **37Aa:** AP/Wide World Photos; **37.8a:** © Boehringer Ingelheim International/photo Lennart Nilsson; **37.10:** © Matt Meadows/Peter Arnold, Inc.; **37.11:** © Chris Harvey/Tony Stone Images

Chapter 38
Opener: © Heather Angel/Biofotos; **38.8 (top):** © Ed Reschke/Peter Arnold, Inc.; **38.8(bottom):** © St. Bartholomew's Hospital/SPL/Photo Researchers, Inc.; **38.9:** © Manfred Kage/Peter Arnold, Inc.

Chapter 39
Opener: © Bales Littlehales/Animals Animals/Earth Scenes; **39.5:** © P. R. Ehrlich/Stanford University/Biological Photo Service; **39.11:** © CNRI/SPL/Photo Researchers, Inc.

Chapter 40
Opener: © CNRI/SPL/Photo Researchers, Inc.; **40.8a:** © J. Gennaro, Jr./Photo Researchers, Inc.

Chapter 41
Opener: © John Allison/Peter Arnold, Inc.; **41.4:** © Linda Bartlett; **41.11a:** © Peter Miller/Photo Researchers, Inc.; **41.11b:** © Lori Adamski Peek/Tony Stone Images; **41.15:** © Dan McCoy/Rainbow

Chapter 42
Opener: © Arthur Tilley/FPG International; **42.4 (both):** © Heather Angel/Biofotos; **42.8:** © Lennart Nilsson/The Incredible Machine; **p. 741, 42A:** Courtesy of Anita L. Zimmerman; **42.13b:** © Prof. P. Motta/Dept. of Anatomy/University "La Sapienza", Rome/SPL/Photo Researchers, Inc.; **42B:** Robert S. Preston/courtesy of Professor J.E. Hawkins, Kresge

Chapter 43
Opener: © Hans Pfletschinger/Peter Arnold, Inc.; **43.2:** © Michael Fogden/OSF/Animals Animals/Earth Scenes; **43.4 (both):** © Ed Reschke; **43.10 (bottom right):** © Ed Reschke/Peter Arnold, Inc.; **(rest):** © Ed Reschke; **43.13:** Courtesy of H.E. Huxley; **43.15:** From "Behold Man", Little, Brown, and Co., Boston. Photo by Lennart Nilsson

Chapter 44
Opener: © Maresa Pryor/Animals Animals/Earth Scenes

Chapter 45
Opener: © Stan Osolinski/FPG International; **45.1:** © Runk/Schoenberger/Grant Heilman Photography; **45.2b:** © Roger K. Burnard/Biological Photo Service; **45.4:** © Wyman Meinzer/Peter Arnold, Inc.; **45.7:** © Biophoto Associates/Photo Researchers, Inc.; **45.10:** © Ed Reschke/Peter Arnold, Inc.

Chapter 46
Opener: © Runk/Schoenberger/Grant Heilman Photography; **46.8a,b:** Courtesy of E.B. Lewis; **46.12a:** Lennart Nilsson, *A Child is Born,* Dell Publishing Company

Chapter 47
Opener: © Gary Braasch/Tony Stone Images; **47.1:** © Frank Lane Agency/Bruce Coleman, Inc.; **47.2 (both):** © R. Andrew Odum/Peter Arnold, Inc.; **47.6:** © Frans Lanting/Minden Pictures; **47.8a:** © Y. Arthus-Bertrand/Peter Arnold, Inc.; **47.8b:** © FPG International; **47.9:** © Jonathan Scott/Planet Earth Pictures; **47.10:** © Susan Kuklin/Photo Researchers, Inc.; **47.11a:** © Oxford Scientific Films/Animals Animals/Earth Scenes; **47.12:** © J & B Photo/Animals Animals/Earth Scenes

Chapter 48
Opener: © G. & M. Kohler/FPG International; **48.3a:** © Paul Janosi/Valan Photos; **48.6a:** © Ted Levin/Animals Animals/Earth Scenes; **48.6b:** © Michio Hoshino/Minden Pictures

Chapter 49
Opener: © Art Wolfe/Tony Stone Images; **49.4a:** © Alan Carey/Photo Researchers, Inc.; **49.5a:** © Runk/Schoenberger/Grant Heilman Photography; **49.5b:** © National Audubon Society/A. Cosmos Blank/Photo Researchers, Inc.; **49.5c:** © Z. Leszczynski/Animals Animals/Earth Scenes; **49.6:** © Hans Pfletschinger/Peter Arnold, Inc; **49.7a-c:** Courtesy of Dr. Daniel Janzen

Chapter 50
Opener: © Scott Camazine; **50.1:** © Gallbridge/Visuals Unlimited; **50.2a:** © Stephen Krasemann/Peter Arnold, Inc.; **50.2b:** © Richard Ferguson; **50.2c:** © Mary Thatcher/Photo Researchers, Inc.; **50.2d:** © Karlene Schwartz; **50A:** Courtesy of C. Oviatt

Chapter 51
Opener: © Steve Solum/Bruce Coleman, Inc.; **51.3:** © Douglas Faulkner/Sally Faulkner Collection; **51.7, 51.8:** © John Shaw/Bruce Coleman, Inc.; **51A:** © John Bennett; **51.10:** © Grant Heilman/Grant Heilman Photography; **51.11:** © Norman Owen Tomalin/Bruce Coleman, Inc.; **51.12:** © E.R. Degginger/Animals Animals/Earth Scenes

Chapter 52
Opener: © Grant Heilman/Grant Heilman Photography; **52.5a,b:** © Dr. John Skelly; **52.6:** © Calvin Larsen/Photo Researchers, Inc.; **p. 898:** Courtesy of Ric Garcia; **52.9:** © Bob Coyle; **52.10:** © G. Prance/Visuals Unlimited; **52.11:** © Nichols/Magnum; **Figure A, p. 906:** © Gary R. Zahm/Bruce Coleman, Inc.

Line Art and Text

Chapter 2
2.4b: Reprinted with permission from *Nature,* Vol. 279, May 17, 1979, page 233. Copyright © 1979 Macmillan Magazines Limited.

Chapter 19
19.17: From Margaret O. Dayhoff and Richard V. Eck, *Atlas of Protein Sequence and Structure, 1967-1968.* Reprinted by permission of National Biomedical Research Foundation, Washington, DC.

Chapter 20
20.3: From D. Hartl, *A Primer of Population Genetics.* Copyright © 1981 Sinauer Associates, Inc., Sunderland, MA. Reprinted by permission. Data from P. Buri, "Gene Frequency in Small Populations of Mutant Drosophila" in *Evolution* 10:367-402, 1956.

Chapter 22
22.2: Redrawn from *Vertebrates, Phylogeny, and Philosophy,* 1986, Contributions to Geology, University of Wyoming, Special Paper 3 (frontispiece and article by Rose and Bown; and Thomas M. Bown and Kenneth D. Rose, "Patterns of Dental Evolution in Early Eocene Anaptomorphine Primates (Omomyidae) from Bighorn Basin, Wyoming," in *Paleontological Society Memoir 23 (Journal of Paleontology,* Vol. 61, supplement to no. 5). Courtesy of Kenneth D. Rose of The Johns Hopkins University, Baltimore, MD; **22.4b:** Reprinted by permission from Alan Walker.

Chapter 28
28.7a: From Stephen Miller and John Harley, *Zoology,* 2d ed. Copyright © 1994 Wm. C. Brown Communications, Inc. Reprinted by permission of Times Mirror Higher Education Group, Inc., Dubuque, Iowa. All Rights Reserved.

Chapter 34
34.3b: (1st From T. Elliot Weier, et al., *Botany,* 6th ed. Copyright © 1982 John Wiley & Sons, Inc., New York, NY. Reprinted by permission of the authors; **34.8:** From Kingsley R. Stern, *Introductory Plant Biology,* 6th ed. Copyright © 1994 Wm. C. Brown Communications, Inc. Reprinted by permission of Times Mirror Higher Education Group, Inc., Dubuque, Iowa. All Rights Reserved; **34.9:** From Kingsley R. Stern, *Introductory Plant Biology,* 6th ed. Copyright © 1994 Wm. C. Brown Communications, Inc. Reprinted by permission of Times Mirror Higher Education Group, Inc., Dubuque, Iowa. All Rights Reserved.

Chapter 35
35.7a: From Kent M. Van De Graaff, *Human Anatomy,* 3d ed. Copyright © 1992 Wm. C. Brown Communications, Inc. Reprinted by permission of Times Mirror Higher Education Group, Inc., Dubuque, Iowa. All Rights Reserved.

Chapter 36

36Bb: From Kent M. Van De Graaff and Stuart Ira Fox, *Concepts of Human Anatomy and Physiology,* 3d ed. Copyright © 1992 Wm. C. Brown Communications, Inc. Reprinted by permission of Times Mirror Higher Education Group, Inc., Dubuque, Iowa. All Rights Reserved.

Chapter 39

39.8 (middle): From John W. Hole, Jr., *Human Anatomy and Physiology,* 5th ed. Copyright © 1990 Wm. C. Brown Communications, Inc. Reprinted by permission of Times Mirror Higher Education Group, Inc., Dubuque, Iowa. All Rights Reserved.

Chapter 40

40.5: From Kent M. Van De Graaff and Stuart Ira Fox, *Concepts of Human Anatomy and Physiology,* 4th ed. Copyright © 1995 Wm. C. Brown Communications, Inc. Reprinted by permission of Times Mirror Higher Education Group, Inc., Dubuque, Iowa. All Rights Reserved.

Chapter 43

43.6: From Kent M. Van De Graaff, *Human Anatomy,* 3d ed. Copyright © 1992 Wm. C. Brown Communications, Inc. Reprinted by permission of Times Mirror Higher Education Group, Inc., Dubuque, Iowa. All Rights Reserved.

Chapter 44

44.7: From Stuart Ira Fox, *Human Physiology,* 4th ed. Copyright © 1993 Wm. C. Brown Communications, Inc. Reprinted by permission from Times Mirror Higher Education Group, Inc., Dubuque, Iowa. All Rights Reserved. Reprinted by permission.

Chapter 45

45.5: From John W. Hole, Jr., *Human Anatomy and Physiology,* 6th ed. Copyright © 1993 Wm. C. Brown Communications, Inc. Reprinted by permission of Times Mirror Higher Education Group, Inc., Dubuque, Iowa. All Rights Reserved; **45.6:** From Kent M. Van De Graaff and Stuart Ira Fox, *Concepts of Human Anatomy and Physiology,* 4th ed. Copyright © 1995 Wm. C. Brown Communications, Inc. Reprinted by permission of Times Mirror Higher Education Group, Inc., Dubuque, Iowa. All Rights Reserved; **45.9a:** From John W. Hole, Jr., *Human Anatomy and Physiology,* 6th ed. Copyright © 1993 Wm. C. Brown Communications, Inc. Reprinted by permission of Times Mirror Higher Education Group, Inc., Dubuque, Iowa. All Rights Reserved; **45.13:** From Kent M. Van De Graaff and Stuart Ira Fox, *Concepts of Human Anatomy and Physiology,* 4th ed. Copyright © 1995 Wm. C. Brown Communications, Inc. Reprinted by permission of Times Mirror Higher Education Group, Inc., Dubuque, Iowa. All Rights Reserved; **TA 45.3:** From John W. Hole, Jr., *Human Anatomy and Physiology,* 6th ed. Copyright © 1993 Wm. C. Brown

Communications, Inc. Reprinted by permission of Times Mirror Higher Education Group, Inc., Dubuque, Iowa. All Rights Reserved.

Chapter 46

46.14: Redrawn from Kent M. Van De Graaff and Stuart Ira Fox, *Concepts of Human Anatomy and Physiology,* 4th ed. Copyright © 1995 Wm. C. Brown Communications, Inc. Reprinted by permission of Times Mirror Higher Education Group, Inc., Dubuque, Iowa. All Rights Reserved.

Chapter 47

47.2: Source: Data from S. J. Arnold, "The Microevolution of Feeding Behavior" in *Foraging Behavior: Ecology, Ethological, and Psychological Approaches,* edited by A. Kamil and T. Sargent, 1980, Garland Publishing Company, New York, NY; **47.7:** Source: Data from G. Hausfater, "Dominance and Reproduction in Baboons (Papio cynocephalus): A Quantitative Analysis" *Contributions in Primatology,* 7:1-150, 1975.

Chapter 49

49.4b: Source: Data from D. A. MacLulich, *Flucuations in the Numbers of the Varying Hare (Lepus americanus),* University of Toronto Press, Toronto, 1937, reprinted 1974.

Chapter 52

52B: From Judith Myers, "Population Outbreaks" in *American Scientist,* May-June 1993, vol. 81, issue #3. Reprinted by permission.

Illustrators

Molly Babich:
2.2c, 4.7 (art), 5.6b, 6.15b, 8.3 (art), 9.6b, 10.9 (art), 10.10b, 10.11a, 12.2(art), 16.8a, 20.2a, 20.5, 22.6, 24.4a, 27.2a1, 28.11, 29.6a2, 20C, 30.12 (art), 32.6 (art), 36.2, 38.9a-c, 45.7a, 45.7 (art), 45.10a

Todd Buck:
9.3, 29.7a, 45.2a

Chris Creek:
37.1, 37.2, 38.5, 39.6, 40.1a-b, 40.5, 43.6

Anne Greene:
42.5, 46.11

Peg Gerrity:
22.14, 29.10a-b, 29.14a-b

Kathleen Hagelston:
5.8c, 17.1, 28.9c, 29.3

Kathleen Hagelston/Carlyn Iverson:
14.1b, 17.8, 36.3

Kathleen Hagelston/Marjorie Leggit:
14.3b, 40.10

Kathleen Hagelston/Rictor Lew:
40.7, 44B

Kathleen Hagelston/Laurie O'Keefe:
37.5

Kathleen Hagelston/Rolin Graphics:
5.14a, 6.6, 6.9, 36.7, 36.8, 36.13, 36.16, 40.9, 43.7, 43.8, 43.9

Kathleen Hagelston/Nadine Sokol:
17.9, 17.11

Illustrious, Inc.
3.1a, 3.2, 3.3, 3.4, 3.5, 3.6, 3.7a, 3.7b, 3.9, 3A, 3B, 3.10, 4.3, 4.6b, 4.9, 4A, 4.13, 4.14, 4.18, 4.19, 5.2, 6.10, 6.11, 7.4, 7.7, 7.11, 10.5a, 10.6a, 10.7a, 10.8a, 11.1, 11.5, 11.7, 12.3, 12.6, 12.7, 13.5, 13.7, 14.9a, 15.6b, 15.7, 16.1, 16.2c, 16.3, 16.5, 16.9a, 18.1, 18.2, 20.1, 20.8, 20.10, 21.4, 28.3, 31A, 35.1, 35.2a, 35.9b, 38.10, 46.2, 46B, 52.1 and miscellaneous text art.

Carlyn Iverson:
1.1a, 4.4, 4A, 4.20, 5.4a, 5.5a, 5.8b, 6.8, 9.1b, 9.2, 11.2, 12.2a, 18.3, 19.6, 21.11, 22.2 (art), 23.1, 25.6a, 25.13, 27A, 28.9b, 30.7b, 30.14a, 30.15, 31.18a, 35.8, 38.8a, 38A, 39.10, 40.8b, 40.11, 41.7, 41.8, 41.12, 42.3, 42.10, 42.11, 42.13a, 43.4a, 45.3, 45.9b, 46.12b, 47.3a, 47.4, 47.5, 48.1, 50.7, 50.9, 50.10, 50.11, 50.12, 51.13

Carlyn Iverson/Rolin Graphics:
31.3, 34.3a

Jak Graphics:
27.13, 34.5

Karen Johnson/Precision Graphics:
32A, 32B

Edward Jones:
27.9

Mark Lefkowitz:
21.2, 34.6, 38.4

Rictor Lew:
44.7a, 46.14

Rictor Lew/Precision Graphics:
1.1, 1.4

Marjorie Leggitt:
22.3a

Mark Lefkowitz:
40.4, 41.4

Steve Moon:
45.13

Diane Nelson:
36B(art)

Laurie O'Keefe:

14.10a-b, 20.12, 22.1b, 23.8a

Precision Graphics:

2.1, 2.3, 2.4, 5.10, 5.13a-c, 5.15 (art), 6.1b-c, 6.2, 6.12, 6.14, 7.2, 7.3, 7.5a-b, 7.6, 7.8, 7.10, 8.2, 8.4, 8.7, 8.9b, 8.10, 9.4, 9.5, 9.8, 9.9, 9.10, 9.11, 10.3, 10.4, 11.9, 12.2 (chart), 13.2, 13.4, 13.6a, 13.6b, 14.2, 14B, 15.1, 15.4, 15.8, 15D, 17.3, 17.5b, 17.6, 17.7, 17A, 19B, 19.17, 20.3, 20.11, 21.8a, 21.16 (art), 21.18, 22.1a, 22.3b, 22.4a-b, 22.8b, 22.9, 22B, 22.11, 23.5, 23.6, 23.8b, 23A, 23B, 23.11, 23.12, 24.1 (art), 24.3, 24.5, 24.6, 24.10c, 25.1, 25.2, 25.4a, 25.7 (art), 25A, 25B, 25C, 25.10a, 25.11 (art), 25.12 (art), 25.14b, 26.1b, 26.3 (art), 26.5 (art), 26.7 (art), 26.9 (art), 26.10 (art), 27.1, 27.3a, 27.5b, 27.6b, 27.7b, 27.12, 27B, 27C, 27D, 28.2, 28.5a, 28.6a, 28.10, 29.8, 29.9d, 29.11 (art), 29.13a, 30.3 (art), 30.4 (art), 30.5, 30.9, 30B, 30.10, 30.13, 31.1, 31.6a, 31.7a, 31.12b, 31.15a (art), 31.16, 32.2 (art), 32.5, 32.8, 32.9a, 32C, 33.7, 33.8,
33.10, 34.2a, 34.3b, 34.8, 34.9, 34.12a, 35.5, 35.9a, 35.11, 36.5, 36.6, 37.7a, 37.9, 37A (art), 38.1, 38.2, 38.3, 39.1, 39.2, 39.3, 39.4, 39.5b, 40.2, 40.3, 40.6, 41.2b, 42.8b, 42.9, 42.12, 43.1, 43.3, 43.15a, 44.1, 44.2, 44.6, 44.7b, 46.1, 46A, 47.2a, 47.3b-c, 47.7, 48.1b, 48.2, 48.3b, 48.5, 48.6 (art), 48.7, 48A, 49.1, 50.3, 52.4, 52B and miscellaneous text art. Comprehensive sketches provided by Kathleen Hagelston.

Rolin Graphics

3.12, 3.13, 4.5, 4.10, 4.15, 4.16, 6.3, 6.4, 6.5, 8.8b, 9.7, 11.3 (art), 11.8, 12.4, 12.8, 12.9, 13.1, 13.8, 13.10, 14A, 15.3, 15.5a, 15A, 16.4, 16.6b, 16.7, 16.12, 17.2, 19.1a, 21.1, 21.5, 21.7, 23.10, 25.5a, 29.1, 29.4b, 29.5b, 31.8 (art), 31.19, 32.1, 32.3, 32.11, 32.12, 33.12, 33.14, 33.15, 34.1, 35.6 (art), 35.10, 36.12a, 36.14, 37.12, 39.7, 41.3, 41.4a-d, 41.5, 42.1, 42.2, 42.6, 43.5b, 43.10 (art), 44.3, 44.4, 44.5, 44.8, 44.9, 45.8, 45.11, 46.6, 46.10, 48.4, 49.2, 49.3, 49.4b, 49A, 50.4, 50.5, 50.6, 51.5, 51.2, 51.4, 51.5, 51.6, 51.9, 51.14, 52.2 and miscellaneous text art.

Shoemaker, Inc.:

4.12, 6.7, 7.9, 8.5, 8.6, 8.9a, 11.6, 18.8, 20.6, 36.11, 38.7, 38.11, 42.7

Nadine Sokol

3.14, 5A (art), 17.10, 18.9, 28.7a, 36.15b, 37.6, 37.8b, 41.14, 45.12, 50.13, 52.3

Scott Williams

27.10a

Tom Waldrop:

41.10a, 41.2a, 45.5, 45.6a-b, 45.9a

Yvonne Walston:

35.7a, 37.4, 41.9, 41.13

A Closer Look Boxes

p. 242: Joyce E. Haines; **p. 516:** Gregory J. McConnell; **p. 539:** Kingsley Stern; **p. 598:** Charles N. Horn; **p. 657:** Joyce E. Haines; **p. 864:** Kenneth R. Hinga; **p. 883:** Joyce E. Haines

INDEX

Dermis (animal), *618,* **619**
Descent with modification, 291, 295
   C. Darwin's research indicating, 297–99
   evidence for, 304–7
   natural selection as mechanism for
      adaptation and, 300–303
Desertification, **900**
Deserts, **882**
Detritus, **860**
Detritus food chains, 863
Deuteromycota (imperfect fungi), **439**
Deuterostomes, **484, 504**
   amniote egg, evolution of, 514–17
   chordate characteristics, evolution of,
      506–7
   homeothermy in, 519
   invertebrate chordates, 507
   jaws, evolution of, 510–11
   limbs, evolution of, 512–13
   mammals, 519–21
   phylogenetic tree of, *508*
   protostomes vs., *484*
   radial symmetry in, 504–6
   vertebrate body plan, evolution of, 509
   wings and feathers, evolution of,
      518, 519
Development
   of behavior, in animals, 828–29
   as characteristic of life, 5
   of plant embryo, 593, 596–97
Development, animal, 803–22
   cell specialization and morphogenesis
      in, 808–10
   human embryo and fetal, 811–16
   human stages of, 817
   stages of, 804–7
Devonian period, 348–49
Diabetes mellitus, **778**
Diaphragm, **687**
Diastole, **634**
Diatoms, **418**
Dicots, 532
   embryo, *593*
   germination in, 597
   leaf, *546*
   monocots vs., 532
   roots of, *536,* 537
   seed germination and development in,
      597
   stems, *541, 542, 543*
Dicotyledons (dicots), **458**
Diencephalon (brain), 725
Diet, 678–80
   cancer prevention and, 273, *274*
   cardiovascular disease and, 638–39
   minerals in, 679 (table), 680
   nutrition labels and, 50
   saturated fats in, 48
   vitamins in, 678, 679 (table)
Differentially permeable, **90**
Differential reproduction, 303

Differentiation, **804,** 808
Diffusion, **91**
   gas exchange by, 684–87, 691
   process of, *91*
   of water (osmosis), 92, *93,* 100 (table)
Digestive gland, 672–73
   hormonal control of, 676
Digestive system, 667–77
   human, 671–77
   nutrition, health, and, 678–80
   types of animal, 668–70
Digits, **756**
Dihybrid crosses, 191–93
   Mendel's law of independent
      assortment derived from, 191,
      192
   problems of, 192
   testcross of, *193*
Dikaryotic stage of fungal reproduction,
   431
Dinoflagellates, **418**
Dinosaurs, 345, 514
   latest research findings on, 346
Diploid (2n) number, **159, 170**
   variations in organisms with, 321
Directional selection, **318,** *319*
Disaccharide, 45
Discontinuous feeders, 669
Disruptive selection, **320**
Distal convoluted tubule, **702**
Distolic pressure, 637
Division, 383
Division Anthocerotophyta (hornworts),
   445
Division Ascomycota (sac fungi), *434,*
   435, *439*
Division Basidiomycota (club fungi), *436,*
   437, 438
Division Bryophyta (mosses), **446,** *447*
Division Cycadophyta (cycads), 345, **456**
Division Deuteromycota (imperfect
   fungi), **439**
Division Equisetophyta (horsetails), **451**
Division Ginkgophyta (ginkgos), **456**
Division Gnetophyta (gnetophytes), **457**
Division Hepatophyta (liverworts), **446**
Division Lycopodophyta (club mosses),
   451
Division Magnoliophyta (angiosperms),
   345, **457–61.** *See also* Angiosperms
   (Magnoliophyta)
Division Pinophyta (conifers), 345, **454,**
   455
Division Psilotophyta (psilotophytes), **450**
Division Pteridophyta (ferns), **452,** *453*
Division Zygomycota (zygospore fungi),
   432–33
DNA (deoxyribonucleic acid), 5, **56,**
   231–44
   activation of, by steroid hormones,
      768–69
   antisense, 286

Chargaff's rules on bases of, 235
chromosomal structure and, *264*
complementary base pairing in, 57,
   236, 238
exons of, 251
gene mutations and changes in, 256,
   269, 312
genetic disorders caused by triplet
   repeats of bases in, 220, 222
   (table)
human vs. ape, 361
introns of, 251
as key genetic material, **232**–34
mapping human migrations through
   analysis of mitochondrial, 289–
   90, 367
model of bases in, 236, *237*
nucleosome structure including, *263*
replication errors, 241
replication of, 238–41, 281–82
sequence-tagged sites (STSs) on, 286
similarity of all, 307
structure of, *56,* 57 (table), 235–36, *237*
structure of, vs. RNA structure, 248
   (table)
transcription and, 248, 250–51
translation and, 248, 252–54
transposons (jumping genes) and, 242
variability of bases in, 236
DNA fingerprinting, **282**
DNA hybridization studies, 388, 389
DNA ligase, **279**
DNA polymerase, **238,** 240, 281
   proofreading of DNA replication by,
      241
DNA probe, **281**
Dominance, genetic
   autosomal, *218,* 220–24
   codominance, 198
   common crosses involving simple, 194
      (table)
   incomplete, *198*
Dominance hierarchies, **831,** 850
Dominant allele, **187**
Donor (electron), 30
Dormancy, 579, 596
Dorsal hollow nerve cord, 506
Dorsal-root ganglion, 721
Double fertilization (angiosperm),
   460–61, 592
Double helix of DNA, *56,* 57, 236, *237*
Down feathers, 519
Down syndrome, 206, 213, 214
Drinking water, pollution in, 896
Drosophila flies, genetics experiments
   with, 202, *203,* 316, 810
Drugs
   antibiotic, 407
   antiviral (acyclovir, azidothymidine-
      AZT), 401
   for cardiovascular disease, 639
   cocaine, 729

effects of, on humans, 728–29
   hallucinogens, 438
   heroin, 729
   marijuana, 728
   medicinal, obtained from plants, 599, 883
   methamphetamine, 729
Duchenne muscular dystrophy, 226–27
Duodenum, **672,** *673*
Duplication, chromosomal, 207
Dutcher, Susan, on behavior in unicellular algae, 415
Dynamic equilibrium organs, 744–45

E

Ear
   anatomy of, 742, *743*
   balance and, 744–45
   hearing and, 745, 746
   inner ear anatomy, *744*
   parts and functions of, 742 (table)
Earth
   atmosphere of, 333, 341
   biomes of (*see* Biomes)
   dynamic crust of, 338–39
   eras, periods, and epochs of, 340–49
   fossils in sedimentary rock of, 336–37 (*see also* Fossils)
   geological time scale of, *340, 356*
   history of, *336*
Earthworms, 491–92
   circulatory system of, *629*
   digestive tract of, *668*
   excretory organs of, 701
   gas exchange in, 686
   locomotion in, *750*
   reproduction in, *787*
Ecdysone (insect), 770
Echinoderms (Echinodermata), **504**–6
Ecological pyramid, **865**
Ecology, **840**
   biological relationships and, 902
   defined, 860, **861**
   of populations, 839–48
Ecosystem(s), 2, **3, 860**
   biogeochemical cycles in, 866–69
   deciduous forest, *862*
   defined, 860
   energy flows in, 863–65
   freshwater pond, *862*
   human food chain vs. natural food web in, 871
   interactions within communities of, 849–58
   living components of, 860
   marine enclosures for study of, 864
   organization of, *6*
   populations in, 6–9, 839–48, 863, 865
   succession in, 860–61
   water (hydrologic) cycle in, 870
Ectoderm, 466, 612, **805,** 813

Ectothermic organisms, 346, **512,** 515
Edema, **650**
Effectors, **721**
Eggs
   algae, 414
   amniote, 514–17
   bryophyte plant, *447*
   hard, in birds, 519
   leathery, in reptiles, 514
   monotreme, 519
   production of human, 176, *177,* 794, *795, 796*
   structure of human, *178*
   vascular plant, *453, 455, 460–61*
Ejaculation, **791**
Electromagnetic spectrum, **120,** *121*
Electrons, **25**
   acceptors and donors of, 30
   atomic configurations and, 28, *29*
   coenzymes as carriers of, 112
   covalent bonding and sharing of, 31–33
   energy levels of, *27*
   ionic bonding and transfer of, 30–31
   movement of, around the nucleus, 27
   orbitals of, 27, *28*
   oxidation and reduction reactions and number of, 33
Electron shells, 27
Electron transport system, ATP synthesis and, **112, 124,** 125, 139, **146**–47
Elements, **24**
   atoms as components of, 25–29
   most common, in living organisms, 2, 24, 25 (table)
Elephantiasis, **480**
Embryo, animal
   cell differentiation and specialization in, 808
   effect of yolk on, 806–7
   genetic control of pattern formation in, 810
   human, 811–16
   morphogenesis of, 809–10
   protecting, 788–89
   vestigial structures in development of vertebrate, *306*
Embryo, plant, **592**
   developmental stages of, 593
   somatic, 600
Embryonic disk, 813
Embryo sac, **589**
Emission, seminal, 791
Emphysema, 693
Endocrine system, 613, 767–84
   behavior and, 827
   cellular metabolism and effects of hormones, 768–69
   defined, **768**
   environmental signals and hormone redefinition, 781–82
   human, 771–81
   insect growth hormones, 770

Endocytosis, 96–97
   evolution of eukaryotic cell and, 412
   receptor-mediated, *97*
Endoderm, 466, 612, **805,** 813
Endodermis, dicot root, **537**
Endolymph, 743
Endomembrane system, 71–74
Endometriosis, 798
Endometrium, **794**
Endoplasmic reticulum (ER), **71**
Endoskeleton, 504, 506, 751
   in humans, 753–58
Endosperm, **592**
Endospore, bacterial, **403**
Endosymbiotic theory, 249, 342, 408, 412
Endothermic organisms, **519**
   dinosaurs as possible, 346
Energy, **4,** 104–6
   biological relationships and, 150
   defined, **27, 104**
   exchange of, 105
   flows of, in ecosystems, 863–65
   intake of, as characteristic of life, 4
   laws of, 105
   as nonrecyclable, 105, *106*
   potential, 27
   pyramid of, *865*
   solar, 75, 120–21
   storage of, in fats, 48–49
Energy balance sheet, 106
Energy of activation, *108*
Entamoeba histolytica, 421
Enterocoelom, 485, 504
Environment. *See also* Ecosystem(s)
   air pollution in, 892–95
   biological relationships and, 902
   effects of increased CO_2 levels in, on photosynthesis, 129, 132
   land degradation and toxic waste in, 898, 899–902
   phenotype and effects of, 200
   polygenic inheritance and effects of, 228
   sustainability and, 902
   water pollution in, 896–97
Environmental resistance, **841**
Environmental signals
   categories of, 781, *782*
   opening and closing of stomates in response to, 556
Enzyme(s), **52,** 107–12
   activation of, by peptide hormones, 769
   amount of, and speed of, 110
   cofactors and coenzymes affecting, 111, 112
   complex of substrate and, 109
   denatured, 110
   digestive, 672, 674 (table)
   effect of temperature and pH on, 110
   energy of activation lowered by, 108
   factors affecting speed of, 110–12

gene specification of, 246
inhibition of, 110–11
intestinal, 674
production of recombinant DNA using, 279
protein function as, 88
Enzyme cascade, 769
Enzyme-substrate complex, 109
Epidermal growth factor, 781
Epidermis
animal, **619**
human, *618*
plant, **537, 533**
Epididymides, 790
Epiglottis, **672, 688**
Epinephrine (adrenaline), 723, 776
Epiphytes, **561**
Epistasis, 199
Epithelial tissue, **612**–13
Epitheliomuscular cells (*Hydra*), 472
Equilibrium species, 844
Equisetophyta (horsetails), **451**
Erection, penile, 791
Ergot (fungi), 435, 438
Erythrocytes (red blood cells), 93, *247*, **641**–42
Esophagus, **672**
Essential plant nutrients, 558 (table)
Estrogen, 780, **795**, 798
role of, in uterine cycle, 796, *797*
Estuary, **876**, *877*
Ethmoid bone, 754
Ethnobotany, 883
Ethylene, **579**, 582 (table)
as plant growth regulator, 576
Eubacteria, **405**, 406–7, 408
cyanobacteria, 406–7
shapes of, *406*
Euchromatin, **263**
as genetically active, 265
Euglenoids (Euglenophyta), **418**, *419*
Eukaryotes
diploid chromosome number of select, 159 (table)
DNA replication in, 241
evolution of, 249, 342, 408, 412–13
messenger RNA (mRNA) processing in, *251*
regulation of gene expression in, 262–67
Eukaryotic cells, **67**–79
in animals, 67 (table), *68*
cell cycle of, 160, *161*
cytoskeleton of, 76–79
endomembrane system in, 71–74
energy-related organelles of, 75–76
evolution of, 249, 342, 408, *412*–13
nucleus of, 70
in plants, 67 (table), *69*
prokaryotic cells vs., 80 (table)
ribosomes of, 71

Evolution, 291, 293–330
adaptation by natural selection as process of, 300–303, 318–21
of amniote egg, 514–17
of animals, 466–68
as basis of biology, 2
causes of, 315–17
chemical, 333–35
convergent, 388
C. Darwin's studies and theory of, 294–95, 297–303
detecting (Hardy-Weinberg law), 313–14
DNA fingerprinting in studies of, 282
of eukaryotes, 249, 342, 408, 412–13
evidence supporting, 304–7
explanation for life's unity and diversity in, **6**, 326–27
of Hawaiian silversword alliance, 326–27
history of life on Earth as, 336–51
human (*see* Human evolution)
of jaws, 510–11
of limbs, 512–13
lineages, 350, 387–91
models of evolutionary change, 351
of nervous system, 712–13
origins of life and, *332, 333*–35
parallel, 388
of plants, 450 (table)
scientific thought prior to Darwin, 295–96
speciation and, 322–25
variations in populations and, 300, 312, 321
A. R. Wallace's studies and theory of, 301
of wings and feathers, 519
world views before and after C. Darwin's studies, 294, 295 (table)
Excretory system, 697–710
homeostasis and, 698–700
human organs of, *698*
human urinary system, 702–7
organs of, 701
Exercise, effects of, on human body, 143, 639, 762
Exhalation, **687**, *689*
Exocrine glands, 613
Exocytosis, **96**
Exon, **251**
Exoskeleton, **493**, *750, 751*
Expanded trinucleotide repeat, 220, 222 (table)
Experimental variable, **16**
Experiments, scientific, 15, 16
Exponential growth, **840**
Expulsion, **791**
Exteroceptors, 734
Extinction, **343**
mass, 343, *348–49*, 514
Extractive reserves, 9

Extraembryonic membranes, 514, **788, 811**
Extrinsic proteins, 87
Ex Vivo gene therapy, *285*
Eye
camera-type, 488
compound, 493, 495, 736
Eye (human), 737–40
anatomy of, *737*
focusing, 738, *739*
function of parts of, 737 (table)
retina of, 738
rods and cones of, *740*
vision problems with, 739–40
Eyespot
green algae, 414
planaria, 474, 736
sea star, 506

F

F1 generation, 186
F2 generation, 186
fitness of, and speciation, 323
Facilitated transport, **94**
Facultative anaerobes, 404
FAD (flavin-adenine dinucleotide), **112**
Family, **383**
Farm animals
bovine growth hormone for, 280, 284
genetically engineered, 284
Fat(s), **48**, *49*
as energy source, 149–50
in human diet, 48, 50
Fatty acid, 44, 48
Feathers, 519
Feedback inhibition (enzyme), **110**, *111*
Feeding, continuous vs. discontinuous, 669
Feeding polyps (*Obelia*), 473
Female reproductive system, 794–98
birth control and, 799 (table)
breasts and milk production, 798
diseases of, 798–800
fertility, 798
fertilization and, 797
hormones, 780, 795–96, *797, 798*
organs, 794 (table)
ovarian cycle, 795, 796 (table)
ovaries and egg production, 176, *177, 795, 796*
side view of, *794*
uterine cycle, 796, *797*
Fermentation, 139, **142**
advantages and disadvantages of, 142
efficiency of, 142
Ferns (Pteridophyta), **452**, 462
adaptation of, 452
fronds of, 452
life cycle of, *453, 459*
uses of, 452
whisk, 450

Garden pea (*Pisum sativum*), Mendel's experiments using, 184, *185*, 186–93
Gart gene, 214
Gases, diffusion of, *91*, 691
Gas exchange, animal
  breathing and, 687, *689*
  internal and external respiration and, *690*, 691
  on land, 686–87
  in water, 684–85
Gas exchange, plant, 533, 546, 556
Gastric glands, 672
Gastric juices, 672–73, 676, 777
Gastric mill (crustacea), 495
Gastropods (Gastropoda), **489**
Gastrovascular cavity (cnidarians), **470**
Gastrula, **805**
Gastrulation, 813
Gawienowski, Margaret, signal transduction in, 575
Gender, sex chromosomes as determiner of, 202–3
Gene(s), **5**, 202–5, 245–76
  altering, in yeast cells, 89
  alternate forms of (*see* Allele(s))
  amino acid coding by, 249
  autosomal, 218–25
  cell division and distribution of, 158
  chromosomes and, 264
  embryo pattern formation controlled by, 810
  evolutionary lineages and, 388–89
  expression of (*see* Gene expression)
  Gart, 214
  homeotic, 810
  interacting (epistasis), 199
  jumping (transposons), 242
  linked, 204–5
  mapping order of, on chromosomes, 205
  mutations in, 256, 269, 312
  nested, 220
  operons of (*see* Operons)
  pleiotropy of, 198
  polygenic inheritance and multiple, 200, *201*
  regulator, 260, *261*
  replacing defective, 285–86
  role of, 246–47
  sex-linked, disorders of, 226–27
  src gene, 270–71
  structural, 260, *261*
  on X chromosomes, 202–3
Gene amplification, 265
Gene cloning, 278–79
Gene expression, 248–55
  cancer as failed regulation of, 268–74
  participants in, 255 (table)
  protein synthesis as result of, 255
  regulation of, in eukaryotic cells, 262–67

regulation of, in prokaryotic cells, 260–61
  role of RNA in, 248
  transcription, 248, 250–51
  translation, 248, 252–54
  transposons and, 242
Gene flow, **315**
  within species, 322
Gene locus, **187**
Gene migration, 315
Gene mutation, 256, 269
  evolution and, 315
  variations in populations caused by, 312
Gene pharming, 284
Gene pool, **313**–14
  gene flow as cause of increasing similarity of, 315
  gene mutations as cause of multiple alleles in, 315
  genetic drift and chance changes in, 316–17
Generative cell (pollen grain), 589
Gene therapy, **285**–86
Genetically engineered microbes (GEMS), 283
Genetic code, 249
Genetic counseling, 218–19
Genetic disorders (human)
  Alzheimer disease, 719
  base triplet repeats as cause of, 220, 222–23
  carriers of, 219
  color blindness, 226
  cri du chat syndrome, 207
  cystic fibrosis, 95, 225, 285
  detection of, 216–17
  Down syndrome, 206, 213, 214
  Edward syndrome, 213
  founder effect as cause of, 317
  Fragile X syndrome, 222, *223*
  gene therapy for, 285–86
  hemophilia, 226, 286
  Huntington disease, 220
  hypercholesterolemia, 285
  Kartagener's syndrome, 415
  Klinefelter, 213, 215
  lysosomal enzyme disorder, 73, 224
  Marfan syndrome, 198
  metabolic diseases, 246
  metafemale, 213, 215
  muscular dystrophy, 226–27
  neurofibromatosis, 220
  nondisjunction as cause of, 213–15
  Parkinson disease, 285
  Patau syndrome, 213
  phenylketonuria (PKU), 225
  Rh factor and blood type, 224
  severe combined immunodeficiency syndrome (SCID), 285
  sickle-cell disease, 221
  Tay-Sachs disease, 224

Turner, 213, 215
  XYY, 213, 215
Genetic drift, **316**–17
Genetic engineering, **278**
  gene cloning and recombinant DNA in, 278–79
  mapping human chromosomes and, 286
  of microbes, 283
  of plants, 602–3
  products of, 280, 283–84
  replacing defective genes (gene therapy) as, 285–86
  replication of DNA in, 281–82
  transgenic organisms produced by, 283–84, 602–3
Genetic recombination
  in eukaryotes (*see* Sexual reproduction)
  meiosis and methods of, 172–75, 179
  in prokaryotes, 403
  variations in populations caused by, 312
Genetics. *See* Cell reproduction; Chromosome(s); DNA (deoxyribonucleic acid); Gene(s); Human genetics; Inheritance
Genetics problems
  of dihybrid crosses, 192–93
  of monohybrid crosses, 188–89
  of X-linked genes, 203
Genital herpes, 800
Genital warts, 800
Genome, altering. *See* Genetic engineering
Genomic imprinting, 220, 222
Genotype, **187**, 208
  calculating probability of (*see* Genetics problems)
  multiple alleles and, 199
  phenotype vs., 187 (table)
  polygenic inheritance and, 200, *201*
Genus, **383**
Geological time scale, 340 (table)
  animals and, 356 (table)
  plants and, 450 (table)
Geology, C. Darwin's study of, 297–98
Germination (seed), **596**–97
Germ layers (ectoderm, mesoderm, endoderm), 466, 612, **805**
Gerontology, **817**
GH (growth hormone), *773*, **774**
Giant panda, relationship to red panda, 388
Giardia lamblia, 422
Gibberellins, **574**, 582 (table)
  as plant growth regulator, 576
Gibbon, *360*, 361
Gills, **685**
Gill slits (tunicates), 507
Gilmour, Thomas, 269
Ginkgo (Ginkgophyta), **456**
Girdling (tree), **562**
Gland cells (*Hydra*), 472
Glaucoma, 738
Global warming, *892*, 893

Globular proteins, 54
Glomerular capsule, **702, 704**
Glomerular filtrate, 704
Glomerulus, **702**
Glottis, **688**
Glucagon, **777**
   insulin levels and, *778*
Glucocorticoids, 776
Glucose, **45**
   cellular respiration and metabolism of, 138–48
   chemical formula for, 29
   storage of, as glycogen, 676–77
Glycerol, 44, 48, *49*
Glycogen, **46**
   storage of glucose as, 676–77
Glycolipids, 86, 88
Glycolysis, 139, **140,** *141*
Glycoproteins, 87, 88
Glyoxysomes, 74
Gnathostomates, **510–11**
Gnetophytes (Gnetophyta), **457**
Goiter, **774**
Golden brown algae (Chrysophyta), 417, **418**
Golgi apparatus, **73**
Gonadotropic hormones (FSH, LH), *773,* **774,** 793, 795
Gonadotropic-releasing hormone (GnRH), 773, 793, 796
Gonads, **787**
Gonorrhea, 800
Good-genes hypothesis of mate selection, 830
Gorilla, *360,* 361
Graafian follicle, 795
Grain (pollen), **454**
Granular leukocytes, 641
Granum (grana), **75,** *122,* **123**
Grasshopper, 498–99
   anatomy of, *498*
   circulatory system of, *629*
Grasslands, *884,* 885
Gravitropism, **569**
Gravity
   animal response to, 742–45
   growth response of plants to, 569
Grazing food chains, 863
Green algae (Chlorophyta), **413**–16, 445
   colonial, 414
   filamentous, 416
   with flagella, 414
   multicellular, 416
Green glands (crustacea), 495
Greenhouse effect, 129, 867, **892**–93
Griffith, Frederick, experiment of, *232,* 233
Ground meristem, 533, 540
Ground tissue (plant), 533, 534
Groundwater, 896
Growth (plant) **804**
   hormonal inhibition of, 579, 582 (table)
   hormonal regulation of, 576, 582 (table)

phytochrome control of, 580–81
of populations, 840–43
research on *Arabidopsis thaliana* and, 578
as response to stimuli, 568–70
Growth factor receptors, 269, 272
Growth factors, 268, 269, 781
Growth hormone (GH), *773,* **774**
Growth hormones, insect, 770
Guanine (G), **235**
Guard cells, **556**
   hormonal regulation of, 579
Gut
   complete and incomplete, 668
   human, 671–77
Guttation, **554**
Gymnomycota (slime mold), **425**–26
Gymnosperms, 345, **454**–57
   adaptation of, 457
   conifers, 454–55
   cycads, 456
   ginkgos, 456
   gnetophytes, *456,* 457
   life cycle of, 454, *455*
   uses of, 457

H

Habitat, **851**
   isolation of species by, 322, 323 (table)
Hagfishes, 509
Hair, 519, 619, 816
Hair cells
   balance and, 744–45
   hearing and, 745
   touch and, 742
Halophiles (bacteria), 405
Haploid (n) number, **159, 170,** 178
Hardy, G. H., 313
Hardy-Weinberg law, **314**
Harvey, William, discoveries of, on blood circulation, 634
Haustoria, 538
Hazardous waste, 899
HCG (human chorionic gonadotropic) hormone, 797, **813**
Hearing, 742–45
   ear anatomy, *743*
   ear parts and functions, 742 (table)
   inner ear anatomy, *744*
   protecting, 746
   sound sense receptors, 745
Heart
   amphibian, 512
   bird, 519
   reptile, 514
Heart, human, **632**–35
   blood movement through, 633
   external anatomy of, *632*
   heartbeat, 634, *635*
   internal anatomy of, *633*
Heart attack, 638–39
Heartwood, 543

Helium atom, **25**
Helper T cells, **658,** 660, 799
Hemichordates (Hemichordata), **506**
Hemocoel, 486, **496,** 498, *629*
Hemocyanin, 486
Hemoglobin, **641, 691**
   globin alleles of, 312
   oxygen transport by, 691
   sickle-cell disease and, *247*
Hemolymph, 628
Hemolytic disease of the newborn (HDN), 645
Hemolytic jaundice, 677
Hemophilia, 226, 286
Hennig, Willi, 391
Hepatic portal system, *677*
Hepatitis, 677
Hepatophyta (liverworts), **446**
Herbaceous plants, **457**
Herbaceous stems, **540,** *541*
Herbivores, **860**
Hermaphroditic animals, **475,** 491
Heroine, 729
Herpes, 401
   genital, 800
Hershey, Alfred, bacteriophage experiment of, *234*
Heterochromatin, **263**
   as genetically inactive, 263–65
Heterogametes (egg, sperm), 414, 424. *See also* Eggs; Sperm
Heterospores, 454, *455*
Heterotrophs, **335**
   anaerobic, 341
   bacterial, 404
Heterotrophy, 2
Heterozygous organism, **187**
   variation in, 321
Hirudin, 492
Histamine, **653**
Histone protein, *263, 265*
HIV (human immunodeficiency virus), **799,** 660. *See also* AIDS (acquired immunodeficiency syndrome)
HMS *Beagle,* voyage of, *294*
Holozoic organisms, 420, 422
Homeobox, 810
Homeostasis, **4, 622**–23, 708
   adrenal cortex maintenance of, 776
   excretory system and, 698–700, 706–7
   exercise and, in human body, 143
   insulin and glucagon levels and, *778*
Homeothermic organisms, **519**
Homeotic genes, 810
Hominids, **361,** 362–70, 371
   archaic Neanderthals, 368
   Cro-Magnon, 368–69
   erect walk of, 362–63
   modern human species, 367, 370
   origin of *Homo* genus, 364
   skull anatomy and tools of, *369*

macroscopic functioning of, 759
microscopic functioning of, 760–62, *763*
skeletal, 616
somatic system and nerves of, 721
Muscle action potentials, **762**
Muscle fiber, 616–17
contraction of, *759,* 761
nerve stimulation of, 721, *762, 763*
skeletal, *760*
sliding filament theory of, *761*
Muscular dystrophy, 226–27
Muscular (contractile) tissue, **616**–17
Musculoskeletal system, 749–66
human skeleton in, 753–58
muscle function in, 759–63
types of skeletal systems, 750–51
Mushrooms (club fungi), *436, 437*
poisonous and hallucinogenic, 438
Mutagens, **256**
Mutations, **232**
cancer and genetic, 269
chromosomal, **206**–7, 216, 220, 222–23
gene, 256
in prokaryotes, 403
viral, 398
Mutualism, 854 (table), **856**
Mycelium (fungi), *430,* **431**
Mycorrhizae, 344, **440,** 538, **561,** 856
Myelin sheath, **714**–15
Myocardium, **632**
Myofibrils, **760**
Myogram, *759*
Myosin, **760,** *761*
Myotonia, 791

N

NAD+ (nicotinamide adenine dinucleotide), **112**
NADH dehydrogenase complex, 147
NADP+ (nicotinamide-adenine dinucleotide phosphate), **112**
NADPH, synthesis of, 112, 124, *125*
Nastic movements in plants, 570–71
Native Americans
hallucinogenic mushrooms used by, 438
mapping migrations of, through mitochondrial DNA analysis, 289–90
Natural selection, 5, **300**–303, 318–21
fitness of organisms and, 300–303, 318
reproductive potential of organisms and, 300
types of, 318–20
variations in populations and, 300, 321
Nature vs. nurture, 228
Neanderthals, **368**
Negative feedback, homeostasis and, **622**
Nematocyst (cnidarians), **470**
Nematoda (roundworms), 478, **479**–80

Nemertea (ribbon worms), **474**
Neogene period, 347
Neoplasia, 268
Nephridia (annelids), **490,** 491, **701**
Nephrons, **702,** *703*
Nerve growth factor, 781
Nerve impulse transmission, 715–17
at synapses, 718
Nerves, 617, 714–18
of peripheral nervous system, **720**
stimulation of muscles by, 762, *763*
Nervous system, 711–32
Alzheimer disease of, 719
arthropod, 493
central, 712, *713,* 724–27
effects of drugs on, 728–29
evolution of, 712–13
formation of, 809
homeostatis controlled by, 622
neurons of, 714–18
peripheral, 712, *713,* 720–23
Nervous tissue, **617**
Nested genes, 220
Nests, dinosaur, *346*
Neural plate, 807
Neural tube, 807
Neurofibromatosis, 220
Neuroglial cells, 617, 715
Neuromuscular junction, **762,** *763*
Neurons, **617, 714**–18
action potential, *716,* 717
Alzheimer disease and abnormal, 719
anatomy of, *714*
nerve impulse transmission, 715–17
resting potential, *716,* 717
synapses, 718
Neurotransmitters, 714, **718**
as environmental signals, 781
types of, 718
Neurula, 807
Neurulation, nervous system produced by, 807
Neutrons, **25**
Neutrophils, **641,** 653
Newborn (human), 816
hemolytic disease of, 645
Newts, 512, 513
Niche, **851**
Nirenberg, Marshall, 249
Nitrification, 868
Nitrogen, cycling of, in ecosystems, 868
Nitrogen-fixation, **405,** 538, **868**
by bacteria, 283, *405,* 560, *561*
Nitrogenous wastes, excretion of, 698, 699 (table)
Node (leaf), 531, 540
Nodules (root), **560,** *561*
Noise, damage to hearing by, 746
Nomenclature, binomial system of, 295, 380–82

Noncompetitive inhibition of enzymes, 110
Noncyclic electron pathway, 124, *125*
Noncyclic photophosphorylation, 126
Nondisjunction, 206
abnormalities caused by, **213**–14, 215
Nongonococcal urethritis (NGU), 800
Nonrandom mating, 315
Nonseptate fungi, **431**
Nonspecific immune defenses, 652–54
Nonvascular plants, 445–48, 459
Norepinephrine (NE), **718,** 723, 776
Nose, smelling sense in, 735
Notochord, **506, 807,** *809*
Nuclear envelope, **70**
Nucleic acid, 44, **56**–57, 58 (table), **232**
Nuclein, 232
Nucleoid, **66, 166,** 402
Nucleolus (nucleoli), **70**
Nucleoplasm, 70
Nucleosome, *263, 264*
Nucleotides, 44, **56**
DNA composition based on, *235, 236, 237*
mutations and changes in sequences of, in genes, 256
Nucleus (atom), 25
movement of electrons about, 27
Nucleus (cell), **70**
cancer, 268
eukaryotic, *264*
Numbers, pyramid of, 865
Nutrition
animal, 678–80
fungal, 430, 431
human (*see* Human nutrition)
plant, 558–63
prokaryote, 404–5
protoctist, 413, 420–21, 422, 425
Nutrition labels on packaged foods, 50
Nutritive-muscular cells (*Hydra*), 472

O

Obelia, 472, *473*
Obligate anaerobes, 404
Obligate intracellular parasites, 398
Observational data, 17
Obstructive jaundice, 677
Occipital bone, 754
Occipital lobe (cerebrum), 726
Occupational hazards, cancer and, 273
Ocean ridge, **339,** 879
Oceans, 878–79
benthic division, 879
global warming and levels of, 893
pelagic division, 878, *879*
pollution of, 896–97
Octopus, 488
Oils, **48**–49
Olfactory cells, **735**
Oligochaetes, **491**–92

Tissue, plant, 533–34
  dicot root, *536, 537*
  epidermal, 533
  ground, 534
  vascular, 534, *535*
Tissue culture (plant), **600**–602
  hormones and, 576, *577*
Tissue fluid, 622, 624
  exchanges between blood and, **642,** *643*
Tissue level of organization, 466, 470
T lymphocytes, 652, **654**
  activation and diversity of, *659*
  characteristics of, 659
  cytotoxic, 658
  helper, 658, 660, 799
  memory, 659, 661
  suppressor, 659
Toads, 512, 513
Tobacco mosaic virus, *397*
Tonegawa, Susumu, research of, on
    antibody diversity, 657
Tonicity, **92**–93, 100 (table)
  regulation of, in humans, 706–7
Tonsils, 651
Tool use by hominids, 365, 366, 369
Torpor state, 512
Torsion (gastropod), 489
Tortoises, Charles Darwin's studies of
    Galápagos Island, 298, *299*
Totipotent cells, **600**
Touch
  communication by, 834
  sensing, 619, 742
Toxic substances, 898, 899
Toxicysts, 421
Toxoplasma gondii, 423
tPA (tissue plasminogen activator), 280
Trachea
  arthropod, **493,** *686*
  human, **672, 688**
Tracheids (xylem), 534, *535,* 552
Transcription, **248,** 250–51
  formation of messenger RNA, 250
  processing of messenger RNA, 251
  regulation of gene expression after,
      262, 266, *267*
  regulation of gene expression at, 262,
      263–66
Transcription factors, **266**
Transduction (bacteria), 403
Transduction of stimuli (plants), 568, 575
Transfer RNA (tRNA), **248,** 252–53
  structure of, *253*
Transformation (bacteria), 403
Transform fault, 339
Transgenic organisms, **283**–84, 602–3
Transitional fossils, *304,* 345, 350
Transition reaction, **144**
Translation, **248,** 252–54
  amino acid transfer in, 252–53
  control of gene expression at, 261

polysome structure and, 252
  regulation of gene expression after,
      262, 267
  regulation of gene expression at, 262, 267
  three steps of, 253–54
Translocation, chromosomal, 207, 214,
    254, 312
Transmission electron microscopy, 64
Transpiration, **555**
Transport systems, animal
  blood and, 640–45, 691
  human, 632–39
  invertebrate, 628–29
  vertebrate, 629, 630–31
Transport systems, plant, *552*
  biological relationships in, 564
  inorganic nutrients, 558–61
  organic nutrients, 562–63
  water, 553–56
  xylem and phloem tissue, 534, *535*
Transport vesicles, 71
Transposons, discovery of, 242
Tree. *See also* Forests
  climate and annual rings of, 539
  effect of acid deposition on, 894, *895*
  girdling of, 562
  paper produced from, 545
  secondary growth and wood of, 542,
      543
Treeless biomes, 882–85
Trematodes, 476
Triassic period, 345, 348–49
Trichinosis, **479**–80
Trichocysts, 421
Trichomonas vaginalis, 422
Trichonympha collaris, 422
Tricuspid valve, 632
Triglyceride, 48–49
Triplet code, **249**
Triplet repeat mutations, 220, 222
    (table), *223*
Triploblasts, **474**
Trisomy, 206, 213, 215 tRNA (transfer
    RNA), **248,** 252, *253* tRNA
    synthetases, 253
Trochophore larva, 490
Trophic levels, **863,** 865
Trophoblast, **812**
Tropical rain forests, 8–9, 886–88
  deforestation of, 900, *901*
  levels of life in, *887*
  productivity of, 886, *888*
  significance of, to humans, 9
Tropisms, **568**–70
Trp operon, 260
True-breeding plants, 184, *185*
Trypanosoma gambiense, 422
Trypanosome, **422**
Trypsin, 674
TSH (thyroid-stimulating hormone), *773,* **774**
Tube cell (pollen grain), 589

Tube feet (sea star), 505
Tuberculosis, 692–93
Tubers (plant), 544
Tube-within-a-tube body plan, **474**
Tubular secretion of urine, 704–5
Tubulin subunits, 77
Tumor, **268**
Tumor angiogenesis factor, 781
Tumor-suppressor gene, 161, **269**
  cancer stopped by, 272
Tundra, **882**
Tunicates (Urochordata), **507**
Turgor pressure, **93**
  plant response to stimuli by changes in,
      570–71
  stomate opening and closing, and guard
      cell, 556
  water transport and, 553
Turner syndrome, 213, 215
Turtles, 517
Tympanic membrane, **742**
Typhlosole, 491

U

Ulcers, 673
Ulna, **756**
Ultraviolet (UV) radiation
  effect of, on skin, 618–19, 621
  as mutagen, 256
Ulva (green algae), *416,* 445
Umbilical cord, **814**
Uniramia (Uniramia), **496**–99
  centipedes and millipedes, 496
  insects, *497,* 498–99 (*see also* Insects
      (Insecta))
United States
  acid deposition in, *895*
  population growth in, 846
Unit membrane model (plasma
    membrane), *84,* 85
Unsaturated fatty acid, 48
Urea, excretion of, **699**
Ureter, **702**
Urethra, **702**
Uric acid, excretion of, **699**
Urinary bladder, **702**
Urine, **702**
  composition of, 705 (table)
  processes in production of, 704, *705*
Urochordata (tunicates), **507**
Useful energy, 105, *106*
Uterine cycle, **796,** *797*
Uterus, **794,** 796–97
  implantation of embryo in, 812–13
Utricle, **743,** *744*

V

Vaccines, **400, 661**
  biotechnological production of, 280
  against viruses, 400–401

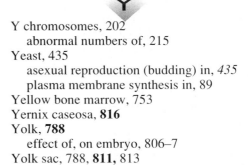